The Cambridge Handel Encyclopedia

George Frideric Handel was born and educated in Germany, flourished in Italy and chose to become British. One of the most cosmopolitan great composers, some of Handel's music has remained in the popular repertory since his lifetime, and a broad variety of his theatre works, from Italian operas to English oratorios, has experienced a dramatic renaissance since the late twentieth century. A large number of publications devoted to Handel's life and music have appeared from his own time until the present day, but *The Cambridge Handel Encyclopedia* is the first resource to gather the full range of present knowledge and leading new scholarship into a single volume for convenient and illuminating reference. Packed with well over 700 informative and accessible entries, both long and short, this book is ideal for performers, scholars, students and music-lovers who wish to explore the Handelian world.

ANNETTE LANDGRAF is a member of the editorial office of the Hallische Händel-Ausgabe based at the Martin-Luther-Universität Halle-Wittenberg, and has edited Handel's *Israel in Egypt* (1999) and the *Anthem for the Funeral of Queen Caroline* (2004). She has published numerous articles about Handel, is currently working on an edition of the 1732 version of *Esther*, specialises in the reception history of Handel's music and has recently published a collection of six oratorio librettos.

DAVID VICKERS was Gerald Coke Handel Foundation scholar at the Open University, teaches at the Royal Northern College of Music in Manchester, and is currently preparing new editions of Handel's *Semele* and *Partenope*. Producer of GFHandel.org and chairman of the annual Stanley Sadie Handel Recording Prize, he is a journalist, author, project consultant and musicologist. He writes essays for most leading classical record labels, is a critic for *Gramophone* and frequently appears on BBC Radio 3.

'An incredible achievement! Articles are extensive, both well documented for scholars and eminently readable. No stone appears to have been left unturned and the result is an amazingly comprehensive A–Z of anyone and anything connected to the great master of the baroque and the legacy with which he has enriched our lives.'

Harry Christophers, conductor of The Sixteen and artistic director of the Handel and Haydn Society, Boston

'The Cambridge Handel Encyclopedia is remarkable: a well-researched, elegantly written, oftentimes witty, cornucopia of Handelian lore and miscellany.'

William Christie, conductor and founder of Les Arts Florissants

'The Cambridge Handel Encyclopedia is a fitting tribute to one of the greatest composers. It is extremely comprehensive, dealing not only with the background to Handel's musical masterpieces, but also with his contemporaries, colleagues, friends and singers who performed in his operas and oratorios. Eighty-eight experts from a range of scholarly disciplines examine Handel's life and work from a wide variety of aspects, and the encyclopedia will serve to emphasise the composer's genius in such a wide range of musical styles. The editors are to be congratulated on producing such an indispensable adjunct to every musical library.'

Sir Charles Mackerras, conductor

'The Cambridge Handel Encyclopedia will be warmly welcomed by all Handelian scholars and performers. The descriptions of musical works are concise and to the point; the numerous biographical entries are especially interesting, and recreate the vivid and colourful musical worlds of Germany, Italy and London that formed the background to Handel's great works.'

Paul McCreesh, conductor and director of the Gabrieli Consort & Players

'What a glorious resource this book is! It is an absolute must for all lovers of Handel's music. It is a terrific mine of information about his music and the fascinating cast of characters who performed it.'

Nicholas McGegan, conductor and artistic director of the Göttingen Handel Festival

'The Cambridge Handel Encyclopedia will never gather dust on my bookshelf. The wealth of information that it contains is so enticing that frequent reference is inevitable, and it is impossible to restrict myself to a single topic of enquiry at any one time. Music lovers, performers and scholars should not be without this book.'

Trevor Pinnock, harpsichordist, conductor and founder of the English Concert

The Cambridge
Handel Encyclopedia

Edited by ANNETTE LANDGRAF and DAVID VICKERS

CAMBRIDGE
UNIVERSITY PRESS

CAMBRIDGE UNIVERSITY PRESS
Cambridge, New York, Melbourne, Madrid, Cape Town, Singapore, São Paulo, Delhi

Cambridge University Press
The Edinburgh Building, Cambridge CB2 8RU, UK

Published in the United States of America by Cambridge University Press, New York

www.cambridge.org
Information on this title: www.cambridge.org/9780521881920

First published 2009

Printed in the United Kingdom at the University Press, Cambridge

A catalogue record for this publication is available from the British Library

Library of Congress Cataloguing in Publication data
The Cambridge Handel encyclopedia / [edited by] Annette Landgraf, David Vickers.
    p.   cm.
Includes bibliographical references.
ISBN 978-0-521-88192-0 (hardback)
1. Handel, George Frideric, 1685–1759 – Encyclopedias.   I. Landgraf, Annette.
II. Vickers, David, 1961–   III. Title.
ML410.H13C23   2009
780.92 – dc22   2009035296

ISBN 978-0-521-88192-0 Hardback

This book is fondly dedicated to Bernd Baselt and Stanley Sadie; both devoted Handelians, great lexicographers and much-missed mentors.

Contents

Illustrations

Contributors

BEVERLY ADAMS
The History of Parliament Trust

DOMENICO ANTONIO D'ALESSANDRO
Conservatorio di Musica 'Lorenzo Perosi', Campobasso

JOHN K. ANDREWS
Independent scholar, London

CLIFFORD BARTLETT
King's Music, Huntingdon

GRAYDON BEEKS
Pomona College, California

TERENCE BEST
The Open University/Hallische Händel-Ausgabe

MELANIA BUCCIARELLI
City University London

MICHAEL BURDEN
University of Oxford

DONALD BURROWS
The Open University

JOHN BUTT
University of Glasgow

NICHOLAS CLAPTON
Royal Academy of Music, London

HANS DIETER CLAUSEN
Independent scholar, Hamburg

DAVID E. COKE
Independent scholar, Ripon

GRAHAM CUMMINGS
University of Huddersfield

KERRY DOWNES
University of Reading

PIERRE DUBOIS
Université François- Rabelais, Tours

ROBIN EAGLES
The History of Parliament Trust

ULRICH ETSCHEIT
Bärenreiter, Kassel

MATTHEW GARDNER
Ruprecht-Karls-Universität, Heidelberg

CHRISTINE GERRARD
University of Oxford

ELIZABETH GIBSON
Independent scholar, Nova Scotia

DANIEL GLOWOTZ
Westfälische Wilhelms Universität Münster

DAGMAR GLÜXAM
Independent scholar, Furth

JOHN GREENACOMBE
Independent scholar, London

WILLIAM D. GUDGER
College of Charleston, South Carolina

BREAN HAMMOND
University of Nottingham

ELLEN T. HARRIS
Massachusetts Institute of Technology

KATIE HAWKS
Independent scholar, Cambridge

JÜRGEN HEIDRICH
Westfälische Wilhelms-Universität Münster

ARTIE HEINRICH
Independent scholar, Bernau

WENDY HELLER
University of Princeton

RAINER HEYINK
Martin-Luther-Universität Halle-Wittenberg

JOHN WALTER HILL
University of Illinois

KATHARINE HOGG
Gerald Coke Handel Collection, The Foundling Museum, London

CHRISTOPHER HOGWOOD
The Academy of Ancient Music, Cambridge

ROBERT D. HUME
Pennsylvania State University

DAVID HUNTER
University of Texas

DAVID ROSS HURLEY
University of Pittsburgh

H. DIACK JOHNSTONE
University of Oxford

BERTA JONCUS
Goldsmiths College, University of London

ANDREW V. JONES
University of Cambridge

ROBERT KETTERER
University of Iowa

MATTHEW KILBURN
University of Oxford

DAVID KIMBELL
University of Edinburgh

RICHARD G. KING
University of Maryland

KLAUS-PETER KOCH
Independent scholar

WALTER KREYSZIG
University of Saskatchewan

HARTMUT KRONES
Universität für Musik und darstellende Kunst, Vienna

ANNETTE LANDGRAF
Martin-Luther-Universität Halle-Wittenberg/Hallische Händel-Ausgabe

FRANCESCO LORA
Università di Bologna

SARAH McCLEAVE
Queen's University, Belfast

THOMAS N. McGEARY
Independent scholar, Champaign, Illinois

CHRISTINE MARTIN
Neue Schubert-Ausgabe, Tübingen

JUDITH MILHOUS
New York City University

TOSHIKI MISAWA
Hokkaido University

PANJA MÜCKE
Philipps-Universität Marburg

KONSTANZE MUSKETA
Händel-Haus, Halle

BUFORD NORMAN
University of South Carolina

SUZANA OGRAJENŠEK
University of Cambridge

HANS-GÜNTER OTTENBERG
Technische Universität Dresden

UTE POETZSCH
Zentrum für Telemann-Pflege und -Forschung, Magdeburg

WERNER RACKWITZ
Independent Scholar, Berlin

GERT RICHTER
Händel-Haus, Halle

JULIANE RIEPE
Martin-Luther-Universität Halle-Wittenberg

LESLIE M. M. ROBARTS
Independent scholar, Powys

JOHN H. ROBERTS
University of California, Berkeley

STEPHEN ROE
Sotheby's, London

JULIAN RUSHTON
University of Leeds

JULIE ANNE SADIE
Independent scholar, Cossington, Somerset

GRAHAM SADLER
University of Hull

†SIEGFRIED SCHMALZRIEDT

DOROTHEA SCHRÖDER
Universität Hamburg

HANNAH SMITH
University of Oxford

RUTH SMITH
University of Cambridge

REINHARD STROHM
University of Oxford

CAROLE TAYLOR
Independent scholar, London

NICHOLAS TEMPERLEY
University of Illinois

ANDREW C. THOMPSON
University of Cambridge

COLIN TIMMS
University of Birmingham

GÖTZ TRAXDORF
Händel-Haus, Halle

DAVID VICKERS
Royal Northern College of Music, Manchester

CARLO VITALI
Centro Studi Farinelli, Bologna

WILLIAM WEBER
California State University

RALF WEHNER
Felix Mendelssohn Bartholdy. Leipziger Ausgabe der Werke

JENS WEHMANN
Händel-Haus, Halle

EDWIN WERNER
Händel-Haus, Halle

JOHN WINEMILLER
Independent scholar, Knoxville

EVA ZÖLLNER
Independent scholar, Hamburg

Translators

ANGELA BAIER
TERENCE BEST

Foreword

We are told that Beethoven pointed at his Arnold edition of Handel and declared 'Handel is the greatest and most capable composer; from him I can still learn'. Today we seem to have lost the art of praising Handel; even our most ardent Handelian anoraks find it difficult to applaud their hero in the sort of terms that for earlier generations were second nature. Faced with The Apotheosis of Handel – that familiar 1787 engraving with the laurel wreath, the supporting angels, the upturned eyes – we simply blush and turn to the critical notes, hoping they will let us off the hook.

During his lifetime Handel was subjected to extremes of both reverence and dismissal – from Goupy's caricature of the glutton seated at the organ, to Roubiliac's sculpture of the great composer which took its place in Vauxhall Gardens alongside Homer and Milton. But Roubiliac immortalised Handel in a remarkably informal pose, relaxed, wearing slippers and free from his wig, as a reminder that, though larger than life, he was still living and, though unique, very human.

> Who cou'd like Handel with such art controul
> The various passions of the warring soul?
> With sounds each intellectual storm assuage,
> Fire us with holy rapture, or with rage?

This question, posed by an anonymous poet writing On the Death of Mr Handel in 1759, was very specifically musical in its praise. A century later the eulogies had become much more generic, more moral than musical:

> this was a man who had done honour to music as much by the nobility of his character as by the sublimity of his genius. He was one of the too few artists who uphold the dignity of art to the highest possible standard. He was the incarnation of honesty. The unswerving rigidity of his conduct captivates even those who do not take him for a model. He worked ceaselessly for the improvement of others without ever feeling weary. He was virtuous and pure, proud and intrepid. His love of good was as unconquerable as his will. He died at his post, working to the last hour of his life. He has left behind him a luminous track and a noble example.

This was the Revd T. Hanly Ball speaking to the Wimbledon Village Club in 1864, whose Victorian superlatives would be more acceptable were we not so aware that they were often used not so much to praise the past, but to slay the present, and criticise (or at least minimise) the products of later writers. 'The works of Haydn, Beethoven, Mozart, Mendelssohn, Spohr, and others – great masters – are performed, and they are admired, and justly so, but they have not the hold upon the taste and feelings (of Englishmen at least) that Handel has', wrote Dean Ramsey in 1862, adding, in a pre-echo of Elvis-mania: 'He is the greatest, and the favourite. He stands alone.' William Crotch agreed: 'The choruses of Mozart and Beethoven are frequently *magnificent*, but seldom sublime', and listening yet again to the opening of *Zadok the Priest*, it is hard to disagree that Handel stands highest.

These comments all come from a century whose essential listening experience was by and large limited to a smallish selection of Handel's oratorios, a few instrumental concertos and his keyboard works. The rediscovery of Handel's operas during the twentieth century initially set the cause back through appearing to demonstrate that, as far as the modern theatre was concerned, they were archaic constructions that failed to hold water and needed drastic surgery and cosmetic changes before they could be presented. To a certain extent this opinion still survives, although some operations are nowadays more sympathetic to the patient than others. 'Critical appraisal' may have faulted some of Handel's librettos, just as 'moral appraisal' had earlier been brought to bear on his liberal 'borrowings' of musical material from others, both living and dead – with similarly negative conclusions – but our awareness of the breadth of Handel's output is now greater than at any previous period, including his own lifetime.

We are also more voluminously informed than ever before on every aspect of his work and life. My own passion for Handel's music was first sparked by the sheer power of the product – rather like an encounter with a vintage 8-litre Bentley – immediately followed by a desire to see under the bonnet, and to admire, if not to understand, the source of this power. I thus have one foot in the 'Handel is the greatest' camp and the other in the critical world of present-day scholarship. On Handel's moral supremacy we are now allowed to be sceptical or noncommittal, but on the nuts-and-bolts approach to composing – at which he wins hands down – we are surrounded by eager and well-informed researchers, and almost overwhelmed with facts and theories demanding our attention. For me (and I hope for you) such a ready-reference volume as the present publication makes the perfect Baedeker.

CHRISTOPHER HOGWOOD
Cambridge

Preface

Soon after Handel's death on 14 April 1759 literature devoted to him began steadily to flow. John Mainwaring's *Memoirs of the Life of the Late George Frederic Handel* (1760) was the first published biography of its kind devoted to a composer, and it remains indispensable for Handelians today. Over the next century or so, further seminal writings about Handel and his music were penned not just in England by Charles Burney and John Hawkins, but also by the French collector Victor Schoelcher and the German musicologist Friederich Chrysander. During the twentieth century an increasing amount of scholarly (and sometimes unscholarly but very popular) literature was produced that explored all kinds of aspects of the composer's life, music, cultural circle and the intellectual context of his career. Books by Otto Erich Deutsch, Winton Dean, and more recently Donald Burrows and Ruth Smith, have provided abundant sources of fascinating information that throws considerable light on our appreciation of Handel's achievements as a composer, performer, businessman and intellectual figure. Many other scholars have also made important contributions with articles, collections of essays, critical editions of scores, conference papers and performance projects. With such a rich legacy of Handelian literature, it is surprising that the present volume is the first ever compendium devoted to the composer. Whilst other musical geniuses of similar stature who worked in the 'long eighteenth century', (his exact contemporary Bach, but also Mozart, Haydn and Beethoven) have all received one or more major dictionary-style publications collecting much valuable information under one roof, this service has not been undertaken for Handel. The celebration of the 250th anniversary of his death in 2009 is a timely opportunity to redress this.

The Cambridge Handel Encyclopedia will by no means supplant some of the seminal writings that have preceded it (for a thumbnail view of these one could do worse than to consult our list of abbreviations below), but we hope that it performs a valuable function for all kinds of readers eager to have an unprecedented range of information about Handelian topics at their fingertips. Performers, teachers, students, music-lovers, and perhaps even scholars, will undoubtedly learn a few useful things from dipping into these pages.

It scarcely requires justification to claim that such an ambitious 'one-stop-shop' for accessible, up-to-date and illuminating information about Handel is necessary and long overdue. This book is devoted to a composer of consistent and significant popularity, and one who has come to epitomise 'European-ness': Handel was born in Saxony in 1685, spent several years pursuing a glittering career in Italy (1706–10), worked in at least two major German cities (Hamburg and Hanover), spent most of his creative life based in London producing a tremendous variety of music (usually for the theatre), and in 1727 became a naturalised British citizen. From a twenty-first-century perspective, Handel has come to represent what it means to be multi-national. His career was almost as dramatic as the plot of one of his operas, and so his life continues to fascinate his legions of admirers, although we know little about his personal life and there are major gaps in our biographical knowledge. Indeed, Handel remains a figure of interest, admiration and affection principally because of the enduring appeal of his music. A remarkably full amount of his works is preserved more or less intact (it seems that only a few early German works are lost, and perhaps some music composed in Italy only survives in fragmentary form). Moreover, a broad variety of the composer's music has never been out of the repertoire since his own lifetime: *Zadok the Priest* has been performed at every British coronation since 1727, festive performances of *Messiah* are a firmly established tradition (though more seldom at Easter, for which Handel and the oratorio's librettist Charles Jennens intended it), and parts of the *Water Music* and *Music for the Royal Fireworks* have entered the public consciousness. Although the renaissance of Handel's operas has taken longer to permeate public awareness, a few popular arias were long admired in arrangements, such as the ubiquitous 'Largo' based on 'Ombra mai fu' (actually marked *larghetto*) from *Serse*. Even the music used in recent years for the UEFA *Champion's League* (both at football matches and on television broadcasts) is a blatant parody of *Zadok the Priest*. Handel is undoubtedly an icon of the Western classical tradition with very few comparable peers, and his music has never been more widely available, performed and appreciated than it is today. John Hawkins, in his epic *A General History of the Science and Practice of Music*, aptly concluded his tribute to Handel (whom he knew):

> The character of an author is but the necessary result of his works, and as the compositions of Handel are many and various, it is but justice to point out such of them as seem the most likely to be the foundation of his future fame. Many of the excellencies, which as musician recommended him to the favour and patronage of the public during a residence of fifty years in this country, he might perhaps possess in common with a few of the most eminent of his contemporaries; but, till they were taught the contrary by Handel, none were aware of that dignity and grandeur of sentiment which music is capable of conveying, or that there is a sublime in music as there is in poetry. This is a discovery which we owe to the genius and inventive faculty of this great man; and there is little reason to doubt that the many examples of this kind with which his works abound, will continue to engage the admiration of judicious hearers as long as the love of harmony shall exist.

It is hoped this book will be read with pleasure and satisfaction by inquisitive Handelians. We have endeavoured to make it much more than a mere dictionary, and anticipate that its discussion of places, people, venues, major musical works and themes associated with Handel will lead readers happily to browse its content for pleasure, whilst also proving an effective tool for those wishing to lay their hands rapidly on essential information for specific purposes. It is inevitable that some of the articles here will contain discussions that might be familiar to some readers already wise to the Handelian world, but many of this book's articles represent the latest research into areas of Handel scholarship that have been shrouded in erroneous received thinking, garbled by misleading popular opinion, or simply under-explored. Plenty of articles provide valuable new information and ideas (for example, iconography, pasticcios, numerous *cantate con stromenti*, venues, audience, cities and reception). Most of the world's leading Handel scholars contribute articles pertinent to their latest research, and we have invited scholars from other musicological fields to write about the connection between their subject and Handel. Moreover, our list of eighty-eight contributors forms a remarkably broad church of different historians (not only musical, but also architectural, military, political, literary etc.).

The book consists of a simple A–Z dictionary, with a few illuminating illustrations, and helpful cross-references (indicated in small capitals). In a few cases we have dispensed with cross-references to topics that are obvious (Italy, London, Handel). Secondary or minor singers and instrumentalists do not all receive their own individual articles, but full cast lists are given for major works. Castrato voices were frequently described in contradictory terms by contemporary eyewitnesses, and could often change pitch over time, so we have taken the liberty of labelling such singers simply as 'Castrato' (although the range of particular singers is indicated in relevant biographical articles, using the Helmholtz system). In Handel's lifetime there was a difference of eleven days between the Julian calendar, still in use in Britain until 2 September 1752, and the Gregorian calendar, already adopted on the continent. Double dates are given only when the person in question was both on the continent and subsequently moved permanently to Britain. Select bibliographies are placed at the end of each article where it has been deemed useful. We petition hunter-gatherer bibliophiles to forgive us for the fact that our indications of further reading must necessarily serve as friendly signposts for the uninitiated. Inquisitive readers are encouraged to investigate excellent reference works such as *The New Grove Dictionary of Music and Musicians*, *The New Grove Dictionary of Opera*, *Die Musik in Geschichte und Gegenwart* (MGG), and the *Oxford Dictionary of National Biography* (ODNB) in conjunction with the present volume. Abbreviations for commonly cited literature have been used throughout the book (see below for a list). Appendices include various helpful lists, not least a select bibliography, chronology, discography and an up-to-date HWV catalogue of Handel's compositions. Reference to the worklist might occasionally be helpful for identifying full titles of songs, cantatas and chamber sonatas referred to only by HWV number in some articles.

Navigating a course through the vast ocean of Handel studies towards a safe harbour is, as opera seria simile arias frequently tell us, difficult to manage without experienced helmsmen and/or guiding stars. Therefore, we particularly wish to thank all of the contributors, both for their articles and their active interest in guiding the book to fruition; Cambridge University Press, and in particular Vicki Cooper, Becky Jones and Mary Worthington, for their enthusiasm and support for our project; and especially Andrew Jones, Elizabeth Gibson, Ruth Smith and Donald Burrows, who gave us plenty of useful advice throughout the project, not least during the early planning stage. Individual articles in this encyclopedia were improved by helpful suggestions from Jeremy Barlow, Clifford Bartlett, Terence Best, Alessandro Borin, Sandra Bowdler, Melania Bucciarelli, David Coke, Pierre Dubois, Eleanor Selfridge-Field, Philippe Gelinaud, John Greenacombe, Anthony Hicks, Richard King, Ursula and Warren Kirkendale, Claudia

Korsmeier, Kurt Markstrom, Thomas N. McGeary, Clarissa Campbell Orr, John Roberts, Lynda Sayce, Giovanni Andrea Sechi, Carlo Vitali, Mark Windisch and Edwin Werner. We received useful assistance from Angela Baier, Stephan Blaut, Brigitte Gaul, Michael Pacholke and Teresa Ramer-Wünsche. Götz Traxdorf and Jens Wehmann shared material from the library of the Händel-Haus in Halle. We are particularly grateful to the Händel-Haus, and to Sarah Bardwell and Martin Wyatt at the Handel House Museum in London, for their generous donation of several illustrations. Rory Lalwan at Westminster City Archives and John Fisher at the Guildhall Library were very helpful with advice about eighteenth-century maps of London. The staff of the Gerald Coke Handel Collection (at the Foundling Museum) deserve our profound thanks for their friendly assistance behind the scenes, which has frequently gone beyond the call of duty. Above all, we offer our heartfelt gratitude to our families for giving us encouragement and tolerating our obsession.

ANNETTE LANDGRAF and DAVID VICKERS

Abbreviations

AMZ	*Allgemeine Musikalische Zeitung*
Bianconi	L. Bianconi and G. Bianconi (eds.), *I libretti italiani di Georg Friedrich Händel e le loro fonti*, 1* & 1** (Florence, 1992)
Burney	Charles Burney, *A General History of Music from the Earliest Ages to the Present Period*, vol. 4 (London, 1789), ed. F. Mercer (London, 1935; repr. 1957)
Burrows	Donald Burrows, *Handel* (Oxford, 1994)
Burrows, *Chapel Royal*	Donald Burrows, *Handel and the English Chapel Royal* (Oxford, 2005)
Burrows and Dunhill	Donald Burrows and Rosemary Dunhill, *Music and Theatre in Handel's World* (Oxford, 2002)
Burrows and Ronish	Donald Burrows and Martha J. Ronish, *A Catalogue of Handel's Musical Autographs* (Oxford, 1994)
Dean, *Operas*	Winton Dean, *Handel's Operas 1726–1741* (Woodbridge, 2006)
Dean, *Oratorios*	Winton Dean, *Handel's Dramatic Oratorios and Masques* (London, 1959)
Dean and Knapp, *Operas*	Winton Dean and John Merrill Knapp, *Handel's Operas 1704–1726* (rev. edn, Oxford, 1995)
Deutsch	Otto E. Deutsch, *Handel: A Documentary Biography* (New York and London, 1955)
EM	*Early Music*
GHB	*Göttinger Händel-Beiträge*
Harris, *Librettos*	Ellen T. Harris (ed.), *The Librettos of Handel's Operas* (New York, 1989)
Hawkins	John Hawkins, *A General History of the Science and Practice of Music* (London, 1776)
HG	Händel-Gesellschaft edition (ed. Friedrich Chrysander)
HHA	Hallische Händel-Ausgabe
HHB i	*Händel-Handbuch*, vol. 1: Siegfried Flesch, *Lebens- und Schaffensdaten*; Bernd Baselt, *Thematisch-systematisches Verzeichnis: Bühnenwerke* (Kassel and Leipzig, 1978)
HHB ii	*Händel-Handbuch*, vol. 2: Bernd Baselt, *Thematisch-systematisches Verzeichnis: Oratorische Werke; Vokale Kammermusik; Kirchenmusik* (Kassel and Leipzig, 1984)

HHB iii	*Händel-Handbuch*, vol. 3: Bernd Baselt, *Thematisch-systematisches Verzeichnis: Instrumentalmusik; Pasticci und Fragmente* (Kassel and Leipzig, 1986)
HHB iv	*Händel-Handbuch*, vol. 4: *Dokumente zu Leben und Schaffen* (Kassel and Leipzig, 1985)
HJb	*Händel-Jahrbuch*
HWV	Thematisch-systematisches Verzeichnis der Werke Georg Friedrich Händels
JAMS	*Journal of the American Musicological Society*
JRMA	*Journal of the Royal Musical Association*
Mainwaring	[John Mainwaring], *Memoirs of the Life of the Late George Frederic Handel* (London, 1760; repr. 1964, 1967)
MGG	*Die Musik in Geschichte und Gegenwart*, 2nd edn (Kassel etc., 1994–2008)
ML	*Music and Letters*
MT	*The Musical Times*
MQ	*Musical Quarterly*
NG	*New Grove Dictionary of Music and Musicians*, 2nd edn, ed. Stanley Sadie and John Tyrrell (London, 2001)
NG Opera	*New Grove Dictionary of Opera*, ed. Stanley Sadie and Christina Bashford (London, 1992)
PRMA	*Proceedings of the Royal Musical Association*
Sartori	*I libretti italiani a stampa dalle origini al 1800*, 7 vols. (Cuneo, 1990–4)
Smith, *Oratorios*	Ruth Smith, *Handel's Oratorios and Eighteenth-Century Thought* (Cambridge, 1995)
Strohm	Reinhard Strohm, *Essays on Handel and Italian Opera* (Cambridge, 1985)

Aachen. See AIX-LA-CHAPELLE

Academy of Ancient (originally 'Vocal') Music. Founded at the CROWN AND ANCHOR
TAVERN in London in 1726, the Academy of Ancient Music performed a wide-
ranging canonic repertory unique in the eighteenth century. Called the Academy
of Vocal Music until 1731, this professional society included foreign singers (the
castrato Pier Francesco Tosi, for example) until dispute over the choice of living
composers led to the new name and a novel focus on works as old as Thomas
Tallis and Giovanni Palestrina. While the membership came chiefly from the
CHAPEL ROYAL, WESTMINSTER ABBEY, and ST PAUL'S CATHEDRAL, a list
from 1730 included William Hogarth, John Perceval (later Earl of EGMONT),
and numerous TORY gentlemen. Early leaders included Bernard GATES and
Johann Christoph PEPUSCH; Agostino STEFFANI was the first president in
absentia. Programmes balanced Italian with English composers, for example,
Luca Marenzio and Thomas Morley. Recent works by Steffani, Handel or John
Travers tended to be conservative in genre or style. Handel was represented
by the *Utrecht Te Deum and Jubilate* in 1731 (TE DEUM, 1), *ESTHER* in 1742 and
the Cannons anthem *My song shall be alway* in 1752 and 1757 (ANTHEMS, 2).
Nothing close to this repertory was performed elsewhere, save perhaps at the
Sistine Chapel, because its learned and specialised nature kept it on the fringes
of London musical life.

   In the 1750s Travers and Benjamin Cooke took the leadership, and by 1770
the repertory was focused on Handel and eighteenth-century British composers.
A few pieces from the old repertory – William Byrd's setting of *Civitas sancti tui*
twice in the early 1770s, for example – were nonetheless still performed. In the
1780s the society became a public concert series at the Freemasons' Hall under
the leadership of Samuel ARNOLD, offering symphonic works, glees, selections
from Handel's oratorios and a few Elizabethan madrigals. The series may have
lasted until 1800, perhaps even to Arnold's death in 1802.   WILLIAM WEBER

J. Hawkins, *An Account of the Institution and Progress of the Academy of Ancient Music* (London, 1770)
W. Weber, *Rise of Musical Classics in Eighteenth-Century England* (Oxford, 1992)

Accademia degli Arcadi. See ARCADIAN ACADEMY

Aci, Galatea e Polifemo ('Sorge il dì'), HWV 72. Sometimes inaccurately described as
a cantata or pastoral opera, it is actually a serenata in two acts for three solo
voices: Aci (high-lying soprano), Galatea (mezzo-soprano or contralto) and
Polifemo (deep bass). The scoring includes recorder, oboes, trumpets, strings
and continuo; either Handel did not provide an overture or it is not extant. He

completed his autograph score in NAPLES on 16 June 1708, adding on it the remark 'd'Alvito'. This hints that the serenata was intended as a celebration of the nuptials between the Duca d'ALVITO and Princess Beatrice di Montemiletto, which took place in Naples on 19 July 1708. The first performance was probably hosted at the Palazzo d'Alvito at Chiaia on the same day or during the following week. The serenata was commissioned by the bride's aunt, Duchess Aurora SANSEVERINO of Laurenzana (whom MAINWARING called 'Donna Laura'), and the libretto was written by her secretary Nicola GIUVO. It was revived (as La Galatea) on 9 December 1711 at the grand hall of the Palazzo Laurenzana in Piedimonte, to celebrate the marriage of the Duchess's son count Pasquale d'Alife to Marie-Magdalene de Croy (from a French ducal family related to the landgraves of Hessen-Darmstadt). On both occasions, Handel's music was part of lavish musical entertainments which included sets of serenatas and operas by different composers (N. Fago, PORPORA, G. A. PERTI, F. Mancini and others). It seems that Giuvo, who authored most of the librettos, followed a plan drawn from OVID's Metamorphoses, dealing with ill-fated couples. Unfortunately, both young bridegrooms died shortly after their respective nuptials, but, Neapolitan superstition notwithstanding, a further revival (as Polifemo, Galatea ed Aci) took place at the Palazzo Reale on 26 July 1713 for the name-day of Countess Anne von Daun, the four-year-old daughter of the Habsburg viceroy of Naples.

The original cast of singers is uncertain. Some authors have speculated that the remarkable role of Polifemo was intended for either Giuseppe Maria Boschi or Antonio Francesco Carli (both of whom later sang for Handel in Venice and London), but these candidates can be discarded: Polifemo was probably tailored for the Neapolitan priest Antonio Manna, who sang in N. Fago's opera È più caro il piacer doppo le pene for the d'Alvito wedding in 1708 and in four serenatas performed at Piedimonte in 1711. He had served as a bass in the Vienna court chapel with the large monthly salary of 100 Gulden (1700–5), and it is significant that he resumed the role of Polifemo in Galatea (different libretto, music by G. Comito) at Naples in 1722. It is unknown who created the roles of Galatea and Aci; for the 1711 revival they were entrusted to castratos from FLORENCE: Domenico Tempesti, who often sang major roles at Naples from 1705 to 1712, and the less renowned Giovanni Rapaccioli.

Metamorphoses (XIII. 738–89) is the original source of the sad story featuring Galatea (daughter of the sea god Nereus) and her beloved shepherd Acis (son of Faunus and the nymph Symaethis). The giant Polyphemus, the same one-eyed brute described in the Odyssey, yearns after Galatea, trying to lure her from Aci and finally to rape her, but to no avail. Then, at the height of his rage, he hurls a huge rock at Acis and crushes him to death. The shepherd's blood, gushing from beneath the rock, is changed by godly intervention into the river Aci; Galatea rejoins him in the Sicilian sea. Giuvo's finely crafted libretto dwells upon the conventional register of crossed love's labours (after Petrarch, a model dear to Aurora Sanseverino in her own verse production), and contrasts it with grotesque horror, while paying tributes to his patroness's name and heraldry with such keywords as 'aurora' (dawn), 'alloro', equivalent of 'lauro' (laurel) for Laurenzana, and 'aquila' (eagle). Themes, word-choice and particular turns of phrase show affinities to the texts of La TERRA È LIBERATA and DUNQUE SARÀ PUR VERO.

Though apparently not conceived for staged performance, *Aci* elicited from Handel a warm response to character design. Polifemo's awe-inspiring range of two octaves and a fifth (D–a′), exploring gigantic intervallic leaps, well become his monstrous nature, as do the cavernous ending phrases and the conjuration through word-painting of a moth fluttering in the nocturnal shade ('farfalla confusa') in his slow aria 'Fra l'ombre e gli orrori'. The same grotesque imbalance, breaking the boundaries of both metric and melodic regularity, emerges in his forceful 'Precipitoso nel mar che freme', while his entrance aria 'Sibilar l'angui d'Aletto', introduced by an unusual obbligato recitative with two trumpets, forces the usual devices of the *aria di sdegno* into the imitation of hissing snakes and barking dogs. Galatea's vocal character appears more defiant than Aci's, whose subdued statements (with the only exception of 'Che non può la gelosia' and 'Dell'aquila gli artigli') mirror his submission to his lower-pitched beloved. In keeping with the pastoral tradition, depictions of tender feelings and nature's beauty prevail throughout in the lovers' parts, emphasised by sophisticated instrumental colour, such as in Galatea's 'Sforzano a piangere' with oboe and 'S'agita in mezzo all'onde' with recorder, or Aci's lyrical birdsong aria 'Qui l'augel da pianta in pianta' with oboe. Aci's plangent death scene ('Verso già l'alma col sangue') is based on quiet chromatic music from *Dixit Dominus* (Italian and Latin CHURCH MUSIC). Ensembles include the opening duet 'Sorge il dì', where the lovers' voices blend intricately, one trio for each act, and a perfunctory final trio.

Handel's later BORROWINGS from *Aci* notably include the trio 'Caro amico amplesso' altered into a lovers' duet in *PORO* (1731), and Polifemo's arias were reused in *RINALDO* (1711), *SOSARME* (1732) and *ATALANTA* (1736). The Neapolitan serenata bears almost no musical resemblance to Handel's CANNONS setting of the same story (*ACIS AND GALATEA*) composed in 1718, although he inserted seven of its numbers into a bilingual version of *Acis* in 1732.   CARLO VITALI

See also PALAZZI, 10–12

A. Furnari and C. Vitali, 'Händels Italienreise. Neue Dokumente, Hypothesen und Interpretationen', GHB IV (1991)
HHB ii
A. Hicks, 'Handel: Aci, Galatea e Polifemo', CD booklet note (Virgin Veritas, 5 45557 2, 2003)
J. Riepe, 'Händel in Neapel', Ausdrucksformen der Musik des Barock. Passionsoratorium – Serenata – Rezitativ, ed. S. Schmalzriedt (Karlsruhe, 2002)
W. Windzus (ed.), Aci, Galatea e Polifemo, HHA I/5 (Kassel, 2000)

Acis and Galatea, HWV 49[a/b]. Handel did not specify a category of genre for this work, and over time it was referred to as a 'little opera', 'pastoral (entertainment)', 'serenata' and 'masque' (the most widely accepted term today). His musical connections with the popular myth, which harks back to a tale from Book XIII of OVID's *Metamorphoses*, spanned almost four decades of his life: his first setting (*ACI, GALATEA E POLIFEMO*) was written for NAPLES in 1708, and he set it to music again ten years later for his patron James Brydges (later 1st Duke of CHANDOS). The libretto of *Acis and Galatea* is of uncertain authorship, but it might have been a close collaboration between the poets John GAY, Alexander POPE and John HUGHES. The story is a love triangle consisting of the 'pure lovers' Acis (a shepherd) and Galatea (a nymph), and the monstrous cyclops Polyphemus, who is spurned by the horrified Galatea. In a fit of jealous rage, Polyphemus kills Acis with a rock, whereupon the grief-stricken Galatea uses her divine powers to transform the dead Acis into a fountain, so that the two lovers can be united for eternity. Two shepherds, Damon and Coridon, contribute advice to the rival male lovers (Damon to Acis; Coridon to Polyphemus).

Although the autograph of this first version of *Acis and Galatea* (HWV 49[a]) is undated, it was written for a private performance at CANNONS in June 1718. It is unlikely that this was a fully staged performance with scenic action, but perhaps costumes and scene decoration were involved. The only singers that can be traced to the 1718 performance are the tenors James Blackley (Acis) and Francis Rowe (Damon). This early version is marked by several musical peculiarities, including the complete absence of the alto register in both instrumental and vocal scoring; the choruses are for soprano, three tenors and bass, and were sung by the soloists. The players of the CANNONS CONCERT probably performed with one single instrument per part, with oboists doubling on recorders (Handel's scoring makes it clear that the different woodwind instruments were not used simultaneously).

The music is certainly Handel's finest early English masterpiece. The sinfonia is joyously extrovert, the choruses are superb (especially 'Wretched lovers', with its contrasting moods of wistfulness and a witty portrayal of the clumsy Polyphemus's arrival on the scene). The songs for each of the three principal roles are imaginatively characterised and charmingly melodic, and cover a wide expressive range from Acis's mellifluous 'Love in her eyes sits playing' and Polyphemus's rustic 'O ruddier than the cherry' (featuring sopranino recorder solo) to Galatea's pastoral 'Heart, the seat of soft delight' (in which two recorders and rolling string figures gently evoke the bubbling fountain which Galatea has transformed from Acis's corpse). There are two fine accompanied recitatives in different styles: Polyphemus's extraordinarily angry rant 'I rage, I melt, I burn!' and a moving death scene for Acis featuring string-writing of remarkable pathos. The songs for Damon and Coridon, in which their sensible moralising advice consistently falls on deaf ears, are also attractive.

There seems to have been at least one more performance at Cannons in late 1718 or early 1719, but more than a decade passed before *Acis and Galatea* was revived for the London public. In 1731 it was performed as a benefit for the tenor Philip Rochetti at the LINCOLN'S INN FIELDS THEATRE, for which occasion Handel might have lent some material. In June 1732, following an independent performance under the direction of Thomas ARNE, Handel introduced a revised version (HWV 49[b]) that had a run of four performances at the KING'S THEATRE. The *Daily Courant* advertised that Handel's performances would be 'performed by a great Number of the best Voices and Instruments', and that 'There will be no Action on the Stage, but the Scene will represent, in a Picturesque Manner, a rural Prospect, with Rocks, Groves, Fountains and Grotto's; amongst which will be disposed a Chorus of Nymphs and Shepherds, Habits, and every other Decoration suited to the Subject' (Deutsch, p. 293). The heavily revised score drew upon material adapted from both the Naples and Cannons versions, as well as borrowing movements from other cantatas, operas and oratorios (including even the 'Wohin' chorus from the BROCKES PASSION). It grew from a two-part English masque into a three-act bilingual serenata, accommodating an expanded orchestra and choir, and featuring eight soloists (including the Italian opera company soloists Anna STRADA del Pò, SENESINO and Antonio MONTAGNANA). Handel simply merged the librettos of the two earlier works, had some of the Cannons songs translated into Italian and added a few more shepherds, whose names would change back and forth over the coming years. Another four performances were given during the 1732–3 season, and *Acis and Galatea* was part of Handel's concert series at OXFORD in July 1733. In May 1734 he directed a single revival which included Italian arias from Il PASTOR FIDO for Giovanni CARESTINI and Carlo SCALZI.

Two years later Handel performed it twice at COVENT GARDEN, with the role of Acis restored to tenor voice for John BEARD. On this occasion all of the singers were capable of singing in English, but, surprisingly, Handel again used a bilingual version. He did not revert to the all-English version close to the Cannons original until the 1739–40 Lincoln's Inn Fields concert season, when the masque was performed five times with the SONG FOR ST CECILIA'S DAY and various concertos (ORCHESTRAL WORKS). For these performances Handel added an elaborate choral conclusion to the duet 'Happy we', featuring a carillon (INSTRUMENTATION, 3). He revived the bilingual version again in 1741, probably to accommodate the castrato Andreoni, but his last revival at DUBLIN in January 1742 used the 1739/40 all-English version (albeit with a shorter version of the chorus 'Happy we' without carillon).

Although Handel never performed *Acis and Galatea* again, it was among the most performed of his works during his lifetime. John WALSH managed five print-runs of a reduced-score version and even published a subscription-based full score in 1743 (see ALEXANDER'S FEAST). The masque version (HWV 49^a) was arranged by luminaries such as MOZART and MENDELSSOHN, but the bilingual 'serenata' revision (HWV 49^b) is practically unknown today.

ARTIE HEINRICH

J. Butt, 'Acis & Galatea HWV 49^a: G. F. Handel – Original Cannons Performing Version (1718)' (CD booklet note, Linn CKD 319, 2008)
Dean, Oratorios
B. Trowell, 'Acis, Galatea and Polyphemus: A "serenata a tre voci"?', Music and Theatre: Essays in honour of Winton Dean, ed. N. Fortune (Cambridge, 1987)
W. Windszus (ed.), Acis and Galatea (1718 version), HHA I/9.1 (Kassel and Leipzig, 1991)
Georg Friedrich Händel. Aci, Galatea e Polifemo Cantata von 1708. Acis and Galatea, Masque von 1718. Acis and Galatea, italienisch–englische Serenata von 1732. Kritischer Bericht im Rahmen der Hallischen Händel-Ausgabe (Hamburg, 1979)

adaptations. A by-product of Handel's unparalleled popularity in the English-speaking world was the number and variety of arrangements of his works. These extend from complete oratorios and concertos to songs, hymns, organ voluntaries and student pieces for instruments. Most famous of all is the 'Largo' from SERSE, which for more than a century was in most people's minds a sentimental violin or piano solo, but was also brought into service in 1920 as the British Honduras National Anthem, with Latin words. 'The HARMONIOUS BLACKSMITH' and the HALLELUJAH CHORUS are to be found in dozens of arrangements, both vocal and instrumental.

Even in the composer's lifetime marches and songs from his operas had been adapted for use in ballad operas. In later times, the new texts imposed on his melodies often reflect the exalted image of him that arose at the time of the WESTMINSTER ABBEY festivals (HANDEL COMMEMORATION). Samuel ARNOLD, first editor of the collected works, was responsible for three large-scale sacred pasticcios based on selected works of Handel (PASTICCIO, 2). One of these, *Redemption* (1786), remained a feature of the London oratorio concerts for more than twenty years, and was published in vocal score in 1814. Two of the most popular 'anthems' by Handel in Victorian times were in fact parodies of opera songs derived from Arnold's *Redemption*: 'Holy, holy, Lord, God almighty', after 'Dove sei' from *RODELINDA*, and 'Lord, remember David', after 'Rendi 'l sereno al ciglio' from *SOSARME*.

The most numerous reworkings of Handel's melodies were in the form of tunes for hymns and metrical psalms. This practice was pioneered by Methodists (NONCONFORMITY), who had no reservations about singing sacred words to tunes with secular associations. CHARLES WESLEY exhorted singers to 'Plunder the carnal lover; Strip him of ev'ry melting strain, Every melting measure, Music in virtue's cause retain, Rescue the holy pleasure'. At first the choice generally fell on tunes whose structure resembled that of a hymn, such as the march from *RICCARDO PRIMO*, adapted by JOHN WESLEY as early as 1742, 'Sin not, O king' from *SAUL* (adapted 1750), and 'See, see the conquering hero comes' from *JOSHUA* (adapted 1754). With the growth of Handel's reputation as a 'religious' composer, arrangers were more willing to make use of some of his most popular love songs and to tailor their form to fit hymn texts. Even Anglicans began to relax their strictures. Richard Langley, organist of Exeter Cathedral, used three Handel melodies in his hymn collection *Divine Harmony* (1774): 'Sin not, O king'; the minuet from the overture to *BERENICE*; and 'Verdi prati' from *ALCINA*. Handel songs were also effectively adapted as charity hymns (that is, fund-raisers) for the London hospitals.

In 1790 Dr Edward Miller, organist of Doncaster, took an adaptation of 'I know that my redeemer liveth' already popular in dissenting circles, and reduced it still more drastically, bringing it down to 'common metre' (8.6.8.6). He set it to five metrical psalms in his widely used Anglican selection, *Psalms of David*, including Psalm 146, 'The Lord who made both heav'n and earth'. The result was a neatly balanced and appealing tune that was quickly adopted in many churches.

The decisive move was made by Arnold and John Wall Callcott in their influential collection *The Psalms of David for the Use of Parish Churches* (London, 1791). The editors, who enjoyed high prestige in musical circles and in the established Church, stated as one of their aims 'the preservation of many excellent pieces of old and foreign music, which were sinking speedily to oblivion'. The adapted pieces set to metrical psalms in the book included no less than twenty-seven by Handel (compared with only fourteen by other composers). With Anglicans as well as the Nonconformists on board, the fashion for the Handel parody hymn gained steam rapidly. Between 1790 and 1820 hymn tunes based on 'Verdi prati' appeared in 38 printed collections, 'See the conquering hero' in 79, 'Sin not, O king' in 111 and 'I know that my redeemer liveth' in 217. In each case, several different versions were in use. The popularity of these pieces was doubtless one of the reasons for the many misleading attributions of other hymn tunes to Handel, which also reached their highest numbers at this time. An example is the splendid tune 'Hanover', which was in fact the work of William CROFT, but was attributed to Handel in countless publications, beginning in 1767. Another is 'JOY TO THE WORLD'. The fashion for Handel arrangements eventually subsided in Britain, but not in the United States, where in 1998 S. DeWitt Wasson found more than forty different Handel parodies in some 500 twentieth-century hymnals. Most popular of all is a melody based on 'Non via piacer' from *SIROE*, which is the standard American tune for 'While shepherds watched their flocks by night'. NICHOLAS TEMPERLEY

See also ARRANGEMENTS

N. Temperley, *The Hymn Tune Index*, vol. 1 (Oxford, 1998)

Addison, Joseph (b. Milston, Wilts. 1 May 1672; d. London, 17 June 1719). Politician, poet, journalist and dramatist who initially intended to pursue a diplomatic career. On his way home from Italy in 1704 he may have met the young Handel in HAMBURG. Addison was a member of the politically, socially and culturally influential Kit-Cat Club, whose circle included Jonathan Swift, William CONGREVE and Richard Steele. His English opera libretto *Rosamond*, set by Thomas Clayton (1707), was produced as a handsome quarto WORDBOOK by Jacob TONSON the first, but its performances in 1707 were poorly received. His tragedy *Cato* (1713) held the stage for decades, but Addison is chiefly remembered for his lively periodical writing, which began with an essay for *The Tatler* in 1709 and flourished when, with Steele, in 1711 he launched the hugely successful journal *The Spectator*. He commented in *The Spectator* on Handel's first London opera *RINALDO*, reflecting on the inherent inconsistencies in and extravagant effects of Italian opera (6 March 1711, *Spectator* No. 5, vol. 1, 18–22). LESLIE M. M. ROBARTS

The Spectator, 2nd edn, 2 vols. (London, 1713)

Adlington Hall. See Elizabeth LEGH

Admeto, Re di Tessaglia, HWV 22. First performed at the KING'S THEATRE on 31 January 1727, *Admeto* was among the most successful of Handel's operas for the Royal Academy of Music (OPERA COMPANIES, 2). GEORGE I reportedly attended all nineteen performances that season; it was also among the works implicated in the much-touted competition between CUZZONI and FAUSTINA Bordoni, which left its mark in contemporary gossip, engravings and printed pamphlets (RIVAL QUEENS). The original cast featured:

Admeto	SENESINO (castrato)
Alceste	Faustina Bordoni (soprano)
Antigona	Francesca CUZZONI (soprano)
Ercole	Giuseppe BOSCHI (bass)
Trasimede	Antonio Baldi (castrato)
Orindo	Anna DOTTI (alto)
Meraspe	Giovanni Battista Palmerini (bass)

George I's interest in *Admeto* might well be a result of the libretto's Hanoverian lineage. Aurelio AURELI's *L'Antigona delusa da Alceste*, set to music by Pietro

Andrea Ziani, was first performed in VENICE in 1660, and dedicated to the two Dukes of Brunswick-Lüneburg: Georg Wilhelm and Ernst August, the father of George I. After a number of Italian revivals, the original version travelled to HANOVER with the young Dukes, and was subsequently adapted by poet Ortensio MAURO and composer Matthio Trento under the title L'Alceste for presentation at the Hanoverian opera in 1679 and 1681. The 1681 Hanover libretto was likely the basis for the revisions made for Handel, which have yet to be securely attributed to either of Handel's usual collaborators, Nicola HAYM and Paolo ROLLI. The Hanover L'Alceste was likely the first opera the young George Ludwig would have seen as a young man; Handel's Admeto of 1727 was also likely the last opera George I attended before his death in June of that year.

The opera retains much of the complexity of plot, irony and playfulness that was Carnival's legacy to Venetian opera. Based loosely on EURIPIDES's The Alcestis, Handel's Admeto, Re di Tessaglia dramatises the tragicomic tale of King Admetus (Admeto) and the death and rebirth of his wife Alcestis (Alceste) who sacrifices her life in order to save that of her husband, is ultimately rescued from the Underworld and returned to her husband by Hercules. Aureli combined this with a secondary plot involving the exiled Trojan Princess Antigona who had been engaged to Admeto prior to his marriage. Admeto's brother Trasimede had become so enamoured of Antigona that he had given his brother a portrait of a woman of inferior beauty; Admeto broke the engagement and married Alceste, while Trasimede continued to swoon over the portrait of Antigona. Much of the opera concerns the complications caused by these games with portraits and identity, which are somewhat simplified in the version set by Handel: Trasimede contends with his love for the portrait and his desire for the woman who resembles that portrait; Admeto, who realises Trasimede's deception, also falls in love with the portrait, and resolves to marry Antigona in the aftermath of his wife's presumed death. Only after Alceste (disguised as a soldier in order to test her husband fidelity) stops Trasimede from killing his brother, is the truth revealed. Admeto chooses – albeit with undisguised ambivalence and at Antigona's urging – to return to his wife, while Trasimede's desires remain unfulfilled, a slightly muted conclusion that eschews the perfect lieto fine, arguably absorbing some of Euripides's play.

The mixture of comedy, intrigue and pathos – combined with more than a touch of the supernatural – inspired Handel to compose a brilliant and varied score. The eponymous hero's music plumbs the full range of human suffering. For example, in the opening scene Admeto's physical pain, inflicted by the knife-thrusting spectres in the 'Ballo di larve' (one of several pantomimic dances in the opera), inspires an extended passage of highly expressive accompanied recitative ('Orride larve') featuring remarkable harmonic juxtapositions and violent shifts in affect and tempo, before giving way to the calm despair of the aria 'Chiudetevi miei lumi'. Admeto's horrors return in II.viii for yet another startling accompanied recitative, 'Quivi tra questi solitari orrori', followed by the contrapuntally rich lament 'Ah, si morrò', in which the King's desire for his own death is captured by an obsessive semiquaver motive. Sung to the sleeping Admeto, Alceste's aria 'Luci care' (I.iii), with the unexpected introduction of the transverse flute at the end of the prima parte, provides an uncanny vision of the afterlife in a moment of extraordinary tenderness, while Antigona laments her lost love for Admeto with the gentle siciliano 'Da tanti affanni' (II.vi). The numerous playful and comedic moments include Trasimede's fantasies about Antigona as Diana in 'Se l'arco avessi', a minuet that invokes the huntress goddess with a pair of horns (I.ix), or the cleverly aborted da capo aria 'Io ti bacio' (III.iv), in which Antigona kisses the portrait of Admeto.

The opera was revived twice under Handel's direction. Nine performances in the 1727–8 season introduced only one new singer, the soprano Mrs WRIGHT, who replaced Anna Dotti's male servant Orindo with a court lady named Orinda, the change in gender necessitating cuts in both plot and music. The most drastic abbreviations were made for the six performances for the 1731–2 opera season. Of the original cast, only Senesino remained, and even his role was cut considerably; Orindo was omitted entirely, and the casting of Alceste with a contralto (Anna Bagnolesi) and Ercole with a tenor (Giovanni Battista PINACCI) necessitated some infelicitous transpositions and cuts. The opera was also adapted for performances in HAMBURG (1729, 1731) and BRUNSWICK (1729, 1732 and 1739).

A third revival in 1754 at the King's Theatre under the direction of Francesco VANNESCHI, without the composer's involvement, marks the final perform-ance of any Handel opera during the composer's lifetime and was, according to Charles BURNEY, received with 'indifference'. It may be this on this occa-sion that the autograph of the opera was lost, for it remains the only one of Handel's extant operas for which no complete autograph survives, and is also one from which relatively few borrowings have been documented. The score was completed on 10 November 1726, but the earliest extant manuscript is from the so-called Malmesbury collection (SOURCES AND COLLECTIONS, 12), which had belonged to Handel's admirer, Elizabeth LEGH. Legh may have been Admeto's first champion. According to her sister Mrs Pendarves (later DELANY), Legh was 'out of her senses' after hearing the first full rehearsal of Admeto. Other important champions of the work include Burney, who provides a vivid description of each number of the opera, and J. J. Quantz, listed as one of the subscribers to the first printed edition, published by CLUER.   WENDY HELLER

S. Aspden, 'The "Rival Queans" and the Play of Identity in Handel's Admeto', Cambridge Opera Journal 18/3 (2006), 301–31
Burney
D. Burrows and R. D. Hume. 'George I, the Haymarket Opera Company and Handel's Water Music', EM 19 (1991), 323–43
Dean, Operas
Harris, Librettos
W. Heller, 'The Beloved's Image: Handel's Admeto and the Statue of Alcestis', JAMS 58/3 (2005), 559–638
S. McCleave, 'Handel's Unpublished Dance Music: A Perspective to His Approach on Composition', GHB VI (1996), 127–42
S. Ograjenšek, 'From Alessandro (1726) to Tolomeo (1728): The Final Royal Academy Operas', Ph.D. dissertation (University of Cambridge, 2005)
Strohm

aesthetics. In the seventeenth century and the first half of the eighteenth century, music was still generally thought of as one of the 'Sister Arts' – alongside poetry and painting – which were all considered imitative. Of all the arts, poetry was considered to be the most excellent. James HARRIS – a friend of

Handel's – noted in his 1744 treatise 'concerning, Music, Painting, and Poetry' that, in the union of poetry and music, 'poetry must ever have the precedence, its utility, as well as dignity, being by far the more considerable'. Consequently, music was as it were in a state of dependence upon poetry and, in vocal music, it was expected to follow the meaning of the words as closely as possible. Though Harris acknowledged that the imitations of music were less precise than those of painting, he still gave credence to the idea that music was basically an imitative art. Such a conception accounts in particular for the common practice of 'word-painting' which consisted in imitating the manifest meaning of the words through musical figurations (e.g. a rising scale on words suggestive of elevation, or a low-pitched note on words suggestive of fall; quick divisions to express a flight or a slow movement and soft tones to express death or sorrow, etc.). Although numerous instances of word-painting are to be found in Handel's works, his art generally reflects a departure from this central tenet of baroque musical aesthetic. Servile imitation was made subservient to the quest for *expression*. Again and again, Handel's works are a plea for the ability of music to rival poetry as the most powerful of all the arts and to express intense, complex passions instead of simply being a graceful accomplice to poetry.

Even before Charles AVISON attempted to formulate a theory of musical expression in his *Essay on Musical Expression* (1751), Handel managed to go beyond the former theories of music that defined it as either a 'science' akin to mathematics, or an imitative art. Handel's music thus corresponded to the new conception of the link between nature and music that was emerging: music was meant to express feelings or passions rather than abstractly formalise – or 'imitate' – the inner workings of the universe.

Furthermore, Handel's art was to be gradually equated with the sublime, an aesthetic category originally borrowed from literature. The main characteristics of his music were thought to be its powerful effects and the fact that irregularity, rather than a strict adherence to the correctness of rules, prevailed in it. In his influential *Philosophical Enquiry into the Origin of our Ideas of the Sublime and Beautiful* (London, 1757), Edmund Burke explained that the sublime resulted from all such excess in size, bulk or power as might create a feeling of terror. The energy, power and vitality of Handel's composition thus came to be associated with the idea of the musical sublime. For example, John Potter admired Handel's 'irregular flights of fancy' and the 'grandeur and sublimity' of his style. As for John MAINWARING, Handel's first biographer, he insisted upon the musician's native 'genius' and explained that 'those who have an inventive genius will depart from the common rules, and please us the more by such deviations'. In this way, Handel could be put on a par with Shakespeare, Homer or MILTON.

All this contributed to the upgrading of music which could now be considered equal, if not superior, to the other arts and literature. Handel's supporters, such as William HAYES, admired him precisely for the unexpected and irregular aspects of his music. The often expressed comparison between Handel and John DRYDEN testified to the fact that, with Handel, music had reached a status equal to that of literature. The great HANDEL COMMEMORATION at WESTMINSTER ABBEY and the Pantheon in 1784 and the following years saw the culmination of that transformation of Handel's art into large, 'sublime' performances which took on overtly patriotic overtones. In his *Account of the Musical Performances in Westminster Abbey and the Pantheon in Commemoration of Handel* (London, 1785), Charles BURNEY wrote that 'Handel was always aspiring at numbers in his scores and in his orchestra; and nothing can express his grand conceptions, but an omnipotent band: the generality of his productions in the hands of a few performers, is like the club of Alcides, or the bow of Ulysses, in the hands of a dwarf'. The distortion in the performance of Handel's works was thus given a theoretical justification. At the beginning of the nineteenth century, William Crotch endeavoured to write a coherent theory of the musical sublime (*Substance of several Courses of Lectures on Music read in the University of Oxford and the Metropolis*, London, 1831) in which he hailed Handel as the greatest composer in this style. Following a now well-established tradition, Crotch considered Handel's sacred oratorios, and in particular their great choral fugues, to be the epitome of sublime music.   PIERRE DUBOIS

C. Avison, *An Essay on Musical Expression*, London 1752, ed. P. Dubois (Aldershot, 2004)

E. Burke, *A Philosophical Enquiry into the Origin of our Ideas of the Sublime and Beautiful* (1757)

W. Crotch, *The Substance of Several Courses of Lectures on Music read in the University of Oxford and the Metropolis* (London, 1831)

P. Degott, *Haendel et ses oratorios: des mots pour les notes* (Paris, 2001)

J. Harris, *Three Treatises, concerning Art; Music, Painting, & Poetry; Happiness* (London, 1744)

P. Kivy, *The Possession and the Possessed: Handel, Mozart, Beethoven, and the Idea of Musical Genius* (New Haven and London, 2001)

J. Potter, *Observations on the State of Music and Musicians* (London, 1762)

C. L. Johnson, '"Giant Handel" and the Musical Sublime', *Eighteenth-Century Studies* 19/4 (Summer 1986), 515–33

Agrippina, HWV 6. Handel's second Italian opera, premiered at VENICE's Teatro SAN GIOVANNI GRISOSTOMO from 26 December 1709 to late January or early February 1710. MAINWARING reports an enthusiastic reception over a run of twenty-seven nights (not an exceptional number for Venice's leading opera house), during which 'The theatre, at almost every pause, resounded with shouts and exclamations of *viva il caro Sassone!* and other expressions of approbation too extravagant to be mentioned'. Further stagings took place in NAPLES' Teatro San Bartolomeo, with substantial cuts and additional music by Francesco Mancini (1713), at HAMBURG's GÄNSEMARKT (1718), and probably in Vienna (1719). The title role refers to Julia Agrippina, the second wife to the Roman Emperor Claudius. The action, set in Rome about AD 50, features the schemes of the ambitious Empress to put the son of her previous marriage, Nerone (Nero), on the throne. Claudio (Claudius), who at first is believed drowned in a shipwreck, names his rescuer Ottone (Otho) as his successor. By seducing the influential freedmen Pallante (Pallas) and Narciso (Narcissus), Agrippina successfully discredits Ottone in the eyes of both his betrothed Poppea (Poppaea), and of Claudio, who secretly covets the same young lady. At Agrippina's instigation, Claudio orders Poppea to marry Nerone, but Ottone renounces the throne in order to claim Poppea as his bride, thus paving the way to Agrippina's triumph. Then the goddess Giunone (Juno) descends from heaven to bless the nuptials. Apart from Juno and the cameo role of the servant Lesbo, all characters are drawn from the histories of TACITUS and SUETONIUS, yet their behaviour is largely fictionalised, as customary in the Venetian opera tradition since

Monteverdi. Erotic intrigue and satire of gullible royals prevail; the general tone is light and non-judgemental, often close to comedy.

Given the contemporary historic context of the War of the SPANISH SUCCESSION, and the strong pro-Habsburg standing of the Grimani family, it is likely that the subject includes some political innuendo. For example, Nero and Otho may have reminded the audience of the competing pretenders, Philippe of Anjou and Charles of Austria. Claudius is described in the libretto's foreword as 'feeble-spirited, all given over to luxury, listless, and amorous' despite his former military conquests. This portrait fits the ageing Louis XIV of France, the leader of the anti-imperial party, much better than Pope Clement XI, whom the Handel literature sometimes mentions in this regard. Madame de Maintenon, then second (secret) wife of Louis, was indeed noted for her informal influence on matters of state, and her possible identification with the opera's protagonist is suggested by her grandfather's name, Agrippa d'Aubigné, an outstanding soldier and statesman similar to Agrippina's grandfather Marcus Vipsanius Agrippa.

This circumstantial evidence may support the traditional attribution of the anonymous libretto of *Agrippina* to the imperial diplomat Vincenzo GRIMANI, who may have met Handel in ROME some time between 1706 and 1708 and at Naples in July 1708. Hiring the budding German composer for his family theatre in Venice for the purpose of political propaganda would have been a brilliant, if daring, move. Nonetheless, the only hard evidence for Grimani's authorship of *Agrippina*, a printing licence published in 1973 by Remo Giazotto, is a manifest forgery, while a similarly politically oriented guess concerning the libretto for *ACI, GALATEA E POLIFEMO* has been refuted by recent research.

Handel's cast of singers was as follows:

Claudio	Anton Francesco Carli (bass)
Agrippina	Margherita DURASTANTI (soprano)
Nerone	Valeriano Pellegrini (castrato)
Poppea	Diamante Maria Scarabelli (soprano)
Ottone	Francesca VANINI-BOSCHI (contralto)
Pallante	Giuseppe BOSCHI (bass)
Narciso	Giuliano Albertini (castrato)
Lesbo	Nicola Pasini (bass)
Juno	? (contralto)

This is confirmed by both the original printed libretto and an anonymous eighteenth-century Venetian manuscript *Indice de' drammi di San Giovanni Grisostomo*, although neither source discloses who sang Juno or the identity of the librettist, and only the latter mentions 'Signore Giorgio Federico Hendel' as the composer. Although the autograph score at the British Library is incomplete, several period sources allow a reliable reconstruction. An early copy of the score now in Vienna suggests that for some performances Durastanti might have been replaced by Elena Croci Viviani, a soprano from Bologna who later sang in London (although not for Handel). Two starring basses such as Carli (with a phenomenal range and a sepulchral low register) and Boschi (more baritone-like in his tessitura, and an energetic actor) were a rare occurrence in the same cast. Handel exploited their duality to humorous effect, as he did with the neatly expressive but restrained soprano of Durastanti versus the coloratura skill of Scarabelli, among the highest-paid female sopranos at the turn of the century. Pellegrini was a high castrato of uncommon merit as to agility and range, at least in the generation preceding CAFFARELLI and FARINELLI. Pasini was an ordinary church bass serving at St Mark's; Francesca Vanini-Boschi, if limited in range, was a specialist in lively trouser roles. Handel's overall satisfaction with the company at San Giovanni Grisostomo is shown by the high rate of his later invitations to London bestowed on them.

Durastanti is a particular case. The fact that she was allowed to sing a suitcase aria from *La RESURREZIONE* ('Ho un non so che nel cor') at a climactic point (I.xviii), her show-stopping virtuosic duel with an obbligato oboe in 'L'alma mia fra le tempeste', her highly dramatic and formally irregular 'Pensieri' (II.xiii), give evidence of Handel's commitment to showing her in the most favourable light as a performer, in apparent continuity with their ideal collaboration earlier at RUSPOLI's in Rome.

Appealing and entertaining as it is, *Agrippina* is hardly a forward-looking work, but it is rather the culmination of a style that would be soon out of date. The variety of short pieces other than full da capo arias (ariosos, ariettas, cavatinas) and of ensembles such as trio, quartet and two choruses, outnumber by far more modern features. Of its 48 arias 41 stem from previous works by Handel himself or are BORROWINGS from different composers. Nevertheless, from the opening sinfonia the instrumental writing is cleverer and grander than contemporary Italian audiences were accustomed to: chromaticism, metre changes, modulation and compelling themes are already Handel at his best. No wonder that Venetian patrons 'were thunderstruck with the grandeur and sublimity of his style' (Mainwaring, pp. 52–3).   CARLO VITALI

Bianconi
G. J. Buelow, 'Handel's Borrowing Techniques: Some Fundamental Questions from a Study of *Agrippina* (Venice, 1709)', GHB II (1986)
Dean and Knapp, *Operas*
Harris, *Librettos*
H. S. Saunders, 'Handel's *Agrippina*: The Venetian Perspective', GHB III (1989)
J. Sawyer, 'Irony and Borrowing in Handel's Agrippina', ML 80/4 (1999), 531–59
Strohm
H. C. Wolff, 'L'opera comica nel sec. XVII a Venezia e l'Agrippina di Händel (1709)', *Nuova rivista musicale italiana* 7 (1973), 39–50

Agrippina condotta a morire. See *DUNQUE SARÀ PUR VERO*

Ah, che troppo ineguali. See CHURCH MUSIC, ITALIAN AND LATIN

Ah! crudel, nel pianto mio, HWV 78. An accompanied cantata for soprano, oboes, violins, viola and basso continuo, *Ah! crudel* is the plaint of a lover whose beloved is cruel and disdainful. It is likely that the cantata was written in ROME for RUSPOLI, but no specific date for its composition is known as a bill for copying the work only appears in the Ruspoli account books on 10 October 1711, long after Handel left Italy. A striking accompanied recitative before the third and final aria depicts the downpours, thunder and lightning of a fierce storm, which the lover compares to the beloved's 'threatening look'.   ELLEN T. HARRIS

W. and U. Kirkendale, *Music and Meaning: Studies in Music History and the Neighbouring Disciplines* (Florence, 2007)

Aix-la-Chapelle (Aachen). German city on the borders of Belgium and the NETHER-LANDS, originally a Roman spa called Aquisgranum. From 768 onwards the favourite residence of Charlemagne (742–814) and the principal coronation site of the Holy Roman Emperor and of German kings from 936 to the 1560s. The most famous building is the cathedral, built 790–805 by Charlemagne (who is buried there).

During Handel's times it was a prosperous imperial free Catholic city, situated in the Duchy of Jülich at the outmost frontiers of Limbourg and widely reputed as a spa. Miraculous recoveries were attributed to its warm springs, even for illnesses where cures in other places had no effect. During the spa season it was also a fashionable place and a destination for many important international visitors, including numerous aristocrats.

According to newspapers Handel stayed in Aix-la-Chapelle in September and October 1737 to recover from his 'paraletick disorder' (HANDEL, 16). MAINWARING and HAWKINS gave the wrong year and the plaque at the Elisenbrunnen fountain incorrectly gives the date for Handel's stay as 1735. Recent research has established that Handel was cured in Burtscheid, a small independent market town near Aix-la-Chapelle, but he played the organ in the 'principal church' (the cathedral) of the city.   ANNETTE LANDGRAF

F. Blondel, *Thermarum Aquisgranensium et Porcetanarum elucidatio thaumaturgia* (Aquisgrani, 1688)
A. Landgraf, 'Aachen und Burtscheid zu Händels Zeit', HJb 50 (2004)
HHB iv, 280–5
K. L. v. Pöllnitz, *Amusemens des eaux d'Aix-la-Chapelle* (Amsterdam, 1736)

Aix-la-Chapelle, Treaty of. See War of the AUSTRIAN SUCCESSION

Alberti, Johann Friedrich (b. Tönning/Schleswig, 11 Jan. 1642; d. Merseburg/Saxony-Merseburg, 14 June 1710). Organist and composer. He studied theology, law and philosophy in Rostock, from 1661 in Leipzig. After later studying music in Leipzig and DRESDEN he became court and cathedral organist in Merseburg around 1665/70 until he suffered a stroke in 1698. Johann Gottfried Walther, Johann MATTHESON and Wolfgang Caspar Printz all praised his counterpoint. A now missing book of manuscript music dated 1698 and bearing Handel's initials included some of his compositions.

KLAUS-PETER KOCH (Trans. ANGELA BAIER)

[W. Coxe], *Anecdotes of George Frederick Handel, and John Christopher Smith* (London, 1799; facsimile edn, ed. P. M. Young, New York, 1979), 6n.
HHB iv
J. Mattheson, *Grundlage einer Ehren-Pforte* (Hamburg, 1740)
Ph. Spitta, 'Art. Alberti, Johann Friedrich', *Allgemeine Deutsche Biographie*, vol. 1 (Leipzig 1875)

Alceste, HWV 45. Incidental music for a play by Tobias SMOLLETT, composed by Handel between 27 December 1749 and 8 January 1750. The song texts were written by Thomas MORELL. The ambitious production was to be designed by Giovanni Niccolò Servandoni, stage architect of the French court, and scheduled to be performed by a large orchestra, actors, singers and dancers, at John RICH's COVENT GARDEN Theatre. The venture was abandoned for unknown reasons. Since the text of the play is lost, the dramatic action can only be reconstructed by consulting the few stage directions in Handel's manuscript score. It is also unclear whether his music for *Alceste* has been preserved in its entirety or whether parts of it are missing. The autograph manuscript is extant only in various fragments, which contain a four-movement overture, a 'Grand Entrée', probably used for a ballet interlude, and seven scenes set to music:

1. A wedding scene, consisting of three choruses and an aria, celebrating the royal couple Alceste and Admetus.
2. An aria sung by the muse Calliope on Admetus's sick bed.
3. A scene sequence in the Underworld beginning with an aria for Charon sung at the banks of the River Styx, followed by a chorus and an aria welcoming Alceste in 'Pluto's Palace' and in Elysium.
4. Another aria for Calliope, who is trying to comfort Admetus.
5. A scene in which a siren appears as Thetis's messenger to her son Alcides.
6. A Symphony and a choir for Alcides's entrance.
7. A final scene in which Apollo announces himself in recitative and exhorts the muses to praise Alcides, followed by a divertissement with dances and a final chorus.

Of the 'Balli', only the first and the last dance have been preserved. It is also unclear when another two-movement overture (later included in *JEPHTHA*) was played. Perhaps it was used as an act tune; scale motifs in its last movement are elsewhere used to accompany the entrances of Apollo and Alcides. Handel notated 'Act IV' into the Styx scene, which suggests that *Alceste* was not intended as a two-act afterpiece (as surmised by Fiske), but a five-act drama modelled on the classical tragedy by EURIPIDES.

In the extant music only the gods, sirens and muses sing; the main characters Alceste, Admetus and Alcides do not. The role of Calliope was written for Cecilia Arne (YOUNG), that of the Siren for her sister Esther YOUNG, that of Apollo for Thomas LOWE and that of Charon for Gustavus WALTZ (the choruses included a second soprano, Miss Faulkner). These were not merely singing actors, but accomplished soloists for whom Handel wrote demanding da capo arias. It is noteworthy that he set Calliope's two arias 'Gentle Morpheus' and 'Come Fancy' twice respectively, although no changes in the cast were planned. The versions resemble each other in form and in the technical demands made upon the singer, but differ markedly in musical style: the original cradling motifs of 'Gentle Morpheus', typical for slumber scenes in baroque opera, are replaced by sentimental sighing motifs in the second version; the rather old-fashioned first version of 'Come Fancy', an Andante larghetto in 12/8 time, is replaced by an energetic Allegro, divided into regular period structures of mostly four bars, in which virtuosity is not expressed by long-winded coloratura but by graceful trill motifs. It seems as if Handel and Morell had worked on different alternatives at the same time since the textual versions of the alternative arias also show slight variations.

Music originally composed for a project that came to grief was later adapted for The *CHOICE OF HERCULES*. Handel reused some pieces from *Alceste* in more or less their original forms (such as the aria 'Enjoy the sweet Elysian grove' and the choruses), although other arias were substantially revised. He included another three numbers in his 1751 revivals of *ALEXANDER BALUS* and *BELSHAZZAR.*

CHRISTINE MARTIN (Trans. ANGELA BAIER)

Dean, *Oratorios*
O. E. Deutsch, 'Poetry Preserved in Music: Bibliographical Notes on Smollett and Oswald, Handel and Haydn', *Modern Language Notes* (Baltimore, Feb. 1948), 657, 679
L. Finscher, 'Händels "Alceste', *Göttinger Händel-Tage 1960* (Göttingen, 1960), 18 ff.
R. Fiske, *English Theatre Music in the Eighteenth Century*, 2nd edn (Oxford, 1986)
HHB ii
R. G. King, 'Who Wrote the Texts for Handel's Alceste?', MT 150/1906 (Spring 2009)

Alchemist, The. Probably the first music composed by Handel to be heard on the London stage, this is an arrangement of nine dance movements that were performed as act tunes in Ben JONSON's comedy *The Alchemist* at the Queen's Theatre (see KING's THEATRE) in 1710. Eight of them were taken from the overture to Handel's *RODRIGO.* The anonymous adaptation (formerly HWV 43) was published by WALSH under the title *Musick in the Play call'd the Alchimist by an Italian Master* in 1710 and again in 1733, together with other incidental music performed in the play, including six opera arias by Handel and works by CORELLI, VIVALDI and GEMINIANI.

CHRISTINE MARTIN (Trans. ANGELA BAIER)

C. A. Price, 'Handel and The Alchemist: His First Contribution to the London Theatre', MT 116 (1975), 787–8

Alcina, HWV 34. Italian opera. The plot originated in cantos 6–7 of Ludovico ARIOSTO's *Orlando furioso*, and concerns the Christian knight Ruggiero's captivity on the enchanted island of Alcina – a beguiling sorceress who discards her lovers by turning them into rocks, wild beasts and trees. Ruggiero's spouse Bradamante (disguised as the soldier 'Ricciardo') and her governor Melisso arrive at the island, fend off Alcina's flirtatious sister Morgana (who is attracted to 'Ricciardo'), and attempt to bring the corrupted and wanton Ruggiero to his senses. After cruelly renouncing Bradamante, Ruggiero is restored to his right mind by Melisso's magic ring, recognises the true horrors and temporal nature of Alcina's decadent realm and is devastated by his recent treatment of Bradamante. The lovers are reconciled, and Ruggiero regains his heroic qualities, whereas Alcina's first taste of rejection causes her powers to crumble. Ruggiero defeats Alcina's soldiers and monsters, and wins the admiration of her long-suffering captain Oronte (who has been ill-treated by his inconstant lover Morgana). Alcina is confronted and openly denounced by the courageous boy Oberto, who seeks his shipwrecked father Astolfo (whom she spitefully turned into a lion), and Ruggiero uses the magic ring to smash the source of Alcina's power, thereby liberating her victims.

The text of Handel's opera was adapted from the anonymous libretto *L'isola di Alcina*, first set to music by Riccardo Broschi for ROME in 1728. Handel might have acquired a copy of the libretto during his trip to Italy in 1729 (HANDEL, 15), but it is not known to what extent he was involved in revising the text for his own setting. No Italian literary collaborator has been identified. Handel completed the score on 8 April, during the middle of a run of five performances of *ATHALIA* (receiving its first London performances). Although *Alcina* seems to have been composed at a rapid pace, the autograph score contains evidence of the composer's self-critical revisions, considerable attention to small musical details, and his concern for dramatic subtleties. There were two completed movements in the score that were discarded during the compositional process, and both feature musical material that was transferred to the contemporary performances of *Athalia*: Ruggiero's virtuoso aria 'Bramo di trionfar' (I.viii) was adapted into a new setting of Josabeth's 'Through the land so lovely blooming', and the energetic first setting of the chorus 'Questo è il cielo di contenti' (sung by Alcina's attendants in I.ii) was reused for the opening movement of the Organ Concerto, Op. 4 No. 4 (ORCHESTRAL WORKS, 5), and replaced in the score of *Alcina* by a gentle 'larghetto'.

John Christopher SMITH SENIOR wrote out the verbal texts of some recitatives into the autograph before the composer proceeded to fill in the vocal and basso continuo parts. Handel's preparation of the music was further aided by his BORROWING musical ideas from various sources. Morgana's 'Tornami a vagheggiar' was based on words and music from his own old Roman cantata *OH, COME CHIARE E BELLE* (composed twenty-seven years earlier), and the chorus 'Dall'orror di notte cieca', in which Alcina's victims are transformed back to life, was modelled on an aria from *La TERRA È LIBERATA* that had originally served to illustrate Apollo's amazement when the nymph Daphne transforms herself into a laurel tree. Alcina's 'Mi restano le lagrime' was based on a musical theme used three years earlier for SENESINO's 'Ecco alle mie catene' in *EZIO*, but with words taken from Handel's sketches for the abandoned opera *TITUS, l'EMPEREUR*. The composer also used ideas from works by other composers: Ruggiero's arias 'La bocca vaga', 'Mi lusinga' and 'Sta nell'ircana' were influenced by material from TELEMANN's cantata collection *Der Harmonische Gottesdienst*, and the second setting of 'Questo è il cielo di contenti' used music from Telemann's *Musique de table*; 'Bramo di trionfar' was based on music by KEISER, and BONONCINI's opera *Xerse* yielded ideas for Bradamante's 'È gelosia' and Alcina's accompagnato 'Ah! Ruggiero crudel'.

Ruggiero's 'Mi lusinga dolce affetto' (II.iii), in which the hero penitently realises his cruelty towards Bradamante, originally had an extended opening ritornello, but Handel's deletion of half a dozen bars focused more immediately upon Ruggiero's sorrowful entry (a falling scale that harks back to the melodic and sentimental qualities of Coridon's 'Would you gain the tender creature' in *ACIS AND GALATEA*). The composer also took particular care over Alcina's C minor lament 'Ah! mio cor' (II.viii), deleting bars, and making copious changes to both vocal and orchestral parts in order to maximise the pathos of the sorceress's awakening experience of rejection. Moreover, Handel superbly conveys the contrast between Alcina's deteriorating powers and the restoration of Ruggiero as a virtuous hero: Ruggiero's acquisition of wisdom and enlightenment is evident in the famous aria 'Verdi prati', in which notably economical and dignified music is used for his (undeniably nostalgic) observation about the evil artifice of the island, whereas Alcina concludes the Act with a complicated soliloquy featuring an extraordinary accompanied recitative ('Ah! Ruggiero crudel!') and an explosive coloratura rage aria ('Ombre pallide') that clearly convey her emotional turbulence and impotent rage. In Act III, Ruggiero's return to heroic stature and action is celebrated with plenty of style in 'Sta nell'ircana' (featuring two horns), whereas two scenes later Alcina's broken-hearted soliloquy

'Mi restano le lagrime' (in the unusual key of F sharp minor, and with a series of unexpected diminished fifths in the violins) privately reveals her unprecedented vulnerability.

Bradamante is the finest role Handel wrote for M. C. NEGRI, and the arias for Morgana, Oronte and Oberto (all written for English singers) are consistently inventive and expressive. Oberto is the only character devoid of hypocrisy, and is also the only character openly to confront and denounce Alcina for her evil-doing in a showpiece aria ('Barbara! io ben lo so', inserted after Handel had completed the rest of the score). The variety of musico-dramatic devices in the opera was expanded by the unusual use of a theatre chorus (in addition to the soloists) and the inclusion of BALLET MUSIC designed for Marie SALLÉ's dancers.

The first rehearsal of the opera, held at Handel's house (MUSEUMS, 2) five days before the first performance, was attended by Mary Pendarves [DELANY], who enthused:

> 'tis so fine I have not words to describe it. Strada has a whole scene of charming recitative – there are a thousand beauties. Whilst Mr. Handel was playing his part I could not help thinking him a necromancer in the midst of his own enchantments.

However, BURNEY's anecdote that CARESTINI initially refused to sing 'Verdi prati' until the enraged Handel threatened to withhold the singer's fees suggests that preparations did not go entirely smoothly. The first performance took place at COVENT GARDEN on 16 April 1735, with the following cast:

Alcina	Anna Maria STRADA del Pò (soprano)
Ruggiero	Giovanni Carestini (castrato)
Bradamante	Maria Caterina Negri (alto)
Morgana	Cecilia YOUNG (soprano)
Oronte	John BEARD (tenor)
Oberto	William SAVAGE (boy soprano)
Melisso	Gustavus WALTZ (bass)

Alcina received eighteen performances during its first run. Apparently 'Verdi prati' was frequently encored, although Sallé's dance as Cupid was hissed at during one performance, but encored on another occasion. The opera attacted critical acclaim, such as a poem in the *Grub-Street Journal* that compared the beguiling spells of the titular sorceress with Handel's weaving of musical charms (8 May 1735), and a discourse in the *Universal Spectator* (5 July 1735) proposed that the opera was an instructive moral allegory. Notwithstanding its success, Handel's only revivals were bowdlerised versions performed in November 1736 and June 1737. The first 'modern' production was at Leipzig in 1928, and the popularity of the opera substantially increased after the Handel Opera Society's London production in 1957. During the last half-century, *Alcina* has been frequently staged and has received seven commercial recordings.

DAVID VICKERS

Burney
   'Sketch of the life of Handel', *An Account of the Musical Performances in Westminster Abbey* (London, 1785)
W. Dean, 'The Making of Alcina', *Con che Soavità*, ed. I. Fenlon and T. Carter (Cambridge, 1995)
   Operas

Deutsch
S. Flesch (ed.), *Alcina*, HHA II/33 (Kassel, 2009)
Harris, *Librettos*
Strohm
D. Vickers, 'Handel's *Alcina*' (CD booklet note, Deutsche Grammophon Archiv 477 737–4, 2009)

Alessandro, HWV 21. This was the opera in which the celebrated FAUSTINA Bordoni made her much-anticipated London debut, and the first of five Royal Academy operas (OPERA COMPANIES, 2) in which Handel wrote for three of the finest singers of the era: SENESINO, CUZZONI, and Faustina. The libretto was adapted by Paolo Antonio ROLLI from Ortensio MAURO and Agostino STEFFANI's opera *La superbia d'Alessandro*, premiered in 1690 at the newly built theatre in HANOVER, and revived there with numerous revisions in 1691 under the title *Il Zelo di Leonato*. Rolli consulted both versions; Handel borrowed from Steffani's score. In adapting the source opera, an important consideration for Rolli and Handel was to balance the parts of Cuzzoni and Faustina so that the ladies usually appeared one after another, and often in contrasting styles; in this way, their vocal abilities were being compared.

At the walls of the Indian city Oxidraca (Malli), Alexander the Great (Alessandro) berates his men for their reluctance to attack, mounts the wall, proclaims his heritage (he considers himself son of Jove), and throws himself within. Inspired by his courage, Alessandro's men breach the walls and the hero is seen alone, defending himself valiantly against a host of enemies. Leonato leads a rescue of Alessandro, and reproaches the conqueror for his recklessness. Alessandro responds that heroes gain immortality through battle. Within sight of the breached wall, Lisaura and Rossane express concern for Alessandro, whom they both love. The Indian King Tassile tells them that the conqueror is safe. The two women celebrate but express their jealousy of each other. Tassile is indebted to Alessandro, but Alessandro is also his rival for Lisaura's heart. Back at Oxidraca, Alessandro is glorified in a rousing chorus. Lisaura and Rossane enter: Alessandro's attraction to Rossane provokes the jealousy of Cleone, who brings Lisaura to the conqueror's attention. Rossane leaves in a huff, Alessandro following, and Lisaura, left alone, resolves to reject him. In an apartment, Rossane bewails her misfortune, and is unconvinced by Alessandro's protestation of love. At the temple of Jupiter, Alessandro receives the adulation of the sycophant Cleone, who prostrates himself to the conqueror. The soldier Clito, outraged at this action, refuses to do the same. Alessandro angrily throws Clito to the ground, forcing him to lie prostrate. The two women urge Alessandro to calm himself and forgive Clito; he ruminates on the conflicting demands of love and glory.

Act II opens with Rossane alone in a shady garden. Alessandro discovers her sleeping, marvels at her beauty and hopes to steal a kiss. Lisaura arrives, unbeknownst to Alessandro, and observes as he sings to Rossane. Alessandro sees Lisaura and attempts to recover the situation, but is overheard by the awakened Rossane. The two women mock Alessandro, each singing back to him the music he has sung to the other. Alessandro rages against this unbecoming treatment. Tassile unsuccessfully tries to convince Lisaura that Alessandro loves only Rossane. In a chamber, Rossane resolves to convince the conqueror to free her and then abandon him, but upon seeing him, realises she cannot leave.

Alessandro offers to free her, which strengthens her love, and he decides to choose Rossane over Lisaura. The rejected Lisaura remains hopeful. Alessandro generously gives all the conquered lands to his men, but Clito again refuses to recognise Alessandro as son of Jove, and rejects the proffered kingdom. Enraged, Alessandro seizes a spear and is about to kill Clito when the canopy of the throne collapses. Suspecting treachery, Alessandro imprisons the innocent Clito. Rossane sees the collapsed canopy, fears the worst and faints. Alessandro revives her and the two pledge their love. Leonato reports a rebellion; Alessandro decides to confront it, and professes his love to Rossane.

Act III opens with Clito in prison. He is freed by Leonato, and they resolve to join the other Macedonians and overthrow Alessandro. In a garden, Lisaura and Rossane agree to abandon their jealousies and allow Alessandro to choose between them. Lisaura confronts Alessandro, demanding to know his choice. He tells her that his friendship with Tassile precludes his choosing her, and Lisaura generously admits defeat. Alessandro tells an overjoyed Tassile of his decision. Rossane urges Alessandro to flee the conspirators, but he resolves to confront them. She begs the gods to save him. The indignant conspirators meet Alessandro, are cowed by his presence, and we learn that it was the rebels of Oxidraca who conspired to kill Alessandro by collapsing the throne canopy. Alessandro grants Clito clemency. In the temple of Jupiter, Rossane and Lisaura pray for an end to civil war. Tassile reports the marvellous effect of Alessandro's presence on the conspirators. The opera ends happily with an extended finale, celebrating the power of love.

Handel finished the score on 11 April 1726; it is not certain when he began composition. Both SCIPIONE and Alessandro were composed during the 1725/6 season. He had apparently written at least as far as Act II.vi in Alessandro by February or early March 1726, for the sinfonia originally composed for this scene was transferred at that time to the opening of the second act of Scipione. Act III of Alessandro was probably composed immediately after Handel finished Scipione. He also wrote two substitute arias for Faustina during the first run of Alessandro. The cast of the first performance was as follows:

Alessandro	Senesino (castrato)
Rossane	Faustina Bordoni (soprano)
Lisaura	Francesca Cuzzoni (soprano)
Clito	Giuseppe Maria BOSCHI (bass)
Tassile	Antonio Baldi (castrato)
Cleone	Anna Vincenza DOTTI (contralto)
Leonato	Luigi Antinori (tenor)

Alessandro had thirteen performances between 5 May (the premiere) and 7 June 1726 at the KING'S THEATRE; further performances were given under Handel's direction during the 1727/8 season with a similar cast. In November 1732 the composer substantially revised Alessandro for six performances: five arias were excised, the recitative was much reduced, and the parts of Cleone and Leonato were eliminated. Alessandro was also performed under the title ROSSANE during three seasons in the 1740s by Lord MIDDLESEX's company, and as Der hochmütige Alexander at HAMBURG (18 and 21 November 1726) and BRUNSWICK (17 and 20 August 1728).

With its intrigues, paired lovers, prison scene and resolution of the plot through virtuous behaviour of the characters on stage leading to a double wedding at the end, *Alessandro* is a typical heroic opera seria. It is also, to some extent, a collection of bravura arias, particularly for the three star singers. Highlights include the Overture, praised by BURNEY; the stirring and dramatic opening scene, which contains a complex of sinfonias, recitatives and an aria ('Tra le stragi') unified by key, metre and theme; the comedy of Act II.ii, in which the two ladies mock Alessandro by singing back to him the love music he has just sung to the other (presaging a celebrated scene in METASTASIO's *Alessandro nell'Indie*); Alessandro's response to the ladies' mocking ('Vano amore'), a magnificent rage aria extraordinary for its length, difficulty and unusual form (the B section brings a change in metre and tempo); and the first scene in Act III, a touching arioso for which Handel provided a lovely obbligato bassoon part. Handel lavished much care upon *Alessandro*: the autograph shows extensive revision and polishing. The result is a magnificent score, full of orchestral pageantry and many fine arias.   RICHARD G. KING

Dean, *Operas*
Harris, *Librettos*
R. G. King, 'Classical History and Handel's *Alessandro*', ML 77/1 (Feb. 1996), 34–63
    'The Composition and Reception of Handel's *Alessandro* (1726)', Ph.D. dissertation
    (Stanford University, 1992)
S. Ograjenšek, 'From *Alessandro* (1726) to *Tolomeo* (1728): The Final Royal Academy Operas',
    Ph.D. dissertation (University of Cambridge, 2005)
Strohm

Alessandro Severo (*Alexander Severus*), HWV A¹³. PASTICCIO opera in three acts by Handel. The first performance was at the KING'S THEATRE on 25 February 1738. Apostolo ZENO's libretto was originally set by Antonio LOTTI for VENICE in 1717.

The third-century Roman Emperor Alessandro Severo is dominated by his mother Giulia Mammaea. She arranges for Alessandro to marry Sallustia but quickly becomes jealous of the new Empress and insists that he divorce and banish her. Sallustia's friend Albina arrives in Rome disguised as a man, pursing Claudio who won her heart in Sicily and then deserted her. She overhears Sallustia's father Marziano plotting with Claudio to murder Giulia, and tells Sallustia. Sallustia warns Giulia not to drink from a cup of poisoned wine but refuses to identify the traitor. When Marziano and his men come to kill Giulia, Sallustia again defends her, moving Giulia to restore her to her rightful place. Marziano and Claudio are pardoned, and Claudio marries Albina.

The cast was as follows:

Alessandro Severo	CAFFARELLI (castrato)
Sallustia	FRANCESINA (soprano)
Giulia	Antonia MERIGHI (alto)
Albina	Maria Antonia MARCHESINI, 'La Lucchesina' (mezzo-soprano)
Claudio	Margherita Chimenti, 'La Droghierina' (soprano)
Marziano	Antonio MONTAGNANA (bass)

There were five performances. WALSH published a set of 'favourite songs', no copy of which has come to light, and the overture.

The principal source for Handel's *Alessandro Severo* is the conducting score, British Library, Add. MS 31569. A single copy of the printed libretto survives in the Schoelcher Collection in the Bibliothèque nationale. Handel took all the set numbers from operas performed in London during the preceding ten years. Most of the music came from the three new operas of the preceding season, *ARMINIO*, *GIUSTINO* and *BERENICE*, suggesting that he may have seen this pasticcio as an alternative to reviving any one of them. The overture and the recitatives were newly composed. In an accompagnato for Giulia, Handel expresses her fear of impending doom with a tremolo effect in the strings indicated by a wavy line, the only time he employed this convention in recitative.

JOHN H. ROBERTS

Alexander Balus, HWV 65. English oratorio. The libretto by Thomas MORELL is based on chapters 11 and 12 of the Apocryphal First Book of Maccabees. The historical backdrop of the plot is the reign of Alexander Balus (or Balas), the pretended son of the Syrian monarch Diadochus Antiochus IV Epiphanes, around 150 to 145 BC. The plot revolves around Alexander's love for his wife Cleopatra, daughter of the Egyptian Diadoch King Ptolomee (Ptolemy IV Philometor). Ptolomee intends to disempower his son-in-law and replace him on the Syrian throne with his rival Demetrius. In addition to the throne, Ptolomee has also promised Cleopatra to Demetrius and has therefore ordered her to be abducted. Alexander then begins a military campaign of vengeance, in the course of which he is betrayed and killed. Alexander's friend and vassal Jonathan, one of the three Maccabaean brothers and, since the death of his brother Judas Maccabaeus (*JUDAS MACCABAEUS*), new leader of the Israelite people, successfully finishes Alexander's campaign, kills Ptolomee and liberates his people from Egyptian rulership. Cleopatra has lost both husband and father and withdraws from the world to mourn.

Alexander Balus was one of two new oratorios for the 1748 COVENT GARDEN oratorio season – the other being *JOSHUA* – and Handel composed it between 1 June and 4 July 1747. *Alexander Balus* was therefore composed before *Joshua*, although *Joshua* was performed first. *Alexander Balus* was first performed on 23 March 1748 with the following cast:

Alexander Balus	Caterina GALLI (alto)
Cleopatra	Domenica Casarini (soprano)
Aspasia	Sibilla Gronamann (mezzo-soprano)
Jonathan	Thomas LOWE (tenor)
Ptolomee	Henry REINHOLD (bass)

It was performed three times, and was revived for two performances in 1754. A revival had been planned for 1751 but was postponed because of the death of FREDERICK, Prince of Wales. In 1754 the only member of the original 1748 cast was Galli, who took over the part of Cleopatra's confidante Aspasia. The new line-up of singers necessitated heavy changes in the score: the title role became a soprano part (probably sung by Christina Passerini) and lost five arias to Aspasia, whose part was considerably expanded. In addition, Jonathan (sung by John BEARD) received three additional arias taken over from the incidental music for *ALCESTE*. The role of Cleopatra was sung by Giulia FRASI. The 1754 WORDBOOK was adapted from old stock printed for the abandoned 1751 revival.

Alexander Balus does not seem to have been popular with Handel's audience. It has remained unfamiliar and unpopular to this day. Dean remarked that 'Act I is perhaps the dullest single act in any of the oratorios', and criticisms levelled at the work include allegations that Morell's textual borrowings from MILTON, POPE, Shakespeare and others are weak, and that the libretto is not ideally suited to a theatrical setting. The dramaturgy and poetry of the piece, if judged according to the standards of classical drama theory, seem botched, with the roles of Alexander, Aspasia and Jonathan insufficiently characterised. However, Dean observed that 'Nowhere in the English oratorios does [Handel] come closer to *opera seria*', and more recent scholarship about *Alexander Balus* has discussed possible allegorical, psychological or political interpretations (Smith, Rosand). Moreover, the score offers several musical delights. None of Handel's other biblical oratorios contains more da capo arias and fewer choral movements, which perhaps indicates that the composer deliberately conceived it as an operatic-style contrast to the contemporaneous *Joshua* and *Judas Maccabaeus*, which both accorded the chorus a more important role and were not structured as narrative dramas. He used a large number of different instrumental textures in the INSTRUMENTATION, especially in the choruses of the Syrians, and other dramatic devices in order to create a markedly oriental atmosphere. He also took BORROWINGS from several old works, most notably using three arias from *La* RESURREZIONE for the title role's 'Fair virtue shall charm me', 'Mighty love now calls to arm' and 'Fury with red sparkling eyes'.

The character of Cleopatra prompted Handel to create some outstanding musical and dramaturgical scenes. For example, her entrance aria in Act I, 'Hark, hark! He strikes the golden lyre' features unusually exotic sonorities from pizzicato cellos, transverse flutes, harp and mandolin (perhaps Handel was recalling her namesake's seductive Parnassus scene in GIULIO CESARE). Also, III.iv is an exceptionally musico-dramatic unit: Cleopatra laments her dire fate in a minor-key accompanied recitative ('Shall Cleopatra ever smile again?', which includes chromatic reminiscenes of the dying lament of the title character in SEMELE), receives the news about Alexander's death in a secco recitative ('Ungrateful tidings'), and reacts emotionally to her husband's murder in a short E minor aria ('O take me from this hateful light', which commences with six bars of unaccompanied voice). Then the intensity of the scene is increased by her receiving news of her father Ptolomee's death in secco recitative, her dignified accompanied recitative 'Calm thou my soul', and her mournful and hushed exit aria 'Convey me to some peaceful shore'. According to Morell, when Handel first read the text of Cleopatra's final aria he 'cried out "D—n your Iambics" '. Apparently he was exasperated at the poet's monotonous use of iambic verses, perhaps because it encumbered rhythmical diversity in the music. Morell then explained to Handel that the metre in the aria could easily be transformed into a trochee and changed it accordingly. By the time he returned with the altered verses, however, Handel had apparently decided that he 'would have them as they were' and had already set the original text to music featuring simple string accompaniment that strongly resembles Bellezza's final renunciation of pleasure in *Il* TRIONFO DEL TEMPO E DEL DISINGANNO. Cleopatra's doleful withdrawal is followed by a sombre conclusion for Jonathan and the Israelites in G minor (the only other oratorio to end with a minor-key chorus is the comparably tragic THEODORA).

DANIEL GLOWOTZ (Trans. ANGELA BAIER)

E. Bénimédourène, 'Contamination et réemploi musical chez Haendel', *Musurgia* 6/1 (1999), 77–87
Burrows and Dunhill
Dean, *Oratorios*
G. Fleischhauer, 'Das "Glockenspiel"-Motiv und seine Bedeutung – ein Beitrag zu Händels Schaffensmethode und Menschenbild', HJb 18/19 (1972/3)
HHB ii
H. J. Marx, *Händels Oratorien, Oden und Serenaten* (Göttingen, 1998)
E. Rosand, 'Handel's Oratorical Narrative', GHB VIII (2000)
Smith, *Oratorios*

Alexander's Feast, HWV 75. Handel finished composing his setting of John DRYDEN's ode on 17 January 1736, and it received its first performance at COVENT GARDEN theatre on 19 February. Dryden's poem was written for musical setting, which was originally composed by Jeremiah Clarke and performed in 1697 for the London celebration of St Cecilia's Day (22 November), one of a chain of such works from the last two decades of the seventeenth century: Dryden had similarly contributed another ode ('From harmony, from heav'nly harmony') a decade previously. Clarke's score for *Alexander's Feast* is lost, but the ode was printed and published at the time, and this was the source from which Newburgh HAMILTON prepared the libretto for Handel. The initiative seems to have come from Hamilton himself, in order to combine 'the united Labours and utmost Efforts of a *Dryden* and a *Handel*'. In the WORDBOOK for Handel's performances (see Figure 1), Hamilton said in his preface that he was 'determin'd not to take any unwarrantable Liberty with that Poem, which has so long done Honour to the nation': 'I therefore confin'd myself to a plain Division of it into *Airs*, *Recitatives*, or *Chorus's*; looking upon the Words so sacred, as scarcely to violate one in the Order of its first Place.' He did, however, add a text of his own for a concluding chorus ('Your voices tune, and raise them high'), taken from his own Cecilian ode *The Power of Music*, which had been composed by Robert Woodcock in 1720. (The score of this is also lost.)

Dryden's full title, retained by Hamilton, was *Alexander's Feast; or, the Power of Musick*, and the subject matter of the ode is a description of the influence that Timotheus had over Alexander the Great, demonstrating that the behaviour of a man who was recognised as one of the world's most powerful and ruthless rulers could be influenced, modified or controlled by 'musick'. (Timotheus has the role of a court bard, accompanying himself on the lyre, so he was presumably responsible for the words of his songs as well.) Part I of the ode describes the celebratory feast in the palace at Persepolis after Alexander's conquest of Persia, at which his present reward is the company of the courtesan Thais. Timotheus begins by tactfully referring to the legend that Alexander was descended from Jove, exciting the adulation of the crowd and encouraging the King's vanity. His next theme, appropriately for the feast, is praise of Bacchus, the god of wine and youth. When the effects of this are in danger of becoming excessive, Timotheus changes the mood by recalling the tragic fate of Darius, the Persian king killed by his own generals and deserted on the battlefield. When Alexander has been

ALEXANDER's *FEAST*;

OR, THE

POWER OF MUSICK.

A N O D E

Wrote in Honour of St. *CECILIA*,

By Mr. *DRYDEN*.

Set to MUSICK by Mr. *HANDEL*.

Hear how Timotheus' *various Lays surprise,*
And bid alternate Passions fall and rise;
While, at each Change, the Son of Libyan Jove
Now burns with Glory, and then melts with Love;
Now his fierce Eyes with sparkling Fury glow,
Now Sighs steal out, and Tears begin to flow;
Persians *and* Greeks *like Turns of Nature found,*
And the World's Victor stood subdu'd by Sound.

Pope's Essay on Criticism.

LONDON:
Printed for J. and R. TONSON in the *Strand*.

MDCCXXXVI.

[Price One Shilling.]

1. *Alexander's Feast*, title page of wordbook, with an inscription from Alexander Pope's Essay on Criticism, published by J. and R. Tonson, 1736.

thus softened, Timotheus turns his thoughts to love, another topic popular with the crowd, and finally 'with wine and love at once oppress'd', Alexander falls asleep on Thais's breast.

At the beginning of Part II Timotheus awakens Alexander with the music of battle and a call for vengeance for the Grecian soldiers killed in the Persian wars. Alexander, actively encouraged by Thais, takes his revenge by burning Persepolis. That brings the narrative to a conclusion, and the remainder of the ode is by way of a commentary: the power of Timotheus's music in pagan days has been superseded by Cecilia's sanctification of the art of music, and the elevation of Alexander through his reputedly divine parentage is contrasted with Cecilia's contribution in bringing the divine art of music down to mortals. In place of the lyre, the organ 'enlarg'd the former narrow bounds, and added length to solemn sounds'; in musical composition, the 'arts unknown before' are represented by Handel in a minor-key contrapuntal chorus. Hamilton's concluding text encourages the audience to follow Cecilia's example by making the evening 'sacred to harmony and love'. (Dryden and Hamilton follow the convention that Cecilia herself was a musician, though the historical accounts of the saint and martyr say only that she 'sang in her heart' as she heard the organ playing.)

Handel composed *Alexander's Feast* at a difficult time in his career. In 1734–5 he had performed his first season at Covent Garden Theatre, in consequence of the occupation of the KING'S THEATRE by the OPERA OF THE NOBILITY. The season had been artistically successful, in the opera programme and in the introduction of a concentrated sub-season of English oratorio performances complemented by organ concertos. However, there was no obvious way ahead: while the rival opera company was in its most popular and vigorous phase, Handel had no prospect of a full opera cast for the next season, and had to remain inactive during the first months. *Alexander's Feast* was the work with which he returned to the theatre: the association with a text from a major English poet marked a new direction for Handel, but the ode was also a practical proposition in his current circumstances because it could be mounted with just three leading singers who were competent in English (the soprano STRADA, tenor John BEARD, and bass Mr ERARD, with a minor role for the second soprano Cecilia YOUNG). There was, however, a problem on account of the two-part structure of Dryden's ode, since theatre audiences were used to the three-act span of operas and oratorios. Handel expanded the evening with two substantial items between the Parts: the orchestral concerto HWV 318 (ORCHESTRAL WORKS, 2) and the Italian cantata *CECILIA, VOLGI UN SGUARDO* (HWV 89). Furthermore, the ode itself was adorned with two further concertos: a Harp Concerto (HWV 294) at the reference to Timotheus's lyre-playing near the beginning, and an Organ Concerto (HWV 289) before the concluding chorus (ORCHESTRAL WORKS, 3; 5). Instrumental colour also compensated for the limitation in the number of soloists: the score includes items featuring horns and recorders, as well as the harp, trumpets and drums, and the lutenist-singer Carlo ARRIGONI was involved in the Italian cantata. In 1739 Handel solved the structural problem by adding a setting of Dryden's shorter St Cecilia ode (*SONG FOR ST CECILIA'S DAY*) as a third act to complement *Alexander's Feast*, opening his season on St Cecilia's day; for his London revivals in 1751–5 *Alexander's Feast* was partnered by The *CHOICE OF HERCULES* instead. At DUBLIN in 1742 he produced a rather unbalanced version by detaching Hamilton's epilogue as a miniature 'Part III'.

Beyond Handel's own performances, *Alexander's Feast* has special significance on account of its printed edition, carefully prepared and 'Publish'd by the Author'. Proposals for the edition were announced in May 1737, and it was published in March 1738; the engraved portrait of Handel by HOUBRAKEN, which was produced specifically to accompany the score and shows the opening scene of the ode below the portrait, was not ready in time and was delivered a month later. The subscribers' list was headed by all seven of King GEORGE II's children. This was the first such score of Handel's to be published in full, with all of the recitatives and choruses in addition to the arias and overture. (The only subsequent publication of its type during Handel's lifetime was John WALSH's edition of *ACIS AND GALATEA* in 1743.) Where the two-part structure had posed a problem for Handel in 1736, the more modest length provided an opportunity for concert performers, in provincial centres as well as in London, and the accessibility of the printed edition ensured that *Alexander's Feast* became one of the most performed of Handel's English oratorio-style works.   DONALD BURROWS

D. Burrows (ed.), *Alexander's Feast*, Novello Handel Edition (London, 1982)
   'The Composition and First Performance of Handel's *Alexander's Feast*', MT 123/1670 (1982), 252–5
   'The Sources of *Alexander's Feast*', ML 66/1 (Jan. 1985), 87–8
W. Dean, 'An Unrecognized Handel Singer: Carlo Arrigoni', MT 118 (1977), 556–7
R. Loewenthal [= Smith], 'Handel and Newburgh Hamilton: New References in the Strafford Papers', MT 112/1545 (Nov. 1971), 1063–6
R. Luckett, 'St Cecilia and Music', PRMA 99 (1972–3), 15–30
R. Smith, 'The Argument and Contexts of Dryden's *Alexander's Feast*', *Studies in English Literature, 1500–1900* 18/3 (Summer 1978), 465–90

Alla caccia ('**Diana cacciatrice**'), HWV 79. An accompanied cantata for soprano, soprano chorus, trumpet, violins and basso continuo, *Alla caccia* appears in the account books of RUSPOLI on 16 May 1707 when ANGELINI submitted his bill for copying it. Because the text concerns hunting and refers to the story of Diana and Actaeon, it was long thought that the work was composed for performance at Ruspoli's estate in Vignanello. Ursula Kirkendale now places the first performance on 22 February 1707 at Cerveteri, Ruspoli's estate on the Tyrrhenian coast. Given that Angelini's copy totalled fifty-two pages, what survives of this cantata must be fragmentary. A recitative belonging to it, 'Tacete, olà tacete', was discovered following the edition of the cantata in the HHA (EDITIONS, 7).
                                                              ELLEN T. HARRIS

B. Janz, 'Schnitzeljagd. Ein neu aufgefundenes Fragment zu Händels Kantate *Diana cacciatrice* HWV 79', GHB X (2005)
W. and U. Kirkendale, *Music and Meaning: Studies in Music History and the Neighbouring Disciplines* (Florence, 2007)

Allegro, il Penseroso ed il Moderato, L', HWV 55. English ode composed between 19 January and 4 February 1740, text selected from John MILTON's separate poems *L'Allegro* ('The Cheerful Man') and *Il Penseroso* ('The Pensive Man'), probably written in the early 1630s soon after the poet left CAMBRIDGE. *L'Allegro* invokes the goddess Mirth to allow the poet to live amid delightful pastoral scenes, then amid 'towered cities' and the 'busy hum of men', and proclaims the pleasures of mirth and theatre comedies. In absolute opposition, Il Penseroso invokes the goddess Melancholy to grant peaceful quiet, studious contemplation in a 'lonely Tow'r', and endorses tragedy, epic poetry and cathedral music.

The idea for Handel to compose a work contrasting the philosophies in Milton's juxtaposed poems was suggested by James HARRIS, one of England's leading aestheticians, to Charles JENNENS at around the end of 1739. Handel responded eagerly to the proposal, and Harris sent a draft of the libretto from SALISBURY to Jennens in London via the Earl of SHAFTESBURY on 6 January 1740. In addition to making numerous recommendations to Handel regarding instrumental scoring, aria type and choice of singer, Harris also explained:

> there is not only one grand contrast which runs through the whole, of <u>Mirth</u> to <u>Melancholy</u>, but that these two have each their several species, which the great poet has elegantly contrived to set in opposition to each other. Mirth he has divided into <u>rural</u> mirth & <u>city</u> mirth[.] In rural mirth you have <u>the singing of the lark</u>, hunting, the <u>scene of plowmen</u>[,] milk-maids, mowers, shepherds &cr[.] In city mirth, you have <u>courts</u> & assemblies, plays and <u>fine music</u>. Melancholy he has divided according to the seasons of the natural day[.] <u>By night</u> we have the <u>nightingale</u>; <u>walking by moonshine</u>, and the <u>contemplation of great & enthusiastic subjects</u> in some solitary tower[.] – In <u>day time</u> we have <u>soft repose</u> in some deep and dark forrest or <u>the attendance upon solemn church music</u>. It tis proper also to observe that each part begins with an <u>execration of it's contrary</u>, and then goes to describing the <u>genealogy of it's own subject</u>.

Jennens and Handel proceeded to refine Harris's draft, and in many cases Milton's original poetry was little changed. On 15 January 1740, Jennens reported to Harris that Handel was not 'perfectly satisfy'd with your division, as having too much of the Penseroso together, which would consequently occasion to much grave musick without intermission, & would tire the audience. He said, he had already resolv'd upon a more minute division, which therefore I left him to make with the assistance of your plan.' By this time, Handel had requested Jennens to add a new third part. The composer thought it could be based on Milton's *At a solemn musick*, but Jennens considered that this was unconnected to the preceding verses, and instead wrote Il *Moderato* in imitation of Milton and Shakespeare (Handel later set lines from *At a solemn musick* in SAMSON). Jennens contrived that 'Moderato' would advise moderation in all things, after which the seemingly incompatible extremes of Mirth and Melancholy could be blissfully reconciled in the duet 'As steals the morn' (based on one of Prospero's speeches in Act V of *The Tempest*).

Four days later Handel commenced composing his score. Most of Harris's modestly expressed suggestions regarding music-setting were superbly realised, such as the division of L'Allegro's part between John BEARD, a boy treble and a bass, whereas the part of Penseroso was allocated exclusively to FRANCESINA. Handel also followed Harris's recommendations concerning the structure of 'Haste thee, nymph' as a song for John Beard leading into a chorus, and that 'Mirth, admit me of thy crew' should be a 'Song for a Base Voice with French Horns', although in fact Handel used only one solo horn for the song. However, he did not compose an overture, despite Harris's instruction and Jennens's petitions. The composer instead wanted to perform two of his recently composed Op. 6 Concerti Grossi (ORCHESTRAL WORKS, 2).

Handel carefully designed the music for Allegro and Penseroso to alternate as if in an argumentative dialogue between the two extremes of extroverted and introverted human nature. They each set out their conflicting views accompanied by (and in rejection of) the musical mood and sonority that will become associated with their opposite. Whilst Allegro opens and closes the first part, the second part begins and finishes with Penseroso. The score is among Handel's most poetic works, full of imitative sounds (e.g. the curfew bell in 'Oft on a plat of rising ground'), humour (the infectious staccato laughter in 'Haste thee, nymph'), onomatopoeic sounds (the melismatic 'busy hum of men' in 'Populous cities') and nature scenes (the flute imitating a nightingale in 'Sweet bird' and a chirping cricket in 'Far from all resort of mirth'). There is robust hunting music, a sensuous evocation of frolicking country folk being lulled to sleep as daylight fades ('Or let the merry bells ring round', which begins in jaunty mood as a solo for the boy treble accompanied by sparkling carillon), a lively visit to the theatre to see comedies by Ben Jonson and William Shakespeare ('I'll to the well trod stage anon'), and a solemn experience of divine sacred music ('There let the pealing organ blow'). The crowning climax of the work is the duet 'As steals the morn', in which the soprano and tenor voices (reinforced respectively by oboes and bassoons) rapturously symbolise a harmonious union that offers reason, enlightenment and the restoration of 'intellectual day'.

The first performance took place at LINCOLN'S INN FIELDS on 27 February 1740, in the midst of a severe winter. The *London Daily Post* advised its readers that 'Particular Care has been taken to have the House secur'd against the Cold, constant Fires being order'd to be kept in the House 'till the Time of Performance'. The cast was as follows:

L'Allegro	John Beard (tenor)
	'The Boy' [anonymous] (treble)
	Henry REINHOLD (bass)
Il Penseroso	Elisabeth Duparc, 'La Francesina' (soprano)
Il Moderato	William SAVAGE (bass)

In addition to two of the Op. 6 Concerti Grossi (perhaps including No. 10, HWV 328), Handel also performed the Organ Concerto, Op. 7 No. 1 (HWV 306) during the ode's first run of five performances (ORCHESTRAL WORKS, 2; 5). An anonymous review in the *Daily Advertiser* on 5 March 1740 praised the Miltonic ode as '*sensible Musick, or, (a Thing long unheard of among us) Musick set to Sense*', although Jennens reported that witty customers at Tom's Coffee House honoured Il *Moderato* with the title 'Moderatissimo'. Handel revived L'*Allegro* in early 1741, with several additions setting hitherto unused lines of Milton's poems but without Il *Moderato*; one of the singers, Andreoni, could not sing in English, and his texts were translated by Paolo ROLLI. Handel reinstated the third part at DUBLIN (1741–2), but in later revivals (1743, 1754 and 1755) replaced it with the SONG FOR ST CECILIA'S DAY.

ANNETTE LANDGRAF and DAVID VICKERS

G. Beeks, 'Some Thoughts on Musical Organization in L'Allegro, il Penseroso ed il Moderato', HJb 51 (2005)

D. Burrows, 'From Milton to Handel: The Transformation of Milton's "L'Allegro" and "Il Penseroso" into a Musical Work for Concert Performance in the London Theatres', Musique et théâtralité dans les îles britanniques, ed. C. Bardelmann and P. Degott (Metz, 2005)

Burrows and Dunhill

Deutsch

A. Hicks, 'Handel: *L'Allegro, il Penseroso ed il Moderato*', CD booklet note (Hyperion, CDA 67283/4, 1999)

R. M. Myers, *Handel, Dryden and Milton* (London, 1956)

R. Smith, 'Handel, Milton, and a New Document from their English Audience', *Handel Institute Newsletter* 14/3 (Autumn 2003)

Alleluia (Alleluia, amen). 'Alleluia' and 'Amen' are terms of Hebrew origin, meaning respectively acclamation and assent; together or separately their normal function is to mark the end of Christian liturgical texts. Their musical setting is given a special prominence, involving a very florid melodic line in monodic compositions, or elaborate contrapuntal treatment in polyphonic ones; this is demonstrated in the many Amens in fugal style in the modern period, or in the Alleluias which usually provide a triumphant conclusion to Latin motets of the Catholic tradition and to the ANTHEMS which are their Anglican equivalent. In the final sequence of chords in choral works, the two words are often set to a plagal cadence. Handel's output includes a number of compositions intended for Anglican services, all for soprano solo and continuo, which set the two words 'Alleluia' and 'Amen' (HWV 266–77): *Amen, alleluja* in D minor (c.1745–7); *Amen* in F major and *Amen, allelujah* in G minor (c.1732–9); *Allelujah, amen* in D minor, G minor and A minor (c.1738–41); *Amen, allelujah* in C major (c.1732–9); *Amen, hallelujah* in F major (c.1743–7); *Halleluja, amen* in F major (c.1745–7); they are unique among Handel's works, and their purpose is uncertain, but it is possible that they were intended as exercises for the study of Italian bel canto (HWV 276–7 could have been composed for the royal princesses). Much more spectacular are the concluding Alleluias of Handel's own anthems: in particular, in those for the CORONATION of King GEORGE II the model was probably the grand motets written by PERTI – and, perhaps, also by ALESSANDRO SCARLATTI – for the MEDICI, as well as by the concerted compositions in 'stile colossale' of the Roman school. Equally majestic is the setting of the words 'Alleluia' and 'Amen' in several of Handel's oratorios: in two famous choruses the use of the two words marks the end of the second and third parts of *MESSIAH*; it is even more interesting, however, to observe how the first scene of *SAUL* imitates the structure (symphony and chorus – three internal musical numbers – shortened repeat of the chorus, with 'Alleluia') of Perti's Florentine motets, culminating in an 'Alleluia' of great theatrical power, whilst the final chorus of *JUDAS MAC-CABAEUS* returns to setting just the words 'Hallelujah! Amen!', giving to this oratorio the same concluding formula as the Anglican liturgical service.

FRANCESCO LORA (Trans. TERENCE BEST)

See also HALLELUJAH CHORUS

Almira (*Der in Krohnen erlangte Glückswechsel, oder: Almira, Königin von Kastilien*), HWV 1. German opera. The libretto by Friedrich Christian FEUSTKING is based on a text by Giulio PANCIERI which was originally set by Giuseppe Boniventi and premiered in autumn 1691 at the Teatro San Giovanni e Paolo in VENICE. Ten years later Boniventi's opera was performed in Vicenza. In 1703 Pancieri's libretto was set by Ruggiero Fedeli and performed at BRUNSWICK, for which a German prose version was written that one year later formed the basis for Feustking's libretto, which was first set by Reinhard KEISER and first performed at WEISSENFELS (probably on 5 August 1704; its full title was *Almira: Der Durchlauchtige Secretarius, Oder: Almira, Königin in Castilien*). At some time later that same year, Handel composed his setting at HAMBURG.

The compositional circumstances are complicated. Gerhard Schott, the director of the GÄNSEMARKT opera house in Hamburg, died in 1702. His widow took over the company's direction in 1703, but soon afterwards leased it to Keiser and Drüsicke. There had been twelve new operas in 1702, but until 1705 there were only three more. It seems that this was not only due to a lack of patrons, but, according to Mattheson, also to restrictive controls over operatic ventures passed by the Senate (documented for 1704). Keiser began composing his setting of Feustking's *Almira* in 1704 for Hamburg, but in the summer he received an opera commission from Weissenfels to honour a visit by the Elector Palatine. This commission was perhaps influenced by the fact that Keiser's birthplace Teuchern lay in the Saxon ducal territories of Saxe-Weissenfels, but it seems to have been issued at short notice, so Keiser staged his *Almira* at Weissenfels instead of Hamburg. But this meant that now there was no new opera ready for the Gänsemarkt theatre, so the nineteen-year-old Handel was commissioned to set the same libretto again. It is unknown whether Keiser or Johannes MATTHESON instigated the commission for Handel's first opera, but it is likely that he composed it whilst regularly discussing the project with Mattheson.

The dates printed in the original wordbooks reveal that the first Hamburg performance of *Almira* was supposed to have taken place in 1704, but it was postponed to 8 January 1705 (maybe the duel between Handel and Mattheson on 5 December 1704 caused delays in the production's preparation; the two were reconciled on 30 December). Handel's opera was popular: MAINWARING claimed that there were thirty consecutive performances, although that improbably high figure was disputed by Mattheson. The cast was as follows:

Almira, Queen of Castile	Madame CONRADI[N] (soprano)
Fernando, a foundling	Johann Mattheson (tenor)
Edilia, a Princess	? (soprano)
Raymondo, King of Mauretania	? (bass)
Osman, his son	Konrad Dreyer (tenor)
Bellante, Princess of Aranda	? (soprano)
Consalvo, Almira's guardian	Gottfried Grünewald (bass)
Tabarco, servant	Christoph Rauch (tenor)

The plot is set in Castile during the Middle Ages, probably between the thirteenth and fifteenth centuries. Almira has come of age and is crowned Queen in succession to her father. She makes her former guardian Consalvo her adviser, appoints his son Osman general, and the foundling Fernando, whom she is secretly in love with, her secretary. Almira's father's dying wish was that she should marry a son of Consalvo. However, Osman is wooing Edilia, who is also loved by Raymondo. Consalvo pays court to Bellante, who in her turn is in love with Osman. This leads to further emotional complications and entanglements, which are finally resolved by the discovery that Fernando is Consalvo's lost son. Almira marries Fernando, and the other couples (Osman and Bellante; Raymondo and Edilia) are also united in matrimony.

After the premiere Feustking's libretto was criticised by Barthold FEIND because of bad rhymes in the first aria 'Almire regiere und führe'. This led to prolonged literary quarrels and finally escalated into a full-blown political dispute. This controversy was one of the reasons why Keiser used Feind's revised Almira libretto when he recomposed the opera for Hamburg two years later (it was the last of the six operas premiered during 1706). However, Feustking's libretto is an improvement on earlier texts used by the Hamburg opera company: it is arguably less stereotypical, less routinely mechanical, and his large-scale scenes are effectively differentiated and colourful.

Handel's music includes fifty-two arias (most of them notably short, and about a third with simple continuo accompaniment), three duets and one ensemble, in addition to four accompanied recitatives and two choruses. Fifteen of the arias have Italian texts. Some arias end with ritornellos between ten and forty bars long, presumably designed to allow scenery changes. All three acts include dance movements. The colourful instrumentation is modelled on Keiser: there are various combinations of two oboes with two violins, viola and continuo, as well as numbers using solo oboe and solo violin and continuo. The score also includes bassoon, viola da braccio, two flutes and three violins, and the first chorus contains three trumpets and timpani. Handel occasionally borrowed musical themes from Almira in his later works until 1737. The only extant complete score is a manuscript copy prepared by TELEMANN for a Hamburg revival in 1732 (for which he made various cuts, inserted two of his own arias and probably added a new overture). It is unclear whether two productions of Almira at Leipzig (1710 and 1714) were based on the earlier Handel or Keiser scores, although the latter was certainly based on Feustking's libretto, which was also set to music by Johann Philipp Käfer for Durlach in 1717.

KLAUS-PETER KOCH (Trans. ANGELA BAIER)

W. Braun, 'Der "Almira"-Stoff in den Vertonungen von Ruggiero Fedeli, Reinhard Keiser und Georg Friedrich Händel', HJb 36 (1990)

R. F. C. Fenton, 'Almira (Hamburg, 1705): The Birth of G. F. Handel's Genius for Characterization', HJb 33 (1987)

K.-P. Koch, 'Das Jahr 1704 und die Weißenfelser Hofoper. Zu den Umständen der Aufführung von Reinhard Keisers Oper "Almira" anläßlich des Besuches des pfälzischen Kurfürsten am Weißenfelser Hof', Weißenfels als Ort literarischer und künstlerischer Kultur im Barockzeitalter, ed. R. Jacobsen (Amsterdam and Atlanta, 1994)

R.-S. Pegah, 'Neues zur Oper Almira', GHB X (2004)

J. H. Roberts, 'Keiser and Handel at the Hamburg Opera', HJb 36 (1990) (see also reply by H. Serwer)

'Zur Entstehung und Aufführungsgeschichte von Händels Oper "Almira". Anmerkungen zur Edition des Werkes in der Hallischen Händel-Ausgabe', HJb 36 (1990)

D. Schröder (ed.), Almira, Königin von Kastilien, HHA II/1 (Kassel, 1994)

Strohm

Alpestre monte, HWV 81. A lover, wandering through wild mountain landscapes, complains about his insensitive 'nymph', anticipates death, and hopes she will visit his grave. The (female) recipient is called Nice, which, besides verse style, links HWV 81 to other arguably 'Neapolitan' cantatas of 1708–9, such as HWV 136 and 161. A desolate obbligato recitative, modulation to remote keys in the first aria ('Io so ben ch'il vostro orrore'), and the interweaving downward spirals between solo soprano and violin in the second ('Almen dopo il fato mio'), enhance the piece's depressive mood.

The same text was set to music by Francesco Mancini, a Neapolitan who is the real author of the spurious *Dal fatale momento* (HWV 101). Mancini's operatic career shows strict and tantalising intersections with Handel's at London's KING'S THEATRE (1710), Aurora SANSEVERINO's court in Piedimonte (1711) and at NAPLES's San Bartolomeo (1713).   CARLO VITALI

Alvito, 5th Duke of (Tolomeo Saverio Gallio) (b. 26 Feb. 1685, Alvito, now in Latium; d. Naples, 26 April 1711). Son of Alfonsa Diez Pimiento Countess de Legard and Duke Francesco, from the Neapolitan branch of the Gallio Trivulzio dynasty, which controlled huge possessions in Lombardy, Spain and the Kingdom of Naples. The lavish celebrations for Tolomeo's wedding with Princess Beatrice Tocco di Montemiletto, held in NAPLES on 19 July 1708, occasioned the composition of Handel's *ACI, GALATEA E POLIFEMO* and the publication in ROME of a verse collection including Paolo ROLLI's earliest known production.

CARLO VITALI

A. Furnari, 'I rapporti tra Händel e i duchi d'Alvito', *Händel e gli Scarlatti a Roma*, ed. N. Pirrotta and A. Ziino (Florence, 1987)

Amadei, Filippo (b. Reggio/Emilia, c.1670; d. Rome, c.1725). Violone player, cellist and composer. Also known as Filippo Mattei or simply called Pipp[in]o, Amadei lived in the household of Cardinal Benedetto PAMPHILIJ in ROME before 1690. After 1689 he was in the service of Cardinal Pietro OTTOBONI as violone virtuoso and composer of operas, oratorios and cantatas. Between April 1708 and March 1710 he was occasionally employed by Francesco Maria RUSPOLI. From 1715 to approximately 1723 he lived in London, gave concerts on his violone and played the cello in the Royal Academy of Music (OPERA COMPANIES, 2) opera orchestra at the KING'S THEATRE. In 1721 he (and not Attilio ARIOSTI) composed the first act of the opera *MUZIO SCEVOLA* (the two following acts were composed by BONONCINI and Handel). Shortly before, he had arranged Giuseppe Maria ORLANDINI's Florentine opera *Amore e Maestà* for the King's Theatre as *Arsace*, which included fourteen newly composed arias, and used a newly adapted text by Paolo ROLLI (first performance 12 February 1721). Both works were also performed in HAMBURG (in 1723 and 1722 respectively). MATTHESON mentions that compositions by Amadei were sent to him from England in 1722 and 1728. After 1723 Amadei returned to Ottoboni's service in Rome.

KLAUS-PETER KOCH (Trans. ANGELA BAIER)

E. Gibson, *The Royal Academy of Music 1719–1728: The Institution and its Directors* (New York, 1989)
H. J. Marx, 'Die Musik am Hofe Pietro Kardinal Ottobonis unter Arcangelo Corelli', *Analecta musicologica* 5 (1968), 104–77
J. Mattheson, *Critica musica* (Hamburg, 1722/3)
    Der musicalische Patriot (Hamburg, 1728)

Amadigi di Gaula, HWV 11. The dedication of the libretto, signed by HEIDEGGER, implies that Handel composed *Amadigi* during his residence at BURLINGTON HOUSE. Since the autograph score does not survive, we cannot be quite sure when, but presumably it was in the spring of 1715, for the premiere at the KING'S THEATRE, Haymarket took place on 25 May. This was exceptionally late in the season, no doubt because NICOLINO's return to London after three years abroad had been delayed. The cast was as follows:

Amadigi	Nicolino (castrato)
Dardano	Diana Vico (alto)
Oriana	ANASTASIA ROBINSON (soprano)
Melissa	Elisabetta PILOTTI-SCHIAVONETTI (soprano)
Orgando	[unidentified] (soprano)

Six performances were given; six more followed in 1716, and a further five in 1717. Even before the premiere, while the company was awaiting the arrival of Nicolino, Handel evidently made extensive alterations to his score, and revisions and additions continued to be made during the three seasons *Amadigi* remained in the repertory. Of the 'two new symphonies' added for an orchestra benefit evening in June 1716 one eventually became the first movement of the Concerto, Op. 3 No. 4 (HWV 315). After 1717 Handel never revived the opera, but it enjoyed some popularity in HAMBURG between 1717 and 1720, when more than a dozen performances of *Oriana*, a German adaptation by KEISER, are recorded. A harlequinade, 'Amadis, a new Dramatick Opera in Dancing' was staged by RICH at LINCOLN'S INN FIELDS in 1718 and 1719.

The last opera Handel wrote before the setting up of the Royal Academy of Music in 1719 (OPERA COMPANIES, 2), *Amadigi* belongs to that still experimental phase when Handel and his colleagues were seeking the best kind of dramatic material to make the new genre attractive for a sceptical clientele. Like its most successful predecessors, *RINALDO* and *TESEO*, it lays much emphasis on magic and spectacle; in fact, like *Teseo*, it is a setting of a libretto adapted from a French *tragédie lyrique*, from *Amadis de Grèce* (1699) by Antoine Houdar de LA MOTTE, with music by Destouches. The Italian adapter is not named, but was probably HAYM. The elimination of the spectacular divertissements of the French original results in a plot that seems sometimes inconsequential. But the essential dramatic ideas come across strongly, and the librettist scores highly in providing a series of aria texts every one of which is the direct expression of powerful emotion.

Act I: Amadigi attempts escape from the sorceress Melissa's enchanted garden under cover of night. But Dardano, secretly a rival for Oriana's love, betrays him. Sunlight floods the scene, and the way is barred by evil spirits. Melissa warns Amadigi against attempting to rescue the imprisoned Oriana, but he defies her fury. As Amadigi and Dardano approach Oriana's prison, Dardano declares himself a rival. Amadigi overcomes Melissa's magic by marching through a flaming gateway, but Dardano is unable to follow. Oriana and Amadigi are reunited. In their felicity they linger too long; Melissa returns with her demons, and Oriana is carried off once more.

Act II: Amadigi comes to what he believes to be the Fountain of True Love. Gazing into it, he sees images of Oriana and Dardano exchanging amorous endearments; he swoons. Melissa leads on Oriana, who mourns him for dead. Amadigi revives, only to denounce her for her infidelity. Oriana flees, leaving him to the mercy of Melissa. Dardano despairs of winning Oriana's love, but is given new hope when Melissa proposes transforming him into the likeness of Amadigi. Before he can take advantage of this metamorphosis he is distracted by a sighting of the real Amadigi, and rushes away to kill him. Instead, he is killed himself. The bewildered Oriana learns all this from Melissa; steadfast in her love for Amadigi, she challenges the enchantress to do her worst.

In Act III, Oriana is awaiting torment and death, but remains serene in spirit; Melissa on the other hand is perplexed. Oriana and Amadigi are led in, each begging for the other to be spared. Unmoved, Melissa invokes the shade of Dardano. He, however, brings from the Underworld only the tidings that the gods are against her. Feeling her powers failing, Melissa stabs herself. The magician Orgando (Oriana's uncle) confirms that the lovers' troubles are over. Pastoral song and dance conclude the opera.

Amadigi has only four important solo roles, all for high voices, and the standard orchestra of oboes, bassoons, strings and continuo is extended only by two recorders in one aria, and by one trumpet in two arias and a sinfonia. Less instrumental music survives to accompany the various *coups de théâtre* than one would anticipate. These factors might lead the casual observer to rank it among Handel's less musically stimulating scores. In fact *Amadigi* fully deserves BURNEY's tribute: 'there is more invention, variety, and good composition, than in any one of the musical dramas of Handel which I have yet carefully and critically examined' (Burney, p. 698). If it wears its musical riches less ostentatiously than *Rinaldo*, that is because all the constituent elements of Handel's mature operatic language are now so imaginatively and freely intermingled.

A glorious array of dance-like arias illustrates the point. The hornpipe-aria 'Sento la gioia' closes the opera with brilliant concerto-like emulation between Nicolino/Amadigi and a solo trumpet; in the siciliana-aria 'Gioie, venite in sen' voice and orchestra share the materials in chamber-music-like intimacy; in the sarabande-aria 'Pena tiranna' obbligato oboe and bassoon transform a melancholy love song into something dark-hued and tragic, even sinister. Admirable too is the way in which the four characters are brought to individual life by Handel's music. Melissa is a notable forebear of Alcina. Her magickings provide much incidental diversion, but first and last – in the *scena* and aria 'Ah mio cor' in the opening scene, and in the *scena* and aria 'Io già sento', another tragic sarabande, in her death scene – she is a doomed lover, and it is in this capacity that she haunts the memory.   DAVID KIMBELL

Bianconi
W. Dean, 'A New Source for Handel's *Amadigi*', ML 72/1 (1991), 27–37
Dean and Knapp, *Operas*
Harris, *Librettos*
D. Kimbell, 'The *Amadis* Operas of Destouches and Handel', ML 49/4 (1968), 329–46
J. M. Knapp (ed.), *Amadigi di Gaula*, HHA II/8 (Kassel, 1971)
Strohm

Amarilli vezzosa ('Il duello amoroso'), HWV 82. In a lonely wood, the exasperated shepherd Daliso (castrato Pasquale Betti in the first performance) demands immediate satisfaction from Amarilli (soprano Margherita DURASTANTI), who has been keeping him on tenterhooks for a while. As she claims her right to free choice of timing, he threatens to use force, but the shepherdess, in a literal 'over-my-dead-body' challenge, offers her breast to his spear. On Daliso's repentant apologies, Amarilli reveals that her arguing was a manoeuvre in order to gain time, since her father Silvano is just approaching. The final duet blends Daliso's bitter reproaches with Amarilli's mocking dismissal of his love.

Handel set to music this witty, though metrically clumsy, text in August 1708, probably for RUSPOLI's Sunday *accademie*. The actual performance took place on 28 October, after the composer had probably left ROME to visit the MEDICI court at FLORENCE. While the scoring (for divided violins in concerto grosso arrangement, plus continuo) is unpretentious, the combination of soprano and alto voice is unique among Handel's Italian cantatas, and the extended form (Sonata–R–A–R–A–R–A–R–A–R–Duo) ranks HWV 82 halfway between a dramatic cantata and an intermezzo. Minuet and siciliano tunes, a soubrette-ish aria and a vivid confrontation of characters may indeed suggest a staged or semi-staged, intermezzo-like, performance. Daliso's 'È vanità d'un cor' was recycled just over a year later in *AGRIPPINA* (Ottone's 'Pur ch'io ti stringo al sen'), and the same character's 'Pietoso sguardo' (borrowed from the previous year's *RODRIGO*), was used again in *RINALDO*, Il *PASTOR FIDO* and *FLAVIO*.

CARLO VITALI

Amelia, Princess (b. Hanover, 30 May/10 June 1711; d. London, 31 Oct. 1786). Second daughter of GEORGE II and Queen CAROLINE, the lively and opinionated Amelia was a key personality at her father's court, particularly after Queen Caroline's death, when she took over her social duties. Although she was considered as a possible bride for Frederick II of Prussia, the match fell through, and she never married. Something of a trendsetter in her youth, she was keenly interested in politics, hunting and, from the 1760s, in landscaping her estate at Gunnersbury, Middlesex. She was taught the keyboard and musical theory by Handel from c.1723 (HANDEL, 20). Amelia became one of Handel's most loyal royal supporters in England, reportedly attending even the unpopular *THEODORA* in 1750. She also subscribed to the publication of Handel's *Grand Concertos* (Op. 6) (ORCHESTRAL WORKS, 2).   HANNAH SMITH

H. Smith, *Georgian Monarchy: Politics and Culture, 1714–1760* (Cambridge, 2006), 202–3

American Handel Festival and **American Handel Society.** See FESTIVALS, 6 and HANDEL SOCIETIES, 1

'Aminta e Fillide'. See *ARRESTA IL PASSO*

Amyand, George (b. 26 Sept. 1720; d. 16 Aug. 1766). Lawyer, British co-executor of Handel's will (HANDEL, 8), MP 1754–66, created baronet 1764. Married 9 April 1746 Anna Maria (b. 1725, d. 30 June 1767), daughter of John Abraham Corteen, a HAMBURG merchant. Their son George (b. 1748, d. 1819) married (1771) Catherine Cornewall, for whom Handel may have stood as a godparent. Their daughter Harriet married (1777) James HARRIS junior.   DAVID HUNTER

Andrews, Henry (b. c.1679; d. 1764). HAWKINS and COXE both state that soon after settling permanently in England Handel spent some months at the house of a 'Mr Andrews' at BARN ELMS in Surrey. Only one Mr Andrews fits this description – Henry Andrews, who had inherited the lease of the mansion called Barn Elms in 1711 on the death of his father, Sir Matthew Andrews, an East Indian Nabob and MP. Educated at Trinity College, CAMBRIDGE, Henry Andrews held the position of Carrier of All Royal Letters and Dispatches between the Court or Palace of Residence of the Monarch and the First Post Stage or Post

Office of the Post Master General from 1705 to 1714. There is no evidence that his association with Handel, whom he could have encountered at court, arose from any particular interest in the composer or his music. It could well be that his arrangements with Handel were commercial rather than social and that the composer's status at Barn Elms was that of a paying tenant, occupying 'apartments' (Hawkins's word) in the house, rather than a guest. The most likely date for Handel's stay at Barn Elms is the summer of 1713, after which he is said to have spent the winter at Andrews's town house in London, the location of which is unknown.   JOHN GREENACOMBE

Angelini, Antonio Giuseppe (fl. 1696–1720, nickname 'Panstufato'). Handel's principal copyist in Rome, he also copied works by Giovanni BONONCINI, Antonio CALDARA and Alessandro SCARLATTI. Several volumes in the Santini Collection in Münster (SOURCES AND COLLECTIONS, 13) are from his hand. He copied Handel's works – cantatas, church music and the Italian oratorios Il TRI-ONFO DEL TEMPO E DEL DISINGANNO and La RESURREZIONE (conducting score) – for PAMPHILIJ, RUSPOLI and OTTOBONI. The earliest surviving bill is from 16 March 1707; the last is dated 24 November 1708. Angelini collaborated with other copyists: Tarquinio LANCIANI and Alessandro Ginelli. His considerable skill at copying from Handel's autographs is evident in corrections that were inserted into his copies.   WALTER KREYSZIG

Burrows
W. and U. Kirkendale, *Music and Meaning: Studies in Music History and the Neighbouring Disciplines* (Florence, 2007)
H. J. Marx, 'The Santini Collection', *Handel Collections and their History*, ed. T. Best (Oxford, 1993)
K. Watanabe and H. J. Marx, 'Händels italienische Kopisten', *GHB* III (1987)

Anglicanism See CHURCH OF ENGLAND

Anne, Princess, of Hanover and Orange (b. Herrenhausen, near Hanover, 2 Nov. 1709; d. The Hague, 12 Jan. 1759). Daughter of GEORGE II and CAROLINE of Ansbach. As pupil, patron and friend, Anne played a significant role in Handel's life and career. Her first documented encounter with the composer occurred on 17 October 1714, when she accompanied her parents to hear him perform at ST JAMES'S PALACE. Anne's lessons with Handel had begun by June 1723 at the latest, and it is likely they commenced before that, perhaps by 1720; how long they continued is not known. Handel was paid a royal pension of £200 per annum to teach the Princesses, and he taught Anne an advanced course of figured bass accompaniment and composition; he also may have served as vocal tutor: Lord HERVEY called Handel Anne's 'singing master' (HANDEL, 20).

The details of Anne's patronage of Handel are largely unknown, but it is clear that she played an important role during the years of the so-called 'Second Academy' (1729–34) (OPERA COMPANIES, 3). In 1732 Anne encouraged Handel to perform ESTHER at the KING'S THEATRE, the first of his public oratorio performances in London. Her patronage of the composer continued after she married William IV, Prince of Orange, in 1734 and left England. Handel composed *This is the day which the Lord has made* (ANTHEMS, 4) for the wedding, and also provided the public celebratory serenata PARNASSO IN FESTA.

Hesse-Cassel on 8 May 1740. All the anthems were performed at ST JAMES'S PALACE in either the CHAPEL ROYAL or the QUEEN'S CHAPEL.

This is the day takes its text from Psalms 45: 13–15, 17 and 118: 24, Ecclesiasticus 26: 1, 3, 16 and Proverbs 31: 25, 26, 28, 29; the full anthem text was published in The *White-hall Evening-Post* for 3–6 November 1733, referring to a rehearsal which took place on 5 November at St James's Palace. The anthem includes nine solo numbers, survives in one complete score (Hamburg, Staats- und Universitätsbibliothek, M C/266) and contains various BORROWINGS from *ATHALIA* (1733) and one from the 'Caroline' Te Deum in D (1714) (TE DEUM, 2).

Sing unto God again draws on the Psalms (41:13; 68:32; 106:48; 128:1–5) and the music has survived in various sources, including some small autograph fragments (Cambridge, Fitzwilliam Museum, MU MS 251). The anthem is made up of six numbers; the elaborate final chorus, featuring taxing coloraturas for tenor soloist (probably John BEARD), was based on the final chorus of *PARNASSO IN FESTA*; some numbers (1, 2, 4) were reused in Il *TRIONFO DEL TEMPO E DELLA VERITÀ* (1737).

For the 1740 anthem the outer movements are taken from the 1736 anthem (Nos. 1, 2 and 4–6) and the middle movements from the 1734 anthem (Nos. 2–4), the only evidence for which is the printed text in The *Daily Gazetteer* for 8 May 1740; no score of the complete anthem is known to exist.

MATTHEW GARDNER

D. Burrows, *Chapel Royal*
 (ed.), *This is the Day*, Novello Handel Edition (2007)
HHB ii, 726–30

5. Funeral anthem, HWV 264

The ways of Zion do mourn, an orchestrally accompanied full anthem without soloists, was written for the funeral of Queen CAROLINE (who died on 20 November 1737). In several movements Handel used quotations of German CHORALES, 'Herr Jesu Christ, du höchstes Gut' and 'Du Friedefürst, Herr Jesu Christ', which perhaps acknowledged the shared Lutheran roots of the composer and his Queen. The text is an encomium of the deceased Queen, and was probably compiled by George CARLETON, using passages from the King James BIBLE and the Book of Common Prayer, some adapted to their new context but others unchanged (see Smith, *Oratorios*, pp. 104–7). The verses paid poignant tribute to the Queen by calling her 'great among the nations', and prominently referred to her 'righteousness', 'judgment', 'kindness' and 'meekness'.

Handel completed his composition on 12 December 1737, (see Figure 2), and in the evening of 17 December the Queen was buried in the crypt of Henry VII's Chapel (also called the Lady Chapel) at WESTMINSTER ABBEY. The anthem was performed after the burial service, and lasted about 45–50 minutes. The choir consisted of singers from the CHAPEL ROYAL, Westminster Abbey, ST PAUL'S CATHEDRAL and Windsor. London newspapers reported that 'several musical Gentlemen of distinction attended in surplices, and sang in the burial service. There were near 80 vocal performers, and 100 instrumental from his Majesty's band, and from the Opera, &.' (Deutsch, p. 444). It is generally

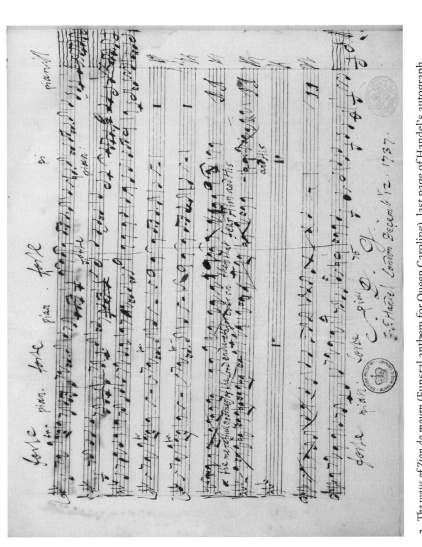

2. *The ways of Zion do mourn* (Funeral anthem for Queen Caroline), last page of Handel's autograph manuscript (R.M. 20.d.9, fol. 48ᵛ, 1737).

accepted that there was a friendly relationship between the Queen and Handel, and we know that she appreciated and promoted his art; so the composition of her funeral music was probably not the mere fulfilling of a commission, but the final acknowledgement of her closeness to him, and the expression of his own grief.

It is clear from the disposition of the autograph that the Symphony was composed last and subsequently added to the manuscript. Handel tried to revive the music of the anthem in a secular theatrical concert context on several occasions: he planned to use an Italian version in his benefit pasticcio oratorio in March 1738 (*An ORATORIO*) until GEORGE II objected, soon afterwards rejected an initial idea to use the anthem as the *Elegy on the Death of Saul and Jonathan* in Act III of *SAUL* (composed 1738), and eventually performed it (with adjusted words) as the first part of his next work *ISRAEL IN EGYPT*. In 1749 he incorporated two choruses into the FOUNDLING HOSPITAL Anthem (ANTHEMS, 8).

ANNETTE LANDGRAF

See also Jacobus GALLUS (HANDL)

Burrows, *Chapel Royal*
A. Landgraf (ed.), *Anthem for the Funeral of Queen Caroline*, HHA III/12 (Kassel etc., 2004)
    'Die Begräbniszeremonie für Queen Caroline', HJB 49 (2003)
Smith, *Oratorios*

6. Dettingen anthem

Orchestrally accompanied anthem *The King shall rejoice* (HWV 265) in five movements, musically distinct from the Coronation Anthem with the same title (ANTHEMS, 3); both begin with settings of Psalm 21 verse 1. Composed between 30 July and 3 August 1743 as a companion-piece to the Dettingen Te Deum (TE DEUM, 5), and probably in anticipation of a state Thanksgiving Service for the recent victory at DETTINGEN but not performed until 27 November, following the King's return to London. Handel transformed musical ideas for three movements from chamber sonatas by TELEMANN, in one case via a chorus movement in *SEMELE*, composed a month previously; the last movement was subsequently used as the finale for *JOSEPH AND HIS BRETHREN*.

Burrows, *Chapel Royal*

7. Anthem on the Peace

Orchestrally accompanied four-movement anthem *How beautiful are the feet* (HWV 266) composed for the service at the CHAPEL ROYAL on the Thanksgiving Day for the Peace of AIX-LA-CHAPELLE, 25 April 1749, and repeated at Handel's FOUNDLING HOSPITAL concert the following month. The next performance, in a reconstruction by Donald Burrows, took place in 1973. Solo movements feature treble and alto singers from the Chapel, matched by flute and oboe. The music of the anthem was recomposed or adapted from movements in *MESSIAH*, the *OCCASIONAL ORATORIO* and the Chapel Royal anthem *I will magnify thee* (HWV 250^b) (ANTHEMS, 4).

See also War of the AUSTRIAN SUCCESSION

D. Burrows, 'Handel's Peace Anthem', MT 114/1570 (Dec. 1973), 1230–2

8. Foundling Hospital anthem

The orchestrally accompanied anthem *Blessed are they that considereth the poor and needy* (HWV 268), first performed by Handel in his concert at the FOUNDLING HOSPITAL on 27 May 1749. It constituted the main item in Part III of the programme and was described in the wordbook as 'The Anthem composed on this occasion'. The music was mainly adapted, though very effectively, from other sources, principally *The ways of Zion do mourn* (ANTHEMS, 5) and a discarded chorus from the recently composed oratorio *SUSANNA*; it concluded with the HALLELUJAH CHORUS from *MESSIAH*, which at that time had only received six performances in London. The original version of the anthem seems to have consisted entirely of choral movements but at some stage, probably in 1751, Handel revised the anthem substantially, adding an aria (composed for GUADAGNI) and a duet for two trebles. This version may have been performed at the official opening of the Hospital Chapel in 1753, and was included in a concert that the Hospital gave in memory of Handel in 1759. DONALD BURROWS

D. Burrows, 'Handel and the Foundling Hospital', ML 58/3 (July 1977), 269–84

'APOLLO E DAFNE'. See *La TERRA È LIBERATA*

Arbace (*Arbaces*), HWV A¹⁰. PASTICCIO opera in three acts, based on Leonardo VINCI's *Artaserse* (Rome, 1730). It was first performed at the KING'S THEATRE on 5 January 1734. Vinci's setting of METASTASIO's libretto was officially the first, although HASSE's setting was performed in Venice seven days later. *Artaserse* became Vinci's most famous opera.

Artabano, commander of the royal guard of Serse (Xerxes), King of Persia, plots to kill him and his sons, Dario and Artaserse, and take the throne for himself. Having murdered Serse, he gives his bloody sword to his son Arbace, telling him to flee, and persuades Artaserse to have Dario executed as the presumed assassin of their father. Caught with the murder weapon in his hand, Arbace says he is innocent but refuses to explain. Semira, Arbace's sister and Artaserse's lover, defends her brother. Mandane, Artaserse's sister and Arbace's lover, demands Arbace's death, though she still loves him. Artaserse is torn by conflicting loyalties to his dead father and Arbace, his dearest friend. After Arbace quells a rebellion led by Artabano's henchman Megabise Artaserse finally becomes convinced of his friend's innocence. Arbace continues to protect his father, but when he prepares to drink from a poisoned cup intended for Artaserse, Artabano stops him and admits his own guilt. Artaserse exiles Artabano, and both pairs of lovers are happily united.

The cast was as follows:

Arbace	Giovanni CARESTINI (castrato)
Mandane	Anna Maria STRADA del Pò (soprano)
Artaserse	Carlo SCALZI (castrato)
Artabano	Margherita DURASTANTI (mezzo-soprano)
Semira	Maria Caterina NEGRI (alto)
Megabise	Maria Rosa Negri (mezzo-soprano)

Handel originally cast the bass Gustavus WALTZ as Artabano, Durastanti as Semira, and Caterina Negri as Megabise, but when Waltz became unavailable

(*SEMIRAMIDE*) the other two singers moved up in the hierarchy, and Caterina Negri's sister took on the remaining role. Unlike the two pasticcios that preceded it in the 1733–4 season, *Semiramide* and *CAIO FABBRICIO*, *Arbace* enjoyed considerable success, running for six nights in January and another three in March. Mrs Pendarves (later DELANY), who knew it was 'an opera of Vinci's', thought it 'pretty enough, but not to compare to Handel's compositions' (Deutsch, p. 361). WALSH issued a small collection of 'favourite songs'.

In preparing his conducting score of *Arbace*, now in the Staats- und Universitätsbibliothek Hamburg, Handel made use of a manuscript that his friend Charles JENNENS had acquired along with the aria collection on which the pasticcio *Caio Fabbricio* is based. Now in, the Sibley Music Library, Eastman School of Music, University of Rochester, USA, it is a complete score of Vinci's opera, containing many pencilled changes and directions in Handel's hand. In the first five scenes he entered the recitative cuts and revisions in Jennens's score. SMITH copied them into the conducting score, but already in Scene iii the copyist began leaving some notes to be filled in by Handel (as he had done in the conducting score of *LUCIO PAPIRIO*), and after the change of cast took effect in Scene vi Handel began writing all the recitative notes in the conducting score himself after Smith had copied the text.

Copying of the conducting score must have begun in October 1733, before the elimination of Waltz, which also required revisions in the score of *Semiramide*, first performed on 30 October. The final version included arias by Hasse and PORTA along with fourteen arias, an arioso, a duet, the final *coro* and three accompagnati from Vinci's score. Carestini had created the part of Arbace for Vinci in ROME, but his voice was now somewhat lower, leading Handel to replace his aria 'Mi scacci sdegnato' and cut the second half of the arioso 'Perché tarda'. As in *Semiramide* and *Caio Fabbricio* an aria for Carestini was inserted just before the final *coro*. Initially he requested 'Son qual nave che agitata', an aria of unknown origin not to be confused with Giay's setting of the same text sung by FARINELLI in Lucca and London, but later he replaced it with a PORTA aria, while 'Son qual nave' was transferred to the end of Act I in place of Vinci's famous 'Vo solcando un mar crudele'. Similarly Scalzi may have intended to replace his Act III aria 'Nuvoletta opposta al sole', which lay too high for him, with an aria from Hasse's *Dalisa* (1730), but instead the pages that had been left blank for it were filled with an aria from Hasse's *Siroe* (1733) and the Dalisa aria went into Act II.

Vinci's overture having been used for *Semiramide*, Handel replaced it with an unidentified sinfonia. He reworked Vinci's secco recitatives in response to the different ranges of some of the characters and the extensively abridged text, but he also copied many of Vinci's notes without change, making it impossible to sort out the two composers' contributions solely on the basis of the conducting score. The printed libretto, which has only recently come to light (copies in Bibliothèque nationale, National Library of Scotland, and University of Texas), represents an earlier version than the conducting score. JOHN H. ROBERTS

H. D. Clausen, *Händels Direktionspartituren ('Handexemplare')* (Hamburg, 1972)

J. H. Roberts, 'Handel and Charles Jennens's Italian Music Manuscripts', *Music and Theatre: Essays in Honour of Winton Dean*, ed. N. Fortune (Cambridge, 1987)

Strohm

Arbuthnot, John (bap. Arbuthnott, Kincardineshire 29 April 1667; d. London 27 Feb. 1735). Scottish physician, mathematician and satirical writer. A graduate of Marischal College, Aberdeen, Arbuthnot later acquired MD degrees from St Andrews and CAMBRIDGE universities. He became physician to Queen ANNE, as well as a fellow of the Royal Society. He collaborated with Jonathan Swift on TORY satirical pamphlets and created the character of John Bull. On the accession of GEORGE I he lost his court appointments but maintained a fashionable private practice. Along with Jonathan Swift, Alexander POPE, John GAY and others, he was a member of the Scriblerus Club, a group of leading writers who despised false taste. He assisted Gay and Pope with the comedy *Three Hours after Marriage* (1717) and contributed verse to the third volume of *Miscellanies* (1731), and was noted for his wit, lively imagination and political satire.

How Arbuthnot met Handel is not known, but by June 1713 he was identified as the composer's 'great patron and friend' who 'has the composer constantly at his house'. Arbuthnot was credited with composing several anthems sung in the CHAPEL ROYAL before Queen Anne, and, although no music survives, he may have been responsible for the paraphrase text of Psalm 42 that Handel used for his first Chapel Royal anthem *As pants the Hart* (HWV 251^a) (ANTHEMS, 1). Arbuthnot probably introduced Handel to the CANNONS Circle through his personal friendship with James Brydges, Earl of Carnarvon (later 1st Duke of CHANDOS), and his brother, the Revd Dr Henry Brydges. At Cannons he may have had a hand in the preparation of the libretto for ESTHER (HWV 50^a). He was a subscriber and director of the Royal Academy of Music (OPERA COMPANIES, 2), which deputed him to negotiate terms with the singer ANASTASIA ROBINSON. Though plagued by poor health in his later years, Arbuthnot continued to publish on medical subjects. Dr Johnson eulogised him as 'a man estimable for his learning, amiable for his life, and venerable for his piety'.

GRAYDON BEEKS and LESLIE M. M. ROBARTS

G. Beeks, '"A Club of Composers": Handel, Pepusch and Arbuthnot at Cannons', *Handel: A Tercentenary Collection*, ed. A. Hicks and S. Sadie (London, 1987)

Arcadia. An ancient Greek district in the Peloponnese (Morea), a wild region traditionally inhabited by herdsmen. In European literature and art, the term denotes the pastoral environment or *locus amoenus* (pleasurable place), providing an alternative location (*utopia*) to that of modern civilisation. Although classical literature (Hesiod, Theocritus, Virgil's *Bucolica*) sometimes place their shepherd folk in Arcadia, our vision of the Arcadian landscape is a Renaissance creation, following Jacopo Sannazaro's poem *L'Arcadia* (Naples, 1504). Following Polybius, the Arcadians were thought to be a peaceful community because they were musical. Music was imagined to be the 'natural' idiom of shepherds, in which speaking and singing coincided. PASTORAL topics abound in solo cantata and opera, where Thyrsis and Chloris represent the modern individuals whose passions are really described. Other re-creations of Arcadia are palace gardens and pleasure groves such as the 'Parrhasian Grove' in ROME, designed for the ARCADIAN ACADEMY by Antonio Canevari (1723). REINHARD STROHM

R. Jenkyns, 'Virgil and Arcadia', *Journal of Roman Studies*, 79 (1989), 26–39
H. Jung, *Die Pastorale. Studien zur Geschichte eines musikalischen Topos* (Berne and Munich, 1980)

R. Strohm, 'Les Sauvages, Music in Utopia, and the Decline of the Courtly Pastoral', Il Saggiatore musicale, 11/1 (2004), 21–49

Arcadian Academy, The (Accademia degli Arcadi). One of the most famous Italian academies, the Arcadian Academy was founded in ROME in 1690 by a circle of literary, artistic and musical men who had originally been gathered together in a group by the exiled Queen Christina of Sweden (who died in 1689). The academy was named after the Greek district ARCADIA and the members adopted Greek PASTORAL names. Among the fourteen founders were the president Giovanni Maria Crescimbeni and Carlo Innocenzo FRUGONI. During the presidency of Crescimbeni (1690–1728), the academy had c.1,000 members, of whom about 600 lived in Rome. The writers Pietro METASTASIO, Apostolo ZENO, Silvio STAMPIGLIA were all members of the academy, and so were all of Handel's patrons in Rome including Benedetto PAMPHILIJ (nicknamed 'Fenicio Larisseo'), Pietro OTTOBONI ('Crateo Ericino'), Prince Francesco Maria RUSPOLI ('Olinto'/'Arsenio'). The composers Arcangelo CORELLI, Alessandro SCARLATTI and Bernardo Pasquini were members.

The Arcadians wished to reform Italian aesthetic and poetic style. In vehement opposition to the widespread ornate style present in recent architecture, art and music, Arcadian texts were influenced by classical Graeco-Roman poetry, conveyed pastoral simplicity with less comical elements than had become familiar in typical late seventeenth-century dramma per musica and used pastoral allusions to suggest that one could model one's own life after the idyllic lifestyle of carefree and innocent shepherds, thus circumventing the difficulties of contemporary socio-political life.

CHRYSANDER proposed that the twenty-three-year-old Handel was too young to become a member of the Arcadian Academy because the minimum age for admission was twenty-four, but this theory has been discredited by Kirkendale, who proved that the age limit was not a serious obstacle to joining. It seems most likely that Handel simply did not desire to become a member. However, many of his CANTATAS were written for academy-member patrons, and perhaps performed at the academy's gatherings. Some were set to poetry written by Pamphilij and Ottoboni, and OH, COME CHIARE E BELLE, also known under the name 'Olinto pastore', was evidently an Arcadian cantata connected with Ruspoli. Later in London, Handel set cantata texts by academy member Paolo ROLLI.   WALTER KREYSZIG

I. Carini, L'Arcadia dal 1690–1890: Memorie storiche (Rome, 1891)
F. Chrysander, G. F. Händel, 2nd edn (Leipzig, 1919), vol. 1
E. T. Harris, Handel as Orpheus (Cambridge, MA, 2001)
W. and U. Kirkendale, Music and Meaning: Studies in Music History and the Neighbouring Disciplines (Florence, 2007)
F. Pierno, 'Crateo, Olinto, Archimede e l'Arcadia: Rime per alcuni spettacoli operistici romani (1710–1711)', Händel e gli Scarlatti a Roma, ed. N. Pirrotta and A. Ziino (Florence, 1987)
F. Santovetti, 'Arcadia a Roma Anno Domini 1690: Accademia e vizi di forma', Modern Language Notes 112 (1997), 21–37
A. M. Giorgetti Vichi (ed.), Gli Arcadi dal 1690 al 1800 (Rome, 1977)

Archbishop of Canterbury. See William WAKE

aria

1. Structures and forms

The aria forms the backbone of many of the genres cultivated by Handel through-out his career: the Italian secular cantatas of his early years, the Italian operas of his middle years, and, with the CHORUS, the English oratorios of his maturity. The most common aria form found in these genres is the da capo aria. This is particularly true of the cantatas and operas. The oratorios include a broader array of forms, but the da capo aria is still the most common type.

The da capo aria is an expanded ternary form. The formal plan of the five-part da capo aria includes an A section consisting of two complete statements by the vocalist of the A section text (A1 and A2), the first typically modulating from tonic to dominant and the second returning to the tonic. In minor-mode A sections the modulation is typically to the relative major (III) rather than the dominant. The B section, which sets the remaining lines of text, offers a change of various musical elements including key and sometimes mode. It is followed by a restatement of the A section, with the singer increasingly ornamenting his or her part.

Not all da capo arias follow the five-part scheme precisely. For instance, the A section may be divided into three parts. 'The Parent Bird' from SUSANNA, an aria in the minor mode, includes a three-part rather than a two-part A section, with an A1 modulating to the minor dominant, an A2 ending in the subdominant, and an A3 cadencing to the tonic. In 'Ah Jealousy, thou pelican' in JOSEPH AND HIS BRETHREN, also in minor mode, there are again three parts in the A section, the first cadencing to the relative major and A2 and A3 both move to the tonic. A3 actually contains two statements of the A text.

The vast majority of arias in the operas are in da capo form, with occasional one-part arias that have the same form as the A section of a da capo A1 and A2 ('Thus let my thanks be pay'd' in SEMELE). There are sometimes exceptions in the operas, such as 'Stille amare' in TOLOMEO, with its unusual ending as Tolomeo falls unconscious instead of completing his da capo, or 'Vaghe pupille', the famous mad scene in ORLANDO. A flexible approach to form is even more common in the oratorios. There are, for example, occasional strophic arias, as in 'Oh Lord, whose mercies numberless', from SAUL, an air sung by David to appease the King. JEPHTHA features a two-tempo aria, 'Farewell, ye limpid springs and floods', that begins with an E minor Larghetto in 12/8 followed by an E major Andante larghetto in common time. The oratorios frequently feature one-part arias, and a related aria type that has the same musical form as the cavatina but uses a new text for A2 ('My soul rejects the thought with scorn' in Saul).

In spite of the larger number of options in the oratorios, Handel still frequently employs da capo form, and even many arias that are not da capos still relate to this form. For example, the 'written-out da capo' has an A section that ends in the tonic, a B section, and a return related to the A section that is different enough to require writing out ('Rejoice greatly' from *MESSIAH*). A 'modified da capo' follows a similar pattern with the significant difference that its first part ends on a key other than the tonic ('Oh sacred oracles of truth' in *BELSHAZZAR*). On rare occasions Handel scores a dramatic effect by setting up the expectation of a da capo and then truncating it, such as 'Leave me, loathsome light' in *Semele*, in which Somnus falls asleep after the B section, without completing his aria. Thus the da capo form and manipulations of it form a common thread running throughout Handel's oeuvre.   DAVID ROSS HURLEY

D. R. Hurley, *Handel's Muse: Patterns of Creation in his Oratorios and Musical Dramas, 1743–1751* (Oxford, 2001)

C. S. Larue, 'Handel and the Aria', *The Cambridge Companion to Handel*, ed. D. Burrows (Cambridge, 1997)

2. Musical rhetoric

The da capo aria format in general provided little text and therefore not many affective changes. Handel's primary interest seems to have been in exploiting to the full all the possibilities offered by the special *dispositio* of words, verses and sentences, in distilling as many facets of meaning and *Affekt* from the text as possible, and in presenting the text in a detailed and nuanced *elaboratio* (RHETORIC).

In the *dispositio* repetitions of words or textual units, either freely composed or conforming to rhetoric patterns, were put to use. *MATTHESON* listed such a rhetorical pattern as: Exordium (introduction), Narratio (statement of facts), Propositio (proposition of the main points), Confirmatio (affirmative proof), Confutatio (refutation) and Peroratio (conclusion). Many of Handel's arias are modelled on this pattern. For example, in the A section of Polifemo's aria 'Non sempre, no, crudele, mi parlerai così' from *ACI, GALATEA E POLIFEMO* the text is heard in its entirety (as *exordium* and *narratio*), then the *propositio* emphasises the essential textual contents: 'no, no, non sempre, mi parlerai così' and 'crudele'. The figures of speech resulting from the repetitions of certain words and changes in the word order, called *epizeuxis* and *parembole*, lead to a heightened intensity in the music as well. The *elaboratio* can also be shown to have been worked out in detail by the inclusion of *exclamatio* and a *quinta deficiens* (as *saltus duriusculus* and symbolising something that is missing). The following part of the speech is an (affirming) *confirmatio* and consequently the singing voice repeats the entire text but, as *hyperbaton*, in a higher range and with enormous *exclamatio* leaps. Then follow more repetitions of words intended as refutation, as *confutatio* ('no, no, no, no, no, no, non sempre, no, crudele'), in addition to other figures of musical rhetoric like *emphasis* (repetition), *suspiratio* (sighing pause), *saltus duriusculus*, *catachresis* ('wrong' turn), *exclamatio* and (beginning) *hyperbaton*. The latter is continued with renewed text repetitions in the *peroratio*, where the words 'mi parlerai così' receive an additional affirmation (*epizeuxis*), which leads to a prolonged *exclamatio* including *pathopoiia* (dissonance). Even the orchestral postlude, repeating a variation of Polifemo's vocal line (as *paronomasia*) and (as *epanalepsis*) the B section of the aria are modelled on rhetorical principles. This B section portrays the 'devilish' giant with numerous *saltus duriusculi* (for example the tritone), while the portrayal of his sufferings for love ('a poco a poco, a poco a poco') calls forth the *passus duriusculus* of the descending chromatic fourths, the most powerful symbol of pain available in the vocabulary of musical rhetoric.

All of Handel's arias draw upon similar artistic devices, although it is not always possible to trace preconceived patterns. But even in arias which primarily use a repetition of the entire text (e.g. 'Open thy marble jaws' in *JEPHTHA*), the internal structure is geared to the principles of narration and confirmation, refutation (of single words) and final repetition. The interpretative elucidation or retracing of the text by musical-rhetoric figures is therefore of continued high relevance.   HARTMUT KRONES (Trans. ANGELA BAIER)

H. Krones, 'Musik and Musikalische Figurenlehre', *Historisches Wörterbuch der Rhetorik* 5, ed. G. Ueding (Tübingen, 2001)
J. Mattheson, *Der vollkommene Capellmeister* (Hamburg, 1739)

3. Ritornellos and orchestration
The ritornello is a regular feature of Handel's arias. His da capo arias typically include ritornellos that appear as introductions and conclusions to the A section, and sometimes there are abbreviated ritornellos after the internal vocal cadence to the dominant (or related key) in the middle of the A section. B sections usually do not feature ritornellos. Sometimes Handel includes a new substitute ritornello for the repeat of the A section opening, achieved through the use of a *dal segno* indication. Very often the opening ritornello includes material that will appear in the vocal body of the aria, described by one author as a 'synopsis before the event'. But sometimes Handel uses material that is distinct from the vocal line.

The extent to which Handel labelled his scores with details of INSTRUMEN-TATION can vary widely. For instance, as Stahura has pointed out, the autograph of *RADAMISTO* is full of carefully marked detail, while most of the movements in his next full opera *FLORIDANTE* do not even have instrumental specifications at their outset. In general, however, Handel used typical baroque orchestration for the bulk of his arias: strings, winds and basso continuo. It is difficult to know the exact instrumentation of Handel's continuo; there may have been a great deal of flexibility. But one can point out certain tendencies. He seems to have used just one harpsichord until the late 1720s and often two harpsichords thereafter. In the oratorios both harpsichord and organ are used (PERFORMANCE PRACTICE).

Handel could use the sparsest orchestration and give it a specific colour, such as arias for voice and continuo alone, with sometimes a full band of string instruments joining for the final ritornello. In his operas in particular it is not unusual to have merely first violins, voice and basso continuo, but in other arias including strings he sometimes has violins divided into first and second parts, violas, voice and basso continuo. Oboes often double the violin part when they do not have an individual parts, but at other times they are used very prominently for orchestral colour, as in Hercules's 'Alcides' name in latest story' (*HERCULES*) which is remarkable for double-reed colour.

In fact, within the limits of baroque practice, Handel was an innovative orchestrator who created many special effects. This is true at least from his

Italian period – some of the cantatas have wonderful effects, such as the sound of oboe and pizzicato strings, or obbligato cello in 'Apollo e Dafne' (*La TERRA È LIBERATA*). In his English years Handel's Italian operas involve a great deal of instrumental effects in spite of their limited instruments. One famous example is 'Scherza infida' from *ARIODANTE*, where he uses two muted violins, muted viola with a soft bassoon part, voice and pizzicato strings on the bass. Recorders and flutes, probably played most often by the double-reed players, add special colouring to many arias, such as 'Softest sounds' in *ATHALIA*, where a solo flute is featured. An unusual aria in *ALEXANDER BALUS* shows just how striking Handel's orchestration can be: 'Hark, he strikes the golden lyre' includes parts for two flutes, violin 1 and 2, viola, cello 1 and 2, harp and mandolin, and a continuo that includes bassoons. Brass instruments are used sparingly but sometimes prominently in Handel's arias; there are several famous examples of trumpet solo, from *ETERNAL SOURCE OF LIGHT DIVINE* to 'Revenge, Timotheus cries' (*ALEXANDER'S FEAST*) to 'The trumpet shall sound' in *MESSIAH*. Handel used solo horn only once in his operas, in the famous 'Va tacito e nascosto' in *GIULIO CESARE*.   DAVID ROSS HURLEY

See also INSTRUMENTATION

P. Brainard, 'Aria and Ritornello: New Aspects of the Comparison Handel/Bach', *Bach, Handel, Scarlatti: Tercentenary Essays*, ed. P. Williams (Cambridge, 1985)
Dean, *Oratorios*
M. Stahura, 'Handel and the Orchestra', *The Cambridge Companion to Handel*, ed. D. Burrows (Cambridge, 1997)

4. Instrumental arrangements

In his lifetime many arrangements for instruments alone were made of Handel's arias. Handel certainly made a few himself; only two, for the harpsichord, survive in his autograph: (1) a shortened version (only 19 bars) of 'Molto voglio' in *RINALDO* (HWV 482¹), and (2) a complete version of 'Sventurato godi, o core abbandonato' in *FLORIDANTE* (HWV 482²); the first is a simple affair, perhaps written as an easy piece for a pupil, but the *Floridante* aria is of great interest and beauty. It has a full keyboard texture, with some changes from the orchestral version; the passages for continuo accompaniment only are beautifully realised, while the voice part is richly ornamented. The word-text is underlaid to the music for its first statement in the A section, as are the first two words of the B section; the internal and concluding ritornellos are marked V. over the upper stave. It is a neat fair copy, so was presumably written for a patron or pupil who admired the aria. Three other arrangements in a similar style are found in manuscript copies of the same period (1721–2), which may be authentic: 'Ombra cara' in *RADAMISTO* (HWV 482³), with the full word-text and an unornamented vocal line, and 'Pupille sdegnose' and 'Come se ti vedrò' in *MUZIO SCEVOLA* (HWV 482⁴ and HWV 482⁵), which are more in the manner of 'Sventurato'.

                    TERENCE BEST

T. Best (ed.), *Einzeln überlieferte Instrumetalwerke II*, HHA IV/19 (Kassel, 1988)

Arianna in Creta, HWV 32. Italian opera. The plot concerns the Athenian prince Teseo's mission to overturn the barbaric tribute of human sacrificial offerings that

Athens must pay to Crete. He accomplishes this by defeating the Minotaur in the labyrinth at Knossos, with the essential aid of his lover Arianna (the daughter of King Minos). The plot is expanded by Arianna's jealous misunderstandings of Teseo's honourable actions, the Cretan warrior Tauride's conceited enmity towards Teseo, and the Athenian victim Carilda's eventual love for her steadfast compatriot Alceste. The action is complicated by Tauride's lust for Carilda, and the latter's unrequited initial love for Teseo.

Pietro PARIATI's libretto *Teseo in Creta* was first set to music by Francesco Bartolomeo CONTI (Vienna, 1715), although none of its aria texts appear in Handel's version. The anonymous London adaptation was based on the revised version *Arianna e Teseo*, set by Leonardo LEO (ROME, 1729). It was also prepared directly from another adapted version of Pariati's libretto that had been used for a pasticcio at NAPLES in 1721. Most aria and duet texts in Handel's version were taken almost without change from the Neapolitan and Roman librettos, although seven of the twenty-eight texts seem to be exclusive to the London setting. It is possible that Handel might have met Leo during the 1729 VENICE Carnival, and perhaps his interaction with Leo, or at least some exposure to Leo's recent work, influenced his decision to set *Arianna* to music in autumn 1733. His trip to Italy in 1729 (HANDEL, 15) certainly influenced the new opera in other direct ways: it was during this journey that Handel first became interested in hiring the castratos Giovanni CARESTINI and Carlo SCALZI for London. He eventually did so after most of the KING'S THEATRE opera company defected to the OPERA OF THE NOBILITY at the end of the 1732–3 season (only STRADA remained loyal to Handel).

After Handel's return from OXFORD to London in summer 1733, he composed *Arianna in Creta* for his new group of singers in advance of the 1733–4 season. The first draft was completed on 5 October 1733, but then he extensively revised the opera. Most of Teseo's highly virtuosic arias had to be transposed down because Handel seems to have made a slight miscalculation about the pitch of Carestini's voice (for example, Teseo's heroic 'Qui ti sfido, o mostro infame', sung as he goes to fight the Minotaur, was transposed down from E major to E flat major). Some other alterations might have been made for artistic reasons. The inserted 'Sdegnata sei con me' (I.xi) exploited a more lyrical aspect of Carestini's singing and also adds tenderness to Teseo's characterisation. 'Bella sorge la speranza' was allocated to Alceste in the original draft of III.ii, but Handel reassigned it to Teseo in the *scena ultima*, where it was transposed down from E flat to D major in order to form the first part of an attractive finale. The duet 'Mira adesso' for Teseo and Arianna (III.vii) was not part of the original draft, but inserted before the first performance.

It is likely that rumours about Handel setting *Arianna in Creta* reached the Opera of the Nobility, whose music director Nicola PORPORA had already composed a setting of Pariati's libretto (Venice, 1727). Handel's competitors responded by producing their own 'Arianna' opera (*Arianna in Nasso*, libretto by Paolo ROLLI) at LINCOLN'S INN FIELDS on 29 December 1733, almost a month before *Arianna in Creta* was premiered at the KING'S THEATRE on 26 January 1734. Handel's cast was as follows:

Arianna	Anna Strada del Pò (soprano)
Teseo, Prince of Athens	Giovanni Carestini (castrato)
Alceste, an Athenian, in love with Carila	Carlo Scalzi (castrato)
Carilda, an Athenian, in love with Teseo	Maria Caterina NEGRI (contralto)
Tauride, a Cretan, in love with Carilda	Margherita DURASTANTI (mezzo-soprano)
Minos	Gustavus WALTZ (bass)
Il Sonno	Waltz

Members of the AUDIENCE were enthusiastic about Carestini. Shortly after Handel's season began with *SEMIRAMIDE*, Lady Bristol wrote that she was impressed by the new castrato, but thought that 'the rest are all scrubbs except old Durastante, that sings as well as ever she did' (Deutsch, 336). The return of Durastanti to the London stage was presumably unexpected: the composer created two show-stealing moments for her character Tauride, the arrogant 'Mirami, altero in volto' (I.i) and 'Qual leon' (III.vi, a splendid showpiece with horns). However, Handel's reduction of 'Qual leon' to only its A section for the performances suggests that his former prima donna's vocal powers were waning. Alceste is the only role that Handel composed for Scalzi; his simile aria 'Son qual stanco pellegrino' (II.xii) features sublime interplay between the soprano voice and a graceful solo cello part written for Francisco CAPORALE. Carilda was the first role that Handel wrote for Negri. BURNEY disparagingly remarked that she 'seems to have possessed no uncommon abilities', but Handel did not always match his own high standards when writing for a new singer for the first time, and his later roles written for her suggest that she was a capable and useful performer. Burney claimed that Waltz had 'a coarse figure, and a still coarser voice'. Even if so, neither attribute is incompatible with the tyrannical Minos.

Arianna in Creta ran for sixteen performances. It was promptly revived the next season (Handel's first at COVENT GARDEN), when some alterations were made: a few arias were abridged or omitted, Alceste was adapted for the tenor John BEARD, and BALLET MUSIC was added for Marie SALLÉ. In the later eighteenth century, *Arianna in Creta* was remembered and admired only by a few connoisseurs: Gottfried van SWIETEN included 'Ariadne' on his shortlist of printed scores requested from James Harris junior in 1777, and Burney judged that Handel 'seems to have exerted his powers of invention, and abilities in varying the accompaniments throughout this opera with more vigour than in any former drama since the dissolution of the Royal Academy of Music in 1728' (pp. 783–5). Modern commentators have been harsh in their criticism of the opera, but it contains plenty of strong dramatic ideas and masterfully crafted music.   DAVID VICKERS

Dean, *Operas*
G. Gronda, *La carriera di un librettista: Pietro Pariati da Reggio di Lombardia* (Bologna, 1990)
Harris, *Librettos*
Strohm
    'Arianna in Creta: Musical Dramaturgy', *Dramma per Musica: Italian Opera Seria of the Eighteenth Century* (New Haven, 1997)
D. Vickers, '*Handel's Performing Versions*: A Study of Four Music Theatre Works from the "Second Academy" Period', Ph.D. dissertation (The Open University, 2007)

Ariodante, HWV 33. Handel composed the opera *Ariodante* for his first season at COVENT GARDEN in 1734–5. The libretto was adapted from Antonio SALVI's *Ginevra principessa di Scozia*, originally set by Jacopo Antonio PERTI and produced at the Medici villa of Pratolino near FLORENCE in 1708: it is possible that Handel saw this production. Salvi's libretto was shortened for the London version, partly in order to make room for the addition of ballets and choruses, but the adaptation was sensitively done, and the plot and characterisations are among the best in any opera seria. The story is taken from Cantos 4–5 of Ludovico ARIOSTO's famous poem *Orlando furioso*, written in the early sixteenth century. The central event – the trick by which Polinesso persuades Ariodante that Ginevra is unfaithful – had also been used by Shakespeare in *Much Ado about Nothing*. Salvi (and Handel) retained Ariosto's location of Edinburgh for the drama; fundamental to the plot is the idea, derived from Ariosto, that in medieval Scotland the death sentence was automatic for unfaithful women. The chivalric background to Ariosto's narrative also accounts for the tournament scene in Act III.

In the opening scenes Ginevra, the King's daughter, rejects the advances of Polinesso, the Duke of Albany, who receives hints that Dalinda, her lady-in-waiting, would be more favourable to him. In the palace garden the King overhears Ginevra and the visiting knight Ariodante pledging their love, and approves the match. Dalinda agrees to Polinesso's request that she should admit him to Ginevra's apartment, dressed in her mistress's clothes, and deflects the attentions of Lurcanio, Ariodante's brother. Act II takes place that evening. Ariodante reacts strongly to Polinesso's taunt that Ginevra is unfaithful, but then sees a woman dressed as Ginevra admitting Polinesso; Lurcanio restrains him from immediate thoughts of suicide. Inside the palace the King is about to announce Ariodante as his heir when the courtier Odoardo brings a report that Ariodante is dead, having thrown himself into the sea. Lurcanio produces a document reporting Ginevra's apparent infidelity, and offers a challenge to anyone prepared to defend her. When Ginevra greets the King she is dumbfounded and confused when he rejects her. In Act III it turns out that Ariodante is not dead; he rescues Dalinda from assassins and learns of Polinesso's plot. At the palace Polinesso offers himself as Ginevra's champion, and the King accepts him in spite of Ginevra's opposition. In the combat Lurcanio mortally wounds Polinesso: apparently the heavens are signalling Ginevra's guilt, but a stranger in a helmet with lowered visor comes to her defence. It is Ariodante, who says he has knowledge of Ginevra's innocence, which he will reveal if Dalinda is promised a pardon. Odoardo reports that the dying Polinesso has confessed his crime, Dalinda accepts Lurcanio as her lover, the King releases Ginevra from her confinement, and the happiness of the two pairs of lovers is celebrated with an entertainment of dancing and singing.

Ariodante was composed in the summer and early autumn of 1734. Handel began the overture on 12 August and drafted the first two acts with his usual rapidity, finishing Act I on 28 August and Act II on 9 September, but then he seems to have laid the score aside and the drafting of Act III was not completed until 24 October. In the meantime there had been some changes in his resources for the following season. Lurcanio was written as a soprano-clef role in the first two acts, but in Act III he is a tenor; when Handel returned to the score he also took the opportunity to incorporate the Covent Garden dancers led by Marie SALLÉ, adding ballet sequences at the end of each act. A further group of subsequent revisions involved the recomposition of Dalinda's music for a soprano instead of a contralto. *Ariodante* came to the stage on 8 January 1735 and ran for eleven performances, a good total in terms of the repertory programmes of the London opera companies. The cast comprised:

Ariodante	Giovanni CARESTINI (castrato)
Ginevra	Anna STRADA del Pò (soprano)
Polinesso	Maria Caterina NEGRI (alto)
Dalinda	Cecilia YOUNG (soprano)
Re	Gustavus WALTZ (bass)
Lurcanio	John BEARD (tenor)
Odoardo	Stoppelaer (tenor)

In *Ariodante* Handel wrote some spectacular arias for Carestini, which displayed his vocal agility and wide range (a–a″), but also contributed powerfully to the delineation of his situation at key moments in the drama: in Act I his joy at the prospective union with Ginevra, in Act II his wretchedness at Ginevra's apparent infidelity and in Act III his realisation that his problems have the prospect of a happy resolution. The music for all of the characters, in Handel's most expansive and exuberant style, shows him at the height of his powers as an opera composer; *Ariodante* also has one of the best librettos that he ever set.

The opera was composed at a difficult time in Handel's career. Not only had he lost the use of London's premier opera theatre, but this was the period of greatest success for the rival company, the OPERA OF THE NOBILITY, who brought FARINELLI and CUZZONI to London to join already popular singers such as SENESINO and MONTAGNANA. Furthermore, dissension in the royal family was running high, affecting the patronage base in London: in the 1734–5 season FREDERICK, Prince of Wales, exclusively supported the Nobility, though the King and Queen remained with Handel. Princess ANNE, formerly the composer's greatest royal supporter but now married to the Prince of Orange, never saw *Ariodante* in the theatre but probably heard Handel play the music at a private preview to the royal family at KENSINGTON PALACE, during a return visit to London.

Handel revived *Ariodante* in a shortened version for two performances in May 1736. The dances were omitted, but the most striking feature was the replacement of Carestini's music with arias by other composers, in order to accommodate the new castrato Gioacchino CONTI in the title role.

DONALD BURROWS

D. Burrows (ed.), *Ariodante*, HHA II/32 (Kassel, 2007)
    'Good for the Garden: The Composition of Handel's *Ariodante*', *'The Stage's Glory': John Rich (1692–1761)*, ed. B. Joncus and J. Barlow (forthcoming)
    'Handel's 1736 Performances of *Ariodante*', *Florilegium Musicae: Studi in onore di Carolyn Gianturco*, ed. P. Radicchi and M. Burden (Pisa, 2004)
    'Perhaps Handel was Right after All: Some Thoughts on Editing *Ariodante*', *MT* 148/1898 (Spring 2007), 35–48
Dean, *Operas*
Harris, *Librettos*
Strohm

Ariosti, Attilio Ottavio (b. Bologna, 5 Nov. 1666; d. London, before 3 Sept. 1729). Italian composer. He probably received musical training at San Petronio in his native Bologna. At the age of twenty he entered the city's monastic Order of Servites, and served as their organist. No record of his ordination as a priest has been found, but he became a deacon in 1692, and was later known as 'Padre Attilio'. BURNEY claimed that Ariosti received special dispensation from the Pope permitting him 'to exercise a secular profession' (p. 724).

A versatile performer of numerous instruments, Ariosti attracted the attention of the Duke of Mantua, who employed him by March 1696. He composed his first complete opera for VENICE in 1697, after which he went to BERLIN. He was master of music to Sophie Charlotte, the Electress of Brandenburg (and sister of the future GEORGE I of Britain). His popularity at the Protestant court displeased his Order, but he stayed in Berlin until 1703, during which time he wrote several operas and the libretto for Giovanni BONONCINI's *Polifemo*. HAWKINS, probably taking his information from MAINWARING, claimed that Ariosti met the young Handel at Berlin in 1698, and that it 'laid the foundation of a friendship, which, notwithstanding a competition of interests, subsisted for many years after' (vol. 19, p. 866).

After six years at Berlin, Ariosti promised his Order that he would return to them, but en route for Italy he stayed in Vienna for seven and a half years. In addition to composing an opera, several oratorios, serenatas and cantatas for Joseph I, the Emperor appointed him imperial minister and agent for all the princes and states of Italy in 1707. Ariosti eventually returned to Bologna as a diplomat in 1708. After the death of Joseph I in 1711 he worked as an agent for the Duke of Anjou (later Louis XV). His political work meant that he was less prolific as a composer than other leading Italian contemporaries, but in 1710 his *Amor tra nemici* (Vienna, 1708) became the first opera sung entirely in Italian on the London stage (albeit renamed *Almahide*, and with only eleven of his forty-three arias preserved).

Ariosti made his London debut playing the viola d'amore during a performance of Handel's *AMADIGI* at the KING'S THEATRE on 12 July 1716. He might have played in the opera orchestra throughout the 1716–17 season, which ended with his first original London opera *Tito Manlio*. The directors of the Royal Academy of Music (OPERA COMPANIES, 2) reputedly attempted to engage Ariosti to compose *Numitore* for the company's opening season (1719–20), but he was too busy (perhaps working as an agent for the Elector Palatine) to accept the commission, and apparently recommended Giovanni PORTA instead. Ariosti's first new opera for the Royal Academy was *CORIOLANO* (1723), which was published in an edition that was unusually almost complete. Ariosti also published selections from his next opera *Vespasiano* (first performed 14 January 1724), a collection of six cantatas and six lessons for the viola d'amore dedicated to George I.

Along with Bononcini and Handel, Ariosti was a highly esteemed and important member of the Royal Academy's trio of principal composers. There is no evidence of antagonistic rivalry between the three composers: it is conceivable that all three had been friends for several decades, and it is possible that they played in the orchestra for each other's operas. However, some of their supporters were partisan: John GAY wrote to Jonathan Swift that 'folks, that could not distinguish one tune from another, now daily dispute about the different styles of Handel, Bononcini, and Attilio'. Ariosti wrote sporadically for the Academy until it collapsed in 1728, but his later operas were less popular, and he seems to have lived his final year in impoverished conditions. Handel's esteem for his colleague's work is perhaps indicated by his revival of *Coriolano* in 1732.

DAVID VICKERS

L. Lindgren, 'Ariosti's London Years, 1716–29', ML 62/3–4 (July–Oct. 1981), 331–51

Ariosto, Ludovico (b. Reggio Emilia, 8 Sept. 1474; d. Ferrara, 6 July 1533). Italian poet and playwright, his major work is the epic poem *Orlando furioso* (published in 1516 with revised editions in 1521 and 1532). Intended to complete Matteo Maria Boiardo's (d. 1494) *Orlando innamorato*, Ariosto's *Orlando* is a chivalric romance in forty-six cantos set in the time of Charlemagne. The numerous fabulous episodes gather around three main topics: the war between Saracens and Christians, which functions as a narrative backdrop; Orlando (Charlemagne's nephew) and his love for Angelica, Princess of Cathay, which climaxes with Orlando's madness when Angelica marries Medoro; and the contrasted love between Ruggiero and Bradamante.

Ariosto's poem, like its rival Torquato TASSO's *Gerusalemme liberata* (1575), received immediate and wide success in Italy and abroad; its octaves were set to music by madrigalists in the sixteenth and seventeenth centuries and it was first translated into English in 1590. Interest in Ariosto, as well as in Tasso, GUARINI and other Italian poets was widespread in London during the late seventeenth and eighteenth centuries, also thanks to the activity of the Arcadian poet Paolo ROLLI (Eulibio Brentiatico), Nicola Francesco HAYM and members of the 'Italian Circle', Antonio Conti, Antonio Cocchi, Scipione Maffei and Giuseppe Riva.

By the time Handel premiered his first Ariosto opera in 1733, episodes and characters from the poem had been the subject of many baroque operas. *ORLANDO* draws the subject from the central episode of Orlando's madness following Angelica and Medoro's idyll (cantos 23–4) and exploits Ariosto's magic and spectacular setting. *ARIODANTE* takes from Ariodante and Ginevra's episode in cantos 4–5, while *ALCINA* stages Ruggiero's escape from Alcina's enchanted isle and his reunion with Bradamante (cantos 6–7).

MELANIA BUCCIARELLI

R. Döring, *Ariostos 'Orlando furioso' im italienischen Theater des Seicento und Settecento* (Hamburg, 1973)

G. E. Dorris, *Paolo Rolli and the Italian Circle in London, 1715–1744* (The Hague and Paris, 1967)

E. Jorgens, 'Handel's *Ariodante*: Scotland and Arcadia', *Dramma per Musica: Italian Opera Seria of the Eighteenth Century* (New Haven, 1997)

'Orlando Metamorphosed: Handel's Operas after Ariosto', *Parnassus* (Fall–Winter 1982), 45–74

Strohm ('Comic Traditions in Handel's *Orlando*', 249–69)

'Armida abbandonata'. See *DIETRO L'ORME FUGACI*

Arminio, HWV 36. *Arminio* had its premiere at COVENT GARDEN on 12 January 1737, with the following cast:

Arminio, a German prince	Domenico ANNIBALI (castrato)
Sigismondo, son of Segeste	Gioacchino CONTI (castrato)

Tusnelda, Arminio's wife, Segeste's daughter	Anna STRADA del Pò (soprano)
Ramise, Arminio's sister	Francesca BERTOLLI (alto)
Varo, Roman general	John BEARD (tenor)
Segeste, a German prince	Henry REINHOLD (bass)
Tullio, Roman captain	Maria Caterina NEGRI (alto)

The opera was composed between 15 September and 14 October 1736, during a gap in the composition of GIUSTINO. Once he had completed it Handel added extra arias for Tullio ('Non deve Roman petto'), Sigismondo ('Non son sempre vane larve'), Arminio ('Fatto scorta') and Ramise ('Voglio seguir'). The first was written when Handel decided to allocate the role to Negri; everything else in Tullio's part had been written for bass voice. Sigismondo's additional number is a scene-setting dream aria focusing attention on a character who at first might seem marginal to the main plot. The extra arias for Arminio and Ramise give more energy to the closing scenes. In the event the opera proved overlong, and several numbers were shortened during the run of performances.

Arminio was much admired in Handel's own circle of acquaintances. Lord SHAFTESBURY found it 'rather grave but correct and labour'd [i.e. cunningly wrought] to the highest degree & is a favourite one with Handel. ... But I fear 'twill not be acted very long. The Town dont much admire it' (Burrows and Dunhill, p. 23). Indeed, it enjoyed only six performances and was never performed again until a German version, Arminius und Thusnelda, was staged in Leipzig in 1935. Arias from Arminio were later introduced into the pasticcios ALESSANDRO SEVERO (1738) and GIOVE IN ARGO (1739); two of its most brilliant numbers, Sigismondo's 'Posso morir' and Arminio's 'Fatto scorta' reappeared in the December 1744 revival of SEMELE.

Arminio marks the return, after a sequence of legendary or magic operas, to more typical opera seria fare. Its text is adapted from one of SALVI's most popular librettos, which had first been set in 1703 by Alessandro SCARLATTI, and which was to retain its currency into the 1740s in settings by HASSE and GALUPPI. Handel's decision to compose may be in some way connected with the recent royal wedding of FREDERICK, Prince of Wales, with Princess AUGUSTA of Saxe-Gotha. Arminio (Hermann) holds in early German history something of the same quasi-mythical status as Boudicca in early English history; and it is surely a remarkable coincidence that an adaptation of the same Salvi libretto should have been made by HAYM for GEORGE I's first visit to the London opera in 1714.

Act I: Tusnelda persuades her husband Arminio to make a tactical retreat before the Roman armies. But he is betrayed by Segeste, and taken prisoner; if he is too proud to accept the pax romana, reflects Segeste, he must be sacrificed. Hearing of Segeste's treachery, Ramise rejects the love of Segeste's son Sigismondo. He is downcast, but when Segeste orders him to forget Ramise and think of the opportunities offered by the new alliance with Rome, his son defies him.

Act II: As Segeste and Tullio discuss what to do with Arminio a letter arrives from the Emperor, ordering his execution. Segeste promises obedience, but is troubled by the effect it will have on Tusnelda. Arminio and Tusnelda in turn scorn Segeste's urging to submit to Rome. Ramise is prevented from killing

Segeste only by the intervention of Sigismondo, who is hopelessly torn between love for Ramise and family ties. Knowing that Varo has fallen in love with Tusnelda, Arminio entrusts her to him before going to face death. Varo resolves not to be outdone in noble conduct.

Act III: Arminio's execution is interrupted by Varo: a warrior should not die like a criminal. Tullio reports another German uprising. Varo orders Arminio back to prison, and takes command of the necessary military measures. The perplexity of the Germans is resolved only when Sigismondo, ordered by Segeste to kill Arminio, releases him. Enraged to find his orders disobeyed, Segeste has Sigismondo and Ramise imprisoned. Tullio reports the death of Varo and the defeat of the Romans. The magnanimity of the victorious Arminio wins over Segeste.

While the Romans and their ally, the 'collaborator' Segeste, feature strongly in the first scene – indeed Segeste is crucial to the intrigue throughout – they are rapidly shifted to the margins, musically speaking, and the focus of attention becomes the clash of patriotic and family loyalties in the minds of the Germans, particularly young Sigismondo.

As the drama becomes more intimate, so the musical style becomes richer. In the first act the spare orchestral writing – predominantly unison violins and continuo – serves to throw into relief a small number of key movements in which the voices are more richly accompanied: the opening duet for Tusnelda and Arminio, in which the presuppositions of the plot are highlighted rather in the manner of a prologue; Arminio's noble chaconne-like aria 'Al par della mia sorte'; and 'Posso morir' for Conti (Sigismondo). In Act II likewise fuller scoring is held in strategic reserve, in this case to bring the act to a musico-dramatic climax in the prison scene. Act III is altogether more richly scored; here are found the only number with brass (Varo's 'Mira il ciel') and the only one with recorders (the duet, 'Quando più minaccia'). The forms are freer too, the second scene of the act containing four consecutive numbers without da capo.

The influence on Handel's style of the latest Italian music is clearest in Sigismondo's arias. It may be seen not only in the sometimes rather two-dimensional virtuosity of the music (notably in the extraordinary voice–oboe duetting in 'Quella fiamma' – Conti was the only operatic castrato for whom Handel wrote a high c''') (SAMMARTINI), but more interestingly in the use of a characteristic that one might describe with the Verdian term *parola scenica*: the sudden adagios that punctuate 'Posso morir', or the silences interrupted by recitative-like self-questioning in 'Il sangue al cor favella'.   DAVID KIMBELL

Burney
Dean, *Operas*
Harris, *Librettos*
Strohm

Arne, Cecilia. See Cecilia YOUNG

Arne, Susannah. See Susannah CIBBER

Arne, Thomas Augustine (b. London, 12 March 1710; d. London, 5 March 1778). Composer, violinist and keyboard player. The son of a London upholsterer, Arne had originally been intended to study law. However, from an early age he showed a keen interest in music and became a pupil of Michael FESTING, who taught him the violin. As a Catholic, he was denied the traditional career of a church musician. Instead, in the early 1730s he turned his attention to the theatre. During this time the Arne family – Arne's father, his brother Richard, his sister Susanna Maria (CIBBER) and Thomas Augustine Arne himself – earned themselves a dubious reputation by putting on an unauthorised stage production of Handel's ACIS AND GALATEA at the LITTLE THEATRE in the Haymarket on 17 and 19 May 1732, announced 'With all the Grand Chorus's, Scenes, Machines, and other Decorations'.

In the following years Arne quickly established an outstanding reputation as a composer of operas, masques and various afterpieces, mostly performed at DRURY LANE, where he held a position as house composer. Among his early successes were a setting of MILTON's Comus (1738) and the masque Alfred (first version 1740). The last-named work also appeared in Arne's later oratorio seasons as being performed 'in the manner of an oratorio'.

In 1738, by now one of the leading figures in London's musical life, Arne was numbered alongside Handel as one of the founding members of the Society of Musicians. Handel's DUBLIN successes in 1742 probably inspired Arne to try his luck there, too, and he spent two seasons in the Irish capital with his wife Cecilia (YOUNG) from 1742 to 1744, performing a number of Handel's oratorios as well as The Death of Abel (1744), the first oratorio from his own pen. A second trip to Dublin followed in 1755–6, but ended disastrously, with Arne returning to London with his pupil Charlotte BRENT, leaving his wife behind.

With the soprano Charlotte Brent he had a number of successes at COVENT GARDEN and Drury Lane in the late 1750s and early 1760s, and he received his doctorate from OXFORD in 1759. However, by the late 1760s, other composers were being preferred and, even though Arne was able to continue his career as a theatrical composer, the last years of his life were marred by continual financial difficulties.   EVA ZÖLLNER

J. Adas, Arne's Progress: An Eighteenth-Century Composer in London, Ph.D. dissertation (Rutgers University, 1993)

M. Burden, Garrick, Arne and the Masque of 'Alfred' (Lewiston, NY, 1994)

J. A. Parkinson, An Index to the Vocal Works of Thomas Augustine Arne and Michael Arne (Detroit, 1972)

R. J. Rabin and S. Zohn, 'Arne, Handel, Walsh, and Music as Intellectual Property: Two Eighteenth-Century Lawsuits', JRMA 120 (1995), 112–45

E. Zöllner, English Oratorio after Handel: The London Oratorio Series and its Repertory, 1760–1800 (Marburg, 2002)

Arnold, Samuel (b. London, 10 Aug. 1740; d. London, 22 Oct. 1802). Composer, organist and music editor. Arnold received his first musical training as a choirboy in the CHAPEL ROYAL under Bernard GATES and James Nares. In 1764, he was engaged by John BEARD as harpsichordist at COVENT GARDEN, where he was also active as house composer, producing and compiling opera pasticcios and other music. In 1769 he took over the lease of Marylebone Gardens, one of London's pleasure gardens. Like VAUXHALL and RANELAGH, Marylebone Gardens were famous for their musical entertainments and in his capacity as proprietor, Arnold arranged and composed a considerable number of short burlettas for performance there.

The late 1760s and 1770s saw a gradual shift in Arnold's musical interests: from 1768 to 1777 he ran the annual Lenten oratorio series at the LITTLE THE-ATRE in the Haymarket and (from 1770) at Covent Garden. In his series Arnold not only offered favourite Handelian works (most importantly MESSIAH, JUDAS MACCABAEUS and SAMSON), but also several new oratorios of his own. In 1777, his already extensive work for the theatre received a new impetus when he was appointed composer and music director of the Little Theatre; his association with this theatre proved extraordinarily long-lived: for about a quarter of a century Arnold provided the managers with almost one hundred operas, musical afterpieces and pantomimes, mostly arrangements and compilations from works of other composers.

However, Arnold does not seem to have been content with a mere career in the theatre: in 1773 he was awarded a doctorate in music from OXFORD, and from the 1780s several prestigious posts followed. In 1783 Arnold succeeded James Nares as organist and composer to the Chapel Royal, he was a governor of the Royal Society of Musicians, and in 1784 he also joined its concert committee, which was responsible for the organisation of the HANDEL COMMEMORATION in WESTMINSTER ABBEY. At about the same time Arnold resumed his work as oratorio manager at DRURY LANE, this time in partnership with the elder Thomas Linley. The programmes were dominated by Handel's oratorios and selections along the lines of the Handel Commemoration festivities.

Arnold's oratorio activities probably inspired him to embark on a gargantuan project, a complete edition of Handel's works (EDITIONS, 2), first advertised in 1786. Even though the project remained unfinished, it secured Arnold lasting fame. By the late 1780s he had become one of the leading figures in London's musical life, holding, among many others, the post of official conductor of the ACADEMY OF ANCIENT MUSIC (1789–94), and (from 1793) that of organist of Westminster Abbey. EVA ZÖLLNER

R. H. B. Hoskins, 'Dr Samuel Arnold (1740–1802), an Historical Assessment', 2 vols., Ph.D. dissertation (University of Auckland, New Zealand, 1982)
  The Theater Music of Samuel Arnold: A Thematic Index (Warren, MI, 1998)
P. J. Rogers, 'A Bibliographic Survey of Arnold's Handel Edition, the First Gesamtausgabe', Music in Performance and Society: Essays in Honor of Roland Jackson, ed. M. Cole and J. Koegel (Warren, MI, 1997), 165–75
E. Zöllner, 'Israel in Babylon or the Triumph of Truth? A Late Eighteenth-Century Pasticcio Oratorio', The Consort 51 (1995), 103–17
  English Oratorio after Handel: The London Oratorio Series and its Repertory, 1760–1800 (Marburg, 2002)

arrangements

1. Joseph Starzer
2. Wolfgang Amadè Mozart
3. Felix Mendelssohn Bartholdy
4. Robert Franz
5. Friedrich Chrysander

1. Joseph Starzer (1727–86)

A composer and violinist in Vienna, Starzer arranged JUDAS MACCABAEUS in 1779 at the instigation of Gottfried van SWIETEN, who also translated the text into German. Starzer was the first composer to arrange one of Handel's oratorios, and, according to Sonnleithner, the success of his performances inspired MOZART (who took over the direction of the van Swieten concerts after Starzer's death). Starzer's arrangement was prepared from a RANDALL edition, but, in accordance with the taste of his time, he added new instrumental parts for oboes and bassoons, and used flutes, horns, drums (but no clarinets) to enrich the colour of the orchestral sound and to fill in the middle of the orchestral texture. Starzer's additions were more sparing than Mozart's later changes.

ANNETTE LANDGRAF

W. Rackwitz, 'Über die Bearbeitung von Händels Judas Maccabaeus durch Joseph Starzer und über ihre Wirkungsgeschichte', GHB IX (2002)
L. von Sonnleithner, 'Ueber Mozart's angebliche Bearbeitung und Instrumentierung des Händel'schen Oratorium Judas Maccabäus', Caecilia 18 (1836), 242–50

2. Wolfgang Amadè Mozart

In 1787 MOZART succeeded Joseph Starzer as director of the concerts organised by Baron Gottfried van SWIETEN, who while in BERLIN had acquired several Handel scores, partly through the agency of his friend James HARRIS, including those of which he commissioned arrangements with a view to making them appeal to a modern Viennese audience. Mozart's four arrangements were of English-language works translated into German. The first was Acis und Galatea, K566 (ACIS AND GALATEA), performed in November 1788. In March and April 1789 Der Messias, K572 (MESSIAH), was performed at the house of Count Johann Baptist Esterházy, the soloists including Mozart's sister-in-law Aloysia Lange and the tenor Valentin Adamberger. In July 1790, unseasonably, came two tributes to St Cecilia, Das Alexanderfest, K591 (ALEXANDER'S FEAST), and the Ode auf St Caecilia, K592 (SONG FOR ST CECILIA'S DAY). The full scores are published within the Neue Mozart Ausgabe.

Mozart's arrangements were designed to render the continuo unnecessary except in simple recitative, and to enrich coloration, in line with contemporary taste formed in part by his own works. Violas are added where Handel used none. Horns sustain, as in the classical orchestra. At the opening of Acis clarinets, perhaps played by Mozart's friends the Stadler brothers, displace the oboes, to delightful effect. Mozart retains oboes for Polyphemus ('Cease to beauty'), and adds nothing to 'O ruddier than the cherry' (but the solo may have been played on a flute, an octave too low). The rapt introduction (clarinets and bassoons) to 'Must I my Acis still bemoan' should be forgiven by even the most purist of Handelians. In Messiah, Mozart's additions to 'The people that walked in darkness', while remote from Handel's aesthetic, are wonderfully expressive. Throughout the arrangements, passages are enhanced tactfully, even delicately, by woodwind counterpoints (as 'He sung Darius', in Alexander's Feast). In the 'What Passion cannot Music raise and quell?' (Song for St Cecilia's Day) the syncopated bassoon counterpoint and pizzicato arpeggios are too far from Handel's language fully to work, without being exquisitely Mozartian. Mozart's trumpeters were unable to cope with clarino-register playing; for 'The trumpet's loud clangour' (Song for St Cecilia's Day) Mozart has recourse to woodwind, whereas in Messiah 'The trumpet shall sound' is translated 'Sie schallt, die Posaun'; nevertheless, the last trump is represented not by a trombone (as in Mozart's Requiem) but by combined horns and trumpets.

In 2001 a hitherto unknown MS full score of *Judas Maccabeus* was discovered in Halifax, West Yorkshire, with wind parts attributed to Mozart. That Mozart arranged this oratorio had long been rumoured, but although this is not the arrangement by Starzer (ARRANGEMENTS, 1), internal evidence is insufficient to confirm the attribution to Mozart. Mozart's *Messiah* formed the basis of later arrangements (e.g. Prout) that continued to be performed into modern times; more recently this and the other arrangements have been revived, sometimes with period instruments. Thus today one great composer's 'take' on another can be enjoyed without damaging our appreciation of the originals.

JULIAN RUSHTON

B. Baselt, 'G. Fr. Händels "Ode for St. Cecilia's Day" und ihre Bearbeitung durch W. A. Mozart', *HJb* 38 (1992)

D. Burrows, 'Gottfried van Swieten and London Publications of Handel's Music', *HJb* 47 (2001)

R. Cowgill, 'An Unknown Handel Arrangement by Mozart? The Halifax *Judas*', *MT* 143 (Spring 2002), 19–36

Dean, *Oratorios*

3. Felix Mendelssohn Bartholdy

On behalf of his teacher Carl Friedrich Zelter, Mendelssohn orchestrated the Dettingen Te Deum (TE DEUM, 5) and *ACIS AND GALATEA* in Mozartian style for the SING-AKADEMIE ZU BERLIN in 1828/9. In these arrangements Mendelssohn intervened heavily in the original structure of Handel's works, cutting da capos and including magnificent parts for woodwind and brass instruments, adding violas (often absent from Handel's original scores). Mendelssohn later abandoned this technique of superficial sound display, and distanced himself from the typical Handel arrangements of his time (particularly those by Ignaz von MOSEL) by propagating the ideal of historically informed performances. This, however, did not mean English-language performances with the original orchestrations, which would have been difficult to realise in the early nineteenth century. But Mendelssohn's arrangements from the 1830s resulted from an intensive study of manuscript sources and of English printed editions of Handel's works. His later interventions in the scores were solely due to performance-related reasons. Depending on the specific performance conditions, he supported the orchestral part with a newly composed organ part or – if no organ was available – with an additional wind band to counterbalance the many singing voices then employed in concerts or music festivals (as in performances of the ANTHEMS *Zadok the Priest* and *O praise the Lord with one consent* in 1836). In addition, prominent trumpet passages, whose performance presented technical problems, were reorchestrated and the parts given to more flexible instruments (mostly oboes, sometimes horns). The organ was used mainly in the accompaniment of choruses, arias and duets, but simple recitative was accompanied by homophonic settings for two cellos and a double bass. In order to preserve the balance of sound between the vocal and the instrumental parts, Mendelssohn, if the premises permitted, had a stair-like tribune constructed with the choir being placed to the left and right and the orchestra seated on a triangular platform which narrowed to the conductor's podium at the front. However, Mendelssohn did not always insist on his own conception of the works, as is shown by the fact that he directed a number of performances

of Mozart's arrangements of *MESSIAH* (1837, 1839) and *ALEXANDER'S FEAST* (1833, 1846).
RALF WEHNER (Trans. ANGELA BAIER)

F. Mendelssohn Bartholdy (arr.), *Dettingen Te Deum* (Leipzig, 1869)
  (arr.), *Acis und Galatea*, ed. A. Rosenmüller (Stuttgart, 2008)

4. Robert Franz

In 1858 Robert FRANZ started to arrange works by Old Masters when he became aware that most preceding editions had been editorial arrangements that did not give musical texts as composers had originally written them. He argued that arrangements should correspond to the 'ideal' sound of the nineteenth century. Franz stated that the bass lines were only sketches and the composer had in his mind how to fill them in using a contrapuntal and polyphonic style on the basis of the bass figures; he also added inner parts where the composer had written rests. Orchestral instruments replaced harpsichord and organ. He considered that the sound of clarinets and bassoons is comparable to the sound of the organ, and treated the woodwind quartet as part of the *bassi* placing it near the first double bass. In his opinion the organ, if available, should only have been used to intensify the sound or to add brilliance at special places. The smooth sounds of horns were used to compensate for the supposed shrillness of the high trumpets; oboes and flutes served to add a special lustre from time to time. Franz made orchestral arrangements to accompany *MESSIAH*, the Utrecht *JUBILATE*, *JUDAS MACCABAEUS* and *L'ALLEGRO*, and thirty-six arias and duets with piano arrangement. Six soprano arias were also arranged with orchestral accompaniment.
ANNETTE LANDGRAF

R. Franz, *Offener Brief an Eduard Hanslick über Bearbeitungen älterer Tonwerke namentlich Bach'scher und Händel'scher Vocalmusik* (Leipzig, 1871)
D. Gutknecht, 'Robert Franz als Bearbeiter Händelscher Werke', *HJb* 39 (1993)

5. Friedrich Chrysander

CHRYSANDER put considerable effort into promoting Handel's music. His vigorous – and at times aggressive – arguments that the composer's works should be performed strictly in accordance with the original score sharpened the consciousness of musicians and audiences for historical performance practice. However, Chrysander sought to find a realistic way to increase the wider acceptance of Handel's compositions. So he remodelled parts of the Anthem for the Funeral of Queen Caroline (ANTHEMS, 5) into a commemoration music for the death of Bismarck, and he rearranged *MESSIAH*, *DEBORAH*, *HERCULES*, the Utrecht *JUBILATE*, *ESTHER*, *ACIS AND GALATEA*, *ISRAEL IN EGYPT*, the *SONG FOR ST CECILIA'S DAY* and *JUDAS MACCABAEUS*.

Chrysander regarded himself as the highest authority concerning Handel, and therefore thought that he knew and understood the composer so well that this approach to arranging his works was justified. Using contemporary modern instruments, Chrysander required his orchestra to emulate the original orchestra of Handel's time, with strings divided into concertino and ripieno groups, but he used a much larger group of wind players (for instance ten trumpets if he had a choir of 300 singers), piano replaced the former continuo instruments for arias, recitatives, orchestral movements, and was also used instead of organ in choruses. He wrote out accompaniments for the basso continuo, and ornaments for the vocal parts, because musicians were no longer able to improvise in an appropriate style. The sung texts were German translations which strove to re-create the musical expression of the original English words.

Chrysander removed elements which he believed were obstacles to the swift dramatic development of action. To achieve his goal, he shifted entire movements or smaller sections to different positions within works, and replaced arias that he thought were dramatically weak with pieces from other works. He replaced choruses in ISRAEL IN EGYPT with arias, and divided Part II and Part III of the original oratorio into three parts. For the final chorus in *Deborah* he encouraged the conductor to transpose the horns downwards because he disliked the way they sounded in the original octave. To compensate for this change, he added trumpets to double the soprano and alto choral parts. Moreover, he adjusted arias to suit the abilities of solo singers or left them out if they were too difficult (much as Handel himself did in his own revivals).

ANNETTE LANDGRAF

A. Landgraf, 'Die Händel-Bearbeitungen Friedrich Chrysanders', HJb 48 (2002)

Arresta il passo ('Aminta e Fillide'), HWW 83. A dramatic cantata for two sopranos, violins, viola and basso continuo, *Arresta il passo* was composed in ROME for RUSPOLI. After its completion, and probably after the first performance, the work was expanded with the addition of two arias and recitatives, which survive separately in autograph. Specific instructions for their insertion appear in the copy of the work made by Angelini that survives in Münster (SOURCES AND COLLECTIONS, 13). A reference to the second aria of the work, 'Fiamma bella', in the Ruspoli account books on 14 July 1708 may provide the date of this expanded version, created for performance when Handel may still have been in NAPLES. Paper evidence, as well as Handel's borrowings from KEISER in the overture and a number of arias, indicates that the original cantata was probably composed early in Handel's Roman period. Ursula Kirkendale suggests that *Arresta il passo* was the first work Handel wrote in Rome, associating it with a bill in the Ruspoli documents submitted on 29 December 1706 for an untitled new cantata for singers and concertino violinists. Handel made use of the musically rich material from this cantata in his early operas, borrowing, for example, the sirens' song in *RINALDO*, 'Il vostro maggio', directly from the fifth aria, 'Se vago rio'.

ELLEN T. HARRIS

W. and U. Kirkendale, *Music and Meaning: Studies in Music History and the Neighbouring Disciplines* (Florence, 2007)

Arrigoni, Carlo (b. Florence, 5 Dec. 1697; d. Florence, 18 Aug. 1744). Italian tenor; also theorbist, violinist and composer. His presence in London, 1731–6, coincided with the lifespan of the OPERA OF THE NOBILITY, which premiered his opera *Fernando* (set to a libretto adapted by ROLLI) at LINCOLN'S INN FIELDS on 5 February 1734. Arrigoni both sang in Handel's cantata *CECILIA, VOLGI UN SGUARDO* and played the lute in Op. 4 No. 6 (ORCHESTRAL WORKS, 3) during the first performances of *ALEXANDER'S FEAST* in 1736.

Handel wrote his name in the conducting score of *ESTHER*, but there is no evidence that he sang in any performances.   JOHN WALTER HILL

W. Dean, 'An Unrecognized Handel Singer: Carlo Arrigoni', MT 118 (1977), 556–7

'Arrival of the Queen of Sheba, The'. Popular name for the sinfonia that today opens Part III of the oratorio *SOLOMON*. This name was first used in a performance and recording of the work by Sir Thomas Beecham in the 1950s. The sinfonia was originally composed a year or two before *Solomon* and may have originally formed part of an earlier oratorio. The movement is in ritornello form alternating between a bustling tutti for full orchestra with contrasting solo sections featuring two oboes.   DAVID ROSS HURLEY

As pants the heart. See ANTHEMS, 1, 2

Atalanta, HWV 35. Italian opera. It celebrated the marriage of Prince FREDERICK of Wales to Princess AUGUSTA of Saxe-Gotha. The story had been used before for operatic entertainments associated with royal weddings in Germany and Italy (Strohm, pp. 71–3). Handel probably knew a version by STEFFANI (*Le rivali concordi*, libretto by Ortensio MAURO) that was performed in 1693 at HANOVER, where a few years later another libretto based on the story was dedicated to GEORGE I's mother. Moreover, the wedding of Frederick and Augusta in April 1736 was celebrated in Gotha with a performance of Stölzel's serenata *L'amore vince l'inganno*, based on a version of the *Atalanta* story produced at Parma in 1694.

Handel's version was anonymously adapted from Belisario VALERIANI's libretto *La caccia in Etolia* (Ferrara, 1715). It is like an extended PASTORAL cantata, and the plot was summarised for Handel's AUDIENCE in the printed WORDBOOK:

> Meleager, King of Etolia, being love in with Atalanta, Daughter of Jason, King of Arcadia, demanded her of her Father in Marriage; but she, not to lose the Pleasure she took in hunting wild Beasts, refused his Crown and Love; and under the Name of Amarillis, went to the Woods among the Nymphs and Shepherds, the better to follow the Chace [*sic*]. Meleager, as a Shepherd, under the Name of Thirsis, follows her to the Woods, where she at last fell in love with him. Nicander, an old Shepherd, in whom Meleager had trusted the Secret, discovers their Births and Characters; whereupon their Nuptials ensue. The Loves of Amintas and Irene are introduced, to give greater Scope to the Drama.

The entire opera is set in 'A large Champaign Country, with a Prospect of Cottages: A Wood on each Side, and a vast Mountain at a Distance', until an elaborate *Deus ex machina* finale in which Mercury 'descends on a Cloud, attended by the Loves and Graces', and leads a *licenza* in praise of Prince Frederick and Princess Augusta.

Handel finished composing *Atalanta* on 22 April 1736. The royal wedding took place on 27 April at the CHAPEL ROYAL; the service included Handel's anthem *Sing unto God* (ANTHEMS, 4). On 29 April the *London Daily Post* reported 'We hear Mr. Handel has compos'd a new opera, on the occasion of his Royal Highness's marriage . . . and as the wedding was solemnized sooner than was expected, great numbers of artificers, carpenters, painters, engineers, &c. are employed to . . . bring it on the stage with the utmost expedition' (Deutsch, p. 405). The cast for the first performance at COVENT GARDEN on 12 May 1736 was as follows:

Atalanta, Princess of Arcadia	Anna STRADA del Pò (soprano)
Meleagro, King of Etolia	Gioacchino CONTI (castrato)
Irene, a shepherdess	Maria Caterina NEGRI (alto)
Aminta, a shepherd	John BEARD (tenor)
Nicandro, an old shepherd, Irene's father	Gustavus Waltz (bass)
Mercurio	Henry REINHOLD (bass)

Atalanta was performed eight times. The OPERA OF THE NOBILITY also contributed to the festivities with four performances of PORPORA's *Festa d'Imeneo* (4–15 May), a serenata that features virtuosic music set to a sycophantic libretto by Paolo ROLLI that lauds the royal newly-weds from its outset. In contrast, *Atalanta* is an affectionate and ironic drama that seems to have been designed to charm rather than to overwhelm. Handel's musical characterisations are finely crafted. Meleagro's cavatina 'Cara selve' (I.i) – simply accompanied by continuo – tenderly conveys his sincere unrequited love for Atalanta, and the singer's sustained first note was an ideal opportunity for Conti to display his *messa di voce*. Meleagro's unshakeable optimism is unmistakable at the end of Act I in 'Non saria poco', which has astonishing virtuoso passages that take the singer up to a high c''', whereas the radiantly beautiful 'M'allontano sdegnose pupille' (II.vii) sweetly conveys his open declaration of love to Atalanta. Her jaunty entrance aria in pursuit of a grisly beast (I.vii) is soon followed by 'Riportai gloriosa palma' (I.viii), in which gleeful coloratura runs suggest that her modesty is less than sincere. However, the opera's dramatic intensity is unexpectedly increased by her extraordinary lament 'Lassa! ch'io t'ho perduta' (II.ii); Handel's richly expressive string scoring, use of a C minor Larghetto, and the sudden jump from secco recitative into the aria without an introductory ritornello, create an unambiguous serious insight into Atalanta's emotional self-doubt, and suggests her sincere love for 'Tirsi'.

The other pair of lovers, Aminta and Irene, are also captivatingly portrayed in excellent music. Irene's 'Come alla tortorella' (I.vi), in which violins represent a dove cooing to its faithful mate, reveals that she is more sensitive than her cruel toying with Aminta has hitherto indicated. Aminta's explosive outburst 'Di' ad Irene' (II.vi) conveys his conflicting emotions using music from LA RESURREZIONE contrasted with softer passages in which the shepherd admits that he still loves Irene. Handel's witty music in 'Diedi il core' (III.ii) shows Aminta mischievously giving Irene a taste of her own medicine when he claims to have found 'Another, and a fairer Maid'. Irene's long-suffering father Nicandro chastises his daughter in 'Impara, ingrata' (I.v), which uses an aria from ACI, GALATEA E POLIFEMO, albeit developed with material borrowed from a Passion setting by GRAUN. Handel also used musical ideas from works by BONONCINI, KEISER, Sarro, Alessandro SCARLATTI and TELEMANN. The bouncy three-part sinfonia, which BURNEY described as 'uncommonly gay and spirited, as the hilarity of the occasion required', has a solo trumpet part that was written for Valentine Snow. The opera's only accompanied recitative was reserved for the arrival of Mercurio, after which the royal nuptials were celebrated with a splendid succession of short choruses and trumpet fanfares accompanied by an indoor fireworks display.

Handel made two significant changes after his completion of the score: Nicandro's short aria 'O trionfar' was omitted prior to the first performance (its opening theme was reused two years later in the overture to *SAUL*), and at some point – perhaps during the performances – Meleagro's brilliant *aria di bravura* 'Tu scolasti il mare infido' in the *lieto fine* was relocated to an earlier scene in Act III (and its words adjusted), and its original position was filled by a new duet ('Cara, nel tuo bel volto') for the principal lovers.

An unusually detailed report of the STAGING of the finale was published in the *London Daily Post* on 13 May 1736:

> a new Set of Scenes . . . took up the full length of the Stage: The Fore-part of the scene represented an Avenue to the Temple of *Hymen*, adorn'd with Figures of several Heathen Deities. Next was a Triumphal Arch on the Top of which were the Arms of the Royal Highnesses, over which was placed a Princely Coronet. Under the Arch was the Figure of *Fame*, on a Cloud, sounding the Praise of this Happy Pair. The names *Fredericus* and *Augusta* appear'd above in transparent Characters.
>
> Thro' the Arch was seen a Pediment, supported by four Columns, on which stood two Cupids embracing, and supporting . . . the Royal Ensign of the Prince of Wales. At the farther end was a View of *Hymen*'s Temple, and the wings were adorn'd with the Loves and Graces bearing Hymenaeal Torches, and putting Fire to Incense in Urns, to be offer'd up upon this joyful Union.
>
> The Opera concluded with a Grand Chorus, during which several beautiful Illuminations were display'd, which gave an uncommon Delight and Satisfaction.

According to one eyewitness, the spectacular fireworks display featured 'a row of blue fires burning in order along the ascent to the temple; a fountain of fire sprouts up out of the ground to the ceiling, and two more cross each other obliquely from the sides of the stage; on the top is a wheel that whirls always about, and throws out a shower of gold-colour, silver, and blue fiery rain' (Deutsch, pp. 410–11). Ironically, the Prince and Princess of Wales chose not to experience this lavish entertainment produced in their honour, and instead went to a revival of Addison's *Cato* and a farce at DRURY LANE. They might have attended Handel's revival on 20 November 1736 (Prince Frederick's birthday), for which only a few minor alterations were made.

Handel reused three arias in *ALESSANDRO SEVERO* (1738) and the hunting chorus 'Oggi rimbombano' was included in *GIOVE IN ARGO* (1739). An inventory made at Covent Garden in the early 1740s shows that the six wings of the stage decoration, probably painted by Joseph GOUPY, still existed. The fireworks display was masterminded by Mr Worman, who replicated his contribution at Cuper's Gardens on 18 July 1741 along with Handel's accompanying music, which was referred to as the 'celebrated Fire Musick'. The finale of *Atalanta* was commonly described as the 'Fire Musick', even at BATH on 6 November 1749 after Handel had created his popular *MUSIC FOR THE ROYAL FIREWORKS*.

John WALSH's subscription score of *Atalanta* had 143 SUBSCRIBERS for 181 copies, and was the most successful printed edition of any Handel opera during the composer's lifetime. The first production since 1736 was staged outdoors at Hintlesham Hall, Suffolk, by Kent Opera in 1970.   DAVID VICKERS

Burney
W. Dean, 'Handel's Atalanta', *Sundry Sorts of Music Books: Essays on the British Library Collection, presented to O. W. Neighbour on his 70th Birthday*, ed. C. Banks, A. Searle and M. Turner (London, 1993)
  Operas
Deutsch
Harris, *Librettos*
Strohm

Athalia, HWV 52. English oratorio. The libretto by Samuel HUMPHREYS was based on Jean RACINE's final play *Athalie* (1691), and Handel's setting is the conclusion to a series of his music theatre works that seem to have been influenced by the French dramatist. The composer completed his autograph score on 7 June 1733. It seems that he wrote the oratorio specifically for his performances at OXFORD in July 1733, although the finely constructed choruses and INSTRU-MENTATION (featuring recorders, flutes, oboes, bassooos, horns and trumpets, strings and basso continuo) are consistent with his contemporary works for the KING'S THEATRE, and therefore suggest that he might have had an eventual London performance in mind. Handel expected that his new oratorio would be performed by his company of opera singers including SENESINO and MONTAGNANA, but at the end of the 1732–3 season most of them defected to the OPERA OF THE NOBILITY. By the time the composer travelled to Oxford it was necessary to find alternative singers for all the roles except Josabeth.

The first performance of *Athalia* was planned for 9 July 1733 at the SHELDO-NIAN THEATRE, but on that day the speeches during the academic ceremony overran, so the premiere was postponed to the next day. The *London Magazine* reported that the oratorio was received by the Oxonian audience 'with the utmost Applause' (Deutsch, p. 329). The cast was as follows:

Athalia, Queen of Judah, grandmother to Joas	MRS WRIGHT (soprano)
Joas, rightful King of Judah	? Goodwill (boy treble)
Joad, High Priest	Walter POWELL (countertenor)
Josabeth, Aunt of Joas, wife of Joad	Anna STRADA del Pò (soprano)
Mathan, Priest of Baal, formerly a Jewish Priest	Philip Rochetti (tenor)
Abner, Captain of the Jewish forces	Gustavus WALTZ (bass)

The WORDBOOK described the chorus as three groups: Israelite/Levite priests, young Levite virgins and Sidonian priests. The biblical sources for the story are 2 Kings 8–11 and 2 Chronicles 22–3. Jerusalem and the people of Judah are ruled by Athalia, daughter of the wicked King Ahab and Queen Jezebel. She has acquired the throne by murdering her grandchildren, and aggressively fosters worship of Baal. In the Temple the Jewish chorus hymns the one true God, and, led by Josabeth, decries tyrannical attempts to suppress the Jewish religion. The High Priest, Joad, laments Athalia's apostasy and suppression of the true faith, and prays for relief. In the palace, Athalia wakes in terror and recounts her nightmare to Mathan, priest of Baal (an apostate Jew), and Abner, commander of the Jewish army: after a terrible warning of God's enmity from a ghastly apparition of her mother Jezebel, a lovely boy dressed as a Jewish priest stabbed her to the heart as she caressed him. Athalia's Baalite attendants fail to reassure her, and Mathan suggests that they investigate the truth of the dream in the Temple. Abner, secretly loyal to the Jewish cause, goes to warn Joad. In the Temple Joad and Josabeth plan to reveal to the Jews the identity of the boy Joas, sole rightful heir to the throne, saved in infancy by Josabeth (his aunt) from Athalia's massacre of all the royal princes. Abner's news overwhelms Josabeth with despair; Joad reminds her that she should trust in God, and his confidence is endorsed by a choral hallelujah.

At the start of Part II the harvest festival (Shavuot) is celebrated with hymns to God's universal bounty. Joad draws from Abner a declaration of loyalty to the true succession. Athalia and Mathan arrive, and Athalia recognises in Joas the boy of her nightmare. Deflecting Josabeth's attempts to protect him, she engages him in conversation, in which (believing himself an orphan) he guilelessly defeats her attempts to discover his identity. She proposes to take care of him henceforth; he denounces her apostasy. Athalia angrily threatens Josabeth with his forcible removal and storms out. Josabeth again despairs, and is comforted in a remarkable duet by a serenely assured Joas and then, in another duet, by her husband. The chorus takes up the theme of God's care of the faithful in expectation of a happy outcome.

Part III opens with Joad, divinely inspired, foretelling the fall and death of Athalia and the restoration of the true faith. He asks Joas which king he would take as a model if he were ever himself on the throne. When Joas names his ancestor David, Joad kneels to him as the rightful ruler, and Josabeth calls on the Jews to recognise him too; they swear allegiance. Mathan makes friendly overtures to Josabeth and Joad which they scorn. Athalia arrives to claim Joas; Joad reveals him to her as the king, who will purge idolatry, and the chorus acclaim him ('Bless the true church and save the king'). Athalia calls on Abner to stamp out treason but he declares his allegiance to Joas, depriving Athalia of military support. Feeling God's vengeance strike, Mathan collapses. Athalia recognises that she is about to die but defies her enemies in the spirit of her mother Jezebel. In the final scene Joad and Josabeth join in a duet of conjugal affection and happiness, and Abner leads the chorus in rejoicing and gratitude to God for their deliverance.

The fact that Athalia is Joas's grandmother and Josabeth is his aunt is mentioned only in the wordbook's list of characters; that Athalia is Josabeth's mother and has murdered all the other royal princes is mentioned nowhere. But the Old Testament story was familiar to Handel's audience, providing a favourite justification of the 1688 Revolution (deposition of a despotic apostate) and a cherished precedent for JACOBITES (restoration of the true heir to the throne). The oratorio could appeal to Hanoverians in its championing of law and liberty, but in the controlling eminence of Joad it flouts Whiggish dislike of priestly power. Perhaps it was an ideal subject for Oxford, which was the English stronghold of Jacobitism, and where the defeat of WALPOLE's Excise

Bill had recently been celebrated with toasts to the Pretender for three nights in succession. However, a story about the bloodline prophesied to lead from King David to the Messiah being protected from extinction had general relevance to audiences of all Christian persuasions.

Athalia contains many apposite dramatic arias, such as Mathan's consoling 'Gentle airs' (featuring a rapturous cello solo) and the doomed Athalia's venomous exit aria 'To darkness eternal'. Handel also composed some superbly crafted choruses: the Israelite celebration of Shavuot is splendidly conveyed in 'The mighty Pow'r' by the unbridled use of the entire orchestral resources and an eight-part choir, with a central contrasting solo section for Joad accompanied only by woodwinds. The composer did not revive *Athalia* in his next London season, probably because he reused most of the music in the serenata PAR-NASSO IN FESTA and anthem *This is the day* (ANTHEMS, 4), which were both associated with the wedding of Princess ANNE. He eventually presented *Athalia* to the London public on 1 April 1735, although this featured an Italian-language part for CARESTINI (Joad) which included extensive Italian arias that had been recently prepared for the castrato in a revival of *ESTHER*; Handel also inserted a new setting of Josabeth's 'Through the land so lovely blooming' (based on an aria discarded from *ALCINA*) and replaced the final chorus with his new Organ Concerto in F major (HWV 292) (ORCHESTRAL WORKS, 5); its fugal conclusion featured a choral 'ALLELUIA'. *Athalia* was revised in 1743 for a prospective revival that never took place, and its last revival under Handel's supervision was a heavily revised version in March 1756.   RUTH SMITH and DAVID VICKERS

S. Blaut (ed.), *Athalia*, HHA I/12.1–2 (Kassel, 2006)
P. Brett and G. Haggerty, 'Handel and the Sentimental: The Case of *Athalia*', ML 68/2 (1987), 112–27
D. Burrows, 'Handel's 1735 (London) Version of *Athalia*', *Music in Eighteenth-Century Britain*, ed. D. W. Jones (Aldershot, 2000)
Dean, *Oratorios*
A. C. Held, 'Händels Oratorium *Athalia* (HWV 52, 1733) und die biblischen Tragödien Racines', *GHB* VIII (2000)
J. Racine, *Athalie* (1691), trans. W. Duncombe (London, 1722; 2nd edn 1726)
Smith, *Oratorios*

audience. From biographer MAINWARING onwards, the audience has been portrayed as both a supporter of and a major enemy to Handel. In the absence until 2000 of any study of who constituted the audience, biographers have been content to retail stories rather than investigate whether those stories are true and accurate. Four areas are considered here.

1. Class
2. Gender
3. Religion
4. Fashion

1. Class

Britain's wealth and power were concentrated in the hands of the ruling royal family, the nobility, the gentry and merchant princes, which, according to a contemporary estimate, numbered 12,670 families. This minuscule 0.8 per cent of the population of England and Wales had annual incomes of £400 or more. By contrast, the labouring and destitute poor, who had annual incomes no greater than £49 and among whom £20 was considered subsistence level, constituted the vast bulk of the population (84.5 per cent).

Handel, with an annual income from the royal family alone of £600 from about 1723, was part of an even more exclusive group, the top 0.3 per cent, or one of only 4,670 families. At his death in 1759 Handel was not only the richest musician by far based in London, having built up stock holdings valued at £17,500, but he was also among the rarified circle of the wealthiest commoners in the land (see HANDEL, GEORGE FRIDERIC, 17). It is within the exclusive group of fewer than 5,000 families that Handel's paying audience is largely to be found. This elite group had the wealth, political connections, local dominance and military, religious or legal standing to exercise control over the rest of the population.

Writers subsequent to Mainwaring have claimed that by turning to oratorios Handel appealed to a 'middle class' audience. As tickets to oratorio cost the same as those for opera (10s. 6d. for pit and box seats), and were the most expensive kind of theatrical entertainment, the claim is easily refuted. The middling sort, defined by historians as families with annual incomes of £50–200, which comprised about 12.1 per cent of the population, and even those in the lower echelon of the elite with incomes of around £200–400 (2.6 per cent) were priced out of regular attendance.

2. Gender

Women have been portrayed as leaders of the opposition to Handel during the 1730s and 1740s. One, Lady Margaret BROWN, had the misfortune to be named and thus has received much opprobrium. By contrast, the numerous male opponents, such as the directors of the OPERA OF THE NOBILITY, English composers and musicians and Italian singers, have not received anything like the degree of criticism. The 'double standard' explanation may apply in this case as in sexual behaviour: men are allowed to oppose (be promiscuous), women are not. Men determine whether an artist is good, bad or indifferent. For a woman or women to organise publicly against Handel seems to have been regarded by writers such as BURNEY and FLOWER as not only an affront to Handel but also to the male arbiters of culture.

3. Religion

Biographer SCHOELCHER brought the religious affiliations of the audience into play by claiming that JUDAS MACCABAEUS, when first performed in 1747, received considerable support from Jews. He based this misjudgement on an interpellation that librettist Thomas MORELL made to a remark addressed by Handel to the banker Sir Thomas Hankey: 'The Jews will not come to it because it is a Christian story; and the Ladies will not come, because it [is] a virtuous one.' First published in Biographia Dramatica in 1782, the remark makes little sense. Not only does it lay the blame for thin houses on marginalised others, it is illogical in terms of the Jews supporting only Israelite oratorios and women supporting only romantic or salacious ones. The contrast (antithesis) is a rhetorical device, simplistic in the extreme. Its most striking omission is the group that ought to be supporting Handel, namely Christian males!

Use of Old Testament stories cannot be regarded as demonstrating a special affection on Handel's part or that of his librettists for Jews. These stories were the common currency of all churchgoers and authors (including RACINE, METASTASIO and ZENO). Nor can the inclusion of Jewish characters in otherwise secular works, such as *ATHALIA* or *ALEXANDER BALUS*, be considered as indicative. Handel was not the unique purveyor of such entertainments: there were performances in London of oratorios on Jewish themes by four other composers from 1732 to 1745. While the portrayal of the Israelites may have had an attraction for contemporary Jews, its absence did not inhibit their subscription to opera scores that had no Jewish characters or to purely instrumental music.

4. Fashion

Handel seems to have recognised the legitimacy of audience behaviour even when it went against him. With the 1744–5 season of oratorios proving financially grave, Handel wrote a letter to the *Daily Advertiser*, published 17 January 1745, noting that he had 'received the greatest Obligations from the Nobility and Gentry' for this and previous seasons but now his 'Labours to please are become ineffectual' and he must offer to return to the season subscribers three-quarters of their subscriptions before expenses overwhelm him. In the event only sixteen subscribers requested the return of their money and Handel restarted his season, acknowledging in a second letter, published in the *Daily Advertiser* of 25 January, the generosity of his subscribers.

Handel also profited from audience enthusiasm. At OXFORD in July 1733, at DUBLIN for the 1741–2 season, and at the benefit held for him on 28 March 1738 at the KING'S THEATRE ('*An ORATORIO*'), his receipts were commented upon admiringly or enviously. Indeed, even without a monetary incentive, an audience could register its support, as on the occasion of his return to directing in January 1738 following his first acute attack of saturnine gout, when a newspaper reported that Handel 'was honour'd with extraordinary and repeated Signs of Approbation'. From the oratorio seasons that Handel promoted after the JACOBITE rebellion of 1745–6, he often made a profit but not always.

The phenomenon of fluctuating success is not dependent upon the aesthetic qualities of works, at least to the extent that high quality could not guarantee high attendance. There is no shame in discerning the cause of both high and low attendance as lying in the operation of fashion. Both we and Handel's contemporaries recognise its action, but neither we nor they know how it works. Thus Miss C. Gilbert, writing to James HARRIS in 1755 was able to remark that Handel is 'most ungratefully neglected this year . . . Fashion in every thing will have most followers.' The following year, Catherine Talbot asked 'how long can even *MESSIAH* remain fashionable?' Quite a long time in the case of the preferred work for the musical fund-raisers held at the FOUNDLING HOSPITAL, but even that run eventually came to an end. Fashion may not always reward the most deserving work or performer, but it never ceases to act.   DAVID HUNTER

See also SUBSCRIBERS

Burrows and Dunhill, 212
Deutsch, 448, 602, 851–3
E. T. Harris, 'Handel the Investor', ML 85/4 (2004), 521–75
D. Hunter, 'George Frideric Handel and the Jews: Fact, Fiction and the Tolerances of Scholarship', *For the Love of Music: Festschrift in Honor of Theodore Front on his 90th Birthday*, ed. D. F. Scott (Lucca, 2002)

'Patronizing Handel, Inventing Audiences: The Intersections of Class, Money, Music and History', EM 28/1 (2000), 32–49

'Margaret Cecil, Lady Brown: "Persevering Enemy to Handel" but "Otherwise Unknown to History" ', Women & Music 3 (1999), 43–58

R. Smith, 'Thomas Morell and his Letter about Handel', JRMA 127 (2002), 191–225

Augusta, Princess of Wales (Princess of Saxe-Gotha) (b. Gotha 19 Nov. 1719; d. London, 8 Feb. 1772). Wife of FREDERICK, Prince of Wales and mother of King GEORGE III. Augusta came to England in the spring of 1736 shortly before her marriage. Handel composed the anthem *Sing unto God* (ANTHEMS, 4) for the wedding service (it was reportedly sung 'wretchedly'), and his new opera *ATALANTA* was part of the public celebrations. Notwithstanding Frederick's patronage of rival composers, the Prince and Princess attended numerous performances of Handel's works. During her married life Augusta faithfully followed her husband's lead in matters of taste; after his death she swiftly identified herself with her father-in-law GEORGE II.   ROBIN EAGLES

F. Vivian, A Life of Frederick, Prince of Wales, 1707–1751: A Connoisseur of the Arts (Lampeter, 2007)

Aureli, Aurelio (b. Murano, first half of the seventeenth century; d. Venice, after 1708). Librettist of *L'Antigona delusa da Alceste*, which in the revision by Ortensio MAURO (HANOVER, 1681) was adapted for the libretto of Handel's London opera *ADMETO, RE DI TESSAGLIA*, first performed at the KING'S THEATRE on 31 January 1727. In 1652 Aureli's first opera, *Erginda*, was produced in VENICE; as a result he became a member of some prestigious Venetian Academies which regularly included librettists: the Accademia Delfica and the Accademia degli Imperfetti. In 1659 he went to Vienna; in 1660 he was again in Venice for the performance of *L'Antigona* with music by Pietro Andrea Ziani. From 1688 he settled in Parma, where he certainly lived until 1693 and was involved with the opening of the new Teatro Ducale. He wrote about fifty opera librettos, in which mythology and history are treated in an unusually bizarre manner; his last works were performed in Venice in 1708.

DOMENICO ANTONIO D'ALESSANDRO (Trans. TERENCE BEST)

C. Mutini, Dizionario biografico degli italiani, vol. 4 (Rome, 1962), 587–8
Strohm

Austrian Succession, War of the (1740–8). The death of the Holy Roman Emperor, Charles VI, in October 1740 triggered conflict. Charles had worked hard in the previous two decades to secure acceptance of the Pragmatic Sanction, enshrining his daughter Maria Theresia's rights to succeed to his Habsburg inheritance, by other European powers. However, his death (and that of the Russian Tsarina) prompted the new King of Prussia, Frederick II, to invade the Habsburg province of Silesia. Prussian victories encouraged other powers to attack Austrian possessions: Bavaria and France invaded Bohemia and Upper Austria. Frederick came to terms with Austria in July 1742, thus enabling Austria, supported by British subsidies, to expel French and Bavarian forces from her territory. Britain was not yet officially at war with France. A conflict, known as the War of Jenkin's Ear, had broken out with Spain over a series of trade disputes in 1739. GEORGE II's position was difficult because he had signed a neutrality agreement with France in 1741 to protect his Hanoverian territories from invasion. Yet there

Tabarco presides over an entry of charlatans). Handel's early operas for London have fewer dances: mermaids dance whilst singing 'Il Vostro Maggio' (a forlana) to seduce the eponymous crusader in RINALDO (1711; II.iii); Athenians dance while the panegyric chorus, 'Ogn'un acclami' is sung during the hero's triumphal entry in TESEO (1713; II.iv); the libretto for AMADIGI (1715) signals a 'Dance of Enchanted Knights and Ladies' to distract Amadigi from rescuing Oriana (I.viii); a 'Dance of Shepherds and Shepherdesses' concludes this opera. RADAMISTO (1720), Handel's first opera for the Royal Academy of Music (OPERA COMPANIES, 2), features entr'acte dances after Acts I (a march, three rigaudons) and II (passacaille, gigue), and a passepied–rigaudon–passepied group within its final, celebratory, scene. The finales of Amadigi and Radamisto employ a formula to which Handel returned in his 1734–5 operas, where the final chorus generates the music for one or more of the dances. ADMETO (1727) features a 'Dance of Bloody Spirits with Daggers' in its opening scene; the nervous musical energy of its repeated dotted figures (with rests) is highly suggestive. Act II of this opera, set in Hades, opens with a French Overture (followed by a fugue) during which dancing furies torment Alceste. All of Handel's 1734–5 COVENT GARDEN operas – Il PASTOR FIDO, ARIANNA IN CRETA, ORESTE, ARIODANTE and ALCINA – have dances, normally at the end of each act. Some of these seem to have been integrated into the scenes, while others presumably functioned as entr'actes. The integral dances normally appeared in celebrations (see the finales of Acts I and II of Il pastor fido; the dances of the captive courtiers in I.ii of Alcina; the Act III finales of all these operas). The innovative dream sequence intended for the end of Ariodante's Act II – where a devastated Ginevra falls asleep, and a sequence of entries for agreeable and disagreeable dreams is followed by a battle – does not seem to have been performed in this opera, but was instead transferred to Act II of Alcina. While the principal performer and choreographer of these was Marie SALLÉ (for whom Handel also wrote TERPSICORE), Leach Glover (d. 1763) – a theatrical dancer who was later to take up a position at court – created some of the group choreographies, including the 'Dance of Sailors' from Oreste (end of Act I) which was later to become a popular entr'acte dance at Covent Garden. Handel's last theatrical dances were for ALCESTE (1750), a work for Covent Garden which was never performed.   SARAH MCCLEAVE

Banqueting House, Whitehall. Built 1619–22 by Inigo Jones for court masques but deemed unusable after the installation of Rubens's painted ceiling in 1635. Designed for a gap between older buildings, it has no end elevations or proper staircase. After the 1698 Whitehall fire it was used as a chapel, for example for the Royal Maundy. Because of its large size the Utrecht Te Deum was rehearsed there on 19 March 1713 and the Dettingen Te Deum in November 1743 (TE DEUM, 5). Restored in 1964.   KERRY DOWNES

Barlocci, Giovanni Gualberto (Gianguelberto) (fl. Rome, eighteenth century). Italian librettist. He adapted older librettos and wrote several new texts, usually for ROME. His libretto for Oreste (1723), originally set to music by Benedetto Micheli (?c.1700–84) was the source for the anonymous adaptation of Handel's pasticcio ORESTE (1734). Handel might have become acquainted with Barlocci's work during his visit to Rome in 1729, but it is also possible that he learned about the opera from Giovanni CARESTINI, who had performed in the original Rome version. WALTER KREYSZIG

Barn Elms. A mansion and grounds on the Surrey side of the Thames, opposite Fulham, where Handel spent a few summer months soon after settling in England as the guest or tenant of the owner, Henry ANDREWS. Though there had been a house there since at least the sixteenth century, the mansion Handel would have known was relatively new, having been substantially remodelled, if not completely rebuilt in the mid-1690s. Andrews may have given up the lease of the house by 1714, but Handel may have renewed his acquaintance with Barn Elms in the late 1720s during its occupation by John James HEIDEGGER. Handel could have attended functions there like the reception given for GEORGE II and Queen CAROLINE in August 1727, when the mansion and grove of trees were 'finely illuminated after the Italian Manner with a vast number of Candles'. The building survived, in a much altered state, until 1954 when it was demolished following a fire. JOHN GREENACOMBE

Barrett Lennard, Henry. See LENNARD, Henry Barrett

Bartolozzi, Francesco (b. Florence, 25 Sept. 1727; d. Lisbon, 2 March 1815). An Italian engraver who stayed in London for nearly forty years, in the service of GEORGE III from 1764. In 1789 he produced a fine stipple engraving *From the Statue in Vauxhall Gardens* after Biagio Rebecca for ARNOLD's edition [EDITIONS, 2].

EDWIN WERNER

See also ICONOGRAPHY

J. Simon, *Handel: A Celebration of his Life and Times 1685–1759* (London, 1985), 274–5
A. Tosi, *Allgemeines Künstler-Lexikon. Die Bildenden Künstler aller Zeiten und Völker*, vol. 7 (Munich and Leipzig, 1993), 299–301

Baselt, Bernd (b. Halle, 13 Sept. 1934; d. Hanover, 18 Oct. 1993). Musicologist. Bernd Baselt studied at the HALLE Conservatory and at Halle University, where he took a doctorate with a dissertation on Philipp Heinrich Erlebach. In 1975 he completed the *Habilitation* with a thesis about Handel's stage works, including a thematic catalogue of Handel's operas. From 1959 he held lecturing positions at the University of Halle, and in 1983 he was appointed Professor and succeeded Walther SIEGMUND-SCHULTZE as director of the musicological institute. Baselt was recognised as a leading expert on Central German music history, and as a scholar of TELEMANN and especially Handel. He was editor of the Händel-Werke-Verzeichnis (HWV), the *HÄNDEL-HANDBUCH* (1978–86) and of the *Händel-Jahrbuch* (1991–3) (JOURNALS, 2). He was general editor of the Hallische Händel-Ausgabe (EDITIONS, 7), and a driving force behind the Halle Händel-Festspiele (FESTIVALS, 4) and Handel conferences. Baselt was also a board member of the Georg-Friedrich-Händel-Gesellschaft (HANDEL SOCIETIES, 3), and served as its vice-president (1971–91) and president (1991–3).

KLAUS-PETER KOCH (Trans. ANGELA BAIER)

W. Dean, 'Bernd Baselt – Eine persönliche Würdigung', HJb 40/1 (1994/5) *Georg Friedrich Händel – ein Lebensinhalt. Gedenkschrift für Bernd Baselt (1934–1993)*, ed. K. Hortschansky and K. Musketa (Halle, 1995)

Bassoon. See INSTRUMENTATION

Bates, Joah. See HANDEL COMMEMORATION

Bath, Somerset (pop. 6,500 c.1750). The most fashionable of England's spa resorts, offering mineral water to drink and hot bathing known to be efficacious in cases of rheumatoid or paralytic afflictions including those caused by lead poisoning. Handel is known to have visited Bath at least twice, in August 1749 and in May 1751. Handel subscribed to two publications by Thomas Chilcot, organist of the Abbey Church, who organised performances of some of the oratorios and other works with the violinist Giuseppe Passerini and his wife Christina, who had been recommended to Handel by TELEMANN. Christina, a soprano, sang for Handel in London in the 1750s. In addition to sacred works performed at the Abbey during a charity concert in 1758, *ALEXANDER'S FEAST*, *L'ALLEGRO*, *JUDAS MACCABAEUS*, *SAMSON* and *MESSIAH* were performed at Wiltshire's Rooms, Simpson's Theatre and the Orchard Street Theatre during the 1750s.

DAVID HUNTER

See also CHELTENHAM

Beard, John (b. c.1717; d. Hampton, 5 Feb. 1791). English tenor (range B–a′). Beard was the first star tenor of the London stage (see Figure 3). Handel greatly aided his career by tailoring roles to his voice and dramatic repertory, featuring Beard in almost every ode, oratorio and music drama – either new or revived – that he composed in English. Beard received musical training as a boy chorister at the CHAPEL ROYAL, and sang the role of Priest Israelite in Bernard GATES's performance of *ESTHER* in February 1732. After his voice broke, Beard did not pursue a career as a choral singer. He was honourably discharged from the Chapel Royal on 29 October 1734. Handel engaged him to sing in his opera company at COVENT GARDEN. During the period 1734–7, Beard sang in Handel's operas (roles included Silvio in the November 1734 revival of Il *PASTOR FIDO*, Lurcanio in *ARIODANTE*, Oronte in *ALCINA*, Aminta in *ATALANTA*, Varo in *ARMINIO*, Vitaliano in *GIUSTINO*, and Fabio in *BERENICE*) and in performances of English works (Mathan in the first London revival of *ATHALIA* and the tenor solos in *ALEXANDER'S FEAST*). He also performed Handel's music as a 'gentleman extraordinary' with the Chapel Royal at the wedding of FREDERICK, Prince of Wales, in 1736 (ANTHEMS, 4), and probably on other occasions.

Beard's growing reputation led DRURY LANE to engage him to sing opposite the theatre's star soprano Catherine CLIVE. Beginning with The Devil to Pay in August 1737, Beard appeared in a string of hit plays. In January 1739 the tenor wedded Lady Henrietta Herbert, and their marriage – the first ever between noblewoman and an actor – caused a furore; the family promptly cut off Lady Henrietta and in polite society she was accused of marrying 'Beard [of] the farces' out of lust. Although Drury Lane continued to use Beard in works previously mounted, it ceased to cast him in fresh roles; at this point it was primarily Handel who broadened his repertory. His compositions for Beard included Jonathan in *SAUL*, the tenor solos in *ISRAEL IN EGYPT*, the *SONG FOR ST CECILIA'S DAY* and *L'ALLEGRO, IL PENSEROSO ED IL MODERATO*, the title

3. John Beard by Thomas Hudson, oil on canvas, c.1743.

role in *SAMSON*, Jupiter in *SEMELE*, Simeon in *JOSEPH AND HIS BRETHREN*, Hyllus in *HERCULES*, the title role in *BELSHAZZAR*, the tenor solos in the *OCCASIONAL ORATORIO*, and the title roles in *JUDAS MACCABAEUS* and *JEPHTHA*. From 1740 Beard sang also in concerts at Hickford's Rooms.

Beard joined the 1743 rebellion against Drury Lane manager Charles Fleetwood and crossed over to Covent Garden, returning to Drury Lane after David Garrick became manager in 1748. That same year he became principal tenor at RANELAGH Gardens, where he regularly performed excerpts from Handel's works, notably *Alexander's Feast* and *L'Allegro*. His involvement with Handel in the late 1740s is unclear – perhaps crises in the legal battles with his wife's family preoccupied him – but from 1751 he donated his services at annual performances of *Messiah* in aid of the FOUNDLING HOSPITAL (he later became one of the charity's governors), and from 1752 he sang regularly in the composer's oratorio concerts.

In 1753 Beard's wife died, reportedly broken by her relatives' heartlessness; not only had her family crippled the Beards financially, but the family of her first husband, the Marquis of Powis, forced her fifteen-year-old daughter to marry the new forty-eight-year-old Earl of Powis to keep Lady Henrietta from obtaining the jointure for which the Beards had fought since 1739. In 1759, the year of Handel's death, Beard received a D.Mus. at OXFORD, married the daughter of Covent Garden manager John RICH and took over management of that theatre in 1761. While mounting musical theatre and operas to showcase himself, Beard also ran oratorio seasons that regularly featured him in renowned Handel roles. In 1764 he was appointed 'Vocal Performer in Extraordinary' to King

GEORGE III, and was granted a life pension of 100 pounds per annum. He retired in 1767 owing to deafness, but attended the HANDEL COMMEMORATION in 1784.

Beard's core repertory was English musical theatre and song. Of his 108 theatre roles, Handel furnished only twenty-eight. However, Handel's music was vital to the tenor's popularity and reputation, and no other singer had such a close working relationship with the composer extending across so many years. The tenor's monument in the church at Hampton has a quotation from the opening vocal part of 'When thou tookest upon Thee to deliver man' from Handel's Dettingen Te Deum (TE DEUM, 5), which surely signifies the importance of Handel and his music in Beard's life (although the extract chosen was not composed for the tenor, but for the Chapel Royal bass John Abbot).

BERTA JONCUS

Burrows, *Chapel Royal*
Dean, *Operas*
Dean, *Oratorios*
N. Jenkins, 'John Beard: The Tenor Voice that Inspired Handel', *GHB* XII (2008)

Beethoven, Ludwig van (bap. Bonn, 17 Dec. 1770; d. Vienna, 26 March 1827). In 1823 Beethoven called Handel 'the greatest composer who ever lived' and said he would 'kneel at his grave'. He owned a portrait of Handel and made copies of some of his works. In 1783, probably inspired by his teacher Neefe, he composed the Fugue for Organ in D major (WoO 31), on the head motif of the Air and Variations in the Suite in E of the 'HARMONIOUS BLACKSMITH'. Beethoven heard numerous performances of Handel's music in Vienna that were organised by the circles around Gottfried van SWIETEN, including *JUDAS MACCABAEUS* (probably on 15 April 1794), and in 1796 he composed *Twelve Variations on a Theme from Handel's oratorio 'Judas Maccabaeus'* ('See the conqu'ring hero comes', originally from *JOSHUA*) for piano and cello (WoO 45). Handelian influences are also evident in the oratorio *Christus am Ölberge* (Op. 85, 1803–4), the *32 Variations for Piano* (WoO 80, 1806), the *Missa solemnis* (Op. 125, 1819–23), and the overture *Die Weihe des Hauses* (Op. 124, 1822).   HARTMUT KRONES (Trans. ANGELA BAIER)

D. MacArdle, 'Beethoven and Handel', ML 41/1 (Jan. 1960), 33–7
Thayer-Deiters-Riemann, *L. van Beethovens Leben*, vol. 4 (Leipzig, 1907), 457–8

Beggar's Opera, The. A ballad opera in three acts. Playbook by John GAY, music arranged by Johann Christoph PEPUSCH. Premiered at LINCOLN'S INN FIELDS, 29 January 1728. The *Beggar's Opera* interspersed well-known airs with dialogue to create a new genre, BALLAD OPERA, which was to remain popular throughout the eighteenth century. Gay's 'Opera' broke all theatrical records: it was performed sixty-two times during its first season, spread immediately from Lincoln's Inn Fields to rival and provincial theatres and has been popular ever since, partly through the adaptation *Die Dreigroschenoper* by Bertolt Brecht and Kurt Weill. Drawing on the lives of celebrated criminals, Gay inverted tropes standard to sentimental comedy, Italian opera and pastorals to suggest parallels between London's underworld and 'the Town' and government. In the plot, Polly, daughter of gang leader Peachum, secretly marries the highwayman Macheath against her parents' wishes. Visiting a brothel, Macheath is betrayed by an ex-lover and imprisoned. He persuades a rival 'wife', the goaler's daughter Lucy, to free him, but is recaptured. Standing at the scaffold he receives an unlikely royal pardon.

Building on the traditions of English broadside ballads, Gay artfully selected tunes whose earlier associations sharpened the satire of his verses. He relied on dances and airs from the editions of the Playfords and their successors, on London theatre music – by Handel and PURCELL among others – and, to a lesser extent, on broadside ballads that had passed into print. These sources became standard for later ballad operas. The work unleashed an unprecedented storm of publicity and a fashion for low-style music, players and afterpieces, leading Handel's supporters erroneously to blame the *Beggar's Opera* for contributing to the demise of the Royal Academy of Music (OPERA COMPANIES, 2).

BERTA JONCUS

J. Barlow, 'The Beggar's Opera in London's Theatres, 1728–1761', 'The Stage's Glory': John Rich (1692–1761), ed. B. Joncus and J. Barlow (forthcoming)

(ed.), The Music of John Gay's The Beggar's Opera (Oxford, 1990)

W. E. Schultz, Gay's Beggar's Opera: Its Content, History and Influence (New Haven, 1923)

Belchier (Belcher, Belchar), John (bap. Kingston, Surrey, 5 March 1706; d. London, 6 Feb. 1785). Eminent surgeon at Guy's Hospital and friend of ROUBILIAC, POPE and Handel, Belchier tried, on Pope's behalf, to persuade Handel to set the poet's *Ode for Music* (previously set by GREENE) and may have been the original owner of Roubiliac's terracotta bust (the 'Copner') of Pope. It is not known whether he served Handel in his professional capacity. Handel left him a bequest of 50 guineas in his will (HANDEL, 8).   ELLEN T. HARRIS

C. Burney, An Account of the Musical Performances in Westminster-Abbey, and the Pantheon . . . in Commemoration of Handel (London, 1785)

W. K. Wimsatt, The Portraits of Alexander Pope (New Haven, 1965)

Belshazzar, HWV 61. English oratorio, libretto by Charles JENNENS, composed between 23 August and 23 October 1744 and first performed at the KING'S THEATRE, 27 March 1745. The setting is Babylon, capital of Assyria, in 539 BC. The River Euphrates runs through the city. In Babylon are King Belshazzar; his mother, Queen Nitocris; Babylonians; captive Jews, deported from Jerusalem fifty years previously by Belshazzar's grandfather Nebuchadnezzar; and Nitocris's counsellor, the Jewish leader and prophet Daniel. Besieging Babylon are Cyrus, ruler of the Medes and Persians; his Persian army; and Gobryas, a Babylonian whose son Belshazzar has murdered. Nitocris meditates on human greed and ambition: empires rise and fall, only God is boundless, unchanging and eternal. She fears the imminent collapse of her heedless son's degenerate kingdom. Daniel confirms that Babylon is doomed and encourages Nitocris's trust in God. The Babylonians look down from their immense walls and laugh at Cyrus's siege. But Cyrus, inspired by a dream in which he was exhorted to conquer Babylon, rebuild Jerusalem and repatriate the Jews, plans with Gobryas to divert the river and enter the city along its dry bed. The invasion is set for the night of the feast of the Babylonian wine-god Sesach, when the Babylonians will all be drunk. Cyrus commits himself and his troops to God. The Persians proclaim the supremacy of God. In the city, Daniel interprets the Scriptures to his fellow Jews: Isaiah's and Jeremiah's prophecies foretelling the fall of Babylon and Cyrus's repatriation of the Jews are about to be fulfilled. In the palace Belshazzar inaugurates the unbridled feast of Sesach, rejecting his mother's plea to refrain from licentious riot. To flaunt the superior power of his gods over Jehovah, he orders that the sacred Jewish temple vessels, captured by Nebuchadnezzar and untouched since, be used as drinking cups for his feast. The Jews, aghast, try to remind him of God's power, as does Nitocris: in vain.

At the opening of Part II, the Persians divert the River Euphrates and enter Babylon along its empty bed. At Belshazzar's feast the King and his wives, concubines and lords drink out of the Jewish temple vessels, celebrating their gods. Belshazzar recklessly challenges the God of Judah to show His hand. Whereupon a hand appears, writing on the wall opposite him. He is terrified; his court is appalled. He summons his wise men to decipher the inscription, but they cannot. Nitocris advises Belshazzar to consult Daniel. Brushing aside the King's offer of great rewards, Daniel interprets God's words: Belshazzar's days are numbered; his kingdom will be given to the Medes and Persians. Nitocris implores her son to repent. In another part of the city, Cyrus attributes his invasion's success to God and orders his companions to refrain from slaughter: he has come to protect, not destroy. The Persians hail him as the ideal of kingship; were all rulers like him, there would be universal peace and freedom.

Part III, like Part I, begins in the palace with a soliloquy by Nitocris. She is tormented by alternate fear and hope. Despite God's warning the King resumes his feast. News arrives that Cyrus's invasion has reached the palace itself. The Jews celebrate God's victory over the Babylonian gods. Belshazzar, fortified by the god of wine, prepares to do battle with Cyrus. At the start of the concluding scene, Belshazzar has been killed. Gobryas is appeased. Cyrus declares an end to war and an amnesty to all but tyrants. Nitocris kneels before Cyrus as his captive but he raises her, guarantees protection to her people, and offers himself as a son to her. Daniel shows Cyrus Isaiah's prophecy of his victory and urges him to complete its fulfilment. Acknowledging the God of Israel, Cyrus vows to rebuild His temple and city at Jerusalem and return the Jews to their homeland. Daniel leads a final hymn of praise to God.

Handel composed *Belshazzar* straight after HERCULES (Dean, *Oratorios*, p. 435: 'the peak of Handel's creative life'). This crowning achievement of his 'opera of the mind' continually offers striking instances of virtuosic formal innovation, notably planning of large dramatic blocks, such as a single scene comprising twelve numbers using simple and accompanied recitative, recitative with chorus, airs by three characters, choruses by three different groups, and a descriptive sinfonia (II.ii, the feast); juxtaposition of entire scenes (Nitocris's two discussions with Daniel, I.i and III.i), and of numbers (Nitocris's duets of conflict with her real son and of conciliation with her better 'son'); exploitation of the freedom of accompanied recitative (eight in all, several with full ritornellos); and choruses of three nationalities (uniquely in the oratorios), with clearly individualising music appropriate to their mentalities, varying from three parts to six, and from five bars to 190, no two alike in design. Countless imaginative details of dramatisation include a suggestion of the Babylonians prancing on horseback on their towering walls (335 feet high and 85 feet wide); the telling interjection of silence, as in the horror-struck opening of the six-part Jews' warning 'Recall O king', itself a cappella and succeeded by a *forte* orchestral entry on the word 'Jehovah'; the directionless runs of Belshazzar's drunken 'Let festal joy', imitated in his mother's reproof ('The leavy honours'); serene joy breaking into excited hope in Daniel's Scripture teaching ('O sacred oracles', 'Thus saith the Lord'); God's utterances given maximum clarity by being unaccompanied (Cyrus's dream, Daniel's interpretation of His hand), and His writing on the wall expressed by a single violin line of staccato quavers moving by semitones; Belshazzar's single cry ('Ah!') as he sees the writing.

Unparalleled first-hand records of *Belshazzar*'s genesis survive, in five letters from Handel to Jennens – the most numerous, longest, most explicit we have from him about any of his compositions, indeed about anything – and three from Jennens to Holdsworth. They must be read to appreciate the work's evolution. His librettist James MILLER having died, Handel patched up his relationship with Jennens, damaged by Jennens's dissatisfaction with *MESSIAH*, and persuaded him to collaborate again. No other Handel libretto draws on so wide a range of sources: the BIBLE (Isaiah, Jeremiah, Ezra, Psalms, Daniel), Josephus, Herodotus, Xenophon, Polybius, Rollin's *Ancient History*, Ramsay's *The Travels of Cyrus* and Bolingbroke's *The Idea of a Patriot King*. Jennens deftly combines his selections to make vivid dramatic sequences, interweaving ideology and characterisation. Two of his comments about Handel to Holdsworth, 'I must take him as I find him, & make the best use I can of him' (7 May 1744), and, in retrospect, 'the truth is, I had a farther view in it' (26 September 1744), point to his personal investment in the libretto, which can be read as a contribution to the many contemporary depictions of the ideal Patriot King (Cyrus, with Belshazzar as the anti-type), as a wishful premonition of the restoration of the exiled JACOBITE supporters to their homeland, and as an anti-DEIST assertion of the validity of Messianic prophecy and Christian revelation (see Smith). Despite his determination, expressed during the rift with Handel over *Messiah*, to 'put no more Sacred Words into his hands, to be thus abus'd' (17 February 1743), Jennens's Bible selections in *Belshazzar* are frequently verbatim, and marginal references show classical history confirming Scripture. The famous 'stage directions' (notably detailed for the moment of the writing on the wall) inspired Handel, and give the audience any prompt needed for their own imaginations (LIBRETTOS, 3; WORDBOOKS).

Jennens delivered the libretto an act at a time over a period of two and half months. Enthused by the first two acts, Handel began composition, then found he had to revise: 'you may believe that I think it a very fine and sublime Oratorio, only it is realy too long, if I should extend the Musick, it would last 4 Hours and more. I retrench'd already a great deal of the Musick, that I might preserve the Poetry as much as I could, yet still it may be shortned' (letter of 2 October 1744). Burrows identifies four stages of revision between start of composition and first performance. Dean identifies nineteen numbers, almost one third of the total, which Handel revised or rewrote (some twice). Of Jennens's 797 lines, 266 were cut, but proportionately from each act. Pushed to exercise his gift for concise expressiveness, Handel produced a condensed, fast-moving drama. As with *SAUL*, their previous dramatic oratorio collaboration, Handel allowed Jennens (uniquely among his librettists) to annotate his autograph (working) score: Burrows identifies Jennens's hand on over twenty pages. Handel's fourth stage of revision was a response to a crisis. The intended cast was:

Belshazzar	John BEARD (tenor)
Nitocris	FRANCESINA (soprano)
Daniel	Susanna CIBBER (alto)
Cyrus	Miss ROBINSON (mezzo-soprano)
Gobryas	Henry Theodore REINHOLD (bass)

But Cibber fell ill, and, instead of replacing her, Handel gave Daniel's part to Robinson and shared out the other male roles, so that at the first performances Cyrus's part was shared between Robinson and Reinhold, and Gobryas between Beard and Reinhold: three singers each singing two roles, four roles shared among three singers, one role being created by a male and a female singer. The audience's reception was frosty. Already distressed by the poor response to his over-ambitious season, which he had halted and then resumed before *Belshazzar*'s premiere, Handel suffered a recurrence of his nervous disorder during the summer and autumn. He made changes to the score in 1748 (probably for a revival that did not take place) and in 1751, when the whole first scene was omitted but a small but significant amount of the text was restored, amplifying Cyrus's role as Patriot King (and perhaps to showcase GUADAGNI). Handel last revived *Belshazzar* in 1758.

BORROWINGS are relatively few, but interesting in range. They include ALESSANDRO SCARLATTI's *Pompeo* for the ground bass of 'Thus saith the lord'; PORTA's *Numitore* (the Royal Academy's first production) for 'Alternate hopes and fears'; the *Postillions* movement from TELEMANN's *Musique de Table* suite in B flat for the 'Allegro Postillions' sinfonia; and self-borrowings ranging from *Clori, Tirsi e Fileno* (*COR FEDELE, IN VANO SPERI*) to *ARIODANTE* and *OTTONE*. The reuse of Chandos anthems 5 and 8 (ANTHEMS, 2) for the concluding choruses seems to have been suggested by Jennens.

Belshazzar's political maturity is unique among Handel's biblical dramas. There is no triumphalism, nationalism or vengeance; the hero's aim is bloodless conquest, peace, liberty and good government; goodness is not the preserve of a single nation or race; generous, courageous, wise people of four different nations collaborate for the benefit of others; at the end all the participants except a wicked tyrant are alive, free and honourably treated, and captives are liberated and repatriated. *Belshazzar* continues to merit Dean's description as a 'work of supreme genius, whose relevance to our times seems to loom larger with every decade'. RUTH SMITH

A. Baier, ' "Jehovah hath redeemed Jacob". *Belshazzar als jakobitisches Oppositionsdrama*',
    GHB XI (2006)
D. Burrows (ed.), *Handel: Belshazzar*, Novello Handel Edition (London, 1993)
Correspondence of Charles Jennens and Edward Holdsworth, Gerald Coke Handel
    Collection, Foundling Hospital Museum
Dean, *Oratorios*
D. R. Hurley, *Handel's Muse: Patterns of Creation in his Oratorios and Musical Dramas, 1743–51*
    (Oxford, 2001)
Smith, *Oratorios*

Beregan, Nicolò (b. Vicenza, 11 or 21 Feb. 1627; d. Venice, 17 Dec. 1713). Librettist of *GIUSTINO*, reworked by Pietro PARIATI (Bologna 1711, with music by Albinoni), and later revised for a Roman production with music by VIVALDI (1724); this version was set by Handel and first performed at COVENT GARDEN on

16 February 1737. Another of his dramas, GENSERICO (1669), was Handel's source libretto of an unfinished opera. Of noble birth, he was among the most respected members of the Venetian legal profession, but between 1656 and 1660 he was exiled for involvement with others in the murder of a Flemish merchant from HAMBURG. In 1660 he was cleared of the charge and returned to VENICE, where he resumed the twin activities of lawyer and man of letters. He was a member of various Accademie: dei Dodonei in Venice, dei Concordi in Ravenna and dei Gelati in Bologna. DOMENICO ANTONIO D'ALESSANDRO (Trans. TERENCE BEST)

Giorgio E. Ferrari, *Dizionario biografico degli italiani*, vol. 8 (Rome, 1966), 804–5
Strohm, 34–79

Berenice, Regina d'Egitto, HWV 38. Composed between 18 December 1736 and 27 January 1737, *Berenice* had its premiere at COVENT GARDEN on 18 May 1737. The cast was as follows:

Berenice	Anna STRADA del Pò (soprano)
Selene	Francesco BERTOLLI (alto)
Demetrio	Domenico ANNIBALI (castrato)
Alessandro	Gioacchino CONTI (castrato)
Arsace	Maria Caterina NEGRI (alto)
Fabio	John BEARD (tenor)
Aristobolo	Henry REINHOLD (bass)

The opera appeared under inauspicious circumstances. In the later stages of the 1736–7 season both Handel's company at Covent Garden and the OPERA OF THE NOBILITY were in a ruinous financial plight, and Handel, in his determination to get the better of his rivals, drove himself beyond exhaustion. The Earl of SHAFTESBURY's Memoirs describe how 'Great fatigue and disappointment, affected him so much, that he was this Spring struck with the Palsy, which took entirely away, the use of 4 fingers of his right hand; and totally disabled him from Playing: And when the heats of the Summer 1737 came on, the Disorder seemed at times to affect his Understanding' (Deutsch, p. 846). Handel was unable to direct performances of *Berenice*, responsibility for which was assumed by John Christopher SMITH JUNIOR. Four performances were given – only *NERO* and, presumably, *SILLA* had fewer. But SCHÜRMANN revived it in BRUNSWICK in 1743; it was the last of Handel's operas to be staged in Germany in his own lifetime.

The libretto is the fifth and last of the texts that Handel took from Antonio SALVI; he may have witnessed its original staging with music by PERTI at Pratolino in October 1709; its dramatic scope is relatively limited. The characters gyrate around the central theme of politically expedient marriage in a bewildering series of twists and turns, hoodwinkings, prevarications and plain falsehoods, creating, by Act II, an almost buffo-like imbroglio.

Act I: Alessandro, an Egyptian prince raised in Rome, has been sent by the dictator Sulla to make a political marriage with Berenice (Queen of Egypt), and falls under her spell. Berenice scorns to marry at Rome's behest, for she loves her Macedonian suitor Demetrio. However, Demetrio is in love with Berenice's sister Selene, and plans with the aid of Mithridates, King of Pontus, to raise her to the throne in place of Berenice. The Romans issue an ultimatum:

unless Berenice agrees at once to marry Alessandro, Demetrio's life is in danger. Berenice tries to arrange a marriage between Selene and Arsace, a client prince. Her disconcerted sister prevaricates: Arsace must first prove his devotion in some bold undertaking. Demetrio is rescued from an Egyptian mob by Alessandro.

Act II: While Berenice is pressing Demetrio to confess his love, she reveals, prompted by another urgent demand from the Roman ambassador Fabio, that Selene is to marry Arsace. Demetrio is outraged. Mistaking the objects of one another's affections, Alessandro and Arsace imagine they are rivals, and under pressure from the *Realpolitik* promptings of the court counsellor Aristobolo, debate the claims of honour and expediency in love. Selene explains to Demetrio why she appeared to have acted unfaithfully. Overhearing this, Berenice brings in Arsace to claim his bride; but he, in the national interest, has surrendered her to Alessandro, who, entering in turn, refuses any marriage not prompted by mutual devotion. Berenice orders Demetrio to be imprisoned and tortured.

Act III: An incriminating letter from Mithridates to Demetrio has been intercepted. Demetrio was to have been released; but when he acknowledges the truth of the letter, and reiterates his unchanging devotion to Selene, Berenice reverses her decision and he is imprisoned once more. The Queen summons an assembly in the Temple of Isis, and tells Fabio she is now ready to accept whichever consort Rome imposes. Selene promises to marry Arsace if he can save Demetrio. As Arsace ponders this challenge, Alessandro charges him to take back to Berenice the royal seal he has been given. He will not marry the Queen as long as she is acting under duress. Still torn by conflicting emotions, Berenice orders Aristobolo to bring Demetrio's severed head to the temple. But Arsace has used the seal entrusted to him to free Demetrio. Berenice finds herself smitten with sudden love for Alessandro; Arsace is moved magnanimously to yield Selene to her true beloved. The conflicts of politics and love are sweetly resolved.

Because of the limitations of the plot, Handel's music for *Berenice* rarely has scope to do more than dress the individual scene. It is chiefly remembered for two numbers: the Minuet from the Overture and Demetrio's aria 'Si tra i ceppi', the music of which was originally written for different words in a different dramatic context (the nuptial altar has been superseded by a torture chamber). The opera is, however, packed with fine arias, and would surely have been regularly revived had it belonged to an earlier phase of Handel's career. Shaftesbury perceived a deepening of the musical expression as the drama unfolded, the first act being 'full of exquisite genteel airs', while the second 'is more in the great taste & may (I think) properly be call'd sublime' (Burrows and Dunhill, p. 29). It is symptomatic of the sorry case of *Berenice*, however, that not all the best music has a context worthy of it (the dramatic significance of what sounds like an exceptionally fine love duet at the end of Act I, for instance, is wholly mysterious), and that several of its finest numbers seem not to have been performed at all: these include the full version of 'Mio bel sol', with its extraordinary closing melisma; the original setting of 'Si tra i ceppi'; and Berenice's 'Avvertite mie pupille', 'the only aria Handel ever wrote in C sharp minor' (Dean, *Operas*, p. 385)

Handel follows Salvi's text more closely than usual, shortening it ruthlessly, but only once making one of his typical creative interventions. In Act III the aria

'Chi t'intende' is transferred from Fabio to Berenice: what had been an observation becomes an experience; and set as a freely designed interior monologue for voice and solo oboe (SAMMARTINI) is transformed into the turning point of the opera.   DAVID KIMBELL

Burney
Burrows and Dunhill
Dean, *Operas*
Harris, *Librettos*
Strohm

Berenstadt, Gaetano (b. Florence, 7 June 1687; bur. Florence, 9 Dec. 1734). Italian castrato (compass: g–eb″). Born of German parents – his father was timpanist to the Grand Duke of Tuscany – he started his singing career in Italy, performing at NAPLES and Bologna. During his first visit to London he sang the role of Argante in the 1717 revival of *RINALDO*. Having returned to Italy he came back to London in 1722 and joined the Royal Academy of Music (OPERA COMPANIES, 2) for two seasons. Handel created for him the roles of Adelberto in *OTTONE*, the title role in *FLAVIO* and Tolomeo in *GIULIO CESARE*. Berenstadt again left for Italy in 1724 and continued to appear on stage until his death in 1734.

                                                                        ARTIE HEINRICH

Dean and Knapp, *Operas*
L. Lindgren, 'An Intellectual Florentine Castrato at the End of the Medicean Era', *Lo stupor dell'invenzione: Firenze e la nascita dell'opera* (Florence, 2001)

Berger, Cyriakus (fl. Halle, 1658–84). Court musician, organist, bass viol player, timpanist. Cyriakus Berger was employed as a court musician at HALLE from 1658 to 1670, and as court organist at the Halle Dom from 1668/9 to 1670. In addition, he was appointed to the post of organist at the Moritzkirche from 1670 to 1684. On 18 October 1658 he married Elisabeth Händel, who was George Frideric Handel's cousin.   KLAUS-PETER KOCH (Trans. ANGELA BAIER)

W. Serauky, *Musikgeschichte der Stadt Halle*, vol. 2 (Halle/Berlin, 1939)

Berlin. It is undocumented whether Handel visited the residential city of Elector Frederick III (from 1701, King Frederick I in Prussia). MAINWARING described the young Handel journeying to Berlin, where he allegedly met Attilio ARIOSTI and Giovanni BONONCINI. However, such a trip would presumably have taken place before the death of Handel's father on 14 February 1697, when neither of the Italian composers was residing in the city. However, it is entirely possible that Handel's father, impressively styled *Churfürstlich Brandenburgischer Cammerdiener von Haus aus*, might have taken his son along to pay his respects to the Elector in Berlin. It is also conceivable that Handel, together with Georg Philipp TELEMANN, might have gone to see Bononcini's opera *Polifemo* in 1702, or have stopped on his way to HAMBURG in 1703 at Lützenburg Palace, a centre for Italian opera.

    Musical life in any residential city was always determined by the demands, the necessities and the inclinations of the residing court. Electress Sophie Charlotte's son Frederick William I was fond of Handel's operas, especially *ALESSANDRO* and *SIROE*, and often had music from those operas performed. In early January 1734, the King's emissary in London, Caspar Wilhelm von

Borcke, thought it necessary to inform His Majesty that the OPERA OF THE NOBILITY had been founded and that it was trying to 'abbaissieren', that is, to debase, Handel. No operas by Handel were performed in Berlin during the composer's lifetime, unlike in BRUNSWICK or Hamburg. The Crown Prince, later Frederick II, found Handel's taste antiquated and his musical inspiration exhausted. Frederick's musical entourage, however, thought highly of him, although in the opinions of Johann Joachim Quantz, Carl Heinrich GRAUN or Carl Philipp Emanuel Bach, Handel's musical style belonged to a different and bygone age. All the same, Frederick II is said to have tried to acquire Handel's manuscript scores from John Christopher SMITH JUNIOR for £2,000 in the 1770s. The music library owned by Frederick's sister Anna Amalia contained an almost complete collection of Handel's works, printed by John WALSH or William RANDALL, together with the Utrecht Te Deum (TE DEUM, 1), twelve overtures and ALEXANDER'S FEAST, copied by Johann Philipp Kirnberger. The first Berlin performance of *Alexanders Fest*, arranged by Christian Gottfried Krause and with a German text by Karl Wilhelm Ramler, took place in Krause's house around 1766.

Krause was a member, along with Johann Friedrich Agricola, Christoph Friedrich Nicolai, Johann Georg Sulzer and Quantz, of the Montagsklub, founded in 1749 and a centre of Berlin Enlightenment circles. In addition to the musical preferences of the court, the emancipation of the middle classes and the related development of public musical life, especially of amateur concerts, in combination with a rising interest in English language and literature, led to the rediscovery of Handel's oratorio works. The concert society *Koncert der Liebhaber der Musik*, founded in 1770 at the suggestion of Nicolai and directed by Friedrich Ernst Benda and Carl Ludwig Bachmann, furthered this trend. Nicolai's amicable connections with Johann Joachim Eschenburg in Brunswick and with Christoph Daniel EBELING and Matthias Claudius in Hamburg made an exchange of performing materials possible. *Attested* performances of *Alexanders Fest* (1770, 1771 and 1776), JUDAS MACCABAEUS (1774, 1777 and 1787), the Utrecht Te Deum (1771/2) and of MESSIAH (1773 and 1775) took place in the musical events organised by the concert society. *The ways of Zion do mourn* (ANTHEM, 5) was performed in February 1780 to commemorate the passing of the Dowager Princess Louise Amalie and, with a newly adapted Latin text, was repeated as funeral music for Frederick the Great (*Trauergesang über den Tod Sr. Majestät Friedrichs II.*) in October 1786.

Carl Friedrich Zöllner translated the libretto of SAUL into Latin and German in 1792; as a textual basis he used the edition by ARNOLD, which King GEORGE III had given as a present to Frederick William II. Baron Gottfried van SWIETEN, at that time imperial envoy at the Prussian court, heard Handel's music in the concert society, as well as in performances commissioned by the Crown Prince and in Princess Anna Amalia's drawing room. In 1785 Johann Friedrich REICHARDT composed his *Cantata in the Prise* [sic] of *Handel*. Under the patronage of the Crown Prince, Johann Adam HILLER performed a heavily adapted *Messiah* at the Berlin Dom on 19 May 1786. In the autumn of 1786 the organist and choral director J. G. G. Lehmann produced a version of the oratorio at the church of St Nicolai which was closer to Handel's original. Like Hiller he used the German translation by KLOPSTOCK and Ebeling. Handel's oratorios were now regarded as 'church music'.

With the SING-AKADEMIE, founded by Carl Friedrich Christian Fasch in 1791, an institutional link into the nineteenth century was established. Carl Friedrich Zelter, Felix MENDELSSOHN BARTHOLDY, Gaspare Spontini, Johann Otto Heinrich SCHAUM and Karl Friedrich Rungenhagen conducted and adapted numerous oratorios in the first half of the nineteenth century and the tradition of oratorio performances was continued into the second half by the Sing-Akademie and other choral societies. Giacomo MEYERBEER included music by Handel in his court concerts.

As early as 1805 Schaum had called for a German edition of Handel's works (EDITIONS) in Berlin; between 1821 and 1825 four volumes of Anthems were published. A four-day Handel festival was celebrated by, among others, Joseph Joachim, Siegfried Ochs and Georg Schumann in 1906. The first staged performance of an opera took place in 1923 with Julius Cäsar, conducted by Franz von Hoeßlin and the first staged performance of an oratorio followed in 1936 with Herakles, produced by Hans Niedecken-Gebhard.

WERNER RACKWITZ (Trans. ANGELA BAIER)

D. Burrows, 'Gottfried van Swieten and London Publications of Handel's Music', HJB 47 (2001)
G. Busch, 'Das "Händel-Dreieck" Braunschweig-Berlin-Hamburg in der Eschenburg-Nicolai-Korrespondenz 1770–1779', GHB VI (1995)
'Alexanders Fest, oder die Gewalt der Musik. Die früheste Berliner und Braunschweiger Händel-Rezeption zur Zeit des jungen Goethe', Händel-Rezeption der frühen Goethe-Zeit, ed. L. Lütteken and G. Busch (Kassel, 2000)
HHB iv
J. A. Hiller, Nachricht von der Aufführung des Händelschen Messias, in der Domkirche zu Berlin, den 19. May 1786 (Berlin, 1786)
A. Monheim, Händels Oratorien in Nord- und Mitteldeutschland im 18. Jahrhundert (Eisenach, 1999)
F. Nicolai, 'An Herrn Bibliothekar Biester. Über einige Nachrichten von J. A. Hiller', Neue Berlinische Monatsschrift, ed. J. E. Biester, 13/1 (1805), 3–31
W. Rackwitz, 'Marginalien zur Händel-Rezeption im Umfeld des brandenburgisch-preußischen Hofes im 18. Jahrhundert', HJB 44 (1998)

Bernacchi, Antonio Maria (b. Bologna, 23 June 1685; d. Bologna, 13 March 1756). Italian castrato. Already famous throughout Europe, he first performed in London in 1716 (in Alessandro SCARLATTI'S Pirro e Demetrio, with three extra arias written for him by Handel). The following year he sang in revivals of Handel's RINALDO (title role), and AMADIGI (Dardano). As primo uomo for the Second Academy (OPERA COMPANIES, 3), he created the title role in LOTARIO (1729) and Arsace in PARTENOPE (1730), and appeared in revivals of GIULIO CESARE and TOLOMEO and the pasticcio ORMISDA. Though ROLLI described Bernacchi as 'quite exceptional' (Deutsch, 246), and he was famed for his virtuosity (in which he once bested even FARINELLI), he returned to Italy after only one season because London audiences preferred SENESINO. Mrs Pendarves (later DELANY) commented: 'Bernachi has a vast compass [it was actually only a–f″], his voice mellow and clear, but not so sweet as Senesino, his manner [of acting] better; his person not so good, for he is as big as a Spanish friar' (Deutsch, p. 247). He retired in 1736, becoming a well-known singing teacher in his native city.

NICHOLAS CLAPTON

Bernardi, Francesco. See SENESINO

Bertolli, Francesca (b. Rome, c.1710; d. Bologna, 9 Jan. 1767). Italian alto. In 1728 she was listed among the singers of the Princess Violante Beatrice di Toscana; in the same year she made her debut in Albinoni's *L'incostanza schernita*. She was engaged by Handel for the KING'S THEATRE, and made her London debut in December 1729 in the premiere of *LOTARIO* (as Idelberto). Between 1730 and 1733 she sang in the premieres of the operas *PARTENOPE* (as Armindo), *PORO* (Gandarte), *EZIO* (Onoria), *SOSARME* (Melo) and *ORLANDO* (Medoro), as well as in those of the oratorios *ESTHER* (Harbonah and Mordecai) and *DEBORAH* (Sisera), of the pasticcio *ORMISDA* (Arsace) and the serenata *ACIS AND GALATEA* (Dorinda); she also took part in revivals of *GIULIO CESARE* (Tolomeo), *SCIPIONE* (Lelio), *RINALDO* (Argante), *RODELINDA* (Unulfo), *TAMERLANO* (Irene), *FLAVIO* (Teodata) and *ALESSANDRO* (Tassile). In the same period she sang also in operas by Attilio ARIOSTI and Leonardo LEO.

In the summer of 1733 she abandoned Handel to perform with the OPERA OF THE NOBILITY, with which she remained until 1736: there she sang in operas of Giovanni BONONCINI, Nicola PORPORA, Pietro Giuseppe Sandoni (CUZZONI) and Francesco Maria VERACINI, as well as in an unauthorised revival of *OTTONE* (as Matilda). From 1737 she sang with Handel again, performing in the premieres of *ARMINIO* (as Ramise), *GIUSTINO* (Leocasta) and *BERENICE* (Selene), as well as in the pasticcio *DIDONE ABBANDONATA* (based on music by Leonardo VINCI). She then left London and returned to Italy, where between 1740 and 1742 she sang in Turin, Vicenza, VENICE and Genoa. After marrying, she abandoned the stage and retired to Bologna.

Bertolli was one of the most frequent performers on the London stage. Her voice was particularly well suited to breeches roles and not especially remarkable for its quality, compass (b♭–e″) and agility. Handel wrote secondary roles, both male and female, in roughly equal numbers for her; Mary Pendarves (later DELANY) was critical of her style and vocal gifts, but praised her physical beauty and elegance on the stage.   FRANCESCO LORA (Trans. TERENCE BEST)

Bible. According to BURNEY ('Sketch', p. 34), Handel 'took offence' at being provided with the words of the Coronation anthems 'by the bishops' (ANTHEMS, 3; William WAKE) because 'he thought it implied his ignorance of the Holy Scriptures', and riposted: 'I have read my Bible very well, and shall chuse for myself.' His HALLE schooling gave him the bases for reading the Bible in Hebrew, Latin and Greek as well as German. The Bible he grew up with was Luther's translation (LUTHERANISM), and he probably wrote some settings of it during his Halle years, but none survives. In Italy he set the Vulgate (CHURCH MUSIC), but the bulk of his biblical settings dates from his years in England. The Bible was the bedrock of Protestantism: the only source of truth and salvation, in favour of which papal authority, the claims of tradition and the solitary revelation of 'inner light' were all to be rejected. In Britain Protestantism was the national religion (CHURCH OF ENGLAND), and Protestantism was a condition of full citizenship. The Bible was supposed to rule even the ruler: a copy was ceremoniously carried in the CORONATION service and presented to the monarch by the Archbishop of Canterbury with an injunction to 'keep all the words of this law to do them' and the words, 'we present you with this book, the most valuable thing that this world affords. Here is wisdom; this is the royal law; these are the lively oracles of God.' As divine revelation the Bible was justified by its account of miracles and fulfilled prophecies. The dawn of biblical criticism in the early eighteenth century brought the authority traditionally accorded to the Scriptures, on the grounds of their being directly inspired by God, under concerted rational attack. The Bible was a topical and debated text in Handel's England. It was also beginning to be valued as great poetry, the authorised King James Version being held up as a model for imitation – yielding scores of paraphrases – and as a source for musical setting and for sacred drama. Its verbatim use in a theatre, however, was liable to raise objection. In his anthems and oratorios Handel set texts taken verbatim from, slightly adapted from, paraphrased from, or based on twenty-four Old Testament and eight New Testament books of the English Bible, including verses from forty-nine psalms in four versions (King James, Coverdale's translation in the Book of Common Prayer, Tate and Brady's versions and MILTON's versions), and five books of the Apocrypha. Fifty of his catalogued works are based on the Bible or Apocrypha, including nineteen oratorios (LIBRETTOS, 3). Of his oratorios about Jesus Christ, *LA RESURREZIONE*, the *BROCKES PASSION* and *MESSIAH*, only the last uses verbatim biblical text. According to HAWKINS, 'In conversation he would frequently declare the pleasure he felt in setting the Scriptures to music; and how much the contemplating the many sublime passages in the Psalms had contributed to his edification.'   RUTH SMITH

See also HANDEL, 12

C. Burney, 'Sketch of the Life of Handel', in *An Account of the Musical Performances . . . in commemoration of Handel* (London, 1785; repr. 2003)
Smith, *Oratorios*

Birthday Ode for Queen Anne. See *ETERNAL SOURCE OF LIGHT DIVINE*

Bishop of London. See Edmund GIBSON

Blessed are they that considereth the poor. See ANTHEMS, 8

Blindness. See HANDEL, 16

Blow, John (b. Newark, c.1649; d. London, 1 Oct. 1708). By c.1670 Blow was considered one of England's finest composers and organists; he held posts at both WESTMINSTER ABBEY and ST PAUL'S CATHEDRAL during his lifetime, and William CROFT and Henry PURCELL were among his pupils. Blow's major works include a considerable quantity of church music, numerous odes and one stage work, *Venus and Adonis*, survives. In 1700 he published a set of secular songs *Amphion Anglicus*. Blow had died by the time Handel arrived in London in 1710. Handel borrowed from the overture to Blow's Ode for St Cecilia's Day, *Begin the Song* (1684) in his overture to *SUSANNA* (1749).   MATTHEW GARDNER

M. Burden, 'Purcell and his Contemporaries', *The Purcell Companion*, ed. M. Burden (London, 1995)

Bononcini, Giovanni (b. Modena, 18 July 1670; d. Vienna, 9 July 1747). Italian composer, active in London between 1720 and 1732. Bononcini was engaged as a composer for the Royal Academy of Music (OPERA COMPANIES, 2) by Lord BURLINGTON, who was in ROME during 1719 with precise instructions to hire him. At that time, Bononcini was in the service of the Viennese ambassador Johann Wenzel, Count of Gallas (1714–19). Previously, he had been in the service of Filippo and Lorenza Colonna (1692–7) in Rome (where he collaborated on numerous serenatas, operas and an oratorio with the poet Silvio STAMPIGLIA), before moving to Vienna (1698–1712). In 1702, due to the disruption caused by the War of the SPANISH SUCCESSION, he led a group of musicians from Vienna to the Prussian court of Sophie Charlotte. According to MAINWARING, Bononcini may have met Handel during this trip.

His most successful opera, *Il trionfo di Camilla Regina de' Volsci* (NAPLES, 1696), reached London in 1706 and was performed (in English) sixty-three times between 1706 and 1709. After a failed attempt to hire Bononcini in 1707, the composer was finally in London in October 1720. His operas, *Astarto*, *L'odio e l'amore* (*Cyrus*) and *MUZIO SCEVOLA* (Act II), *Crispo* and *GRISELDA*, dominated the first two Academy seasons and were highly successful. The success of Bononcini's operas in London was matched by the success of his *Cantate and Duetti* (published with an astonishing list of 237 subscribers) and the commission of the funeral anthem for the Duke of MARLBOROUGH (1722). Bononcini's presence at the Royal Academy of Music served to diversify the programme; his light, natural and tuneful vein was often opposed to Handel's virtuosic and dramatic style. Despite their distinct musical qualities, Handel must have appreciated Bononcini's music as he borrowed extensively from his rival's compositions, especially from *Il Xerse* (Rome, 1694), in his own *SERSE* and in several other works (BORROWINGS).

Bononcini's Italian and Catholic heritage brought him closer to other Italians in London such as diplomat Giuseppe RIVA, poet Paolo ROLLI and the castrato Francesco Bernardi, known as 'Il SENESINO', as well as to English Roman Catholics such as the Earl of PETERBOROUGH and his wife ANASTASIA ROBINSON, and to well-known JACOBITES such as the Duchess of Buckingham and Francis Atterbury, the Dean of Westminster. The arrest of Atterbury in relation to the failed JACOBITE plot to assassinate members of the Hanoverian family in 1722 coincided with the decline of Bononcini's public favour, as he was not re-engaged by the Royal Academy directors until the 1723–4 season (*Farnace*, *Calfurnia*). In summer 1723 and 1724 he was in Paris, where plans to produce an Italian opera (probably his *Erminia*, produced in Rome 1719 and London, March–May 1723) with singers from the Royal Academy failed to materialise. The 1723–4 season would have concluded Bononcini's career in London, had he not been offered an annual stipend of £500 by the Duchess of Marlborough, on 14 May 1724, to relieve him from his duties at the Royal Academy of Music and direct performances of his own music at the Duchess's private concerts. He enjoyed her patronage until 1731; Bononcini's only opera for the Academy during this period (following the success of *Camilla*'s revival at LINCOLN'S INN FIELDS in 1726) was *Astianatte* (1727) based on RACINE's *Andromaque*, via Antonio SALVI's libretto of 1701. *Astianatte* remains famous for the fight that erupted in the theatre between the supporters of Francesca CUZZONI and FAUSTINA Bordoni (RIVAL QUEENS).

Bononcini was a member of the ACADEMY OF ANCIENT MUSIC from 1726 to 1731, when the composer and his friend Maurice GREENE found themselves at the centre of a scandal concerning the authorship of Antonio LOTTI's *In una siepe ombrosa* (from *Duetti, terzetti e madrigali*, VENICE, 1705), which had been performed at the Academy in 1727 or 1728 as Bononcini's work. Bononcini left London for Paris in 1732. After travelling to Madrid in 1733 and Lisbon, he returned to Vienna in 1736, where he spent his last years.

MELANIA BUCCIARELLI

A. Ford, 'Music and Drama in the Operas of Giovanni Bononcini', PRMA 101 (1974–5), 107–20

L. E. Lindgren, 'A Bibliographic Scrutiny of Dramatic Works Set by Giovanni and His Brother Antonio Maria Bononcini', Ph.D. dissertation (Harvard University, 1972)

J. H. Roberts (ed.), *Handel Sources: Materials for the Study of Handel's Borrowing*, vol. 8 (New York, 1986)

Bordoni, Faustina. See FAUSTINA

Borosini (Borrosini), Francesco (b. Modena, c.1680; fl. 1708–30; d. ?Vienna, ?after 1747). Tenor (range G–a′). Born to a musical family, he was a pupil of his father, the noted tenor Antonio Borosini. After an early appearance at Reggio Emilia in Ballarotti's *Ottaviano in Sicilia* (1692), possibly still as a boy treble, he apparently made his adult debut rather late, in LOTTI's *Il vincitor generoso* at VENICE in 1708. In Italy, his modest theatrical career developed until 1729 in his native area (Reggio, Parma and Milan) over half a dozen stagings. In 1712, he succeeded his father at the Imperial Chapel in Vienna, continuing his service there until 1731 and singing lead roles at the court theatre (1719; 1722–4). During his engagement at London's KING'S THEATRE in the 1724–5 season, he created the Handel roles of Bajazet in *TAMERLANO* and Grimoaldo in *RODELINDA*. Moreover, Handel rewrote for him the soprano part of Sesto in *GIULIO CESARE*, with much new music. In the same company, Borosini also appeared in ARIOSTI's *Dario* and VINCI's *ELPIDIA* alongside the soprano Rosa D'Ambreville, a fellow Modenese whom he had married in 1720 or early 1721 and who equally served at the Emperor's musical household in Vienna from 1721 to 1740 with a substantially higher salary than her husband. His London reappearance during the 1746–7 season, in Paradies's *Fetonte* and Terradellas's *Bellerofonte*, passed almost unnoticed.

Endowed with an imposing yet pleasant appearance, Borosini was suited to performing roles of 'noble fathers', tyrants and villains. His voice had a near-baritone quality, as shown in the parts written for him by Fux, which are notated in the bass clef. He excelled in a forceful style of singing, with wide leaps and energetic syllabic declamation, mingled with elaborate arpeggiato passages. The roles Handel wrote for him exploit a compass from c′ (occasionally A) to a′ and a central range between g and e′. Besides Allegros featuring spectacular agility (like 'Ciel e terra' for Bajazet or 'Io già t'amai' and 'Tuo drudo è mio rivale' for Grimoaldo) they also include some of the composer's finest dramatic accompanied recitatives and several lyrical slow arias. Evidence from the autograph of *Tamerlano* suggests that Borosini's arrival in London in September 1724 induced the composer to revise radically the role of Bajazet for the tenor, who had sung the character in GASPARINI's *Il Bajazet* at Reggio in 1719.

CARLO VITALI

borrowings. Handel frequently based his compositions on earlier music by himself or other composers. His borrowings can be divided into five broad types:

(1) Transfer of an entire piece with little or no change except perhaps in text or key. Handel did this only with his own music, though in a few cases he did allow singers to insert arias by other composers into a revival or pasticcio (*ARIODANTE*, *PORO*, *GIOVE IN ARGO*). Beginning in 1730 he frequently interpolated numbers from other works into revivals of his operas and oratorios.

(2) Adaptation of an existing piece or substantial section. Again he adopted this approach primarily with his own music, but he did adapt a number of fugal sections by other composers for choruses in the later anthems and oratorios.

(3) Modelling a new piece on an old one. Although Handel most often employed models by other composers, he also used his own music in the same way. Frequently he followed the model very inexactly, with few if any obvious quotations. For this reason such relationships can easily be overlooked or their full extent underestimated.

(4) Fragmentary borrowing. He might take an entire ritornello, an initial or internal idea, a contrapuntal subject or two or more isolated passages, usually related. Slender relationships can sometimes be confirmed by the proximity of other borrowings from the same source.

(5) Use of stock figures, ideas that even though originally derived from some external source, recurred so frequently in Handel's music that they became in effect part of the composer's working vocabulary.

In practice the boundaries between these types can blur, at least from an analytical point of view. Very often, moreover, Handel combined material from several sources in one piece, and we have no way of knowing (except with straight transfers) whether we have found all the relevant ancestors. For these reasons, any attempt to categorise pieces according to the type of borrowing they contain must come to grief.

Apart from including popular favourites in revivals and pasticcios, Handel's self-borrowing seems primarily to have been driven by a desire to save himself trouble by reusing music that his current audience had not yet heard. Thus in his Venetian opera *AGRIPPINA* he drew heavily on scores composed for ROME, FLORENCE and NAPLES, and his first two London operas, *RINALDO* and Il *PASTOR FIDO*, consisted largely of arias already performed in various Italian cities. Similarly, the privately mounted *SILLA* and the abandoned incidental music for Smollett's *ALCESTE* served as sources for *AMADIGI* and the *CHOICE OF HERCULES*. The novelty principle likewise governed his choice of models and sources by other composers. Borrowing from KEISER in Rome or TELEMANN in London would have passed unnoticed by most listeners. We have no reason to suppose that Handel expected any of his quotations to be understood as meaningful allusions, except possibly in the Funeral Anthem for Queen Caroline (ANTHEMS, 5). Most of his external borrowings were quite conscious and deliberate. He regularly perused certain collections and large-scale works in search of material, sometimes jotting down promising ideas or transcribing extended passages. Among the dozens of composers laid under contribution he seems to have particularly favoured Giovanni BONONCINI, GASPARINI, Keiser, LOTTI, Alessandro SCARLATTI, and Telemann.

Because most of the music Handel composed in HALLE and HAMBURG is lost, we cannot be sure what role borrowing played in the works of his first twenty years, though some transformative imitations of Keiser have been found in ALMIRA. In Italy, however, he immediately began drawing heavily on German sources, and from that point onwards borrowing remained a constant and important part of his creative process. Around 1735 we see an increase in the size and exactness of his appropriations from other composers, perhaps in response to deteriorating health. Yet even in his last works his methods remain predominantly transformative.

In reusing his own compositions as opportunity permitted Handel's methods were typical of his time. His willingness to rely upon sources or models by other composers was also by no means exceptional. It is not true, as sometimes stated, that external borrowing was universally accepted among his contemporaries; in fact it was often criticised, especially in Germany, and Handel himself took care to cover his tracks after borrowing from VINCI's Didone abbandonata. But numerous treatises and prefaces make it clear that such practices were very widespread, especially among Italian composers, and examples have been discovered in the music of VIVALDI and GLUCK among others. It would appear, however, that Handel's external borrowing was unusually systematic and extensive. He probably also went beyond most of his leading contemporaries in the degree to which his compositional process depended on the use of old material of whatever origin. It is hard to escape the conclusion that he lacked some facility in the invention of original ideas.

As early as 1722, MATTHESON chided Handel in print for taking melodic ideas from arias by Lotti and himself, but it was not until the nineteenth century that the borrowings became the subject of widespread public discussion. Some British writers, equating any sort of borrowing with plagiarism, condemned him on moral grounds, and Sedley Taylor adopted a prosecutorial stance in his useful compendium of parallel passages (1906). In recent years a more historically enlightened view has taken hold, even as many additional relationships have been brought to light. It has increasingly been recognised that rather than posing a threat to Handel's reputation his famous habit can help us understand more fully the complexity and creative power of his extraordinary musical mind.   JOHN H. ROBERTS

G. Buelow, 'The Case for Handel's Borrowings: The Judgment of Three Centuries', Handel: Tercentenary Collection, ed. S. Sadie and A. Hicks (London, 1987)
J. H. Roberts, Handel Sources, 9 vols. (New York, 1986)
  'Why Did Handel Borrow?', Handel: Tercentenary Collection, ed. S. Sadie and A. Hicks (London, 1987)
  'Handel and Vinci's "Didone abbandonata": Revisions and Borrowings', ML 68/2 (1987), 141–50
S. Taylor, The Indebtedness of Handel to Works by Other Composers (Cambridge, 1906)

Boschi, Giuseppe Maria (b. Mantua or Viterbo, c.1687; fl.1703–44). Italian bass singer, whose operatic career probably began at Genoa in 1705. In 1707–9 he sang in VENICE, where he played Pallante in Handel's AGRIPPINA, and soon afterwards he came to London, taking the role of Argante in RINALDO; his wife, the contralto Francesca VANINI, also sang in both productions. He returned to Italy and joined the choir of St Mark's, Venice, obtaining leave to sing in operas at Turin and DRESDEN. Handel probably re-engaged him for the newly formed Royal Academy of Music (OPERA COMPANIES, 2) during his visit to Dresden in 1719, and Boschi returned to London, where he sang in all thirty-two of the Academy's operas between 1720 and 1728, including thirteen by Handel. Thereafter he returned to Italy. He had a wide vocal range (G to g') and Handel's music for him is usually lively and forceful, though the arias are sometimes (as in *RICCARDO PRIMO*) graced with a contrapuntal accompaniment.

DONALD BURROWS

Boyce, William (b. London, bap. 11 Sept. 1711; d. London, 7 Feb. 1779). One of the foremost English composers of his time, he was a chorister at St Paul's, and apprenticed to Maurice GREENE. Though he soon became almost deaf, he was appointed composer to the CHAPEL ROYAL, organist and composer of the King's Chapel and conductor at the Three Choirs Festival (FESTIVALS, 1). His vocal works with orchestral accompaniment and short dramatic works (*David's Lamentation, Pindar's Ode, Peleus and Thetis, The Chaplet, The Shepherd's Lottery, The Secular Masque*) fitted within the contemporary 'Handelian' oratorio style. His 'seranata' *Solomon*, loosely based on the Song of Songs, was a small-scale oratorio in all but name, at the crossroads between various genres, reconciling entertainment and moral edification. His twelve Sonatas for two violins and a bass proved extremely popular. In 1755, he became Greene's successor as conductor of the festival of the SONS OF THE CLERGY at St Paul's and Master of the King's band. In this capacity, he produced two odes each year, the overtures to which formed the basis of his celebrated Eight Symphonies (1760). As his deafness increased, Boyce retired to edit his *Cathedral Music* (1760, 1768, 1773) from the manuscripts bequeathed to him by Greene, which made the wealth of the English choral tradition better known. Boyce was admired by his contemporaries both because his style, a model of balance, 'strength, clearness, and facility, without any mixture of styles, or extraneous and heterogeneous ornaments' (BURNEY) was close to Handel's and because his music was perceived as specifically and originally English. PIERRE DUBOIS

Boyle, Richard. See 3rd Earl of BURLINGTON

Brady, Nicholas (b. London, 1659; d. London, 1726). Anglican priest and poet. He provided the text for Henry Purcell's ode *Hail, bright Cecilia* (1692), and assisted Nahum TATE in the preparation of *A New Edition of the Psalms of David* (London, 1696), which provided texts for a number of ANTHEMS set by Handel.

WALTER KREYSZIG

R. A. Leaver, 'The Failure that Succeeded: The New Version of Tate and Brady', *The Hymn* 48 (1997), 22–31

Brahms, Johannes (b. Hamburg, 7 May 1833; d. Vienna, 3 April 1897). Composer. He was interested in Handel's music, and his *Variations and Fugue on a Theme by Handel* (Op. 24, written in 1861) for solo piano is based on a theme from the Suite for harpsichord HWV 434. Brahms performed *MESSIAH* in Detmold, the Dettingen

Te Deum (TE DEUM, 5), *SAUL*, *ALEXANDER'S FEAST* and *SOLOMON* in Vienna between 1872 and 1875. He wrote piano accompaniments for CHAMBER DUETS (HWV 183, 185, 188, 191,193, 196, 197) AND TRIOS (HWV 201 and 202) for the edition of the Deutsche Händel-Gesellschaft (EDITIONS, 5) published in 1870, based on Thomas Smart's arrangements for the Handel Society (EDITIONS, 3). Brahms made some corrections to the accompaniments and arranged HWV 179, 181, 186, 189, 190 and 192 for CHRYSANDER's new 1880 edition of the chamber duets.   WERNER RACKWITZ (Trans. ANGELA BAIER)

I. Fellinger, 'Das Händel-Bild von Brahms', GHB III (1989)

J. Neubacher, 'Ein neuer Quellenfund zur Mitarbeit Johannes Brahms' an Friedrich Chrysanders Ausgabe von Händels "Italienischen Duetten und Trios" (1870)', *Die Musikforschung* 51 (1998), 210–15

W. Rackwitz, 'Anmerkungen zum Verhältnis Friedrich Chrysanders zu Johannes Brahms und Joseph Joachim', *Brahms-Studien* 12 (1999), 41–60

H. Serwer, 'Brahms and the Edition of Handel's Chamber Duets and Trios', HJb 39 (1993)

W. Siegmund-Schultze, 'Händel und Brahms', HJb 39 (1993)

Breidenstein, Carl Heinrich (b. Steinau/Hesse, 28 Feb. 1796; d. Bonn, 12 July 1876). Music teacher, director and lecturer. He studied law and philosophy in BERLIN and Heidelberg, and music with Anton Friedrich Justus THIBAUT in Heidelberg. In 1822 he became Director of Music at Bonn University, where he became the first musician to occupy a professorship in musicology in Germany (in 1826). Breidenstein was probably influenced by Thibaut's enthusiasm for Handel, and he was the first German editor to publish a vocal score of *ISRAEL IN EGYPT*. Breidenstein wanted to make the work popular, and sought to make his edition faithful to Handel's original score (in contrast to earlier arrangements by Ignaz MOSEL and others), although this ambition was contradicted by a later article offering advice to perform the oratorio with additional accompaniments and contemporary instruments. He was particularly interested in music aesthetics, but was unsure how to classify tone-painting in Handel's compositions.   ANNETTE LANDGRAF

K. Breidenstein, 'Israel in Aegypten, Oratorium von G. F. Händel. Uebersetzung und Klavierauszug von K. Breidenstein', *Berliner Allgemeine Musikalische Zeitung* 30 (1827), 240–2; 31 (1827), 247–9; 32 (1827), 257–9

(ed.), *Israel in Egypten* (Bonn and Cologne, 1826)

Brent, Charles (b. 1692/3; d. 1770). Countertenor and fencing master, created the part of Hamor in the first performance of Handel's *JEPHTHA* at COVENT GARDEN in 1752, and is known to have sung at RANELAGH Gardens.

Brent, Charlotte (b. London, 17 Dec. 1734; d. London, 10 April 1802). Soprano, daughter of Charles Brent. A pupil of Thomas Augustine ARNE, she made her first appearance on stage as Liberty in Arne's *Eliza* at DUBLIN in 1755. When Arne returned with Brent from Dublin in 1756, he left his wife behind. According to BURNEY, Brent remained with Arne, to whom she was articled as a student, and appeared in several of his works in ensuing years. She was engaged by John BEARD at COVENT GARDEN, where she was celebrated as Polly in the 1759 revival of *The BEGGAR'S OPERA* (1759), and made a name for herself as a concert and oratorio singer. In 1766 she married the violinist Thomas Pinto. It has been suggested that she sang for Handel in 1759, but this seems unlikely, as she is not included in the cast of singers of that season as given in the HARRIS papers.   EVA ZÖLLNER

Burrows and Dunhill

Briani, Francesco (b. Venice; fl. 1709–10). Italian librettist. Two of his librettos were set to music by Antonio LOTTI for Venice in 1710: *Il vincitor generoso*, which was dedicated to King Frederick IV of Denmark, and *Isacio tiranno*, which was dedicated to the Duke of MARLBOROUGH. The latter libretto was adapted by Paolo ROLLI for Handel's *RICCARDO PRIMO*. Margherita DURASTANTI had sung the role of Pulcheria in the original Venetian production, and perhaps she suggested Briani's libretto as a suitable project for the Royal Academy of Music (OPERA COMPANIES, 2) before she left London in 1724. Alternatively, somebody connected with the Marlboroughs might have recommended Briani's text.   WALTER KREYSZIG

A. Groppo, *Catalogo di tutti i drammi per musica recitati ne' teatri di Venezia* (Venice, 1745)
E. Selfridge-Field, *Pallade veneta: Writings on Music in Venetian Society, 1650–1750* (Venice, 1985)

Bristol. Though never visited by Handel (as far as is known), the city can lay claim to a couple of notable Handel firsts. The earliest recorded public performance of his music in the English provinces took place here in 1727, when excerpts from *ACIS AND GALATEA* were given, and it was in Bristol, on 17 August 1758, that *MESSIAH* was heard for the first time in an English Cathedral. John WESLEY, who was present, doubted 'if that congregation was ever so serious at a sermon as during this performance'. Two years earlier, on 14 January 1756, *Messiah* had been chosen to open the New Musick Room in Prince Street.

It may be more than a coincidence that the 1st Duke of CHANDOS, for whom *Acis and Galatea* was originally written, had property in Somerset, including a mansion at Keynsham, now on the outskirts of Bristol, where tradition has it that Handel played the organ in the parish church. A street there is named after him.

The Revd Thomas BROUGHTON, who wrote the libretto for *HERCULES*, was Vicar of St Mary's Redcliffe, and is buried in the north choir aisle where there is a memorial to him. Above it is the 'Handel window', installed in the composer's memory on the centenary of his death in 1859 to commemorate his supposed associations with the church. As at Keynsham there is a tradition that Handel played the organ at St Mary Redcliffe.   JOHN GREENACOMBE

British Library and British Museum. See SOURCES AND COLLECTIONS

Brockes, Barthold Heinrich (b. Hamburg, 22 Sept. 1680; d. Hamburg, 16 Jan. 1747). One of the most important German poets of his age. He came from a wealthy family background and was provided with a demanding and extensive education. He was a pupil of the Johanneum and the Akademisches Gymnasium in HAMBURG; after finishing his education he travelled to DRESDEN and Prague. He studied in HALLE (1700–2), where he met HANDEL and TELEMANN. After a probationary period of six months at the Wetzlar Imperial Chamber Court, he went to Italy, Switzerland and Paris to complete his education and graduated as a Licentiat in Leyden in 1703. From 1704 he lived in Hamburg, where his independent financial means enabled him to adopt an aristocratic lifestyle and to cultivate his interests in music, painting and poetry. He became a Senator in 1720 and later held various other public posts. Brockes was co-founder of the Teutschübende Gesellschaft (a society concerned with the propagation of the German language, founded in 1715) and a member of the Patriotische Gesellschaft ('Patriotic society', founded in 1724), which published the enlightenment periodical Der Patriot. An independently minded man, Brockes was respected for his translations of Italian, French and English poetry. His cantatas, occasional poems, lyric reflections on Christian morality and his nature poetry are notable for their refined form and creativity in both art and language. His poetical works were published in the nine-volume collection Irdisches Vergnügen in Gott (1721–48). The first performance of his passion oratorio Der für die Sünde der Welt gemarterte und sterbende Jesus, set by Reinhard KEISER (1712), took place in his house. Handel set the same libretto to music in about 1716 (BROCKES PASSION). The composer and the poet probably remained friendly long after Handel left Hamburg, and in about 1724 he composed nine aria texts from Irdisches Vergnügen (GERMAN ARIAS).

UTE POETZSCH (Trans. ANGELA BAIER)

W. Braun, 'Händel und der Dichter Barthold Heinrich Brockes', Händel und Hamburg (Hamburg, 1985)

B. H. Brockes, Irdisches Vergnügen in Gott. Naturlyrik und Lehrdichtung, ed. H.-G. Kemper (Stuttgart, 1999)

Werke, Band 1. Selbstbiographie. Verteutschter Bethlehemitischer Kindermord. Gelegenheitsgedichte. Aufsätze, ed. J. Rathje (Dresden, 2008)

H.-G. Kemper, U.-K. Ketelsen and C. Zelle (eds.), Barthold Heinrich Brockes (1680–1747) im Spiegel seiner Bibliothek und Bildergalerie (Wiesbaden, 1998)

H.-D. Loose (ed.), Barthold Heinrich Brockes (1680–1747). Dichter und Ratsherr in Hamburg (Hamburg, 1980)

Brockes Passion (Brockes Oratorium), HWV 48. Handel's only German-language oratorio, composed in London, is a setting of Barthold Heinrich BROCKES's libretto Der für die Sünde der Welt gemarterte und sterbende Jesus. It belongs to the genre of the passion oratorio, in which the passion narration, central to Christian faith, is poetically paraphrased, affectively dramatised and extended by the inclusion of lyrical reflections. MATTHESON regarded the 'description of the sufferings of Christ', that is the PASSION, as the 'most dignified content' of an oratorio imaginable (Mattheson, Kern melodischer Wissenschaft, p. 106). Passion oratorios were concert works, performed in private residences or in concert halls, and Der für die Sünde der Welt gemarterte und sterbende Jesus made the HAMBURG poet Brockes famous: from 1712 there were numerous reprints of the text, and the poet included it in some of his other publications; in 1730 it was even translated into Swedish. He modelled his elevated style of poetry on predecessors such as Giambattista Marino, whose Strage degli Innocenti he translated into German and published as Verteutschter Bethlehemitischer Kindermord (1715).

It is not known why or for what occasion Handel set the 1713 version of the libretto text to music, but he composed it in London in about 1716. Perhaps the idea arose from correspondence with either Brockes or Mattheson. In 1717 Handel's score reached Mattheson in Hamburg, although its first documented performance did not take place until 3 April 1719. In the following years there were further performances in the city, for example at the Maria-Magdalenen-Kirche; Mattheson also reports a performance in Lüneburg. There were a number of concert series in Hamburg in which the different settings by Keiser, TELE-MANN, Mattheson and Handel were performed; a pasticcio arranged from the four versions was also popular. Handel's autograph score is lost but a number of contemporary copies have survived, which demonstrate that the fame of his *Brockes Passion* spread beyond Hamburg. One of these copies was in part pre-pared by Johann Sebastian BACH, another of English provenance later belonged to Joseph HAYDN.

The libretto of the passion oratorio is remarkable for the extraordinary power of its language and its profound grasp of the subject. Brockes's multi-layered imagery is supposed to stimulate strong responses from the reader or listener to Christ's suffering and dying. An Evangelist (tenor) narrates the story. In addition to Jesus (bass), the cast of characters includes the apostles Petrus (tenor), Judas, Johannes, Jakobus (altos), Maria, three maidservants (sopranos), the basses Caiphas, Pilatus, a *Kriegsknecht* (i.e. a mercenary soldier), and choruses of apostles, Jews and servants. Spiritual reflection upon the events of the passion story is contributed by the Tochter Zion ('Daughter of Zion', soprano) and by soprano, alto, tenor and bass representatives of the *Gläubige Seelen* ('Christian Faithful'). Affective reflections and meditations are particularly important, and unfold in nine soliloquies allocated to the Tochter Zion, the Gläubige Seelen, Petrus, Jesus, Judas and Maria, which resemble solo cantatas.

Handel's oratorio commences with a three-movement sinfonia with a con-certato middle movement. The introductory chorus 'Mich vom Stricke meiner Sünden zu entbinden' alternates solo passages, with dynamically reduced accompaniment, and tutti sections with full chorus. It is reminiscent of a French opera chorus, and French influences can also be detected in Jesus's words, enforced by the instrumental basses, in his exchanges with the apostles 'Erwacht! / Wer ruft?', which Handel embeds in a quasi-ostinato trio setting for two violins and basso continuo. Generally, Handel utilises the available spectrum of musical means and stylistic elements in a subtle manner. The arias have syllabic text declamation; only chosen rhyming words or words with a par-ticular affect attached to them are accentuated by coloratura writing. The music for the *Turbae* ('crowd' choruses), allocated only recitative in the text, is set in arioso style. In order to conjure up an association of massed groups of people, Handel uses different techniques of imitation, interlinks the voice parts, and sometimes has different choral sections declaiming different text passages. The four CHORALE movements – called 'Coro' like the other tutti movements and the *Turbae* music – are four-part cantional settings, in which Handel tastefully decorates conventional hymn melodies.

The instrumentation is string-based and has additional oboes. Often the violins are used without the violas; the oboe sometimes appears as solo instru-ment, such as in Petrus's 'Heul, du Schaum der Menschenkinder', or reinforces the vocal line, such as in the Tochter Zion's aria 'Wisch ab der Tränen scharfe Lauge'. There are obbligato arias with continuo accompaniment and large-scale, Italian-style operatic arias with lavish instrumentation like Petrus's aria 'Gift und Glut'. In addition to the da capo aria, Handel uses strophic and through-composed musical forms. Although his use of onomatopoetic effects is restrained, he employs them to palpable effect in the Gläubige Seelen's 'Brich brüllender Abgrund', and in the ensemble for the Tochter Zion and chorus 'Eilt, ihr angefochtnen Seelen'. The keys used are also characteristic for the subject matter's expressivity: B flat and minor keys dominate, in addition to F and B flat major and G minor there are a number of pieces in E flat major and C minor; unusual and highly affective keys are A flat major (used once), the melancholy F minor (used three times, including the duet for Jesus and Maria and the trio for the Christian Faithful 'O Donnerwort'), as well as the gloomy F sharp minor for the Tochter Zion 'Laß doch diese herbe Schmerzen'.

Handel responded elegantly to the complex structure of Brockes's poetic imagery. He borrowed a number of arias from earlier compositions including Roman CANTATAS, the oratorio Il TRIONFO DEL TEMPO E DEL DISINGANNO, the Utrecht Te Deum (TE DEUM, 1), the ode ETERNAL SOURCE OF LIGHT DIVINE and from ANTHEMS composed at around the same time. He never performed his passion oratorio, presumably because he had little use for it in England. However, he did borrow from numerous arias and choruses in his later English oratorios ESTHER, ATHALIA and DEBORAH. Some music found its way into RADAMISTO (HWV 12^a), GIULIO CESARE and SERSE. The sinfonia was included in Op. 3 No. 3 (ORCHESTRAL MUSIC, 2).

UTE POETZSCH (Trans. ANGELA BAIER)

Dean, *Oratorios*
HHB ii
HHB iv
J. Kremer, 'Händels *Brockespassion* – eine Passion für den Galant-Homme?', HJb 55 (2009)
J. Mattheson, *Kern melodischer Wissenschaft* (Hamburg, 1737)
F. Schroeder (ed.), *Passion nach Barthold Heinrich Brockes*, HHA I/7 (Leipzig, 1965) (Kritischer Bericht, Leipzig, 1973)
H. E. Smither, *A History of the Oratorio*, vol. 2: *The Oratorio in the Baroque Era: Protestant Germany and England* (Chapel Hill, NC, 1988)

Brook Street. See MUSEUMS, 3

Broschi, Carlo. See FARINELLI

Broughton, Thomas (b. London, 5 July 1704; d. Bristol, 21 Dec. 1774). English priest, author and librettist of Handel's HERCULES. He was educated at Eton College (1716–20), St Paul's School (1720–3) and Gonville and Caius College, CAMBRIDGE (BA 1727, ordained 1728, MA 1730), where he specialised in mathematics and modern languages. In 1727 he was appointed Reader to the Temple Church, London. A staunch upholder of the established Church, in 1732 he published *Christianity Distinct from the Religion of Nature*, a three-volume rebuttal of DEISM. His *Bibliotheca historico-sacra* (1737, 1739), a thousand-page encyclopedia of world religions, was twice reissued and was translated into Hungarian. A conscientious minister, he was appointed in 1744 to the valuable SALISBURY prebendary of the BRISTOL vicarages of Bedminster and St Mary Redcliffe. He married Anne Harris, daughter of the parish schoolmaster; they had seven children. Broughton was a diverse, lucid, lively and modest author with a distinct narrative gift, contributing 120 articles to *Biographia Britannica* (1747–50) and editing DRYDEN's miscellaneous works (1743). As a priest (notably in *Fifteen*

Sermons on Select Subjects, 1778) he promoted Christian virtue at its most generous. He was a lover of Handel's music, and subscribed to his *ATALANTA*.

RUTH SMITH

R. Smith, 'Handel's English Librettists', *Cambridge Companion to Handel*, ed. D. Burrows (Cambridge, 1997)

Brown, Lady Margaret (b. 12 June 1692; d. 13 Feb. 1782). Daughter of Robert Cecil, MP, and granddaughter of the 3rd Earl of Salisbury. She married Robert Brown in 1725 and returned with him to VENICE where he was a merchant banker. There her musical interests were strengthened and she made the acquaintance of singers such as FARINELLI. On their return to England in 1735, following her husband's receipt of a baronetcy and a seat in Parliament, Lady Brown became active in soliciting subscriptions for the opera seasons and in the early 1740s (if not before) held concerts on Sundays at her house. Though stigmatised by BURNEY as 'a persevering enemy to Handel' there is little evidence for her direct opposition. Her husband's brother James Brown (d. 1743) married Catherine, the eldest daughter of Colley CIBBER.

DAVID HUNTER

D. Hunter, 'Margaret Cecil, Lady Brown: "Persevering Enemy to Handel" but "Otherwise Unknown to History"', *Women and Music* 3 (1997), 43–58
'Puppet Politics: Tobias Smollett, Charlotte Charke, and Theatrical Opposition to Handel', *Theatre Notebook* 48 (2004), 7–17

Brunswick. The Brunswick opera house was founded by Duke Anton Ulrich of Brunswick-Wolfenbüttel in 1690, and until 1864 it was located at what is today the Hagenmarkt. The theatres of HAMBURG and Brunswick exchanged repertoire and performers on a regular basis. Between 1723 and 1743 twelve operas by Handel were performed: *OTTONE* (1723, 1725), *GIULIO CESARE IN EGITTO* (1725, 1733), *ALESSANDRO* (1728), *RICCARDO PRIMO* (1729, 1734, ?1739), *ADMETO* (1729, 1732, 1739), *SIROE* (1730, 1735), *PARTENOPE* (1731–3), *PORO* (1732), *ARIANNA IN CRETA* (1737/8), *ALCINA* (1738), *GIUSTINO* (1741) and *BERENICE* (1743). Some of them received more than one performance. The operas were performed (sometimes under different titles, but often shortly after they had been premiered in London) either during the winter fair (February) or during the summer fair (August) by the Wolfenbüttel Hofkapelle, until 1730 under the direction of Georg Caspar SCHÜRMANN (Hofkapellmeister from 1707 to 1751). The operas were performed complete, mostly in Italian, less frequently in German; sometimes the aria texts remained in the original Italian whereas recitatives and choruses were translated into German and set to new music (often by Schürmann). KLAUS-PETER KOCH (Trans. ANGELA BAIER)

See also SALZDAHLUM; WOLFENBÜTTEL

R. Brockpähler, *Handbuch zur Geschichte der Barockoper in Deutschland* (Emsdetten, 1964)
F. Chrysander (ed.), 'Geschichte der Braunschweig-Wolfenbüttelschen Capelle und Oper vom sechszehnten bis zum achtzehnten Jahrhundert', *Jahrbücher für musikalische Wissenschaft*, vol. 1 (Leipzig 1863)

Brydges, James. See 1st Duke of CHANDOS

Buckingham Palace. In the first half of the eighteenth century Buckingham House was owned by the Dukes of Buckingham. It was bought by GEORGE III in 1761 for his wife Queen Charlotte to use as a comfortable family home across GREEN PARK from the court at ST JAMES'S PALACE. In the 1820s George IV commissioned John Nash to rebuild the house as a palace, and the State and semi-State Rooms contain many pieces of art and furniture that were moved from CARLTON HOUSE. The palace did not become the official London residence of the British monarchy until Queen Victoria settled there in 1837. The Royal Music Library, containing many of Handel's autographs and manuscript copies, was housed in the Palace by the mid-nineteenth century (SOURCES AND COLLECTIONS, 1). During the 1870s, Friedrich CHRYSANDER frequently visited the palace in order to study the Handel autographs in preparation of his edition (EDITIONS, 5).

WALTER KREYSZIG

R. G. King, 'New Light on Handel's Musical Library', MQ 81/1 (1997), 109–37
'The Royal Music Library at Buckingham Palace', *Musical Times and Singing Class Circular* 43 (1902), 451–5

Buckley, Samuel (d. 1741). London printer and publisher, active from late 1690s, who for many years edited and published The *Daily Courant*, London's first successful daily newspaper. In 1711 he undertook the printing of the earliest issues of the *Spectator*, in which venture he was soon joined by others, including Jacob TONSON. Based 'at the Dolphin in Little-Britain', near St Bartholomew's Hospital, Buckley had a reputation as 'a learned printer' and an 'excellent linguist'. In 1713 he published the wordbook for Handel's TESEO, one of the least impressive in appearance of the early wordbooks, the Italian and English versions of the title page and the dramatis personae being both crammed onto single sides. This was his sole foray into the world of opera, though he did publish a few play texts in association with others such as Tonson.

JOHN GREENACOMBE

A. King and J. Plunkett (eds.), *Popular Print Media, 1820–1900*, vol. 2 (2004), 332–3

Burlington, 3rd Earl of (Richard Boyle, 4th Earl of Cork) (b. London, 25 April 1694; d. Chiswick, 3 Dec. 1753). Architect, collector, patron of the arts and probably host to Handel c.1713–16. Aged ten, he inherited his titles and London property including BURLINGTON HOUSE, Piccadilly, a country seat at Chiswick, near London, and vast estates in Yorkshire and Ireland. A disciple of Inigo Jones and Palladio, his realised projects include York Assembly Rooms and Chiswick House. Through his designs, his protégés, and publications based on his magnificent collection of architectural drawings, Palladianism became the premier mid-eighteenth-century style of English grand architecture. Music was an even more constant passion, especially Italian opera. During some of Handel's stay at Burlington House the Earl was in Italy (1714–15), whence he brought back the CASTRUCCI brothers and AMADEI. A director (1719–28) of the Royal Academy of Music (OPERA COMPANIES, 2), pledging £1,000 rather than the required £200, he was chiefly responsible for securing BONONCINI as one of its composers. It was to Burlington that Handel reported his progress in securing singers for the Academy (Deutsch, 93–4). Although Burlington was a founder member of the OPERA OF THE NOBILITY, he continued to support Handel's performances. 'Burlington's belov'd by ev'ry Muse' (Gay, *Trivia*, 1716): he was a generous patron of writers, subscribing to ninety-seven publications, and it was probably at Burlington House that Handel became acquainted with GAY, ARBUTHNOT and POPE. RUTH SMITH

T. Barnard and J. Clark (eds.), *Lord Burlington: Architecture, Art and Life* (London, 1995)
Mainwaring
J. Simon (ed.), *Handel: A Celebration of his Life and Times* (London, 1985), 92–4

Burlington House. One of several Restoration mansions fronting Piccadilly, begun c.1664 by Sir John Denham and sold on to the 1st Earl of Burlington. This plain brick house, with a spacious forecourt and extensive gardens (which a street-name remembers) may have been Handel's base c.1712–16. The young 3rd Earl of BURLINGTON, who succeeded in 1704, subsequently learned architecture and became the brains of the Palladian movement. Shortly after his majority in 1716 he engaged Colen Campbell to encase the house in stone. Its skeleton survives in the present academic complex (1866–9) with the upstairs 'fine rooms' designed by William Kent in the 1720s. KERRY DOWNES

Burney, Charles (b. Shrewsbury, 7 April 1726; d. Chelsea, London, 12 April 1814). Musician, historian and author who held conflicting feelings about Handel. Born in 1726, Burney had occasional contact with the composer as a young musician, watching him 'bestride our musical world like a colossus'. Although Burney admired Handel's organ music greatly, he did not become closely involved with the evolving Handelian repertory for some time. In his memoirs he indicated that his taste was shaped instead by 'traveled and heterodox gentlemen, who were partial to the Music of the more modern composers they heard in Italy'. Burney sought fame as a man of letters with some success by turning the 'polite' language epitomised by Anthony Ashley Cooper, 4th Earl of SHAFTESBURY towards new Italian opera and German instrumental music.

Yet Burney became involved with Handel deeply by writing a book memorialising the 1784 HANDEL COMMEMORATION. He was quick to propose a volume – including a short biography and an overview of the festival – to the aristocratic organisers but then found himself sucked into a world of what he called 'Handelomaniacs'. While Burney welcomed speaking at length with King GEORGE III, he came under severe pressure to write only what Handel's 'insatiable and exclusive admirers' wanted. In his eyes the craze for Handel threatened to overshadow the music of opera composers from the generation after Handel he admired – Johann Adolf HASSE, Giovanni Pergolesi or Francesco Feo, whose pieces were performed at the Concert of Antient Music. A compromise can be seen in his declaration that the overture to *MESSIAH* seemed 'dry and uninteresting' compared with Handel's other efforts in the genre. But in the last volume of the *General History of Music* (1789), Burney went in a new direction in discussing Handel's operas in detail and with great awe. He nonetheless spent little time on the oratorios, odes or masques. WILLIAM WEBER

C. Burney, *An Account of the Musical Performances in Westminster Abbey* (London, 1785)
  A General History of Music from the Earliest Ages to the Present Period, 4 vols. (London, 1776–89)
  Memoirs of Dr. Charles Burney, 1726–1769, ed. Slava Klima, Garry Bowers and Kerry S. Grant (Lincoln, NE, 1988)
  Music, Men and Manners in France and Italy, 1770, ed. H. Edmund Poole (London, 1974)

Bussani, Giacomo Francesco (b. Cremona, fl. 1673–80). Italian librettist, and Canon regular of the Lateran Congregation at the Carità in VENICE. He wrote seven librettos for Venetian theatres between 1673 and 1680, five of which were set to music by Antonio Sartorio for the Teatro San Salvatore. The other two were written for the Teatro San Giovanni e Paolo and Teatro San Giovanni Grisostomo, which were owned by Giovanni Carlo and Vincenzo GRIMANI.

Bussani wrote the libretto of *GIULIO CESARE IN EGITTO*, which was first set by Sartorio for Venice in 1677. The text was also used for Johann Sigismund KUSSER's *Cleopatra* at BRUNSWICK in 1691. Handel might have become aware of Bussani's libretto as a result of Sartorio's close association with the Court of HANOVER in his position as Kapellmeister to the Duke Johann Friedrich of Brunswick-Lüneburg.   WALTER KREYSZIG

C. Monson, '"Giulio Cesare in Egitto" from Sartorio (1677) to Handel (1724)', ML 66/4 (1985), 313–43
Strohm
V. Vavoulis, 'Antonio Sartorio – Giacomo Francesco Busani: Two Makers of Seventeenth-Century Venetian Opera', Ph.D. dissertation (University of Oxford, 2002)

Buxtehude, Dieterich (b. ?Helsingborg, ?1637; d. Lübeck, 9 May 1707); Danish composer and organist. In 1668 he became organist at St Mary's Church, LÜBECK. He was praised not only as a virtuoso but also for the *Abendmusiken* (concert performances of cantatas or oratorios with large forces) which attracted even Johann Sebastian BACH in 1705. Today, he is best known as the greatest exponent of the 'North German Organ School'.

Much has been made by later writers of Handel's encounter with Buxtehude on 17 or 18 August 1703. Together with Johann MATTHESON, he had been invited to Lübeck by the wealthy politician and music-lover Magnus von Wedderkop to apply for the post of an assistant organist who might eventually become Buxtehude's successor. They performed on various keyboard instruments and heard Buxtehude play in St Mary's Church but neither of them delivered an official audition. According to Mattheson they drew back because the assistant was obliged to marry Buxtehude's eldest daughter Anna Margaretha, then twenty-eight years old. Yet, considering their juvenile age and modest experience, it is possible as well that the churchwardens did not regard them as serious candidates. It may even be asked if they conversed with Buxtehude at all; Mattheson's conspicuous silence on any comments from the latter's side suggests that he and Handel took their Lübeck excursion mainly as a musical pleasure trip at Wedderkop's expense but saw their future clearly in the realm of opera instead of church music.   DOROTHEA SCHRÖDER

Mainwaring
J. Mattheson, *Grundlage einer Ehrenpforte* (Hamburg 1740, repr. Kassel, 1969)
K. Snyder, *Dieterich Buxtehude: Organist in Lübeck* (Rochester, NY, 2007)

Byrom, John (b. Broughton, 29 Feb. 1692; d. Stockport, 26 Sept. 1763). Poet, hymn writer and creator of a system of shorthand. Byrom, who became a landed gentleman on the death of his elder brother in 1740, loved music but disliked Italian opera. He is noted for his verse written in response to conflict between the partisans of Handel and BONONCINI in May 1725:

Some say, compar'd to Bononcini,
That Mynheer Handel's but a Ninny;
Others aver, that he to Handel
Is scarcely fit to hold a Candle.
Strange all this difference should be
'Twixt Tweedle-dum and Tweedle-dee!

Byrom attended the fireworks display in GREEN PARK in April 1749, and described the occasion in a letter to his wife, but made no comment on Handel's *MUSIC FOR THE ROYAL FIREWORKS.*   DAVID HUNTER

Deutsch

C

Caffarelli or Caffariello (Gaetano Majorano) (b. Bitonto, Apulia, 12 April 1710; fl. 1726–55; d. Naples, 31 Jan. 1783). Castrato (range c′–c‴). His operatic career, stretching over twenty-nine years and some eighty stagings, developed in the shade of his fellow Apulian and close contemporary FARINELLI, with whom he shared training at PORPORA's school in NAPLES. Caffarelli's Roman debut in 1726 (as Alvida, a female role, in Sarro's *Valdemaro*) immediately projected him to nationwide stardom. During the following decade, he appeared in VENICE, Turin, Milan, ROME, FLORENCE, Genoa, Naples and Bologna, singing operas by PORPORA, HASSE, Lampugnani, Pollarolo and others, often in primo or secondo uomo roles and commanding huge salaries. Highlights in this period were two Hasse operas also starring Farinelli: *Siroe* at Bologna's Malvezzi (Spring 1733) and *Artaserse* at Venice's San Giovanni Grisostomo (Carnival, 1734). In 1735, a new stay in Naples won him the post of primo soprano in the Chapel Royal, succeeding the aged Matteuccio and superseding the absent Farinelli, on whom that post had been formerly bestowed by Emperor Charles VI.

In the 1737–8 season, he stayed in London at HEIDEGGER's invitation, professedly to replace Farinelli in the public's favour. At the KING'S THEATRE, besides the title roles in Handel's *FARAMONDO* and *SERSE*, Caffarelli sang as primo uomo in AMADEI's *Arsace*, VERACINI's *Partenio* and Pescetti's *La conquista del vello d'oro*. In 1739, at Farinelli's invitation, he followed him to Madrid, performing in court festivals. Caffarelli's late career centred mostly on Naples, with visits to Vienna (1749) and the royal courts at Versailles and Lisbon (1753–5). After that, he went on singing well into his fifties in church festivals and occasional serenatas, lauded by observers (among them David Garrick and Charles BURNEY) for his untarnished angelic colour and moving expression. He died rich and decorated with a noble title.

Caffarelli's notorious loftiness, laziness in attending rehearsals, propensity to scandalous quarrels with colleagues and noble patrons, was a major hindrance to his career. Evidence from reports and extant scores profile him as more inclined towards a fluid and refined cantabile than huge leaps or spectacular coloratura. Clarity, perfect utterance, trills and chromatic scales were his strong points. Handel seems to have made the most of his mezzo-soprano tessitura, avoiding his (dangerously uneven) upper octave.   CARLO VITALI

R. Celletti, *Storia del bel canto* (Florence, 1986)
S. Mamy, *Les grands castrats napolitains à Venise au XVIIIe siècle* (Liège, 1994)

Caio Fabbricio (*Gaius Fabricius*), HWV A⁹. PASTICCIO opera in three acts, based on Johann Adolf HASSE's *Cajo Fabricio* (ROME, 1732). It was first performed at the

KING'S THEATRE on 4 December 1733. The libretto was originally written by Apostolo ZENO for Vienna and set by Antonio CALDARA in 1729.

Pirro (Pyrrhus), King of Epirus, is leading the Tarentines and other Italian Greeks in their war with Rome. Following a major Greek victory Rome sends the high-minded statesman Caio Fabbricio to negotiate with him. Among Pirro's captives is Fabbricio's daughter Sestia, of whom he has become enamoured. After attempting unsuccessfully to bribe Fabbricio with treasure Pirro proposes that he marry Sestia, an idea Fabbricio indignantly rejects. Pirro's betrothed Bircenna, in disguise, allies herself with Turio, a Tarentine who hates Pirro for interfering with local customs. Turio approaches Fabbricio with an offer to betray Pirro; Fabbricio tells him to put it in writing. Sestia's betrothed Volusio, who was believed to have died in battle, also plans to kill Pirro. Volusio is unmasked when he intervenes to save Pirro from an attempted assassination arranged by Bircenna and Turio. Turio helps Sestia and Volusio escape, but Fabbricio returns her to Pirro, and Volusio is captured. Forced by Pirro to act as Volusio's judge, Fabbricio condemns him to death and all appears lost until Fabbricio hands Pirro Turio's letter revealing his plans to poison him. In response Pirro frees Sestia, Volusio and the other Roman captives and even hints at future reconciliation with Bircenna.

The cast was as follows:

Pirro	Giovanni CARESTINI (castrato)
Sestia	Anna Maria STRADA del Pò (soprano)
Bircenna	Margherita DURASTANTI (mezzo-soprano)
Volusio	Carlo SCALZI (castrato)
Turio	Maria Caterina NEGRI (alto)
Fabbricio	Gustavus WALTZ (bass)
Cinea	Maria Rosa Negri (mezzo-soprano)

Caio Fabbricio was Handel's third offering in his first season competing with the OPERA OF THE NOBILITY. He may have planned to open the season with this opera, using all seven of his singers, but if so, he was prevented by the temporary unavailability of Waltz (*SEMIRAMIDE*). When *Caio Fabbricio* was performed in December it fared no better than *Semiramide*, achieving only four performances. None of the music was published.

Handel based his score on a manuscript that had recently been acquired by his friend and future librettist Charles JENNENS. This manuscript, now in the Newberry Library, Chicago, contains all twenty-eight of Hasse's arias (attributing Volusio's 'Nocchier che teme assorto' to PORPORA) but lacks the overture, two choruses and the recitatives. Pencil markings by Handel indicate transpositions and cuts. At first Handel intended to use most of Hasse's arias, but ultimately he was able to retain only thirteen, while seven arias by Albinoni, Francesco Corselli, Hasse, LEO and VINCI were added by the singers. Carestini sang two of the arias Vinci had composed for CAFFARELLI but replaced three others and inserted one in the last scene, as he had done in *Semiramide*. The title role, originally sung by the castrato Domenico ANNIBALI, was sadly curtailed for the vocally inferior Waltz, who sang only a single aria; another had to be eliminated because in the meantime it had been inserted in *Semiramide*. At an early stage Durastanti and Caterina Negri exchanged roles, Durastanti having probably objected to being cast in the dramatically less important role of Turio, though as Bircenna she still got only three arias, while Negri was reduced to two. The overture (represented only by its bass line) and the final chorus remain unidentified. As in *Semiramide*, Handel composed entirely new recitatives, which include many deft dramatic touches. The libretto was printed before some of the arias were replaced. The conducting score is in the Staats- und Universitätsbibliothek Hamburg. JOHN H. ROBERTS

H. D. Clausen, *Händels Direktionspartituren ('Handexemplare')* (Hamburg, 1972)
J. H. Roberts, 'Handel and Charles Jennens's Italian Music Manuscripts', *Music and Theatre: Essays in Honour of Winton Dean*, ed. N. Fortune (Cambridge, 1987)
Strohm

Caldara, Antonio (b. Venice, c.1670; d. Vienna, 28 Dec. 1736). Italian composer and cellist. Caldara spent his youth in VENICE and served from 1699 to 1707 as *maestro di capella* of the Duke of Mantua. He then moved to ROME at the beginning of 1708. From the beginning of 1709 until May 1716 he held the post of *maestro di cappella* in the service of the Prince Francesco Maria RUSPOLI, and was occasionally employed by other important Roman patrons of Handel's, such as Cardinal Pietro OTTOBONI and the CARMELITE ORDER. As Caldara and Handel moved in the same musical circles in Rome, there was undoubtedly personal contact between the two composers, and perhaps an exchange of musical ideas and styles. Handel probably heard Caldara's operas *Sevaggio eroe* and *La Partenope* when he was at Venice for the 1707/8 Carnival, and in 1730 he used the latter opera's libretto as the source text for PARTENOPE. He might have heard Caldara's oratorio *Il martirio di Santa Caterina* performed for Cardinal OTTOBONI during Lent in 1708. DAGMAR GLÜXAM (Trans. ANGELA BAIER)

D. Burrows, 'The "Carmelite" Antiphons of Handel and Caldara', *HJb* 46 (2000)
U. Kirkendale, *Antonio Caldara. Life and Venetian – Roman Oratorios* (Florence, 2007)
W. and U. Kirkendale, *Music and Meaning: Studies in Music History and the Neighbouring Disciplines* (Florence, 2007)
H. J. Marx, 'Die Musik am Hofe Pietro Kardinal Ottobonis', *Analecta Musicologica* 5 (1968), 104–77

Cambridge. Handel had no direct personal contact with the City or University of Cambridge, and the appointment of Maurice GREENE as Professor there in 1730 may have prompted him to perform in OXFORD three years later. Greene's successor John Randall had taken part as a chorister in the Chapel Royal production of *ESTHER* in 1732, and in 1759 he gave a performance of *MESSIAH* at the Senate House in memory of Handel, inaugurating a series of annual oratorio performances. In 1816 Cambridge University received seven volumes of Handel's musical autographs as part of the bequest of Viscount FITZWILLIAM's music library. The detailed descriptions of the autographs in the *Catalogue of the Music in the Fitzwilliam Museum* (1893) were contributed by Arthur Henry Mann, the organist of King's College, who also conducted an authentic-scale performance of *Messiah* and facilitated the acquisition of the Lennard Collection (SOURCES AND COLLECTIONS, 4), with the 'Handel bookcase', for the FITZWILLIAM MUSEUM. A series of staged performances of Handel's oratorios in the 1930s was significant in reviving interest in some lesser-known works; the productions of the Cambridge Handel Opera Group began in 1985. DONALD BURROWS

Campioli, Antonio Maria (birth name: Gualandi) (b. Bologna, 3 Aug. 1682; d. Bologna, 10 July 1739). Italian castrato (range: a–d″), and elder brother of the successful soprano Margherita Campioli. He sang in operas by Antonio CALDARA, Handel (*GIULIO CESARE* in HAMBURG), Johann Adolf HASSE and Georg Caspar SCHÜRMANN. He was engaged by Handel in 1731–2, and took part in revivals of *TAMERLANO* (title role), *PORO* (Gandarte), *ADMETO* (Trasimede) and *FLAVIO* (title role), and also in the premiere of *SOSARME* (Argone) and in the pasticcio *LUCIO PAPIRIO DITTATORE* (Azzio Tullio).

FRANCESCO LORA (Trans. TERENCE BEST)

G. Erdmann, '"Eghiptens jamar": Über den beschwerlichen Einsatz italienischer Sänger in Graupners Kirchenmusik', *Mitteilungen der Christoph-Graupner-Gesellschaft* 2 (Dec. 2005), 3–29

M. Fürstenau, *Zur Geschichte der Musik und des Theaters am Hofe der Kurfürsten von Sachsen und Könige von Polen* (Dresden, 1862)

Campistron, Jean Galbert de (b. Toulouse, 1656; d. Toulouse 11 May 1723). French librettist. Known for his successes with conventional *tragédie*, with Jean RACINE as his mentor, in 1686 Campistron wrote the pastorale *Acis et Galatée* for the Duc de Vendôme, which was set to music by Jean-Baptiste LULLY. After the retirement of Philippe QUINAULT, Lully commissioned Campistron to complete the libretto of *Achille et Polyxène* (1687). The poet became a member of the Académie Française in 1701. His *tragédie Arminius* likely served as the source for Antonio SALVI's opera libretto *ARMINIO* (Florence, 1703).

WALTER KREYSZIG

Strohm

Campra, André. See HANDEL, 19

Cannons. Country residence of James Brydges, first Duke of CHANDOS (1674–1744). Chandos's taste was refined but cautious; he preferred opulence to the innovative style of VANBRUGH's great houses. After several false starts he employed the young James Gibbs, whose Roman training and natural talents equipped him to suit a design to any patron's wishes. Formal gardens, planted avenues and an ornamental lake were the setting for a square courtyard house adorned with giant half-columns on two adjacent sides, set diagonally so that both faced the approaching visitor – an example of baroque illusionism using real constituents.

Cannons was Handel's base in 1717–19; in 1718 *ACIS AND GALATEA* was probably composed there (legends claim that it was enacted on the terrace), and *ESTHER* was possibly first performed at the house in about 1719. The chapel (completed 1720) was collegiate but, like St LAWRENCE'S, Whitchurch, had an organ and music gallery behind the altar and the Duke's gallery at the other end.

The garden statues included a gilt lead equestrian George I. The Timon of Alexander POPE's 1731 satire on Taste was widely, but wrongly, identified with Chandos. By then his expenditure on old master pictures and modern ceiling paintings had led to retrenchment. Managing his own finances less skilfully than the army's, he left his heir the estate and all its debts. Cannons was promptly sold and demolished for the materials.

KERRY DOWNES

Cannons Concert, The. The musical establishment maintained by James Brydges, Earl of Carnarvon and 1st Duke of CHANDOS. It consisted of a mixture of professionals – generally players of the second and third rank from the Italian opera orchestra – and household servants, all of whom were paid quarterly salaries and provided with food and lodging. It must also have been possible to call upon the services of occasional guests. Brydges began hiring musicians in late 1715 beginning with the cellist and composer Nicola Francesco HAYM. In September 1716, the ensemble consisted of two treble singers, a small number of string players, an oboist and a flautist. By August 1717 it had grown to include recorder and bassoon, together with tenor and bass singers, and by mid-1718 had added a second oboe (perhaps only temporarily) and two more tenor singers. There seems to have been no regular viola player until late 1719. By New Year's Day 1721 the total was six violins and single lower strings, with trumpet, oboe and bassoon, and three trebles, one 'Contra alto', two 'counter tenors', one tenor and two basses.

Brydges lost a great deal of money in the collapse of the SOUTH SEA COMPANY in 1720, leading to the release of his 'professors' (i.e. professional musicians) from mid-1721 and the retention of only those musicians who were also household servants. Most of the furloughed players found employment in the orchestra of the Royal Academy of Music (OPERA COMPANIES, 2), to which Brydges had been a subscriber as early as May 1719, and several of the singers found positions in the CHAPEL ROYAL and/or WESTMINSTER ABBEY choirs. Some musical activity was maintained until 1725, with Johann Christopher PEPUSCH supplying musicians from London in the last two years or so. Handel, Haym and Pepusch all composed music for the Cannons Concert.   GRAYDON BEEKS

See also John KYTCH

G. Beeks, 'Handel and Music for the Earl of Carnarvon', *Bach, Handel, Scarlatti: Tercentenary Essays*, ed. P. Williams (Cambridge, 1985)

Cannons Anthems, Jubilate and Te Deum. See ANTHEMS, 2; JUBILATE; TE DEUM, 3

cantatas for voice and continuo. Exactly how many continuo cantatas Handel composed cannot be stated with complete certainty, because of unresolved questions about the status of works that exist in different versions: do transpositions and/or variants carry his authority, or are they the result of a singer's preference, or of scribal choice or error? In our present state of knowledge, the total number (including alternative versions emanating from the composer) is probably about eighty. Handel composed roughly two-thirds of them in ITALY during his residence there (1706–10) and most of the remainder in London; several of the latter were revisions of earlier works (Mayo, 'Einige Kantatenrevisionen'). *Nice, che fa, che pensi?* was probably composed in HANOVER in 1710. Most (just over sixty) are scored for soprano and continuo, though in two cases the voice might more accurately be described as mezzo-soprano (HWV 145 and 172); about sixteen are for alto; probably only HWV 136[a] was originally for bass.

The continuo cantatas are among the least known of Handel's compositions and the least studied by scholars, though significant contributions have been made in recent years. The only one that has gained some currency is 'Lucrezia' (*O numi eterni*), and this is untypical in most respects. To regard them as apprentice works whose chief value was as sources for borrowings is to overlook their intrinsic musical quality. In his early twenties Handel was already an accomplished composer; he learnt much from older Italian composers, especially ALESSANDRO SCARLATTI and CORELLI, but he quickly found his own voice: many of the audacious turns of melody and harmony heard in more familiar works composed fifteen or more years later had already appeared in the cantatas.

Handel's most important patron in Italy was the Marquis Francesco Maria RUSPOLI (later Prince of Cerveteri). He was a member of the ARCADIAN ACADEMY in ROME, whose participants, drawing inspiration for their discussions from the romance *Arcadia* by Jacopo Sannazaro (1456–1530) and from the poetry of Theocritus and Virgil, adopted pastoral names; Ruspoli's was Olinto, the name of one of the characters in Handel's accompanied cantata *OH, COME CHIARE E BELLE*. He held his weekly *conversazioni* on Sundays, from the late afternoon to the early evening, and it would have been on these occasions that many of Handel's continuo cantatas were first heard: settings of stylised pastoral poems performed in front of a small gathering of aristocratic, cultivated amateurs. The soprano Margarita DURASTANTI, who arrived in Rome probably at about the same time as Handel, undoubtedly sang many of them, accompanied by the composer. Copyists' bills survive that give a *terminus ante quem* for certain cantatas. Among the copyists who can be identified are ANGELINI, Ginelli and LANCIANI.

While it would be misleading to dismiss all the cantata texts as elaborate variants on a single theme – the agony of love – this is certainly the commonest subject, caused usually by separation from the beloved, or by unrequited love, or by the infidelity (real or imagined) of the loved one. A few texts treat the subject differently: cynically (HWV 86), light-heartedly (HWV 155), even optimistically or joyfully (HWV 107, 115, 135, 169), occasionally as a danger to be avoided (the *lezione amorosa*: HWV 102 and 172; and the pair HWV 176 and 175; see Jones, 'Handel's *Amore ucellatore* Cantata'). Handel's masterpiece, 'Lucrezia' (*Oh numi eterni*), is unique among the continuo cantatas in treating a historical subject: the rape of Lucretia by Tarquin. The setting is usually pastoral. The poet might address the natural world, as in HWV 88: 'Care selve, aure grate, erbette e fiori, / che l'aspre mie querele, / compagne al dolor mio, sì spesso udite' ('Dear woods, welcome breezes, grasses and flowers, who so often hear my harsh complaints, the companions of my grief'), or he might imagine his emotions reflected in nature, as in HWV 127: 'L'aura, che intorno spira, / è figlia del mio cor, che ognor sospira; / e del ruscello son l'onde correnti / parto degli occhi miei sempre piangenti' ('The air that blows around is the daughter of my heart, who is always sighing; and the flowing ripples of the stream are the offspring of my ever-weeping eyes').

The case for a homosexual interpretation of certain cantata texts is surely unproven, notwithstanding the impressive arguments advanced by Harris. The strongest hint, perhaps, is in the B section of the second aria in *Stelle, perfide stelle*: 'Ma di scoprir l'ardor / mio cor non lice' ('But my heart is not allowed to reveal my love'). Whatever may be imagined to lie hidden beneath their surface, many cantata texts explicitly express heterosexual love. The characters might be named – the female names most frequently encountered are Clori, Nice and Fille/Filli; the only male names are Fileno and Tirsi – or the gender might be revealed by the inflection of adjectives or nouns related to them. In *Sarei troppo felice* the singer is named as Clori and the beloved as Fileno; adjectives referring to the former have feminine endings, and to the latter masculine endings. *Manca pur quanto sai* is addressed to 'Tirsi inconstante'; the unnamed singer is female ('Benché tradita io sono'). *Menzognere speranze* contains no proper names, but the singer describes herself as 'delusa', and the object of her unreciprocated love as a 'vago garzoncello'; in *Nel dolce tempo* the singer is male ('son pago') and the beloved female ('ninfa', 'pastorella'). The avoidance of gender-specific words by means of synecdoche (e.g. the heart, signifying the person) could be a matter of convenience: it allows the cantata to be sung by a man or a woman; and gender might be 'disguised' simply because some frequently used words do not inflect, for example, 'amante', 'felice', 'idolo', 'incostante', 'tesoro'.

For only a tiny handful of Handel's continuo cantatas is the poet known. Cardinal Benedetto PAMPHILIJ wrote the text of HENDEL, NON PUÒ MIA MUSA and possibly of *Sarei troppo felice* (he also wrote the libretto of Handel's oratorio Il TRIONFO DEL TEMPO E DEL DISINGANNO and of the accompanied cantata TRA LE FIAMME, as well as providing texts for cantatas by ALESSANDRO SCARLATTI, including one on a subject that Handel also set: *Lucrezia romana*.) Kirkendale has plausibly suggested that the text of *Udite il mio consiglio* might have been written by Abbé Francesco Mazziotti, tutor of Ruspoli's eldest son, Bartolomeo, and that, moreover, it contains topical allusions. The texts of three of the cantatas that Handel wrote in London are by Paolo ROLLI; they were printed in *Di canzonette e di cantate libri due* (London, 1727) as numbers 22, 3 and 17 respectively: *Deh! lasciate e vita e volo*, *Ho fuggito Amore* and *Son gelsomino* (which exists in versions for soprano and alto). Handel modified the text of the first considerably; the second was set also by Giovanni Rolli, Paolo's brother. Handel used the first aria of Rolli's 'Soffri mio caro Alcino' in his cantata *Dolc'è pur d'amor l'affanno*.

The musical structure of Handel's continuo cantatas is almost always determined by that of the poetry. Roughly half follow the standard pattern of RARA (recitative, aria, recitative, aria) and about a quarter the pattern ARA. Among the variety of patterns found in the remaining cantatas, the commonest is RARARA. Recitatives are characterised by lines of seven or eleven syllables (the *settenario* and *endecasillabo*), as established by Petrarch in the fourteenth century; rhymes might occur at any point, but are virtually standard in the final couplet. Syllable counts are more varied in arias: anything from four to ten syllables per line; five (*quinario*) and eight (*ottonario*) are popular. The two semistrophes of the text provide the A and B sections of the characteristic da capo aria; rhyme schemes such as *abc abc* or *aab ccb* are quite common. Handel's occasional abandonment of da capo structure might have been prompted in two cases by the syntactical incompleteness of the first semistrophe: A2 in 'Ah, che pur troppo è vero' and A1 in 'Aure soavi'.

In some cases a cantata ends in the same key in which it began, for example, HWV 112, 114, 115, 129 and 151; it might be significant that in none of these texts do the speaker's situation and outlook change from beginning to end. The move from G minor to G major in *Care selve, aure grate* adds a note of optimism that is only latent in the poetry. *Oh numi eterni* ('Lucrezia') begins and ends in F minor, but Handel achieves a powerful effect through contrasting keys and forms within the cantata. The drama is entirely internal: Lucretia vents her fury after her rape by Tarquin. After the raging second aria, 'Il suol che preme' in C minor, structural patterns and keys become more fluid, reflecting Lucretia's unstable mind. All the remaining text is recitative, but out of it Handel creates a mournful G minor aria, 'Alla salma infedel', of irregular design (it has the character but not the strictness of a ground bass – a favourite device of Handel's), and a serene arioso in E flat major as Lucretia prepares to kill herself. These are separated and followed by secco recitative, but for the last eight lines of text the musical style is that of an accompagnato – a brilliant dramatisation of Lucretia's desire for vengeance. It is more common for Handel's cantatas (unlike those of many of his contemporaries and predecessors) to end in a different key from that in which they began. In a significant number, A1 (the second movement) adopts the key in which R1 had started, as if Handel wanted to establish an opening key firmly. There is occasionally a relationship between such an opening key and the concluding key of the cantata: HWV 84 moves from major to relative minor, and HWV 125 from minor to relative major. Handel's key schemes usually operate within fairly close relationships, and sometimes are carefully planned. *Dalla guerra amorosa* (the soprano version is probably the original) features two relative major/relative minor groups: R1 moves from D major to B minor, A1 is in D major, and R2 starts and ends in B minor; A2 is in F sharp minor and A3 (with short recitatives at the beginning and end) in A major. Occasionally a change of thought in the text might have suggested a more varied tonal scheme. In the first two movements of *Del bel idolo mio*, for example, the poet imagines searching for the soul of his dead lover, Nice, in Hades; R1 begins and ends in B minor, A1 is in E minor – both sharp-side keys. In R2 he wonders what he will do if he does not find her; the music modulates to G minor; the text ends with a question, as usual set to an imperfect (Phrygian) cadence. The thought changes in A2 and A3: his tears will be symbols of fidelity; he prays to the gods to return Nice to him; the keys now are on the flat side: G minor and B flat major.

Though uniform in texture, the arias display great variety in the nature of the two-point counterpoint between voice and bass. *Ne' tuoi lumi, o bella Clori* illustrates something of the range of Handel's technique. In A1 the voice borrows motifs from the bass, the latter suggesting features of ground bass; the voice becomes more independent in the B section while the ostinato patterns continue below. The bass is much more instrumental in A2; in contrast to its vigorous semiquavers and tumbling quaver arpeggios, the voice presents sustained lyrical phrases. In A3 bass and voice share the same character, and intertwine smoothly in imitative counterpoint.

Of fundamental importance is the relationship between text and music. Handel's response to words is sensitive, imaginative and resourceful; there is nothing to suggest that he found the supposedly monothematic and cliché-ridden poetry a constraint. Most striking to modern ears are the flashes of chromatic harmony, the startling dissonances, and the unexpected twists of harmony or melody that convey heightened emotion. Handel had the power to convey every nuance of feeling between the darkest grief (e.g. A1 in HWV 116, A1 in HWV 126, A2 in HWV 146) and the most exuberant joy (e.g. A2 in HWV 88, A2 in HWV 107, A2 in HWV 129). The change from optimism to despair at the second semistrophe of A2 of *Nice, che fa?* is reflected in a dramatically contrasted B section: in its tempo (from Allegro to Adagio), metre (6/8 to 3/4), mode (major to minor), and harmonic style (stable to unstable).

While individual arias from Handel's operas and oratorios are frequently performed in isolation, divorced from the dramatic context that gives them meaning, the continuo cantatas are neglected. This is ironical since the latter are in essence self-contained, free-standing operatic scenes in which, even without the support of a plot, characters and emotions spring vividly to life. The continuo cantatas are a treasure trove waiting to be discovered.

ANDREW V. JONES

See also CHAMBER DUETS AND TRIOS

M. Boyd, 'Handel's Italian Cantatas: Some New Sources', *Handel Tercentenary Collection*, ed. S. Sadie and A. Hicks (London, 1987)

E. T. Harris, *Handel as Orpheus: Voice and Desire in the Chamber Cantatas* (Cambridge, MA, 2001)
  'Handel's London Cantatas', GHB I (1984)
  'Paper, Performing Practice, and Patronage: Handel's Alto Cantatas in the Bodleian Library MS Mus.d.61–62', *Festa musicologica: Essays in Honor of George J. Buelow*, ed. T. J. Mathieson and B. Rivera (New York, 1995)

A. V. Jones, 'Handel's *Amore ucellatore* Cantata', HJb 52 (2006)

W. and U. Kirkendale, *Music and Meaning: Studies in Music History and the Neighbouring Disciplines* (Florence, 2007)

H. J. Marx and S. Voss, 'Unbekannte Kantaten von Händel, A. Scarlatti, Fago und Grillo in einer neapolitanischen Handeschrift von 1710', *Studi in onore di Agostino Ziino in occasione del suo 65° compleanno*, ed. B. M. Antolini and T. M. Gialdroni (Lucca, 2004)

J. Mayo, 'Handel's Italian Cantatas', Ph.D. dissertation (University of Toronto, 1977)
  'Einige Kantatenrevisionen Händels', HJb 27 (1981)

R. Strohm, 'A Book of Cantatas and Arias Bought in Florence, 1723', *British Library Journal* 12 (1995), 184–201

K. Watanabe, 'The Music-Paper Used by Handel and his Copyists in Italy 1706–1710', *Handel Collections and their History*, ed. Terence Best (Oxford, 1993)

K. Watanabe and H. J. Marx, 'Händels italienische Kopisten', GHB III (1989)

Cantate con strumenti (cantatas with additional instruments). See individual entries

Capece, Carlo Sigismondo (Capeci) (b. Rome, 1652; d. Polistena, 1728). A doctor of law, secretary to Maria Casimira, widow of Jan Sobieski, King of Poland, in Rome from at least 1703 to 1714. For her palace theatre and other Roman venues, he wrote *drammi per musica*, prose comedies and other dramatic works. Handel set his oratorio La RESURREZIONE in 1708. Capece's librettos for Maria Casimira were usually set by Domenico SCARLATTI, for example *Amor d'un ombra e gelosia d'un'aura* (Rome, 1714; revived in London, 1720, as *Il Narciso*). Handel's TOLOMEO (1728) is based on Capece's *Tolomeo et Alessandro, ovvero la corona disprezzata*, and ORLANDO (1733) on his *L'Orlando, ovvero la gelosa pazzia*, both set by Domenico Scarlatti for Maria Casimira in 1711.

A member of the ARCADIAN ACADEMY (under the name of Metisto Olbiano), Capece was a libretto reformer, but more in matters of moral content than dramatic structure. He wrote the first libretto pair on the Iphigenia myth (*Ifigenia in Aulide* and *Ifigenia in Tauri*, both 1713); his later works, including *Telemaco* (1718), influenced METASTASIO. Capece often highlights praiseworthy attitudes of self-sacrifice, reconciliation and purification, for example in *La clemenza d'Augusto* (1697) and *Tito e Berenice* (1714); he also likes pastoral settings. Both tendencies are found in the two dialectically related librettos which Handel later set in dramatically enriched versions. Nicola HAYM revised *Tolomeo*: stylistic reasons also suggest his contribution to a revision of *Orlando*, shortly before his death (31 July 1729) – implying that this opera may originally have been planned for 1729–30.   REINHARD STROHM

Strohm
R. Strohm, *Dramma per Musica: Italian Opera Seria of the Eighteenth Century* (New Haven, 1997)

Caporale, Francisco (Francis) (d. London, 15 April 1746). Italian cellist and composer. According to BURNEY, he was in London by the autumn of 1733 when Handel composed the aria 'Son qual stanco pellegrino' (*ARIANNA IN CRETA*) 'to display the abilities of Caporale, just come over' (Burney, p. 784). He was a principal in Handel's orchestra and performed lyrical obbligato parts in *ALCINA*, *ALEXANDER'S FEAST* and the *SONG FOR ST CECILIA'S DAY*. He subscribed to the FUND FOR THE SUPPORT OF DECAY'D MUSICIANS and contributed an unidentified cello solo at a benefit performance of *PARNASSO IN FESTA* for the Fund on 14 March 1741 (Deutsch, pp. 459, 514). Though not possessed of 'a very powerful hand', he was, said Burney, 'always heard with great partiality, from the almost single merit, of a full, sweet, and vocal tone (p. 1003). His death, reported in the *Daily Advertiser* on 21 April 1746, was mentioned by THOMAS HARRIS, who had played the cello alongside him at the Castle Musical Society. Caporale bequeathed his instruments to his eldest son, 'Nichola' (Nicola), who was with him in London, 'having a good opinion of his Skill'. His other children were still in Naples, perhaps his native city.
JOHN GREENACOMBE and WALTER KREYSZIG

Burrows and Dunhill
B. Matthews, *The Royal Society of Musicians of Great Britain, List of Members, 1738–1984* (London, 1985), 32
National Archives, Will of Francis Caporale (PROB 11/746)

Carco sempre di gloria, HWV 87. Composed of borrowed movements, *Carco sempre di gloria* exists as a discrete work only in the ARNOLD edition, from which source CHRYSANDER took it. Not published as a separate work in HHA, the putative cantata consists of the recitative 'Carco sempre di gloria', recomposed for alto from *CECILIA VOLGI UN SGUARDO*, the aria 'Sei del ciel' (an additional song in *ALEXANDER'S FEAST* for the alto castrato ANNIBALI in 1737) and the aria 'Sei cara' from *Cecilia volgi un sguardo* transposed down a fourth and apparently without the obbligato violin part. Annibali may have sung these movements between the parts of *Alexander's Feast* in 1737.   ELLEN T. HARRIS

Carestini, Giovanni Maria Bernardino ('Il Cusanino') (b. Filottrano, near Ancona, 13 Dec. 1700; fl. 1721–58; d. Bologna, May 1760). Italian castrato (range b–c‴) who studied in Milan from the age of about twelve under the patronage of Cardinal Agostino Cusani (from whom the singer gained his nickname). His first known performance was a female role in CALDARA's *Oratorio di Santo Stefano* at San Severino in June 1714, and he made his opera debut at Milan during the 1719–20 Carnival. A year later he performed at ROME alongside his teacher BERNACCHI in Alessandro SCARLATTI's *Griselda* (February 1721). During the next decade he sang in operas by composers such as PORPORA, VIVALDI, PORTA,

VINCI and HASSE at Rome, Prague, Vienna, VENICE, Parma, FLORENCE and NAPLES.

Handel attempted to hire Carestini for the Second Academy (OPERA COMPANIES, 3) during his trip to Italy in 1729 (HANDEL, 15), but the singer did not come to London until autumn 1733. He made his debut for Handel in the pasticcio *SEMIRAMIDE*, but the first role the composer wrote for him was Teseo in *ARIANNA IN CRETA*. Teseo's highly virtuosic arias show that Carestini was a gifted performer of brilliant fast arias, but most of Teseo's music was composed before the singer had reached England: after hearing him sing, Handel realised that his new primo uomo was equally talented at performing slower sentimental arias, and added the lyrical aria 'Sdegnata sei con me'. The pathetic passions suitable for Carestini's voice were most fully realised in Handel's music for the title hero in *ARIODANTE* (e.g. 'Scherza infida') and Ruggiero in *ALCINA* ('Mi lusinga dolce affetto'), although both roles also contain notable heroic music requiring astonishing agility and technique (e.g. Ariodante's 'Doppo notte' and Ruggiero's 'Sta nell'Ircana').

The castrato also performed the role of Mirtillo in an expanded revision of Il *PASTOR FIDO*, and was given some spectacular new music to sing as Apollo in *PARNASSO IN FESTA*. However, he was uncomfortable singing in English, and was given Italian parody texts for Barak's arias in the 1734 revival of *DEBORAH*, and newly composed Italian insertions to sing in the 1735 revival of *ESTHER* (which were repeated a few weeks later in a revival of *ATHALIA*). As with his predecessor SENESINO, it seems likely that Carestini's working relationship with Handel could be difficult. BURNEY claimed that the castrato disliked the simply constructed aria 'Verdi prati' (*Alcina*) and refused to learn it, and that Handel angrily refused to pay Carestini's wages unless the star castrato relented. By 10 July 1735, only a week after the last performance of *Alcina*, Carestini had quit: the London Daily reported that 'Yesterday Signor Carestina, a celebrated Singer in the late Opera's in Covent Garden Theatre, embarqued on Board a Ship for Venice'. It is not clear whether the female version of Carestini's name was a printer's error or deliberate sarcasm.

By September 1735 Carestini had returned to Italy, where he spent the next few years singing in operas by GIACOMELLI, Hasse, LEO and GALUPPI. He returned to London for some concerts in 1740 (but not with Handel). During the 1740s he sang in operas by GLUCK (Milan) and Jommelli (Padua), and frequently worked with Hasse (particularly at DRESDEN, 1747–9). The castrato performed in five GRAUN operas at BERLIN (1750–3), and sang at St Petersburg in 1755. He gave his final public performance on 10 July 1758 at Naples. According to Burney:

> [Carestini] was tall, beautiful, and majestic. He was a very animated and intelligent actor, and having a considerable portion of enthusiasm in his composition, with a lively and inventive imagination, he rendered every thing he sung interesting by good taste, energy, and judicious embellishments. He manifested great agility in the execution of difficult divisions from the chest in a most articulate and admirable manner. It was the opinion of Hasse, as well as of many other eminent professors, that whoever had not heard Carestini was unacquainted with the most perfect style of singing. (pp. 782–3)

DAVID VICKERS

Burney, 'Sketch of the life of Handel', *An Account of the Musical Performances in Westminster Abbey* (London, 1785)

C. Korsmeier, *Der Sänger Giovanni Carestini (1700–1760) und 'seine' Komponisten. Die Karriere eines Kastraten in der ersten Hälfte des 18. Jahrhunderts* (Eisenach, 2000)

F. W. Marpurg, *Historisch-kritische Beyträge zur Aufnahme der Musik*, I. Band, Drittes Stück (Berlin, 1754), 'II. Lebensläuffe, A: Herrn Johann Joachim Quantzens Lebenslauf, von ihm selbst entworfen', 234–5

D. Vickers, 'Handel's Performing Versions: A Study of Four Music Theatre Works from the "Second Academy" Period', Ph.D. dissertation (The Open University, 2007)

Carey, Henry (b. ?Yorkshire, 27 Aug. 1687; d. London, 4 Oct. 1743). English composer and librettist, he composed music for DRURY LANE Theatre from 1723 to 1731, including songs, incidental music for plays, pantomimes, masques and comic operas. Notwithstanding the fact that many of his theatrical works mock the Italian opera tradition, Carey subscribed to several of Handel's works during the 1720s. His strong support of native theatre and opera can be seen not only through his two librettos for English operas, *Amelia* (1732, set by LAMPE) and *Teraminta* (1732, set by J. C. SMITH junior, and by John STANLEY in c.1754) but also in his joint venture with Lampe, *The DRAGON OF WANTLEY* (1737).   MATTHEW GARDNER

J. N. Gillespie, 'The Life and Works of Henry Carey, 1687–1743', Ph.D. dissertation (University of London, 1982)

Carillon. See INSTRUMENTATION

Carissimi, Giacamo (b. Marino, near Rome; bap. 18 April 1605; d. Rome, 12 Jan. 1674). Italian composer of many motets, cantatas and Latin oratorios, from 1629 *maestro di capella* at the German College in ROME. Handel might have been acquainted with Carissimi's treatment of Belshazzar (*Baltazar*) or, more likely, Solomon (*Judicium Salomonis*), and he certainly knew Carissimi's most celebrated oratorio, *Jephte*. Composed by 1649, but never published, *Jephte* circulated in many manuscript copies, and its final chorus was printed and praised in Kircher's *Musurgia universalis* (Rome, 1650).

The chromatic recitative 'He chose a mournful muse' in *ALEXANDER'S FEAST* borrows from Jephte's lament 'Heu mihi! filia mea'. In composing *SAMSON*, Handel made three BORROWINGS from Jephte. 'With thunder arm'd' is based on 'Fugite, cedite' and 'Et ululantes'. The more extensive borrowing refashioned Carissimi's final chorus 'Plorate filiae Israel' as 'Hear, Jacob's God'. The modal harmony gives the Israelites a solemn sound, and Carissimi's six-part scoring is retained.

The sequence of numbers 'See, the conquering hero' (in *JOSHUA*, later in *Judas Maccabaeus*) apparently models its depiction of a procession coming from a distance on Carissimi's scene beginning with 'Incipite in tympanis', where the texture is increased from solo to duet, then trio, and finally full chorus. Handel's *JEPHTHA* treats the same subject as Carissimi's *Jephte*, but there are no musical borrowings.   WILLIAM D. GUDGER

Dean, *Oratorios*

W. D. Gudger, 'Handel's Use of Borrowings: Overlooked Examples from Georg Muffat and Carissimi', unpublished paper, American Musicological Society (Minneapolis, 1978)

G. Massenkeil, 'Zum Verhältnis Carissimi – Händel', *HJb* 28 (1982)

Carleton, George (b. c.1685; d. Hastings 15 Dec. 1746). Carleton was a member of London's leading choral establishments (CHAPEL ROYAL from 1713, WESTMINSTER ABBEY from 1727, ST PAUL'S CATHEDRAL 1706–28), but within these his principal role was as a Priest, and he was appointed Sub-Dean of the Chapel Royal in August 1732. He was probably responsible for the selection of the text of the *Anthem for the Funeral of Queen Caroline* (ANTHEMS, 5); as a result of an ambiguity in a letter of 18 December 1737 to the Duke of CHANDOS, this has sometimes been attributed to Edward Willes, Sub-Dean of Westminster Abbey. The sister of Carleton's wife was married to the musician Maurice GREENE.

DONALD BURROWS

Carlton House. Built c.1709 for Henry Boyle (later Baron Carleton), the house was located on Pall Mall, a short distance from ST JAMES'S PALACE, and only just around the corner from the KING'S THEATRE on the Haymarket. Boyle bequeathed the house to his nephew Lord BURLINGTON, who sold it in March 1733 to FREDERICK, Prince of Wales. It became the Prince's principal residence. According to BURNEY, Handel held rehearsals of his oratorios at Carlton House (probably during the latter half of the 1740s), and 'if the prince and princess were not exact in coming into the Music-Room, he used to be very violent'. After Frederick's death, his widow AUGUSTA lived at the house, and in the 1780s it was elaborately expanded and remodelled by the Prince of Wales (later George IV). The house was demolished in the 1820s, when the capitals of the portico columns were salvaged for the National Gallery.

DAVID VICKERS

C. Burney, 'Sketch of the Life of Handel', *An Account of the Musical Performances in Westminster Abbey* (London, 1785)
G. Thomas, 'Burney on Handel: A New Source', *The Handel Institute Newsletter* 6/2 (Autumn 1995)

Carmelite Order. A Catholic religious order. The psalm settings *Laudate pueri* (HWV 237) and *Nisi Dominus*, the motet *Saeviat tellus* and the antiphons *Haec est Regina virginum* and *Te Decus virgineum* were composed by Handel, on commission from the COLONNA family, for the feast of the Madonna del Carmine (the Blessed Virgin of Mount Carmel), and performed in ROME, in the church of Santa Maria di Monte Santo on 15 and 16 July 1707, during first and second vespers. These works do not constitute a complete self-contained vespers; their composition was separate from that of the *Dixit Dominus*, which was written in the previous April, probably for the Easter ceremonies.

FRANCESCO LORA (Trans. TERENCE BEST)

See also Italian and Latin CHURCH MUSIC

D. Burrows, 'The "Carmelite" Antiphons of Handel and Caldara', HJb 46 (2000)
W. Shaw and G. Dixon, 'Handel's Vesper Music', MT 126 (July 1985), 392–7

Carnarvon, Earl of. See Duke of CHANDOS

Caroline Elizabeth, Princess (b. Hanover, 30 May/10 June 1713; d. London, 28 Dec. 1757). Third daughter of GEORGE II and Queen CAROLINE. Caroline never married, partly because of her poor health, but played a considerable role in raising her younger sisters, MARY and LOUISA. She retired from public life completely in the 1750s, although she retained some philanthropic interests. She was taught keyboard and musical theory by Handel from c.1723

(HANDEL, 20), and shared her family's interest in his work. Her letters to Princess ANNE comment on Handel's difficulties in attracting audiences in c.1734–5. Caroline also subscribed to the publication of the *Grand Concertos* (Op. 6) (ORCHESTRAL WORKS, 2).   HANNAH SMITH

Caroline, Queen (Princess of Hanover, Princess of Wales) (b. Ansbach in Germany, 1 March 1683; d. Hampton Court, 20 Nov. 1737). Daughter of the Margrave Johann Friedrich von Brandenburg-Ansbach and his second wife, Princess Eleonore Erdmuthe of Saxe-Eisenach. In 1705 Caroline married her cousin, the Electoral Prince Georg August von Braunschweig-Lüneburg, later Elector of HANOVER and King GEORGE II of Great Britain. She spent her youth mostly in DRESDEN, and in BERLIN at the court of Frederick I, King of Prussia, and Sophie Charlotte, his second wife and sister of GEORGE I. Caroline was musical and known for her fine voice, and she also loved literature and philosophy. She maintained a lively correspondence with Gottfried Wilhelm Leibniz whom she met at Berlin in 1704. Leibniz helped her to reject a marriage contract with Charles III (later Charles VI, Holy Roman Emperor), which would have required her to convert to Roman Catholicism. In October 1727 George II and Caroline were crowned King and Queen Consort of Great Britain (CORONATION), and Caroline became one of the most popular queens in the history of the British monarchy. She had a considerable influence over George II's government and was made 'Guardian of the Kingdom of Great Britain, and His Majesty's Lieutenant within the same during His Majesty's absence'. The Queen was known for her tolerance and cleverness as much in politics as in her marriage. She supported the Prime Minister Sir Robert WALPOLE, who pursued a consistent policy of peace abroad, and under whom Great Britain prospered economically. Caroline bore the King three sons and five daughters. She died at HAMPTON COURT as the result of a rupture from which she had suffered since the birth of Princess LOUISA. Her death was a bitter loss not only for George II, but for the British nation. She was buried at WESTMINSTER ABBEY. King George II had ordered that his coffin should be placed in the stone sarcophagus in which Queen Caroline was laid to rest, and that the side-panel of the coffin should be removed, so that their remains might lie next to each other as in a double bed.

The Queen's connection with Handel went back to 1710 when Handel was appointed Kapellmeister to the Elector of Hanover. It is likely that Handel composed some of the CHAMBER DUETS for her, for instance HWV 178, 185, 194, 197 and 199, although it is unlikely that she sang them herself. She was not a performer, but a patron. In London, Handel was music master to her daughters, and the royal couple personally commissioned him to compose anthems for their coronation service (ANTHEMS, 3). It is generally accepted that there was a friendly relationship between the Queen and Handel, and we know that she appreciated and promoted his art. There is no evidence that the Te Deum in D major, the so-called 'Caroline' Te Deum (TE DEUM, 2) was composed for Caroline. The composer's personal affection for Queen Caroline is clearest in the mournful choral anthem *The ways of Zion do mourn* that he composed for her funeral service on 17 December 1737 (ANTHEMS, 5).   ANNETTE LANDGRAF

D. Burrows, 'Handel and Hanover', *Bach, Handel, Scarlatti*, ed. P. Williams (Cambridge, 1985)
A. Landgraf (ed.), *Anthem for the Funeral of Queen Caroline*, HHA III/12 (Kassel, 2004)

castrato. Castration had been practised since antiquity, but the practice of castrating and then training talented young boys for their potential as virtuoso singers was practised primarily in ITALY, Spain and Portugal beginning in the 1550s. Documentary evidence shows that in late sixteenth-century ROME both Cappella Giulia and Cappella Sistina hired 'pueri' (boys), 'eunuchi' and 'Spagnuoli' (Spaniards) to sing the treble parts in polyphonic settings. There were arguably both Spanish falsettists and Spanish castratos who masqueraded as falsettists pretending to command secret techniques of voice production. Then Italians took the lead. Writing in 1640, the Roman scholar Pietro della Valle unfavourably compared 'the falsettists of those times with the castratos' natural soprano, which we have in great store nowadays'.

Until their extinction in the early twentieth century, church music was the main career opportunity for castratos; however, from the early seventeenth century the most virtuosic became highly paid and famous international solo singers in opera seria and as chamber recitalists in royal or noble households. In opera, they were typically employed for a combination of heroic, princely, male lovers while tenors and basses mostly impersonated older men, such as fathers, tyrants or wise counsellors. This convention lasted until the first decade in the nineteenth century, when castratos abruptly disappeared from the operatic stage.

Castration eliminated the major source of the androgen hormone (testosterone) produced by the Leydig cells. The removal of the male testicles before puberty produces *primary hypogonadism*, which causes numerous developmental abnormalities by the time adulthood is reached. Without testosterone, the adult castratos had an infantile penis, no beard growth and an absence of the usual male distribution of auxiliary hair. Lacking testosterone at the time of puberty, the long bones in the arms and legs continued to grow longer relative to the torso. Castratos grew very tall, knock-kneed, and splay-footed; these features ('eunuchoid appearance') are noticeable in the large caricature galleries drawn by Antonio Maria Zanetti and Pier Leone Ghezzi. Castration resulted in a relatively and abnormally large amount of oestrogen. Hence, the castratos developed the secondary sexual characteristics of females: noticeable development of subcutaneous fat deposits on the hips, buttocks and breast; female pattern of pubic hair; and pale, soft, waxy skin. Hence, castratos very effectively performed female roles, especially in operas produced in Rome where female singers were prohibited. The idea – spread by satires of castratos and the movie *Farinelli* (FILMS) – that castratos were capable of extraordinary sexual prowess is likely based on a confusion between adults castrated as young boys ('cut out for singing' before puberty) and adults castrated as slaves or captives, who may have retained sexual function for some time afterwards. Equally unsupported is the popular assumption that they were *ipso facto* inclined to homosexuality.

Most significantly, the absence of testosterone prevents the enlargement of the male's vocal cords, resulting in high-pitched voices in the female range. An adult male's vocal cords are about 12–16 mm in length; an adult female's, about 8–11.5 mm. The vocal cords of a castrato remained at their prepubescent length of about 7–8 mm. As a result, the castrato's voice had a female's naturally high range, the vocal clarity of a young boy and the strength provided by the lung capacity of a full-grown male. The strength of the castrato's voice is suggested by the legendary duets between castratos and trumpet players, which the castratos won. Boys who were suited for musical careers received extraordinarily intensive vocal training, and excelled at improvisation, ornamentation and astonishing feats of breath control.

Almost all of the leading male roles in Handel's operas (as well as, on a minor scale, some parts in cantatas and oratorios, including English oratorios) were sung by Italian castratos, with vocal ranges from alto to soprano. The most important castratos who sang for Handel in Italy were Pasquale Betti and Stefano Frilli, and in London were NICOLINO, SENESINO, BERENSTADT, PACINI, BERNACCHI, CARESTINI, SCALZI, CONTI ('Gizziello'), ANNIBALI, CAFFARELLI and GUADAGNI. Carlo Broschi ('FARINELLI') sang for the rival OPERA OF THE NOBILITY, but sang arias by Handel on several occasions.

THOMAS N. MCGEARY and CARLO VITALI

P. Barbier, *The World of the Castrati: The History of an Extraordinary Operatic Phenomenon* (London, 1996)

N. Clapton, *Moreschi: The Last Castrato* (London, 2004)

F. Haböck, *Die Kastraten und ihre Gesangskunst* (Berlin and Leipzig, 1927)

A. Heriot, *The Castrati in Opera* (London, 1956)

S. Mamy, *Les grands castrats napolitains à Venise au XVIIIe siècle* (Liège, 1994)

E. R. Peschel and R. E. Peschel, 'Medicine and Music: The Castrati in Opera', *Opera Quarterly* 4/4 (Winter 1986/7), 21–38

E. Rizzuti and C. Vitali, 'Anamnesi versus autopsia? Appunti per una possibile sintesi, ovvero il caso Farinelli', *Il Farinelli e gli evirati cantori*, ed. L. Verdi (Lucca, 2007)

Castrucci, Pietro (b. Rome, 1679; d. Dublin, 7 March 1752). Italian violinist and composer; one of the most important representatives, together with Francesco GEMINIANI and Giovanni Stefano Carbonelli, of the Italian violin-playing and compositional tradition in England. Pietro Castrucci was a pupil of the highly esteemed Arcangelo CORELLI and, from early 1705 at the latest, worked, together with his father, the harpsichordist Domenico Castrucci, as violinist, principle *cameriere* and music copyist in the household of the Marchese Francesco Maria RUSPOLI (while Handel was there; Castrucci copied some of his works) and for Cardinal Pietro OTTOBONI. When Richard Boyle, Earl of BURLINGTON (who, since 1713 at the latest, had been in contact with Handel in London), travelled to Italy for the first time in 1714/15, Castrucci entered his service in January 1715 (and stayed until 1721). After they had returned to London on 1 May 1715, Castrucci gave his first (benefit) concert on 23 July 1715. Soon after he became concertmaster in Handel's opera orchestra; he remained in the employment of the Royal Academy of Music (OPERA COMPANIES, 2) until 1737 and his solo playing became highly popular. For example, Castrucci played the violin solos in 'Sposo ingrato' (*RADAMISTO*) and 'Se in fiorito' (*GIULIO CESARE*). According to BURNEY, Castrucci invented the so-called Violetta marina (INSTRUMENTATION, 22), for which Handel composed two parts in the aria 'Già l'ebro mio ciglio' in *ORLANDO* (1733). In 1752 he moved to DUBLIN but soon after died in poverty. At his funeral on 10 March 1752 the DEAD MARCH from Handel's oratorio *SAUL* was performed.

Castrucci, Prospero (b. ?Rome, 1690; d. ?London, 1760). Violinist and composer. Like his brother Pietro, Prospero (presumably also a pupil of Arcangelo Corelli) worked in Rome for Ottoboni as musician and then entered the service of Lord Burlington (and stayed until 1720). In London he first played in Handel's orchestra and then succeeded Talbot Young as director of the Castle Society of Music (also known as 'Phillarmonica Club'), which organised amateur concerts at the Castle Tavern in Paternoster Row. The Castrucci brothers are mentioned in a number of autograph manuscripts by Handel.

DAGMAR GLÜXAM (Trans. ANGELA BAIER)

B. Boydell, *A Dublin Musical Calender 1700–1760* (Dublin, 1988)
Burney
Dean, *Oratorios*
Dean and Knapp, *Operas*
Hawkins
HHB i
W. and U. Kirkendale, *Music and Meaning: Studies in Music History and the Neighbouring Disciplines* (Florence, 2007)
H. J. Marx, 'Die Musik am Hofe Pietro Kardinal Ottobonis', *Analecta Musicologica* 5 (1968), 104–77

Catholicism. See HANDEL, 12

Catone (*Cato*), HWV A⁷. PASTICCIO opera in three acts, based on Leonardo LEO's *Catone in Utica*. It was first performed at the KING'S THEATRE on 4 November 1732. METASTASIO originally wrote his libretto for ROME, where it was first performed in the setting of Leonardo VINCI in 1726. Leo set a second version revised by the author. The opera opened the Carnival season of 1729 at the Teatro SAN GIOVANNI GRISOSTOMO in VENICE on 26 December 1728.

Having defeated the followers of the murdered Pompeo (Pompey) at Thapsus, Cesare (Julius Caesar) comes to Utica seeking reconciliation with Catone, last defender of the republican cause. Catone's daughter Marzia, who has been Cesare's lover, has hopes of renewing their intimacy, but Catone rejects all Cesare's overtures and wants her to marry his ally Arbace, prince of Numidia, who loves her passionately. Pompeo's widow Emilia blames Cesare for his death and is intent on revenge. When Catone tries to force Marzia to wed Arbace immediately she declares her love for Cesare. Catone intervenes to save Cesare from an attempted assassination led by Emilia but then challenges him to single combat. Their duel is interrupted by news that Cesare's men have attacked the city. After exacting from Marzia a promise to marry Arbace and hate Cesare, Catone commits suicide offstage. Marzia announces his death and repulses the victorious Cesare.

The cast was as follows:

Catone	SENESINO (castrato)
Marzia	Anna Maria STRADA del Pò (soprano)
Emilia	Celeste GISMONDI (soprano)
Arbace	Francesca BERTOLLI (alto)
Cesare	Antonio MONTAGNANA (bass)

Lord HERVEY, supposing the opera to be Handel's, complained it was 'long, dull, and consequently tiresome' (Deutsch, p. 296). It nonetheless survived for five performances and was favoured by WALSH with a small collection of 'favourite songs'.

Handel based his arrangement on a copy of Leo's opera belonging to Sir John Buckworth, now in the Royal Academy of Music, London. Of the twenty-six arias in the manuscript, nine were apparently inserted in the opera by the singers, above all FARINELLI, making his VENICE debut. Farinelli's part contains two arias composed for him in his brother's L'isola d'Alcina and Vinci's Medo (both 1728), and Boschi's 'Il tuo affanno ed il tuo sdegno' is a parody of an aria Handel had composed for him in the December 1720 version of RADAMISTO, 'Con la strage de' nemici'. Handel's aria was supplied with new upper instrumental parts, presumably because Boschi only had a copy for voice and bass. Leo's authorship of the overture in the Buckworth score is also in doubt. That manuscript and Handel's conducting score in the Staats- und Universitätsbibliothek Hamburg have both been published in facsimile.

In London, Catone underwent much more drastic changes than had GIACOMELLI's LUCIO PAPIRIO in the previous season. Bertolli and Montagnana could not be expected to sing any of the arias sung by Farinelli and Gizzi in Venice, and the newcomer Gismondi seems to have insisted on singing only arias she already knew. The London insertions included arias by HASSE, PORPORA, Vinci and VIVALDI. As in his other early tragedy DIDONE ABBANDONATA, Metastasio had ended Catone with a recitative, but in London Strada sang as a 'last song' the famous aria 'Vò solcando un mar crudele' from Vinci's Artaserse (1730). In the end the only set numbers retained from the Buckworth score were nine arias, a sinfonia consisting of the ritornello of the chorus 'Già ti cede il mondo intero', and the overture.

In revising the recitatives Handel adopted a somewhat different approach than he had followed in Lucio Papirio. First SMITH copied the revised text into the conducting score. Then Handel, having marked the Buckworth score to show the cuts and some crucial stage directions, pencilled into the conducting score all the notes that needed to be altered, after which Smith inked them over and copied the rest of the notes from the Buckworth score.   JOHN H. ROBERTS

Catone, arr. G. F. Handel, ed. H. M. Brown (New York, 1983)
H. D. Clausen, Händels Direktionspartituren ('Handexemplare') (Hamburg, 1972)
L. Leo, Catone in Utica, ed. H. M. Brown (New York, 1983)
Strohm

Cecilia, volgi un sguardo, HWV 89. Italian cantata, first performed before the second part of ALEXANDER'S FEAST on 19 February 1736 at COVENT GARDEN. The solo parts were sung by tenor Carlo ARRIGONI and soprano Anna STRADA del Pò. Handel had probably already composed an extended accompanied recitative and aria for tenor voice as a suitable interpolation (LOOK DOWN, HARMONIOUS SAINT), but Arrigoni's involvement in Alexander's Feast as a lute player might have influenced the composer to utilise the Florentine musician's voice. In contrast to the richly scored ode and its associated concertos, Handel used a simple orchestration of violins, violas and basso continuo.

The introductory recitative petitions St Cecilia to glance towards Britain in order to witness the celebrations in her honour, and the tenor lyrically extols virtue in the arias 'La virtute è un vero nume' (a gentle Largo) and 'Splenda l'alba in oriente' (a graceful Andante allegro, full of demanding coloratura, based on *SPLENDA L'ALBA IN ORIENTE*). Handel initially planned to conclude with a simple recitative for soprano and a lively duet ('Tra amplessi innocenti'), but he expanded Strada's contribution by inserting an extra recitative and the substantial aria 'Sei cara, sei bella' (a parody of 'Sweet accents' from the discarded *Look down, harmonious saint*): its breezy A section is contrasted with a ravishing slower middle part ('Un puro ardor'), which Hicks compares to 'the rapt, heavenward-gazing image of Cecilia found in many Renaissance paintings'. In 1737 'Sei cara, sei bella' was probably replaced by the new shorter aria 'Sei del ciel' for the castrato ANNIBALI. DAVID VICKERS

See also *CARCO SEMPRE DI GLORIA*

A. Hicks, 'An Ode for St Cecilia's Day / Cecilia, volgi un sguardo' (CD booklet note, Hyperion CDA67463, 2004)
H. J. Marx (ed.), *Kantaten mit Instrumenten*, HHA V/3, vol. I (Kassel, 1994)

Cerveteri. See *ALLA CACCIA*; Francesco Maria RUSPOLI

Cesarini, Carlo Francesco (b. San Martino-Sassocorvaro/Pesaro-Urbino, around 1666; d. Rome, after 2 Sept. 1741). Violin virtuoso, composer and *maestro di musica* in the household of Cardinal Benedetto PAMPHILIJ in Bologna and ROME in the 1690s. Cesarini probably met Handel during the latter's interaction with the Cardinal in Rome in 1707. Cesarini arranged and adapted the score of Handel's *Il TRIONFO DEL TEMPO E DEL DISINGANNO* for revivals in March 1708 and February 1709. On 26 February 1708, before Handel first arrived in London (in late 1710), the QUEEN'S THEATRE produced the pasticcio *Love's Triumph* (libretto by Peter Anthony Motteux after Pietro OTTOBONI), for which the first act was composed by Cesarini (the following two acts were by Giovanni Lorenzo Lulier and Giovanni Battista BONONCINI respectively); however, none of the composers were present in London for the performance.

KLAUS-PETER KOCH (Trans. ANGELA BAIER)

Deutsch
HHB iv
U. Kirkendale, *Antonio Caldara: Life and Venetian – Roman Oratorios* (Florence, 2007)
H. J. Marx, 'Die "Giustificazioni della casa Pamphilj" als musikgeschichtliche Quelle', *Studi musicali* 12 (1983), 121–87
L. Montalto, *Un mecenate in Roma barocca: Il Cardinale Benedetto Pamphilj (1653–1730)* (Florence, 1955)

Cesti, Pietro Antonio (b. Arezzo; bap. 5 Aug. 1623; d. Florence, 14 Oct. 1669), Italian composer and tenor. He started his career as a church musician in Tuscany and in 1637 joined the Franciscan order in FLORENCE. He was *maestro di cappella* of Volterra Cathedral until 1649, and then sang at Pisa Cathedral for six months before he became an opera singer in Florence and Lucca. In 1651 his first opera was performed in VENICE. Cesti received patronage from the MEDICI and GRIMANI families. In 1652 he was appointed director of the *Kammermusiker* at the court of Archduke Ferdinand Carl in Innsbruck. Seven years later he was released from his monastic vows, and in 1666 became 'honorary chaplain and director of theatrical music' at the court of Emperor Leopold I in Vienna. Cesti was one of the leading cantata composers of his time: Handel made

BORROWINGS from Cesti's secular two-voice cantata *Cara e dolce libertà* in *La Resurrezione, Aci, Galatea e Polifemo, Ah! Crudel, nel pianto mio, Agrippina*, an Air in A major for harpsichord (HWV 468) and *Joshua*.

WALTER KREYSZIG

D. L. Burrows, 'Antonio Cesti on Music', MQ 51/3 (July 1965), 518–29
A. Hicks, 'Handel's Early Musical Development', PRMA 103 (1976–7), 80–90
S. Taylor, *The Indebtedness of Handel to Works by Other Composers* (Cambridge, 1906)

chamber cantatas. See CANTATAS FOR VOICE AND CONTINUO

chamber duets and trios, HWV 178–201. Handel composed twenty chamber duets and two chamber trios; two more duets are attributed to him (HHB ii, 605–25). The authenticity of HWV 195 is doubtful. HWV 183 was composed by Reinhard KEISER, and first printed in Keiser's *Divertimenti serenissimi* (Hamburg 1713), although several contemporary copies attribute it to Handel, which may be due to a mix-up with the doubtlessly authentic duet HWV 182, composed on the same text. The duets and trios were composed – often in pairs – in four periods, distributed over a space of time of nearly four decades. There is no information about any specific occasions for their composition but they were certainly in demand at the courts in ROME, HANOVER and London, where they were used for teaching and studying purposes as well as for advanced domestic music-making. Only five of the late duets and one trio are dated; the dating of the others is based on the study of the manuscript sources (see Table 1).

The ten compositions known as 'Hanover' duets (HWV 194, 198, 184, 180, 199, 178, 191, 196, 185, 197) have been extant as a collection since c.1710/12 – together with the two trios – in a fair copy prepared by the copyist 'Hanover B', and are preserved in the same order in numerous other copies. However, at least half of these duets as well as the trios and two further duets were already composed during Handel's Italian years. In the 1720s Handel composed two more, and between 1740 and 1745 he wrote six more duets and a second version of HWV 182 (unfinished). The genre of the chamber duet had developed from diverse and sometimes homophonic compositions consisting of small musical units, and duets such as those by Agostino STEFFANI reached their zenith of popularity in about 1700. By the time Handel wrote his last chamber duets, the genre had already gone out of fashion, but some of the musical material in the later duets became well known because he borrowed from them in MESSIAH and other oratorios.

Handel's chamber duets normally consist of two or three duet movements (without solo passages), which alternate between common and triple time and have basso continuo accompaniment. They stand at the summit of the genre's development, are musically demanding and their counterpoint is carefully wrought: the early duets are more rigid, scholarly and lengthy, but impeccable in their compositional execution, whereas the later duets are conceived on a more generous yet more compact plan. Most early duets are composed for a high and a low singing voice, that is, as two-part compositions, whereas Handel arranged the later ones in trio style by having two high voices engage with the basso continuo in an equal conversation.

Handel was inspired not only by Steffani's duets but also by Giovanni Maria Clari and Pietro Torri, from whom he borrowed text and musical motifs for HWV

Table 1

	Italy, 1706–10	Hanover, 1710–12	London, 1720s	London, 1740/5
Duets	HWV 182[a], S/T/B.c.			HWV 182[b], A/A/B.c.
	HWV 187, S/B/B.c.			
'Hanover'		HWV 194, S/A/B.c.		
Duets		HWV 198, S/A/B.c.		
	HWV 184, S/B/B.c.			
	HWV 180, S/S/B.c.			
	HWV 199, S/S/B.c.			
		HWV 178, S/A/B.c.		
	HWV 191, S/B/B.c.			
	HWV 196, S/B/B.c.			
		HWV 185, S/A/B.c.		
		HWV 197, S/A/B.c.		
Duets			HWV 188, S/A/B.c.	HWV 192, S/S/B.c., 1 July 1741
			HWV 193, S/A/B.c.	HWV 189, S/S/B.c., 3 July 1741
				HWV 181, S/A/B.c., 31 Oct.1742
				HWV 190, S/A/B.c., 3 Nov. 1742
				HWV 186, S/A/B.c.
				HWV 179, S/S/B.c., 31 Aug. 1745
Trios	HWV 201, S/S/B/B.c., 12 July 1708			
	HWV 200, S/S/B/B.c.			

188 (text by Giuseppe Domenico de Totis). His duets also feature BORROWINGS from Dieterich BUXTEHUDE (HWV 192) and Antonio CALDARA (HWV 189).

The authors of most of the texts that Handel used are unknown. The authors of the early Roman duets probably belonged to the environment of the ARCADIAN ACADEMY, and Bartolomeo Ortensio MAURO might have contributed texts for those composed in Hanover. HWV 181 is based on the 'Beatus ille' by Quintus Horatius Flaccus. HWV 187 and 196 (after 'Amor dorme' by Francesco de Lemene) are composed on the same texts as works by Benedetto MARCELLO. Handel sometimes set the same text twice.

All duets except HWV 198 and 199 are extant in autograph form in two collections located in English libraries: the FITZWILLIAM MUSEUM in CAMBRIDGE has all of the extant autographs for the 'Hanover' duets (MU.MS. 253, HWV 178 and 191 fragmentary); the remaining duet autographs are in the British Library in London (R.M.20.g.9, HWV 193 fragmentary). The autograph for the trio HWV 201 is in the possession of an anonymous private collector. Most known manuscript copies of this trio and all printed editions to date only reproduce a shortened version, where the original tripartite setting of the first movement is reduced to the A section only.

The 'Hanover' duets and the trios were often copied, and were printed by WALSH's successors William RANDALL and Robert Birchall – together with the duets from the 1720s and Keiser's HWV 183 – in 1777 (duets) and 1784 (trios), but most of the duets located in the British Library only circulated in a few manuscript copies. Although the autograph volume had been consulted by Felix MENDELSSOHN BARTHOLDY in 1829 and by Henry Smart when preparing his edition in 1852, both made no use of their findings. Friedrich CHRYSANDER knew about this source by at least 1870; however, he did not use it for volume 32 of his *Gesamtausgabe* and only included the missing duets in a new edition in 1880 (HG vol. 32a). The forthcoming new critical edition (HHA V/7) will rectify the mistakes contained in the previous editions and will also include HWV 201 in its complete form. KONSTANZE MUSKETA (Trans. ANGELA BAIER)

K. Musketa, 'Die Duetti und Terzetti da camera von Georg Friedrich Händel', Ph.D. dissertation (University of Halle, 1987) (abbreviated version: HJb 36 (1990))
'Exempel von "geistreicher und schöner Art": Händels Kammerduette', HJb 54 (2008)

chamber music. In Handel's time there were two principal types of instrumental chamber music: sonatas or suites for a melody instrument and basso continuo, commonly known both then and today as solo sonatas or suites (actually a misnomer, since at least two instruments are involved), and works for two melody instruments and continuo, correctly called trio sonatas. Handel composed many fine works in both categories.

1. Solo sonatas
2. Trio sonatas

1. Solo sonatas
Sixteen solo sonatas which are undoubtedly authentic have survived; fourteen have survived in Handel's autograph, and the authenticity of the other two can be safely affirmed on stylistic grounds. The earliest of them must date from his Italian period, and the latest was one of his last instrumental compositions, written about 1750; but the majority are from the mid-1720s. These works are characterised by Handel's usual compositional fluency, with graceful melody and a strong contrapuntal interaction between the upper part and the bass.

Only two works are **Flute sonatas** for the transverse flute, or 'German flute', as it was called in England at this time. The first, in D (HWV 378), was written early in the Italian period, about 1707. The only source is a manuscript copy in the Conservatoire Royal in Brussels, with the title *Sonata XXX Traversa Solo e Basso Continuo del Sr Weisse*. According to evidence elsewhere in the manuscript, this must be Johann Sigismund Weiss (c.1690–1737), brother of the famous lutenist

Silvius Leopold WEISS. Scholars are agreed, however, that the attribution to him is incorrect, and that the sonata is clearly an early work by Handel. The only other sonata specifically designated for the flute dates from about 1728, in E minor (HWV 379), headed in the autograph *Sonata a Travers. e Basso*. It consists entirely of reworkings of movements from other sonatas: one from HWV 378, and two each from works composed earlier in the 1720s, HWV 359ª for violin and HWV 360 for recorder. The adaptations from HWV 359ª and 360 are skilfully made to suit the technique of the flute, so the oft-stated belief, based on the frequent ambiguities in contemporary publishers' title pages, that composers of this period were indifferent to which instruments their sonatas were played on, is clearly untrue in Handel's case.

There are three **Oboe sonatas**. The earliest, in B flat (HWV 357), headed *Sonata pour l'Hautbois Solo* in the autograph, was composed between 1707 and 1710. The paper on which it is written is part of a small batch which Handel used when he was in HANOVER in 1710, but this paper may have been in his possession earlier. The autograph of the next sonata, in C minor (HWV 366), headed *Hautb Sol*, lacks the last movement, but the text of that is supplied by other sources; the sonata was composed in Handel's first year in England (1711–12). The third sonata, in F (HWV 363ª), probably belongs to the same period or a little later, certainly before 1716. The autograph is lost, but several good copies survive.

When Handel used the word 'Flauto', it always meant the recorder: the transverse flute he called 'Traversa' (INSTRUMENTATION). There are six **Recorder Sonatas**: the surviving autographs of four of them are beautifully written fair copies, dating from 1725–6: HWV 360 in G minor, HWV 362 in A minor, HWV 365 in C, and HWV 369 in F. The autograph of HWV 365 has lost its first leaf, which probably had the same title as the others, *Sonata a Flauto e Cembalo*. This title suggests that the tradition of having at least two continuo instruments, usually harpsichord and violoncello, does not apply here (in contrast with HWV 379, which has *Sonata a Travers. e Basso*). The mid-1720s were a time when Handel was music master to the royal princesses, daughters of the future GEORGE II, and it is conceivable that these fair copies were written for them, possibly as exercises in continuo-playing, as their basses are very fully figured (the word 'exercises' should not be understood pejoratively – they are all supremely beautiful works). Two more sonatas from the same period, in D minor (HWV 367ª) and in B flat (HWV 377), have no indication of instrument on the autographs, so the attribution to the recorder is less certain, but is suggested by the compass of the upper part; and one manuscript copy of HWV 367ª has *Sonata iii a Flauto e Cembalo*.

There are five **Violin sonatas**. The earliest is in G (HWV 358), and exists only in autograph. It is written on the same paper-type as the oboe sonata HWV 387, but the awkwardness of some of its passages must suggest an early date, c.1707. There is no indication of instrument: one scholar has suggested that it is for recorder, but some very high notes near the end (b‴–e⁗) could be played only on the violin. The upper part goes no lower than g′, which might indicate that the work is for some kind of violino piccolo.

To the period 1724–6 belong three very fine mature sonatas, in D minor (HWV 359ª), A (HWV 361) and G minor (HWV 364a). The autograph of HWV 364ª is headed *Violino Solo*; at the foot of first page Handel copied out the first bar a second time, with the solo part an octave lower in the alto clef, and the words *Per la Viola da Gamba*, showing an alternative scoring for the work (HWV 364ᵇ). In this gathering HWV 359ᵃ follows in the middle of a page, with the heading *Sonata 2*, with no indication of instrumentation, but the context and the compass of the solo part show that it must also be for violin. HWV 361 is headed *Violino Solo*: it is a virtuosic work, with some double-stopping; the finale is a reworking of that of the recorder sonata HWV 377.

The grandest of Handel's solo sonatas is the magnificent one in D (HWV 371), which was written about 1750, and is one of his last instrumental compositions. The autograph, the only source, is headed *Sonata a Violino Solo e Cembalo di G. F. Handel*, so again the implication is that the continuo is for harpsichord alone, an interpretation supported by the rapid semiquaver figuration in the second and fourth movements, comfortable on a keyboard, but less so on the violoncello.

Handel's solo sonatas are an impressive contribution to the genre, but for 250 years the texts of many of them in print were in confusion, largely because of the disreputable practices of the publisher John WALSH in the early 1730s, which the later editors ARNOLD and CHRYSANDER were unable to sort out. Around 1730–1, having acquired copies of ten of the sonatas, Walsh published them in a pirated edition with a fake Jeanne Roger title page, even though she had died in 1722, before most of the sonatas were written (Estienne ROGER). Walsh was faced with a problem: the German flute was by this time one of the most popular instruments for amateurs, yet none of the Handel sonatas of which he had copies was for the flute; so he transposed three of them into 'sharp' keys suitable for the instrument, and printed them with the indication *Traversa Solo*: HWV 359ᵃ appears in E minor (HWV 359ᵇ), HWV 363ᵃ in G (HWV 363ᵇ), and HWV 367ᵃ in B minor (HWV 367ᵇ). The violin sonata HWV 364ᵃ is allocated to *Hoboy Solo*. Three sonatas have movements missing or printed in the wrong work, and, worst of all, to make up a set of twelve he included as his numbers X and XII two violin sonatas, in A and E, which are undoubtedly spurious (HWV 372, 373). The British Library copy of the edition has an annotation in a contemporary hand over sonatas X and XII 'NB. This is not Mːʳ Handel's.' Walsh reprinted it about a year later, this time with his own title page, and a comment at the bottom 'Note: *This is more Corect [sic] than the former Edition.*' The transpositions for the flute remained unaltered, as did the designation of HWV 364ᵃ as an oboe sonata, but many other errors were corrected, including those which involved missing or misplaced movements; the two spurious violin sonatas were also removed, but, astonishingly, to make up the set of twelve he replaced them with two others, in G minor and F (HWV 368, 370), which are even less likely to be Handel's work than their predecessors: the composition of HWV 368 is particularly feeble. One of the British Library copies of this issue also has a contemporary handwritten comment on each of these two sonatas (not in the same hand as in the previous edition) 'Not Mːʳ Handel's Solo'. The sonatas HWV 357, 358, 377, 378 and 379 were not included in either of Walsh's issues, and of course HWV 371 was not yet written. The Walsh edition was retrospectively advertised as Op. 1.

When Arnold published his edition in about 1793, he knew only the first Walsh issue with the Roger title page; in 1879, when Chrysander came to publish the sonatas, he had access only to the second Walsh issue and Arnold's edition, as well as the autographs of HWV 362, 371 and 379 in the British Museum;

unfortunately the autographs of the others (except HWV 363ᵃ and 378, which are lost), are in the Fitzwilliam Museum collection, which Chrysander never saw. Consequently he reproduced Walsh's transposed versions, and his four spurious violin sonatas, added HWV 379 at the beginning of his volume (as no. 1a; HWV 359b is no. 1b), and numbered the set Op. 1 Nos. 1–15; the correct texts of these works remained unpublished until late in the twentieth century. Chrysander printed the D major violin sonata (HWV 371) for the first time (his Op. 1 No. 13), but even here the unfortunate fate which bedevilled these sonatas in print struck again. Not long after writing HWV 371, Handel was composing the oratorio JEPHTHA (1751–2); in the third act he needed a 'Symphony' to herald the arrival of the Angel, and for this purpose he used the last movement of the yet unpublished violin sonata. It needed shortening for its new situation, so he indicated cuts in pencil in the autograph, totalling 18 bars; Smith copied the new text into the performing score of the oratorio, and Handel entered a viola part in his own hand. When Chrysander came to print the sonata using the autograph as his copy-text, he incorporated the cuts, perhaps not recognising they were relevant only to the *Jephtha* version of the piece; it was not until 1952 that the full original text was published.

In the later decades of the twentieth century the sonatas have appeared in their correct form in several critical editions; in these and in other studies the full history of the earlier corruptions and confusions is examined, and the unauthentic works identified; the latter include three flute sonatas attributed to Handel (HWV 374–6) which Walsh published with three by other composers, in 1730: the first and third are unauthentic, the second has the first two movements of the C minor oboe sonata, HWV 366, clumsily transposed to E minor, a spurious third movement and a version of the keyboard minuet HWV 434/4. Two single movements for violin and continuo (HWV 408, 412) from the 1720s, and a violin solo (HWV 407) dated 1738, also survive in the composer's autograph.

2. Trio sonatas

The texts of Handel's trio sonatas have not been so affected by publishers' corruptions as the solo sonatas were, although paradoxically far fewer of the autographs have survived. The most common instrumentation of baroque trio sonatas was for two violins and continuo, and in the following account it is to be understood that this is the case with Handel's, unless indicated otherwise.

There are sixteen unquestionably authentic works, composed between c.1699 and 1739. Two sets were published by Walsh as Op. 2 (six sonatas), and Op. 5 (seven sonatas); the others remained in manuscript.

The first of Handel's trio sonatas may well be his earliest extant composition. It is in G minor (HWV 387, Op. 2 No. 2), and shows many signs of immaturity: it appears among others in a later copy written by S2 (COPYISTS) about 1732, a manuscript from the Aylesford Collection owned by Charles JENNENS (SOURCES AND COLLECITONS, 3). At the head of this sonata Jennens wrote 'Compos'd at the Age of 14'. Jennens could have acquired such information only from Handel himself, so if the composer's memory was reliable we have a date of c.1699 for this work. The opening of the finale is a first version of a gambit that Handel was to use many times in later years.

Three sonatas belong to the early part of the Italian period, c.1707. One in F (HWV 392) may even have been written when the composer was still in HAMBURG: it has many of the quirky features which Handel employed at this time as he struggled to find his true voice, including an extraordinary passage at the end of the second movement, where the music is suddenly interrupted in full flow, followed by seven concluding bars with strange chromatic harmonies. The other early sonatas are in G minor (HWV 391, Op. 2 No. 6), and in F (HWV 405): the latter is for two recorders and continuo, written on the same paper-type as the solo sonatas HWV 357 and 358; the autograph is incomplete, but there is a set of manuscript parts with the whole text.

Four sonatas, whose autographs are lost, were probably composed at the time of Handel's engagement at CANNONS, about 1717–19. These are fine works: one of the most powerful is HWV 386, which exists in two forms: (1) in C minor (HWV 386^a), which is certainly the original, and is found in most of the manuscript sources, two of which assign the upper part to the oboe: this is the most likely instrumentation, since the third movement, in 3/2, has a solo for the upper part over repeated chords, very like the oboe solos in several works composed about this time, including AMADIGI; (2) in B minor (HWV 396^b, Op. 2 No. 1), with the upper part for flute; the transposition required some awkward redistribution of notes in the second and fourth movements. This is the text of Walsh's edition, and it might seem to be another of his unauthentic transpositions for the flute; but two later manuscript copies also give this version, so he may not have been responsible. In HWV 388, in B flat (Op. 2 No. 3) three movements have material in common with the overture in ESTHER (c.1719): which came first is still a matter of conjecture. One copy has this sonata for two oboes and bassoon, another has the flute for the upper part. HWV 389, in F (Op. 2 No. 4) has the upper part for flute in Walsh: one copy has violin, another oboe, and the recorder is also a possibility. HWV 390, in G minor (Op. 2 No. 5) is the last of this group, and is of the same high quality as the others.

The Op. 2 edition was first published about 1730–1 with a fake Roger title page, but with a more reliable text than that of Op. 1. There are a few errors, and Walsh reprinted it about 1733 with corrections and his own title page (in French). Again there is a footnote 'Note: *This is more Correct than the former Edition.*' As with Op. 1, Arnold reprinted the 'Roger' version, and Chrysander the second issue; but Chrysander caused confusion by printing not six but nine sonatas as Op. 2, because he included three which were unknown to Walsh and Arnold (HWV 392–4), but instead of simply adding them at the end of Walsh's six, he printed the early sonata HWV 392 as No. 3, so displacing Walsh's 3–6 to become 4–7. HWV 393 and 394, both of doubtful authenticity, followed as 8 and 9. His reason for this may be that HWV 393 and HWV 388 begin with a similar phrase, so he felt that they were connected: that is true, of course, since in his usual way Handel was reworking old material.

The edition of Op. 5 (HWV 396–402) was produced under more ideal circumstances. In 1736 the elder John Walsh died, and was succeeded in the business by his son John. Handel had a better relationship with the son than he had had with the father, and one of the early fruits of this collaboration was the publication on 28 February 1739 of seven sonatas Op. 5, for which there is no doubt that the composer provided the copy. He mostly recycled old material, which included ballet music written for the operas of the mid-1730s – ARIANNA IN CRETA, ARIODANTE, TERPSICORE, Il PASTOR FIDO, ALCINA, PARNASSO IN FESTA and ORESTE, and instrumental movements from the Chandos Anthems (ANTHEMS, 2)], which were particularly suitable for trio sonata treatment in that they had no viola part; there was also some newly composed music.

Autographs of two of the Op. 5 sonatas survive, No. 5 in G minor (HWV 400), but lacking the last two movements, and No. 6 in F (HWV 401). In HWV 401 the second and third movements are reworkings of those in the early sonata HWV 392: in both movements Handel shortened and tightened the structure, but in the first of them he retained the extraordinarily dramatic passage at the end (see above), slightly modified; perhaps the middle-aged composer felt a fondness for this piece of youthful exuberance. The fifth and final movement of this sonata in the autograph is a version of the variation movement which concludes the organ concerto Op. 4 No. 1 (HWV 289) (ORCHESTRAL WORKS, 5) which Walsh had published in October 1738; for the Op. 5 edition it was replaced by a minuet, presumably to avoid a clash. Chrysander and modern editions give both movements.

At about the time that Op. 5 was being prepared Handel composed a large-scale trio sonata in C, HWV 403: the autograph is the only source, and the four movements were reworked into the oratorio SAUL in 1738: three became the overture, and the fourth served as the 'Wedding Symphony' in Act II.

Some trio sonatas traditionally attributed to Handel are of doubtful authenticity and are probably spurious: (1) Of the three sonatas added by Chrysander to Op. 2, HWV 394 in E is undoubtedly spurious. (2) HWV 393, in G minor, is a fine work, often performed today; it has some stylistic affinity with the sonatas of the Cannons period, and is accepted as genuine by some scholars; however, some features make it suspect, and no consensus has yet been reached. (3) A sonata in E minor for two flutes and continuo (HWV 395) is also very doubtful: Hasse has been suggested as a likely composer. (4) Six sonatas for oboe, violin and continuo (HWV 380–5), which on unreliable evidence from one eighteenth-century witness have been attributed to the twelve-year-old Handel, are almost certainly unauthentic.   TERENCE BEST

T. Best, 'Handel's Chamber Music – Sources, Chronology and Authenticity', EM 13/4 (Nov. 1985), 476–99

D. Burrows, 'Walsh's Editions of Handel's Opera 1–5: The Texts and their Sources', Music in Eighteenth-Century England, ed. C. Hogwood and R. Luckett (Cambridge, 1983) HHA IV/3 (rev. edn), IV/4 (rev. edn), IV/9, IV/18, IV/19

D. Lasocki and T. Best, 'A New Flute Sonata by Handel', EM 9/3 (July 1981), 307–11

R. Mellace, Johann Adolf Hasse (Palermo, 2004)

Chamberlain, Lord (of Great Britain). The Lord Chamberlain held virtual dictatorial power over the theatre companies, actors and musicians in Great Britain. Due to attacks on the government from the stage, Parliament passed in 1737 the Licensing Act, which required that copies of all plays and entertainments intended to be performed in Great Britain be submitted to the office of the Examiner of Plays for a licence a fortnight before presentation.

Since the act covered operas and oratorios, Handel or his librettists submitted to the Lord Chamberlain's office manuscript or printed copies of his works for the stage. Copies of most of Handel's post-1737 dramatic works submitted for a licence are now found (some with MS revisions) in the Larpent Collection at the Henry E. Huntington Library and Art Gallery, San Marino, California.

THOMAS N. MCGEARY

D. MacMillan, *Catalogue of the Larpent Plays in the Huntington Library* (San Marino, CA, 1939)
V. J. Liesenfeld, *The Licensing Act of 1737* (Madison, WI, 1984)

Chandos Anthems and Te Deum. See ANTHEMS, 2; TE DEUM, 3

Chandos, 1st Duke of (James Brydges) (b. Dewsall, Herefordshire, 6 Jan. 1674; d. Cannons, 9 Aug. 1744). Politician and patron of the arts. Descended from a baron and a successful merchant, Brydges was educated at Westminster School, New College, OXFORD and WOLFENBÜTTEL, where he made useful contacts at the court of HANOVER. Returning to LONDON, he won friends in commerce and politics, at court and in the Royal Society and musical circles. In 1705 he was appointed paymaster to Queen ANNE's army abroad during the War of the SPANISH SUCCESSION. In eight years he amassed £600,000 by short-term high-interest investment of money passing through his hands – too novel a procedure to be illegal, and government payment in arrears was endemic. With peace in 1713 he resigned, bought the CANNONS estate from his late wife's family, remarried and set about rebuilding. His early Hanover contacts enabled him to secure the earldom of Carnarvon from GEORGE I in October 1714.

He then embarked on a career as a patron of the arts, rebuilding the Tudor manor house at Cannons as a grand Palladian mansion and furnishing it appropriately. He also rebuilt the parish church of ST LAWRENCE, Little Stanmore ('Whitchurch'), and had it decorated in the Italian baroque style. Uniquely among his peers, Brydges maintained a sizeable musical establishment. He began hiring musicians for his 'CANNONS CONCERT' in late 1715 and by New Year's Day 1721 the membership numbered some twenty-four singers and instrumentalists. In April 1719 he was made 1st Duke of Chandos in recognition of his services to the state. From the middle of 1721 he reduced his musical establishment in response to his losses in the collapse of the SOUTH SEA COMPANY. Some sort of regular musical activity was maintained until 1725. After that date references to music and musicians are rare, although Brydges was a member of the Society of the Gentlemen Performers of Musick in 1732 when *ESTHER* was performed by them with singers from the CHAPEL ROYAL.

Handel is first reported at Cannons in mid-August 1717, presumably as an artist-in-residence, and by Christmas of the same year Johann Christoph PEPUSCH was also there. Handel wrote eleven anthems and a Te Deum for Brydges between August 1717 and February 1719 (ANTHEMS, 2; TE DEUM, 3), and *ACIS AND GALATEA* by midsummer 1718. The date of composition of 'The Oratorium' (*ESTHER*, HWV 50^a) has not been established, but it was certainly completed after Handel's trip to DRESDEN in 1719. Pepusch also composed anthems for the Cannons Concert, together with various occasional pieces. He was appointed director of music in 1719, a post he retained until the end of 1725, in the latter years on a part-time basis. His second collection of *Six English Cantatas*, published in May 1720, was dedicated to Brydges.

Brydges attempted to recoup his financial losses during the 1720s and 1730s by investing in business ventures that were rarely successful. By the time of his death his second and surviving son, Henry, who would become 2nd Duke of Chandos, had spent his inheritance and was deeply in debt. Within four years the estate of Cannons was sold and the house pulled down and sold for furnishings. The contents of the library, excluding music, were sold at auction. About a third of the musical holdings were apparently inherited by Brydges's granddaughter Lady Caroline Brydges Leigh and have survived (SOURCES AND COLLECTIONS, 6).   GRAYDON BEEKS

C. H. C. Baker and M. I. Baker, *The Life and Circumstances of James Brydges, First Duke of Chandos, Patron of the Liberal Arts* (Oxford, 1949)

G. Beeks, 'Handel and Music for the Earl of Carnarvon', *Bach, Handel, Scarlatti: Tercentenary Essays*, ed. P. Williams (Cambridge, 1985)

"A Club of Composers": Handel, Pepusch and Arbuthnot at Cannons', *Handel Tercentenary Collection*, ed. S. Sadie and A. Hicks (London, 1987)

S. Jenkins, *Portrait of a Patron: The Patronage and Collecting of James Brydges, 1st Duke of Chandos (1674–1744)* (Aldershot, 2007)

J. Johnson, *Princely Chandos: The Life of James Brydges, 1st Duke of Chandos* (Gloucester, 1984)

Chapel Royal, The. The term refers both to a British institution and to some specific architectural sites. The English Chapel Royal originated in Anglo-Saxon times, as a body of priests and servants who ministered to the spiritual needs of the sovereign and travelled about with the court. By the mid-thirteenth century the Chapel employed professional singers and the first known appointment of a Master of the Children dates from the 1440s. The Chapel became the principal choral institution of the court, managed by a Dean and Sub-Dean within the Lord Chamberlain's jurisdiction. During the period of Handel's association the musical establishment of the Chapel Royal comprised twenty-six Gentlemen in Ordinary including ten priests (some of whom nevertheless undertook musical functions) and ten choristers, complemented by the offices of Organists, Composers, Master of the Children, Lutenist, Violist and Organ-Blower. The Gentlemen's routine duties involved a rota system with half of them in service at any time; however, the leading singers (principally altos and basses) came to occupy two places requiring service throughout the year, and most of the Gentlemen combined Chapel Royal offices with similar posts at WEST-MINSTER ABBEY, ST PAUL'S CATHEDRAL and St George's Chapel, Windsor. These institutions provided the principal employment for professional singers in LONDON apart from the theatres; the offices of Organist and Composer were also central to the careers of Maurice GREENE and William BOYCE. The altos Richard Elford and Francis Hughes turned to the Chapel from the theatres during the first decade of the century, as Italian opera and castrati gained ground.

From the sixteenth century onwards the Chapel became less nomadic and a chapel room in one of the royal palaces became their principal centre. Soon after her accession in 1702 Queen ANNE adopted ST JAMES'S PALACE as her London residence and the Chapel Royal moved to the chapel there, a modest space that had been acquired and decorated in King Henry VIII's reign, possibly the former dining hall of the original leper hospital. Strictly, however, any place where the monarch worshipped was still a 'Chapel Royal', especially when

141

accompanied by the court's ecclesiastical and musical staff. Nevertheless the term was most often applied to the Chapels within royal palaces, as for example at KENSINGTON and HAMPTON COURT where the Hanoverians often resided for the summer. Rather confusingly, there were a number of parallel Chapel Royal establishments (French, Dutch and German Lutheran) to serve various groups of court servants and these functioned in various other 'chapel' spaces at St James's. The 'French Chapel' in which the wedding of Princess Anne took place (with Handel's music) in 1734 is a building at St James's Palace designed by Inigo Jones which was currently otherwise given over to use by the 'French' Chapel Royal (QUEEN'S CHAPEL).

The musical institution of the Chapel is important not only because of the associated repertory of Handel's English church music (ANTHEMS; TE DEUM), but also because the developments that led to Handel's first London theatre oratorio performances in 1732 were initiated by a private production of *ESTHER* that Bernard Gates prepared with the Chapel Royal choristers; the Gentlemen and boys of the Chapel also provided Handel with chorus singers in later oratorio performances. The Chapel was regularly associated with the string players of the Royal Musicians in performances of the annual court odes as well as special royal church services.   DONALD BURROWS

Burrows, *Chapel Royal*

Chapel Royal Anthems. See ANTHEMS, 1, 3–7

Charities. See FUND FOR THE SUPPORT OF DECAY'D MUSICIANS; FOUNDLING HOSPITAL; Corporation of the SONS OF THE CLERGY

Cheltenham. Spa town in Gloucestershire developed around several scattered, mainly saline, springs discovered in the second decade of the eighteenth century. Drinking the waters was held to be beneficial for internal and constitutional complaints, especially digestive troubles, and for rheumatism. The early spa buildings were relatively unsophisticated, but by the 1740s the town was attracting about 650 annual visitors, including persons of quality. It is not unlikely that Handel was among them, but information is scanty. According to a newspaper report Handel returned to London from Cheltenham on 13 June 1751. His trip must have been quite brief and was combined with a visit to BATH, where he had arrived on 3 June (HHB iv, p. 452).   ANNETTE LANDGRAF

See also HANDEL, 15–16

B. Little, *Cheltenham* (London, 1952)

Chester, Cheshire. On his way to DUBLIN in November 1741, Handel spent several days in Chester as the packet-boat from Parkgate was delayed due to contrary winds. BURNEY tells a story about *MESSIAH* being rehearsed and a bass singer's sight-reading difficulties, but the legend was debunked by Charles Cudworth.   DAVID HUNTER

See also HANDEL, 15

C. Cudworth, 'Mythistorica Handeliana', *Festskrift Jens Peter Larsen*, ed. N. Schiørring, H. Glahn and C. E. Hatting (Copenhagen, 1972)

Choice of Hercules, The, HWV 69. English ode, called a 'Musical Interlude' in Handel's autograph score. It was conceived as a new third part for a revival of *ALEXANDER'S FEAST* at COVENT GARDEN on 1 March 1751. The soloists were probably:

Hercules	Gaetano GUADAGNI (castrato)
Pleasure	Giulia FRASI (soprano)
Virtue	Caterina GALLI (mezzo-soprano)
Attendant on Pleasure	Thomas LOWE (tenor)

Handel quickly assembled the ode between 28 June and 5 July 1750, using a large part of his unperformed incidental music for *ALCESTE* and BORROWING material from a 'Gloria' by Antonio LOTTI (formerly HWV 245). The libretto was most probably provided by Thomas MORELL, who had written the words for the *Alceste* songs. Handel notated some of the changes for *The Choice of Hercules* directly into the autograph score of *Alceste*, although he substantially recomposed some of the pieces. The plain recitatives, one aria ('There the brisk sparkling nectar drain') and the trio and following accompanied recitative and aria ('Where shall I go?' and 'Mount, mount the steep ascent') were newly composed.

The young Hercules meets two female figures, Pleasure and Virtue, who both try to win the hero. Pleasure tries to entice him with love and all the delights of the senses in a pastoral bower of bliss, but Virtue reminds the demi-god of his higher destiny and exhorts him to virtue and heroic deeds. Hercules is at first unsettled by the tempting promises made by Pleasure and her Attendant but in the end opts for the chance of eternal glory and undertakes the 'steep ascent' pointed out by Virtue.

Hercules's choice was familiar throughout early modern Europe as an epitome of moral decisions about how to live one's life; as an allegory for the soul's choice of virtue over sin (Hercules was traditionally a type of Christ); and as a reminder to absolutist sovereigns of their responsibilities to their subjects. The ode's source, acknowledged by the wordbook, is the versification of part of Xenophon's *Memorabilia* (memoirs of Socrates) by the OXFORD Professor of Hebrew Robert LOWTH, published in 1743. Lowth's poem reached a wide British public in 1747, when the Oxford Professor of Poetry, Joseph Spence, reprinted it as the culmination of the chapter on classical heroes in his *Polymetis*. The subscription list of this folio volume on classical Roman visual art and literature is full of Handel's friends. The Harris papers (Burrows and Dunhill, pp. 81–2, 208) show several of them hoping as early as 1739 that Handel would do a Choice of Hercules setting. The 4th Earl of SHAFTESBURY had been brought up literally in the shadow of the painting of the Choice of Hercules commissioned by his father from Paolo de Matteis. That image was used in the 3rd Earl's influential philosophical works, and became so famous that it was reproduced even on fans and snuffboxes.

Although Handel self-borrowed much of the music in *The Choice of Hercules*, and the incidental purpose of most of the source material is apparent in the new context, the piece is skilfully organised and does not show any arbitrariness. The first part of the work is apparently balanced, first Pleasure and then Virtue each having three solos, the last in each case endorsed by a connected chorus. But there are distinctions. Pleasure (named 'Sloth' in Lowth's original poem) begins with an extended accompanied recitative, her first air has soft triplet motifs and a pleasant dance-like melody, and her lively (newly written) air, 'There the brisk sparkling nectar drain', with obbligato horns suggesting outdoor sports, provides a contrast of mood with the languor of her first; her third air and its chorus use the same material as her first (making her three airs themselves a da capo structure). But Virtue begins with a plain recitative, and has different material for each solo; her first air ('This manly youth's exalted mind', featuring solo flute and violin passages) is the only da capo number in the ode, and her third solo 'So shalt thou gain immortal praise' is only a short four-bar introduction to a chorus.

Virtue then keeps silent while Pleasure again appeals to Hercules with a further air and chorus, and a following recitative to which, at last, Hercules responds with 'Oh, cease, enchanting siren, cease thy song! / I dare not, must not join thy festive throng', and an exquisite E major air, *largo e mezzo piano*, suggestive of intense longing ('Yet can I hear the dulcet lay'). Pleasure's Attendant adds the pressure of another air ('Enjoy the sweet Elysian grove', to the same words as in *Alceste*, but reduced to only its A section), and Hercules's 'Where shall I go?' inaugurates the dramatic apex of the work, a trio for Hercules, Pleasure and Virtue. It halts with Hercules still unresolved, but Virtue leads straight into an accompanied recitative, air and chorus which urge Hercules, with an increasing suggestion of triumphant resolution, to 'Mount, mount the steep ascent'. This inspires him to take his destined path to his immortal future, and a determined acceptance of his responsibilities and hardships can be heard in the D minor of his last aria, and also in the transposition of the material of the final chorus from its original G major into the relative minor. The choice of Lotti's 'Gloria' as a source for this chorus befits the words, which project Hercules into a sacred sphere: 'Virtue will place thee in that blest abode, / Crown'd with immortal youth, among the Gods a God.'

Handel revived *The Choice of Hercules* in the 1753 and 1755 Lenten oratorio seasons, inserted between the two parts of *Alexander's Feast*. After Handel's death there were few eighteenth-century performances of the ode, although it was performed at Vienna in 1793, perhaps with a German-language text.　　　　CHRISTINE MARTIN (Trans. ANGELA BAIER)

K. Beißwenger, 'Eine Messe Antonio Lottis in Händels Notenbibliothek', *Die Musikforschung* 42 (1989), 353–6

Burrows and Dunhill

Dean, *Oratorios*

R. Fiske, *English Theatre Music in the Eighteenth Century*, 2nd edn (Oxford, 1986)

M. Gardner, 'Handel and Maurice Greene's Circle at the Apollo Academy: The Music and Intellectual Contexts of Oratorios, Odes and Masques', Ph.D. dissertation (Ruprecht-Karls-Universität Heidelberg, 2007)

HHB ii

A. Hicks, 'The Choice of Hercules HWV 69' (CD booklet note, Hyperion CDA67298, 2002)

H. J. Marx, *Händels Oratorien, Oden und Serenaten* (Göttingen, 1998)

W. Rackwitz, 'Die Herakles-Gestalt bei Händel', *Festschrift zur Händel-Ehrung der DDR 1959* (Leipzig, 1959)

W. Sandberger, 'Zum Motiv und zur Dramaturgie des Herkules auf dem Scheidewege bei Bach (BWV 213) und Händel (HWV 69)', GHB XI (2006)

Choir. See CHORUS; PERFORMANCE PRACTICE

chorale. Handel would have been exposed to the Lutheran chorale repertory at church and school in HALLE (HANDEL, 13), so it is likely to have played a formative role in his melodic invention. Chorales make sporadic appearances in Handel's later compositions: the *BROCKES PASSION* uses four and *The ways of Zion do mourn* (ANTHEMS, 5) contains unequivocal references to two (possibly in acknowledgement of Queen Caroline's Lutheran origins). Chorale references can also be found in several other oratorios and odes during the ensuing years. The 'HALLELUJAH CHORUS' of *MESSIAH* has long been trawled for its references to chorales, particularly 'Wachet auf'. One of the most spectacular examples is the blazing prominence of 'Gott ist heilig' in the climactic final section of 'Praise the Lord' in *SOLOMON*. John H. Roberts has made two interesting observations about Handel's use of chorales: first, many of them may derive from compositions by others (perhaps in the famous 'commonplace' book he possessed), that Handel used as inventive stimulus. Thus attributing a specific significance to a chorale and its original text needs to be done with the utmost caution. Secondly, there is evidence that Handel sometimes used chorales as a catalyst for improvisations within his organ concertos. This suggests a practice he retained from his earliest years (an incomplete chorale working moreover suggests that he may have used chorale settings as a method of teaching composition).

JOHN BUTT

J. Roberts, 'German Chorales in Handel's English Works', HJb 42/3 (1996/7)

chorus. Handel's upbringing in schools and churches in HALLE would have introduced him to a variety of conceptions of the 'chorus'. The singing of Lutheran chorales and other songs would have been a fundamental element of both musical and spiritual education, the better pupils learning part-singing through more elaborate chorale settings and traditional motet repertoire. Modern vocal music, in the more elaborate 'concerto' style, would have brought a rather different conception of the 'chorus': the principal singer of each line would have been an advanced pupil ('concertist') and the line may have been doubled by a less experienced singer in chorus sections ('ripienist'). Thus, Handel's foremost conception of a chorus in his own early compositions would have been as an extension of the solo sections, something that could be sung by soloists throughout or doubled by one or more extra singer. This German practice was, in fact, borrowed from Italy and there is some evidence that this is just what Handel did in his Italian psalm settings of 1707 (Italian and Latin CHURCH MUSIC]. This choral practice was exactly that of Italian opera too, where the closing choruses were led, if not exclusively sung, by the principals. Indeed, there was no chorus – in the modern sense – in the first two Italian oratorios, the choruses at the end of each part of *La RESURREZIONE* being sung by the five principal singers together.

While English choral foundations did not follow the Italianate practice directly, there was some analogy to the concertist–ripienist divide in the way the verse anthem repertory was sung, by which there was an alternation between soloists as 'verse' (singing singly or in groups) and the sections designated as 'full' (in which the 'verse' singers also participated). One particular feature of cathedral and collegiate practice was the splitting of the choir on two sides of the church, thus laying the foundations not only for double-choir practice, but also for a choral effect in which the voices in each line did not always come from the same direction. In all, Handel experienced no difficulties in adapting his choral style to English practice, and, just as on the continent, the chorus could be expanded as the occasion demanded. When working for James Brydges (later 1st Duke of CHANDOS) at CANNONS in 1717–18, he prepared anthems that were sung by two singers to a part, at most; some of these pieces were adaptations of anthems previously written for the larger forces of the CHAPEL ROYAL, while others were new works which were themselves later adapted for more singers (ANTHEMS, 2). In preparing music for large state occasions, when several of the London choirs sang together, Handel might have encountered forces that were among the largest in Europe. The funeral anthem for Queen Caroline in 1737, *The ways of Zion do mourn*, involved over fifty singers (ANTHEMS, 5).

It is obviously in the Oratorios that Handel's writing for chorus has been most celebrated, but it is important to keep in mind his fundamental adherence to English and continental practices. First, surviving parts suggest that the soloists continued to sing in the choruses, thus creating some sense of continuity, in both timbre and technique, between choruses and arias. However, it is likely that in many, if not all, cases the soloists were situated as a group away from the remainder of the singers (this was also typical of the concertist/ripienist practice in Germany). Secondly, Handel may sometimes have borrowed aspects of English practice, as in *ESTHER* in 1732 when the chorus was advertised as being placed as if for a 'Coronation Service'; this may have involved situating the chorus in two facing blocks. A similar division of forces was presupposed in the great double-chorus oratorios of *ISRAEL IN EGYPT* and *SOLOMON*. Although there are no extensive records of the number of singers participating in the choruses of Handel's oratorios, the FOUNDLING HOSPITAL accounts for the 1754 performance of *Messiah* include twenty-two singers, including the five soloists. This might thus represent a reasonable average number of singers, which was presumably somewhat higher in double-choir works.

The textures of Handel's choruses are extremely varied, although almost always excellently suited to forces of varying ability and flexible enough to withstand a variety of circumstances. As the early psalm settings attest, the choruses are not always less virtuosic than solo writing; indeed, the origin of some of the most florid choruses of *Messiah* in virtuoso Italian CHAMBER DUETS attests to the lack of an obvious barrier between the writing for solo and massed voices. On the other hand, the large tableaux articulated by the choruses that are characteristic of such works as *SAUL* are clearly of a monumental style that is very much Handel's own. It clearly borrows much from German and English choral traditions in both its sturdy counterpoint and its hymn-like melodic style. Yet there is always a tremendous dramatic pacing and also a subtlety of subject position, which brings the drama alive to the listener in remarkable ways. The choruses in Part I of *Saul* seem to come right from within the world of the action, whether in a generic articulation of praise (the opening chorus) or the delightfully naive hymn of welcome to David. In the darker atmosphere of Part II, the chorus seems more to articulate emotions from outside the action as if to draw us into the emerging moral of the story. 'Envy! Eldest born of hell!' sounds almost like a grotesque parody of an English anthem, a striking lesson from the Hebrew world now presented in a theatrical context. Similarly, the closing chorus, 'Oh fatal consequence', begins as a severe fugue darkly coloured by its diminished fifth and merging into dramatic homophony, as if the emotion cannot be held within the static musical world of counterpoint. Part III sees the chorus return more to the scene of the action, but as part of a formal elegy that has the shape of a rite, which might or might not take place in the real time of the drama. Thus having heard the chorus commenting on the events from our side of the stage, we now hear it doing the same within the world of action; but we are somehow drawn into the depths of mourning through our prior identification with the chorus.

Handel's flexible model for the oratorio chorus was to have historical repercussions that he could not possibly have anticipated, having a profound influence on the amateur choral culture of the modern age. Moreover, the fact that Handel wrote his choruses with a great deal of performance flexibility in mind and also carefully planned the changing role of the chorus as representing massed viewpoints from both on and off the stage, meant that he had essentially defined a new genre of musical drama. JOHN BUTT

See also COUNTERPOINT; PERFORMANCE PRACTICE

Chrichley, J. London printer and publisher, active 1732–43, 'at the London Gazette' near Charing Cross. He published bilingual WORDBOOKS for most of the operas and other Italian entertainments performed at the KING'S THEATRE in the late 1730s and early 1740s, including three operas produced by Handel in 1738 – *FARAMONDO, ALESSANDRO SEVERO* and *SERSE*. His first theatre wordbook was for LAMPE's English opera *Dione* (1733); his first Italian opera wordbook was *SIROE*, for the OPERA OF THE NOBILITY (1736), and his last was *Meraspe* (1742). In 1741 he published the wordbook for Handel's last opera, *DEIDAMIA*, which was not, however, performed at the King's Theatre. JOHN GREENACOMBE

Chrysander, Friedrich (b. Lübtheen in Mecklenburg, 8 July 1826; d. Bergedorf, now part of Hamburg, 3 Sept. 1901). Musicologist, biographer and editor. Being one of five children in a poor family, Chrysander had no access to higher education. He took part in a teacher training in Ludwigslust 1847–9. In 1850 he began working as a teacher in Schwerin, where he came in contact with musical circles and encountered Handel's music. He resigned from his post to focus on Handel activities. Without having studied, he got a doctorate from the Universität Rostock in 1855.

Chrysander wrote an extensive biography, *G. F. Händel* (1858–67), the second biography of Handel that met high musicological standards after Victor SCHOELCHER's work. Though having planned three parts, Chrysander abandoned the work unfinished after two and a half volumes as the complete edition of Handel's works, known as *Ausgabe der Deutschen Händelgesellschaft* (HG), became his main project (EDITIONS, 5). In 1856 he was one of the founders of the Deutsche Händel-Gesellschaft, whose main purpose was to publish the HG, but by 1860 the directorate of the Gesellschaft disintegrated. More or less working on his own, Chrysander continued the editorial work and travelled to Britain regularly once a year to study Handel sources. Furthermore, he acquired Handel's newly discovered conducting scores from Victor Schoelcher for the Hamburger Stadtbibliothek in 1868, which were of major importance for his work. As supplements to the HG edition, Chrysander added six volumes of sources of Handel's BORROWINGS, thus laying the foundations for future research on this topic. He also published vocal scores, which were of a poorer musicological quality.

After the withdrawal of the HG's publisher Breitkopf & Härtel (Leipzig) from the directorate of the Händelgesellschaft, Chrysander set up a printing workshop in the premises of his own garden in Bergedorf. He employed several engravers and printers over the years. They also produced printing plates for different kinds of music for Schott & Co. in London. To increase his income, Chrysander also ran a gardening business.

During 1869 and the following years Chrysander was one of the main protagonists in a musical feud, which manifested itself in articles often printed in the *Allgemeine Musikalische Zeitung* (a journal edited by Chrysander 1868–71 and 1875–82). Opposing Robert FRANZ and his circle, Chrysander pleaded for a maximum of historical exactness in the editing and performance of Handel's (and other) works (ARRANGEMENTS, 5). Chrysander explored historic musical instruments in order to develop a performing practice for Handel's music. When the conductor Hans von Bülow received a donation of 10,000 Marks in 1890, he gave it to Chrysander, who spent the money on a collection of baroque musical instruments for the Museum für Kunst und Gewerbe in Hamburg.

During the 1890s Chrysander was involved in preparing Handel performances, notably of the *Händelfeste* in Mainz. In addition to making arrangements of numerous works, he also helped to choose the singers. The HG edition was almost complete by the time of Chrysander's death. His son Rudolph (1865–1959), who had been one of Bismarck's personal doctors, continued to publish and sell vocal scores of Handel's works. Rudolph was involved in plans for a Handel and Hasse Festspielhaus at Bergedorf that never came to fruition. JENS WEHMANN

B. Baselt, 'Beiträge zur Chrysander-Forschung I: Friedrich Chrysander und Hans von Bülow – eine Dokumentation', HJb 15/16 (1969/70)

Katalog zu den Sammlungen des Händel-Hauses; 9. Teil: Nachlässe und Teilnachlässe; Band 2: Briefe aus dem Teilnachlass Friedrich Chrysander. ed. G. Traxdorf et al. (Halle, 2001)

A. Landgraf, 'Die Händel-Berarbeitungen Friedrich Chrysanders', HJb 48 (2002)

H. J. Marx, 'Das Händel-Bild Friedrich Chrysanders', HJb 48 (2002)

K. Musketa, 'Friedrich Chrysanders Briefwechsel mit dem Verlagshaus Schott & Co. in London. Dokumente aus dem Chrysander-Nachlass des Händel-Hauses', HJb 48 (2002)

P. v. Reijen, 'Die Händel-Klavierauszüge Friedrich Chrysanders und seiner "Nachfolger"', HJb 48 (2002)

W. Schardig, *Friedrich Chrysander. Leben und Werk* (Hamburg, 1986)

W. R. Vollbach, 'Friedrich Chrysanders Briefe an Fritz Vollbach', *Die Musikforschung* 13 (1960), 143–59, 280–99

church music, English. See ANTHEMS; JUBILATE; TE DEUM

church music, German. Seven sacred cantatas by Handel, presumably composed at HALLE before 1704, are listed in a catalogue that once belonged to Adam Meißner (a former organist of the Ulrichskirche in Halle). The catalogue contains an index of 276 pieces of church music, and Handel's pieces are listed under the heading *Sieben hallesche Kirchenkantaten* (HWV 229$^{1-7}$). None of them has survived. Perhaps they were the results of his early training in composition with Friedrich Wilhelm ZACHOW, specifically in the writing of the older German church cantata on biblical texts. If so, Handel may have used the same scoring (twelve to fifteen vocal and instrumental parts) that is evident in Zachow's surviving pieces dating from 1690 until 1710. WALTER KREYSZIG

B. Baselt, 'Handel and his Central German Background', Handel: Tercentenary Collection, ed.
 S. Sadie and A. Hicks (London, 1987)
HHB ii
W. Serauky, Musikgeschichte der Stadt Halle, vol. 2, 1. Halbband (Halle/Berlin, 1939)

church music, Italian and Latin. Handel composed church music all his life but it seldom took centre stage in his compositional activities. He seems to have composed his first sacred music while studying with Friedrich Wilhelm ZACHOW, organist at the Marktkirche in HALLE, but this early music is entirely lost. Whether Handel wrote any music for the Calvinist-orientated Dom in Halle during his time as organist there in 1702/3 – incidentally the only post as church musician he ever held – is highly doubtful. There is, however, an estate inventory list prepared after the death of Adam Meißner, organist at the Ulrichs-Kirche, which includes seven German-language sacred cantatas attributed to Handel (German CHURCH MUSIC). The majority of Handel's church music was composed for the Anglican liturgy between 1713 and 1751. Dated in between are almost all his Latin and Italian church works, mostly composed during Handel's stay in Italy. As far as quantity goes, they constitute only a small part of the works he composed in Italy but they are nevertheless of great artistic importance if placed within the overall context of his oeuvre.

Handel's first preserved work for the church is *Laudate pueri dominum* (HWV 236), his first setting of Psalm 112. The composition in F major, extant in an autograph version, is scored for solo soprano, two violins and basso continuo. Judging from the evidence of the paper-type and musical style of the piece, it seems that it was probably composed during Handel's time in HAMBURG between 1703 and 1705. The *Laudate pueri dominum* is commonly regarded as the earliest surviving musical autograph by Handel. The occasion for and the circumstances surrounding the composition are unknown; it has been surmised that the work was submitted as part of an application for a so-called 'Organistenprobe', an organists' audition (for example in LÜBECK in August 1703), or that it was intended as a sample of Handel's compositional skills for potential patrons with regard to his planned journey to Italy. Stylistically, the psalm setting with its virtuoso solo soprano part is dependent on the modern Italian *stile concertato*.

Handel's other Latin- and Italian-language church music was for the most part commissional work for particular occasions and festivities in the Roman Catholic liturgy and was composed during his stay in ROME in 1707/8, while he was busy as organist, harpsichordist and composer of cantatas and oratorios. There is music for the Divine Office – that is, the prayers for the Roman Catholic canonical hours – (three psalm settings and three antiphons), devotional music (four motets) and two Marian cantatas.

Probably the first sacred work to have been composed by Handel in Rome is the double-choir psalm setting *Dixit Dominus* (HWV 232, Psalm 109) for two

soprano part at all, instead distributing the vocal parts evenly over the other voice ranges; only the antiphon *Te decus virgineum* calls for a solo contralto voice.

Three of Handel's sacred works were written for his Roman patron Francesco Maria RUSPOLI, for whom he had been composing since May 1707 at the latest. On 30 June 1707, Ruspoli's account books record a payment to the copyist Angelini 'per due Motetti parte con V.V.' and 'per una Salve parte e V.V. e Violone'. This probably refers to the Latin motets *O qualis de coelo sonus* (HWV 239) and *Coelestis dum spirat aura* (HWV 231), both on non-biblical texts, and the Marian antiphon *Salve Regina* (HWV 241); all three compositions have an almost identical scoring: solo soprano, two violins, violoncello and basso continuo. They were composed for performance at Ruspoli's country seat in Vignanello in May/June 1707; the venue was probably the local church of S. Sebastiano. *O qualis de coelo sonus* and *Salve Regina* survive in autograph versions, whereas the autograph of *Coelestis dum spirat aura* is lost. However, the copy in Angelini's handwriting, for which Ruspoli was billed, has been preserved. This copy includes information about when and for what occasion the work was composed, 'In festo S. Antonij de Padua . . . 1707', which probably indicates that *Coelestis dum spirat aura* was performed on 13 June 1707 for the Feast of St Anthony of Padua. Since St Anthony was the patron saint of Vignanello and the year 1707 saw the 475th anniversary of his canonisation, the 1707 feast was lavishly celebrated in S. Sebastiano. The liturgical context of Handel's other compositions can be determined on the basis of the texts that were used: the Whitsuntide motet *O qualis de coelo sonus* was probably performed on 12 June 1707 (Whit Sunday) and the *Salve Regina* on Trinity Sunday (19 June). *Coelestis dum spirat aura* and *O qualis de coelo sonus*, on newly written Latin texts, have similar compositional structures. After a one-movement introductory sonata, the four text sections are set alternately as recitatives and da capo arias and finish with a brilliant Alleluia. The text of *Salve Regina* is divided into four sections as well and, apart from the third section – an aria featuring obbligato organ, resembles a sacred Lamento. The soprano soloist in all of the above works might have been the highly paid Margherita DURASTANTI, who countersigned Angelini's bill for the performing materials.

It was once believed that the autograph of *Ah, che troppo ineguali* (HWV 230) for solo soprano, two violins, viola and basso continuo is a fragment of a larger Marian cantata, but recent research has shown that it is a complete work probably composed for Cardinal Pietro OTTOBONI and perhaps performed in the Palazzo della Cancelleria (PALAZZI, 6) on 17 August 1707; the plea for peace explicitly mentioned in the text might refer to political and military events connected with the War of the SPANISH SUCCESSION, into which the Papal States had entered as allies of the French. In June 1707, imperial troops entered the territories of the Papal States, ransacked the Roman Campagna and marched on to NAPLES, only narrowly missing Rome. In keeping with the subject matter, the cantata is set in the 'French' funeral key of B minor and in the aria ritornello the motivically demanding composition is fraught with endless dissonant sequences.

The large-scale Marian cantata *Donna che in ciel* (HWV 233) for solo soprano, four-part choir, two violins, viola and basso continuo – with a French OVER-TURE and a closing movement in two parts for solo and chorus – has been preserved in a contemporary copy, for the most part in Angelini's handwriting, marked 'Anniversario della Liberatione di Roma dal Terremoto nel giorno della Purif.ᵉ della Beat.ma V.ⁿᵉ'. Handel's cantata was therefore probably composed to commemorate the terrible earthquakes which shook central Italy in the winter of 1702/3; the most serious one on 2 February 1703 cost the lives of many thousands of people in the vicinity of Rome. In gratitude for the fact that the Eternal City itself had been spared, Pope Clement XI ordered annual thanksgiving services to be celebrated on 2 February (incidentally also Candlemas Day) and it is likely that Handel's cantata was performed as part of these festivities. However, again there is no documentation about who commissioned the work and where and when it was first performed.

The lengthy motet *Silete venti* (HWV 242), preserved in an autograph version, for solo soprano, two oboes, bassoon, two violins, viola and basso continuo is generally thought to have been composed in London around 1724, based on the evidence of Handel's handwriting style and the type of paper used. It has a French-style introductory sinfonia and the text alternates between accompanied recitative and aria. The final 'Alleluia' section is a reworking of the conclusion to *Saeviat tellus*, which had probably been composed for Cardinal Carlo Colonna, but there is no evidence to support the theory that *Silete venti* was intended as a gift for the cardinal and presented to him during Handel's visit to Rome in 1729.   RAINER HEYINK (Trans. ANGELA BAIER)

See also *GLORIA IN EXCELSIS DEO*

G. Beeks, 'The Roman Vespers of 1707' (review of music edition), EM 14/2 (May 1986), 277–81
    'Handel's Sacred Music', *The Cambridge Companion to Handel*, ed. D. Burrows (Cambridge, 1997)
D. Burrows, 'The "Carmelite" Antiphons of Handel and Caldara', HJb 46 (2000)
G. Dixon, 'Handel's Vesper Music – Towards a Liturgical Reconstruction', MT 126/1709 (July 1985), 393–7
    'Handel's Music for the Carmelites: A Study in Liturgy and Some Observations on Performance', EM 15/1 (Feb. 1987), 16–29
    'Handel's Music for the Feast of Our Lady of Mount Carmel', *Händel e gli Scarlatti a Roma*, ed. N. Pirrotta and A. Ziino (Florence, 1987)
J. M. Knapp, 'Handel's Roman Church Music', *Händel e gli Scarlatti a Roma*, ed. N. Pirrotta and A. Ziino (Florence, 1987)
H. J. Marx, 'Händels lateinische Kirchenmusik und ihr gattungsgeschichtlicher Kontext', GHB V (1993)
G. Poppe, 'Beobachtungen zum Laudate pueri F-Dur HWV 236 vor dem Hintergrund der Gattungsgeschichte und von Händels Hamburger Situation', HJb 51 (2005)
J. Riepe, 'Kirchenmusik im Rom der Zeit Händels: Institutionen, Auftraggeber, Anlässe. Einige Anmerkungen', HJb 46 (2000)
W. Shaw, 'Handel's Vesper Music – Some MS Sources Rediscovered', MT 126/1709 (July 1985), 392–3
    'Some Original Performing Material for Handel's Latin Church Music', GHB II (1986)

Church of England, The. Both the established religion and the religion of the establishment during the time Handel lived in London. Because it was the Church of the aristocracy and other persons of wealth and influence, it was assured of a certain quality of life, but this came at the price of theological dullness. After the seventeenth-century politico-religious storms, Anglican clergy of the eighteenth century were keen to tread a moderate, uncontroversial path between Calvinism and Catholicism and steer away from high politics. They sought to reconcile reason and religion; they played down dogmatism and matters of ecclesiastical organisation, and emphasised good works as a way to salvation, rather than God's grace. This 'latitudinarianism' ensured the Church's health in the face of DEISM, NONCONFORMITY and atheism, and it permeates Handel's oratorios. Another important aspect of the Church was its employment of ceremonial and liturgical music, which occasioned Handel to write ANTHEMS and TE DEUMS for institutions such as ST PAUL'S CATHEDRAL, WESTMINSTER ABBEY, and the CHAPEL ROYAL. KATIE HAWKS

See also HANDEL, 12

Smith, *Oratorios*
G. R. Cragg, *The Church and the Age of Reason (1648–1789)* (London, 1960)
F. L. Cross (ed.), *The Oxford Dictionary of the Christian Church* (Oxford, 1958)

Cibber, Colley (b. London, 6 Nov. 1671; d. London, 11 Dec. 1757). Actor, manager and playwright. Interested in the theatre from an early age, Cibber made his debut as an actor at DRURY LANE in September 1690. His breakthrough came when he stepped in for Edward Kynaston at short notice in a performance of CONGREVE's *The Double Dealer* in 1694. Two years later he took to writing plays himself, with only moderate success. In 1730 Cibber was made Poet Laureate to GEORGE II. His son Theophilus (1703–58) married Susannah Maria Arne in 1734. EVA ZÖLLNER

Cibber, Susannah Maria, née Arne (bap. London, 28 Feb. 1714; d. London, 30 Jan. 1766). Actress and contralto, sister of Thomas Augustine ARNE. First taught by her brother Thomas, Susannah Arne made her debut as a singer in John Frederick LAMPE's *Amelia* (1732) to great acclaim. On 17 May of that year she also appeared in a pirated performance of Handel's *ACIS AND GALATEA*, organised by her father and brother. In 1733 she joined Theophilus Cibber's group of players at the LITTLE THEATRE in the Haymarket, and subsequently at DRURY LANE, where she was active as a singer and a dramatic actress. She became one of the most famous tragediennes of her day. In 1734 she married Theophilus Cibber (son of Colley CIBBER) but the marriage was not a success, ending in a much publicised scandal in 1738, with her husband suing her for adultery. However, it was revealed that Cibber himself had persuaded his wife to enter a relationship with his friend, a William Sloper, having the couple followed and observed afterwards in order to collect evidence against her. The court cases (Cibber sued his wife again in 1739) attracted unwelcome publicity, and Susannah went to live with Sloper and temporarily retired from the stage. By late 1741, the scandal forgotten, she went to DUBLIN, appearing there as an actress at the Aungier Street Theatre. She sang in Handel's Dublin concert series, including 'He was despised' in the first performances of *MESSIAH*. Back in London, she sang for Handel for two further seasons in 1742–3 and 1744–5, also successfully re-establishing her career as an actress there. She did not have a sustained working relationship with the composer, and there is no record of any particular close friendship between them, but he created prominent roles for her in *SAMSON* (Micah), *HERCULES* (Lichas) and *BELSHAZZAR* (Cyrus), and made substantial revisions to accommodate her as Jael in the November 1744 revivals of *DEBORAH*. EVA ZÖLLNER

Civitavecchia. See ROME; Francesco Maria RUSPOLI

Clari, Abate Giovanni Carlo Maria (b. Pisa, 27 Sept. 1677; d. Pisa, 16 May 1754). Italian composer. From 1691 to 1695 he studied in Bologna with Giovanni Paolo Colonna (1637–95). Clari was *maestro di cappella* in Pistoia (1703–24) and Pisa, and in 1697 he was elected as a member of the Accademia Filarmonica. He composed two operas, Il *savio delirante* (Bologna, 1695) and Il *principe corsaro* (Florence, 1717), twelve oratorios, church music and chamber music. Handel's THEODORA features numerous BORROWINGS from Clari's chamber duets (published Bologna, 1720): the Allegro in the overture (*Quando col mio s'incontra*), Septimius's air 'Descend, kind Pity' (*Quando tramonta il sole*), the duet 'To thee, thou glorious son of worth' (*Dov'è quell'usignolo*), and the choruses 'Come, mighty Father' (*Cantando un dì*), 'Blest be the hand' (*Cantando un dì* and *Fuoco è la chioma bionda*) and, 'How strange their ends' (*Lontan dalla sua Fille*). CHRYSANDER published Clari's *Duetti e terzetti da camera* as Supplement 4 to HG.

ANNETTE LANDGRAF

Clarinet. See INSTRUMENTATION

Clavecin. See INSTRUMENTATION; KEYBOARD MUSIC

Clerici, Roberto (b. ?Parma; fl. 1711–48, Vienna, Venice, Naples, London, Portugal, Paris and Parma). Theatre painter and machinist. Clerici was probably born in Parma and is documented as having worked in Vienna (1711), VENICE and NAPLES (1712–16) and London (1716–19), later also in Portugal (1735–8), Paris and Parma (1739–48). He caused a sensation with his perspective view of a royal palace, reportedly measuring more than 1,000 yards, for one of the London performances of Alessandro SCARLATTI's opera *Pirro e Demetrio* at the KING'S THEATRE in 1716. The same stage scenery was used a year later for the pasticcio *Clearte*. In 1719 an obviously different theatre painting by Clerici, exceeding the former one by 30 feet – depicting triumphal scenes – was used for a concert in the King's Theatre. According to the printed libretto, he also designed the production of Giovanni PORTA's opera *Il Numitore*, which opened the first season of the Royal Academy of Music (OPERA COMPANIES, 2) in 1720. At that time Clerici could also have been responsible for designing the stage scenery of some of Handel's operas.

KLAUS-PETER KOCH (Trans. ANGELA BAIER)

Deutsch
J. Eisenschmidt, *Die szenische Darstellung der Opern Georg Friedrich Händels auf der Londoner Bühne seiner Zeit* (Wolfenbüttel, 1940) (new edn by H. J. Marx (Laaber, 1987)) (British Library, Add. MS 322249)
HHB iv

Clive, Catherine ('Kitty') (b. London, 15 Nov. 1711; d. Twickenham, 6 Dec. 1785). English soprano (g–b‴), comedienne and occasional author. She studied singing with Henry CAREY, who composed and wrote plays for her. She rose to success in BALLAD OPERA, establishing DRURY LANE as the home of the genre. Her early repertory also included high-style music such as airs by Handel, and from 1732 her appearances in vehicles by Henry Fielding helped establish her as a top-ranking comedienne. Handel composed theatre SONGS for her in The *Universal Passion* – adapted 1737 from Shakespeare by Handel's later librettist

James MILLER – and CONGREVE's *The Way of the World* (1740). She replaced an indisposed singer in Handel's first run of *L'ALLEGRO, IL PENSEROSO, ED IL MODERATO* (1740), and sang in a performance of *ALEXANDER'S FEAST* at Drury Lane (1742). In 1743 she sang Dalila in the first run of *SAMSON* and a brief arioso section ('But lo') after the pastoral symphony in the London premiere of the *MESSIAH*. Following a falling out with John RICH in 1744–5, Clive never again appeared at COVENT GARDEN. Her largest oil portrait (1740) attests to her reputation as a leading Handel interpreter; in the painting she holds 'Sweet Bird' from *L'Allegro*. Clive's own *The Rehearsal, or Bayes in Petticoats* (1753), one of three benefit farces she wrote for herself, featured an early burletta by William BOYCE and her perennially popular 'taking off' of Italian prima donnas. BERTA JONCUS

B. Joncus, 'Handel at Drury Lane: Ballad Opera and the Production of Kitty Clive', JRMA 131 (2006), 179–226

Kitty Clive, Goddess of Mirth: Creating a Star through Song (1728–1765) (forthcoming)

Clori, mia bella Clori, HWV 92. An accompanied cantata for soprano, violins and basso continuo, *Clori, mia bella Clori* was composed in ROME, probably for RUSPOLI. A bill for copying a 'Cantata à voce sola con VV' that appears in the Ruspoli account books on 28 August 1708 might refer to this work (its former association with *AH! CRUDEL* is unlikely given that cantata's larger accompanimental forces). In the anonymous text covering four recitative–aria pairs, the lover at first bemoans his separation from Clori, but then worries about her fidelity; the cantata ends in a burst of jealous passion. ELLEN T. HARRIS

'Clori, Tirsi e Fileno'. See *COR FEDELE, IN VANO SPERI*

Cluer, John (b. London, late seventeenth century; d. London, Oct. 1728). Music publisher and printer. In his 'Printing Office' in Bow Church Yard, London, Cluer printed and sold music scores and books, often in association with Bezaleel Creake, and dealt in medicines. Cluer printed the first volume of the *Suites de Pièces pour le Clavecin* (1720) for Handel, which was sold by Richard MEARES and John Christopher SMITH SENIOR. In 1724 he produced a small-size full score of *GIULIO CESARE*. Until 1728 Cluer printed seven more Handel operas, whereas Handel's other music was done by Walsh. After Cluer's death, his widow Elizabeth continued the business together with his foreman Thomas Cobb, whom she married. In 1730 they published *LOTARIO*. JENS WEHMANN

D. Flower, 'Handel's Publishers', English Review 62 (1936), 66–75

Hawkins

C. Humphries and W. C. Smith, *Music Publishing in the British Isles from the Earliest Times to the Middle of the Nineteenth Century: A Dictionary of Engravers, Printers, Publishers and Music Sellers, with a Historical Introduction* (London, 1954)

F. Kidson, *British Music Publishers, Printers and Engravers* (London, 1900)

'Handel's Publisher, John Walsh, his Successors and Contemporaries', MQ 6/3 (1920), 430–50

W. C. Smith with C. Humphries, *Handel: A Descriptive Catalogue of Early Editions* (London, 1960)

Coelestis dum spirat aura. See Italian and Latin CHURCH MUSIC

Coke, Gerald (b. London, 25 Oct. 1907; d. Bentley, Hants., 9 Jan. 1990). Gerald Coke described himself as 'a willing victim of the collecting bug'. He amassed a major collection of Handel material during the greater part of the twentieth century, as well as a significant collection of porcelain. The Gerald Coke Handel Collection (SOURCES AND COLLECTIONS, 7) includes manuscripts and printed scores, books, art works and ephemera, reflecting Coke's interests in all aspects of Handel. His network of friends among music libraries and dealers allowed him to create a collection remarkable for its depth in the number of variant publications collected, as well for its breadth in encompassing items as varied as commemorative medals, a tobacco jar and a musical box, as well as the scholarly resources which form the core of the collection. Coke married Patricia Cadogan in 1939 and used success in his business career to support their joint contributions to music and gardening; an avid encourager and enabler of the arts, he supported excellence amongst professional performers as well as encouragement for aspiring musicians. He was a founder of the Glyndebourne Arts Trust, and a director of the Royal Opera House and the Royal Academy of Music. His collection was enthusiastically shared with scholars at his home in Hampshire, and it is currently accessible to the public at the FOUNDLING MUSEUM.

KATHARINE HOGG

collections. See SOURCES AND COLLECTIONS

Colman, Francis (d. Pisa, 20 April 1733). A manuscript 'Opera Register from 1712 to 1734' now at the British Library (Add. MS 11258) is attributed to Colman. Since the register continues into a period when he was in Italy, he is likely not to be the compiler of the register. The register, often our only source of documentation about certain opera productions, records the titles, dates of performance and singers of operas performed in London, beginning with Il PASTOR FIDO (26 November 1712) and concluding with PORPORA's Enea nel Lazio (11 May 1734). Interspersed are comments about the theatres, sets and costumes, singers, ticket prices, subscriptions, attendance and reception of the operas.

THOMAS N. MCGEARY

K. Sasse, 'Opera Register from 1712 to 1734 (Colman-Register)', HJb 5 (1959)

Colonna, Carlo (b. Rome, 17 Nov. 1665; d. Rome, 8 July 1739). Italian Cardinal and patron. He was born into one of ROME's most important aristocratic families. The Roman Palazzo Colonna on Piazza SS Apostoli had its own theatre at least since the 1680s, where operas by Bernardo Pasquini, among others, were performed. From 1692 Giovanni BONONCINI, later Handel's colleague and 'rival' in London, was for a few years in the service of Connestabile Filippo Colonna, the Cardinal's brother. As dedicatee or commissioner of music, Cardinal Colonna was linked to musicians such as Arcangelo CORELLI, Alessandro and Domenico SCARLATTI, and Antonio CALDARA; in 1727 he recommended the young FARINELLI to Bologna. As papal maggiordomo the Cardinal was responsible for the performance of the annual Christmas cantata in the Palazzo Apostolico from 1696. At least since 1699 Colonna celebrated the annual feast of the Madonna del Carmine in the Roman church of S. Maria di Monte Santo by providing festive music for the first and second vespers and for mass (CARMELITE ORDER). Handel composed some of his vesper music for this festival, either in 1707 (when it is documented that he directed the music for first Vespers on 15 July) or in 1708: the antiphons Haec Est Regina and

Te Decus Virgineum, the motet *Saeviat Tellus* and maybe *Laudate Pueri* (HWV 237) and *Nisi Dominus* (Italian and Latin CHURCH MUSIC). In the summer of 1707 Handel performed in Colonna's house on a number of occasions. According to MAINWARING, Handel was invited by Colonna again when he stayed in Rome in 1729 but declined because the 'Pretender' to the British throne (JACOBITES) was present. JULIANE RIEPE (Trans. ANGELA BAIER)

H. J. Marx, 'Händels lateinische Kirchenmusik und ihr gattungsgeschichtlicher Kontext', GHB V (1993)

Commemoration of Handel. See HANDEL COMMEMORATION

compositional processes. The compositional process through which a musical work is developed out of sketches, fragments and drafts into a musical event or into the last version of the score sanctioned by the composer is a fascinating subject, but also one that can never be entirely or precisely grasped. In the case of Handel, the extant performing scores document his later revisions to his dramatic works fairly well, whereas there is relatively little evidence about the early compositional stages, in particular about early sketches. Most of Handel's compositions have been handed down to the present only in the form of the finished score. It is not even known whether the pre-compositional collecting of musical ideas took place mainly in Handel's mind, on the keyboard or with the help of sketches jotted down on music paper. Sometimes there are records of a starting point and/or an intermediary stage in the compositional process: there might be a model, either by Handel himself or by someone else, a sketched motif or an autograph passage showing cuts or revisions. These materials present the most important sources for understanding Handel's compositional method. But the insights gained from the study of them cannot be applied to the great majority of his works for which no such sources are extant. On the contrary, it should rather be assumed that the works for which records of the compositional process are extant – such works constituting only a small part of Handel's output – are exceptional in that they perhaps presented difficulties while being composed and had an atypical compositional course.

As is perhaps to be expected, least is known about the phase in the creative process which begins before anything is fixed in written form, that is, with the first idea, the 'inspiration'. On the basis of letters by Handel's contemporaries it can be assumed that he was inspired by dramatic situations (report about a reading of MILTON's *Samson Agonistes*; Burrows and Dunhill, p. 80). Also, the rhythm and sound of certain initial text lines seem to have triggered an immediate creative impulse within him (report of the librettist Thomas MORELL about a meeting with Handel; Deutsch, p. 851). The creative seed sown in situations like these probably fell on fertile ground: Because of Handel's custom of including dates in his autographs, the time which he needed to write down an opera or an oratorio can be estimated at an average of about one month. It is assumed that he was only able to write down his larger scores in such a short space of time because he had spent the preceding rehearsal- and performance-free months collecting and improvising on a stock of his own and of borrowed themes and motifs at the keyboard. This primary supply of musical ideas was still malleable and could be adapted to different dramatic requirements if a specific commission or text arrived. The particulars of these collecting phases and the way the collected ideas were moulded into their final form and destination cannot be reconstructed today.

However, if there are sketches extant or if a musical idea remained a fragment because the composer discarded it and began anew, it is possible to draw conclusions about the compositional process by comparison with the finished score. The same is possible by consulting Handel's many corrections in his autographs. Most alterations are in the form of cuts or additions, of changes in the melody (especially in the vocal lines), of the strengthening or weakening of cadenzas, of changes in the rhythmic structure and of metrical reorganisation. Most changes affect more than one of these parameters. Various reasons for these changes can be identified: a work might be too long for performance, dramaturgy might require adjustments, performance conditions might change (especially singers might require changes in their parts), the balance between the various parts of a musical setting might need to be refined (for example, concerning length, musical key, distribution of strong and weak cadenzas, addition or reduction of overlappings, melodic diversity, predictability, symmetry or word-setting). Again, more than one reason might apply in any given case so that the identification of the decisive reason for an alteration in the musical material is often difficult.

Cuts in the autographs sometimes allow us to draw conclusions about Handel's first phase of writing a score, the draft phase. It is generally known that in his draft scores Handel did not yet notate all the parts but left room so that he could complete them later on. In so doing he did not need to write a new score in his second phase but could instead 'fill up' the draft score. What a draft score originally looked like is therefore only discernible in the parts which were cut after the first phase and therefore not filled up. What is interesting about these drafts is that they allow a glimpse into Handel's compositional process, namely which parts of the composition he immediately wrote down in fixed form and which parts he left for the second phase. As a rule, he first notated at least the basso continuo (with numbers if he did not want to forget a particular harmonic turn) and a vocal or instrumental melody. Replacing the continuo or in addition to it, in bass arias or choral settings he sometimes notated the vocal bass line as well, presumably because he wanted to fix the distribution of the text right away. In polyphonic choral settings, all vocal parts are sometimes notated into the draft score, also an instrumental melody in cases where musical motifs overlap between voices and instruments. If he notated more than two upper parts immediately, the instrumentation presumably seemed especially important to him. This method of organising the compositional process apparently helped him to write as fast as possible while at the same time guaranteeing that a maximum number of musical ideas was safe from being forgotten somewhere along the way.

Abraham is of the opinion that the starting point for Handel's compositions lies in the composer's abilities in the field of improvisation, as attested by many of his contemporaries. In the pre-compositional phase, that is, in the phase where a stock of musical material was collected, the variations and combinations explored in improvisation were probably very important for Handel.

However, Abraham conveys the impression that the actual compositional pro-cess was a spontaneous act of creation with little or no preconceived ideas about structure ('ex improviso'). This assumption can safely be discarded simply by looking at some of Handel's aria ritornellos, which include motifs that only become important in the aria's later progression. Such ritornellos ('synopsis ritornellos') and their variations were studied in detail by Brainard, who com-pared Handel's and Johann Sebastian BACH's compositional methods and came to the conclusion that Handel's musical language was characterised by 'its high degree of segmentation, the discrete nature of its individual phrases being so pronounced as to permit, on occasion, a reshuffling of the very order in which they are presented'.

Diligent in his methodology and circumspect in his conclusions, Hurley studied Handel's compositional method by looking at revisions in some of the oratorios. He was able to show the diversity of the techniques and revisional methods employed by Handel (often for the sake of increasing the dramatic impact). However, there are some generalising conclusions, again drawn by comparing Handel to Bach: Handel's method of composing is described as paratactic (*Handel's Muse*, p. 145, *passim*) and Bach's as hypotactic; Handel is said to compose in 'short, discrete, autonomous units' (*Handel's Muse*, p. 279) which are combined in an 'additive' fashion. Hurley regards Handel's revisions as attempts to conceal this structure by 'hiding the seams or rendering a paratactic surface more hypotactic' (*Handel's Muse*, p. 146).

For further scholarship in this field metaphorical terms like 'additive', 'parat-actic' or 'surface' will only be of use if they can be defined in relation to music so that their application to musical facts gains a precise significance. In the present use of these terms their interpretational value seems limited and cannot adequately describe the techniques employed by Handel in rendering his musi-cal language flexible. It remains a desideratum to study the repercussions of his interventions on the entire organism of a musical setting and to evaluate their share in the uniqueness of Handel's musical language.

HANS DIETER CLAUSEN (Trans. ANGELA BAIER)

G. Abraham, 'Some Points of Style', *Handel: A Symposium* (London, 1954)
P. Brainard, 'Aria and Ritornello: New Aspects of the Comparison Handel/Bach', *Bach, Handel, Scarlatti: Tercentenary Essays* (Cambridge, 1985)
D. R. Hurley, *Handel's Muse: Patterns of Creation in his Oratorios and Musical Dramas, 1743–1751* (Oxford, 2001)
C. S. LaRue, 'Metric Reorganisation as an Aspect of Handel's Compositional Process', *Journal of Musicology* 8 (1990), 477–90

Comus, HWV 44. John MILTON's *Maske presented at Ludlow Castle*, written for the Earl of Bridgewater in 1634 and published in 1637, became popular under the title *Comus* when adapted for the London stage by John Dalton and Thomas Arne in 1738. The story tells of a young lady getting lost in the woods and meeting the magician Comus, son of Bacchus and Circe. Comus and his followers try to seduce the virgin with all possible forms of sensual pleasure. She remains firm and is liberated by her two brothers under the guidance of an Attendant Spirit, with final assistance from the river goddess Sabrina. Handel wrote new music – three arias and a repeated chorus for two sopranos, a bass, two-part violins, two oboes and basso continuo – for another adaptation of the masque, created for his friend the Earl of GAINSBOROUGH and performed privately in the composer's presence at the Earl's country seat in Exton, Rutland, in June 1745. Several pieces of music by Handel were included, and the newly composed sequence, headed 'Serenata a 9' and 'Serenata' in the two manuscript copies that survive (the autograph may have been lost in the fire that destroyed Exton Hall in 1810), ended the work. Lord Gainsborough himself played Comus and sang Handel's new music with his two daughters, who also appeared as Sabrina and the Attendant Spirit; his son was one of the Bacchantes. The text set by Handel is adapted from the final speech of the Attendant Spirit in the original masque (lines 984–1011), describing the heavenly realms, blessed by perpetual summer, to which he will return. The chorus 'Happy plains' is repeated after each of the three arias, so that the whole sequence forms an independent little cantata, distinct from the rest of the masque. The arias themselves are short and simple, out of consideration for the amateur performers, but delicately characterised; the chorus, set predominantly in homophonic fashion, is lightened up by a few moderately contrapuntal sections. The style of the entire Serenata, not least the choir's repetitious 'Happy, happy', is reminiscent of ACIS AND GALATEA. Within a year Handel had reworked the music of all four of the Comus numbers in his OCCASIONAL ORATORIO, performed in February 1746, with some loss of its original delicacy.   CHRISTINE MARTIN (Trans. ANGELA BAIER)

B. Matthews, 'Unpublished Letters Concerning Handel', MT 40 (1959), 261–8 (see also
       406–7, letter from W. Dean)
HHB i
A. Hicks, 'Handel's Music for Comus', MT 117 (1976), 28–9
       'The Shaftesbury Collection', Handel Collections and their History, ed. T. Best (Oxford, 1993)
C. Timms and A. Hicks (eds.), Music for Comus (London, 1977)
F. B. Zimmerman, 'G. F. Händels neu entdeckte Musik aus "Comus"', HJb 20 (1974)
       (ed.), Serenata: There in blissful shades (Musica Da Camera no. 58; London, c.1982)

concerti a due cori, concerti grossi and concertos. See ORCHESTRAL WORKS

Congreve, William (b. Bardsey Grange, Yorkshire, Jan. 1670; d. London, 19 Jan. 1729). English author, poet and playwright of four comedies, The Old Batchelour (1693?), The Double Dealer (1693), Love for Love (1694) and The Way of the World (1698), one tragedy, The Mourning Bride (1697) and many poems and translations.

Congreve had a lifelong interest in music. Henry PURCELL set the songs in The Old Batchelour, and Congreve later worked closely with John ECCLES, who wrote music for all of his other plays, and for whom he wrote the text of Hymn to Harmony. Active in promoting English-language opera, he wrote the libretto of Judgment of Paris for a 'prize' competition in 1701, and collaborated with VANBRUGH in founding the QUEEN'S THEATRE, Haymarket, for which he and Eccles wrote Semele c.1705–6. Thereafter he retired from the stage, but lived long enough to see Handel and Italian opera dominate musical taste in London. He was buried in Poets' Corner at WESTMINSTER ABBEY, close to where Handel was later interred.

The moral laxity of Congreve's plays was sharply criticised by Jeremy Collier in A Short View of the Immorality and Profaneness of the English Stage (1698), and Handel's decision to set SEMELE to music nearly half a century later met with similar disapproval from Charles JENNENS. Handel's song 'Love's but the frailty of the mind' (HWV 218) was sung by Kitty CLIVE at a revival of Congreve's *The Way of the World* at DRURY LANE on 17 March 1740.   JOHN K. ANDREWS

W. Congreve, *The Complete Works of William Congreve*, ed. M. Summers (London, 1923)
J. Eccles, *Semele: An Opera*, ed. R. Platt (London, 2000)

Conradi(ne), Madame (b. Dresden, c.1680; d. after 1719). German soprano. Daughter of a Dresden barber, by 1700 she was employed as a singer at the GÄNSEMARKT in HAMBURG. Handel might have composed the title role in ALMIRA for her. Johann Gottfried Walther praised her as 'not only a virtuoso singer but also a magnificent actress'. Johann MATTHESON stated that she 'possessed an almost complete personal beauty and in addition also an exceptionally beautiful voice, which extended uniformly strong from a to d'''. This made her the most outstanding singer.' Mattheson also claimed that he 'sang everything to her each day until she could retain . . . [the melody] in her memory', which suggests that perhaps she was unable to read music and thus depended on memorisation. She retired from the stage in 1709, and two years later married Count Gruzewska.   WALTER KREYSZIG

F. Chrysander, *G. F. Händel*, 3 vols. (Leipzig, 1858–67)
Mainwaring
J. Walther, *Musikalisches Lexikon oder musikalische Bibliothek* (Leipzig, 1732)

Conti, Francesco Bartolomeo (b. Florence, 20 Jan. 1682; d. Vienna, 20 July 1732). Italian composer and theorbo player. He was initially in the service of the Prince-Cardinal Francesco Maria de' Medici. In March 1701 he went to the Habsburg court in Vienna as deputy theorbo player; he was later promoted to the rank of first instrumentalist (1708) and to that of court composer (1713). As a virtuoso on the theorbo and the mandolin, Conti was acclaimed also in London, where in 1707 he played for Queen ANNE. In the prevailing musical conservatism in the court of the Emperor Charles VI, and in direct contact with Johann Joseph Fux and Antonio CALDARA, he was significant also as a composer of operas, intermezzos, cantatas, oratorios and dance music, following the Roman and Neapolitan stylistic model of the early 1700s. As well as in Vienna, his operas were produced in HAMBURG, BRUNSWICK, Bratislava, Copenhagen and DRESDEN: his stage masterpiece, *Don Chisciotte in Sierra Morena*, had performances between 1719 and 1738. He worked with librettists such as Silvio STAMPIGLIA, Pietro PARIATI, Apostolo ZENO and Pietro METASTASIO, and with scene designers such as Ferdinando, Giuseppe and Antonio Galli-Bibiena. The parts of his oratorios (for example those of *Dio sul Sinai*, 1719) end with fugal choruses which set them apart from the Italian tradition of madrigals or monorhythmic ensembles, and anticipate the English practice adopted by Handel. Handel included music by Conti in his pasticcio ORMISDA.

FRANCESCO LORA (Trans. TERENCE BEST)

H. W. Williams, *Francesco Bartolomeo Conti: His Life and Music* (Aldershot, 1999)

Conti, Gioacchino ('Gizziello') (b. Arpino, 27 Feb. 1714; d. Rome, 25 or 26 Oct. 1761). Italian castrato. The son of the tanner Marcantonio Conti, he derived his nickname from Domenico Gizzi, his singing teacher and benefactor. According to later accounts, he had a triumph in ROME in Leonardo VINCI's *Artaserse*, in the role of Arbace composed for Giovanni CARESTINI (1730); but it is more likely that his first success was in NAPLES in Giovanni Battista Pergolesi's *Salustia*, in which he replaced NICOLINI, and in Mancini's *Alessandro nelle Indie* (1732). Until 1735 he performed in Naples, Vienna, VENICE and Genoa, in operas and oratorios by Leonardo LEO, Nicola PORPORA, Giuseppe Di Majo, Johann Adolf HASSE, Francesco Araja, Antonio CALDARA, Pietro Vincenzo Ciocchetti and Gaetano Maria Schiassi. Engaged by Handel for LONDON in 1736, his first appearance was in a revival of *ARIODANTE* at COVENT GARDEN (although with an unusual agreement by Handel he substituted all the original arias by others from his own Italian repertory). A week later, he created the part of Meleagro in *ATALANTA*. In the next season he sang in the new operas *ARMINIO* (as Sigismondo), *GIUSTINO* (Anastasio), *BERENICE* (Alessandro) and took part – with new or adapted arias – in the revivals of *ALCINA* (Ruggiero), *PARTENOPE* (Ormindo) and *PORO* (Alessandro), as well as the oratorio *ESTHER* (with Italian arias prepared two years earlier for Carestini), and in the pasticcio *DIDONE ABBANDONATA*. Going back to Italy, he perfected his technique at BERNACCHI's academy, and from 1738 to 1752 he returned to the stage in ROME, Turin, Padua, Siena, FLORENCE, Fano, Venice, Parma, Lucca, Reggio, Milan and especially Naples (1746–8), in operas by Giuseppe Arena, Nicola Bonifacio Logroscino, Leo, Giovanni Battista Lampugnani, Baldassare GALUPPI, Andrea Bernasconi, Pergolesi, Giuseppe Sellitti, Giuseppe Scarlatti, Nicola Conti (no relation), Rinaldo da Capua, Matteo Capranica, Niccolò Jommelli, Egidio Romualdo Duni, Hasse, Giovanni Battista Pescetti, Di Majo, Gaetano Latilla, Girolamo Abos, Antonio Caputi, Gioacchino Cocchi, Antonio Gaetano Pampani. Subsequently he worked at the courts of Lisbon (1752–5: operas by David Perez and Antonio Mazzoni) and Madrid (1756: cantatas by Nicola Conforto and FARINELLI). A singer skilled in the pathetic and graceful (unlike his rival CAFFARELLI), and personally courteous and modest, Conti had also an exceptionally flexible voice with a wide range: the arias composed for him reach the highest notes – c''' and c♯''' – ever written by Handel for a castrato.   FRANCESCO LORA (Trans. TERENCE BEST)

V. Fucci, 'Gioacchino Conti detto Gizziello, *musico* del secolo XVIII', Ph.D. dissertation (University of Bologna, 2006)

continuo. See INSTRUMENTATION

Cooper, Anthony Ashley. See 4th Earl of SHAFTESBURY

copyists. Before the recent developments of computer setting and the photocopier, musical performance relied crucially on the hand-copying of scores and performing parts. Like many composers, and especially those working in the theatre, Handel passed his autograph scores to copyists, sometimes even before the complete work had been drafted, so that fair copies could be made, partly for practical use in the production of part-books for players and singers and partly to ensure the secure preservation of the contents. Copyists were then further employed in the maintenance of running revisions to scores and parts as they were modified for the initial performances and subsequent revivals. The patchwork appearance of the performing scores for many of Handel's works, with deletions, insertions and revisions, is eloquent testimony to the composer's reliance on an industrial organisation of supporting scribes. Although few of the original performers' parts survive, it seems that Handel was sufficiently well-off to delegate such work, in contrast to the situation found, for example, with the court odes of William BOYCE, where the composer had to undertake a proportion of the labour himself. Copyists were of further significance for their role in producing archive copies for patrons who had commissioned the music (as in the case of the Italian cantatas for RUSPOLI), or for supporters in England who wanted complete scores of operas, oratorios and other works for their libraries. (The early published editions of Handel's music mainly served a market that required anthologies of individual arias and sets of parts for instrumental works, rather than complete scores.)

There is little direct documentation of Handel's working relationship with his copyists, but much can be inferred, particularly about the activity in London, from the manuscripts themselves; it is, however, sometimes difficult to judge the nature of the relationship with the composer that a particular copy represents. Handel's corrections or interventions in manuscript copies from his Italian years indicate associations with the copyists Antonio ANGELINI, Alessandro Ginelli and Francesco LANCIANI in ROME; there is little comparable evidence relating to his work in HAMBURG, HANOVER or indeed the other Italian cities. The various phases of Handel's London career have left a rather bewildering variety of manuscript copies to be considered, but it seems probable that the most authoritative material is best understood in terms of a circle of copyists managed for the composer in his early London years by D. LICNIKE (forename unidentified) and then, from the beginning of the Royal Academy period, by John Christopher SMITH SENIOR). While the processes for the generation of performing scores and part-books can be inferred from the needs of Handel's successive theatre seasons, the relationship between this activity and the production of 'library scores' from the same team of scribes is more difficult to determine. It may be no coincidence that Elizabeth LEGH's series of manuscripts (now the Malmesbury Collection) began at a rather slack time in the Haymarket operas, and that major work on the volumes of the Granville and Lennard collections took place as Handel's performances were moving towards shorter oratorio-based seasons (SOURCES AND COLLECTIONS).

The identification of copyists' hands is a hazardous matter, and many casual misattributions have occurred in descriptions of manuscripts of Handel's music. The foundation of modern scholarship on the Handel copyists is the review of sources that was included in Jens Peter Larsen's book on *Messiah*; this built on techniques that were currently being developed by scholars working on the music of J. S. BACH. From the performing scores now in Hamburg, the manuscripts of the Granville, Lennard and Smith collections in England, and a number of other early copies, Larsen identified the handwriting of the principal copyists from the 'Smith scriptorium', allocating a series of 'S' codes (S1, S2 etc.). It is unlikely that many of the copyists, even the most prolific, will ever be identified by name; it has been suggested that two of them might have been Smith's daughters, but it seems more probable that the major copyists were underemployed musical performers. (Linicke was an orchestral viola player, as was possibly Smith himself, and Larsen's 'S6' was the oboe player William

Teede.) Larsen's initial classification has been refined and modified by other studies, including those by Hans Dieter Clausen on the performing scores and by Winton Dean on the early London copyists. Also, research on watermarks and rastra in music manuscripts has enabled more precise dates of origin to be ascertained, with the opportunity of identifying sequences of changes in the handwriting of long-serving copyists; the 'Handel copyists' also need to be related to wider contexts of music copying in eighteenth-century Italy and England. Better understanding of copyists' activities relies on systematic and comprehensive reference to a sprawling mass of eighteenth-century musical sources; in practice, it is difficult to resolve this ideal with the immediate need to interpret a particular manuscript or a particular work of Handel's.

DONALD BURROWS

H. D. Clausen, *Händels Direktionspartituren (Handexemplare)* (Hamburg, 1972).
W. Dean, 'Handel's Early London Copyists', *Essays on Opera* (Oxford, 1990)
J. P. Larsen, *Handel's Messiah: Origins, Composition, Sources* (London, 1957)
K. Watanabe, 'The Music-Paper Used by Handel and his Copyists in Italy 1706–1710', *Handel Collections and their History*, ed. T. Best (Oxford, 1993)
K. Watanabe and H. J. Marx, 'Händels italienische Kopisten', *GHB* III (1989)

copyright. England's first copyright law, the Statute of Queen ANNE of 1710, granted to 'the Author of any Book or Books . . . and his Assignee or Assigns' the exclusive right to print copyrighted books for a renewable term of fourteen years. The Act was crafted chiefly to protect the financial interests of booksellers (i.e. publishers) against unauthorised editions. Its relevance to music and music publishing was initially unclear. The first known lawsuit concerning music and copyright was filed in 1741, when Thomas ARNE unsuccessfully claimed that two LONDON printers had illegally published some of his works. In 1777, however, J. C. Bach prevailed in a similar dispute, when the court held that published music could be copyrighted. Before then, royal patents served the function of copyrights for music, prohibiting reproduction of scores without authorisation. Three such royal privileges for the exclusive publication of Handel's music were issued: in 1720 to Handel, and in 1739 and 1760 to John WALSH, Handel's publisher.

The legal issue in both the Arne and Bach lawsuits, as well as that behind the protection afforded by royal patents, concerned the right to publish and derive income from publication. The use of pre-existent material in the creation of new works, such as Handel's BORROWING, was not an issue of copyright law in the eighteenth century. Likewise, the performance of musical compositions was not subject to copyright protection. Indeed, composers were occasionally forced to compete against their own works, as in 1732 when Handel revived *ACIS AND GALATEA* to compete with a version mounted by Arne. Only later did the concept of copyright expand to protect not just the publication of musical composition, but also the use and performance of musical ideas.

JOHN T. WINEMILLER

D. Hunter, 'Music Copyright in Britain to 1800', *ML* 67/3 (July 1986), 269–82
R. J. Rabin and S. Zohn, 'Arne, Handel, Walsh, and Music as Intellectual Property: Two Eighteenth-Century Lawsuits', *JRMA* 120 (1995), 112–45

Cor fedele, in vano speri ('Clori, Tirsi, e Fileno'), HWV 96 This cantata in two parts was copied for RUSPOLI on 14 October 1707, thus probably premiered shortly before the composer's departure to FLORENCE for staging *RODRIGO*. As to dramatic form, it draws from 'egloga rappresentativa', a Renaissance genre typically staged or semi-staged, while the musical setting hints at a serenata. For subject matter, style and versification, characters and their names, it appears to be the sequel to a pair of serenatas by Silvio STAMPIGLIA (libretto) and Giovanni BONONCINI (music): *La nemica d'Amore* (1692) and *La nemica d'Amore fatta amante* (1693), both lavishly performed with large attendance in the courtyard of Palazzo Colonna, ROME, on commission of Prince Filippo, the elder brother of Cardinal Carlo COLONNA. Although by 1707 Stampiglia lived in Vienna in the Emperor's service, on stylistic grounds the libretto of *Cor fedele* may be attributed to him (or a competent follower).

Shepherds Tirsi (soprano) and Fileno (alto) compete for the love of Clori, a shepherdess (soprano). Though in principle more inclined towards Tirsi, she wouldn't dispense with Fileno, either. So she takes an oath of faithfulness to both, but her intrigue is discovered in the end. A comparison of the fragmentary autograph in LONDON with the only complete copy in Münster suggests that Handel devised two different finales: one with both rivals joining to desert the flirtatious girl, the other showing the three characters striking a deal for peaceful coexistence, since suffering from the beloved's unfaithfulness doesn't rule out obtaining some 'mercé' (erotic satisfaction).

The light plot provides the backbone for a row of diverse numbers (an ouverture, thirteen arias, three duets, one trio, many dialogues in recitative) which – also because of the wide range of 'affetti' and the styles conveying them – amount to more than a comic intermezzo and a little less than an opera. The rich scoring stipulates recorders and oboes in pairs, a solo violin, strings, theorbo and continuo. For Self-BORROWINGS see *RODRIGO*, *AGRIPPINA*, *ACIS AND GALATEA* (1732 version).   CARLO VITALI

Coram, Thomas (b. Lyme Regis, Dorset, ?1668; d. London, 29 March 1751). A British sea captain and philanthropist who returned to London after years in the American colonies, Coram was appalled at the dead and dying children he saw abandoned in the streets. He spent seventeen years petitioning the aristocracy for support to open a children's home in an age when supporting illegitimate children was seen to be condoning or encouraging the immoral behaviour of their mothers. After Coram enlisted the support of the ladies of the aristocracy, the Royal Charter for the FOUNDLING HOSPITAL was finally granted in 1739, and the Hospital took in the first foundlings in 1741. Coram chose a board of directors with money and influence to ensure the success of the Hospital, and this led to his own removal from the Board of Governors in 1741; in spite of his skills and persistence as a lobbyist, he was neither a gentleman nor an aristocrat, and lacked the political skills for administration which his fellow governors brought to the task. He continued personal visits to the Hospital and was buried beneath the altar of the Hospital chapel.   KATHARINE HOGG

G. Wagner, *Thomas Coram, Gent: 1668–1751* (Woodbridge, 2004)

R. K. McClure, *Coram's Children. The London Foundling Hospital in the Eighteenth Century* (New Haven, 1981)

Corelli, Arcangelo (b. Fusignano, 17 Feb. 1653; d. Rome, 8 Jan. 1713). Italian composer and violinist. Corelli is attested as living in ROME from 1675, where he soon gained considerable recognition as violinist, composer, *maestro* of the orchestra and violin teacher. Through his connections with the Cardinals Benedetto PAMPHILIJ and Pietro OTTOBONI, Corelli came in contact with Handel (PALAZZI, 5–6). Presumably Corelli, as one of the most important Roman violin virtuosos, played the solo violin part in most of Handel's works composed in Rome, such as the cantata *QUAL TI RIVEGGIO, OH DIO* or the Sonata a 5, HWV 288 (ORCHESTRAL WORKS, 6). He led the orchestra in the two Roman oratorios *Il TRIONFO DEL TEMPO E DEL DISINGANNO* and *La RESURREZIONE*, and was probably also involved in the performances of Handel's antiphons HWV 235 and 243 and the psalms HWV 237 and 238 (Italian and Latin CHURCH MUSIC). Handel borrowed thematic material from Corelli's Op. 5 (Sonata No. 10, F major) for his opera *AGRIPPINA*.

Corelli was immensely popular in England and Handel's later music sometimes bears traces of Corellian style. Examples of this can be found in the trio sonatas, Op. 5 (CHAMBER MUSIC, 2) and especially in the Concerti grossi, Op. 6 (ORCHESTRAL WORKS, 2), where the use of the *concertino* and the *concerto grosso*, the scoring for strings and continuo and the formal structures echo Corelli's Concerti grossi, Op. 6.   DAGMAR GLÜXAM (Trans. ANGELA BAIER)

O. Edwards, 'The Response to Corelli's Music in Eighteenth-Century England', *Studia Musicologica Norvegica*, vol. 2 (1976), 51–96

L. Finscher, 'Corelli als Klassiker der Triosonate', *Nuovi studi corelliani* (Florence, 1978)

W. and U. Kirkendale, *Music and Meaning: Studies in Music History and the Neighbouring Disciplines* (Florence, 2007)

Mainwaring

H. J. Marx, 'Die Instrumentation in Händels frühen italienischen Werken', *GHB* II (1986)

   'Händels "Grand Concerto" op. 6 Nr. 4 und seine italienischen Vorbilder', *GHB* VII (1998)

Coriolano. Italian opera by Attilio ARIOSTI. The libretto was adapted by Nicola HAYM from a text by Pietro PARIATI that was first set to music by CALDARA (Vienna, 1717). Haym dedicated the wordbook to the Duchess of Newcastle, and some political allegory was suggested by his comparison between the Duke of MARLBOROUGH and how Caius Marcius Coriolanus preserved the freedom of the Roman Republic. The action is set at ROME in 485 BC, and the printed WORDBOOK explains the complicated plot:

> Caius Marcius, who was after sirnam'd Coriolanus from the Conquest of Corioli over the Volsci, Enemies to Rome, not being able to brook the excessive Ambition of Sicinius, one of the Tribunes of the Commons, and sworn Enemy to the Patricians, did publickly accuse him, and that so vigorously, that Sicinius, who intirely govern'd the Minds of the People, made them believe that Coriolanus aim'd at the Destruction of the Common Liberties: Upon which he was summon'd to make his Defence; but refusing to do it, was . . . unjustly banish'd. He retir'd into the Country of the Volsci, and was generously receiv'd by Attius Tullus, their Prince, with whom he had contracted a strict Friendship, after the Peace concluded between the Romans and the Volsci. At this Time great Numbers of the Volsci gathering in Rome, upon occasion of the Solemn Games, which were then to be celebrated, and being mortally hated by Sicinius, for the harbouring of

Coriolanus, were, by contrivance of the same, without Regard to the establish'd Peace, most shamefully turn'd out, not only of Publick Theatres, but of Rome. This Affront did so much enrage the Volsci, that they resolv'd to revenge themselves by raising a new War against the Romans: Their chief Commanders were Attius Tullus with Marcius Coriolanus, whose Mind was chiefly bent on curbing the popular Insolence, and taking away those Abuses which had crept in, to the Prejudice of the Senate and Nobility. The War being declar'd, they led up their Forces towards the Roman Territories, and after many Conquests encamp'd under the Walls of Rome, threatening it with utter Ruin. Not that brave Coriolanus did wish it, his only Design being to force the stubborn People to their due Obedience, and check the Haughtiness of the Tribune. The Commons, by Instigation of Sicinius, persisting in their Endeauvours to oppress the Nobility, did so incite the conquering Coriolanus, that he was just upon the Point of storming his native City, which was then full of Terror and Confusion. Upon this Account Ambassadors were sent to him with Proposals for an Accommodation, but had no Success; neither could the Prayers of the Consul, nor even of his own Wife, in the least move Coriolanus. At last, his Mother went to him, and . . . her Petition did so prevail on his Filial Duty, that he withdrew his Forces, and Sav'd his Country from impending Ruin: In Memory of which a Temple was Consecrated to Woman's Fortune.

Ariosti's setting was composed for the Royal Academy of Music's (OPERA COMPANIES, 2) fourth season, and first performed at the KING'S THEATRE on 19 February 1723, following the first run of Handel's *OTTONE*. The cast was as follows:

Coriolano	SENESINO (castrato)
Volunnia, in love with Coriolano	Francesca CUZZONI (soprano)
Veturia, mother of Coriolano and Claudia	Margherita DURASTANTI (mezzo-soprano)
Claudia, in love with Tullo	Anastasia ROBINSON (contralto)
Tullo, Prince of the Volsci	Alexander GORDON (tenor)
Furio, Volunnia's father	Giuseppe BOSCHI (bass)
Sicinio, Tribune, in love with Volunnia	Gaetano BERENSTADT (castrato)

Coriolano ran for thirteen performances, and it proved to be one of the Royal Academy's most successful operas. Ariosti's satisfaction with it is evident in his supervision of an almost complete edition of the score published by Richard MEARES. Durastanti chose it for her own lucrative benefit nights in both the 1722–3 and 1723–4 seasons. In particular, the title role was one of the finest heroic parts written for Senesino in London. Coriolano's prison scene (III.viii) has a long chromatic accompanied recitative ('Spirate, o iniqui marmi') followed by a magnificent da capo aria in F minor ('Voi d'un figlio tanto misero'), which is marked 'largo e piano sempre', but has an agitated B section marked Presto. The scene was admired by RAMEAU, and praised by HAWKINS as 'wrought up to the highest degree of perfection that music is capable of'. It reputedly drew 'tears from the audience at every representation'.

The quality of Senesino's contribution probably influenced Handel to revive the opera for five performances by the Second Academy (OPERA COMPANIES,

3) in March and April 1732 (directly after the first run of SOSARME). Senesino was the only remaining member of the original cast. It was unprecedented for Handel to perform an old opera composed by one of his former Royal Academy colleagues, but it contributed to the remarkable diversity of the music theatre works offered during his 1731–2 season, and the respectable success of the revival probably encouraged him to repeat the experiment for a revival of BONONCINI's GRISELDA in the 1732–3 season.   DAVID VICKERS

A. Ariosti, Il Coriolano, ed. G. Vecchi (facsimile of 1723 Meares edition) (Modena, 1984)
E. Gibson, The Royal Academy of Music 1719–1728: The Institution and its Directors (New York, 1989)
Hawkins
L. Lindgren, 'Ariosti's London Years, 1716–29', ML 62/3–4 (July–Oct. 1981), 331–51
J. P. Rameau, Génération harmonique ou Traité de musique théorique et pratique (Paris, 1737), 154

Cork. In the mid-eighteenth century, Cork was Ireland's second-largest city and it can lay claim to three performance 'firsts' concerning MESSIAH: the oratorio's first performance outside DUBLIN and LONDON, during Advent, and in consecrated space. A poem by James Delacourt published in Faulkener's Dublin Journal 22–6 December 1744, and republished in the London Daily Gazetteer of 1 January 1745 records the event which took place at St Finbarr's Cathedral, 6 December 1744.   DAVID HUNTER

D. Hunter, 'Messiah in Cork in 1744', Handel Institute Newsletter 12 (2001)

Corneille, Pierre (b. Rouen, 1606; d. Paris, 1684). French dramatist who established French 'classical tragedy' with works such as Le Cid (1637), Horace (1640), Pompée (1644, not the model for Giulio Cesare in Egitto) and Héraclius Empereur d'Orient (1647). Many of his tragédies were turned into drammi per musica by Italian librettists. Handel's oeuvre overlaps with Corneille's only in NORIS's Flavio Cuniberto, revised by HAYM as FLAVIO (1723), a work drawing on Le Cid, and in SALVI's RODELINDA (1710), derived from Corneille's tragédie Pertharite (1651). Both dramas employ episodes from the Longobard history of PAULUS DIACONUS. While correcting certain dramaturgical weaknesses of Pertharite, Salvi developed the heroic allures shown by the French protagonists into a unique blend of despair, pride and passion, especially in the female lead (the change of title is significant). Corneille's Théodore, vierge et martyre (1645–6) was one of Thomas MORELL's sources for THEODORA. Pierre's brother **Thomas Corneille** (b. Rouen, 1625; d. Les Andelys, 1709) was similarly widely imitated by Italian librettists, including Salvi. METASTASIO combined elements of his tragédies Maximien and Stilicon in his EZIO.   REINHARD STROHM

R. Strohm, Dramma per Musica: Italian Opera Seria of the Eighteenth Century (New Haven, 1997)

cornetto. See INSTRUMENTATION

Coronation of King George II and Queen Caroline. This took place on 11 October 1727. The church service in WESTMINSTER ABBEY, at which Handel's four Coronation Anthems (ANTHEMS, 3) were performed, was followed by a secular celebration in Westminster Hall; the procession to the Abbey began at midday, and the royal family left Westminster Hall at 8 p.m. Although the ceremonial of British coronations was regulated by precedents of ancient authority, the constitutional and religious circumstances of the most recent coronations had all been different, and this was the first coronation of a King and Queen Consort of Great Britain. The immediately preceding coronations had been those of William II and Mary (as joint sovereigns) in 1689, Queen ANNE in 1702 (without any specific recognition of her husband, Prince George of Denmark), and GEORGE I in 1714 (as the first King of Great Britain, following the Act of Union in 1707). It is probable that Handel had attended the 1714 coronation though he did not contribute any music, presumably on account of his foreign status at the time. The 1727 coronation was more lavish in its arrangements, and more significant as a social event, than the two preceding ones: Lord HERVEY said that it was 'performed with all the pomp and magnificence that could be contrived', and that the Queen's dress was 'as fine as the accumulated riches of the City and suburbs could make it'. Archbishop William WAKE annotated on his copy of the printed order of service that *The King shall rejoice* was 'in Confusion: All irregular in the Music'. William BOYCE later described the 1727 service as the 'first grand musical performance'. Contemporary reports of rehearsals of Handel's music comment on the size of the performing group, one estimate putting the numbers at 40 singers and 160 orchestral players; in practice, his orchestra for the *MUSIC FOR THE ROYAL FIREWORKS* in 1749 may have been larger, but he probably never had a more numerous ensemble of singers.   DONALD BURROWS

Burrows, *Chapel Royal*
    'Handel and the 1727 Coronation', MT 118/1612 (June 1977), 469–73

Corri (Cori), Angelo Maria (fl. London, 1735–42). Italian librettist. He is documented as having worked at the KING'S THEATRE from April 1735 to June 1737, and was employed by the MIDDLESEX OPERA COMPANY from December 1739 until the 1741–2 season. He wrote opera librettos and arranged texts by Pietro METASTASIO for the OPERA OF THE NOBILITY's productions of operas by Pietro Sandoni, Francesco Maria VERACINI (*Adriano in Siria*, 1735, *La clemenza di Tito*, 1737), Egidio Romoaldo Duni and Giovanni Battista Pescetti. He sometimes also wrote the printed librettos' dedications.

                                        KLAUS-PETER KOCH (Trans. ANGELA BAIER)

Costa, Sir Michael (Andrew Agnus) (b. Naples, 4 Feb. 1808; d. Hove, 29 April 1884). Conductor, composer. Costa, in Britain since 1829, built up a reputation as conductor. In 1848 he was elected conductor of the Sacred Harmonic Society from which the later Handel Festivals emanated, and from 1857 to 1880 he presided over the Handel Festival in the CRYSTAL PALACE. According to the taste of the time he composed additional accompaniments for Handel's oratorios and his were among the best known and widely played. They were heavily overloaded with brass and percussions, and it was reported: 'It is possible to make too much mere noise even on the central transept, and Sir Michael Costa gave, on this occasion another proof of the fact.'   ANNETTE LANDGRAF

See also FESTIVALS, 2

The Musical Times and Singing Class Circular, 1 July 1880, 339; 1 June 1884, 321–3

counterpoint. By the age of ten, Handel had embarked on a formal study of music and composition under ZACHOW, the renowned organist in HALLE. According to

Mainwaring's account, 'the first object of [Zachow's] attention was to ground him thoroughly in the principles of harmony'. If contemporary methods are any indication, this would have involved traditional contrapuntal study, based around intervals, but also issues of syllabic stress and metre. Thus, the principles of counterpoint were intimately connected to matters relating to singing.

With this in mind, MATTHESON's comment that the young Handel was stronger than the Leipzig cantor KUHNAU at improvised fugue, but weaker in singable melody, takes on a new resonance. If counterpoint was central to Handel's talent, perhaps the supremely strong melodic style he eventually developed was somehow grounded in this. Indeed, when we consider counterpoint as something much broader than its specialised sense of 'academic', canonic composition, it can be seen as informing most aspects of baroque style. After all, much of the strength that Handel eventually acquired as a melodist came from the way his vocal lines combine with others, particularly the basso continuo.

A large proportion of Handel's arias are similar in texture to the Italianate trio sonata, the two melodic lines shared between the voice and the massed violins. Moreover, individual vocal lines often show a richness that could well derive from the experience of combining voices. This is overt in, say, the 'Gloria' of the early *Dixit Dominus* (Italian and Latin CHURCH MUSIC), in which the countersubject to the text 'et spiritui sancto' consists of a sequence of falling sevenths. In contrapuntal terms, this is a monodic adaptation of two lines singing in Fuxian 'fourth species' counterpoint (i.e. suspensions). In Handel's mature vocal style such melodic sweeps – when judiciously used – can join up the registers of the voice in order to generate a melody that is not only rich in its range, but also sonorous in timbre.

If counterpoint as a means of generating fine melody and flow of voices is absolutely central to Handel's achievement, he was clearly much less interested in counterpoint as a technique fostered for its own sake. Obviously, if he required stricter counterpoint for a particular mood, he was prepared to devote considerable effort to achieving the satisfactory development of the texture (such as his renowned sketches for the strettos in the 'Amen' fugue of *MESSIAH*). Contrapuntal textures provided a good way of capitalising on the church background of the combined choirs in his oratorio performances. Counterpoint may have had a specifically Christian resonance too, if the choruses in *THEODORA* are anything to go by. Here the music for the pagan Romans tends to be homophonic, dance-like or even positively hedonistic, while the Christian music is marked by its comparative sophistication and contrapuntal integrity (some of it very striking in mood, such as the chorus 'How strange their ends').

More often than not, Handel's contrapuntal writing is directed towards dramatic effect, the natural build-up of voices in fugue leading to a sense of climax, which can often thereafter turn into blatant homophony or freer figuration. This is obvious in his concerto style, where a fugal exposition can form part of a ritornello, providing a sense of order between virtuosic episodes. Handel's improvisatory talent in fugue is implied by the *Six Fugues or Voluntarys* (1735, composed c.1717), which show a fluent texture (generally in three parts) that one could imagine being extended or shortened as necessary; these are often arrested by a closing 'Adagio'. The late organ concerto, Op. 7 No. 3 (ORCHESTRAL WORKS, 5), contains an indication for an 'ad libitum' movement, 'Adagio e Fuga', which implies that the ageing Handel continued to improvise exactly as he had in his youth.   JOHN BUTT

countertenor. The medieval Latin word *contratenor*, literally meaning 'against the "tenor"' (the part 'holding' the tune), originally denoted polyphonic function and range rather than voice-type or a particular vocal technique. In Handel's day the term was on different occasions used to describe both a CASTRATO and a female contralto: CARESTINI had the 'finest and deepest counter-tenor that has perhaps ever been heard' (Burney, p. 369), and Antonia MERIGHI was described as 'A Counter Tenor' (*Daily Journal*, 2 July 1729). Handel's first English alto soloists at the CHAPEL ROYAL, Richard Elford and Francis Hughes, for whom he wrote in both treble G and alto C-clefs, had a combined range of f–d″ (compare Carestini: a–a″ and Merighi: a–f′). They were elsewhere described variously as 'tenors' and 'countertenors'. All male voices at this time used some falsetto-like production in the upper register. In today's colloquial usage, countertenor generally denotes a mainly falsettist singer, who may use his 'modal' speaking range for low notes, with a certain amount of 'register overlap', more or less cunningly disguised.

Pace the modern use of such voices, in his oratorios Handel originally intended most of his male roles in the alto range for women. In the first performances of *MESSIAH* in 1742, he employed Susannah CIBBER alongside the countertenors William Lamb[e] and Joseph Ward (lay clerks at DUBLIN's two cathedrals). Though listed as chorus members, their ranges and share of the solos were roughly equal to Cibber's, and Handel described them as 'very good' (Deutsch, 530; an antidote to the historically poor reputation of the cathedral alto). Handel used church-based altos on other occasions, notably Walter POWELL (the first Joad in *ATHALIA*, 1733), Mr RUSSELL (the first David in *SAUL*, 1739) and Charles BRENT (the first Hamor in *JEPHTHA*, 1752). The case of William SAVAGE is singular in its versatility: he sang for Handel, in both opera and oratorio, as treble, boy alto and/or countertenor, tenor and bass.

It is likely that a censorious attitude from the Anglican establishment (usually their only employer) towards other public performance played a large part in the countertenors' absence from the wider musical scene. One who escaped such censure was Daniel SULLIVAN, whose career was entirely secular – he created Athamas in *SEMELE* and the title role in *JOSEPH AND HIS BRETHREN* (both 1744).

Since the appearance of Alfred Deller in the late 1940s the countertenor has enjoyed an enormous renaissance, satisfying a public taste for dramatic verisimilitude in both opera and oratorio. Modern 'superstar' countertenors (all primarily falsettists) have probably made this fashion unstoppable, though, in Handel opera at least, it has no historical basis: on stage, the composer never substituted a countertenor of any kind for a castrato, always preferring a theatrically trained female singer of similar range.   NICHOLAS CLAPTON

G. M. Ardran and D. Wulstan, 'The Alto or Countertenor Voice', ML 48/1 (1967), 17–22
L. E. DeMarco, 'The Fact of the Castrato and the Myth of the Countertenor', MQ 86/1 (2002), 174–85
J. Potter, 'The Tenor–Castrato connection, 1760–1860', EM 35/1 (Feb. 2007), 97–112
N. Zaslaw, 'The Enigma of the Haute-Contre', MT 115/1581 (Nov. 1974), 939–41

Covent Garden Theatre. Built in 1732 at a cost about £6,000 as a new home for the patent theatre company that had operated at LINCOLN'S INN FIELDS since 1714. Detailed descriptions of the design and internal configuration of the theatre survive in Chancery records because the company's owner/manager John RICH sued the architect, Edward Shepherd. Happily, an architectural plan and section of the theatre exist (dated 1774, but representing something close to the original state of the building, not altered in major ways until 1782). A modern reconstruction by Richard Leacroft gives an excellent sense of both stage and auditorium, which had a maximum capacity of c.1,400. Because Rich featured (and performed in) elaborately staged pantomimes, the theatre was fitted for fancy scenic display. Rich's repertory heavily emphasised music and dance; his theatre, unsurprisingly, was acoustically good for music.

The origins of Rich's friendship with Handel are obscure, but Rich was definitely a lover of music. He was among the subscribers for the score of *RODELINDA* in 1725, for *SCIPIONE* in 1726, for *ADMETO* in 1727, and in 1740 he subscribed for three sets of *Twelve Grand Concertos* (Op. 6) (ORCHESTRAL WORKS, 2). Rich has a reputation as a curmudgeonly and anti-cultural skinflint, but when Handel was forced out of the KING'S THEATRE, Haymarket, after the season of 1733–4, Rich welcomed him and his opera company at Covent Garden – a more modern building fully competitive in acoustics and stage machinery.

The terms of Handel's tenancy at Covent Garden are not known. He says in a letter of 1734 that he is 'engaged with Mr. Rich to carry on the Operas at Covent Garden' (Deutsch, p. 369). Handel is known to have paid Rich rent and house charges for use of the house two nights a week during opera seasons of varying length. But though the opera venture was financially separate from the theatre company, Rich apparently went shares with Handel in some fashion in accepting financial liability for offerings that were artistically distinguished but financially unsuccessful (OPERA COMPANIES, 4). In March 1737, in the third and last season of the arrangement, Rich wrote to the Duke of Bedford about arrears in his payment of the ground rent for the theatre, saying that the operas have occasioned such 'Severe Losses' that he was unable to pay the rent but would endeavour to do so within a year.

Six of Handel's Italian operas and a pasticcio received their premieres at Covent Garden during the 1734–5, 1735–6 and 1736–7 seasons. These were *ORESTE* (the pasticcio, 1734), *ARIODANTE* (1735), *ALCINA* (1735), *ATALANTA* (1736), *ARMINIO* (1737) *GIUSTINO* (1737) and *BERENICE* (1737). Between 1736 and 1757 Handel premiered fifteen of his odes and oratorios there: *ALEXANDER'S FEAST* (1736), *Il TRIONFO DEL TEMPO E DELLA VERITÀ* (1737), *SAMSON* (1743), *SEMELE* (1744), *JOSEPH AND HIS BRETHREN* (1744), the *OCCASIONAL ORATORIO* (1746), *JUDAS MACCABAEUS* (1747), *JOSHUA* (1748), *ALEXANDER BALUS* (1748), *SUSANNA* (1749), *SOLOMON* (1750), The *CHOICE OF HERCULES* (1751), *JEPHTHA* (1752), and The *TRIUMPH OF TIME AND TRUTH* (1757). Between 1738 and 1742 Handel organised his operas and oratorios in other theatres, but his relationship with Rich and Covent Garden remained cordial. Handel is generally associated with the King's Theatre, but Covent Garden offered him a very satisfactory alternative venue. Handel installed his own organ in the theatre and left it to John Rich in a codicil to his will (HANDEL, 8).   JUDITH MILHOUS and ROBERT D. HUME

R. Leacroft, *The Development of the English Playhouse* (London, 1973)
J. Orrell, 'Covent Garden Theatre, 1732', *Theatre Survey* 33 (1992), 32–52
F. H. W. Sheppard, *Survey of London*, vol. 35: *The Theatre Royal Drury Lane and The Royal Opera House Covent Garden* (London, 1970)

Coxe, William (b. London, 6 March 1748; d. Bemerton, 8 June 1828). CHURCH OF ENGLAND clergyman and writer. His parents were William Coxe (c.1710–1760), physician to the King's household, and Martha, daughter of Paul (d.1732) and Elizabeth D'Aranda. Martha Coxe married John Christopher SMITH JUNIOR in about 1761 and the long-time widower became stepfather to six young children. Both of Coxe's parents had a prior marriage; in 1741 his father had married Barbara Clark; his mother had married Charles Henry Lee in September 1743 but he died of smallpox the following January. All three of Martha's spouses had connections with the royal court. Charles Lee was Gentleman Usher to Princess AMELIA and Master of the Revels. Smith, in addition to carrying on Handel's oratorios, was appointed music master to Dowager Princess Augusta.

Coxe wrote a slim book based on the anecdotes about Handel that his stepfather had written or related, added anecdotes about Smith, and included thirty-four pages of Smith's music excerpted from several oratorios. Little new information about Handel emerges from the anecdotes though the mention of the possible betrothals is significant. The Coxe family became owners of the DENNER portrait of Handel (ICONOGRAPHY). William passed it to his brother Peter, who passed it to his sister Martha, who had married Revd Sir Peter Rivers, Bt. Following her death in about 1835 the portrait became the property of the Sacred Harmonic Society and then of the National Portrait Gallery.

DAVID HUNTER

See also HANDEL, 10

[W. Coxe], *Anecdotes of George Frederick Handel and John Christopher Smith* (London, 1799; facsimile edn, P. M. Young, New York, 1979)
H. Pettit, 'Edward Young and the Case of Lee vs. D'Aranda', *Proceedings of the American Philosophical Society* 107 (1963), 145–59

Croft, William (bap. Nether Ettington, Warwicks., 30 Dec. 1678; d. Bath, 14 Aug. 1727). The most important English composer and church musician at the time of Handel's arrival in London, and one of the few plausible direct links to the music of Henry PURCELL, who had died only fifteen years previously. Croft had been a CHAPEL ROYAL chorister under Purcell and John BLOW, and after briefly contributing music for London's theatre plays he followed a career in church music, succeeding as Composer, Organist and Master of the Children at the Chapel Royal, as well as Organist of WESTMINSTER ABBEY, following the deaths of Jeremiah Clarke and Blow in 1707–8. In 1713 he received the degree of Doctor of Music from OXFORD University, his exercise comprising settings of English and Latin odes celebrating the Peace of Utrecht (War of the SPANISH SUCCESSION).

Most of Croft's compositions are organ-accompanied English anthems for the routine services at the Chapel Royal and the Abbey, but he was also a significant composer of orchestrally accompanied anthems and canticle settings, overlapping with Handel's first English contributions to these genres. He composed four such anthems between 1714 and 1720, including the only orchestrally accompanied item for King GEORGE I's coronation in 1714. Of particular interest is his setting of the Te Deum and Jubilate in D major, developing the famous model from Purcell's 1694 setting with trumpets and strings. The Te Deum was composed for a service at the Chapel Royal on a national Thanksgiving Day in February 1709 and it saw several subsequent performances, in particular at another Thanksgiving Day service in ST PAUL'S CATHEDRAL in January 1715 that was attended by the King; for that occasion Croft revised his music substantially, influenced by the style of Handel's 'Utrecht' settings from 1713 (TE DEUM, 1). Croft's Te Deum received a further revival at the Chapel Royal in 1720, but in his last years the initiative for such music passed to Handel.   DONALD BURROWS

Crown and Anchor Tavern. The building in the Strand from c.1678, sometimes referred to as the Crown Tavern, was described as 'a large and curious House, with good Rooms and other Conveniences fit for Entertainment'. It was the place for the meetings of the Philharmonic Society and the ACADEMY OF ANCIENT MUSIC (founded there in 1726). Bernard GATES performed ESTHER (HWV 49ᵃ) at the tavern on 23 February, 1 and 3 March 1732; Handel attended possibly one of the performances. The tavern hosted the academy's performances of the Chandos Te Deum (TE DEUM, 3) (23 March 1737), parts from ISRAEL IN EGYPT (10 May 1739), SAUL (24 April 1749), ESTHER (24 February 1743) and MESSIAH (16 February 1744). The FUND FOR THE SUPPORT OF DECAY'D MUSICIANS was founded at the Tavern in 1738. It was rebuilt in 1790 but has since been demolished.   ANNETTE LANDGRAF

HHB iv
H. C. Shelley, *Inns and Taverns of Old London* (Boston, 1909)
J. Simon (ed.), Handel: *A Celebration of his Life and Times 1685–1759* (London, 1985)
J. Strype, *Survey of London* (1720), (online) (hriOnline, Sheffield). (Accessed: 22 Feb. 2008), book 4, chap. 7, 117

Crudel tiranno amor, HWV 97ᵃ⁻ᵇ. The original version of this cantata for soprano, two violins, two oboes *colla parte*, viola and continuo (HWV 97ᵃ) was probably composed in 1721 for Margherita DURASTANTI, and it might have been one of the two cantatas performed in a benefit concert at the KING'S THEATRE on 5 July 1721 (HHB iv, 100). The autograph of this version is lost, but Handel used all three arias in FLORIDANTE. An autograph manuscript of an alternative version for voice, possibly violin, and keyboard (HWV 97ᵇ) dating from c.1738 was recently discovered in Munich (Bayerische Staatsbibliothek), which is the only extant source to transmit a fully figured basso continuo realisation in the hand of the composer. This version is set a tone higher than the original composition, the vocal part is rewritten (possibly from memory) and the right hand of the keyboard accompaniment is adopted from the violin part of the *cantata con stromenti*, with some adjustment of melody and rhythm.
                                                           WALTER KREYSZIG

D. Burrows, 'Two More Musical Autographs by Handel', GHB XI (1998)

H. J. Marx (ed.), *Kantaten mit Instrumenten I*, HHA V/3 (Kassel, 1994); *Kantaten mit Instrumenten III*, HHA V/5 (Kassel, 1999)

B. Over, 'Ein neu aufgefundenes Händel-Autograph in der Bayerischen Staatsbibliothek: Crudel tiranno Amor (HWV 97)', HJb 51 (2005)

Crystal Palace. In 1851 the Crystal Palace was erected for the London World Exposition (the architect was Joseph Paxton) and it was moved from HYDE PARK to Sydenham in 1854. Consisting of glass and steel it had a surface area of 79,212 sq. m, and was built as a tourist attraction, a type of indoor pleasure garden that hosted all types of exhibitions and other diversions. The first so-called 'Grand Handel Festival' (FESTIVALS, 2) took place there in the Central Transept on 19 June 1857, and demand for further festivals followed the outstanding success of the first event. Altogether the Crystal Palace hosted twenty-three Handel festivals. The festivals were organised by the Sacred Harmonic Society, an organisation run by the then manager of the Palace (Sir Michael COSTA).

The acoustics in the Crystal Palace were very problematic because it was not built as a concert hall and was not at all suitable for soloists; the voices sounded rather weak, only the choruses had a good effect. The Palace played an important role in the development of musical life in Britain, especially in the second half of the nineteenth century, because it attracted a large number of amateurs and audiences from a new stratum, from the rising middle classes. The Crystal Palace was regarded as 'a temple of music' because of Saturday concerts, the Handel Festivals and special performances that were given on a scale possible nowhere else. The Crystal Palace was destroyed by fire on 30 November 1936, ten years after the last Handel Festival.   ANNETTE LANDGRAF

C. Friemert, *Die Gläserne Arche, Kristllpalast London 1851 und 1854* (Dresden, 1984)

A. Landgraf, 'Der Kristallpalast und seine Bedeutung für die Aufführung von Händels Musik', HJb 55 (2009)

M. Musgrave, *The Musical Life of the Crystal Palace* (Cambridge, 1995)

P. R. Piggott, *The Palace of the People: The Crystal Palace at Sydenham 1854–1936* (London, 2004)

'Cuckoo and the Nightingale, The'. See ORCHESTRAL WORKS, 5

Culloden, Battle of. See JACOBITES

Cumberland, Duke of. See Prince WILLIAM

Cuopre talvolta il cielo, HWV 98. Accompanied by violins and basso continuo, *Cuopre talvolta il cielo* is one of only two instrumental cantatas Handel wrote for bass voice. It was composed in 1708 in NAPLES, at the same time as *ACI, GALATEA E POLIFEMO*. The opening accompanied recitative and aria describe the violence of a cruel storm, which is compared in the second recitative to the torment caused by the beloved's angry face. Handel represents the storm with slashing violins against a rumbling bass, an effective combination he borrowed from the setting of a tempest in 'Armida Abbandonata' (*DIETRO L'ORME FUGACI*), written the year before in ROME; he used the accompaniment again in London to represent the waters overwhelming the Egyptians in *ISRAEL IN EGYPT*.

ELLEN T. HARRIS

Cuzzoni, Francesca (b. Parma, 2 April 1696; fl. 1718–40; d. Bologna, 19 June 1778). Soprano (range c′–c′′′). Daughter to a professional violinist employed at the

Parma court, she studied in her native town under Francesco Lanzi and made her debut there in July 1714, in an unnamed serenata performed at the ducal gardens in Colorno for the entertainment of the Earl of PETERBOR-OUGH. Cuzzoni's early career brought her to Bologna, FLORENCE, Siena, Genoa, Mantua, Reggio Emilia, Milan, Turin and Padua, singing in operas by GASPARINI, ORLANDINI, VIVALDI and Pollarolo. Her Venetian debut season at the Teatro SAN GIOVANNI GRISOSTOMO (1718–19) projected her to stardom. It also marked her first appearance with Faustina BORDONI (RIVAL QUEENS) and led to an invitation to sing before Emperor Charles VI in Vienna. She sang in five more operas at VENICE (1721–2) before the Royal Academy of Music (OPERA COMPANIES, 2) engaged her to sing in London on a salary of 1,500 guineas (the same amount allotted to SENESINO).

She made her London debut as Teofane in Handel's *OTTONE* on 12 January 1723. According to MAINWARING, she refused to sing the slow aria 'Falsa imagine' until Handel threatened to throw her out of the window. BUR-NEY claims that the aria subsequently 'fixed her reputation as an expressive and pathetic singer'. Further roles that Handel composed for Cuzzoni include Emilia (*FLAVIO*), Cleopatra (*GIULIO CESARE*), Asteria (*TAMERLANO*), the title role in *RODELINDA*, Berenice (*SCIPIONE*), Lisaura (*ALESSANDRO*), Antigona (*ADMETO*), Costanza (*RICCARDO PRIMO*), Laodice (*SIROE*) and Seleuce (*TOLOMEO*). During the same period Cuzzoni also appeared in operas by ARIOSTI and BONONCINI, and during summer 1724 she travelled with most of the company (except Senesino) to Paris, engaging in unstaged performances of *Ottone* and *Giulio Cesare* and singing sacred pieces by Bononcini for King Louis XV and the French court. On her return to London, she married the composer and keyboard virtuoso Pier Giuseppe Sandoni (probably on 12 January 1725). The addition of Faustina Bordoni to the Royal Academy's company of singers in spring 1726 resulted in a passionate division between the partisan supporters of each diva.

In October 1728 Cuzzoni left England, but she returned in April 1734 to join the OPERA OF THE NOBILITY, for whom she performed in five operas by PORPORA, plus others by Sandoni, HASSE, Orlandini, VERACINI, Ciampi, the pasticcio *Orfeo*, and a revival of Handel's *Ottone*. She left in June 1736, but made her final visit to London in 1750–1 for some unsuccessful benefit concerts. Burney heard her on 18 May 1751, and claimed that her 'thin cracked voice' was only the shadow of its former splendour. Before Cuzzoni's career came to that melancholy end, she had experienced many reversals of fortune on the continent. Between 1729 and 1739, she commanded huge salaries at opera houses in Venice, Bologna, NAPLES, Florence, Genoa and Turin. She and Sandoni visited Vienna in 1728–9 and 1739, but the couple probably parted soon after: two daughters were born to them, but their unhappy marriage was plagued by debts, gambling and mutual misdemeanour. Cuzzoni sang at Hamburg in 1740, visited Amsterdam in 1741–2, was employed as a court and church singer at Stuttgart in 1745–7 and sang in Paris before Queen Maria Leszczyńska in early 1750. There is circumstantial evidence that during the last stage of her career she suffered imprisonment for debts both in the Netherlands and in England, although press rumours that she had been sentenced to death in Venice for poisoning her husband were mere gossip. After 1751, now an impoverished widow, she

4. Francesca Cuzzoni, engraving from Hawkins, 1776.

retired to Bologna, where she appears to have been friendly with the music scholar Padre Martini. There is no evidence to support the tradition that she eked out a living as a button-maker.

According to Marpurg, Quantz heard Cuzzoni in 1727, and credited her with 'a very agreeable and *clear soprano* voice; a pure intonation and a fine shake' (i.e. trill), and a style of singing both 'innocent and affecting' that was enhanced by 'tender and touching expression'. Her shortcomings were 'not great rapidity of execution, in allegros' (Quantz) and an unpleasant physical appearance: 'short and squat, with a doughy cross face, but fine complexion; . . . not a good actress; dressed ill' (reported by Burney, pp. 318–19; see Figure 4). G. B. Mancini, who performed with her at Leghorn in 1738, lauded her 'angelic voice', refined utterance, equality of registers, sophisticated extempore coloratura and masterly use of rubato time. The singing theorist P. F. Tosi, writing in 1723, extolled Cuzzoni in 'the pathetic' and Bordoni in 'the allegro', suggesting that a blend of both singers would amount to perfection. Handel may have held a similar viewpoint when, starting in late 1726, he composed for Cuzzoni such florid allegros as 'Se 'n vola lo sparvier' and 'La sorte mia vacilla' in *Admeto*, whilst continuing to give her arias with the sensual lilt of those that had peppered her earlier roles (e.g. Cleopatra's 'V'adoro, pupille' and Rodelinda's 'Ritorna o cara'). CARLO VITALI

Burney

P. L. Franco, 'Francesca Cuzzoni (1696–1778): lo stile antico nella musica moderna', MA dissertation (University of Pavia, 2000–1)

C. S. Larue, *Handel and his Singers: The Creation of the Royal Academy Operas, 1720–1728* (Oxford, 1995)

Mainwaring

F. W. Marpurg, *Historisch-kritische Beyträge zur Aufnahme der Musik*, 1/3 (Berlin, 1754), 'II. Lebensläuffe. A) Herrn Johann Joachim Quantzens Lebenslauf, von ihm selbst entworfen', 240

S. Ograjenšek, 'From *Alessandro* (1726) to *Tolomeo* (1728): The Final Royal Academy Operas', Ph.D. dissertation (University of Cambridge, 2005)

Da quel giorno fatale ('Il delirio amoroso'), HWV 99. Bereft of her beloved Tirsi, who did not yield to her desire, Clori falls prey to insane fantasies. She imagines that she descends to Hades (where 'ungrateful' souls are supposed to dwell) in order to rescue him from his deserved punishment. At first, Tirsi keeps avoiding her, but, after many laments and prayers, he condescends to mount on a barge sailing to Lethe and the Elysian Fields, the seat of the Blessed. There, among flowers, songs and music, both will enjoy everlasting love and bliss.

This extended cantata in ten movements is scored for solo soprano, recorder, oboe, three violins, viola, cello and continuo. The oboe, then a novel instrument in Italian orchestras, is allotted a prominent role both in the opening Sonata and in the finale, where dance movements (gigue, minuet) and French-style ceremonial lilt (entrée) come to the fore (DANCE FORMS). More Italianate features are to be found in the concertato passages for voice and violin or cello, as in the first and second arias ('Un pensiero' and 'Per te lasciai'). Cardinal PAMPHILIJ, who provided the text, hosted the premiere in his Roman palazzo in May 1707, some three months after composition (PALAZZI, 5). That a castrato took the (narrative/dramatic) solo part should not be overstated, since Pamphilij's household records never mention any female singers, either resident or invited. For self-borrowings see *RODRIGO*, *JEPHTHA*.   CARLO VITALI

Dalrymple, Sir David (1st Baronet of Ha[l]les) (b. c.1665; d. 3 Dec. 1721). Scottish politician and solicitor-general to Queen ANNE. Dalrymple's letter to Hugh Campbell dated 27 May 1718 describes his recent visit to CANNONS, and remarks that the Duke of CHANDOS 'has a Chorus of his own, the Musick is made for himself and sung by his own servants, besides which there is a Little opera now a makeing for his diversion whereof the Musick will not be made publick. The words are to be furnished by M^rs. POPE & GAY, the musick to be composed by Hendell. It is as good as finished, and I am promised some of the Songs by Dr ARBUTHNOT who is one of the club of composers' (HHB iv, 76). This is the earliest known information about *ACIS AND GALATEA* (HWV 49^a), and implies that the masque was staged or semi-staged.   WALTER KREYSZIG

dance forms. Dances are genres established, and distinguished, by characteristic rhythmic patterns within certain metres. In Handel's work, dance rhythms appear in four contexts: (over seventy) choreographed theatrical dances for his operas (BALLET MUSIC); dozens of minuets published by John WALSH in the 1720s and 1730s for the London social dance scene; instrumental pieces (not intended for dancing) written for solo, chamber or orchestral forces; and arias within his cantatas, operas and oratorios.

Most of Handel's instrumental dances are in binary form. Exceptions include his danced rondeaux in ALMIRA (1705) and ARIODANTE (1735), as well as some twenty chaconnes and passacaglias – which are variations on a ground bass. Most of these were written for harpsichord, with the most extensive being HWV 442, No. 2 (sixty-two variations). Within his instrumental music, the more notable departures from conventional dance forms were written to accommodate opera scenes involving supernatural characters. Thus Handel wrote a French overture (complete with fugue) for the dancing furies in his ADMETO (1727, II.i), and a suite of contrasting character pieces for the entries and interactions of the pleasant and baleful dreams in his Ariodante. Other dances which vary from the binary norm are the forlana 'Il vostro Maggio' which was sung and danced by seductive mermaids in RINALDO (1711), and the minuet-chorus of singing and dancing Athenians in II.iv of TESEO (1713, 'Ogn'un acclami'). These sung dances are in da capo form, characteristic of the ARIA.

Most – but not all – of Handel's choreographed theatrical dances follow eighteenth-century convention in having phrases based on four-bar units (or multiples thereof). Within the harpsichord suites and partitas, Handel's phrase lengths are more varied, with chaconnes, passacaglias and sarabandes being the most regular; minuets sometimes admit six-bar phrases; allemandes, courantes and gigues typically observe irregular structures (sections with odd numbers of bars). Handel's arias with dance rhythms (see Telle), follow the conventions of aria regarding melodic development and phrasing. For example, binary instrumental dances often observe an internal formal procedure where a shorter characteristic rhythmic gesture (normally one or two bars in length) is established and repeated at the beginning of each refrain – this gesture is then fragmented and developed (Mather). Within the da capo aria, dance rhythms were subjected to more intense manipulation, involving the techniques of repetition, contraction and expansion, as well as the insertion of vocal coloratura. Although it is usually only non-danced pieces which are referred to as 'stylised' in scholarly literature, it can be argued that as all dances observe a certain style (Fairfax), so does their music.

Handel composed in most of the then-current dance genres, many of which were of French origin. Notable exceptions include his Venetian forlana in Rinaldo (discussed above), and his eight (mainly orchestral) English hornpipes. Dances of early seventeenth-century origin such as the allemande and courante were generally early works (harpsichord being the most popular medium), while he returned to mid-baroque genres such as the gavotte and minuet throughout his career. His sole tambourin (ALCINA, 1735) is a dance type which originated in the eighteenth century. Handel's sarabandes can be divided into two broad categories. The first of these is in 3/2 metre, and makes a feature of repeated notes in its melody (Best, 'Handel and the Keyboard', p. 213). Handel wrote in this style whilst in HAMBURG, and during his first years in London; this type of sarabande is found in his KEYBOARD MUSIC (see HWV 432, No. 4; HWV 437, No. 4; HWV 439, No. 3; HWV 450, No. 4 and HWV 455, No. 2), in two dances in his first opera, Almira, and in Almirena's aria, 'Lascia, ch'io pianga', from Rinaldo

(II.iv). His later sarabandes are in 3/4 metre, and do not feature the melodic lines or rhythms characteristic of the earlier pieces. His fifty-six marches, found both in his operas and in his unstaged oratorios, were invariably used to evoke a military atmosphere.

Handel did not always record generic labels in his autographs. Sometimes the dance type evoked is obvious (for example, the 'Entrée des songes agréables' from Alcina is clearly a minuet), but at least twelve of his opera dances defy any attempts at categorisation; the notated social dance repertory and the operas of his peers contain many examples of non-generic dances.

Many of Handel's opera or oratorio overtures end with a movement in dance rhythm; the minuet was the most favoured (twenty-nine examples), with the gigue (ten), and gavotte (seven) also being fairly prominent. Dance rhythms (sometimes in hybrid combinations) can be detected in many of his arias; it has been argued (Telle) that Handel used dance to evoke certain moods or affects. This approach to understanding Handel's music accords with our knowledge of the baroque doctrine of affections. An intensive musical study of baroque dances has been undertaken by Meredith Little and Natalie Jenne, as well as Betty Bang Mather.

Handel's self-BORROWINGS suggest that he saw music written for different contexts as interchangeable. Thus many of his dances from the 1734–5 COVENT GARDEN operas were to appear in later trio sonatas (HWV 396–400; HWV 402) (CHAMBER MUSIC, 2), while the sprightly dance in common time from Act II of his ORESTE first appeared as the final movement of LOTARIO's overture (1729). ARIANNA IN CRETA (Covent Garden revival, November 1734), Ariodante and Alcina (1735) each had an overture movement which later featured (in the same opera) as a choreographed dance. That this practice was not exclusive to Handel is apparent when we consider which of his pieces was to enter the notated dance repertory: 'Non è si vago e bello', an opera aria in bourrée rhythm from GIULIO CESARE (I.vii) was choreographed by Anthony L'Abbé (Little and Marsh (Danse Noble, No. 6980); L'Abbé also choreographed the march from SCIPIONE (I.i; ibid., No. 7180), under the title 'Queen Caroline' (the dance was composed for Her Majesty's 1728 birthday).   SARAH MCCLEAVE

T. Best, 'Handel and the Keyboard', The Cambridge Companion to Handel, ed. D. Burrows (Cambridge, 1997)

E. Fairfax, The Styles of Eighteenth-Century Ballet (Lanham, MD, and Oxford, 2003)

M. Little and N. Jenne, Dance and the Music of J. S. Bach (Bloomington and Indianapolis, 2001)

M. Little and C. G. Marsh, La Danse Noble: An Inventory of Sources (New York, 1992)

B. B. Mather, with D. M. Kearns, Dance Rhythms of the French Baroque: A Handbook for Performance (Bloomington and Indianapolis, 1987)

K. Telle, 'Tanzrhythmen in der Vokalmusik Georg Friedrich Händels', Beiträge zur Musikforschung 3, ed. R. Hammerstein and W. Seidel (Munich and Salzburg, 1977)

Dandridge, Bartholomew (b. London, bap. 17 Dec. 1691; d. London, c.1754). English painter, studied at KNELLER's Academy and at the St Martin's Lane Academy under John Vanderbank and Louis Chéron. Some portraits of influential members of the high society (e.g. FREDERICK, Prince of Wales) attest to the popularity of his French-influenced style. The portrait of Handel attributed to him was presumably painted about 1725 (although all of his known large-scale portraits date from after 1731).   EDWIN WERNER

Daphne (Die verwandelte Daphne). See *FLORINDO*

De Fesch, Willem (b. Alkmaar, bap. 26 Aug. 1687; d. London, 3 Jan. 1761). The Dutch-born composer and violinist Willem De Fesch worked in Amsterdam (c. 1708–25) and at Antwerp Cathedral (1725–31) before moving to London where he initially worked as a concert violinist and organist. His first oratorio *Judith* (1733) was probably written owing to Handel's successful revival of *ESTHER* the previous year. Although associated with members of the OPERA OF THE NOBILITY, he stayed out of their conflicts with Handel and in 1746 he was 'first fiddle' in Handel's orchestra (Deutsch, 629–30). During the 1740s he wrote two larger-scale works, *Love and Friendship* (1744) and *Joseph* (1745), before retiring from public life in 1750.   MATTHEW GARDNER

R. L. Tusler, *Willem de Fesch 'An excellent musician and a worthy man'* (The Hague, 2005)
E. Zöllner, 'Murder most Virtuous: The Judith Oratorios of De Fesch, Smith and Arne', *Music in Eighteenth-Century Britain*, ed. D. W. Jones (Aldershot, 2000)

Dead March. Handel's 'Dead March in *SAUL*' achieved surprising popularity in Britain as an item for concerts or sombre ceremonies. It is a movement in C major, headed 'La Marche' and scored for trombones, timpani, flutes, strings and organ, composed in 1738 to precede the Elegy for Saul and Jonathan in Act III of the oratorio. In 1741 Handel wrote a different movement, with similar scoring but in D major and this time headed 'Dead March', in his autograph of *SAMSON*, but this was abandoned, perhaps because the trombone players had left London before the oratorio came to performance in 1743. Rather confusingly, for a subsequent revival of *Samson* Handel rewrote the *Saul* march in a D major version with horns replacing the trombones. He also wrote a version of the *Samson* march for trombones and timpani alone, and yet another (for orchestra with trumpets, horns and timpani) to represent the wedding procession in *JOSEPH AND HIS BRETHREN*.   DONALD BURROWS

D. Burrows, 'Handel, the Dead March, and a Newly Identified Trombone Movement', *EM* 18/3 (Aug. 1990), 408–16

Deborah, HWV 51. English oratorio. Handel composed *Deborah* following the success of his expanded versions of *ESTHER* (HWV 50^b) and *ACIS AND GALATEA* (HWV 49^b) in 1732. The libretto was newly written by Samuel HUMPHREYS based on a story in the Old Testament Book of Judges. The choice of subject may have been suggested by Maurice GREENE'S *Song of Deborah and Barak* of the previous year. Like *Esther* the new oratorio featured a Jewish heroine, and the libretto was dedicated to Queen CAROLINE.

In Act I Deborah, a prophetess and Judge of Israel, summons Barak to lead the Israelite army against the Canaanites and their commander Sisera. She then prophesies that Sisera will die by the hand of a woman. Jael, the wife of Heber the Kenite (an ally of Sisera), laments the horrors of war, but Deborah assures her that she will perform a virtuous deed that very day and thereby become a heroine of her people. Barak is encouraged by his supporters, who include his aged father Abinoam, before a messenger from Sisera suggests a parley. The Israelites accept the offer.

In Act II Sisera enters with the priests and worshippers of Baal, the Canaanite deity, and they face off against the followers of Jehovah. The chorus represents both parties. The Israelites are represented by the rich harmonies and intricate counterpoint of Handel's church anthems while the Priests of Baal sing music in a simpler style based largely on dance rhythms. Deborah refuses to pledge her allegiance to Sisera who departs with his followers. The Israelites then predict the defeat of the Canaanites.

In Act III the Israelites return from their victory bringing with them the priests of Baal among their prisoners. Jael describes how she lured Sisera into her tent and killed him while he slept by driving a nail through his temple. The Israelites rejoice at the news and Deborah pronounces that Jael has fulfilled her destiny.

Handel completed the composition of *Deborah* on 21 February 1733 (the day after he directed the last performance of *ORLANDO*). Perhaps his busyness during this period explains why about two-thirds of *Deborah* was drawn from works he had written in ITALY or England that had not been heard publicly in LONDON, including *Dixit Dominus* (Italian and Latin CHURCH MUSIC), *ACI, GALATEA E POLIFEMO, Il TRIONFO DEL TEMPO E DEL DISINGANNO*, the Ode for Queen ANNE's Birthday (*ETERNAL SOURCE OF LIGHT DIVINE*), several of the Cannons anthems (ANTHEMS, 2), and the *BROCKES PASSION*. He also included the two Coronation anthems (ANTHEMS, 3) he had not used in *Esther* (i.e. *Let thy Hand be Strengthened* and *The King shall Rejoice*). It seems likely that Handel selected some of the music to match text written by Humphreys, but that the librettist also wrote new words to fit music the composer had earmarked for reuse. This latter pattern is particularly evident in some of the borrowings from the Cannons anthem *O Praise the Lord with One Consent*, which was set to a rhyming text from TATE and BRADY's metrical version of the Psalms. However, it is evident from the score that Handel's choice to 'borrow' from his own old works did not make his task easy, but instead required him substantially to rewrite several movements. There is also a good deal of newly composed music, including all the recitatives, several fine arias (such as Barak's 'How lovely is the blooming fair' and 'In the battle fame pursuing'), two duets for Deborah and Barak, and some impressive choruses (including 'Doleful tidings', an unexpectedly moving lament sung by the Baalite Priests upon hearing news of Sisera's assassination). Many of the choruses are in five or eight parts, and Handel's indications for varying their accompaniments are unusually detailed. There is no evidence that an overture was part of *Deborah* until its last revival under the composer in 1756, and it is possible that it had hitherto commenced with the first chorus 'Immortal Lord of earth and skies'.

Deborah was first performed at the KING'S THEATRE on 17 March 1733 in the course of a mixed season of opera and oratorio. The cast was as follows:

Deborah	Anna Maria STRADA del Pò (soprano)
Barak	SENESINO (castrato)
Jael	Celeste GISMONDI (soprano)
Abinoam	Antonio MONTAGNANA (bass)
Sisera	Francesca BERTOLLI (alto)
Israelite Woman	Gismondi
Israelite Priest	Montagnana
Baalite Priest	[unidentified] (bass)
Herald	[unidentified] (tenor)

The chorus apparently consisted of about twenty singers in addition to the soloists, and the orchestra may have included as many as seventy-five players, including three horns, three trumpets and two organs. Three days after the first performance, the *Daily Advertiser* reported that 'The Pit and Orchestre were cover'd as at an Assembly, and the whole House illuminated in a new and most beautiful manner'.

Handel clearly made a mistake in attempting to charge higher ticket prices for the first performance, which provoked a protest on the part of the subscribers to his season, but *Deborah* was generally well received in the composer's lifetime. He revived it during his OXFORD visit in the summer of 1733 and again in London in each of the two following years. There seems to have been an aborted revival in 1737, and a good deal of the music appeared the following year in Handel's benefit concert (An ORATORIO). The complete oratorio was performed again in 1744, 1754 and 1756, the latter two seasons after Handel's blindness. In 1734 and 1735 some of the music was sung in Italian.

Deborah fell out of favour after about 1780 and was performed rarely in the nineteenth and twentieth centuries. Some commentators, especially Winton Dean, have complained about its bloodthirsty story and patchwork nature, but performances and recordings from the 1990s have shown it to be a stronger and more appealing work than many had previously thought.   GRAYDON BEEKS

D. Burrows, 'Handel's 1738 "Oratorio": A Benefit Pasticcio', *Georg Friedrich Händel: ein Lebensinhalt. Gedenkschrift für Bernd Baselt (1934–1993)*, ed. K. Hortschansky and K. Musketa (Halle and Kassel, 1995)
Dean, *Oratorios*
H. Serwer, 'In Praise of Handel's *Deborah*', *American Choral Journal* 27/2–3 (1985), 14–19
D. Vickers, 'Handel's Performing Versions: A Study of Four Music Theatre Works from the "Second Academy" Period', Ph.D. dissertation (The Open University, 2007)

Deidamia, HWV 42. Handel's last opera, composed between 27 October and 20 November 1740. The libretto, by Paolo ROLLI, appears to be an original composition, not derived from an earlier libretto as was usually the case with Handel's operas. It is Rolli's best work for Handel, well paced, with effective characterisation of the two principals, and language free from affectation. The plot is based on the story of Achilles's boyhood according to one of the traditions of Greek mythology: the high priest Calchas declared that without Achilles Troy could never be taken, but an oracle predicted that he would die in the campaign. His parents sought to forestall this outcome by sending him, dressed as a girl, to Lycomedes, King of the island of Skyros, where he was hidden under the name of Pyrrha among Lycomedes's daughters, one of whom was Deidamia. He became her lover, and was the father of Pyrrhus. Ulysses was sent to Skyros to find him.

At the beginning of the opera, Ulisse, under the false name of Antioco, and Fenice, an ambassador, arrive amid grand ceremony. Ulisse accuses Licomede of harbouring Achille, and so betraying Greece; Licomede denies the charge and invites Ulisse to search for the boy. Deidamia is with her companion Nerea; when Achille appears she complains that he prefers hunting to being with her, but he denies it. Nerea reports to Deidamia the arrival of the Greek ambassadors; Ulisse explains to Deidamia why the Greeks must make war on Troy, and left alone she vows to protect Achille.

At the beginning of Act II Achille is impressed by Ulisse's soldierly appearance. Ulisse makes amorous advances to Deidamia; Achille, who has overheard the conversation, is jealous and accuses her of infidelity. Nerea announces that Licomede has arranged a hunting party to entertain the visitors, and that Fenice has paid compliments to her. She and Deidamia agree to encourage these amorous approaches in order to protect Achille; Deidamia fears she may lose his affections because of their recent quarrel. A chorus celebrates the joy of hunting. In the forest Fenice tells Ulisse to join in the hunt, while he continues his courting of Nerea. Ulisse reports seeing a girl who is an impressive hunter. He suspects that it is Achille, and that the boy is Deidamia's lover; he is sure the pair will give themselves away. Ulisse pretends to court 'Pirra', who resists him playfully, saying that love is not for 'her', and that Deidamia is listening. Ulisse departs and Deidamia angrily rebukes Achille for breaking his promise to keep away from the Greeks. She leaves in distress, and he returns to the hunt. Fenice pretends to admire 'Pirra', who repeats that 'she' is keen only on hunting, not love; Fenice is sure that this is no girl. The hunting chorus is repeated in shortened form.

In Act III a gallery is set out with gifts brought by the Greeks: these are mostly clothes and ornaments for the women, but among them are weapons. Deidamia invites 'Pirra' to choose first; Achille says he would rather have a bow and arrows for hunting. Ulisse says they have thought of that, and shows them to him with a shield, a sword and a helmet. Achille joyously puts on the helmet and brandishes the sword; in despair Deidamia tries to stop him, when a trumpet call is heard. Ulisse says it is an attack by villains; Achille declares he will defend them. Ulisse challenges him to say who he is: Greece needs him. Achille admits his identity and says he is ready for war. Deidamia is in despair and bitterly blames Ulisse; she then pleads with her father, who says that he knew she loved Achille, but that the young man must do his patriotic duty. Achille tries to comfort her by saying he will marry her before he leaves; in her distress she says she loves 'Antioco'. Achille tells Ulisse that he can have her, Ulisse reveals his true identity, and says his behaviour was a pretence: let Achille and Deidamia be joined. Achille scorns the warnings of the oracle and is sure he will return, but she knows that he will not. Fenice proposes to Nerea, who accepts him. Licomede agrees that Deidamia and Achille shall marry. After a duet by Ulisse and Deidamia, the chorus sings of the joys of faithful love.

The scene in which Achilles is tricked into revealing his identity was a favourite with painters from the sixteenth to the nineteenth centuries, and the story was the subject of several librettos between 1641 and 1736 (see Heller, 'Reforming Achilles').

The 1740–1 season was Handel's second at the Theatre Royal in LINCOLN'S INN FIELDS. After performances of IMENEO in November and December, Deidamia was premiered on 10 January 1741. The cast was:

Deidamia	Elizabeth Duparc ('la FRANCESINA') (soprano)
Nerea	Maria Monza (soprano)
Achille	Miss Edwards (soprano)
Ulisse	Giovanni Battista Andreoni (castrato)

Fenice   William SAVAGE (bass)
Licomede   Henry REINHOLD (bass)

There were three performances, the third of them at the LITTLE THEATRE in the Haymarket – the last opera ever performed under Handel's direction: his future lay in the composition of non-staged works in English.

Deidamia has much of the best music: she is sympathetically drawn as a woman in love who is terrified of losing the boy she adores, yet is exasperated by his behaviour ('Va, perfido!'), and both enraged and griefstricken by Ulisse's deception, which deprives her of her happiness ('M'hai resa infelice'). In the end she knows that she can do nothing to alter Achille's destiny, and accepts the sacrifice she has to make. Achille is a young boy, impetuous and thoughtless, with no deep feelings except for a love of hunting: he is amused when Ulisse pays court to him in his girl's disguise, and is too immature to understand Deidamia's anger at his irresponsibility in teasing Ulisse; his jealousy when he thinks that Deidamia is unfaithful is mere childish petulance, and he has a boy's delight in brandishing weapons. BURNEY considered that 'the sum total of fine airs in this opera is so considerable, that . . . it may be numbered among the happiest of Handel's dramatic productions', and expressed astonishment at 'the fertility and vigour of [Handel's] invention'. Most later commentators have been harsher in their criticism, but Deidamia is very effective on the stage, and in 1955 it was the first work to be performed by the Handel Opera Society in London.   TERENCE BEST

T. Best (ed.), Deidamia, HHA II/41 (Kassel, 2001)
Burney
Dean, Operas
Harris, Librettos
W. Heller, 'Reforming Achilles: Gender, Opera Seria and the Rhetoric of the Enlightened Hero', EM 26/4 (Nov. 1998), 562–81
HHB iv

deism. Lord Herbert of Cherbury (d. 1648) asserted that God exists, and should be worshipped with virtue and repentance, for which He will reward/punish us. Not, perhaps, too threatening to the CHURCH OF ENGLAND, but others developed accompanying views that 'Christianity [was] Not Mysterious' (a famous deist title); religion should be accessible to everybody through reason; priestly practices were highly suspect; revelation, so important in the BIBLE, was but an aid to rational discovery; the connection of Old Testament to New was flimsy. Deism foundered after the 1730s, largely because of a spirited defence by mainstream Anglicans (heard in MESSIAH and Handel's other oratorios).   KATIE HAWKS

See also HANDEL, 12

Smith, Oratorios
G. R. Cragg, The Church and the Age of Reason (1648–1789) (London, 1960)

Delany, Mary (née Granville, former married name Pendarves) (b. Coulston, Wilts., 14 May 1700; d. Windsor, 15 April 1788). Mary Granville was from her earliest years groomed for a place at court but never obtained one. At the age of eight she was sent to live with her aunt Ann (née Granville) Stanley, who had been maid of honour to Queen Mary, and her husband, Sir John Stanley, secretary to the Lord

CHAMBERLAIN. She first met Handel in 1710, when he and HEIDEGGER came to pay their respects to her uncle. As supporters of the Stuarts, the Hanoverian Succession reversed the fortunes of her branch of the Granville family, and in 1717, for financial and political reasons, Delany was forced by her uncle George Granville, Lord Lansdowne, into a loveless marriage with the much older Alexander Pendarves. With Pendarves's death in 1725, she gained social independence as a widow. After this time, Delany, who had excellent training in music and a strong ability at the keyboard, frequented the operas of Handel with her brother Bernard GRANVILLE and her many friends. She was an avid letter-writer, especially to her sister Ann DEWES, and the preservation of these letters, despite Delany's requests that they be destroyed, provides a wellspring of information about Handel's music and its reception.

From 1733, she lived near Handel in Upper Brook Street, and within the period of one month, her letters tell of her hearing *DEBORAH* (4 April 1734); of hosting a party at which 'Mr. Handel was in the best humour in the world, and played lessons and accompanied STRADA and all the ladies that sung from seven o' clock till eleven' (12 April); and attending *SOSARME*, a 'charming' opera, 'and yet I dare say it will be almost empty! 'Tis vexatious to have such music neglected' (30 April). In 1743, against her brother's wishes, she married Patrick Delany, an Irish Anglican cleric. Whilst living in Ireland, she continued to follow Handel's career and learned to play his new compositions from WALSH prints, writing, for example, on 16 November 1751 that she and her friend Anne DONNELLAN, were taking 'great pleasure in thrumming over the sweet songs' of *THEODORA*. After Patrick Delany's death in 1768, she returned to London, where her intellectual and artistic accomplishments continued to bring her the friendship and admiration of many outstanding figures of her day. In 1785, GEORGE III gave Mrs Delany a pension and a house at Windsor, where she lived the remaining years of her life.   ELLEN T. HARRIS

Mary Delany, will of, PROB 11/1165, fol. 335, The National Archives
R. Hayden, *Mrs Delany: Her Life and Flowers* (2nd edn, London, 1992)
M. Laird and A. Weisberg-Roberts (eds.), *Mrs Delany and her Contemporaries* (forthcoming)
Lady Llanover (ed.), *The Autobiography and Correspondence of Mary Granville, Mrs Delany*, 1st ser., 3 vols. (London, 1861), 2nd ser., 3 vols. (1862)

'delirio amoroso, Il'. See *DA QUEL GIORNO FATALE*

Denner, Balthasar (b. Altona near Hamburg, 15 Nov. 1685; d. Rostock, 14 April 1749) German painter. He had art lessons from an early age, but in 1701 his parents apprenticed him to a trading house in HAMBURG for six years. He might have already become aware of Handel, because he cultivated a friendship with Barthold Heinrich BROCKES and was very interested in music. In 1707 Denner was accepted at the BERLIN Academy of Art. There he communicated with many foreign artists especially from Paris and Holland. In 1715 he stayed in London for six weeks. In 1720 he went to HANOVER where he met many English lords and ladies who invited him to England. He eventually took his family to London in 1721, where his miniatures were already highly regarded and was welcomed by the aristocracy. In about 1726–8 Denner painted his well-known portrait of Handel (now in the National Portrait Gallery; Figure 5), but the artist was

5. A portrait of Handel attributed to Balthasar Denner, oil on canvas, 1726–8.

always in fragile health and could not tolerate the smog in London. He returned to Altona in 1728.   EDWIN WERNER

See also ICONOGRAPHY

H. Börsch-Supan, 'Georg Friedrich Händel und Balthasar Denner', GHB II (1986)
W. Schroeder, Balthasar Denner, 1685–1749, Portrait Artist (Winnipeg, 1994)

Der beglückte Florindo. See FLORINDO

Der für die Sünden der Welt gemarterte und sterbende Jesus. See BROCKES PASSION

Der in Kronen erlangte Glückswechsel. See ALMIRA

Dettingen, Battle of (27 June 1743). The battle was fought between a French army under Marshal Noailles and the similarly sized Pragmatic Army of GEORGE II (so-called because of its avowed aim of defending the Pragmatic Sanction that was designed to allow Maria Theresia to succeed to all her father's Habsburg territories) (War of the AUSTRIAN SUCCESSION). George's forces included contingents from Britain, Hanover, Hessen and Austria. It was to be the last occasion on which a reigning British monarch personally led his forces into battle. George, whose military ambitions had been largely frustrated, was nearly sixty at the time of the battle but he managed to inflict a serious defeat on the French. Contemporary reports noted the King's courage during the battle, personally urging his troops on, sword in hand. The victory was celebrated in a variety of ways and Handel composed his Dettingen Te Deum to mark the King's safe return to London (TE DEUM, 5). George initially enjoyed increased popularity because of the victory, although stories that he had favoured his Hanoverian troops over his British led to a swift change of public mood and a backlash against the Hanoverian connection.   ANDREW C. THOMPSON

W. Handrick, Die Pragmatische Armee, 1741–1743 (Munich, 1991)

Deutsch, Otto Erich (b. Vienna, 5 Sept. 1883; d. Vienna, 23 Nov. 1967). Deutsch took his university degree in the history of literature and art, but later devoted his life entirely to the study of the history of music. After the First World War, he worked as journalist and bookseller and was Anthony van Hoboken's librarian from 1926 to 1935. In 1939 he emigrated to England and became a British citizen in 1947. In CAMBRIDGE he collaborated on The British Union Catalogue of Early Music and compiled his Verzeichnis der Werke Franz Schuberts. In his Documentary Biography of Franz Schubert, first published in 1946, he wished to portray the composer's life and work objectively on the basis of a chronological and annotated collection of all available contemporary documents concerning Schubert, thereby dispensing with fictional myth-making and subjective biographers' opinions.

Handel: A Documentary Biography was published as 'a companion' in 1955, dedicated 'To England his second fatherland'. In this book Deutsch collected original sources like documents, records, letters and diaries by Handel and his contemporaries, as well as newspaper reports and pictures, about the composer's life and works. The biography has remained an indispensable reference work for Handel scholarship until the present day. In 1952 Deutsch returned to Vienna and worked, among other places, at the Salzburg Mozarteum.

CHRISTINE MARTIN (Trans. ANGELA BAIER)

See also HÄNDEL-HANDBUCH

Deutsch
   'Handel's Will', Antique Collector (Jan.–Feb. 1941)
   'Handel and Cambridge', Cambridge Review, 7 March 1942
   'Handel's Hunting Song', MT 83/1198 (Dec. 1942)
W. Gerstenberg, J. La Rue and W. Rehm (eds.), Festschrift Otto Erich Deutsch zum 80. Geburtstag
   (Kassel, 1963) (includes list of publications)
HHB iv

'Deutsche Arien, Neun'. See GERMAN ARIAS

Deutsche Händel Gesellschaft. See Friederich CHRYSANDER; EDITIONS, 5

Devoto, John (Giovanni) (fl. 1708–52; of French descent). Theatre painter. Devoto is documented as having worked at DRURY LANE (1723–33), Goodman's Field Theatre (1735–46) and also at New Wells (Clerkenwell, London) and in Norwich, painting scenery for pantomimes and plays. His opera drawings, possibly intended for LOTARIO, were stolen and advertised in the Daily Post in 1728, complete with offers of a reward. According to Lindgren, the drawings now in the British Museum might have been intended for a production of Handel's EZIO at the KING'S THEATRE. Devoto probably also painted the new stage scenery for the operas PORO and ORLANDO. He also designed the admission tickets for HERCULES and SAMSON. KLAUS-PETER KOCH (Trans. ANGELA BAIER)

E. Croft-Murray, John Devoto: A Baroque Scene Painter (London, 1953)
L. Lindgren, 'Die Bühnenausstattung von Händels Opern in London', Händel auf dem
   Theater. Bericht über die Symposien 1986 und 1987, ed. Hans Joachim Marx (Laaber,
   1988)
   'The Staging of Handel's Operas in London', Handel Tercentenary Collection, ed. S. Sadie and
   A. Hicks (London, 1987)

Dewes (var. D'Ewes, née Granville), Ann (b. 1707, d. 1761). Younger sister of MARY DELANY, Dewes lived until her marriage in 1740 with their parents in Gloucester, and afterwards at her husband's family estate in Warwickshire, but her sister wrote to her of social, artistic and political events in London. Her oldest son, Court Dewes (1742–93), sent his aunt Delany a poem on Handel's death, about which Delany wrote, 'I was very much pleased with Court's lines on Mr. Handel; they are very pretty and very just' (5 May 1759).   ELLEN T. HARRIS

Lady Llanover (ed.), *The Autobiography and Correspondence of Mary Granville, Mrs Delany*, 1st ser., 3 vols. (London, 1861); 2nd ser., 3 vols. (1862)

'Diana cacciatrice'. See *ALLA CACCIA*

Didone abbandonata (Dido abandoned), HWV A^{12}. PASTICCIO opera in three acts, based on Leonardo VINCI's *Didone abbandonata* (ROME, 1726). It was first performed at COVENT GARDEN on 13 April 1737. METASTASIO's libretto was first set by Domenico Sarro for NAPLES in 1724 and revised especially for Vinci.

The action begins as the affair between Didone, Queen of Carthage, and the Trojan hero Enea (Aeneas) is coming to an end. Despite his continuing love for Didone, Enea intends to leave Carthage in order to pursue the destiny ordained for him by the gods. The barbaric king of the neighbouring Moors, Iarba, posing as his own envoy Arbace, offers Didone his master's hand, which she contemptuously refuses. Iarba then makes common cause with Didone's treacherous confidant Osmida and tries unsuccessfully to kill Enea. Iarba's confidant, Araspe, falls in love with Didone's sister Selene, who secretly loves Enea. When Didone asks Enea to kill her or give his blessing to her marrying Iarba he can do neither. Iarba challenges Enea to a duel; Iarba falls, but Enea spares his life. As Enea sails away Iarba sets fire to Carthage and Didone throws herself into the flames devouring her palace.

The cast of the first performance was as follows:

Didone	Anna STRADA del Pò (soprano)
Enea	Gioacchino CONTI, 'Gizziello' (castrato)
Iarba	Domenico ANNIBALI (castrato)
Selene	Francesca BERTOLLI (alto)
Osmida	Maria Caterina NEGRI (alto)
Araspe	John BEARD (tenor)

This was the first pasticcio arrangement of another composer's opera Handel had made since the 1733–4 season, and it would be his last. *Didone* had only a short run of three nights in April with a fourth performance on 1 June. Lord SHAFTESBURY found the opera 'very heavy' (Burrows and Dunhill, p. 26). It was probably after the second performance on 20 April that Handel suffered an attack of paralysis that threatened for a time to end his performing career. Beard may have been replaced in some later performances, perhaps by SAVAGE, who apparently filled in for him in *BERENICE* that spring (Dean, *Operas*, p. 392); Araspe's two arias in the printed libretto were both cut in the conducting score along with the preceding solo scenes. None of the music of *Didone* was published.

In preparing his version of the opera Handel made use of a copy of Vinci's score belonging to his friend Charles JENNENS. This manuscript, which is now in the Newberry Library, Chicago, and has been published in facsimile, contains numerous annotations by Handel relating to his arrangement. Apparently because no copy of the Rome libretto was available in London, the anonymous librettist based his revised text primarily on the Naples libretto of 1724. The conducting score, British Library, Add. MS, London 31607, contains a note by Samuel ARNOLD describing its relationship with the lost keyboard score, which he owned. Most of the leaves on which Handel wrote his changes ended up in the keyboard score.

At least thirteen of Vinci's original arias were retained in the final version along with his overture and a sinfonia in Act III. Also saved was Dido's emotional final scene ending in recitative. Handel interpolated nine arias, probably chosen by the singers; the composers include GIACOMELLI, HASSE, Vinci and VIVALDI. An aria by Ristori, 'Quel pastor che udendo al suono', referred to by Handel in the Fitzwilliam Museum, Cambridge, MU.MS. 258, pp. 89–90, was retexted as 'Mi tradì l'infida sorte' in Act III Scene ii. Unusually, three of the interpolated arias were sung to texts from the Naples or Rome librettos, 'Sono intrepido nell'alma', 'A trionfar mi chiama' and 'Cadrà fra poco in cenere'. Before deciding to stage Vinci's opera Handel had borrowed musical ideas from it in his GIUSTINO and ARMINIO, composed in August–October 1736. As a result he felt obliged to cover his tracks by making revisions and cuts in several of Vinci's arias, most notably by extensively recomposing Didone's 'Se vuoi ch'io mora'. He also reworked Vinci's secco recitatives, but only to the extent required by the altered ranges of the singers and textual alterations.   JOHN H. ROBERTS

H. D. Clausen, *Händels Direktionspartituren ('Handexemplare')* (Hamburg, 1972)
J. H. Roberts, 'Handel and Vinci's "Didone abbandonata": Revisions and Borrowings', ML 68/2 (1987), 141–50
Strohm, 164–211
L. Vinci, *Didone Abbandonata*, ed. H. M. Brown (New York, 1977)

Die durch Blut und Mord erlangte Liebe. See NERO

Die verwandelte Daphne. See FLORINDO

Dietro l'orme fugaci ('Armida abbandonata'), HWV 105. Deserted by her lover Rinaldo, despite much useless beseeching, the sorceress Armida watches his ship sailing away, complains about his disloyalty, wishes him to sink and be devoured by sea monsters, but soon repents since she cannot stop loving him. She realises that only the god of love can deliver her from her pangs. While drawing the plot from TASSO's *Gerusalemme Liberata* (Canto XVI, vv. 36, 63–7), the unidentified lyricist closely relies on the rhetoric pattern provided by Rinuccini's celebrated *Lamento d'Arianna*, incorporating individual keywords and line fragments thereof. Handel set the cantata for Marquis RUSPOLI in May–June 1707, probably for the benefit of the household soprano Margherita DURASTANTI, who would later star in AGRIPPINA at VENICE, then in further Handel roles for the Royal Academy of Music (OPERA COMPANIES, 2).

A tense dramaticism, enhanced by the extended use of the accompagnato recitative, prevails throughout the cantata, which provides many time-honoured devices of opera proper. Such are the first aria 'Ah, crudele' – a lament whose florid singing line is based on repeatedly descending lines – and the concluding Siciliana 'In tanti affanni miei', with its (Neapolitan-style) finely nuanced textures, and during which the eloquent cantabile supported by unison violins in the A section gives way to subdued stepwise phrases accompanied by continuo only in the B section. The accompagnato recitative 'O voi, dell'incostante', marked *Furioso*, introduces the second aria, whose vigorous octave leaps would customarily hint to warlike or vengeful feelings (*aria di sdegno*). Nevertheless, its text 'Venti, fermate' ostensibly proclaims Armida's forgiveness – a study in psychological ambivalence announcing the great dramatist.   CARLO VITALI

Direktionspartituren. See SOURCES AND COLLECTIONS, 2

Dixit Dominus. See CHURCH MUSIC, ITALIAN AND LATIN

Doctorate, Honorary. See OXFORD

Dod, Benjamin (bap. London, 2 April 1707; d. London, ?Aug. 1765). Dod was a stationer, trade publisher and bookseller to the Society for Promoting Christian Knowledge. His name appears in the imprints of oratorio WORDBOOKS for Handel published by John WATTS: Dod sold Watts's books in the City. Dod probably supervised the publication of the wordbook for a revival of *JOSEPH AND HIS BRETHREN* in 1757 when Watts was ill.   LESLIE M. M. ROBARTS

L. M. M. Robarts, 'A Bibliographical and Textual Study of the Wordbooks for James Miller's *Joseph and his Brethren* and Thomas Broughton's *Hercules*, Oratorio Librettos Set to Music by George Frideric Handel, 1743–44', Ph.D. dissertation (University of Birmingham, 2008)

Dom, Halle. On 13 March 1702 Handel – although a 'Lutheran subject' – was engaged on trial for one year by HALLE's reformed community as organist for their 'Königliche Schloss- und Domkirche'. An organ by Christian Förner (built 1667) was available for his playing in the two daily church services on Sundays and feast days. He presumably quit his post during the first half of 1703. The church, which to this day has no towers, had been built by Dominican monks around 1300. It came to be known as the 'Dom' from 1523, when Cardinal and Archbishop Albert of Brandenburg made it his *Stiftskirche*. Later, when Samuel SCHEIDT was organist, the Lutheran administrators of the former archbishopric of Magdeburg used it as their private church. After 1680 the new sovereign Prince, the Elector of Brandenburg, relinquished the church to reformed German-speaking refugees.   GÖTZ TRAXDORF (Trans. ANGELA BAIER)

M. Filitz, *Dom Halle* (Regensburg, 2006)
HHB iv
K. Musketa, 'Händel als Organist am Dom zu Halle: neue Quellenfunde', HJb 55 (2009)

Donna, che in ciel. See CHURCH MUSIC, ITALIAN AND LATIN

Donnellan (*var.* Donellan, Donalen, Donnalan), Anne (b. ?1700; d. 1762). Daughter of Nehemiah Donnellan, Lord Chief Baron of the Exchequer of Ireland (d. 1705), her mother later married Philip Percival, who brought the family to London. A close friend of Mary DELANY and Bernard GRANVILLE, she was greatly admired for her singing ability. Probably introduced to Handel by Delany, she maintained her friendship with him in later years when she lived nearby on Charles Street,

Berkeley Square. Delany writes of hearing Handel play at Donnellan's house. Handel left her 50 guineas in his will (HANDEL, 8). At her death, Donnellan bequeathed a portrait (now lost) of Handel set in gold to the British Museum.

ELLEN T. HARRIS

Anne Donnellan, will of, PROB 11/875, The National Archives
P. Kelly, 'Anne Donnellan: Irish Proto-Bluestocking', *Hermathena: A Trinity College Dublin Review*, 154 (1993), 39–68
Lady Llanover (ed.), *The Autobiography and Correspondence of Mary Granville, Mrs Delany*, 1st ser., 3 vols. (London, 1861), 2nd ser., 3 vols. (1862)

Dotti, Anna Vincenza (b. Bologna, c.1695; d. after 1728). Italian contralto (compass a–e″). Her debut might have been 1711 at Bologna. In 1716 she sang in VENICE and from 1717 to 1720 in Naples, where she played Almirena in a version of Handel's *RINALDO* with additions by Leonardo LEO (October 1718). She was a member of the Royal Academy of Music (OPERA COMPANIES, 2) in London for three seasons from autumn 1724. Roles created for her include Irene in *TAMERLANO* and Eduige in *RODELINDA*. She sang in revivals of *GIULIO CESARE* and *OTTONE*; in *ALESSANDRO* and *ADMETO* she played male roles. Anna Dotti left England (and the stage) in spring 1728.   ARTIE HEINRICH

Dragon of Wantley, The. A burlesque opera in three acts by John Frederick LAMPE set to a libretto by Henry CAREY and based on a local legend in the Rotherham area of Yorkshire. Act I opens with a description of the 'wretched Havock' which the Dragon (bass, Henry REINHOLD) is causing before a maid, Margery (soprano ISABELLA YOUNG), and her father Gaffer Gubbins (tenor, John Laguerre) decide to ask the 'valiant Knight' Moore (tenor, Thomas Salway) to rid them of the Dragon. Moore accepts in exchange for the favours of Margery, causing Mauxalinda (soprano, ESTHER YOUNG), Moore's mistress, to grow jealous. As Act II begins Margery is recovering from a dream where Moore was killed by the Dragon; Mauxalinda is intent on revenge but is stopped by Moore. In Act III Moore slays the Dragon and is reunited with Margery.

The first performance was on 16 May 1737 at the LITTLE THEATRE, in the Haymarket. The work was extremely popular, running to sixty-nine performances in its first season alone. *The Dragon of Wantley* bears some similarities to Handel's opera *GIUSTINO*, first performed three months earlier on 16 February 1737. However, this is likely to be a coincidence given that Carey finished the text two years earlier. A further link between the two works is that Henry Reinhold sang in both their premieres. *The Dragon of Wantley* was essentially, as with many burlesque operas of the time, designed as a parody on Italian opera, for example, Salway – who had sung small parts for Handel in operas and oratorios at COVENT GARDEN in 1735 – came on stage dressed as the castrato FARINELLI.

MATTHEW GARDNER

R. Fiske, *English Theatre Music in the Eighteenth Century* (Oxford, 1973)
H. C. Wolff, 'Eine Englische Händel-Parodie: "The Dragon of Wantley" (1737)1', HJB 29 (1983)

dramaturgy. The art of creating and performing a drama. It is a parallel to RHETORIC, the art of creating and performing an oration. It also overlaps with poetics, not least because dramas are often written in verse.

Based on ancient Greek precedent and on Aristotle's *Poetics* as the fundamental text, 'classical' dramaturgy with its various rules and precepts had functioned since the sixteenth century as an enabling doctrine for dramatists, but was increasingly regarded as restrictive, despite modifications and reinterpretations. Its use implied the values of classicism, the aesthetic hegemony of the genre of spoken tragedy, and the self-legitimatory interests of courtly society. Thus its application to the musical theatre (opera and oratorio) and generally to 'modern' society was contestable. The *Querelle des anciens et des modernes*, sparked by Charles Perrault's defence of Philippe QUINAULT's and Jean-Baptiste LULLY's *Alceste* (1674), a successful *tragédie en musique* which had been attacked by the classicists Nicholas Boileau-Despréaux and Jean RACINE, spread to other countries, involving such critics as Lodovico Antonio Muratori, Barthold FEIND, Johann MATTHESON, John Dennis and Joseph ADDISON.

A respected formulation of classicist dramaturgy was Pierre CORNEILLE's treatise *Trois discours sur le poème dramatique* (1660). He describes the three so-called 'Aristotelian unities' of time, place and action; the six hierarchically ordered *parties integrantes* (inherent parts) of subject, character/ethos, sentiment/passion, diction, music and decoration; and poetic forms such as prologue, epilogue, division into acts and scenes. Corneille prefers dramatic probability (verisimilitude) to absolute historical truth; he rejects miracle (*le merveilleux*) and accident as dramaturgical expedients, and emphasises the overall ideals of morality and good taste (*bienséances*). Debates arose about how far these precepts could be applied to the *dramma per musica* – a genre that fulfilled similar socio-artistic functions in Italy as spoken tragedy did elsewhere. Italian seventeenth-century librettists endlessly transgressed Aristotelian precepts (often excusing themselves in their prefaces), but the libretto reformers of Handel's generation by and large adopted them. Similar rules were applied to the Latin and vernacular oratorio in Arcangelo Spagna's *Discorso dogmatico*, a preface to his oratorio text publication of 1706.

Handel undoubtedly participated in discussions about the *Regeldrama*, already in HAMBURG and ROME; but his many settings of 'classicist' dramatic texts by Antonio SALVI, Carlo Sigismondo CAPECE, Domenico LALLI, Agostino PIOVENE, Apostolo ZENO and Pietro METASTASIO are counterbalanced by several opera librettos (for example by Aaron HILL, Nicola Francesco HAYM and Silvio STAMPIGLIA) featuring magic, comical traits and/or formal freedom. The dramaturgy of *ORLANDO* is non-Aristotelian ('Ariostean', perhaps), although Capece had tried to narrate the story according to classicist principles. Handel's musical decisions often subvert the dramaturgy of his 'classicist' texts. His later ORATORIOS could for structural reasons not equally be subjected to unifying dramaturgical principles, but in this genre, too, magic and romantic traditions (as found, for example, in English drama) competed with the classicist influence of Corneille and Racine. REINHARD STROHM

Strohm
R. Strohm, *Dramma per Musica: Italian Opera Seria of the Eighteenth Century* (London and New Haven, 1997), 119–251

Draper, Somerset (bap. Wandsworth, Surrey, 1 April 1706; d. London, 1756). Draper, son of a brewer, was a relative of the stationer Jacob TONSON, whose publishing firm employed Draper as its financial agent and negotiator of terms with authors. Draper's name appears in the imprints of several wordbooks published by Tonson for Handel's oratorios, the first being *HERCULES* in 1745 and the last a revival of *JOSHUA* in 1754. In return for Draper's loyalty, Tonson redeemed the mortgage on the Draper brewery.   LESLIE M. M. ROBARTS

Dresden. With his conversion to Catholicism and the acquisition of the Polish crown, the Saxon Elector Frederick Augustus I (King of Poland as Augustus II; also called Augustus the Strong) established his residential city of Dresden as one of the leading European courts. Music, since the foundation of the Electorate of Saxony an integral part of court culture, and other arts were flourishing as never before in the era of Augustus the Strong (1694–1733) and his son Frederick Augustus II (1733–63), earning their reigns the title of 'Dresden's Augustan Age'. The Hofkapelle, on triple duty in opera, church and chamber, counted musicians of exceptional abilities among its ranks and the ensemble of singers was among the best in Europe.

On 14 May 1719 Handel received a commission from the Royal Academy of Music (OPERA COMPANIES, 2) to engage singers for the 1720/1 season. Travelling on from HALLE, he reached Dresden in July and began negotiating for singers (according to a letter from Handel to Lord BURLINGTON dated 15 July 1719). Revivals of Antonio LOTTI's *Giove in Argo* (3 September), *Ascanio* (7 September) and the premiere of *Teofane* (13 September) in celebration of the marriage of Crown Prince Frederick Augustus and Archduchess Maria Josepha in September 1719, afforded Handel opportunities to hear singers who were considered for London: SENESINO, Margherita DURASTANTI and Giuseppe Maria BOSCHI (the latter two already known to Handel from his Italian years) as well as Maddalena SALVAI and Matteo Berselli. Moreover, it seems highly likely that his encounter with Lotti's *Teofane* later influenced his decision to compose his own setting of the libretto (*OTTONE*). Handel, who had 'exhibited his skills before His Royal Majesty and His Royal Highness the Crown Prince' (perhaps on a fortepiano by Cristofori), received 100 ducats for this performance, and left Dresden in November 1719. There is no documentary evidence for a longer stay or a renewed visit in early 1720.

Most of the singers Handel had his eye on had their contracts extended by the Dresden court (only Durastanti left Dresden early to be able to perform in the premiere of *RADAMISTO* on 27 April 1720), which meant that they were not available for London until autumn 1721. However, it seems that Senesino instigated an intrigue – including particularly unreasonable behaviour during rehearsals of Heinichen's *Flavio Crispo* – to provoke Augustus the Strong into sacking them before the termination of their contracts. By way of these schemes, the singers were able to come to London in the course of the year 1720.

Italian opera in Dresden was revived a few years later under Giovanni Alberto Ristori with new young singers (and charmed, among others, the Prussian Crown Prince, later Frederick II, to such an extent that he immediately ordered the foundation of his own Italian opera company when he acceded to the throne), but it only established its pan-European dominance under Johann Adolf HASSE from 1731 to 1734. There were no performances of Handel's operas at Dresden during the eighteenth century: as a matter of principle, the court opera performed only works by its own Hofkapellmeisters until 1763. When the opera company also started performing works composed elsewhere, opera seria of the Handelian type had gone out of fashion.

The Dresden court was notable for collecting instrumental music by non-local composers like VIVALDI, TELEMANN and Fasch. These were built up over long periods of time, and included about 120 sources of Handel's instrumental works preserved in scores and parts, such as overtures, orchestral suites, concerti grossi and trio sonatas (including some works of doubtful authenticity like HWV 393–4). The works could have been performed as 'table music' and in chamber concerts; later they may have been part of the *Graduale instrumentaliter* in the Catholic court services. Overtures were often extended by newly added introductions or movements, and were rescored to take advantage of the rich sonorities of the Dresden Hofkapelle orchestra. Many of the Dresden Handel sources come from the estate of the Hofkapelle's concertmaster Johann Georg Pisendel. Copies of overtures, suites and other instrumental works were probably made from the WALSH editions. Some works, such as the contrafactum 'Huc pastores properate' (after the aria 'Son confusa pastorella' from *PORO*; possibly prepared under Zelenka's supervision), are unique.

There were radical changes in the musical life at the Dresden court in the aftermath of the SEVEN YEARS WAR, and changes in the Electorate's rulership led to further relocation of court music-making into the domestic sphere, especially as far as instrumental music was concerned. According to the biannual calculations of financial expenditure on court music drawn up from October 1777, among many other works, Handel's keyboard music was acquired and may have been used by Elector Frederick Augustus III, an accomplished keyboard player, for music-making and studying purposes.

Handel's oratorios began to be performed quite late, and predominantly in bourgeois circles, mainly by the so-called *Dreyßigsche Singakademie*. In addition to some sporadic performances in the 1820s, *JUDAS MACCABAEUS* (from 1820), *MESSIAH* (from 1822) and ten other oratorios were performed by the Singakademie under the direction of the court organist Johann Gottlob Schneider, in the majority of cases including the forces of the *Königliche Kapelle* and often for the benefit of charities. Some transcriptions of Handel's works (1868/73) by the Dresden-based cellist and composer Friedrich Grützmacher were very popular in their day.

Handel's operas began to be occasionally performed at Dresden after 1920, with productions of *SERSE* (1924), *GIULIO CESARE* (1934), *ARIANNA IN CRETA* (1953), *ALESSANDRO* (the opera's first German performance, 1959) and *DEIDAMIA* (1969). His orchestral and chamber music was included regularly in the symphonic concerts of the *Königliche Kapelle* and in performances given by the Tonkünstler society. Gradually a steady tradition of Handel performance emerged, and since the 1970s has been reinvigorated by the early music scene. HANS GÜNTER OTTENBERG (Trans. ANGELA BAIER)

I. Burde, *Die Werke Georg Friedrich Händels in Überlieferung und Praxis der Dresdner Hofmusik des 18. Jahrhunderts*, MA dissertation (Technical University of Dresden, 2000)

F. Chrysander, *G. F. Handel*, vol. 2 (Leipzig, 1860), 18

M. Fürstenau, *Zur Geschichte der Musik und des Theaters am Hofe zu Dresden* (Dresden, 1861/2)

J. Gress, 'Händel in Dresden (1719)', HJb 9 (1963)

O. Landmann, 'Einige Überlegungen zu den Konzerten nebenamtlich komponierender Dresdner Hofmusiker in der Zeit von etwa 1715–1763', *Die Entwicklung des Solokonzerts* (Blankenburg, 1983)

Drums. See INSTRUMENTATION

Drury Lane Theatre. The first Drury Lane Theatre was erected by the King's Company in 1674. According to John DRYDEN's prologue for the opening, it was a 'Plain Built House', and it turned out to be better suited to spoken drama than to opera. The architect has been speculatively identified as Sir Christopher Wren. Capacity has been variously estimated, but was probably originally c.600–800 and gradually expanded to c.2,300 by 1762. Drury Lane was a patent theatre used principally for spoken drama, though it did BALLAD OPERA in the 1730s, and Berta Joncus has recently demonstrated that its incidental music included large amounts of Handel (almost entirely uncredited) in the 1730s and 1740s. The theatre was rebuilt on a grander scale by Sheridan in 1794.

JUDITH MILHOUS and ROBERT D. HUME

B. Joncus, 'Handel at Drury Lane: Ballad Opera and the Production of Kitty Clive', *JRMA* 131 (2006), 179–226

F. H. W. Sheppard, *Survey of London*, vol. 35: *The Theatre Royal Drury Lane and The Royal Opera House Covent Garden* (London, 1970)

Dryden, John (b. Aldwincle, Northants., 9 Aug. 1631; d. London, 1 May 1700). Dryden is a major figure in seventeenth-century British culture. Born into a staunch Parliamentarian family, his lifelong and scholarly interest in Greek and Roman literature began at Westminster School and continued at Trinity College, CAMBRIDGE. Formerly employed as a clerk for Oliver Cromwell's Lord Chamberlain, he wrote an enthusiastic Royalist poem *Astraea Redux* (1660) to celebrate the restoration of the monarchy, after which he turned to writing stage comedies and tragedies. Dryden was appointed Poet Laureate in 1668. In the same year he wrote an essay *Of Dramatick Poesie*, which explores dramatic theory, dramatic practice and the comparative merits of blank verse and rhyming couplets.

Absalom and Achitophel (1681), partly co-authored with Nahum TATE, has long been thought Dryden's most famous poem, but there is little doubt that the *Aeneid* in English couplets is his masterpiece. In 1674 he wrote an operatic libretto based on MILTON's *Paradise Lost*. A decade later he drafted an ambitious operatic project on the subject of King Arthur, the prologue of which was fashioned into the masque-like *Albion and Albanius*, with music by Louis Grabu. This proved unfortunate at its eventual staging in 1686, because it coincided with the closure of London's theatres in response to the Duke of Monmouth's challenge to the throne of James II. After the Glorious Revolution of 1688, Dryden, having become a Roman Catholic and refusing to recant, was stripped of his court positions. He became dependent on his writing, which included adapting texts for the theatre. Dryden had reservations about the compromises that music forced upon a poet's expression. Nevertheless, impressed by Henry PURCELL, he wrote a preface for the printed score of Purcell's *The Prophetess, or Diocletian* (1691). At this time he collaborated with Purcell on the opera *King Arthur*, using text based on his earlier Arthurian material, and during the early 1690s the composer supplied incidental music for revivals of several of Dryden's plays.

The poet's interest in the relationship between music and poetry is particularly apparent in his two St Cecilia 'odes', the SONG FOR ST CECILIA'S DAY (1687), set to music by Giovanni Draghi, and ALEXANDER'S FEAST, OR, THE POWER OF MUSIQUE, written for celebrations of music's patroness in 1697 and set by Jeremiah Clarke (music now lost). The complexity of the poetry in these two odes challenges composers to prove that vocal music can approach poetry's capability to achieve the sublime. *Alexander's Feast* was Handel's first setting of a major work by a leading English writer and was adapted from Dryden's poem by Newburgh HAMILTON in 1736. Edward Holdsworth in a letter to Charles JENNENS noted the taxing nature of Dryden's poetry. On hearing that Handel had set *Alexander's Feast*, Holdsworth wrote that 'tho' 'tis very musical to read, yet the words . . . are very difficult to set . . . I hope [Handel's] superior genius has surmounted all difficulties' (9 March 1736: HHB iv, pp. 260–1). Handel's music for *Song for St Cecilia* followed in 1739. The popularity enjoyed by Handel's settings of these 'odes' undoubtedly sustained Dryden's reputation during the eighteenth century.   LESLIE M. M. ROBARTS

R. M. Myers, *Handel, Dryden and Milton* (London, 1956)
J. A. Winn, *John Dryden and his World* (New Haven, 1987)
D. Vickers, 'Music for a While: John Dryden and Henry Purcell', *Goldberg* 44 (2007), 42–53

Dublin. Capital of Ireland (pop. 100,000 in Handel's time). From biographer John MAINWARING's account of Handel's visit to Ireland, one might think that the decision to leave London was a whim or at least made with considerable nonchalance. Given Handel's characteristic caution this seems unlikely. While we have no direct knowledge of what caused him to spend a season in the capital city of Britain's nearest colony, we do know that he had among his friends in London several Anglo-Irish persons, including the Earl of EGMONT, his brother Philip PERCIVAL and his wife Martha, and Frances, the wife of John Christopher SMITH JUNIOR. Mary Pendarves (later DELANY), had spent several years there in the 1730s. John Clegg, the Irish virtuoso violinist, played in his band, and he also knew Matthew DUBOURG, who led the Irish State Music and Trumpets in Dublin. The actor James Quin, another of Handel's friends, may also have been involved and he played at the Aungier Street Theatre from the summer of 1741.

With the discovery of an advertisement for a poem by Laurence Whyte, the title of which appears to indicate that Handel was invited to Dublin by the Lord Lieutenant, William Cavendish, Duke of Devonshire, biographers have assumed that Handel received an actual invitation. In fact there was no necessity for an invitation (one was not needed to obtain a passport, to hire musicians or a hall, to rent a house or to advertise). The use of the word is a trope that attributes generosity and care to the leader of the land. From the Irish point of view, the visit could not be portrayed as providing Handel with a convenient bolt hole. The trope makes the visit appear mutually pleasing. In contrast, the view from London, at least as voiced by POPE and by early Handelian commentators, was that Handel was driven from England. For BURNEY, whose genre was supposedly non-fiction, a withdrawal from London would take Handel and his works 'out of the range of enmity and prejudice', thereby suggesting a psychological motive.

Handel arrived in Dublin (from Holyhead) on 17 November 1741 and left on 13 August 1742 (returning via Parkgate, near CHESTER). His venture was primarily a commercial one. The initial plan appears to have been for a single six-performance concert series at NEALE'S MUSICK HALL (23 December 1741–10 February 1742), funded by subscription. Handel gave two performances each of *L'ALLEGRO*, *ACIS AND GALATEA* (including the *SONG FOR ST CECILIA'S DAY*) and *ESTHER*. Success prompted a second series (17 February–31 March 1742), which included two performances of *ALEXANDER'S FEAST*, another performance of *L'Allegro*, two performances of *Hymen* (a revised version of *IMENEO*, promoted to Dubliners as a 'serenata'; these were Handel's last performances of one of his operas, albeit unstaged). After the second series concluded with another performance of *Esther*, Handel gave the premiere of *MESSIAH* on 13 April; Philip Percival was on the Board of Mercer's Hospital and it may well have been he who suggested to Handel the possibility of holding a fund-raising concert. This was followed by two further performances (not for charity) of *SAUL* (25 May) and *Messiah* (3 June).

The solo singers included Signora AVOGLIO, a soprano who accompanied Handel to Dublin, Susanna CIBBER, contralto, and two members of the Dublin cathedral choirs. Some of the other cathedral men filled out the chorus. Mrs Cibber arrived in Dublin at the request of Quin, who wished to aid her in recovering her place on the stage, which she had been forced to leave as a result of the scandal surrounding two adultery cases brought by her husband. Whether Handel actively encouraged either Mrs Cibber or Quin in this plan or simply took advantage of it is unknown. In the event, Mrs Cibber's performance in *Messiah* supposedly caused Dean Delany (not yet the husband of Mary Pendarves) to exclaim, 'Woman, for this, be all thy sins forgiven.'

Handel, as a well-seasoned impresario, would not have embarked on such a trip, especially one supposedly designed to restore his fortunes, without some assurances from reliable sources such as Dubourg, Percival or Clegg concerning the musicians he would need for his orchestra. The instrumental musicians that he employed in Dublin primarily comprised the members of the Irish State Music and Trumpets, led by Dubourg. Almost all the eleven State Musicians had been professionals for at least ten years and nearly half for twenty-five or more before Handel's visit. They were probably supplemented by a few independent musicians. The performances were given by smaller instrumental and choral resources than was usual in London, but Handel was well satisfied with the musical standard and the commercial profit of his Dublin expedition. He mentioned in a letter to Jennens the possibility of returning to Ireland but it never happened.   DAVID HUNTER

See also CORK; HANDEL, 15

D. Burrows, *Handel: Messiah* (Cambridge, 1991)
    'Handel's Dublin Performances', *Irish Musical Studies*, vol. 4, ed. P. F. Devine and H. White (Dublin, 1996)
D. Hunter, 'Inviting Handel to Ireland: Laurence Whyte and the Challenge of Poetic Evidence', *Eighteenth-Century Ireland* 20 (2005), 156–68
    'The Irish State Music from 1716 to 1742 and Handel's Band in Dublin', *GHB* XI (2006)

Dubourg, Matthew (b. London, 1703; d. London, 3 July 1767). Violinist and composer, pupil of Francesco GEMINIANI. Dubourg made his debut solo appearance at LINCOLN'S INN FIELDS in 1715. His first documented appearance with Handel was in a benefit concert at Hickford's Room in James Street (near the Haymarket) on 18 February 1719, which, according to the *Daily Courant*, included an unidentified new concerto 'Compos'd by Mr. Hendel, and perform'd by Mr. Matthew Dubourg' (Deutsch, 83–4). In 1727 he married Frances, the daughter of Bernard GATES, and the following year he was appointed Master and Composer of State Music in Ireland. He led the orchestra for Handel's DUBLIN concerts (including the first performances of *MESSIAH*), and at COVENT GARDEN during the 1743 oratorio season, in which he performed violin solos between parts of works such as *SAMSON* and *L'ALLEGRO*. Dubourg, who participated in numerous Irish performances of Handel's works, received a bequest of £100 from Handel (HANDEL, 8). DAGMAR GLÜXAM (Trans. ANGELA BAIER)

Deutsch
A. Mann, 'An Unknown Detail of Handel Biography', *Bach: The Journal of the Riemenschneider Bach Institut*, 25 (1994), 59–62
R. E. Seletsky, '18th-Century variations for Corelli's Sonatas, op. 5', EM 24 (1996), 119–30
N. Zaslaw, 'Ornaments for Corelli's Violin Sonatas, op 5', EM 24 (1996), 95–115

DuBurk (Duburk, Duburg, Duburgh, De Bourk), John (d. ?1772). Handel's primary manservant from 1757, DuBurk took over this responsibility after the death of his uncle Peter LeBlond, as attested by Handel in the second codicil of his will (HANDEL, 8). Handel bequeathed him £500 and all his wearing apparel. DuBurk apparently attended Handel at concerts; he is the highest-paid servant on the bills for performances of *MESSIAH* at the FOUNDLING HOSPITAL in 1758 and 1759. When Handel's will was proved (24 April 1759), DuBurk attested to the authenticity of Handel's handwriting, and after all the stated bequests were made and an inventory taken, he bought the remaining items in Handel's house for £48. He also took tenancy of the house and lived there from 1759 to 1772. ELLEN T. HARRIS

Deutsch
J. Greenacombe, 'Handel's House: A History of No. 25 Brook Street, Mayfair', *London Topographical Record* 25 (1985), 119
G. F. Handel, will of, PROB 1/14 (autograph), The National Archives
HHB iv

Ducas (or Doukas), Michael (c.1400–1462). Byzantine historian, author of the *Historia Byzantina* which served as a source for the libretto of Handel's *TAMERLANO*. Ducas probably occupied a position of esteem under Constantine XII, the last Emperor of Constantinople. After the city's capture by Sultan Mohammed II in 1453, Ducas sought refuge with the Prince of Lesbos, Dorino Gateluzzi, and was entrusted with a number of diplomatic missions. In 1455 and 1456, Ducas returned to Constantinople with Gateluzzi's son and successor Domenico to pay homage to the Sultan. WALTER KREYSZIG

W. Plate, 'Ducas', *Dictionary of Greek and Roman Biography and Mythology*, ed. W. Smith, 3 vols. (London, 1844–59)

Duel. See Johann MATTHESON

'Duello amoroso, Il'. See *AMARILLI VEZZOSA*

Duets. See CHAMBER DUETS AND TRIOS

Dunque sarà pur vero ('Agrippina condotta a morire'), HWV 110. Conceived in a traditional seventeenth-century form of 'lamento' – as shown, *inter alia*, by several
ariosos interweaving with the recitatives and overweighing arias proper – this
cantata for solo soprano, two violin parts and continuo features a fictional
monologue of the Roman Empress mother Julia Agrippina (AD 15–59), just
moments before her assassination ordered by her son Nero. The grim event,
reported by the historians TACITUS, SUETONIUS and Dio Cassius, took place
in Baiae, Gulf of NAPLES. This circumstance, allied with precise and extended
textual correspondences with GIUVO's libretto for *ACI, GALATEA E POLIFEMO*,
suggests the work to have originated around 1708 within the Neapolitan circle
of Aurora SANSEVERINO.

    The aria 'Se infelice', conveying Agrippina's menace to return as a haunting
ghost, seems both a textual and musical precedent to Cleopatra's 'Piangerò la
sorte mia' in *GIULIO CESARE*. This, plus Agrippina's twice-repeated prediction
about her remains being denied a decent burial, and the final offer of her 'seno'
('breast', euphemistic for the original 'uterus' and 'venter' in Tacitus) to the
stabbers, are the only motives drawn from these classical narratives. The rest is a
whirlpool of conflicting attitudes: despair, curses, prayers to Jupiter for revenge,
repentance on experiencing a backfiring of motherly love, resignation and proud
defiance. Handel set this peculiarly asymmetric cantata libretto, totalling 134
lines but only four arias, by putting a premium on expressive depth and flexible
phrasing rather than on vocal acrobatics. A strong unifying drive is provided
by the bass section, while the violins, by turns unison or divided, add dramatic
and psychological momentum into the texture. This happens particularly in the
long central section, framed by a recurring arioso. For self-BORROWINGS see
TESEO, ESTHER.   CARLO VITALI

Duparc, Elisabeth. See La FRANCESINA

Durastanti, Margherita (b. c.1685; fl. 1700–34; d. Rome? after 1753). Soprano (range
b–a″, tessitura d′–g″), later mezzo-soprano (range f–g″ tessitura c′–g″). She
experienced a working relationship singing newly composed music across a
longer number of years than any other singer with whom Handel worked, even
the tenor John Beard. The opera-loving Carlo Ferdinando Gonzaga, Duke of
Mantua, supported her debut at VENICE's Teatro San Salvatore in 1700 and
employed her in his court theatres at Mantua and Casale Monferrato until his
deposition in 1703. From January 1707 to October 1708 she served at RUSPOLI's
household in ROME, where she first encountered Handel. From Autumn 1709
to February 1713 she was engaged at Venice's Teatro SAN GIOVANNI GRISOS-
TOMO, where she sang in nine operas by LOTTI and C. F. Pollarolo, and the
title role in Handel's *AGRIPPINA*. During the same period, and over the next
two years, she appeared in Bologna, Genoa, FLORENCE and lesser operatic
centres in northern Italy. In late September 1715, Durastanti arrived in NAPLES
and stayed there until at least Carnival 1717, performing operas and serenatas at

the Royal Palace, the Teatro San Bartolomeo and in various noble households (including Aurora SANSEVERINO's).

While there, she met and married Casimiro Avelloni, an impoverished count who apparently shared her subsequent tours to DRESDEN (1719), London (1720–1; 1722–4), Munich (1721) and Paris (1724). Avelloni was involved in trading art and financial speculations, with scanty success. In the late 1720s the couple settled down in Rome, although the husband sometimes hid at Naples to escape creditors. Their marriage proved largely fruitful; King George I and the Princess Royal even served as godparents to a daughter in March 1721, when the couple lived at Golden Square, Soho. The Venetian painter A. M. Zanetti, who lodged there in the summer, sketched her sturdy profile and large jaw, an image which corresponds with BURNEY's later description of her as 'coarse and masculine'. However, despite physical disadvantage and frequent pregnancies, she learned and performed a new opera about every six weeks during each London season, as well as singing for the royal family and occasional employers. From the initial £1,100 per season, contracted by Handel on behalf of the Royal Academy (OPERA COMPANIES, 2) in 1719, her salary ascended to 1,200 guineas. She earned more than £1,000 for her benefit night on 17 March 1724, during which she performed a farewell cantata on an English text by Alexander POPE. Although at this point a critic described her as 'old' and her voice 'both mediocre and worn-out', she returned much later to sing in Handel's company during the 1733–4 season (his first in competition with the OPERA OF THE NOBILITY). Lady Bristol reported that Durastanti sang 'as well as ever she did' in the pasticcio SEMIRAMIDE (Deutsch, 336), but Handel's abridgement of Tauride's 'Qual leon' in the first run of ARIANNA IN CRETA was perhaps a sensitive precaution that avoided presenting his ageing ex-prima donna in an unflattering vocal light. Then, after a busy theatrical career developing over thirty-four years and nearly sixty documented productions, Durastanti disappeared. There is circumstantial evidence that she still lived, in financial distress, in early 1753.

Among the non-operatic roles Handel wrote for her, one may arguably include some solo cantatas for the Ruspoli accademie, such as DIETRO L'ORME FUGACI, CLORI, MIA BELLA CLORI, ALLA CACCIA, Nella Stagion che di Viole e Rose and La Lucrezia. Durastanti's appearance at Ruspoli's as Maria Maddalena in the first performance of La RESURREZIONE (1708) attracted a reprimand from the Pope that led to her substitution with a castrato for the second performance. In addition to the title role in Agrippina, Handel composed numerous important operatic roles for Durastanti: RADAMISTO (title role, 1720); Clelia (Muzio Scevola, 1721); Rossane (FLORIDANTE, 1721); Gismonda (OTTONE, 1723); Vitige (FLAVIO, 1723); Sesto (GIULIO CESARE, 1724); Tauride (ARIANNA IN CRETA, 1734); Calliope (PARNASSO IN FESTA, 1734). The analysis of extant scores shows that she started as a low-lying soprano who later added a few lower notes and substantially downpitched her tessitura. The turning point in the process may have been around 1721 (see CRUDEL TIRANNO AMOR). The voice-shift seems to have increased her ability both to perform extended coloratura passages and leaping intervals, while energetic syllabic singing and fine chromatic nuances remained her strong points throughout. In fact, roles in Handel's Royal Academy operas are more virtuosic than anything she had sung previously in her career. Her acting versatility is suggested by the wide dramatic variety of her roles, from strong female characters to a full range of trouser roles, from juvenile through heroic to villainous.   CARLO VITALI

L. Lindgren, 'Musicians and Librettists in the Correspondence of Gio. Giacomo Zamboni', *Royal Musical Association Research Chronicle*, 24 (1991)

Düsseldorf. Residence of the Elector Johann Wilhelm (Jan Wellem) of Pfalz-Neuburg (1690–1716). He was a cousin of the Elector of HANOVER. Handel stayed at the Düsseldorf court which had its own court orchestra and court opera (since 1659) on three separate occasions. Agostino STEFFANI seems not to have procured invitations. After Handel had been appointed Kapellmeister in Hanover (June 1710) and was given holiday leave, he travelled first to HALLE then via Düsseldorf (autumn 1710) to London. In the summer of 1711 he left London for Hanover again, travelling via Düsseldorf (June 1711) (WEISS). After the Royal Academy of Music (OPERA COMPANIES, 2) was founded in February 1719, Handel had to travel to the continent again to hire singers. He first returned to Düsseldorf (May 1719) to engage the soprano castrato Benedetto Baldassari, then travelled to DRESDEN via Halle. From there he returned to London in early November 1719, bringing with him a set of Italian singers. A hundred years later, in 1820, Düsseldorf and the Lower Rhine music festivals saw the beginnings of a Handel renaissance (RECEPTION HISTORY) with a series of memorable performances of Handel's oratorios under the direction of the likes of Felix MENDELSSOHN BARTHOLDY, Julius Rietz, Ferdinand Hiller, Robert Schumann and Julius Tausch.   KLAUS-PETER KOCH (Trans. ANGELA BAIER)

K. W. Niemöller, 'Die Händel-Pflege auf den niederrheinischen Musikfesten', HJb 44 (1998)
    'Die Händelüberlieferung im historischen Notenarchiv des Musikvereins Düsseldorf: Zur Händelpflege des 19. Jahrhunderts im Umkreis von Mendelssohn und Schumann', *Georg Friedrich Händel – ein Lebensinhalt: Gedenkschrift für Bernd Baselt (1934–1993)*, ed. K. Hortschansky and K. Musketa (Halle, 1995)

Ebeling, Christoph Daniel (b. Garmissen near Hildesheim, 20 Nov. 1741; d. Hamburg, 30 June 1817). Scholar, librarian. He translated *MESSIAH* together with Friedrich Gottlieb KLOPSTOCK in 1775; their version in turn formed the textual basis for later translations by Johann Adam HILLER and Georg Gottfried GERVINUS. Around the same time Ebeling also translated the Utrecht Te Deum (Berlin, Staatsbibliothek Preussischer Kulturbesitz Mus T 1429) (TE DEUM, 1). Later he used parts of his German text of *JUDAS MACCABAEUS*, based on the version by Eschenburg, for a cantata featuring music by Handel, *Der vierzehnte Julius 1790*. His German-language version of *SAUL*, which has a metre and rhyme scheme that is close to the English original, was published in 1786. In the *Lobgesang auf die Harmonie* (Berlin, Staatsbibliothek Preussischer Kulturbesitz Mus. ms. autogr. C. F. G. Schwenke 4), set to music by Christian Gottlieb Schwenke, Ebeling celebrated the 'unrivalled' Handel.

WERNER RACKWITZ (Trans. ANGELA BAIER)

Ch. D. Ebeling, 'Versuch einer auserlesenen musikalischen Bibliothek', *Unterhaltungen*, vol. 10, parts 4 and 10 (Hamburg, 1770)

M. Marx-Weber and H. J. Marx, 'Der deutsche Text zu Händels "Messias" in der Fassung von Klopstock und Ebeling', *Beiträge zur Geschichte des Oratoriums seit Händel*, Festschrift Günther Massenkeil, ed. R. Cadenbach and H. Loos (Bonn, 1986)

W. Rackwitz, 'Händeliana in Briefen Chrysanders an Heinrich Bellermann', HJb 45 (1999)

Ebner, Johann Wolfgang (b. Augsburg, 1612; d. Vienna, 11/12 Feb. 1665). Organist, harpsichordist, Kapellmeister, composer. Ebner was organist at the Vienna Stephansdom before 1634–?1637. Later he became court organist (1637–65) and Kapellmeister (1663–5). He composed harpsichord, ballet and church music. Together with Johann Jacob FROBERGER he established the so-called Wiener Klavierschule. Handel copied compositions by him into the now missing book of manuscript music dated 1698. KLAUS-PETER KOCH (Trans. ANGELA BAIER)

[W. Coxe], *Anecdotes of George Frederick Handel and John Christopher Smith* (London, 1799; facsimile edn, ed. P. M. Young, New York, 1979), 6n.

Eccles, John (b. ?London, c.1668; d. Hampton Wick, 12 Jan. 1735). The first evidence of the English composer's activities is a published collection of songs from 1691. He worked as a composer at the Theatre Royal and DRURY LANE from 1693, during which time he produced a large amount of music for masques and plays. Having taken part in the Prize Musick Competition of 1701 to set William CONGREVE's libretto *The Judgment of Paris*, Eccles turned again to a Congreve text in 1706 when he composed *Semele: An English Opera* (the text of which was later set by Handel (*SEMELE*). When plans to stage *Semele* failed, the disillusioned Eccles left the theatre but continued with his duties as Master of the Queen's Musick, which required him to compose odes for the royal family until his death. In this capacity he was also involved in performances of Handel's music; for example, Eccles received travel expenses for himself and twenty-two of the Queen's musicians to perform the Utrecht Te Deum at Windsor on 19 November 1713; Handel may also have been present at this time.   MATTHEW GARDNER

Burrows, *Chapel Royal*, 93
S. Lincoln, 'The First Setting of Congreve's *Semele*', ML 44/2 (April 1963), 103–17
R. Platt (ed.), *Semele: An Opera*, Musica Britannica edition (London, 2000)

Echeggiate, festeggiate, Numi eterni, HWV 119. This large-scale cantata for five soloists and an orchestra of recorders, oboes, strings and basso continuo, can, on the basis of its autograph and subject, be dated soon after Handel's arrival in London at the end of 1710. A reference in the anonymous text to Charles III, King of Spain, points to contemporary English negotiations to end the War of the SPANISH SUCCESSION. Charles, however, was declared Emperor of the Habsburg Empire on 17 April 1711 following the death of his brother, Joseph I, which event forestalled him ever being named King of Spain. The composition of the cantata must, therefore, pre-date this event, falling into the very narrow period of the first three months of 1711. Significant BORROWINGS from earlier Italian cantatas suggest the work may have been composed hurriedly. There is no record of its performance, but as the text relates to the peacemaking of Queen ANNE, it could possibly be the 'fine Consort . . . being a Dialogue in Italian, in Her Majesty's praise, set to excellent Musick by the famous Mr. Hendel' on the occasion of her birthday on 6 February 1711.

ELLEN T. HARRIS

editions

1. Early editions
2. Arnold
3. Handel Society
4. Schaum
5. Chrysander (HG)
6. Novello
7. Hallische Händel-Augabe (HHA)

1. Early editions
Most of Handel's London theatre works were published in full or reduced score during his lifetime. Such contemporary editions usually contained the overture, arias and duets (with the original singers named), but usually excluded recitatives, choruses and short orchestral movements (e.g. battle music or sinfonias). Some works, such as *RINALDO* and *ISRAEL IN EGYPT*, were first represented in print by anthologies of 'favourite' songs, with more comprehensive collections only coming later. Notable exceptions of entire works published in complete form are *ALEXANDER'S FEAST* (printed in 1738) and *ACIS AND*

GALATEA (issued in 1743). Chamber music and orchestral concertos (e.g. the 'Twelve Grand Concertos', Op. 6 (ORCHESTRAL WORKS, 2)) were issued as sets of parts rather than in full score. Other printed music issued during Handel's life – not necessarily with much involvement from him – included anthologies of overtures and collections of aria arrangements for flute, oboe or violin with figured bass for keyboard accompaniment. Some pieces published under Handel's name (e.g. some sonatas or various SONGS) have been passed on only through early prints, but most of these are certainly spurious.

Scores of favourite arias from particular operas or oratorio-style works were usually advertised shortly after the first performance. Most early printed editions were produced by John WALSH SENIOR in connection with John and Joseph HARE, although during the 1720s he infringed Handel's Royal Privilege (COPYRIGHT) of 1720 by producing some pirate editions of KEYBOARD MUSIC and CHAMBER MUSIC with faked title pages of the Amsterdam music publisher ROGER. During this decade, some of Handel's works were published by John CLUER, Richard MEARES (senior and junior) and Benjamin Cooke, but from 1730 Handel seems to have cultivated a close business partnership with John WALSH JUNIOR. After 1766 Walsh's successors were William RANDALL and John Abell, and the original Walsh printing plates passed via Elizabeth Randall to H. WRIGHT. After 1783 some of Handel's works (excluding operas) were issued by Harrison & Co., and these scores increasingly contained editorial contributions from Dr Samuel ARNOLD, who shortly afterwards started his own project to publish a complete collected edition of Handel's works (EDITIONS, 2).

See also SUBSCRIBERS, 2

2. Arnold

On 22 June 1783 the music publisher R. Birchall proposed that there should be a 'uniform and complete' subscription edition of Handel's works in score, and such an idea was repeated by Charles BURNEY on the occasion of the 1784 HANDEL COMMEMORATION. These impetuses might have inspired Samuel Arnold to commence his own edition. Notwithstanding some of William Randall's complete editions (such as the first published score of *MESSIAH* in 1767), the majority of Handel's works had never been fully published, access to the compositions was limited, and even the large-scale vocal works were often only available as aria collections. Arnold aimed to publish Handel's complete works including all instrumental movements, recitatives and choruses. He issued a number of first editions of works which had not been performed since Handel's death, and which were only known by a few experts.

It was conceived as a complete collected edition on a subscription basis, and Arnold produced scores covering a representative cross-section of Handel's oeuvre, but eventually it included only five operas. The edition was terminated after 180 numbers of forty-eight pages each had been issued (there is not a set number of volumes). The first instalment was probably sent to the subscribers in July 1787, and by 1788/9 Arnold had 369 subscribers, so the print-run might have started with about 400 copies. But after working on his edition for eleven years, on 22 September 1797 Arnold published a memorandum stating that he was forced to abandon his edition because it lacked enough subscribers. He was aware that his edition was not always correct, and hoped to revise it in 1801/2, but died before he could start the new undertaking.

The practical edition contains just the musical works without any additional information. It is based on early prints and, to a smaller extent, on manuscript copies and autographs. It seems that Arnold had access to sources which are now missing, such as, possibly, the performing score of AGRIPPINA, but he found it difficult to produce clear versions of works that Handel had altered often. Arnold's scores therefore usually offer a mix of different versions.

3. Handel Society

An organisation founded in 1843 on the suggestion of Tommaso Rovedino. Its objective was to publish 'a superior and standard edition' of Handel's complete works at an annual subscription cost of one guinea. The prospectus dated 7 March 1843 sets forth that the 'Council will commence its labours so soon as Five Hundred Subscriptions shall be received. Should the number of members amount to a thousand, it is presumed that at least four hundred pages will be delivered annually.' The members of the first Council were Rovedino (secretary), R. Addison (treasurer), William S. Bennett, Sir Henry R. Bishop, William Crotch, James W. Davison, Edward J. Hopkins, George A. Macfarren, Ignaz Moscheles, Thomas M. Mudie, Edward F. Rimbault, Sir George Smart, Henry Smart and James Turle. The auditors were F. W. Collard, T. F. Mackinlay and R. Mills. Some Council members were also editors; MENDELSSOHN edited Israel in Egypt. By January 1848 lack of subscribers had led to the dissolution of the Handel Society, but the publishers Cramer, Beale & Co. continued to issue more volumes until 1858 with title pages stating 'Printed for the Handel Society'.

Editors consulted the original manuscripts, and their editions were moderately adapted to the taste of the nineteenth century. One goal was the careful collation of all the existing versions, and another that the scores would serve the needs of both amateurs and professionals. The volumes contain pianoforte adaptations of the instrumental parts (Israel in Egypt contains an editorial organ part), and a preface with an introduction about the history of the work, a short description of the principles of the edition, and the libretto. The sixteen volumes published by the Handel Society included:

> Coronation Anthems (vol. 1, 1843/4; includes Prospectus), ed. W. Crotch
> L'Allegro, il Pensieroso ed il Moderato (vol. 2; 1843/4), ed. I. Moscheles
> Esther (vol. 3; 1844/5), ed. C. Lucas
> Ode for St. Cecilia's Day (vol. 4; 1844/5), ed. T. M. Mudie
> Israel in Egypt (vol. 5; 1845/6), ed. F. Mendelssohn Bartholdy
> The Dettingen Te Deum (vol. 6; 1846/7), ed. Sir G. Smart
> Acis and Galatea (vol. 7; 1846/7), ed. W. S. Bennett
> Belshazzar (vols. 8, 9; 1847/8), ed. G. A. Macfarren
> Messiah (vols. 10, 11; 1850), ed. E. F. Rimbault
> Chamber Duets and Trios (vol. 12; 1852), ed. H. Smart
> Samson (vol. 13; 1853), ed. E. F. Rimbault
> Judas Maccabaeus (vol. 14; 1855), ed. G. A. Macfarren
> Saul (vol. 15; 1857), ed. E. F. Rimbault
> Jephtha (vol. 16; 1858), ed. G. A. Macfarren

4. Schaum

In 1805 Johann Otto Heinrich SCHAUM published an article in which he argued that there was a need for a collected Handel edition with text underlay in the German language. He published only four volumes between 1822 and 1825. These were based on Arnold's edition, but with most of the earlier printing errors eliminated, and Schaum added accompaniments for pianoforte or organ. All four volumes contained ANTHEMS:

Volume 1: HWV 253 and 251[b]
Volume 2: HWV 255 and 256[a]
Volume 3: HWV 248 and 252
Volume 4: HWV 254 and 249[b]

5. Chrysander (HG)

Friedrich CHRYSANDER's 'Ausgabe der Deutschen Händel-Gesellschaft' (1858–94), issued in Britain as 'The Works of G. F. Handel', is the most comprehensive and voluminous Handel edition yet produced. It was planned as a collection of 100 volumes, and the first edition published in 1858 was *SUSANNA*. When Chrysander died in 1901 only two volumes had not been issued: *Messiah* (vol. 45, which was edited by Max Seiffert in 1902) and a miscellaneous anthology (vol. 49, prepared but never published). Chrysander's average annual output was two volumes, and the HG edition eventually comprised ninety-three volumes of Handel's works and six supplements containing sources of Handel's borrowings from composers ERBA, URIO, STRADELLA, CLARI, MUFFAT and KEISER. Volumes 2 and 6 were edited by Seiffert. During the early years of the project Chrysander was supported by G. G. GERVINUS, and he also received financial support from George V of Hanover from 1859 to 1866 until the kingdom was annexed to Prussia. Afterwards he had to fund the HG edition himself: he ran a market garden on his land in Bergedorf, and also had a small workshop for music printing, with engravers he employed from Leipzig.

The volumes are in full score with an added accompaniment for pianoforte, the original text and a German translation. In most cases Chrysander's preface included short critical notes and the libretto with a German translation. His music texts were largely accurate, but gave different versions as 'A', 'B' or 'C' without any explanation of their historical context. Nor did he clearly signal where he made editorial changes different from the texts of his primary sources. Chrysander collated most of the known important manuscripts and printed sources including the Arnold and Handel Society editions, and frequently visited Britain to see Handel's original autograph manuscripts in BUCKINGHAM PALACE. However, he based his editions primarily on the performing scores, whereas autographs only served as the primary source if the performing score was not extant (SOURCES AND COLLECTIONS, 1, 2). At present numerous works have still only been commercially published in Chrysander's edition because the Hallische Händel-Ausgabe is not yet finished.   ANNETTE LANDGRAF

6. Novello

The music publishing house of Novello was founded by J. Alfred Novello in 1830, initially to promote works composed and edited by his father, the London musician Vincent Novello. Beginning with *Messiah* in 1846–7, Novello published a series of Handel's works, mainly English oratorios and church music, in octavo-size vocal score format. Appearing under the nominal editorship of Vincent Novello, these made the music available at a modest cost, and in a form that was aimed at audiences and students as well as performers. In connection with the inauguration of the CRYSTAL PALACE Handel Festivals, the vocal scores of nine oratorios and *Alexander's Feast* were republished as a 'Centenary Edition' at 2 shillings each; comparable folio-size vocal scores had cost about ten times that amount only a few years previously. To complement the vocal scores Novello printed full scores of a few works, including *Messiah*, from old plates, some of them of Walsh origin. Under the management of Arthur Henry Littleton the promotion of the vocal scores continued to flourish in the second half of the nineteenth century, supported by the growth in choral singing in Britain; special vocal scores were also printed for the miscellaneous programmes of the Crystal Palace Handel Festivals. Shortened versions of oratorios subsequently appeared, reflecting the performing conditions of provincial music festivals, and the addition of new works became sporadic. Watkins SHAW's edition of *Messiah*, published in 1959 to replace Ebenezer Prout's version of 1902, marked the introduction of modern standards of scholarship, and led to the inauguration of a new series as the Novello Handel Edition, in which twenty-one additional works have appeared (to 2009). DONALD BURROWS

7. Hallische Händel-Ausgabe (HHA)
The new collected critical edition of Handel's works is based on a comprehensive study of the surviving sources, and is intended to serve both scholarly and practical needs. The original impetus for the HHA came from Karl Vötterle, the owner of the Bärenreiter publishing house in Kassel, and the goal was a selected edition of Handel's works, which was not intended to compete with the Chrysander edition. The contract between Bärenreiter and the city of Halle for the project was signed during the Second World War in 1943, and two years later the vocal score of *DEIDAMIA* was issued. After the war, the Hallische Händel-Gesellschaft was founded in 1948, and one of its objectives was to create a new and comprehensive critical edition of Handel's works (HANDEL SOCIETIES, 3). The first volume of the 'revived' HHA was published in 1955, but it was originally planned as a practical edition based on Chrysander, adding works missing from the old HG edition and several unknown works. However, during the second half of the twentieth century the idea of an entirely new critical edition based on modern philological and editorial standards was gradually established, not least because many new sources have been found since the Chrysander edition was finished.

The HHA aims to reproduce all of Handel's alternative compositional and performing versions of a work, although the main text of each volume is normally Handel's complete and unabridged first performance version. Each volume contains a detailed preface, facsimiles of interesting musical pages and the original WORDBOOKS of vocal works, a German translation of the libretto (the English text is usually included in the facsimile of the wordbook, if not the HHA provides one), the music texts and a critical report (featuring a detailed description and evaluation of the sources). The HHA is planned to comprise 116 volumes and ten supplements.   ANNETTE LANDGRAF

See also Ignaz (von) MOSEL

T. Best, 'From Walsh to the Hallische Händel-Ausgabe: Handel Editions Past and Present', Handel Studies: A Gedenkschrift for Howard Serwer, ed. R. G. King (Hillsdale, NY, 2009)

D. Burrows, 'John Walsh and his Handel Editions', Music and the Book Trade from the Sixteenth to the Twentieth Century, ed. R. Myers, M. Harris and G. Mandelbrote (New Castle, DE and London, 2008)

'Making the "Classic" Accessible: Vincent Novello's Vocal Scores of Handel's Oratorios', HJb 53 (2007)

V. Cooper, The House of Novello: Practice and Policy of a Victorian Music Publisher, 1829–1866 (Aldershot, 2003)

J. M. Coopersmith, 'The First Gesamtausgabe: Dr. Arnold's Edition of Handel's Works', Notes 4 (1947), 277–91, 439–49

'Handel Society', Gentleman's Magazine (1842), 407

P. Hirsch, 'Dr. Arnold's Handel Edition (1787–1797)', Music Review 8 (1947), 106–16

A. Landgraf, 'Die Händelausgabe von Samuel Arnold', Händel Haus-Mitteilungen 2/23 (1993)

W. C. Smith, Handel: A Descriptive Catalogue of the Early Editions (London, 1960)

Egmont, John Percival, 1st Earl of (b. Burton, County Cork, Ireland, 12 July 1683; d. London 1 May 1748). Politician and diarist. A noted music-lover, Egmont (as he became in 1733, having been made Baron Perceval in 1715, and Viscount in 1723) was one of the initial directors of the Royal Academy of Music (OPERA COMPANIES, 2). He also subscribed to the ACADEMY OF ANCIENT MUSIC, founded in January 1725, and to the Philharmonic Society. Egmont held concerts at his home in Pall Mall where family, friends and professional musicians (including his children's teachers) performed vocal and instrumental music in front of friends. He served as an MP for Harwich 1727–34. As the first president of the Georgia Society (1732–42), Egmont did much to secure financial support for the American colony and had a hand in sending the WESLEYs there. Egmont's unpublished correspondence with this brother Philip PERCIVAL sheds much light on the Irish State Music.   DAVID HUNTER

D. Hunter, 'The Irish State Music from 1716 to 1742 and Handel's Band in Dublin', GHB XI (2006)

Elbing (Polish: Elbląg). Polish city, former member of the Hanseatic league, Polish fiefdom from 1466 to 1772, continually in the spheres of interest of other Baltic sea states in the seventeenth and eighteenth centuries. A large number of English tradesmen lived in Elbing. Hiob Adolph Dieterich, assistant to the Kantor of the local Gymnasium, performed two operas by Handel there, Il FLORIDANTE in 1731 and Emilia (probably FLAVIO) in 1732. In 1737 a Handel pasticcio, HERMANN VON BALCKE, was performed there. It has been suggested that Handel stayed in Elbing (after taking the waters in AIX-LA-CHAPELLE) with John Christopher SMITH SENIOR in 1737 on the basis of a missing and probably spurious letter dated 15 October 1737.

KLAUS-PETER KOCH (Trans. ANGELA BAIER)

K.-P. Koch, 'Händel-Rezeption bis zum Ende des 18. Jahrhunderts in östlichen Gebieten Europas', Bach-Händel-Schütz-Ehrung der DDR 1985, ed. W. Siegmund-Schultze and B. Baselt (Leipzig, 1987)

J. Müller-Blattau, 'Händels Festkantate zur Fünfhundertjahrfeier der Stadt Elbing 1737',
  Elbinger Jahrbuch 11 (1933), 239–53; repr. as 50 Jahre Göttinger Händel-Festspiele. Festschrift,
  ed. Walter Meyerhoff (Kassel etc., 1970) 120–32

L'Elpidia, ovvero Li rivali generosi (Elpidia, or the Generous Rivals), HWV A¹. PASTICCIO opera in three acts. It was first performed at the KING'S THEATRE on 11 May 1725. The libretto is an adaptation of Apostolo ZENO's *I rivali generosi*, first set for VENICE by Marc'Antonio Ziani in 1697.

In the sixth century, the Byzantine Emperor Justinian sent his general Belisarius (Belisario) to reconquer Italy, then ruled by Witiges (Vitige), King of the Ostrogoths. As the opera opens Belisario is laying siege to the Ostrogoth capital Ravenna. Two Greek princes fighting under him, Olindo and Arminio (Ormonte in the score), are rivals for the love of Elpidia, Princess of Puglia. Although her heart belongs to Olindo, she declares she will marry whichever of them is most valiant in battle. Vitige also has his eye on Elpidia and has her abducted, while Arminio captures Vitige's daughter Rosmilda, who immediately falls in love with him. Olindo surrenders himself to Vitige to win Elpidia's release. Arminio then rescues Olindo, forcing him out of gratitude to let Arminio have Elpidia. But when Olindo clears Arminio of a false charge of treason Arminio renounces his claims to Elpidia and agrees to marry Rosmilda instead.

The cast of the first performance was as follows:

Belisario	Giuseppe Maria BOSCHI (bass)
Olindo	SENESINO (castrato)
Arminio	Andrea PACINI (castrato)
Elpidia	Francesca CUZZONI (soprano)
Vitige	Francesco BOROSINI (tenor)
Rosmilda	Benedetta Sorosina (mezzo-soprano)

The first pasticcio presented by the Royal Academy of Music (OPERA COMPANIES, 2), Elpidia was remarkably successful, running for a total of eleven nights at the end of the 1724 5 season. Five more performances followed at the beginning of the next season (November–December 1725), with Antonio Baldi, Luigi Antinori and Anna DOTTI replacing Pacini, Borosini and Sorosina. WALSH eventually published the overture and a total of nineteen vocal numbers, an unusually high total for a pasticcio.

The libretto printed for the first London performance attributes the music of Elipidia to 'Signor Leonardo Vinci, except some few Songs by Signor Giuseppe Orlandini'. As Reinhard Strohm discovered, most of the arias came from three operas composed for the Carnival season of 1724–5 at the Teatro SAN GIOVANNI GRISOSTOMO in Venice, VINCI's *Ifigenia in Tauride* and *Rosmira fedele* and Orlandini's *Berenice*. Strohm assumed that Elpidia was a free pasticcio compiled by Handel and that he had composed the secco recitatives and perhaps several other movements. But letters from the former London theatre manager Owen SWINEY published by Elizabeth Gibson in 1989 indicate the score was originally assembled in Venice. In the absence of BONONCINI, who had withdrawn from the Royal Academy in 1724, the directors may have asked Swiney, their agent in Italy, to provide them with additional repertory. Swiney probably chose the libretto (which he may have revised himself) and selected the arias based on his knowledge of the singers in the London company. The distinctive style of the recitatives reveals they were composed by Vinci. It must also have been Vinci who composed two new duets on texts from Zeno's original libretto and the three accompanied recitatives and turned a duet from his *Ifigenia* into the final chorus.

The score Swiney sent to London was probably entirely by Vinci and ORLAN-DINI, but before the first performance the opera underwent considerable modification as several singers inserted favourite arias attributed to Capelli, Peli, Sarro and Vinci. As copied, the role of Belisario was destined for a tenor, perhaps Alexander GORDON, but Boschi re-emerged in time for the first performance. Handel's role in the revision is uncertain. Presumably he led the performances since he owned the conducting score (British Library, Add. MS 31606), but that manuscript contains no verifiable traces of his hand. At most he altered some of Vinci's recitatives and made minor cuts in one Vinci aria. For the revival many of the arias were replaced with others by GIACOMELLI, LOTTI, Orlandini, Sarro and Vinci, mainly to accommodate the new singers; we cannot be sure exactly what was performed because no copy of the printed libretto has survived.

The main musical source for *Elpidia* is the conducting score, which was used in both runs of the opera. It lacks some of the music, but the losses can be partly made good from the Walsh editions. Modern editions of the 1697 and 1725 librettos were published by Bianconi.   JOHN H. ROBERTS

Bianconi
H. D. Clausen, *Händels Direktionspartituren ('Handexemplare')* (Hamburg, 1972)
E. Gibson, *The Royal Academy of Music, 1719–1728: The Institution and its Directors* (New York, 1989)
J. H. Roberts, 'Vinci, Porpora and the Royal Academy of Music', *Chigiana* 46 (forthcoming)
Strohm, 164–211

Erard. German bass who sang in Handel's short 1736 season at COVENT GARDEN. Little is known about him, though he may be the Erhard (Erhardt) who sang in operas by TELEMANN in Germany in 1730–5. His first London appearance was in the premiere of *ALEXANDER'S FEAST*. Next he sang Polifemo in a revival of the bilingual *ACIS*, for which Handel composed a new scene, and then Haman in *ESTHER*. Finally he sang Polinesso in Handel's hurried revival of *ARIODANTE*. Thereafter he disappears from the scene. A member of the audience at *Alexander's Feast* wrote in his wordbook against one of the bass arias, 'O for Seneseno [sic]', presumably as a comment on Erard's singing. But the music Handel composed for him in *Acis* suggests that his vocal accomplishments were by no means negligible.   JOHN GREENACOMBE

A. Hicks, 'Acis and Galatea in 1736', *Handel Institute Newsletter* 15/1 (2004)
Dean, *Operas*, 303

Erba, Dionigi (d. Milan, 29 Nov. 1730). Italian composer. Based at Milan, he was appointed *maestro di cappella* at S. Francesco in 1692, and from 1697 he was *maestro di cappella* at S. Maria presso San Celso. Handel made a fragmentary copy of Erba's *Magnificat* in 1738 and borrowed from it extensively for Parts II and III of his new oratorio *ISRAEL IN EGYPT*: 'He rebuked the Red Sea', 'The Lord is my strength', 'He is my God', 'The Lord is a man of war', 'The depths have cover'd them', 'Thy right hand, O Lord' / 'Thou sentest forth thy wrath', 'And with the blast of thy nostrils', 'Who is like unto thee' / 'The earth hath swallowed them' and 'Thou in thy mercy' all use material taken from Erba's music. The most striking borrowing is the section 'Thou sentest forth thy wrath', in which Handel retained most of Erba's choral parts and merely adapted the rhythm to fit the new text.   ANNETTE LANDGRAF

'Ero e Leandro'. See QUAL TI RIVEGGIO, OH DIO

Esther, HWV 50^{a-b}. English oratorio. Some early manuscript copies usually feature the simple title Oratorium, perhaps used because it was the only work of its kind yet written in England. Handel composed Esther for James Brydges, the Earl of Carnarvon (later 1st Duke of CHANDOS). The oratorio was probably first performed at CANNONS, but precise details of its composition and early performance history are unknown. The score might have been initially drafted and performed in 1718, but new research by John Roberts has proved that Handel extensively recomposed it after returning from DRESDEN (between the end of 1719 and before 25 March 1720). It is likely that this version of Esther, later called Haman and Mordecai by CHRYSANDER, was performed in midsummer 1720. The cast is unknown, but probably included the tenor James Blackley. Some solo parts, and the soprano choral lines, could have been have been sung by boys trained by Johann Christoph PEPUSCH (music director at Cannons from mid-1719).

The authorship of the libretto is uncertain. In 1732 it was rumoured to be the work of Alexander POPE, who never confirmed or denied the attribution, but the text could have been a collaboration between several members of the Cannons circle, which also included John ARBUTHNOT and John GAY. It is based on Thomas Brereton's Esther; or Faith Triumphant (1715), which was a close adaptation of RACINE's play Esther (1689). The Cannons version (HWV 50^a) only partially portrays the story in the BIBLE and the Apocrypha. A brief summary of the Scriptural context fills several gaps in the plot of the oratorio: King Assuerus of Persia (the same historical person as the title character in SERSE, and named Ahasuerus in the King James Bible) celebrated the third year of his reign by holding a lavish feast, during which he ordered his wife Vashti to join him. Her refusal angered Assuerus, and she was repudiated. He searched for a new wife, and the Jew Mordecai took Esther to the King's house, but kept their ethnicity and religion secret. Esther pleased Assuerus, and twelve months later she became Queen, but continued to keep her faith and origin hidden. Mordecai saved the King from an assassination plot.

The remainder of the story is sketchily told in Handel's oratorio. Assuerus appoints the arrogant bully Haman as his right-hand man. Haman wishes to force everybody to 'reverence' him, but Mordecai refuses. In revenge, Haman tricks the King into arranging a decree that the Jews must be executed as enemies of the kingdom. Mordecai urges Esther to intercede with Assuerus on their behalf, but it is forbidden to enter the King's inner court without having first obtained his personal invitation. All who break this law are condemned to death, unless Assuerus recognises the person, and holds out his golden sceptre towards them as an indication that they may approach him. Esther bravely visits the King unbidden. She is spared by his love for her, and Esther requests that

Assuerus and Haman join her at a banquet (the Bible reveals that Haman exults in being invited to a banquet with the royal couple, and has tall gallows built especially for Mordecai). At the banquet, Esther exposes Haman's treachery against Mordecai and her people, and Haman – despite showing remorse in Handel's version – is hung upon his own gallows. Mordecai is honoured by the King. The Israelites celebrate their narrow escape from genocide, and look forward to their future return to Jerusalem, where they shall rebuild the Temple.

Notable music in Handel's score includes an elaborate harp obbligato part in the Israelite aria 'Praise the Lord with chearful noise', and the extravagant Purcellian verse-anthem finale ('The Lord our enemy has slain'), which has sections for solo voices and continuo linked by orchestral sections and choral refrains featuring a solo trumpet. Assuerus's 'O beauteous Queen' contains musical BORROWINGS from works by LOTTI and Johann David Heinichen that Handel probably heard at Dresden in September 1719, and the 1st Israelite's 'Tune your harps' was based on material from KEISER's *Nebucadnezar* (1704). Nine numbers reused musical ideas from the recent *BROCKES PASSION* (including several key dramatic moments such as the duet 'Who calls my parting soul from death' and Haman's penitent 'Turn not, O Queen'), and Handel also quoted part of the *WATER MUSIC* in the splendid arioso and chorus 'Jehovah crown'd' (which features two horns).

Esther had minimal influence on Handel's London theatre career until a dozen years later. His forty-seventh birthday was celebrated in February 1732 by a performance of the oratorio at the CROWN AND ANCHOR TAVERN featuring singers from the CHAPEL ROYAL directed by Bernard GATES. Viscount Percival (later 1st Earl of EGMONT) wrote in his diary that 'This oratoria or religious opera is exceeding fine, and the company were highly pleased'. Perhaps this inspired Handel to ponder the potential of English oratorio entertainments, but he was stimulated into action on or before 17 April 1732 when a 'pirate' performance of *Esther* was given without his consent. Perhaps the composer's ire was provoked by unwelcome local competition prepared to use his own music against him, and he acted quickly. On 19 April the *Daily Journal* announced:

> At the King's Theatre in the Hay-Market, on Tuesday the 2nd Day of May, will be performed, The Sacred Story of ESTHER: an Oratorio in English. Formerly composed by Mr. *Handel*, and now revised by him, with several Additions, and to be performed by a great Number of the best Voices and Instruments. N.B. There will be no Action on the Stage, but the House will be fitted up in a decent Manner, for the Audience. The Musick to be disposed after the Manner of the Coronation Service.

By prominently advertising that *Esther* had been revised, and emphasising the superiority of his singers and players, Handel's transparent effort to reclaim his own work prompted his pioneering of the English oratorio genre. The composer required the poet Samuel HUMPHREYS to redesign the libretto in order to expand the slender Cannons oratorio into a full-scale entertainment in three acts suitable for an evening at the theatre. Judging from the amount of recycled music added in 1732, Humphreys's contributions were probably in accordance with Handel's specific instructions. A substantial new opening scene was designed to introduce Esther at her coronation as Queen of Persia, containing music arranged from the motet *Silete venti* (Italian and Latin CHURCH MUSIC), an aria adapted from *La RESURREZIONE*, and the CORONATION anthem *My heart is inditing* (ANTHEMS, 3). The additional music also included two numbers adapted from the ode *ETERNAL SOURCE OF LIGHT DIVINE*, the coronation anthem *ZADOK THE PRIEST* (given parody words, and abridged slightly, in order to fit the end of Act II), three newly composed arias and a new duet. Most of the original Cannons score was retained, although some of it was altered to suit the singers at Handel's disposal. The orchestration of the final chorus was enlarged to include two more trumpets, bassoons and timpani, and its verse anthem sections were replaced by solo 'Alleluia' passages (the WORDBOOKS imply that these were for Mordecai, but Handel almost always assigned the solos to the leading male singer performing Assuerus).

According to BURNEY, the Bishop of London (Edmund GIBSON) refused to grant permission for Gates's staged production of *Esther* to be transferred to the KING'S THEATRE. However, there is no proof that Handel wanted to perform it with scenic action; it is likelier that he wanted to mount a lavishly decorated concert performance, as had been done for his Roman oratorio *La Resurrezione* (1708), and which he would do in subsequent seasons for *DEBORAH* (1733) and *PARNASSO IN FESTA* (1734). The new version of *Esther* (HWV 50^b) was first performed on 2 May 1732, and ran for six performances. The cast was:

Assuerus	SENESINO (castrato)
Esther	Anna Maria STRADA del Pò (soprano)
Haman	Antonio MONTAGNANA (bass)
Mordecai	Francesca BERTOLLI (contralto)
Israelite Woman	Ann Turner-ROBINSON (soprano)
Israelite	Mrs Davis (soprano)
Harbonah / Officer / Israelite	? (tenor)

Handel revived the oratorio, with minor alterations for an almost identical cast, in April 1733, and performed it twice more with a different cast at OXFORD three months later. He continued to perform *Esther* throughout the rest of his life, but never in exactly the same version from one revival to another. Different singers available to him necessitated different solutions: in 1735 CARESTINI required several Italian insertions (some of which were impressive arias recycled from the rest of *Silete venti*), and this bilingual version was also useful for accommodating the castrati ANNIBALI and CONTI in 1737. In the meantime, the 1736 revival was probably an English version similar to 1733, but with the role of Assuerus reverting to a tenor (sung by John BEARD). Handel made further practical changes for a revival in 1740 (the 'Alleluia' solos were removed from the final chorus), at DUBLIN in 1742 he performed a stripped-down version with limited forces (the two coronation anthems were omitted), and more alterations were made for a single performance in March 1751. The last revival during his lifetime was prepared with considerable assistance from John Christopher SMITH JUNIOR in 1757, and featured the new duet and chorus 'Sion now her head shall raise' (possibly Handel's last original composition, dictated to Smith). ANNETTE LANDGRAF and DAVID VICKERS

Dean, *Oratorios*
Deutsch

A. Landgraf, 'Esther: von der Bibel über Brereton zu Händel', *HJb* 52 (2006)

J. Roberts, 'The Composition of Handel's *Esther*, 1718–1720', *HJb* 55 (2009)

H. Serwer (ed.), *Esther* (first version, HWV 50ᵃ), HHA I/8 (Kassel, 1995)

Smith, *Oratorios*

D. Vickers, 'Handel's Performing Versions: A Study of Four Music Theatre Works from the "Second Academy" Period', Ph.D. dissertation (The Open University, 2007)

Eternal source of light divine, HWV 74. English ode. During the late seventeenth century it became customary for the Royal Musicians and singers of the CHAPEL ROYAL to perform celebratory odes on New Year's Day and the monarch's birthday. The tradition continued until the death of GEORGE III in 1820. During the early years of Queen ANNE's reign such odes were composed by John ECCLES, the Master of the Queen's Musick, but in 1711 Handel and NICOLINO gave the Queen a concert of unspecified Italian music for her birthday (perhaps instead of the customary English ode), and the castrato (without Handel) provided a similar concert the following year.

Handel's only court ode was probably composed for Queen Anne's forty-eighth birthday on 6 February 1713. His autograph of *Eternal source of light divine* is undated, but its text by Ambrose Philips repeatedly praises 'The day that gave great Anna birth, Who fix'd a lasting peace on earth', which seems to be a reference to the Queen's role as a peacemaker in the end of the War of the SPANISH SUCCESSION. Handel might have received the text for the ode soon after completing the Utrecht Te Deum on 14 January 1713 (TE DEUM, I), and perhaps he temporarily ceased work on the Utrecht JUBILATE in order to compose the ode and organise its performance.

John Eccles was paid travelling expenses for himself and the Queen's Musicians to Windsor for 'attendance there on Her said Majesties Birthday Febr[uar]y the 6, 1713' (he was not paid his usual fee for composing and copying a new ode, which further suggests that a performance of Handel's ode was being planned), but the Queen was actually at ST JAMES'S PALACE on her birthday, suffering severely from gout, and made only a brief public appearance to play cards in the Great Presence Chamber while a ball took place in the adjoining room. Perhaps Handel's ode was heard on this occasion, or cancelled owing to the Queen's ill health, or postponed until her next birthday in 1714 when she hosted a ball and 'splendid entertainment' at Windsor.

The ode is Handel's loveliest early English composition, and shows traces of his recent exposure to English music by composers such as Henry PURCELL. The opening arioso describing the dawning sun was written for the Chapel Royal alto Richard Elford, whose melismatic vocal part is accompanied by sustained strings and gently echoed by a solo trumpet. Each different choral statement of 'The day that gave great Anna birth' is connected to its preceding solo movement, and the concluding chorus 'United nations shall combine' features a division between the choir and a Purcellian echo (maybe sung by the soloists). There are hints of Italianate opera in 'Let envy there conceal her head' (intended for the bass Bernard GATES) and the eloquent duet 'Kind health descends on downy wings' (intended for the theatre singers ANASTASIA ROBINSON and Jane Barbier). Alas, the poetry's wish for the last of the Stuart monarchs to enjoy good health was ill-fated, but Handel recycled 'Kind health descends' in his first public performances of ESTHER (1732, HWV 50ᵇ), which also featured a new movement based on the ostinato bass of the duet 'Let rolling streams'. Music from the ode was also reused in *ACIS AND GALATEA* (1732 version, HWV 49^b) and *DEBORAH*.   DAVID VICKERS

O. Baldwin and T. Wilson, 'Music in the Birthday Celebrations at Court in the Reign of Queen Anne: A Documentary Calendar', *A Handbook for Studies in 18th-Century English Music*, ed. M. Burden, 19 (2008)

Burrows, *Chapel Royal*

D. Burrows, 'Eternal Source for Speculation: Handel's Birthday Ode for Queen Anne', *Handel Institute Newsletter* 20/2 (2009)

M. Custodis, 'Kunst und Karriere: Georg Friedrich Händels Ode "Eternal Source of Light Divine" ', *Archiv für Musikwissenschaft* 65 (2008), 225–41

J. A. Winn, 'Style and Politics in the Philips–Handel Ode for Queen Anne's Birthday, 1713', *ML* 89/4 (2008), 547–61

Euripides (b. 480s BC; d. 406 BC). Athenian playwright. He wrote about ninety plays that display an impressive dramatic range: Aristotle called him 'the most tragic' of the tragedians (*Poetics*, 1453a10). The strong, sometimes shocking emotions that motivate his characters' speeches and monodies influenced later writers like OVID and Seneca, who were important vectors for bringing Euripidean subjects and emotions to the Western tradition. The Hercules in Euripides's *Alcestis* and *Herakles* influenced presentation of that character in Handel's *ADMETO*, *HERCULES* and *The CHOICE OF HERCULES*. The pasticcio *ORESTE* and the oratorio *JEPHTHA* were adapted respectively from *Iphigenia in Tauris* and *Iphigenia at Aulis*.   ROBERT KETTERER

K. Nott, '"Heroick Vertue": Handel and Morell's "Jephtha" in the Light of Eighteenth Century Biblical Commentary and Other Sources', *ML* 77/2 (1996), 194–208

W. Heller, 'The Beloved's Image: Handel's *Admeto* and the Statue of Alcestis', *JAMS* 58/3 (2005), 559–637

Ezio, HWV 29. Italian opera. After Handel abandoned work on *TITUS L'EMPEREUR*, he composed *Ezio* from about November 1731 until the beginning of January 1732 (the last folio of his autograph score, on which he would have signed and dated the opera upon its completion, is missing). The opera was first performed at the KING'S THEATRE on 15 January 1732. The cast was as follows:

Ezio, General of the Imperial Forces	SENESINO (castrato)
Valentiniano III, Emperor of Rome	Anna Bagnolesi (alto)
Massimo, Roman Patrician	Giovanni Battista PINACCI (tenor)
Fulvia, Massimo's daughter	Anna STRADA del Pò (soprano)
Onoria, the Emperor's sister	Francesca BERTOLLI (alto)
Varo, Prefect of the Praetorian Guard	Antonio MONTAGNANA (bass)

The libretto was anonymously adapted from a text by Pietro METASTASIO, which had been first set fully by Pietro Auletta for ROME in December 1728 (a month after PORPORA had opportunistically performed a version at VENICE altered by LALLI). Handel might have collected the libretto during his journey to Italy in 1729 (HANDEL, 15). The plot was loosely based on historical characters described in Book III of Procopius's *De Bellis*, and has parallels with Thomas CORNEILLE's *Maximien* and Jean RACINE's *Britannicus*. The action is set in Rome, in AD 451, during the final years of the reign of Emperor Valentinian III (r. 425–55). The WORDBOOK summarises the plot:

> Aetius, an illustrious General . . . returning from the famous Victory of the
> Catalonian Fields, where he defeated and put to Flight Attila King of the
> Huns, was unjustly accused to the jealous Emperor, and by him condemned
> to die. The Author of this treachery against the innocent Aetius, was
> Maximus a Roman Patrician, who being displeased before at Valentinian for
> attempting the Chastity of his Wife endeavoured, though ineffectually, to
> engage the Assistance of Aetius to murther [sic] the Emperor, artfully
> concealing his own Desire of Revenge; but knowing that the Loyalty of
> Aetius was the greatest Obstruction to his Design, he fix'd upon him the
> Imputation of Treason, and solicited his Death, intending (as he afterwards
> did) to make the Populace mutiny against Valentinian, by accusing him of
> the Ingratitude and Injustice, to which he himself had induced him. All this
> is historical, and the rest within the Bounds of Probability.

Metastasio's *lieto fine*, with the loyal Ezio and his friend Varo nobly protecting the tyrant Valentiniano from Massimo's attempted coup, obscures the grisly historical truth that three years later (AD 454) Aetius was murdered by Valentinian III, who was in turn murdered by Maximus the following year (however, the politically inept Maximus reigned less than two months because he offended the Vandals, and, when they sacked Rome, was killed by his own angry citizens). The later Roman chronicler Marcellinus Comes believed that this sequence of assassinations, starting with that of the much-loved Aetius, brought about the fall of the western empire.

Several fictional dramatic aspects of Metastasio's drama are dilemmas concerning romantic fidelity, filial duty, political loyalty and moral integrity: Fulvia is forced to cope with her dishonest father's machinations, the unwelcome lustful attention of the corrupt Emperor, and the unjust imprisonment (and seemingly the execution) of her lover Ezio; Onoria exploits the political turmoil as an opportunity to win Ezio's love (the historical figure Honoria reputedly offered herself in marriage to Attila the Hun), but she becomes uncomfortable with her brother's tyranny; Valentiniano is gradually revealed as a fickle tyrant whose envy of Ezio's popularity deceives him into naively accepting counsel from his secret enemy Massimo (who seems increasingly out of touch with reality and reason as the opera progresses); Varo is the hero of the opera's final act when he disobeys Valentiniano's petulant order to assassinate the innocent Ezio, and instead saves his friend's life. The drama is a tense intrigue in which every character's actions spin relentlessly in conflict with each other.

These intense confrontations and reactions are strongly conveyed in Handel's music, which is consistently inventive and masterful. He incorporated some music from the abandoned *Titus*, and used material from KEISER's *Claudius* and *L'inganno fedele* and Alessandro SCARLATTI's *Pompeo* (BORROWINGS). The autograph score contains numerous examples of Handel's meticulous attention to dramatic subtlety and characterisation, and he wrote out all of Metastasio's full stage directions in his score even though these were not printed in the London wordbook. Moreover, *Ezio* has some outstanding arias. In 'Caro padre' (I.iii), which features a plaintive flute part and meticulously controlled dynamics, Fulvia pleads with her father not to force her to commit treason. Ezio's trial on trumped-up charges is a tense moment worthy of a political thriller, and the injustice and personal strain upon Fulvia lead to 'La mia costanza' (II.xii), with Handel's

Neapolitan-influenced music perfectly illustrating her passionate defiance of both her father and the Emperor. In III.xii, her accompanied recitative and aria 'Misera, dove son? . . . Ah! non son io che parlo' is a powerful lament in which she simultaneously fears for Ezio, is shamed by Massimo, and is angry at Valentiniano (it is the only operatic text in Handel's works that was also set by MOZART).

The title character ranks as one of the noblest virtuous heroes Handel wrote for Senesino, and the prison scene at the conclusion of Act II ('Ecco alle mie catene', in the unusual key of F sharp minor) was tailor-made for the castrato's renown for singing in the 'pathetic' style. It is Ezio's first opportunity to convey his private feelings of despair and vulnerability, and three years later Handel reused its musical style, mood, rhythm and key to portray Alcina's loneliness in 'Mi restano le lagrime' (ALCINA). The heroic musical climax of the final act is sung by Varo: 'Già risonar' (III.xiii) features lively interplay between a solo trumpet and a pair of oboes, and, although it seems long for a military aria marking a supposedly hasty departure, the splendid music occurs at the decisive turning point in the plot when Massimo's treachery has eventually been discovered (VIVALDI). Varo's status as the heroic protagonist of the *lieto fine* is emphasised by Handel's decision to give him the last solo – proclaiming the importance of a noble heart – in the vaudeville-style final chorus. There are no other ensembles or duets during the opera, but the arias for the other three characters are finely designed to convey their personalities: the vengeful Massimo, jealous Valentiano, and the lovelorn Onoria all have superb music.

One of Handel's finest serious operas, Ezio was one of his worst failures at the box office. Performed only five times during its first run, it was probably an expensive disaster: the author of the so-called Colman's *Opera Register* wrote that although 'Clothes & all ye Scenes' were new, it 'did not draw much Company' (Deutsch, 282). Handel never revived the opera, although he reused a few of its numbers in a revival of Il PASTOR FIDO (HWV 8^c), and in his self-pasticcios ALESSANDRO SEVERO and GIOVE IN ARGO. BURNEY admired 'its musical merit', but Ezio was not performed again until a German adaptation was staged at GÖTTINGEN in 1926. The opera is not often staged, but it was phenomenally popular in the former East Germany, where there were at least 362 performances of 23 different revivals between 1954 and 1983.   DAVID VICKERS

Burney
G. Buschmeier, 'Metastasio-Bearbeitungen im 18. Jahrhundert am Beispiel der Ezio-Opern von Händel und Gluck', HJb 45 (1999)
Dean, *Operas*
Harris, *Librettos*
M. Pacholke (ed.), *Ezio*, HHA II/26 (Kassel, 2008)
M. Rätzer, *Szenische Aufführungen von Werken Georg Friedrich Händels vom 18. bis 20. Jahrhundert: Eine Dokumentation* (Halle, 2000)
D. Schröder, 'Envy, Betrayal and Disaffection: A Roman Drama on the London Opera Stage', CD booklet note (Deutsche Grammophon, 477 8073, 2009)
Strohm
  'Handel, Metastasio, Racine: The Case of Ezio', MT (Nov. 1977), 901–3
A. R. Thöming, 'Produktion und künstlerische Gestaltung bei Metastasios drama per musica Ezio, dargestellt am Beispiel der Opernfassungen von Hasse (1730 und 1755), Händel (1732) und Graun (1755)', Ph.D. dissertation (Rostock University, 1999)

F

Fabri, Annibale Pio ('Annibalino' or 'Ballino') (b. Bologna, 1697; d. Lisbon, 12 Aug. 1760). Italian tenor (range B to a') and composer. He studied with the famed castrato Pistocchi in his native Bologna, and sang in eighty documented operatic roles over thirty-five years. His stage debut was as a boy treble in CALDARA intermezzos at RUSPOLI's palace at ROME in the 1711 Carnival. During the 1710s he sang in operas at Mantua, VENICE, Rome and Milan, and composed oratorios for Bologna (1719–20), where he was granted membership of the illustrious Accademia Filarmonica. By the early 1720s he was much in demand as an opera singer, performing regularly at NAPLES and FLORENCE, and working with leading composers including Bassani, GASPARINI, VINCI and Alessandro SCARLATTI. In 1716 he started a long-standing association with VIVALDI, for whom he regularly sang strongly dramatic roles until 1729.

Handel probably recruited Fabri at Bologna in 1729, when seeking new singers for the Second Academy (OPERA COMPANIES, 3). The tenor worked in London for two seasons (1729–31). After hearing him sing for the first time, Mrs Pendarves (later DELANY) described his voice as 'sweet, clear and firm . . . he sings like a gentleman, without making faces, and his manner is particularly agreeable; he is the greatest master of musick that ever sang upon the stage' (Deutsch, p. 247). Paolo ROLLI conceded that 'Fabri is a great success. He really sings very well. Would you have believed that a tenor could have had such a triumph here in England?' (Deutsch, pp. 249–50). Fabri's popularity was such that Viscount Percival (later Earl of EGMONT) employed the singer as music master for his daughters.

Handel composed three fine roles for Fabri: Berengario (the tyrant in *LOTARIO*), Emilio (the hapless warlike lover in *PARTENOPE*) and Alessandro (the noble hero Alexander the Great in *PORO*). Fabri also sang prominent parts in revivals of *GIULIO CESARE* (Jan.–Feb. 1730), *RINALDO* (April–May 1731) and *RODELINDA* (May 1731), and the title roles in the pasticcios *ORMISDA* and *VENCESLAO*. His wife Anna Bombaciari (a professional contralto) presumably accompanied him to London, but never sang in any of Handel's productions.

In January to March 1733, Fabri sang in Vienna for Emperor Charles VI, who stood as godfather (by proxy) to his daughter Carolina Elisabetta. During the mid-1730s he sang across Italy, and, on FARINELLI's invitation, in some court serenatas and operas by D'Astorga and HASSE in Spain (1738–9) and Portugal (1740–2). He revisited the role of Alexander the Great for performances of *Alessandro nell'Indie* at Madrid (1738, music by Francesco Courcelle) and Lisbon (1740, probably based on a version by Hasse). His last known stage appearance

was at Brescia (1749), after which he sang at the royal chapel in Lisbon until his
death.   DAVID VICKERS and CARLO VITALI

Dean, *Operas*
Dean and Knapp
C.Vitali and F. Boris (eds.), *Carlo Broschi Farinelli: La solitudine amica: lettere al conte Sicinio Pepoli*
(Palermo, 2000)

Faramondo (HWV 39). The last of Handel's opere serie of the heroic type. Its eponymous hero Faramondo, legendary first King of France, belongs to the world
of Arthurian legend and received a first literary tribute in *Faramond, ou l'histoire
de France* by Gautier de Costes de la Calprenède (1610–63). De la Calprenède's
romance was the basis for Apostolo ZENO's libretto *Faramondo*, which is set
during the migration period of the fifth century AD and focuses on a conflict between the tribes of the Cimbri and the Franks over a switched child.
Teobaldo, general of the Cimbrian King Gustavo, has exchanged Gustavo's
son Sveno for his own son Childerico in order to seize the throne for his own
clan. This plan goes wrong because the Franconian King Faramondo slays Gustavo's alleged son in battle, while Sveno, the real heir to the throne, is raised
as Teobaldo's son under the name of Childerico. Gustavo then swears an oath
promising the Cimbrian throne and his daughter Rosimonda to whoever kills
Faramondo. When Rosimonda falls in love with Faramondo, she is assailed by
moral qualms since she believes Faramondo to be the murderer of her brother
and therefore feels bound to her father's oath. The Suevic King Gernando,
Faramondo's friend and vassal, enters into an alliance with Gustavo to destroy
Faramondo but is resolutely rebuffed by Rosimonda. There is also a second
love plot: Adolfo, another of Gustavo's sons, is in love with Faramondo's sister
Clotilde, who is also the object of desire of King Gustavo himself. Faramondo
undertakes various attempts to solve both conflicts and is of course victorious
in the end. Adolfo and Clotilde as well as Faramondo and Rosimonda are paired
off, Gernando is pardoned, the guilty Teobaldo is exiled and Childerico is identified as Gustavo's son and heir. The opera's final chorus celebrates the victory
of Faramondo's moral virtue over emotions like love and hatred in the usual
fashion.

    Faramondo was composed after Handel had returned refreshed from his stay
at the health resort AIX-LA-CHAPELLE in the autumn of 1737. While Handel
had been away, John Jacob HEIDEGGER had assembled a new Italian opera
ensemble for the 1737–8 season at the KING'S THEATRE from the remaining
singers of the two bankrupt Italian opera companies; he commissioned Handel
to provide three entertainments, which were *ALESSANDRO SEVERO*, *SERSE* and
Faramondo. The composer began the score of *Faramondo* on 15 November 1737
and finished it on 24 December 1737, interrupting work on the opera from 4 to
17 December in order to compose and perform the Funeral Anthem for Queen
CAROLINE (ANTHEMS, 5), who had died on 20 December 1737. *Faramondo* was
premiered on 3 January 1738 with the following cast:

Faramondo	CAFFARELLI (castrato)
Adolfo	Margherita Chimenti, 'La Droghierina' (soprano)
Gernando	Antonia MERIGHI (contralto)
Gustavo	Antonio MONTAGNANA (bass)

Rosimonda	Maria Antonia MARCHESINI (mezzo-soprano)
Clotilde	FRANCESINA (soprano)
Teobaldo	Antonio Lottini (bass)
Childerico	William SAVAGE (?soprano and tenor clef)

Caffarelli and Francesina were new to Handel, and Savage's voice seems to have broken at around this time. Handel cut the roles of Teobaldo and Childerico in later performances, presumably because Savage and Lottini were no longer available. The private correspondence of the Wentworth family reveals that the opera was initially a success. The publisher John WALSH reacted quickly and offered a subscription edition of the score as early as 7 January 1738; it was then published on 4 February. Handel never revived the opera, although he used some arias and the overture between 1745 and 1758.

Faramondo is Handel's only original setting of a libretto by Zeno. It is striking how close Handel keeps to older settings of the same text: Zeno's libretto was first set to music by Carlo Francesco Pollarolo (VENICE, 1699) and this version in turn formed the basis for settings by Nicola PORPORA (NAPLES, 1719) and Francesco GASPARINI (ROME, 1720). Gasparini's setting was the most important source for Handel's version, since almost all arias, duets and the final chorus contain borrowings from it. Handel had already borrowed from Gasparini's Faramondo in GIUSTINO (1736), so he presumably knew the score very well, and perhaps admired some of Gasparini's dramaturgical solutions. Handel also borrowed, albeit only short musical sections, from KEISER's La forza della virtù, Francesco Antonio Massimiliano Pistocchi's Narciso, Giovanni BONONCINI's Xerse and ALESSANDRO SCARLATTI's operas Marco Attilio Regolo, Dafni and Griselda.

There is no doubt that Faramondo was composed in haste. The fluctuating quality of the music and dramaturgical inconsistencies suggest that perhaps Handel was occasionally a bit unfocused. The opera has often been criticised for faults such as a weak libretto and unbalanced characterisation of the protagonists. Gasparini had already made various cuts to Zeno's complicated but coherent libretto, leading to slight problems in the structure and comprehensibility of the plot, but these were aggravated by the further abbreviations to recitatives and parts of some arias made for Handel's setting. The end result was that the plot was almost unintelligible and four of the dramaturgically central roles (Gernando, Gustavo, Teobaldo and Childerico) never come into focus, thereby causing imbalance in the dramatic structure of Faramondo. However, among the many musical riches of the opera are the virtuoso da capo arias of the title character, sung by Caffarelli, and the music for the two leading ladies. Faramondo's aria di bravura, 'Voglio che sia l'indegno', is an outstanding depiction of his moral dilemma in being torn between fear for Rosimonda and fury at her father Gustavo; the descending scales, chromatic arpeggios and sudden breaks in the melodic line draw an impressive picture of the character's wavering state. Rosimonda is also facing a conflict in having to choose between loyalty to her father's oath and her love for Faramondo, voiced musically in her aria 'Vanne, che più ti miro', whereas her 'Sì, l' intendesti, sì' shows her rebuffing Gernando's advances using Handel's typical musical formula for conveying contempt. Clotilde's arias made considerable technical demands upon the flexible voice of 'La Francesina', most notably the spectacular *aria di bravura* 'Combattuta da due venti' (later reused in *GIOVE IN ARGO*).

DANIEL GLOWOTZ (Trans. ANGELA BAIER)

A. L. Bellina, 'Filologia fra testo e musica: L'opera in Arcadia, "Faramondo" e "Siface"', *Lettere italiane* 45/2 (1993), 218–43
Burrows and Dunhill
W. Dean, *Handel and the opera seria* (Berkeley, 1969)
    Operas
Harris, *Librettos*
R. M. Mason, D. Hunter, 'Supporting Handel through Subscription to Publications, the Lists of *Rodelinda* and *Faramondo* compared', *Notes* 56/1 (1999), 27–93
R. Strohm, 'Francesco Gasparini, le sue opere tarde e G. F. Händel', *Francesco Gasparini (1661–1727): Atti*, ed. F. Piperno, F. della Seta (Florence, 1981)

Farinel, Jean-Baptiste (Giovanni Battista Farinelli) (b. Grenoble, 15 Jan. 1655; d. Venice, c.1725). French violinist and composer. He was Konzertmeister at the HANOVER court from 1680. In 1689, he married the actress and singer Vittoria TARQUINI, and subsequently worked at Osnabrück (1691–5). He returned to his post at Hanover until 1713, and was responsible for managing the court musicians during a period that coincided with Handel's appointment as Kapellmeister. He was ennobled by the Elector of Hanover (later GEORGE I), and between 1722 and 1724 travelled several times to Grenoble as a self-described *commissaire du roi d'Angleterre*.

WALTER KREYSZIG

Burrows
Mainwaring

'Farinelli' (Carlo Broschi) (b. Andria, Apulia, 24 Jan. 1705; d. Bologna, 16 Sept. 1782). Castrato (range c–d'''). After receiving early training from Nicola PORPORA, his public career began in NAPLES in 1720. In following years his international fame grew as he sang in ROME and in the major cities of northern ITALY, Munich and Vienna, and for composers including Porpora, LEO, VINCI, HASSE, GIACOMELLI, CALDARA and his brother Riccardo Broschi, who provided him with carefully tailored showpieces.

After declining several invitations to travel to England, including Handel's attempt in 1729 to engage him for the Second Academy (OPERA COMPANIES, 3), in 1734 Farinelli accepted an invitation to join the OPERA OF THE NOBILITY in London, where he sang for three seasons. He arrived in London on 26 September 1734, and the following month sang twice before the royal family, when he sang at sight several Handel arias, accompanied at the harpsichord by Princess ANNE.

His first benefit concert on 15 March 1735 was one of the most celebrated musical events of the century. One ecstatic listener cried, 'One God, One Farinelli'. His salary was 1,502 guineas per season; but with a benefit night, private concerts and gifts from admirers, his income could have approached £4,000 that season. He sang in one Handel opera, a revival of *OTTONE*, although it was produced by the rival Opera of the Nobility. Farinelli sang not the leading role, but that of Adelberto. Of his seven arias, five were taken from other Handel operas, *RICCARDO PRIMO*, *LOTARIO* and *PARTENOPE* (the others are unidentified).

In summer 1737, he travelled to Paris, and instead of returning to London for another season, went on by royal invitation to Madrid, where he sang before the melancholic King Philip V. At royal command, he broke his contract with the Opera of the Nobility and remained in Spain for twenty-two years (continuing through the reign of Ferdinand VI), where he directed operas and lavish court festivals. He held the official position of 'criado familiar de su Majestad' (i.e. 'His Majesty's familiar servant'), as which he was answerable only to the King, and had free access to royal chambers at any time. He retired in 1760 to a villa outside Bologna, which he had purchased in 1732 and improved with his accumulated wealth, living as a gentleman-farmer and fêted by the local nobility. Furnished with his musical instruments, and a large collection of scores and paintings (including portraits of European monarchs he had befriended), his villa became a site for visiting travellers, including GLUCK, MOZART, BURNEY, Casanova and international Grand Tourists. THOMAS MCGEARY and CARLO VITALI

P. Barbier, Farinelli: le castrat des lumières (Paris, 1994)

S. Cappelletto, La voce perduta: Vita di Farinelli evirato cantore (Turin, 1995)

F. W. Marpurg, Historisch-kritische Beyträge zur Aufnahme der Musik, I. Band, Drittes Stück (Berlin, 1754), 'II. Lebensläuffe, A: Herrn Johann Joachim Quantzens Lebenslauf, von ihm selbst entworfen', 233–4

T. McGeary, 'Farinelli in Madrid: Opera, Politics, and the War of Jenkins' Ear', MQ 82 (1998), 383–421

    'Farinelli's Progress to Albion: The Recruitment and Reception of Opera's "Blazing Star"', British Journal for Eighteenth-Century Studies 28 (2005), 339–60

J. Milhous and R. D. Hume, 'Construing and Misconstruing Farinelli in London', British Journal for Eighteenth-Century Studies 28 (2005), 361–85

C. Vitali and F. Boris (eds.), Carlo Broschi Farinelli: La solitudine amica: lettere al conte Sicinio Pepoli (Palermo, 2000)

Faulkner, George (b. ?1703; d. Dublin, 29 Aug. 1775). Irish printer and bookseller who published WORDBOOKS for Handel's DUBLIN season of 1741–2, including the first edition of MESSIAH. Faulkner was the best-known and most important Irish bookseller of the eighteenth century. Jonathan Swift called him the 'Prince of Dublin Printers', but Charles JENNENS was not best pleased with his Messiah wordbook, finding it 'full of Bulls'. A second impression corrected some of these errors but introduced new ones. Whether or not Jennens had seen a copy and transmitted his views to Handel in time for the performance of SAUL on 25 May 1742, Faulkner's wordbook for that work is a great improvement. His successful bi-weekly newspaper, the Dublin Journal, which he had started in 1725, is an important source for Handel's activities during his time in Ireland, and for the performances of his music in Dublin in succeeding years. The dramatist John O'Keeffe described Faulkner in later life as 'a fat little man with a large well powdered wig and brown clothes'. He had a wooden leg, having lost one to amputation about 1730.

Faulkner's adopted daughter and reputed niece, Anna Maria Fa(u)lkner (d. 1796/7), was a soprano for whom Handel composed a part in his incidental music for the unperformed ALCESTE (1749/50). She may have sung some of the music when Handel recast it as the CHOICE OF HERCULES (1751). Arias by

6. Faustina Bordoni by Bartolomeo Nazari, oil on canvas, c.1734.

Handel often featured in her concerts, and at her benefit concert in April 1751 she performed arias from *ALEXANDER'S FEAST* to great acclaim.

JOHN GREENACOMBE

'Faustina' (Faustina Bordoni) (b. Venice, 30 March 1697; d. Venice, 4 Nov. 1781). Italian soprano (see Figure 6). She probably made her operatic debut in Carlo Francesco Pollarolo's *Ariodante* in VENICE in 1716. In the following fifteen years she sang in opere serie by Italy's most eminent opera composers, such as Antonio LOTTI, Tomaso Albinoni, Giovanni BONONCINI, Francesco GASPARINI, Giovanni PORTA, Domenico Sarro and Leonardo VINCI, at the most famous Italian opera houses, for example in Venice at the Teatro SAN GIOVANNI GRISOSTOMO, in NAPLES and Bologna. Outside Italy she was heard in Pietro Torri's *Griselda* (Munich, 1723) and in operas by Antonio CALDARA and Johann Joseph Fux (Vienna, 1725–6). From March 1726 to May 1728 she sang for the Royal Academy of Music in London (OPERA COMPANIES, 2). Handel's roles for her included Rossane (*ALESSANDRO*), Alceste (*ADMETO*), Pulcheria (*RICCARDO PRIMO*), Emira (*SIROE*) and Elisa (*TOLOMEO*). She also sang in revivals of *RINALDO* and *RADAMISTO*, and in operas by Bononcini and Attilio ARIOSTI. Her supposed rivalry with Francesca CUZZONI was the talk of the town, but recent research has shown that the popular story about their onstage fight during a performance of Bononcini's *Astianatte* in 1727 is untrue (RIVAL QUEENS).

After she married Johann Adolf HASSE in 1730, Bordoni predominantly sang in her husband's operas. The two of them were engaged by the DRESDEN court and Bordoni remained its prima donna until she retired from the stage in 1751. On extended tours she presented herself on many European stages (from November 1734 to January 1737 and again from September 1738 to early 1740 in Italy, 1744 in Vienna, from summer 1746 to spring 1747 in Munich and Italy, from May 1748 to early 1749 in Italy, summer 1750 in Paris, March 1753 in BERLIN and from 1756 to 1763 in Naples, Warsaw, Venice and Vienna). Bordoni was one of the most important female singers of her time and had a voice range of nearly two octaves (b♭ to g″, in her Handel parts c′ to a″). The arias composed for her include coloratura passages in diatonic scales, *scalette di salti di terza*, martellati, register changes, wide interval leaps, rhythmic variations and sequences of trills, showing her voice to have been not only highly virtuosic and very agile but also demonstrating that she had perfect breath control and an extremely secure intonation. Her contemporaries – for example Johann Joachim Quantz – especially praised her immaculate articulation, her excellent trills and her command of the martellato technique, the latter ability being effectively showcased by Handel in the aria 'Alla sua gabbia d'oro' in *Alessandro*.

PANJA MÜCKE (Trans. ANGELA BAIER)

Dean, *Operas*

C. S. LaRue, *Handel and His Singers. The Creation of the Royal Academy Operas, 1720–1728* (Oxford, 1995)

F. W. Marpurg, *Historisch-Kritische Beyträge zur Aufnahme der Musik*, I. Band, Drittes Stück (Berlin, 1754), 'II. Lebensläuffe, A: Herrn Johann Joachim Quantzens Lebenslauf, von ihm selbst entworfen', 240

P. Mücke, *Johann Adolf Hasses Dresdner Opern im Kontext der Hofkultur* (Laaber, 2003)

S. Ograjenšek, 'From *Alessandro* (1726) to *Tolomeo* (1728): The Final Royal Academy Operas', Ph.D. dissertation (University of Cambridge, 2005)

S. Woyke, 'Faustina Bordoni-Hasse – eine Sängerinnenkarriere im 18. Jahrhundert', *GHB* VII (1998)

Feind, Barthold (b. Hamburg, 23 Nov. 1678; d. Hamburg, 14 Oct. 1721). Poet, librettist. He studied law at the universities of Wittenberg (1699–c.1701) and HALLE (c.1701–1703) and graduated as a *Licentiat*. It is not known whether he and Handel, who was also studying law in 1702, met during Feind's stay in Halle. Feind later settled in HAMBURG, probably practising as a lawyer, and became the most important librettist of the GÄNSEMARKT opera between 1705 and 1716. His librettos were set to music by Reinhard KEISER and Christoph Graupner. However, he made life difficult for himself by becoming involved in political controversies concerning the opera. He criticised Friedrich Christian FEUSTKING's libretto of *ALMIRA*, which Keiser set for WEISSENFELS in 1704 and Handel for Hamburg in 1705, because he disagreed with Feustking's poetological views. He rewrote *Almira* for Keiser, who set the new version for Hamburg in 1706. He did the same with Feustking's libretto for Handel's *NERO* (1705), which became *Octavia* and was set by Keiser (also in 1705). He translated the Italian libretto of Handel's *RINALDO* for a production at Hamburg in 1715. KLAUS-PETER KOCH (Trans. ANGELA BAIER)

G. Dünnhaupt, 'Barthold Feind d. J.', *Personalbibliographien zu den Drucken des Barock*, vol. 2 (Stuttgart, 1990)

B. Feind, *Deutsche Gedichte: bestehend in musicalischen Schau-Spielen, lob-glückwünschungsverliebten und moralischen Gedichten, ernst- und scherzhafften Sinn- und Grabschrifften, Satyren, Cantaten und allerhand Gattungen, sammt einer Vorrede von dem Temperament und Gemüthsbeschaffenheit eines Poeten und Gedancken von der Opera . . . Erster Theil* (Stade, 1708)

HHB iv

S. Stompor, 'Die deutschen Aufführungen von Opern Händels in der ersten Hälfte des 18. Jahrhunderts', HJb 24 (1978), 31–89

Fernando. See *SOSARME*

Festing, Michael Christian (b. London, 29 Nov. 1705; d. London, 24 July 1752). English composer and virtuoso violinist, taught by Richard Jones and Francesco GEMINIANI. In 1731 Festing co-founded the Apollo Academy with Maurice GREENE after the BONONCINI–LOTTI controversy at the ACADEMY OF ANCIENT MUSIC. In 1738 he was one of the founders of the FUND FOR THE SUPPORT OF DECAY'D MUSICIANS and their Families, of which Handel became a member. Festing was musical director of RANELAGH Pleasure Gardens from their opening in 1742 until his death.   MATTHEW GARDNER

festivals

1. Three Choirs Festival
2. Triennial Handel Festival
3. Göttingen Handel Festival
4. Halle Handel Festival
5. London Handel Festival
6. Maryland Handel Festival
7. Karlsruhe Handel Festival
8. Handel Festival Japan (HFJ)

1. Three Choirs Festival

One of the oldest and most important annual choral festivals in Britain, it is held in turn in the cathedrals of Hereford, Gloucester and Worcester. It is difficult to determine exactly in which year the festivals began; the first documented events are those in Worcester in 1719, Hereford in 1720 and Gloucester in 1721. It was not organised as a 'Handel Festival' but particularly in the eighteenth century the programmes tended to be dominated by Handel's music. The first documented performance of one of his compositions at the festival was a TE DEUM on 18 August 1736. In following years the cathedrals introduced performances of English-language works such as *ALEXANDER'S FEAST* (1739), *ACIS AND GALATEA* (1745), *SAMSON* (1748), *L'ALLEGRO* (1751), *JUDAS MACCABAEUS* (1754), *MESSIAH* (1757) and the Coronation Anthems (ANTHEMS, 3). *Messiah* was performed at nearly every festival, as a whole or in parts, until 1963. In 1800 the musical forces comprised forty-four singers and forty-seven instrumentalists, but by the middle of the nineteenth century the number of performers had increased considerably up to c.220 choristers and more than 100 instrumentalists. The three choirs also participated in the triennial festivals at the CRYSTAL PALACE.

2. Triennial Handel Festival

The British tradition of Handel festivals started with the HANDEL COMMEMORATION at WESTMINSTER ABBEY in 1784, which established a grand precedent for large-scale celebrations of Handel's music. During the nineteenth century these were most famously typified by the colossal oratorio performances at the CRYSTAL PALACE, which had something like a carnival atmosphere: in 1883 there were approximately 3,900 performers, and the 1885 festival had 87,796 visitors. The first Handel festival at the venue took place in 1857, and included MESSIAH, JUDAS MACCABAEUS and ISRAEL IN EGYPT. The programme of the 1859 festival fixed the running order for the rest of the nineteenth century: rehearsals were on Saturday, Monday was devoted to Messiah, Wednesday featured 'Selections' from various works, and Israel in Egypt – which had usually the largest audience – concluded the festival on Friday. From 1859 to 1883 the festival was held every three years, but the pattern was broken for a bicentenary festival in 1885. The festivals were again held every three years until 1912, after which they were interrupted by the First World War. Three more Triennial Handel festivals took place at Crystal Place between 1920 and 1926.

ANNETTE LANDGRAF

3. Göttingen Handel Festival

Founded by Oskar HAGEN, whose production of a heavily adapted version of RODELINDA on 26 June 1920 jump-started the interest in Handel's musico-dramatic works, not only at GÖTTINGEN but also in HANOVER and Münster. The chorus singers were students recruited from Georg-August-Universität, and the 'festival orchestra' consisted of musicians from the Akademische Orchestervereinigung. The official organiser was the Universitätsbund, the Society of Friends of the Göttingen University. According to Hagen's artistic aims, the festival concentrated on Handel's operas: after Rodelinda came Hagen's versions of OTTONE (1921), GIULIO CESARE (1922), SERSE (1924) and EZIO (1926). These productions usually took place in the Stadttheater with occasional staged open-air performances in the city park (for example ACIS AND GALATEA in 1934).

Hanns NIEDECKEN-GEBHARD was the festival's principal assistant director intermittently from 1922 until his death in 1954. Paul Thiersch (1879–1928) and later Heinrich Heckroth (1901–70) designed scenery and costumes. In 1931 the Göttinger Händel-Gesellschaft (HANDEL SOCIETIES, 4) was formed. During the turbulent years of the Second World War the Göttingen Handel Festival continued, albeit on a smaller scale, with interruptions, and hard-pressed by the Nazi Party's attempts to exert ideological influence. The first prestigious post-war era was ushered in by the appointment of conductor Günther Weißenborn as artistic director. The festival gained new momentum and an international profile when British period-instrument specialist John Eliot Gardiner was made artistic director in 1980. In contrast to the festival's early tradition of adapting Handel's scores in order to bring them 'up to date' and make them 'fit for the stage', Gardiner assumed the artistic credo of striving for historically informed PERFORMANCE PRACTICE, and concentrated on performing dramatic oratorios with internationally renowned soloists. Under its present artistic director Nicholas McGegan (since 1991), the festival has returned to its roots by focusing on the revival of lesser-known Handel operas. In recent years there has been a deliberate policy to explore different approaches to STAGING, from baroque-style productions (e.g. ATALANTA in 2005 and ORLANDO in 2008) to modern conceptual spectacles (e.g. Igor Folwill's *RINALDO* in 2004 and *GIULIO CESARE* in 2007). Recent festivals have included an increasing number of smaller concerts around the vicinity of the old university town and across the southern part of Lower Saxony. Numerous oratorio and opera productions since the 1980s have been documented on critically acclaimed commercial RECORDINGS.   JÜRGEN HEIDRICH (Trans. ANGELA BAIER)

4. Halle Handel Festival

There were occasional Handel events at HALLE an der Saale from 1859 onwards, and festivals devoted to Handel from 1922. The annual Handel festival was founded in 1952: consisting of twenty-two performances, the newly initiated festival endeavoured to establish Handel's birthplace as a cultural institution in East Germany, and to promote Handel's less popular works; another objective was to provide a forum for scholarly research and musical performance. Between 1972 and 1989 it was called the Händelfestspiele der DDR, but was renamed the Händel-Festspiele in Halle an der Saale in 1990. The city organises the festival, held each June, in coordination with the Georg-Friedrich-Händel-Gesellschaft (HANDEL SOCIETIES, 3). The Händel-Haus (MUSEUMS, 1) is a central meeting point during the festival, hosts an annual academic conference, and is home to the Hallische Händel-Ausgabe (EDITIONS, 7).

From the beginning of the festival it established traditions like a wreath-laying ceremony at the Handel Memorial, featuring a concert given by young musicians. For some years the opening ceremony included the award of the Händel-Preis: from 1959 until 1993 a prize for both individuals and collective work, but since 1993 it has been awarded only to individuals for special services to Handel's music and research. The final event of the festival is traditionally an open-air concert with an impressive firework display in the Galgenbergschlucht.

In the early years of the festival performers were from the Halle region and the former GDR, but since the 1959 commemoration year international performers were also involved. During the 1970s and 1980s leading international baroque specialists participated in festival concerts, and foreign academics became increasingly involved in the conferences. Nowadays performers from Halle and nearby cities remain involved, but there is additionally an excellent programme of operas, oratorios and concerts by internationally renowned baroque specialists from all over the world. Performances take place at locations associated with Handel (e.g. the Marktkirche, the Dom and some smaller chamber music events at the Händel-Haus), in the recently built Georg-Friedrich-Händel Halle (opened 1999), the opera house (the 'Stadttheater' before 1991) and at the historic Goethe Theater in Bad Lauchstädt. Since 1999 the festival has been extended to run for ten days. The event involves the whole city of Halle and is an important opportunity for Handel enthusiasts, Handel scholars, music-lovers and musicians to meet up regularly once a year.   ANNETTE LANDGRAF

5. London Handel Festival

Founded by the conductor Denys Darlow in 1978, the festival takes place annually between March and April. Performances include oratorios at Handel's parish church, ST GEORGE'S, Hanover Square (which also include an annual performance of Bach's St Matthew Passion) and staged opera productions at the Royal

College of Music's Britten Theatre. The resident London Handel Orchestra and London Handel Choir were formed in 1981, and consist of leading specialist musicians. During the 1990s festival concerts were frequently conducted by Paul Nicholson (associate director, 1994–7) and Laurence Cummings, who succeeded Darlow as the festival's artistic director in 2002. A small nucleus of regular principal members of the orchestra formed the London Handel Players in 2000.

The festival specialises in promoting lesser-known works, such as recordings of The Triumph of Time and Truth and Silla (both under Darlow), the modern premiere of the 1732 version of ESTHER (HWV 50^b) in 2002 (under Cummings), and the revival of rarely staged operas (e.g. SOSARME, EZIO, TOLOMEO, PORO, ATALANTA and ALESSANORO, 2004–9). The festival is an important showcase for conservatoire postgraduate students to gain experience of working alongside professional musicians: the festival inaugurated the Handel Singing Competition in 2002, and numerous finalists now have successful careers.

6. Maryland Handel Festival

Founded in 1981 by the musicologist Howard Serwer and conductor Paul Traver, the festival presented a variety of choral, solo, chamber, opera and orchestral concerts at the University of Maryland, College Park (USA), usually in connection with academic conferences organised by the American Handel Society (AHS) (HANDEL SOCIETIES, 1). In 1982 the festival embarked on a twenty-year project to perform all of Handel's English dramatic oratorios in order of their composition and in the version of their first performance. All of these were conducted by Paul Traver, who thus became the first musician since Handel to direct performances of all of the composer's oratorios. Many of these were works seldom performed on the American continent. At the conclusion of the oratorio project in 2001, the festival was renamed the American Handel Festival, and continues to be held at other venues in conjunction with the biennial AHS conferences.   DAVID VICKERS

7. Karlsruhe Handel Festival

In 1977 the 'Händel-Tage' was founded by Günter Könemann (director of the Badisches Staatstheater), and this was expanded into a festival in 1985 (the tercentenary of Handel's birth). Around that time, it was also decided that historically informed performance practice was mandatory, and that an orchestra playing on period instruments was needed: the 'Deutsche Händel-Solisten' started out as a group of baroque specialists assembled in a rather ad hoc fashion but within a few years it developed into a professional baroque orchestra. One of the main goals of the festival is the performance of little-known operas. At least half of the Handel operas performed at Karlsruhe have seldom been staged since the eighteenth century, such as LOTARIO (2006), a production which was notable for its investigation of baroque acting techniques (gestures, action, costumes and lighting).

†SIEGFRIED SCHMALZRIEDT (Trans. ANGELA BAIER)

See also INTERNATIONALE HÄNDEL-AKADEMIE

8. Handel Festival Japan (HFJ)

Held every winter in Tokyo, the festival was founded in 2003 by the scholar Toshiki Misawa to introduce Japanese music-lovers to a wide range of Handel's vocal and instrumental music. HFJ's choir and orchestra, the Cannons Concert Chamber Choir and Orchestra, focuses mainly on works never or rarely performed in Japan, such as ACIS AND GALATEA (2003), La RESURREZIONE (2004), Concerti grossi, Op. 6 (ORCHESTRAL WORKS, 2) and The CHOICE OF HERCULES (both 2006), HERCULES (2007) and others. In 2006 HFJ started two separate projects: 'Handel Vocal Seminars' are organised for scholars and performers to study and perform Handel's vocal works, and the series 'Handel's Church Music' promotes performances of the composer's works, such as the Chapel Royal and Chandos Anthems (ANTHEMS, 1–2), that are little known in Japan. TOSHIKI MISAWA

See also RECEPTION; Appendix 7 – An overview of fifty Handel performers, 1959–2009

A. Boden, Three Choirs: A History of the Festival (Gloucester, 1992)
W. Meyerhoff, 'Chronik der Göttinger Händel-Festspiele 1920–1970', ed. H.-P. Hesse, 60 Jahre Göttinger Händel-Festspiele (Göttingen, 1980)
H. Motel, 'Chronik der Göttinger Händel-Festspiele 1971–1979', ed. H.-P. Hesse, 60 Jahre Göttinger Händel-Festspiele (Göttingen, 1980)
M. Musgrave, The Musical Life of the Crystal Palace (Cambridge, 1995)
W. Relikopf, 'Oskar Hagen. Begründer der Göttinger Händelfestspiele', Göttinger Jahrbuch 30 (1982)
G. Richter, 50 Jahre Händel-Festspiele in Georg Friedrich Händels Geburtsstadt Halle an der Saale (Halle, 2001)
W. Shaw, The Three Choirs Festival (London, 1954)
W. Siegmund-Schultze, 'Die Hallischen Händel-Festspiele 1952–1954', HJb 1 (1955)

Feustking, Friedrich Christian (b. Stellau near Stormarn/Schleswig-Holstein, 1678; d. Tolk near Flensburg/Schleswig-Holstein, 3 Feb. 1739). Librettist for the GÄNSEMARKT opera in HAMBURG and theologian. He wrote librettos for Johann MATTHESON (Cleopatra, 1704), Reinhard KEISER (Almira, version for WEISSENFELS, 1704) and Handel (ALMIRA and NERO, both 1705). His texts for Almira and Nero occasioned a long and bitter literary dispute with Barthold FEIND and Christian Friedrich HUNOLD.

KLAUS-PETER KOCH (Trans. ANGELA BAIER)

F. Chrysander, G. F. Händel, vol. 1 (Leipzig, 1858), 105–15
HHb iv, 23–6
H. J. Marx and D. Schröder, Die Hamburger Gänsemarkt-Oper: Katalog der Textbücher 1678–1748 (Laaber, 1999)

Figlio d'alte speranze, HWV 113. Set for soprano, violins and basso continuo, the anonymous text tells of the changing fortunes of King Abdolonymus, born to greatness, reduced to being a gardener and restored to the throne of Sidon. Composed on paper of Venetian manufacture, it may be one of the earliest pieces Handel wrote in Italy, pre-dating his arrival in ROME. Throughout the cantata Handel emphasises the image of the wheel of fortune, using distinct turning motives in each of the three arias. The word [So]nata on the first page of the autograph has led to the hypothesis that Handel planned to begin the cantata with an instrumental introduction and, further, that this was specifically the 'Sonata a

5' (HWV 288) (ORCHESTRAL WORKS, 6). As the word is crossed out, however, it may simply mean that the paper was at first intended for a different work than the cantata, or that Handel, if he originally planned to open the cantata with a sonata, changed his mind.   ELLEN T. HARRIS

films. Since 1942 a number of Handel films have been produced which fall into two main categories: portrayals of Handel (biographical films and side roles) and documentaries about his life or works. The following list aims to include the major Handel films or documentaries that are known to exist at present.

1942   *The Great Mr Handel*, GB, dir. Norman Walker (biopic, Wilfred Lawson as Handel)

1960   *Georg Friedrich Händel*, DDR (VEB DEFA-Studio für Wochenschau und Dokumentarfilm) dir. Wernfried Hübel (documentary)

1963   *A Cry of Angels* ('Hallmark of Fame'), GB, dir. George Schaefer (biopic / part of a TV series, Walter Slezak as Handel)

1985   *Honour, Profit, Pleasure*, GB, dir. Anna Ambrose (biopic, Simon Callow as Handel)

1985   *God rot Tunbridge Wells*, GB, dir. Tony Palmer (biopic, Trevor Howard, Dowe Griffiths, Christopher Bramwell and Ronald Neilson as Handel)

1988   *The Italian Connection*, US, Films for the Humanities and Sciences (documentary/educational)

1988   *The Voice of Britannia*, US, Films for the Humanities and Sciences (documentary/educational)

1994   *Farinelli: Il castrato*, F, dir. Gérard Corbiau (portrayal, side role, Omero Antonutti Jeroen Krabbe as Handel)

1995   *Handel's Last Chance*, Canada/Slovakia, dir. Milan Cheylov (biopic, Leon Pownall as Handel)

1996   *A Night with Handel*, GB, dir. Alexander Marengo (music with work introductions and some biography)

1998   *George Frideric Handel*, US, Films for the Humanities and Sciences (documentary/educational)

1999   *Journey through Time: Handel*, GB (Wales HTV), producer, Hefin Owen (documentary)

2003   *Handel's Water Music: Recreating a Royal Spectacular*, GB (BBC), dir. Suzy Klein (documentary)

2005   *Famous Composers: George Frideric Handel*, US (Kultur Video) (documentary)

2006   *Händel in Rom*, D, dir. Olaf Brühl (documentary)

2007   *Georg Friedrich Händel – Das Geheimnis eines Genies* ('Geschichte Mitteldeutschlands'), D (MDR), dir. Dirk Otto (documentary/portrayal, Manfred Erwe as Handel)

2008   *Barockstar: Georg Friedrich Händel*, D (MDR/Arte), dir. Ulrich Meyszies (documentary)

2009   *Händel – Der Film*, D (Seelmannfilm/NDR), dir. Ralf Pleger (documentary/portrayal, Matthias Wiebalck, Sebastian Madyda and Levi Wessel as Handel)

2009   *Handel – The Conquering Hero* ('The Birth of British Music 2'), GB (BBC), dir. Andy King – Dabbs (documentary)

Several of these productions can be considered as films to commemorate a specific stage of Handel's life; for example, 1985, which saw two films in English, was the tercentenary of Handel's birth. More recently Olaf Brühl directed a documentary to coincide with Handel's arrival in ROME 300 years earlier (1706) and by mid-2009 one English and two German productions have been released in commemoration of the 250th anniversary of Handel's death. The first Handel film to be produced in 1942 can also be related to a commemorative year, the bicentenary of the first performance of *MESSIAH*, and it is on the production of this work that this film focuses. Although much of the information presented is historically incorrect, the film offers valuable insights into Britain in 1942; for example, the film delivers the message that a bad situation (Handel's financial difficulties/wartime Britain) can be overcome (Handel's recovery to wealth/a successful resolution to the Second World War).

The two biographical films from 1985 are contrasting: the witty *Honour, Profit, Pleasure* is set as a play within a play in the frame of a baroque theatre with a narrator. *God rot Tunbridge Wells* on the other hand depicts an aged Handel looking back on his life. In *Farinelli: Il castrato* (1995) Handel, who is a secondary role, is seen in several confrontations between himself and the castrato FARINELLI, and is cast as someone who will do everything necessary to ruin his rival (but also as a supreme composer of greater talent than his rivals at the OPERA OF THE NOBILITY).

The documentaries and educational films about Handel's life are, as the list above shows, more numerous than biographical films and portrayals. Throughout the 1980s and 1990s, several films in this category were produced in the United States and Great Britain, before Olaf Brühl's 2006 *Händel in Rom* for German television (ZDF and 3Sat). The earliest documentary known is also a German production, the 1960 *Georg Friedrich Händel*, which is an interesting piece of evidence in terms of Handel's music in the former DDR and also performance practice in the 1960s.

In all the films and documentaries, Handel's music is frequently used, focusing on his more 'well-known' works such as *Messiah*, *MUSIC FOR THE ROYAL FIREWORKS* and *WATER MUSIC*. It is, however, noteworthy that a considerable number of films, documentaries, commercials and television series on subjects other than Handel have also used his music.   MATTHEW GARDNER

E. T. Harris, 'Twentieth-Century Farinelli', MQ 81/2 (1997), 180–9
J. C. Tibbetts, *Composers at the Movies: Studies in Musical Biography* (New Haven, 2005)
British Film Institute, www.bfi.org.uk/research.html
The Internet Movie Database, www.imdb.com/

'Fireworks Music'. See *MUSIC FOR THE ROYAL FIREWORKS*

Fischer, Johann Caspar Ferdinand (b. Schönfeld (Krasno) near Karlsbad (Karlovy Vary)/Bohemia, probably 6/7 Sept. 1656; d. Rastatt/Baden, 27 Aug. 1746). Organist, keyboard player, Kapellmeister and composer. His compositional style was influenced by Jean-Baptiste LULLY. He was *Hofkapellmeister* at the court of the Dukes of Saxe-Lauenburg (late 1680s to 1692 in Schlackenwerth (Ostrov)), then at the court of the Margraves of Baden (1692–1715 in Schlackenwerth, 1715–41 in Rastatt). Out of his extensive work the collection of preludes and fughettas *Ariadne musica* especially influenced Johann Sebastian BACH and Handel (the subject of the fugue in F sharp minor as prototype for the subject of Handel's F minor fugue HWV 433).   KLAUS-PETER KOCH (Trans. ANGELA BAIER)

M. Seiffert, 'Händels Verhältnis zu Tonwerken älterer deutscher Meister', *Jahrbuch der Musikbibliothek Peters für 1907*, vol. 14 (Leipzig, 1908), 41–57

R. Walter, *Johann Caspar Ferdinand Fischer: Hofkapellmeister der Markgrafen von Baden* (Frankfurt am Main etc., 1990)

Fishamble Street. See DUBLIN

Fitzwilliam Museum. Founded in 1816 when Viscount FITZWILLIAM left his extensive collection of art, printed and manuscript music, and £100,000 to CAMBRIDGE University. A considerable part of the Fitzwilliam bequest included printed Handel works as well as autograph manuscripts which had been collected by the Viscount, comprising of volumes left by Handel to J. C. SMITH SENIOR that did not go via J. C. Smith junior and King GEORGE III to the British Museum. In 1902 a valuable addition to the Fitzwilliam Museum's Handel collection was acquired through a gift made by Francis Barrett LENNARD. The present Fitzwilliam Museum building was not complete until 1848.   MATTHEW GARDNER

See also SOURCES AND COLLECTIONS, 1; 4

C. Winter, *The Fitzwilliam Museum, Cambridge* (London, 1958)

Fitzwilliam of Merrion, 7th Viscount (Richard Fitzwilliam) (b. Richmond, Surrey, 1 Aug. 1745; d. London, 4 Feb. 1816). Benefactor and collector of art and music, educated at Charterhouse School and Trinity Hall CAMBRIDGE where he showed interest in music, studying harpsichord with Jacques Duphly in Paris after graduation in 1764. He made numerous tours to the continent and was one of the eight executive directors of the Concerts of Antient Musick in London (1788–1806). He played a role in the 1784 HANDEL COMMEMORA-TION, showing a keen interest in Handel's music, which is also evident from the large collection of printed and manuscript music he had acquired by his death (bequeathed to Cambridge University and now held by the FITZWILLIAM MUSEUM).   MATTHEW GARDNER

C. Cudworth, 'A Cambridge Anniversary: The Fitzwilliam Museum and its Music-Loving Founder', *MT* 107/1476 (Feb., 1966), 113–14, 117

W. Weber, *The Rise of Musical Classics in Eighteenth-Century England* (Cambridge, 1992)

Flavio, HWV 16. The composition of the opera, at first called *Emilia*, and still so entitled in the autograph, was completed on 7 May 1723. It had its premiere at the KING'S THEATRE a week later, on 14 May. The cast was as follows:

Flavio, King of Lombardy	Gaetano BERENSTADT (castrato)
Guido, son of Ugone	SENESINO (castrato)
Emilia, daughter of Lotario	Francesca CUZZONI (soprano)
Vitige, in love with Teodata	Margherita DURASTANTI (soprano)
Teodata, daughter of Ugone	ANASTASIA ROBINSON (alto)
Ugone, counsellor	Alexander GORDON (tenor)
Lotario, counsellor	Giuseppe Maria BOSCHI (bass)

The opera was only modestly successful, a run of eight performances taking it through to the end of the season. It was never revived during the Royal Academy years (OPERA COMPANIES, 2), but had a very brief rerun for the Second Academy in 1732 (OPERA COMPANIES, 3).

Act I: While Vitige and Teodata are lovers in secret, Emilia and Guido are formally betrothed. The two fathers propose to introduce their daughters at court. Ugone presents Teodata to the King. Lotario invites Flavio to the forthcoming marriage of Emilia and Guido, but is outraged when Ugone rather than himself is appointed governor of Britain. Flavio shares his thoughts on Teodata's beauty with Vitige, who, to hide his alarm at the King's admiration of his own beloved, affects indifference. Meeting his old father, who is smarting from the assault of the jealous Lotario (a slapped face), Guido undertakes to defend the family honour, even at the risk of losing Emilia.

Act II: As Teodata and Flavio are conversing, Ugone bursts in, still bewailing his lost honour. Believing her father to be talking about her own amour with Vitige, Teodata confesses all, so giving him further cause to deplore his fate. Vitige is appalled to be charged with the task of telling Teodata how the King dotes on her. And since Ugone now knows of their affair, they agree to get married without delay. In the meantime Teodata must be charming but non-committal with Flavio. As she departs to prepare for her tricky role, Vitige struggles with jealous forebodings. Meanwhile Emilia's wedding preparations are interrupted by Lotario, insisting that she break off all relationship with Guido. Guido defeats Lotario in a duel. Emilia finds her father mortally wounded.

Act III: Flavio's love-sick musing is interrupted by Emilia and Ugone, both crying out for justice; the King needs time to resolve so difficult a matter. When Vitige introduces Teodata the King is so overcome by her beauty that he requires Vitige to 'explain to her his flame', with ambiguous consequences. Vitige and Teodata are reconciled just as Flavio arrives to claim her as his new queen. Philosophically putting this setback behind him, the King resolves the Emilia–Guido dilemma with Solomon-like sagacity; Vitige and Teodata's union is given royal blessing; Ugone is dispatched to govern Britain.

The libretto is adapted by HAYM from NORIS's *Flavio Cuniberto* (VENICE, 1682), as it had appeared in a ROME recension of 1693, composed by Luigi Mancia. Its plot is, as Haym observed, a double one. Of the two pairs of young lovers, Vitige and Teodata have to overcome the potential rivalry of the King, while the love of Guido and Emilia is crossed by the claims of affronted honour. The first is a subject from Dark Age Lombard history, the second from Pierre CORNEILLE's great tragicomedy *Le Cid*. Noris's original libretto had been a masterly specimen of the late seventeenth-century Venetian style, witty yet somehow world-weary. Haym shortened it drastically, sometimes to reduce a character's garrulousness, sometimes in the interests of propriety; the comic intermezzi that punctuated and commented on the action are eliminated, and the whole is formally regularised.

Critics dispute what exactly these changes have done to the tone of the opera: how much of its ironic comedy survives; whether a number of ludicrous incidents should somehow be absorbed into the framework of a typical dynastic drama, or whether they are intended as satirical puncturings of heroic decorum. *Flavio* is an elusive opera; but a classical poise pervades all its emotional ambiguities and cross-currents. The design of the first act illustrates this well. First come two contrasting tableaux for the two pairs of lovers, almost entirely without dramatic action: for Teodata and Vitige an illicit nocturnal assignation and love duet (no other Handel opera begins in this way); then, for Emilia and Guido a formal engagement in the bright light of day, sealed with two grand and rather public arias. The intrigue begins in the third tableau, when Teodata is introduced to court, and Flavio decides to dispatch Ugone to govern Britain. Here Haym's adaptation does not match Noris's original for clarity, plausibility or wit. The final tableau is a different matter, however, demonstrating far more eloquently than Noris had done the consequences of the incipient intrigue for the emotional lives of the principal characters, and giving Handel the opportunity to round off the act with the two splendid arias, 'L'armellin vita non cura' and 'Amante stravagante'. With English words by CAREY, 'See, see, my charmer flyes me', this latter aria was the nearest thing to a hit song in Flavio.

The music is true to the tone of the drama. Its orchestration is exceptionally 'spare and delicate' (Dean and Knapp, p. 471). Brass is not employed at all, and where flute or recorder are used to vary the standard string and oboe scoring, they function not as independent obbligato instruments, but simply double a violin part and give it a touch of distinctive colour. Throughout the opera, even in the Overture, tutti scoring à 3 is more frequent than à 4. The rhythmic cast is delicate too: a third of Flavio's numbers are in the light-footed 3/8 metre.

The two sets of lovers, in both cases one soprano, one alto (with Teodata and Vitige the man has the higher voice), are nicely differentiated. The music of Emilia and Guido is more characteristic of the grand Royal Academy manner; for the others Handel generally adopts a simpler, more tuneful style, though as the ironies of the plot become more painful Vitige's music too becomes more heroically vehement.   DAVID KIMBELL

Bianconi
Burney, 723–4
H. D. Clausen, 'Der Einfluß der Komponisten auf die Librettowahl der Royal Academy of
    Music (1720–1729)', Zur Dramaturgie der Barockoper. Bericht über die Symposien der
    Internationalen Händel-Akademie Karlsruhe 1992 und 1993, ed. H. J. Marx (Karlsruhe, 1994)
Dean and Knapp, Operas
Harris, Librettos
J. M. Knapp (ed.), Flavio, HHA II/13 (Kassel, 1993)
Strohm

Flörcke, Johanna Friederike. See HANDEL, 9

Florence. A city in central Italy and the capital of the Grand Duchy of Tuscany, which occupied most of present-day Tuscany except the Republic of Lucca and the Principality of Massa. At the turn of the seventeenth century, Florence had c.80,000 inhabitants. It is estimated that there were 385 noble families concentrated in the capital, numbering some 2,000 people, who were thus 2.5 per cent of the city's population and a scarce 0.4 per cent of the entire state.

During the long reign (1670–1723) of Grand Duke Cosimo III Medici, a policy of strict neutrality between Spain and the Empire, coupled with a formal leaning towards France, successfully prevented war. On the other hand, subjects lamented the sovereign's personal bigotry, which resulted in the excessive power of the clergy and monastic orders. Clerical near-monopoly over education facilities (whether elementary or higher, such as the famed University of Pisa), the enforcement of strict Catholic morals and traditionalist thought through the civil courts frequently caused discontent.

The economy was also ruled by protectionism and monopolies. High taxation, the decline in production of prized textiles (formerly the backbone of Tuscan export) and increased public debt were criticised by observers. Some relief was provided by the seaport at Leghorn, a major centre for shipping and finance, mainly due to the privileges allotted to a thriving Jewish community. As big fortunes tended to shift from commerce and banking to the landed interest, the traditionally sober lifestyle of the ruling class became increasingly prone to conspicuous consumption. Besides the ruling Medici dynasty, the Riccardi, Salviati and Corsini families lived in a princely manner and were noted for their patronage of the arts. According to Rogissart's period handbook for grand tourists, Florence boasted a great number of magnificent palaces, 52 churches, 89 convents and 22 hospitals. The average Florentines were described as hard-working, sober, lively spirited and hospitable to strangers; particularly to scholars, whom they held in high esteem. Their less desirable qualities were alleged to be a stricter segregation of women than elsewhere in Italy and an embarrassing inclination towards elaborate ceremonies.

The MEDICI household was the largest musical employer: their tenured *musici ordinari* can be regarded as a secular music establishment. Other court musicians were hired on a temporary basis, while church musicians (the two functions often overlapped) were mostly administered by trade guilds, convents, vestries and a large number of lay confraternities, whose high-class production of oratorios was an outstanding feature in Florence's musical life. The Cathedral of Santa Maria del Fiore had downsized operations to organ playing or little more, while large-scale performances, in connection with court worship or dynastic festivals, took place at the churches of L'Annunziata and Santa Felicita. The network of *accademie* or *conversazioni* (Sorgenti, Immobili, Infuocati etc.) were involved in opera production. At the time of Handel's travels in Italy (HANDEL, 2; 15), the Teatro della Pergola had been dormant since 1689, but operas were performed in a variety of smaller urban venues, most notably in the 506-seat Teatro del Cocomero, and in the suburban residences of the Medici princes. Violinists Francesco Veracini and his son Antonio entertained only casual ties with the Medici, but ran an influential private music school, whose most successful pupil Francesco Maria (Antonio's nephew) made his debut c.1708 (VERACINI). CARLO VITALI

See also PALAZZI; *RODRIGO*

W. Kirkendale, *The Court Musicians in Florence during the Principate of the Medici: With a Reconstruction of the Artistic Establishment* (Florence, 1993)

Le Sieur de Rogissart, *Les delices de L'Italie, qui contiennent une description exacte du pays, des principales villes . . .* (Leyden, 1706, 2nd edn 1709)

F. Lora, 'I mottetti di Giacomo Antonio Perti per Ferdinando de' Medici principe di Toscana: ricognizione, cronologia e critica delle fonti', Ph.D. dissertation (University of Bologna, 2005–6)

R. L. Weaver and N. W. Weaver, *A Chronology of Music in the Florentine Theater: Operas, Prologues, Farces, Intermezzos, Concerts, and Plays With Incidental Music*, 2 vols. (Detroit, 1978–93)

Floridante, Il, HWV 14. Libretto after Francesco SILVANI's *La Costanza in trionfo* (VENICE, set by Marc'Antonio Ziani, 1696). The only surviving daughter of the dethroned former king has been passed off by the usurper as his own child and has been promised in marriage to the usurper's General, a Prince of a friendly neighbouring country, if the latter should gain military victory. While the General triumphs in naval battle, the usurping villain changes his mind and now wants to marry his ward himself in order to bestow legitimacy upon his own kingship. Silvani's story claims to be authentic Scandinavian history but in reality lacks any historical foundation.

Paolo ROLLI, the opera company's Italian secretary, entirely rewrote the text and changed the setting to ancient Persia. Handel probably had no choice but to work with him and therefore had to make do with the dramaturgic weaknesses of the libretto: the main action is interrupted again and again only to bring on the secondo uomo and the seconda donna. Since theatrical conventions made it necessary for a singer to leave the stage after his or her aria, it was the librettist's task to construct the plot in such a way as to make these exits seem dramatically motivated. In this Rolli often failed.

Handel had to interrupt his composition after one and a half acts because at that time the news reached London that his female lead Margherita DURAS-TANTI (soprano) had fallen ill. After the directors of the Royal Academy of Music (OPERA COMPANIES, 2) had substituted her with ANASTASIA ROBINSON (alto, originally supposed to sing Rossane), Handel was forced to revise his score by transposing the part of Elmira to fit Robinson's alto range and by rewriting or substituting Rossane's arias for Maddalena SALVAI, a soprano. He had a new conducting score copied for the first act which partly includes autograph recitatives. He found the changes in the part of Elmira problematic: Anastasia Robinson's voice was not only too low for the part but also lacked the necessary range. Neither did she possess the agility and security of pitch needed for the fast arias. Handel therefore simplified the part but continued to cling to his original conception of the role instead of, as was usual in cases like this, composing a whole new set of arias. The belated arrival of the castrato Benedetto Baldassari, who was to sing Timante, necessitated further changes to the score. Handel took his abilities and status within the company into consideration and composed a new version of one of his arias ('Amor comanda') and added an additional scene at the beginning of Act III. *Floridante* was first performed on 9 December 1721 with the following cast:

Oronte, King of Persia	Giuseppe BOSCHI (bass)
Rossane, his daughter	Maddalena SALVAI (soprano)
Elmira, his supposed daughter	Anastasia ROBINSON (alto)
Floridante, Prince of Thrace, Oronte's general, betrothed to Elmira	SENESINO (castrato)
Timante, Prince of Tyre, prisoner of war under the name of Glicone, betrothed to Rossane by letter	Benedetto Baldassari (castrato)
Coralbo, a Persian satrap	?Lagarde (bass)

Floridante was Handel's only new opera for the season and was performed fifteen times until 26 May 1722. Giovanni BONONCINI's two new operas for the season were more successful with thirty-four performances altogether. The audience seemed to prefer his pleasant, song-like arias. Handel on the other hand, while making concessions to public taste in the minor roles, retained his strongly dramatic style for the principal heroic characters. The opera's principal attraction rests on the contrast between the heroic couple Floridante/Elmira (with their tragic farewell duet 'Ah, mia cara') and the amorous couple Timante/Rossane (with the duet 'Fuor di periglio', which includes horns imitating cooing doves). Handel shows Elmira's pride and steadfastness in a fast and fiery aria with contrasting ritornello motifs ('Ma pria vedrò le stelle') but also develops the character's very human side in a nocturnal scene where she wavers between hope and fear (arioso and accompagnato 'Notte cara'). Floridante is characterised as heroic but also tender in an important aria with flowing triplet coloratura passages ('Bramo te sola') and even more in his moving Siciliano ('Se dolce m'era già'). Shorter and more song-like arias characterise the second couple. The happy prisoner Timante sings only cheerful arias ('Dopo il nembo e la procella'), whereas Rossane captivates the listener with her coquettish naivety ('Sospiro, è vero') and her unswerving devotion to Elmira, whom she once thought her sister ('Se risolvi abbandonarmi'). King Oronte is presented as boastful of his Machiavellian ruling powers at first, in unison with bass or orchestra ('Finché lo strale'). Later, in desperation ('Che veggio, che sento'), he forces himself to a defiant acceptance of his own defeat. Handel recognised that the usual da capo form would not express this transformation satisfactorily and therefore gave the aria a bipartite structure.

A contemporary account (HHB iv, p. 102) reports that parts of the action were understood to take an oppositional stance against King GEORGE I and therefore applauded. It is conceivable that Rolli, influenced by conservative aristocrats, had in fact intended such a meaning and had used Handel, who was always loyal to the King, to convey it.

The overture and arias were printed by Walsh in London soon after the first performance, 'publish'd by the Author'. In this case the addition was no meaningless phrase: Handel seems to have corrected the proofs meticulously. He had the duet 'Ah, mia cara', which he had been forced to rewrite as a concession to the changes in his cast, printed in the original version.

There were a number of revivals under Handel's direction. There were seven performances between 4 December and 26 December 1722 (no libretto extant). Durastanti, recovered from her illness, took over the part of Rossane, not that of Elmira originally intended for her. Rossane was therefore upgraded to the prima donna part: she received one additional aria and three others were exchanged. The new arias come from the cantata CRUDEL TIRANNO AMOR, which Handel had probably composed for Durastanti in the summer of 1721. Timante was now sung by the castrato Gaetano BERENSTADT, for whom Handel recomposed one aria and transposed the rest.

The opera was next revived for two performances on 29 April and 2 May 1727, probably as a substitute because Francesca CUZZONI fell ill. FAUSTINA Bordoni sang Rossane (and received yet one more aria). In order to keep the balance within the ensemble, SENESINO also received a new aria. This performing version is documented by a libretto printed in 1721 but containing handwritten additions dating from 1727. Handel last revived Floridante for seven performances during his 1732–3 season (cast unknown), again as a substitute, but this time because STRADA had fallen ill. The newly printed libretto contains a number of mistakes.   HANS DIETER CLAUSEN (Trans. ANGELA BAIER)

H. D. Clausen, 'Die Entstehung der Oper Floridante', GHB IV (1991)
   (ed.), Il Floridante, HVW 14, HHA, Series ii/11 (Kassel, 2005)
Dean and Knapp, Operas
Harris, Librettos
Strohm

Florindo (Der beglückte Florindo), HWV 3. Der beglückte Florindo and its sequel Die verwandelte Daphne are operatic settings of a pastoral-mythological text by HINSCH. The familiar myth of Apollo and Daphne, later the subject of Handel's cantata masterpiece La TERRA È LIBERATA, is interwoven with the pastoral fiction of a love-match between Daphne and Florindo, son of the river god Enipheus. According to the libretto and MATTHESON's catalogue of HAMBURG operas (in Der musikalische Patriot) the operas were staged in 1708; since they are the first items in Mattheson's list for that year, they are assumed to have been performed, perhaps under the direction of Graupner, early in 1708 when Handel was in Italy. Performances of Daphne were adorned with an interlude, Die lustige Hochzeit, by KEISER and Graupner.

The preface of the libretto to Florindo purports to explain the double opera format, and usefully summarises their plots:

> Since the splendid music with which this opera was adorned has turned out really rather too long, and might have put the audience out of humour, it has been deemed necessary to arrange the whole work into two parts: of these the first presents the Pythian Festival ordained in honour of Apollo and, happening on the same day, the betrothal of Florindo and Daphne. From this important part of the action it takes the name Der glückliche Florindo. The second part will treat of Daphne's stubbornness in the face of Phoebus's [= Apollo's] love, also how she came to abhor all love, and finally her metamorphosis into a laurel tree. From this it takes the name Die verwandelte Daphne.

However, with six carefully designed acts and some hundred texts for arias and ensembles, Florindo and Daphne are surely not a single opera opportunistically cut in two. It seems more likely that composer and librettist began work on the assumption that they could fit the Apollo and Daphne myth, elaborated with subplots and 'human interest', into a single evening, but found, as the drama took shape, that the double-opera scheme was more practicable. That must have happened before Handel left for Italy in 1706, well over a year before the premieres. Any last-minute rearrangement of the kind suggested in the libretto would have been a substantial task, and could only have been undertaken by Keiser or Graupner themselves. No Italian model has been discovered, though the fact that a third of the aria texts are in Italian suggests there will have been one. An abundance of choral singing and dancing testifies to the continuing influence of French opera in Hamburg.

No music survives in anything like its original form. Three orchestral suites (HWV 352, 353, 354) can be confidently linked with *Florindo* and *Daphne*, either as simple copies or as transcriptions. Two unattached overtures, HWV 336 and 453, may also originate in these operas. Instrumental parts for four movements attributed to *Florindo* are found in the Flower Collection (SOURCES AND COLLECTIONS, 8), but lacking vocal parts or headings they cannot be more nearly identified.

DAVID KIMBELL

See also LIBRETTOS, I

B. Baselt, 'Wiederentdeckung von Fragmenten aus Händels verschollenen Hamburger Opern', *HJb* (1983)
Dean and Knapp, *Operas*
Harris, *Librettos*
HHB iii
J. H. Roberts, 'A New Handel Aria, or Hamburg Revisited', *Gedenkschrift für Bernt Baselt (1934–1993)* (Halle, 1995)
H. C. Wolff, *Die Barockoper in Hamburg, 1678–1738* (Wolfenbüttel, 1957)

Flower, Sir (Walter) Newman (b. Fontmell Magna, Dorset, 8 July 1879; d. Blandford, 12 March 1964). Writer, editor and collector. After initial training as a writer on popular journals, he joined the publishing firm Cassell & Co. in 1906, and purchased the company in 1927. He wrote a biography on Handel, which was also translated into German. However, it seldom hits the standards of modern scholarship. Flower built up an important collection of manuscripts and early prints of Handel's works (SOURCES AND COLLECTIONS, 8). He was knighted in 1938.

WALTER KREYSZIG

N. Flower, *George Frideric Handel: His Personality and his Times* (London, 1923)
W. C. Smith, *A Handelian's Notebook* (London, 1965)

Flute. See INSTRUMENTATION

Flute sonatas. See CHAMBER MUSIC

Food and Drink. See HANDEL, 10

'Forest Music' ('Waldmusik'). A three-movement suite attributed to Handel. There is a legend that he wrote this piece for Lady Dorothy Vernon at Clontarf Castle during his stay in DUBLIN in 1742. Neither the composer nor the arranger is known. The piece originated in WALSH's *Forest Harmony*, second book, a collection of sixty minor pieces for two instruments in treble clef (among them are three movements from Handel's *WATER MUSIC*). None of the pieces is ascribed to a special composer. Three of them were later arranged as a keyboard piece and put together under the title *Handel's Forest Music*. It has been published in four different and independent arrangements by C. Lonsdale (1856), Chester Kingsbury (1963), Percy Young (1970) and Daniel Pinkham (1972).

ANNETTE LANDGRAF

Deutsch
W. H. G. Flood, 'Dublin, from 1741 to 1777', *Sammelbände der Internationalen Musikgesellschaft*, XIV, H. 1 (1912), 53
W. C. Smith, 'Catalogue of Works', *Handel. A Symposium*, ed. G. Abraham (Oxford, 1954)

Fougeroux, Pierre-Jacques. French diarist. In April 1728 Fougeroux visited London and wrote six long and detailed letters (now in the Gerald Coke Handel Collection) (SOURCES AND COLLECTIONS, 7) describing the city and its society and culture, including his visits to hear Handel's operas *SIROE*, *TOLOMEO* and *ADMETO*. His observations, though occasionally inaccurate, give an insight into the constitution of Handel's opera orchestra, and are the only documentation that Handel used two harpsichords and an archlute in simple recitative, in which, he notes, the sound of each chord was cut off. He noted the brilliance of the orchestra and its 'grand fracas' (PERFORMANCE PRACTICE).

THOMAS N. MCGEARY

W. Dean, 'A French Traveller's View of Handel's Operas', *Essays on Opera* (Oxford, 1990) (see also Burrows, *Handel*, Appendix E: 'A London Opera-Goer in 1728')

Foundling Hospital, The. Opened in 1739 for the 'education and maintenance of exposed and deserted young children'. The children's home was founded by the campaigning philanthropist Thomas CORAM, and was supported by William HOGARTH, who donated works of art and encouraged fellow artists to do the same. The Hospital became in effect the first public art gallery in Britain, as visitors came to see the art and to make donations for the upkeep of the foundlings. Handel offered a benefit concert for the Hospital in 1749, to pay for the completion of the Chapel building, and he also donated an organ for the Chapel. The concert, for which he composed the anthem *Blessed are they that considereth the poor* (ANTHEMS, 8) was a great financial success and Handel went on to give a benefit concert every year. The performance of *MESSIAH* in 1750 was over-booked and a second performance was hastily arranged. Handel raised over £7,000 for the Hospital during his lifetime, and in a codicil to his will he bequeathed a copy of the score and parts of *Messiah* to the charity (HANDEL, 8). The Hospital moved out of London in 1926 and the buildings were demolished, although the front gates and part of the grounds can still be seen and now enclose a children's playground. It closed as an institution in 1953, but continues today as the childcare charity Coram Family. It still has an annual fund-raising concert on Handel's birthday, its extensive archives record details of Handel's association with the charity, and Handel-related materials are exhibited with the charity's art collection in the Foundling Museum (MUSEUMS, 3).

KATHARINE HOGG

D. Burrows, 'Handel and the Foundling Hospital', ML 58/3 (1977), 269–84
R. H. Nichols and F. A. Wray, *The History of the Foundling Hospital* (London, 1935)
B. Nicolson, *The Treasures of the Foundling Hospital* (Oxford, 1972)

'Francesina' (Elisabeth Duparc) (b. ?1698; d. 1773 or 1778). French soprano, hence her nickname 'La Francesina' (range c–b″). Trained in Italy, she came to London in 1736 to sing for the OPERA OF THE NOBILITY. On her first appearance in England Duparc sang before Queen CAROLINE and most of the royal family at KENSINGTON PALACE (15 November 1736), 'and met with a most gracious reception . . . after which, *The Francesina*, performed several Dances to the entire Satisfaction of the Court' (Deutsch, 417). After that company's demise, she was engaged by Handel to sing in his pasticcio *ALESSANDRO SEVERO*, also premiering Clotilde in *FARAMONDO* and Romilda in *SERSE* (1737–8 season). From

7. Elizabeth Duparc, know as 'la Francesina', mezzotint engraving by John Faber after Knapton, 1737.

this time she was almost exclusively a Handel singer, his leading soprano at the KING'S THEATRE (January–April 1739 and 1744–5), LINCOLN'S INN FIELDS (for the seasons of 1739–40 and 1740–1) and COVENT GARDEN (February–March 1744 and 1746). In 1739, she sang in the first performances of SAUL (Michal), ISRAEL IN EGYPT, the SONG FOR ST CECILIA'S DAY and (probably) the pasticcio, GIOVE IN ARGO. She took part in the first performances of L'ALLEGRO, IL PENSEROSO ED IL MODERATO the following year, and, in the 1740–1 season, sang Rosmene in IMENEO and the title role in DEIDAMIA. She did not join the composer in his DUBLIN 'season' (1741–2), nor did she sing for him in London in 1743, but thereafter created the title role in SEMELE and Asenath in JOSEPH AND HIS BRETHREN (both 1744) Nitocris in BELSHAZZAR and Iole in HERCULES (both 1745), and was the soprano soloist in the OCCASIONAL ORATORIO (1746). During this period, she also sang in numerous oratorio revivals, including DEBORAH, SAMSON (both in 1744) and MESSIAH (1745). Her only other documented performances of Handel's music were in London concerts in 1752.

BURNEY described her as a second-class singer, but also wrote of her 'natural warble and agility of voice which Handel seems to have great pleasure in displaying' (p. 421), and of her 'lark-like execution'. Therefore it is little wonder that Handel wrote several 'bird' songs for her, such as 'Nascondi l'usignol' (Deidamia), described by Burney as 'a light, airy, pleasing movement, suited to the active throat of the Francesina' (p. 434). In the many fine parts Handel composed for Duparc, she was clearly a worthy successor to STRADA, and on many occasions his writing for her resembles his music for CUZZONI. The role of Semele, for example, contains tests of her Cuzzonian agility ('No, no, I'll take no less': as Mrs DELANY remarked 'there is something in her running-divisions that is quite surprizing. She was much applauded', Deutsch, 582) alongside demonstrations of her *sostenuto* ('Oh, sleep why dost thou leave me?') and dramatic abilities ('Ah, me! Too late I now repent').

She was also a painter, as well as being that rare commodity, a French singer trained in the Italian manner, to which she added a proficiency in English (two-thirds of the Handel works she sang were in this, her third language); altogether a most accomplished woman (see Figure 7).   NICHOLAS CLAPTON

Franz, Robert (b. Halle, 28 June 1815; d. Halle, 24 Oct. 1892). Composer and conductor of the HALLE Singakademie (1842–67). He arranged works by Handel (ARRANGEMENTS, 4) and J. S. BACH for performance between 1858 and 1882, published anthologies of opera arias for soprano and alto voices, and a collection of twelve duets taken from the operas and the CHAMBER DUETS. He directed the Singakademie in performances of the Dettingen Te Deum (TE DEUM, 5), *JUDAS MACCABAEUS, JOSHUA, SAMSON, MESSIAH, ISRAEL IN EGYPT, JEPHTHA, L'ALLEGRO, IL PENSEROSO ED IL MODERATO* and the Utrecht JUBILATE, in some cases regularly. He was an active supporter of proposals to erect a statue of Handel in Halle (MONUMENTS).

WERNER RACKWITZ (Trans. ANGELA BAIER)

J. Böhme, 'Händel's *L'Allegro, il Pensieroso ed il Moderato* in der Bearbeitung von Robert Franz', HJb 39 (1993)

K. Sasse, *Beiträge zur Forschung über Leben und Werk von Robert Franz 1815–1892* (Halle, 1986)

Frasi, Giulia (fl. 1740–c.1772). Italian soprano (range b to a''), probably born in Milan, where she studied with G. F. Brivio. She joined the opera company at the KING'S THEATRE in the Haymarket in 1742, and sang in Italian operas there until 1760–1, missing only one opera season. She sang in the MIDDLESEX OPERA COMPANY's production of *ROSSANE* (based on Handel's *ALESSANDRO*) in 1743 and 1747–8, taking male roles, and in the Handel pasticcio *Lucio Vero* in 1747, as well as in a 1754 production of *ADMETO*. During the period 1744–6 she sang a number of male roles, which has misled some scholars into identifying a 'Signor Frasi' as the singer of those parts. But she more typically sang female roles. Her accomplishments as an Italian opera singer were noteworthy. BURNEY, who taught her (presumably singing), remarked of her participation in a 1745 performance of the pasticcio *L'incostanza Delusa* that Count St Germain's 'Per pietà bell'idol mio' was sung by 'Frasi, first woman, and encored every night'.

Frasi possessed certain qualities that made her ideal for English oratorio. Burney wrote that 'having come to this country at an early period of her life, she pronounced our language in singing in a more articulate and intelligible manner than the natives', and praised her 'sweet and clear voice' and 'smooth and chaste style of singing' (p. 841). Handel engaged Frasi to sing in a revival of *JUDAS MACCABAEUS* in 1748, and employed her regularly from 1749; she created a number of roles, including the title role in *SUSANNA*, the two queens in *SOLOMON*, the title role in *THEODORA*, and Iphis in *JEPHTHA*. Burney's claim that she was 'cold and unimpassioned' is puzzling in light of the many passionate arias that Handel composed for her. This is true from the first time he wrote original music for her; while preparing the scores of *Solomon* and *Susanna* Handel transferred some expressive music from the tenor characters, ultimately sung by Thomas LOWE, to soprano, including the music that eventually became 'Will the sun forget to streak' and 'Faith displays her rosy wing'. It seems likely that he did so with Frasi's expressive powers in mind, as these changes are in keeping with the styles he typically wrote for her. She continued to appear in all oratorio seasons under Handel and his successors until about 1768, singing in all of his oratorios except *SEMELE*. DAVID ROSS HURLEY

Dean, *Oratorios*

D. R. Hurley, *Handel's Muse: Patterns of Creation in his Oratorios and Musical Dramas, 1743–1751* (Oxford, 2001)

A. Rees, *The Cyclopaedia; or, Universal Dictionary of Arts, Sciences, and Literature*, vol. 15 (Philadelphia, c.1820)

Sartori, vol. 2

Frederick, Prince of Wales (Frederick Louis; Electoral Prince of Hanover) (b. Hanover, 20/31 Jan. 1707; d. London, 20 March 1751), the eldest son of King GEORGE II and Queen CAROLINE. He remained in HANOVER when his grandfather (George I) became King of England, and did not join his parents in England until 1728. He and Handel no doubt became acquainted at Hanover, and later when Handel attended at the English court giving music instruction to Frederick's two eldest princesses (HANDEL, 20).

Frederick himself played the cello and was an amateur composer. As a way of cultivating his image and projecting his patriotism, Frederick undertook various forms of arts patronage. He collected paintings, patronised writers, gave annual subsidies to the opera companies, formed a musical establishment at his court, and regularly hosted series of concerts (and later rehearsals of operas and oratorios) at his various homes. His patronage also extended to architects, gardeners, artisans and craftsmen who built and decorated his several residences.

The idea that Frederick bore personal animosity against Handel derives from passages in John, Lord HERVEY's *Memoirs*, where Hervey reports that to spite his sister Frederick 'set himself at the head' of the OPERA OF THE NOBILITY. Hervey's account was amplified by later writers into the fictions that Frederick at the head of the political opposition to Robert WALPOLE founded the Opera of the Nobility as a way of opposing Handel, and that members of the royal family and LONDON society exclusively patronised one opera company or the other. Hervey's memoirs are biased and inaccurate: he held a personal grudge against Frederick (the two had a falling out over a mistress) and as Vice Chamberlain of the Household and favourite of the Queen, took her side in the family feuds.

Frederick's household accounts show that he gave bounties to Handel's company for the 1731, 1732, 1733 and 1736 seasons. It is not clear why no payments are recorded for the 1734 and 1735 seasons, but this gap should not be over-dramatised into a personal antagonism against Handel. The composer's wedding anthem *Sing unto God* (ANTHEMS, 4) and opera *ATALANTA* were part of the celebrations of Frederick's marriage to Princess AUGUSTA of Saxe-Gotha in 1736. Although the Prince did not attend the premiere of either, there are regular records of his payments for attendance at Handel's operas and oratorios in the following years. Numerous anecdotes report Handel's frequent attendance at musical events at the Prince's court, where the composer occasionally held oratorio rehearsals (CARLTON HOUSE). Handel's programme of concerts at COVENT GARDEN in 1751 was curtailed by theatre closures following the Prince's unexpected death.   THOMAS N. MCGEARY

John, Lord Hervey, *Some Materials towards Memoirs of the Reign of King George II, by John, Lord Hervey*, ed. R. Sedgwick, vol. 1 (London, 1931), 273–4

T. McGeary, 'Handel, Prince Frederick, and the Opera of the Nobility Reconsidered', GHB VII (1998)

K. Rorschach, 'Frederick, Prince of Wales (1707–51) as Collector and Patron', *Walpole Society*, vol. 55 (1989/90)

C. Taylor, 'Handel and Frederick, Prince of Wales', MT 125/1692 (Feb. 1984), 89–92

F. Vivian, *A Life of Frederick, Prince of Wales, 1707–1751: A Connoisseur of the Arts*, ed. R. White (Lewiston, NY, 2006)

Froberger, Johann Jacob (b. Stuttgart, bap. 19 May 1616; d. Héricourt, France, 6 or 7 May 1667), German composer, organist and keyboard virtuoso. His harpsichord music, blending German traditions with Italian and French traits, was popular until well into the early eighteenth century. Handel owned a now missing book of manuscript music dated 1698 (last seen in the collection of John Christopher SMITH JUNIOR's stepdaughter, Lady RIVERS), containing exemplary pieces by (among others) Froberger. Yet there are no known BORROWINGS from Froberger in his own keyboard music.   DOROTHEA SCHRÖDER

[W. Coxe], *Anecdotes of George Frederick Handel and John Christopher Smith* (London, 1799; facsimile edn, ed. P. M. Young, New York, 1979), 6n.

HHB iv, 17

'From Harmony, from heav'nly Harmony'. See *SONG FOR ST CECILIA'S DAY*

Frugoni, Carlo Innocenzo (b. Genoa, 21 Nov. 1693; d. Parma, 20 Dec. 1768). Poet and librettist. Of noble birth, the young Carlo Innocenzo was entered by his parents into the Congregazione dei Somaschi, where he remained with varying fortunes until 1733 (although he did not become a lay priest until 1743). In 1716 he joined the ARCADIAN ACADEMY, but it was the intellectual and social circles in Bologna (1720–1) that were decisive for his vocation as a poet, and were the reason for his progressive distancing of himself from the Somaschi. In 1729 he revised Apostolo ZENO's *LUCIO PAPIRIO DITTATORE* for a production at Parma which was set to music by Geminiano GIACOMELLI. This score was slightly adapted by Handel, and the pasticcio was premiered at the KING'S THEATRE on 23 May 1732.

DOMENICO ANTONIO D'ALESSANDRO (Trans. TERENCE BEST)

Strohm

G. F. Vercellone, *Dizionario biografico degli italiani*, vol. 50 (Rome, 1998), 622–7

Fuchs, Aloys (b. Raase, Moravia, 22 June 1799; d. Vienna, 20 March 1853). Austrian musicologist and collector. In 1824 he began working as an assistant to Raphael Georg KIESEWETTER in Vienna, and five years later was appointed to the Board of the Gesellschaft der Musikfreunde. He accumulated 1,400 music autographs as well as a large collection of manuscripts and early prints. Among these were some Handel scores copied from autographs, including *ACI, GALATEA E*

POLIFEMO, Nisi Dominus and Dixit Dominus (Latin and Italian CHURCH MUSIC), and also arrangements and piano reductions (e.g. ten movements from *La RESURREZIONE*). WALTER KREYSZIG

F. W. Riedel, 'Über die Aufteilung der Musiksammlung von Aloys Fuchs', *Die Musikforschung* 15 (1962), 374–9

Zur Bibliothek des Aloys Fuchs: Ergänzungen und Berichtigungen', *Die Musikforschung* 16 (1963), 270–5

R. Schaal, 'Zur Musiksammlung Aloys Fuchs', *Die Musikforschung* 15 (1962), 49–52

Fugue. See COUNTERPOINT

Fund for the Support of Decay'd Musicians. The first British society for aid to aged and infirm musicians, their widows and orphans, was founded under this title in 1738. Led by a dozen governors (the violinist Michael FESTING most prominently), the 'friendly' society had 248 paying subscribers when it was enrolled in Chancery Court in 1740. Handel played a central role in development of capital, organising concerts focused on *ALEXANDER'S FEAST, PARNASSO IN FESTA*, the first London performance of *MESSIAH* and concertos he composed for the concerts. He left £1,000 to it at his death (HANDEL, 8), and the HANDEL COMMEMORATION of 1784 contributed £6,000. The centrality of Handel's music in such concerts encouraged GEORGE III to grant the fund a charter as the Royal Society of Musicians in 1790. WILLIAM WEBER

B. Matthews, *Royal Society of Musicians of Great Britain: List of Members, 1738–1984* (London,1985) (includes P. Drummond, 'The Royal Society of Musicians in the Eighteenth Century', ML 59/3 (1978), 268–89)

Funeral Anthem for Queen Caroline. See ANTHEMS, 5

G

Gainsborough, 4th Earl of (Baptist Noel) (b. May 1708; d. 21 March 1750). English lord and the brother of the Earl of SHAFTESBURY's wife Susanna. In June 1745 Handel visited Lord Gainsborough's home at Exton in Rutland (now Leicestershire), and provided music for a domestic performance of MILTON's masque *COMUS*. Handel afterwards travelled to SCARBOROUGH.   WALTER KREYSZIG

HHB iv, 393

Galli, Caterina (b. ?Cremona, 1719/24; d. Chelsea, 23 Dec. 1804). Italian mezzo-soprano (range a–g″). Little is known of her early life before her first recorded appearance at Bergamo in spring 1742. She relocated to England that year, and appeared with the MIDDLESEX OPERA COMPANY in London as a singer of male roles in the 1742–3 season, but was not rehired. Her big break came when Handel engaged her to appear in his oratorios in 1747, first in revivals of the *OCCASIONAL ORATORIO* and *JOSEPH AND HIS BRETHREN*. She appeared in the first performance of *JUDAS MACCABAEUS* (Israelite Man, Second Israelite Woman), in which, according to BURNEY, her rendition of ' 'Tis Liberty' was a smash hit and established her reputation (Rees, *The Cyclopedia*, vol. 16). She subsequently created a number of Handelian roles, often of male characters, including Othniel in *JOSHUA* (1748), the title role in *ALEXANDER BALUS* (1748), Joacim in *SUSANNA* (1749), the title role in *SOLOMON* (1749), Irene in *THEODORA* (1750) and Storgè in *JEPHTHA* (1752). Dean asserts that she probably appeared as Virtue in *THE CHOICE OF HERCULES* (1751), and she also appeared in a number of revivals. She sang for Lord Middlesex's opera again in 1747–8, appearing in the Handel pasticcios *LUCIO VERO* and *ROSSANE* as well as in operas by HASSE and Vincenzo Ciampi. In 1754 Galli returned to her homeland, but by 1773 she was back in England, appearing in a revival of *MESSIAH*. She was engaged in the 1773–5 seasons of the opera. Thereafter she appeared sporadically until 1799, when she sang 'He was despised' at COVENT GARDEN to a polite audience. She died in her lodgings in Chelsea just two days before Christmas in 1804. Her obituary identified her as 'the last of Handel's scholars'.   DAVID ROSS HURLEY

Dean, *Oratorios*
A. Rees, *The Cyclopedia: or, Universal Dictionary of Arts, Sciences and Literature*, vol. 16 (Philadelphia, c.1820)

Galliard, John Ernest (b. ?Celle, 1666 or 1687; fl. ?; d. Chelsea, bur. 18 Feb. 1747). German-born composer and oboist. The son of a French wig-maker, he was trained as an oboist at the Celle court orchestra. From 1706 he worked in London as a chamber musician. In 1710 he was appointed organist at SOMERSET

HOUSE, and soon afterwards started writing English anthems and canticles. From 1712 he also became a well-known composer and performer in London's leading theatres. He played the oboe (and probably also the recorder) in the opera orchestra at the Queen's Theatre (KING'S THEATRE), and frequently wrote music for John RICH's theatrical entertainments at LINCOLN'S INN FIELDS and COVENT GARDEN. In 1736 he composed the theatre song 'The early horn', which became a popular favourite regularly sung by the tenors John BEARD and Thomas LOWE. He was a founding member of the ACADEMY OF ANCIENT MUSIC and the FUND FOR THE SUPPORT OF DECAY'D MUSICIANS, and translated Pier Francesco Tosi's famous treatise on singing into English. Handel composed noteworthy obbligato parts for Galliard in *TESEO* (Medea's arias 'Dolce riposo' and 'Morirò, ma vendicata'), and oboe parts in *SILLA* and *AMADIGI* were probably composed for him. Handel subscribed to the printed score of Galliard's *Hymn of Adam and Eve* (based on MILTON's Paradise Lost) in 1728.   DAVID VICKERS

See also INSTRUMENTATION, 13

Gallus (Handl), Jacobus (b. Duchy of Krain (Slovenia), c.26 July 1550; d. Prague, 18 July 1591). Renaissance composer. He worked at Melk, Obrowitz (Zábrdovice) near Brno, and Olomouc, among other places. His major works are twenty masses, the *Opus musicum* (374 motets in four volumes), and 100 madrigals. Handel borrowed from Gallus's Passiontide motet (for Holy Saturday) *Ecce quomodo moritur justus* (*Opus musicum*, II:13) when setting the words 'but their name liveth evermore' for the chorus 'Their bodies are buried in piece' in *The ways of Zion do mourn* (ANTHEMS, 5).   HARTMUT KRONES (Trans. ANGELA BAIER)

E. Škulj, *Gallusovi predgovori* (Gallus' Vorworte) (Ljubljana, 1991)
   Clare vir. Ob 450-letnici rojstva Iacobusa Gallusa (Ljubljana, 2000)

Galuppi, Baldassarre ('il Buranello') (b. Burano by Venice, 18 Oct. 1706; d. Venice, 3 Jan. 1785). Italian composer. After a disastrous debut as opera composer in Vicenza (1722), around 1726–7 he served as harpsichordist at the Teatro della Pergola and the MEDICI court in FLORENCE. Then, thanks to the lessons of Antonio LOTTI, he enjoyed a second start at VENICE's Teatro Sant'Angelo (1728–9). In 1740 he was appointed *maestro del coro* at the Ospedale dei Mendicanti; in 1741 his schoolmate G. B. Pescetti, music director of the KING'S THEATRE, invited him to join Lord MIDDLESEX's company. Galuppi's *Penelope, Scipione in Cartagine, Enrico, Sirbace* and *Ricimero* were produced in London until 1756, although he probably was already back to Venice in late 1743.

   In 1745 he wrote his first buffo opera, thus starting a new spectacular career that brought him as far as St Petersburg, where he worked for Catherine the Great (1765–8). Meanwhile, he ascended the ranks of Venice's state chapel at St Mark's until the appointment as *primo maestro* (1762). After his return from Russia, he served there and at the Ospedale degli Incurabili until his death, composing a flood of sacred music. His growing fame in this field even induced copyists to smuggle others' works (e.g. Vivaldi's) under his name. Besides seventeen buffo operas on librettos by Carlo Goldoni, he set to music 109 operas in both buffo and serio genres (including pasticcios and dubious attributions); eight para-operatic works (serenatas, intermezzos, farces) and twenty-seven oratorios. Some 125 keyboard pieces and a number of orchestral and chamber works further witness to his astounding productivity.

CARLO VITALI

Gänsemarkt. HAMBURG developed a flourishing cultural and musical life during the seventeenth century. This culminated in the foundation of a public opera house designed after Venetian models. It was believed that an opera house would increase the city's attractiveness: Johann MATTHESON made the connection between a prospering economy and city theatres when he claimed 'where there are the best banks, there are also the best opera houses'. The opera house was situated near the Alster, between the Gänsemarkt ('goose market') and the Dammtor. It was a very high and long building with a deep stage. The complicated stage machinery allowed for spectacular stage effects. Pit, boxes and gallery together could hold about 2,000 people. The theatre was inaugurated on 2 January 1678 with an opera by Johann Theile. It developed into an intellectual centre which attracted musicians, composers, painters, stage technicians, poets and translators. The opera house developed its own style with highly individual aesthetic rules, albeit influenced by French and especially Italian models. One of the leading composers was the theatre's music director Reinhard KEISER, who was succeeded after 1721 by TELEMANN. The last of the 300 or so operas to be performed there was Telemann's *Sancio* in February 1738. The theatre was demolished in 1757.

Handel played the violin in the Gänsemarkt opera orchestra, but also directed from the harpsichord. He composed and performed four German-language operas: *ALMIRA*, *NERO*, *FLORINDO* and *Die verwandelte Daphne*. Long after he left Hamburg, his music continued to feature in the theatre's seasons. Fourteen of his Italian operas were revived there between 1715 and 1737. The librettos of these were adjusted, sometimes to a form close to the original source text on which Handel's opera had been based. Recitatives were translated into German and set to new music (by Keiser, LINICKE, Mattheson or Telemann). Arias and instrumental pieces were taken from the scores printed by John CLUER and John WALSH. Aria texts were not translated, and the instrumental parts were substantially retained, but castrato vocal parts were transposed downwards because the vogue in Hamburg was for 'natural voices'. The operas performed (and the dates of the first Hamburg performances) were: *RINALDO* (1715), *AGRIPPINA* (1718), *RADAMISTO* (renamed *Zenobia*) (1722), *FLORI-DANTE* (1723), *MUZIO SCEVOLA* (1723), *TAMERLANO* (1725), *GIULIO CESARE* (1725), *OTTONE* (1726), *ALESSANDRO* (*Der hochmütige Alexander*) (1726), *RIC-CARDO PRIMO* (*Der mißlungene Braut-Wechsel oder Richardus I*) (1729), *ADMETO* (1730), *PORO* (*Triumph der Großmut und der Treue oder Cleofida*) (1732), *PARTENOPE* (1733) and *RODELINDA* (1734). Some of the operas, such as *Giulio Cesare* and *Admeto*, were especially popular with the public and were performed during consecutive seasons. UTE POETZSCH (Trans. ANGELA BAIER)

G. Cummings, 'Handel, Telemann and Metastasio, and the Hamburg *Cleofida*', HJb 46 (2000)

C. Floros, H.-J. Marx and P. Petersen (eds.), *Hamburger Jahrbuch für Musikwissenschaft, 3: Studien zur Barockoper* (Hamburg, 1978)

A. Koch, 'Die Bearbeitungen Händelscher Opern auf der Hamburger Bühne des frühen 18. Jahrhunderts', Ph.D. dissertation (University of Halle, 1982)

H.-J. Marx and D. Schröder, *Die Hamburger Gänsemarkt-Oper. Katalog der Textbücher (1678–1748)* (Laaber, 1995)

J. Mattheson, *Der Musicalische Patriot* (Hamburg, 1728)

M. Rätzer, *Szenische Aufführungen von Werken Georg Friedrich Händels vom 18. bis 20. Jahrhundert. Eine Dokumentation* (Halle, 2000)

Gardyner, J. Printer, of Carey Street, Lincoln Inn Fields, active in the first two decades of the eighteenth century. In 1712 Gardyner produced the WORDBOOK for Handel's second London opera, Il PASTOR FIDO (HWV 8ᵃ), and for another opera *Dorinda* (music by Alessandro SCARLATTI and others), also produced at the Queen's Theatre in 1712 (See KING'S THEATRE).   JOHN GREENACOMBE

Gasparini, Francesco (b. Camaiore near Lucca, 19 March 1661; d. Rome, 22 March 1727). Italian composer and teacher. He might have studied with Bernardo Pasquini and CORELLI in ROME, where he received patronage from Cardinal PAMPHILIJ and Cardinal OTTOBONI. Between 5 June 1701 and April 1713 he was *maestro di coro* at the Ospedale della Pietà in VENICE, during which time he became the dominant opera composer in the city. He travelled to Milan, FLORENCE and Genoa before finally settling in Rome: he succeeded CALDARA as Francesco Maria RUSPOLI's *maestro di cappella* in July 1716, and in 1718 became one of the few musicians to become a member of the ARCADIAN ACADEMY. Gasparini's works were performed outside Italy, in places such as HAMBURG, Vienna and London, where his Venetian operas *Antioco* and *Ambleto* (both 1705) were the models for pasticcios staged at the Queen's Theatre during the 1711–12 season (See KING'S THEATRE).

The development of Handel's Italian style was presumably influenced by his encounters with Gasparini's operas at Venice. Handel's London settings of *TAMERLANO* and *FARAMONDO* were both closely modelled on earlier homonymous operas by Gasparini (*Tamerlano*, Venice, 1711; *Il Faramondo*, Rome, 1720), and he significantly recomposed his version of *Tamerlano* after studying Gasparini's different later setting *Il Bajazet* (Reggio Emilia, 1719) (BOROSINI). He borrowed musical material from the London publication of songs from *Ambleto* in several works, most notably *DEIDAMIA* and *ALEXANDER BALUS*, and owned a manuscript copy of Gasparini's *La fede tradita e vendicata* (Turin version, 1719; it was incorrectly catalogued as a pasticcio entitled *Ernelinda* by its later owner Victor SCHOELCHER), from which he borrowed musically in several operas written between 1731 and 1736 (*EZIO*, *ORLANDO*, the November 1734 revision of Il *PASTOR FIDO*, *ARIODANTE* and *GIUSTINO*).

DAGMAR GLÜXAM (Trans. ANGELA BAIER)

Dean and Knapp, *Operas*

J. H. Roberts, 'Handel and Gasparini: The Ernelinda Borrowings', *HJb* 49 (2003)

   (ed.), *Handel Sources: Materials for the Study of Handel's Borrowing* (New York, 1986)

Strohm

Gates, Bernard (b. The Hague, 23 April 1686; d. North Aston, Oxon., 15 Nov. 1773). Gates's father (also Bernard) was presumably involved with the preparations for King William III's removal from the Hague to London. Bernard junior was a chorister at the CHAPEL ROYAL, and succeeded as a Gentleman in 1708; he was one of the Chapel's leading bass-voice singers by the time that Handel came to

London. As with many of the Gentlemen, he also served with the choir at WEST-MINSTER ABBEY. At the Chapel he became Master of the Children following the death of William CROFT in 1727, and was appointed to a second Gentleman's place in 1737; he also became Master of the Choristers at Westminster Abbey in 1740. He is named by Handel as a bass singer in several works, including the court ode ETERNAL SOURCE OF LIGHT DIVINE (1713) and the CORONATION Anthems (ANTHEMS, 3). He lived in James Street, Westminster from 1728; there he gave occasional concerts (including a performance of the Coronation Anthems in 1730) and prepared a production of ESTHER with the Chapel Royal Children in 1732, starting a process that led Handel to introduce his own performances of the oratorio at the KING'S THEATRE. His house was also used for Handel's rehearsals of royal wedding anthems in 1736 and 1740. He seems to have been a strong supporter of Handel in a contentious period during the 1730s and was certainly responsible for supplying treble voices from his choristers for Handel's later oratorio seasons. In 1757 he resigned his Masterships and retired to Oxfordshire.   DONALD BURROWS

Gay, John (b. Barnstaple, c.30 June 1685; d. London, 4 Dec. 1732). English playwright and poet. Characteristic of Gay's career and output was a tension between the opposed poles of dependence and independence. He belonged to the Scriblerus Club led by Alexander POPE, a circle fiercely critical of the WHIG establishment, yet sought patronage indiscriminately. Gay's ally Aaron HILL probably introduced him to Handel during the production of RINALDO (1711). The composer wrote one of his earliest English theatre SONGS, ''Twas when the sea was roaring', for Gay's farce The What d'ye Call It (1715). Gay's verses to Lord BURLINGTON in praise of Handel (Trivia, 1716) indicate that Handel and Gay both belonged to Burlington's circle. Gay might have been involved in supplying the libretto for Handel's ACIS AND GALATEA (1718), composed for James Brydges (later 1st Duke of CHANDOS). In the BEGGAR'S OPERA (1728), Gay used ''Twas when the sea' and the march from Rinaldo (III.ix), and the banned sequel to the Beggar's Opera, Polly (published 1729, first performed 1777) included three other tunes by Handel. The Beggar's Opera was Gay's greatest success and became the prototype for the genre BALLAD OPERA. Among the targets of Gay's satire in the Beggar's Opera and Polly was Italian opera, through allusions to the recent rivalry between CUZZONI and FAUSTINA (RIVAL QUEENS), to the caprices of prime donne and to operatic conventions such as the simile arias, the prison scene and the deus ex machina. That his supporters were among the greatest advocates of Italian opera highlights Gay's equivocal position.   BERTA JONCUS

B. Joncus, 'Handel at Drury Lane: Ballad Opera and the Production of Kitty Clive', Journal of the Royal Musical Association 131 (2006), 179–226

D. Nokes, John Gay: A Profession of Friendship (Oxford, 1995)

Geminiani, Francesco (Saverio) (Xaverio) (bap. Lucca, 5 Dec. 1687; d. Dublin, 17 Sept. 1762). Italian composer, violinist and music theorist. He worked at ROME (April 1704–Dec. 1706), NAPLES (1706–7) and Lucca (1707–9), and arrived in London in 1714. His first patron in England was Baron Johann Adolf KIELMANSEGG, to whom he dedicated his Op. 1 violin sonatas. Kielmansegg also arranged a joint appearance by Geminiani and Handel, who played the harpsichord, before

GEORGE I. It is unknown if Geminiani ever returned to Italy; from 1732 until his death he worked as a violinist, teacher, composer, music theorist, concert impresario and art dealer in London, Paris and DUBLIN.

Geminiani was one of the most famous violinists of his age. His contemporaries compared him as a composer to Handel and CORELLI; works by the three composers were sometimes performed together in concert (such as the St Cecilia festival concerts in London on 6 and 7 October 1756). Together with Handel's own Concerti grossi (ORCHESTRAL WORKS, 2), Geminiani's Concerti grossi, Op. 2 (1732) and Op. 3 (1733), and his concerto grosso arrangement of Corelli's Op. 5 sonatas, were at the core of the genre's immense popularity in England. He was also much sought after as teacher and among his pupils were Joseph Kelway (c.1702–1782), an organist held in high esteem by Handel, and the violinist Matthew DUBOURG.   DAGMAR GLÜXAM (Trans. ANGELA BAIER)

E. Careri, 'Händel e Geminiani: "The Rubens and Titian of Music"', Studi musicali 20 (1991), 141–53

Francesco Geminiani (1687–1762) (Oxford, 1993)

Genserico, HWV A². Opera fragment. In about late 1727 Handel worked on an opera seria based on the libretto Il Genserico by Nicolò BEREGAN. The story about Genserich, the King of the Vandals who sacked Rome in AD 455, had already been set to music by Antonio CESTI (VENICE, 1669) and Christian Heinrich Postel had produced a German version (HAMBURG, 1693). It is not known why Handel broke off his composition after reaching Act I Scene ix. The overture, an introductory chorus and six arias up to this point are fully set, whereas the secco recitatives only have the verbal text without music. The original pages of the Genserico overture found their way into the score of TOLOMEO, where the introductory chorus was cancelled out, but used as a basis for the final ensemble. All six arias were reused during Handel's composition of SIROE: two arias were given new texts, three others provided material for newly composed arias and the last one was inserted but later omitted. Genserico is sometimes referred to as Olibrio, because the libretto text used in the fragment was wrongly attributed to Apostolo ZENO as part of his Flavio Olibrio.   ARTIE HEINRICH

Dean, Operas

HHB iii

George I, King (Georg Ludwig, Elector of Hanover) (b. Hanover, 28 May 1660; d. Osnabrück, 11/22 June 1727). The eldest son of Ernst August, Elector of HANOVER, and his wife Sophia, George inherited the electoral title in 1698, and succeeded to the British crown in 1714 after the death of Queen ANNE. While George had a hereditary claim to Anne's throne through his mother's grandfather, James VI and I, his title was essentially a parliamentary one, enshrined in the Act of Settlement of 1701 to ensure that Anne's successor was a Protestant, and not her Catholic half-brother, James, whose supporters, the JACOBITES, opposed the Hanoverian succession.

George's parents had been patrons of STEFFANI and Torri in the 1690s, and George inherited their musical enthusiasms, although he was forced to close the court opera after his father's death for financial reasons. Despite such exigencies, he employed a Konzertmeister, Jean-Baptiste FARINEL, along with an orchestra of sixteen. Handel joined this establishment as Kapellmeister in 1710, and George permitted him leave of absence to travel, principally to London, soon afterwards. Handel's Utrecht Te Deum (TE DEUM, 1) and JUBILATE written for the official British celebrations for the Peace of Utrecht in 1713, ran counter to George's opposition to the Peace (War of the SPANISH SUCCESSION). This might have strained the relationship between the Elector and his absconded Kapellmeister, but Handel returned to George's favour on his accession to the British crown the next year, and the composer appears to have provided the 'Caroline' Te Deum (TE DEUM, 2) to celebrate the royal family's arrival in England. The King was, famously, delighted with the WATER MUSIC of 1717 and Handel was pensioned as 'Composer of Musick' to the English CHAPEL ROYAL in 1723.

George I was a leading patron of the Royal Academy of Music (OPERA COMPANIES, 2), founded in 1719. He acted as the Academy's principal subscriber, laying out £1,000 per annum, and took an interest in its activities, with Handel as its director of music. George had attended the opera in London prior to the establishment of the Academy, and the King's keen interest in Handel's operatic music was acknowledged by the composer in 1720 when he dedicated RADAMISTO to the King, noting that he had given 'particular Approbation' to it.

George married his cousin, Sophia Dorothea of Celle in 1682, a union which produced two children, George Augustus (later GEORGE II) and Sophia Dorothea (later the mother of Frederick II of Prussia) but, in personal terms, proved disastrous, and led to divorce and the imprisonment of George's wife. The King lived for the rest of his life with his mistress Melusine von der SCHULENBURG. While George took a considerable interest in national politics, he nevertheless remained something of a distant figure to many of his British subjects, and his uneasy and, at times, estranged relationship with his son and heir proved politically destabilising. He continued to be deeply attached to Hanover and frequently spent time there. He was en route to Hanover in 1727 when he was suddenly taken ill and died. He was buried at Hanover.   HANNAH SMITH

Burrows, *Chapel Royal*
R. Hatton, *George I: Elector and King* (London, 1978)

George II, King (George Augustus, Prince of Wales, Prince of Hanover) (b. Hanover, 30 Oct. 1683; d. London, 25 Oct. 1760). The only son of GEORGE I and Sophia Dorothea of Celle, George was raised in HANOVER. He married CAROLINE of Brandenburg-Ansbach in 1705 and although he was often unfaithful to her, she wielded enormous emotional and political influence over him. He was devastated by her death in 1737 and somewhat retreated from court life thereafter. They had seven surviving children: FREDERICK, Prince of Wales, ANNE, AMELIA, CAROLINE ELIZABETH, WILLIAM, MARY and LOUISA. George accompanied George I to England in 1714, and succeeded him in June 1727. George had been notoriously at odds with his father, and this pattern was repeated in George's relationship with his eldest son, Frederick, whom he banished from the royal palaces in 1737. George was a keen Hanoverian patriot and although his devotion to Hanover brought him unpopularity in Britain, he spent considerable periods of time there on both business and pleasure. It was here in

1735 that he met Amalie von Wallmoden who remained his companion until his death.

George II was an enthusiastic supporter of Handel, and the composer wrote some of his most well-known works for the key royal and state events of the reign, commencing with the Coronation Anthems (ANTHEMS, 3). A keen soldier, George had fought with distinction for the Allied cause at Oudenarde in 1708 during the War of the SPANISH SUCCESSION, and in June 1743, he led his army to victory against the French at the Battle of DETTINGEN (the last British monarch to do so personally) to great popular acclaim. The success was commemorated by Handel in his 'Dettingen' music (TE DEUM, 5; ANTHEMS, 6), and the composer also celebrated the Peace of Aix-la-Chapelle (War of the AUSTRIAN SUCCESSION) with his *MUSIC FOR THE ROYAL FIREWORKS* (1749). As well as commissioning works for royal occasions, George II was also a fierce supporter of Handel's operas and there may well be some truth in HERVEY's famous assertion that the fiery-tempered George was so partisan that 'an anti-Handelist was looked upon as an anti-courtier' (Burrows, p. 180). George's appreciation of oratorio was much more limited, but he seems to have continued to assist Handel, for instance allowing him to borrow the 'great kettledrums' of the Artillery for use in some oratorio performances.

Unlike his wife and children, George II was no musician, and his interest in music declined after the death of Caroline. But odes by John ECCLES, Maurice GREENE and William BOYCE for the King's birthday and New Year's Day were still performed at court. George continued to make known his rather bluff musical tastes. It was reported that the King demanded that the *Music for the Royal Fireworks* consisted of 'no fid[d]les', and indeed that he wanted 'no kind of instrument but martial instruments' (Burrows, p. 297). George II's own ideas about kingship also had an impact on the performance of Handel's royal music. George's desire for a monarchy that was less sacral and more frugal in tone led to him shunning major, public religious ceremonies of the type that characterised Anne's reign. Although it was speculated after Dettingen that the victory would be celebrated with a high-profile thanksgiving service at ST PAUL'S CATHEDRAL, in the event Handel's music was performed more privately at the CHAPEL ROYAL to mark the King's safe return to England. Royal concern with expenditure dominated George's relations with Handel at the time of the celebrations for the Peace of Aix-la-Chapelle, and the King was angered when Handel proved reluctant to let his music be rehearsed at VAUXHALL GARDENS in exchange for the crown being lent equipment by the Vauxhall manager Jonathan TYERS to stage the spectacular. George II had few cultural interests; his enthusiasm for Handel was the major exception. HANNAH SMITH

H. Smith, *Georgian Monarchy: Politics and Culture, 1714–1760* (Cambridge, 2006)

George III, King (b. London, 24 May 1738; d. Windsor, 29 Jan. 1820). Second child and eldest son of FREDERICK, Prince of Wales, and AUGUSTA of Saxe-Gotha. He had a great love of music and from his earliest years was an enthusiastic admirer of Handel, who died the year before George acceded to the throne in 1760. The King often recalled an early encounter with the composer when Handel allegedly remarked of the Prince: 'While that boy lives, my music will never want a protector.' The monarch amply fulfilled this prediction. Throughout the

King's long reign Handel was effectively posthumous court composer in perpetuity. The King took an active interest in the music performed at Windsor and elsewhere and from the few surviving details of the concerts, some of them in George's handwriting, it is clear that the programmes were strongly Handelocentric, mixing overtures from operas or oratorios with arias and choruses and instrumental music. In general, and by contrast to Queen Charlotte, the King's musical taste was conservative and he steadfastly retained his affection for his first love, Handel.

He did much to further the composer's reputation. The King acquired a large collection of the composer's autograph manuscripts which became the focal point of the Royal Music Library (SOURCES AND COLLECTIONS, 1). This is a significant event in the history of collecting: a monarch seeking to preserve the output of a relatively modern composer. He owned the famous ROUBILIAC bust originally made for Handel himself and one of Handel's harpsichords was a prized possession, though there is some debate as to the identity of the instrument. George patronised and was the prime mover behind the Handel centenary celebrations, which took place a year early in 1784 (HANDEL COMMEMORATION). He read in manuscript BURNEY's *Account of the Musical Performances in Westminster Abbey and the Pantheon in Commemoration of Handel* (1785), providing a number of comments, suggestions and 'improvements'. Subsequently, the King took an interest in the later annual celebrations. Samuel ARNOLD's monumental edition of Handel's works (EDITIONS, 2) was dedicated to George III: Arnold's preface underlines the King's role in preserving the reputation of the composer through his munificence and support. The Royal Library also contained more publications of Handel than of any other composer.

The King actively proselytised Handel's works and a visiting musician would receive approbation if he took into account the royal taste. Thus the young MOZART performed some music by Handel for the King during his London visit (1764–5), and HAYDN received a manuscript copy of the BROCKES PASSION from the King and Queen Charlotte in 1795 which he took back to Vienna with him. But the younger composers never supplanted the place of Handel in the King's heart.   STEPHEN ROE

S. Roe, 'Music at the Court of George III and Queen Charlotte', *The Wisdom of George III*, ed. J. Marsden (London, 2005)

German arias ('Deutsche Arien'), HWV 202–10. The nine German arias for soprano, obbligato solo instrument and basso continuo are among Handel's few extant settings of German texts. These texts were taken from the first volume of Barthold Heinrich BROCKES's anthology *Irdisches Vergnügen in Gott*. Handel used the second edition (1724) but did not set any of Brockes's *Sing-Gedichte* in their entirety; instead he chose single aria texts from different cantatas, among them one entitled *Die unsere Seele, durchs Gesicht, zur Ehre Gottes aufmunternde Schönheit der Felder im Frühlinge* (The beauty of the fields in spring, the sight of which elevates our souls and exalts the Lord). This title expresses the poet's general intention well: under the influence of English Physico-Theology the beauties of nature and their effect on humans are portrayed as symbolising the perfection of God's creation.

The sequence of the arias dates back to the order in which the autograph arias were bound together as a collection at the end of the eighteenth century. Handel did not envisage the nine arias as a cycle. They were originally preserved in six autograph fascicles; HWV 209 even had its own page numbers in Handel's handwriting. HWV 204 used to form the flyleaf of the omnibus volume and therefore might be the first aria to have been composed. Only HWV 202–3 and HWV 206–7 were written down together and might have been composed as pairs. In 1727 Brockes collected all nine arias into three new cantatas in the second volume of his *Irdisches Vergnügen* because 'the world-famous virtuoso, Herr Hendel, has set those same arias to music in an incomparable way' and had them performed in his house concerts. Handel's German arias must therefore have been composed between 1724 and 1727.

This assumption is further supported by the use of musical material that also appears in operas composed at around the same time (*GIULIO CESARE, TAMERLANO* and *RODELINDA*). The arias also share formal and thematic links with Handel's Italian CANTATAS, namely HWV 202 with *La bianca rosa* (HWV 160c), and HWV 210 with *Sento là che ristretto* (HWV 161). With the exception of HWV 209, the German arias are in da capo form but they are shorter and simpler than their Italian counterparts. Handel generally eschewed virtuoso coloratura writing in the voice parts, and he seems to have paid special attention to text comprehensibility in the dialogues between singer and solo instrument (probably intended for violin, although perhaps a flute or oboe might have been used for some songs in domestic performance; we cannot rule out the possibility that Handel envisaged it as a 'tutti unisoni' part for a larger group of instruments).

Handel avoided blatantly obvious onomatopoeia when setting Brockes's nature descriptions to music, but the texts certainly inspired him to evoke musical imagery. For example, in HWV 204 wide interval leaps symbolise the falling flower petals and the soaring of the soul. A permanently modulating and dissonance-rich sequence featuring the main motif in HWV 208 represents the changing colours of the dusky sky. A musette bass line evokes a rural scene in HWV 206 ('wenn er Bäum' und Feld beblümet' (when He makes trees and fields prosper))'. The 'süße Stille' (sweet tranquillity) in HWV 205 is made palpable through marked pauses in the music, and the quaver motifs reminiscent of birdsong evoke associations with a *locus amoenus*. The composer responded imaginatively to 'Meine Seele hört im Sehen': after being delayed by the punctuated first note, the theme erupts suddenly into exuberant coloratura representing the soul's delight in the divine creation. With settings such as these, Handel succeeds in making the abstract reasoning in the *Irdisches Vergnügen in Gott* tangible.   CHRISTINE MARTIN (Trans. ANGELA BAIER)

B. H. Brockes, *Land-Leben in Ritzebüttel, als des Irdischen Vergnügens in Gott Siebender Theil*, 3rd edn (Hamburg, 1748), 213–14; 223–4

D. Burrows (ed.), *Neun deutsche Arien* (Wiesbaden, 2003)

Burrows and Ronish

H. P. Fry, 'Händel und der Dichter Barthold Heinrich Brockes', *Händel und Hamburg. Ausstellung anläßlich des 300. Geburtstages von Georg Friedrich Händel*, ed. H. J. Marx (Hamburg, 1985)

D. Vickers, 'Neun deutsche Arien' (CD booklet note, Hyperion CDA67627, 2007)

A. Weidenfeld, 'Die Sprache der Natur. Zur Textvertonung in Händels "Deutschen Arien"', GHB IV (1991)

Gervinus, Georg Gottfried (b. Darmstadt, 20 May 1805; d. Heidelberg, 18 March 1871). Historian, author, and member of the 'GÖTTINGEN Seven'. He initiated a German Handel society and a complete edition of the composer's works (EDITIONS, 5). He was a member of the society's board of directors (1856–64). After the publishing house Breitkopf & Härtel withdrew from the project, Gervinus and CHRYSANDER were alone responsible for the Handel edition. Gervinus translated and revised the texts of vocal works for the first thirty-nine volumes and translated part of the texts for volumes 40–4. His relationship with Chrysander became strained over differences in opinion concerning issues such as the singability of his translations and the equal status of vocal and instrumental music. WERNER RACKWITZ (Trans. ANGELA BAIER)

W. Ebling, *Georg Gottfried Gervinus (1805–1871) und die Musik* (Munich, 1985)
G. G. Gervinus, *Händel und Shakespeare. Zur Ästhetik der Tonkunst* (Leipzig, 1868)
   Händels Oratorientexte, ed. V. Gervinus (Berlin, 1873)
   'Nomen est omen. Händel über Händel', AMZ 6 (1871), 688–93, 705–8, 721–5, 737–41
M. Miller, 'Gervinus und Händel', *Georg Gottfried Gervinus 1805–1871* (Heidelberg, 2005)

Giacomelli (Jacomelli), Geminiano (b. Piancenza, c.1692; d. Loreto, 25 Jan. 1740). Italian composer. After receiving musical training in Parma from the cathedral's *maestro di cappella* Giovanni Maria Capelli (1648–1726), Giacomelli's first opera *Ipermestra* was performed at VENICE in 1724. From 1719 to 1727 he was *maestro di cappella* at the court of Francesco Farnese, Duke of Parma, and at the church of Madonna della Steccata. He worked at the church of San Giovanni in Piacenza (1727–32), but returned to his old job at Parma until 1738, when he obtained a position at the church of Santa Casa in Loreto.

Handel might have attended a performance of Giacomelli's *LUCIO PAPIRIO DITTATORE* at Parma in May 1729. Set to a text by Carlo Innocenzo FRUGONI, in turn adapted from a libretto by Apostolo ZENO, Handel revived the opera at the KING'S THEATRE on 23 May 1732. Handel also included arias by Giacomelli in his pasticcios *L'ELPIDIA*, *VENCESLAO* and *DIDONE ABBANDONATA*.

WALTER KREYSZIG

C. Anguisola, *Geminiano Ciacomelli e Sebastiano Nasolini, musicisti piacentini* (Piacenza, 1935)
Strohm

Gibson, Edmund (bap. Bampton, 16 Dec. 1669; d. Bath, 6 Sept. 1748). Bishop of London; low church polemicist. Appointed Dean of the CHAPEL ROYAL in 1721 and Bishop of London in 1723, Gibson was also deeply involved in the voluntary reform societies and the charity schools movement. Dubbed WALPOLE's 'pope' because he wielded political authority on behalf of the WHIG ministry, Gibson was also involved in approving Handel's compositions for the CORONATION of King GEORGE II in 1727. The Bishop held moral objections towards the staging of sacred music and there is a rumour that he blocked the stage performance of *ESTHER* in 1732. As a formidable administrator, however, Gibson may also have had concerns about the effectiveness of the Chapel Royal, not wishing the choristers to be distracted from their formal duties. BEVERLY ADAMS

Burrows, *Chapel Royal*
N. Sykes, *Edmund Gibson, Bishop of London, 1669–1748: A Study in Politics and Religion in the Eighteenth Century* (Oxford, 1926)

Gideon. See PASTICCIO, 2. ORATORIOS

Giebichenstein. Located north of HALLE and near the banks of the Saale river, the village is situated by the ruins of a former castle of the Magdeburg bishops, Burg Giebichenstein, from which it also takes its name. It was officially annexed to Halle in 1900. Handel's grandfather Georg Taust (1606–85) was pastor in the village church of St Bartholomaeus (Saint Bartholomew), where he performed the marriage of his daughter Dorothea to the official Giebichenstein surgeon Georg Händel on 23 April 1683 (HANDEL, 9). In 1738 the nave of the Romanesque church was torn down and replaced by a baroque central-plan building. Only the plain angular tower was left standing; encased in its weather vane the remains of a poem by Georg Taust were discovered in 2000.

GÖTZ TRAXDORF (Trans. ANGELA BAIER)

Archives of the Evangelische Bartholomaeus-Gemeinde Halle, Giebichenstein

Giove in Argo (*Jupiter in Argos*), HWV A^{14}. PASTICCIO opera in three acts, primarily by Handel. It was first performed at the KING'S THEATRE on 1 May 1739. The libretto was originally written for DRESDEN by Antonio Maria LUCCHINI in 1717 and set by Antonio LOTTI. Handel heard a performance of Lotti's opera there in 1719 and later borrowed from one of the arias. Handel's opera was long referred to by its English title, but this had more to do with the fragmentary nature of the sources than with the character of the work, which is entirely in Italian.

A typical pastoral rather than any sort of serious drama, *Giove in Argo* is based very loosely on OVID's accounts of Jupiter's affairs with two mortal women, Callisto and Io, here given the name of the Egyptian goddess Isis (Iside). The action takes place in a forest in Argos with most of the characters disguised as shepherds. Calisto's father Licaone, tyrant of Arcadia, has killed Inaco, father of Iside. Giove, calling himself Arete, presses Iside to accept his love, offering to kill Licaone. Calisto renounces love and joins the goddess Diana's band of virgins, but this does not deter Arete from making advances. Iside's betrothed Osiri, under the name Erasto, comes in search of her but denounces her after being told by Arete that she has been carrying on with a handsome shepherd. She goes insane. Catching Calisto in a compromising moment with Arete, Diana sentences her to death. She is saved by Giove, who reveals his true identity and restores Iside's sanity, though not before Osiri rescues her from a bear and she stabs Licaone.

Handel had resigned himself to performing only unstaged works at the King's Theatre in 1738–9, but when an opera company was formed at COVENT GARDEN under the patronage of Lord MIDDLESEX he decided to launch his own opera season after Easter, beginning with *Giove in Argo*. Initially he apparently intended to use his regular singers, including FRANCESINA (Iside), Mrs Arne (Calisto) (Cecilia YOUNG) and Lucchesina (Diana). The unexpected arrival of the Italian mezzo-soprano Costanza Posterla and her family in mid-April, however, led him to engage Posterla and her youthful daughter for the roles of Iside and Diana, transferring the role of Calisto to Francesina. No singers are named in the printed libretto. The most likely cast would be as follows:

Arete (Giove)	John BEARD (tenor)
Iside	Costanza Posterla (mezzo-soprano)
Erasto (Osiri)	William SAVAGE (bass)?
Diana	Posterla (daughter) (soprano)
Calisto	Elisabeth Duparc, 'Francesina' (soprano)
Licaone	Henry REINHOLD (bass)?

Savage had just sung the alto arias in ISRAEL IN EGYPT as a falsettist, so he may have been familiar with Erasto's three arias, all taken from alto roles. Alternatively the two bass parts could have been played by Reinhold and Gustavus WALTZ or even Savage and Waltz. Giove drew favourable comments from some of Handel's supporters (Burrows and Dunhill, pp. 69–70), but it lasted for only two performances, perhaps partly because of Posterla's abrupt departure from England.

Although Giove in Argo is properly classified as a pasticcio, it includes considerably more new music than Handel's other operatic pasticcios. Most of the numbers were borrowed from nine operas he had written between 1712 and 1738, the serenatas ACIS AND GALATEA (1732 and 1734) and PARNASSO IN FESTA (1734), and the oratorio Il TRIONFO DEL TEMPO E DELLA VERITÀ (1737). Two of Iside's arias, 'Ombra che pallida' and 'Questa d'un fido amore', came from Francesco Araja's Lucio Vero (Venice, 1735), together with her accompanied recitative 'Iside, dove sei?' These insertions must have been requested by Posterla, who had sung under Araja in St Petersburg. Handel not only composed the secco recitatives but also provided twelve new numbers: six arias (three of them based on arias in his opera IMENEO, left unfinished in September 1738), two ariosos, three accompagnati and the final chorus. Undoubtedly he invested as much effort as he did in the score because of the change of cast and demands of the singers.

Giove in Argo is the only one of Handel's Italian operas of which no complete score has survived. Fortunately all the newly composed numbers are preserved in manuscripts in the Fitzwilliam Museum, Cambridge, the British Library, the Gerald Coke Handel Collection, Foundling Museum, London and Henry Watson Music Library, Manchester, and Handel's draft of the Act I recitatives before the change of cast is in the Fitzwilliam Museum, but the secco recitatives for Acts II and III are lost except for two bars linking the two accompagnati in Iside's mad scene. The two Araja arias were identified by the present author in 2001. In 2002 he undertook to reconstruct the opera for the HHA, and a preliminary version of this edition, with the missing recitatives supplied by the editor, was performed by Alan Curtis and Il Complesso Barocco in GÖTTINGEN, HANOVER and HALLE in May–June 2007. An alternative reconstruction by Thomas Synofzik and Steffen Voss with recitatives partially based on Lotti's setting was performed in Bayreuth in September 2006.

Conceived in the waning days of Handel's operatic career, Giove in Argo showed the influence of the increasingly popular genre of ORATORIO in its numerous choruses – more than in any other Handel opera – and the inclusion of two organ concertos in the original performances. The newspapers and the printed libretto described it as 'a dramatical composition', and it has been suggested that, like the 1732 *Acis and Galatea* and *Parnasso in Festa*, it was presented 'with costumes and scenery but no action' (Dean, *Operas*, p. 396). But since Handel and our three contemporary witnesses all called it an opera, we can safely assume that it was fully if simply staged. While *Giove in Argo* occasionally betrays signs of its hurried and complicated genesis and necessarily lacks the coherence of Handel's best original operas, it nonetheless contains a wealth of charming music and some dramatically potent scenes for Iside and Calisto. Its failure to win favour in 1739 is attributable primarily to the changing taste of the London public. JOHN H. ROBERTS

B. Baselt, 'Georg Friedrich Händels "Jupiter in Argos" und seine quellenmässige Überlieferung', *HJb* 33 (1987)

W. Dean, 'Handel's *Jupiter in Argos*', *Handel Studies: A Gedenkschrift for Howard Serwer*, ed. R. G. King (Hillsdale, NY, 2009)

J. H. Roberts, 'The Story of Handel's *Imeneo*', *HJb* 47 (2001)
 'Reconstructing Handel's *Giove in Argo*', *HJb* 54 (2008)

Gismondi, Celeste (d. London, 11 March 1735). Italian soprano (compass: b♭–b♭″). She was probably the comic intermezzo singer Celeste Resse, who performed at NAPLES between 1725 and 1732 and seems to have been responsible for intermezzo plots during that time. She might have had some influence on the role of Dorinda that Handel created for her in *ORLANDO* (Strohm, pp. 249–69). In 1733 she also sang in *DEBORAH*, but later that year defected to the OPERA OF THE NOBILITY, for whom she appeared under her married name Hempson until 1734. ARTIE HEINRICH

Giulio *Cesare* in Egitto, HWV 17. Italian opera. The story is based on historical action which took place during the Alexandrine War between September 48 and March 47 BC. The WORDBOOK summarises the action:

> Julius Caesar Dictator, having subdued the Gauls, and not being able thro' the Interest of Curius a Tribune to obtain the Consulship, carried so far his Resentment to the Subversion of the Latine Liberty, that he shew'd himself more like an Enemy than a Citizen of Rome. The Senate being apprehensive of his growing Power, in order to check it, sent the Great Pompey against him with a numerous Army, which was defeated by Caesar in the Pharsalian Fields. Pompey after this Rout, remembering the good Services he had done to the House of Ptolomey, thought it best to shelter himself there with Cornelia his Wife, and his Son Sestus; in the very time that Cleopatra and Ptolomey (the young and licentious King) forgetting their Affinity of Blood, were like inveterate Foes, arm'd against each other in Contention for the Crown. . . . Caesar being sensible, that nothing but the entire Destruction of Pompey could establish him Emperor of Rome, pursued him even into Egypt. Ptolomey naturally cruel and void of Honour, in hopes to ingratiate himself with Caesar, and procure his Assistance against Cleopatra, presented him with the Head of Pompey, whom he had murdered at the Instigation of Achilla. Caesar wept at the horrid Sight, taxing Ptolomey of Treachery and Barbarity; who not long after, at the Insinuation of the same wicked Counsellor, infringing upon the Sacred Laws of Hospitality, attempted privately to take away his Life; which Caesar narrowly escap'd by throwing himself from the Palace into the Water, where he saved himself by

swimming; upon this, arm'd with Fury and Resentment, he turn'd his
Forces against the bloody Tyrant, who was soon after kill'd in the Heat of
Battle. Caesar falling in Love with Cleopatra, plac'd her upon the Throne of
Egypt, he being at that time Master of the World, and first Emperor of
Rome.

The printed libretto cites some classical sources for this history, and notes that
several authors affirm 'that Ptolomey was vanquish'd by Caesar, and slain in
Battle; but how, was uncertain. Whereupon it was thought necessary in the
present Drama to make Sestus the Instrument of Ptolomey's Death in Revenge
for his Father's Murder, varying from History only in Circumstances of Action.'
The opera begins with Achilla's presentation of Pompeo's decapitated head to
Cesare, but most of its plot is fictional. The characterisation of Cesare as a courageous military hero and ardent lover implies a more youthful figure than his
historical counterpart (who was fifty-four when he met Cleopatra), and it is likely
that some members of Handel's AUDIENCE accepted the incongruity between
the operatic Giulio Cesare (the epitome of wisdom, magnanimity, courage and
virility) and the historical Julius Caesar (whose scheming, fornicating and murdering his way into political power had been described by influential classical
historians such as SUETONIUS).

The libretto for Handel's opera was adapted by Nicola Francesco HAYM
from a text by Giacomo Francesco BUSSANI (first set to music by Antonio
Sartorio for VENICE in 1677), and also on a revised version which was performed at Milan in 1685. Haym extensively restructured and rewrote the drama:
he removed the frequent use of disguise and cross-dressing, thereby purging
comic elements from Cornelia and Sesto, and transforming them into serious characters. Two important new scenes were added to Act III (the dying
Achilla's defection to the Romans; Cleopatra's lament whilst in chains). For the
Parnassus scene in which Cleopatra seduces Cesare whilst dressed as Virtue –
surely an ironic situation – Haym took much of the dialogue and stage directions from the 1685 Milanese libretto, but skilfully mingled it with the aria text
'V'adoro pupille' from the original 1677 Venetian text. Haym also astutely transferred texts from one character to another: 'Tu sei il cor' was a conventional
love duet for Cesare and Cleopatra (Milan, 1685), but for London it became
an ideal text to convey Achilla's frustrated and menacing attempt to seduce
Cornelia. However, most arias in Handel's setting have no known literary
antecedents.

Giulio Cesare was the first major work that Handel composed after moving into
his house in Brook Street, near Hanover Square (MUSUEMS, 2), perhaps during
the summer (he only wrote 'Anno 1723' on the final page of his autograph
manuscript; Figure 8). His score has a particularly rich INSTRUMENTATION:
two recorders, flute, two oboes, two bassoons, four horns, strings – sometimes
in five parts – and a continuo group including viola da gamba and harp. He seems
to have been meticulously self-critical about musico-dramatic details during the
COMPOSITION PROCESS of this opera, which was subjected to at least seven
different stages of revision. The character of Cleopatra's cousin Berenice was
removed, and her aria 'Va tacito e nascosto' transferred to Cesare, whereby
the text in which Berenice advised her cousin to stealthily entrap Cesare using

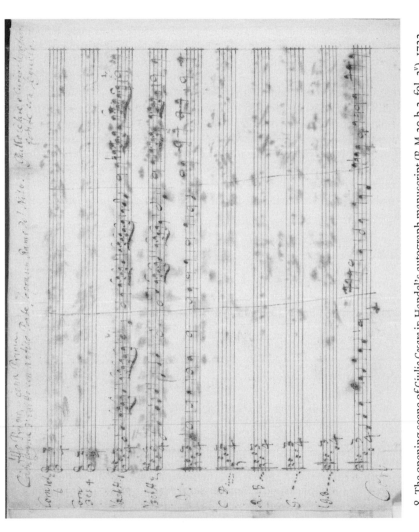

8. The opening scene of *Giulio Cesare* in Handel's autograph manuscript (R.M.20.b.3, fol. 3ᵛ), 1723.

her amorous powers of persuasion became instead Cesare's veiled first-person description of his cunning political manoeuvring with Tolomeo. Cleopatra's accompanied recitative 'Che sento? oh Dio' was originally short and led quickly into the powerful lament 'Se pietà', but Handel inserted a new contrasting second part to the recitative. He completely rewrote an unusually high number of arias (e.g. Cesare's opening aria 'Presti omai'), and carefully re-evaluated the contribution of Sesto and Cornelia, relocating their anguished duet 'Son nata a lagrimar' from just after they have witnessed Pompeo's head to their enforced separation at the end of Act I. The duet's initial position was instead filled by Handel's refined version of Cornelia's 'Priva son d'ogni conforto'. Likewise, the composer strengthened the pathos of Cleopatra's prison scene – the emotional climax and heart of the opera – by replacing her original F minor siciliano 'Troppo crudele siete affanni' with the sublime E major lament 'Piangerò la sorte mia'. Such compositional revisions greatly enhanced the quality of the music drama. Handel also used BORROWINGS from some of his old compositions: 'Va tacito' was based on an aria from *Vedendo amor* (HWV 175), Sesto's 'Cara speme' was borrowed from the BROCKES PASSION, and Tolomeo's vindictive 'L'empio, sleale' was originally composed for SENESINO to sing in a benefit performance of *OTTONE* on 26 March 1723.

Giulio Cesare was first performed at the KING'S THEATRE on 20 February 1724. The cast was as follows:

Giulio Cesare, first emperor of the Romans	Senesino (castrato)
Cleopatra, Queen of Egypt	Francesca CUZZONI (soprano)
Cornelia, widow of Pompeo	ANASTASIA ROBINSON (contralto)
Sesto, son of Pompeo and Cornelia	Margherita DURASTANTI (mezzo-soprano)
Tolomeo, her brother and King of Egypt	Gaetano BERENSTADT (castrato)
Achilla, General and Tolomeo's counsellor	Giuseppe Maria BOSCHI (bass)
Curio, Tribune of Rome	John Lagarde (bass)
Nireno, Cleopatra's confidant	Giuseppe Bigonzi (castrato)

Handel's popular new opera ran for thirteen performances. A French visitor to London attended a performance, and reported that 'Cenesino and Cozzuna shine beyond all criticism . . . The house was just as full at the seventh performance as at the first. In addition to that the squabbles, between the Directors and the sides that everyone is taking between the singers and the composers, often provide the public with the most diverting scenes' (Deutsch, p. 160). But not everyone was enamoured with the opera: John BYROM wrote to his wife that 'it was the first entertainment of this nature that I ever saw, and will I hope be the last, for of all the diversions of the town I least of all enter into this' (Deutsch, p. 158).

Handel revived Giulio Cesare thrice. The first revival in January 1725 (ten performances) was largely unchanged except for the role of Sesto, which was recast for the tenor Francesco BOROSINI. The roles of Curio and Nireno were cut, although for the last few performances Handel reinstated Nireno, but gave him a sex change ('Nerina'). The other two revivals were both given by the Second Academy (OPERA COMPANIES, 3) after one of Handel's new operas had flopped (eleven performances after *LOTARIO* in January–February 1730, and four performances after *EZIO* in February 1732). The first modern revival was by Oskar HAGEN at GÖTTINGEN in 1922, but the complete first-performance version, with all voices at the correct pitch and in Italian, was first revived at the Barber Institute of Fine Arts, Birmingham, on 20 January 1977. Although it is the most frequently staged Handel opera in modern times, performances are rarely uncut, and seldom adhere to the original three-act structure.

DAVID VICKERS

W. Dean and S. Fuller (eds.), *Giulio Cesare* (Oxford, 1998)
Dean and Knapp
Harris, *Librettos*
HHB i
R. Ketterer, *Ancient Rome in Early Opera* (Urbana and Chicago, 2009)
C. Monson: '"Giulio Cesare in Egitto": From Sartorio (1677) to Handel (1724)', ML 66/4 (Oct. 1985), 313–43

Giustino, HWV 37. *Giustino* was drafted between 14 August and 7 September 1736. After composing *ARMINIO*, Handel returned to *Giustino*, filling out the score between 15 and 20 October. The opera received its premiere at COVENT GARDEN on 16 February 1737, with the following cast:

Giustino, peasant and hero	Domenico ANNIBALI (castrato)
Anastasio, Emperor	Gioacchino CONTI (castrato)
Arianna, Empress	Anna STRADA del Pò (soprano)
Leocasta, Anastasio's sister	Francesca BERTOLLI (alto)
Amanzio, general	Maria Caterina NEGRI (alto)
Vitaliano, tyrant, Giustino's brother	John BEARD (tenor)
Polidarte, Vitaliano's captain	Henry REINHOLD (bass)
Fortuna	William SAVAGE (?treble)

Like Tullio in *Arminio* the role of Amanzio was first written for bass then adapted for Negri with an additional aria, 'Dall'occaso' in Act III. Other revisions made before the premiere include the addition of brilliant oboe solos in the Overture and in Arianna's 'Quel torrente' in Act II. Nine performances were given between February and June 1737. Handel never revived the opera, but drew on it heavily for the pasticcio *ALESSANDRO SEVERO* in 1738; Anastasio's arias 'Non si vanti' and 'Verdi lauri' were used again in the December 1744 revival of *SEMELE*.

The libretto of *Giustino* had originally been written by Niccolò BEREGAN for LEGRENZI in 1683. Handel would have known it since 1706, when a German version with music by Schieferdecker was staged in HAMBURG. Subsequently the libretto was modernised by Pietro PARIATI on at least two occasions, and it was his 1724 revision, made for VIVALDI, that Handel used for his opera. The drastic abbreviation of the Beregan–Pariati text was probably made by ROSSI. The characters are historical figures from sixth-century Byzantium, but the story is almost entirely fictitious. With its ploughboy-to-emperor trajectory, its dreams, supernatural visions and monsters, it more resembles a fairy tale than a historical drama. LAMPE and CAREY's *Dragon of Wantley*, staged at Covent

Garden in October 1737, and much enjoyed by Handel himself, appears to aim its satirical thrusts particularly at *Giustino*.

Act I: Amid the acclamations of the people, the widowed Arianna crowns Anastasio as her new imperial consort. Polidarte brings a demand from Vitaliano: the hand of Arianna as the price of peace. Outraged, Anastasio prepares for war. Working at his plough Giustino dreams of glory; when he rests and falls asleep, a vision of Fortune and her attendant genii inspires him to bid his fields farewell. He rescues Leocasta from a bear; she proves to be the Emperor's sister and takes Giustino back to the palace. Amanzio harbours secret designs on the throne. Gladly accepted into Anastasio's service, Giustino is at once charged with a mission to resue Arianna, who has been captured by Vitaliano's men. Since she rejects Vitaliano's amorous advances, he commands that she be exposed to 'that savage monster that fills the fields around with abundant slaughter'.

Act II: Anastasio and Giustino are shipwrecked on the same rocky coast where Arianna is exposed to the monster. Giustino kills the monster, and the happy party re-embark for home. Vitaliano, regretting his hasty decision to have Arianna devoured, just misses them; seeing the dead monster he hopes she may have escaped. Leocasta muses on her love for Giustino. To Amanzio's jealous indignation, the Emperor loads Giustino, who has brought in Vitaliano prisoner, with thanks and honours. While Giustino leaves to give the *coup de grâce* to the Emperor's enemies, the chained Vitaliano is shown to Arianna, to whom he continues to avow his love.

Act III: Vitaliano escapes from prison, and rouses his troops for another attack on Anastasio. Meanwhile Amanzio has succeeded in arousing the Emperor's suspicions about the loyalty of the 'peasant' Giustino. Anastasio is persuaded to denounce his wife as faithless, condemn Giustino to death as a traitor and transfer the command of the army to Amanzio. Thanks to Leocasta Giustino escapes. But when Vitaliano discovers him asleep at the foot of a mountain, he sees the perfect opportunity to kill his most formidable enemy. His hand is held when the mountain splits asunder, and the voice of his dead father thunders forth, declaring Giustino and Vitaliano to be brothers. Joyfully reunited they set out to defeat the treacherous Amanzio. Amanzio's triumph is cut short: Anastasio recognises his error; Vitaliano is welcomed as an ally, Giustino as co-regent; and the happy reunion is to be sealed with his marriage to Leocasta.

Giustino is one of the operas in which Handel's interest in the music of his younger contemporaries is most apparent. The prevalence of major keys, of lively tempos, of common time (almost two-thirds of the numbers are in 4/4 time), and such *galant* mannerisms as short repeated phrases, syncopated rhythms, orchestral accompaniments in which slowly moving harmonies derive their vitality from chord repetition rather than the free contrapuntal movement of the voices, are all features that, for a connoisseur of the modern style like BURNEY, made *Giustino* 'one of the most agreeable of Handel's dramatic compositions' (Burney, p. 809). It is amusing to note that several passages he held up for particular commendation rank among Handel's more flagrant 'BORROWINGS', from VINCI in 'Mio dolce amato sposo' and 'Zeffiretto che corre nel prato', from GRAUN in the A major version of 'Nacque al bosco' and in 'Dell'occaso'.

The opera is more richly scored than its neighbours, Arminio and BERENICE, and includes in Giustino's first aria, 'Può ben nascer', one of Handel's most notable pieces of dramatic-cum-psychological orchestration. The scene has moved from the court to the countryside, where Giustino is discovered labouring at the plough but dreaming of glory. The orchestra that introduces the aria consists of recorder consort with solo oboe and viola; in the postlude, the same material is reworked for full orchestra with the addition of two horns. This aria sets off a remarkable sequence of nine linked movements, only the last of which is a da capo aria, and two of which, the goddess Fortune's aria and the chorus of genii that attend on her, are propelled on the same ostinato bass, treated with characteristic Handelian freedom.   DAVID KIMBELL

Burney
Dean, *Operas*
Harris, *Librettos*
J. H. Roberts, 'Handel and Vinci's *Didone abbandonata*: Revisions and Borrowings', ML 68/2 (1987), 141–50
(ed.), *Handel Sources: Materials for the Study of Handel's Borrowing*, vols. 5 and 7 (New York, 1986)
Strohm
'Vivaldi's and Handel's settings of Giustino', *Music and Theatre: Essays in Honour of Winton Dean*, ed. N. Fortune (Cambridge, 1987)

Gloria in excelsis Deo in B flat major, for soprano, strings and continuo. In 2000 this unusual and attractive solo *Gloria*, preserved in a manuscript score and parts in the Royal Academy of Music, London, was hailed by Hans Joachim Marx as an unknown early work of Handel. His claims prompted extensive scholarly debate, Anthony Hicks strongly contesting Handel's authorship. Based on the evidence and argument offered to date, the attribution to Handel must be regarded as doubtful. Nonetheless, the *Gloria* is tied to Handel in two significant ways: he borrowed musical ideas from it, most notably in the opening movement of the *Laudate pueri* in D major, HWV 237 (Italian and Latin CHURCH MUSIC); and the manuscripts containing it came from collection of William SAVAGE, who probably copied and performed it while he was singing for Handel as a boy soprano in 1735–7.   JOHN H. ROBERTS

G. Barnett, 'Handel's Borrowings and the Disputed *Gloria*', EM 24/1 (2006), 75–92
C. Bartlett, A. Hicks, H. J. Marx and M. Talbot, 'The "Handel" Gloria Reconsidered', EM 30/2 (2002), 252–62
H. J. Marx, 'A Newly Discovered Gloria by Handel', EM 29/3 (2001), 342–52
'Ein neuentdecktes "Gloria"', GHB IX (2002)

Giuvo (Giovo, Giovio, Juvo), Nicola (Nicolò) (b. Naples, c.1680; d. Naples, in or after 1758). Italian man of letters. After legal studies, he had taken minor clerical orders (*abate*) by 1704; later, between 1708 and 1711, he enlisted in the ARCADIAN ACADEMY (nickname: Eupidio Siriano). Sometimes inaccurately described in contemporary sources as 'marquis of Landskron', Giuvo made a living as secretary and librarian to various aristocratic households in NAPLES, acquiring a local reputation as librettist for para-operatic genres (i.e. oratorios and serenatas for weddings and politico-dynastic celebrations). Rather than public theatres, his customers were religious brotherhoods, the viceregal court and the nobility. His career in this capacity, stretching from 1704 to 1740, culminated in the official appointment of court poet to the new Bourbon dynasty during the late 1730s. Giuvo's long-standing association with Aurora SAN-SEVERINO and her husband included his collaboration with Handel on *ACI, GALATEA E POLIFEMO* and possibly on the cantatas *DUNQUE SARÀ PUR VERO, Nel dolce tempo, Nell'affricane selve, Sento là che ristretto* and the chamber trio *Se tu non lasci amore*. His *Agrippina* for PORPORA (Naples, 1708) is unrelated to Handel's.

CARLO VITALI

Gluck, Christoph Willibald (b. Erasbach, Upper Palatinate, 2 July 1714; d. Vienna, 15 Nov. 1787). Austrian composer, born in Bohemia. After a period in Italy where he composed a number of serious operas, he came to London in 1745. *La caduta de' giganti* was performed at the KING'S THEATRE on 7 January 1746, its subject an anticipatory celebration of the defeat of Charles Edward STUART by forces loyal to GEORGE II. *Artamene* followed in March. Each opera had only a short run of performances. Before returning to Germany Gluck met Handel, for whom he was later to express profound admiration; but reports of their encounter are anecdotes published long after the event. Reichardt's revision of Gerber's *Historisch-biographisches Lexicon der Tonkünstler* has Handel tell Gluck that he took too much trouble for English audiences: 'You must write something striking, going straight into their ears; then your opera is sure to please.' According to BURNEY (1785), Handel said that Gluck 'knows no more of contrapunto, as mein cook, Waltz', which was perhaps not as harsh a criticism as it sounds (Gustavus WALTZ). To Burney, in 1772, Gluck claimed to have 'studied the English taste . . . finding that plainness and simplicity had the greatest effect upon them, he has, ever since that time, endeavoured to write for the voice, more in the natural tones of the human affections and passions, than to flatter the lovers of deep science or difficult execution'. Such directness and simplicity are attributes more of Handel's oratorio choruses than his operas. In the following decades Gluck composed in many forms (opera seria, opéra comique, ballet), where the influence of the older composer could hardly intrude. But he made simplicity and directness the watchword in the Viennese reform operas *Orfeo, Alceste* (where the choruses are especially fine) and *Paride ed Elena*, and in his last works, composed for Paris in 1774–9. JULIAN RUSHTON

See also GUADAGNI

C. Burney, *The Present State of Music in Germany and the Netherlands* (London, 1773) (see also P. A. Scholes, *Dr Burney's Musical Tours in Europe* (2 vols., London, 1959))

P. Howard, *Gluck: An Eighteenth-Century Portrait in Letters and Documents* (Oxford, 1995)

Gopsall. See Charles JENNENS

Gordon, Alexander (b. Aberdeen, c.1692; d. South Carolina, 1754 or 1755). Scottish tenor (compass: d–a'). In 1720 he created the role of Tiridate in the first version of *RADAMISTO* (HWV 12^a), and in 1723 he sang Ugone in *FLAVIO*. A famous anecdote cites that Gordon threatened to jump on Handel's harpsichord during a rehearsal; it is said that the composer replied: 'Oh! Let me know when you will do that and I will advertise it. For I am sure more people will come to see you jump than to hear you sing.' After his singing career he became a scholar, author and publisher.   ARTIE HEINRICH

C. Morey, 'Alexander Gordon, Scholar and Singer', ML 46/4 (Oct. 1965), 332–5

Göttingen. German town first documented in 953 as Gutingi. Its earliest traces of institutionalised musical life were the Latin schools in the early fourteenth century. After the Reformation, the town's musical activities were dominated by the municipal town music and, after the establishment of a garrison (1632), by military music. The town's musical life gathered momentum after GEORGE II founded the town's university in 1734. Similar to Leipzig, a Collegium musicum was established in 1735 to hold weekly concerts. The integration of historical musicology into the university's core subjects was led by Johann Nikolaus Forkel (the pioneering biographer of J. S. BACH), who started lecturing at Göttingen in 1772, and became the first academic Director of Music in 1779. Part of his academic duties was organising winter concerts and playing the organ at the university church, where Wilhelm Friedemann BACH (at Forkel's invitation) performed on the organ in 1773. Forkel also maintained a lively correspondence with C. P. E. Bach. His successor Johann August Günther Heinroth (from 1818) founded the Singakademie, assembled a large orchestra and organised a concert series of symphonic works and oratorios. Carl Maria von Weber, Louis Spohr, Niccolò Paganini and Franz Liszt all performed at Göttingen. In 1855 Julius Otto Grimm was appointed conductor of the newly founded Cäcilienverein, and arranged appearances by performers such as Clara Schumann and Johannes BRAHMS; the latter's affair with Agathe von Siebold, daughter of a Göttingen gynaecologist, became famous.

The foundation of the Göttinger Konzertverein (1885), of the Freibergsche Gesangverein (1887) and the opening of the Göttingen Stadttheater (1891) were also important steps on the way to consolidating and expanding public concert life. In 1920 the Göttingen Handel Festival (FESTIVALS, 3) was founded, and the Göttinger Symphonie-Orchester was established by Günther Weißenborn in 1951. The editorial office of the Neue Bach-Ausgabe was in Göttingen until the project was completed in 2006.   JÜRGEN HEIDRICH (Trans. ANGELA BAIER)

M. Staehelin, *Musikwissenschaft und Musikpflege an der Georg-August-Universität Göttingen* (Göttingen, 1987)

Göttinger Händel-Gesellschaft. See HANDEL SOCIETIES, 4; JOURNALS, I

Goupy (Goupée), Joseph (b. London, 1689; d. London, 1769). Scene designer. Born in London of French Catholic heritage, Goupy specialised in making copies and etchings of old master paintings; he was, according to John HAWKINS, one of Handel's two intimate friends. They were in ROME at the same time, and in London their careers quickly took parallel tracks: Goupy had ties to BURLINGTON HOUSE in the early 1710s and received commissions from Baron KIELMANSEGG in 1717 and James Brydges (Duke of CHANDOS) in 1718. He carried out various projects for GEORGE I, and in the mid-1720s became involved creating sets for the Royal Academy of Music (OPERA COMPANIES, 2); he is specifically credited with the sets for *RICCARDO PRIMO*. Around 1740, both

9. *The Charming Brute* by Joseph Goupy, black and coloured chalks on paper, c.1743.

he and Handel enjoyed the hospitality and patronage of the art collector Henry Furnese, MP (after 1688–1756). Appointed cabinet (personal) painter to FREDERICK, Prince of Wales in 1736, Goupy tried, on behalf of the Prince and other aristocratic patrons in 1743, to persuade Handel to compose or revise a work for the MIDDLESEX OPERA COMPANY. Handel's refusal apparently led Goupy to paint an image of the composer as a hog playing the organ and trampling underfoot 'pension, benefit, nobility [and] friendship' (Figure 9). After Goupy distributed this image as an etching, Handel never forgave him. With the unexpected death of Prince Frederick in 1750, Goupy lost his patronage and leaves no significant artistic work after this date. In 1755 he sold his copper plates to John Boydell, and in 1765 he auctioned a good deal of his art collection, including his own works. He died in restricted circumstances in 1769.   ELLEN T. HARRIS

See also ICONOGRAPHY

E. T. Harris, 'Joseph Goupy and George Frideric Handel: From Professional Triumphs to Personal Estrangement', *Huntington Library Quarterly* 71/3 (2008)
J. Simon, 'New Light on Joseph Goupy', *Apollo* 139 (Feb. 1994), 15–18

Gowland, John (bap. 1704, d. 1776). Apothecary on New Bond Street to whom Handel bequeathed £50 (HANDEL, 8). Gowland moved from York to St George Hanover Square in the mid-1720s. For a period of about a year around 1735, Handel's friend Joseph GOUPY rented rooms from him. He was named apothecary to FREDERICK, Prince of Wales, by 1741 and apothecary to His Majesty, GEORGE III, by 1763. He is probably the apothecary mentioned by James SMYTH who attended Handel in his last illness.   ELLEN T. HARRIS

John Gowland, will of, PROB 11/1022, fd. 277, The National Archives
T. Mortimer, *The Universal Director: or, the Nobleman and Gentleman's true guide to the Masters and Professors of the liberal and polite arts and sciences, and of the mechanic arts, manufactures . . . established in London and Westminster, and their environs, etc.* (London, 1763)
P. J. and R. V. Wallis, *Eighteenth-Century Medics* (Newcastle upon Tyne: Project for Historical Biobibliography, 1988), pp. xviii–xix

Granville, Bernard (b. 1698/9; d. 1775). Called 'a sober musical thing' by his sister, Mary DELANY (22 October 1734), Granville, who never married, inherited two great fortunes, one in 1736 and the other in 1752. In 1738 he purchased Calwich Abbey, a large estate in Staffordshire, and divided his residence between it and London. Handel advised him on the purchase of an organ and gave him music books from his own collection. Granville gave Handel a painting identified as a Rembrandt, and in his will Handel bequeathed to Granville this and another he had purchased (HANDEL, 8). Granville's large manuscript collection of Handel's works is preserved in the British Library (SOURCES AND COLLECTIONS, 9).

ELLEN T. HARRIS

D. Burrows, 'The 'Granville' and 'Smith' Collections of Handel's Manuscripts', *Sundry Sorts of Music Books*, ed. C. Banks, A. Searle and M. Turner (London, 1993)
M. T. Fortescue, *The History of Calwich Abbey* (London, 1914)
R. Granville, *The History of the Granville Family* (Exeter, 1895)
Lady Llanover (ed.), *The Autobiography and Correspondence of Mary Granville, Mrs Delany*, 1st ser., 3 vols. (London, 1861), 2nd ser., 3 vols. (1862)
H. McLean, 'Bernard Granville, Handel and the Rembrandts', *MT* 126/1712 (1985), 593–601
'Granville, Handel and "Some Golden Rules"', *MT* 126/1713 (1985), 662–5
R. A. Streatfeild, 'The Granville Collection of Handel Manuscripts', *The Musical Antiquary* 2 (1910–11), 208–24

Graun, Carl Heinrich (b. Wahrenbrück, 1703/4; d. Berlin, 8 Aug. 1759). German composer. He received his musical training at the Kreuzschule in DRESDEN, where he might have been a choral singer when Handel visited the city in 1719. In February 1725 he was employed as a tenor and composer at the court of Duke August Wilhelm of Brunswick-Wolfenbüttel. In 1735 he was invited to

Prussia, and he was appointed Hofkapellmeister at BERLIN in 1740. Graun was sent to Italy to engage singers for the Prussian court opera, and he composed passion oratorios, church music, Italian cantatas and operas. Handel borrowed musical ideas from Graun's Brunswick Passion oratorio *Kommt her und schaut* (c.1729) in *ALEXANDER'S FEAST, ATALANTA, BERENICE, GIUSTINO* and *Il TRIONFO DEL TEMPO E DELLA VERITÀ* (all written 1736–7), and later in *JUDAS MACCABAEUS* and the Foundling Hospital Anthem (ANTHEMS, 8).

In the 1740s some of Graun's Berlin operas were revived at SALZDAHLUM and BRUNSWICK, including those on the same subjects as pasticcios that Handel performed in London during the previous decade (*CATONE IN UTICA* and *GIOVE IN ARGO*). At the beginning of the nineteenth century A. B. Marx complained that the annual Berlin performances of Graun's passion cantata *Der Tod Jesu* (1754) were edging out Handel's *MESSIAH*.   WALTER KREYSZIG

A. Feltz, 'Georg Friedrich Händels Entlehnungen aus der "Grossen Passion" von Carl Heinrich Graun: Ein Beitrag zu Händels Kompositionsweise in der Mitte der 1730er Jahre', HJb 35 (1989)

J. H. Roberts (ed.), *Handel Sources: Materials for the Study of Handel's Borrowing*, vol. 5 (New York, 1986)

Green Park. A triangular piece of the royal parks in central London west of ST JAMES'S PALACE, and north of what is now BUCKINGHAM PALACE. Green Park was the site of the grand fireworks display on 27 April 1749 before which Handel's *MUSIC FOR THE ROYAL FIREWORKS* was performed. The King and his entourage watched the event from the Queen's Library (demolished about 1825), which housed the late Queen CAROLINE's extensive music collection.

DAVID HUNTER

P. Daub, 'Queen Caroline of England's Music Library', *Music Publishing & Collecting: Essays in Honor of Donald W. Krummel*, ed. D. Hunter (Champaign, IL, 1994)

Greene, Maurice (b. London, 12 Aug. 1696; d. London, 1 Dec. 1755). English composer, organist and sometime friend of Handel. When 'the great Saxon Timotheus' first came to London, Greene was still a pupil of Richard Brind whom, in March 1718, he succeeded as organist of ST PAUL'S CATHEDRAL. According to BURNEY, Handel was particularly fond of the organ there which, after evensong, he often played (with young Greene acting as his bellows-blower). When, some years later, Handel discovered that Greene was also paying court to Giovanni BONONCINI, he is said to have dropped him, and never again to have spoken of him 'without some injurious epithet'. As organist of St Paul's, Greene was responsible for the music at the annual SONS OF THE CLERGY festival at which, from 1731 onwards, Handel's TE DEUM settings and some of his anthems were regularly performed. Greene also composed a number of orchestrally accompanied anthems for the same occasion, and one of these, *O praise the Lord, ye angels of his*, was subsequently published by Friedrich CHRYSANDER as the work of Handel (and is now catalogued as HWV 257). Though Greene had also been Organist and Composer to the CHAPEL ROYAL since 1727, his anthem for the wedding of Princess ANNE in 1734 was, in the event, displaced by one of Handel's (HWV 262) (ANTHEMS, 4). Whenever the interests of the royal family were involved, it was Handel who was called on to hymn the event; Greene was thus fobbed off with the lesser events and, as Master of the King's Musick from

1735, the thankless task of composing the biannual odes to celebrate the King's birthday and the New Year.   H. DIACK JOHNSTONE

H. D. Johnstone, 'Handel and his Bellows Blower (Maurice Greene)', GHB VII (1998)
'The Chandos Anthems: The Authorship of no. 12', MT 117 (1976), 601–3 and 998; also 129 (1988), 459

Grimaldi, Nicolo. See 'NICOLINO'

Grimani, Vincenzo (b. 26 May 1652 or 1653, Venice; d. Naples, 26 Sept. 1710). Italian diplomat, clergyman and theatrical manager. Son of Antonio Grimani, a member of the wealthiest Venetian patriciate, and Elena Gonzaga di Palazzolo, a relative to the dukes of Mantua. As a diplomatic agent of Emperor Leopold I, he negotiated an alliance between the Duchy of Savoy and the Empire in 1690. On France's complaint, this entailed his banishment from VENICE and an attempt on his life in Milan. In 1697, on the Emperor's recommendation, he was promoted to the rank of cardinal. He then obtained a pardon from Venice, later serving as Vienna's representative before the Holy See (1700–2, 1706–8) and imperial viceroy of NAPLES from June 1708 until his death.

From 1678 he built and ran Venice's leading opera house SAN GIOVANNI GRISOSTOMO in association with his elder brother Giovanni Carlo. His correspondence provides copious evidence of his negotiations for singers with several courts in Italy and in Germany, which were possibly also a front for his diplomatic activities because Venetian laws limited social intercourse between patricians and foreigners. His authorship of three librettos for the family theatre, first suggested in Bonlini's catalogue (1730), is unsupported in the original sources: these are Elmiro for Pallavicino (1686), Orazio for Tosi (1688) and AGRIPPINA for Handel (1709).   CARLO VITALI

Griselda. Opera in three Acts by Giovanni BONONCINI, text by Paolo Antonio ROLLI after Apostolo ZENO (VENICE, 1701); first performance: KING'S THEATRE, 22 February 1722. The ancient tale of the humble Griselda was known in Europe through the elaborations of Petrarch, Boccaccio, Chaucer, Hans Sachs, Thomas Dekker, Lope de Vega, a number of sixteenth- and seventeenth-century English and Italian dramas, Zeno's libretto (and its numerous revisions), Luigi Riccoboni's dramatisation of 1717 (written around 1705) after Zeno and the English ballad of Patient Grissel, which circulated in print during the 1720s and was linked to Bononcini's opera.

Rolli's libretto diverges significantly from both Zeno's original of 1701 and Carlo Sigismondo CAPECE's revised libretto for Alessandro SCARLATTI's Griselda (ROME, 1717) – a possible source for Rolli's adaptation. The names of Costanza, Ottone and Roberto are changed into Almirena, Rambaldo and Ernesto, while Corrado is eliminated altogether. According to Rolli himself, the alterations that were made were in part caused by the use of an older (unidentified) drama he was asked to utilise.

The opera was first performed during the Royal Academy of Music's 1721–2 season with great success (OPERA COMPANIES, 2). It received sixteen performances over a four-month period. The overture and all the arias from the opera were printed by WALSH in 1722. Griselda and Crispo were praised in Richard Steele's play The Conscious Lovers as performed at DRURY LANE on 7 November

1722 (translated by Rolli, *Gli amanti interni*, 1724, who also comments on the popularity of Bononcini and his *Griselda*). BURNEY reports that the opera 'seems to have been regarded as Bononcini's best theatrical production in this country', and observes that 'Handel's bold and varied style, rich harmony, and ingenious contrivance, had made such an impression on the public, as to render it necessary for Bononcini, in setting this opera, to quit *his ambling nag*, and to mount his great horse, accoutred in all his trappings, and endeavour to move with unusual pomp and stateliness' (Burney, pp. 719–21). ANASTASIA ROBINSON (alto) sang in the title role; Francesco Bernardi, known as 'Il SENESINO' (alto castrato), was Gualtiero; Maddalena SALVAI (soprano) was Almirena; Giuseppe BOSCHI (bass) was Rambaldo and Benedetto Baldassari (soprano castrato) was Ernesto. The role of the meek Griselda was particularly suited to Robinson; she made a specific reference to it in a letter (undated, but probably written in autumn 1722) concerning the role of Matilda in Handel's *OTTONE*.

The subject, markedly anti-heroic, was new to the London operatic stage and focused around, not a queen or a princess, but an ordinary, vulnerable shepherdess whose patience and submissiveness overcomes the persecution and humiliation she is undeservedly subjected to. The general tone of the opera is sentimental and, as Lindgren observes, its success may well reflect the 'changing tone of the age' as much as Steele's *The Conscious Lovers* did. Bononcini's sustained pathetic music and natural style, often opposed to Handel's, was particularly suitable to the subject (as it was to that of *Crispo*, performed during the same season) and is well exemplified in one of the most popular arias (also praised in Steele's comedy), 'Dolce sogno, deh le porta' for Gualtiero (II.viii). 'Dolce sogno' is a delightful aria in a lulling 3/8 time ('Lento e piano sempre'). The limited compass and the relatively low register (b–c♯″) are perfectly suited to Senesino's range, with short and contained coloraturas that allow numerous *messe di voce*. The natural semi-syllabic setting is characterised by brief and regular motives in stepwise motion on the weak beat, compensated by longer phrases of larger intervals. This aria exemplifies Bononcini's typical musical style and lends itself to a comparison with the aria 'Si già sento l'ardor che m'accende', in which the hero fakes passion for Almirena (I.v). This aria is an 'Allegro assai' in F major, and is characterised by a bold and accentuated virtuosity based on the contrast between opposing dynamics, instrumental groupings, tempi and rhythmic figures. Trills, long and fast coloraturas, large and sometimes dissonant intervals, and a wide compass that forces Senesino up to g″, very high for him, engage the singer from the very beginning of the aria, and it provides a good example of Bononcini's more virtuosic writing that might have spurred Burney's observations. Handel revived *Griselda* on 22 May 1733 with the Second Academy (OPERA COMPANIES, 3), possibly at Senesino's instigation (the only singer from the 1722 production, who retained the role of Gualtiero).

MELANIA BUCCIARELLI

See also *CORIOLANO*

M. Bucciarelli, 'From Venice to London: On the Trail of Luigi Riccoboni and Italian Opera', *Opera Subjects and European Relationships*, ed. N. Dubowy et al. (Berlin, 2007)

L. E. Lindgren, 'A Bibliographic Scrutiny of Dramatic Works Set by Giovanni and His Brother Antonio Maria Bononcini', Ph.D. dissertation (Harvard University, 1972)

Guadagni, Cosimo Gaetano (b. Lodi, 16 Feb. 1728; d. Padua 11 Oct. 1792). Italian castrato (range in Handel g–e″) who came to London in 1748 as first *amoroso* in Croza's comic opera company. Described by BURNEY (who helped him with his English pronunciation) as 'a wild and careless singer', he nevertheless became well known for his fine technique (never a singer to sacrifice simplicity of utterance for the purposes of mere display, his *messa di voce* was especially famous), and for his acting (Garrick coached him in 1755, when he appeared in J. C. SMITH JUNIOR's *The Fairies* at COVENT GARDEN). Guadagni worked for Handel from 1750 to 1755, taking part in revivals of *SAUL, SAMSON, JUDAS MACCABAEUS, BELSHAZZAR, ALEXANDER'S FEAST* (including the new insertion *CHOICE OF HERCULES*), *ESTHER, L'ALLEGRO, JOSHUA, JOSEPH AND HIS BRETHREN* and *JEPHTHA*. He created the role of Didymus in *THEODORA* in 1750, but Guadagni's best-known Handel solos were the several arias recast for him in *MESSIAH*, including 'But who may abide' and 'How beautiful are the feet'.

Horace Walpole named a horse after Guadagni, but the singer is best remembered as the creator of *Orfeo* for GLUCK (Vienna, 1762), in which role he achieved European fame. He returned to England from 1769 to 1771, appearing in J. C. Bach's pasticcio of *Orfeo*, for which he was arrested and tried for participation in an illegal opera production. During the last decade of his life, in Padua, he sang in a series of adaptations and other versions of the Orfeo story, his performances of which revealed the influence of Handel – he was criticised for making these operas sound like oratorios.   NICHOLAS CLAPTON

Gualandi, Antoni. See 'CAMPIOLI'

Guarini, (Giovanni) Battista (b. Ferrara, 10 Dec. 1538; d. Venice, 7 Oct. 1612). Italian poet, dramatist and diplomat. He was in service of Alfonso II d'Este, Duke of Ferrara, as ambassador between 1567 and 1588; he also succeeded TASSO as the court poet in 1577. He spent the years 1588 to 1595 estranged from the Ferrara court and continued to move from one court to another. His most important work is the pastoral play *Il pastor fido* (completed by 1585), which laid the grounds for the genre of *tragicommedia pastorale* and prompted the vogue for pastoral subjects.

Guarini was the poet with the single greatest influence in music history of the late Renaissance and baroque. His poetry, rich in possibilities for expressing emotion in music, had a decisive influence on madrigal composers, notably Claudio Monteverdi and Philippe de Monte. Similarly, he exercised great influence on librettists up to and including METASTASIO, most notably with *Il pastor fido*, which set the model for the code of elegance and gallantry. The play was used for intermedi, and became a source for an inexhaustible number of madrigals and monodies, and later for cantatas and intermezzos. Handel's setting of *Il PASTOR FIDO* is the first of four known operas based on it. The other three were composed by C. L. P. Grua (1721), Apolloni (1739) and Salieri (on a libretto by Da Ponte, 1789).   SUZANA OGRAJENŠEK

Dean and Knapp, *Operas*
E. T. Harris, *Handel and the Pastoral Tradition* (London, 1980)
A. Hartmann, jr., 'Battista Guarini and Il Pastor Fido', MQ 39/3 (July 1953), 415–25

Guernsey, Lord. See 3rd Earl of AYLESFORD

H

Haarlem. Handel visited this city in the NETHERLANDS during September 1740, probably on his way back to London after a journey on the continent. He visited the Grote Kerk (St Bavo), where he heard the organist Henricus Radecker perform on the newly built organ. Handel then played the instrument himself, and expressed great admiration for the elaborate instrument built by Christian Müller in 1735–8 and already known (as it still is) as one of the finest organs in the Netherlands (three manuals, pedal, sixty stops). On 27 August 1750 Handel was in Haarlem again, travelling home from his final visit to Germany. On this occasion he asked Radecker to play the organ for him because he had suffered injuries from a coach accident some days previously.   DOROTHEA SCHRÖDER

See also HANDEL, 15

HHB iv

Habermann, Franz Johann (b. Königswart, near Eger (now Cheb), Bohemia, 20 Sept. 1706; d. Eger, 8 April 1783). Bohemian composer from a musical family that also included two brothers and at least one son. After travels to Italy, Spain and France, he returned to Bohemia and worked in Prague and Eger. In 1747 he published six masses under the title 'Philomela pia' (SATB, two violins, two trumpets and organ). From these part-books Handel copied themes and scored portions of five masses, found now in the FITZWILLIAM manuscripts. Handel made extensive use of Habermann's material in 1751: in the Organ Concerto, HWV 308 (early January) (ORCHESTRAL WORKS, 5) and the oratorio *JEPHTHA* (which occupied him intermittently through August). About a dozen movements in *Jephtha*, including most of the choruses, borrow from Habermann.

WILLIAM D. GUDGER

See also BORROWINGS

D. Burrows, 'A Good Day's Work: Composition and Revision in the First Movement of
    Handel's Organ Concerto HWV 308 (Op. 7 No. 3)', HJb 42/3 (1996/7)
Dean, *Oratorios*
W. D. Gudger, 'Handel's Last Compositions and his Borrowings from Habermann', *Current
    Musicology* 22 (1976), 61–72; 23 (1977), 28–45
F. J. Habermann, *Missa Sancti Wenceslai, Martyris*, ed. W. D. Gudger (Madison, WI, 1976)

Haec est regina virginum. See Italian and Latin CHURCH MUSIC

Hagen, Oskar (b. Wiesbaden, 14 Oct. 1888; d. Madison, WI, 5 Oct. 1957). Art historian, musicologist and initiator of the GÖTTINGEN Handel Festival (FESTIVALS, 3). After studying composition with Carl Adolph Schuricht and Engelbert

Humperdinck, Hagen received degrees in musicology and history of art at the universities of BERLIN and HALLE, where Hermann Abert kindled his interest in Handel's operatic works. From 1918 to 1924 the art historian, who had by then received his postdoctoral qualification as a lecturer, was assistant professor at the University of Göttingen. In addition to his teaching duties, Hagen completed a plan he had initially conceived in Halle: the rediscovery of Handel's operas. As arranger, translator of the librettos (into German), director and conductor he presented a selection of operas, such as *RODELINDA* (1920), *OTTONE* (1921), *GIULIO CESARE* (1922) and *SERSE* (1924). The stage settings and costumes were designed by the architect Paul Thiersch and from 1922 Hagen began to direct his productions in collaboration with a university friend from Hallensian days, Hanns NIEDECKEN-GEBHARD. The performances, semi-professional according to modern standards, featured established singers and students; they were received very well by the general public and critics. Hagen's arrangements included cuts in the score, changes in the original order of arias, transpositions of the castrato parts and modifications in tempi and dynamics; the staging and general performance character was influenced by expressionist theories, Wagnerian music drama and notions about baroque music shaped by its reception in the Romantic Age. Hagen's productions were aimed at pleasing the contemporary audiences and chimed in with the *Zeitgeist* then prevalent. They stand at the beginning of the ongoing modern reception of Handelian music theatre. Because his professional career did not really take off in Göttingen, Hagen left the city in 1924 and from then on taught at the University of Madison (Wisconsin, USA). He stayed true to his Handelian operatic mission and gave talks advocating the performance of the operas. He also maintained amicable relations with Werner Josten (Smith College, Northampton, Massachusetts, USA), who supported the American premieres of Hagen's arrangements of *Giulio Cesare, Serse* and *Rodelinda*. ULRICH ETSCHEIT (Trans. ANGELA BAIER)

W. Boetticher, 'Die frühe Göttinger Händelrenaissance. Versuch einer Würdigung', GHB II (1986)

U. Etscheit, *Händels "Rodelinda". Libretto–Komposition–Rezeption* (Kassel, 1998)

K. Schneider, 'Aus der Zeit – für die Zeit. Oskar Hagen und die Göttinger Händel-Festspiele', *Paul Thiersch und die Bühne*, Exhibition catalogue, Halle (1995), 18–21

M. Staehelin, 'Siebzig Jahre Göttinger Händel-Festspiele. Zu den Anfängen der Göttinger Händel-Renaissance', GHB IV (1991)

R. Steglich, 'Händels Oper Rodelinde und ihre neue Göttinger Bühnenfassung', *Zeitschrift für Musikwissenschaft* 3 (1920/1), 518–43

Hall Collection. See SOURCES AND COLLECTIONS, 10

Halle (Saale). Handel's native town, first documented in 806, owes its name and early economic development to the local brine springs; the salt harvesters, called 'Halloren', formed the settlement's first guild. From 961 Halle belonged to Magdeburg (an archbishopric from 968). Sovereign princes resided at Halle until 1680 (first at the GIEBICHENSTEIN castle, then from 1503 at the Moritzburg, and from the 1520s also at the 'New Residence'). From c.1513 the town's cultural life began to flourish under Archbishop Albert of Hohenzollern-Brandenburg (1490–1545). In 1680 Halle fell under the dominion of Brandenburg-Prussia. Plague epidemics and fires decimated the population but the influx of reformist refugees from France and from the Palatinate helped to re-establish a prospering economy after 1685. In the mid-nineteenth century Halle developed into a large city because of its coal and potash salt industry; until 1990 it was an important chemical industry location and had as many as 330,000 inhabitants. Today it is the largest city in Saxony-Anhalt (with a population of approximately 240,000), and is regarded as the region's cultural capital.

The Augustinian monastery of Neuwerk was founded north of Halle in 1116 and came to occupy a leading position in the intellectual, spiritual and musical life of the region. When the town council first engaged jugglers and players as Stadtpfeifer in 1461, they had to provide music but were also expected to serve as watchmen: in case of danger, they had to give signals from the Hausmann towers of the Marienkirche (this continued until 1916, and the tradition has now been revived of placing wind players on a bridge linking the towers to play twice a week). In 1520 Albert of Brandenburg founded the so-called Neue Stift on the premises of a former Dominican monastery, and it soon replaced the Neuwerk monastery as most important centre for church music. The Stiftskirche (now the DOM) was an early Gothic hall church, which was remodelled and redecorated in the Renaissance style. In 1531 Albert received a papal privilege authorising him to found a Catholic university in Halle. The Dom provost Michael Vehe (d. 1539) edited *Ein New Gesangbüchlein Geystlicher Lieder* in 1537: one of the earliest printed Catholic songbooks, it also contains songs by the court organist Wolff Heintz (c.1490–c.1552). However, Albert ran into financial difficulties because of his immoderate expenditures, and was forced to leave Halle and dissolve the Neue Stift in 1541. Soon after Halle became Protestant (LUTHERANISM), and Heintz became organist at the newly built church of ST MARIEN (the 'Marktkirche').

In 1565 the three parochial schools of St Marien, St Ulrich and St Moritz were united in the former Franciscan monastery and became the Stadtgymnasium; the school choirs were also united and became the Stadtsingechor, which mainly sang in services at three of the town's principal churches. The choir's *Kantors* were always teachers at the Gymnasium and taught music theory and practice for four hours every week. On special feast days the Stadtsingechor performed solemn church music at the Marktkirche, together with the Stadtpfeifer instrumentalists. The choristers also went around the town singing, which supported their livelihoods.

The Hallensian composer and organist Samuel SCHEIDT worked as court organist from 1609, and from 1619 he was Hofkapellmeister. In 1625 the Hofkapelle was dissolved, and in 1628 Scheidt was employed by the town as *Director musices* until he lost his post two years later because of a dispute with Christian Gueinzius (headmaster of the Gymnasium). Duke August of Saxony became the city's new administrator in 1638, and promoted German-language culture. German operas were performed under Philipp Stolle to celebrate occasions such as ducal weddings and birthdays, and in 1660 David Pohle (1624–95) arrived in Halle and soon became Hofkapellmeister. Duke August inherited the Duchy of Saxe-Weissenfels in 1656 but continued to reside in Halle. Only in 1680 did his descendants leave Halle, which now, according to a provision made in the Peace of Westphalia, belonged to Brandenburg-Prussia. Among the court musicians was the instrumentalist and composer Johann Philipp KRIEGER, who later became Hofkapellmeister at WEISSENFELS.

From 1684 to 1712 Friedrich Wilhelm ZACHOW was organist at the Markt-kirche. A small organ by Georg Reichel (built 1664) was available, but Zachow died by the time a new organ by Christoph Cuntzius – about which J. S. BACH had been asked to give his professional opinion – was inaugurated in 1716. Handel is undoubtedly the most important of Zachow's many pupils: he was born in the house called 'Zum Gelben Hirschen' ('The Yellow Stag') and bap-tised the following day in the Marktkirche. He probably attended the Lutheran Gymnasium (HANDEL, 13) and was taken occasionally to the Weissenfels court by his father.

The city's intellectual and cultural climate at that time was shaped by an aspir-ing bourgeoisie and HALLE UNIVERSITY (founded 1694), which was among the most modern educational institutions in Germany: Handel enrolled in 1702, the year in which he also became organist at the Dom. The reformed church services were rather meagre from a musical point of view, and Handel probably only had to accompany the community songs sung out of the hymnbook by Lobwasser (1573). On Sundays and feast days, however, he also had at his disposal the so-called *Oboisten-Companie* of the Hyntzsch family (Michael Hyntzsch and his son Johann George had formerly been employed as ducal shawm players at the court of Duke August). Even though Handel apparently reminisced that in his Hallensian youth he had composed 'like the Devil', none of his extant works can be dated to this early period of his life with any certainty. In 1703 he permanently left his native town and later only returned to visit.

In 1746 WILHELM FRIEDEMANN BACH took over the post of organist at St Marien from the deceased Gottfried Kirchhoff (a former pupil of Zachow), and held the office until 1764. Later (from 1787) Daniel Gottlob Türk (1750–1813) became the St Marien organist: an esteemed keyboard teacher, he received permission to lecture on music theory and composition at the university in 1779. With the foundation of a Collegium musicum, he introduced a public concert series, and in 1803 directed the first performance of a Handel oratorio in Halle (*MESSIAH* in MOZART's arrangement). He was encouraged in this by Johann Friedrich REICHARDT, who had settled in Giebichenstein after losing his post as Royal Prussian Hofkapellmeister (Reichardt's house became a meeting-point for numerous devotees of literature, music and the sciences). In 1808 Türk became the director of the Stadtsingechor after the Lutheran Gymnasium was dissolved, and taught many pupils including the ballad composer Carl Loewe (1796–1869).

From the nineteenth century Halle developed a reputation for cultivating Handel's music. Music festivals in 1829 and 1830 involved significant oratorio performances, and from 1842 the Singakademie began to flourish under Robert FRANZ, who contributed substantially to the success of the Handel anniversary celebrations in 1859, when a bronze statue of Handel, designed by the BERLIN sculptor Hermann Heidel, was erected in the market square (MONUMENTS). The statue was financed by benefit concerts, among which were performances of *SAMSON, ISRAEL IN EGYPT* and *Messiah*. More anniversary celebrations were held in 1885. The following year a new theatre opened, and was reckoned to be among the most modern in Europe: it had electric lighting and, measured according to contemporary standards, sophisticated stage machinery. It was destroyed in the Second World War but later rebuilt, and is now the city's opera house.

A proper Institute of Musicology at the university was only founded by Hermann Abert in 1913. The first Halle Handel Festival took place in 1922, and included a production of ORLANDO (FESTIVALS, 4). From the mid-1930s the festivals were ideologically distorted by the fact that the Nazis partly used them for propaganda purposes, although in 1937 the city of Halle purchased the house in which Handel was born. It was turned into the Händel-Haus museum (MUSEUMS, 1), although the war delayed its opening until 1948. The Händel-Haus is currently home to the Georg-Friedrich-Händel-Gesellschaft (HANDEL SOCIETIES, 3), the editorial office of the Hallische Händel-Ausgabe (EDITIONS, 7), and the office of the Halle Handel Festival (which became annual in 1952).

KONSTANZE MUSKETA (Trans. ANGELA BAIER)

K. Musketa, *Musikgeschichte der Stadt Halle, Führer durch die Ausstellung des Händel-Hauses* (Halle, 1998)
W. Serauky, *Musikgeschichte der Stadt Halle*, 2 vols. (Halle and Berlin, 1935–42)

Halle University. The university's registers show that Handel enrolled on 10 February 1702, shortly before his seventeenth birthday. The Friedrichs-Universität had been founded eight years previously (on 11 July 1694) after a few years' preparation. Since the university's funds were limited, the erection of new buildings was out of the question. Therefore the city of HALLE provided the old Waage building (1575) on the market square, which had been used up to then for festivals and marriages. Most professors lectured at their own homes, some of which were located in the nearby Große Märkerstraße. Only in 1834 did Halle University receive its own representative college building. The Waage building was destroyed in the last days of the Second World War.

GÖTZ TRAXDORF (Trans. ANGELA BAIER)

Hallelujah Chorus. The concluding movement of Part II of *MESSIAH* is Handel's most famous 'Hallelujah' chorus, though there are several other chorus movements that combine the word with other texts (ALLELUIA, AMEN). A letter from 1780 related an anecdote that the practice of standing for the chorus began at the first London performance of the oratorio in 1743 in the King's presence, at the words 'For the Lord God omnipotent reigneth', but the veracity of this is uncertain. It is possible that the practice began in 1749, when FREDERICK, Prince of Wales, attended a concert at which the FOUNDLING HOSPITAL Anthem (which also concludes with the chorus) was performed (ANTHEMS, 8). In 1750 a member of the audience at one of Handel's performances of *Messiah* noted that 'at some of the chorus's the company stood up'.

DONALD BURROWS

Hallische Händel-Ausgabe (HHA). See EDITIONS, 7

'Haman and Mordecai'. See *ESTHER*

Hamburg. When Handel arrived in Hamburg in 1703, he found a cosmopolitan city which was the equal of any German rivals in its intellectual and cultural life. The city is reputed to have been founded by Charlemagne. The so-called Hammaburg was built on the left bank of the Alster river in 831/2, and tradesmen and craftsmen began to settle underneath the Burg (Castle). The same year saw the establishment of a bishopric which was united with the bishopric of Bremen in 848. In 1188 Count Adolph III of Holstein had a new commercial settlement built on the right bank of the Alster. This new settlement received various privileges such as free shipping on the Elbe, fishing and grazing rights and exemption of the citizens from having to defend their country in arms. The two settlements united in the early thirteenth century. The city's situation near the mouth of the Elbe, and the privileges granted to its inhabitants, encouraged its development into an important commercial and trading centre. There was a substantial economic boom when the city came under the government of the Counts of Schauenburg (from 1227).

In the fourteenth century Hamburg became a member of the Hanseatic League, after which the city successfully defended itself against proliferating piracy in the North Sea. When the last Count of Schauenberg died in 1459, the city, which by now had 15,000 inhabitants, came under the dominion of Denmark. However, the mayor refused to pay tribute to the new territorial masters, which prompted the development of the city's political independence. Although never officially recognised by the Danish, Hamburg's imperial city-state status was eventually granted and made irrevocable in 1618. Until modern times Hamburg successfully conducted and maintained a finely honed diplomatic policy of neutrality.

The city's first public contact with the Lutheran Reformation (LUTHERANISM) in 1523 proved to be of the utmost importance: at first the Council was in opposition but soon the citizens called for taxation of clergy members and independent elections of priests by the parish officials. In February 1529 the *Lange Rezeß*, an official written agreement, fundamentally redesigned the city's constitution, especially the relationship between Council and citizens and their political organs. Part of the *Rezeß* was Johannes Bugenhagen's Lutheran 'Christian Order'. This new order was the basis for the establishment of the municipal church and school administration, and for the organisation and administration of charitable giving to the poor.

In 1536 Hamburg became a member of the Schmalkaldic League, a league of Lutheran cities and rulers opposed to the Counter-Reformationist endeavours of Emperor Charles V. The city's commercial classes had extensive international trading relationships, and many foreigners made their homes in Hamburg. There were especially close ties with the NETHERLANDS and with England. The population had grown to about 40,000 by c.1660. The influx of immigrants, many of them political refugees from various European regions, brought with it new opportunities for trading relationships and technologies as well as general learning and culture. The city's stock exchange was founded in the sixteenth century, and its first bank opened in 1619. Its port became one of the most important trading centres in Europe. Extensive urban development in the first decades of the sixteenth century led to further growth and fortification so that the city was able to resist numerous sieges during the Thirty Years War. The population continued to grow in the following decades so that Hamburg numbered 75,000 inhabitants in 1710. The city's location remained attractive even though participation in self-government was restricted to established Lutheran citizens. Hamburg's political neutrality made it an important diplomatic centre and a popular place of residence and exile for noblemen.

The seventeenth century also saw the beginnings of the city's flourishing cultural life, with music forming an integral part. Houses were designed or rebuilt to modern standards. Scholars prepared students of the Lateinschule Johanneum for university education at the Akademisches Gymnasium (founded 1623). From the seventeenth century onwards Hamburg had its own newspapers, publishing houses and a developing book trade. Musical life was cultivated in religious and municipal institutions and in private settings. The GÄNSEMARKT opera house opened in 1678.

In 1703 Handel left HALLE to pursue a musical career in Hamburg, where he met and befriended Johann MATTHESON, in whose parents' house he often stayed; he played violin and harpsichord in the Gänsemarkt opera orchestra, which at times led to conflict with Mattheson. He also made numerous other contacts, such as Reinhard KEISER and probably Gian Gastone de' MEDICI, and visited BUXTEHUDE at LÜBECK. As an organ virtuoso Handel was presumably attracted by the fine organs in the city's churches (such as the famous instrument at the Maria-Magdalenen-Kirche). Little of Handel's music written in Hamburg has survived. His first setting of the psalm *Laudate Pueri* (HWV 236) might have been composed in the city, and only one of his four operas for the Gänsemarkt opera house survives in an almost extant form (*ALMIRA*).

It is not known if Handel revisited Hamburg during his later continental travels, but he maintained a friendship with its resident Georg Philipp TELEMANN, and perhaps he returned to the city in the autumn of 1750. The Handel scholarship initiated by Friedrich CHRYSANDER gained Hamburg the reputation of an important Handelian centre. UTE POETZSCH (Trans. ANGELA BAIER)

See also Johann Heinrich BROCKES; SOURCES AND COLLECTIONS, 2

F. Kopitzsch, *Grundzüge einer Sozialgeschichte der Aufklärung in Hamburg und Altona*, 2nd edn (Hamburg, 1990)

H.-D. Loose (ed.), *Hamburg. Geschichte der Stadt und ihrer Bewohner*, vol. I: *Von den Anfängen bis zur Reichsgründung* (Hamburg, 1982)

H. J. Marx (ed.), *Händel und Hamburg* (Hamburg, 1985)

D. Schröder, 'Eine Stadt im Wandel: Hamburg am Ende des 17. Jahrhunderts', *Aspekte der Musik des Barock. Aufführungspraxis und Stil*, ed. S. Schmalzriedt (Laaber, 2006)

Hamilton, Newburgh (b. County Tyrone, Ireland, c.1692; bur. St George's, Hanover Square, 19 Sept. 1761). Librettist. Educated at Trinity College, DUBLIN, Hamilton moved to London, where he was the playwright of the farce *The Petticoat-Plotter* (1712) and the comedy *The Doating Lovers* (1715). Neither theatrical venture was successful, but in 1720 his St Cecilia's Day ode *The Power of Musick* was published. It was dedicated to the son of the commander-in-chief of the Pretender's fleet, and from 1725 until at least 1754 Hamilton was employed as steward to the JACOBITE Earl of Strafford (d. 1739), his widow and their son.

In 1736 Hamilton arranged John DRYDEN's ode *ALEXANDER'S FEAST* into recitatives, arias and choruses, and in his WORDBOOK dedication explained that he had been 'determin'd not to take any unwarrantable Liberty' with Dryden's text, and that his principal intention was 'not to lose this favourable Opportunity' of promoting 'the united Labours and utmost Efforts of a *Dryden* and a *Handel*'. However, the text of the last chorus 'Your voices tune' was taken from Hamilton's own *The Power of Musick*, which also provided the source text for the companion piece CECILIA, VOLGI UN SGUARDO (adapted from LOOK DOWN, HARMONIOUS SAINT).

In 1741 Hamilton collaborated with Handel on a skilful adaptation of John MILTON's tragedy *Samson Agonistes* as SAMSON. He dedicated the 1742 first edition of the libretto to FREDERICK, Prince of Wales, who was at that time the figurehead of the patriot opposition against his father and his administration. In his preface, Hamilton stated enthusiastically that in Handel's oratorios 'the Solemnity of Church-Musick is agreeably united with the most pleasing Airs of the Stage', and explained how he had prepared the libretto by abridging Milton's original poem and taking some texts from Milton's other poems and psalm paraphrases. Some of the libretto was composed by Hamilton himself.

The similar method of using old William CONGREVE poems to flesh out SEMELE suggests that Hamilton might have compiled this text for Handel as well. However, the only other verified collaboration between them is the OCCASIONAL ORATORIO (1745/6), which uses verses by Milton and Edmund Spenser as a pro-government prayer for military victory against the Catholic Young Pretender (Charles Edward STUART).

Hamilton called Handel 'my friend' in the preface to *Alexander's Feast*, and it seems that the composer appreciated Hamilton's willingness and ability to accommodate his wishes regarding the adaptations and alterations of texts for his librettos. A long-standing friendship may be assumed from Handel's will, in which he bequested £100 to 'Mr Newburgh Hamilton of Old Bond Street who has assisted me in adjusting words for some of my Compositions' (Deutsch, p. 776) (HANDEL, 8).   HANS DIETER CLAUSEN (Trans. ANGELA BAIER)

Dean, *Oratorios*
R. Loewenthal [— Smith], 'Handel and Newburgh Hamilton. New references in the Strafford
    Papers', MT 112 (1971), 1063–5
Smith, *Oratorios*

Hampton Court. Begun by Cardinal Wolsey, extended by Henry VIII and always appreciated for its consciously old-fashioned picturesqueness. William and Mary commissioned Wren to build two sides of a large new palace which would impress the visitor arriving from London (in a similar manner to CANNONS) by road or river. The palace could accommodate the court and was therefore more than a country retreat with deer parks. There is no evidence that Handel went there, but Queen ANNE's court travelled regularly to Windsor and Hampton Court. GEORGE I commissioned apartments for the Prince of Wales, who as GEORGE II frequented the palace until Queen CAROLINE's death there in 1737; no monarch has lived there since.   KERRY DOWNES

Händel, Christian Gottlieb (b. ?Weissenfels, 1714; d. Copenhagen, ?22 March 1757–4 Aug. 1757). An oboist based at Copenhagen by about 1750, he was the son of the surgeon Georg Christian Händel and grandson of Carl Händel (George Frideric Handel's half-brother from their father Georg Händel's first marriage). Christian was named as a beneficiary of Handel's will dated 1 June 1750 (HANDEL, 8). He was still named in the second codicil dated 22 March 1757, but it seems that he had died by the time that the third codicil was added on 4 August 1757, when he was replaced in the will by his two sisters in Goslar and Pless (Polish: Pszczyna), Silesia. KLAUS-PETER KOCH (Trans. ANGELA BAIER)

See also Appendix 3 – Handel's Family Tree

B. Hofestädt and L. Bense, 'Vom Händelschen Familiensinn', *Die Familie Händel und Halle. Zum Stadtjubiläum 1200 Jahre Halle*, ed. Hallische Familienforscher "Ekkehard" e.V. (Halle, 2006)

Händel, Georg (Handel's father). See HANDEL, 9

Handel, George Frideric

1. Halle and Hamburg (1685–1705)
2. Italy (1706–1710)
3. From Hanover to London (1710–1713)
4. London and the Royal Academy years (1714–1728)
5. The Second Academy and Covent Garden years (1729–1759)
6. Transition and oratorio (1737–1751)
7. Last years (1751–1759)
8. Last Will and Testament
9. Family and relationships
10. Character
11. Sexuality
12. Religion
13. Education
14. Languages and nationality
15. Journeys
16. Health
17. Finances
18. Handel the art collector
19. Handel's library
20. Handel the music teacher
21. Handel's reputation and influence

1. Halle and Hamburg (1685–1705)

Handel was born on 23 February 1685 in a house near the centre of the city of HALLE, to a family with a professional background in medicine and the Church; he was baptised (as Georg Friederich Händel) the following day in the nearby Marktkirche (ST MARIEN). His father, who held offices as a surgeon to the successive Saxon and Prussian courts associated with Halle, had been widowed in 1682; young Georg was a child of his second marriage and his musical training was initiated as a result of a journey with his father to visit his half-brother at the WEISSENFELS court. (This story, and the one concerning Handel's surreptitious practice on a clavichord that had been smuggled into the attic of the family home, derive from John MAINWARING's biography of the composer, published in 1760, which remains the major – if sometimes unreliable – source for the incidents of Handel's early career.) Despite some hesitation from his father, Handel became a pupil of Friedrich Wilhelm ZACHOW, organist of the Marktkirche and a competent composer. A few days before Handel's twelfth birthday, his father died at the age of seventy-five: the previous year, the two may have visited the Prussian court in BERLIN. In 1701 Handel took his first communion at the Marktkirche, and the following year he gained his first professional appointment, as organist to Halle's Domkirche (DOM), which at that time was used by a Calvinist congregation serving Huguenot immigrants. The duties there were fairly light, and compatible with Handel's role of a student at HALLE UNIVERSITY, where he registered (probably to study law) in February 1701. Meanwhile, he developed contacts with musicians in the Halle region, including TELEMANN at Leipzig. It also seems probable that through a network of local connections he made contact with Reinhard KEISER, who had been born near Weissenfels and educated in Leipzig, but was now composer and musical director for the operas in HAMBURG; in the summer of 1703 Handel left Halle, to pursue a musical career there.

At Hamburg he found a new musical friend in Johann MATTHESON, four years his senior, and while waiting for the opening of the next opera season they travelled together to LÜBECK where, probably not entirely seriously, they considered the prospect of succeeding Dieterich BUXTEHUDE in his organist's post. Their friendship was, however, attenuated by professional jealousy as Handel's career advanced. In spring 1704 the opera theatre had closed briefly, and Keiser returned to Weissenfels for a time, leaving the next season in the hands of the younger men. Employed initially as a back-desk violinist, Handel soon assumed a role as accompanist-director from the harpsichord, which on one occasion brought him into physical conflict with Mattheson. He also took up the new libretto of ALMIRA that had been prepared for Keiser, and composed it himself; this came to performance in January 1705, and was followed by operas on two other librettos, one of which proved so extensive that it had to be divided into two (FLORINDO). Only the score of Almira survives in a reasonably complete state. Although no autographs survive, most of Handel's early KEYBOARD MUSIC seems to have been written in Hamburg, some of it possibly in connection with teaching activities.

2. Italy (1706–1710)

Handel's experiences in the Hamburg opera house brought him into contact with a more cosmopolitan European outlook, and he seems to have absorbed new musical influences very quickly. But the new perspectives that opened up, particularly in relation to the modern Italian operatic style, could only be explored to a limited extent in Hamburg, where the situation of the opera company had also changed again on Keiser's return. An Italian visitor to Hamburg suggested that Handel might benefit from a move to ITALY, probably reinforcing what he himself had been thinking for some time. Travelling 'on his own bottom' – that is, without the limitations imposed by attendance on a particular patron – Handel made the journey in the autumn of 1706, though his route and itinerary are uncertain. He was to be based in Italy until early 1710, though it is possible that he made at least one return visit to Hamburg during that time.

In 1707–9 he moved around various musical centres in Italy, as opportunities presented themselves. The best evidence for his activity in these years relates to

ROME, the city which probably formed the base in which he spent the longest time, and from which he made seasonal visits to other places. There was currently no working opera house in Rome, but there were supportive patrons in Marquis (subsequently Prince) RUSPOLI and the Cardinals PAMPHILIJ and OTTOBONI, whose concerts promoted their social and political status in the city community. Thus Handel's creative energies were diverted from opera in the theatre to oratorios in private concert performance: Il TRIONFO DEL TEMPO E DEL DISINGANNO (1707) and La RESURREZIONE (1708) are major works owing much to operatic models. La Resurrezione, performed against a sumptuous and specially constructed scenic background in Ruspoli's Roman palace (PALAZZI), attracted a papal rebuke for the representation of Mary Magdalene by a female singer, who had to be replaced by a castrato for the second performance. Hardly less significant were the regular private concerts for which Handel composed a substantial repertory of continuo-accompanied Italian CANTATAS, effectively short operatic scenes in the mode of pastoral poetry that was then fashionable at Rome. There were also cantatas of a more specifically dramatic nature, with two or more characters represented and a larger instrumental ensemble. The concerts probably also featured Handel as a composer and performer of instrumental music; a few sonatas with solo instruments may have originated at this time, though it seems probable that as a keyboard player he relied on his accumulated repertory and his fluency in improvisation. CORELLI led the orchestra for both of Handel's oratorios, but he was not the only prominent violinist in Rome, where there was a pool of good players for both stringed and woodwind instruments.

In comparison with Almira, the Italian works show that Handel quickly developed a broader and more lyrical style in the composition of arias, with the music of ALESSANDRO SCARLATTI and GASPARINI as particularly powerful influences. Hardly less remarkable, however, is the technical confidence and liveliness that is displayed in the Latin CHURCH MUSIC which he composed in 1707 for church services performed at Ruspoli's country estate of Vignanello near Rome, and for services of the CARMELITE order that were produced under the patronage of Cardinal COLONNA. Dixit Dominus displays a skill in composition for vocal ensembles that had presumably been nurtured in previous musical experience (of which we know nothing specific) at Halle and Hamburg. The performances probably involved a chamber-sized orchestral ensemble and solo vocalists (though on the autograph of one of the Latin psalm settings Handel refers to 'capella'), but nevertheless we find here the first hints of the grand chorus style that would become significant for his later career in London.

Opportunities for opera performance took Handel to FLORENCE (RODRIGO, 1707) and VENICE (AGRIPPINA, 1709). Encouragement from the MEDICI family may have been one of the factors that prompted Handel's move from Hamburg to Italy; Rodrigo was performed under Medici patronage, but it may also mark the end of this relationship. It seems probable that Handel visited Venice for the Carnival season in the years before he was given an opportunity to contribute to the city's operatic programme. According to Mainwaring, Handel's first face-to-face encounter with Alessandro Scarlatti took place in Venice; Mainwaring also relates an anecdote about a contest in keyboard-playing between Handel and DOMENICO SCARLATTI (at which honours were more or less even on the harpsichord, but Handel was recognised as superior on the organ), which he places in Rome, but may have taken place in Venice.

One major southwards excursion from Rome is known: a visit to NAPLES in the summer of 1708, where Handel composed the extended cantata *ACI, GALATEA E POLIFEMO* for a wedding celebration, at least one other Italian cantata and an Italian vocal trio with continuo accompaniment. The journey must have involved some diplomatic finesse, for Naples had been taken by imperial forces in 1707 and was thus on the opposite side from Rome in the current Italian aspect of the War of the SPANISH SUCCESSION. Political alliances are reflected in the cantata-type works that Handel composed in Rome to French and Spanish texts (the latter set with a guitar accompaniment) (SONGS). His close association with Ruspoli in particular made it difficult for him to avoid identification with politically defining events; he even travelled with Ruspoli's entourage on an excursion to the seaport of Civitavecchia, as part of the promotion of a particular naval policy relating to the war.

3. From Hanover to London (1710–1713)
It was probably in Venice that Handel made the personal contacts that would set up the next stages of his career: English visitors who informed him about London's fledgling Italian opera company (OPERA COMPANIES), and representatives from the court of HANOVER who had regular theatre boxes for the opera seasons. *Agrippina* enjoyed a resounding success into the first weeks of 1710, but by then Handel had apparently already decided that he was not going to return to Rome: it seems, indeed, that he regarded the Italian phase of his career as closed, and that he needed now to find an environment that would provide employment suitable to his talents and ambitions. There were several such possibilities at German courts, and he had probably already been approached by Hanover: he was to be found there by the beginning of June, and was appointed Kapellmeister to the Elector on 16 June.

During the 1690s the Hanover court had supported its own Italian opera company, with Agostino STEFFANI as the principal composer; Handel may well have met Steffani, who had now taken up careers in the Church and international diplomacy, in Italy. In 1710 there was no immediate prospect of a revival of the Hanover opera and Handel's musical duties for the court seem to have involved mainly instrumental music and continuo-accompanied Italian CHAMBER DUETS, with an occasional Italian cantata accompanied by the court's chamber orchestra. Soon after Handel's arrival in Hanover the dowager Electress Sophia wrote enthusiastically about Handel's harpsichord playing in a family letter, and referred to a rumour that he had been involved in a love affair with the soprano singer Victoria TARQUINI, who was married to the Hanover court's Konzertmeister (orchestral leader) (FARINEL). Victoria had taken part in recent opera seasons at Venice, presumably with the approval of the Hanover court, and Handel seems to have made a similar arrangement for leave of absence to seek experience as an opera composer elsewhere. A possible opening at DÜSSELDORF came to nothing, but another opportunity in London may have received particular encouragement in Hanover, since the Electoral family stood in prospect of immediate succession to the British throne on the death of Queen ANNE. Less than six months after introducing himself at Hanover, Handel was in London.

The establishment of Italian opera in London had come about through a tortuous series of developments in the theatre companies during the first decade of the eighteenth century, involving rival managers and various venues. By 1710, however, all of the essential elements were in place: a management recognised by the LORD CHAMBERLAIN, a designated venue (the Queen's Theatre in the Haymarket; later the KING'S THEATRE), a good-quality company of singers including a leading Italian CASTRATO, and an established orchestra of about twenty-five players, many of them first-rate musicians from continental Europe. The company had only recently given its first production entirely in Italian. Preparations for Handel's first London opera were fairly lavish, with spectacular scenic effects and a specially written libretto. *RINALDO* was first performed on 6 February 1711 and ran for fifteen performances; Handel had probably returned to his Hanover duties before the run was completed.

The opera house formed a relatively closed community that did not seek close integration with local cultures, even musical ones, but in Hanover Handel made an effort to learn the English language, and on his return to London in 1712 he seems to have formed social relationships with English musicians, in particular the professional singers who served the choirs at the CHAPEL ROYAL, WESTMINSTER ABBEY and ST PAUL'S CATHEDRAL. (The new building at St Paul's was currently approaching a recognisable state of completion.) He also made contacts with influential people associated with the London court, and had even performed before the Queen in a private concert with performers from the opera during his first visit. In parallel with the composition of a couple of new operas, Il *PASTOR FIDO* and *TESEO*, his attention towards the end of 1712 turned towards English church music, in just the same way that his Latin psalms had accommodated the local culture at Rome in 1707. (In terms of religious practice, Handel probably found the Church of England an easier environment than Romanism.) He tried his hand first at an English anthem with organ accompaniment (HWV 251ª), and then in the early months of 1713 he composed an English setting of the Te Deum and Jubilate for voices and orchestra, reinterpreting the spirit of Purcell's famous 'St Cecilia' setting from 1694 in terms of his own grand style. This music was performed at the state Thanksgiving Service for the Peace of Utrecht at St Paul's Cathedral in July 1713, marking an unusual acceptance of a 'foreign' composer for such an occasion. (TE DEUM, I; JUBILATE)

4. London and the Royal Academy years (1714–1728)

The Elector of Hanover acceded as King GEORGE I of Great Britain in August 1714 on the death of Queen Anne. Strictly, Handel's extended period of residence in London had broken the terms of his leave of absence from Hanover, and a pension of £200 per annum granted by Anne in December 1713 seems to have been a recognition that the composer was not planning to resume his career there. It may have taken some time to sort out the formal situation regarding the termination of his Hanover employment, but the new King confirmed the continuation of his British pension and Handel's music was performed in the Chapel Royal at the first Sunday services after the arrival of members of the royal family from Hanover. Although Handel was supported consistently by the Hanoverians, he seems to have remained surprisingly independent of both the benefits and drawbacks of association with the 'German' elements at court, and there is little sign that he received especial royal favour in the early years of George I's reign. His productivity for the opera house was also rather thin, with only one new opera, AMADIGI (1715); the other major composition of these years is the German BROCKES PASSION, apparently supplied from London for performance in Hamburg.

The London opera company suffered gradual attrition through managerial and financial problems, and a dispute between the King and the Prince of Wales (later GEORGE II) in 1717 divided the patronage base, so that it was impossible to continue. Handel was placed in a difficult position both by the elimination of his principal public career and by the situation at court, where choices had to be made between support for the King or the Prince. The WATER MUSIC river party in July 1717 was part of a programme of social assertion on the King's behalf, but Handel probably tried to avoid becoming further involved, and found an alternative base for his activities with a private patron. James Brydges, subsequently Duke of CHANDOS, employed a group of musicians at CANNONS, his estate in Edgware, about 10 miles north-west of central London, and it was here that he took up the composition of English-language works: church music (originally performed at ST LAWRENCE'S church adjoining the Cannons estate) and his first English musical drama, ACIS AND GALATEA (1718). ESTHER, his first English oratorio, was also probably composed for Brydges, though the circumstances are obscure. In 1718 he also probably turned his attention to the preparation of a set of keyboard suites that came to publication in 1720.

During the second half of 1719 the royal dispute proceeded slowly towards a political resolution and moves were afoot to establish a new opera company. The circumstances of Britain's constitutional monarchy did not allow the creation of a 'court opera' on the continental model and the new institution, the Royal Academy of Music, was created within the legal framework of a commercial joint-stock company, authorised by a royal charter giving the right to perform for twenty-one years, and with the King as a major subscriber. Handel was nominated as 'Master of the Orchestra' for the company and was dispatched to Europe to secure the best singers available. His success was incomplete in the short term because many of those he approached, in particular the castrato SENESINO, were already bound by other commitments, but nevertheless sufficient voices were secured for the new company to open in April 1720. The opening production was not Handel's newly composed opera RADAMISTO, but this followed on 27 April, as the first event attended by both the King and the Prince of Wales after their political (though not personal) reconciliation. However, it came near the tail-end of London's theatre season, and by the time the first full season opened the following November Senesino had been incorporated into the company.

The opera seasons of the following years provided the most secure base for Handel's theatre career in London, and he contributed a regular succession of new scores to the repertory, all based on adaptations of LIBRETTOS of operas that had already been set by other composers in Italy. Composition was, however, only one facet of Handel's musical responsibilities with the opera company, as he was also heavily involved with the musical preparation of the productions. Furthermore, in the early years he had to share his role with other London-based composers, including Giovanni BONONCINI, though he gradually emerged as the dominant figure. The years 1723–5 saw a particularly rich crop of new opera scores from him – *TAMERLANO, GIULIO CESARE* and *RODELINDA*. Various other events from the same period indicate that his long-term career was now settled in London: in July 1723 he moved into the London house in Brook Street that was to be his home for the remainder of his life (MUSEUMS, 2), and earlier the same year he had been appointed Composer to the Chapel Royal, a largely honorific office that carried another £200 pension, to which a further £200 was added for his role as music master to the royal princesses. There were no public events in the later years of George I's reign that required large state celebrations: Handel's compositions for the Chapel Royal were for Sunday services marking the King's safe return from visits to Hanover. The death of the King on his way to Hanover in June 1727 did not substantially alter Handel's position, since he remained in favour with his successor, and indeed re-established his wider public reputation with the four anthems for the CORONATION of King George II and Queen CAROLINE in October 1727 (ANTHEMS, 3). In spite of his title as Chapel Royal Composer, Handel's leading participation in this event might have been in some doubt but for a number of contributory circumstances, including the death of the senior English Chapel Royal Composer William CROFT in the summer of 1727, and Handel's inclusion in an Act of Naturalisation in February, by which he had become a British subject.

By the time of the coronation, however, the opera company was beginning to face serious trouble. It had exhausted its initial financial capital, and the novelty of the opera genre had faded. Audience interest focused on the performers rather than the operas themselves, which brought its own problems. Senesino was still the leading man, but satirical complaints about expensive foreign singers and 'foreign opera' were growing in strength, and were to appear among the peripheral targets of *The BEGGAR'S OPERA*. The company had been well served by a succession of leading ladies: Margherita DURASTANTI in the early years and then Francesca CUZZONI. In 1726 Cuzzoni was joined by another soprano, FAUSTINA Bordoni, and Handel's scores took full advantage of the opportunities provided by two ladies with contrasted personalities. However, the sopranos generated partisan rivalry among members of the audience which led to disorders that even closed the theatre at one performance in June 1727 – though, as it happened, on a night when the repertory opera was by Bononcini (RIVAL QUEENS). After one more season the Royal Academy in its original form came to an end, having apparently run its course; an attempt to set up a further opera season for 1728–9 came to nothing.

5. The Second Academy and Covent Garden years (1729–1737)

Not surprisingly, those most closely affected by the collapse of the opera company were reluctant to accept the situation as final. Handel was faced with the potential collapse of his central career in London and John Jacob HEIDEGGER, the manager of the KING'S THEATRE, was left with a useless building. The two men therefore collaborated in a scheme to revive the opera company under their own management, and secured the essential physical elements: the right to use the theatre (granted for five years) and the stock of scenery and costumes that was the accumulated property of the Royal Academy. (The Academy as a legal entity continued for its full span, and was the nominal recipient of the annual royal bounty.) Early in 1729 Handel set off for Italy to collect a new group of singers: he was unsuccessful in his reputed quest to sign FARINELLI, but he assembled a serviceable company around the castrato BERNACCHI, the soprano STRADA and the tenor FABRI. The King's Theatre season under the new management opened on 2 December: for the season Handel composed two new operas (*LOTARIO* and *PARTENOPE*) and filled out the season's repertory with revivals of his own operas, supplemented by the pasticcio *ORMISDA* in which he drew on music by various contemporary composers, including LEO, VINCI and HASSE.

The second season saw the return of Senesino and a continuation of the same type of repertory programme. Just before the end of 1730 Handel's mother died, severing a direct link with the past, but he maintained correspondence with the family through his brother-in-law. The company survived two further seasons, and the bass MONTAGNANA was added to the company, but once again the impetus gradually flagged and tensions mounted between Handel and his performers. New operas were introduced, but the most significant development was the introduction of *Esther* and *Acis and Galatea* in concert-style performances on the end of the 1731–2 opera season; a new oratorio, *DEBORAH*, was one of the new offerings in the following season. By then, however, the Handel–Heidegger management was facing serious difficulties from the formation of a rival opera company supported by younger opera patrons and FREDERICK, Prince of Wales. On the last night of the 1732–3 season Senesino announced his intention to transfer to the other company, and it transpired that the OPERA OF THE NOBILITY had drawn away all of the major singers apart from Strada. Handel, however, found some short-term consolation in a successful series of performances at OXFORD during the University's 'Act' celebrations in July 1733, giving an all-English programme comprising *Esther*, *Deborah*, *Acis and Galatea* and his new oratorio *ATHALIA*.

Handel was left with one further season at the King's Theatre and managed to assemble a creditable cast, including the castrato Giovanni CARESTINI, with whom he presented a full programme including the new opera *ARIANNA IN CRETA*, probably in conscious response to an 'Arianna' opera by PORPORA which the rival company gave at LINCOLN'S INN FIELDS Theatre. His other major new stage work of the season, *PARNASSO IN FESTA* was a full-length operatic-style serenata in celebration of the wedding of Princess ANNE (the King's eldest daughter, and Handel's pupil) to Prince William of Orange; he also contributed an anthem to the wedding ceremony, as the first of a series of anthems for events in the royal family during the 1730s (ANTHEMS, 4). By the end of the 1734–5 season Handel had come to an agreement with the theatre manager John RICH, enabling him to present operas at Rich's new theatre in COVENT GARDEN. Adding the young English tenor John BEARD to his existing cast based on Carestini and Strada, he produced an attractive season including the new operas *ARIODANTE* and *ARIANNA*, making good use of Covent Garden's troupe of dancers (led by Marie SALLÉ); the opera performances had, however, to be interleaved with the theatre's regular repertory of plays. In March and April 1735 he diversified the programme with a substantial run of oratorios, accompanied by the new attraction of organ concertos. The rival company now held London's regular opera theatre, and added to their competitive advantage by expanding their cast with the return to London of Cuzzoni and, above all, the incorporation of Farinelli along with Senesino. Two further seasons of messy competition followed. In 1735–6 Handel could not initially assemble a viable Italian opera company; he eventually began performances in February 1736 with English concert works, including a new setting of DRYDEN's ode ALEXANDER'S FEAST, and eventually managed to run a short series of operas featuring a new young castrato, Gioacchino CONTI. The new opera was ATALANTA, for the wedding season of the Prince of Wales: once again Handel also provided the anthem for the wedding, but the Prince did not attend Handel's opera. For the 1736–7 season Handel composed three new operas (ARMINIO, GIUSTINO and BERENICE) and presented an ambitious programme; towards the end of the season his health suffered and he had to travel to the continent for a cure. Meanwhile, the publication of a handsome full score of *Alexander's Feast* had made one of his English works unusually accessible to the musical public, and two events in 1738–9 indicated a remarkable broadening in the appeal of Handel's music beyond the opera house: the statue of the composer at VAUXHALL GARDENS, and his portrait in Hickford's new concert room.

6. Transition and oratorio (1737–1751)

By the summer of 1737 the future of Italian opera in London was uncertain: Farinelli and Senesino left, never to return, and Handel's friends were anxious about his capacity to continue his former lifestyle. An opera cast was created from the remnants of the Nobility company and a group of opera patrons, mainly from the Nobility group, managed to run a season at the King's Theatre in 1737–8, commissioning two opera scores from Handel. SERSE and FARAMONDO were performed in 1738, but it is doubtful that the composer had much to do with the performances. The writing of the scores, interleaved with the anthem for the funeral of Queen Caroline (ANTHEMS, 5) which took place at Westminster Abbey on 17 December 1737, showed, however, that he had regained his physical stamina as a composer.

The opera subscription failed for 1738–9, and there followed three rather ragged seasons in which Handel performed whatever repertory his circumstances allowed, while the opera directors, now led by Lord MIDDLESEX, attempted to maintain some performances but did not have resources for a proper opera programme. Handel took the King's Theatre himself for a series of oratorio-style performances beginning in January 1739, featuring two major new oratorios, SAUL and ISRAEL IN EGYPT. By the end of the season in May these had been accompanied by revivals of *Alexander's Feast* and a new version of his Italian oratorio *Il trionfo del Tempo*; when a couple of newly arrived Italian sopranos were added to the cast there was even something approaching an opera in GIOVE IN ARGO, a 'dramatical composition' in Italian that may have been semi-staged. For the next two seasons Handel moved to Rich's old theatre at Lincoln's Inn Field. In 1739–40 he for the first time gave an all-English programme (including his new setting of Dryden's SONG FOR ST CECILIA and the MILTON-derived L'ALLEGRO, IL PENSEROSO ED IL MODERATO), but this was largely by default, since he did not have the cast for Italian operas: in 1740–1, when he did have suitable singers, he reverted to a mixed Italian/English programme, productions of the new operas IMENEO and DEIDAMIA being interleaved with revivals of English oratorios. Imeneo had in fact been drafted in September 1738, but its production was delayed by the unpropitious circumstances of the ensuing seasons. With Deidamia on 10 February (performed, for some reason, at the LITTLE THEATRE in the Haymarket) Handel gave his last performance of an Italian opera in London. His persistence no doubt reflected his own lingering attachment to the genre, but he may also have felt some personal obligation in view of his involvement with the foundation of the Royal Academy of Music, with its brief to perform operas for twenty-one years. By the summer of 1741 the Middlesex group had at last managed to set up a new company of their own to restore a full Italian opera season at the King's Theatre.

Between 22 August and 29 October 1741 Handel drafted two major new oratorio scores, MESSIAH and SAMSON, most likely in anticipation of the next London season, but his plans were modified by an invitation to perform in DUBLIN, at a new music room inaugurated by a concert society. He left the score of Samson unfinished, and attended (with some amusement) the Middlesex company's first performance before setting off for Dublin, where his first subscription series of six English oratorio-type works, beginning on 23 December, was well received. He presented a second series, incorporating two performances of Imeneo (probably in a concert format) with the English works, possibly stimulated by a new situation that arose when the actress Susannah CIBBER was added to his company. In Dublin he found a workable group of orchestral musicians but had some difficulty with the ecclesiastical authorities over the employment of singers from the cathedral choirs; the restrictions were relaxed, however, with a charity performance that he initiated after the completion of the second subscription, at which Messiah received its first performance.

Back in London in the autumn of 1742, Handel talked of returning to Dublin (though he never did so) and was guarded about revealing his immediate plans, but he made an arrangement with John Rich for a season of oratorio performances at Covent Garden in 1743, concentrating his performing nights on the Wednesdays and Fridays during Lent, when plays were not performed, and repeating the Dublin scheme of six-performance subscriptions. He managed two successful subscriptions, with Samson (which had not been given in Dublin) as the major attraction; the inclusion of Messiah attracted some controversy in the newspapers, and also some criticism from the librettist Charles JENNENS, which may have contributed to a recurrence of Handel's medical disorder. However, by the summer he had returned to his routine, composing two major scores (SEMELE and JOSEPH AND HIS BRETHREN) in anticipation of another Covent Garden season in 1744, along with a Te Deum and an anthem intended for the celebration of the military victory at DETTINGEN, though in fact that event had long passed by the time the occasion for the performance arose (ANTHEMS, 6; TE DEUM, 5). He was approached by the opera directors and initially indicated some willingness to compose for them, but eventually decided against this, though he seems to have made his old score of ALESSANDRO available to them. His persistence in pursuing independent performances seems to have exacerbated the already difficult relations with the opera supporters, especially since the 'Middlesex' project was again approaching financial and artistic exhaustion.

When the opera company failed in the summer of 1744, Handel took the King's Theatre himself and planned an extensive season, to include BELSHAZZAR and HERCULES as the new scores, with twenty-four performances of English works beginning in November 1744. This scheme proved over-ambitious, and was undermined by opposition from the 'opera party': some of the early performances were cancelled, and in January 1745 Handel announced his intention to abandon the season: however, enough support was forthcoming to enable his performances to struggle on as far as April, with sixteen concerts in all. From the summer of 1745 all plans were disrupted by the JACOBITE rebellion, though the re-formed Middlesex company resumed operas at the King's Theatre (with GLUCK as a house composer) in January 1746, and in February Handel gave three performances of his OCCASIONAL ORATORIO at Covent Garden in order to compensate the shortfall on the previous season. He then returned to the general plan that had worked in 1743 and 1744, of giving English works at Covent Garden on the available nights of Lent, but now with individual ticket entry rather than subscriptions. JUDAS MACCABAEUS met with sufficient success in 1747: further Lenten repertory seasons followed in 1748 and 1749, with JOSHUA, ALEXANDER BALUS, SUSANNA and SOLOMON as the new works.

The end of the oratorio season in March 1749 was followed by two other major events about a month apart. In April the London celebrations for the peace of Aix-la-Chapelle (War of the AUSTRIAN SUCCESSION) involved Handel in his last music for the Chapel Royal (HWV 266) and, more publicly, the provision of MUSIC FOR THE ROYAL FIREWORKS in GREEN PARK: although estimates vary, there is no doubt that the latter occasion, with the preceding rehearsal in Vauxhall Gardens, resulted in the largest audience of his career. Soon after that, he offered a concert performance to the FOUNDLING HOSPITAL, a charity for the 'maintenance and education of exposed and deserted young children' that had been inaugurated ten years previously and was currently involved in a large building programme. The concert, held in the Hospital's as yet unfinished chapel and in the presence of the Prince of Wales, took place on 27 May: the programme included the Fireworks Music and the 'Foundling Hospital Anthem' (ANTHEMS, 8). Handel followed up the concert by offering to present an organ to the Hospital and a year later, after the end of the Covent Garden oratorio season, he marked the 'opening' of the organ with a performance of Messiah in the chapel. The organ itself was not completed in time, but the demand for tickets was such that the Messiah performance had to be repeated a fortnight later. Thus started a pattern that was to be repeated throughout the last decade of Handel's life: the Lenten season of oratorios at Covent Garden, followed by one or two performances of Messiah at the Hospital after Easter.

In the 1750 oratorio season Handel had presented one new oratorio, THEODORA; in the summer he reworked and supplemented some incidental music that he had written for a planned production of SMOLLETT's play ALCESTE at Covent Garden, into a one-act drama The CHOICE OF HERCULES, ready for the next oratorio season. Then he left London for what was to become his last visit to the continent; he had also made his will on 1 June. He was involved as a passenger in a coach accident abroad, but apparently recovered quickly, and was reported as playing the organ to the Prince and Princess of Orange at The Hague (NETHERLANDS). He was back in London by December, when he took up a correspondence with Telemann in Hamburg; in the first days of 1751 he composed a new organ concerto and on 21 January began the score of his major new oratorio for the forthcoming season.

7. Last years (1751–1759)

The 1751 oratorio season began on 22 February, but by then Handel had only composed half of the score of JEPHTHA, which he had laid aside because of problems with his eyesight. The season was curtailed on account of the closure of the London theatres following the death of the Prince of Wales in March, though by then Handel had performed The Choice of Hercules. There were reports that Handel had lost his sight in one eye, but he managed to give two performances of Messiah at the Foundling Hospital, and in early June he travelled to BATH hoping to improve his health. On his return to London he managed to finish Jephtha, but in circumstances of difficulty, and J. C. SMITH junior was invited back to assist with the management of his future oratorio seasons. The 1752 season included Jephtha, and the only other musical autograph from this time is a page of revisions to an aria from Joshua: with quickly deteriorating eyesight and a return of his 'paralytic disorder', Handel's creative days were over, at least on paper (see Figure 10 for the last portrait of him, painted in 1756 after he had gone completely blind). The routines of the annual oratorio seasons were maintained; from time to time Handel is reported as performing on the organ at the performances, or taking some part in the management of the singers. Various new movements were added to the oratorio scores, but his involvement in their composition is uncertain. It seems probable that there were times when he was more active and could take some part in suggesting or initiating new musical developments, for example in the early months of 1757, when a final and expanded English version of his first Italian oratorio was produced as The TRIUMPH OF TIME AND TRUTH for that year's oratorio season. On the whole, however, the existing repertory provided enough works to fill the Lenten seasons. In 1759 Handel managed to attend at least some of the oratorio season, which concluded with Messiah on 6 April. He planned to travel to Bath, but was too ill to do so; he died at his house in Brook Street on 14 April and was buried at Westminster Abbey six days later. He left a considerable estate, which was distributed according to the provisions of his will and the subsequent codicils: among the bequests added a few days before his death was £1,000 to the FUND FOR THE SUPPORT OF DECAY'D MUSICIANS AND THEIR FAMILIES.

DONALD BURROWS

8. Last Will and Testament

Handel wrote his will on 1 June 1750 (see Figure 11). He remembered family members in Germany, named his niece Johanna Friederike Flörcke (HANDEL, 9) as executor, and left significant gifts to Peter LeBlond (his manservant), John Christopher SMITH SENIOR, and James HUNTER. Four codicils dictated and signed by him (6 August 1756, 22 March 1757, 4 August 1757 and

10. A portrait of Handel by Thomas Hudson, oil on canvas, 1756.

11 April 1759) amend and expand the original document. In the first three, he appointed George AMYAND, a London merchant with HAMBURG connections, co-executor with his niece; adjusted for the death of his 'old servant' Peter LeBlond; and bequeathed paintings from his collection (HANDEL, 18) to Charles JENNENS and Bernard GRANVILLE, as well as a fair copy of the score and parts of *MESSIAH* to the FOUNDLING HOSPITAL. Three days before his death, Handel added bequests to those who helped prepare the codicils and to others who assisted him in his final illness, and he remembered neighbours and friends. He also made a gift to the FUND FOR THE SUPPORT OF DECAY'D MUSICIANS AND THEIR FAMILIES, and asked permission of the Dean and Chapter of Westminster to be buried in WESTMINSTER ABBEY, leaving 'not more than' £600 for a monument. The will was proved in the Prerogative Court of Canterbury on 26 April 1759. The legatees were:

Servants
    Peter LeBlond ('clothes and linnen' and £500, predeceased Handel)
    John DuBURK ('all my wearing apparel' and £500)
    Thomas Bramwell (£100)
    Other servants ('a year wages')

I give and bequeath to my Cousin Christian Gottlieb Handel of Coppenhagen one hundred Pounds sterl:

Item I give and bequeath to my Cousin Magister Christia[n] August Rotth of Halle in Saxony one hundred Pounds sterl:

Item I give and bequeath to my Cousin the Widow of George Taust, Pastor of Giebichenstein near Halle in Saxony three hundred Pounds sterl: and to Her six Children each two hundred Pounds sterl: All the rest and residue of my Estate in Bank Annuitys or of whatsoever kind or Nature, I give and bequeath unto my Dear Niece Johanna Friderica Flöerken of Gotha in Saxony (born Michaelsen in Halle) whom I make my Sole Execut.rix of this my last Will. In witness Whereof I have hereunto set my hand this 1 Day of June 1750

George Frideric Handel

11. Handel's will, dated 1 June 1750.

German family and friends

Christian Gottlieb HÄNDEL (£300, predeceased Handel)

Sisters of Christian Händel: Christiana Susanna Handel (£300) and sister at Pless (£300)

Christian August Rotth (£100, predeceased Handel)

Widow Rotth or her surviving children (£200)

Widow Taust (£300, predeceased Handel)

Taust children (£300 each [4])

Johanna Friderica Flörcke (residuary legatee)

Professional colleagues and contacts

Christopher Smith (large harpsichord, little house organ and £500)

John RICH (great organ)

Thomas MORELL (£200)
Newburgh HAMILTON (£100)
Charles Jennens (paintings)
Matthew DUBOURG (£100)
Society for Decayed Musicians (£1,000)
Mr. REICHE, Secretary for the affairs of Hanover (£200)
Foundling Hospital (copy of score and parts to *Messiah*)
Westminster monument (£600)

Witnesses of will
George Amyand (£400)
Thomas HARRIS (£300)
John Hetherington (£100)

Surgeon
John BELCHIER (£50)

Friends and neighbours
James Hunter (£500, predeceased Handel)
James SMYTH (£500)
Benjamin MARTYN (50 guineas)
John GOWLAND (apothecary) (£50)
Mrs. PALMER (£100)
Mrs. MAYNE (50 guineas)
Mrs. DONELLAN (50 guineas)
Bernard Granville (paintings)

ELLEN T. HARRIS

D. Burrows (ed.), *Handel's Will: Facsimiles and Commentary* (London, 2009)
The National Archives, PROB 11/845 (Prerogative Court of Canterbury Copy)
The National Archives, PROB 1/14 (autograph copy)
Royal College of Music, MSS 2190–2 (original papers relating to the final distribution to
   Handel's German relatives)
W. C. Smith, 'More Handeliana', ML 34/1 (1953), 11–24

9. Family and relationships

Handel's direct ancestors originally hail from Breslau (now Wrocław, Poland). Since Handel's great-great-grandfather (Valten Händel, fl. 1544) the family had traditionally been blacksmiths and coppersmiths. Whereas the great-grandfather Valentin senior still worked in Breslau, Handel's grandfather Valentin junior (1582–1636) emigrated to the West: he lived in Eisleben until 1608 and then moved to HALLE in 1609. Valentin had five sons (Valentin, Christoph, Samuel, Gottfried and Georg) and a daughter (Barbara), all of whom lived in Halle. Christoph's daughter married the musician Cyriakus BERGER, and Barbara's daughter the musician Christoph Conrad RÜDEL.

Georg Händel (b. 24 Sept. 1622; d. 14 Feb. 1697) became a surgeon and barber. After years as an apprentice and journeyman which took him to northern Germany and even as far as Portugal, he returned to Halle in 1642 and married Anna Oettinger (a surgeon's widow) in 1643. He became a citizen of Halle in 1643, and two years later was appointed as the departmental surgeon of Giebichenstein by the Halle-based administrator of the Archbishopric of Magdeburg, Duke

August of Saxe-Weissenfels (r. 1638–80). Due to his medical skills he became *Geheimer Kammerdiener* (private valet) and *Leibchirurg* (personal surgeon) of the Duke in 1660. He lost his positions when the Archbishopric of Magdeburg fell to the House of Brandenburg in 1680, but the Elector awarded him a pension for life after he distinguished himself as a doctor during years of plague (1681–3), and he was appointed *Leibchirurg* in 1688 by Duke JOHANN ADOLF I of Saxe-Weissenfels (the son of the last administrator). In 1683, after the death of his first wife, with whom he had three sons (Gottfried, Christoph, Carl) and three daughters (Dorothea Elisabeth, Anna Barbara, Sophie Rosina) he married Dorothea Taust (1651–1730), a clergyman's daughter who bore him two more sons – among them George Frideric Handel – and two daughters (Dorothea Sophie, Johanna Christiana). A granddaughter from his first marriage, Maria Sophia Pfersdorff, later married Caspar Mangold (d. 1725), and their son was Georg Caspar MANGOLD.

When his father died in 1697, Handel still had living half-siblings from his father's first marriage: Carl, *Kammerdiener* and *Leibchirurg* in WEISSENFELS, and Sophie Rosina Pfersdorff, née Händel, who lived in Langendorf near Weissenfels. His two natural sisters, Dorothea Sophia Michaelsen, née Händel, and Johanna Christiana, lived in Halle. All of the sisters and half-sisters were dead by 1728. Handel's mother, whom he had visited on various occasions during his stays in Germany, died in 1730. Handel returned to his native city in 1710, 1711, 1716, 1719, 1729 and probably in 1750. He corresponded with his brother-in-law, the lawyer Michael Dietrich Michaelsen (1681–1748), husband of Handel's sister Dorothea Sophia (d. 1718), until shortly before Michaelsen's death. He remained in contact also with the Taust family, his mother's relations. The original version of his will dated 1750 included among the beneficiaries his nephews Christian Gottlieb HÄNDEL (a Copenhagen oboist) and *Magister* Christian August Rotth in Halle, Dorothea Elisabeth Taust, née Pfersdorff (widow of Georg Taust, Handel's maternal uncle) and her six children, and especially his niece Johanna Friederica Flörcke, née Michaelsen (1711–71) in Gotha.

Descendants of Handel's family still live in Halle and its surrounding area, and have spread to Goslar in Lower Saxony, Pirmasens in the Rhineland-Palatinate and Pless in Silesia.   KLAUS-PETER KOCH (Trans. ANGELA BAIER)

See also Appendix 3: Handel's Family Tree

L. Bense, 'Neue Erkenntnisse zu den verwandtschaftlichen Zusammenhängen zwischen den Familien Taust, Rotth und Händel', *Ekkehard* 2 (1995)
  'Georg Friedrich Händels Mutter: Dorothea Händel geb. Taust (10. Februar 1651 Dieskau – 27. Dezember 1730 Halle)', *Händel-Hausmitteilungen* 2 (2005), 11–17; 1 (2006), 15–20
Die Familie Händel und Halle. Zum Stadtjubiläum 1200 Jahre Halle, ed. Hallische Familienforscher "Ekkehard" e. V. (Halle, 2006)
K.-P. Koch, 'Handel's German Relatives', *Handel's Will: Facsimiles and Commentary'*, ed. D. Burrows (London, 2009)
W. Piechocki, 'Die Familie Händel in der Stadt Halle. 1. Der Kupferschmied Valentin Händel (1582–1636)', *HJb* 33 (1987)
  'Die Familie Händel in der Stadt Halle. 2. Der Wundarzt Georg Händel (1622–1697)', *HJb* 36 (1990)
Stadtarchiv Halle (ed.), *Georg Friedrich Händel, Abstammung und Jugendwelt* (Halle, 1935)

10. Character

Mainwaring points to Handel's 'noble spirit of independency, which possessed him almost from his childhood, [and] was never known to forsake him, not even in the most distressful seasons of his life'. 'Independency' does not fit with what we know about Handel's completion of obligations and his unwillingness to jump at the latest offer. He served out his contracted time at Halle, at Hamburg and at Florence before moving on to the next assignment. His employment by the Hanoverians and travel to London were not just career moves on his part.

If this characterisation of 'independency' is Handel's own, it is a deliberate falsehood or wishful thinking. Without the active support of royal and noble patrons, Handel's life and career would not have been successful, profitable or pleasant. If the characterisation is Mainwaring's, we should regard it as a narrative device or theme that allows him to foreshadow, to highlight the image of the solitary artistic genius, and also to excuse actions or attitudes that could as readily be described as stubborn, arrogant, self-important or wrong.

As Mainwaring notes concerning Handel's relationship with Senesino, Handel created and prolonged enmities when he did not need to, notably among performers but also among friends of long standing, such as Joseph GOUPY and John Christopher Smith senior. Able to speak and write in four languages (HANDEL, 14), and be humorous and curse in all of them, he seems to have been unwilling to flatter.

BURNEY, who worked with Handel in the 1740s, reported that 'Handel wore an enormous white wig, and, when things went well at the Oratorio, it had a certain nod, or vibration, which manifested his pleasure and satisfaction. Without it, nice observers were certain he was out of humour.' Confirming the serious cast Handel's face usually assumed, Burney wrote that 'Handel's general look was somewhat heavy and sour; but when he *did* smile, it was his sire the sun, bursting out of a black cloud. There was a sudden flash of intelligence, wit, and good humour, beaming out of his countenance, which I hardly ever saw in any other.'

Though as a lover Handel apparently romanced the singer Vittoria Tarquini while in Italy and was interested enough in two other women for marriage to be discussed with their families (according to COXE), he remained single. Whether this should be explained as a lack of sociability or a fear of commitment, as the result of the demands of his profession, or, as has been suggested more recently, due to a homosexual predisposition, cannot at present be determined.

DAVID HUNTER

11. Sexuality

Handel was a lifelong bachelor, which later biographers justified or rationalised in various ways on the grounds of his devotion to music or lack of social affections.

In the climate of gay studies in the 1990s, scholars began enquiring into the sexuality of artists and musicians, often for ulterior political reasons. Although they tentatively included Handel among the homosocial or homosexual men of eighteenth-century England, the claim that he was a gay man gained public notice in a 1990 lecture and later published essay by Gary Thomas. Thomas interrogated statements of Handel's biographers and interpreted their avoidance of the discussion of Handel's sexuality as evidence the biographers were hiding the fact Handel was gay; biographical evidence about those associated with the circle of Lord BURLINGTON in the years 1715–18 was claimed to indicate Handel was part of a homosexual circle at BURLINGTON HOUSE and Chiswick. Ellen Harris followed up Thomas's claim in *Handel as Orpheus* (2001), in which she avoids claiming that Handel was gay, but asserts contemporaries 'associated' him with homosexuality through comparisons with Orpheus, and that there are homosexual allusions or association in texts he set to music.

Thomas's biographical claims about the sexual orientation of persons at Burlington House and Chiswick are refuted by readily available documentary evidence; and no amount of homosexual readings of literary texts can overcome the fact that there is no evidence at all of Handel's homosexual orientation or contemporaries' awareness of it. Contrary to Thomas and Harris's statements, contemporaries were not reluctant to discuss sodomy or Handel's sexuality, and several anecdotes report Handel had mistresses, including a report that reached the Hanoverian court in 1710 of an affair in Italy with the singer Vittoria TARQUINI.

THOMAS N. MCGEARY

C. Burney, 'Sketch of the Life of Handel', in *An Account of the Musical Performances in Westminster Abbey and the Pantheon . . . in Commemoration of Handel* (London, 1785)

E. T. Harris, *Handel as Orpheus: Voice and Desire in the Chamber Cantatas* (Cambridge, MA, 2001)

G. C. Thomas, '"Was George Frideric Handel Gay?" On Closet Questions and Cultural Politics', *Queering the Pitch: The New Gay and Lesbian Musicology*, ed. P. Brett, E. Wood and G. C. Thomas (New York, 1994)

12. Religion

Religion was a defining element of identity and citizenship in Handel's worlds. Descended on his mother's side from Lutheran pastors and theologians, Handel grew up in an increasingly tolerant and religiously diverse society. Huguenot and Calvinist refugees could settle in Halle and Jews were readmitted in 1692. Halle and its university (founded 1694) were enriched by the teaching of the internationally influential pietist A. H. Francke and humanist jurist Christian Thomasius. However the scope of Handel's first job, at the Domkirche, was restricted because the congregation was predominantly Calvinist. According to Mainwaring (pp. 64–5), in Italy efforts were made to convert Handel to Catholicism, but 'he replied, that he . . . was resolved to die a member of that communion, whether true or false, in which he was born and bred', and he also refused mere 'outward conformity'. British naturalisation required conformity to Anglicanism, 'which he was not such a bigot as to decline', while 'he would often speak of it as one of the great felicities of his life that he was settled in a country where no man suffers any molestation or inconvenience on account of his religious principles' (Hawkins, vol. 2, pp. 910–11). He left no explicit verbal testimony to his faith, but according to HAWKINS, throughout his life he manifested 'a deep sense of religion', and in his final years could regularly be seen at ST GEORGE'S Hanover Square 'on his knees, expressing by his looks and gesticulations the utmost fervour of devotion'.

RUTH SMITH

See also BIBLE; CHURCH OF ENGLAND; DEISM; LUTHERANISM; NONCON-FORMITY

13. Education

The musical tuition that Handel received from ZACHOW in Halle included training in composition as well as in organ-playing: according to Mainwaring, 'he shewed him the different styles of different nations . . . and, that he might equally advance in the practical part, he frequently gave him subjects to work, and made him copy, and play, and compose in his head'. In addition to learning keyboard skills (applicable to harpsichord and clavichord as well as organ), Handel seems to have become proficient on the violin, and possibly also the oboe. Of his general school education in Halle we have no specific details (STADTGYMNASIUM), but it provided him with sufficient grounding to sign on as a student at the University in 1702; it seems probable that his parents had provided a supportive environment for his education, expecting that he would follow a professional career, most likely in Civil Law. Circumstantial evidence from later in his career suggests a lively critical interest in literature. Halle was a flourishing intellectual centre at the time: the new university gained a reputation for progressive thinking in theology, philosophy and the law under the leadership of Christian Thomasius, sometimes involving lively controversy with August Hermann Francke, a pietistic pastor who was Professor of Theology and Classical Languages. Francke also founded a complex of schools, the buildings for which, near the city centre, were under construction during Handel's youth: these included a charity school that Handel would have remembered later in life during his association with the Foundling Hospital.

14. Languages and nationality

By the time he registered as a student at Halle University, Handel probably already had some fluency in Latin and French as well as German; Italian was acquired in Hamburg and in Italy itself, and in a letter written (in French) during his return visit to Hanover in 1711–12 Handel mentioned that he had 'made some progress' with the English language. According to one eighteenth-century description, when conversing with Handel 'it was requisite for the hearer to have a competent knowledge of at least four languages: English, French, Italian and German; for in his narratives he made use of them all' (Dr Quin to Burney, 16 July 1788). His surviving letters in English, French and German are idiomatic, and his treatment of Italian texts in his operas indicates an intimate understanding of their content and expression. This versatility no doubt contributed to the success of his career: French was the formal language of European courts, while Italian and English were the languages of the main genres in which he composed, and the principal languages of the performers with whom he had professional day-to-day business. He may have retained some German inflection in his speech, but many anecdotes about his pronunciation of English are clearly caricatures. He had an 'ear' for language, as for music, and some of his letters reflect the lively and humorous manner that some contemporaries described.

Though born at a time when Halle was in Prussian territory, he referred in his will to 'Halle in Sachsen', and probably regarded the identity of his parentage as 'Saxon'. His legal status was changed by the inclusion of his name in a Naturalisation Act of 1727, by which he became a British subject. At this point he chose his nation, and he was already established as a Londoner, but he

Based on *Charte fuer die Geschichte der Jahre 1660–1722*/draft by J. Rupp, lithography by W. Winckler

* Handel is alleged to have visited these places, but there is no hard evidence

12. Map of places Handel visited.

remained open to, and in contact with, European influences that maintained the breadth of his outlook.

DONALD BURROWS

15. Journeys

Handel travelled for the same reasons we do today (education, employment, family and friends, health), though he was one of very few in his day for whom international travel was necessary and could be afforded (see Figure 12). His first visits beyond the borders of the Electorate were to the German cities of BERLIN (?1696, ?1697, ?1702) and HAMBURG (1703). Whether undertaken by coach, chaise or on horseback, any long-distance travel was an arduous prospect not only in terms of the discomfort of vehicles and inns but also from the danger of highwaymen, accidents and breakdowns.

The prospect of life and work in ITALY must have been sufficiently alluring to cause Handel to travel roughly 890 miles (1,430 km) from Hamburg to FLORENCE in 1706. The Brenner Pass, south of Innsbruck, presumably was the route he took over the Alps. Certainly on the return to Germany in 1710 he travelled that way. In all likelihood, Handel used this same route for the recruiting trip he made to VENICE, BOLOGNA and ROME from London in 1729, a journey of over 1,000 miles (1,600 km). While in Italy 1706–10 Handel spent considerable periods in FLORENCE, Venice, Rome and NAPLES, composing and performing for his noble patrons.

At the age of twenty-five Handel made the first of nineteen sea crossings, all but two (to and from DUBLIN) probably on the Harwich–Hellevoetsluis route taken by packet boats. The light ships, while relatively fast, were not built for passenger comfort. The limited number of cabins meant that most passengers had to remain on deck for the duration of the journey, regardless of the season and the weather. During times of war the boats were liable to seizure by enemy vessels or privateers. Dispatched in 1719 by the Royal Academy of Music (OPERA COMPANIES, 2) to recruit star singers, Handel travelled to DRESDEN via Halle.

In search of private spa treatment to restore his health, Handel visited the warm baths at Borset/Burtscheid near AIX-LA-CHAPELLE (Aachen) in September–October 1737, and again in 1740, when he also visited HAARLEM, HANOVER, Berlin and Halle. On his visit to the continent in 1750, Handel stayed with Princess ANNE and her husband, the Dutch stadholder, at Deventer and Het Loo (NETHERLANDS), and also visited Haarlem, The Hague, Hanover and HALLE. In September 1751 he travelled to Spa, Belgium.

In addition to his visit to Dublin (1741–2), when Handel travelled via CHESTER and Holyhead, and via Parkgate on the return, Handel also visited other British towns. These included the spa resorts of TUNBRIDGE WELLS (1735, 1737, 1758), SCARBOROUGH (1745), BATH (1749, 1751), and CHELTENHAM (1751). He also spent time in the towns of OXFORD (1733), SALISBURY and Southampton (1739). During the summers of 1734 and 1744 he was in 'the country' but we know not where. Handel stayed with his noble friends the Cowpers at Cole Green, Hertfordshire (1738), the SHAFTESBURYs at Wimborne St Giles, Dorset (1739), and with the Gainsboroughs at Exton, Rutland (1745).

J. Black, *The British Abroad: The Grand Tour in the Eighteenth Century* (New York, 1992)
I. Trinder, *The Harwich Packets, 1635–1834* (Colchester, 1998)

16. Health

From early 1737 (if not before) Handel suffered repeated periods of incapacitation due to headaches, irritability, rheumatic pains, colic (acute abdominal pain), cognitive dysfunction (notably loss of speech and/or language comprehension) and localised paralysis. Eventually he became blind. These symptoms can be diagnosed as peripheral neuropathy, transient ischemic attacks (small strokes) or plumbism; all are the consequence of lead poisoning. In addition, he probably suffered from what is now called binge-eating disorder, which contributed to or perhaps even caused his obesity. His friends urged him to moderate his diet in the belief that excessive consumption of wine and rich food would kill him, though they had no idea of the direct link between wine, food and lead poisoning. In 1743 George Harris wrote to his brother James (HARRIS) that he had been told that Handel 'would probably recover his health again, were he not so much of the epicure' (Burrows and Dunhill, p. 166). There was no cure for lead poisoning but spa treatments could and did reduce the lead burden temporarily, thereby delaying the next painful attack of rheumatism, colic or palsy. Samuel Sharp diagnosed Handel's sight problems in 1751 as a *gutta serena*, that is amaurosis (loss of sight due to disease of the optic nerve) and inoperable. Nonetheless, two other eye specialists, William Bromfield and John Taylor, both diagnosed cataracts and operated accordingly, without success.

DAVID HUNTER

D. Hunter, 'Miraculous Recovery? Handel's Illnesses: The Narrative Tradition of Heroic Strength and the Oratorio Turn', *Eighteenth-Century Music* 3 (2006), 253–67
'Handel's Ill-Health: Documentation and Diagnoses', *RMA Research Chronicle* 41 (2008)

17. Finances

It is only possible to trace Handel's finances with accuracy after his arrival in London. He journeyed with the economic security of a salaried position at the Hanoverian court, and although he did not receive his first year's wages until summer 1711, he earned money in the English capital through the composition of opera and, perhaps, as a result of private patronage. In 1713, he lost the position in Hanover, but was granted an annual pension of £200 by Queen Anne. The pension was continued when George I succeeded Anne in 1714, and the King also saw to it that the composer received his full back salary from Hanover in October 1715. With these payments and significant income from the opera, Handel began a lifetime of successful investing by purchasing £500 of stock of the SOUTH SEA COMPANY. He seems to have sold his shares profitably before the collapse of this stock in 1720, as his name appears on none of the subscription lists of that year.

Handel apparently reinvested as quickly as he could, purchasing £150 of South Sea Annuities in June 1723, the year George I doubled the pension he had been given by Queen Anne. In December 1727, when his purchases in this account had accumulated to £600, he sold the entire amount, only to reopen a new account in South Sea annuities in June 1728 with a purchase of £700. His secure financial situation between 1728 and 1732 is apparent from his purchase of £2,400 of stock during these years. In June 1732, however, he terminated the account, using £2,300 to create a cash account in October. Over the next six and a half years, he slowly depleted this account without making a single deposit, closing it out in March 1739.

He did not invest again until the early months of 1743, when he purchased £1,600 of South Sea Annuities. After this time, he withdrew funds from his stock accounts only for the purpose of reinvestment in stronger issues. He reopened a cash account in 1744, apparently because his financial situation necessitated maintaining cash reserves. Between February 1744 and May 1745, he reduced this account to zero on three occasions, but he never sold stock and even purchased £1,300 of 3 per cent Annuities in April 1744. After 1747, Handel was able regularly to transfer funds from his cash account into stock without making any cash withdrawals.

In 1750 Handel consolidated all of his stock accounts worth £7,700 into a single 4 per cent Annuity, and typically added funds each year at the end of his oratorio season. In 1757 and 1758 the deposits were made into the cash account, but in May 1758 this account was closed, and all his monies moved into stock. When Handel died in 1759, he held £17,500 in 3 per cent Consolidated Annuities.

ELLEN T. HARRIS

E. T. Harris, 'Handel the Investor', ML 85/4 (2004), 521–75

D. Hunter, 'Royal Patronage of Handel in Britain: The Rewards of Pensions and Office', Handel Studies: A Gedenkschrift for Howard Serwer, ed. R. G. King (Hillsdale, NY, 2009)

18. Handel the art collector

Handel 'had a great love for painting; and, till his sight failed him, among the few amusements he gave into, the going to view collections of pictures upon sale was the chief' (Hawkins, vol. 2, p. 912) From purchases at auction, and no doubt from dealers and directly from artists, he built a collection of upwards of 145 prints and paintings, plus his own portraits. At one auction he bought a Rembrandt for £39 18s.

His eclectic collection was that of a connoisseur: it covered all genres and national schools. He had still lifes, hunting and battle scenes, conversation pieces and seascapes. Close to half of his collection were views and landscapes. Handel seemed fond of scenes with ruins, which would have been reminders of the transience of fame and grandeur. Especially valued by Handel would have been Balthasar DENNER's pair The Old Man's head and the Old Woman's head, willed to Charles Jennens. The prints in his collection were reproductive engravings of landscapes or art works in Roman churches. The latest rococo style was represented by two paintings by Watteau.

The highest genre of painting was histories. Handel had paintings or prints of mythological subjects of the Rape of Proserpine, Diana on the Hunt, Venus and Adonis, Narcissus, the Loves of Jupiter, and Bacchus and Ariadne. Of biblical subjects, there were Hagar and Ishmael, the Finding of Moses, Samson and Delilah, and the Flight into Egypt. By Joseph GOUPY, he had two watercolours (gouaches), the blind Belisarius, and Mucius Scaevola before Porsinna (for both, examples by Goupy still survive).

Our knowledge of Handel's collection derives from the single surviving copy of a posthumous auction sale catalogue (at the Frick Art Library, New York). Surprisingly, the sale catalogue lacks any portraits of Handel, his friends or colleagues. These may have been dispersed prior to the sale, as certainly were the paintings bequeathed to Jennens and Bernard Granville (HANDEL, 8).

THOMAS N. MCGEARY

A. M. Hughes and M. Royalton-Kisch, 'Handel's Art Collection', Apollo 146 (1997)

T. McGeary, 'Handel as Art Collector: His Print Collection', GHB VIII (2000)

'Handel's Art Collection', EM 37/4 (Nov. 2009)

H. McLean, 'Bernard Granville, Handel and the Rembrandts', MT 126 (Oct. 1985), 593–601

19. Handel's library

His music library comprised a large amount of printed and manuscript music, including both an archive of his own compositions (e.g. his autograph manuscripts and performing scores) and also numerous works by other composers. A French traveller claimed in his memoirs that he met Handel and saw his library, describing it as 'hardly extensive, but carefully chosen in every genre'. Allegedly Handel collected manuscripts 'of every opera performed in Italy', 'all LULLY's operas, and those of [André] Campra . . . those of RAMEAU', Rameau's keyboard music and Jean-Marie Leclair's 'symphonies and his opera Scylla [et Glaucus]'. According to the memoirs, Handel wished to acquire motets by Jean-Joseph Cassanéa de Mondonville.

Perhaps he also possessed other works that he took BORROWINGS from, such as Alessandro STRADELLA's serenata Qual prodigio è ch'io miri?, TELEMANN's cantata collection Harmonischer Gottes-Dienst, and compositions by CARISSIMI, KEISER, MUFFAT, Alessandro SCARLATTI, and others (although he also used music from manuscripts belonging to acquaintances such as Charles JENNENS). Handel certainly made his own manuscripts of sacred music by LOTTI, ERBA and URIO, and there is evidence that he owned copies of STEFFANI's duets and Johann KRIEGER's Anmuthige Clavier-Übung. His name appears in subscription lists for printed scores of music by John Bennett, William BOYCE (including the serenata Solomon), Thomas Chilcot of Bath, William Felton, John Ernest GALLIARD, Elisabetta de Gambarini, Barnabus Gunn, Musgrave Heighington, John Christian Mantel, James Nares, J. C. Smith junior, Telemann (Musique de table) and Elizabeth Turner.

Handel was also interested in literature. His name is on subscription lists for editions of poems by Henry CAREY, John GAY and Joseph Mitchell, and he subscribed to works by Aaron HILL, James MILLER, Richard Rolt, John Pine's edition of Quinti Horatii Flacci Opera, J. Rowell's translation of The Marchioness de Lambert's Letters to her Son and Daughter, on True Education and Joseph Stanglini's Nouvelle Méthode pour appendre La Langue Italienne. Otherwise we know little about the books that Handel owned or read, but he probably obtained WORDBOOKS of Italian operas, upon which some of his own operas were based, and during the early 1730s he seems to have been interested in setting music dramas connected to the plays of Jean RACINE.

Handel bequeathed his 'Musick Books', among other things, to J. C. Smith senior. These were passed on to J. C. Smith junior, who later gave most of the autograph manuscripts to GEORGE III. The rest of Handel's library seems to have been passed down to Smith junior's family (COXE and RIVERS), and the remaining music was sold in the early 1850s. In 1856 the BRISTOL bookseller Thomas KERSLAKE sold remnants of Handel's music library to Victor SCHOELCHER, and it is known to have contained more than the performing scores (now at Hamburg); however, the other items are no longer traceable. ANNETTE LANDGRAF

See also SOURCES AND COLLECTIONS, 1–2

D. Charlton, S. Hibberd, '"My father was a poor Parisian musician": A Memoir (1756) Concerning Rameau, Handel's Library and Sallé', JRMA 128 (2003), 161–99
R. King, 'New Light on Handel's Musical Library', MQ 81 (1997), 109–38
J. Simon, 'Handel's Library: The Evidence of Book Subscription Lists', Handel: A Celebration of his Life and Times 1685–1759, ed. J. Simon (London, 1985)

20. Handel the music teacher

It is probable that teaching played a significant part in Handel's life while he was in Hamburg: it would have brought him into contact with influential families (German and foreign) in the city, and provided a secure source of income while he sought advancement in the opera house. Later on such considerations did not apply, and his teaching activities were restricted to a few favoured pupils. In the 1720s he became music master to the royal princesses (the grandchildren of King George I). His duties in this office were probably quite light and intermittent, but he seems to have taken seriously the musical talents of Anne, the eldest princess, and committed himself accordingly. His other principal pupil was John Christopher SMITH JUNIOR; their professional relationship developed as Smith's status gradually changed from an apprentice to a colleague. Handel's activities with these students were concentrated into about a decade from 1723; a course of instruction in figured bass and counterpoint seems to be represented in a group of Handel's autographs from the period.

21. Handel's reputation and influence

By the time of Handel's death his works had an established position in English musical life. His oratorios continued to be performed in London theatre seasons during the 1760s, ZADOK THE PRIEST was included in King GEORGE III's coronation service, and his music – arias, concertos and complete oratorios – formed an essential repertory for provincial music clubs, societies and festivals. The impetus for the sustained performance of his music was renewed in the last quarter of the eighteenth century by the London festivals that began with the HANDEL COMMEMORATION in 1784, involving large audiences and large numbers of performers, many of them from provincial cities. More remarkably still, Handel's music was taken up in other continental centres – Berlin and Hamburg, but also Vienna, where MOZART adapted the scores to local conditions. A sustained performance tradition was complemented by other manifestations of the continuing, and rising, status of Handel's music, particularly in the publication of full scores, culminating in the attempt at a collected library edition of his works under the editorship of Samuel ARNOLD.

This remarkable situation was, however, based almost entirely on the English-language part of the repertory by which Handel had been known in his later years: oratorio-type works, and orchestrally accompanied church music. In England this provided a repertory of major works that was memorable in performance and practical for concert production: as singing developed as a recreation for amateurs during the nineteenth century, the music also proved surprisingly adaptable to circumstances involving large festival choirs and orchestras. Composers and critics sometimes voiced resentment about the 'dominance' of Handel, but his music proved to be a difficult model to avoid for English choral composers, and it was difficult to deny that his works deserved a continued place in the programmes of the burgeoning provincial festivals. *Messiah, Judas Maccabaeus* and *Israel in Egypt* formed the staple of the repertory. Meanwhile, the other aspect of the continuing regard for Handel's music was represented in the nineteenth century by the new collected editions of scores attempted first by the Handel Society in London and then accomplished over a period of more than forty years by Friedrich CHRYSANDER in Germany.

Although the large-scale choral movement in Britain did not survive the changes wrought by the period of the First World War, Handel's oratorios and church music continued to be part of the repertory for the leaner musical institutions of the twentieth century. The focus, however, shifted gradually to a revival of Handel's Italian operas, which had not featured in the performed repertory (apart from isolated arias as concert items) since the 1740s, though Arnold's edition had included four opera scores and Chrysander's edition had covered all of them. There were some pioneer productions of operas and staged oratorios in the first half of the twentieth century, but the second half saw the comprehensive restoration of Handel's operas in performance and recording, and their absorption into the mainstream programmes of major opera houses. With this came also the revival of other genres from Handel's earlier repertory – the Italian oratorios and cantatas and the Latin church music. Throughout these major changes, however, Handel's instrumental music – concertos and keyboard music – also maintained a modest constant presence, and some operatic movements (most notably 'Handel's Largo') achieved popularity in instrumental arrangements.

Handel's personal image underwent changes that to a large extent followed the fortunes of his music. He was almost immediately given a place in the cultural pantheon of great national figures, and thereafter rather taken for granted; critical assessment of his music depended on whether the taste of the assessor favoured 'ancient' or 'modern' music. As the oratorio performances became more ritualised, and moved away from theatre venues, so Handel himself became interpreted as a primarily 'religious' composer. As the dramatic power and musical quality of the operas was rediscovered, he was seen as a secular figure with a primarily theatrical career. It still remains a challenge to take in the full breadth of his musical personality and achievement.

DONALD BURROWS

See also RECEPTION

Handel and Haydn Society, Boston. See HANDEL SOCIETIES

Handel Commemoration, The. A festival in 1784 that honoured the twenty-fifth anniversary of the composer's death and the centenary of his birth (based on the inaccurate date of 1684), offering three concerts of unusual scale and pivotal importance. Though the programmes were devoted entirely to his music, they followed a careful patterning of contrasting genres then called 'miscellany'. The first event, held at noon in WESTMINSTER ABBEY on Wednesday, 26 May, was focused on sacred works, chiefly the Dettingen Te Deum (TE DEUM, 5) and Funeral Anthem for Queen Caroline (ANTHEMS, 5), but opened with the overture to *ESTHER* and concluded with 'The Lord shall reign' from *ISRAEL IN EGYPT*. The second concert, secular in nature, occurred at 8 p.m. the next day, in the large hall on Oxford Street called the Pantheon. The programme included four concertos, eleven vocal pieces from nine operas by Handel, and four choruses from three oratorios; yet it concluded with *My heart is inditing*, the anthem written for the CORONATION of King GEORGE II in 1727 (ANTHEMS, 3). The performance of *MESSIAH* in the Abbey on Saturday, 29 May, drew the

largest crowd, and 525 musicians supposedly participated in the two performances there. The festival drew so prodigious a response, bringing in £12,726,
that the first and last programmes were repeated on 3 and 5 June. A similar
festival was held in most of the succeeding seven years, the last one involving
1,068 musicians. Large-scale oratorio performances were done widely in Germany and the United States directly upon the model of the commemoration
(RECEPTION).

GEORGE III and Charles BURNEY were deeply involved in the festival, which
was organised by the directors of the Concert of Antient Music, the first public
concerts in Europe to establish a canonic repertory. The festival occurred just
after an election won by William Pitt the younger, at the culminating point of
the crisis between monarchy and Parliament in effect since the early 1770s.
The commemoration helped clear the air politically, thanks to the presence of
Opposition figures among the directors of the Antient Concerts. Still, criticism
was directed at preference for 'indifferent' English singers over the Italians
in town and at the absence of the Prince of Wales, whose WHIG supporters
derided the commemoration as a partisan undertaking. Charles Dibdin used
their rhetoric to deplore the 'blind and bigoted admiration of a *German modern*'
instead of honouring 'English ancients' or living local composers.

WILLIAM WEBER

C. Burney, *An Account of the Musical Performances in Westminster Abbey* (London, 1785)

[C. Dibdin], *The Bystander* (London, 1790)

H. Diack Johnstone, 'A Ringside Seat at the Handel Commemoration', MT 125/1701 (1984),
632–6

W. Weber, 'The 1784 Handel Commemoration as Political Ritual', *Journal of British Studies* 27/4
(1989), 43–70

Handel editions. See EDITIONS

Händel-Handbuch (HHB). Four volumes published 1978–86 by the VEB Deutscher Verlag
für Musik Leipzig and the Bärenreiter Verlag Kassel. It is a reference work and a
supplement to the Hallische Händel-Ausgabe (EDITIONS, 7) which is intended
to serve the needs of both scholars and performers. The content of the first
three volumes was conceived by Bernd BASELT. It starts with a chronology of
Handel's life by Siegfried Flesch, and the main part is Baselt's 'HWV' catalogue
of Handel's works in systematic order. The fourth volume is a documentary
biography with documents in their original language, based on the *Documentary
Biography* by Otto Erich DEUTSCH, but with commentary in German. A fifth
volume containing a bibliography was originally planned but this has never
been published. ANNETTE LANDGRAF

HHB i–iv

Händel-Haus (Halle) and **Handel House (London).** See MUSEUMS

Handel Institute, The. Registered charity founded by a group of British scholars in
1987 to promote the study and appreciation of the music and life of Handel
and his contemporaries and associates, and to support and publish the fruits of
research into such areas. The Handel Institute organises academic conferences
in London (approximately every three years), and nominates members to the

boards of the Hallische Händel-Ausgabe (EDITIONS, 7) and the Gerald COKE Handel Foundation. It awards grants in support of research into Handel and his contemporaries, and publishes a newsletter twice a year containing short research articles.   DAVID VICKERS

The Handel Institute Newsletter, Spring 1990

Händel-Jahrbuch and **Handel Journals.** See JOURNALS

Handel monuments (inc. statues). See MONUMENTS

Handel Opera Society. See Appendix 7: An overview of fifty Handel performers, 1959–2009

Handel Revival, The. See RECEPTION and Appendix 7

Handel Singing Competition, The. See FESTIVALS, 5

Handel Societies

> 1. American Handel Society (AHS)
> 2. Czech Handel Society
> 3. Georg-Friedrich-Händel-Gesellschaft (GFHG e.V)
> 4. Göttinger Händel-Gesellschaft
> 5. Handel and Haydn Society (Boston, Massachusetts)
> 6. The Handel Institute Japan (HIJ)
> 7. Händel-Gesellschaft Karlsruhe

1. American Handel Society (AHS)
Founded in 1985 by Howard Serwer, Paul Traver and J. Merrill Knapp in emulation of similar societies in England and Germany to encourage the study of Handel's life, works and times, and to support the performance of his music. The society is governed by a board of directors that has included professional and amateur scholars and musicians with special interest in the society's missions. General membership in the AHS is open. From 1985 to 2001, the society sponsored an academic conference in conjunction with the Maryland Handel Festival (FESTIVALS, 6). After the cessation of the Maryland Festival, the society has continued to convene the American Handel Festival every two years at different venues, including Iowa City, Iowa (2003), Santa Fe and Albuquerque, New Mexico (2005), Princeton, New Jersey (2007) and Danville, Kentucky (2009). These festivals continue to combine an academic conference with performances of works by Handel and his contemporaries. The Howard Serwer Lecture (formerly the American Handel Society Lecture), delivered by a distinguished scholar or critic, has been a central feature of the festivals since 1987.

The AHS nominates two members to the Editorial Board of the Hallische Händel-Ausgabe (EDITIONS, 7). In pursuit of its goals to promulgate scholarship and performance, it offers an annual a grant in honour of J. Merrill Knapp to a young scholar to support work in Handel studies or related fields. The *Newsletter of the American Handel Society* has appeared three times annually since 1986. From 1991 to 1998 the society awarded the American Handel Society Recording Prize.   ROBERT KETTERER

2. Czech Handel Society

Founded at Prague in 1990, the society was organised to encourage the positive development of Handel performances and research both in the Czech Republic and internationally. A monograph about Handel written by founder member Pavel Polka was published in October 1990, and the performance project 'Masterworks of Baroque Opera' (1996–2004) staged six Handel operas.

DAVID VICKERS

3. Georg-Friedrich-Händel-Gesellschaft (GFHG e.V.)

Founded in HALLE on 23 April 1955 as conceptual successor to the Deutsche Händel-Gesellschaft (founded in 1859), the Neue Deutsche Händel-Gesellschaft (1925–35) and the Hallische Händel-Gesellschaft (founded 1948 and directed by Max Schneider). The initial statutes laid down the following objectives: 'To study Georg Friedrich Händel's life and works comprehensively and to distribute and deepen knowledge of his work, especially by publishing new editions and by promoting the performance of his works throughout the world. The society, in collaboration with the city of Halle, will organize a Handel festival in Handel's birthplace Halle [FESTIVALS, 4]. The society will also publish the annual Händel-Jahrbuch [JOURNALS, 2] and promote the Hallische Händel-Ausgabe (HHA) [EDITIONS, 7].'

The first general meeting elected Max Schneider as president, the musicologist Rudolf Steglich as vice-president, and Walter SIEGMUND-SCHULTZE as academic secretary. Other members of the board were Horst-Tanu Margraf (the conductor and main initiator of the Halle Handel Festival), Karl Vötterle (an important initiator of the Hallische Händel-Ausgabe and director of the publisher Bärenreiter), Georg Engelmann (representative of the Leipzig-based Deutscher Verlag für Musik), the composer and musicologist Ernst Hermann Meyer (president, 1967–88) and biographer Walter Serauky. The society's hope to gain an international character was indicated by the inclusion of board members Jens Peter Larsen (Danish musicologist), William C. Smith (Assistant Keeper of the British Museum) and the British conductor and organist Arnold Goldsborough. Honorary memberships were awarded to the English musicologist Edward Dent, Friedrich CHRYSANDER's daughter-in-law Berta Chrysander and Romain ROLLAND's widow Marie Rolland.

The society's activities were financed by the GDR but their eventual success in becoming truly international was largely due to the dedication of its members during a difficult period of political isolation. Information about the society's work and proceedings of its annual academic conferences – organised in collaboration with the Halle Institute of Musicology – are published annually in the Händel-Jahrbuch. The ambitious four-volume HÄNDEL-HANDBUCH (containing the three-volume HWV catalogue) was published between 1978 and 1986. The HHA has also progressed steadily, albeit not without difficulties: the communist Socialist Unity Party (Sozialistische Einheitspartei Deutschlands, SED) tried to influence board decisions until the reunification of Germany in 1989/90. Presently the society counts 700 members from fourteen countries; its seat has always been the Händel-Haus (MUSEUMS, I). Later presidents have been Ernst Hermann Meyer (1967–88), the former academic secretary

Walther Siegmund-Schultze (1989–91), Bernd BASELT (1991–3), Wolfgang Ruf (1995–2009) and Wolfgang Hirschmann (since 2009).

GERT RICHTER (Trans. ANGELA BAIER)

4. Göttinger Händel-Gesellschaft

An incorporated society registered by the city of Göttingen on 12 March 1931. The society's objective is to cultivate the musical works of Handel and to make them accessible. In order to realise this objective, the society has organised and sponsored the Göttingen Handel Festival (FESTIVALS, 3) ever since taking over these duties from the Universitätsbund (the Society of Friends of the Göttingen University). There was no institutional support for the festival in its early days and it kept going mainly by the dedication and initiative of individuals. Festivals had to be cancelled when its founder Oskar HAGEN left in 1925, and when Alfred Bertholet, chairman of the festival's board of trustees, did the same in 1929. The festival was briefly financed by the Händel-Festspiel-Gemeinde, but the common wish to have festivals at regular intervals with professionally organised performances led to the official foundation of the society as it stands today.

The society's first president was Walther Meyerhoff, who held the post until his death in 1976. The next presidents were Friedrich Riethmüller and Hans-Ludwig Schreiber (from 1993). Among the society's honorary members are Jens Peter Larsen, Winton Dean, Günther Weißenborn and Donna Leon. Since autumn 2007 the festival has been financed by an independent, non-profit-making 'Festspiel GmbH' (a limited company). The objective of the society remains the organisation of the festival, but it also supports scholarly publications such as the Göttinger Händel-Beiträge (JOURNALS, 1), and organises the early music concert series 'Göttinger Reihe Historischer Musik', which promotes young musicians and holds an annual musical competition.

JÜRGEN HEIDRICH (Trans. ANGELA BAIER)

5. Handel and Haydn Society (Boston, Massachusetts)

A choral society founded in 1815 by a group of merchants, with the intention of honouring the greatest 'old' composers (Handel) and the most important of the 'new' (HAYDN). One of the oldest performing groups in North America, the Society gave the American premiere of MESSIAH (1817), and has performed it annually since 1854 (RECEPTION). It also gave the American premieres of Haydn's The Creation (1819) and BACH's B minor Mass (1887).   DAVID VICKERS

6. The Handel Institute Japan (HIJ)

An organisation of scholars, performers and music-lovers founded in 1998 by Professor Keiichiro Watanabe (a pioneer of Handel studies in Japan and an international Handel scholar), aiming to study and perform Handel's works, mainly opera stagings with baroque gesture. HIJ has performed ORESTE (2000), RINALDO (2002), La RESURREZIONE (2004) and others.   TOSHIKI MISAWA

7. Händel-Gesellschaft Karlsruhe

Founded in 1989 by citizens of Karlsruhe, local politicians and patrons to secure a broader basis of support for the Karlsruhe Handel Festival (FESTIVALS, 7) and the INTERNATIONALE HÄNDEL-AKADEMIE, and also to commemorate

Handel's life and works. Under its presidents Erwin Sack (1989–99), Siegfried Schmaltzriedt (1999–2007) and Peter Overbeck (since 2007), the society and its board of trustees have promoted young musicians, and award scholarships and travel allowances to music students from Eastern Europe. The society holds the annual 'Händel-Jugendpreis' competition, and a concert given by award winners takes place during the festival.

†SIEGFRIED SCHMALZRIEDT (Trans. ANGELA BAIER)

See also HANDEL INSTITUTE; Appendix 8: Handel organisations and websites

Handl, Jacobus. See Jacobus GALLUS (HANDL)

Hanover. City in North Germany, situated on the River Leine; capital of Lower Saxony. Handel was appointed Kapellmeister to the court on 16 June 1710 but spent fewer than twelve months there in total before settling in London in 1712.

The rise of Hanover began in 1636, when Duke Georg of Calenberg – one of two branches of the house of Brunswick-Lüneburg – established his residence there. Under the fourth of his sons, Ernst August (r. 1679–97), the house was reunited and the duchy grew in stature, becoming an electorate in 1692. Ernst August and his consort, Sophie of the Palatinate (granddaughter of James I of England), were Lutherans, but their taste was French and they loved music. Taking advantage of the library, which was supervised by Leibniz, Sophie encouraged intellectual and artistic pursuits. Ernst August established a LULLY-style orchestra under Jean-Baptiste FARINEL and appointed Johann Anton Coberg music teacher to the family, including his talented daughter, Sophie Charlotte. Operas and French plays were staged in a 408-seat 'Comoedienhaus', opened in 1678, but in 1687–9 Ernst August built a magnificent new 1,300-seat opera house, 'the best painted and the best contriv'd in all Europe' (Toland). The period 1689–97 was the heyday of baroque opera in Hanover; most of the ten new works produced were settings by Agostino STEFFANI of librettos by Ortensio MAURO, and most were revived promptly in HAMBURG.

Ernst August's son, Georg Ludwig (r. 1697–1714, later GEORGE I), closed the opera but encouraged chamber music. The ensemble grew to embrace 'an excellent band of oboists' from BERLIN (Mattheson, *Grundlage einer Ehrenpforte*). The young TELEMANN admired the French style of the Hanover orchestra, which in Handel's day numbered eighteen. It is here that Handel appears to have completed 'Apollo e Dafne' (*La TERRA È LIBERATA*) and, according to MAINWARING, to have composed chamber duets to verses by Mauro, as Steffani had done. When Handel was dismissed, in 1713, his successor was Francesco Venturini. After Georg Ludwig's accession to the throne of Great Britain, Hanover was ruled by a regent but declined in importance for Handel.   COLIN TIMMS

See also HERRENHAUSEN

D. Burrows, 'Handel and Hanover', *Bach, Handel, Scarlatti: Tercentenary Essays*, ed. Peter Williams (Cambridge, 1985)
R. Hatton, *George I, Elector and King* (London, 1978)
H. Sievers, *Die Musik in Hannover* (Hanover, 1961)
J. Toland, *An Account of the Courts of Prussia and Hannover, sent to a Minister of State in Holland* (London, 1705)

R. E. Wallbrecht, *Das Theater des Barockzeitalters an den welfischen Höfen Hannover und Celle* (Hildesheim, 1974)

Hanover Square. See ST GEORGE'S Hanover Square

Hare, John and Joseph. The Hares were musical instrument makers, sellers and music publishers. John Hare (b. London, 1672; d. London, July 1725) established his business as an instrument maker near the Royal Exchange in Cornhill, and as a music seller in St Paul's Churchyard. These latter premises were taken over by Richard MEARES, another music publisher and instrument maker, in 1706. By 1703 Hare had entered into a partnership with John WALSH as a music publisher, and the association continued into the second generation with Joseph Hare, ending about November 1730. Walsh and Hare dominated the music-publishing trade in London. As Walsh held the office of 'Musical Instrument-maker in Ordinary' to the monarch the arrangement presumably resulted in Hare instruments being supplied regularly to the King's Musick.

Joseph Hare (b. London, c.1700; d. London, July 1733) set up his own music business making and selling instruments and scores, near Birchin Lane in Cornhill. DAVID HUNTER

See also EDITIONS, I

'Harmonious Blacksmith, The'. A spurious title for the Air and variations in the Suite in E (HWV 430), No. 5 in the 1720 collection of *Suites de Pièces pour le Clavecin* (KEYBOARD MUSIC). The piece was first published under this title about 1822, and an absurd legend was invented about Handel taking shelter in a forge and being inspired by the sound of the blacksmith's hammer on the anvil.

TERENCE BEST

Harp and Harp Concerto. See INSTRUMENTATION; ORCHESTRAL WORKS, 3

Harris, James (b. ?Salisbury, 25 July 1709; d. Salisbury, 22 Dec. 1780). Author, public servant, music-lover and patron, friend and collaborator of Handel. Educated at SALISBURY Cathedral School and Wadham College, OXFORD, on his father's death (1731) he inherited substantial property and (1732) toured the Low Countries, Germany and France. He settled in the family home in Salisbury Cathedral Close (now Malmesbury House) and in 1745 married Elizabeth Clarke (1722–81). Three of their children survived: their diplomat son James, later 1st Earl of Malmesbury, and their daughters Gertrude and Louisa, for whom Harris continued his own father's practice of providing a literary and musical education. He served as a Salisbury magistrate, MP for Christchurch (1761–80), a Lord of the Admiralty and the Treasury (1763–5), a Trustee of British Museum (1765–80) and secretary and comptroller to Queen Charlotte (1774–80). As a philosopher, aesthetician and philologist with a national and European reputation, Harris transmitted the ethical and aesthetic principles of his uncle the 3rd Earl of Shaftesbury, especially in *Three Treatises* (1744) on art, music, painting and poetry, and happiness. He had 'a genius for friendship based on common interests' (Burrows and Dunhill), and was the focal point of the 'brother Handelists' – his brothers Thomas and George William, his cousin the 4th Earl of SHAFTESBURY, his KNATCHBULL relations, Charles JENNENS, Lord Guernsey

(3rd Earl of AYLESFORD) and the 4th Earl of Radnor. His other musical correspondents included Charles BURNEY, Maurice GREENE, Greene's librettist John Hoadly, John HAWKINS, John Lockman, John Marsh, J. C. SMITH SENIOR and Gottfried van SWIETEN (seeking to acquire scores by Handel). Harris was a principal organiser of musical life in Salisbury. The annual Salisbury Festival, with distinguished visiting soloists, and royalty and aristocracy among the audience, frequently featured Handel's work, including the first performance of SAUL outside London. Harris contributed pasticcios for which he wrote words to existing music (including Handel's), sometimes himself composing the recitatives. David Garrick produced Harris's pastoral pasticcio Daphnis and Amaryllis as The Spring, an afterpiece, at DRURY LANE THEATRE in 1762. A devotee of MILTON's poetry, Harris was the initiator of Handel's L'ALLEGRO and made the first draft of the libretto, specifying several features which Handel implemented, such as solos for John BEARD including 'Let me wander' as a siciliano, the distinction between a light (boy) soprano for L'Allegro and a mature soprano (FRANCESINA) for Penseroso, and 'Mirth, admit me' set for 'a Base Voice with French Horns'. He contributed the list of Handel's works to the biography by MAINWARING.   RUTH SMITH

See also Elizabeth LEGH

Burrows and Dunhill

Harris, Thomas (b. 1712; d. 1785). Brother of James HARRIS, lawyer and cellist. He attended the rehearsal of the *MUSIC FOR THE ROYAL FIREWORKS* at VAUXHALL GARDENS with his brother George as well as numerous other performances. He witnessed the first three codicils to Handel's will and received a legacy of £300 (HANDEL, 8). He owned the MERCIER portrait of Handel, which he bequeathed to his nephew James Harris junior.   DAVID HUNTER

See also John HETHERINGTON

Burrows and Dunhill

Hasse, Johann Adolf (bap. Bergedorf near Hamburg, 25 March 1699; d. Venice, 16 Dec. 1783). One of the most successful German-born composers of Italian opera seria, he wrote more than sixty operas, predominantly using librettos on historical subjects by METASTASIO and the DRESDEN court librettists PALLAVICINI, Giovanni Claudio Pasquini and Giovanni Ambrogio Migliavacca. After initially studying music with his father, he went to HAMBURG in 1714, where he was taught singing by MATTHESON and joined the GÄNSEMARKT opera as a tenor in 1718. A year later he was engaged to sing at the opera in BRUNSWICK, where his first opera, Antioco, was performed in 1721. Hasse then travelled to Italy; he stayed in VENICE, Bologna, FLORENCE and ROME. By 1726 he had settled at NAPLES, where he converted to Roman Catholicism, reputedly studied with Alessandro SCARLATTI, and rapidly became one of the city's most successful composers. In 1730 he married the soprano FAUSTINA Bordoni at Venice. At around this time he was appointed Hofkapellmeister of the prestigious musical establishment at Dresden, but he did not arrive at the Saxon capital until July 1731. His official duties did not prevent him from often spending extended periods living and working across Italy, and developing long associations with the Habsburg court at Vienna, the Prussian court at BERLIN, and the Ospedale degli Incurabili in Venice. From the 1740s he cultivated an affectionate collaborative friendship with Metastasio. The cultural life of the court at Dresden was decimated during the SEVEN YEARS WAR, and Hasse moved to Vienna in 1764. He and Faustina retired to Venice in 1773, where they lived quietly near the church of S. Marcuola (in which they are buried).

Hasse might have met Handel at Naples in 1729, although there is no evidence that the two composers knew each other personally. He never visited London, although early biographers erroneously reported him to have done so. However, his music was performed by Italian singers working in the British capital: arias from operas composed for Naples, Venice, Rome, Milan and Bologna were featured in Handel's PASTICCIOS *ORMISDA* (1730; five arias), *VENCESLAO* (1731; five arias), *CATONE* (1732; six arias), *SEMIRAMIDE* (1733; seven arias), *ARBACE* (1734; three arias) and *DIDONE ABBANDONATA* (1737; three arias). Moreover, Handel's production of *CAIO FABRICIO* (1733) retained thirteen arias from Hasse's setting (Rome, 1732), although it was initially planned to use more. Also, FARINELLI sang arias by Hasse to popular acclaim in the OPERA OF THE NOBILITY's 1734 production of *Artaserse* (a pasticcio based on Hasse's setting for Venice, 1730). PANJA MÜCKE (Trans. ANGELA BAIER)

F. Lippmann (ed.), *Colloquium 'Johann Adolf Hasse und die Musik seiner Zeit'* (Laaber, 1987)
R. Mellace, *Johann Adolf Hasse* (Palermo, 2004)
  L'autunno del Metastasio: Gli ultimi drammi per musica di Johann Adolf Hasse (Florence, 2007)
P. Mücke, *Johann Adolf Hasses Dresdner Opern im Kontext der Hofkultur* (Laaber, 2003)
Strohm
R. Wiesend (ed.), *Johann Adolf Hasse in seiner Zeit. Bericht über das Symposium vom 23. bis 26. März 1999 in Hamburg* (Stuttgart, 2006)

Haugwitz, Count Heinrich Wilhelm (b. 30 May 1770; d. Namiescht on the Oslawa (Czech: Náměšť nad Oslavou), Moravia, 19 May 1842). Austrian Count, music patron and cloth manufacturer, who was introduced to Handel's music by Salieri. He learned to play the violin in Vienna, where he might have encountered Handel's music in concerts organised by Gottfried van SWIETEN. Haugwitz regularly had musical works performed at his palace in Náměšt and at his summer residence Schönwald (Czech: Šumná) by his court orchestra (which in 1830 consisted of a Kapellmeister, 31 instrumentalists, 9 solo singers and 24 choristers). The repertoire was mainly recent Viennese music, but from 1820 he uniquely pioneered a Handel revival in Bohemia. Between April and August 1837 he organised a concert series of twelve Handel oratorios and cantatas. He arranged the music and translated the English texts himself, and his library contained fifty-seven works by Handel.

KLAUS-PETER KOCH (Trans. ANGELA BAIER)

R. Angermüller, 'Händel-Übersetzungen des Grafen Heinrich Wilhelm von Haugwitz', HJb 38 (1992)
J. Racek, 'Oratorien und Kantaten von Georg Friedrich Händel auf dem mährischen Schlosse von Náměšt', HJb 6 (1960)

Have mercy upon me. See ANTHEMS, 2

Hawkins, John (b. London, 29 March 1719; d. London, 21 May 1789). Author of an astute sketch of Handel's career in *A General History of the Science and Practice* *of Music* (1776). Born in 1719, set up as attorney by 1742, Hawkins went on to become chairman of the Quarter Sessions and Justice of the Peace for Middlesex. While his musical interests grew out of the clerical tradition of 'ancient' music, they also owed much to the linguistic empiricism of Dr Samuel Johnson, on whom he wrote the first biography. A friend and admirer of Handel, Hawkins wrote a subtle narrative of how the composer wielded influence over many areas of London's free-wheeling musical world. 'He was not a proud man, but he was capricious,' wrote Hawkins concerning Handel's efforts to give the composer authority over the singer, especially during the 'civil discord' between him and SENESINO. Hawkins respected Handel's opera oeuvre but despised the 'ridiculous character of the opera connoisseur' whose thinking lacked discipline. The concertos put him off, seeming 'made in a hurry' due to the expectations left by the Corellian canon. He looked ahead to nineteenth-century musical values in declaring that, through the oratorios, Handel 'could attach to him the real lovers and judges of music'. WILLIAM WEBER

Hawkins
B. H. Davis, *A Proof of Eminence: The Life of Sir John Hawkins* (Bloomington, 1973)
W. Weber, 'Intellectual Origins of Musical Canon in Eighteenth-Century England', JAMS 47/3 (1994), 488–520

Haydn, Joseph (b. Rohrau, Lower Austria, 31 March 1732; d. Vienna, 31 May 1809). Austrian composer. Haydn was compared to Handel as early as 1775, on the occasion of the performance of his oratorio *Il Ritorno di Tobia*. He had received some training from Handel's one-time rival PORPORA, and might have heard newly orchestrated ARRANGEMENTS of Handel's works in Vienna during the 1780s. But Haydn only became fully acquainted with the impact of Handel's oratorios during his first stay in England (1791–2), particularly during the HANDEL COMMEMORATION concerts at WESTMINSTER ABBEY in June 1791, at which he heard *ZADOK THE PRIEST*, extracts from several oratorios, and *MESSIAH*. After hearing the 'HALLELUJAH CHORUS' he is said to have wept and exclaimed: 'He is the master of us all!' In 1795 Queen Charlotte (wife of GEORGE III) presented Haydn with a manuscript copy of the *BROCKES PASSION*.

Some Handelian influences can be detected Haydn's two late Viennese oratorios set to librettos prepared by Gottfried van SWIETEN: *Die Schöpfung* (*The Creation*) (adapted from a poem by an unidentified English poet called 'Lidley', which was in turn based on the BIBLE and on MILTON's *Paradise Lost*) and *Die Jahreszeiten* (*The Seasons*) (based on James Thomson's pastoral poems). Haydn told his early biographer Griesinger that 'Handel was great in choruses but mediocre in song', but it is reputed that his aversion to setting the croaking of frogs to music in *Die Jahreszeiten* was overcome when Swieten reminded the composer about Handel's onomatopoetic setting of the jumping frogs in *ISRAEL IN EGYPT*. HARTMUT KRONES (Trans. ANGELA BAIER)

D. W. Jones (ed.), *The Oxford Companion to Haydn* (Oxford, 2002)
J. P. Larsen, 'Händel und Haydn', HJb, 28 (1982)

Hayes, William (b. Gloucester, bap. 26 Jan, 1708; d. Oxford, 27 July 1777). Heather Professor of Music in OXFORD, organist, composer and a prominent member of the Catch Club. He collected numerous musical compositions of past masters, published by his son Philip after his death. A devotee of Handel, he contributed to the dissemination of his music in the provinces, where he conducted many of his oratorios. A committed apostle of ancient music, he wrote a few scathing pamphlets to vent his anger at anything he considered too 'modern'. In his 'Remarks on Mr Avison's Essay on Musical Expression' (1753), he took issue with Charles AVISON about Handel and stated his attachment to strict principles of composition, linking the rules of the 'science' of music with questions of morality.   PIERRE DUBOIS

Haym, Nicola Francesco (b. Rome, 6 July 1678; d. London, 31 July 1729). Italian composer, cellist, poet, theatre manager and antiquarian. He enjoyed the patronage of Cardinal Pietro OTTOBONI from 1694 until 1700 and taught cello at the Seminario Romano. Lindgren suggests that all of Haym's earliest known compositions, which include two oratorios, might have been commissioned by Ottoboni and that he may have played in the orchestra at the Teatro Capranica, which staged the first two operas Haym later adapted for London, Alessandro SCARLATTI's Pirro e Demetrio (1694) and Giovanni BONONCINI's Il trionfo di Camilla (1698). In 1701 he arrived in London, initially as the accompanist of violinist Nicola Cosimi, to serve as master of chamber music to Wriothesley Russell, 2nd Duke of Bedford (d. 1711), who hired Cosimi whilst in ROME during 1698–9. He was involved in the production of Italianate operas at DRURY LANE and the Queen's Theatre (KING'S THEATRE) as continuo cellist, and worked as composer and manager for the singer Joanna Maria, Baroness Linchenham (d. 1724). In addition, he created the two most successful adaptations of the decade, Camilla (1706) and Pyrrhus and Demetrius (1708), which marked Nicola Grimaldi's (known as 'NICOLINO') debut in London.

Haym probably adapted both text and music for many pasticcios produced in London from 1711 onwards. He certainly reworked Etearco, Dorinda, Creso and Lucio Vero, and perhaps Almahide, Ernelinda, Arminio and Vincislao. He began his collaboration with Handel in 1713, with the adaptation of the libretto for TESEO, followed perhaps by AMADIGI and RADAMISTO. He may also have provided ARIOSTI with Tito Manlio. Between 1715 and 1718 Haym enjoyed the patronage of James Brydges, Earl of Carnarvon (later 1st Duke of CHANDOS), for whom he wrote six anthems in 1716.

He is listed as one of two continuo cellists in the plans for the orchestra of the Royal Academy of Music (OPERA COMPANIES, 2) that were drawn up about 15 February 1720; from autumn 1722 until spring 1728 he also served as secretary of the academy, adapting librettos and working as stage manager for all productions. He adapted texts for Handel (OTTONE, FLAVIO, GIULIO CESARE, TAMERLANO, RODELINDA, SIROE, TOLOMEO and perhaps ADMETO and the pasticcio ELPIDIA), Ariosti (Caio Marzio CORIOLANO, Vespasiano, Artaserse and perhaps Aquilio consolo, Dario, Elisa, Lucio Vero and Teuzzone) and Bononcini (Calfurnia and Astianatte).

Haym's practical approach to adapting librettos for the Royal Academy reflects Giuseppe RIVA's description of the task. In his letters to Lodovico Antonio Muratori (1725–6), Riva explained how a libretto for London had to be adapted to the cast and how any libretto from Italy had to be 'reformed, or rather deformed, in order to encounter favour: they must have few lines of recitative and many arias, and this is why some of the best operas of Apostolo [ZENO] will never be done and why the two most beautiful by METASTASIO, *Didone* and *Siroe*, will suffer the same fate'. Haym's librettos focus on dramatic action and although the loss of much recitative from the original librettos occasionally obscures characters' motivation, Haym's adaptations were well received by his audiences, singers and composers (with the possible exception of Bononcini).

When he died, Haym was probably helping Handel and HEIDEGGER plan for the opening season of the so-called 'Second Academy' (OPERA COMPANIES, 3), and it has been speculated that he might have already revised the librettos for *PARTENOPE*, *ORMISDA* and *VENCESLAO* (all produced 1730–1). His obituary remembers him for his 'Genious for Musick . . . indefatigable Industry . . . uncommon Modesty, Candour, Affability and all amiable Virtues of Life'.

MELANIA BUCCIARELLI

See also LIBRETTO, 2

L. Lindgren, 'The Accomplishments of the Learned and Ingenious Nicola Francesco Haym (1678–1729)', *Studi Musicali* 16 (1987), 247–380

Haymarket Theatre. See KING'S THEATRE; LITTLE THEATRE

Hebestreit (Hebenstreit), Pantaleon (b. Kleinheringen, now Bad Kösen/Saxony-Anhalt, 27 Nov. 1668; d. Dresden, 15 Nov. 1750). Violinist, dancing master and composer. In about 1694 he redesigned the dulcimer as the instrument which would later bear his name (the 'Pantaleon') and went on extended concert tours playing it. He probably met Handel at WEISSENFELS, where he was engaged as dancing master from 1698 until 1705/7. He composed two arias for Reinhard KEISER's opera *Octavia* (1707), one of which Handel borrowed in *ALLA CACCIA*.

KLAUS-PETER KOCH (Trans. ANGELA BAIER)

B. Baselt, 'Händel auf dem Wege nach Italien', *G. F. Händel und seine italienischen Zeitgenossen*, ed. W. Siegmund-Schultze (Halle, 1979)

J. Mattheson, *Grundlage einer Ehren-Pforte* (Hamburg, 1740)

Heidegger, John Jacob (later James) (b. Zurich, 13 June 1666; d. Richmond, 5 Sept. 1749). Swiss opera and masquerade impresario. Little is known of him before 1707, when he began to participate enthusiastically in the long process of acclimatising English audiences to Italian opera. He selected arias for the pasticcio *Thomyris* (1707) and probably translated *Clotilda* (1709). According to a letter to the *Tatler* in January 1710, 'Count Hideacre has been able to get 2 or 3000 guineas an Opera subscribd' (Bond, *New Letters*, pp. 96–8), evidence of how successfully he mingled with the upper strata of society. He assisted Owen SWINEY in management at the Queen's Theatre and took over the opera company when Swiney fled, bankrupt, in 1713. Heidegger probably began direct sponsorship of his famous (and morally controversial) masquerade balls about this time, though there is no firm evidence. He also adapted, translated or produced various operas between 1713 and 1717, including Handel's *AMADIGI* (1715). Optimistic at the accession of King George, Heidegger leased the theatre (now renamed the KING'S THEATRE) in 1716 for £400 per annum. Until 1739, he managed the premises for various companies and did it so responsibly that no lawsuits resulted and little financial detail survives. Masquerades helped balance the books, since a profit of £300 to £500 per event was possible. As one of the 'directors' of the Royal Academy of Music, Heidegger probably helped promote subscriptions, and he exercised his diplomatic skills trying to keep peace among fractious singers like FAUSTINA Bordoni and Francesca CUZZONI in 1727. After the Royal Academy collapsed in 1728, Heidegger and Handel jointly operated the 'Second Academy' from 1729 until 1734, when Handel moved to COVENT GARDEN and Heidegger rented the theatre to the OPERA OF THE NOBILITY for three seasons. Handel returned to the King's Theatre for 1737–8 where he joined forces with the opposition, after which Heidegger shut down the company. In the 1740s Heidegger rented the King's Theatre to Lord MIDDLESEX for his opera, no longer participating in management. Famous for his physical ugliness, Heidegger was also known for his generosity and charity. He left his building lease to his illegitimate daughter, Elizabeth Pappet, later Davis, whose husband sold it in 1767.   JUDITH MILHOUS and ROBERT D. HUME

See also OPERA COMPANIES, 1–3, 5

R. P. Bond (ed.), *New Letters to the Tatler* (Austin, TX, 1959)

J. Milhous and R. D. Hume, 'Heidegger and Opera Management at the Haymarket, 1713–1717', *EM* 27/1 (1999), 65–84

F. H. W. Sheppard, *Survey of London*, vols. 29–30: *The Parish of St. James Westminster, Part I: South of Piccadilly* (London, 1960)

'Heilig, heilig'. See 'HOLY, HOLY'

Heins, John Theodore (formerly Dietrich) (b. ?Germany, c.1697; d. Norwich, ?1756). Portrait painter who came to Norwich not later than 1720, where he painted

13. A portrait of Handel by John Theodore Heins, oil on canvas, 1740.

numerous portraits of members of prominent local families but also of singers and musicians. Not all of his portraits are of consistent quality. Many of his finer works were commissioned by the Astley family of Melton Constable; among them the well-known *Musical Party* (1734). Some of his paintings were published as engravings by George Vertue and Jacobus HOUBRAKEN. His portrait of Handel (1740) was unknown until 2005, when it was auctioned in Cologne (Figure 13).   EDWIN WERNER

T. Fawcett, 'Eighteenth-Century Art in Norwich', *Walpole Society* 46 (1976–8), 92–243
R. Jeffree, 'Heins, John Theodore', *Grove Dictionary of Art* (New York, 1996)

Hendel, non può mia Musa, HWV 117. Handel is lauded for his excellence in music, and is favourably compared to Orpheus. If the mythical singer could move beasts, rocks and trees, Handel has performed a greater wonder in reviving the poet's Muse, who had hung her plectrum 'upon an ancient tree' (apparently quoting from Psalm 137: 'We hanged our harps upon the willows'). A choral praise of Harmony is called for in the concluding aria. Cardinal PAMPHILIJ, then aged fifty-five and Vatican chief librarian since 1704, improvised this short cantata, possibly – MAINWARING guesses – to prove Handel's steadiness 'against the assaults of vanity'. Handel's autograph setting for soprano and continuo, dated 1708, was copied four times for RUSPOLI until 1711, thus witnessing its popularity. Its overt caricature of formulaic word-painting in both arias may suggest embarrassment and/or a defiant reaction from the composer (cf. his much later description of the librettist as an 'old fool').   CARLO VITALI

W. Dean, 'Charles Jennens's Marginalia to Mainwaring's Life of Handel', *Essays on Opera* (Oxford, 1990)

Hercules, HWV 60. By the time Handel composed his secular musical drama *Hercules* he had made a major shift in the focus of his creative life. During the 1720s and 1730s he was known to London audiences primarily as an impresario and composer of Italian operas for the London stage; but by the time he went to Ireland in 1741, he had made the decision not to compose any more operas. His DUBLIN concerts consisted of biblical oratorios, notably *MESSIAH*, as well as some secular works, and these programmes were successful. When he returned to England he may have contemplated similarly presenting each season a new oratorio as well as a new secular work to be performed in the manner of an oratorio. Thus in 1744 he presented the new biblical oratorio *JOSEPH AND HIS BRETHREN* as well as the new secular work *SEMELE*, and in 1745 his new offerings were *BELSHAZZAR*, based on the Old Testament, and the secular musical drama *Hercules*. But soon Handel abandoned this plan and concentrated in subsequent seasons on the creation of biblical oratorios alone.

The wordbook for *Hercules* was published without its author's name, but its authorship can be confidently attributed to Revd Thomas BROUGHTON, noted for his 1742 publication *An Historical Dictionary of all Religions* but also active in a number of literary efforts, including an edition of John DRYDEN's works. His wordbook for *Hercules* acknowledges as its source the *Trachiniae* (*The Women of Trachis*) by Sophocles and OVID's *Metamorphoses*. While these works constitute the main influences on the libretto as a whole, individual scenes and numbers of the drama draw upon a wealth of other materials, the most important being

Hercules Oetaeus. As it is presented by the libretto, which represents a synthesis of the sources as well as new material provided by Broughton, the plot of *Hercules* concerns the homecoming of the long-absent Hercules. He has just sacked the city of Oechalia and the Princess Iole is among the spoils of war he carries home. His wife Dejanira mistakenly comes to believe that Hercules is in love with Iole. Uncertain what to do at first, she eventually decides to send her husband a robe given her by the centaur Nessus after he was mortally wounded by Hercules. Nessus had assured her that the garment would 'revive the expiring flames of love'. The garment is actually poisoned, and leads to the death of Hercules. Dejanira reacts with self-horror in a mad scene, and Hercules is received on Olympus. The priest of Jupiter reveals that it is the divine will that Hercules's son Hyllus should wed Iole, which has been Hyllus's desire through much of the oratorio.

The wordbook differs from the plays of Sophocles and Seneca, who portray an adulterous Hercules who destroyed Oechalia in order to gain Iole. Ovid ascribes Dejanira's jealousy to rumours she has heard, and it is not clear if they are justified. Broughton goes so far as to clean up Hercules's past, making him a hero who deserves to be raised to the 'starry mansions' because of his virtue. As a result, much emphasis is thrust upon Dejanira and her unfounded jealousy.

Handel began drafting the score on 19 July 1744, completing the three acts in turn on 30 July, 11 and 17 August, and finished filling in details a few days later. Before the first performance on 5 January 1745 he expanded the part of the herald Lichas, originally a minor tenor role, for the celebrated singer and actor Susanna CIBBER. After the conducting score was copied, Handel decided to omit Dejanira's 'Cease ruler of the day to rise'. The intended first cast was as follows:

Hercules	Henry REINHOLD (bass)
Dejanira	Miss ROBINSON (mezzo-soprano)
Iole	FRANCESCINA (soprano)
Hyllus	John BEARD (tenor)
Lichas	Susanna Cibber (alto)

Miss Robinson, who created the challenging role of Dejanira, does not seem to have performed in any other season.

Hercules was not particularly successful in its first performance, and there are several reasons for this. First, Cibber became ill and was unable to sing on the first performance; some of her arias were given to other characters and certain of her lines of recitative were read by bass Gustavus WALTZ, whether spoken or sung we are not sure, in a miserably hoarse voice (Cibber was able to sing the second and last performance for the season one week later). Secondly, Handel took advantage of the collapse of a rival Italian opera company and rented the King's Theatre, where his Italian operas had been performed. *Hercules* was considered to be an attempt on Handel's part to win over the opera audience. Some of the supporters of the Italian opera actively opposed Handel's performances by luring his audience away to other entertainments. Attendance was indeed poor; Charles JENNENS reported that Handel 'had scarce half a house the first night, much less than half the second; & has been quiet ever since' (HHB iv, p. 386). Despite the fact that the musicians told the Earl of SHAFTESBURY that they admired Hercules (Burrows and Dunhill, p. 210), Handel never again wrote a full-scale secular dramatic work.

Although Handel seems to have avoided the term oratorio for Hercules and Semele, they share many characteristics with that genre, including English texts, elaborate choruses, and concert rather than staged performances. But there are certain operatic features, such as the secular text based on mythology, and in Hercules in particular, a heavy use of operatic forms such as the da capo aria (a three-part aria in the form ABA) and the cavatina (a one-part form). Though these are found in other oratorios they are particularly abundant in Hercules. This formal unity makes two contrasting scenes particularly striking in context: first, the scene in which Hercules dons the robe and the pains of death make him larger than life; and secondly, Dejanira's celebrated mad scene 'Where shall I fly?' These scenes stand apart from the typical forms and represent the climax of the drama. There are also several grand choruses in widely contrasting characters, from the festive dance-like character of 'Crown with festive pomp the day' to the famous 'Jealousy, infernal pest'.

Handel presented Hercules in two later seasons, 1749 and 1752, and in both he eliminated the character Lichas, although he transferred much of his music to other characters. In 1749 he shortened the work by eliminating several pieces, and in 1752 he made further cuts, even abridging Dejanira's mad scene, but adding 'Still caressing and caress'd' from Alceste.   DAVID ROSS HURLEY

D. Burrows, 'The Composition is as good as possible', CD booklet essay (Deutsche Grammophon Archiv, 469 532–2, 2002)
Burrows and Dunhill
Dean, Oratorios
D. R. Hurley, 'Dejanira and the Physicians: Aspects of Hysteria in Handel's Hercules', Musical Quarterly 80/3 (1996), 548–61
'Dejanira, Omphale, and the Emasculation of Hercules: Allusion and Ambiguity in Handel', Cambridge Opera Journal 11/3 (1999), 199–214
L. M. M. Robarts, 'A Bibliographical and Textual Study of the Wordbooks for James Miller's Joseph and his Brethren and Thomas Broughton's Hercules, Oratorio Librettos Set to Music by George Frideric Handel, 1743–44', Ph.D dissertation (University of Birmingham, 2008)
Smith, Oratorios

Herder, Johann Gottfried (b. Mohrungen, East Prussia, 25 Aug. 1744; d. Weimar, 18 Dec. 1803). Poet, clergyman and philosopher. In his writings on music aesthetics, he used Handel's large-scale vocal works (especially ALEXANDER'S FEAST) as examples for his discussions about questions of expressivity and on musical settings featuring the use of Affekte. He praised the musical depiction of the 'movements of the human heart' but attacked what he perceived as acoustic imitations.   HARTMUT KRONES (Trans. ANGELA BAIER)

J. G. Herder and J. G. Müller, Früchte aus den sogenanntgoldenen Zeiten des achtzehnten Jahrhunderts (Stuttgart and Tübingen, 1830)
H. Krones, 'J. G. Herder, die Affektenlehre und die Musik', Ideen und Ideale. J. G. Herder in Ost und West, ed. P. Andraschke and H. Loos (Freiburg i.B., 2002)

Hermann von Balcke. German pasticcio. All wordbooks and music are now lost, but until 1945 two wordbooks existed in ELBING, containing a libretto by Georg Daniel Seyler about the foundation of the town by Hermann von Balcke, a regional Master of the Teutonic Knights. In 1868 Döring claimed that Handel wrote this opera for the quincentenary commemoration of the Elbing's founding, but this is certainly false. One of the wordbooks contained the comment that the arias were by Handel and Johann Jeremias du Grain (who set all of the recitatives to music), and the other provided evidence that it was performed on 28 November 1737 by the town's *Kantor* Christian Lau. In 1926 Leux identified that sixteen of the opera's forty aria texts were taken from seven Handel operas, with their original Italian texts preserved. In 1933 Müller-Blattau proposed that many of the German aria texts were fitted to Handel arias with similar metres and dramatic affections.   KLAUS-PETER KOCH (Trans. ANGELA BAIER)

I. Leux, 'Über die "verschollene" Händel-Oper "Hermann von Balcke"', *Archiv für Musikwissenschaft* 8 (1926), 441–51

J. Müller-Blattau, 'Händels Festkantate zur Fünfhundertjahrfeier der Stadt Elbing 1737', *Elbinger Jahrbuch* 11 (1933), 239–53; repr. *50 Jahre Göttinger Händel-Festspiele. Festschrift*, ed. W. Meyerhoff (Kassel, 1970)

Herrenhausen. Palace and gardens outside HANOVER, in Handel's day the summer residence of the electoral family. Established by Johann Friedrich (r. 1649–65), they were enlarged by Ernst August (r. 1679–97); the architect was Giacomo Querini (or Quirini), the painter Tommaso Giusti, the sculptor Pieter van Empthusen and the landscape gardener Martin Charbonnier. The first garden theatre to incorporate perspective was built in the grounds in 1689–92. The court resided at Herrenhausen from May to October, and Ernst August's widow, Sophie, retired there. His son Georg Ludwig (later GEORGE I) continued improving both palace and gardens, which drew admiration from Toland. He planted an avenue of 1,300 lime trees (the Herrenhausen *allée*) in 1725 and opened the gardens to the public.   COLIN TIMMS

J. Toland, *An Account of the Courts of Prussia and Hannover, sent to a Minister of State in Holland* (London, 1705)

Hervey, Lord John (b. London, 15 Oct. 1696; d. Ickworth, Suffolk, 5 Aug. 1743). Courtier and writer. Hervey's highly partisan *Memoirs* (published 1848) misled numerous biographers into writing that FREDERICK, Prince of Wales, opposed Handel in the 1730s, as a way of distancing himself from his father, GEORGE II, and his sister Princess ANNE. Writers have claimed that the OPERA OF THE NOBILITY was a significant part of Frederick's campaign. In fact, the Prince and his father not only supported financially but also attended the Nobility Opera. Hervey's jealousy of the Prince caused him to severely misjudge Handel's relationships with members of the royal family.   DAVID HUNTER

Hetherington, John (b. ?1697; d. 1778). Lawyer, who witnessed the first and second codicils to Handel's will and received a legacy of £100 under the fourth codicil (HANDEL, 8). He dined with George and Thomas HARRIS, Handel and Charles JENNENS at the latter's London house 29 May 1756. He was tutor to Lord John Russell (1710–71) on his grand tour 1730–1 (Russell unexpectedly succeeded his brother in 1732 as 4th Duke of Bedford).   DAVID HUNTER

Burrows and Dunhill

J. Ingamells, *A Dictionary of British and Irish Travelers in Italy, 1701–1800* (New Haven, 1997)

Hill, Aaron (b. London, 10 Feb. 1685; d. London, ?8 Feb. 1750), author, entrepreneur and theatre impresario, played a seminal role in Handel's early career in England. In November 1710 Hill was appointed by William Collier to direct opera at the Queen's Theatre, Haymarket (KING'S THEATRE), after actors' strikes forced Collier out of DRURY LANE. The Haymarket company, starring the famous castrato NICOLINO, capitalised on the growing London vogue for Italian opera. Hill probably met Handel in London towards the end of 1710 and they collaborated on *RINALDO*, giving the company its first real critical success. Hill, working with Giacomo ROSSI, produced a libretto to fit round Handel's score, some of it drawn from Handel's earlier work in Europe. *Rinaldo*'s dazzling stage effects, involving fire-breathing dragons, moving mountains and waterfalls, contributed to the opera's popular acclaim but also inspired satirical attacks in ADDISON and Steele's *Spectator*. Collier sacked Hill after only three performances (probably for his financial extravagance) and he never had the chance to work with Handel again.

Hill's patriotic preface to the printed libretto of *Rinaldo* optimistically prophesied that Italian opera in England would inspire native English opera, but by 1730 he had become ambivalent about the imported genre because the taste for it thwarted any possibility of serious English opera. He joined a chorus of disapproval attacking the effeminacy and degeneracy of Italian opera, and in 1732 he championed the short-lived vogue for English operas such as CAREY and LAMPE's *Amelia*. Hill was almost certainly the author that year of the anonymous pamphlet *See and Seem Blind* which, among other targets, attacked Handel's popular oratorios and dismissed *ESTHER* as a 'religious farce' rendered incomprehensible by Italian singers. Hill wanted instead fully fledged sacred dramas performed by English actors. In December 1732 he wrote to Handel pleading with him to change the tide in national musical taste, and to 'deliver us from our Italian bondage; and demonstrate that English is soft enough for Opera'. He also implored Handel to create music theatre 'reconciling reason and dignity . . . [that] would charm the *ear*, and hold fast the *heart*, together' (Deutsch, 299). Hill's conviction that Handel could single-handedly accomplish this feat, captured by his eulogistic *Ode, on Occasion of Mr Handel's Great Te Deum at the Feast of the Sons of the Clergy, on Feb, 1732*', shows an admiration for Handel that, despite their differences, he never lost.   CHRISTINE GERRARD

C. Gerrard, *Aaron Hill: The Muses' Projector 1685–1750* (Oxford, 2003)
A. Hill (attr.), *See and Seem Blind: Or, A Critical Dissertation on the Publick Diversions, etc.*, ed. R. D. Hume (Los Angeles, 1986)
J. Milhous and R. D. Hume, 'The Haymarket Opera in 1711', *EM* 17/4 (Nov. 1989), 523–38

Hiller, Johann Adam (b. Wendisch Ossig (Osiek Łużycki), 25 Dec. 1728; d. Leipzig, 16 June 1804). Composer and music historian. His performances of *MESSIAH* contributed to the development of German bourgeois concert life. For his heavily adapted version performed in the BERLIN Dom in 1786, he used the translation by KLOPSTOCK and EBELING, from which recitatives and arias were translated into rather bad Italian by D. Gasperini. In the same year, Hiller performed *Messiah* at Leipzig, this time using his own translation of the libretto, and repeated this policy for an uncut version in 1787. Hiller later thought of Handel as a distant giant of a 'bygone era' and regarded his oratorios primarily as church music.   WERNER RACKWITZ (Trans. ANGELA BAIER)

H. Grimm, 'Hillers Berliner Messias-Aufführung im Kontext seines Schrifttums', *Händel-Rezeption der frühen Goethe-Zeit*, ed. L. Lütteken and G. Busch (Kassel, 2000)
J. A. Hiller, *Mein Leben: Autobiographie, Briefe und Nekrologe*, ed. M. Lehmstedt (Leipzig, 2004)
M. Marx-Weber, 'Johann Adam Hiller als Bearbeiter Händelscher Werke', HJb 39 (1993)

Hinsch, Heinrich (b. Stade, c.1650–60; d. Hamburg, 5 May 1712). German poet and librettist. After studying theology and law, he moved to HAMBURG, where he became one of the most productive librettists associated with the GÄNSEMARKT opera house. In his preface to *Claudius* (1703, set to music by Reinhard KEISER), Hinsch advocated that operas should entertain the senses of an audience 'without attempting to address their reason or understanding'. He wrote a lengthy libretto (*FLORINDO*) for Handel, but it is likely that he intended it to be divided into two connected operas: *Der beglückte Florindo* and *Die verwandelte Daphne* (the music of both is lost).   WALTER KREYSZIG

See also LIBRETTOS, I

H. Rupp and C. L. Lang (eds.), *Deutsches Literatur-Lexikon*, vol. 7 (Berne and Munich, 3rd edn, 1979)
H. Schröder, *Lexikon der hamburgischen Schriftsteller*, vol. 3 (Hamburg, 1857)

Hoare, William ('Hoare of Bath') (b. near Eye, Suffolk, c.1707; d. Bath, 12 Dec. 1792). English painter and printmaker. His parents sent him to London to study with Giuseppe Grisoni. In 1728 he went with Grisoni to Italy, where he stayed for nine years. Then he settled in BATH and came into vogue as a portraitist for the city's notable visitors.   EDWIN WERNER

See also ICONOGRAPHY; Appendix 4

M. Holbrook, 'Painters in Bath in the Eighteenth Century', *Apollo* 98 (1973), 375–84

Hogarth, William (b. London, 10 Nov. 1697; d. London, 25 Oct. 1764). A leading British artist during the first half of the eighteenth century, and of particular significance as a history painter and portraitist. He is best known for his satirical paintings and engravings in which he made observations about his cultural peers and different sectors of contemporary London life; his attacks included the adulation received by Italian opera singers. In his early print *Masquerades and Operas* he shows CUZZONI singing in a benefit performance, while a nobleman pours out a sack of gold coins in front of her. She holds a rake, so literally rakes in the money. Handel and Hogarth had mutual friends such as Thomas MORELL, but there is no direct evidence that they were close acquaintances. They were united by their respective efforts to support the FOUNDLING HOSPITAL through donating their artistic talents, and one of Hogarth's finest paintings is the full-length, seated portrait of the hospital's founder, Thomas CORAM. Hogarth painted a small portrait sketch that is traditionally said to represent Handel.   EDWIN WERNER

J. Barlow, *The Enraged Musician: Hogarth's Musical Imagery* (Aldershot, 2005)
D. Bindman, *Hogarth* (London, 1981)
J. Uglow, *William Hogarth: A Life and a World* (London, 1997)

'Holy, holy' ('Heilig, heilig'). An ADAPTATION of the aria 'Dove sei' from *RODELINA*, with words in English or German. It was very popular as a recital item for concerts in the nineteenth century, and is also known under the title *Prayer / Gebet*.   ANNETTE LANDGRAF

Horn. See INSTRUMENTATION

Houbraken, Jacobus (b. Dordrecht, Holland, 25 Dec. 1698; d. Amsterdam, 14 Nov. 1780). The leading portrait engraver in eighteenth-century Holland. In 1737 he engraved a portrait of Handel that was originally intended to be included for the subscription of *ALEXANDER'S FEAST* (Figure 14). However, it was also used in subsequent publications and was sold by Handel himself from his house on Brook Street (MUSEUMS, 2). The portrait with a scene taken from Hubert François Gravelot on the lower part of the plate (depicting Timotheus playing to Alexander the Great and Thais, as described in *Alexander's Feast*) is based on an unknown original.   EDWIN WERNER

J. Simon, *Handel: A Celebration of his Life and Times 1685–1759* (London, 1985)

How beautiful are the feet. See ANTHEMS, 7

Howlatt, Thomas. Printer and publisher, of Silver (now Barter) Street, Bloomsbury, active in the second decade of the eighteenth century, who produced the WORD-BOOK for Handel's first London opera, *RINALDO* (1711). On the title page Howlatt described himself as 'Printer to the *House*' – that is the Queen's Theatre (KING'S THEATRE) in the Haymarket – but *Rinaldo* was, in fact, his only wordbook for this theatre. Wordbooks for the other operas during the 1710–11 season were published by Jacob TONSON. Howlatt's only other recorded wordbook was for a production of ECCLES's setting of Motteux's *Acis and Galatea* at LINCOLN'S INN FIELDS. Howlatt was named in Aaron HILL's lawsuit against the managers of the Queen's Theatre as one of the tradesmen (the only one to be named) who conspired with the management to defraud Hill by making him responsible for bills which should have been covered by the subscriptions.

JOHN GREENACOMBE

Hudson, Thomas (b. Devon, perhaps Bideford, ?1701; d. Twickenham, 26 Jan. 1779). Portrait painter. He trained under Jonathan Richardson (1665–1745), later marrying his daughter. From 1745 until 1755 he was the most successful London portraitist and was praised for having the ability to catch a likeness. He painted members of the royal family, other persons of the nobility and Handel twice: in 1748/9 (see Figure 15), and 1756 (see Figure 10). A large number of his portraits were engraved, his first Handel portrait by Andrew Miller (1748) and John Faber (1748/9). Hudson supported Thomas CORAM's FOUNDLING HOSPITAL, of which Handel was also a governor. The artist also formed a collection which contained the terracotta model of Roubiliac's statue of Handel for VAUXHALL GARDENS (now in the FITZWILLIAM MUSEUM).   EDWIN WERNER

See also ICONOGRAPHY; MONUMENTS

14. A portrait of Handel, engraving by Jacobus Houbraken after an unknown original, 1738.

15. A portrait of Handel by Thomas Hudson, oil on canvas, 1748–9.

Hughes, John (b./bap.? Marlborough, 29 Jan. 1678; d. London, 17 Feb. 1720). English poet. Hughes is remembered for his encouragement of composers to set English rather than foreign texts. To this end he wrote texts for *Ode in Praise of Musick* (1703), which was set by Hart, *Calypso and Telemachus* (1712) set by GALLIARD, and the masque *Apollo and Daphne* (1716), set by PEPUSCH. Hughes wrote a cantata text, *VENUS AND ADONIS* (c.1710), which was published in London in 1735 as 'A Cantata set by Mr. Handel'. Handel may indeed have set Hughes's text, but no autograph survives, and the two airs existing in a manuscript copy may not be by him.   LESLIE M. ROBARTS

Burrows
J. M. Knapp, 'A Forgotten Chapter in English Eighteenth-Century Opera', ML 42/1 (1961), 4–17

Humphreys, Samuel (b. c.1698; d. Canonbury, London, 11 Jan. 1737). English writer. From 1730 he was Handel's main literary assistant at the KING'S THEATRE, providing the text for the expanded version of *ESTHER* (1732), the librettos of *DEBORAH* and *ATHALIA*, and the English translations for the wordbooks of *PORO* (1731), the revised *RINALDO* (1731), *EZIO* (1732), *SOSARME* (1732) and *ORLANDO* (1732), and for the pasticcio *VENCESLAO* (1731) and LEO's *CATONE IN UTICA* (1732), both produced by Handel. He was also the librettist of *Ulysses* (1733) by J. C. SMITH *JUNIOR*. Almost nothing is known of his life. He wrote poems praising the Duke of CHANDOS ('Cannons', for which he received £20) and Sir Robert WALPOLE, and a life of the 'TORY martyr' poet Matthew Prior, prefacing an edition of his poems (1733). According to the *London Magazine*, he took up translating to survive financially, and his most popular work, his translation from the French of Thomas-Simon Gueullette's *Peruvian Tales* (1734, completed by Samuel Kelly), enjoyed eight editions in the eighteenth century. He also translated *Spectacle de la nature* by Antoine Noël, abbé de la Pluche (1733) and works by Boccaccio, Crébillon and La Fontaine. His most substantial work was his three-volume *The Sacred Books of the Old and New Testament, Recited at Large* (1735), compiled from the major commentaries with additional remarks of his own, some of them political, which yields interesting glosses on many biblical oratorio subjects.   RUTH SMITH

R. Smith, 'Handel's English Librettists', *Cambridge Companion to Handel*, ed. D. Burrows
    (Cambridge, 1997)
    Oratorios

Hunold, Christian Friedrich ('Menantes') (b. Wandersleben, Thuringia, 29 Sept. 1681; d. Halle, 6 Aug. 1721). German author. Educated at Arnstadt and Weissenfels, in 1700 he moved to HAMBURG, where he joined an intellectual circle connected to the GÄNSEMARKT opera. He wrote novels in the *galant* genre, edited and published the poetic theories of Erdmann Neumeister, wrote the libretto of the first German-language oratorio-style PASSION (Hamburg, 1704), and developed a poetics of opera librettos in his *Theatralische Gedichte*, which criticised the libretto of Handel's *NERO* (1705). In 1708 he settled in HALLE.

UTE POETZSCH (Trans. ANGELA BAIER)

HHB iv
Menantes, *Theatralische, Galante und Geistliche Gedichte* (Hamburg, 1705)
    Ein Dichterleben zwischen Barock und Aufklärung, ed. C. Hobohm (Jena, 2006)

Hunter, James (b. London, 17 Dec. 1711; d. London, between July and Oct. 1757). Born into a wealthy Huguenot family, Hunter became a recognised international trader before he was twenty. He subscribed to the publications of *ALEXANDER'S FEAST* (1738) and the Op. 6 Concerti grossi (1740) (ORCHESTRAL WORKS, 2), and is also reputed to have acquired a collection of Handel's works in manuscript. The original volumes in the Barrett LENNARD collection (compiled c.1736–41) may preserve this set, their discontinuation coinciding with Hunter being declared bankrupt (SOURCES AND COLLECTIONS, 4). For a few years around this time he copied music for Handel, and is the scribe previously known as S7 (COPYISTS). In 1745 Hunter purchased a dye house in Old Ford and made a financial success of selling scarlet-dyed wool to the East India Company. Handel left him £500 in his original will of 1750 (HANDEL, 8). When the will was proved, Handel's servant John DUBURK testified 'that he well knew the said James Hunter' and that he 'died in the Life time of the said Mr. Handel'.

ELLEN T. HARRIS

D. Burrows, '"Something necessary to the connection": Charles Jennens, James Hunter and
    Handel's *Samson*', *Handel Institute Newsletter* 15/1 (2004), 1–3
E. T. Harris, 'James Hunter, Handel's Friend', *HJb* 46 (2000)

HWV (Thematisch-systematisches Verzeichnis der Werke Georg Friedrich Händels). A thematic-systematic catalogue of Handel's works compiled by Bernd BASELT, published as the *HÄNDEL-HANDBUCH* (vols. 1–3). Previous attempts to organise a worklist of Handel's compositions had been made by Jacob Maurice Coopersmith and A. Craig Bell, but the HWV was a landmark achievement because it created a coherent structure for the classification and identification of Handel's vast compositional output.

The HWV lists works systematically by genre; within genres works are presented in chronological order (e.g. OPERA and ORATORIO). For categories in which chronological order cannot be adequately established works are arranged alphabetically by title (e.g. Italian CANTATAS and SONGS). Numerous instrumental works which cannot be dated are arranged by keys. Each catalogue entry contains incipits of every movement (in the style of a vocal score), and has information about known compositional dates and performances under Handel. Different music related to alternative authentic versions is listed in an appendix for each relevant entry, and references are given to editions by CHRYSANDER and the HHA (EDITIONS, 7). Each entry also lists manuscript and printed sources (e.g. autographs, copies, early editions, WORDBOOKS), BORROWINGS and literature. Scholarly progress since 1986 means that the HWV will need to be fully revised after the HHA is completed.

ANNETTE LANDGRAF

See also Appendix 1 – Worklist

Hyde Park. In 1536 Henry VIII confiscated the manor of Hyde from WESTMINSTER ABBEY to extend his hunting ground from ST JAMES'S to Hampstead Heath. Limited public access began c.1630; after the Restoration the park was circled with a brick wall and became a place of promenade, carriage driving and military reviews, but also of duels and muggings. It was nearer than St James's Park to Handel's home on Brook Street (MUSEUMS, 2), and he may have walked there regularly. Landscaping began c.1730 when a stream was expanded into the 'Serpentine River'. The park was the original location of the CRYSTAL PALACE (built 1851), which was moved to Sydenham in 1854.   KERRY DOWNES

See also LONDON

Hymen. See IMENEO

hymns, HWV 284–6. Handel wrote three fine hymn tunes (c.1746–7), all settings of hymns by Charles WESLEY (1703–88), to whom he is thought to have been introduced by Priscilla Rich (the wife of John RICH). His source for the words was probably *24 Hymns for the Great Festivals and Other Occasions*, published in 1746 with tunes by another German musician, Johann Friedrich LAMPE. Handel's tunes are on a single page of manuscript at the FITZWILLIAM MUSEUM, and are set for voice and figured bass with interludes. They were discovered there, arranged and published in 1827 by Charles WESLEY's son, the composer Samuel Wesley (1766–1837). They have been known by the names 'Cannons', 'Fitzwilliam', and 'Gopsal'. The last-named is in widespread use in conjunction with its original text, 'Rejoice, the Lord is king'. However, Handel's three original hymns are dwarfed in popularity by the many ADAPTATIONS from his other works.   NICHOLAS TEMPERLEY

I will magnify thee. See ANTHEMS, I; II

iconography. There are about five hundred known depictions of Handel (a selection is listed in Appendix 4). Among the numerous preserved paintings and sculptures created during his lifetime and shortly after his death, there are more than twenty that can be regarded as authentic and probably capture a real likeness of the composer (painted from about 1710). In the last twenty-five years doubts have been cast on the authenticity (i.e. the identity of sitters and artists) of many more, often on account of gaps in the documentation of their provenance. However, to discard depictions lacking proper documentation can seem overly pedantic in the search for authentic portraits giving real likenesses. The decisive question to be asked when evaluating a portrait should therefore be whether the physiognomical characteristics of the sitter resemble the known 'authentic' portraits, whereas questions about possible attributions or artistic 'worth' are of less immediate importance.

The first portrait generally regarded as authentic and giving a real likeness of Handel is a miniature by (Johann or Jacob?) Christoph PLATZER (Figure 23). The provenance of this youthful portrait can only be traced back as far as 1920 but it does reproduce, in close comparison with other known portraits, certain particular physiognomical characteristics of the sitter. The next portrait is an anonymous oil painting dating from around 1720. Its original attribution to James Thornhill (1675–1734) seems unsustainable, but a comparison of this picture with the undoubtedly authentic portrait of Handel by Philip MERCIER (c.1730) yields the certain conclusion that the sitter is indeed the same person. These two portraits, in addition to a few sculptures by Louis-François ROUBIL-IAC (especially the 1739 terracotta bust in the Thomas Coram Foundation) and a portrait of Handel attributed to Bartholomew DANDRIDGE (possibly painted between 1725 and 1732) are among the few portraits that depict the composer without a wig. They all reproduce similar facial features and resemble each other closely in their depiction of the form of the head, ears and earlobes. The assumption that the sitter is indeed Handel is further strengthened by the fact that on his left cheek the traces of a mole can be distinguished. This mole is also discernible on Jacobus HOUBRAKEN's 1737/8 engraving (where it is side-inverted) (Figure 14), on the terracotta bust by Roubiliac and in a portrait by John Theodore HEINS (1740; see Figure 13), which indicates that the so-called 'Thornhill' portrait might have been painted from life. However, it is still difficult to determine for which painters Handel really 'sat'; for example, the composer's eye colour varies even between 'authentic' portraits.

Between 1725 and 1728 Handel seems to have been portrayed a number of times. The well-known portrait by DENNER (Figure 5) dates from around 1727/8. There is also a highly expressive anonymous engraving (where Handel is wearing the same wig as in the Denner portrait), which was probably copied from another art work. The 'Denner wig' also appears in a small portrait sketch by William HOGARTH, presumably dating from the years between 1725 and 1728 as well. A number of other contested 'Handel' portraits by Balthasar Denner, or at least attributed to him, have survived, but, since the artist spent only a limited amount of time in London, it is difficult to assess their authenticity. The *Deutsches Historisches Museum* in Berlin has a portrait of Handel signed by Denner and dated 1733. The fact that the painting is signed would alone make it one of the 'most genuine' portraits, but it has not usually been counted among the Handel depictions considered as authentic. Another anonymous painting (in Knole House) is signed, dated and attributed to Denner in an inscription on the frame but the signature seems to be spurious. The sitter in this portrait resembles that in another Handel portrait, painted by John Theodore HEINS in 1740 and only made accessible to a larger public in 2005. Even if the portrait in Knole House is not by Denner, there can be little doubt that it is indeed an authentic depiction of the composer.

Georg Andreas WOLFGANG junior also portrayed Handel in London, probably in 1737. His preparatory sketch in pencil and sepia was formerly in the possession of the Musikbibliothek Peters. This sketch seems to have been the model for his well-known miniature and an engraving by Johann Georg Wolfgang senior (1662–1744). A third painting attributed to G. A. Wolfgang junior is now in the Musikmuseet in Stockholm. It is said to have been painted in 1731 and might be the missing portrait formerly in the collection of Charles BURNEY.

Following the commission issued to Louis-François Roubiliac for a marble statue of Handel to be erected in VAUXHALL GARDENS (Figure 24; (MONUMENTS), the sculptor prepared, among other works, a terracotta bust of Handel (1739), which was regarded by contemporary spectators as resembling the living Handel closely. It is therefore one of the most important 'reference points' in determining the authenticity of other portraits of the composer. In 1737 Jacobus Houbraken engraved a large print with a portrait of Handel; shortly afterwards, in 1740, John Theodore Heins portrayed Handel again (both depictions portray similar physiognomical characteristics). Another well-known, though unsigned, portrait of Handel, probably dated around 1745, was formerly attributed to Thomas HUDSON and, since the mid-1970s, is now thought to have been painted by Francis van der Myn (1719–83). Probably one of the best-known portraits of Handel, painted by Hudson in 1748/9 (Figure 15), shows the composer in a statesmanlike pose wearing precious robes and holding a score of *MESSIAH*. This depiction has been often reproduced in other prints and engravings since the beginning of the twentieth century. According to historical sources, Handel took the Hudson portrait with him when he visited his relatives in Halle for the last time in 1750. About ten years later Hudson painted another portrait of Handel, who in the meantime had gone blind.

More works by Roubiliac probably capture the external appearance of Handel even better. They show Handel shortly before and after his death, and can be likened to the great Hudson portraits with the exception that Roubiliac's Handel is now an old man. Perhaps Roubiliac's greatest work – for which his other portraits seem to have functioned as preliminary studies – is the magnificent monument (Figure 31) in WESTMINSTER ABBEY (MONUMENTS). Possibly the most precious Handel relic of all, the so-called 'death mask', is privately owned. It was undoubtedly the basis for further works by Roubiliac and has therefore been attributed to him. The mask shows Handel with his eyes open, and may not be a 'death mask' at all, but some scholars, *inter alios* Victor SCHOELCHER, believe that Roubiliac took a cast of the composer's face 'on the very day' of his death, and afterwards retouched it by opening the eyes.

In addition to the 'authentic' portraits of Handel, or at least to those now regarded as authentic, there are a number of further depictions of Handel, of which it is not (yet) known whether they were painted from life or, indeed, whether the sitter is in fact Handel. (See Appendix 4 for a selected list). Among them is a portrait by William HOARE of Bath, which is certainly of Handel. It is conceivable that it was painted between 1737 and 1751 during a visit by the composer to the artist's home city (BATH).

Another unsigned portrait from the estate of Handel's sister, which, like the 1748/9 Hudson portrait, shows the composer sitting at a table dates from after 1750 and is still family-owned. Possibly members of Handel's family commissioned this portrait from a local painter after they had been given the famous Hudson portrait by Handel himself in 1750. Countless depictions were made after Handel's death: there are innumerable busts, sculptures, monuments, paintings and especially engravings that are more or less successful at portraying the composer, as well as adaptations of known authentic portraits for medals, invitations and so on.

Even though they are not 'portraits' in the strict sense of the word, there were also caricatures and satiric depictions of Handel and the circles in which he moved. Probably the best known of these is a gouache by Joseph GOUPY, c.1743 (Figure 9), now in the FITZWILLIAM MUSEUM, which also circulated in a number of engraved copies. It depicted Handel, probably in allusion to his great appetite for food, as an organ-playing *Charming Brute*. It is unsurprising that Handel's and Goupy's friendship is said to have ended over this caricature.

EDWIN WERNER (Trans. ANGELA BAIER)

See also APPENDIX 4: HANDEL ICONOGRAPHY

H. Börsch-Supan, 'Georg Friedrich Händel und Balthasar Denner', GHB II (1986)

The Gerald Coke Handel Collection: Exhibition, Jenkyn Place, Bentley, Hampshire, 1985

J. W. Goodison, *Catalogue of Paintings in the Fitzwilliam Museum, Cambridge*, vol. 3: *British School* (Cambridge, 1977)

J. F. Kerslake, *Early Georgian Portraits* (London, 1977)

H. J. Marx, 'Händel', MGG

D. Saywell and J. Simon, *Complete Illustrated Catalogue, National Portrait Gallery* (London, 2004)

W. Schenkluhn, 'Zwischen Repräsentation und Selbstdarstellung – Die späten Händelporträts von Thomas Hudson', HJb 49 (2003)

J. Simon (ed.), *Handel: A Celebration of his Life and Times 1685–1759* (London, 1985)

W. C. Smith, *A Handel Iconography*, unpublished typescript (Gerald Coke Handel Collection, Lfom 1627)

E. Werner, 'G. F. Händel freundlich und gelassen . . . ', *Händel-Hausmitteilungen* 15 (2006)

Illness. See HANDEL, 16

Imeneo, HWV 41. Handel's penultimate Italian opera, first performed during his season at LINCOLN'S INN FIELDS Theatre in 1740–1, and revived as a 'Serenata' at Fishamble Street Music Room, DUBLIN in 1742, his last public performances of an Italian work. The libretto was derived from a two-part *componimento drammatico* for a wedding celebration at NAPLES in 1723, with a libretto by Silvio STAMPIGLIA and music by Nicola PORPORA. A version of this as a three-act opera was performed at VENICE in 1726, but Handel's libretto seems to have been expanded independently by an unidentified literary collaborator in London, and his score went through an unusually extended process of revision before it came to performance.

The story of the opera, set in ancient Athens, concerns the choice that Rosmene has to make between two rival suitors. Tirinto, to whom she is betrothed, laments that she has gone with other virgins to take part in the rites in honour of the goddess Ceres. It is rumoured that their ship has been captured by pirates, but it turns out that Imeneo, who had travelled with the virgins disguised as a woman in order to be near Rosmene, has slaughtered the pirates while they were sleeping. As a reward he claims the hand of Rosmene; he is supported by the senator Argenio (whose daughter Clomiri was also on board the ship), but Tirinto is horrified at the proposal. Clomiri is upset because she has fallen in love with Imeneo herself, but he seems indifferent to her. Faced with the rival claims of Imeneo and Tirinto, Rosmene gives non-committal answers.

In Act II Argenio tells Rosmene that she should favour Imeneo, even though this means breaking faith with Tirinto; he announces that the Athenians support Imeneo, but the choice is left to her. Both Imeneo and Tirinto urge her to make her choice, and renew the pressure on her at the beginning of Act III. Rosmene says that her heart is torn between them, and Imeneo declares that he will marry no one but Rosmene, to Clomiri's disappointment. Rosmene resolves to announce her choice and, feigning a trancelike state, enacts a descent to Hades where the judge Radamanto 'cleaves away' her heart with his sword, whereupon she faints into the arms of the two men, but then reassures them that she is not really delirious. Saying that she is like a ship coming to anchor, she gives her hand to Imeneo, and asks Tirinto to accept the situation calmly.

According to the Argument that summarises the background to the story in the printed wordbook for the opera, Hymen (Imeneo) 'liv'd happily with her for the rest of his Life'. Rosmene's dilemma had been between 'love' and 'duty', and her choice (the opposite path from that apparently promoted in ORLANDO) apparently turned out well. Handel's musical treatment of the story has an ironic twist, for Tirinto's music, especially the showpiece aria 'Sorge nell'alma mia', is clearly in the opera seria tradition of dominant, heroic, castrato roles, while Imeneo is a baritone: there is no doubt, on the basis of musical signals, about which of the men an ambitious girl ought to choose. Another unconventional feature of *Imeneo* is the simplicity of the plot: Rosemene's dilemma takes more than two acts to resolve. This may be attributed to the inflation of the original two-part libretto, but in practice the drama is diversified with a variety of incidents and cross-currents, and it is presented through some attractive, accessible music, in chorus movements as well as arias.

The first performance of Imeneo took place on 22 November 1740, and was one of the few occasions in Handel's later career for which we have evidence of King GEORGE II's attendance. The cast was as follows:

Imeneo   William SAVAGE (baritone)
Tirinto   Andreoni (castrato)
Rosmene   FRANCESINA (soprano)
Clomiri   Miss Edwards (soprano)
Argenio   Henry REINHOLD (bass)

Only five years previously Savage had sung in Handel's ALCINA as a boy treble. Miss Edwards was a young protégée of the actress Kitty CLIVE. In a modification to suit the relative ages of the cast, Argenio was Clomiri's father, instead of her brother as in the source libretto. A performance was announced for 29 November but cancelled on account of Francesina's indisposition, and only one further presentation followed, on 13 December. Handel curtailed the run on account of cold weather, but he did not take up Imeneo again when he resumed his performances nearly a month later. The Lincoln's Inn Fields theatre may have been particularly suited to the intimate drama of Imeneo, which required only one stage setting, 'A Pleasant Garden'.

The score had a curiously extended history before it came to the stage. Handel originally drafted the opera, without the music for most of the recitatives, the choruses or a proper conclusion, in September and October 1738, between the composition of SAUL and ISRAEL IN EGYPT. Whatever his hopes at that time, he did not have the resources to present the opera in the following season, when he gave oratorio-style works at the King's Theatre, apart from the 'Dramatical composition' GIOVE IN ARGO at the end of the season, an Italian pasticcio largely drawing upon his previous music and without a castrato in the cast. Towards the end of his all-English 1739–40 season at Lincoln's Inn Fields he had hopes of introducing an opera and pulled out the score of Imeneo again, subjecting it to a thoroughgoing revision which reached the opening scenes of Act III, whereupon he had to abandon the project again. In 1740–1 he finally had a cast that would make the production possible. Most of his programme consisted of English works, but with Imeneo and then DEIDAMIA (produced in January and February 1741) he made his final farewell to Italian opera in London.

The Dublin version was, at most, semi-staged, and the score was reworked to suit the singers at his disposal. Imeneo was taken by the baritone Calloghan McCarty, Mrs CIBBER played Tirinto and Christina AVOGLIO played Rosmene; the role of Clomiri was reduced, possibly to vanishing-point, and the identity of the bass singer for Argenio is unknown. The new score was coherent, but some of the revisions removed the dramatic edge from the story: 'Sorge nell'alma mia' was given to Imeneo, and a duet from SOSARME was introduced at the end to indulge the musical combination of Avolio and Cibber, with rather curious effect since Rosmene had just rejected Tirinto.   DONALD BURROWS

D. Burrows (ed.), Imeneo, HHA II/40 (Kassel, 2002)
Dean, Operas
Harris, Librettos
J. H. Roberts, 'The Story of Handel's Imeneo', HJb, 2001
Strohm

In the Lord put I my trust. See ANTHEMS, II

instrumentation

1. General characteristics of Handel's use of instruments
2. Bassoon
3. Carillon
4. Clarinet
5. Continuo
6. Cornetto
7. Drums
8. Flute
9. Harp
10. Harpsichord
11. Horn
12. Mandolin
13. Oboe
14. Organ
15. Recorder
16. Theorbo, lute and guitar
17. Trombone
18. Trumpet
19. Viol
20. Viola
21. Violin
22. Violetta marina
23. Violoncello
24. Violone

1. General characteristics of Handel's use of instruments

Handel's standard orchestra, like that of his contemporaries, was the four-part band with first and second violins, viola, basso continuo, with oboes sometimes doubling the string parts. According to different semantic contexts, this line-up could be reinforced by various woodwind, brass and other less usual instruments. He sometimes divided the orchestra into concertino and concerto grosso, soli and tutti, into two instrumental choirs of equal musical value, or split smaller ensembles from the main band to play on or behind the stage. A prospective list for the Royal Academy of Music's orchestra (OPERA COMPANIES, 2) and contemporary eyewitness descriptions of performances at the KING'S THEATRE suggest that Handel's ensemble consisted of about twenty violins, perhaps three or four violas, four cellos, two double basses, two harpsichords, an archlute, two to four oboes and three or four bassoons. The large number of violins, typical of Handel's age, is in keeping with the rising importance of the violin group within the orchestra. The band frequently included two horns and one trumpet. Further instruments like recorders and flutes were apparently played alternatingly by other members of the orchestra (most likely the oboists), not by specialists. The size of the orchestra in general was variable and could be adjusted to particular venues or occasions.

Basso continuo. See Continuo

2. Bassoon

Since c.1700 the bassoon had been a four-jointed double-reed instrument (wing joint, boot, bass joint and bell) with a conical bore. The bocal connected the reed, held in the mouth, to the wooden body of the instrument. The addition of three tone holes (F, D, B flat) extended the bassoon's range from the original C major scale to a chromatic scale.

In his opera scores, Handel usually calls the bassoon *Basson*, sometimes *Fagotto* or *Bassoon*. The range does not exceed the usual C to g′, and the bassoon parts are usually notated in the bass or tenor clef. Handel used the bassoon only rarely in his Italian works (but especially in *RODRIGO* and *La RESUR-REZIONE*) because the instrument was not widely known in Italy. However, in London it became a standard member of the orchestra. Handel usually had bassoons doubling the basso continuo line, but sometimes gave them independent (sometimes divided) and concertante parts (*RINALDO*, *AMADIGI*, *ARIO-DANTE*, *ALEXANDER'S FEAST* with two bassoons and *Fagotto III ripieni*) or assigned them the bass line in oboe trios (*ALMIRA*, *Rinaldo*, *ATHALIA*, *SAUL* and several Concerti a due cori (*ORCHESTRAL WORKS*, 1)). The use of oboes and bassoons on stage in *Ariodante* is noteworthy. The timbre of the bassoon lent a special tone colour to tragic, sombre or pastoral scenes, such as accompanied recitatives in *OTTONE*, *Saul* and *RODELINDA*, and the Cave of Sleep in *SEMELE*. Handel used contrabassoon (*basson grosso*, *double basson*) in *L'ALLEGRO* and the *MUSIC FOR THE ROYAL FIREWORKS*, in the latter work together with eight Fag. I and four Fag. II.

3. Carillon

The carillon, also called *Glockenklavier* in contemporary sources, should be in G and have a range of two to three octaves. Handel used it in the lavishly scored *Saul* (1739), which also included three trombones, kettledrums and a harp, and for performances of Il *TRIONFO DEL TEMPO E DELLA VERITÀ* on 3 March 1739, *ACIS AND GALATEA* in December 1739 and *L'Allegro* in February 1740. The carillon, like the trombones, was heard by London audiences for the first time in *Saul*, but was not used by Handel after 1740. Charles JENNENS reported in a letter that Handel had commissioned 'a very queer instrument which he calls carillon (Anglice, a Bell) . . . 'Tis played upon with keys like a Harpsichord, and with this Cyclopean instrument he designs to make poor Saul stark mad.' Since this particular instrument has not survived and nothing further is known about it, the carillon part in *Saul* is nowadays played by a Celesta or a *Lyra-Glockenspiel* (Bell-Lyra).

Cello. See Violoncello

4. Clarinet

The chalumeau, a single-reed instrument of predominantly cylindrical bore and two keys, whose (still unclear) relationship to the clarinet has been the subject of many controversial and learned disputes to date, had a range of f′–c‴. Handel used two chalumeaux in *RICCARDO PRIMO*. In the conducting score of *TAMERLANO* Handel calls for a *Clar:* or *Clarin* in the aria 'Par che mi nasca in seno'; this might refer to the same chalumeau instrument or to a genuine clarinet (6. CORNETTO).

5. Continuo

The exact composition of the basso continuo group in the works of Handel, as in those of his contemporaries, is still somewhat of a mystery due to missing specifications and merely general statements concerning the instruments involved (such as *Bassi*, *Bassi tutti* and the like). Sometimes certain instruments can be identified as belonging to the basso continuo group through negative directions such as *Senza Cembalo e Bassons*, *Senza Violoncello e Contrabasso* and so on. In accordance with the performance practice of his time, Handel used, in addition to the harpsichord (or two harpsichords), the violoncello, double bass, bassoon and theorbo in his continuo group. Organs were used in oratorios (two organs in Saul, ISRAEL IN EGYPT), but their general role remains obscure, and it seems that they were never used in operas. In ESTHER (1732) and in DEBORAH (1733) Handel specified the use of two harpsichords and two organs. There was probably some continuo contribution from the harp when the instrument was available for performances of *Esther* and *Saul*.

The theorbo is regularly mentioned in the opera scores after 1720, but disappears after 1739. However, the sole fact that an instrument is not mentioned specifically in a score cannot be taken as confirmation that it was not included in the orchestra during the actual performance, and Handel certainly used a lute in his 1744 revival of *Deborah* (Burrows and Dunhill, p. 206). This is especially true for the double basses, which are not mentioned in numerous operatic scores but whose presence in the orchestra can be regarded as fairly certain, as well as for the bassoons. These instruments might not have needed explicit mentioning, either because their presence in the continuo group was regarded as a matter of course, as in the case of the bassoons (however, not in Italian orchestras, since the bassoon was rarely used in Italy) and the double basses, or because their pausing during vocal sections (or sections marked *piano*) was just as self-evident. As a general rule, the full basso continuo group probably played during tutti (or *forte*) sections in independent instrumental movements, choruses and aria ritornellos and, for reasons of musical balance (for example in the *Sonata a Violino Solo e Cembalo*, HWV 371), a reduced continuo group was employed during solo passages (i.e. instrumental and vocal solos), arias with obbligato or soft-sounding instruments and in secco recitatives.

The assumption that a bass or tenor clef in the score generally indicates the presence or the pausing of the double basses is questionable. The compositional context seems to be the decisive factor here since a reduction of the bass group was always connected to a reduction in the scoring of the upper parts (*Tutti*, *Solo* or *Soli*, vocal sections) in baroque performance practice.

6. Cornetto

The cornetto is an instrument widely used in baroque music (especially church music) and is tube-like in form, hexagonal or octagonal in cross-section and normally has six finger-holes on the front and one thumb-hole on the back side, giving the instrument a range between a and c'''. The cornetto is usually made of two curved wooden pieces wrapped in black parchment or leather. Handel calls for *Cornetti 1 et 2* (range c' to c''') in the aria 'Par che mi nasca in seno' in the autograph score of *Tamerlano*, but there is some doubt as to exactly what he meant by 'Cornetti'. Otherwise, there is no evidence that Handel ever used the instruments.

Double bass. See Violone

7. Drums

Eighteenth-century kettledrums or timpani usually consisted of two bowls of different sizes, made from copper, brass, silver or copper-coloured wood. The bowl was covered with a drumhead or membrane of tanned animal skin of an even thickness (mostly calf but also donkey, goat, sheep, horse or dog); the instrument was tuned using screws. The drumsticks, until the end of the eighteenth century rarely covered with a polstered tip, were made from different, well-dried types of wood like ebony, cherry tree, boxwood, beech tree and so on. Since the kettledrums were always used by Handel and in baroque compositional practice in general as foundation or bass part to the trumpet parts, their music is always notated with the trumpets (and sometimes horns). Handel used drums tuned to DA or CG and normally called them *Timpani, Kettel[drums]* (*Rinaldo*) or *Tamburi* (*Riccardo Primo*). They appear only rarely in Handel's operas (*Almira, Rinaldo, Riccardo Primo, Atalanta, DEIDAMIA*) but regularly in his church music (for example the Dettingen Te Deum (TE DEUM, 5)) and oratorios (especially *Saul, Israel in Egypt, SAMSON, JUDAS MACCABAEUS, JOSHUA* and *SOLOMON*). Handel's use of kettledrums with two oboes and strings in the accompagnato 'Lascia, Berardo' in *Riccardo Primo* is very unusual. Kettledrums are used without trumpets in *Israel in Egypt* ('But the waters overwhelmed their enemies', in imitation of the roaring sea) and *Semele* (in imitation of thunder). In *Saul* Handel used, for the first time, large kettledrums tuned an octave lower. The description *Timpani scordati* (*PARNASSO IN FESTA*) presumably refers to muted drums, such as were normally used in funeral ceremonies.

8. Flute

A transverse flute in 1700 still consisted of three sections. From 1720 they began to be made in the improved four-joint-type with a divided heartpiece. This new flute could be better adapted to different tunings by as many as seven exchangeable joints. Handel first used the transverse flute, which he called *Flauto traverso* or *Traversa* and notated in the treble clef (range d' to d'''), in his early Italian works (e.g. *La RESURREZIONE*). In his London theatre works (starting with *Il PASTOR FIDO*), the transverse flute seldom appears as a solo instrument, although 'Ombre, piante' (*Rodelinda*) and 'Sweet bird' (*L'Allegro*) are fine exceptions to the rule. The flute was normally used to double the vocal or the violin parts (for example *Radamisto*). The *Traversa Bassa* in B flat (needed in *Riccardo Primo*) is a transposing flute with a lower sound. The transverse flute was usually played by an oboist; the first genuine flautist to be engaged by Handel was Carl Friedrich WEIDEMANN in *Tamerlano* (1724).

9. Harp

From the mid-seventeenth century the harp became established as a chromatically tuned instrument with two ranks of strings (*Harpa doppia*) and a range between C and c'''. It was used by Handel in one opera and in four oratorios; he also wrote the *Concerto per la Harpa*, Op. 4 No. 6 (HWV 294) for the instrument

(ORCHESTRAL WORKS). In *Giulio Cesare* he used a harp with a range of C to a″ as part of the stage music in the 'Parnassus' scene (II.ii). The harp appears as a solo instrument in *Esther* and *Saul*, and there is an unusual combination of a harp (ranging up to e‴) and a mandolin in *ALEXANDER BALUS*.

10. Harpsichord

In Handel's time the harpsichord was a keyboard instrument with one, two or sometimes three manuals and two 8-foot-pitch registers, sometimes also with 4- and 16-foot-pitch registers and an overall range from C to c‴ (with a short octave and a full chromatic range from F to f″). Although Handel was a renowned harpsichordist, he primarily used the instrument in public to perform as part of the basso continuo group, although it is seldom mentioned explicitly in the score.

Handel's works composed for Hamburg and in his larger vocal works for Rome probably featured only one harpsichord, but for his London operas it seems that the composer used two harpsichords (and a theorbo). The need for two harpsichords, not unusual at that time, perhaps increased when the orchestra was divided into concertino and concerto grosso because both orchestral sections needed their own harpsichord. In Tutti sections both harpsichords played. The duet 'Tu caro sei il dolce' in *SOSARME* suggests that at least from the early 1730s Handel alternated the two harpsichords to accompany the different voices in duets. He rarely used harpsichord as an obbligato instrument (*Aci, Galatea e Polifemo* and, most famously, 'Vo' far guerra' in *Rinaldo*).

Baroque composers generally used the direction *Senza Cembalo(-i)* to indicate a dynamic reduction in the accompaniment to vocal parts, in arias with concertante plucked instruments (for example the direction *con la Theorba e Basso pizzicati senza Bassons e Cembalo* in *PARTENOPE*), other soft instruments (such as flutes, bassoons or violins), or in arias scored only for strings or woodwind instruments. It was typical to omit the harpsichord when the strings played pizzicato. The direction *tasto solo*, which appears now and then in the scores, indicates that the bass line was performed without chords.

11. Horn

The horn, a brass instrument consisting of a metal tube coiled into a circular shape and a flared bell at the base, is first mentioned by Handel in a stage direction in the autograph score of *Il pastor fido* (1712). He composed his first genuine horn parts in the *WATER MUSIC*, but soon reworked these parts in his first oratorio *Esther* (c.1719). From *Radamisto* onwards he used horns in many of his operas and oratorios, mostly horns in F, although sometimes in C, G, D, A or B flat. They appear as transposing and non-transposing instruments and their music is notated in the treble clef; Handel usually called the horn 'Corno'. He usually used horns in pairs, predominantly in choruses and instrumental movements, but during the early 1730s he increasingly used them to notable effect (*ORLANDO* and *ARIANNA IN CRETA*), sometimes with a contrasting pair of recorders (*PORO* and *Sosarme*), or with a complementary pair of oboes (*Partenope*), but less often with trumpets (*Deidamia*). Handel used horns to double the trumpet parts (albeit sounding an octave below) in choruses in his 1754 FOUNDLING HOSPITAL performances of *Messiah*. He occasionally used more than two horns, such as three in *Deborah* and four in the *Concerto a due cori* (HWV

333–5^b). *Giulio Cesare* is unusual in calling for four differently tuned horns (one each in A and D, G and D), and also features a solo part for a single horn ('Va tacito'). Handel's only other solo obbligato horn part is 'Mirth admit me of thy crew' in *L'Allegro*. Handel used nine horns in the *Music for the Royal Fireworks* (with each of the three notated parts played by three instruments).

12. Mandolin

The mandolin was used by early eighteenth-century composers including Alessandro SCARLATTI, Francesco Mancini, F. B. Conti, VIVALDI, LOTTI, GASPARINI and VINCI. Its wooden body is about 40 to 65 centimetres long and shaped like a pear. It is round-backed and has a flat soundtable with a carved rosette and a neck like a small lute, where the strings are attached. At first, a six-stringed mandolin was in use (tuned g–b–e'–a'–d''–g'') but in about 1740 the so-called Neapolitan Mandolino (tuned g–d'–a'–e'') became widely accepted. Handel wrote a part for mandolin (ranging up to e''') in Cleopatra's aria 'Hark! He strikes the golden lyre' in *Alexander Balus* together with a harp, in a two-part notation on a single stave.

13. Oboe

The oboe rose rapidly in popularity as a solo and orchestral instrument in France, Italy and Germany after 1700. Handel, encouraged by great oboists such as Ignazio Rion (1704–22), John KYTCH, John LOEILLET, John Ernest GALLIARD and Giuseppe SAMMARTINI, left a large number of works for the oboe or including oboe parts. After *Almira* and various cantatas including oboes composed in Italy, Handel wrote, especially between 1717 and 1720, highly demanding oboe parts in works such as the trio sonata HWV 404, the Cannons Anthems with three oboe solos (ANTHEMS, 2), and *Acis and Galatea*.

In the eighteenth century the oboe was a three-jointed instrument consisting of a lower joint, an upper joint and a slightly flared bell. Handel called it either *Oboe* or *Hautbois* and always notated its music in the treble clef. Its usual range is between c' and c''', but higher notes are possible. In *FLAVIO* and *Tamerlano* Handel used oboes with exchangeable joint pieces as transposing instruments. As was usual at the time, Handel's oboes often doubled the ripieno violins, played independent orchestral parts, or formed part of an oboe trio, consisting of two oboes and a bassoon (*Rinaldo, Amadigi, Radamisto, Israel in Egypt, Concerto a due cori*, HWV 332), or as a solo instrument in instrumental movements (the overture to *Rinaldo*, and several of the Concerti grossi, Op. 3 and *Concerti a due cori*, HWV 333–4) and opera arias (*Almira, Agrippina, TESEO, AMADIGI, Radamisto*). There are no oboe solos in Handel's operas between 1724 and 1737; the oboes did, however, continue to double the violins and remained an integral part of the orchestra, and there are oboe solos in the oratorios *Deborah* and *Athalia* (both 1733). The availability of Sammartini in 1737 seems to have encouraged Handel to compose remarkable oboe solo parts for arias in *ARMINIO, GIUSTINO* and *BERENICE*.

Depending on the character of the composition itself (or rather the character or importance of the upper parts), unison oboes were either doubling the first violins or the oboe group was distributed between the first and second violin groups. Whether oboes doubled the first violin or both the first and second violin is often ambiguous in the operas, though Handel seems to be more specific in the oratorios. Even if the oboes are not explicitly mentioned in all of Handel's scores, it cannot be safely assumed that they were not present in the orchestra. If not otherwise indicated, the oboes probably played in the ripieno sections (ritornellos), but if there was an additional vocal line, passages marked *piano*, or arias that included acoustically weak instruments, the oboes (often) paused in order to maintain a pleasing orchestral balance. The differentiation between woodwind *solo* and *ripieno* suggests that the use of more than one oboe per part was normal practice if the string ensemble was large enough (according to J. J. Quantz, four oboes if there were twelve violins; see Quantz, *On Playing the Flute*, 214). However, the *Music for the Royal Fireworks* with its twenty-four oboes (twelve Ob. I, eight Ob. II and four Ob. III) was unusual. The use of solo oboes or an oboe trio in accompanied recitatives (*Athalia*, *Saul*), and of oboes and bassoon on stage in *Ariodante*, was uncommon. The direction *ad libitum* in an aria featuring a solo oboe in *Berenice* indicates that the cadenza should be improvised, as was standard baroque performance practice.

DAGMAR GLÜXAM (Trans. ANGELA BAIER)

14. Organ

The organ is the principal keyboard continuo instrument in Handel's sacred vocal music, including the English anthems written for CANNONS and the CHAPEL ROYAL. In the Italian oratorio Il *TRIONFO DEL TEMPO E DEL DISIN-GANNO* (1707) a Sonata with a brilliant organ obbligato leads into an aria that also has solo organ. A similar organ obbligato is found in 'In the battle fame pursuing' in *Deborah* (1733). From 1735 Handel featured solo organ concertos (ORCHESTRAL WORKS) in his ode and oratorio performances. In the word-book for *Samson* Newburgh HAMILTON wrote that in Handel's oratorios 'the Solemnity of Church-Musick is agreeably united with the most pleasing Airs of the Stage' (Deutsch, p. 559). The solemn sound was the chorus supported by the organ, the principal way it was used in Handel's oratorios, though the organ also served as a bass instrument in arias or accompanied recitatives (*tasto solo*).

Handel's composing and conducting scores usually contain few directions for the organist. But the scores which do have indications (notably *Saul*), plus copies of an authentic organ part for *Alexander's Feast*, show that in England Handel adopted the nomenclature used by British organists and organ-builders. Handel mainly used a one-manual organ without pedals, which had a compass beginning with G″ and A″ continuing chromatically to d‴. The low bass compass (below the usual C′ on modern instruments) allows for doubling the bass in octaves (*tasto solo all'octava bassa*). In doubling the chorus, whether scored chordally or in fugal entries, the organ is marked by Handel as 'organo pieno' ('full organ') or 'loud': the full ensemble of flue ranks at 8′, 4′, 2 2/3′, 2′ (and perhaps 1 3/5′). 'Soft organ' was the Open and Stopped Diapasons combined (Principal 8′ and Gedackt 8′), such as in the introductory bars of *ZADOK THE PRIEST*.

The organ's flute-like stops, sounding in two octaves, also could reinforce flutes or recorders or provide a bass for these instruments. Additionally the organ is encountered in 'exotic' scorings involving those instruments and the harp or lute, including the only mention of the organ in an opera score, *TERPSICORE* ('Tuoi passi'). WILLIAM D. GUDGER

15. Recorder

Until around 1700 the recorder had seven finger-holes at the front, a thumb-hole at the back and a wide and cylindrical bore, producing a rather unobtrusive sound. Around 1700, however, the bore became conical, the cut-up was made smaller and the labium broadened.

These changes in the structure of the recorder extended the instrument's range and its sound in the upper ranges became more brilliant and with that the recorder's popularity rose considerably. All the same, the instrument continued to be used primarily by Handel and his contemporaries as an obbligato instrument in lyrical or melancholy (love) scenes or in pastoral nature depictions (for example in *Aci, Galatea e Polifemo*). The recorder, called *Flauto* (*Flauti*) or *Flauto dolce* by Handel, is notated in the treble or alto clef (*COR FEDELE IN VANO SPERI*) and its range is between f′ and f″. Handel used recorders as early as in *Almira* and later included them, solo or in pairs, in instrumental movements (for example, with a solo bassoon in the Overture to *Rinaldo*) and arias in twenty-four operas, nine oratorios (for example in *La Resurrezione*), cantatas (*La TERRA È LIBERATA*, *ECHEGGIATE, FESTEGGIATE, O numi eterni, TRA LE FIAMME*), church works (*O come let us sing*, HWV 253, Te Deum in B flat major, HWV 281) and instrumental sonatas (CHAMBER MUSIC, 3). In performance, the recorder parts were probably played by the oboists.

Apart from the recorder, Handel sometimes used – predominantly in imitation of birdsong – the piccolo flute (so-called flageolet, *Flagioletto*; for example in *Rinaldo*, *Acis and Galatea*, *Riccardo Primo*, *Alcina*, and in the *Water Music*, which calls for a transverse flute and two *flauti piccoli*. He also used a bass recorder (*Basso de[i] flauti*) in *Giustino*. In the 1730s the recorder began to disappear from orchestras and was gradually replaced by the transverse flute.

16. Theorbo, lute and guitar

The *Arciliuto* and the *Tiorba* are both members of the lute family. The theorbo had been used in the baroque orchestra in opera and oratorio since the early seventeenth century; it played in the basso continuo group or in arias with a pastoral context. From about 1680 the arciliuto (the archlute, also liuto or leuto) became popular as a continuo instrument initially in Rome, but later elsewhere in Europe.

The theorbo, which is different from a lute in having a larger body, an extended neck and a re-entrant tuning of its stopped strings, usually had six double courses – tuned A–d–g–b–e′–a′ – and a number of diatonic basses (diapasons) typically tuned G_1–A_1–B_1–C–D–E–F–G. These run alongside the neck and end in a second peg-box, and are only plucked as open strings. The archlute has a smaller body and shorter string length and therefore the first two double courses preserve the tuning of the Renaissance tenor lute – G–c–f–a–d′– g′, with unfretted diatonic basses running downwards from F.

In his early Italian works, Handel only calls for archlutes and theorbos in the oratorio *La Resurrezione* and the cantata *Cor fedele, in vano speri*. In London the theorbo was a standard member of Handel's orchestra, even though it is seldom mentioned explicitly in the opera and oratorio scores. As with the harpsichord, oboes or bassoons, the simple fact that the theorbo is not mentioned in the score does certainly not mean that it was not present in the orchestra. When Handel writes Liuto (as in Violonc. soli e Cemb. e Liuto in the arioso 'Due bell'alme' in Deidamia) or Lute (as in senza Lute in ORESTE and Ariodante) he seems to mean an archlute or a theorbo. An interesting phenomenon in Venetian music, Viennese opera scores and Handel's music is the instrumentation of the accompanying parts for a lute (theorbo, archlute) and the violins or strings playing pizzicato (Partenope, Terpsicore). The latest documented use of a lute in Handel's theatre orchestra is the 1744 revival of Deborah.

The chitarra spagnuola, which Handel calls for in the Spanish cantata 'NÒ SE EMENDERÁ JAMAS', is a five-course instrument (tuned A–d–g–b-e'), which was unusual even in Handel's time. The music for the chitarra is notated in a grand staff system with the bass line playing colla parte with the basso continuo, but where this descends to F and G below the instrument's range the guitarist might have instead strummed appropriate harmonies.

17. Trombone

The trombone probably developed out of the so-called slide trumpet, which had been popular in court and municipal music since the sixteenth century because of its agility but declined in popularity in Italy (after 1630) and in Vienna and England (after 1700). Handel does not mention any trombones in his Italian works; however, a trombonist received payment after the performances of La Resurrezione. Possibly the trombone was used to double other instruments and was not explicitly mentioned, as was the custom in church music. Later Handel only wrote for trombones between 1739 and 1741, in his oratorios Israel in Egypt and Saul (in the latter oratorio, three trombones playing together with two trumpets and kettledrums); they appear in scenes of triumph, divine sublimity or deep mourning. He originally intended to include trombones in Samson but decided to dispense with them when he revised the work in 1742, presumably because there were no trombonists available.

18. Trumpet

The trumpet, until the mid-nineteenth century a natural trumpet constructed of a thin brass, copper or silver tube bent into a spiral with a cylindrical bore, was used by Handel for ceremonial music, typical martial or triumphal scenes, and in arie di furore. The trumpets Handel used (called Clarin or Principal, later Tromba) were mostly in D, sometimes in C and infrequently in G. On a natural trumpet all the pitches in the overtone series can be played; Handel required his trumpets to reach a″, in later works c‴. The earliest extant aria to feature trumpet is from Aci, Galatea e Polifemo, and solo trumpet occasionally appears in his Italian works (the cantata Alla caccia and a couple of flamboyant arias in La Resurrezione). Two trumpets and kettledrums are used in Agrippina.

Trumpets are included in twenty-two of Handel's London operas, although in most cases they appear only once or twice in the course of the opera (only in Partenope and Atalanta they can be heard five times respectively; the latter opera also features a fine sinfonia with a solo trumpet part written for Valentine Snow). It was common in Italian opera of the time to contain stage directions specifying that trumpeters should appear on stage with no corresponding music to be found in the score, and this is evident in some of Handel's works (Rinaldo, I.ii; Teseo,

II.iv; *Partenope, scena ultima*). The trumpeter presumably played a conventional fanfare on or behind the stage.

Oratorio scores regularly feature trumpets, which appear predominantly (sometimes together with horns) in choruses and instrumental movements (such as sinfonias in *Saul*). Like Bach, Handel normally used trumpets in pairs or in trios, but he used four trumpets and kettledrums in *Rinaldo* and nine trumpets (three trumpet trios) in the *Music for the Royal Fireworks*. He occasionally composed an Italian-style trumpet aria, as pioneered by STRADELLA, Carlo Pallavicino and Antonio Draghi, and there are prominent solo obbligato parts for the instrument in *ETERNAL SOURCE OF LIGHT DIVINE*, *SILLA*, *Amadigi*, *Radamisto*, *Lotario*, *Ezio*, *Alexander's Feast*, *Giustino*, *Messiah*, *Samson* and *Joshua* (among others).

19. Viol

The viola da gamba of Handel's age was a fretted, six-stringed instrument tuned to D (or C)–G–c–e–a–d'. Possibly Handel got to know the viol through the violist Ernst Christian Hesse (1676–1762), whom he met in Hamburg and who played in Italy around 1708. While in Italy, Handel frequently used the viol as a solo instrument, as bass instrument in the concertino or in the basso continuo group (for example in *La Resurrezione* and *Tra le fiamme*); his music for the viol is notated in the alto and bass clef. In London he only used it in *Giulio Cesare* (notated in the tenor and bass clef). The usual range is between D or C (for the C the lowest string was perhaps tuned down) and d″ (c″).

20. Viola

Even though the viola was always present in four-part orchestral settings by Handel and other contemporary composers, it generally had a harmonising function only. In vocal works the viola sometimes played the bass line ('bassetto' technique) or it was omitted altogether. Virtuoso viola parts (like the one in Zoroastro's bass aria 'Sorge infausta una procella' in *Orlando*) are rare and, when called for, the part-writing mostly has violas and violins playing in unison. The only solo appearance by a viola in all of Handel's works occurs in *Almira* (*Viola da Braccio Solo*).

Handel used the usual violas in c–g–d'–a' with a range between c and d″, sometimes up to e♭″. He usually called the instrument *Viola* but sometimes *Violetta*, which seems to have been used as a synonym, and appears in the printed London scores of opera arias. The viola was also sometimes called *Tenor violin* in early eighteenth-century London. Its music is usually notated in the alto clef; in the early Italian works (e.g. *Dixit Dominus*) the second viola is notated in the tenor clef. If the part-writing for the viola is *colla parte* or doubling the bass line, the tenor or bass clefs were used, but when nothing was specified they usually played an octave higher. There are divided violas in some works (for example in *Laudate pueri*, Rome 1707, *SUSANNA*, *Solomon*); the use of 4 *Viole* in *Sosarme* is exceptional.

21. Violin

Handel used violins as orchestral instruments in opera, oratorio, church music or orchestral music. He also composed demanding solo and trio sonatas for violin(s) and continuo (CHAMBER MUSIC). The regular violin tuning was g–d′–a′–e″ and the violin parts are notated in the treble clef or in the alto clef (when playing in unison with the violas). He almost always called the instrument Violino, sometimes adding specifications like ripieno, del Concerto grosso, solo or concertino. Violins appear in Handel's orchestra either divided or in unison, as was usual at the time, but he also used the northern German way of dividing the violins into three groups (for example in Almira, and occasionally in later operas and oratorios like Messiah). The third violins either play their own violin part or double the violas, of which there were always few. The character of the violin parts, ranging between g and b♭‴–c‴, later e‴, is that of the customarily Italianate style of string-playing, and includes demanding passage work, rapid tirate, split chords, stile concitato, tremolo, pizzicato, con sordino playing and so on.

Collaboration with violinists in Italy, especially with Arcangelo CORELLI and Matteo Fornari in Rome, presumably influenced Handel's violin writing. As is evident in Il trionfo del Tempo e del Disinganno, the cantata Da quel giorno fatale and the Sonata a 5 (HWV 288), the violin became an important and highly virtuosic solo instrument in Handel's Roman works. Later on in London, Handel continued to have excellent violinists at his disposal such as Pietro CASTRUCCI (for whom he wrote solo parts in Radamisto, Giulio Cesare, Alcina and Alexander's Feast) and Matthew DUBOURG.

22. Violetta marina

The Violetta marina resembles the viola d'amore and is a bowed string instrument with sympathetic strings developed by the Castrucci brothers. Two violette marine with a range of c to e♭″ are featured as concertante instruments in Orlando. It is unclear whether the violetta marina was also used in Sosarme or whether it is identical to the so-called 'English violet'.

23. Violoncello

The violoncello became established as a part of the standard orchestra in Italy, Vienna and Germany by the late seventeenth century, so it is likely that Handel used it in Almira. However, he first mentioned it explicitly in his early Italian works. In Handel's age the violoncello normally had four strings, less frequently five (C–G–d–a and C–G–d–a–e′), and music written for it was notated in the bass or tenor clef. The usual range of Handel's orchestral cello parts rarely exceeds C to g′ or a′ (Berenice); the solo cello parts with the top notes b♭″ (Arianna in Creta) and b′ (Berenice) are less extensive in range than the parts in arias composed by Antonio CALDARA, Giuseppe Porsile or Georg Reutter for Vienna which take the soloist up to e″.

The cello was part of the basso continuo group; in the concertino it played the bass line. In the figured bass notation the cello part (whether the instrument was used in the basso continuo group or in concertino style) was often notated on its own (for example in Almira, though without specifying the instrument) or colla parte with the bassoon (for example in Deidamia). According to the performance practice of Handel's time, the cello probably also accompanied the secco recitative.

Handel used obbligato cello in his early Italian and later English works. The respected cellists Filippo AMADEI, Francisco Godsens (d. 1741) and Francisco CAPORALE all played in Handel's orchestra at one time or another. The direction *ad libitum*, which is included in the arias with a solo cello part in *Athalia*, *Arianna* and *Alexander's Feast*, indicates that a cadenza was improvised. The direction *Violonc. soli* (for example, at the beginning of the aria 'Due bell'alme' in *Deidamia*) should not be taken to mean that there is a solo cello part but, in accordance with performance practice of the time, that the cello group should be scaled down in size or volume.

24. Violone

Handel usually called the 16' bass bowed string instrument *Violono*, *Violone grosso* or *Contrabasso*; all terms probably refer to a double bass. This could be either a six-stringed instrument (tuned to G–C–F–A–d–g) or a four-stringed one (tuned to C–G–D–A). Handel's music rarely requires bowed bass players to go lower than C – the exception is a B♭ in *Rinaldo* – or higher than d' or e' (with the exception of a b♭' in *Atalanta* and a b' in *Berenice*). As was usual in baroque performance practice, Handel notated music for violone like the violoncello, although it sounded an octave lower. He first mentioned the instrument explicitly in the autograph score of *Agrippina*, but he had probably used the instrument earlier because it was a member of the standard basso continuo group in Germany and Italy. The violone is not always mentioned in Handel's scores, but it was expected that it would play the same part as the rest of the basso continuo group (but possibly not in secco recitatives). The direction *Solo* (e.g. *La terra è liberata* and *Rinaldo*) or *Soli* (Maria Maddalena's 'Per me già di morire' in *La Resurrezione*, Handel had employed five double basses) might not indicate a solo appearance, but rather a reduction in volume or size of the bass group, such as was often done at the time in order to maintain a musical balance with the upper parts (for example in Armida's 'Ah! Crudel, il pianto mio' in *Rinaldo*, which is for oboe, bassoon and *Violone grosso solo*).   DAGMAR GLÜXAM (Trans. ANGELA BAIER)

D. Burrows, 'Handel's London Theatre Orchestra', EM 13 (1985), 349–57
   'Of Handel, London Trumpeters, and Trumpet Music', *Historic Brass Society Journal* 11 (1999), 1–9
B. Cooper, 'The Organ Parts to Handel's *Alexander's Feast*', ML, 59/2 (April 1978), 159–79
W. Dean, *Handel and the Opera Seria* (Berkeley, 1969)
D. Glüxam, *Instrumentarium und Instrumentalstil in der Wiener Oper zwischen 1705 und 1740* (Tutzing, 2006)
B. Haynes, *The Eloquent Oboe: A History of the Hautboy 1640–1760* (Oxford, 2001)
C. Hogwood, 'Handel's Use of Timpani and Percussion Instruments', *Michaelsteiner Konferenzberichte 75: Perkussionsinstrumente in der Kunstmusik vom 16. bis zur Mitte des 19. Jahrhunderts* (Michaelstein and Blankenburg, forthcoming)
H. J. Marx, 'The Instrumentation of Handel's Early Italian Works', EM 16 (1988), 496–505
D. Möller, *Besetzung und Instrumentation in den Opern Georg Friedrich Händels* (Frankfurt, etc., 1989)
   'Die Holzblasinstrumente in den Opern G. F. Händels', *Concerto* 10 (1993), 14–22
J. J. Quantz, *On Playing the Flute*, trans. E. R. Reilly, 2nd edn (London, 1985)
J. Spitzer and N. Zaslaw, *The Birth of the Orchestra. History of an Institution, 1650–1815* (Oxford, 2004)
M. W. Stahura, 'Handel and the Orchestra', *The Cambridge Companion to Handel*, ed. D. Burrows (Cambridge, 1997)
J. Tyler, 'The Italian Mandolin and Mandola 1589–1800', EM 9 (1981), 438–46

Internationale Händel-Akademie, Karlsruhe. An institute founded to support the Karlsruhe Handel Festival (FESTIVALS, 7) in 1986 by Günter Könemann, director of the Baden State Theatre, and Fany Solter, Dean of the Karlsruhe College of Music. The academy has been directed by the harpsichordist Christine Dax-elhofer since 2000, and offers vocal and instrumental courses. Papers and discussions from the academy's symposiums on musicology and art history are regularly published in the *Veröffentlichungen der Internationalen Händel-Akademie Karlsruhe*. The lecturers Margit Legler and Sigrid T'Hooft have pioneered ground-breaking revivals of baroque acting techniques.

†SIEGFRIED SCHMALZRIEDT (Trans. ANGELA BAIER)

investments. See HANDEL, 17

Israel in Babylon. See PASTICCIOS, 2

Israel in Egypt, HWV 54. English oratorio. It was Handel's first oratorio based solely on scriptural texts (BIBLE). In Part I, *The Lamentation of the Israelites for the Death of Joseph*, the Israelites pay tribute to Joseph and mourn the greatness of their loss; they find consolation and confidence from their trust in God. The entire *Lamentation* is taken from the anthem *The ways of Zion do mourn* (ANTHEMS, 5), which Handel had composed for the funeral of Queen CAROLINE in 1737. Only a few words were changed in order to make lines mourning the late Queen of Britain refer instead to the prophet Joseph. Part II, *Exodus*, recounts the mission of Moses and Aaron to liberate the Israelites from Egyptian bondage. Its text is arranged from Exodus (1–2, 7, 9–10, 14–15) and Psalms (78, 105, 106), and includes depictions of the ten plagues sent by God to curse Egypt until Pharaoh relented and allowed the Hebrews to leave. Part III, *Moses' Song*, is taken from Exodus 15:1–21, and conveys an extended Israelite hymn of thanksgiving to God, who has delivered them safely through the Red Sea and drowned the pursuing Egyptian army.

The libretto of Parts II and III is anonymous. *Moses' Song* is an almost verbatim setting of the biblical source, but the preparation of the text for *Exodus* would have required greater literary effort. A correspondent to the *London Daily Post* in April 1739 had been told that 'the Words were selected out of the Sacred Writings by the Great Composer himself' (Deutsch, pp. 481–3), but it is plausible that this task was undertaken by Charles JENNENS. Perhaps the concept for *Israel in Egypt* was developed by Handel and Jennens whilst they collaborated on *SAUL*. On 1 October 1738, only three days after completing *Saul*, Handel began setting *Moses' Song* (completed 11 October). He proceeded to compose *Exodus* between 15 and 20 October.

Each of the oratorio's three parts is in the style of an anthem. The *Lamentation* was performed as an entirely choral full anthem. There are only a few movements for soloists in Parts II and III, and none of the arias have da capos. The oratorio contains an unusually high proportion of choral music that covers an impressive variety of styles, including many double choruses and several peculiar recitative-like passages for the choir (notably 'He sent a thick darkness'). Handel's fondness for tone painting is especially prominent during *Exodus*: an Evangelist-like tenor announces that God turned the Egyptian waters into blood, an alto aria with springing string figures onomatopoeically illustrates how 'The land brought forth frogs' and a succession of powerful choruses narrate the plagues of flies, lice and locusts ('He spake the word'), hail and fire ('He sent them hailstones'), and how God 'smote all the first-born of Egypt'. *Moses' Song* features an unusual bass duet ('The Lord is a man of war'), the lovely alto solo 'Thou shalt bring them in', and gripping choruses such as 'The people shall hear' and the extended finale 'The Lord shall reign for ever'.

Handel's INSTRUMENTATION makes bold use of trumpets and drums and three trombones (which he also used in Saul). His score includes several Lutheran CHORALES, and the opening of Exodus is shaped in the style of a German passion oratorio. The work is full of extensive BORROWINGS from works by other composers (including STRADELLA, ERBA, KERLL and URIO), and Handel also reused some of his own previous compositions, most notably two keyboard fugues in minor keys (HWV 605 and 609) for 'He smote all the first-born of Egypt' and 'They loathed to drink of the river'.

Israel in Egypt was first performed on 4 April 1739 at the KING'S THEATRE. The soloists were:

Elisabeth Duparc, 'La FRANCESINA'	(soprano I)
? (boy)	(soprano II)
William SAVAGE	(alto I)
Robinson (boy)	(alto II)
John BEARD	(tenor)
Henry REINHOLD	(bass I)
Gustavus WALTZ	(bass II)

Handel played organ concertos during both intervals, including 'The cuckoo and the nightingale' (HWV 295) (ORCHESTRAL WORKS, 5) after the first part (the other concerto has not been identified). The oratorio was given twice more during that season (11 and 17 April), on which occasions the composer inserted a recitative and three arias in Italian for Francesina (who had already sung them in An Oratorio a year earlier, although they were transpositions of music composed for CARESTINI in the 1735 revival of ESTHER). There was another single performance of Israel in Egypt on 1 April 1740. The oratorio was not revived again until 1756, when the Lamentation was replaced by a new first part compiled with assistance from John Christopher SMITH JUNIOR, and that used pieces from SOLOMON, the OCCASIONAL ORATORIO and the 'Anthem on the Peace' (ANTHEMS, 7). This version was performed twice (17 and 24 March 1756), and was the model for further revivals on 4 March 1757 and 24 February 1758.

Some biographers and scholars claim that Israel in Egypt was a failure because Handel changed the score after the first performance and seldom performed it in later seasons. Mrs DELANY regretted that the 1756 revival was unpopular because it was 'too solemn for common ears' (Deutsch, 771). However, contemporary documents reveal that some members of the AUDIENCE appreciated the oratorio, and in 1753 William HAYES praised the fact that the score shows its composer to have 'discovered an inexhaustible Fund of Invention, the greatest Depth of Learning, and the most comprehensive Talent in expressing even inarticulate Nature' (Deutsch, 733). Perhaps Handel chose not to perform the oratorio more frequently because he valued the original conception of the oratorio – a symbiosis of English and German church music (chorale, passion and anthem) – highly enough to prefer not to perform it regularly instead of making unwelcome compromises. Practical circumstances were rarely advantageous for an ideal revival: he might have disliked the structural damage done after the first performance to accommodate more arias for Francesina; perhaps the 1740 revival was only possible because the countertenor Mr RUSSELL could take the part originally performed by Savage (whose voice had broken and settled as a bass in the meantime); from October 1742 there were no trombonists available in London. Moreover, the period of time when the oratorio could be performed was limited if Handel wished to correspond with the liturgical calendar: he always performed the oratorio in or around the Holy Week; Exodus 15:1–22 is the First Lesson for the morning service on Easter Monday in the Book of Common Prayer, and the use of the chorale 'Christ lag in Todesbanden' in the first chorus of Part II ('And the people of Israel sigh'd') further suggests that the oratorio was connected to Easter. Alternatively, the predominantly choral anthem style of the oratorio might have seemed strange to theatre audiences more accustomed to Italian opera.

Since Handel's lifetime *Israel in Egypt* has become established as one of his most popular works, and its large portion of choruses made it especially suitable for the Handel Festivals at CRYSTAL PALACE from 1857 onwards (FESTIVALS, 2). The trombone parts were lost for many years, until they were restored by CHRYSANDER (who found them at the end of the performing score). For a long time the oratorio was mistakenly thought to be a two-part work because the autograph and the performing score consist only of *Exodus* and *Moses' Song*. The original three-part 1739 version was first revived by the Sine Nomine Singers and Baroque Orchestra, conducted by Harry Saltzman, at New York in 1985, and has since received seven complete commercial recordings.

ANNETTE LANDGRAF

Burrows and Dunhill
Dean, *Oratorios*
Deutsch
HHB ii
A. Landgraf (ed.), *Israel in Egypt*, HHA I/14.1 (Kassel, 1999) (contains first-performance version)
  (ed.), *Israel in Egypt*, HHA I/14.2 (Kassel, 1999) (contains changes and additions for second performance on 11 April 1739 and revivals in 1756–7)
  'Israel in Egypt: Ein Oratorium als Opfer der Politik', HJb 42/3 (1996/7)
M. A. Parker-Hale, 'Handel's Choral Recitatives', GHB II (1986)
Smith, *Oratorios*
S. Taylor, *The Indebtedness of Handel to Works by other Composers: A Presentation of Evidence* (Cambridge, 1906)

Italy. At the outset of the eighteenth century, following a row of plague epidemics, wars and famines, Italy had barely recovered the population level of a hundred years earlier (13.5 million), while the rest of Europe had experienced a growth of around 35 per cent. In an age when demography was still the key factor to the wealth of nations, this may account for the general stagnation of economy. Although larger cities retained high standards of culture and lifestyle, the gap between town and country and the relative impoverishment of the labouring classes, particularly in the South, touched a historic depth. Also the semi-colonial rule of Spain, as sealed by the peace of Westphalia (1648), is traditionally considered one major cause for backwardness. Spain held sway over an area of 140,000 square kilometres, or a good half of the present territory of the Italian Republic, including the Duchy of Milan and the vice-kingdoms of NAPLES, Sicily and Sardinia, plus a chain of naval bases along the coast of Tuscany. Within the remaining jigsaw puzzle of states and statelets, only the Republic of VENICE and the Duchy of Savoy were able to pursue some degree of self-rule by bargaining their support to the European powers competing with Spain (notably France and the Empire) for territorial and commercial advantages. Savoy, controlling strategic areas on both sides of the western Alps, built a strong army that played a crucial role during the War of the SPANISH SUCCESSION. Besides their historical significance at large, the vicissitudes of this conflict on the Italian theatre make the backdrop to Handel's sojourn in Italy and may, to a certain extent, shed light on his moves through the peninsula.

Two cousins from the house of Savoy faced one another on opposing sides: Prince Eugene, the Empire's field-marshal, and Duke Vittorio Amedeo, commander-in-chief of the Franco-Spanish forces. Then a reversal of alliances took place and both Savoys sided with the Empire. In September 1706, the decisive battle was waged around the mighty bulwarks of Turin. The Bourbon forces suffered a bloody defeat; within a mere twelve months the Viennese hegemony replaced that of Madrid in Italy. On 24 September 1706 the imperial army entered Milan. In summer 1707, an expeditionary corps of 8,000 led by Count von Daun crossed the Papal States passing close to a terrified ROME, pierced the Spanish lines on the river Garigliano and fought its way to Naples, where the first Habsburg viceroy, Count von Martinitz, was enthroned on 7 July. In the next three years, he was succeeded first by von Daun himself, then by Cardinal Vincenzo GRIMANI. In 1708 the Gonzaga Duke of Mantua, declared a felon to the Empire, was ousted by Prince Philip of Hesse-Darmstadt, another veteran of the Neapolitan raid. Both Prince Philip and Grimani earned a seat in the musical hall of fame as patrons of VIVALDI and Handel, respectively. In September 1708, backed up by the British fleet, the Habsburgs seized Sardinia from Philip V of Spain. Also in 1708, Emperor Joseph I (a lukewarm Catholic in comparison to his father Leopold I, whom he had succeeded in 1705) ordered von Daun to invade the Papal States from the north as a warning to Pope Clement XI, who was reluctant to desert the Franco-Spanish party. Paying no heed to excommunication, Daun defeated the Roman troops led by General Marsigli and forced the Pontiff to sign a dishonourable peace on 15 January 1709. From this moment on, the *pax austriaca* – eventually confirmed in 1713 by the Treaty of Utrecht – spared the Italian peninsula further warfare.

Seeking to account for Handel's decision to visit Italy, MAINWARING quotes 'The number of schools and academies for Music subsisting in the different quarters of this country, and the vast encouragements afforded to those who excel in the Art' as the factors conspiring 'to render it the most eminent part of the world for its Composers, Singers, and Performers'. It is not easy to assess what hopes and goals Handel had in mind and to what extent he realised them. He stayed there for about three and a half years, far too long for a simple tourist. It is clear, however, that he wished to project the image of a gentleman travelling with some kind of servant or secretary, not of a professional musician seeking employment. If Mainwaring is to be believed, he preferred to decline an allowance from the Grand Prince of Tuscany, instead drawing on his own pocket money of 200 ducats. Nevertheless, at Rome, Naples and 'most other places' he reportedly had 'a palazzo at command, and was provided with table, coach, and all other accomodations'. The RUSPOLI accounts suggest that he consumed – probably not alone – a terrific amount of victuals, the fare of a distinguished guest. The testimonial written on his behalf by Grand Prince Ferdinando to his brother-in-law, the Elector Johann Wilhelm, lauds his 'civility of manners, fullness of honest feelings and a full command of several tongues', if at the expense of his talent for music, defined only as 'more than middling'.

Witnesses by non-musicians (diarist Valesio, Duke Salviati) style him in the first line as 'sonatore di Clavicimbalo' (harpsichord player); probably this was how he liked to be regarded. If his prime interest had been opera, he would have spent more time in Venice or Naples and less in Rome, where opera houses were closed since 1698 by a papal ban, renewed after the 1703 earthquake and maintained until 1709. Despite incomplete data, during the war decade 1700–10 a rough survey yields more than hundred opera stagings in Venice, some forty in Naples, fifty in Florence and half that figure even in Bologna, where Roman policies set the trend. Handel may have considered taking a position at a court or in a noble household, such as CORELLI held from OTTOBONI, but hardly any suggestion of becoming a *maestro di cappella* to a church, since he declined to abjure LUTHERANISM. Nevertheless, his remarkable output of sacred music for the Catholic service may have triggered such offers, probably from Cardinals COLONNA and PAMPHILIJ, or Agostino STEFFANI, who was a veteran of missionary activity in Germany.   CARLO VITALI

See also HANDEL, 2; 15

Burrows
A. Hicks, 'Handel's Early Musical Development', PRMA 103 (1976–7), 80–9
W. and U. Kirkendale, *Music and Meaning: Studies in Music History and the Neighbouring Disciplines* (Florence, 2007)
N. Pirrotta and A. Ziino (eds.), *Händel e gli Scarlatti a Roma* (Florence, 1987)
R. Strohm, 'Händel in Italia: nuovi contributi', *Rivista Italiana di Musicologia* 9 (1974), 152–74
C. Vitali, 'Italy – Political, Religious and Musical Contexts', *The Cambridge Companion to Handel*, ed. D. Burrows (Cambridge, 1997)

Italy, residences in. See PALAZZI

J

Jacobites (Jacobus = Latin James). Supporters of the Catholic King James II of England (James VII of Scotland), deposed 1689, and his family, the Stuarts. James was succeeded by his two Protestant daughters but the next nearest Protestant, GEORGE I of HANOVER, was only fifty-eighth in line (according to Stuart loyalists). Parliament nevertheless chose the Hanoverians for the British throne, in order to safeguard the CHURCH OF ENGLAND. Restoration plots by the exiled Stuarts (living in France and ITALY) and their supporters in France, Spain and Britain continued into the 1750s and resulted in actual rebellions in 1715 and 1745. In 'the 1745' Charles Edward STUART led his army as far south as Derby, apparently justifying the fear of Jacobitism fomented by the British government, and giving rise to Handel's patriotic SONGS 'Stand round, my brave boys' (performed at Drury Lane Theatre, 14 November 1745) and 'From scourging rebellion' and his *OCCASIONAL ORATORIO* and *JUDAS MACCABAEUS*. Jacobite support was strongest in Scotland, the Stuarts' homeland, and reprisals there in the wake of the 1745, under Prince WILLIAM, the Duke of Cumberland, were brutal. The Stuarts' Catholicism fragmented their British support, and Charles Edward converted to Anglicanism, but too late for success. Jacobitism still has some adherents.   RUTH SMITH

See also NON-JURORS; Appendix 5 – Genealogical table of the ruling houses of Britain and Hanover

B. P. Lenman, *The Jacobite Risings in Britain 1689–1746* (London, 1980)
P. K. Monod, *Jacobitism and the English People, 1688–1788* (Cambridge, 1989)

Jennens, Charles (b. (?)Gopsall, Leicestershire, 1699/1700; d. Gopsall, bur. 20 Nov. 1773). English landowner, patron, author, art collector and editor (see Figure 16). Grandson and heir of a wealthy Birmingham iron magnate, Jennens was educated at Balliol College, OXFORD, and subsequently divided his time between the 736-acre Leicestershire estate of Gopsall purchased by his grandfather, and London (Queen Square and later (Great) Ormond Street, Bloomsbury).

The guiding principles of Jennens's life were Protestant Christianity and the STUART cause. As a NON-JUROR and an ideological but not pro-active JACOBITE, he excluded himself from public office. He devoted much of his time and wealth to vigorous engagement in, and patronage of, arts and letters. He had catholic but decisive musical tastes and was a devotee of Handel's music. From 1725 a constant subscriber to Handel's publications, he amassed the largest contemporary collection of the composer's works (SOURCES AND COLLECTIONS, 3), which he bequeathed to his kinsman the Earl of AYLESFORD.

16. Handel's friend and librettist Charles Jennens, portrait by Thomas Hudson, oil on canvas, c.1744.

He also acquired part of Cardinal OTTOBONI's music library and other Italian music MSS (lending them to Handel, who used them for BORROWINGS); and he encouraged contemporary English composers by subscribing to and collecting their works. He acquired a 'Piano-forte Harpsichord' from FLORENCE in 1732, and had an organ made to Handel's specification.

Jennens was one of Handel's most interesting librettists. He first offered Handel a libretto in 1735; he wrote for no other composer. MESSIAH was not only his libretto but his brainchild (conceived in 1739). His librettos of SAUL and BELSHAZZAR have strong dramatic structure and characterisation and deploy political analogies adroitly. A member of the HARRIS circle, Jennens prompted James Harris to draft the libretto of L'ALLEGRO ED IL PENSEROSO, himself supplying the words for the concluding Il moderato at Handel's request. He also possibly compiled or advised on the text of ISRAEL IN EGYPT. During the composition of Saul Handel incorporated some crucial alterations which Jennens suggested. Handel's letters to Jennens about Belshazzar (HHB iv, pp. 376–9) provide vivid insight into the evolution of a Handel oratorio. Both men were strongly opinionated and touchy, and their relationship could be tempestuous (as when Jennens first heard, and was disappointed by, Messiah), but they remained good friends, Jennens commissioning Thomas HUDSON's 'Gopsall' portrait of Handel (1756) and Handel bequeathing Jennens two paintings.

During his lifetime Jennens was better known for amassing one of the largest picture and sculpture collections in England. It manifested his religious commitment, his loyalty to the deposed Stuart royal family, his enthusiasm for Italian art and his patronage, in later life, of English artists. At Gopsall, which he inherited in 1747 (with thirty-four other properties in six counties), he spent twenty years laying out the garden and its buildings (reputedly at a cost of £80,000) and transforming the Jacobean house into a magnificent late Palladian mansion (demolished 1951). Dominating the grounds was the monument (1764) to his close friend and fellow non-juror Edward Holdsworth (1684–1746), a classical scholar whose work on Virgil Jennens had nurtured: an Ionic rotunda (rediscovered 1992) over a cenotaph was surmounted by ROUBILIAC's *Religion* or *Fides Christiana* (cenotaph and statue Belgrave Hall Museum, Leicester). The composition is subtle and complex, the inscription eloquent of Jennens's non-juring principles, and the statue unique in Roubiliac's output.

Jennens was sensitive and depressive, possibly manic-depressive. He never married. His shyness and irascibility, coupled with his great wealth, earned him resentment. Posthumous derogation derives mainly from abusive allegations by the mendacious critic George Steevens, who justifiably envied Jennens's scrupulous and forward-looking editions of *King Lear*, *Hamlet*, *Othello*, *Macbeth* and *Julius Caesar* (1770–4), the first appearance of each play in a single volume and with textual variants in footnotes. Jennens's superb library, particularly rich in classical and theological publications and Shakespearian incunabula, was dispersed in an abysmally catalogued sale in 1918.

Jennens's monument at Nether Whitacre Church, Warwickshire, records his generous bequests to religious charities. His portraits, such as the splendid Hudson (1745) at the Handel House Museum (MUSEUMS, 2), preserve the privacy which he seems to have preferred to the ostentation which his detractors attributed to him; they barely suggest his strong character and abilities. His correspondence with Holdsworth (preserved in the Gerald COKE Handel collection) is a valuable source of information about Handel.   RUTH SMITH

W. Dean, 'Charles Jennens's Marginalia to Mainwaring's Life of Handel', *Essays on Opera* (Oxford, 1990)

A. Hicks, 'Handel, Jennens and Saul: Aspects of a Collaboration', *Music and Theatre: Essays in Honour of Winton Dean*, ed. N. Fortune (Cambridge, 1987)

J. H. Roberts, 'The Aylesford Collection', *Handel Collections and their History*, ed. T. Best (Oxford, 1993)

R. Smith, 'Making Use of Handel: Charles Jennens (1700–73)', *Atti del XIV congresso della Società Internazionale di Musicologica* (Bologna, 1990)

Oratorios

'The Achievements of Charles Jennens', *ML* 70/1 (1989), 161–90

R. Smith and R. Williams, 'Jennens, Charles', *The Dictionary of Art* (New York, 1996)

Jephtha, HWV 70. Handel's last new English oratorio, composed 21 January–27 February and 18 June–30 August 1751, and premiered on 26 February 1752 at COVENT GARDEN theatre, with three performances in a six-week season that also included *JOSHUA*, *HERCULES*, *SAMSON*, *JUDAS MACCABAEUS* and *MESSIAH*. The original cast was as follows:

Jephtha	John BEARD (tenor)
Storgè	Caterina GALLI (mezzosoprano)
Iphis	Giulia FRASI (soprano)
Hamor	Charles BRENT (countertenor)

Zebul	Wass (bass)
Angel	[unidentified] (boy treble)

The libretto by Thomas MORELL is based on the biblical book of Judges (10–12). The Jewish Gileadites, in the promised land after the exodus from Egypt, have forfeited God's protection by adopting the idolatry of neighbouring heathen tribes. Worsted by the child-sacrificing Ammonites, they determine to renew their faith in God and recall from exile the great commander and patriot Jephtha, who agrees to lead the nation. His sensitive wife, Storgè, his lively daughter Iphis and his prospective son-in-law, Hamor, manifest similar patriotic selflessness. Meditating alone, Jephtha feels the spirit of God. He vows that, if granted victory, he will sacrifice to God the first thing he meets on his return. Summoning the Gildeadites, he leads them in prayer. Storgè is frightened by nightmares of danger threatening Iphis, who reassures her mother. A peace mission to the Ammonites is rebuffed. Jephtha and the Gileadites invoke God's aid for battle.

In Part II Hamor returns with news of divinely assisted victory. Iphis prepares to give her father a hero's welcome. Jephtha arrives, also attributing victory to God, and to his horror, first meets Iphis leading her festive procession to greet him. Distraught, he sends her away and explains to his dumbfounded brother, wife and prospective son-in-law that his beloved only child must die as the result of the vow which has brought them freedom. They join in an anguished quartet, Jephtha refusing to break his pledge to God. Iphis, having learned her fate, courageously accepts it, content that the vow resulted in her country's salvation. Jephtha is overcome by her goodness and his predicament. The Gileadites attempt to fathom God's decrees.

In Part III the sacrifice is prepared. Jephtha prays that angels will carry Iphis to heaven. Iphis encourages the hesitant priests to execute her and looks forward to a brighter afterlife. The priests pray to God for guidance. An angel appears and explains that the vow of sacrifice did not require Iphis's death, which God would abhor. She is to be devoted to God as a perpetual virgin, and will be eternally honoured. The Holy Spirit dictated Jephtha's vow and approves his faith. Relief is tempered by Hamor's loss of his bride, Iphis's of her husband, and Storgè's of a future family. Jephtha's and Iphis's courage and faith are hymned, and the final chorus celebrates Gilead's regained liberty.

Jephtha's immediate predecessors, *ALEXANDER BALUS* and *THEODORA*, had unfamiliar stories, ended unhappily, and were unenthusiastically received. By contrast Jephtha's story was one of the best known in the Old Testament. It was also one of Judaeo-Christianity's prickliest nettles, agonised over from the earliest days of biblical scholarship, and especially during the Enlightenment. For it too ended unhappily, apparently with the daughter's death, implicating God as a sadist, and raising the question of why Jephtha is honoured by the New Testament (Epistle to the Hebrews). Morell's alternative ending, current since medieval times in biblical apologetics, enabled him to justify God's ways to man. Excessive self-reliance (Jephtha's first air), and the pervading belief in unalterable 'fate' (the nihilistic 'Whatever is, is right'), are shown to be dead ends, unlike faith in God's Grace (Jephtha's 'Waft her, angels' and Iphis's 'Brighter scenes'), and, above all, the power of prayer. The double plot enabled Morell to write within the topical genre of pathetic patriot drama, whose theme was the tragic conflict of private and public commitments. (If Morell intended Jephtha, like Hoadly's Jephtha, to celebrate Prince FREDERICK as leader of the Patriot Party, Frederick's recent death must have made the opening scene of desperate need for a patriot leader sadly relevant for the first audience.)

Previous settings of the story included CARISSIMI's oratorio Jephte (which Handel knew), Pellegrin's and Montéclair's opera (1732 and often revived) and Maurice GREENE's oratorio (libretto John Hoadly, published 1737). Morell drew on Hoadly, on George Buchanan's Latin play Jephthes, sive Votum (1554), and on EURIPIDES, whose two Iphigenia plays yielded dozens of operas in the baroque and classical eras. Morell's voluminous reading of European literature is traceable in many quotations, some but by no means all indicated in the WORD-BOOK. Handel's score is also richly derivative. Seven choruses cull six masses by HABERMANN (published 1747), and Handel also took musical ideas from Antonio LOTTI's Missa Sapientae (BORROWINGS). Handel's most recent sources were GALUPPI's serenata La vittoria d'Imeneo (1750) for the duet 'These labours past', and his own recent D major Violin Sonata (HWV 371; CHAMBER MUSIC), for the Angel's Symphony, which also uses 'Lascia omai' from 'Delirio amoroso' (1707) (DA QUEL GIORNO FATALE). The most poignant recollection is of the wronged Ginevra's farewell to her father (ARIODANTE) in Iphis's 'Happy they'. But this oratorio gives no sense of tiredness or decline of inspiration. For many it is Handel's profoundest work. It is marked by fertility and concision; by formal innovation (e.g. the quartet 'O spare your daughter'); by mastery of structure (e.g. the tonal organisation of the central section of the work, which constitutes one of Handel's most original compositional spans); by range, intensity and inwardness of emotion (there is little added orchestral 'colour'). There are seven accompanied recitatives, Jephtha's anguished 'Deeper and deeper still' passing through 15 keys in 44 bars before staggering into silence. Handel harvests his whole repertory of choral expressiveness (chromatic anxiety, hymnal ardour, 'devout' orthodox counterpoint, word-painting of sublime effects of untrammelled nature and the supernatural), and extends it for 'How dark, O Lord', developing five distinct ideas within 183 bars as the chorus casts around for a way to make sense of the world, ending with a cry of humanity facing implacable fate. Handel experienced the start of his own blindness while setting 'All hid from mortal sight', recording in his autograph score (in German): 'Got as far as this on Wednesday 13 February 1751, unable to continue because the sight of my left eye is so weakened' (Figure 17). It is unknown whether Handel or Morell initiated the change, made during composition, of 'What God ordains is right' to 'Whatever is, is right' (quoting Alexander POPE's Essay on Man). Jephtha keeps in play till the denouement conflicting ideas of God: personal, moral, protector and judge; Jansenist 'hidden' God ('In glory high'); immutable fate (Jephtha in the quartet); Newtonian, cosmic, indifferent watchmaker ('How dark'). Two-thirds of the concerted numbers are entirely or partly in triple time, several with pastoral overtones appropriate to the innocent simplicity of the early Israelite landowners in general and Iphis in particular, her songs before the crisis being mainly in dance rhythms. In moving from radiant girlhood to inspired nobility Iphis is the culmination of Handel's lifelong portrayals of blameless women whose predicament brings out their heroism (a line begun in English oratorio with the very first, Esther). Storgè is the last in the line of Handel's

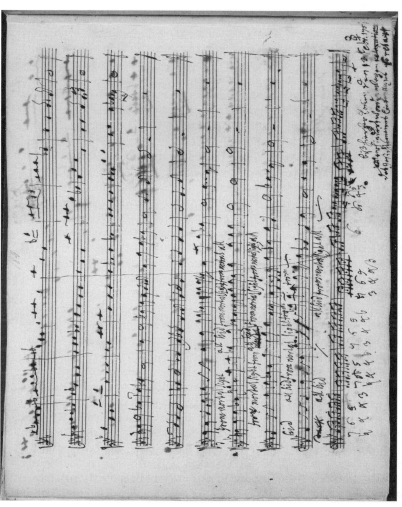

17. 'How dark are thy decrees' from Handel's autograph manuscript of *Jeptha* (R.M.20.e.9, fol. 91ᵛ), 1751. Upon reaching the bottom of this page, Handel noted that the onset of blindness was forcing him to take a rest from composing.

passionate wronged women, begun forty-five years before in his Italian cantatas. Jephtha's rise from blinkered confidence through inexpressible torment to true courage and faith is unerringly explored in his pat 'Virtue my soul', his heart-stopping 'Open thy marble jaws, O tomb' (a heroic effort to keep a grip on sanity in the form of a da capo air), his anguished 'Deeper and deeper still', and his apprehension of heaven, the soaring 'Waft her, angels' (on which see Hurley).

Handel revived Jephtha in 1753, 1756 and 1758. In 1756 (helped by J. C. SMITH JUNIOR) he added an air for Zebul adapted from *AGRIPPINA* and replaced Hamor's and Iphis's final airs with a duet leading into a quintet for all the principals.   RUTH SMITH

D. Burrows, 'Handel's Last Musical Autograph', HJb 40–1 (1994–5)
Dean, *Oratorios*
T. Goleeke, '"These labours past": Handel's Look to the Future', GHB VI (1996); HHB ii
D. R. Hurley, *Handel's Muse: Patterns of Creation in his Oratorios and Musical Dramas, 1743–1751* (Oxford, 2001)
T. Morell, *Jephtha*, MS libretto, Larpent Collection, Huntington Library, San Marino, CA
K. Nott, '"Heroick Vertue": Handel and Morell's *Jephtha* in the Light of Eighteenth-Century Biblical Commentary and Other Sources', ML 77/2 (1996), 194–208
K. Nott (ed.), *Jephtha*, HHA I/32 (Kassel, forthcoming)
R. Smith, *Handel's Oratorios and Eighteenth-Century Thought* (Cambridge, 1995)
    'Thomas Morell and his Letter about Handel', JRMA 127/2 (2002), 191–225
R. Smith, 'Why Does Jephtha Misinterpret His Own Vow?', *Handel Studies: A Gedenkschrift for Howard Serwer*, ed. R. G. King (Hillsdale, NY, 2009)

Johann Adolf I, Duke See Duke of SAXE-WEISSENFELS

Johannespassion. A St John Passion manuscript preserved anonymously in BERLIN was attributed to Handel by CHRYSANDER and published in HG and HHA. Its authenticity was questioned as early as 1905, and in recent years it has generally been regarded as spurious, though in 2003 Rainer Kleinertz sought to reinstate it in the Handel canon. Close reading of a long critique of the work in MATTHESON's *Critica Musica* (1724) points to Reinhard KEISER as the composer. He probably composed it in 1697 for the Jacobi-Kirche in HAMBURG.
                                                                    JOHN H. ROBERTS

R. Kleinertz, 'Zur Frage der Autorschaft von Händels "Johannespassion" ', HJb 49 (2003)
J. H. Roberts, 'Placing "Handel's St. John Passion" ', HJb 51 (2005)

Jonson, Benjamin (b. ?London, 11 June 1572; d. London, mid-Aug. 1637). Jonson, poet, playwright and bricklayer, was a soldier in the Low Countries before he turned to writing and directing plays. In 1598, Shakespeare acted in Jonson's *Every Man in his Humour*, and his company performed Jonson's tragedy *Sejanus* (1603). Jonson also produced masques for the King. Noted for their wit, delightfully convoluted plots, sagacity and learning, Jonson's comedies include The *ALCHEMIST*, a revival of which in 1710 had the overture from Handel's *RODRIGO* as its incidental music.   LESLIE M. M. ROBARTS

Joseph and his Brethren, HWV 59. In Part I of this sacred drama or oratorio, Joseph, released from an Egyptian prison, interprets Pharaoh's dreams. He forecasts harvests followed by famines and advises the storage of grain. For this wisdom, and to public acclaim, Pharaoh makes him first minister and marries him to

Asenath, the chief priest's daughter. We are to understand at the start of Part II that Joseph's brothers have appealed to Joseph for food but have not recognised him. He has imprisoned Simeon to ensure that the brothers return to Egypt with Benjamin. When Benjamin arrives, Joseph rejects the brothers' entreaties for food. In Part III Joseph frames his youngest brother in order to separate him from the others. This abuse of authority torments Joseph, because in spite of his anger towards his older brothers for having conspired to kill him years before, he has no desire to hurt either his father or Benjamin, or abuse Pharaoh's trust. Failure to confide in his wife makes his predicament worse. The brothers' earnest pleas for mercy, and Joseph's consciousness that he has made Benjamin suffer needlessly, undermine his resolve and he reveals his true identity. Asenath tells the reunited brothers that Pharaoh has given permission for their father and them to live in Egypt.

The librettist, James MILLER, derived Parts II and III of the libretto from Apostolo ZENO's *Giuseppe*, an oratorio libretto prepared for Antonio CALDARA in Vienna in 1722, which was itself an adaptation of *Joseph*, a play by Abbé Genest and first performed in 1711. Miller intercalated verse from his own plays into Parts II and III, and to provide a three-part structure for Handel invented Part I, selecting events from Genesis to present Joseph as a hero. Thus in Parts II and III Joseph becomes an anti-hero. Miller provided a synopsis of Joseph's story in the wordbook, which is essential reading if an audience is to make sense of the plot.

Joseph was one of the new oratorios written for the 1744 season, the other being the secular SEMELE. Handel dated and signed Part I of *Joseph* on Friday, 26 August 1743 and Part II on Monday, 12 September 1743. Part III is unsigned because Handel ignored Miller's ending and concluded the oratorio with a chorus, with its prose text, from the recently composed Dettingen Anthem (ANTHEMS, 6).

Handel spiritedly seized the opportunities afforded by Miller's libretto to explore acute psychological and moral dilemmas. Of particular note is the music's portrayal of Joseph's inner turmoil as he harbours a personal desire for revenge while holding publicly affirmed scruples. The oratorio presents a man who administers Egypt wisely but who struggles to govern his own feelings. The emotional tensions generated by Joseph's duplicity and the distressing effect on the brothers, Simeon and Benjamin in particular, situate the oratorio firmly in the theatre of tears and make *Joseph* a notably sentimental work. In achieving this effect of anguish and pain it contains some very fine dramatic recitatives and extended scenes, of which two are outstanding. In the opening prison scene Joseph wrestles for self-control as he burns with bitterness at the injustice of his false imprisonment, an episode of charged emotion that is later paralleled by Simeon's indignation at his own unwarranted incarceration.

Most of Part I takes place in the public arena, while Parts II and III occupy a domestic and interior world. Handel also makes clear distinctions between the principals, of whom Asenath has more airs than Joseph, though Joseph dominates the simple and accompanied recitatives. In the air 'Ah Jealousy, thou Pelican', Handel finely captures Asenath's desperation and fear that Joseph is defensive of a grievance he will not share with her. The air's reference to the mother pelican's sacrifice for her young is now an obscure image but in Miller's time was a literary and theological commonplace. Handel sets pleasing duets for Joseph and Asenath when they are to be married and when all is resolved at the end of the oratorio.

But it is Simeon who is Handel's most finely drawn character, and the music powerfully portrays him as a guilty victim. Accompanied recitatives considerably heighten dramatic tension as we hear Simeon as a man of injured decency appealing for Joseph to respond sympathetically to fatherly tenderness, brotherhood and kinship. These extended pieces contain some of Handel's sharpest musical insights into human misery, and they tug at the heartstrings. In stark contrast to Simeon's passionate outbursts are Joseph's aching nostalgia in 'Ye departed Hours' and the subsequent air 'The Peasant tastes' and Benjamin's heartfelt appeal for clemency, 'Thou hadst, my Lord'. The inevitable but long-delayed collapse of Joseph's pretence occurs when he recognises that he can no longer suppress his true feelings, and in a succinct resolution to the oratorio he confesses and seeks forgiveness, and the work closes with brief Hallelujahs.

Supporting the principals are two finely contrasted groups of choruses, Egyptians and Joseph's brothers. The Egyptians are celebratory, whereas the brothers' choruses are 'learned' and ecclesiastical in style, particularly the concluding chorus to Part II, 'O God, who in thy heav'nly Hand'. Of the three sections to this chorus, the second is based on a poignant chorale tune (also used in BWV 616), and the third, beginning 'O Lord' as the brothers place their trust in God, is in the moving style of an Anglican psalm.

Joseph was first performed at COVENT GARDEN on 1 March 1744, with the cast:

Joseph	Daniel SULLIVAN (countertenor)
Asenath	FRANCESINA (soprano)
Simeon	John BEARD (tenor)
Judah	John Beard
Pharaoh	Henry REINHOLD (bass)
Reuben	?Henry Reinhold
Benjamin	[?Samuel Champness] (treble)
Phanor	Esther YOUNG (alto)

Mary DELANY reported that 'The oratorios fill very well', and Handel banked £250 after *Joseph*'s first night. *Joseph* received further hearings on 7, 9 and 14 March 1744 and was performed again in 1745, 1747, 1755 and 1757. *Joseph* was revived by J. C. SMITH JUNIOR in the 1760s but then disappeared from the repertory. It is rarely performed nowadays, perhaps because of mistrust of sentimental drama and misunderstanding of Miller's libretto.

LESLIE M. M. ROBARTS

D. Chisholm, 'New Sources for the Libretto of Handel's *Joseph*', *Handel Tercentenary Collection*, ed. S. Sadie and A. Hicks (Basingstoke, 1987)

Dean, *Oratorios*

L. M. M. Robarts, 'A Bibliographical and Textual Study of the Wordbooks for James Miller's *Joseph and his Brethren* and Thomas Broughton's *Hercules*, Oratorio Librettos Set to Music by George Frideric Handel, 1743–44', Ph.D. dissertation (University of Birmingham, 2008)

Joshua, HWV 64. English oratorio. The libretto, rhymed throughout, was adapted from Exodus 12, Leviticus 23, Numbers 9, 13, 14, Joshua 1, 3–11, 13–15 and Psalm 114. The librettist is unknown. In Part I the Ark of the Covenant, carried by priests, miraculously opens up a passage through the River Jordan, enabling the Israelites, led out of the Sinai desert by Joshua and Caleb – the only truly righteous surviving members of the previous generation – to take possession of the promised land of Canaan. A commemorative monument is erected. An angel foretells the fall of Jericho and its heathen 'tyrant king' to the Israelites, and at the call to arms (the first, and thrilling, use of brass) the young Othniel leaves his beloved Achsah, Caleb's daughter, to join up. Part II depicts the fall of Jericho, achieved by carrying the Ark seven times round the city while blowing trumpets, and followed by massacre of its hostile (but not its hospitable) inhabitants. The feast of Passover is instituted and celebrated. News comes of Israelite defeat, the result of complacency. Joshua rouses the nation from despair. Othniel is discovered by Caleb enjoying some respite with Achsah and, moved to valour, joins Joshua and his other comrades in battle. Divinely inspired, Joshua halts the sun and moon in their courses, enabling the Israelites to push home their victory. Part III rejoices in the conquest of Canaan; Joshua divides the country among the Israelite tribes, rewarding Caleb's devoted service. Caleb offers Achsah as a prize for conquest of the one city still in Canaanite hands, a challenge eagerly accepted by Othniel. His success is greeted with 'See, the conqu'ring hero comes'. His union with Achsah, and denunciation of lawless and irreligious tyrants, lead to concluding praise of Jehovah.

Handel composed this oratorio between 19 July and 19 August 1747 for his 1748 season at COVENT GARDEN theatre (first performance 9 March), which also included *ALEXANDER BALUS* and *JUDAS MACCABAEUS*. Compared with his other biblical oratorios it is short, and Handel premiered it with a 'new Concerto', probably the *Concerto a due cori* in B flat major, No. 1 (ORCHESTRAL WORKS, 1). The first cast was as follows:

Joshua	Thomas LOWE (tenor)
Caleb	Henry Theodore REINHOLD (bass)
Othniel	Caterina GALLI (mezzo-soprano)
Achsah	Domenica Casarini (soprano)
Angel	[unidentified] (tenor)

Handel revived *Joshua* in 1752, expanding the one-movement introduction with two movements from *SOLOMON's* overture, and in 1754, when he cut four numbers and inserted five. There were several performances by others in the 1750s. 'See, the conqu'ring hero comes' was inserted into *JUDAS MACCABAEUS* after its first season, and found a permanent home there.

Joshua immediately became a favourite with Handel's public, 'O had I Jubal's lyre' continuing to the present as a popular concert piece. The unassuming charm of many of the solos sets off the grandeur of choruses such as 'Glory to God' (the fall of Jericho), which so impressed HAYDN in 1791. Several choruses are distinctively introduced by an unaccompanied precentor- or cantor-like solo line. Brass and drums are zestfully deployed, the festive 'See the conqu'ring hero' bearing the memorable marking for military side drum 'ad libitum; the second time warbling'. Detailed and imaginative musical enactment evokes the halting of the sun and moon, heard first to rise and then, with held notes over increasingly full orchestral bars, to stand still.

Like most of the biblical oratorios, *Joshua* is a lesson. God helps those who help themselves. Miracles are supplied to the chosen people, but have to be earned. National moral failing causes a setback, is corrected by repentance and followed by renewal of faith and courage, and success results. As always, Old Testament moral behaviour is improved on by the librettist. Unusually, the exploration of the Israel–Britain analogy is cemented by an insistent sense of history, whether looking forward to times when the present will be remembered or looking back to the nation's prehistory (the librettist evidently knew that Passover involves recounting the deliverance from Egypt, the Israelites' theme in 'Almighty Ruler').

Joshua gains meaning from its historical context. It was a panacea for national pride, coinciding with the most disastrous months of the War of the AUSTRIAN SUCCESSION. The rapid siege of Jericho in the oratorio was counterpointed in real life by the drawn-out siege of Bergen op Zoom, which ended in Allied defeat. The citizen militia in *Joshua* responds to the rallying cry with patriotic fervour – a quotation from *Henry V* makes the point – and a young hero is formed; in real life, the professional army was being ineptly commanded and there was royal concern at the decline of popular patriotism. The portrait of Joshua himself may honour Prince WILLIAM, Duke of Cumberland. In celebrating the laws and liberty of the Israelites, and the tyranny of their enemies, *Joshua* reminded its audiences of reasons for their own country's war against the absolutist Catholic powers. The oratorio also tapped the concerns of contemporary political and religious debates. For example, the colonising of Canaan was a fiercely con-tested political precedent: did it justify imperial conquest (a gain of the war in 1748), being divinely decreed, or was it fanatical aggression against innocent natives? *Joshua* sides with religious orthodoxy. It shows the Israelites taking root in equitably shared-out land; their territorial claims are their entitlement; their war is defensive, protecting citizen liberty, property and the rule of law – the signal benefits enjoyed by the new nation, recently released (as they are repeat-edly reminded) from Egyptian bondage. The miraculous Ark of the Covenant, containing the Israelites' God-given laws, is a potent symbol for the cherished British constitution – a commonplace analogy of the time, but here raised to a remarkable pitch. RUTH SMITH

[Anon.], *Joshua*, MS libretto, Larpent Collection, Huntington Library, San Marino, CA
D. Burrows, 'Handel's Last Musical Autograph', HJb 40–1 (1994–5)
Dean, *Oratorios*
Smith, *Oratorios*

journals

1. Göttinger Händel-Beiträge (GHB)
2. Händel-Jahrbuch (HJb)

1. *Göttinger Händel-Beiträge* (GHB)

Published irregularly since 1984, and normally every two years, this is an important journal series in international Handel scholarship. Volumes con-tain festival lectures and papers presented at the annual symposium which takes place during the GÖTTINGEN Handel Festival (FESTIVALS, 3), scholarly articles, reviews and a cumulative bibliography of Handel literature. The GHB is edited by Hans Joachim Marx (since 2006 in partnership with Wolfgang Sandberger). Volumes I–V were published by Bärenreiter, but from Volume VI (1996) the GHB has been published by the Göttingen publishing house Vandenhoeck & Ruprecht.   JÜRGEN HEIDRICH (Trans. ANGELA BAIER)

2. *Händel-Jahrbuch* (HJb)
Originally edited by Rudolf Steglich on behalf of the Händel-Gesellschaft (based in Leipzig, founded in 1925) and published by Breitkopf & Härtel from 1928 to 1933, since 1955 the new series has been published almost annually by the Georg-Friedrich-Händel-Gesellschaft e.V. (HANDEL SOCIETIES, 3) under the editorship of the academic secretary. It contains reports, documentations, bibliographies, reviews and independent scholarly articles from the field of Handel scholarship. Between 1967/8 and 1975/6 the HJb included papers given at academic conferences during the HALLE Handel Festival (FESTIVALS, 4) sporadically, but since 1989 this practice has been customary. From 1955 until 1991 the HJb was published by the Deutscher Verlag für Musik (Leipzig), by Studio (Cologne) from 1992 to 1995, and since 1995 it has been published by Bärenreiter.   KONSTANZE MUSKETA (Trans. ANGELA BAIER)

Journeys. See HANDEL, 15

'Joy to the world'. One of the most popular Christmas carols in the United States since the mid-nineteenth century, and recently in Britain as well. Its tune 'Antioch' was often attributed to Handel on the grounds of a chance resemblance of the opening phrase to both 'Lift up your heads' in *MESSIAH*. Other hymnals credited the tune to Lowell Mason (1792–1872), who introduced it to America in 1836 as 'arranged from Handel'. But in 1986 the late John Wilson showed that it was first published in two English collections, one firmly dated 1833 (for details see *Bulletin* No. 166 of the Hymn Society of Great Britain and Ireland).

NICHOLAS TEMPERLEY

Jubilate (Latin: 'Jubilate Deo'). One of the two morning prayer canticles frequently used in Thanksgiving liturgies (the other canticle is 'TE DEUM laudamus'). Handel set the English text 'O be joyful in the Lord' (from Psalm 100) in spring 1713 for his Utrecht Jubilate (HWV 279), which was performed together with the Utrecht Te Deum (TE DEUM, 1) on 7 July 1713 at ST PAUL'S CATHEDRAL in celebration of the Peace of Utrecht (War of the SPANISH SUCCESSION). The first movement was borrowed from the first movement of *Laudate pueri*, HWV 237 (Latin and Italian CHURCH MUSIC). In c.1717 Handel rearranged the Utrecht Jubilate as the anthem *O be joyful in the Lord* (HWV 246) (ANTHEMS, 2) for the small forces of the CANNONS CONCERT. He added an instrumental introduction and drastically reduced the scoring: the original large four- to eight-voice chorus was brought down to three solo voices with an orchestra comprising oboes, two violins and bassi, whereas the original Utrecht version was scored for an orchestra containing three violins, violas and two trumpets. The music in each version reveals the influence of Henry PURCELL's Te Deum

and Jubilate (1694), although Handel probably also studied William CROFT's
settings from 1709.   WALTER KREYSZIG

Burrows, *Chapel Royal*

Judas Maccabaeus, HWV 63. English oratorio. Thomas MORELL had completed the
libretto (his first for Handel) by the end of 1745. Handel set it between 8 or 9
July and 11 August 1746, and gave the first performance at COVENT GARDEN
on 1 April 1747. Morell derived his material from the two Books of Maccabees in
the Apocrypha and from Book 12 of Flavius Josephus's *The Antiquities of the Jews*.
The background is the persecution of the Jews of Judaea by their overlords, the
Syrian Seleucid dynasty, in the reign of Antiochus IV Epiphanes. The oratorio is
a condensed version of the Jewish Hasmonean revolt during 166–161 BC led by
the Maccabees – Mattathias and his five sons, of whom three, Judas, Simon and
Eleazar, figure in the oratorio.

At the opening of Part I, Jerusalem has been ravaged and the Temple defiled,
the Jews are in flight, and Mattathias has died. Intense grief for the loss of both
home and father-figure begins to lift in response to Simon's reminder of the
Jews' responsibility as God's people. They offer up a prayer. Divinely inspired,
Simon nominates Judas as the new leader. Judas joyfully accepts the challenge,
disclaiming ambition for power. The nation rallies behind him to attempt
'unequal war' with the goals of liberty and peace, praying that God will heed
their call for aid. In Part II two great victories, against the generals Apollonius
and Seron, have been achieved and are recalled, and Judas is celebrated. But a
new armed threat plunges the Jews into despair as intense as at the opening.
Once more Judas calls them to arms and they rally to fight for 'laws, religion,
liberty'. Again they renew their faith, and this time they forswear apostasy. In
Part III Simon and a group of Jews have recovered the sanctuary of the Temple
and rededicate it, instituting the Feast of Lights, Chanuka (dedication), with a
prayer for peace. News of victories over the Syrian generals Lysias and Nicanor
is followed by the return of Judas himself and the army, and all join in a hymn
of gratitude to God. Judas leads an elegy for the fallen, who include his brother
Eleazar. The Jewish ambassador to Rome, Eupolemus, brings word of a secure
future: Rome guarantees Judaean independence in a defensive alliance. The
oratorio ends in celebration of the blessings of peace and with praise of God, to
whom the Jews owe their safety.

The libretto is dedicated to, and celebrates, in the person of the Jewish
hero Judas, a British hero, Prince WILLIAM, Duke of Cumberland. But when
Morell wrote it, Cumberland was only just beginning to drive the JACOBITE
rebellion back to Scotland; and by the time the oratorio was first performed,
he had returned to his command against France on the continent, where the
War of the AUSTRIAN SUCCESSION was going badly for the British alliance.
The scenario of the Jews instigating a rebellion is in any case not a very good
parallel to the British repressing one. In fact the parallel is more complex, and
better. In 166 BC the Jews under the (religiously Hellenic) Syrians were, like
the British in 1745, disunited. A section of powerful Jews and their followers
had absorbed their overlords' Hellenism, secured special treatment from the
Syrians by disowning their membership of the Jewish nation, and caused a
civil war with the conservative Jews, which prompted the Syrian repression of

the faithful. The parallels are as follows. The Jewish nation disrupted from within by apostate Hellenisers = the British nation disrupted from within by Catholic Jacobites. The Hellenising Jews enlisting the support of the foreign, Hellenising, expansionist Syrians = British Jacobites enlisting the support of the foreign, Catholic, expansionist French. The Jewish nation uniting behind the leadership of Judas defeats and repels the armed apostate and foreign element (Hellenised Jews and Syrians) = the British nation uniting behind the leadership of Cumberland defeats and repels the armed apostate and foreign element (Jacobites and their sponsors, the French). Morell dexterously supplies just enough genuine historical names and incidents to make the parallels credible and few enough to allow the themes of integrity, courage, freedom, unity and peace – topical and universal – to occupy centre stage. *Judas Maccabaeus* is a drama of emotion not character; of a nation not individuals; of spiritual development not personal interaction.

Handel magnificently realises the libretto's aims. His treatment of the relation between soloists and CHORUS, unique among the oratorios, presents an audible image of individuality meshing in national unity. The Jewish people form the main character. No Handel oratorio apart from *ISRAEL IN EGYPT* has so many concerted numbers. The largest individual roles are those of the Israelite man and woman, the equivalent of the chorus leaders of Greek tragedy. The brevity of many of the choruses, and their interleaving with the solo voices, heightens the sense of national togetherness. The pattern of the work's structure, the rise from an initial low point followed by collapse and a second, greater, rise, is marked by Handel's use of C minor for both the opening chorus of grief and the return to despair in Part II. He differentiates the several laments, all haunting: 'Mourn, ye afflicted children' a muffled funeral march; 'From this dread scene' expressing anguished fear; 'For Sion' conveying inward-looking, obsessive, misery with a rocking barcarolle rhythm, creeping chromaticism in the individual voice parts, and 'choked' pauses; and 'Ah! wretched Israel' a desolate continuo aria with sympathising solo cello swelling to a chorus over a ground bass – a traditional motif of unavoidable disaster – with silences and a postlude suggesting grief too strong for words. The battle recalled at the start of Part II ('Fall'n is the foe') is frighteningly vivid, in the ominous key of D minor. Contrasted themes, one sickeningly imitating the fall of soldiers, the other the hacking 'warlike sword', in seemingly unpredictable dispersed entries evoke the bewildering swirl of movement on a battlefield. Surprise is heightened by the sudden clearing of air and space on the quiet 'fall'n' as the fact of death impinges, only to be swept aside in the welter of action. Handel is equally alive to the drama of spiritual renewal. In the final number of Part II he unmistakably points up the contrast between paganism and true faith with a startling silence, an equally startling change from G minor to C major, and a move from a phrase in insistent quavers suggesting the mindless ritual of idol worship to a great block statement in minims, followed by the grandeur of a double fugue in 'church mode'. At the rededication of the Temple, the expansive, rapt melody of 'Father of Heaven' makes this act of worship the spiritual centre of the work, eloquent of reconciliation with God, and of the serenity of having come home. Throughout, Handel's unerring orchestral colouring particularises and intensifies: bassoons adding characteristic plangency to 'For Sion'; trumpets and drums withheld until two-thirds of the way through 'Sound an alarm', itself halfway into the work, and then used to thrilling effect; the trumpet obbligato giving the A minor elegy 'With honour' a cast of antique heroism; flutes creating a sense of pastoral plenty in 'O lovely peace'.

Judas Maccabaeus is one of Handel's most compact oratorios, all its movements relatively short; his own timings in the autograph make it 105 minutes. The first performances included 'a new concerto', probably the *Concerto a due cori*, No. 3 in F (ORCHESTRAL WORKS, 1). The cast in the first season was:

Judas Maccabaeus	John BEARD (tenor)
Simon / Eupolemus	Henry Theodore REINHOLD (bass)
Israelitish Woman	Elisabetta de Gambarini (soprano)
Israelitish Man	Caterina GALLI (mezzo-soprano)

Judas Maccabaeus immediately became, and remained, immensely popular. Handel revived it every year except 1749. He made numerous revisions, beginning before the first performance, making additions during the first season, and making further changes and additions in later revivals. The non-specific nature of much of the text lent itself to adaptation. Two of the most famous numbers were not in the score as first performed: 'O Liberty', which Handel extracted from Morell's libretto and put into the preceding OCCASIONAL ORATORIO, and the chorus and duet 'See, the conqu'ring hero comes' with its march, which originated in JOSHUA. 'Flowing Joys' and 'Sion now' were also later additions, the latter originally composed for ESTHER in 1757, and perhaps Handel's last authentic composition. RUTH SMITH

M. Channon (ed.), *Judas Maccabaeus*, Novello Handel Edition (London, 1998)
Dean, *Oratorios*
R. Smith, *Oratorios*
   'The Meaning of Morell's Libretto of Judas Macccabaeus', ML 79/1 (1998), 50–71
   'Thomas Morell and his Letter about Handel', JRMA 127/2 (2002), 191–225

Julius Caesar. See *GIULIO CESARE*

Jupiter in Argos. See *GIOVE IN ARGO*

K

Karlsruhe. See FESTIVALS, 7; HANDEL SOCIETIES, 7; INTERNATIONALE HÄNDEL-AKADEMIE

Keiser, Reinhard (bap. Teuchern near Weissenfels, 12 Jan. 1674; d. Hamburg, 12 Sept. 1739). German composer and opera director. One of the leading figures in HAMBURG musical life for over forty years, he arrived at the city's GÄNSEMARKT opera via Leipzig (where he attended the Thomasschule) and BRUNSWICK (where he composed chamber music and operas from 1694 to 1697). Keiser took over the direction of the Gänsemarkt opera from the widow of Gerhard Schott in spring 1703, and proceeded to influence the Gänsemarkt style profoundly. He remained the company's director until the turn of the year 1706/7. During this time he was responsible for the first performances of fourteen operas, including two by Handel (*ALMIRA* and *NERO*). Keiser worked in Hamburg for nearly all of the rest of his life, even becoming *Domkantor* in 1728 (seven years after TELEMANN had established himself in the city), although during the years 1718–23 he worked at Gotha, Eisenach, Stuttgart and Copenhagen.

After moving from HALLE to Hamburg, Handel played second violin in the Gänsemarkt opera orchestra, and, later on, the harpsichord. He had first-hand experience of seven premieres of operas by Keiser, and his BORROWINGS show that he closely studied at least ten operas (including some dating from Keiser's time in Brunswick) and three pieces of the older composer's vocal chamber music. Handel's borrowings from Keiser, already noticed by MATTHESON in 1722 and Johann Adolph Scheibe in 1739, were drawn from works that date between 1694 (*Procris und Cephalus*, first performance in Brunswick) and 1714 (the printed collection *Musicalische Land-Lust*). These borrowings can be divided into two groups: the first group includes works dated 1694–1705 which were only available to Handel in manuscript form. Among them are the operas *Claudius* (first performed in February 1703, and still in the repertoire when Handel arrived in Hamburg), *Nebucadnezar* (1704) and *Octavia* (1705). Handel probably played in the orchestra for at least most of these works. There are no borrowings from Keiser's opera *Masagniello*, premiered in June 1706, which perhaps indicates that Handel had left for Italy by that time. The second group of works which he borrowed from includes printed scores dated 1713–14, which he presumably had access to in England. The works that Handel most frequently borrowed from are *Claudius* and *Octavia*, especially in numerous works composed in Italy (1707/8), although he continued to use material derived from Keiser throughout his creative career, even including his last oratorio The TRIUMPH OF TIME AND TRUTH (1757): in sixteen operas, twenty-seven oratorios, church music, cantatas and instrumental music. Sometimes Handel used the same source material for different works in different genres.

Friedrich CHRYSANDER evaluated Keiser's life and work negatively, and his (unsupportable) claim that Keiser and Handel had personal difficulties prevented a fair appreciation of Keiser during the nineteenth and twentieth centuries. The general attitude towards Keiser's achievements only began to change to a more objective one with Heinz Becker's fresh approach in the mid-twentieth century. The origins of ALMIRA and of Handel's NERO and Keiser's counterpart Octavia (all 1704/5) suggest that the two composers had an amicable relationship. The delay to the first performances of Handel's FLORINDO and DAPHNE until January/February 1708 was not Keiser's fault, but caused by political controversy in Hamburg. Moreover, Keiser arranged RINALDO (first Hamburg performance 27 November 1715) and PARTENOPE (first performance 28 October 1733), even though by 1733 he was already Domkantor and had no financial need to produce operas any more. It is not known if Keiser was personally responsible for arranging AMADIGI for Hamburg in 1717 as Oriana, but it certainly included some of his own arias.

KLAUS-PETER KOCH (Trans. ANGELA BAIER)

W. Dean, 'Handel and Keiser: Further Borrowings', Current Musicology 9 (1969), 73–80

H. Frederichs, Das Verhältnis von Text und Musik in den Brockespassionen Keisers, Händels, Telemanns und Matthesons (Munich and Salzburg, 1975)

H. J. Marx, 'Handel's Years as an Apprentice to Reinhard Keiser at the Gänsemarkt Opera House in Hamburg (1703–1705)', Handel Studies: A Gedenkschrift for Howard Serwer, ed. R. G. King (Hillsdale, NY, 2009)

J. Mattheson, Critica musica, vol. 1, Part 1 (Hamburg, 1722)

Grundlage einer Ehren-Pforte (Hamburg, 1740)

J. H. Roberts, 'Handel's Borrowings from Keiser', GHB II (1986)

(ed.), Handel Sources: Materials for the Study of Handel's Borrowing, vols. 1–3 (New York, 1986)

'Keiser and Handel at the Hamburg Opera', HJb 36 (1990) (also contains reply by H. Serwer)

J. A. Scheibe, Critischer Musikus (Leipzig, 1745)

Kensington Palace. William III disliked Whitehall and bought the Jacobean Nottingham House as easily adaptable for a London residence, ordering large additions from his Office of Works. Apart from Hawksmoor's King's Gallery (1695), the state rooms, replacing the Jacobean core, were designed probably by Colen Campbell, and decorated in diverse styles by William Kent for GEORGE I, who often lived there in the summer. The gardens were extended eastwards into HYDE PARK. GEORGE II made Kensington his principal residence but was the last sovereign to live there. Handel often visited as music teacher to the princesses (HANDEL, 20), and private concerts featuring newly arrived Italian opera singers were often given there, such as a sneak preview of the Second Academy singers in October 1729 (OPERA COMPANIES, 3), and a private performance by the OPERA OF THE NOBILITY's castrato FARINELLI in October 1734.

KERRY DOWNES

Kerll, Johann Kaspar (von) (b. Adorf, Vogtland, 9 April 1627; d. Munich, 13 Feb. 1693). German organist and composer. He started his career as organist with Archduke

Leopold Wilhelm in Vienna and maybe in Brussels and Olmütz (Olomouc) (he also found time to travel to ROME). From 1656 to 1673 he was Hofkapellmeister in Munich, from 1673 to 1683 court organist in Vienna and in 1683/4 he returned to Munich where he remained until his death. His keyboard music influenced Johann Sebastian BACH and Handel. In 1698 Handel entered compositions by Kerll into his book of manuscript music, now lost. He later borrowed material from Kerll's *Modulatio organica* in *ISRAEL IN EGYPT* and *MESSIAH*, and from Kerll's unprinted manuscript scores in the organ concerto HWV 295 (ORCHES-TRAL WORKS, 5).   KLAUS-PETER KOCH (Trans. ANGELA BAIER)

[W. Coxe], *Anecdotes of George Frederick Handel and John Christopher Smith* (London, 1799; facsimile edn, ed. P. M. Young, New York, 1979), 6n.
W. D. Gudger, 'A Borrowing from Kerll in Messiah', MT 118 (1977), 1038
J. Mattheson, *Grundlage einer Ehren-Pforte* (Hamburg, 1740), 135–7

Kerslake, Thomas (b. Exeter, July 1812; d. Clevedon, Somerset, 5 Jan. 1891). BRISTOL secondhand and antiquarian bookseller and publisher. He purchased the collection of manuscript scores used by Handel at his own performances and containing much autograph material, which are now in the HAMBURG Staats- and Universitätsbibliothek (SOURCES AND COLLECTIONS, 2). Kerslake purchased the 'conducting scores' at an auction following the death in 1851 of the Revd Sir Henry Rivers, whose mother Lady Rivers (née COXE), had inherited them in 1795 from her stepfather, John Christopher SMITH JUNIOR. There was apparently little interest in the manuscripts, and Kerslake secured them for a paltry sum – less than £10 – but sufficient to save it from 'the waste-paper market'. In 1856 he offered the collection for sale for 45 guineas, describing it in his catalogue as 'Handel's Autograph Scores, of many of his Oratorios, Operas . . . c. . . . altogether above 200 vols., some in folio some in oblong 4to'. It also included works and pasticcios produced after the composer's death by John Christopher Smith. The collection was purchased from Kerslake by Victor SCHOELCHER, who commented that 'The MSS of great men cannot be the property of any one man exclusively: they belong to the archives of that humanity which they glorify', and tried to dispose of it to the British Museum. In 1860 a disastrous fire at Kerslake's premises resulted in the loss of many rare books and manuscripts, including Handel's autograph setting of the 'Gloria' composed in ROME which closes his setting of the psalm *Nisi Dominus* (HWV 238) (Italian and Latin CHURCH MUSIC).   JOHN GREENACOMBE

[Anon.], *Programme Book for the Tenth Triennial Handel Festival* (London, 1891)
A. H. King, *Handel and his Autographs* (1967)
V. Schoelcher, *The Life of Handel* (London, 1857)

keyboard music. Whether the story told by MAINWARING about the young Handel playing a clavichord in secret in the attic is true or fanciful, the boy must have been involved with keyboard instruments from the beginning of his musical training. The world of his first teacher, ZACHOW, was that of the seventeenth-century German Protestant organist, whose art was based on the solemn COUNTERPOINT of the Lutheran CHORALE, fugues, cantatas and variations on chorale tunes. Handel studied, among others, the works of FROBERGER, Pachelbel, JOHANN KRIEGER and Zachow himself, and he became proficient in playing the organ and the harpsichord. Stylistic evidence suggests that some of his surviving keyboard music dates from his early years before 1706, in HALLE and especially in HAMBURG, where he supplemented his income from the opera house by giving harpsichord lessons, and presumably composed music for his pupils (HANDEL, 20). These early works show a growing confidence and mastery of compositional technique; for example, the large-scale suite in G minor (HWV 439), which must belong to this period, has many passages of fluent and graceful keyboard writing, and a sophisticated combination of counterpoint and *style brisé* which suits the sonorities of the harpsichord perfectly.

Handel spent the next four years in Italy, where he was involved in composing CANTATAS, OPERA and (for a short time) CHURCH MUSIC, so it is no surprise that we have little evidence of harpsichord music being written down: only the Sonata in G for a two-manual instrument (HWV 579) may be dated to the Italian period on stylistic grounds. Yet he often played the harpsichord and the organ, and amazed everyone with his virtuosity. He was described by one Italian as 'eccellente suonatore di cembalo', and later by the Electress of HANOVER as 'Handel qui joue à merveille du clavecin'.

After he settled in England in 1712 he seems to have written a few harpsichord pieces, but he returned seriously to keyboard composition only about 1717, when he was engaged at CANNONS. His style had now matured, and the Italian experience which had so broadened his horizons shows in this area of his work as well as in his vocal music. He composed seven suites, and a set of eleven fugues which display a remarkable variety of techniques, from smooth counterpoint with predominantly quaver movement, as in the one in B flat (HWV 607), to the extrovert one in F minor (HWV 433/2), with entries of the subject in full chords which create a thrilling effect on the harpsichord. Friends of the composer must have wanted copies of the music, and early in 1718 an important manuscript containing a large selection of these works (as well as some from the earlier period), commissioned by Elizabeth LEGH, was compiled by a group of Handel's COPYISTS. Another manuscript with a smaller selection, but with largely similar texts, was copied at the same time.

Handel seems not to have contemplated publication at this stage, but the London publisher John WALSH forced his hand. Having acquired copies of thirty-nine pieces, he printed them, probably in 1719 or 1720, with a title page *PIECES | à un & Deux Clavecins | COMPOSÉES | Par M.*[R] *HENDEL | A AMSTERDAM | Chez Jeanne Roger | N.° 490*; there may have been some collusion with the ROGER firm, since the serial number fits correctly in their sequence, and the edition was later reprinted by Le Cène. It is not clear exactly when the volume was issued, but in June 1720 Handel took out a Royal Privilege (COPYRIGHT) which protected his work for fourteen years, and in November 1720 he issued an authoritative edition of his own, *Suites de Pieces | pour le Clavecin | Composées | par G.F. Handel. | PREMIER VOLUME*. The volume was engraved and printed by J. CLUER, and it seems to be a riposte to the pirated edition, for in a prefatory note the composer wrote:

> I have been obliged to publish Some of the following lessons because Surrepticious and incorrect copies of them had got abroad. I have added several new ones to make the Work more usefull which if it meets with a favourable reception: I will Still proceed to publish more reckoning it my

duty with my Small talent to Serve a Nation from which I have receiv'd so Generous a protection.

The 1720 edition, now known as the 'first set of suites' (HWV 426–33), became one of the best-known collections of harpsichord music published in the eighteenth century. Handel composed seven new movements for it, and revised and reordered many of the existing ones, which included sixteen that appear in the Roger/Walsh edition. It represents the best of his music for the harpsichord, because in spite of the promise to 'publish more', he wrote little more of significance for the instrument. The volume has a remarkably wide range of styles, reflecting the cosmopolitan nature of Handel's musical experience up to that time. Although the word 'Suites' occurs on the title page, and stands at the head of each work ('Suite première pour le Clavecin'), there is no attempt at presenting a consistent pattern of the baroque suite such as we find in BACH. There are indeed some of the traditional movements, Allemande, Courante, Sarabande and Gigue, but there are also fugues (five of them were included), movements in the Italian concerto style called simply 'Allegro' or 'Andante', and sets of variations (*THE HARMONIOUS BLACKSMITH*). The collection shows Handel's originality and independence of mind, and his gift for drawing on different musical influences and unifying them by the power of his genius.

There were many pieces that he had composed by 1720 which do not appear in the edition, including twenty-three of those printed in the Roger/Walsh volume. Some of these are of excellent quality, such as the Suite in B flat (HWV 434), while there are also less mature works which originated in the pre-1706 period. Perhaps Handel really did intend to prepare a second volume with some new music, but in the event he wrote very little: only a fine suite in D minor (HWV 436), written about 1724–6, and a few unimportant single pieces were forthcoming before Walsh again went in for a pirated edition. His 'Second Volume' of suites first appeared about 1731–2: it contains all but three of the pieces from his earlier edition which Handel had not used in 1720, together with the D minor suite (HWV 436), a suite in G of very dubious authenticity (HWV 441), and an obviously very early Chaconne (HWV 442/2). It is a scrappy production, 'full of errors in the coppying', as a contemporary commented; the text not only reproduces the errors of the earlier edition, but adds many more. Having first engraved his imprint at the foot of the title page, Walsh had it blocked out when the few copies were printed, perhaps because of Handel's Privilege. After a reissue about 1732 the edition was reprinted about 1733–4, with changes in the order of the pieces, and the imprint revealed (HWV 434–42).

In 1735 Walsh issued the six fugues HWV 606 (HWV 605–10) which were those left over from the eleven written in 1717, the other five having appeared in Handel's 1720 volume. Except for two small but exquisitely crafted suites composed about 1739 for the Princess LOUISA (HWV 447, 452), Handel's interest in writing harpsichord music had come to an end. He had begun to compose oratorios, and his keyboard skills were now employed in organ concertos to be performed with those works (ORCHESTRAL WORKS, 5).

TERENCE BEST

T. Best, 'Handel's Harpsichord Music: A Checklist', *Music in Eighteenth-Century England*, ed. C. Hogwood and R. Luckett (Cambridge, 1983)

'Die Chronologie von Händels Klaviermusik', HJb 27 (1981)

'Handel and the Keyboard', *The Cambridge Companion to Handel*, ed. D. Burrows (Cambridge, 1997)

(ed.), *Klavierwerke I*, HHA IV/1 Neuausgabe (Kassel, 1993); *Klavierwerke II*, HHA IV/5, Neuausgabe (Kassel, 1999); *Klavierwerke III*, HHA IV/6 (Kassel and Leipzig 1970); *Klavierwerke I–IV. Kritischer Bericht* HHA IV/7 (Kassel, 2000); *Klavierwerke IV*, HHA IV/17 (Kassel and Leipzig, 1975); *Einzeln überlieferte Instrumentalwerke II*, HHA IV/19 (Kassel and Leipzig, 1988)

Kielmansegg, Baron Johann Adolph von (b. Iburg, 30 Sept. 1668; d. London, 14 Nov. 1717). Courtier and diplomat in the Hanoverian service, in 1701 married Sophia Charlotte von Platen und Hallermund, officially the daughter of Franz Ernst, Baron von Platen, and his wife Clara, but really Clara's child with Ernst August (d. 1698), Elector of HANOVER, and thus half-sister of the reigning Elector Georg Ludwig, later GEORGE I. He shared the interests of Georg Ludwig and his brother Ernst August in music and opera. According to MAINWARING, Kielmansegg met Handel on a visit to VENICE in 1710 with Ernst August; Mainwaring represents Kielmansegg as suggesting that Handel travel to Hanover, and as intermediary between Handel and the Elector in determining the terms by which Handel became Kapellmeister. He was involved in mitigating the effects of Handel's dismissal from his post in 1713. Kielmansegg and his wife came to London in 1714, following George I. He paid for the waterborne concert on the Thames at Chelsea on 17 July 1717 for which Handel wrote the *WATER MUSIC*. After his death, George I recognised his widow's family connection by making her Countess of Darlington and Leinster; many in Britain assumed she was, like Ehrengard Melusine von der SCHULENBURG, the King's mistress.

MATTHEW KILBURN

R. Hatton, *George I: Elector and King* (London, 1978)

Kiesewetter, Raphael Georg (b. Holleschau [now Holešov], 29 Aug. 1773; d. Baden near Vienna, 1 Jan. 1850). Austrian musicologist, collector of music manuscripts, civil servant. He studied philosophy at the University of Olmütz (Olomouc) and law at the University of Vienna without graduating, and he studied musical instruments, singing and music theory. Johann Georg Albrechtsberger was one of his teachers. Kiesewetter organised concerts in his own house in Vienna and performed music from the sixteenth to the eighteenth centuries. For his concerts he gathered a collection of old scores, including the music of Handel (SOURCES AND COLLECTIONS, 11). His activities attracted other musicians, authors and also collectors of sources (e.g. Aloys FUCHS). WALTER KREYSZIG

H. Kier, *Raphael Georg Kiesewetter (1773–1850). Wegbereiter des musikalischen Humanismus* (Regensburg, 1968)

King Henry's Chapel. See WESTMINSTER ABBEY

King shall Rejoice, The. See ANTHEMS, 3; 6

King's Theatre, Haymarket (Queen's Theatre until 1714). Designed and built by John VANBRUGH. Conceived as a home for a dual theatre-opera company, it opened in 1705 as a venue for spoken drama. After the theatre union of 1708 it presented Italian opera translated into English; following a series of managerial upheavals and some remodelling, it became in 1711 exclusively an opera house with performances in Italian, which it remained until the original building burnt in 1789. It proved acoustically good for music, and during the first half of the eighteenth century the theatre was relatively elegant. It also served as the venue for the posh, very expensive and decidedly scandalous masquerade balls initiated in 1711 and managed for many years by J. J. HEIDEGGER, who leased the building from Vanbrugh in 1716 and retained control of it until his death in 1749.

The total cost of the building is unguessable, though Vanbrugh is known to have found thirty backers who put up £100 each in return for free admission rights. No early architectural plan of the theatre survives, but the plan and section G. P. M. Dumont published in *Parallèle de plans des plus belles salles de spectacles d'Italie et de France*, dated 1774, are generally accepted as a fair representation of the early state of the theatre. It could hold c.670 comfortably and c.940 jam-packed, though far more auditors could be accommodated with stage and backstage seating for concerts. The documentable capacity of pit and boxes in 1710 was 482. Scene changes were effected with wings and shutters in the standard fashion of eighteenth-century European theatres. For operas and oratorios alike admission to pit and boxes was 10s. 6d.; a gallery seat was 5s.; servants of patrons were allowed free entry into the second gallery.

Handel was closely associated both with the Haymarket Theatre and with Heidegger from the time of his arrival in London into the 1740s. *RINALDO* (his first opera in England) was premiered there in 1711, as were twenty-seven others of the thirty-six original London operas. When the Royal Academy of Music (OPERA COMPANIES, 2) was founded in 1719 the King's Theatre was naturally the venue, and Handel was employed as a principal composer. After the Academy went out of business in 1728, it leased its property to Handel and Heidegger, who jointly ran the 'Second Academy' until 1734 (OPERA COMPANIES, 3), when Handel moved in with John RICH at COVENT GARDEN, and the recently formed rival company (now commonly known as 'The OPERA OF THE NOBILITY') became Heidegger's tenants at the King's Theatre. Handel appears to have joined forces with the remnants of the Nobility Opera, returning to the King's Theatre for 1737–8 and premiering *FARAMONDO* and *SERSE* there that season. Several oratorios received their premieres at the theatre: *DEBORAH* (1733), *SAUL* (1739), *ISRAEL IN EGYPT* (1739) – and in his last, over-ambitious 1744–5 oratorio season, *HERCULES* and *BELSHAZZAR* (both 1745). Afterwards he always organised his public theatre concerts at Covent Garden.

JUDITH MILHOUS and ROBERT D. HUME

See also STAGING, 1

G. F. Barlow, 'Vanbrugh's Queen's Theatre in the Haymarket, 1703–9', EM 17/4 (1989), 515–22

K. Downes, *Vanbrugh* (London, 1977)

J. Milhous, 'The Capacity of Vanbrugh's Theatre in the Haymarket', *Theatre History Studies*, vol. 4 (1984), 38–46

F. H. W. Sheppard, *Survey of London*, vols. 29–30: *The Parish of St. James Westminster*, Part I: 'South of Piccadilly' (London, 1960)

M. W. Stahura, 'Handel's Haymarket Theatre', *Opera in Context*, ed. M. Radice (Portland, OR, 1998)

Klopstock, Friedrich Gottlieb (b. Quedlinburg, 2 July 1724; d. Hamburg, 14 March 1803). Essayist, hymnist, poet, playwright, satirist. Prompted by his interest in literature as early as the 1740s, with special enthusiasm for the reading of Homer, Virgil, MILTON, and the BIBLE, Klopstock decided to create a great religious epic poem, *Der Messias*, in 1742. The last of the twenty cantos was published in 1773. He finished the work after he had heard Handel's *MESSIAH* at HAMBURG in 1772 under the direction of Michael Arne. In 1775 he and Christoph Daniel EBELING created the first German translation for Handel's *Messiah*, which was performed on 21 December under the direction of Carl Philipp Emanuel Bach. It became the basis for the later text versions by Johann Adam HILLER and Georg Gottfried GERVINUS. In his nationalistic ode *Wir und Sie* (1769), a comparison between Britain and Germany, he chose Handel of all German composers: 'Wen haben sie, der, kühnen Flugs, / Wie Händel, Zaubereyen tönt? / Das hebt uns über sie!' (Whom do they have, who with bold flight / Like Handel magical sounds? / This raises us above them!)

WALTER KREYSZIG

H.-J. Kreutzer, '"The Sublime, the Grand, and the Tender", über Händels *Messiah* und Klopstocks *Messias*', GHB XI (2006)

M. Marx-Weber and H. J. Marx, 'Der deutsche Text zu Händels Messias in der Fassung von Klopstock und Eberling', *Beiträge zur Geschichte des Oratoriums seit Händel. Festschrift Günter Massenkeil zum 60. Geburtstag*, ed. R. Cadenbach and H. Loos (Bonn and Bad Godesberg, 1986)

W. Siegmund-Schultze, 'Über die ersten Messias-Aufführungen in Deutschland', HJb 6 (1960)

Knatchbull, Sir Wyndham, 5th Baronet (b. ?Mersham Hatch, 26 Nov. 1699; d. Bath, 23 July 1749) (assumed the surname Wyndham 1746). Friend and supporter of Handel, married (1730) to Kathcrine, half-sister of James HARRIS. He was the recipient of Handel's earliest known personal letter in English (1734), declining an invitation to visit him in Kent. From 1736 he was a regular subscriber to Handel's published works. One of his wife's lively letters reports at first hand Handel's plans for *SAUL* and *ISRAEL IN EGYPT*; another mentions Handel sitting for his portrait ('which is what he is very shy of') at her request (in ivory, untraced; Burrows and Dunhill, 99).

RUTH SMITH

Kneller, Sir Godfrey or Gottfried von Kniller (b. Lübeck, 8 Aug. 1646; d. London, 19 Oct. 1723). Painter and draughtsman. After study in Leiden, Amsterdam, ROME and VENICE, he settled in England in 1674. In 1680 he was appointed Principal Painter to the Crown and later was knighted by William III. In 1711 Kneller founded the first proper academy of art in England. In his studio he produced many portraits on an almost industrial scale. His major works include *The Chinese Convert* (1687), a series of ten reigning European monarchs, portraits of John DRYDEN (1693 and 1697) and forty-eight portraits of members of the Kit-Cat-Club (in a so-called 'kit-cat' format of 36 by 28 inches), including William CONGREVE. Two Handel portraits were attributed to Kneller, but although one of them (now in the FOUNDLING MUSEUM) might show Handel, it was not painted by Kneller, and it is uncertain that the sitter in the other (a genuine Kneller now in private possession) was Handel.

EDWIN WERNER

See also ICONOGRAPHY

C. Baker, 'Kneller, Godfrey', *Allgemeines Lexikon der Bildenden Künstler von der Antike bis zur Gegenwart*, vol. 20 (Leipzig, 1953)

Kreienberg (Kreyenberg), Friedrich Christoph. Hanoverian diplomatic resident in London from 1710 to 1714. He was involved in the matter of Handel's dismissal from the court in HANOVER when Handel had overstayed his leave, which secured him the favour of the future GEORGE I. WALTER KREYSZIG

Burrows
HHB iv

Krieger, Johann (bap. Nuremberg, 1 Jan. 1652; d. Zittau/Saxony, 18 July 1735). Organist, Kapellmeister, composer. Younger brother of Johann Philipp KRIEGER. Hofkapellmeister in Greiz (1678–80), in Eisenberg 1680/1 and musical director and organist in Zittau (1681–1735). It is not known for sure whether Handel entered works by Johann or by Johann Philipp into his book of manuscript music in 1698. Johann MATTHESON thought Johann Krieger and Handel were equals as far as the composition of double fugues was concerned. According to Friedrich CHRYSANDER, Handel took Krieger's published collection *Anmuthige Clavier-Übung* (1699) to London. As late as 1746 Handel borrowed from Krieger's *Neue musicalische Ergetzlichkeit* (1684) in his *OCCASIONAL ORATORIO*.

Krieger, Johann Philipp (bap. Nuremberg, 27 Feb. 1648; d. Weissenfels, 7 Feb. 1725). Organist, Kapellmeister, composer. He was chamber organist and Hofkapellmeister in Bayreuth (1670–6/7), during this time he also travelled to Italy. In 1677 he became chapel organist, then Vizekapellmeister of the court orchestra in HALLE; after the court moved to WEISSENFELS he was made Hofkapellmeister (1680–1725). It is probable that he met the young Handel in Weissenfels. Handel entered works by a 'Krieger' into his 1698 book of manuscript music (it is unclear whether this refers to Johann Philipp or to his brother Johann KRIEGER). Between 1736 and 1759 Handel borrowed the theme from Krieger's *Cembalo-Aria mit 24 Variationen* in B flat major in numerous works (*BERENICE*, Concerto for Trumpet and Horn HWV 375ª, *MUSIC FOR THE ROYAL FIREWORKS, SOLOMON*). He also used the theme from an organ fugue by Krieger in *The ways of Zion do mourn* (ANTHEMS, 5).

KLAUS-PETER KOCH (Trans. ANGELA BAIER)

F. Chrysander, *G. F. Händel*, vol. 1 (Leipzig, 1919)
W. Coxe, *Anecdotes of George Frederick Handel, and John Christopher Smith* (London, 1799; facsimile edn, ed. P. M. Young, New York, 1979)
W. Felix, 'Johann Philipp Krieger und die Hofoper in Weißenfels', *HJb* 36 (1990)
HHB ii; iii
J. Mattheson, *Critica musica*, vol. 1 (Hamburg, 1723)
Grundlage einer Ehren-Pforte (Hamburg, 1740)
H. Reich, 'Händels Chorbearbeitung einer Orgelfuge von Johann Philipp Krieger', *Musik und Kirche* 36 (1966), 172–7

Kuhnau, Johann (b. Geising/Saxony, 6 April 1660; d. Leipzig, 5 June 1722). Organist, *Kantor*, composer, writer, jurist. He was a pupil at the Kreuzschule in DRESDEN, later attended the Gymnasium in Zittau – where he returned as temporary *Kantor* in 1681/2 – and studied law in Leipzig in 1682. He stayed on in Leipzig as organist (1684–1701) and as *Kantor* of the Thomaskirche and university music director (1701–22). His contemporaries, among them MATTHESON and Johann Adolph Scheibe in HAMBURG, praised his mastery of fugue and especially double fugue technique. Handel regularly borrowed material from Kuhnau's sonata collection *Frische Clavier-Früchte* (1696) from 1708 (*La RESURREZIONE*) to 1757 (*The TRIUMPH OF TIME AND TRUTH*). He used the borrowed material in oratorios (*SAUL* and *SUSANNA*), church music and vocal chamber music, and also in orchestral music and instrumental chamber music.

KLAUS-PETER KOCH (Trans. ANGELA BAIER)

E. Derr, 'Thematic Material by Kuhnau in Handel's Resurrezione and Opus 1',
  Bach-Händel-Schütz-Ehrung der Deutschen Demokratischen Republik 1985 (Leipzig, 1987)
J. Mattheson, *Der Vollkommene Capellmeister* (Hamburg, 1739)
  Grundlage einer Ehren-Pforte (Hamburg, 1740)
J. A. Scheibe, *Critischer Musikus* (Leipzig, 1745)
M. Seiffert, 'Händels Verhältnis zu Tonwerken älterer deutscher Meister', *Jahrbuch der Musikbibliothek Peters für 1907*, vol. 14 (Leipzig, 1908)

Kusser (French: Cousser), **Johann Sigismund** (bap. Pressburg (Slovak: Bratislava), 13 Feb. 1660; d. Dublin, Dec. 1727). Composer and Kapellmeister. After training with Jean-Baptiste LULLY in Paris between 1676 and 1682, Kusser worked at the BRUNSWICK court opera from 1690 to 1694 and at the GÄNSEMARKT opera in HAMBURG (1694–5); in both instances he was succeeded by Reinhard KEISER. Between 1700 and 1704 he was Hofkapellmeister in Stuttgart. He later worked as a private tutor in London (1704–7) and then moved to DUBLIN, where he became highly esteemed as 'Chappel-Master of Trinity College' (from 1711), 'Chief Composer' and 'Master of the Musick, attending His Majesty's State in Ireland' (from 1716). While in Hamburg, Handel got to know the interpretational innovations Kusser had introduced about ten years before, such as a new Italianate style of singing. In Dublin Kusser subscribed to four Handel opera scores (containing arias only, 1725–7).

KLAUS-PETER KOCH (Trans. ANGELA BAIER)

H. E. Samuel, 'Johann Sigismund Cousser in London and Dublin', ML 61 (1980), 158–71
  'A German Musician comes to London in 1704', MT 122 (1981), 591–3
D. Schröder, 'Die Einführung der italienischen Oper in Hamburg durch Johann Georg Conradi und Johann Sigismund Kusser (1693–1696)', *Il melodramma italiano in Italia e in Germania nell'età barocca* (Como, 1995)
T. J. Walsh, *Opera in Dublin, 1705–1797: The Social Scene* (Dublin, 1973)

Kytch, John Christian (b. ?Netherlands; fl. London, 1708–38; d. London, 1738). Oboist, bassoonist and flautist. He probably played from 1708 in the Queen's Theatre (KING'S THEATRE) opera orchestra as a bassoonist, and in about 1712 he became second oboist. In 1711 Handel wrote an obbligato bassoon part in *RINALDO* ('Ah! crudel') for Kytch, who probably played oboe solo parts in most of the composer's orchestrally accompanied CHAPEL ROYAL anthems (and perhaps occasionally flute parts). In 1719–20 Kytch was the highest-paid instrumentalist employed at CANNONS, but his presence there is not documented before 1719, so it is uncertain if the oboe solos in Handel's Cannons anthems (ANTHEMS, 2) and *ACIS AND GALATEA* were written for him. However, it is likely that Kytch played the lyrical solo oboe part in 'Tune your harps' (*ESTHER*).

From 1719 he played in public concerts, mostly at Hickford's Room, in which he performed his adaptations of Handel's arias. He was named on the original orchestra list for the Royal Academy of Music's opening season (OPERA COMPANIES, 2), but was apparently replaced by John LOEILLET before the season started. During the early 1720s Kytch rejoined the opera orchestra, and in 1729 he was described as 'first hautboy to the Opera', but during the mid-1730s his reputation as London's leading oboist faded and he became overshadowed by SAMMARTINI. During the 1737–8 season he got into financial difficulties. After his death in 1738 the destitution of his family led to the foundation of the FUND FOR THE SUPPORT OF DECAY'D MUSICIANS AND THEIR FAMILIES.

ANNETTE LANDGRAF and DAVID VICKERS

Burney
Burrows, *Chapel Royal*
B. Haynes, *The Eloquent Oboe: A History of the Hautboy from 1640 to 1760* (Oxford, 2001)

L

L'Allegro, il Penseroso ed il Moderato. See *ALLEGRO, IL PENSEROSO ED IL MODERATO, L'*

L'Epine, Francesca Margherita de ('La Margherita') (b. Tuscany, c.1680; d. London, 8 Aug. 1746). Italian soprano (compass: c'–b♭" but d'–a" in the parts Handel wrote for her). She sang at VENICE and Mantua before moving to London in 1702, where she performed at LINCOLN'S INN FIELDS and DRURY LANE (1703–8). Until 1714 she sang in almost all of the opera productions at the Queen's Theatre (KING'S THEATRE), including most of Handel's early London operas. The parts composed for her include Eurilla in Il *PASTOR FIDO* (HWV 8ᵃ), Agilea in *TESEO* and possibly Flavia in *SILLA*. She also played the male part of Goffredo in the 1712 and 1713 revivals of *RINALDO* (HWV 7ᵃ). It is said that she was 'an excellent Musician being not only an accomplished singer but an extraordinary performer on the Harpsichord' London, British Library (Add. MS 32249, fol. 186). In about 1718 (the exact date is unsure) she married the composer John Christopher PEPUSCH, whom she had joined at Drury Lane in 1715. Although she retired in 1719, she appeared briefly during the first season of the Royal Academy of Music (OPERA COMPANIES, 2), replacing the sick Ann Turner ROBINSON as Polissena in a performance of *RADAMISTO* on 22 June 1720. ARTIE HEINRICH

Burney, IV
D. F. Cook, 'Françoise Marguérite de l'Epine: The Italian Lady?', *Theatre Notebook* 35 (1981), 58–73; 104–13
Hawkins

La Motte, Antoine Houdar de (b. Paris, 17 Jan. 1672; d. Paris, 26 Dec. 1731). French poet, dramatist and critic, member of the Académie Française. He took the side of the Moderns in the Quarrel of Ancients and Moderns, beginning a new phase of the quarrel with his version of Homer's Iliad adapted to contemporary taste (1714). His works set to music include cantatas for Jacquet de la Guerre and librettos for ballets and operas by Campra, Destouches and Marin Marais. RAMEAU outlined his views on opera in a famous letter to La Motte in 1727, in an unsuccessful attempt to obtain a libretto from him. Among his most successful works were the tragedy *Inès de Castro* (1723) and the libretto for Campra's *L'Europe galante* (1697), the first opéra-ballet. His libretto for Destouches's *Amadis de Grèce* (1699) was adapted into Italian for Handel's *AMADIGI*. BUFORD NORMAN

La Resurezzione. See *RESURREZIONE*, La

La terra è liberata. See TERRA È LIBERATA, LA

Lacy, Michael Rophino (b. Bilbao, 19 July 1795; d. London, 20 Sept. 1867). Violinist, composer, actor and playwright. A child prodigy, Lacy settled in London in 1820, and thereafter was active in theatres as violinist, musical director, conductor, arranger, composer and playwright. His greatest theatrical success was his adaptation of Rossini's *La Cenerentola* (1830), which held the stage in both England and America for decades.

Handel and his music often occupied Lacy during the final decades of his life. In 1833 Lacy wrote a pasticcio oratorio, *The Israelites in Egypt, or The Passage of the Red Sea*, a staged mix of Rossini's *Mosè in Egitto* and choruses from ISRAEL IN EGYPT, which he conducted at Covent Garden (22 February), and the Park Theater in New York (31 October 1842). Lacy's interest in staged performances of Handel's oratorios led him to create a second pasticcio, *Jephtha's Vow* (1834), which was never performed; nor was his pasticcio opera *Ginevra of Sicily* (n.d.), based on ARIODANTE. Lacy directed a series of 'Handelian Operatic Concerts' at London in May and June 1847, designed to introduce the public to Handel's then little-known operas; and in the 1850s collaborated with Victor SCHOELCHER on the latter's biography of Handel and unpublished catalogue of the composer's works. Copies of Handel's music in Lacy's hand at the British Library and the Bibliothèque nationale show a wealth of annotations that are notable for their identifications of Handel's BORROWINGS and exploration of his compositional process. Lacy also published numerous arrangements of Handel's music.

RICHARD G. KING

R. G. King, 'Victor Schoelcher's Manuscript Handel Biographies and Catalogues', *HJb* 48 (2002)

V. Schoelcher, *The Life of Handel* (London, 1857)

B. Trowell, 'Michael Rophino Lacy and *Ginevra of Sicily*: A 19th-Century Adaptation of Handel's *Ariodante*', *Handel Institute Newsletter*, 6/1 (Spring 1995)

Lady Chapel. See WESTMINSTER ABBEY

Lalli, (Benedetto) Domenico (actually Niccolò Sebastiano Biancardi) (b. Naples, 27 March 1679; d. Venice, 9 Oct. 1741). Italian librettist. He wrote *drammi per musica*, oratorios, spoken dramas, poetry and prose works. Having fled from NAPLES in 1706 to avoid an embezzlement scandal, Lalli settled in VENICE in 1710. From c.1725 he was resident poet of the S. GIOVANNI GRISOSTOMO theatre and simultaneously court poet to the Bavarian elector. Handel's RADAMISTO is based on Lalli's *L'amor tirannico* (Venice, 1710) as revised for FLORENCE, 1712. The libretto is derived from a *tragicomédie* by Georges de SCUDERY (1638).

REINHARD STROHM

M. Bucciarelli, *Italian Opera and European Theatre, 1680–1720* (Turnhout, 2000)

Lampe, John Frederick (b. Brunswick, winter 1702–3; d. Edinburgh, 25 July 1751). The German composer and bassoonist first arrived in London between 1725 and 1726, having previously studied Law at the University of Helmstedt (1718–20) and lived in HAMBURG (1720–5). Soon after his arrival in England he was playing the bassoon in Handel's opera orchestra and began working as a composer and music teacher.

From 1732 Lampe became a key player in the attempts to produce English opera at the LITTLE THEATRE in the Haymarket. Within a year he wrote three English operas, *Amelia*, *Britannia* and *Dione*, of which only fragments survive. None of these works was particularly successful; however, a fourth work, *The Opera of Operas, or Tom Thumb the Great* enjoyed greater popularity and helped to establish Lampe's reputation in London. In 1737 he produced his most successful work with his friend Henry CAREY, *The DRAGON OF WANTLEY*; the sequel, *Margery, or A Worse Plague than the Dragon* (1738) was not as popular. One of Lampe's most successful later works was the burlesque *Pyramus and Thisbe* (1744) based on an extract from Shakespeare's *A Midsummer Night's Dream*; the title page of the published score refers to the work as 'A Mock Opera' and Lampe includes parodies of Handel's style. Between 1748 and 1750 he was in Dublin where both *The Dragon of Wantley* and *Pyramus and Thisbe* enjoyed further success.

MATTHEW GARDNER

See also ISABELLA YOUNG (I)

R. Fiske, *English Theatre Music in the Eighteenth century*, 2nd edn (Oxford, 1986)
D. R. Martin, *The Operas and Operatic Style of John Frederick Lampe* (Detroit, 1985)

Lanciani, Francesco Antonio (fl. Rome, 1690–1726). Music copyist, composer and singer. He is probably the same Lanciani who appeared as bass singer in S. Lorenzo in Damaso in ROME in 1690, but he is known principally for his work as copyist of works by Alessandro SCARLATTI, CALDARA, GASPARINI and Handel. He copied cantatas by Handel (according to an extant bill at least twenty-one works) on behalf of the Prince RUSPOLI between 1709 and 1711, long after Handel had stayed with Ruspoli in 1707–8. These copies were apparently intended as gifts. Lanciani is the copyist 'Anonymous Mü III' in the collections of the Santini library in Münster (SOURCES AND COLLECTIONS, 13]. There is another copyist sharing Francesco's last name, Tarquinio Lanciani. They collaborated on copies of HWV 47 and HWV 170.

KLAUS-PETER KOCH (Trans. ANGELA BAIER)

W. and U. Kirkendale, *Music and Meaning. Studies in Music History and the Neighbouring Disciplines* (Florence, 2007)
H. J. Marx, 'The Santini Collection', *Handel Collections and their History*, ed. T. Best (Oxford, 1993)
K. Watanabe and H. J. Marx, Händels italienische Kopisten', *GHB III* (1989)

***Languia di bocca lusinghiera*, HWV 123. Consisting of a single recitative–aria pair, this cantata for soprano, oboe, violin and basso continuo seems to be a fragment. Paper evidence places its composition in HANOVER in 1710. The aria 'Dolce bocca' looks backward and forward in Handel's career, deriving in part from the first aria in the Roman continuo cantata *HENDEL, NON PUÒ MIA MUSA*, and then becoming the model for the aria 'Finte labbra!' in *Il PASTOR FIDO* (HWV 8^a).

ELLEN T. HARRIS

'Largo'. See ADAPTATIONS; *SERSE*

Laudate pueri Dominum. See Italian and Latin CHURCH MUSIC

LeBlond, Peter. See HANDEL, 8

Leclair, Jean-Marie. See HANDEL, 19

Legh, Elizabeth (bap. Prestbury, 25 July 1694; bur. London, 20 Aug. 1734). Daughter of John and Lady Isabella Legh of Adlington Hall in Cheshire. She was an accomplished musician and played the harpsichord well. She was born severely crippled, and a contract exists, dated 20 October 1709, between her father and Rachel Ormston of London, for the girl to be manipulated so that the worst features of her disability might be corrected; there is no record of how successful this was. By 1715 she was in the capital city regularly, eventually living in the Leghs' house, near Handel's in the parish of ST GEORGE'S, HANOVER SQUARE. She was a fanatical admirer of Handel's music and must have known him well.

From 1715 until her death in 1734 she assembled an invaluable collection of manuscript scores of Handel's music, commissioned from his copyists: it is the earliest such collection and one of the most important (SOURCES AND COLLECTIONS, 12). In a draft will dated 1731 she wrote: 'I desire all my Musick books that are composed by Mr Handel may be put in some Library or publick Roome at Cambridge, there to be seen or copied.' This will was apparently never proved, and the collection did not go to CAMBRIDGE. After her death it passed to a second cousin, John Robartes, who later became Lord Radnor. In 1741 he presented the collection to James HARRIS, who was the father of the first Earl of Malmesbury, and the collection has been in the possession of the Malmesbury family ever since. In the copy of *OTTONE* in the collection, the air 'Spera sì, mi dice' is annotated 'the Pidgeon Song' in Elizabeth's hand: the anecdote relates that a pigeon used to fly to Elizabeth's window whenever she played the air on the harpsichord.

Her younger brother Charles also became a firm friend of Handel's. The text of a *Hunting Song* 'By C. L. Esq:' was published in the *Gentleman's Magazine* for January 1747, and was first set to music by Mr Ridley, the organist at Prestbury, near Adlington. In 1751 Handel set it himself (SONGS) and the autograph is preserved at Adlington. Whether the composer ever went there is uncertain.

TERENCE BEST

Burrows and Dunhill
W. Dean, 'The Malmesbury Collection', *Handel Collections and their History*, ed. T. Best (Oxford, 1993)
Deutsch
HHB iv

Legrenzi, Giovanni (b. Clusone near Bergamo, Italy; bap. 12 Aug. 1626; d. Venice, 27 May 1690) Italian composer. He was organist at Bergamo (1653), *maestro di cappella* at Ferrara (1656–65) and *maestro di musica* at Venice (1670–90). He composed at least eighteen operas, seven oratorios, masses, over one hundred motets, and a sizeable body of instrumental pieces. In 1683 Legrenzi set Nicolò BEREGAN's libretto *Giustino*, but Handel's later setting of the same story (1738) was based on a revised libretto by Pietro PARIATI (1711). Handel's chamber duet *Và speme infida* (HWV 199) contains several borrowings from Legrenzi's Op. 12 collection of cantatas (1676), and he incorporated ideas from Legrenzi's motet *Intret in conspectu tuo* (which survives only in a copy in Handel's hand) in the chorus 'O first created beam' in *SAMSON*.

WALTER KREYSZIG

R. Emans, 'Händels Kammerduett "Và speme infida" (HWV 199) – eine Reminiszenz an Giovanni Legrenzis op. 12?', GHB III (1987)
Strohm

Lennard, Henry Barrett (b. London, 28 May 1818; d. Brighton, 31 Aug. 1899). The last owner of an important collection of Handel manuscripts presented to the FITZWILLIAM MUSEUM in CAMBRIDGE in 1902; the collection, which he purchased between 1847 and 1855, still bears his name (SOURCES AND COLLECTIONS, 4). He lived first in Central London, then moved to Hampstead in 1876. His career was in business in the City, but he was also an amateur musician: in a letter from A. H. Mann, organist of King's College, Cambridge, written on 5 March 1902 to the director of the Museum, he is described as 'a well known Handelian Scholar'. His son Francis arranged the donation of the collection through Mann, at whose house it was deposited before it was transferred to the Museum, and Mann later made a handwritten catalogue.

CHRYSANDER knew Barrett Lennard, and had access to the collection: in the English text of the Preface to volume 48 of his edition (1894), which has miscellaneous instrumental works, he wrote concerning a manuscript volume of Handel's early keyboard music (now lost), whose contents he printed: 'This book is to be found in the most valuable musical library of Henry Barrett Lennard Esq. of Hampstead, who with great kindness and liberality permitted me to use his magnificent MS. collection of Handel's works for my edition.' The collection is the source of a group of instrumental pieces called 'Sinfonie diverse', also printed in HG 48, as well as of the keyboard volume. TERENCE BEST

D. Burrows, 'The Barrett Lennard Collection', Handel Collections and their History, ed. T. Best (Oxford, 1993)

Leo, Leonardo (b. San Vito degli Schiavoni (today: San Vito dei Normanni, Province of Brindisi/Puglia), 5 Aug. 1694; d. Naples, 31 Oct. 1744). Italian composer, teacher and *maestro di cappella*. In October 1718 Leo performed Handel's RINALDO in the Palazzo Reale in NAPLES for the birthday celebrations of Emperor Charles VI. He composed an additional prologue and included some of his own music in the score. The success of his early opera *Sofonisba* (Naples, 1718) made him a much sought-after composer, and his works were also performed regularly in VENICE, ROME, Turin and FLORENCE. Leo's popularity is attested to by the inclusion of his stage and church music in many manuscript collections all over Europe, and also by the number of arrangements of his works that were produced by other composers. Handel included arias by Leo in his London PASTICCIOS; for example, 'Tuona il ciel' from Leo's *Argeno* (Venice, 1728) found its way into the second act of ORMISDA (1730), and 'Vorrei da lacci sciogliere' from Leo's *Il Demetrio* (Naples, 1732) into the third act of CAIO FABBRICIO (1733).

Handel based the pasticcio CATONE IN UTICA (1732) on Leo's opera of the same name (Venice, 1729), which he might have heard at the Teatro S. GIOVANNI GRISOSTOMO, with FARINELLI in the cast. He used a score of Leo's opera belonging to Sir John Buckworth (London, Royal Academy of Music, MS 75), who might have brought it back from Venice. Handel's version of the opera retained nine of Leo's arias. On 31 October 1741 Handel might have attended a performance of GALUPPI's opera pasticcio *Alessandro in Persia* (MIDDLESEX OPERA COMPANY), which also included music by Leo.

DAGMAR GLÜXAM (Trans. ANGELA BAIER)

Let God Arise. See ANTHEMS 1 (HWV 256^b); 2 (HWV 256^a)

'Let the bright Seraphims'. See *SAMSON*

Let thy hand be strengthened. See ANTHEMS, 3; CORONATION OF KING GEORGE II

librettos

1. Opera librettos in Hamburg and Italy
2. Italian opera librettos in London
3. English librettos

1. Opera librettos in Hamburg and Italy

In HAMBURG, Handel set two librettos by Friedrich FEUSTKING (*ALMIRA* and *NERO*) and two by Heinrich HINSCH (*FLORINDO* and *Daphne*, a single libretto divided in two due to its length). These German-language librettos consist of pervasively rhymed text that integrates arias, little differentiated from recitative in verse length or rhyme, within the scene; there is a prominent use of entrance arias. Where Italian aria texts are interspersed (there are none in *Nero*), these are predominantly da capo exit arias; German-texted arias use various formal structures. Chorus and dance play a significant role in all four librettos, especially at the beginnings and ends of acts, starting with the opening scene.

In the Italian librettos *RODRIGO* and *AGRIPPINA* arias are typically in da capo form and occur at the end of a scene, leading to the character's exit. Scenes are carefully constructed using the *liaison de scène*, or the continuation of at least one character on stage between scenes in the same set location. Entrance arias are rare: *Rodrigo* contains only two; in contrast, the Hamburg *Nero* contains seven in Act I alone. Chorus and dance play no role. Whereas recitative consists largely of *versi sdruccioli*, unrhymed seven- and eleven-syllable lines, a rhymed couplet immediately precedes most arias, serving both as punctuation for the scene (much as in Shakespeare's plays) and a bridge to the rhymed arias in shorter verses.

The subjects of these librettos are typical of Handel's later practice. *Almira*, *Nero*, *Rodrigo* and *Agrippina* are of the domestic-dynastic type, in which questions about succession or alliances become entangled in personal issues. *Florindo* and *Daphne*, by contrast, present the mythological story of Apollo and Daphne. Both *Almira* and *Rodrigo* are adaptations of older librettos.

2. Italian opera librettos in London

Handel's thirty-six opera librettos in London can be divided into four periods of differing lengths: the early, somewhat experimental years (1711–15); the heroic and historical librettos of the Royal Academy of Music (OPERA COMPANIES, 2) and the years immediately following (1720–32); the period of intense operatic competition leading to a return of magical and pastoral texts (1732–6); and the final years, also somewhat experimental, as Handel turned away from Italian opera (1736–41).

In the first period, Handel seems to have been trying out different types of librettos. *RINALDO*, probably the only newly written libretto set by Handel in London, reflects English semi-opera in its epic subject matter and spectacular effects, while Il *PASTOR FIDO* represents a pastoral drama in the Italian style, and *TESEO*, adapted from QUINAULT's libretto for LULLY's Thésée, is Handel's only opera to employ the French pattern of five acts. *SILLA* is the closest in this period to the Italian historical and dynastic type of libretto Handel had already set in Rodrigo (Florence, 1707) and that would became standard during the Royal Academy period. *AMADIGI*, like Teseo adapted from a French libretto, is modified into the Italian three-act form but retains a significant use of chorus and dance.

For all their differences, the early librettos possess features in common. Excepting Il pastor fido, all use spectacular scenic effects and massed scenes that require a wide range of 'extras', ranging from 'a dreadful Host of Spirits' to 'a great Company of Knights and Ladies'. Although scenic construction is not fully standardised in terms of the liaison de scène or the placement of arias at the end of scenes leading to an exit, the da capo aria form predominates, using repetitive or symmetrical verse patterns for the two strophes (such as, abc/abc or aab/ccb). Nicola HAYM and Giacomo ROSSI were his two librettists during this period, but Handel's participation can be assumed from the reuse of arias from his Italian period complete with text. Excepting Silla, the printed librettos contain English translations on facing pages. A complete English version of Rinaldo was prepared by Aaron HILL; the other librettos provide a full translation of the recitatives but only an aphoristic rendition of the arias.

The central and longest period of Handel's operatic composition in London runs from the opening of the Royal Academy of Music in 1720 through the first years of its continuation in the so-called Second Academy (OPERA COMPANIES, 3). The nineteen librettos Handel set during this 'Academy' period share many features. All are based on pre-existent librettos: four derive from librettos by Antonio SALVI (*RODELINDA*, *SCIPIONE*, *LOTARIO* and *SOSARME*) and three from Pietro METASTASIO (*SIROE*, *PORO* and *EZIO*). The texts typically depict dynastic concerns of succession and conquest intertwined with personal issues (especially parental, sibling or marital relationships). Although *ADMETO* stands apart by its use of mythology, the story engages many of the same concerns. The librettos share a scenic construction based on the liaison de scène and scene-ending exit aria in da capo form, against which regularity exceptions become all the more remarkable.

Handel worked primarily with two librettists in this period: Haym (*OTTONE*, *FLAVIO*, *GIULIO CESARE*, *TAMERLANO*, Rodelinda, Siroe, *TOLOMEO*) and Paolo ROLLI (*MUZIO SCEVOLA*, *FLORIDANTE*, Scipione, *ALESSANDRO*, *RICCARDO PRIMO*). Whereas Haym's librettos are typified by vivid dramatic situations (Giulio Cesare, Tamerlano), Rolli's provide more lyrical outlets in recitative refrain structures and recurring aria texts (Scipione, Alessandro).

In the third period, beginning with *ORLANDO* in 1732, Handel's librettos turn back towards epic romance and myth. Orlando, *ARIODANTE* and *ALCINA* are based on ARIOSTO's epic poem Orlando furioso. *ARIANNA IN CRETA* and *ATALANTA* are mythological, as are the serenata *PARNASSO IN FESTA* and the pasticcio *ORESTE*. Many librettos of this period employ magical effects and the kind of visual display and machinery that marked Handel's first London period. Further, *Ariodante* and *Alcina* contain choral movements for the first time since *Amadigi* (1715). BALLET also plays a significant role: Handel composed a danced prologue, *TERPSICORE*, for his revision of *Il pastor fido*; *Arianna* was revived with ballet, and *Oreste*, *Ariodante* and *Alcina* included ballet from the start. Despite added spectacle, choruses and ballets, however, the basic scene construction of the librettos remains largely intact. The disruptive effects of madness in *Orlando* and the interrupted duet of *Ariodante* only make their effect in contrast to these normative patterns. The librettos, like those of the previous period, are all based on pre-existent texts; their librettist adapters are unknown.

The seven librettos of the final period illustrate a *mélange* of style characteristics. The first four, *ARMINIO*, *GIUSTINO*, *BERENICE* and *FARAMONDO*, return to the dynastic, political subjects of the 'Academy' period; nevertheless two of these, *Giustino* and *Faramondo*, as well as the last three librettos, *SERSE*, *IMENEO* and *DEIDAMIA*, continue to include choral movements. Except for *Imeneo*, they call for extensive visual display: *Arminio* and *Serse* need eight different stage sets; *Deidamia* uses nine, and *Giustino*, *Berenice* and *Faramondo* have ten. Spectacle and stage machinery play a particularly important role in *Giustino*. A particular characteristic of this group is the loosening of scenic construction. In *Deidamia*, the first act has thirteen arias, but only five scenes, illustrating the decreasing use the exit aria tied to the end of a scene. Concomitant with this change is a decreasing use of the da capo. The importance of this shift can be seen in the printed librettos of *Faramondo*, *Serse* and *Imeneo*, where none of the arias (regardless of its form) is indicated as a da capo.

As in the first period, Handel seems to be experimenting with different styles and approaches. In addition to the historical plots and use of spectacle in the first four librettos, *Imeneo* tells a mythological story, while *Serse* and *Deidamia* contain striking comic elements. All of the librettos are based on pre-existent texts. Rolli is named as the librettist adapter for *Deidamia*, the first time a librettist is named in a printed libretto of one of Handel's operas since *Tolomeo* (1728).

In 1719 the Royal Academy of Music was chartered for a term of 'one and Twenty years'. This was an obligation Handel might have taken seriously even after the academy apparently dissolved in 1728. From 1732, operatic competition and a growing interest in English oratorio led him away from the types of librettos typical of the 'Academy' period and ushered in a relaxation in the strict forms of opera seria. It was only in 1741, however, 'one and Twenty years' after the opening of the Royal Academy in 1720, that Handel gave up writing Italian opera for the London stage.   ELLEN T. HARRIS

Dean, *Operas*
Dean and Knapp, *Operas*
Harris, *Librettos*
Strohm

3. English librettos
During Handel's years in England the 'civic humanist' view of art was the accepted norm: the artist should serve society; good art can be polemical, and should be instructive; public art has a duty to teach religion, morality, good citizenship and good leadership, by engaging the emotions as a route to the

mind; art should be uplifting, inspiring, sublime; in order to strike home it should depict humanity's inmost workings. All these principles are reflected in Handel's English librettos, which between them explore the relationship of the individual with society, with nature, with God and with other individuals; the effect of art and the role of the artist; British identity, national unity and disunity, monarchy, conquest, empire, trade, war and government; and the authority and validity of religion and of the BIBLE. They reflect the intellectual, emotional, political and spiritual preoccupations, anxieties, pride, questions and solutions of eighteenth-century authors and their public.

Apart from *ETERNAL SOURCE OF LIGHT DIVINE* and the first versions of *ACIS AND GALATEA* and *ESTHER*, all Handel's English librettos were provided to him for public performance in a theatre, and were first performed in London except *ATHALIA* (OXFORD) and *MESSIAH* (DUBLIN). All but the *SONG FOR ST CECILIA'S DAY* were adapted or newly written texts. These are chiefly for three types of work: odes, oratorios and secular dramas. All consist of recitative, solo numbers and choruses. Other than the odes and *ISRAEL IN EGYPT*, *Messiah* and the *OCCASIONAL ORATORIO*, all have a cast of named characters, but none performed in public was written by Handel to be staged with action. Following opera practice, for all theatre performances of Handel's English works the audience could buy printed librettos (WORDBOOKS), usually with those parts of the text not set, or not performed, placed in inverted commas. There is no one authoritative text for any of the librettos, since Handel usually changed the work for a revival, sometimes with the librettist's involvement, and sometimes even making it macaronic (as for *Acis and Galatea* in 1732).

The two types of dramatic libretto originated at CANNONS. *Acis and Galatea* – like the later *SEMELE*, *HERCULES* and *CHOICE OF HERCULES* – drew on classical myth. *Esther* set the pattern of Handel's biblical dramas: a newly written text dramatising the biblical or apocryphal narratives (sometimes paraphrasing Scripture, sometimes inventing incidents). The use in *Esther* of an intermediary source (RACINE's *Esther*, which also provided a precedent for a chorus in the style of ancient classical drama) was followed for some later librettos, for example *SAMSON*. The anthems inserted in the 1732 version of *Esther* represent another and less frequent strain of libretto composition, using actual Scriptural text. Only *Israel in Egypt* and *Messiah* consist entirely of biblical words or the versions of them in the Book of Common Prayer. *THEODORA*, based on a seventeenth-century English novella about an early Christian martyr, is unique. But the choice of theme was seldom wholly novel. Precedents for the librettists' subjects (besides their immediate sources) exist among Italian oratorios and sacred cantatas, German Passions, European sacred drama, recent and contemporary English drama and verse and, once Handel had introduced oratorio, English oratorios by other composers. Some topics were mooted in poems of praise addressed to Handel, or in critiques of his work. The Old Testament librettos invoke the traditional analogy of the biblical Israelites and modern Britons.

In choosing English texts Handel does not appear to have had a long-term 'vision'. He did not have to be involved in the start or even the progress of a libretto's composition for it to be acceptable. *Messiah* was Jennens's idea, and he compiled the libretto before offering it to Handel. *L'ALLEGRO* was suggested to Handel, then drafted when he responded positively, then developed by him, then further developed by one of the librettists, then enlarged at his suggestion. He did not accept everything offered him; he turned down at least two *Paradise Lost* librettos. A scribbled note about Elijah (Dean, *Oratorios*, p. 87) suggests that he thought up possible subjects, but we have no record of his suggesting a libretto which he then composed. The most substantive contribution which we know him to have made is the proposal for a third part to *L'Allegro*, where, however, his own suggestion of another Milton text was superseded by the librettist.

Handel's choices suggest his concern to 'please the town' (reportedly his aim in *L'Allegro*) but also to satisfy himself by pushing out the boundaries of known forms and means of expression. With his librettists he originated oratorio in English and used it for writing profound and spectacular choruses without precedent in English music – something which he was reported as also doing entirely for his own pleasure in 1745 (Burrows and Dunhill, p. 220). Adopting a large and prominent chorus as a fixed element of his English theatre works had major consequences for the compilation of any libretto, and fulfilled contemporary calls in literary circles to revive the use of the chorus in drama.

Nearly a third of Handel's English texts still do not have a firmly attributed librettist. Handel did not, so far as we know, compile or write the words himself; and while he went back to authors who provided him with workable texts, there is no indication of his having a programme for selecting librettists. Once oratorio was a recognisable form, Handel's librettists seem to have come to him of their own accord, or were suggested to him by others, and the majority who volunteered or agreed to write for him were admirers of his music, or members of his circles of acquaintance, or both.

The collaboration often took place at a distance, and Handel appears to have given his librettists considerable scope, while pressing them to match his own usually faster pace, which could leave them out of step. Writing to Jennens about BELSHAZZAR, he is prepared to begin composing without having seen the whole text; to accede to his librettist's plan for the relative proportions; to consider making alterations to an existing work (*Messiah*) according to his librettist's judgements; and to adapt his ideas, even jettisoning his music, to accommodate the librettist's plan (the last a feature confirmed by his autograph scores). Jennens's letter about SAUL (Burrows, pp. 202–3) shows him debating the placing of a 'grand' chorus with Handel, an argument which Jennens won. Once a topic was agreed, Handel was concerned about extent, structural balance (variation of solo roles, disposition of solo, ensemble and chorus numbers, and proportions of recitative to aria), and metrical variety. But his response to Jennens about *Belshazzar* suggests that he wanted to draw inspiration from his librettos as well.

Initially the principal providers were professional writers (Gay, Humphreys). Later librettists were all 'men of letters', but most had other occupations. Of the known authors only Jennens had a private income. It is unclear to what extent libretto writing was a money-earning activity, but Handel's gratitude to Jennens for *Belshazzar*, 'so generous a Present', suggests that it normally was. Libretto writing for hire was publicly dismissed as 'an undertaking . . . in which . . . little or no credit is to be gained' (Morell; quoted in Smith, *Oratorios*, p. 28), and only the professional theatre writers among Handel's librettists acknowledged their authorship on wordbooks. But for a writer with something to say to elite culture's audience, Handel's music could be an ideal vehicle. The theatre was a favourite arena for authors with a message, and serious music theatre works were less vulnerable to censorship than stage plays. One librettist at least saw himself using Handel and not the other way round: 'I must take him as I find him, & make the best use I can of him' (Jennens; quoted in Smith, *Oratorios*, p. 34).

Yoking Handel's sublimity to great literature – the Bible, Sophocles, Dryden, Milton – was recognised as a worthy undertaking. In his preface to ALEXAN-DER'S FEAST, Hamilton rejoiced that 'it is next to an Improbability, to offer the World any thing in those *Arts* more perfect, than the united Labours and utmost Efforts of a *Dryden* and a *Handel*'. Great national art resulted: Hamilton's preface to *Samson* celebrated Handel's having 'added new Life and Spirit to some of the finest Things in the *English* Language, particularly that inimitable Ode of Dryden's, which no Age nor Nation ever excell'd'. Handel reflected this appeal in his most substantial artistic testament, written to his public when his 1745 season was failing: 'As I perceived, that joining good Sense and significant Words to Musick, was the best Method of recommending this [music] to an English Audience; I have directed my Studies that way, and endeavour'd to shew, that the English Language, which is so expressive of the sublimest Sentiments is the best adapted of any to the full and solemn Kind of Musick' (Deutsch, 602).

RUTH SMITH

See also John ARBUTHNOT; Thomas BROUGHTON; John DRYDEN; John GAY; Newburgh HAMILTON; James HARRIS; Samuel HUMPHREYS; Charles JENNENS; James MILLER; John MILTON; Thomas MORELL; Alexander POPE

D. Burrows, '"Reading the Metre": Verse Forms in Oratorio Librettos Written for Handel by Charles Jennens and Thomas Morell', *Musique et Littératures: Intertextualités* (Anglophonia xi), ed. A.-M. Hermat (Mirail, 2002)

Dean, *Oratorios*

R. Smith, 'Intellectual Contexts of Handel's English Oratorios', *Music in Eighteenth-Century England*, ed. C. Hogwood and R. Luckett (Cambridge, 1982)

Oratorios

'Handel's English Librettists', *Cambridge Companion to Handel*, ed. D. Burrows (Cambridge, 1997)

Lincoln's Inn Fields Theatre. The 'third' Lincoln's Inn Fields Theatre (LIF) was built in 1714 for a patent theatre company. Maximum capacity is estimated at c.1,400. From 1723 it flourished by presenting elaborately staged pantomime in which the manager and principal owner John RICH ('Lun') performed as Harlequin. The theatre featured a lot of dance and music and premiered *The BEGGAR'S OPERA* in 1728. In 1732, LIF was replaced by COVENT GARDEN and became an occasional and temporary venue. English opera was staged there briefly by a nonce company in 1732–3. LIF was occupied by the OPERA OF THE NOBILITY for 1733–4 and rented by Handel for the seasons of 1739–40 and 1740–1. In the former season he gave first performances of the SONG FOR ST CECILIA'S DAY and L'ALLEGRO, IL PENSEROSO ED IL MODERATO, and revivals of several English oratorios. In the latter he premiered his last Italian operas, IMENEO and DEIDAMIA. The building went out of theatrical use in 1744.

JUDITH MILHOUS and ROBERT D. HUME

P. Sawyer, *The New Theatre in Lincoln's Inn Fields* (London, 1979)

Linicke (Lynike, Linikey, Leneker, Linniker, Liniken, Linikin, Lunecan, Lunican, Lunicon, Unican), D. (fl. 1707; d. London, ?winter 1725–6). COPYIST, viola player. Linicke was probably of German origin and perhaps related to a family of musicians from WEISSENFELS. He played the viola in the orchestra at the KING'S THEATRE in London from 1708 to 1717, and from 1720 for the Royal Academy of Music (OPERA COMPANIES, 2). In 1711 he copied the score and possibly the parts for the first performance of *RINALDO* in 1711 (now lost), and, among others, the score of *TESEO* (1717) now in the Malmesbury Collection (SOURCES AND COLLECTIONS, 12) The surviving Handel manuscripts copied by Linicke date from 1712 to 1721.   ANNETTE LANDGRAF

W. Dean, 'Handel's Early London Copyists', *Bach, Handel, Scarlatti: Tercentenary Essays* (Cambridge, 1985)

Little Theatre, Haymarket. Built by John Potter in 1720 near the KING'S THEATRE, the Little Haymarket operated in Handel's time without a licence or patent. Small and plain, it probably seated fewer than 600 for plays but more for concerts. Potter rented it out for amateur performances, nonce companies (including Henry Fielding's in the 1730s), French and Italian *commedia dell'arte* troupes, concerts and English operas by Thomas Augustine ARNE and J. F. LAMPE. In the 1750s the Little Haymarket began to function regularly as a summer theatre; Samuel Foote received a summer patent for it in 1766. The theatre ceased operations in 1820.   JUDITH MILHOUS and ROBERT D. HUME

W. J. Burling and R. D. Hume, 'Theatrical Companies at the Little Haymarket, 1720–1737', *Essays in Theatre* 4 (1986), 98–118
J. Milhous and R. D. Hume, 'J. F. Lampe and English Opera at the Little Haymarket in 1732–3', ML 78/4 (1997), 502–31

Livy (Titus Livius) (59 BC–AD 17). Roman historian. The surviving portions of his *History of Rome*, describing the legendary origins of the city, the age of kings and the early republic, and the Second Punic War, were a popular source for drama. Handel set only two strictly Livian operas, *MUZIO SCEVOLA* and *SCIPIONE*. But Livy's claim that history best supplied 'evidence for every kind of behaviour displayed as on a splendid monument', teaching us 'what to emulate, what to avoid' supplied the rationale for all historical drama of Handel's age. The cantata *Lucrezia* is also based on a story from Livy (CANTATAS).   DAVID KIMBELL

Loeillet, John (Jean Baptiste) (b. Ghent, bap. 18 Nov. 1680; d. London, 19 July 1730). Oboist, flautist, harpsichordist, teacher and composer. He settled in London c.1705, was a member of the Drury Lane orchestra in 1707. From 1708 he played oboe in the Queen's Theatre opera orchestra, and became its principal oboist and flautist a year later. He was included in the orchestra list for the Royal Academy of Music (OPERA COMPANIES, 2) in 1719 and was probably the company's principal oboist until KYTCH took over in the early 1720s. The oboe solo parts in *RADAMISTO* ('Quando mai spietata sorte') in *MUZIO SCEVOLA* ('Deggio dunque' and possibly 'Volate più dei venti') were probably written for Loeillet. He tested a new organ at St Dionis Backchurch in 1722 with Handel, CROFT and others.   ANNETTE LANDGRAF

B. Haynes, *The Eloquent Oboe: A History of the Hautboy from 1640 to 1760* (Oxford, 2001)

London. Capital and principal city of Great Britain, first visited by Handel in 1710–11, from 1712 his place of abode, and where he died in 1759. By far the greater part of his musical output was written for and first performed in London.

The London which Handel first encountered was a relatively small and compact city developed around two ancient centres. To the east was the City of London, the commercial heart, substantially rebuilt after the Great Fire of 1666 with its forest of 'Wren' churches and dominated by the new, but still unfinished, ST PAUL'S CATHEDRAL. To the west was the adjoining City of Westminster, the seat of government and the court, which had been much enlarged during the seventeenth century but still hardly extended beyond Soho and ST JAMES'S. There was only one bridge over the Thames – the medieval London Bridge, connecting the City with the old suburb of Southwark, site of Shakespeare's playhouses. A second bridge at Westminster was opened in 1750. Further out were a number of old 'villages', such as Chelsea (RANELAGH), Kensington, Marylebone and Battersea, now of course all part of a continous built-up area but then separated from the centre by a buffer zone of fields, market gardens and open spaces.

When Handel settled in London the city was on the verge of great physical changes. The signing of the Peace of Utrecht (1713) (war of the SPANISH SUCCESSION) and the crushing of the first JACOBITE rebellion (1715) created a period of relative stability which encouraged enterprise and speculation, and the owners of land around the built-up areas began to let it for new developments, particularly at the west end, and to the north in Bloomsbury and Marylebone (see Figure 18). This spate of new building was partly a response to the city's growing population, which rose from about 630,000 (1715) to 740,000 (1760). It was not evenly spread, however. A steady increase up to about 1725 was followed by stagnation, then growth again in the 1750s. Another factor in this physical expansion was the inexorable movement of fashion westwards, partly out of the fear of disease in more crowded districts. Daniel Defoe in 1725 even talks of depopulation in the older parts: 'The City does not increase, but only the Situation of it is a going to be removed, and the Inhabitants are quitting the old Noble Streets and Squares where they used to live, and are removing into the Fields for fear of Infection.' Handel's own house in Brook Street (MUSEUMS, 2) was built in the early 1720s during the first of the great building booms of the eighteenth century of which Defoe has left a vivid description:

> I passed an amazing Scene of new Foundations, not of Houses only, but as I might say of new Cities. New Towns, new Squares, and fine Buildings, the like of which no City, no Town, nay, no Place in the World can shew; nor is it possible to judge where or when, they will make an end or stop of Building.

Then as now, the process of development and renewal was continuing. The building of Mayfair, where Handel lived, started before he moved there and was still not quite finished when he died. Private ownership and private finance ruled. Such 'town planning' as there was depended on the taste of individual landowners, who often looked no further than the boundaries of their own estates. No British monarch had successfully interfered in the planning of London since Charles I at Covent Garden in the 1630s. Charles II's wish for a

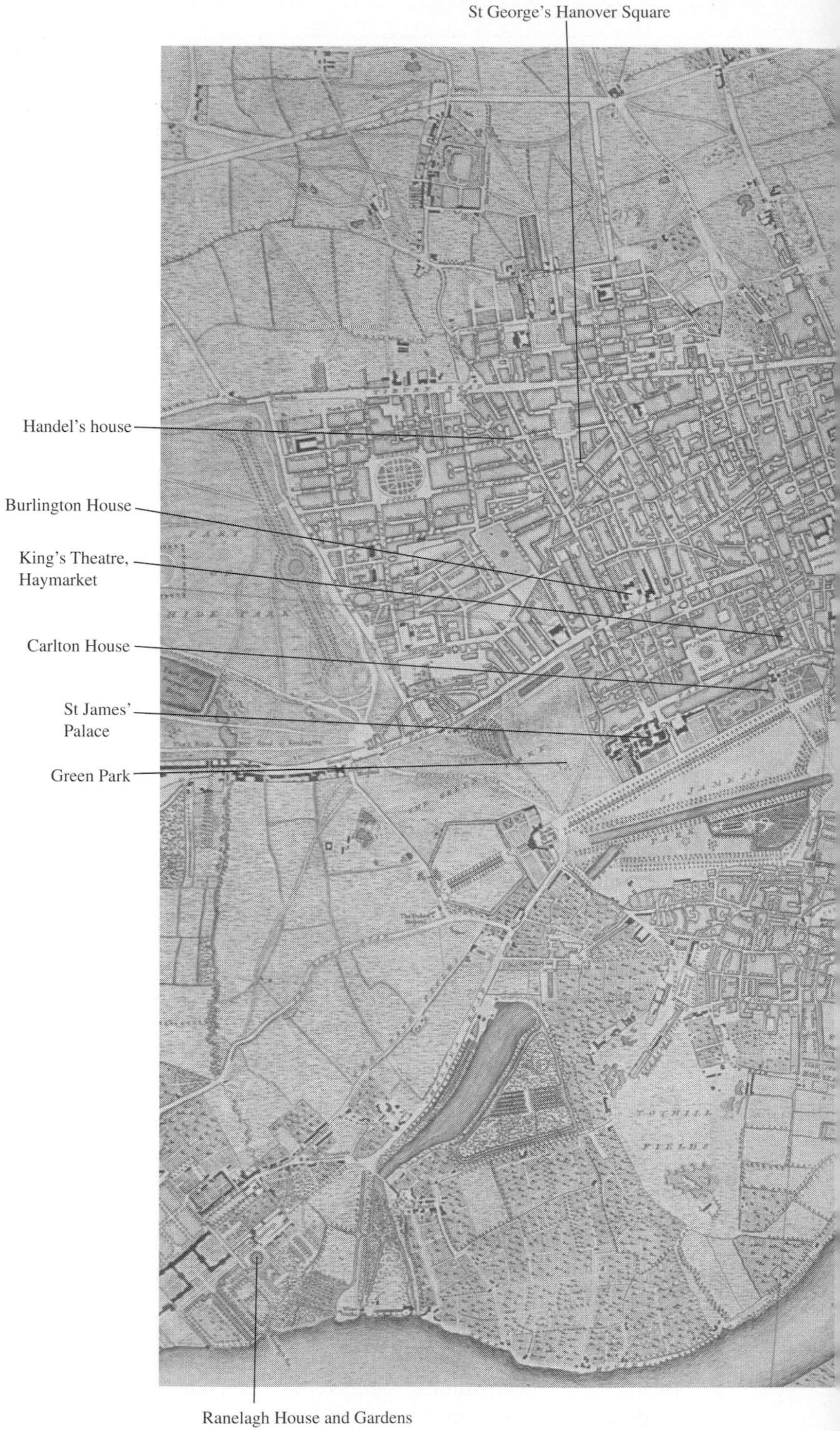

St George's Hanover Square

Handel's house

Burlington House

King's Theatre,
Haymarket

Carlton House

St James'
Palace

Green Park

Ranelagh House and Gardens

18. Map of Handel's London, based on Pine & Tinney's 1763 reprint of John Rocque's *Survey of London and the Country near Ten Miles Round* (1746).

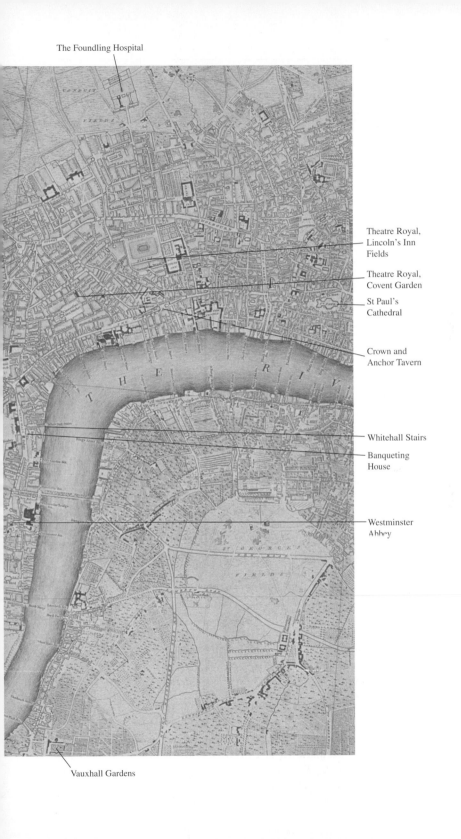

The Foundling Hospital

Theatre Royal,
Lincoln's Inn
Fields

Theatre Royal,
Covent Garden

St Paul's
Cathedral

Crown and
Anchor Tavern

Whitehall Stairs

Banqueting
House

Westminster
Abbey

Vauxhall Gardens

wholesale replanning of the City after the Great Fire was successfully thwarted by private property interests and the medieval street pattern was largely reinstated. London during the reigns of George I and George II was essentially a bourgeois city.

It is perhaps significant that after a decade of living here, Handel chose to acquire a house of his own in a smart new area, among the sort of people on whose support and patronage his English career depended, rather than in the more raffish districts of Covent Garden and Soho traditionally associated with artists and theatrical people. While there was a huge gulf between rich and poor in the city, the slums and areas of poverty and degradation, brilliantly and savagely characterised by HOGARTH in engravings like *Gin Lane*, were sometimes only a stone's throw from the fine new squares and houses of the gentry. Handel – who did not keep a horse or carriage – must have witnessed some fairly harrowing sights when walking the streets. Private charities provided some relief. The FUND FOR DECAY'D MUSICIANS, which Handel supported, was set up when the oboist KYTCH's destitute children were discovered driving donkeys through the Haymarket after their father's death. The sight of so many abandoned children moved a retired sea captain, Thomas CORAM, to establish the FOUNDLING HOSPITAL, an institution for which Handel showed especial sympathy. His annual concerts in the hospital chapel from 1749 raised considerable sums of money for the charity.

In contrast with many continental capitals the physical presence of the court in London was relatively low-key. The British monarchy were denied the huge and splendid palaces of the *anciens régimes*. Both Whitehall and St James's Palaces were old and ramshackle, and the monarch occupied the more modern, but still very modest KENSINGTON PALACE, built for William III far away from the Thames, which aggravated his asthma. GEORGE II's estranged son FREDE-RICK, Prince of Wales, set up his own rival establishment in 1717 in a large rented house on the north side of Leicester Square, where he remained for ten years. In 1733 the Prince moved to CARLTON HOUSE in Pall Mall, which he had purchased from Lord BURLINGTON. It was the nobility rather than the monarchy who occupied the grand mansions of early to mid-Georgian London. In the 1750s one of these, Montagu House in Bloomsbury, was purchased for the newly established British Museum, which opened its doors there in January 1759, just three months before Handel's death. Its former owner, the 2nd Duke of Montagu, who as Master General of he Ordnance was responsible for the fireworks in GREEN PARK in 1749, had moved to another house in Whitehall, where in 1747 Handel was a dinner guest, and was served asparagus grown at the Duke's villa at Blackheath.

London's theatres, the most important buildings in Handel's professional life, were mostly to be found around Covent Garden and the Haymarket. The oldest was the Theatre Royal in DRURY LANE, founded in 1660, used mainly for plays and never by Handel himself. His principal venues were the opera house – KING'S THEATRE – in the Haymarket built in 1704–5 (where Her Majesty's now stands), and the Theatre Royal in COVENT GARDEN, erected in 1731–2 on the profits of *The BEGGAR'S OPERA* next door to London's principal fruit and vegetable market. The theatre in LINCOLN'S INN FIELDS, used by Handel in 1740–1, was built in the seventeenth century. Other concert venues, not used by Handel himself though his music was often performed there, include Hickford's Room in Soho, the CROWN AND ANCHOR TAVERN in the Strand which hosted the concerts of the ACADEMY OF ANCIENT MUSICK, and the Castle Tavern in Paternoster Row in the City used by the eponymous Castle Music Society.

Not all the music Handel wrote for London was intended to be heard in the theatres. Some pieces were first performed in St Paul's Cathedral and WEST-MINSTER ABBEY, and other Chapels Royal, and some in the open air. The instrumental WATER MUSIC was performed on barges on the Thames and the MUSIC FOR THE ROYAL FIREWORKS in Green Park. Some were intended for performance in one or other of London's many pleasure gardens, of which the most famous was VAUXHALL GARDENS, on the south side of the Thames near the Archbishop of Canterbury's London residence, Lambeth Palace. Not only were Handel's songs performed there (and the *Fireworks Music* rehearsed), but, from 1738, the attractions of the gardens included an admired statue of the composer by L.-F. ROUBILIAC, commissioned by the grateful proprietor Jonathan TYERS. The opening of Westminster Bridge in 1750 made access to this fashionable and popular venue very much easier.

Inevitably much of the physical fabric of Handel's London has long since disappeared. He would still recognise much of the layout of the streets and squares in the West End and Bloomsbury, and in some places stretches of eighteenth-century terrace houses survive which he would have known, and may even have seen being built. Great Ormond Street in Bloomsbury, where his librettist Charles JENNENS had a large house, is a good example (though Jennens's own house has gone). The Mayfair homes of his great friend Mrs DELANY and her brother 'Bunny' GRANVILLE are both still standing, the former much altered. The churches of Handel's day have fared better, though the interior of his own parish church, ST GEORGE'S, HANOVER SQUARE, looks very different now from how it appeared in 1725. Every one of the theatres where he performed his operas and oratorios has been either demolished or rebuilt (sometimes more than once). In fact, the only places in London where his music can still be performed in the surroundings where it was first heard are St Paul's Cathedral, Westminster Abbey, the chapels in St James's Palace (CHAPEL ROYAL and QUEEN'S CHAPEL), the BANQUETING HOUSE in Whitehall, and the open-air sites. The public houses and taverns and other concert venues have long since disappeared, as have the premises of Handel's long-time music publisher WALSH, in Catherine Street, Strand (now under the Aldwych). All of the numerous pleasure gardens have vanished under bricks and mortar; so have most of the mansions of the nobility. One notable exception is BURLINGTON HOUSE in Piccadilly, where Handel lived for a while, probably in 1714, before Lord Burlington embarked on his Palladian remodelling. The great Foundling Hospital building is no more, though the institution itself survives. St James's and Kensington Palaces still stand, as does Handel's own house, now a museum in his honour.   JOHN GREENACOMBE

London, Bishop of. See Edmund GIBSON

London Handel Festival. See FESTIVALS, 5

Look down, harmonious Saint ('The Praise of Harmony'), HWV 124. English cantata for tenor, strings and continuo. Perhaps only a fragment, it consists of an accompanied recitative and the aria 'Sweet accents', which has some of Handel's most virtuosic coloratura writing for tenor voice. The text is taken from Newburgh HAMILTON's *The Power of Musick*. It might have been composed for John BEARD to sing as an interlude in the first performances of *ALEXANDER'S FEAST*, but abandoned in favour of the longer Italian cantata *CECILIA, VOLGI UN SGUARDO*, in which the musical material of 'Sweet accents' appears as the soprano aria 'Sei cara, sei bella'. DAVID VICKERS

Lord is my light, The. See ANTHEMS, 2

Lotario, HWV 26. Composed in the autumn of 1729 (Handel signed off his autograph on 16 November) and first staged at the KING'S THEATRE in the Haymarket on 2 December, *Lotario* was the first opera to be put on at Handel's and HEIDEGGER's so-called Second Academy (OPERA COMPANIES, 3). The cast was as follows:

Adelaide, Queen of Italy	Anna STRADA del Pò (soprano)
Lotario, King of Germany	Antonio BERNACCHI (castrato)
Matilde, wife of Berengario	Antonia Margherita MERIGHI (mezzo-soprano)
Idelberto, son of Berengario	Francesca BERTOLLI (alto)
Berengario, Duke of Spoleto	Annibale Pio FABRI (tenor)
Clodomiro, Berengario's general	Johann Gottfried RIEMSCHNEIDER (bass)

Paolo ROLLI, unlikely to flatter, was patronising about Bernacchi and Riemschneider, found Merighi an excellent actress, cast an approving eye over Bertolli's beauty, and had to admit that in the soprano Strada and the tenor Fabri Handel had discovered two real stars (Deutsch, pp. 249–50). Fabri did not stay for long, but Strada became the leading lady of the second half of his operatic career, for whom he was to write a series of magnificent roles.

The libretto is an adaptation, apparently by Giacomo ROSSI, of Antonio SALVI's *Adelaide*, originally written as a festive opera for the Munich court in 1722, and frequently reset in the following years. Its immediate model was the 1729 VENICE version, with music by ORLANDINI, which Handel is likely to have heard during his visit to the city that year. As usual, the recitative is ruthlessly and not always felicitously abbreviated; unusually, however, *Lotario* does have more set pieces than its model, including no fewer than seven metaphor arias – evidently Rossi was undismayed by GAY's satirical targeting of metaphor texts in *The BEGGAR'S OPERA*. The most significant alteration is the expansion of the role of Matilde, to bring the virtuous and malevolent forces into a better matched confrontation. Historically Lotario is the German Emperor Otto the Great (912–73). His name was changed from Ottone to Lotario during composition, presumably because Handel had already composed one *OTTONE* (whose hero was the son of Lotario-Ottone).

Act I: Berengario has led an uprising against the King of Italy, and acquired a half share of the kingdom. Unsatisfied, he has the rightful King poisoned, and now aims to reinforce his claim to the whole kingdom by marrying his son

Idelberto to the widowed Queen, Adelaide, who is immured in the city of Pavia. But Lotario, long an admirer of Adelaide, has been summoned to assist her. A meeting between Adelaide and Lotario, who has managed to get into the city in disguise, gives the Queen confidence to reject the marriage proposal presented on behalf of Idelberto.

Act II: While Lotario is defeating Berengario on the battlefield, the imprisoned Adelaide, emotionally browbeaten by Matilde, is only saved from taking poison by the intervention of Idelberto; he, though a mere political pawn in his parents' scheme, genuinely dotes on Adelaide. On the plain below the city walls, Lotario, with Berengario his prisoner, confronts Matilde on the ramparts above, with Adelaide as her hostage. Idelberto, to help ensure Adelaide's safety, goes over to Lotario's side. Berengario is sent into the city to negotiate.

Act III: Once Berengario is back in the city, he and Matilde try to trick Adelaide into making demands of Lotario on their behalf. She refuses, and they decide to brave Lotario once more in battle. On the verge of a second victory, Lotario halts the assault on the city when Matilde orders Adelaide to be used as a human shield. But by threatening to execute both his hostages, Berengario and Idelberto, Lotario finally overcomes Matilde's determination. Rage and despair bring her to the brink of suicide, from which she is saved by Idelberto. Adelaide is happy to marry Lotario, and asks that Idelberto, whose own plea has saved his parents from condign punishment, should succeed to their throne.

Handel and Heidegger will have hoped to launch the Second Academy with an opera that impressed London opera-goers as favourably as his first Royal Academy (OPERA COMPANIES, 2) opera, RADAMISTO, nine years earlier. Lotario was certainly grand enough as a spectacle; the costumes were evidently admirable, and Handel had composed a great deal of fine music, especially the big virtuoso arias. One striking symptom of the care he took is the finely wrought quality of what one might describe as the musical framing. Lotario is the first opera for which Handel provided instrumental sinfonias to introduce both Acts II and III; it has a concerto-like, four-movement Overture, including a second movement which brilliantly combines the traditional fugal style with extended passages of ground bass. The first act begins with an 'arioso' which enunciates the leading thought of the drama (rather as was to happen in some of Handel's later oratorios), and the last act closes with an exhilarating finale, 'Gioie e serto', in which, while the singers rejoice in a typical gavotte-like chorus, the violins simultaneously play a *double* on the same melody. Outstanding too are the arias that close the first two acts, both of them settings of metaphor texts. Adelaide's 'Scherza in mar' (Act I) is one of Handel's most thrilling seascapes: it includes a notable passage of sequential modulation at the start of the B section, carrying the music from G major to C sharp minor in four bold steps. In Lotario's 'Non disperi peregrino' (Act II) the verses describe a pilgrim overtaken by night, and Handel masterfully sustains a quiet confident tread that moves the music forward despite all the groping melismas and tangles of counterpoint.

For all its musical riches, Lotario did not take. Ten performances were given in December and January 1729–30, then it dropped from the repertory and was never revived. Instead, an unusually large number of its arias, thirteen of them, were taken up in revivals of other operas over the next few seasons. Particularly favoured was Berengario's brilliant aria from Act II, 'D'instabile fortuna', which reappeared in revivals of *RINALDO* (1731), *Ottone* (1733), *ARIANNA IN CRETA* (1734) and in an OPERA OF THE NOBILITY staging of *Ottone* (also in 1734).

DAVID KIMBELL

Burney
Dean, *Operas*
Deutsch
Harris, *Librettos*
M. Pacholke (ed.), *Lotario*, HHA II/23 (Kassel, 2003)
Strohm

Lotti, Antonio (b. Hanover, 1666; d. Venice, 5 Jan. 1740). One of the most highly reputed Italian opera and church composers of his age. He wrote twenty-three operas, eight oratorios and a large quantity of secular and sacred vocal music. The esteemed composer worked at St Mark's in VENICE throughout his career, rising through the ranks of the basilica's musical establishment from alto singer to organist, eventually becoming *primo maestro di cappella* in 1736. An influential teacher, his pupils included GALUPPI and MARCELLO. Handel probably became acquainted with Lotti at Venice during his first Italian journey (HANDEL, 15).

In 1717 Lotti was invited to DRESDEN, where he produced *Giove in Argo* (1717), *Ascanio in Alba* (1718) and *Teofane* (1719); all three featured his wife, the prima donna Santa Stella. When Handel visited Dresden in summer 1719, all three operatic entertainments were performed as part of the marriage celebrations for Crown Prince Frederick August and Archduchess Maria Josepha. Handel used the same librettos for his own *OTTONE* (1723) and *GIOVE IN ARGO* (1739). Some arias in *Ottone* ('Dal minacciar del vento', 'Le profonde vie dell'onde', 'Bel labbro formato' and 'Diresti poi così') share slight motivic links or portray affects akin to the homonymous arias in Lotti's settings, and he included an aria from *Teofane* in the pasticcio *L'ELPIDIA* (1725). In 1731 Handel used the overture and two arias from Lotti's *Alessandro Severo* (Venice, 1717) in the pasticcio *VENCESLAO*.

BURNEY, who heard Lotti's music performed at St Mark's in 1770, later considered that it unites 'all the Science and learned regularity of the old school' to 'grave and pathos', judged that it is 'at once solemn and touching', and claimed that HASSE regarded Lotti's compositions 'as the most perfect of their kind' (Burney, p. 534). Lotti's contrapuntal church music was certainly admired by BACH, who copied several works including the *Missa Sapientiae*. Handel copied out parts of the same mass in about 1749, and borrowed from it several works: the Gloria (formerly classified as HWV 245) provided material for the final chorus of *The CHOICE OF HERCULES*; 'Qui tollis peccata mundi' was Handel's source for the opening section of 'He saw the lovely youth' in *THEODORA*, and in the same oratorio 'Blest be the hand' was influenced by Lotti's 'Domine Deus, Agnus Dei'; part of the final chorus in JEPHTHA ('Freed from war's destructive sword') was based on the middle movement of the Kyrie. Perhaps Handel also examined Charles JENNENS's manuscript of Lotti's *Confitebor tibi* in A (London, British Library, Add. MS 39816).

DAGMAR GLÜXAM (Trans. ANGELA BAIER)

See also BORROWING

K. Beisswenger, 'Eine Messe Antonio Lottis in Händels Notenbibliothek. Zur Identifizierung des Kyrie in g-moll (HWV 244) und des Gloria in G-Dur (HWV 245)', *Die Musikforschung* 42 (1989), 353–6

Dean and Knapp, *Operas*

F. McLauchlan, 'Lotti's *Teofane* (1719) and Handel's *Ottone* (1723): A Textual and Musical Study', *ML* 78/3 (Aug. 1997), 349–90

J. Roberts, *Handel Sources: Materials for the Study of Handel's Borrowing*, vol. 5 (New York and London, 1986)

Strohm

Louisa, Princess (Queen of Denmark) (b. London, 7 Dec. 1724; d. Copenhagen, 19 Dec. 1751). Youngest daughter of GEORGE II and Queen CAROLINE. Louisa married Prince Frederick (later Frederick V) of Denmark in 1743. She had five children prior to her early death, which was caused by a botched hernia operation. Louisa was probably not taught by Handel, but he may have written two compositions for her in c.1739 (HWV 447 and 452). One of her last reported engagements in England was attending a rehearsal with her sisters of Handel's Dettingen music (TE DEUM, 5).   HANNAH SMITH

Lowe, Thomas (b. ?London, c.1719; d. London, 1 March 1783). English tenor (range c–a′). In August 1740 he took part in ARNE's masque *Alfred*, and a month later he made his debut as a singing actor at DRURY LANE. He played minor parts in plays, and he was particularly associated with GALLIARD's song 'The early horn'. He frequently sang in BALLAD OPERAS, and also participated in more serious works, such as Arne's *Comus* (1738). He was a popular performer at VAUXHALL GARDENS, and in 1763 he ceased working in leading theatres and bought the lease of Marylebone pleasure gardens. His voice and fortune swiftly declined. He sold Marylebone to Samuel ARNOLD in 1769, after which he sang intermittently at Sadler's Wells. He died destitute.

Lowe first sang for Handel in 1743, taking the roles of Philistine and Israelite Man in *SAMSON*. Handel wrote two patriotic SONGS for Lowe during the JACOBITE rebellion (1745–6), and the tenor was a regular member of the composer's COVENT GARDEN company in 1748–51. Roles composed for Lowe include the title role in *JOSHUA* and Jonathan in *ALEXANDER BALUS* (both first performed in 1748), the First Elder in *SUSANNA* and Zadok in *SOLOMON* (both 1749), Septimius in *THEODORA* (1750) and Apollo in *ALCESTE* (written in 1750, but never performed). He also sang in numerous oratorio revivals during these seasons, and in Handel's 'Anthem on the Peace' and the FOUNDLING HOSPITAL Anthem (ANTHEMS, 7; 8). He spent much of his career replacing or being replaced by John BEARD in London's leading theatres, and the two tenors both became well known for the role of Macheath in The BEGGAR'S OPERA. Charles Dibdin claimed that Lowe was a more naturally gifted singer than Beard in love songs, but claimed that 'Lowe lost himself beyond the namby-pamby poetry of Vauxhall; Beard was at home everywhere'. Burney belived that Lowe had 'the finest tenor voice I ever heard in my life', but criticised him because 'for want of diligence and cultivation, he could never be safely trusted with any thing better than a ballad, which he constantly learned by his ear'. However, Burney's assessment might be unfair: some of the florid music Handel tailored for Lowe's abilities, such as Joshua's 'Haste, Israel haste', Zadok's 'Golden columns' and

Septimius's 'Dread the fruits of Christian folly', demands an excellent vocal technique.   DAVID VICKERS

C. Dibdin, *A Complete History of the English Stage*, vol. 5 (London, 1800)

Lowth, Robert (b. Winchester, 27 Nov. 1710; d. London, 3 Nov. 1787). Biblical commentator, poet and priest; he studied at OXFORD from 1729 to 1737 and may have been present during Handel's concert series in July 1733. From 1741 Lowth was Professor of Poetry at OXFORD; during this time he wrote his poem *The Judgment of Hercules* which was first published anonymously in 1743 and later formed the foundation for Thomas MORELL's libretto *The CHOICE OF HERCULES* set by Handel in 1750.   MATTHEW GARDNER

M. Gardner, 'Handel and Maurice Greene's Circle at the Apollo Academy: The Music and Intellectual Contexts of Oratorios, Odes and Masques', Ph.D. dissertation (Ruprecht-Karls-Universität Heidelberg, 2007)

Lübeck. German Hanseatic city on the Baltic Sea. Handel and Johann MATTHESON went to Lübeck on 17 August 1703 after an invitation from the politician and music-lover Magnus von Wedderkop (1637–1721). He proposed that both of them should apply for the post of an assistant to Dieterich BUXTEHUDE. They played various organs and harpsichords, were well entertained by Wedderkop and had a pleasant time which Mattheson later enthusiastically remembered.
                                                        DOROTHEA SCHRÖDER

Mainwaring
J. Mattheson, *Grundlage einer Ehrenpforte* (Hamburg, 1740, repr. Kassel, 1969)

Lucchesina, La. See Maria Antonia MARCHESINI

Lucchini (Luchini), Antonio Maria (fl. 1716–30). Italian librettist. In 1717 he moved from VENICE to DRESDEN with Antonio LOTTI. Engaged by the Dresden court, Lucchini wrote several opera librettos, including Lotti's opera *Giove in Argo* (1717), which Handel used for a self-pasticcio in 1739 (*GIOVE IN ARGO*). Lucchini was forced to leave Dresden suddenly when he was involved in a scandal with a woman, and thereafter he wrote librettos for Venice and ROME.
                                                        WALTER KREYSZIG

J. M. Coopersmith, 'The Libretto of Handel's "Jupiter in Argos"', ML 17 (1936), 289–96

Lucio Cornelia Silla. See *SILLA*

Lucio Papirio dittatore (Lucius Papirius dictator), HWV A^6. Opera in three acts by Geminiano GIACOMELLI, revised by Handel for a version first performed at the KING'S THEATRE on 23 May 1732. The libretto was originally written by Apostolo ZENO for Vienna and set by Antonio CALDARA in 1719. Giacomelli composed his setting for Parma, where it was first performed in the spring of 1729 with an all-star cast including FARINELLI, BERNACCHI, BOROSINI and FAUSTINA. For Parma the libretto was revised by the court poet Carlo Innocenzo FRUGONI.

Lucio Papirio, dictator of Rome, on the eve of battle against the Samnites in 325 BC, is warned by diviners to return to Rome and conciliate the gods. He leaves Quinto Fabio in command with strict instructions not to attack the enemy, but Fabio does attack and achieves a great victory. For this disobedience

Lucio Papirio sentences him to death, though the Roman populace favours Fabio. Fabio's father Marco Fabio and his wife Papiria, the dictator's daughter, are torn by conflicting loyalties. Fabio's sister Rutilia persuades him to beg for mercy from Papirio in private, but Papirio humiliates him by showing him to the people on his knees, causing Fabio to reject any pardon. Only when presented with the people's will by the tribune Servilio does Papirio finally yield and pardon Fabio.

The London cast was as follows:

Lucio Papirio dittatore	Giovanni Battista PINACCI (tenor)
Marco Fabio	Antonio MONTAGNANA (bass)
Papira	Anna Maria STRADA del Pò (soprano)
Rutilia	Francesca BERTOLLI (alto)
Quinto Fabio	SENESINO (alto)
Servilio	Anna Bagnolesi (alto)
Cominio	Antonio CAMPIOLI (alto)

Lucio Papirio ran for only four nights – 'it did not take', reports the Colman *Opera Register* (Deutsch, p. 292; HHB iv, p. 201) – while concurrent performances of Handel's oratorio *ESTHER* were well attended. No excerpts were published.

Lucio Papirio was the first in a series of operas by other composers that Handel adapted for the London stage between 1732 and 1737. He altered it less drastically than any of the others, replacing only two of the original arias, although many others were transposed or cut altogether. Thus it cannot be considered a PASTICCIO but is more accurately described simply as an arrangement. The two inserted arias were sung by Montagnana, for whom they had been composed by PORPORA. In making his arrangement Handel probably made use of a score of GIACOMELLI's opera belonging to Sir John Buckworth, now in the Royal Academy of Music, London. Our main source for the music of the London version is the conducting score in the Staats- und Universitätsbibliothek Hamburg. Handel revised Giacomelli's recitatives using a method he rarely employed elsewhere. He apparently gave SMITH SENIOR a copy of the libretto showing the intended cuts, and had him copy the original recitatives along with the arias, leaving blank those passages that he thought Handel might want to alter, including most of the vocal lines of Quinto Fabio and Rutilia. Handel then pencilled in the missing notes, later inked over by Smith, and made various additional changes. The result was a mixture of Handel and Giacomelli (whose bass notes were often retained even when the voice part was rewritten) with occasional touches of Smith.   JOHN H. ROBERTS

H. D. Clausen, 'The Hamburg Collection', *Handel Collections and their History*, ed. T. Best (Oxford, 1993)
Strohm, 164–211

'Lucrezia, La'. See CANTATAS

Lully, Jean-Baptiste (b. Florence, 28 Nov. 1632; d. Paris, 22 March 1687). Giovanni Battista Lulli came to France in 1646 and soon began to dance in and then compose music for ballets at the court of Louis XIV. Surintendant of the King's music in 1661, he founded the Académie Royale de Musique in 1672. With his librettist Philippe QUINAULT, he created operas (*tragédies lyriques*) which feature airs and dances in lavishly staged divertissements but for characterisation and emotion rely more on music that follows the inflections of the poetry.

Handel's library contained scores of Lully's operas (HANDEL, 19), and several eighteenth-century sources pointed out that Handel frequently adopted French musical styles, especially in the slow sections of his overtures. He probably heard Lully's music in HAMBURG and in HANOVER, where French influence was strong, and his earliest operas, such as ALMIRA and RODRIGO, contain strings of French dances, a form which enjoyed great popularity in England early in the eighteenth century (DANCE FORMS).

Lully was admired at BURLINGTON HOUSE, where Handel perhaps composed TESEO and AMADIGI, both using librettos based on French originals and on subjects of Lully operas (Thésée, 1675; Amadis, 1684). Teseo, with its French overture, five acts, spectacular scenic effects, relatively few exit arias and dance-like instrumental music, is the closest to the French model, though the vocal music remains more Italian than French. It also contains several numbers which feature the five-part string texture characteristic of Lully's music (e.g. 'Le luci del mio bene'), a texture Handel used in several other overtures but rarely elsewhere.

Lully's influence seems especially strong in other works on subjects that both composers set to music, such as the overture and Grande Entrée to ALCESTE and the overture to ADMETO. It is also strong in Handel's works during his collaboration with the dancer Marie SALLÉ in the mid-1730s, such as ARIODANTE, ALCINA and TERPSICORE. There are similarities in the treatment of the songes agréables and songes funestes in Ariodante and in Lully's Atys , but it is difficult to determine to what extent there is a specific influence of Lully, as opposed to that of French dance music of Handel's time.   BUFORD NORMAN

B. Baselt, 'Einflüsse der französischen Musik auf das Schaffen G. F. Handels', Der Einfluß der französischen Musik auf die Komponisten der ersten Hälfte des 18. Jahrhunderts (Blankenburg, 1982)

D. Charlton and S. Hibberd, 'My father was a poor Parisian musician', JRMA 128 (2003), 161–99

H. Schneider, 'Händel und die französische Theatermusik in ihren dramatisch-szenischen Aspekten', HJb 37 (1991)
    'Wie französisch ist Händels Teseo', Alte Musik als ästhetische Gegenwart: Bach, Händel, Schütz, vol. 1 (Kassel, 1987)

Lustig, Jacob Wilhelm ('Wohlgemuth, Conrad') (b. Hamburg, 21 Sept. 1706; d. Groningen, 17 May 1796). Composer, organist, theorist and translator. He held a position as organist in HAMBURG, completed his musical training with several of Handel's contemporaries (including MATTHESON and TELEMANN), and attended a performance by Johann Sebastian BACH in Hamburg's Katharinenkirche in November 1720. In 1728 he was appointed as an organist at Groningen. He went to London in 1732 or 1734, where he heard Handel's operas, and in the April 1756 issue of his periodical Samenspraaken over muzikaale Beginselen he acknowledged his fondness for Handel's music in a comparison of it with works by KUHNAU, KEISER and TELEMANN. He gives the only historical evidence about the early compositional date of HWV 442, 481 490, 574 and 577 (KEYBOARD MUSIC) published by Witvogel in 1732.   WALTER KREYSZIG

T. Best, 'Handel's Keyboard Music', MT 112 (Sept. 1971), 845–8

A. Dekker, 'Bach, Lustig en Hamburg', *Mens en Melodie* 24 (1969), 45ff.

J. du Saar, *Het leven en de werken van Jacob Wilhelm Lustig* (Amsterdam, 1948)

Lute. See INSTRUMENTATION

Lutheranism. At the heart of Lutheranism was the 'priesthood of all believers': Jesus was the sole mediator between man and God; by faith in him, and an understanding of Scripture, everyone could find salvation. The disputatious seventeenth century led many Lutheran pastors astray in arcane theological debates, but towards the eighteenth century, personal faith was restated by the Pietist movement, emphasising devotion to and love of Christ. Pietist ideas of individual religious and moral responsibility influenced the development of the German Enlightenment (the University of HALLE was influenced by Pietism), and can be seen in, for example, the works of BROCKES. KATIE HAWKS

See also HANDEL, 12

M

MacSwiney, Owen. See Owen SWINEY

Mainwaring, John (b. Drayton Bassett, Staffs., 4 Aug. 1724; d. Cambridge, 15 April 1807). CHURCH OF ENGLAND clergyman, author and traveller. Married Anne Wilding (1763–95) on 22 November 1788.

Mainwaring's biography of Handel, the first of its kind to treat the life and works of one musician at length, was published in 1760 as *Memoirs of the Life of the Late George Frederic Handel*. The book did not carry its author's name, but letters from the publisher Dodsley and references in contemporary publications leave no doubt that Mainwaring was responsible. He received the assistance of several acquaintances who may have originated the idea: Robert Price (c.1720–61), John Christopher SMITH JUNIOR, Benjamin Stillingfleet, James HARRIS and Fisher Littleton (c.1730–1800). Smith's recollections provided the bulk of the material for the opening biographical section. Harris is thought to have compiled the list of works. Price is quoted directly in the last section, in which the music is discussed, and Stillingfleet may also have contributed to it. Smith and Price were close friends. Littleton was the younger brother of Sir Edward, Mainwaring's friend from their days at St John's College, Cambridge. Fisher Littleton knew Handel during the 1750s and may have been responsible for introducing Mainwaring to the circle who wished to memorialise the great man in print.

Excerpts from the work appeared in the *Gentleman's Magazine* (April and May 1760), the *London Chronicle* (June 1760), the *Universal Magazine* (June 1760) and the *Annual Register* (1760). A translation by MATTHESON, Handel's erstwhile colleague in HAMBURG, with additional comments, appeared in 1761. The book received favourable published reviews; the Earl of SHAFTESBURY and Charles JENNENS kept their adverse comments private. All biographers and readers are indebted to Mainwaring, whose outline and anecdotes have provided a relatively secure base upon which to build more sophisticated studies.   DAVID HUNTER

G. Beeks, 'Memoirs of the Reverend John Mainwaring: Notes on a Handelian Biographer', *Festa Musicologica: Essays in Honor of George J. Buelow*, ed. T. J. Mathiesen and B. V. Rivera (Stuyvesant, NY, 1995)

W. Dean, 'Charles Jennens's Marginalia to Mainwaring's Life of Handel', *Essays on Opera* (Oxford, 1990)

Malmesbury Collection. See SOURCES AND COLLECTIONS, 12

Malmesbury House. See James HARRIS; SALISBURY

Manchester, Charles Montagu, 1st Duke of (b. c.1662; d. London, 26 Jan. 1722). Army officer, diplomatist. A member of the Kit-Kat Club and subscriber to VANBRUGH's Queen's Theatre in the Haymarket (KING'S THEATRE), Manchester was active in securing for London the services of Italian musicians and artists. He negotiated, unsuccessfully, with Giovanni BONONCINI, but the painters Marco Ricci and Giovanni Antonio Pellegrini returned with him on his recall from VENICE in 1708, and the castrato NICOLINO also made the journey. According to MAINWARING, Manchester met Handel in Venice, probably during Carnival 1707–8, and suggested to the composer that he visit London. Manchester was one of the initial directors of the Royal Academy of Music (OPERA COMPANIES, 2). DAVID HUNTER

Mangold, Georg Caspar (b. 1693; d. Weissenfels, 1749). German cellist. He was the son of Handel's half-niece Maria Sophia Pferstorff (HANDEL, 9) and Caspar Mangold, a steward in the service of the Dukes of Saxe-Weissenfels near Langendorf and later mayor of WEISSENFELS. He was a cellist in the Weissenfels Hofkapelle (1722–46), and from 1732 was Silberdiener (a valet entrusted with important keys). His son of the same name was court organist from 1741 until before 1746. KLAUS-PETER KOCH (Trans. ANGELA BAIER)

See also Appendix 3: Handel's Family Tree

B. Hofestädt and L. Bense, 'Vom Händelschen Familiensinn', *Die Familie Händel und Halle. Zum Stadtjubiläum 1200 Jahre Halle*, ed. Hallische Familienforscher 'Ekkehard' e.V. (Halle, 2006)

E. M. Ranft, 'Zum Personalbestand der Weißenfelser Hofkapelle', *Beiträge zur Bach-Forschung* 6 (1987), 5–36

Manns, Sir August Friedrich (b. Stolzenburg, near Stettin, 12 March 1825; d. Norwood, 1 March 1907). Musician, conductor. He was conductor of the CRYSTAL PALACE orchestra from October 1855, and succeeded Michael COSTA as artistic director of the Crystal Palace Handel FESTIVALS (from 1883 until 1900). Manns improved the technical standards of the performances, included female orchestral players (from 1891), and introduced novelties from lesser-known Handel works for the Selection Day of the festival, mostly arranged in a chronological order. ANNETTE LANDGRAF

'Mr. August Manns', *The Musical Times and Singing Class Circular*, 1 March 1898, 153–159; see also 1 June 1888, 362–3

Manuscripts, Music. See SOURCES AND COLLECTIONS

Marcello, Benedetto Giacomo (b. Venice, 24 July 1686; d. Brescia, 24 July 1739). Italian nobleman, composer and author of an infamous satire on early eighteenth-century Venetian opera (*Il teatro alla moda*, 1720). He was encouraged by his parents to cultivate musical pursuits. Marcello might have met Handel during a trip to FLORENCE in 1707. Both composers used the same texts for their CHAMBER DUETS *Giù nei Tartarei regni* (text by Ortensio MAURO) and *Tacete, ohimè, tacete* (text by Francesco de Lemene), and also both composers set the cantata *O numi eterni* ('La Lucrezia'). During the 1710s Marcello taught the soprano FAUSTINA Bordoni, and in July 1720 he received a copy of Handel's *ACI, GALATEA E POLIFEMO* from Philipp von Hessen-Darmstadt (the governor of Mantua). In

Academy (OPERA COMPANIES, 3) in 1729, she was described by the Daily Journal as 'a Woman of a very fine Presence, an excellent Actress, and a very good Singer – A Counter Tenor'. In December 1729 she made her London debut in the first performance of LOTARIO (as Matilda), and in 1730 and 1731 she took part in the first performances of PARTENOPE (Rosmira) and PORO (Erissena). She also sang in revivals of GIULIO CESARE (Cornelia), SCIPIONE (Armira), RINALDO (HWV 7[b], Armida), RODELINDA (Eduige) and in the pasticcio ORMISDA (Palmira). After an interlude in Italy she returned to London in 1736 to take part in the last season of the OPERA OF THE NOBILITY. During the next 1737–8 season she sang in the premieres of FARAMONDO (Gernando) and SERSE (Amastre), and in the pasticcio ALESSANDRO SEVERO

19. A portrait of Handel by Philip Mercier, oil on canvas, c.1730.

(Giulia). Mary Pendarves (later DELANY) wrote of her that 'her voice is not extraordinarily good or bad, she is tall and has a very graceful person, with a tolerable face; she sings easily and agreeably'.

FRANCESCO LORA (Trans. TERENCE BEST)

Messiah, HWV 56. English oratorio. Handel's most famous work, his third oratorio about Christ (the others are *La* RESURREZIONE and the BROCKES PASSION), owes its existence to Charles JENNENS, who compiled the libretto and gave it to Handel apparently by December 1739, hoping that Handel would make it his greatest composition. But, wishing at that time 'to please the Town with something of a gayer turn' (L'ALLEGRO), Handel put it on the shelf, until 1741, when he composed its initial version in twenty-four days (22 August–14 September). He took the score with him to DUBLIN and gave the first performance as a charity matinée on 13 April 1742 at the New Musick Room, Fishamble Street (NEALE'S MUSICK HALL), following two successful subscription series of six concerts each. In all he gave two public rehearsals and two performances of *Messiah* in Dublin, to capacity audiences, receiving resounding praise for his own and his colleagues' generosity and for his composition, 'which in the opinion of the best Judges, far surpasses anything of that Nature, which has been performed in this or any other Kingdom' (*Dublin News Letter*, 10 April 1742). According to Edward Synge, Bishop of Elphin, the audience, including 'the young & gay of both Sexes' who made up a large part of it, appeared 'thoroughly engag'd from one end to the other'. Of the soloists only the soprano, AVOGLIO, came with Handel from England; Susanna CIBBER (alto) was in Dublin as a theatre actress, and the men, two altos, a tenor and two basses, were recruited from the Dublin cathedral choirs.

During the remainder of his life Handel produced thirty-six performances of *Messiah*. He introduced it to England on 23 March 1743, as the ninth performance of two subscription series of six concerts each at COVENT GARDEN Theatre. In London Handel normally performed his works in a theatre, but in this case the venue, with its associations of low life and questionable subject matter, prompted a press debate about appropriateness. But there was no criticism of the music or the concept, and Handel included two more performances in his 1743 season. His soloists were Avoglio, Kitty CLIVE, Miss Edwards (soprano), Cibber, John BEARD and Thomas LOWE (tenor), and William SAVAGE and Henry Theodore REINHOLD (bass), though Beard seems to have sung at most only one performance, his music then being transferred to Avoglio. The orchestra, as in Dublin, was led by Matthew DUBOURG. Handel gave further performances at Covent Garden in 1745, 1749, 1750, 1752 and thereafter as the final performance of his theatre season each year – usually within the fortnight before Easter, in accordance with the design of his librettist, who had intended it for Passion week. But *Messiah* became established as Britain's favourite oratorio through its performances at the FOUNDLING HOSPITAL, where the HALLELUJAH chorus was included in Handel's charity concert in 1749 (as part of the 'Foundling Hospital Anthem'). The initial complete performances there on 1 and 15 May 1750 drew a total audience of nearly 2,000. *Messiah* became an annual Foundling fund-raising event, and Handel bequeathed a score and performing parts to the Hospital.

R. Luckett, *Handel's Messiah: A Celebration* (London, 1992)

J. H. Roberts, 'Christ of the Playhouse: Indirect Narrative in Handel's *Messiah*', *HJb* 55 (2009)

W. Shaw, *A Textual and Historical Companion to Handel's 'Messiah'*, Sevenoaks: Novello, 1965, repr. 1982

Smith, *Oratorios*

J. Tobin, *Handel's 'Messiah': A Critical Account of the Manuscript Sources and Printed Editions* (London, 1969)

Metastasio, Pietro (Antonio Domenico Bonaventura) (b. Rome, 3 Jan. 1698; d. Vienna, 12 April 1782). Italian poet and librettist. He established a considerable reputation as a fine poet and dramatist at the age of twenty-six with his first original drama, *Didone abbandonata*, set by Domenico Sarri for NAPLES in 1724. From 1724 to 1730 opera impresarios in both his home city of ROME and VENICE vied with each other for the privilege and financial success of being the first to present a new drama by this young poet. Two composers, Leonardo VINCI and Nicola PORPORA were particularly associated with six librettos that Metastasio wrote during this period. Vinci composed the first settings of five of these, all except one being premiered at the Teatro delle Dame, Rome. This success and accumulated reputation secured for him the post of Caesarian poet at the Habsburg court in Vienna. From 1730 Metastasio held this position for the rest of his life, becoming something of a European poetic institution.

Particularly through the dramas that he wrote between 1724 and 1740, Metastasio's librettos came to be regarded as the epitome of court opera. In many of these he presented 'a drama of moral forces personified by specified characters who are differentiated by emotionally charged actions and reactions that drive them towards either personal moral victory or moral self-defeat . . . At court performances, the moral hero [or heroine] served to set before the monarch the ideal of the morally inspired ruler' (D. Neville, 'Metastasio', *NG Opera*).

Handel was not a prolific composer of Metastasio's dramas. '[He] perhaps felt that his art was not compatible with the libretti of the highest literary quality. Zeno was the librettist who attracted him least, and Zeno, like Metastasio, regarded his poetical texts as independent dramas' (Strohm, 231). Indeed, Handel set only three of the poet's librettos: *SIROE, Rè di Persia* (1728), *PORO, Rè dell'Indie* (1731) (based on Metastasio's *Alessandro nell'Indie*) and *EZIO* (1732). Judged on the number of their London performances, the first two were amongst the most successful of his operas; the third much less so. Handel's choice of *Alessandro nell'Indie* and *Ezio* may also have been influenced by the knowledge that their Metastasian texts had their individual origins in two *tragédies* by Jean RACINE, in whose work Handel seems to have had a keen interest in the early 1730s.

From 1732, Handel's only direct contact with Metastasio's works was through four PASTICCIOS that he introduced into three of his opera seasons between 1732 and 1737. However, it is likely that these operas were selected as much for the composers of their principal source scores as for Metastasio's poetry, since they feature music by Vinci, HASSE and LEO, Handel's preferred opera composers. They comprise *CATONE IN UTICA* (1732), *SEMIRAMIDE RICONOSCIUTA* (1733), *ARBACE* (1734, based on Metastasio's *Artaserse*) and *DIDONE ABBANDONATA* (April 1737).   GRAHAM H. CUMMINGS

M. Burden, 'Metastasio on the London Stage: Adaptations and Permutations', *Studies in Music from the University of Western Ontario*, 16 (1997), 111–34

E. Hilscher and A. Sommer-Mathis (eds.), *Pietro Metastasio (1698–1782), 'uomo universale'* (Vienna, 2000)

S. T. Knight and M. Burden (eds.), 'Metastasio: 1698–1782', *EM* 26/4 (Nov. 1998)

D. Neville, 'Metastasio and the Image of Majesty in the Austro-Italian Baroque', *Italian Culture in Northern Europe in the 18th Century*, ed. S. West (Cambridge, 1999)

Methodism. See NONCONFORMITY; WESLEYS

Meyerbeer, Giacomo ('Meyer Beer') (b. Tasdorf near Berlin, 5 Sept. 1791; d. Paris, 2 May 1864). Composer. He became acquainted with Handel's music when he joined the SING-AKADEMIE ZU BERLIN in 1805, and came to regard Handel, GLUCK and MOZART as role models for his own compositions. He heard Handel's music performed at Berlin, Vienna, VENICE and London, and oratorio performances directed by Johann Nepomuk Schelble in Frankfurt left a lasting impression on him. Meyerbeer owned and studied scores of Handel's works (including *ACIS AND GALATEA, ALEXANDER'S FEAST, THE CHOICE OF HERCULES, JEPHTHA, JOSHUA* and *MESSIAH*), and in 1845 he orchestrated the recitative and aria 'Lascia ch'io pianga' from *RINALDO*. In 1850 he arranged the recitative and air 'Leave me, loathsome light' from *SEMELE*. He also included music by Handel in concerts at the Prussian court, and was a board member of the *Deutsche Händel-Gesellschaft* between 1856 and 1862. He unsuccessfully attempted to stage Mozart's arrangement of *Acis and Galatea* as a fund-raiser for the statue of Handel (MONUMENTS) to be erected in HALLE.

WERNER RACKWITZ (Trans. ANGELA BAIER)

B. Baselt, 'Miscellanea Haendeliana 3', *Der Komponist und sein Adressat*, ed. S. Bimberg (Halle, 1976)

Juden Bürger Berliner. Das Gedächtnis der Familie Beer-Meyerbeer-Richter, ed. S. Kuhrau, K. Winkler and A. Uebe (Berlin, 2004)

G. Meyerbeer, *Briefwechsel und Tagebücher*, ed. H. Becker (vols. 1–2), H. and G. Becker (vols. 3–4) and S. Henze-Döring (vols. 5–8) (Berlin, 1960–2006)

W. Rackwitz, '"Jephta: eines seiner herrlichsten Werke". Die Händelbeziehungen von G. Meyerbeer', *GHB* XII (2008)

Mi palpita il cor, HWV 132[a–d]. An unnamed male character depicts his love distress in the most vivid terms: heart-throbbing, anguish, chest pain, fear of death. This quasi-clinical approach, far more eloquent than in most similar lyrics of the period, sinks into a conventional blaming of both the insentive Clori and Cupid, who is asked to wound her heart with 'equal arrow'. Under this condition, the singing Ego would pay Cupid humble worship and recover his own health. The uneven literary quality is probably explained through evidence in the sources for a multi-stage composition, with continuo cantata HWV 106 (Dimmi, o mio cor) as the earliest version originated in Italy, then enlarged and adapted to changing combinations of forces during Handel's first years in London. A parallel shift of poets is envisageable.

Although the apparently last version for alto, flute, oboe and continuo (HWV 132[d]) achieves more nuanced colour, each of the previous ones has its particular merit. The opening sequence recitative–arioso–recitative, providing most opportunity for dramatic expression through great rhythmic and harmonic liberty, later found its way into *SAMSON*.

CARLO VITALI

Michaelsen. See HANDEL, 9

Middlesex, Earl of (Charles Sackville; later 2nd Duke of Dorset) (b. 6 Feb. 1711; bap. St Martin-in-the-Fields, London, 25 Feb. 1711; d. London, 6 Jan. 1769). Lord Middlesex made two visits to Italy (grand tour 1731–3; and 1737–8). He directed Italian opera in London between 1739 and 1748, finding himself initially competing with Handel to attract London's 'quality' audience. As well as opera, Middlesex was a leader of the Society of Dilettanti. Middlesex's early years of 'serious play' put him in debt and contributed to a long and bitter quarrel with his father which hurt his political career. He did not succeed to the dukedom until 1767, so sat in the House of Commons for most of his life. He supported the government until 1747, when he joined FREDERICK, Prince of Wales, in Opposition. After the Prince died in 1751 Middlesex's politics became once again more mainstream. CAROLE TAYLOR

John Ingamells (comp.), A Dictionary of British and Irish Travellers in Italy 1701–1800 (New Haven, 1997)

R. Sedgwick, 'Sackville, Charles, (1711–69) Earl of Middlesex', History of Parliament, House of Commons, 1715–1754, vol. 2 (London, 1971)

Middlesex Opera Company. Lord MIDDLESEX was principal director of Italian opera in London between 1739 and 1748. In the summer of 1743 he offered Handel £1,000 to write two operas for the company. Handel wavered but ultimately refused. In so doing he angered the opera party and hurt some of his friends, notably J. C. SMITH SENIOR who had got caught up in the negotiations. In light of this, Handel's production of the operatic SEMELE in his oratorio season the following spring was perceived by Middlesex's supporters as an unforgivable act of competitive defiance. The closest Middlesex came to producing anything by Handel was a revival of ALESSANDRO, produced as ROSSANE in 1743–4, presumably with the composer's permission. Middlesex was luckier in his efforts to bring native Italian talent to London, including composers GALUPPI (in 1741), Lampugnani (in 1743), GLUCK (in 1745), the castrato Angelo Maria Monticelli (in 1741) and others. Middlesex always lacked the princely sums necessary to sustain Italian opera's financial fortunes. In 1743 matters worsened when he alienated his major subscribers by suing them for deficit payments many felt should have been avoided. Taste for Italian opera was in decline in the 1740s, and this period marks the end of an era of London opera production. CAROLE TAYLOR

See also Francesco VANNESCHI

C. Taylor, 'From Losses to Lawsuit: Patronage of the Italian Opera in London by Lord Middlesex, 1739–1745', ML 68/1 (Jan. 1987), 1–25

'Handel's Disengagement from the Italian Opera', Handel: A Tercentenary Collection, ed. S. Sadie and A. Hicks (London, 1987)

Miller, James (b. Bridport, 11 Aug. 1704; d. London, 27 April 1744). English author and priest, librettist of JOSEPH AND HIS BRETHREN. He studied at Wadham College, OXFORD, was ordained, and served as a preacher at Trinity and Roehampton chapels, London. As a writer of comedies he was initially successful, but his strong poetic satires of degenerate taste, political corruption and religious slackness damaged his career, while gaining him respect from fellow authors and moralists including POPE. Initially critical of Handel for writing Italian opera, Miller praised him for his oratorios in the 1735 edition of *Harlequin Horace* and in *The Art of Life* (1739). His comedy *The Universal Passion* (1737) included a song by Handel, 'I like the am'rous youth that's free' (SONGS). *Pigeon-Pye*, a skit on Miller, associates him with Handel's music and singers. Handel subscribed to his *Miscellaneous Works* (1741).   RUTH SMITH

B. Joncus, 'Handel at Drury Lane: Ballad Opera and the Production of Kitty Clive', *JRMA* 131/2 (2006), 179–226

R. Smith, 'Handel's English Librettists', *Cambridge Companion to Handel*, ed. D. Burrows (Cambridge, 1997)

Oratorios

Milton, John (b. London, 9 Dec. 1608; d. Chalfont St Giles, Bucks., 8 Nov. 1674). English poet. His father John Milton senior was a scrivener and an amateur composer, and music-making was an important aspect of the poet's childhood. He attended St Paul's School and received a classical humanist education at Christ's College in CAMBRIDGE (1625–32). His early poetry is composed in Latin, Italian and English. In 1638–9 he went on a Grand Tour to France and Italy, where he met Galileo and collected music by Marenzio, Gesualdo and Monteverdi. Upon his return to London he became an active polemicist. During the English Civil War his political sympathies were with the Puritans and Republicans, and during the Commonwealth he advocated civil rights, freedom of the press and divorce on the grounds of incompatibility. He was Oliver Cromwell's secretary in the Council of State from 1649, but by 1652 the onset of his complete blindness was exacerbated by an eye disease. After the Restoration he was imprisoned. Fortunate to avoid execution, he withdrew from public life. Scorned by his embarrassed daughters, Milton's disappointment at the failure of the English Revolution and personal anguish may be regarded as decisive influences in his late masterpieces *Paradise Lost* (1658–63) and the classically inspired tragedy *Samson Agonistes* (published 1671, but possibly written much earlier).

By the time Handel was established in London Milton had become established as a revered British literary hero, and in 1737 a monument to the poet was belatedly erected in WESTMINSTER ABBEY. Handel's first documented encounter with Milton's poetry was a reading of *Samson Agonistes* at the Earl of SHAFTESBURY's in 1739, and a few months later the composer set Milton's youthful poems *L'Allegro* and *Il Penseroso* (?1631) in *L'ALLEGRO, IL PENSEROSO ED IL MODERATO*. Many contemporaries quickly came to regard the combination of Handel's music and Milton's poetry as an ideal 'sublime' pairing. In 1741, Newburgh HAMILTON adapted *Samson Agonistes* for Handel's *SAMSON*, which also incorporated texts adapted from at least fifteen of Milton's lesser-known early poems. The powerless and blind title hero had been likened to the old Milton by contemporary and later readers; a similar identification was later made between Milton, Samson and the elderly blind Handel (HANDEL, 16).

During a visit to Lord GAINSBOROUGH at Exton in 1745 Handel set three epilogue songs for a domestic performance of Milton's *Maske presented at Ludlow Castle* (*COMUS*), which the poet had originally written in 1634 for a collaboration with Henry Lawes (whose music is lost). Also in 1745, Hamilton again adapted Milton's psalm paraphrases for Handel's *OCCASIONAL ORATORIO*. However,

Handel refused to set librettos based on *Paradise Lost* by Mrs DELANY (1744) and John Upton (1746).   HANS DIETER CLAUSEN (Trans. ANGELA BAIER)

Burrows and Dunhill
D. Danielson (ed.), *The Cambridge Companion to Milton* (Cambridge, 1989)
R. M. Myers, *Handel, Dryden and Milton* (London, 1956)
R. Smith, 'Handel, Milton, and a New Document from their English Audience', *Handel Institute Newsletter* 14/3 (Autumn 2003)

Minato, Niccolò (b. Bergamo, c.1630; d. Vienna, 28. Feb. 1698). Italian poet and librettist. Many of his librettos were first set by Antonio Draghi, and among other composers who used them were LEGRENZI, BONONCINI, HASSE and TELEMANN. Minato's *Xerse* was set by Francesco Cavalli and performed in VENICE in 1655; it is typical of mid-seventeenth-century librettos, having many characters and a mixture of styles, with comic scenes for servants. Later in the century the more concentrated plots of the opera seria became the fashion, and in 1694 *Xerse* was rewritten by STAMPIGLIA and set by BONONCINI. This version was the source for Handel's *SERSE*, but many of the aria texts were unchanged from Minato, including the famous 'Ombra mai fu'.   TERENCE BEST

Mondonville, Jean-Joseph Cassanéa de. See HANDEL, 19

Montagnana, Antonio (b. Venice or the Veneto, fl. 1730–50). Italian bass singer (F–f′). He sang in the Handel/HEIDEGGER company at the KING'S THEATRE for two seasons (1731–3), during which he performed the roles of Varo in *EZIO*, Altomaro in *SOSARME* and Zoroastro in *ORLANDO*, as well as taking parts in revivals of several other Handel operas and English works: *ESTHER* (Haman), *ACIS AND GALATEA* (Polyphemus) and *DEBORAH* (Abinoam). At the end of the second season he left Handel's company to join the newly formed OPERA OF THE NOBILITY, remaining with them for four seasons and continuing in London for the season of 1737–8 at the King's Theatre, when he performed in *FARAMONDO* and *SERSE*. Thereafter he left London and during the 1740s was a court musician at Madrid. He had performed in operas by PORPORA in Rome and Turin during 1730–1, and his association with the composer was renewed in London with the Nobility operas. He probably joined with SENESINO in promoting some contention within Handel's company during 1732–3, and the strong role of Zoroastro in *Orlando* may have been designed to reduce his disaffection. His final Handel role, as Ariodate in *Serse*, is not entirely flattering.

DONALD BURROWS

Montagu, John Montagu, 2nd Duke of (b. Boughton, 29 March 1690; d. London, 6 July 1749). Army officer, politician, opera-lover. Montagu was a director of the newly formed Royal Academy of Music (OPERA COMPANIES, 2) and a subscriber to the MIDDLESEX OPERA COMPANY in the 1740s. As master-general of the Ordnance, he was responsible for the fireworks display in celebration of the peace that ended the War of the AUSTRIAN SUCCESSION. When Handel baulked at holding the rehearsal of his *MUSIC FOR THE ROYAL FIREWORKS* at VAUXHALL GARDENS, the Duke had the King's concurrence with the substitution of another composer's music if Handel did not comply. Montagu's daughter Isabella (d. 1786) married William Montagu, 2nd Duke of Manchester (1700–39).   DAVID HUNTER

D. Hunter, 'Rode the 12,000? Counting Coaches, People, and Errors en route to the Rehearsal of Handel's *Music for the Royal Fireworks* at Spring Gardens, Vauxhall in 1749', *London Journal* (forthcoming)

monuments. In 1738 Louis-François ROUBILIAC was commissioned to sculpt a marble statue of Handel to be erected in VAUXHALL GARDENS. It portrayed the composer as a mythical figure from one of his own works. The public regarded Handel as the legitimate successor of Henry PURCELL and compared him to Orpheus or Apollo, but the statue is also a life-size realistic portrait of the composer. Roubiliac also sculpted the monument to Handel in WESTMINSTER ABBEY, towards the cost of which Handel bequeathed £600 in the fourth codicil to his will (HANDEL, 8).

In 1806 the sculptor Johann Gottfried Schadow (1764–1850) was commissioned by Crown Prince Ludwig of Bavaria to design a number of busts to be erected in the Walhalla Hall of Fame near Donaustauf on the River Danube. Schadow executed a plaster mask of Handel on the basis of a drawing in 1815/16, and the marble bust was then carved by Ridolfo Schadow (1786–1822) in ROME.

The erection of a monument in HALLE was suggested to commemorate the centenary of Handel's death, and this suggestion was eagerly responded to by Hallensians and Handelians in the rest of Germany and England. The monument by Hermann Rudolf Heidel (1810–65) was unveiled in a festive ceremony on 1 July 1859.

In the Grand Foyer of the Paris Opera four musicians represent the music of four great European nations. *Haendel* (including a Hallensian coat of arms), designed by Jean-Jules Salmson, represents English music. Handel is also 'immortalised' in London's Albert Memorial (in HYDE PARK), where he is included in an illustrious circle of national and European personalities in the field of intellectual history. He can be seen among the musicians and poets on the podium frieze.   EDWIN WERNER (Trans. ANGELA BAIER)

See also ICONOGRAPHY

S. Aspden, '"Fam'd Handel Breathing, tho' Transformed to Stone": The Composer as Monument', *JAMS* 55/1 (2002), 67–90

D. Bindman, M. Baker, *Roubiliac and the Eighteenth-Century Monument: Sculpture as Theatre* (New Haven, 1995)

H. Mackowsky, *Die Bildwerke Gottfried Schadows* (Berlin, 1951)

W. Piechocki, 'Zur Geschichte des Händel-Denkmals in Halle', *HJb* 31 (1985)

K. Sproxton, 'Bach and St. Pancras', *MT* 91 (Aug. 1950), 315–16

Morell, Thomas (b. Eton, Bucks., 18 March 1703; d. Turnham Green, Middx., 19 Feb. 1784). English classicist, priest and author (see Figure 20). He studied at Eton College and King's College, CAMBRIDGE (ordained 1725, BA 1726, MA 1730, DD 1743). Notwithstanding his humble origins (his father was a saddler), his education, qualifications and abilities promised distinction in academia or the Church. He attempted both but progressed in neither: improvident, easy-going and insouciant, he was ill equipped for career-building. He began hopefully as sub-curate of the Chapel of St Anne, Kew Green, where Queen CAROLINE was

T. MORELL, S.T.P · S.S.A.

20. Thomas Morell, engraving by James Basire after William Hogarth, 1762.

patron. At her instigation he wrote a commentary on John Locke's *Essay concerning Human Understanding*, but to his mortification she preferred the ignorant 'thresher poet' Stephen Duck as librarian of her Hermitage. His other church appointments were as rector of Buckland, Hertfordshire (a poor King's College living which he held from 1737 but where he resided only until 1742), Fairchild lecturer (1768–83) and chaplain to the Portsmouth garrison (1776–82).

Wholeheartedly dedicated to teaching Christian doctrine, Morell enjoyed a reputation as a useful visiting preacher, catching James Boswell's admiration with a sermon against Methodists at the Temple Church in 1769 (NONCONFORMITY). His surviving sermons include one on the parallel between Old Testament Israel and modern Britain in time of war, and a Three Choirs FESTIVAL sermon in defence of cathedral music. His religious verses (2nd edn, 1736) contributed to the defence of orthodox Christianity against freethinking and shed interesting light on his librettos.

Morell worked principally as a freelance scholar and author. He had a typically eighteenth-century scholar's enquiring mind and was indefatigably industrious. Elected a fellow of the Society of Antiquaries in 1737, he became one of its two secretaries (a post created for him) in 1768, when he also became a Fellow of the Royal Society. He was esteemed as a philologist and classicist, producing editions of Aeschylus, Sophocles and Euripides, a translation with commentary of Seneca's epistles, a thesaurus of Greek prosody still in use in the nineteenth century and revisions of the standard Greek and Latin dictionaries. His edition of Ainsworth's Latin dictionary enlarged it by over 6,000 words; his abridged version (1774) was still being issued in the 1880s. He was deeply read in English literature, as his librettos show; his specimen publication (1737) of part of the *Canterbury Tales* earned him a place in the history of Chaucer scholarship. Some of his political verse (supporting the opposition party of Prince FREDERICK) was published by the *Gentleman's Magazine*.

Morell's long and contented marriage to the socially superior Anne Barker of the Grove, Chiswick, brought him into contact with the family of Lord BURLINGTON, whose property adjoined his in-laws'. By at least 1736 the Morells were living in a quite sizeable house at Turnham Green (north-west Chiswick). Here Morell established a large circle of friends who valued his good humour, narrative talent, camaraderie, affectionate banter and willingness to be helpful. They included William HOGARTH (whose *Analysis of Beauty* he helped to finish), David Garrick and James Thomson.

Morell may have heard a Handel oratorio as early as 1733, when he took an OXFORD MA while Handel was performing at the Encaenia. He recorded that he began writing for Handel in response to a request from the composer backed by the Prince of Wales; but this account (Cambridge University Library, Add. MS 4251:979), written late in life, is not wholly reliable. His first libretto for Handel, *JUDAS MACCABAEUS*, celebrated the Duke of Cumberland's suppression of the 1745 JACOBITE Rebellion (Prince WILLIAM); Cumberland gave him £20 for the dedication. He subsequently wrote the librettos for *ALEXANDER BALUS*, *THEODORA* and *JEPHTHA*, text for the vocal numbers of the unperformed *ALCESTE*, possibly the libretto of The *CHOICE OF HERCULES*, and the new text required for The *TRIUMPH OF TIME AND TRUTH*. Handel bequeathed him £200. For J. C. SMITH JUNIOR he confected librettos to existing music by Handel: *Nabal* (1764), *Tobit* (?1764) and *Gideon* (1769) (PASTICCIOS, 2). His command of biblical, classical and English literature, facility for turning verses, musical ability (his chief 'attributes' in Hogarth's portrait of him are books and an organ), aural sensitivity (attested by a letter in King's College Cambridge Modern Archives and by his careful underlaying of text for Smith's pasticcios), as well as his amiability and constant need of cash, made him a good choice as librettist.   RUTH SMITH

R. G. King, 'John Christopher Smith's Pasticcio Oratorios', ML 79/2 (1998), 190–218
    'Who Wrote the Texts for Handel's *Alceste*?', MT 150/1906 (Spring 2009)
R. Smith, 'Thomas Morell and his Letter about Handel', JRMA 127/2 (2002), 191–225

Moritzburg. See HALLE

Mosel, Ignaz (von), (b. Vienna, 1 or 2 April 1772; d. Vienna, 8 April 1844). Composer, music historian, conductor and Viennese court secretary. Ennobled in 1817, he became vice-director of the court theatre in 1821, and from 1826 he also directed the Vienna Burgtheater until he became first custodian of the court library in 1829. On 29 November 1812 he directed a performance of *ALEXANDER'S FEAST* featuring 590 musicians and singers, which was referred to as the 'Monsterkonzert'. Mosel included Handel's music in festivals of the *Gesellschaft der Musikfreunde* until 1816, and made ARRANGEMENTS of eight oratorio-style works using a similar procedure to Mozart's, including SAMSON, ISRAEL IN EGYPT, JEPHTHA, DEBORAH (never performed; Mosel's arrangement is now lost), SOLOMON, HERCULES, BELSHAZZAR and ATHALIA. Three of these editions and several of his oratorio translations were published. He also arranged the Utrecht Te Deum (TE DEUM, 1) and single pieces from other works, which he often inserted into the oratorios. His 'Mass in D' is a compilation of pieces taken from several Handel psalm settings.

HARTMUT KRONES (Trans. ANGELA BAIER)

Th. Antonicek, I. von Mosel (1772–1844). Biographie und Beziehungen zu den Zeitgenossen, Ph.D. dissertation (University of Vienna, 1962)

I. Mosel, 'Erklärung wegen der angekündigten Herausgabe der Händel'schen Oratorien Jephta, Salomon etc.', AMZ 32 (1830), 788

Mozart, (Johann Chrysostom) Wolfgang Theophilus (Gottlieb, Amadeo, Amadè) (b. Salzburg, 27 Jan. 1756; d. Vienna, 5 Dec. 1791). Austrian composer and keyboard virtuoso. As child prodigies, Mozart and his sister were taken round Europe, and were in London for a year (1764–5), meeting the Handel-loving King GEORGE III, and musicians such as J. C. Bach and BURNEY. It is likely that he heard a good deal of Handel's music, mainly oratorio and choral repertoire, and that some published keyboard music (certainly including fugues) was purchased and taken home to Salzburg. Mozart's early maturity was governed by repeated failure to find better employment away from Salzburg. There he worked in the cathedral, producing numerous works for the Catholic liturgy as well as serenades, symphonies and concertos; but he had little chance to write operas. Mozart visited Italy three times (1769–72), presenting three serious operas in Milan. Munich later offered two commissions, the second, Idomeneo (1781), Mozart's magnificent contribution to the reform of Italian opera seria (the resonant choruses owe something to GLUCK who, in turn, was indebted to Handel). During 1781 Mozart broke free of the Archbishop of Salzburg and settled in Vienna as a freelance. He was patronised by the Emperor and nobility, held a court appointment from 1787, and before he died had been nominated as the next organist at St Stephan's Cathedral. After the German opera Die Entführung aus dem Serail (1782), his work initially centred on the piano (teaching, performing and composing concertos). He later experienced financial problems, despite being invited to compose several operas (three Italian comedies, Die Zauberflöte and La clemenza di Tito).

Soon after settling in Vienna Mozart began to frequent the house of the imperial librarian and censor Baron Gottfried van SWIETEN, an enthusiast of music by Handel and the BACHs. This led not only to Mozart's Handel ARRANGEMENTS (2) but to a more general intensification of his musical language. Some of the resultant compositions, notably fugues, were not saleable and survive as fragments (they may have been finished as improvisations). Mozart composed part of a suite (K399/385i) often dubbed 'in Handelian style', although other influences, notably J. S. and C. P. E. Bach, are also apparent. It consists of a 'French overture' in C major (a noble Grave and brisk fugue), an Allemande in C minor, a Courante in E flat and an unfinished Sarabande in G minor.

Like Handel, Mozart was trained in Italian styles and indeed studied counterpoint formally with Martini in Bologna. In his early sacred music, his contrapuntal writing usually resembles Handel's more than Bach's, but this was not necessarily the outcome of any direct influence. In Vienna, opportunities to compose choral music were limited, but his cantatas for the Freemasons and the unfinished C minor Mass possess Handelian gravity and directness as well as Bachian intensity and, particularly the Mass, Mozartian lyricism; the Mass was reworked as a very un-Handelian oratorio, *Davidde penitente*, in 1785. Mozart's last work, the unfinished Requiem, is much indebted to Handel. The Introit uses the *The ways of Zion do mourn* (ANTHEMS, 5) as a compositional model and stimulus, and the 'Alleluia' double fugue from the Dettingen Te Deum (TE DEUM, 5; also used in *JOSEPH AND HIS BRETHREN*) provided the subject and countersubject ('Kyrie eleison, Christe eleison').　JULIAN RUSHTON

D. Burrows, 'Performances of Handel's Music during Mozart's Visit to London in 1764–5', HJb 38 (1992)
C. Eisen, 'The Mozarts' Salzburg Music Library', *Mozart Studies* 2, ed. C. Eisen (Oxford, 1997)
J. Rushton, *Mozart* (New York, 2006)
C. Wolff, *Mozart's Requiem: Historical and Analytical Studies* (trans. M. Whittall, Berkeley and Los Angeles, 1994)

Muffat, Gottlieb (bap. Passau, 25 April 1690; d. Vienna, 9 Dec. 1770). Vienna court organist. He composed mostly organ and keyboard works, among them six suites and a ciaccona which were published (probably in 1736) under the title *Componimenti Musicali per il Cembalo*. Handel borrowed eighteen movements from this collection, in their entirety or in parts, for the *SONG FOR ST CECILIA'S DAY*, several of the Concerti grossi, Op. 6 (ORCHESTRAL WORKS, 2), *JOSHUA*, *THEODORA*, *JUDAS MACCABAEUS*, *SOLOMON* and *SAMSON*. Muffat in turn used Handel's harpsichord suites for teaching purposes and added his own ornamentation.　HARTMUT KRONES (Trans. ANGELA BAIER)

H. Krones, 'Gottlieb Muffat und Georg Friedrich Händel: zwei Meister – drei Stile', HJb 50 (2004)

Münster. See SOURCES AND COLLECTIONS, 13

museums

1. Händel-Haus (Halle)
2. Handel House Museum
3. Foundling Museum

1. Händel-Haus (Halle)

The house in which Handel was born is first recorded in 1558 as a 'municipal leasehold'. On 30 June 1666 Handel's father, Georg Händel, bought it for 1,310 guilders from Susanne Bley, who had lived in the stately building 'Zum gelben Hirsch' (The yellow stag) since 1654. After Georg Händel's death in 1697, the property passed to his widow and children (HANDEL, 9). Handel lived here until his departure for HAMBURG in 1703. After the death of his mother in 1730, his niece Johanna Friederike Michaelsen presumably lived in the house with her husband Dr Johann Ernst Flörcke from 1755. She died in 1771, leaving the property to her second daughter, Dorothea Luise. In 1783 the property was publicly auctioned off.

The house was established as the civic music museum of HALLE between 1937 and 1948. It was intended from the beginning as a Handel memorial, but also as a more general music museum for the city, and as a museum in its literal sense (i.e. a place where the muses abide), where music should be researched, edited, taught and performed. Accordingly the museum continues to concentrate on three main activities: Handel, the musical history of the region and historical instruments; each aspect is presented in permanent exhibitions. The Händel-Haus organises an annual programme of concerts and recitals, which reaches its high point during the annual Handel FESTIVALS. The museum houses the offices of the Hallische Händel-Ausgabe ('HHA'; EDITIONS, 7) and the Georg-Friedrich-Händel-Gesellschaft (HANDEL SOCIETIES, 3). In 2008 the Händel-Haus was transformed into a public trust.   EDWIN WERNER

2. Handel House Museum

Handel's London home for the final thirty-six years of his life opened as a museum in November 2001 following a nine-year campaign initiated by Stanley Sadie. The importance of 25 Brook Street is clear: Handel composed much of his best-loved music and died there. The house also provides context for many of the anecdotes associated with him. Some of the surviving portraits – the unflattering GOUPY images and the WOLFGANG the Younger miniature – offer corroboration for the instruments he is known to have owned. The inventory of his effects and the sale catalogue of his art collection (HANDEL, 18) provide further insights, particularly into the manner of his later life.

Handel was the first resident of the terraced house at 25 Brook Street, but never the owner. He occupied the whole of it and it was the centre of his working life. Not only did he compose there, he rehearsed his singers, entertained his friends and conducted business – according to the *London Daily Post* and the *Craftsman* from the late 1730s he even sold copies of his music and from the 1740s subscriptions to his oratorio performances.

At present, the museum occupies the upper floors of both 23 and 25 Brook Street, which are now interconnected. The drawing room on the second floor and Handel's bedroom on the third are furnished with period furniture. The museum owns modern copies of a two-manual Ruckers harpsichord, a one-manual Smith harpsichord, and a chamber organ similar to those Handel kept at the house. The Handel House Collection includes original portraits, manuscripts, early editions of his music and biographies as well as a library of related eighteenth-century literature and performance history, commemorative objects and other memorabilia.

The Museum hosts regular concerts and exhibitions. The British Harpsichord Society meets there monthly. Handel House Museum is exceptional among composer museums for its innovative programme of educational events and activities, some involving a composer- and an ensemble-in-residence. Since 2006, the Museum has sponsored an annual Stanley Sadie Memorial Lecture. In 2007 the Trustees succeeded in acquiring a 999-year lease on the ground and lower-ground floors of No. 25 with the intention of enlarging the museum.

JULIE ANNE SADIE

3. The Foundling Museum

In the centre of London's Bloomsbury, the museum tells the story of the FOUNDLING HOSPITAL and of its founders and governors, who included the campaigning philanthropist Thomas CORAM, the artist William HOGARTH and Handel. The museum traces the history of London's first children's charity from the eighteenth century to the present day, and holds a significant collection of works by artist supporters, including Hogarth, Gainsborough and Reynolds, displayed in interiors preserved from the original Foundling Hospital building. The Gerald Coke Collection (SOURCES AND COLLECTIONS, 7) now housed in the museum complements the Handel materials from the original Foundling Hospital, which include a bust of the composer by ROUBILIAC, manuscripts of the 'Foundling Hospital Anthem' annotated by the composer (ANTHEMS, 8), and the score and parts of *MESSIAH* bequeathed to the Hospital by Handel. The museum now hosts several musicological conferences and has a regular concert programme, as well as providing study facilities for the Handel collection.

KATHARINE HOGG

J. Greenacombe, 'Handel's House: A History of No. 25 Brook Street, Mayfair', *London Topographical Record* 25 (1985), 111–30

J. Riding, D. Burrows and A. Hicks, *Handel House Museum Companion* (London, 2001)

J. A. Sadie and S. Sadie, *Calling on the Composer: A Guide to European Composer Houses and Museums* (New Haven, 2005)

K. Wedd, *The Foundling Museum*, ed. R. Harris (London, 2004)

E. Werner, *The Handel House in Halle: History of the Building and Museum and Guide to the Handel Exhibition* (Halle, 2006)

Music for the Royal Fireworks, HWV 351. Orchestral suite. *Musick for the Royal Fireworks* was the propaganda title (Handel simply called it *Ouverture*) for a display commissioned by the worried British government to prop up the ineffectual Treaty of AIX-LA-CHAPELLE (present-day Aachen) after the War of the AUSTRIAN SUCCESSION, and to bolster the royal image. Although Horace Walpole complained that 'there has not been the least symptom of public rejoicing' (Walpole to Horace Mann, 24 October 1748), nevertheless tens of thousands turned out on 27 April 1749 to watch this most lavish public show of the eighteenth century (and none commented on Handel's music).

Visual symbolism was the real significance of the show; public fireworks with music was a long-standing European tradition; Italian and German 'pleasure fires' had been the delight of European courts since the sixteenth century. While fireworks would be the focus for a single evening, 'the Machine' with its emblems – described as 'The Temple of Peace' – stood for several months in GREEN PARK, in the centre of London (Figure 21). This theatrical contrivance was designed by the Chevalier Servandoni (originally Jean-Nicholas Servandony), who had previously worked for the KING'S THEATRE as a scene painter for Handel's operas during the 1720s, while the fireworks were devised and controlled by Gaetano Ruggieri and Giuseppe Sarti, both from Bologna.

First estimates of the expected musical forces were exaggerated; The *London Magazine*, 14 January 1749 claimed:

> The band of musick that is to perform at the fire-works in the green-park, is to consist of 40 trumpets, 20 French horns, 16 hautboys, 16 bassoons, 8 pair of kettle-drums, 12 side-drums, a proper number of flutes and fifes; with 100 cannon to go off singly at intervals, with the musick.

Handel's inclusion in the scheme, which came later, resulted in the reduced forces. His autograph manuscript is scored for 9 trumpets, 9 horns, 24 oboes,

21. 'A Perspective View of the Magnificent Structure erected in Green Park for the Royal Fire Works', c.1749.

12 bassoons, contra-bassoon, serpent, timpani and side-drums. There would have been no continuo or strings for the outdoor version, and all instruments were utilised en masse, with no solos indicated. Four-part strings were added later, probably for a concert performance at the FOUNDLING HOSPITAL.

The opening Overture was originally marked 'Concerto' and 'Adagio' (both erased by Handel), suggesting that the work had begun before the fireworks commission arrived; the opening theme derives from a keyboard *Aria* by Johann Philipp KRIEGER (1649–1725) and had already been used in the two concertos HWV 335a/b associated with the 'military' oratorios (ORCHESTRAL WORKS, 7). At the cadence before the Allegro, a *battaglia* in all but title, Handel indicated 'Bruit de Guerre', probably supplied by eighteen cannon. Otherwise no fireworks coincided with the music.

After a Bourrée for winds alone, La Paix, a pastoral siciliano (with BOR-ROWINGS from TELEMANN's *Musique de table*) has 'Tr.' added to the oboes as an afterthought; the notes are beyond the capacity of the natural trumpet, and Handel's marking certainly indicated flutes (i.e. *traversi*). La Réjouissance began as a simple symbolic fanfare for trumpets and percussion alone, to which Handel added winds (and later strings). The opening theme is found in other composers, including Giovanni PORTA's *Numitore* (the opera which had opened the Royal Academy of Music's (OPERA COMPANIES, 2) first season in 1720), and RAMEAU in *Naïs* (also written to celebrate the Peace). Handel had already written the second of the final Menuets as the third movement of the Overture to the *OCCASIONAL ORATORIO*.

The public rehearsal in VAUXHALL GARDENS on 21 April 1749 attracted 'an audience of above 12,000 [1,200 is more probable] persons... So great a resort occasioned such a stoppage on *London-Bridge*, that no carriage could pass for 3 hours.' On 27 April the royal family inspected the construction in Green Park and 'The whole Band of Musick (which began to play soon after 6 o'clock) perform'd at his Majesty's coming and going, and during his stay in the Machine'. The fireworks then *followed* the music once daylight had faded. The *Gentleman's Magazine* reported:

> At half an hour after eight, the works were begun by a single rocket from before the library, then the cannon within the chevaux de frize were fired; two rockets were afterwards discharg'd at the front camera of the inclosure, when 101 pieces of cannon placed on *Constitution-hill*, were discharged; after which a great number of rockets of different sorts, balloons, &c. were discharged, to surprising perfection.

The royal family watched the display from the Queen's Library. The event lasted about nine hours. The widely predicted mass fatalities did not materialise, but one accidental fire in a pavilion was quickly extinguished, and the temple's designer Servandoni threw a tantrum and drew his sword on the event's manager Charles Frederick (he was imprisoned until he apologised the following morning). Handel's music (or part of it) was heard again at the FOUNDLING HOSPITAL on 27 May 1749, with strings (and presumably reduced winds) probably with the 'Allegro ma non troppo' of the Concerto in D, HWV 335a, used as a finale after *La Paix*. The music was published in parts by John WALSH in June 1749, and featured the additional string parts, although the viola, second bassoon and contrabassoon parts were omitted. Handel's music was not printed in full score until Samuel ARNOLD's edition in 1788.   CHRISTOPHER HOGWOOD

T. Best and C. Hogwood (eds.), *Music for the Royal Fireworks*, HHA IV/13 (Kassel, 2007)

C. Hogwood, *Handel: Water Music and Music for the Royal Fireworks* (Cambridge, 2005)

(ed.), *Music for the Royal Fireworks* (facsimile of autograph score) (Kassel, 2004)

Muzio Scevola, HWV 13. Italian opera. Paolo ROLLI adapted the libretto from a text by Silvio STAMPIGLIA that was first set to music by BONONCINI for Vienna in 1710, although it had much earlier roots in a text written by Niccolò MINATO (first set by Cavalli for VENICE in 1665). Versions of the story were also set to music by STRADELLA (1679), KEISER (1695), MATTHESON (1702) and LOTTI (1712). The WORDBOOK of the Royal Academy of Music's (OPERA COMPANIES, 2) sixth opera production was dedicated by Rolli to GEORGE I, which suggests that perhaps the libretto was chosen in order to serve as a topical metaphor for patriotism and reconciliation. Moreover, the decision for each of the three Acts to be written by different composers provided an opportunity for the recently established opera company to show off its musical assets. The opening act was written by Filippo AMADEI, Act II was composed by Bononcini (who might have suggested the libretto to the Royal Academy, but did not recycle any music from his previous settings), and Handel provided the music for Act III. Operas created by a panel of colleagues were not unusual in Italy. Perhaps it was believed that a collaboration between the three contributors was a public demonstration of unity, but it was perceived by some of the London AUDIENCE as a competitive gesture between 'rivals': an eyewitness reported to a friend in Dresden that Handel 'easily triumphed over the others' (Deutsch, p. 126), and BURNEY later claimed that there was 'a premeditated plan, to try their several abilities, and determine pre-eminence'.

The complicated, convoluted and frequently implausible plot is based on events described in Book II of LIVY's *History of Rome*. The centrepiece of each Act is a renowned example of Roman bravery connected with King Porsena of Etruria's unsuccessful schemes to restore the exiled King Lucius Tarquinius to the throne of Rome in 508 BC. Act I features the heroic resistance of Horatius Cocles (Orazio) against the Etruscan invaders at the Sublician Bridge (other scenes during Amadei's third of the opera show Mucius Scaevola (Muzio) preparing to lead an attack against the Etruscan army, and his lover Cloelia (Clelia) attempting to engage the reluctant Porsena in single combat). Act II contains a scene in which Muzio undauntedly burns his own right hand as a self-imposed penance for his failure to assassinate Porsena (thus earning the respect of Porsena, who in Bononcini's Act proceeds to offer Rome a truce in exchange for taking Clelia and her female companions hostage). In Handel's Act III the heroine Cloelia and her companions escape by leaping into the Tiber and swimming across. The drama was substantially fleshed out with 'intermix'd amours'. Muzio and Porsena both desire Clelia (described at one point as 'a Roman Amazon'), but at the conclusion of the opera the enemy gallantly withdraws his suit for Clelia's hand in marriage, and decides that he would like nothing better than a Roman son-in-law (Orazio) to wed his daughter Irene and thereby inherit his kingdom. The villain Tarquinio has no arias and contributes little to proceedings.

Handel completed writing his contribution to *Muzio Scevola* on 23 March 1721. Its first performance at the KING'S THEATRE on 15 April was interrupted with loud applause when news was brought to George I that his grandson Prince WILLIAM had been born. The cast was as follows:

Muzio	SENESINO (castrato)
Orazio	Matteo Berselli (castrato)
Clelia, a Roman virgin	Margherita DURASTANTI (soprano)
Larte Porsena, King of Etruria	Giuseppe BOSCHI (bass)
Irene, Porsena's daughter	Anastasia ROBINSON (alto)
Fidalma, Irene's confidante	Maria Maddalena SALVAI (soprano)
Lucio Tarquinio	Caterina Galerati (soprano)

The opera ran for ten performances. Handel's third of the opera includes a two-movement French overture, eleven arias, two duets, a battle symphony, four accompanied recitatives and an amply orchestrated final chorus. Orazio's only aria 'Come, se ti vedrò' (III.vi) is a beautiful siciliano that contains an unusually high number of *ad libitum* markings that presumably allowed Berselli considerable freedom to embellish his part. It tenderly portrays Orazio's reluctant departure from his lover Irene, whose 'Ah dolce nome' (sung when captured by the cruel Tarquinio in III.ix) is an emotionally compelling B minor sarabande; the joyous 'Vivo senza alma' for Irene and Orazio (III.x) is an ideal contrast to the duet 'Mà come amar?' in the next scene, which conveys Muzio gradually winning back his offended lover Clelia. Muzio was the first part that Handel wrote for Senesino: 'Il confine della vita' (III.iv) was ideally suited to the castrato's 'pathetic' singing as an afflicted virtuous lover, whereas 'Per Roma giuro' (*scena ultima*) showed the singer's skill at heroic accompanied recitative.

Clelia's fast G minor aria 'Dimmi, crudele amore' (III.iii) is preceded by a passionate accompanied recitative that illustrates her feisty pride; her lively triplet-laden aria 'Lungo pensar' (III.i) features musical material borrowed from Lotti's *Giove in Argo*. Porsena's 'Volate più dei venti' (III.iv) is an animated D minor evocation of raging winds, and its middle section (in F major, larghetto, with an oboe solo) was an imaginative reworking of a theme that Handel had already adopted from Keiser in Il TRIONFO DEL TEMPO and AGRIPPINA. A beautiful first setting of Fidalma's 'A chi vive di speranza' (III.viii) redeveloped music from La TERRA È LIBERATA, but it was replaced by a jauntier alternative before the first performance (both are missing from CHRYSANDER's unreliable edition (EDITIONS, 5)).

The role of Fidalma was cut when *Muzio Scevola* was revived in November 1722 (three performances) to initiate the Royal Academy's third season. Handel never performed it again, but transferred seven of its numbers to revivals of *SCIPIONE* (1730), *ADMETO* (1731), *OTTONE* (1733) and *PARTENOPE* (1737). An all-Italian version revised by KEISER was staged at HAMBURG in 1723. The first modern revival of Handel's Act III was at Essen in 1928. The music by Amadei and Bononcini has never been published, but an abridged concert version of all three Acts was performed at OXFORD in 1977, and the complete second and third Acts were performed at the 2001 London Handel Festival (FESTIVALS, 5).

DAVID VICKERS

Burney
Dean and Knapp
Harris, *Librettos*
N. Rossi, 'Handel's *Muzio Scevola*', *Opera Quarterly* 3/3 (1985), 17–38
Strohm

My heart is inditing. See ANTHEMS, 3

My song shall be always. See ANTHEMS, 2

Nabal. See PASTICCIO, 2

Naples. A seaport on the Tyrrhenian sea and the capital of the Kingdom of Naples, roughly comprising the present regions of Campania, Abruzzi, Molise, Basilicata, Apulia and Calabria. During the first decade of the eighteenth century, Naples numbered some 220,000 inhabitants against 3 million in the whole kingdom. Naples thus ranked as the largest city in Italy and the third largest in Europe after Paris and London. The hypertrophic head of a rural country, it was a city of harsh social contrasts, where consumption by far outweighed production. It is estimated that bureaucracy and the forensic class accounted for one fifth of its population, while the clergy, running to roughly the same proportion, shared most of the available wealth with the royal court and the nobility. Arts and crafts flourished mainly to their benefit. According to Rogissart's period handbook for Grand Tourists, which extols the architectural beauties of Naples over those of Paris, ROME and VENICE, the whole kingdom counted 935 feudal lords (including 119 princes, 156 dukes and 173 marquises), most of them 'coming to Naples in order to eat out their revenues' despite strict anti-luxury regulations. On the other side, as various travellers report, a significant number of urban plebs lived on casual street trades and food distributions from the rich convents. More than any population in Italy, Rogissart wrote, Neapolitans 'are very languid and lazy'. Their inclination towards pleasure and passions would push the lower classes to 'crimes of every sort', therefore 'prisons are always crowded, and a common saying goes that Naples is a paradise inhabited by devils'. Nevertheless, their inordinate devotion, belief in miracles and 'the most outward appearances of religion' fill the city's churches with treasures.

Although retaining the (formally separate) vice-kingdom of Sicily, in summer 1707 Spain had yielded control over the city and kingdom of Naples to the Habsburg Empire (ITALY). The new viceroy (and operatic Venetian impresario) Cardinal Vincenzo GRIMANI arrived there on 30 June 1708. It is plausible to count him among the many 'principal persons' who, according to MAINWARING, bestowed their invitations and assignments on Handel, who tarried in Naples during mid-April–mid-July. The viceroyal household patronised music performances of operas and serenatas both in the royal palace and at the Teatro San Bartolomeo. The core forces for these activities were provided by the Chapel Royal, boasting outstanding composers, vocalists and instrumentalists, and also escorting the viceroy during church services at the cathedral or other official appearances.

Francesco Mancini led it for some months in 1708, then was superseded in December by Alessandro SCARLATTI, whom Grimani summoned back from Rome. Since 1706, the private Teatro dei Fiorentini had also shifted from Spanish drama to opera seria, while opera buffa – as distinct from comic intermezzos customarily interpolated within seria, was still in its prime. Domenico Sarro, Nicola PORPORA, Francesco Fago and Giuseppe Vignola were among the emerging composers of the day, much in demand among the noble households who lavishly celebrated dynastic festivals and family events with music performances, as did some hundred major churches and convents for their patron saints with high masses, sundry devotional services, oratorios and the like. The considerable amount of personnel needed for that thriving music industry was trained at the four male conservatories (Poveri di Gesù Cristo, Pietà dei Turchini, Sant'Onofrio a Porta Capuana and Santa Maria di Loreto) plus their female counterpart l'Annunziata. Conservatories were the cradle of the renowned Neapolitan school, attracting pupils from beyond the kingdom's boundaries and re-exporting them all over Europe, particularly composers and castrati. CARLO VITALI

See also *ACI, GALATEA E POLIFEMO*; *CUOPRE TAL VOLTA IL CIELO*; PALAZZI, 10–12

Le Sieur de Rogissart, *Les delices de l'Italie, qui contiennent une description exacte du pays, des principales villes . . .* (Leyden, 1706, 2nd edn, 1709)

National Socialist arrangements. During the Third Reich the National Socialists adapted music to support their ideology. Known by its progenitors as the *Händeloratorien-Renaissance*, the 'Aryanisation' of Handel's oratorios produced entertainments that were regarded as a timeless and idealised image of the 'musical *Volksschauspiel* [folk drama] of the future', and as the model for the future festivals of the *Volksgemeinschaft* (people's community of the Third Reich). The oratorios were shortened, texts from Old Testament sources were purged of all Jewish references, and the plots were usually replaced by stories fitting the prevalent political sentiments. Works that presented a hero leading his brave people to victory over the inferior foe with the help of God were used to draw parallels with Germany and German heroism.

The oratorio most frequently adapted by the Nazis was *JUDAS MACCABAEUS*, the best-known version was *Der Feldherr* (The War-Lord/The General) (1939; 155 performances). It was the third revision by Hermann Stephani, who had already made alterations in 1904. His second attempt, under the title of *Judas Maccabaeus. Vaterländisches Oratorium*, followed in 1914 and included cuts and rearrangements. The fictional plot of the 1939 version was set in the first year of the Second World War. The title *Der Feldherr* is an allusion to the Führer Adolf Hitler, and the dramatis personae was reduced to 'Der Feldherr' (tenor), 'Der Seher' (The Seer) (bass), 'Frauen aus dem Volke' (Women of the people) (soprano, alto) and 'Männer aus dem Volke' (Men of the people) (tenor, bass). The oratorio commences with the Fatherland defeated and the people in despair, but the Seer rouses them to fight for their Fatherland and freedom. The Feldherr conquers the foes; victory is assured through the spirit of self-sacrifice, heroism and the help of God.

An earlier rearrangement of *Judas Maccabaeus* had been commissioned in 1935 from Hermann Burte by the *Reichsstelle für Musikbearbeitung* (an office of the Propaganda Ministry, run mainly by Hans Joachim Moser). This version was entitled *Held und Friedenswerk* (Hero and labour of peace), and glorified Hitler. A year later, C. G. Harke and Johannes Klöcking created a so-called secular version, *Wilhelmus von Nassauen*. William of Orange defeats the tyrannical superpower of Spain, personified by the Duke of Alba, and a small Low German tribe, trusting in God, rises to heroic greatness and heralds a new era. The plot was meant as an allusion to the current National Socialist Germany under the Führer, and this version was first performed when German troops reoccupied the Rhineland on 7 March 1936. Another version, called *Freiheitsoratorium* (Freedom oratorio), was arranged by Ernst Wollong. The names of characters were changed to 'Der Führer des Volkes' (The leader of the people), 'Ein Heerführer' (A General), 'Bote' (messenger), 'Ein Mädchen und eine Frau aus dem befreiten Land' (a girl and a woman from the liberated country), 'Chor des Volkes und Chor der Jugend' (Chorus of people and chorus of the youth). The plot, intended as an analogy to contemporary political events, portrayed the people faithfully following their leader in the battle for freedom.

The *Fest-Oratorium* (1935) was an arrangement of the OCCASIONAL ORATO-RIO by Fritz Stein. First performed during the Berlin Olympic Games in 1936, Handel's original was shortened and its plot completely changed. Used for propaganda, it was about pain, fights, rebellions and the ultimate victory of a nation. Stein thought it especially suitable for national celebrations. A comparable reworking of JEPHTHA by Hermann Stephani retitled *Das Opfer* (1941) contained the roles 'Der Feldhauptmann' (The Captain), 'Der Heerführer' (The General), 'Die Mutter' (The Mother), 'Die Tochter' (The Daughter), 'Eine Vertraute' (A confidante) and 'Engel' (Angel). Stephani's plot concentrated on the 'super-personal', the 'super-national' and the 'super-temporal', and his adaptation was intended to convey that the entire German nation would uphold a solemn vow.

The *Reichsstelle für Musikbearbeitung* commissioned Harke and Klöcking to make an arrangement of ISRAEL IN EGYPT called *Der Opfersieg bei Walstatt* (The self-sacrifice for victory on the battlefield). It is set at the Battle of Liegnitz (Silesia) in 1241, when Duke Henry II attempted to halt the Mongol invasion of Europe; he was killed and his army defeated. Despite victory the Mongols did not penetrate any further into Europe, but instead returned to Asia because of political destabilisation caused by the death of the Mongol Emperor Genghis Khan. However, in *Opfersieg* the Mongols honourably withdraw because they are impressed by the Germanic bravery of Henry's army. The arrangement included all three parts of Handel's first performance version, renamed *Vorspruch* (Prologue), *Die Schlacht* (The Battle) and *Das Danklied* (The Song of Thanks), and with an entirely new text reminiscent of Richard Wagner's *Nibelungen*. It was hoped that *Opfersieg* would be performed at Breslau in autumn 1944 to encourage the Silesian people, but it was never performed because of the collapse of the Third Reich.

Klöcking's arrangement of JOSHUA was called *Die Ostlandfahrer*. He intended to create a counterpart to the Jewish conquest of Canaan, and chose the foundation of Lübeck as a German settlement by Adolf II, Count of Schauenburg and

Holstein. The publisher Kistner & Sigel agreed to print it in 1944, but there is no information about its performance. Werner Menke's attempt to adapt SAM-SON as the Wieland-Oratorium (1943) used the story from the Nordic Nibelungen Saga of Wieland the Smith, who tried to fly with artificial wings attached to his arms. Moser proposed that the story be changed to Daedalus and Icarus, but it seems that the project was not finished.   ANNETTE LANDGRAF

See also RECEPTION, 2

A. Landgraf, 'Der Opfersieg von Walstatt: Das Oratorium Israel in Egypt von Georg Friedrich Händel im nationalsozialistischen Gewand', Musikkonzepte – Konzepte der Musikwissenschaft, vol. 2, ed. K. Eberl and W. Ruf (Kassel, 2000)
P. M. Potter, 'The Politicization of Handel and his Oratorios in the Weimar Republic, the Third Reich, and the Early Years of the German Democratic Republic', MQ 85/2 (2001)
F. K. Prieberg, Musik im NS-Staat (Frankfurt, 1989)
W. Rackwitz, Geschichte und Gegenwart der Hallischen Händel-Renaissance. 2. Teil: 1929–1976 (Halle, 1979)
K. Roters, Bearbeitungen von Händel-Oratorien im Dritten Reich (Halle, 1999)

naturalisation. See HANDEL, 14

Neal(e)'s Musick Hall, DUBLIN. Commissioned by the music publisher William Neal(e) (d. 1769), and built down Fishamble Street from Christ Church Cathedral, the relatively unadorned room for musical performances was opened on 2 October 1741. Handel held his two series of subscription concerts there from 23 December 1741 to 7 April 1742, and gave the first performance of MESSIAH in it as a fund-raiser for three charities on 13 April. All that survives is part of a wall in the courtyard of an apartment building.   DAVID HUNTER

B. Boydell, A Dublin Musical Calendar, 1700–1760 (Blackrock, 1988)

Negri, Maria Caterina (b. Bologna, c.1705; d. after 1744). Italian contralto (compass: a–e″); sister of the mezzo-soprano Maria Rosa Negri. Her debut was probably at Modena in 1720. She sang at numerous Italian opera houses over the next four years, and worked in Prague from 1724 to 1727. She then sang in VIVALDI's operas at VENICE and NAPLES. In 1733 the Negri sisters joined Handel's opera company in London. Maria Caterina sang in all of his opera, pasticcio and oratorio performances during the next four seasons (Rosa, in contrast, was seldom required, which suggests that she was an unexceptional singer). Handel composed a mixture of male and female roles for her: Carilda (ARIANNA IN CRETA), Clori (PARNASSO IN FESTA), Polinesso (ARIODANTE), Bradamante (ALCINA), Irene (ATALANTA), Tullio (ARMINIO), Amanzio (GIUSTINO) and Arsace (BERENICE). She also sang in Handel's expanded 1734 version of Il PASTOR FIDO (HWV 8ᶜ). She left London in summer 1737, and continued to have an active singing career in Italy until at least 1744.   ARTIE HEINRICH

Nel dolce dell'oblio ('Pensieri notturni di Filli'), HWV 134. An accompanied cantata for soprano, recorder and basso continuo, this delicate work describes 'adored Filli (Phyllis)' dreaming of her beloved in her sleep. The text bears a relationship to Notte placida e cheta, in which a lover hopes to sleep so that he can dream of Fille (Phyllis), and it may be that Notte placida was written in response to Nel dolce dell'oblio. Both begin with arias in F major but then diverge harmonically: Nel *dolce dell'oblio* ending with a final aria in C major, and *Notte placida* concluding with arias in C minor and G minor. A shared motivic relationship between the C major and C minor arias, however, also connects the two works. Both cantatas were composed in ROME, *Nel dolce dell'oblio* can be tentatively dated to 1707, and *Notte placida* within the same year or shortly later.   ELLEN T. HARRIS

Nero, HWV 2. The premiere in HAMBURG on 25 February 1705 of Handel's second opera, *Die durch Blut und Mord erlangete Liebe, oder Nero* followed the premiere of ALMIRA by less than two months. There was time for at most three performances before the theatre closed for Lent, and the opera was never revived, maybe because KEISER's *Octavia*, with a rather similar cast of characters, proved more popular. Handel's music is lost, though much of it will surely have been reused in later works. The role of Nero provided MATTHESON with his swansong as Hamburg's leading tenor, which may have coloured his later assessment of it as a 'model tragic opera'.

The libretto, again by FEUSTKING, covers much of the ground of Monteverdi's *L'incoronazione di Poppea*, and with comparable disregard for moral niceties. Nero fancies Poppea and, in order to make her his empress, contrives spurious pretexts to get rid of his lawful wife Octavia; this essential dramatic action is cluttered with minor characters and subplots. In many respects it is a typical Hamburg libretto with rhymed recitative and a very large number of aria and ensemble texts, many in strophic form; unusually for this date, none of them is in Italian. During the controversy which *Nero* occasioned among rival Hamburg librettists, HUNOLD seemed to be paraphrasing Handel's own comments when he wrote, 'How shall a musician create something beautiful when he has no beautiful words? . . . there is no spirit in the poetry, and it was a vexation to set it to music.'   DAVID KIMBELL

Dean and Knapp, *Operas*
Harris, *Librettos*
HHB i
J. H. Roberts, 'Keiser and Handel at the Hamburg Opera', HJb (1990)
S. Stompor, 'Die deutschen Aufführungen von Opern Händels in der ersten Hälfte des 18. Jahrhunderts,' HJb (1978)
H. C. Wolff, *Die Barockoper in Hamburg, 1678–1738* (Wolfenbüttel, 1957)

Netherlands. Handel never lived or worked in the Netherlands, but his travels to and from the continent beginning in 1710 involved passing through the Low Countries, and after 1734, when his pupil Princess ANNE took up residence at the Dutch court, he had good reason to dwell there. Handel is reported by contemporaries to have travelled through the Netherlands in 1710 and 1737; he likely did so in 1711, 1712, 1716, 1719 and 1729 as well (HANDEL, 15). On 20 September 1740 he played the organ of the Groote Kerk at HAARLEM. In 1750, during his final trip to the continent, Handel returned to hear again that organ (27 August), apparently after his reported injury in a coach accident between Haarlem and the Hague; nothing more is known of the accident. Handel then visited Anne, performing for the Dutch court at Deventer on 8 September and twice at The Hague (2 and 7 December) before departing for London on 8 December.   RICHARD KING

R. G. King, 'Handel's Travels in the Netherlands in 1750', ML 72/3 (1991), 372–86

'Neun Deutsche Arien'. See GERMAN ARIAS

New Theatre in the Haymarket. See LITTLE THEATRE

Newman Flower Collection. See SOURCES and COLLECTIONS, 8

'Nicolino' (Grimaldi, Nicola) ('Nicolini', 'Nicolò') (bap. Naples, 5 April 1673; fl. 1697–1730; d. Naples, 1 Jan. 1732). Castrato, earlier soprano, then alto (range a–e″/f′). His stellar career, stretching well over a hundred stagings in the space of three decades, developed mainly in NAPLES, where he debuted at twelve in Provenzale's *Stellidaura vendicante*, and in VENICE, where he lived for long periods and in 1705 was awarded the knightly Cross of St Mark – hence his nickname 'Cavalier Nicolino'. His last Venetian triumph, in 1730, was the role of Artabano in the epoch-making *Artaserse* by HASSE, with FARINELLI and CUZZONI in the company.

On SWINEY's invitation, he spent a first period in London in 1708–12, with a short visit to DUBLIN in 1711 and a concert at court for Queen ANNE's birthday in 1712. He debuted at the Queen's Theatre (KING'S THEATRE) on 14 December 1708 in a bilingual revival of Alessandro SCARLATTI's *Pirro e Demetrio*, and sang primo uomo parts with overwhelming acclaim. *RINALDO*, marking Handel's operatic debut in London and the spectacular ascent of Italian opera seria there, owed much to Nicolino's contribution in the title role (February–June 1711; revived January–April 1712). The success was renewed in 1715–17 with the first run of *AMADIGI DI GAULA* (title role, May–July 1715; revivals in 1716 and 1717), plus a further revival of *Rinaldo*, January–June 1717). While in Great Britain, Nicolino also appeared in operas and pasticcios with music by BONONCINI, Mancini, GASPARINI and Scarlatti. In the roles Handel wrote for him, the central register goes c′–c″. Elegant and fluid melodies in syllabic writing, further developed in short flourishes, prevail (e.g. Rinaldo's 'Cara sposa'); but there are also instances of livelier movements, such as Rinaldo's 'Abbrugio, avvampo' and 'Or la tromba'.

In 1718, at Naples's Royal Palace, Nicolino revived the title role in Handel's *Rinaldo* with additional music by LEO. In fact, he pioneered the tendency to take the same characters over and over, irrespective of the music setting. Quantz – who heard him in 1726, thus past his vocal heyday – found him a middling singer but an excellent actor (see Marpurg, *Historisch-kritishe Beyträge*); the latter part of the judgement was enthusiastically shared by a host of British observers, such as Colley CIBBER, ADDISON, Richard Steele and BURNEY. It seems, however, that his ornate singing style rapidly grew out of fashion. Writing to FARINELLI in 1749, METASTASIO quotes 'Nicolino's and Matteuccio's stale catherine wheels' as a paragon of the 'bad old taste' allegedly embraced by CAFFARELLI.

Nicolino should not be confused with his colleagues Nicola Paris, alias Nicolino di Brunswick (castrato, fl. 1688–1705), Nicola Grimaldi from Senigallia (fl. c.1740), Niccolò Grimaldi (a Neapolitan buffo, fl. 1753–86). CARLO VITALI

E. Faustini-Fasini, 'Gli astri maggiori del bel canto napoletano: Il cavaliere Nicola Grimaldi, detto "Nicolino"', *Note d'archivio* (1935), 297–316

F. W. Marpurg, *Historisch-kritische Beyträge zur Aufnahme der Musik*, I. Band, Drittes Stück (Berlin, 1754), 'II. Lebensläuffe, A: Herrn Johann Joachim Quantzens Lebenslauf, von ihm selbst entworfen', 231

J. Milhous and R. D. Hume, 'Heidegger and Opera Management at the Haymarket, 1713–1717', EM 27/1 (1999), 65–84

Niedecken-Gebhard, Hanns (b. Ober-Ingelheim, 4 Sept. 1889; d. Michelstadt, 7 March 1954). Stage director of operas and plays. He studied music at the Leipzig Conservatory, and history of art and music in Lausanne, Leipzig and HALLE. At a seminar given by Hermann Abert in Halle he met Oskar HAGEN, who was later to found the GÖTTINGEN Handel Festival (FESTIVALS, 3). He organised small Handel festivals at theatres in Hanover and Münster, and styled himself *Director of Dancers and Masses in Movement* with his monumental stagings of Handel's oratorios. In 1922 he was invited by Hagen to stage *GIULIO CESARE* at Göttingen, which was so successful that he was asked to stage new productions of *RODELINDA*, *OTTONE* and *SERSE* (1923–4). Four years later, however, the dance style he had developed in collaboration with renowned specialists in Modern Dance had gone out of fashion, and his production of *EZIO* (BERLIN, 1928) was a failure. After working at the Metropolitan Opera in New York, he returned to Germany in 1933 and again staged works at Göttingen (1935–8). He was a member of the Nazi Party, and used his experience as a stage director for massive National Socialist festivals. After the war he returned for a third time to Göttingen, where he taught theatre studies.

ULRICH ETSCHEIT (Trans. ANGELA BAIER)

B. Helmich, *Händel-Fest und 'Spiel der 10.000'. Der Regisseur Hanns Niedecken-Gebhard* (Frankfurt, 1989)

'Nine German Arias'. See GERMAN ARIAS

Nisi Dominus. See Italian and Latin CHURCH MUSIC

No se emendará jamás, HWV 140. The only Spanish cantata composed by Handel, this is also unique in its setting for guitar and continuo (violoncello) and the use of anachronistic white notation in the score. In its text, the singer hopes his love is equal to his beloved. A bill for copying the work appears in the RUSPOLI account books for 22 September 1707. ELLEN T. HARRIS

See also INSTRUMENTATION, 16

Nonconformity, or 'dissent'. The 1662 Act of Uniformity required everyone to conform to the state religion, the CHURCH OF ENGLAND: religious uniformity meant political stability. But the seventeenth century had given birth to other Christian denominations, notably Presbyterians, Baptists and Quakers. From c.1730, these were joined by the Methodists, founded by John and Charles WESLEY. Nonconformists disagreed with the Church on matters of ceremony, organisation and doctrine, and refused to conform to the Act. They were denied public offices, but sympathy from the WHIGS gained them toleration. Handel's oratorios are partly a reaction to nonconformists (many of whom disapproved of music). KATIE HAWKS

See also HANDEL, 12

G. R. Cragg, *The Church and the Age of Reason* (1648–1789) (London, 1960)
Smith, *Oratorios*

non-jurors. Term coined to describe those Britons, mainly high-church Anglicans, who refused to forswear loyalty to the deposed STUART King James II and his descendants, and swear allegiance to the Hanoverians; they included Handel's friend and librettist Charles JENNENS. Most public appointments required oaths of allegiance to the crown and so were closed to non-jurors. Non-juring clergy continued to be ordained by non-juring bishops and minister to fellow adherents until the late eighteenth century. Some but by no means all non-jurors were also JACOBITES. RUTH SMITH

R. D. Cornwall, *Visible and Apostolic: The Constitution of the Church in High Church Anglican and Non-Juror Thought* (Newark, DE, 1993)

Noris, Matteo (b. Venice, 1640; d. Treviso, 6 Oct. 1714). A Venetian librettist of vast productivity and reputation. His *Flavio Cuniberto* (VENICE, 1682), in a revised version for ROME (possibly by Silvio STAMPIGLIA, 1696) was the source libretto for Handel's *FLAVIO*. Noris's *Nerone fatto Cesare* (Venice, 1693) influenced the libretto of Handel's *AGRIPPINA*. His *Tito Manlio* (Pratolino, 1696), revised by Nicola Francesco HAYM, was set by Attilio ARIOSTI for London in 1717. REINHARD STROHM

N. Dubowy, "'Un riso bizzarro dell'estro poetico": Il "Flavio Cuniberto" (1681) di Matteo Noris e il dramma per musica del secondo Seicento', *Musica e Storia* 12 (2004), 401–24

Notte placida e cheta, HWV 142. This cantata for solo soprano, two violins and continuo sets the undramatic complaint of a lover about his cruel belle, called 'Fille'. All he asks for is satisfaction in a dream. However, on being awakened, he concludes – in the typical mood of 'cantata morale' – that life is but a dream. The unidentified poet drew keywords and script from a favourite passage in TASSO's *Gerusalemme liberata* (VII/4), possibly with an eye on ARIOSTO's *Orlando Furioso* (XLIV.61) and a row of three sonnets entitled 'Sogno' in G. B. Marino's *Amori* (1614). Handel builds up the lyrical character of the first part through a pair of similar arias, both in F major and 3/8 metre. The ensuing 'dream scene' – a slow aria framed by two accompagnato recitatives – stands consistently in the minor keys, then abruptly gears into an energetic four-part fugue, whose leaping theme seems related to the first aria in *TU FEDEL? TU COSTANTE*. A likely date for composition is 1707–8. CARLO VITALI

Novello. See EDITIONS, 6

O be joyful in the Lord. See JUBILATE

O come, let us sing unto the Lord. See ANTHEMS, 2

O numi eterni ('La Lucrezia'). See CANTATAS

O praise the Lord with one consent. See ANTHEMS, 2

O praise the Lord, ye angels of his. See Maurice GREENE

O qualis de coelo sonus. See Italian and Latin CHURCH MUSIC

O sing unto the Lord a new song. See ANTHEMS, 1

Oboe. See INSTRUMENTATION, 13

Oboe concertos and Oboe Sonatas. See ORCHESTRAL WORKS, 4; CHAMBER MUSIC, 1

Occasional Oratorio, HWV 62. English oratorio. Handel's 1744–5 season had been abandoned before all of the promised performances were given, and in autumn 1745 he experienced serious health problems. He needed to produce a new oratorio for the coming season, and also had to make up for the missing three performances of the previous season that were owed to his subscribers. The *Occasional Oratorio* was originally designed for four soloists (two sopranos, a tenor and a bass) but contemporary documents make it clear that Handel had only three soloists for the first performance at COVENT GARDEN on 14 February 1746: Elisabeth Duparc, 'La FRANCESINA' (soprano), John BEARD (tenor) and Henry REINHOLD (bass). The orchestra was led by the violinist Willem DE FESCH, but Handel struggled to organise his band because the MIDDLESEX OPERA COMPANY would not permit members of the opera orchestra to participate. The oratorio was repeated on 19 and 26 February, but was poorly attended. It was revived on 6, 11 and 13 March 1747, when Caterina GALLI probably sang, and Francesina was replaced by Elisabetta de Gambarini.

In Part I, Handel borrowed the Menuet II from the *MUSIC FOR THE ROYAL FIREWORKS* for the overture, and the air 'Fly from threat'ning vengeance' was based on a 1745 addition to *SAMSON* ('Fly from the cleaving mischief'). Part II contains the chorus 'May God, from whom all mercies spring' from *ATHALIA*, and three numbers from *COMUS*. For Part III Handel transferred another from *Comus*, four movements from *ISRAEL IN EGYPT*, one from *Athalia*, and the last chorus is an adaptation of *ZADOK THE PRIEST*, which had already been parodied in the 1732 version of *ESTHER* (HWV 50^b). The air 'O liberty' was taken from Thomas Morell's libretto for JUDAS MACCABAEUS, which had not yet been set to music.

Apart from texts reused from other oratorios, Newburgh HAMILTON compiled the libretto from John MILTON's paraphrases of Psalms 2, 3 and 5, and various works by Edmund Spenser: *The Tears of the Muses, Melpomene* (lines 115–20), *An Hymne of Heavenly Beauty* (141–7, 155–61) and *The Faerie Queene* (Book 1, Canto VIII, vv. 1, 1–4). The libretto presents no dramatic action, but is a patriotic text in support of the Hanoverian monarchy during the period of deep crisis in 1745–6 caused by the JACOBITE rebellion led by 'Bonnie Prince Charlie' (Prince Charles Edward STUART) to restore the Stuart dynasty to the British throne. Bonnie Prince Charlie raised his standard at Glenfinnan on 19 August 1745, and on 21 September his assembled army defeated the British forces at Prestonpans, after which the government took the invasion more seriously. Londoners started panicking and prepared for defence. Thomas ARNE composed 'God save great George our King', now the British national anthem, and Handel contributed *A Chorus Song made for the Gentlemen Volunteers of the City of London* (SONGS). The Prince entered England on 8 November 1745, continued his march to London and reached Derby on 4 December. Two days later the leaders of his forces persuaded him to retreat to Scotland. They were pursued by a force led by the Duke of Cumberland (Prince WILLIAM), on 16 April 1746 the Jacobites were crushed at the Battle of Culloden and Bonnie Prince Charlie hid in the Highlands before escaping to France.

The *Occasional Oratorio* was hurriedly prepared between January and February 1746 (the autograph is not precisely dated) in the midst of the crisis. Handel's entertainment was intended as support and encouragement for the nation. George Harris referred to it as 'expressive of the rebells flight & our pursuit of 'em'. The text is a political-religious allegory that expresses hope for victory and peace. It implies that George II reigns by the grace of God, and therefore God will not suffer that the rebellious Jacobites will be successful: even if there is a great number of foes, God will help the people who trust in Him and punish the offender. So Part I ends with the optimistic prediction: 'God found them guilty, let them fall, / by their own counsels quell'd. / Push'd them in their rebellions all, / for against him they had rebell'd.'

Part II starts with the praise of liberty, and again presents optimism: 'Who trusts in God shou'd never despair, / the just are still the care of Heav'n.' It refers clearly to the religious aspect of the conflict by reusing a text from *Athalia*: 'Bless the true church, [i.e. Anglican, not Catholic] and save the King! [George II, not 'Charles III'].' God will support his faithful people, and 'After long storms and tempest overblown' shall lead them to victory. This is a similar situation as the Exodus of the Israelites from Egypt, and the parallel is emphasised by Handel's choice to begin Part III of the *Occasional Oratorio* with *Moses' Song*, the final part of *Israel in Egypt* (albeit without the *Introitus* 'Moses and the children of Israel'). The parallel between the ancient Israelites and Handel's contemporary British audience runs through the whole part. Hamilton fitted the new texts to movements taken from *Israel in Egypt*: 'Who is like unto thee, O Lord' is given a new final line, and 'He gave them hailstones for rain' and 'The enemy said' are used in a new context to describe God's military triumph over the enemies of righteousness. It was surely deliberate that Handel and Hamilton chose to conclude the *Occasional Oratorio* with *Zadok the Priest*, which had been specifically composed for the Anointing of the King in the CORONATION ceremony, which represents the sovereign's election and legitimisation through God.

ANNETTE LANDGRAF

Burrows, *Handel*
Burrows and Dunhill, 223–5
M. Channon (ed.), *Occasional Oratorio*, HHA I/23 (Kassel, forthcoming)

'Ode for St Cecilia's Day'. See *SONG FOR ST CECILIA'S DAY*

'Ode for the Birthday of Queen Anne'. See *ETERNAL SOURCE OF LIGHT DIVINE*

Oh, come chiare e belle ('Olinto pastore, Tebro fiume, Gloria'), HWV 143. An expansive work, which includes three soloists and an accompanimental band of concertino and ripieno strings with trumpet in the final aria and coro. Its text refers directly to the War of the SPANISH SUCCESSION and highlights Ruspoli's own role in recruiting and equipping a large regiment to support the papal forces in the defence of Ferrara against the Habsburgs. The serenata opens with a dialogue between the shepherd Olinto (Ruspoli's own adopted name in the ARCADIAN ACADEMY, sung by the soprano DURASTANTI), and Tebro fiume (castrato Gaetano Orsini), the River Tiber as a personification of Rome. Olinto predicts new glory for Rome, but Tebro sees only bad omens. The arrival of Glory (soprano Anna Maria de Piedz) convinces Tebro that Olinto is correct, and all three close the cantata with praise of the 'astro clemente' (one of the text's numerous allusions to Pope Clement XI) that leads them forward. The serenata was performed in the evening of 9 September 1708 after the massing of Ruspoli's troops in the Piazza SS Apostoli earlier in the day. Three hundred librettos were printed at the Marchese's expense, in which the full heading is *Olinto pastore arcade alle Glorie del Tebro Serenata a tre Voci. Fatta cantare dal Sig. Marchese Ruspoli la sera delli 9. Settembre 1708*. Handel borrowed from this occasional piece in his later works; for example, Gloria's aria 'Tornami a vagheggiar' reappears in *Alcina*.

ELLEN T. HARRIS

W. and U. Kirkendale, *Music and Meaning: Studies in Music History and the Neighbouring Disciplines* (Florence, 2007)

Opera. Handel composed more than forty operas, and for some thirty years (not continuous) the opera house was the principal focus for his activity as composer, musical director and sometimes impresario.

There was no opera in HALLE, but friendship with TELEMANN, who ran the Leipzig opera, and family links with WEISSENFELS provided Handel with early experience of two flourishing local centres of German opera. Three years in HAMBURG, where he was befriended by MATTHESON and stimulated by the brilliant example of KEISER, will have taught him all there was to learn there, and he had composed four German operas probably before his twenty-second birthday.

In ITALY, based principally in ROME, he rapidly mastered the Italian style thanks to his close association with such men as Alessandro SCARLATTI and CORELLI, with the finest singers and instrumentalists of the age, and through the regular production of cantatas for his Roman patrons. Rome had no opera at the time, but Handel was able to spend part of the theatre season in FLORENCE or VENICE, and for both cities he was commissioned to compose operas. Following the success of his Venice commission, *AGRIPPINA*, he was encouraged to go to London, where attempts were being made to establish an Italian opera house.

In London opera was still at an experimental stage; for audiences educated on Purcellian semi-opera did not automatically embrace the all-sung Italian type of music drama. The emphasis on spectacle, enchantment and pastoral in Handel's first London operas shows him and his collaborators duly attentive to English sensibilities. With the establishment of the Royal Academy of Music (OPERA COMPANIES, 2) in 1719, however, all seemed set to provide London with a repertory of Italian operas in the modern heroic style, based usually on historical themes drawn from Italian models. In the Academy's best years, with Handel composing some of his greatest music for the finest singers and one of the best orchestras in Europe, London became an operatic capital to match NAPLES, Venice or Vienna. Fashion did not develop into a sustained enthusiasm, however; and party rivalry, personal animosities, difficulties in finding new singers, perhaps even the satirical thrusts of the The *BEGGAR'S OPERA* all contributed to the collapse of the Royal Academy in 1728.

Handel then joined the impresario HEIDEGGER in setting up the so-called Second Academy (OPERA COMPANIES, 3). Opera seasons began to change character. Starting with subjects in the same vein as those of the Royal Academy, Handel was, by 1733–4, moving into the worlds of romance and legend; challenged by rival organisations performing opera in English, he put on English oratorios and odes; pasticcios introduced music in the latest Italian style. The growing hostility of some Italian singers to Handel's imperious manner, and squabbles in royal and aristocratic circles which split his supporters and patrons into opposing parties, led to the setting up of a rival company, the OPERA OF THE NOBILITY.

For three seasons Handel was driven from the KING'S THEATRE and moved into John RICH's well-equipped new theatre in COVENT GARDEN, where he found compensation for the loss of most of his best singers in the small chorus and ballet troupe that now stood at his disposal. Of his Covent Garden seasons, the first (1734–5), when *ARIODANTE* and *ALCINA* were the new operas, was artistically one of the most glorious of his career: the last (1736–7) was the most frantic. Under financial pressure that could not possibly be long sustained he produced three new operas; a pasticcio; eight revivals of operas, odes and oratorios. The frenzy ruined his health and he was too unwell to direct *BERENICE*, the last opera of the season (HANDEL, 16).

Berenice was followed by a period of some four years during which Handel's involvement with opera gradually loosened. His last Italian works were lighter in style and freer in form. A deepening commitment to oratorio and ode in English affected his musical language, and he will not have been deaf to the charms either of the comic burlettas staged by the Opera of the Nobility or of the new 'English' lyricism of ARNE.

Of Handel's German operas only *ALMIRA* has survived; so his operatic work is almost exclusively Italian, and it belongs to a period when Italian opera was undergoing momentous change. Seventeenth-century opera, at its most characteristic in Venice, had been a popular and sometimes bizarre entertainment pulsating with theatrical vitality. By Handel's time a reform movement was making itself felt, and under the influence of French classical drama, opera was becoming a more high-minded and literary form. While the new spirit was less evident in such operatic outposts as Hamburg, he could certainly not escape it in Italy. During the Royal Academy years, this new style of *dramma per musica* was perfected by METASTASIO, the finest Italian poet of the century, and almost at once Handel began to have some of Metastasio's texts adapted for performance in London. He also took a keen interest in the music of the younger Italian composers who set them. In the long run, however, these new fashions were more characteristic of his pasticcios than of his own operas.

It is convenient to think of Handelian opera in terms of this contemporary Italian *dramma per musica*, an intricately plotted poetic drama on a heroic theme; the greater part of the verse is written as recitative, but the 'realistic' passing of time is regularly suspended for the 'full music', usually arias, where characters express their passions, or reveal traits of personality more intimately, or reflect on the action. However, this aesthetic applies only to the central, Royal Academy phase of Handel's operatic career, and even there it is in practice transformed because most of the audience knew little Italian, and any literary subtleties were simply wasted on them. Librettos were drastically abbreviated, sometimes with serious consequences for the finer points of plotting or motivation; the role of the composer vis-à-vis the poet expanded correspondingly.

But in any case (leaving aside the operas composed in Italy for Italian audiences) Handel approached this *dramma per musica* aesthetic only gradually, starting from the different aesthetic traditions of Hamburg, which were eclectic, and England, where music had a central but different role in the native tradition of theatre. From *Orlando* onwards he retreated from it again. In both his earlier and his later operas music's role is less stereotyped, its forms more varied. The dramatic tone is more fanciful, sometimes more humorous. It is a striking feature of Handel's operas that so many of them go back to seventeenth-century models. And that suits his musical language, for however easily he adopted the urbane melodiousness of an Arne or a VINCI, he never lost his old-fashioned contrapuntal way of thinking or the sophisticated rhythmic energy that went with it.

The structure of the libretto results in a musical work in which conventional simple recitative alternates with musical numbers in which Handel deploys with supreme musico-dramatic acumen virtually all the expressive and technical resources of his age. All operas have at least one duet, and occasionally more complex and dramatic ensembles, but the overwhelming majority of these numbers are arias, mostly in da capo form (ARIA). Their stylistic variety is prodigious. Some resemble concerto movements, with brilliant vocal episodes framed by ritornellos for full orchestra; others are conceived as dance-songs, in the manner of minuets or gavottes or sarabandes (DANCE FORMS); in others again the orchestra is pared down to give the aria the intimacy of chamber music. For a small number of important dramatic monologues Handel writes accompanied recitatives; sometimes these provide the starting points for more extensive scene complexes in which recitative, aria and instrumental music are freely intermixed to create some of the most remarkable episodes in eighteenth-century opera. The operas are introduced by overtures, almost always in the French style, and

2. Royal Academy of Music (1719–1728)

On 27 July 1719 the Royal Academy of Music was incorporated as a joint-stock company under Letters Patent. The company was underwritten by a group of no less than seventy-three wealthy aristocrats, most of whom subscribed to the extent of £200 for a single share entitling them to a single vote in the election of directors. If the subscribers anticipated some financial gain, the founding charter leaves little doubt that the primary purpose of the Academy was to underwrite and stage Italian operas. The King granted the Academy an annual bounty of £1,000.

In contrast to the pre-Academy years, Handel's involvement in the 1720s was continuous and central. As 'Master of the Orchester' (for which he was paid a salary) he conducted a band of about thirty-five musicians from the first harpsichord. He composed fourteen operas between 1719–20 and 1727–8. The most famous of these are GUILIO CESARE (1723–4), and TAMERLANO and RODELINDA (1724–5), but several other operas of remarkable quality were popular, such as RADAMISTO (1720), OTTONE (1723) and ADMETO (1727). Giovanni BONONCINI, Atilio ARIOSTI and Giovanni PORTA (whose NUMITORE opened the first season on 2 April 1720) also composed for the Academy. Initially the balance between different composers was spread evenly, but from 1725 Handel's operas increasingly dominated the company's repertoire. The Italian poets Paolo ROLLI and Nicola HAYM arranged librettos for the Academy, generally on dramatic, dynastic themes drawn from works produced originally in Italy. Musically the operas are characterised by virtuoso arias and rich, varied orchestration.

Handel also took a prominent role in the recruitment of singers. Designated 'Master of musick' in a warrant issued by the LORD CHAMBERLAIN on 14 May 1719, he was sent to the continent to negotiate contracts. The warrant stipulated only that Handel secure SENESINO (who was engaged to perform at the court opera in DRESDEN); otherwise he was to exercise his own judgement about which cities to visit and whom to hire. Senesino was the star Italian during the first two Academy seasons. The company's leading lady was initially Margherita DURASTANTI, but in 1722 the diva Francesca CUZZONI joined the company, followed by FAUSTINA Bordoni in 1726. The Academy's composers were obliged to feature the talents of the two 'RIVAL QUEENS' onstage in equal measure. The rivalry peaked in 1728, goaded by opposing camps in the audience. Other important singers during this period were ANASTASIA ROBINSON, ANN TURNER ROBINSON, Alexander GORDON, Giuseppe BOSCHI, Gaetano BERENSTADT, Francesco BOROSINI, Andrea PACINI and Anna DOTTI.

In a state of disarray and some ignominy, the Academy closed its doors for a season (1728–9). The company had run out of money, and its leading singers had returned to Italy. By April 1728, twenty-one calls (99.5 per cent of the money pledged in 1719) had been made to the shareholders. A profit was declared just once, in 1724. Another scheme had to be implemented if Italian opera was to be carried on.

3. The 'Second Academy' (1729–1734)

Late in the spring of 1728 the Royal Academy subscribers handed over the management (and arguably a good deal of the direction) of Italian opera to

Heidegger and Handel, including what was described as the 'loan' of costumes and theatrical stock. The terms of the arrangement remain unclear but for three seasons noble patronage of opera in London receded into the shadows. What has come to be described by historians as the 'Second Academy' continued to enjoy the King's annual bounty of £1,000.

In 1728 and 1729 Heidegger and Handel embarked on separate journeys to Italy. Pushed by necessity in the absence of sufficient noble involvement, Handel also corresponded with agents on the continent and negotiated with diplomats in London to procure singers and other musicians for the London opera. Such divergence from courtly continental norms may have influenced FARINELLI, the most celebrated castrato at the time, to refuse to meet with Handel when he sought out the singer in VENICE. In subsequent seasons, the intercession on the continent by Giovanni Giaccomo Zamboni on Handel's behalf considerably eased the recruitment process. Farinelli did ultimately make the journey to London in 1733–4 but under commission of the OPERA OF THE NOBILITY.

A new cast of singers headed by the castrato Antonio BERNACCHI and soprano Anna Maria STRADA del Pò opened the 1729–30 season at the King's Theatre. Bernacchi suffered comparisons with Senesino, whose former supporters clamoured for his return, and when Senesino rejoined the company in 1730–1, he did so to great acclaim. A crisis occurred in 1733–4 when, for the second time in five years, Handel had to rebuild his company after all his singers – except the loyal Strada – went over to LINCOLN'S INN FIELDS with the Nobility Opera. The renowned castrato Giovanni CARESTINI joined Handel at the King's Theatre in 1733–4 and stayed with him at COVENT GARDEN through 1734–5. Other members of Handel's company during this period included Francesca BERTOLLI, Annibale FABRI, Antonia MERIGHI, Johann RIEMSCHNEIDER, Antonio MONTAGNANA, Giovanni PINACCI, Celeste GISMONDI, Maria Caterina NEGRI and Carlo SCALZI. In 1733–4 Durastanti returned to Handel's company after a nine-year absence from London, and the London-based Gustavus WALTZ was recruited as well.

Since 1723 performances of new operas by Handel had far outpaced performances by other Royal Academy composers, and the trend continued. However, Handel was now solely responsible for providing the repertoire for each season. He composed seven new Italian operas for the Second Academy, most notably PARTENOPE (1730), PORO (1731), SOSARME (1732), ORLANDO (1733) and ARIANNA IN CRETA (1734). The company regularly produced PASTICCIOS, and Handel revived many old Royal Academy operas, even including Bononcini's GRISELDA and Ariosti's CORIOLANO. It was also during this period that Handel began to experiment with English oratorio concerts during his theatre seasons, including ESTHER (1732) and DEBORAH (1733).

During the Second Academy period Handel produced an unprecedented variety of music theatre works, but it is not known who adapted most of the librettos. It was unfortunate that the obvious favourite, Nicola Haym, died in 1729. Handel might have arranged many of the works for resident singers and contributions appear to have been made by Giacomo Rossi. It is unlikely that Paolo Rolli adapted librettos for the Second Academy, but reports are scanty. The libretto of the serenata PARNASSO IN FESTA (1734) is anonymous, but the English oratorio librettos were prepared by Samuel HUMPHREYS.

4. Covent Garden (1734–1737)

Handel was eminently suited to the role of composer-manager of Italian opera production but in the eyes of some subscribers he overstepped the boundaries of this role. He dominated the repertoire of the Second Academy with his own works and his authoritarian handling of the company led to a clash of wills with the leading castrato, Senesino.

Handel had remained at the King's Theatre in 1733–4 but competition from the Nobility company was too strong, and he was obliged to move to COVENT GARDEN in 1734–5. Other than the fact that he was leaving the theatre primarily associated with Italian opera, the move was not a bad choice. Covent Garden Theatre had recently opened under John RICH, the impresario whose production of The BEGGAR'S OPERA at Lincoln's Inn Fields Theatre had overshadowed Italian opera in 1728. Rich and Handel were veterans of London's theatre world and the partnership was probably thought by both to be a reasonable gamble. Handel wrote ARIODANTE, ALCINA, ALEXANDER'S FEAST, ATALANTA, ARMINIO, GIUSTINO and BERENICE for Covent Garden, and revived several oratorios there during the mid-1730s (including the first London performances of ATHALIA in 1735, and Il TRIONFO DEL TEMPO E DELLA VERITÀ in 1737). In 1734–5 he wrote music for the leading French dancer Marie SALLÉ, in hopes of competing against the draw of Farinelli at the Nobility's opera. Sallé danced in performances of Ariodante and Alcina but the attraction did not last.

Like Handel, his singers adapted to the uncertainties of performing on the London stage. FRANCESINA, for example, joined the Nobility in 1736–7, moved over to Handel in 1737–8, then subsequently went on to become one of the composer's favourite oratorio singers. The situation was more difficult for the leading singers. Audience enthusiasm for Senesino in 1733–4, followed by Farinelli's rapturous reception in 1734–5, undoubtedly contributed to Carestini's decision to leave London; he was replaced by Gioacchino CONTI, although in autumn 1736 the company engaged the additional primo uomo Domenico ANNIBALI. During this period Handel started to use English singers in his opera performances, including John BEARD and Cecilia YOUNG, and Italian singers such as Carestini, Negri and Annibali sang arias in their native tongue during oratorio performances.

Handel's stretch at Covent Garden ended on a relatively quiet note. The severe financial losses by both companies could no longer be ignored, Handel experienced serious health problems (HANDEL, 16), and the faction against him had cooled. He returned to the King's Theatre in 1737–8 and the two rival companies effectively became one.

5. The final years (1737–1741)

Between 1737–8 and 1740–1, Handel see-sawed between seasons of Italian operas and English theatre works as he struggled to find the niche that led him to forgo Italian opera altogether. In 1737–8, in a pattern reminiscent of his pre-Academy years, he joined Heidegger's company alongside Giovanni Battista Pescetti and Francesco Maria VERACINI. Handel composed two new operas, FARAMONDO and SERSE, and his role in the musical direction of the season may have been slight. In addition to the remnants of the rival Nobility Opera and Covent Garden companies, the castrato CAFFARELLI was also hired.

Due to another ebb in patronage support, no Italian opera was offered at the King's Theatre for the next two seasons, and most of the principal singers at the Haymarket, including Cafarelli, left London.

Handel travelled to the continent in the summer of 1740 where he is assumed to have hired the castrato G. B. Andreoni and the soprano Maria Monza, who joined Francesina as leading singers for his last new operas for the London stage, *IMENEO* and *DEIDAMIA*. The 1740–1 season was mounted at Lincoln's Inn Fields Theatre rather than at the King's Theatre, an example of the flux and change that characterised Handel's final opera seasons as he continued to experiment with new styles and old forms. After 1740–1, despite overtures by supporters of the Italian opera, notably from Lord MIDDLESEX, Handel shunned the genre in favour of his own invention, the English oratorio.

CAROLE TAYLOR

D. Burrows, 'Handel and the London Opera Companies in the 1730s: Venues, Programmes, Patronage and Performers', GHB X (2004)

E. Gibson, *The Royal Academy of Music 1719 1728: The Institution and its Directors* (New York, 1989)

R. D. Hume, 'Handel and Opera Management in London in the 1730s', ML 67/4 (1986), 347–62

C. Taylor, 'Handel's Disengagement from the Italian Opera', *Handel Tercentenary Collection*, ed. S. Sadie and A. Hicks (London, 1987)

Opera of the Nobility. The term adopted by modern scholars to describe a coterie of performers and opera-goers who joined together in London in the mid-1730s in opposition to Handel's 'dominion' of Italian opera. The term may connote a more well-defined, even institutionalised, contemporary body than actually existed. The company was formed in direct response to a rupture in relations between Handel and the castrato singer SENESINO, which led the singer to announce his withdrawal from Handel's company in the spring of 1733. Relations between Handel and an influential faction of his former subscribers from the Royal Academy of Music (OPERA COMPANIES, 2) were also strained. In these circumstances the so-called Opera of the Nobility was formed with a view to putting Handel to rout. For four seasons, 1733–4 to 1/36–7, the two companies rivalled one another, often on the same nights.

The eponymous Nobility were led by, among others, John West, 7th Baron Delaware, Sir John Buckworth, Thomas Coke, Baron Lovel, Richard Boyle, 3rd Earl of BURLINGTON and William, 2nd Earl Cowper. Their chief aims appear to have been twofold: to regain aristocratic control of the direction of Italian opera which had drifted over into the hands of HEIDEGGER and Handel, and to produce an opera company which would maintain parity with other major continental capitals. To fulfil these aims, the Nobility reclaimed a more active role in recruiting singers and composers currently in vogue on the continent. In 1733–4, they hired Paolo ROLLI to oversee the words and Nicola PORPORA to direct the music and compose. All Handel's Italian singers, save STRADA, followed Senesino and his influential backers to the LINCOLN'S INN FIELDS THEATRE. Such was the prestige of noble patronage that the company quickly established itself as a formidable rival to Handel at the KING'S THEATRE, the traditional home of Italian opera in London.

In 1734–5, in circumstances that remain unclear, the Nobility took over the King's Theatre and Handel moved to COVENT GARDEN. Considerations of the steep costs of mounting a second Italian opera company were put to one side in the heat of faction in 1733; in any event the Nobility undoubtedly thought they would defeat Handel. It seems that Handel was bowed but not deterred by this development, although his position was further weakened when the legendary castrato singer FARINELLI joined Senesino's company in the autumn of 1734. Faction was nothing if not fickle, however, and by the end of 1735–6 critical censure against Handel abated somewhat, particularly among genuine lovers of music who encouraged both companies. The Nobility and Handel offered broadly similar programmes of Italian operas (new and revived works) plus pasticcios. Unlike Handel, the Nobility did not attempt works in English and they departed from traditional fare just once with the oratorio *David e Bersabea* mounted in 1733–4 and revived in 1734–5.

FREDERICK, Prince of Wales, long assumed to have taken a leading role in the formation of the Nobility company, is now known to have patronised Handel as well in precisely the same period. We will probably never know the full story, but this would have been wholly consistent with the Prince's political stance of party ambiguity in the same period. After two seasons the competition was largely spent and the two companies struggled to attract an audience barely large enough to keep one going. In 1737–8, the companies consolidated and Italian opera was resumed under one roof, at the King's Theatre (OPERA COMPANIES, 4).   CAROLE TAYLOR

D. Burrows, 'Handel and the London Opera Companies in the 1730s', GHB X (2001)
R. D. Hume, 'Handel and Opera Management in London in the 1730s', ML 67/4 (1986)
T. McGeary, 'Handel, Prince Frederick, and the Opera of the Nobility Reconsidered', GHB VII (1998)
J. Milhous, 'Händel und die Londoner Theaterverhältnisse im Jahre 1734', Gattungskonventionen der Händel-Oper. Bericht uber die Symposien der Internationalen Händel-Akademie Karlsruhe 1990 und 1991, ed. H. J. Marx (Karlsruhe, 1992)
C. M. Taylor, 'Italian Operagoing in London, 1700–45', Ph.D. dissertation (Syracuse University, 1991)

oratorio. Musico-dramatic entertainments set to sacred or religious texts developed into a genre during the early 1600s that in Italy became known as 'oratorio' ('oratory', i.e. chapel). In particular, the genre was cultivated by composers such as CARISSIMI in ROME, and by other composers (e.g. STRADELLA) throughout the rest of Italy, and it gradually became popular across much of continental Europe during the seventeenth century. From its early origins as extended dramatic motets (often in Latin), oratorios developed in conjunction with contemporary operatic style, becoming longer and featuring librettos in the vernacular language.

Handel's first oratorios were composed in Rome: Il *TRIONFO DEL TEMPO E DEL DISINGANNO* (1707; first performance undocumented) and La *RESURREZIONE* (Easter 1708) were both written and first performed during a short period in which there was a papal ban on public performances of secular opera in Rome; each work features an Italian libretto divided in two parts and music that is stylistically close to contemporary operatic style (with few choruses, always sung by the soloists, and a wide assortment of strongly characterised da capo arias). There were numerous venues where oratorios were performed in Rome, such as the Collegio Clementino, the Jesuit's Seminario Romano, S. Girolamo della Carità, the Chiesa Nuova, and also in private palaces belonging to patrons such as Cardinal OTTOBONI and the Marchese RUSPOLI.

When Handel arrived in England in late 1710 a native tradition of extended dramatic oratorio had not yet developed, although during the previous century some composers had written short narrative pieces depicting incidents from biblical stories (most notably Henry PURCELL's In guilty night, a vivid account of King Saul's visit to the Witch of Endor). Handel subsequently became the principal creator of English oratorio, although the first oratorio-style work that he composed in London was the BROCKES PASSION (c.1716–17), which might have been intended for HAMBURG and is his only German-language oratorio. There is no documented performance of the Brockes Passion under the composer's own direction, but he recycled music from it in his first English oratorio ESTHER, a compact work in six scenes that he probably started composing in 1718 for CANNONS, and for which he wrote more music in 1720 after returning from a trip to DRESDEN.

During the 1720s Handel was almost solely preoccupied with Italian operas for London, but he belatedly returned to the oratorio genre in 1732 when he revised and considerably expanded Esther for his Second Academy (OPERA COMPANIES, 3) company's 1731–2 season at the KING'S THEATRE. Advertised in newspapers as 'The Sacred Story of Esther: an Oratorio in English' (Deutsch, pp. 288–9) in order to bring attention to its novelty, the 1732 version of Esther established the general form of the new genre: the works were divided in three acts or parts, and designed to be long enough to fill an evening at the theatre for an audience accustomed to Italian drammi per musica. Handel connected the musical styles and forms of opera and English sacred choral music (and also drew on his Lutheran musical roots (CHORALE)), and large CHORUS movements sung by extra singers drafted in from London's leading professional ecclesiastical establishments formed a prominent feature of his oratorio performances. From 1732 oratorio-style works became an integral part of his theatre seasons alongside operas, and were frequently performed during Lent whilst secular entertainments such as opera were forbidden. Most oratorio librettos were based on the BIBLE, so the new genre was a practical business opportunity to promote morally acceptable entertainments, especially when Handel's competitors were unable to offer rival attractions on the same nights (although the first London performances of MESSIAH in 1743 triggered an article attacking the apparently profane misuse of 'God's Word' in the theatre). Moreover, his expanding English repertory was to prove highly useful for a concert series at OXFORD in July 1733 that included revivals of Esther, the masque ACIS AND GALATEA (not an oratorio, but sometimes included in Handel's 'oratorio' seasons), DEBORAH (recently premiered in London), and which culminated in the first performance of the new oratorio ATHALIA.

Oratorios also provided Handel with opportunities to experiment with musico-dramatic conventions. In particular, his early English oratorios feature a broad variety of distinctive ideas regarding INSTRUMENTATION, musical styles and imaginative responses to the literary ideas and subject matter contained in diverse LIBRETTOS. During the mid-1730s it was necessary for Handel to produce oratorios in bilingual versions to accommodate Italian opera singers such as CARESTINI who were uncomfortable singing in English (even those more confident, such as BERTOLLI in the 1732 Esther, had aroused ridicule from some commentators). Between late 1733 and early 1738 Handel did not produce any new English oratorios, probably because he did not have an ideal group of singers for such a project, but instead revised his first Roman oratorio and performed it under the title Il TRIONFO DEL TEMPO E DELLA VERITÀ (1737) with his opera singers. Moreover, since 1735 the composer had increased the musical novelty of his revivals of Esther, Deborah and Athalia by introducing organ concertos (ORCHESTRAL WORKS, 5). These were not part of the action, but played between the acts or parts; although his next English composition, the ode ALEXANDER'S FEAST (1736) incorporated concertos into its narrative. He continued to include organ concertos and concerti grossi in his performances of oratorio-style works, but never did so in his late Italian operas. His other oratorio entr'acte compositions are the three Concerti a due cori (ORCHSTRAL WORKS, 1), which were performed with JUDAS MACCABAEUS, JOSHUA and ALEXANDER BALUS during the 1747–8 seasons.

After February 1741, Handel never composed or performed another Italian opera in London, and for the rest of his career he concentrated almost entirely on writing, revising and performing oratorio-style works. The majority of these were performed at COVENT GARDEN theatre (Handel only returned to the KING'S THEATRE for his over-ambitious 1744–5 season), and all of them were performed in the manner of a concert without scenery, costumes or stage action, although the soloists were presumably mindful of the dramatic nature of their contributions in most works. They were probably placed at the front of the platform, with the chorus and the orchestra positioned behind them. It seems that on some occasions the venue was specially decorated: it was announced in London newspapers that for Handel's 1732 performances of Esther 'There will be no Action on the Stage, but the House will be fitted up in a decent Manner, for the Audience' (Deutsch, p. 289), and it was reported that at the first performance of Deborah 'The Pit and Orchestre were cover'd as at an Assembly, and the whole House illuminated in a new and most beautiful manner' (Daily Advertiser, 20 March 1733). Perhaps such efforts were emulating the lavish decoration that Handel had witnessed in Rome for his performances of La Resurrezione, and they certainly compensated visually for the missing elements of opera STAGING that the London AUDIENCE was accustomed to. It is not known if such efforts to decorate the theatre for oratorio nights were continued in subsequent seasons.

From 1738 Handel frequently produced two new oratorio-style works per season that distinctly contrasted in style and subject matter: the epic drama SAUL was followed promptly by the anthem-like ISRAEL IN EGYPT (1738), and other such striking pairs of English-language music theatre works included SAMSON and MESSIAH (1743 season; although Messiah had been premiered a year earlier at Neal's Musick Hall in DUBLIN), JOSEPH AND HIS BRETHREN and SEMELE (1744 season; the latter not an oratorio, but called 'The Story of Semele' in the WORDBOOK and its performance advertised in newspapers as 'After the manner of an Oratorio'), BELSHAZZAR and HERCULES (1745 season; the latter called 'A new Musical Drama'), JOSHUA and ALEXANDER BALUS (1748 season), and SUSANNA and SOLOMON (1749 season). His final original oratorio, JEPHTHA, was composed in two periods during 1751, as he began to suffer irrevocably from blindness (HANDEL, 16), and was first performed in 1752.

During the early 1750s Handel developed a tradition for repeating *Messiah* at the chapel of the FOUNDLING HOSPITAL after the end of his Covent Garden season, but by the middle of the decade his declining health and blindness led to his oratorio seasons being conducted (and perhaps largely prepared) by John Christopher SMITH JUNIOR. Some of the new music included in the 1757 revival of *Esther* may have been composed by Handel, dictating his ideas to Smith, but the younger musician presumably had a considerable role in shaping The *TRIUMPH OF TIME AND TRUTH* (1757), an English version of *Il trionfo del Tempo* that arguably qualifies as the last 'new' work produced during oratorio seasons under Handel's control. After his death Smith junior continued Lenten oratorio seasons at Covent Garden in collaboration with John STANLEY, with repertory dominated by revivals of Handel's oratorios and works arranged from his lesser-known old compositions (PASTICCIOS, 2).

Most of Handel's oratorios are dramatic works based on the Old Testament or the Apocrypha (only *THEODORA* is set in early Christian times). The Scriptural anthologies *Israel in Egypt* and *Messiah* are notably atypical exceptions. Likewise, his first Roman oratorio *Il trionfo del Tempo e del Disinganno* (and its subsequent London revisions) is an allegorical morality play, and the *OCCASIONAL ORATORIO* is a peculiar celebratory work written to celebrate the Hanoverian victory over the 1745 JACOBITE rebellion that uses texts taken from both Scripture and poems by MILTON and Spenser. The criterion for classifying Handel's oratorios is often confused by modern writers, musicians and audiences. The masque *Acis and Galatea*, DRYDEN's Cecilian odes *Alexander's Feast* and *SONG FOR ST CECILIA'S DAY*, the 'moral cantata' *L'ALLEGRO, IL PENSEROSO ED IL MODERATO*, the concert drama *Semele*, Greek tragedy *Hercules* and the allegorical *CHOICE OF HERCULES* are all secular works that were included in Handel's 'oratorio' seasons, but fall outside neat classification. They cannot all be accurately described as 'English music dramas', and it is inaccurate to call them 'secular oratorios'. An ideal solution seems to be that Handel's diverse settings of English librettos intended for unstaged concert performance in a theatre can be understood loosely as 'oratorio-style works', or more simply as 'English music theatre works'.   ANNETTE LANDGRAF and DAVID VICKERS

Burrows
D. Burrows (ed.), *The Cambridge Companion to Handel* (Cambridge, 1997)
Dean, *Oratorios*
HHB ii
A. Hicks, 'The Late Additions to Handel's Oratorios and the Role of the Younger Smith', *Music in Eighteenth-Century England: Essays in Memory of Charles Cudworth*, ed. C. Hogwood and R. Luckett (Cambridge, 1983)
D. R. Hurley, *Handel's Music: Patterns of Creation in his Oratorios and Musical Dramas, 1741–1751* (Oxford, 2000)
Smith, *Oratorios*
D. Vickers, 'Handel's Performing Versions: A Study of Four Music Theatre Works from the "Second Academy" Period', Ph.D dissertation (The Open University, 2007)
E. Zöllner, *English Oratorio after Handel* (Marburg, 2002)

Oratorio, An. A concert of music by Handel, presented by the composer at the KING'S THEATRE on 28 March 1738 and advertised as 'An Oratorio. With a Concert[o]

on the Organ, For the Benefit of Mr. Handel'; the title of the wordbook for the occasion reads 'An Oratorio ... Compos'd by Mr. Handel'. Benefit nights for actors and authors (and occasionally charitable causes) featured quite often in the programmes of DRURY LANE and COVENT GARDEN theatres, mainly towards the end of performing seasons; the beneficiary received the proceeds of the performance after the theatre charges and performers had been paid, and the right to a benefit was often part of an actor's contractual agreement with the management of the theatre company. However, benefits were not a regular practice of the opera companies and their occurrence indicated unusual circumstances; a benefit for Handel was advertised on only one other occasion, a performance of *TESEO* in 1713 that was probably part of a scheme to salvage an income for the leading performers during a financial crisis. Most likely, the 1738 benefit night was part of the agreement that Handel had made with the managers of the 1737–8 opera season, to supplement the £1,000 that he is reported to have received for providing them with two new opera scores (*FARAMONDO* and *SERSE*). He may have been prompted to insist on this condition by the recollection of the lavish financial and social advantages that had come to FARINELLI through his benefit nights with the OPERA OF THE NOBILITY in March 1735 and March 1736. Burney's later description of Handel's benefit is remarkably similar to the reports of Farinelli's in 1735: 'besides every part of the house being uncommonly crouded, when the curtain drew up, five hundred persons of rank and fashion were discovered on the stage, which was formed into an amphitheatre'. Handel's income from the performance was variously reported: the Earl of EGMONT, who was present, estimated that there were 1,300 people in the audience, excluding the galleries, and that Handel made £1,000.

For his benefit night Handel had the current resources of the King's Theatre at his disposal, including the opera company and the orchestra. The programme for a concert performance of comparable length to a three-act opera posed some problems, however: of the seven singers in the opera company, only two (FRANCESINA and MONTAGNANA) had experience of singing in English, a complete performance of one of his operas was probably impractical, and in any case Handel would have wanted to present a broader range of his music than was available from the present repertory of operas. So he brought in extra performers, including John BEARD as a soloist, a number of English chorus singers and probably some additional orchestral players: the Earl of SHAFTESBURY, following a conversation with Handel about the preparations for the concert, reported that 'There are to be six heautboys I remember: Five singers to a part & about a hundred & thirty instruments playing in all'. The situation was helped somewhat by repertory of Italian arias (and Italian translations of pre-existing movements) that Handel had included in his English oratorios in recent years. Part II of the programme consisted of a compressed version of the oratorio *DEBORAH*, with nine English choruses, six English arias, three Italian arias and one Italian duet. English choruses and Italian arias (from Handel's cantatas and the recent oratorio repertory) provided the material for the remainder of the programme, which aimed for variety and the best use of the performers, rather than any dramatic structure. The programme opened with a revised version of the CHAPEL ROYAL anthem *As pants the hart* (ANTHEMS, I), and ended with two movements from *ZADOK THE PRIEST*, to the words 'Blessed are all they that fear the Lord'. William HAYES from OXFORD took part as a chorus singer, and the leading Italian soloist was CAFFARELLI, the first man from the opera company, who presumably had to learn a lot of new music for the occasion. It is possible that the shortened version with Italian text of the Funeral Anthem for Queen Caroline (ANTHEMS, 5) that is found in Handel's autograph was part of Handel's plan for this concert, but was abandoned following disapproval from the King.   DONALD BURROWS

D. Burrows, 'Handel's 1738 Oratorio: A Benefit Pasticcio', *Georg Friedrich Händel – Ein Lebensinhalt: Gedenkschrift für Bernd Baselt (1934–1993)*, ed. K. Hortschansky and K. Musketa (Kassel and Halle, 1995)

Oratorio per la Resurrezione di Nostro Signor Giesù Cristo. See La *RESURREZIONE*

'Oratorium, The'. See *ESTHER*

orchestra. See INSTRUMENTATION

orchestral works

     1. *Concerti a due cori*, HWV 332–334
     2. Concerti grossi, HWV 312–330
     3. Harp Concerto, HWV 294
     4. Oboe concertos, HWV 287, 301–302^a
     5. Organ concertos, HWV 289–300, 306–311
     6. Violin Concerto, HWV 288
     7. Miscellaneous

1. *Concerti a due cori*, HWV 332–334
Orchestral concertos for three instrumental choirs: two woodwind and brass choirs featuring two horns, oboes and a bassoon each and a four-part string choir. Given their name by Friedrich CHRYSANDER for his collected edition of Handel's works (EDITIONS, 5), the *Concerti a due cori* were composed between early 1746 and early 1748 as entr'acte music for performances of the oratorios *JUDAS MACCABAEUS*, *JOSHUA* and *ALEXANDER BALUS* during the 1747–8 season. In order to provide interesting entertainment during the oratorio intervals, Handel set the demanding *Concerti a due cori* for large orchestral forces and employed the *Coro spezzato* technique, unusual for his time. This compositional technique is based on polychoral or antiphonal music-making which had developed in VENICE during the late sixteenth century; perhaps Handel's familiarity with the style increased while he stayed in Italy between 1706 and 1709, but he may have been emulating a later model which has not yet been identified. The *coro spezzato* technique was ideal for adapting vocal as instrumental music, and the concertos HWV 332 and HWV 333 are based on musical material borrowed from popular oratorio choruses from *MESSIAH*, *ESTHER*, *BELSHAZZAR*, *SEMELE* and the *OCCASIONAL ORATORIO*. Only the third Concerto a due cori (HWV 334) is entirely new, although the opening 'Ouverture' shares some material with the overture for two clarinets and corno da caccia (HWV 424); the last movement is an arrangement of the hunting aria 'Io seguo sol fiero' from *PARTENOPE*, and it was later rearranged as an organ concerto (HWV 305$^{a/b}$).

All three concertos have survived in autograph form and their compositional circumstances and first performance venues can be determined quite precisely. HWV 334 was the first to have been composed and it was performed at the premiere of *Judas Maccabaeus* as an opening sinfonia for the third act. HWV 333 and HWV 332 (called *Concerto made from Choruses* in the autograph) were probably those advertised in London for the premieres of *Alexander Balus* and *Joshua* and possibly played as sinfonias opening the respective second acts. All three *Concerti a due cori* have at least four movements and begin with a French-style overture. One might argue that they represent the end point of Handel's development as an orchestral composer because they stand at the crossroads between the earlier concerto grosso type and the later eighteenth-century symphonic orchestral works in sound as well as in style.

2. Concerti grossi, HWV 312–330

Concertos for different instrumental solo groups and orchestra. The six Concerti grossi, Op. 3 (HWV 312–17) were the first orchestral works published in England under Handel's name. Printed by John WALSH JUNIOR in 1734, probably without the composer's approval, the edition united six concertos into a collection. No autograph scores have survived, but closer study reveals that Walsh's edition is a chaotic arrangement of different instrumental works composed by Handel between 1712 and 1722 for diverse ensembles and occasions. Perhaps they were selected, adapted and organised into so-called 'concerti grossi' by musically accomplished copyists or engravers in Walsh's publishing house. Most of the musical material in Op. 3 is based on instrumental movements from *OTTONE*, *AMADIGI*, Il *PASTOR FIDO*, the Chandos Anthems (ANTHEMS, 2) and a number of keyboard fugues. That Op. 3 was a haphazard collection is also obvious by its irregular tonal disposition and the uneven instrumentation of the solo group, with solo instruments sometimes changing from one movement to the next within the same concerto. A handwritten note on one of the surviving copies of the 1734 first edition calls them *Oboe Concertos*, but, although oboes are present in all six concertos, this term is incorrect because there are other instruments with obbligato solo appearances such as violins, recorders and a bassoon.

The title page of the first edition states that these concertos were performed on the occasion of the wedding festivities for Princess ANNE and the Prince of Orange on 13 and 14 March 1734. If Op. 3 is connected to these marriage celebrations, maybe some of the concertos were included as entr'acte music in the serenata *PARNASSO IN FESTA*. However, such performances are not verifiable. Walsh omitted such claims from the second edition of Op. 3 published in 1735, which differs from the first edition on a number of points. For example, No. 5 (HWV 316) received three additional movements, and the concerto printed as No. 4 in the first edition (which turned out be a spurious work not composed by Handel) was replaced by HWV 315, probably because Handel himself had intervened. Walsh's second edition of Op. 3 was more popular than the first and became the basis for all further editions of these concertos. That the collection was a great financial success is also attested by the fact that there were twenty-eight, partly revised, reprints until 1760.

The original idea to publish the concertos of Op. 3 as a collection therefore probably originated with Walsh's mercantile instincts, which had awakened after similar Concerto grosso editions by Arcangelo CORELLI and Francesco GEMINIANI had sold very well on the English markets. Perhaps similar considerations lay behind the publication of Handel's twelve Concerti grossi, Op. 6 (HWV 319–30), printed by Walsh under the title *Twelve Grand Concertos*. This time the composer was fully involved, writing new concertos specifically for the publication. According to the dates on the surviving autographs, almost completely preserved, the concertos were composed between 29 September and 30 October 1739, and the collection was offered to the public on a subscription basis. It is surely not coincidental that Handel's Op. 6 closely resembled Corelli's Concerti grossi, Op. 6 in scope, title, number of concertos, and style (i.e. multi-movement concerti grossi for string orchestra with a concertino group and the possible addition of oboes). Corelli's Op. 6 concertos had been known in London since 1695, and available in printed editions since 1715. Their enthusiastic reception in England and Ireland might reflect the fact that they, like Handel's Op. 3 and Op. 6, were more suitable for concert societies and proficient amateur musicians than the brilliant virtuoso solo concertos of the Vivaldian type. It is possible that Handel regarded the composition of Op. 6 as an artistic challenge and wanted to create a collection rivalling Corelli's set, and this may account for the relatively long time that it took him to finish the concertos. However, he also envisaged that concertos from Op. 6 would be useful for his 1739–40 season at LINCOLN'S INN FIELDS: ten of them were performed during the season (Nos. 9 and 11, both based on recent organ concertos, were probably not used). Moreover, the availability of concertos from Op. 6 meant that Handel did not compose an overture for *L'ALLEGRO, IL PENSEROSO ED IL MODERATO*.

In their formal design the Op. 6 concertos are multi-faceted. There are French overtures next to Italian, French and English dances, church sonata movements, vocal forms like arias or accompanied recitatives, character pieces, fugues or fugati and two-movement sonatas. Instrumental pieces in orchestral settings without solo parts alternate with solo concerto-style movements and strict concerti grossi (with a 'concertino' group of two violins and cello working in combination with the 'ripieno' orchestra of strings and basso continuo), and Handel seems to have deliberately mixed together strictly defined formal types of church concerto and chamber concerto. The large range of variation in the concertos is perhaps also created by his BORROWING of musical material from his own older works (e.g. *AGRIPPINA, GIULIO CESARE* and *IMENEO*) and from other composers: Op. 6 contains borrowings from a harpsichord suite by his boyhood teacher Friedrich Wilhelm ZACHOW, from Domenico SCARLATTI's *Esercizi per Gravicembalo* and numerous parts of Gottlieb MUFFAT's *Componimenti Musicali*.

The *Twelve Grand Concertos* was enthusiastically received by its 100 subscribers, which included members of the royal family and friends such as Charles JENNENS, James HARRIS and the Earl of SHAFTESBURY. Subscribers also included professional musicians and musical organisations. The set became known as 'Opus 6' when the second edition was published in 1741, and further editions were published between 1746 and 1760. Some of the concertos were included in the HANDEL COMMEMORATION concerts in 1784. To this day, the collection is considered as one of the highlights of baroque instrumental music.

HWV 318, known as the 'Concerto in *Alexander's Feast*', is Handel's only other concerto grosso apart from Op. 6 which has a trio concertino group. The composition was finished on 25 January 1736 and played as an introductory sinfonia to the second part of *ALEXANDER'S FEAST* at its premiere on 19 February 1736. In 1741 it was published in Walsh's *Select Harmony Fourth Collection*. For this concerto Handel drew musical inspiration from TELEMANN's *Musique de table, Première Production* (1733) and from VIVALDI's Concerto Op. 8 No. 6 ('Il piacere', RV 180).   DANIEL GLOWOTZ (Trans. ANGELA BAIER)

3. Harp Concerto, HWV 294

The harp concerto in B flat major was composed for performance in the ode *Alexander's Feast*, premiered on 19 February 1736. It was played after the recitative 'Timotheus plac'd on high', representing playing of the Greek bard Timotheus. The sound of the harp and pizzicato bass suggest the bard plucking the lyre. The wordbook for the ode designates the concerto 'for the Harp, Lute, Lyrichord and other Instruments' while an organ continuo part calls for 'Liuto e l'Harpa'. According to John HAWKINS, the solo harp part was composed for William Powell the younger. The lute (played by Carlo ARRIGONI) and lyrichord (a keyboard operated on the hurdy-gurdy principle) presumably were part of a special continuo group. The concerto was published as No. 6 in Handel's Op. 4 organ concertos (1738). Handel himself performed at least the first movement on the organ as solo instrument.   WILLIAM D. GUDGER

4. Oboe concertos, HWV 287, 301–302^a

None of the three authentic Italian-style solo oboe concertos has survived in the composer's autograph. All three are composed in the four-movement Italian church concerto form (with slow–fast–slow–fast movements). No. 3 (HWV 287) was the first to have been composed. Its authenticity is established through stylistic characteristics and a northern German source discovered in the 1990s (Poppe). If the dating to 1703 on the title page of the Leipzig first edition (Schuberth, 1863–4) is to be trusted, it might be Handel's earliest surviving concerto, and is probably a pioneering work from Handel's HAMBURG days that pre-dates the oboe concertos by Telemann, Albinoni, Giuseppe Valentini and Alessandro Marcello, which were all composed after 1710.

The dating of the other two concertos, No. 1 (HWV 301) and No. 2 (HWV 302^a) is more problematic. They were first printed anonymously in John Walsh's *Select Harmony Fourth Collection* (1741), which united six concertos by Handel, Giuseppe Tartini and Francesco Maria VERACINI. For stylistic reasons, No. 1 is thought to have been composed while Handel lived in Hamburg or Italy. No. 2 contains a number of borrowings from orchestral movements or instrumental introductions from Chandos Anthems 5 and 8, which suggests that it must have been composed c.1718.   DANIEL GLOWOTZ (Trans. ANGELA BAIER)

5. Organ concertos, HWV 289–300, 306–311

Handel impressed audiences in Italy with his organ-playing. In the Italian oratorio Il *TRIONFO DEL TEMPO E DEL DISINGANNO* (1707) a Sonata with a brilliant organ obbligato leads into an aria also with solo organ. A similar organ obbligato is found in 'In the battle fame pursuing' in *DEBORAH* (1733). In London, the organ became a regular instrument in

Handel's oratorio orchestras. The organ supported the singing of the chorus, drawn from the London choirs used to such accompaniment, especially in the music Handel reused in his oratorios from the Coronation Anthems (ANTHEMS, 3). Handel normally used a one-manual organ, sometimes playing it himself. At COVENT GARDEN it became the centrepiece of the stage set-up. Handel probably improvised on the organ during the intervals at oratorios before writing concertos as such.

Handel introduced organ concertos with himself as soloist in March and April 1735 at revivals of *Esther*, *Deborah* and ATHALIA. The Concerto in B flat major (HWV 290) was associated with *Esther*, its last movement published as 'The Minuet in *Esther*'. The Concerto in G minor (HWV 291) has violin and cello solos as in a concerto grosso, with solo organ in only one movement in its first version. Much of the music of the early concertos is derived from chamber pieces; the Concerto in F major (HWV 293) is an orchestrated version of the recorder sonata, Op. 1 No. 11 (HWV 369). The Concerto in F major (HWV 292) has more extended organ solo writing and originally continued into an 'Alleluja' chorus in *Athalia*.

For the 19 February 1736 premiere of *Alexander's Feast* Handel composed three concertos, including the Harp Concerto and Concerto grosso (HWV 318) (see above), and the Organ Concerto in G minor/G major (HWV 289), which represented the organ-playing of St Cecilia mentioned in the ode. The music of the ode was published in March 1738 without the concertos. On 4 October 1738 Handel's 'Opera Quarta' (Op. 4) was published by John Walsh junior; it included the five organ concertos composed in 1735–6, plus the harp concerto as a sixth organ concerto. The newspaper advertisement refers to a 'spurious' edition which has not been identified, and Handel evidently gave Walsh his conducting scores from which to work: 'These Six Concerto's were publish'd by Mr. Walsh from my own Copy corrected by my self, and to him only I have given my right therein' (Deutsch, 467). HWV 289 has pride of place as Op. 4 No. 1. Walsh issued a keyboard score that could be used for unaccompanied performance on the harpsichord or organ, or as the solo organ part with the separately issued orchestral parts. The keyboard part of Op. 4 was never out of print until well into the nineteenth century.

During his 1739 season Handel introduced organ concertos made from the instrumental movements in SAUL at the oratorio's second performance (22 January). A new Concerto in A major (HWV 296^a) was introduced with *Alexander's Feast* in March, and the F major concerto (HWV 295), 'The cuckoo and the nightingale', composed on 2 April, was heard at the premiere of ISRAEL IN EGYPT on 4 April. HWV 295 and HWV 296^a were rescored as concerti grossi (Op. 6 Nos. 9 and 11, HWV 327 and 329) in October 1739, but were also published by Walsh in November 1740 as keyboard solos along with four other concertos transcribed from Op. 6 ('A second set of six concertos for the harpsicord and organ'). However, instrumental parts for HWV 296^a and 295 did not appear until January 1760. Around 1738–9 Handel wrote a single-movement Concerto for Two Organs, HWV 303, and a 'Chaconne Concerto', HWV 343^b, which contains improvised keyboard variations with a final orchestral ritornello.

The remainder of Handel's organ concerto output was less than one new concerto per season. These concertos were not intended for publication: they required entire movements and/or the last solo of a movement to be improvised. Most of these concertos were collected posthumously into 'Opus 7', under the supervision of John Christopher SMITH JUNIOR, published on 23 February 1761 both in keyboard reduction and orchestral parts. The concertos in Op. 7 begin in order of composition with the B flat concerto (HWV 306) composed in 1740 for the premiere of L'Allegro, il Penseroso ed il Moderato at LINCOLN INN FIELDS, where Handel had a two-manual organ with pedals. The A major concerto (HWV 307) was composed in 1743 and first heard at the premiere of SAMSON.

In the period 1746–8 Handel's organ concertos were even less complete. The D minor concerto (HWV 304) was overlooked for Op. 7 and not published until Arnold's edition (EDITIONS, 2), which also tried to sort out the complicated sources for an organ concerto in F major (HWV 305[a]), based on the Concerto a due cori, HWV 334. A single-movement Allegro così così was based on an extensive Telemann borrowing. In Op. 7 it is part of Concerto No. 4 (HWV 309), along with a version of the Concerto for Two Organs and the second movement of the concerto Op. 3 No. 6 (HWV 317). The Concerto in B flat, Op. 7 No. 6 (HWV 311) is related to music for the premiere of JOSHUA in 1748.

The Concerto in G minor, Op. 7 No. 5 (HWV 310) was completed on 31 January 1750 and first performed with the premiere of THEODORA (G minor its main key) on 16 March. The B flat major concerto, Op. 7 No. 3 (HWV 308) was composed between 1 and 4 January 1751, with Handel drafting two versions of the opening movement, based on a borrowing from Franz Johann HABERMANN, as is the second movement. This concerto was first performed on 1 March at a performance of Alexander's Feast, the third concerto Handel had designed to represent St Cecilia playing the organ.

In his blindness Handel still performed organ concertos. According to BURNEY he improvised between ritornellos by the orchestra; a fragmentary score for such a performance survives in the hand of Smith junior (facsimile in HHA IV/8, 287–91). The tradition Handel established with the organ concerto was continued in Britain by Thomas Augustin ARNE, John STANLEY, William Felton, James Hook, Charles and Samuel Wesley and others.   WILLIAM D. GUDGER

6. Violin Concerto, HWV 288

Handel's only so-called violin concerto is described in his autograph as Sonata a 5, identifying it as an instrumental piece for five parts, that is, for solo violin and a four-part string and oboe orchestral accompaniment. Its form is that of the three-movement ritornello concerto of the fast–slow–fast Vivaldian solo concerto type. On the basis of the autograph score the concerto can be dated to Handel's Italian years. It is possible that Handel wrote the solo part for Corelli, who had played in the Roman performances of La RESURREZIONE and Il trionfo del Tempo e del Disinganno. There is no evidence that this concerto is the same as the one performed by Matthew DUBOURG at Hickford's Room in London on 18 February 1719, but Handel did reuse the elegant opening movement for the CHAPEL ROYAL anthem I will magnify thee (ANTHEMS, 1).

7. Miscellaneous

There are a number of other concertos and overtures which mostly survive in autograph form that are not precisely datable: HWV 331 (c.1722) is an arrangement of two movements from the WATER MUSIC. The Concerti for Trumpets and French Horns (HWV 335^{a-b}, c.1746–8) resemble the Concerti a due cori in style and contain musical material subsequently used in the MUSIC FOR THE ROYAL FIREWORKS. Some scholars have suggested that the overture in B flat (HWV 336; probably an early Italian composition) might have been the original sinfonia of Il trionfo del Tempo e del Disinganno (1707), but this is doubtful. The two-movement overture HWV 337 seems to be the torso of a three-movement concerto, whose first movement Handel had included in Act I of Ottone (1722). The sinfonia HWV 338 (c.1706–10), the sonata HWV 404 (c.1718–20) and the overture HWV 424 (c.1740–2) are orchestrated trio sonatas.

DANIEL GLOWOTZ (Trans. ANGELA BAIER)

See also INSTRUMENTATION; OVERTURE

T. Best and W. D. Gudger (eds.), Orgelkonzerte I – Op. 4, HHA IV/2 (rev. edn) (Kassel, 2001)

D. Burrows, 'Handel as a Concerto Composer', The Cambridge Companion to Handel (Cambridge, 1997)

'Walsh's Editions of Handel's Opera 1–5: The Texts and their Sources', Music in Eighteenth-Century England, ed. C. Hogwood and R. Luckett (Cambridge, 1983)

C. Cudworth, 'The English Organ Concerto', The Score 8 (1953), 51–60

E. Derr, 'Handel's Use of Scarlatti's "Essercizi per gravicembalo" in his opus 6', Gedenkschrift für Jens Peter Larsen (1902–1988), ed. H. J. Marx (Kassel, 1989)

R. Fiske, 'Handel's Organ Concertos: Do They Belong to Particular Oratorios?', Organ Yearbook 3 (1972), 14–22

S. Flesch, W. Stockmeier, E. Gerlach and I. Schneider (eds.), Orgelkonzerte II, HHA IV/8 (Kassel, 1989)

W. D. Gudger, 'Handel's Harp Concerto', American Harp Journal 6/3 (1978), 14–22

HHB iii

P. Holman, 'Did Handel Invent the English Keyboard Concerto?', MT 144/1883 (Summer 2003), 13–22

B. Lam, 'The Orchestral Music', Handel. A Symposium, ed. G. Abraham (Oxford, 1954)

A. Mann, Handel: The Orchestral Music (New York, 1996)

H. J. Marx, 'The Origins of Handel's Opus 3', Handel Tercentenary Collection, ed. S. Sadie and A. Hicks (London, 1987)

'Händels "Concerti a due cori" (HWV 332–334) und ihre kompositionsgeschichtlichen Grundlagen', HJb 42/3 (1997)

R. Maunder, The Scoring of Baroque Concertos (Woodbridge, 2004)

G. Poppe, 'Eine bisher unbekannte Quelle zum Oboenkonzert HWV 287', HJb 39 (1993)

S. Sadie, Handel Concertos (London, 1972)

Oreste, HWV A^{II}. PASTICCIO opera in three acts. Giovanni Gualberto BARLOCCI's libretto L'Oreste was first set to music by Benedetto Micheli for Rome in 1723, in which CARESTINI had sung the part of Pilade. Perhaps the castrato influenced Handel's choice to use the libretto in London. It was first performed at COVENT GARDEN on 18 December 1734, and repeated on 21 and 28 December. The cast was:

Oreste	Giovanni Carestini (castrato)
Ermione	Anna STRADA del Pò (soprano)
Ifigenia	Cecilia YOUNG (soprano)
Pilade	John BEARD (tenor)
Toante	Gustavus WALTZ (bass)
Filotete	Maria Caterina NEGRI (contralto)

The story is based on EURIPIDES's *Iphigeneia in Tauris* (c.414 BC), but there are also features from Sophocles's *Electra*, the *Eumenides* by Aeschylus, ideas from Herodotus's *Histories*, Book IV and OVID's *Epistulae ex Ponto* as well as Cicero's *Laelius de Amicita*.

Oreste, son of Clytemnestra and Agamemnon, goes mad after he killed his mother and Aegisthus, and is pursued by the Furies. Accompanied by his friend Pilade, he has made his way to Tauris to undergo 'the sacrifice to Diana' in order to be set free from his mad delusions. Ifigenia, his sister, is a priestess in the temple of Diana in Tauris, where she had been brought by the goddess years before, when her father wanted to sacrifice her. Toante is King of Tauris, and it has been prophesied that he shall be killed by Oreste. Since he cannot recognise Oreste, Toante has issued a precautionary decree that all foreigners arriving on Tauris be sacrificed in the Temple of Diana. Ifigenia finds Oreste in the sacred grove of Diana, does not realise that he is her brother, but wishes to save him from death. Filotete, Toante's captain, is in love with Ifigenia, and supports her in order to win her. In the meantime Ermione, Oreste's wife, reaches the harbour of Tauris in her search for her husband. She encounters Pilade, and both are arrested by Filotete. Toante propositions Ermione, but she rejects him. Oreste is in a great court of the temple when Pilade is dragged in by the guards. Oreste intercedes on his behalf, but Toante orders him to be killed too. Oreste is ready to fight, but Ifigenia forbids it, and he gives himself up. Ifigenia takes advantage of Filotete's love to free Oreste, who hesitates to escape without his friend Pilade. Ermione finds Oreste, but Toante interrupts their embrace and imprisons both.

Toante offers them liberty on condition that Ermione will be his, but she refuses. Toante urges Ifigenia to sacrifice Oreste on the altar. Ermione demands that she be sacrificed instead, but is removed from the temple. Pilade pretends to be Oreste in order to die in his place, but Oreste will not let his friend be sacrificed, so both claim to be Oreste. Ermione is not willing to identify her husband, and Ifigenia reveals that she is Oreste's sister. The scene results in a fight, and Toante is killed. The libretto of Handel's version does not identify the stabber, but Barlocci's original libretto clearly reports that it is Oreste (thereby fulfilling the prophecy which Toante had sought to prevent). At the end of the opera, Oreste and Ermione are reunited, brother and sister have been brought together, and Oreste has overcome the tormenting furies.

Perhaps Barlocci's libretto was adapted for Handel by Giacomo ROSSI or Angelo CORI, but we cannot discount the possibility that the composer was involved in organising the text. Barlocci's recitatives were abridged. Some suitable movements were transferred directly from Handel's former operas without changes to the sung texts, whereas other arias were provided with new words to suit their new dramatic context. Six of Barlocci's aria texts were adapted so that they would fit to music from Handel's old operas: 'Io ti levo' from *PARTENOPE* became Ermione's 'Io sperai', 'Se discordia' from *SOSARME* became Pilade's 'Vado intrepido' (Pilade), 'Finchè lo strale' from *FLORIDANTE* was changed to 'Pensa, ch'io sono', 'Figlia mia' from *TAMERLANO* was turned into Pilade's 'Caro amico', 'Non chiedo' from Partenope changed to Filotete's 'Qualor tu paga sei' and 'Baccia per me la mano' from *RICCARDO PRIMO* became Ermione's

'Piango dolente il sposo'. Handel selected his music primarily from his London operas RADAMISTO, Floridante, OTTONE, Tamerlano, Riccardo primo, SIROE, LOTARIO, Partenope and Sosarme, although he also took one aria each from AGRIPPINA and RODRIGO. The final chorus 'Bella sorge la speranza' was taken from ARIANNA IN CRETA, and several ballet numbers were from TERPSICORE and Arianna (both works which had been performed prior to Oreste during the 1734–5 season). The overture is a revised version of the sinfonia to the cantata COR FEDELE, and Handel composed two new ballet movements. Handel effectively chose numbers from works spanning a period of twenty-seven years, and skilfully combined them in a homogeneous and dramatically convincing new opera.   ANNETTE LANDGRAF

B. Baselt (ed.), Oreste, HHA II/Supplement vol. 1 (Kassel, 1991)
A. Landgraf, 'Händel: Oreste' (CD booklet note, Dabringhaus und Grimm MDG 609 1273–2, 2004)

Organ and **Organ concertos.** See INSTRUMENTATION and ORCHESTRAL WORKS, 5

Orlandini, Giuseppe Maria (b. Florence, 4 April 1676; d. Florence, 24 Oct. 1760). Prolific Italian opera composer, especially noted for his comic intermezzi. Although Orlandini worked principally in FLORENCE, Bologna and VENICE, and is not known to have travelled outside ITALY, his arias were incorporated into pasticcios and operas ascribed to other composers in many cities in northern Europe. Pasticcios arranged by Handel for London theatres contain arias from Orlandini's Adelaide, Antigona, Arsace, Berenice, Ifigenia in Tauride, Lucio Papirio and Ormisda.

                                                              JOHN WALTER HILL

W. Kirkendale, The Court Musicians in Florence during the Principate of the Medici (Florence, 1993)

Orlando, HWV 31. Composed probably in October and November 1732 (the score is dated 20 November 1732), Orlando was premiered at the KING'S THEATRE in the Haymarket on 27 January 1733, with the following cast:

Orlando	SENESINO (castrato)
Angelica, Queen of Catai	Anna STRADA del Pò (soprano)
Dorinda, a shepherdess	Celeste GISMONDI (soprano)
Medoro, an African prince	Francesca BERTOLLI (alto)
Zoroastro, a magician	Antonio MONTAGNANA (bass)

Senesino was singing his last Handel role. Ten performances were given during the season, but Handel never revived the opera.

Orlando was the first of three superb Handel operas based on stories from ARIOSTO's Orlando furioso, and it marked an important change of direction in his operatic career. After years of composing mainly historical operas, he turned again to legendary, magical and pastoral themes, rather like those he had composed during his first years in London.

The text is adapted from a libretto by Carlo Sigismondo CAPECE, first set by Domenico SCARLATTI and privately performed in ROME in 1711. Handel transformed it radically, cutting out one pair of authentic Ariostan lovers and replacing them by Zoroastro, a magician-philosopher, who severely but benignly watches over the passion-tossed mortals and finally steers Orlando through his madness, via a 'psychological breakdown involving remorse, grief and reconciliation' (Strohm, 66), to self-mastery. The 'Argument' in the 1733 WORD-BOOK offers a characteristic moral, pointing out that the drama demonstrates 'the imperious Manner in which Love insinuates its Impressions into the Hearts of Persons of all Ranks, and likewise how a wise Man should be ever ready with his best Endeavours to re-conduct into the Right Way, those who have been misguided from it by the Illusion of their Passions'.

Act I: Zoroastro reads signs in the heavens that Orlando will not always be 'a rebel to glory'. He conjures up for Orlando a vision of heroes enervated by love, and urges him to follow the path of glory. But Orlando, madly in love with Angelica, is not yet ready for such wisdom. In Dorinda's cottage in the woods Angelica and Medoro, both of whom have been sheltering there, declare their love for one another. They are unable to conceal it from Dorinda, who is saddened because she too loves Medoro.

Act II: Zoroastro warns Angelica and Medoro not to let love blind them to the danger they are in, and they reluctantly decide that they must leave the forest. Orlando rushes in; his frantic pursuit of Angelica ends only when Zoroastro carries her away in a cloud. In Orlando's deranged mind, she becomes Proserpina, and he imagines himself descending into Hades to snatch Medoro from her protecting arms. As he makes to enter the underworld through a cave, Zoroastro bears him away in a flying chariot.

Act III: In turn Medoro, Orlando and Angelica all come to Dorinda's cottage. Orlando's arrival alarms her: still mad, he first mistakes her for Venus and woos her ardently, then for a hated enemy, to be defeated by swordplay or wrestling. Learning more of the power of love from Angelica, Dorinda decides to have nothing more to do with it. Zoroastro looks forward to restoring Orlando to his senses. But in the meantime Orlando has destroyed Dorinda's cottage, and in it, it seems, Medoro is buried alive. Angelica prepares for death at Orlando's hand, but a sudden transformation scene turns the cave into a temple, where she is protected by genii, and Orlando is overcome by soothing sleep. When he awakes, his mind restored, he is appalled to learn from Dorinda that he is responsible for the deaths of Angelica and Medoro. He is prevented from killing himself by the appearance of the two lovers. Zoroastro explains that he subjected Orlando to these trials because he was 'the jealous guardian of his honour'; all join in celebrating the hero's self-conquest.

Handel revised the form of the libretto as thoroughly as its contents, so that the structure of the opera mirrors the turmoil in the minds of the protagonists. The number of extraordinary pieces is greater than in any other Handel opera: accompanied recitatives, arias in irregular form (one of them, the sleep aria in which Orlando's senses are restored, hauntingly accompanied by two violette marine (INSTRUMENTATION, 22) and continuo), ensemble numbers split up between the characters in unconventional ways, a profusion of instrumental sinfonias accompanying the often supernatural events on stage. The tendency climaxes in the great mad scene at the end of Act II, which BURNEY, not on the whole very fond of this opera, described as painting Orlando's madness admirably 'in accompanied recitatives and airs in various measures'. He continued, 'Handel has endeavoured to describe the hero's perturbation of intellect by fragments of symphony in 5/8, a division of time which can only be borne in such a situation' (Burney, p. 778). The centrepiece of the mad scene is a gavotte '*en rondeau*' with two strongly contrasting episodes, one a lament, the other an outbreak of violence. The gavotte theme 'Vaghe pupille', in which Orlando makes to console the weeping Proserpina/Angelica derives a slightly weird hollowness from the fact that it consists simply of a tune, played by all instruments in unison with the voice (in octaves at the second and third occurrences) with continuo bass. The lament episode is a richly textured series of eight variations over a chromatic ground. The pattern of episodes and refrains continues into the orchestral postlude, accompanying one of the opera's many spectacular *coups de théâtre*: Orlando first rages to the accompaniment of vigorous concerto-like music, and is then borne through the heavens in Zoroastro's arms, as the gavotte theme recurs for the last time, now fully harmonised.

Orlando, an opera that plays entirely in the open air, is notable for a fine series of arias in pastoral mode. Of these, 'Verdi allori' and 'Verdi piante', sung by Medoro and Angelica respectively as they leave the forest in Act II rank with Handel's supremely beautiful pages. The arias 'Lascia Amor' (Zoroastro) and 'O care parolette' (Dorinda), both from Act I, were reused in the pasticcio *ALESSANDRO SEVERO*. DAVID KIMBELL

M. Bucciarelli, 'From Rinaldo to Orlando, or Senesino's Path to Madness', *Il trionfo d'Italia: Italian Voices and European Practice*, ed. J. Boer and R. Strohm (Utrecht, 2008)
Burney
Dean, *Operas*
Deutsch
Harris, *Librettos*
S. Flesch (ed.), *Orlando*, HHA, II/28 (Kassel, 1969)
D. Kimbell, 'Heldinnen aus Ariost', *HJb* 54 (2008)
Strohm

Ormisda, HWV A³. Pasticcio opera in three acts. First performed at the KING'S THEATRE on 4 April 1726. The libretto is an adaptation of *Ormisda* (1721) by Apostolo ZENO as revised for Bologna in 1722 and set by Giuseppe ORLANDINI.

Artenice, Queen of Armenia, was promised in marriage to the son and heir of Ormisda, King of Persia. Ormisda has two sons, Cosroe and Arbace. Artenice loves Arbace, but Cosroe as the first-born is the rightful heir. Ormisda's second wife Palmira urges him to favour her son Arbace and enlists the courtier Erismeno in a plot to take Cosroe's life. Convinced by the false testimony of Erismeno that Cosroe has threatened to kill Palmira, Ormisda has him thrown in prison. Erismeno comes to kill Cosroe but is prevented by Arsace, who instead frees the prisoner. When Cosroe is vindicated by Erismeno's dying confession he repays his debt to Arsace by renouncing his claim to Artenice. Arsace and Artenice will reign in Armenia, Cosroe in Persia.

The cast of the first performance was as follows:

Artenice	Anna Maria STRADA del Pò (soprano)
Ormisda	Annibale Pio FABRI (tenor)
Arsace	Francesca BERTOLLI (alto)
Erismeno	Johann Gottfried RIEMSCHNEIDER (bass)
Palmira	Antonia MERIGHI (alto)
Cosroe	Antonio BERNACCHI (alto)

Although Mrs Pendarves (DELANY) found *Ormisda* 'very heavy' compared to Handel, it ran for fourteen nights in April to June 1730 – longer than either of

Handel's new operas, *LOTARIO* and *PARTENOPE* – and it returned for a further five performances in November to December, with SENESINO taking over the role of Cosroe. A total of twelve songs were published by WALSH.

Ormisda has usually been described as a pasticcio assembled by Handel, but he appears to have had little or nothing to do with its compilation. The opera almost certainly derives from one sent to the Royal Academy (OPERA COMPANIES, 2) by Owen SWINEY from VENICE in late 1725. It was to have been performed early in the season, prior to the anticipated arrival of Faustina BORDONI in March, but it arrived in London too late for the Academy's purposes. This delay probably contributed to Handel's decision to break off work on *ALESSANDRO*, intended for Faustina's debut, and start composing *SCIPIONE*. Because *Ormisda* contained no role for Faustina, it could not be staged during the remaining lifetime of the Royal Academy, but when Handel and HEIDEGGER launched the Second Academy (OPERA COMPANIES, 3) in 1729, they included it in their first season. It seems likely that Swiney's *Ormisda* was a pasticcio, perhaps based on Orlandini's setting, but little of the music of this version can have been retained in 1730. Most of the arias sung in London came from operas dating from 1726 or later, and the recitatives were newly composed to a heavily abbreviated and revised text. The libretto was probably adapted for London by Giacomo ROSSI.

The arias, most of which were identified by Strohm, seem to have been chosen largely if not entirely by the singers. Bernacchi and Merighi sang only arias that had been composed for them, though since Bernacchi's all belonged to Orlandini's *Ormisda* they could have been part of the score sent by Swiney. Strohm believed that Handel composed the recitatives, but this possibility must be discounted on the basis of style. Whoever the composer was, he must also have written the recitatives for the pasticcio *VENCESLAO*, prepared around the same time as *Ormisda* but deferred till the following season. The primary architect of the London pasticcio may have been Heidegger, who had overseen the compilation of several pasticcios in earlier years. It may be significant that the overture and final chorus originally copied into the performing scores were eventually replaced by those from *Clotilda*, a pasticcio arrangement of an opera by Francesco Bartolomeo CONTI put together by Heidegger in 1709.

As first performed, *Ormisda* contained arias by Fiorè, Giay, HASSE, Orlandini, PORPORA, Sarro and VINCI. For the performance of 21 April, a benefit for Strada, ten arias, the final chorus and probably the overture were replaced, and there were additional changes for the revival. Senesino sang a new set of arias, apparently because he wished to avoid direct comparison with Bernacchi; he saw no reason to change any of the Bernacchi arias in *Venceslao*, which opened a few weeks later. Handel owned the two performing scores, implying that he directed the performances, but neither manuscript shows traces of his hand. The main musical source is the conducting score, London, British Library, *Add. MS* 31551.   JOHN H. ROBERTS

H. D. Clausen, *Händels Direktionspartituren ('Handexemplare')* (Hamburg, 1972)

E. Gibson, *The Royal Academy of Music, 1719–1728: The Institution and its Directors* (New York, 1989)

Strohm

C. Timms, 'Handelian and Other Librettos in Birmingham Central Library', ML 65/2 (1984), 141–67

W. Williams, *Francesco Bartolomeo Conti: His Life and Music* (Aldershot, 1999)

Ottoboni, Pietro (b. Venice, 2 July 1667; d. Rome, 28 Feb. 1740). Italian Cardinal, patron and librettist. At the age of twenty-two Ottoboni was created cardinal by his great-uncle, Pope Alexander VIII, and given the post of vice-chancellor of the Church. The income from this post and from other benefices turned Ottoboni into one of ROME's richest men. That he was nevertheless no longer considered creditworthy by 1700 was mainly due to the fact that the Cardinal spent enormous sums of money on music. In 1690 he had a small theatre constructed in his residence, the Roman Palazzo della Cancelleria (PALAZZI, 6); in 1709 a new theatre, based on designs by Filippo Juvarra, was opened. Ottoboni wrote the librettos of several operas that were performed there, and also numerous oratorio and cantata texts. With respect to the oratorio performances that he financed in his own house and elsewhere, Ottoboni was one of the most important Roman musical patrons in early eighteenth-century Rome. Among the musicians in his service were Arcangelo CORELLI and the singer Andrea Adami. Part of Ottoboni's large music collection was later purchased by Charles JENNENS (SOURCES AND COLLECTIONS, 3). Handel performed in the Cardinal's Palazzo in August and September 1707. According to both Jennens and MAINWARING, Handel composed a number of works for Ottoboni; so far it has not been possible to identify them with certainty, but it seems likely that they included *Ah! che troppo ineguali* (Italian and Latin CHURCH MUSIC) and *QUAL TI RIVEGGIO*. 						JULIANE RIEPE (Trans. ANGELA BAIER)

S. La Via, 'Il cardinale Ottoboni e la musica: Nuovi documenti (1700–1740), nuove lettere ed ipotesi', *Intorno a Locatelli: Studi in occasione del tricentenario della nascita di Pietro Antonio Locatelli (1695–1764)*, ed. A. Dunning (Lucca, 1995)

H. J. Marx, 'Die Musik am Hofe Pietro Kardinal Ottobonis unter Arcangelo Corelli', *Analecta musicologica* 5 (1968), 104–77

'Ein Beitrag Händels zur Accademia Ottoboniana in Rom', *Hamburger Jahrbuch für Musikwissenschaft* 1 (1974)

F. Matitti, 'Il cardinale Pietro Ottoboni mecenate delle arti: Cronache e documenti (1689–1740)', *Storia dell'arte* 84 (1995)

Ottone, Re di Germania, HWV 15. Italian opera. The libretto was adapted by Nicola Francesco HAYM from Stefano Benedetto PALLAVICINI's *Teofane*, which was first set to music by Antonio LOTTI for DRESDEN, as part of the marriage celebrations for Frederick August of Saxony and Archduchess Maria Josepha of Austria. Handel was probably among the audience at the first performance of Lotti's *Teofane* on 13 September 1719, when he was at Dresden to engage singers for the Royal Academy of Music (OPERA COMPANIES, 2). Three of them (SENESINO, DURASTANTI and BOSCHI) sang in Handel's version of *Ottone* four years later. Handel started composing his setting of the opera in about July 1722, and completed his score on 10 August. The unusually long gap before the first performance on 12 January 1723 at the KING'S THEATRE was due to the fact that twenty-five-year-old CUZZONI (who was to sing Teofane) only arrived in London in December 1722. The first cast was as follows:

Ottone	Francesco Bernardi, 'Senesino' (castrato)
Teofane	Francesca Cuzzoni (soprano)

Gismonda	Margherita Durastanti (soprano)
Adelberto	Gaetano BERENSTADT (castrato)
Matilda	Anastasia ROBINSON (contralto)
Emireno	Giuseppe Maria Boschi (bass)

The historical background is the marriage between Otto II and Theophanu, niece of the Byzantine Emperor, which was negotiated by the Archbishop of Cologne. The marriage took place in ROME on 14 April 972, and Otto was crowned emperor a year later. The marriage was intended to strengthen Germany's influence in Italy and to create a West–East alliance in Europe. The events described in the opera take place shortly before the marriage.

The ambitious Gismonda, widow of the former Langobard King in Rome, wants her son Adelberto to become emperor instead of Ottone. When Teofane arrives in Rome, Adelberto, in concordance with his mother's wishes, pretends to be Ottone, who has not yet arrived. Teofane, at first confused that her portrait of Ottone does not match the man in front of her, eventually sees through this deceit. Adelberto allies the Romans with the Saracens (led by Emireno), and they rebel against Ottone's troups. The latter prevail, however, and Adelberto and Emireno are imprisoned. Matilda, still in love with Adelberto, pleads for mercy from Ottone, but he remains adamant. The prisoners manage to escape in a boat on the Tiber, taking Teofane hostage. A storm forces them back to shore. Emireno and Teofane discover that they are brother and sister, and Emireno then hands over Adelberto as prisoner to Teofane. Back in Rome the plot resolves: Teofane's appearance placates everyone; Ottone pardons Adelberto; Ottone and Teofane as well as Adelberto and Matilda are united in marriage; Gismonda and Emireno duly repent.

The opera has many magnificent arias, especially for Teofane, Gismonda and Matilda, but also for Ottone. There are tender love songs, for example when Ottone sings about his love for Teofane in the siciliano 'Ritorna, o dolce amore', or when Matilda muses about her feelings for Adelberto in the Larghetto 'Diresti poi cosi?' There are ironic melodies (Adelberto's feigned declaration of love to Teofane, the sarabande 'Bel labbro') and some imperious music for Gismonda when she orders her son Adelberto to court Teofane ('Pensa ad amare'), although she is also capable of tenderness when she pities her son in 'Vieni, o figlio' (marked Larghetto e piano). Teofane's continuo aria 'Falsa immagine' aptly conveys her disappointment on first meeting the man pretending to be her future spouse. The aria became very popular, and Cuzzoni sang it at her last London concerts nearly three decades later, although an anecdote alleges that she had initially refused to sing it until Handel threatened to fling her out of the window (Mainwaring, pp. 110–11). BURNEY calls the opera full of 'favourite songs'; many of them became very popular in England. The composer borrowed from a number of his own works (BORROWINGS), including motets and cantatas written in Italy during 1707–8, AGRIPPINA, TESEO and ESTHER (HWV 50ᵃ). He later reused musical material from Ottone in works such as GIULIO CESARE (a heroic aria composed for Senesino to sing in the performance of Ottone on 26 March 1723, but which was possibly unused, was converted into Tolomeo's villainous 'L'empio sleale') and THEODORA (Ottone's 'Affanni del pensier' provided material – albeit with changed tonality and time signature – for Irene's 'As with rosy steps').

Ottone was one of Handel's successful operas. It had a first run of fourteen performances during the fourth season of the Royal Academy of Music. There were six more performances during the 1723–4 season, and Handel revived the opera again in February–March 1726 (ten performances) and in April 1727 (two performances). His last revival was with the Second Academy (OPERA COMPANIES, 3) in November 1733 (four performances). In December 1734 the OPERA OF THE NOBILITY produced a heavily rearranged version of the opera without Handel's involvement, although the cast included Senesino and Cuzzoni reprising their original roles, and also FARINELLI as Adelberto (but with none of Handel's original arias for that part).

Handel's opera was performed at BRUNSWICK in August 1723 (the version is not known, although another revival took place in February 1725), and it was adapted for HAMBURG by TELEMANN, who used a German libretto by Johann Georg Glauche. In some respects Glauche's libretto is closer to Pallavicini's original text than Haym's because he reinstated seven scenes, five aria texts, and the comic character of Isaurus/Isauro (all of which had been cut by Haym). Telemann's version for the GÄNSEMARKT, retitled *Otto*, retained a majority of Handel's arias (four were omitted or shortened), but it is arguably a pasticcio because it has ten new added arias, two instrumental interludes, newly composed recitatives, and includes one aria by Fortunato Chelleri and another by Leonardo VINCI. This was performed at Hamburg in May 1726 (three performances), and revived in September 1726, May 1727 and January 1729 (at least one performance each time). KLAUS-PETER KOCH (Trans. ANGELA BAIER)

Bianconi
Dean and Knapp, *Operas*
S. Flesch, 'Händel, Ottone und Anastasia Robinson', *Bach-Händel-Schütz- Ehrung der DDR 1985*, ed. W. Siegmund-Schultze and B. Baselt (Leipzig, 1987)
Harris, *Librettos*
R. D. Lynch, 'Händels "Ottone": Telemanns Hamburger Bearbeitung', HJb 27 (1981)
F. J. McLauchlan, 'A Recently "Discovered" Early Copy of Handel's Opera "Ottone" (1723): The "Barnby" Manuscript', HJb 45 (1999)
    Handel's Opera Ottone (1723): The Composition and Performance History during the Composer's Lifetime', Ph.D. dissertation (University of Cambridge, 1995)
    'Lotti's *Teofane* (1719) and Handel's *Ottone* (1723): A Textual and Musical Study', ML 78/3 (Aug. 1997), 349–90
    (ed.), *Ottone*, HHA II/12.1–2 (Kassel, 2008)
Strohm

overture. In a very general sense, an overture is an instrumental introduction to multi-movement and often large-scale compositions. It introduces stage works (ballets, operas, masques) and unstaged concert and chamber-music works (oratorios, cantatas, serenatas). Overtures also open suites of instrumental movements (suites, partitas) scored for different instruments (strings, woodwind and brass instruments, mixed ensembles) or for keyboard instruments.

In a more restricted sense, the term overture is used to denote an instrumental introduction to a vocal work in a characteristic form developed by LULLY. This 'French' overture is based on the model of the two-movement Venetian opera sinfonia, which consists of a slow and then a fast movement. The concept of the

Lullian overture lies in the strict differentiation between those two movements or sections – the first is characterised by dotted, staccato rhythms, 'tirades' and a compact setting in common, or *alla breve*, time and the second by imitations and a more transparent composition (alternating solo and tutti sections, trio passages) in triple or compound time. Both movements are repeated and end in a short repetition of the slow introductory movement which acts as a kind of 'coda'. The French overture is therefore a symmetrical and well-proportioned five-movement musical piece.

Outside France it was received particularly intensively in Germany, also in England (Henry PURCELL) and by a few Italian composers (for example Agostino STEFFANI). Around 1700 German composers refined the overture into the so-called overture-suite (overture with additional movements or 'side movements', suite), a highly complex chamber-music genre. The first composers to combine the French Lullian overture with a suite of airs were Johann Sigismund KUSSER and Gottlieb MUFFAT, who had both trained in France. MATTHESON regarded the French-style overture as the most important instrumental genre of the early eighteenth century (Mattheson, pp. 171–2). The most famous composer of overture(-suite)s outside France was TELEMANN (more than 100 extant compositions). According to Johann Joachim Quantz, Telemann and Handel surpassed even Lully in the composition of overtures (Quantz, 316). Like Telemann, Handel continued writing overtures until the end of his life – Telemann's last overture (including a suite) is dated 1765, Handel's last overture is the one for the oratorio The TRIUMPH OF TIME AND TRUTH (1757); his earliest essays in the field are an overture composed during his HAMBURG days (HWV 336) and the overture to the opera ALMIRA (1705).

In addition to the French overture, there was another type of introduction to multi-movement or cyclical compositions: the sinfonia of Italian origin and tradition and the related sonata and concerto forms, also developed in Italy. Harpsichord/keyboard music (suites, partitas) could also be opened with an allemande, a *prélude* or an introduction, whereby these introductory movements were sometimes closely related to the characteristic style and the expressivity of the French overture. Instrumental introductions, whether overture, sinfonia, sonata, *introduzione* or *prélude*, did not only open entire works but were also used to open acts or scenes. Sometimes arias, especially opera arias, begin with a short sinfonia-like prelude of only a few bars.

With one exception, Handel used overtures to open all of his operas. He kept to the type of overture developed by Lully, that is, the dynamic two-movement format with a dignified and rhythm-based first part of 'elevated' character contrasting with a second part, livelier and written in *fugato* style. Although conforming to the Lullian form, Handel's imagination made full use of all options and freedoms possible in this demanding genre (interesting fugues, imitatative sections and virtuosic parts for solo obbligato instruments). Only the Venetian opera AGRIPPINA begins with a sinfonia and the instrumental introduction to the Florentine opera RODRIGO is an overture including dance movements. There are also other cases where the overture is followed by one or more dance movements; Handel seldom left an overture on its own as an isolated movement.

Most of Handel's cantatas and serenatas composed in Italy dispense with an instrumental introduction although both ARRESTA IL PASSO and COR FEDELE,

IN VANO SPERI have an overture and *DA QUEL GIORNO FATALE* an Introduzione. The sacred cantata *Donna, che in ciel di tanta luce splendi* begins with
an *Introduzione*, the second part of which is composed in *fugato* style (Italian
and Latin CHURCH MUSIC). The Italian oratorios are introduced by *Sonate*,
the German passion oratorio by an Italian-style Sinfonia. The large-scale London serenata *PARNASSO IN FESTA* has a French-style overture, and from 1744
(*SEMELE*) Handel's oratorios open with French overtures. The terms *Symfony*
or *Symphony* often refer to French overtures as well (*MESSIAH, JOSEPH AND
HIS BRETHREN*). Handel called the introduction to *JOSHUA* an 'Introduzione
a tempo di Ouverture'. A few English-language works (*DEBORAH, L'ALLEGRO*)
have no instrumental introduction in the composer's autograph and performing
scores. *ALEXANDER'S FEAST* and the *SONG FOR STCECILIA'S DAY* have French
overtures; the overture of the *Song for St Cecilia's Day* has two additional minuets. The musical interlude *The CHOICE OF HERCULES* begins with an incisive
'Symphony'.

French overtures also open the *WATER MUSIC* suites and the splendid *MUSIC
FOR THE ROYAL FIREWORKS*. Handel's only suite for a wind ensemble (HWV
424) also has an overture. The introductory movements to some of the Concerti grossi and *Concerti a due cori* are French overtures, although for these
works Handel is happy to recycle introductory music used before in oratorios or earlier versions of operatic overtures. Some ANTHEMS begin with a two-
movement *Symphony*, modelled on the overture, less frequently with a Sonata or a
Sinfonia.

The variety of introductory movements Handel used – the *prélude*/preludio,
the allemande, the allegro fugato, the adagio and also the French overture – is
paralleled in his KEYBOARD MUSIC, which consists of mostly cyclical works
like suites and partitas with a few interspersed preludes and chaconnes standing
on their own.

Handel was very sensitive to the design and also the appellation of his introductory movements; his use of the different available styles and compositional
techniques is highly deliberate. His youth and early training north of the Alps
made him familiar with the Italian as well as the French style, which became
popular in Germany around 1700. Handel used French compositional and performance styles even in Italy, as is reported by MAINWARING in an anecdote:
when CORELLI admitted to being unfamiliar with the French style, Handel
replaced the original overture for *Il TRIONFO DEL TEMPO E DEL DISINGANNO*
with an Italian-style *Sonata dell'Overtura* (Mainwaring, pp. 48–9). As is evident in
his late oratorios, Handel, like many of his contemporaries, continued to have
a soft spot for the French overture until the end of his life.

UTE POETZSCH (Trans. ANGELA BAIER)

See also ORCHESTRAL WORKS

D. Burrows, 'Handel as a Concerto Composer', *The Cambridge Companion to Handel*, ed.
    D. Burrows (Cambridge, 1997)
J. Mattheson, *Das Neu-eröffnete Orchestre* (Hamburg, 1713)
J. J. Quantz, *On Playing the Flute* (1789), trans. E. R. Reilly, 2nd edn (London, 1985)

Ovid (Publius Ovidius Naso) (b. 43 BC, Sulmo, Italy). Roman poet, spent most of
his career in ROME, but died in exile in AD 17 on the Black Sea. His abundant

writing in hexameter and elegiac metre, including *Metamorphoses*, *Amores* and *Ars Amatoria*, were a source of romantic diction and imagery from the Middle Ages onward. His mythic narratives that combine eroticism with pastoral landscapes were part of opera from its inception, and his *Heroides* (Heroines) an important source for female lament. Obvious Handelian borrowings from Ovid include 'Apollo e Dafne' (*La TERRA È LIBERATA*) and *ACIS AND GALATEA*, but many Graeco-Roman mythical topics in Handel show Ovidian influence.

ROBERT KETTERER

Oxford. English city some 60 miles north-west of London and an ancient seat of learning. Its population was approximately 8,000 at the time of Handel's visit there in July 1733 (but this went up somewhat when, in term, students at the university there were in residence). The so-called 'Act' in which Handel and his London troupe of singers and instrumentalists took part was a formal degree-giving ceremony which, when celebrated publicly as it was on this occasion, usually involved special music, and a company of stage players who, in 1733, were apparently denied access to the city, and had perforce to perform in Abingdon, a small country town about $6\frac{1}{2}$ miles to the south. Given that Oxford had long been a TORY stronghold (and safe haven for many closet JACOBITES), as also the fact that Handel might then have been considered an emissary of the ruling WHIG faction, the 1733 Act – the first for twenty years – had obvious political overtones. The first news of Handel's impending visit is to be found in *Applebee's Original Weekly-Journal* of 7 April where it is said that the university was intending to honour him with an honorary 'Degree of Doctor of Music'. But either the rumour was wrong and no such offer was ever made, or Handel turned it down – on the grounds, some say, that he had no wish to follow in the footsteps of his erstwhile friend and CHAPEL ROYAL associate, Maurice GREENE, who, three years earlier, had taken a doctorate of music at Cambridge and shortly afterwards been appointed professor there.

It was probably on Wednesday, 4 July, that Handel and his 'lowsy Crew' of 'forreign fidlers'– referred to thus by the irascible Oxford antiquary, Thomas Hearne – set out from London. In addition to a large band of instrumentalists (mostly it seems 'from the Opera') were six well-known singers: Signora STRADA and Mrs WRIGHT (sopranos), Signor Rochetti and Mr Salway (tenors), Messrs WALTZ (bass) and 'Roe' (alto). The latter we may safely assume to have been Francis Rowe, a member of the WESTMINSTER ABBEY choir. On arrival, they were joined by the local countertenor, Walter POWELL, who, in addition to his academic duties as Superior Bedel of Divinity, sang with them in all seven of their Oxford performances. Five of these were given in Wren's splendid SHELDONIAN THEATRE (1669), one in the great Hall at Christ Church and the other in St Mary's, the University church. Also taking part were one 'Mr Mattis' (presumably the violinist John-Nicola Matteis) and Thomas Jones (harpist to the Duke of Chandos) together with a consortium of the most accomplished boys and men from the four main collegiate choirs (Christ Church, Magdalen, New College and St John's) who must have provided the chorus. Among those present on the occasion were Thomas MORELL (whose Cambridge Master of Arts degree he incorporated at Oxford) and Charles JENNENS.

Handel and his team kicked off on the evening of 5 July with a performance of *ESTHER* which was heard again two days later, the Friday (and most of Saturday) having been given over to academic ceremonial. On Sunday (the 8th), the Utrecht Te Deum (TE DEUM, I) and *JUBILATE* and two anthems were performed in St Mary's, the Te Deum and one anthem at Matins, the Jubilate and the other anthem at Evensong. On Monday, the 'Act' as such was resumed, but the proceedings evidently dragged on so long that the scheduled first performance of *ATHALIA*, specially written for the occasion, had to be postponed to the following day. The next morning (11 July), the 1732 polyglot version of *ACIS AND GALATEA* was done in the hall at Christ Church with a repeat performance of *Athalia* (back in the Sheldonian) later the same day. A performance of *DEBORAH*, the final event in this week-long Handel-*Fest*, followed on the Thursday, and on Friday, the 13th, the composer and his colleagues, exhausted no doubt, returned in triumph to the capital.

The Oxford visit had been an immense success, both artistically and financially, with Handel having been allowed the use of the Sheldonian Theatre free of charge in return for the lustre which he and his troops had brought to the formal university 'Act', not to mention the public interest they had generated. The city was evidently packed, and according to one report, 'Almost all our Houses ... are taken up for Nobility, Gentry, and others'; 'we are so hurry'd about Lodging', says *Read's Weekly Journal* of 7 July 'that almost all the Villages within three or four miles of this City, make a good Hand of disposing of their little neat Tenements on this great Occasion'. Other London papers, reporting on the first performance of *Athalia*, speak of 3,500 auditors, but this simply cannot be, given that the theatre is now licensed for 1,000 and can seat no more than 1,500 at most. It seems more likely therefore that these figures refer not to this one performance but to the aggregate of all five performances in the Sheldonian. H. DIACK JOHNSTONE

H. D. Johnstone, 'Handel at Oxford in 1733', EM 31/2 (2003), 248–60
S. Wollenberg, *Music at Oxford in the Eighteenth and Nineteenth Centuries* (Oxford, 2001)

Pacini, Andrea ('Il Lucchesino') (b. Lucca, c.1690; d. Lucca, March 1764). Italian castrato (compass: a–e″). He made his debut in Albinoni's *Astarto* (VENICE, 1708) in a cast that also featured SENESINO. During the next sixteen years Pacini sang at major opera houses all over Italy, including appearances in operas by Alessandro SCARLATTI and BONONCINI. In 1724 Pacini came to London, where he sang as secondo uomo to Senesino for the Royal Academy of Music's 1724–5 season (OPERA COMPANIES, 2). Handel composed the title role in *TAMERLANO* and the part of Unulfo in *RODELINDA* for Pacini, who also sang Tolomeo in the 1725 revival of *GIULIO CESARE*. Later that year he returned to Italy, where he continued to sing in operas until at least 1732. After his retirement from the stage he became a priest.   ARTIE HEINRICH

palazzi. There are numerous Italian palaces and residences in which Handel is known or suspected to have stayed between 1706 and 1710. They are discussed here in order of Handel's visit to each major city.

  1. Palazzo Pitti (Florence)
  2. Parco e Villa Demidoff (Comune di Vaglia, Florence, previously Parco e Villa di Pratolino)
  3. Palazzo Grimani/Palazzo Morosini (Venice)
  4. Palazzo Colonna (Rome)
  5. Palazzo Doria-Pamphilij (Rome)
  6. Palazzo della Cancelleria (Rome)
  7. Palazzo della Provincia (Rome, previously Palazzo Bonelli, then Palazzo Valentini)
  8. Castello Ruspoli di Vignanello
  9. Palazzo Ruspoli di Cerveteri
  10. Palazzo Alvito and Palazzo Gaetani di Laurenzana (Naples)
  11. Palazzo Ducale di Piedimonte d'Alife
  12. Palazzo Ducale di Alvito

1. Palazzo Pitti (FLORENCE)

John MAINWARING wrote that Florence was Handel's first destination in Italy, and that the composer visited the Grand Prince Ferdinando de' MEDICI, 'to whose palace he had free access at all seasons, and whose kindness he experienced on all occasions'. Handel's first stay in Florence, therefore, was probably in the autumn of 1706. Scholars once believed that *RODRIGO*, the twenty-two-year-old Handel's first Italian opera, was performed privately in October 1707 at Ferdinando de' Medici's residence, the Palazzo Pitti, but there is no clear evidence that any actual performance of the opera took place before it was given at the Teatro di Via Cocomero the following November and December.

The building of the Palazzo Pitti was begun in 1448 by the wealthy Florentine banker Luca Pitti, but later, as a result of the decline of his family, the still unfinished building was acquired in 1549 by the Medici – bitter enemies of the Pitti – who remained rulers of the Grand Duchy of Tuscany until 1737. From the fifteenth to the nineteenth centuries this grand and sumptuous Florentine residence was home to three reigning dynasties, and during that time it had numerous extensions; it was here, most probably, that Handel came to know Vittoria TARQUINI, a favourite of the Grand Prince who sang the role of Isabella in Giacomo Antonio PERTI's *Dionisio re di Portogallo* (produced in the Pratolino theatre in September 1707). Perhaps the amorous episode between Handel and Vittoria mentioned by Mainwaring, about which gossip reached even the distant court of HANOVER, took place in the magnificent surroundings of the Palazzo Pitti.

2. Parco e Villa Demidoff (Comune di Vaglia, Florence, previously **Parco e Villa di Pratolino**)

In 1872 Prince Paolo Demidoff acquired the park and villa of Pratolino, which had first belonged to the Medici, then to the Lorena family after the Medici dynasty died out with the Grand Duke Gian Gastone de' Medici. The princely theatre at Pratolino was Ferdinando de' Medici's favoured location for opera performances; it was here, in mid-September 1708, that Handel was present at the performance of PERTI's *Ginevra principessa di Scozia*, and perhaps, on 30 September 1709 – just before his return to Germany via VENICE – at the performance of the same composer's *Berenice regina d'Egitto*.

3. Palazzo Grimani/Palazzo Morosini (VENICE)

According to Mainwaring, the production of *RODRIGO* in Florence was followed by a visit to Venice for the Carnival of 1707/8, and in either January or February 1708 Handel met the Duke of Manchester in the city. He returned to Venice in the Carnival season of 1709–10 for the production of the opera *AGRIPPINA*, which had twenty-seven consecutive performances at the Teatro SAN GIOVANNI GRISOSTOMO. It was during one of Handel's two visits to Venice that he met Domenico SCARLATTI at a masked ball. According to Mainwaring's account, Handel was playing the harpsichord masked, and his identity was revealed by Scarlatti, who 'affirmed that it could be no one but the famous Saxon, or the devil'. The episode may perhaps be assigned to Handel's second stay in Venice, after the famous contest on the harpsichord and on the organ between him and the young Scarlatti which took place in ROME in the residence of the Cardinal Pietro OTTOBONI. So we may speculate that the masked ball of the 1709–10 Carnival happened in the palace of the GRIMANI family: Giovanni Carlo and his brother Cardinal Vincenzo Grimani were the proprietors of the theatre where *Agrippina* was produced. Another hypothesis is that Ferdinando de' Medici recommended Handel to the influential Alvise Morosini, in order to open the doors of the palaces of the Venetian nobility to the German musician, as had happened for Domenico Scarlatti in 1705. If this is so, the Palazzo Morosini is among the Venetian palaces which could have played host to Handel and the carnival celebrations reported by Mainwaring.

4. Palazzo Colonna (ROME)

Situated between Piazza Santi Apostoli, Via Nazionale, Via IV Novembre and Via della Pilotta, the majestic and imposing palace has belonged to the Colonna family for twenty-three generations. The stages of its construction stretched from the thirteenth to the nineteenth centuries, incorporating various small buildings inherited or erected by the ancient Roman family, in a unique and ambitious architectural complex. Unlike the other properties of the Colonnas, this palace was lived in by the cardinals of the family from 1241, and was spared for political reasons by the mercenary troops of Charles V during the sack of Rome on 6 May 1527. At the beginning of the seventeenth century a theatre was built with an adjoining garden, and the library contained at that time a valuable collection of more than 7,000 volumes. The most famous wing of the palace, the Galleria Colonna, is still home to one of the most important art collections in Rome. An extraordinary example of baroque architecture, the Galleria was opened in 1703, a few years before Handel's arrival in the city. According to Mainwaring and Annibale Merlini, Handel was 'often' at the palace of the Cardinal Carlo COLONNA (1665–1739), playing there 'continually' at the end of September 1707. Colonna commissioned the music which Handel composed for the second vespers of the feast of the Madonna del Carmine, celebrated in Rome on 16 July 1707 in the Carmelite church of Santa Maria di Monte Santo in the Piazza del Popolo.

5. Palazzo Doria-Pamphilij (Rome)

The Pamphilij family, originally from Gubbio, owed its fortune to Pope Innocent X, who was Giovan Battista Pamphilij. Following the traditional nepotism of Renaissance popes, Innocent X appointed as cardinal his nephew Camillo, who after barely three years abandoned the purple to marry the extremely wealthy Olimpia Aldobrandini, a widow of the Borghese and the only heir of the Aldobrandini. Of the five sons of this marriage, Cardinal Benedetto PAMPHILIJ (1653–1730) was an amateur author and in charge of the library of the Archivio Segreto Vaticano from 1704. In January 1684 he opened the new theatre which had been built in his palace in the Corso by Carlo Fontana, and which signalled the beginning of Arcangelo CORELLI's service with him. As Mainwaring relates, Handel was 'often' at the Cardinal's palace in the Via del Corso, where the idea probably originated of having the Saxon musician compose the music for Pamphilij's libretto Il *TRIONFO DEL TEMPO E DEL DISINGANNO* and the cantata *HENDEL, NON PUÒ MIA MUSA*. In 1763 Pope Clement XIII granted the members of the Doria family the title, the coat of arms and the property of the Pamphilij family, by virtue of the marriage of Giovanni Andrea III Doria with Anna Pamphilij, with whom the illustrious dynasty came to an end.

6. Palazzo della Cancelleria (Rome)

It was newly built between 1485 and 1513 in Renaissance style for Cardinal Riario, who was Vice-Chancellor of his uncle, Pope Sixtus IV. For this reason the palace has always been the seat of the Pontifical Chancellery. Cardinal Pietro

OTTOBONI (1667–1740), the famous patron of art, music and theatre, and member of the ARCADIAN ACADEMY, set up a small theatre there for concerts and plays, and engaged Filippo Juvarra as architect and scene designer. Mainwaring described Ottoboni as 'a person of taste, and princely magnificence. Besides a fine collection of pictures and statues, he had a large library of Music, and an excellent band of performers, which he kept in constant pay. The illustrious Corelli played the first violin, and had apartments in the cardinal's palace.' In Cardinal Ottoboni's residence Handel came to know Alessandro and Domenico Scarlatti, and it was in this palace that the famous musical competition with the younger Scarlatti took place. Whilst the contest on the harpsichord was more or less equal, with some giving preference to the Neapolitan, Handel's superiority on the organ was clear to all present, and Scarlatti himself acknowledged the skill of his opponent.

7. Palazzo della Provincia (Rome, previously Palazzo Bonelli, then Palazzo Valentini)

The construction of the palace began at the end of the sixteenth century on the initiative of Cardinal Michele Bonelli, nephew of Pope Pius V, with its elegant façade on to the Piazza Santi Apostoli. At the beginning of the eighteenth century the palace was let to distinguished persons of the time; among these was the Marchese di Cerveteri Francesco Maria RUSPOLI, who lived there between 1705 and 1713, and made it one of the most splendid theatres of the age, giving concerts and stage performances by the most important musicians living in the papal city.

Much of Handel's music written between 1706 and 1709 whilst he was at Ruspoli's disposal was probably composed and performed at the Palazzo Bonelli. The composer's first commission for Ruspoli at the palace might have been ARRESTA IL PASSO (?25 December 1706). Numerous secular CANTATAS were produced for Sunday 'conversazioni' hosted by Ruspoli, and the first performance of La RESURREZIONE was given at the palace on 8 April 1708.

In 1713 Francesco Maria Ruspoli, who for military reasons had been raised by Pope Clement XI to the rank of Prince of Cerveteri in 1709, acquired the Palazzo dei Caetani in Via del Corso and set up his new residence there. In 1827 the Palazzo Bonelli was acquired by the banker Vincenzo Valentini, consul of the King of Prussia, in order to set up his own home there. In 1873 the building was sold to the Deputazione Provinciale (the present-day Provincia) of Rome, which chose it as its headquarters.

8. Castello Ruspoli di Vignanello

Situated between Viterbo and Rome, Vignanello (Julianellum) was the feudal domain of the Marescotti until the beginning of the seventeenth century. After the marriage of Sforza Vicino Marescotti with Vittoria Ruspoli, by the desire of Bartolomeo Ruspoli, brother of the bride, his nephews assumed the surname of the house of Ruspoli. The domain of Vignanello enjoyed its greatest splendour between 1688 and 1731, with Alessandro Marescotti Ruspoli Capizucchi, and above all with his son Francesco Maria Ruspoli, who inherited all the properties and the titles of the Marescotti, Capizucchi and Ruspoli families. In May and June 1707 Handel stayed in this chateau of his Roman patron, and there, according to the receipts of the copyist Antonio Giuseppe ANGELINI, he composed and performed two Latin motets: one for the day of Pentecost (12 June, HWV 239) and the other for the Feast of Saint Anthony of Padua (13 June, HWV 231). At Vignanello he also wrote the antiphon *Salve Regina*, and part of the music for the second vespers of the Feast 'Per Nostra Signora del Carmelo', celebrated in Rome in the CARMELITE church of Santa Maria di Monte Santo on 16 July under the auspices of Cardinal Carlo Colonna (Italian and Latin CHURCH MUSIC).

9. Palazzo Ruspoli di Cerveteri

On 4 September 1705 Franceso Maria Ruspoli, after various legal battles, was able to add to his titles that of Marchese di Cerveteri. There, on 23 February 1707, Handel performed for the Marchese Ruspoli the cantata ALLA CACCIA, which he had composed to celebrate the opening of the annual stag hunt. Then with the Marchese's party he visited the port of Civitavecchia, where on 18 March at the banquet which Ruspoli gave the governors of the town on his brigantine, Handel performed the cantata Udite il mio consiglio (HWV 172), which alludes to the 'advice' about the war against the Austrians which the Marchese di Cerveteri gave on that occasion to those present.

10. Palazzo Alvito and Palazzo Gaetani di Laurenzana (NAPLES)

Handel left Rome around the end of April or the beginning of May 1708 and went to Naples, presumably taking advantage of the summer holiday of the Ruspolis in Vignanello. On 16 June he completed ACI, GALATEA E POLIFEMO, which is connected with Tolomeo Saverio Gallio (the Duke of ALVITO), of a Roman family whose members belonged to the Arcadian Academy. On 19 July 1708 the Duke married Beatrice Tocco, daughter of the Prince of Montemiletto; the ceremony took place in Naples in the Palazzo Tocco di Montemiletto, in the very central Strada Toledo (today No. 148). The bride's aunt, the Arcadian Aurora SANSEVERINO, commissioned Handel's serenata as part of the nuptial festivities. Donna Aurora ('Lucinda Coritesia' in the Arcadian Academy) was famous both for her beauty and for her generosity towards men of letters, musicians and painters. We may conjecture that Aci, Galatea e Polifemo was performed in the palace of the Duke of Alvito – situtated in the Chiaia area – before the wedding, as part of the customary musical-political activities of the Gallios: either because on the evening of the wedding (19 July) at the Alvito palace, during the sumptuous wedding festivities, another serenata, also with a text by Giuvo, was performed (with music by Nicola Fago, known as Il Tarantino: È più caro il piacer dopo le pene), or because the libretto set by Handel – which deals with the tragic story of the humble Acis, the unfortunate Galatea and the evil Polyphemus – was not entirely suitable for a wedding! Another possibility, perhaps more likely, is that Handel's work was performed in the Palazzo Gaetani di Laurenzana. This was the sumptuous Neapolitan residence of Don Nicola Gaetani (noble of the Seggio di Nido) and of Donna Aurora Sanseverino, located at the time of their marriage (1686) in the Port'Alba area, not far from the modern Conservatory of Music 'San Pietro a Majella', but later transferred to the palace 'in the Galitta', today the Via Santa Brigida (which runs alongside the Galleria Umberto I, between Via Toledo and the Piazza Municipio). An inventory of the family's personal property shows that the palace was a private seventeenth/eighteenth-century dwelling, rich in every kind of art, with at least 700 paintings (inventoried after the death of Duke Nicola in 1741) on pictorial subjects especially favoured by the patrons who commissioned them: Andromeda and Galatea, Venus and Aurora, Hercules and Adonis, these were the allegorical figures which principally filled the display rooms and the gallery.

11. Palazzo Ducale di Piedimonte d'Alife

The feudal domain of Piedimonte d'Alife (now Piedimonte Matese), not far from Caserta, with the many other lands in the upper Caserta region at the foot of the Massiccio del Matese, overlooking the upper valley of the Volturno, was the property of the Gaetani of Aragon from the end of the fourteenth century. Piedimonte was elevated to a princedom in 1715 and confirmed as the domain of the Gaetani. The Ducal Palace was rebuilt at the beginning of the eighteenth century and sumptuously furnished with many works of art. To further their musical interests the Dukes of Laurenanza built a theatre in which dramatic-musical activity flourished, with singers and performers from all parts of Italy. In this theatre in 1711 there was a revival of Handel's serenata Aci, Galatea e Polifemo with the title La Galatea favola per musica . . . Dall'abbate D. Nicolò Giuvo fra gli Arcadi detto Eupidio in Piedimonte MDCCXI . . . In the cantata Nel dolce tempo (HWV 135ᵃ), the line 'Al bel Vulturno in riva' may indeed allude to the Caserta properties of the Dukes of Laurenanza, for Mainwaring tells us that during his stay in Naples, Handel 'received invitations from most of the principal persons who lived within reach of that capital'.

12. Palazzo Ducale di Alvito

The Alvito feudal domain in Terra di Lavoro, in the diocese of Sora, situated on the border of the Kingdom of Naples and the Papal States – now in the province of Frosinone, on the border with the Abruzzi – was acquired in 1597 by Cardinal Tolomeo Gallio, secretary of state to Pope Gregory XIII, who bought it from Matteo di Capua, Prince of Conca. The Cardinal's great-nephew Francesco Gallio and his son Tolomeo Saverio restructured the palace, extending the atrium and building a grand staircase (1686). The former throne-room was converted into a spacious theatre which still today, after various vicissitudes and much restoration, hosts the productions of the local dramatic society, while the rest of the ducal palace houses the Town Hall. For this palace and its theatre we could also suppose a visit by Handel, according to Mainwaring's evidence quoted above.   DOMENICO ANTONIO D'ALESSANDRO (Trans. TERENCE BEST)

See also ITALY

P. L. Ciapparelli, Due secoli di teatri in Campania (1694 1896). Teorie, progetti e realizzazioni (Naples, 1999)

W. and U. Kirkendale, Music and Meaning: Studies in Music History and the Neighbouring Disciplines (Florence, 2007)

G. Labrot, Italian Inventories 1. Collections of Paintings in Naples 1600–1780 (Munich, 1992)

N. Pirrotta and A. Ziino (eds.), Händel e gli Scarlatti a Roma (Florence, 1987)

R. Strohm, 'Händel in Italia: Nuovi contributi', Rivista Italiana di Musicologia 9 (1974), 152–74

C. Vitali and A. Furnari, 'Händels Italienreise – neue Dokumente, Hypothesen und Interpretationen', GHB IV (1991)

E. Zanetti, 'Roma città di Haendel', Musica d'Oggi 2 (1959), 434–41
    'Händel in Italia', L'Approdo Musicale 3/12 (1960), 3–46

Pallavicini, Stefano (Benedetto Pallavicino) (b. Padua, 22 March 1672; d. Dresden, 16 April 1742). Italian librettist. The son of composer Carlo Pallavicini, he was appointed as court opera librettist at DRESDEN in 1688; he stayed until 1695, when he entered the service of the Elector Palatine Johann Wilhelm in DÜSSELDORF. In 1716 he returned to Dresden as court secretary and poet, and retained these posts until his death. A highly esteemed librettist and member of the ARCADIAN ACADEMY, Pallavicini supplied texts for musical works at Dresden for more than two decades which were set to music by Antonio LOTTI, Giovanni Alberto Ristori, Jan Dismas Zelenka and Johann Adolf HASSE. A four-volume edition of his *Opere* edited by Francesco Algarotti was published in VENICE in 1744.

Handel attended a performance of Pallavicini's *Teofane* (set by Lotti) at Dresden on 13 September 1719; three years later he and Nicola Francesco HAYM used its libretto for *OTTONE*: eighteen arias, an accompanied recitative and two duets were adapted directly from Pallavicini's original, some characters were eliminated (Isauro, Felicita, Germania, a Naiad), and the recitatives were abridged. HANS-GÜNTER OTTENBERG (Trans. ANGELA BAIER)

M. Fürstenau, *Zur Geschichte der Musik und des Theaters am Hofe zu Dresden*, 2 vols. (Dresden, 1861/2; repr. Leipzig, 1971)

Palmer (née Peacock), Elizabeth (b. London, 6 Feb. 1722; d. ?London, ?1764). Married to Ralph Palmer, cousin to Ralph, 1st Lord Verney, in February 1747, little is known of Mrs Palmer herself. From 1746, the Palmers lived near Handel in a double house on Curzon Street. When her husband died in 1755, Palmer moved briefly to the corner of Park Street and Alford (formerly the 'Chappel Street' mentioned in Handel's will) and thereafter to Chelsea. She sold the Curzon Street house to Ralph, 2nd Lord Verney in 1758. Her final account at the Bank of England was closed on 18 June 1764. Handel left her a bequest of £100.

ELLEN T. HARRIS

See also HANDEL, 8

Pamphilij, Benedetto (b. Rome, 25 April 1653; d. 22 March 1730). Italian Cardinal, patron and librettist. He was renowned among his contemporaries as a patron of the arts, especially of music, and as a poet. A great-nephew of Pope Innocent X, Pamphilij held various high offices and had enormous funds at his disposal which enabled him to engage a number of musicians and to finance numerous performances of oratorios. Among the *maestri di musica* in his service were Alessandro Melani (c.1676–c.1681), Giovanni Lorenzo Lulier (1681–90) and Carlo Francesco CESARINI; Arcangelo CORELLI dedicated his Op. 2 to Pamphilij in 1685 and was the Cardinal's principal violinist until 1690. The Cardinal's account books record payments to musicians such as Alessandro SCARLATTI, Bernardo Pasquini and Filippo AMADEI. Pamphilij not only hosted weekly *accademie* in his own house but also organised and financed oratorio performances in venues such as the Roman Collegio Clementino and the oratory of the Arciconfraternita del SS Crocifisso (both institutions were under his protection), the Collegio Romano and the Chiesa Nuova.

A keen amateur poet, Pamphilij was a member of the Accademia degli Umoristi and the ARCADIAN ACADEMY. His cantata texts and oratorio librettos were set to music by Giovanni BONONCINI, Cesarini, Vittorio Chiccheri, Francesco GASPARINI, Lulier, Melani, Giovanni Claudio Pasquini, Domenico Sarri and Alessandro Scarlatti. Handel composed several cantatas (HWV 99, 117, 157, 170) and the oratorio Il TRIONFO DEL TEMPO E DEL DISINGANNO on texts by Pamphilij. Payments for performing materials for the cantata 'Il delirio amoroso' (DA QUEL GIORNO FATALE) and for Il trionfo del Tempo are recorded in the Cardinal's account books; that Pamphilij had these two works performed is therefore very probable but no documents giving definite information about those performances have yet surfaced. It is also unclear to what extent Pamphilij acted as Handel's patron. Possibly the Cardinal, who was 'arciprete' of S. Giovanni in Laterano, enabled Handel to perform as organ virtuoso at the Basilica in January 1707. According to Charles JENNENS, Handel later referred to Pamphilij as an 'old fool' for flattering him in the text of the cantata HENDEL, NON PUÒ MIA MUSA (see Figure 22).   JULIANE RIEPE (Trans. ANGELA BAIER)

See also PALAZZI, 5

H. J. Marx, 'Händel in Rom: seine Beziehungen zu Bendetto Cardinal Pamphilj', HJb 29 (1983)
    'Die "Giustificazioni della Casa Pamphilj" als musikgeschichtliche Quelle', Studi musicali 12 (1983)
L. Montalto, Un mecenate in Roma barocca: Il cardinale Bendetto Pamphilj (1653–1730) (Florence, 1955)

Pancieri, Giulio (anagrams: Louigi Carenpi, Luigio Rincepa, C. G. F. P.) (b. Milan?; fl. 1669/70–1692). Italian librettist, described in several of his librettos as 'Milanese'. He wrote several librettos that were first set to music for VENICE, including L'Almira (music by Giuseppe Boniventi; staged at SAN GIOVANNI GRISTOSTOMO in November 1691). This was Friedrich Christian FEUSTKING's literary source for the libretto of Handel's first opera ALMIRA.

WALTER KREYSZIG

E. Selfridge-Field, A New Chronology of Venetian Opera and Related Genres, 1660–1760 (Stanford, 2007)

Pariati, Pietro (b. Reggio Emilia, 27 March 1665; d. Vienna, 14 Oct. 1733). Italian poet and librettist. He lived in Venice (1699–1714) and was imperial court poet (1714–29). He wrote drammi per musica, intermezzi comici and other dramatic works, several in collaboration with ZENO. Handel's ARIANNA IN CRETA (1734) uses Pariati's most celebrated libretto (premiered Vienna, 28 August 1715, as Teseo in Creta; music by Francesco Bartolomeo CONTI). The text of Handel's GIUSTINO (1738) reflects a revision by Pariati (1711) of a libretto by BEREGAN.

REINHARD STROHM

G. Gronda, La carriera di un librettista: Pietro Pariati da Reggio di Lombardia (Bologna, 1990)
    (includes essays by B. Dooley, H. Seifert and R. Strohm)
Strohm

Parnasso in festa, per li sponsali di Teti e Peleo, HWV 73. Handel's only celebratory serenata (or festa teatrale) for London. Such festive operatic entertainments were popular in Italy for commemorating special occasions such as royal weddings,

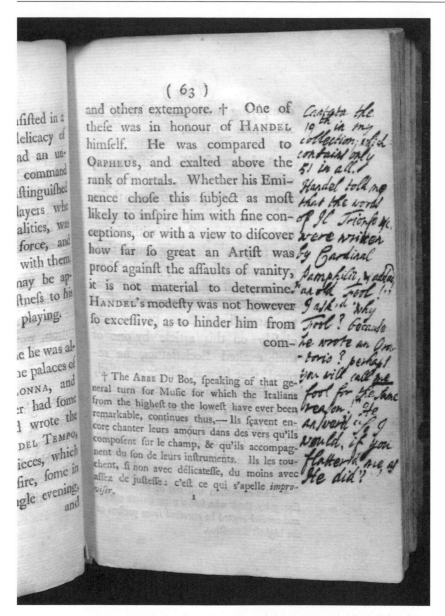

22. Charles Jennens's anecdote about Handel describing Cardinal Pamphilij as an 'old fool' in his copy of Mainwaring's *Memoirs of the Life of the Late George Frederic Handel*, 1760.

and *Parnasso in festa* celebrated Princess ANNE's marriage to Prince William of Orange. The court attended the first performance of Handel's serenata at the KING'S THEATRE on 13 March 1734, and the wedding ceremony took place the following day at the QUEEN'S CHAPEL. It was the first royal wedding held in London since 1683, and GEORGE II organised a lavish ceremony, which included Handel's anthem *This is the day which the Lord hath made* (HWV 262) (ANTHEMS, 4).

The libretto of *Parnasso in festa* is anonymous, and no older Italian model for the text has been identified (the 1734 WORDBOOK was translated into English by George Oldmixon). The action is set on Mount Parnassus, a mountain in central Greece (just north of Delphi). The ancient Greeks associated Mount Parnassus with Apollo, the god of the Arts and a renowned musician, and believed it to be the home of the nine sacred Muses (granddaughters of Zeus who each preside over a particular art or science). In Handel's serenata, Calliope (literally 'beautiful voice', the Muse of epic poetry, and mother of Orpheus), Clio (literally 'celebrate', the Muse of history), Euterpe (literally 'well-pleasing', the Muse of flutes), their leader Apollo, his son Orpheus, Mars (god of War) and the huntress Clori gather at the feast celebrating the nuptials of the mortal King Peleus (one of Jason's Argonauts) and the sea-nymph Thetis. The wedding feast was an auspicious occasion in Greek mythology: the uninvited goddess of Discord, Eris, threw out the golden apple that led to the contest judged by the Trojan Prince Paris; Peleus and Thetis were the parents of Achilles.

The mythological setting of a wedding feast on Mount Parnassus with contributions from various immortals in differing sentiments and contrasting musical moods was an attractive foundation for the serenata, which the *Daily Journal* (11 March 1734) defined as 'an Essay of several different Sorts of Harmony'. Handel borrowed a considerable amount of the score from *ATHALIA* (OXFORD, 1733), which had not yet been revived in London, but also composed nine impressive new numbers, such as Apollo's charismatic aria 'Torni pure', the charming pastoral 'Non tardate, Fauni, ancora', and the spectacular finale 'Lunga serie d'alti eroi' (which BURNEY appraised as having 'great fire and spirit'). The chorus 'S'accenda pur' skilfully grafts choral parts onto the Passacaglia from *RADAMISTO*. Several items taken from *Athalia* are substantially reworked (Apollo's first aria 'Gran tonante' is a considerable reworking of 'Jerusalem, thou shalt no more'). Several fit their new Italianate contexts effectively without much musical alteration: Calliope's 'Già le furie vedo ancor' uses the apostate priest Mathan's 'Hark! his thunders round me roll' to convey adeptly the furies plaguing Orpheus, Orfeo's expression of grief over his lost Euridice ('Ho perso il caro ben') uses the lamenting solo and chorus 'O Lord whom we adore', and the pagan chorus 'The gods who chosen blessings shed' is perfectly refitted as 'Coralli e perle', with its horns now representing conch-blowing Tritons. In addition to the usual scoring of strings, oboes, bassoons and basso continuo, Handel made plentiful use of flutes, recorders, horns, trumpets and timpani (which are marked *timpani scordati*, i.e. muted or muffled like a funeral drum, in the chorus 'Nel petto sento' that opens Part II).

The *Daily Journal* (11 March 1734) anticipated that the entertainment was to be an extraordinary event:

> There is one standing Scene which is Mount Parnassus, on which sit Apollo and the Muses, assisted with other proper Characters, emblematically dress'd, the whole Appearance being extreamly magnificent. The Musick is no less entertaining, being contrived with so great a variety . . . the celebrated Mr. Handel having exerted his utmost Skill in it.

The cast of singers was as follows:

Apollo	Giovanni CARESTINI (castrato)
Clio	Anna STRADA del Pò (soprano)
Orfeo	Carlo SCALZI (castrato)
Calliope	Margherita DURASTANTI (mezzo-soprano)
Clori	Maria Caterina NEGRI (alto)
Euterpe	Maria Rosa Negri (mezzo-soprano)
Marte (Mars)	Gustavus WALTZ (bass)

The huntress Clori was mistakenly printed as 'Cloride' in CHRYSANDER's edition (which also featured the incorrect title 'Il Parnasso in Festa'). The 'Chorus of Nymphs and Shepherds' described in the libretto were most likely the soloists mentioned above, in accordance with customary operatic practice. The soprano and alto lines probably had no further reinforcement, but additional tenors and basses were probably hired to form a balanced chorus (perhaps with three singers to each chorus part). *Parnasso in festa* received four performances. According to *The Bee*, it 'was received with the greatest Applause; the Piece containing the most exquisite Harmony ever furnish'd from the Stage, and the Disposition of the Performers being contriv'd in a very grand and magnificent Manner'. It was most likely an unstaged concert in costume, although an attractive visual element was evidently a significant aspect of the serenata's appeal.

Two months later some of the new choral numbers were incorporated into a revival of Il PASTOR FIDO (HWV 8ᶜ). In 1736 Handel adapted the finale for the conclusion to Sing unto God, an anthem performed at the wedding of Prince FREDERICK (ANTHEMS, 4). *Parnasso in festa* was revived for two performances at COVENT GARDEN in March 1737, and a single performance was given at LINCOLN'S INN FIELDS in November 1740 (the *London Daily Post* advised the public that 'Perticular Care has been taken to air the House well, and keep it warm'). On 14 March 1741 (Princess Anne's seventh wedding anniversary), a charity performance of the serenata was given at the King's Theatre in aid of the FUND FOR DECAY'D MUSICIANS; apparently the original scenery and costumes had been preserved and were reused. *Parnasso in festa* was not performed again until the Handel Opera Society's revival in 1971. An unbiased reception of the work's charms has been assisted by occasional revivals at the London Handel Festival (1984 and 1997) (FESTIVALS, 5), GÖTTINGEN (2005) and, most recently, a commercial recording by the King's Consort (2008).

DAVID VICKERS

Burney
Deutsch
A. Hicks, 'Handel and Il Parnasso in festa', MT 112/1538 (April 1971), 339–40
K. Hortschansky, 'Ein verkapptes Orpheus-Drama? Händels Hochzeits-Serentata Il Parnasso in festa per gli sponsali di Teti e Peleo für Prinzessin Anne und Prinz Wilhelm von Oranien (HWV 73)', HJb 49 (2003)
D. Vickers, 'Handel: Parnasso in Festa', CD booklet note (Hyperion, CDA67701/2, 2008)

Partenope, HWV 27. Italian opera. The libretto was written for NAPLES in 1699 by Silvio STAMPIGLIA, whose story is simple but offers plenty of scope for emotional intensity, insightful characterisation, wit, sexual innuendo and profound despair: Partenope is Queen of the newly founded city of Naples, and is loved by three suitors; Arsace, Armindo and Emilio. Arsace is her chosen favourite, although she is fond of Armindo too. Emilio is the military-minded leader of a neighbouring kingdom, and wishes to command Partenope to love him instead (he is humiliatingly rejected and later defeated in the ensuing battle). When 'Eurimene' arrives at Partenope's court, 'he' claims to have been shipwrecked, and is granted sanctuary by the generous Queen. Arsace recognises that Eurimene is actually his fiancée Rosmira (whom he has abandoned), disguised as a man. He becomes confused about which woman he loves, and privately confronts Rosmira, who forces him to swear a vow of secrecy: Arsace must never reveal her true identity if he hopes to be forgiven for his infidelity.

Throughout the rest of the opera Rosmira uses several tactics to wreak chaotic revenge upon Arsace. Her thirst for vengeance eventually leads to her revealing his infidelity to Partenope, who orders that 'Eurimene' (believed to be Rosmira's champion) and the dishonoured Arsace must face each other in mortal combat (supervised over by Ormonte, the Captain of Partenope's Guards). Arsace, who has desperately sought to avoid open conflict with Rosmira, and has realised that he truly loves her, cunningly reveals her true identity by insisting that they must fight bare-chested. Unable to comply, Rosmira confesses her deception. The estranged lovers are reconciled, Partenope makes peace with the reformed Emilio, and she chooses the gentle Armindo as her husband.

Stampiglia's libretto was set to music many times during the early eighteenth century. Handel probably attended a performance of CALDARA's *Partenope* at the VENICE Carnival in 1708 (Caldara's music is lost). This version of the libretto was the model that Handel chose for his own setting over two decades later, despite his familiarity with at least two more recent adaptations including VINCI's *La Rosmira Fedele* (Venice, 1725). It seems that the directors of the Royal Academy of Music (OPERA COMPANIES, 2) rejected a proposal to include *Partenope* in their 1726–7 season featuring CUZZONI and FAUSTINA (RIVAL QUEENS), perhaps influenced by the indigant opinion of the theatre agent Owen SWINEY, who complained that:

> it is the very worst book (excepting one) that I ever read in my whole life: Signor Stampiglia (the author of it) endeavours to be humourous and witty, in it: If he succeeded in his attempt, on any stage in Italy, 'twas meerly, from a depravity of Taste in his audience – but I am very sure that 'twill be received with contempt in England ... if it is to be done, 'twill bring more scandal & lesse profit, than any opera, that has been, yet, acted to The Hay-Market Theatre.

It cannot be coincidental that a few years later Handel chose to compose his setting of *Partenope* shortly after assuming artistic control of producing Italian operas in London: it seems that the libretto had appealed to him since his first encounter with it in 1708, that he admired other settings of it during the mid-1720s, that he wanted to produce his own version in 1726 and, when this opportunity was denied, he composed his own version as soon as possible afterwards. He finished composing *Partenope* on 12 February 1730, and it was first performed at the KING'S THEATRE on 24 February. The cast was as follows:

Partenope	Anna STRADA del Pò (soprano)
Arsace	Antonio BERNACCHI (castrato)
Rosmira	Antonia Margherita MERIGHI (mezzo-soprano)
Armindo	Francesca BERTOLLI (alto)
Emilio	Annibale Pio FABRI (tenor)
Ormonte	Johann Gottfried RIEMSCHNEIDER (bass)

The opera ran for only seven performances. Handel revived it twice in later seasons. The first revival commenced on 12 December 1730 and ran for seven performances: the role of Arsace was adjusted for SENESINO (including the substitution of Partenope's final aria 'Sì, scherza, sì' for Arsace's 'Seguaci di Cupido' in the *scena ultima*), but otherwise Handel made only a few alterations. Drastic revisions were made to allow ANNIBALI (Arsace) and CONTI (Armindo) roles of equal musical prominence in the opera's last revival under the composer's direction in 1737 (four performances).

Partenope is probably Handel's finest serious comedy, and the score is consistently engaging and memorable. 'Qual farfalletta' (II.vii) perfectly conveys the title heroine's whimsically beguiling nature, although there is plenty in both the libretto and her music to suggest that she enjoys all of the attention she gets from various rival suitors, and is not to be trifled with: she is assertive, enigmatic, seductive and vindictive in equal measure. Armindo's 'Nobil core' (III.v), featuring a solo flute, is a charming portrait of unbridled joy at discovering requited love. Rosmira's 'Io seguo sol fiero' (with robust hunting horns and oboes) is a spectacular conclusion to Act I, and suits the mock bravery of 'Eurimene', but several other moments reveal her tenderness about love ('Se non ti sai spiegar', I.iv) or her own bruised emotions ('Arsace, o Dio!', III.ii). Arsace's climax to Act II ('Furibondo spira il vento') shows him dangerously close to madness, and 'Ch'io parta?' (III.iv) conveys his broken heart through devastatingly economical music of notable beauty and sincerity; they show how far his character has progressed from the conceited lover we meet at the beginning of Act I. Emilio's 'Anch'io pugnar saprò' (I.x) wittily conveys his naive optimism that Partenope will love him, but his prison scene ('Barbaro fato, sì', II.ii) powerfully communicates his loss of hope and anguished self-reproach. 'La gloria in nobil alma' (III.ix) marks his rehabilitation as a reformed gentleman. It can be argued that each of the five protagonists (Partenope, Arsace, Rosmira, Armindo and Emilio) experiences a vital lesson of love that makes them wiser. In this respect, *Partenope* is a bitter-sweet school for lovers comparable with MOZART's *Così fan tutte*.

Dent remarked that '*Partenope* is perhaps the best libretto that Handel ever set', and suggested that the drama possesses a Shakespearian atmosphere. Dent's claim requires clarification: *Partenope* does not resemble the Shakespearian characteristics familiar from the tragedies and histories that have obvious kinship with early eighteenth-century opera seria, but is Handel's equivalent of *Twelfth Night*, including use of disguise, cross-dressing and confusion over identity. Handel's opera is an amused examination of humanity, and adopts an honest approach to depicting a world in which humour, sadness, ridicule, pity, grief and reconciliation all play a vital part.   DAVID VICKERS

Dean, *Operas*

E. J. Dent, 'The Operas', *Handel: A Symposium* (Oxford, 1954)

R. Freeman, 'The Travels of Partenope', *Studies in Music History: Essays for Oliver Strunk*, ed. H. Powers (Princeton, 1968)

Harris, *Librettos*

Strohm

D. Vickers, 'Handel's Performing Versions: A Study of Four Music Theatre Works from the "Second Academy" Period', Ph.D. dissertation (The Open University, 2007)

'The Good, the Bad, and the Ugly: Amorous Representation at the Court of Queen Partenope', *HJb* 49 (2003)

Passion. A term used in the eighteenth century to describe human emotions (affects) (RHETORIC) or bodily and mental suffering. In the general Christian sense, 'The Passion' is the suffering which Jesus Christ had to endure from the night of his betrayal until he was laid in his grave (see Neumeister, p. 492). The biblical Passion narration set to music for liturgical use is a genre that flourished in the Lutheran Church from the Reformation until the late 1700s. The eighteenth-century Passion unites the declamation of the Scriptural text in recitative with contemplating or affective arias and chorales. For a long time it was erroneously believed that Handel composed a 'St John Passion' (*JOHANNESPASSION*) which has aria texts by the librettist Christian Heinrich Postel. In the early eighteenth century poetical and affective retellings of the Passion were popular in HAMBURG (*BROCKES PASSION*).   UTE POETZSCH (*Trans.* ANGELA BAIER)

B. Baselt, 'Händel und Bach. Zur Frage der Passionen', *Johann Sebastian Bach und Georg Friedrich Händel – zwei führende musikalische Repräsentanten der Aufklärungsepoche*, ed. W. Siegmund-Schultze (Halle, 1976)

W. Braun, 'Deutsche Passionen und europäische Musikkultur', *Jahrbuch des Staatlichen Instituts für Musikforschung Preußischer Kulturbesitz* (Stuttgart, 1998)

E. Neumeister, *Geistliches Abel* (Hamburg, 1734)

pasticcio

1. Operas
2. Oratorios

1. Operas

The term pasticcio, Italian for 'jumble' or 'hotchpotch', denotes an opera consisting primarily of music originally composed for another context and reused with little or no change. This usage can be found as early as 1720, in a letter from Paolo ROLLI that speaks of SENESINO as being opposed to making 'pasticci d'arie vecchie' (Gibson, 139). There are two principal types: the pasticcio arrangement, in which an existing score is adapted for a new cast mainly by inserting pieces taken from other works by various composers; and the free pasticcio, where a score is compiled using existing pieces by one or more composers, while the recitatives and perhaps a few additional numbers are newly composed. In either case the singers often played a large role in the choice of arias. Operas written collaboratively by several composers, such the AMADEI–BONONCINI–Handel *MUZIO SCEVOLA* (1721), should not be considered pasticcios. Nor should that word be applied to arrangements in which the additions consist mostly of arias newly composed by the reviser, such as the SCARLATTI–HAYM *Pirro e Demetrio* (1709) or the ORLANDINI–Amadei *ARSACE* (1721). It is often difficult to determine from the printed libretto or even the score of an opera whether it is a pasticcio and where any borrowed music came from.

Prior to Handel's arrival in 1710 most of the Italian operas performed in London were pasticcios, and this remained true until the collapse of the opera company in 1717. As far as we know he had nothing to do with these compilations. Contrary to what was once believed he did not devise the pasticcio *Ernelinda*, first mounted in 1713, though he did later borrow from the 1719 version of GASPARINI's setting of ZENO's libretto. During the first five seasons of the Royal Academy of Music (OPERA COMPANIES, 2) no pasticcios were presented, but after the withdrawal of Bononcini in 1724, the directors obtained a series of pasticcio operas from their agent Owen SWINEY in VENICE. Only two were actually staged, *ELPIDIA* (1725) and *Elisa* (1726), mainly by VINCI and PORPORA, respectively. Handel was probably involved in revising *Elpidia* after it reached London, and he may also have had a hand in the lost *Elisa*; in the absence of the performing scores we have no way of knowing.

Two more pasticcios probably deriving in some way from scores sent earlier by Swiney were offered in the first two seasons of the Second Academy (OPERA COMPANIES, 3), *ORMISDA* (1730) and *VENCESLAO* (1731). The recitatives were composed by someone other than Handel, who may only have led the performances. Beginning in 1732, however, he arranged and performed six operas by GIACOMELLI, HASSE, LEO and Vinci: *LUCIO PAPIRIO DITTATORE* (1732), *CATONE* (1732), *SEMIRAMIDE RICONOSCIUTA* (1733), *CAIO FABBRICIO* (1733), *ARBACE* (1734) and *DIDONE ABBANDONATA* (1737). Except for *Lucio Papirio*, which contains only two inserted arias, all qualify as pasticcios. From the conducting scores and the manuscripts belonging to Sir John Buckworth and Charles JENNENS on which Handel based his arrangements (only his source for Vinci's *Semiramide* remains unknown) it is possible to establish much about how they took shape, and Reinhard Strohm has identified most of the interpolations. Three of these pasticcios were brought out in quick succession within a three-month period at the start of the 1733–4 season, Handel's first in competition with the OPERA OF THE NOBILITY. Strohm (p. 183) thinks he was trying to beat Porpora, the director of the new company, at his own game by staging operas by superior representatives of the latest Italian style, Vinci and Hasse. Alternatively Handel may simply have been filling in as best he could while waiting for the chance to do his own new opera *ARIANNA* in conjunction with the wedding of Princess ANNE, which kept being postponed from October onwards (he finally performed it in late January 1734, more than two months before the royal nuptials). Be that as it may, only *Arbace* was well received, *Semiramide* and *Caio Fabbricio* falling as flat as *Lucio Papirio* and *Catone* had before them, and Handel evidently concluded that he needed to adopt other strategies to vanquish his rivals. Only in the spring of 1737, as an afterthought, did he put on *Didone*, which once again failed.

In arranging operas by other composers Handel functioned primarily as the musical director of an opera company. His main reason for making revisions was to accommodate the score to his singers, whose ranges and vocal styles often differed from those of the original cast, and to adapt the opera to local taste, above all by greatly abridging the recitatives. He generally changed as little as he could, and the interpolated arias usually came from the repertories of the individual singers. When his source was a complete score, he reworked the old recitatives as necessary; when, as in *Semiramide* and *Caio Fabbricio*, it was an aria collection he composed new ones. Only very rarely did he substantively recompose an aria, most notably Vinci's 'Saper bramate' in *Semiramide* – a sharp contrast with his normal transformative methods in borrowing from other composers – and never did he insert arias from his own operas. Nonetheless when he did function as a composer in preparing these arrangements it was with his usual skill and dramatic acuity.

Between 1734 and 1739 Handel also created three pasticcio operas based on his own earlier works, *ORESTE* (1734), *ALESSANDRO SEVERO* (1738) and *GIOVE IN ARGO* (1739), often referred to by its English title, *Jupiter in Argos*. They differ from his other operas, even those containing large amounts of self-borrowing like *AGRIPPINA*, *RINALDO* and *Il PASTOR FIDO*, in that most of the numbers were already known to the audience and were reused without significant change. In *Oreste* and *Alessandro Severo* Handel composed only the secco recitatives and a few other movements, but in *Giove in Argo*, undertaken in response to unexpected competition and then rapidly overhauled to take advantage of newly arrived singers, he produced considerably more new music, as well as inserting two arias by Francesco Araja for the visiting prima donna, Costanza Posterla. *Giove in Argo* is preserved only in fragments, but a reconstruction by John H. Roberts will appear in the HHA. Although these three pasticcios inevitably lack the expressive subtlety and power of Handel's best operas, they merit more critical attention and more frequent performance than they have thus far received.   JOHN H. ROBERTS

H. D. Clausen, *Händels Direktionspartituren* ('Handexemplare') (Hamburg, 1972)

E. Gibson, *The Royal Academy of Music, 1719–1728: The Institution and its Directors* (New York, 1989)

L. Lindgren, 'Venice, Vivaldi, Vico and Opera in London, 1705–17: Venetian Ingredients in English Pasticci', *Nuovi studi vivaldiani: Edizione e cronologia critica delle opere*, ed. A. Fanna and G. Morelli (Florence, 1988)

J. H. Roberts, 'Handel and Charles Jennens's Italian Music Manuscripts', *Music and Theatre: Essays in Honour of Winton Dean*, ed. N. Fortune (Cambridge, 1987)

'Vinci, Porpora and the Royal Academy of Music', *Chigiana* 46 (forthcoming)

Strohm

2. Oratorios

Handel presented one pasticcio oratorio, announced as *An ORATORIO*, as a benefit concert at the KING'S THEATRE in 1738. When John Christopher SMITH JUNIOR and John STANLEY took over Handel's COVENT GARDEN oratorio series in 1760, they tried to vary the otherwise exclusively Handelian fare with a few new oratorios of their own. However, by 1763 they reverted to the accustomed all-Handel programmes because 'no other Oratorios are ever well attended', as John Stanley himself conceded. In order to continue to provide some novelty, pasticcios compiled mainly from Handel's works were occasionally given. Smith was very active in this field, producing three new pasticcios: *Nabal* (1764), *Gideon* (1769) and *Tobit* (c.1764?), all using librettos provided by Thomas MORELL. *Nabal* is based on the story of the pagan Nabal, his beautiful wife Abigail and David, as related in 1 Samuel 25; *Gideon* tells the story of the liberation of the Israelites, led by Gideon, from their Midianite oppressors (Judges 6–7). In *Tobit*,

Morell combined incidents from the Apocryphal Book of Tobit. Smith does not seem to have regarded his pasticcios as substitutes for 'genuine' oratorios, or as hastily assembled selections which had to be put on when nothing else was readily to hand, but instead the wide range of Handel's music presented in the pasticcios suggests that considerable time and energy went into these works. *Nabal* contains music from fifteen operas, four oratorios and some other sacred works. For *Gideon*, Smith's interest evidently focused on Handel's earlier works: the airs and choruses were selected from fewer original compositions, but among these were pieces from as early as 1707 (*RODRIGO*) and 1708 (*ACI, GALATEA E POLIFEMO* and *La RESURREZIONE*), to which Smith added a few excerpts from his own *Feast of Darius* (c.1758). *Nabal* and *Gideon* were sometimes even advertised as 'new' oratorios by Handel.

Smith also gave *ISRAEL IN EGYPT* a pasticcio-like treatment. He had assisted the blind Handel with revivals of the oratorio between 1756 and 1758, and from 1765 onwards Smith performed it 'with Considerable Alterations and Additions' at Covent Garden. There are slight discrepancies between several extant word-books and manuscript scores of Smith's version, but these sources show that he moved away from Handel's original structure for *Israel in Egypt* as three anthems mainly consisting of choral movements. He instead drastically changed the overall complexion of the work by inserting new recitatives and arias from operas including *RODELINDA, Arianna, ARIODANTE, EZIO, TAMERLANO* and *ORLANDO*, as well as music from some of his own compositions. Perhaps the revised libretto was provided by Morell. Smith's version of *Israel in Egypt* not only influenced later performances in Britain but also reached Germany via MENDELSSOHN who mistakenly believed that Smith's revisions were evidence of an otherwise lost authentic version by Handel.

ANNETTE LANDGRAF and EVA ZÖLLNER

R. King, 'New Light on Handel's Musical Library', MQ 81/1 (Spring 1997), 109–38
    'John Christopher Smith's Pasticcio Oratorios', ML 79/2 (1998), 190–216
A. Landgraf (ed.), Israel in Egypt, HWV 54, HHA I/14.1; 14.2 (Kassel, 1999)
E. Zöllner, 'Israel in Babylon or The Triumph of Truth? A Late Eighteenth-Century Pasticcio
    Oratorio', The Consort 51/2 (Autumn 1995), 103–17
    English Oratorio after Handel: The London Oratorio Series and its Repertory, 1760–1800 (Marburg,
    2002)

pastoral. Handel found a rich vein of inspiration in all forms of the pastoral. Through the siciliano, he expressed both deeply felt emotion ('Affanni del pensier', *OTTONE*), and religious sentiments relating to the Good Shepherd ('How beautiful are the feet of them', *MESSIAH*). He also used the DANCE form of the musette to depict a pastoral ambience (Overture, *ALCINA*; 'He shall feed his flock', *Messiah*). The 'Pifa' from *Messiah* refers specifically to the Italian tradition of shepherds who processed through town at Christmas time playing shawms (piffari) and bagpipes. Beyond these specific pastoral idioms, Handel also excelled in portrayals of nature ranging from birdsong ('Sweet bird', *L'ALLEGRO, IL PENSEROSO ED IL MODERATO*) and violent storms ('Venti, turbini', *RINALDO*) to the plagues in *ISRAEL IN EGYPT*. Among the biblical oratorios, many of which are imbued with pastoral imagery, *SOLOMON* and *SUSANNA* particularly stand out for such movements as 'The Nightingale Chorus' ('Let no rash intruder', *SOLOMON*) and 'Ask if yon damask rose' (*Susanna*).

Literary forms of the pastoral also played a significant role in Handel's music. The Italian chamber CANTATAS are largely based on the tradition of pastoral poetry descended from Theocritus and Virgil, and many, such as ARRESTA IL PASSO, can be associated with the ARCADIAN ACADEMY in ROME, which sought to return to classical idioms through the pastoral. Pastoral drama, originating in Il pastor fido by Giambattista GUARINI, found an important place in Handel's work as well. He set a libretto based directly on Il PASTOR FIDO, and ACIS AND GALATEA is a model of the English neoclassical pastoral. Revisions and expansions of these two pastorals in the early 1730s mark an important shift away from the heroic operas of the 1720s, a trend that continued especially in the pastorally infused trilogy of operas based on ARIOSTO's Orlando furioso: ORLANDO, ARIODANTE and ALCINA. ELLEN T. HARRIS

E. T. Harris, Handel and the Pastoral Tradition (Oxford, 1980)

H. Jung, Die Pastorale: Studien zur Geschichte eines musikalischen Topos (Berne and Munich, 1980)

M. R. Wade, The German Baroque Pastoral 'Singspiel' (Berne, 1990)

pastor fido, Il (HWV 8). Italian opera. Handel composed the first, shortest version of the opera (HWV 8ᵃ) in the autumn of 1712 for the Queen's Theatre in London (see KING' THEATRE), following an absence from the city which lasted over a year. The libretto by Giacomo ROSSI was based on Battista GUARINI's famous tragicommedia pastorale of the same title. Handel might have known an Italian setting of the play, kept at the Elector's library at HANOVER and written for Duke Johann Friedrich. Rossi's libretto condenses the play from five acts involving eighteen characters to three acts involving six. The result is a bare skeleton of the plot, with the background and the motivation of characters remaining largely unexplained. In addition, numerous lines of recitative remained unset by Handel and were printed in the libretto annotated with commas, rendering the recitatives as short as possible and providing the absolute minimum of information to make the plot intelligible.

The setting of the opera is the mythological ancient region ARCADIA. The Argomento in the libretto explains how, plagued by anger of the goddess Diana, Arcadians had to sacrifice to her a virgin of their country every year. An oracle announced that the goddess would not be appeased 'till two of Heavenly Race unite in Love, and that the exalted Passion of a Faithful Shepherd cancels the ancient Crime of a perfidious Maid'. This led Titiro and Montano, both of divine descent, to plan a marriage between their children, Silvio and Amarilli. It is not explained that Diana's anger was brought on by a maid who scorned the goddess's favourite priest, Aminta. The goddess also imposed the law demanding a death sentence for every unfaithful wife. This law is fundamental to the plot because Silvio and Amarilli do not love each other. He abhors the idea of love and is only interested in hunting. She, however, loves and is loved by the shepherd Mirtillo. Act I opens with Mirtillo and Amarilli lamenting their love for each other. Mirtillo overhears Amarilli's declaration of love, and wishes to embrace her. She, however, is resolved upon fulfilling her duty to her country and sends him away. Mirtillo wishes to stab himself, but is stopped by Eurilla, Amarilli's confidante, who secretly loves him. She promises to help him win Amarilli, but aside declares she will use deceit to obtain him for herself. Silvio is hunting in the forest, pledging himself to the goddess Diana and spurning

Dorinda's advances. In Act II, Eurilla undertakes her fraud. Finding Mirtillo asleep, she puts a garland in his hand. Mirtillo awakes and reads the sign on the garland: 'Mi fian cari i tuoi voti, e là t'attendo' ('Thy Vows at last are heard, and I expect thee'). Believing it to be a message from Amarilli, he rejoices and kisses the garland. Eurilla convinces Amarilli, who has observed a part of the scene, that Mirtillo loves another. Dorinda vainly pleads her love with Silvio. Next, Eurilla tells Mirtillo that Amarilli is awaiting him in the cave; she also tells Amarilli that Mirtillo is meeting the other woman there and advises her to hide herself in the cave to observe them. Eurilla's plan is for the lovers to be caught together, which will lead to Amarilli's being condemned to death. In Act III Silvio mistakes Dorinda, who is hiding in the bushes, for a wild animal and wounds her. Her misery now finally moves him and he declares his love for her. Meanwhile, Amarilli and Mirtillo have been caught. She is about to be sacrificed and Mirtillo asks to die instead of her. They confirm their love. As the ministers are taking Amarilli away, Diana's High Priest Tirenio stops the proceedings. He announces that Diana has been appeased: Mirtillo is the faithful shepherd of the oracle, of a divine race (it remains unexplained that he is Silvio's brother) and his exalted passion has cancelled the ancient crime. Diana commands that Mirtillo marry Amarilli and Silvio marry Dorinda; Eurilla is forgiven.

Though little is known about the circumstances of the composition, it appears that it was influenced by the precarious state of finances of the Queen's Theatre company in late 1712 (OPERA COMPANIES, 1). The opera is on a shorter scale than Handel's other operas and was perhaps intended as a stopgap. It contains a large proportion of continuo arias and extensively draws on Handel's Italian CANTATAS. The result is a charming score with an appropriately PASTORAL atmosphere. Mirtillo's music for most of the time carries an air of melancholy; the parts of Amarilli and Dorinda sometimes touch on tragic. In contrast, the characterisation of Silvio is gently caricatured. The most notable character, however, is Eurilla, with her dynamic characterisation which befits her role of the agent of the drama: she has a high proportion of bravura arias, bright, brilliant and more lavishly orchestrated than those for other characters. Another notable feature of the first version of the opera is the extensive overture, a full-scale concerto in six movements, which probably originated as an earlier composition. The score was finished on 24 October 1712, but the first performance did not take place until 22 November, and the opera was given outside the regular subscription.

The cast comprised the following:

Mirtillo	Valeriano Pellegrini (castrato)
Silvio	Valentino Urbani (castrato)
Amarilli	Elisabetta PILOTTI-SCHIAVONETTI (soprano)
Eurilla	Francesca Margherita de L'EPINE (soprano)
Dorinda	Jane Barbier (alto)
Tirenio	Richard Leveridge (bass)

The company's finances dictated modest staging with old sets and costumes and no scenic spectacle. After the splendour of RINALDO this was an anticlimax, summarised by the comment in the COLMAN Opera Register: 'Ye Habits were old. – ye Opera Short.' According to the Register the opera, which saw seven performances, never drew a full house; it was replaced with a similarly fated pastoral pasticcio *Dorinda* by HAYM, which shared its scene and costumes.

Handel also produced two substantially revised and expanded versions in 1734 (HWV 8ᶜ). The first revival, performed at the KING'S THEATRE, enjoyed a run of thirteen performances between 18 May and 6 July 1734. The opera was expanded and three-quarters of the musical numbers were borrowed from Handel's other works (*LOTARIO*, *EZIO*, *RICCARDO PRIMO*, *TESEO*, *RODELINDA* and *PARNASSO IN FESTA*). Certain features of the plot were accommodated, sometimes unconvincingly, to bring in the chorus of shepherds and hunters respectively. The parts of Mirtillo and Amarilli were augmented for CARESTINI and STRADA, but the part of Eurilla was reduced for DURASTANTI.

The third version was chosen to open Handel's first season at COVENT GARDEN on 9 November 1734. It ran for five performances. One of the main attractions at Covent Garden was the French ballet troupe led by Marie SALLÉ. This influenced the third version of *Il pastor fido*, which was advertised as 'With several Additions, Intermix'd with Chorus's. Which will be preceded by a new Dramatic Entertainment (in Musick) call'd Terpsichore.' The *opéra-ballet* prologue (*TERPSICORE*) was designed to show off Sallé's skills by presenting her as the muse of dance and miming various emotional states. Dance suites were also added at the end of each act (Act I: dance of huntsmen; Act II: dance of shepherds and shepherdesses; Act III: general dance). Furthermore, two new singers had to be accommodated in the tenor John BEARD (Silvio) and the contralto Rosa Negri (Eurilla), and there were further changes in musical content, the distribution of arias, and small details in various scenes. The revivals in 1734, put on at a difficult time when Handel had to contend with the OPERA OF THE NOBILITY and a war of factions among the members of the royal family, perhaps show Handel's confidence in pastoral subjects as an attraction for his audience – especially considering the close proximity of the *ACIS AND GALATEA* revivals in 1732 and 1734.   SUZANA OGRAJENŠEK

Bianconi
Dean and Knapp, *Operas*
E. T. Harris, *Handel and the Pastoral Tradition* (Oxford, 1980)
    Librettos
Strohm

Paulus Diaconus (Paul the Deacon) (b. Cividale del Friuli, c.720; d. Montecassino, c.799). Italian historian, poet and religious author. Famous for the refinement of his style and the vast range of his cultural interests, he worked at the court of the Longobard kings Rachi, Astolphus and Desiderius. After the fall of the Longobard kingdom, he retired to the monastery of Montecassino, but then went to France at the behest of Charlemagne. He returned to Italy, and in the last years of his life he devoted himself to writing the *Historia Langobardorum*, conceived as a logical continuation of the *Historia Romana*; this masterpiece of narrative historiography is the earliest source of the stories on which the librettos of *RODELINDA* and *FLAVIO* are based. Also attributed to Paulus Diaconus is the text of the hymn 'UT queant laxis REsonare fibris', from which are derived the names of musical notes in the Romance languages.

FRANCESCO LORA (Trans. TERENCE BEST)

'Peace Anthem'. See ANTHEMS, 7

Pendarves, Mary. See Mary DELANY

'Pensieri notturni di Filli'. See *NEL DOLCE DELL'OBLIO*

Pepusch, Johann Christoph (b. Berlin, 1667; d. London, 20 July 1752). The German composer and theorist Pepusch was initially active at the Prussian court (c.1681–97) before travelling through the NETHERLANDS, arriving in London soon after 1697. After working as a viola player and harpsichordist at DRURY LANE Theatre from 1704, he moved to the Queen's Theatre (KING'S THEATRE) in 1708 as a violinist and harpsichordist. He returned to Drury Lane in 1714 as musical director, settling two years later in a similar position at LINCOLN'S INN FIELDS (1716–31).

Between about December 1717 and 1718 Pepusch was a guest at CANNONS, the country house of James Brydges (later Duke of CHANDOS), which Handel also visited in April 1718. Pepusch may have been present at the first performance of Handel's *ACIS AND GALATEA* at Cannons. Although he was back in London for the 1718–19 season, he was a frequent visitor at Cannons from mid-1719 as musical director, producing numerous church anthems for Brydges until 1721 and occasional music until 1725; it is likely that he was present at, and possibly played in, the first performances of Handel's *ESTHER* (c.1718–1720).

Pepusch was a founding member of the ACADEMY OF ANCIENT MUSIC in 1726, with which Handel was involved from 1731. He provided the overture and possibly arranged some of the airs for John GAY's The *BEGGAR'S OPERA* (1728), and from around the same time he began subscribing to Handel's works. During his career Pepusch wrote over 100 violin sonatas and several masques or afterpieces himself; he retired from composition in 1729 to study ancient music. MATTHEW GARDNER

D. F. Cook, 'The Life and Works of Johann Christoph Pepusch (1667–1752) – with Special Reference to his Dramatic Works and Cantatas', Ph.D. dissertation (University of London, King's College, 1983)

R. Fiske, *English Theatre Music in the Eighteenth Century*, 2nd edn (Oxford, 1986)

H. J. Marx, *Händels Oratorien, Oden und Serenaten* (Göttingen, 1998)

Percival, Philip (b. King's Weston, Glos., 13 Nov. 1686; d. London, 26 April 1748). Irish office holder and MP; brother of Sir John, Earl of EGMONT; violist. Percival was appointed (without salary or pension) Director and Supervisor of the Irish State Music and Trumpets in 1716. At that time John Sigismond KUSSER was leader of the musicians and composer. Percival sought and obtained the appointment of Matthew DUBOURG as Kusser's replacement. Percival and his wife Martha (widow of Nehemiah Donnellan, Lord Chief Baron of the Irish Exchequer) resided in London from 1728 to 1735, and again from 1739. They had the misfortune to be living in Albemarle Street next door to the banker and economist Richard Cantillon whose house was set on fire in 1734. They lost many of their possessions in the conflagration. Earlier that year, Mary Pendarves (later DELANY) reported that an evening party she hosted included the Percivals and Handel. One of her closest correspondents was Anne DONNELLAN, Percival's stepdaughter. Percival was a composer, a friend of FREDERICK, Prince

of Wales, and on the Board of Mercer's Hospital in DUBLIN when the annual
fund-raising concerts were begun in 1736.   DAVID HUNTER

D. Hunter, 'The Irish State Music from 1716 to 1742 and Handel's Band in Dublin', GHB XI
    (2006)

performance practice. Sources of information about 'performance practice' (i.e. how
music of the past was interpreted by its performers) are diffuse and inadequate,
and interpretation of them often depends (for good or ill) on preconceptions
and taste. Whatever can be learnt from scholarship, ultimately performers have
to absorb all the available information and then engage with the music itself.
Both 'performance' and 'practice' imply action, and over the last half-century
the idea has become widely accepted that action based on knowledge about how
the music of past composers was performed enriches modern performances
and audiences' experiences of them.

   The earlier modern books that suggested how early music might be played
(from Dannreuther and Dolmetsch to Donington) covered a very wide period,
and the post-war, modern-instrument chamber orchestras played in a similar
generic way, except that French music was understood to have different conventions. There followed an increased chronological and geographical awareness,
though even as recently as the Purcell anniversary of 1995, many specialists failed
to realise how different were the conventions affecting his music from those
appropriate for Handel. There certainly was a common, late-baroque language:
Handel moved with little apparent difficulty from Germany to Italy, back to
Germany and then to England, and the professional musicians that he knew in
London were an international mix from Italy, Germany, the Netherlands, France
and elsewhere. But we have no information from which to surmise whether
there was a London 'sound', and whether the same band played differently
for Handel than it did for BONONCINI. By whatever means Handel controlled
his forces (probably not with anything like modern conducting technique), he
seems to have been a strong personality and we may presume that he would
have imposed his own style on his players. From RINALDO to JEPHTHA lies a
period of forty years, during which he probably established a strong performing
tradition.

   As was usual for composers before the nineteenth century, Handel not only
wrote music, but organised and directed its performance. His autograph scores
convey most of the necessary information; most of the difficulties we find would
have caused no problems to his musicians, but it is useful for us to study the
sources in order to find plausible and effective solutions.

   1. Orchestra
   2. Continuo
   3. Pitch
   4. Notational conventions
   5. Voices
   6. Ornamentation

1. Orchestra

One might distinguish orchestral music from chamber music by assuming that
the former has more than one string player per part. The difference, however, is

often not apparent from the score, and may not always have mattered: Handel played his Concerti grossi, Op. 6 (ORCHESTRAL MUSIC, 2) with his theatre orchestra, but by writing them initially without oboes and publishing them thus, he probably realised that they would often be played by one-to-a-part ensembles. On the other hand, trio sonatas could also be played orchestrally. The most precise and largest string body known from Handel's Italian visit was for the 1708 performances in Rome of La RESURREZIONE, with twenty-two violins, four violas, six cellos and five basses. This, however, was a special event, and there were fewer upper strings for Il TRIONFO DEL TEMPO E DEL DISINGANNO the previous year. Moreover, it is difficult to compare the evidence of the number of players booked (1708) and the number of parts copied (1707): the modern practice of two players per desk was not necessarily universal in the eighteenth century. In 1720 the Royal Academy of Music (OPERA COMPANIES, 2) specified first, second and third violins (8, 5, 4), 2 violas 4 cellos and 2 basses; a decade later there were a few more violins and violas. The most detailed information comes from payment lists of the 1750s. Lists of payment to musicians for performances of MESSIAH at the FOUNDLING HOSPITAL show that the parts were shared in the modern way and gives a string strength that tallies with payments made to players in 1758: 6 each of first and second violins, 3 violas and 3 cellos; 2 double-bass players were paid, but the parts are missing (in 1754 there were three more violins and two more violas).

There is no evidence from Handel's autograph and performing scores that he varied the number of players in separate sections within a work. The occasional solo violin or cello is marked explicitly, though the indication 'solo' may sometimes have other meanings. Perhaps players followed a convention that *piano* indicated 'back desks tacet', cancelled by *forte*, as seems to have guided the use of oboes in accompanimental sections of arias; but there is no evidence, and one would have expected Handel to give an occasional hint about this in his autograph scores. The only exceptions occur in 1749, when he added cues for ripieno strings. The inclusion of these in modern editions of *Messiah* has given the idea undue prominence, since they seem to apply only to that season. Handel had three or four oboes in his orchestra in Italy and London. In his operas, the indication of their presence in the autographs is sketchy, it being not uncommon for the only clue in an aria being V[iolino], implying 'senza hautboys', when the voice enters. Occasionally, the oboes divide and double both first and second violins, sometimes they all double the first violins. This is not always clear, and the editor or conductor has to make his own decision when there is no mention of oboes. Some ritornellos look ungrateful for the instrument or are too dependent on notes outside the oboe's range (though players could be trusted to bend a few notes an octave at cadences), and some may seem more suited to a quieter string sound. The scores of the oratorios are a little more precise. No sets of orchestral parts from Handel's own performances survive except the Foundling Hospital *Messiah* copies (probably based on Handel's practice, though of a work with, unusually, no mention of oboes in the autograph score). Instrumental parts were copied to accompany the scores that were produced for Charles JENNENS, often from the autographs, by one of Handel's main copyists in the 1740s; but these derive from scores rather than

Handel's performing material; if they give any information at all about Handel's use of oboes, it is only for the 1740s, and not backdated to his operatic career. Other instruments (recorders, horns, trumpets, viola da gamba) were used for specific purposes, often symbolic as well as colouristic.

2. Continuo

Operas were customarily directed jointly by the composer on the harpsichord and the principal violinist (i.e. concertmaster). Pictures showing opera performances in various parts of Europe have the players placed across the pit, half with their back to the audience, half facing it, with a harpsichord at each end. Handel might have played from what is often called the 'conducting score' (SOURCES AND COLLECTIONS, 2). The harpsichord parts that exist for some operas were intended for the second harpsichordist; these show the whole work and do not indicate if the second player was sometimes silent. The archlute is occasionally specified, but the current practice of it playing continuo throughout each work right up to music of the 1750s is not documented. There is no evidence of the presence of an organ in Handel's London performances until the mid-1730s. Handel's playing of organ concertos between the acts was a selling point for oratorio performances, but there is no clear evidence that he used the instrument for continuo. Some scholars have extrapolated from the rare surviving organ part (for ALEXANDER'S FEAST, 1736) that the instrument chiefly doubled the bass part during choruses at 8- and 16-foot pitch. That may have been what another player did. But a letter from Jennens (19 September 1738) stated that Handel had just bought a new organ so that 'instead of beating time at his oratorios, he is to sit at the organ all the time with his back to the Audience'. Whether it was this instrument or another, it is also reported by Charles BURNEY that Handel used a harpsichord with a keyboard from which an organ could be played. There was perhaps no need for Handel to write in his score what he was playing himself, so at least for the latter part of his career we can expect no clues about what instrument he played: specific instructions concerning keyboard might have been intended for the player of the second instrument. Jennens's letter also gives a clue that the orchestra was placed on stage for oratorio performances.

Bassoons (almost invariably named in the plural) are only mentioned on the rare occasions when they have individual lines or when they are to be tacent. The modern belief that they always played when the oboes played and were tacent otherwise is an oversimplification and probably wrong. The only bassoon parts that may derive from Handel's practice are the posthumous Foundling Hospital *Messiah* parts; perhaps these show what his bassoonists played in the latter part of his life, and it includes bassoons in arias without oboes.

Secco recitatives were presumably accompanied by two harpsichords; the surviving material gives no indication that these were in dialogue as they accompanied separate singers. Nor does it confirm that a cello played as well and, if it did, how long notes were sustained and whether cadences were ever delayed. The cellist may have read the same part as the harpsichordist, which would have enhanced their musical coordination (see the entertaining description by Michel Corrette in NG). There is scant evidence for the use of the double bass in recitative.

3. Pitch

Although there were various pitch standards across Europe, they were stepped in semitones relating to A = 440 (i.e. modern 'concert' pitch). Roman pitch was a tone lower; we are less certain about Venetian pitch, but it might have been A = 440. However, English pitches were out of kilter. Around 1700, English secular pitch was about A = 403 but rose by 1720, perhaps under the influence of Italian musicians, to around A = 415 (a semitone below A = 440 and currently the customary all-purpose pitch for baroque instruments). Handel's tuning fork at the Foundling Hospital is at A = 423, a typical pitch for organs through the century, including the organ at CANNONS; adaptations of Chandos Anthems for the CHAPEL ROYAL involved transposing the notation down a tone to allow for the higher pitch (ANTHEMS, 1–2). The organs of WESTMISTER ABBEY and ST JAMES PALACE were around A = 474, somewhat over a semitone above A = 440, and it is probable that the organ at ST PAUL'S CATHEDRAL was too. It is likely that wind and string players found it convenient to use different sets of instruments because frequent retuning by a tone would have made it difficult to keep instruments in tune.

4. Notational conventions

Players needed to observe certain unnotated conventions, which made writing and reading music easier, despite a lack of precision. The opening sections of French Overtures, with the length of the main notes and upbeats often being approximate, are easily sorted out in rehearsal, especially if the music is played in two rather than in four (or even eight!). Elsewhere, pairs of quavers may alternate or coincide with dotted quaver and semiquaver; generally the performance is the same, though it may be a clue for inégalité, especially if on at least some occasions the violins are slurred. It should be remembered that Handel composed at enormous speed, and did not need to spell out every detail: it is not uncommon for clues to the phrasing of the opening of an aria to be given only in the final ritornello. Sometimes, two separate themes come together in contradictory rhythms; they should not be adjusted. Handel often notated rhythms more precisely for instruments than for singers.

Trills at cadences are rarely notated but should always be performed. The usual rule is to begin on the upper note, which is prolonged and treated as an appoggiatura; however, the function of the appoggiatura is to be a discord, and there are times when having the main note on the beat is effective. A short upbeat to the final note should usually be added even if it is not notated. In recitatives, at feminine cadences the strong beat should be sung a note higher than the resolution (unless the preceding note is a fourth higher, in which case that note is repeated); the continuo should play a chord on the beat, not delaying the accompaniment until the voice has finished. Sometimes modern performers might prefer to de-emphasise a cadence by not including an appoggiatura.

5. Voices

For most of his career, Handel worked with the most famous singers in Europe. Much of his music was tailor-made for them, and the extensive changes to operas for revivals was largely to make the music suit subsequent singers. High voices were favoured, and included both soprano and alto castratos. The gradual transition from opera to oratorio led to a higher proportion of English singers in Handel's performances, and it seems that some of these were less virtuosic than their Italian counterparts but more sensitive to English words, which was presumably a greater priority for musical entertainments in the vernacular (although the audience still purchased the WORDBOOK so that they could follow the text). The tenor voice, only occasionally given leading roles in Handel's operas, featured more prominently in oratorios during the 1740s, perhaps because of the popularity of John BEARD.

Choirs were quite small; the Foundling Hospital *Messiah* performances featured about a dozen adults, including soloists, and up to six boys. It is clear from the part-books that soloists sang in choruses: the chorus supplemented the soloists rather than replaced them. There is no detailed evidence about the choir in theatre oratorio performances, but they were probably similar. Handel only rarely used a small extra chorus of singers in his operas (such as those premiered at COVENT GARDEN, 1734–5). Otherwise, opera choruses were usually performed by the soloists alone.

6. Ornamentation

Professional performers, both vocal and instrumental, were expected to embellish the written notes. The standard vocal form, the da capo ARIA, was designed or evolved to enable singers to show off their skill. The A section could be sung more or less as written, apart from the pause in the antepenultimate bar of the singer's part, where the music usually paused. Singers now often do nothing, but if not even a short cadenza is added, perhaps the pause should be virtually ignored. The B section is usually less virtuosic, and it would have been bad taste to ornament it too much. But at the da capo, the singer was presumably granted carte blanche to show off his/her skill and style, finishing with a more elaborate cadenza at the pause. Some examples survive, including a few in Handel's hand for OTTONE. But it is difficult to know whether these are examples of what leading singers might have sung or if they were written for less experienced singers needing the composer's guidance. Ideally, ornaments were improvised, but they were possibly (as now) worked out, whether orally or on paper, by repetiteurs or musical advisers. Bearing in mind that some people attended the whole run of performances, there may well have been attempts by singers to outdo what they did last time. Solo instrumentalists were also expected to embellish and add appropriate cadenzas. A principle for cadenzas (no doubt often broken) was to keep them within one breath. CLIFFORD BARTLETT

See also CHORUS; INSTRUMENTATION

Burrows, *Chapel Royal*

D. Burrows, 'Who Does What, When? On the Instrumentation of the basso continuo and the Use of the Organ in Handel's English oratorios', *Handel Studies: A Gedenkschrift for Howard Serwer*, ed. R. G. King (Hillsdale, NY, 2009)

W. Dean (ed.), *G. F. Handel: Three Ornamented Arias* (Oxford, 1976)
'Vocal Embellishment in a Handel Aria', *Essays on Opera* (Oxford, 1990)

B. Haynes, *A History of Performing Pitch: The Story of 'A'* (Lanham, MD, 2002)

W. and U. Kirkendale, *Music and Meaning: Studies in Music History and the Neighbouring Disciplines* (Florence, 2007)

R. Maunder, *The Scoring of Baroque Concertos* (Woodbridge, 2004)

Perti, Giacomo Antonio (b. Bologna, 6 June 1661; d. Bologna, 10 April 1756). Italian composer. He was trained in the Bolognese and Roman musical style, and was *maestro di cappella* in Bologna from 1690 to 1756. In his long life he composed a vast quantity of liturgical and devotional music (most of which has survived), as well as operas for the public theatres in Bologna, Modena, ROME and VENICE. His cantatas were favourites of Aurora SANSEVERINO, who also commissioned from him the serenata *La Leucotee* (the libretto and the music are lost) which was performed to celebrate the same occasion as Handel's *ACI, GALATEA E POLIFEMO* in 1711. Prince Ferdinando de' MEDICI preferred Perti to Alessandro SCARLATTI, not only for the composition of the sumptuous grand motets for the birthdays of the princes of Tuscany (1704–9), but also for the operas in his own Pratolino theatre (1700–10) (PALAZZI, 2): the music is lost, but Antonio SALVI's librettos for Perti's *Dionisio* (*SOSARME*), *Ginevra* (*ARIODANTE*), *BERENICE* and *RODELINDA* were later set by Handel. It is unlikely that Perti met Handel at Pratolino, but there is a strong probability that Handel knew Perti's compositions for the Prince: the final fugue in *Let thy hand be strengthened* (ANTHEMS, 3), for example, has a more than casual thematic and contrapuntal similarity to that of the Florentine motet *Alleluia* (1709).

FRANCESCO LORA (Trans. TERENCE BEST)

M. Fabbri, 'Nuova luce sull'attività fiorentina di Giacomo Antonio Perti, Bartolomeo Cristofori e Giorgio F. Haendel', *Chigiana* 21 (1964), 143–90

F. Lora, 'I motetti di Giacomo Antonio Perti per Ferdinando de' Medici principe di Toscana: Ricognizione, cronologia e critica delle fonti', Ph.D. dissertation (University of Bologna, 2005–6)

J. Riepe, 'Gli oratorii di Giacomo Antonio Perti: Cronologia e ricognizione delle fonti', *Studi musicali* 22 (1993), 115–232

C. Vitali and A. Furnari, 'Händels Italienreise: neue Dokumente, Hypothesen und Interpretationen', *GHB* IV (1991)

Peterborough, Charles Mordaunt, 3rd Earl of (b. 1658?; d. Lisbon, 21 Oct. 1735). Army officer, diplomatist, politician. A larger-than-life character whose exploits included accompanying Prince William of Orange on his journey to London in 1688, Peterborough was smitten by Anastasia ROBINSON when she performed the title role in BONONCINI's *GRISELDA* (1722). They were in Paris together during the summer of 1723. A subscriber to the Royal Academy of Music (OPERA COMPANIES, 2) for the 1723–4 season, Peterborough was the dedicatee of the libretto of the first opera of that season, Bononcini's *Farnace*. SENESINO insulted Anastasia during a public rehearsal of ARIOSTI's *Vespasiano* in January 1724 and was caned by Peterborough who forced him, kneeling, to acknowledge her virtue and beauty. As with his first wife, Peterborough married Anastasia in secret, probably towards the end of 1723. Contrary to myth, he was never a Roman Catholic.

DAVID HUNTER

Pilotti-Schiavonetti, Elisabetta ('La Pilotti') (d. Hanover, 5 May 1742).Italian soprano (compass: c'–c'''). She made her London debut at the Queen's Theatre (KING'S THEATRE) in November 1710, and continued to sing in the opera company there until 1717. During that time Handel composed roles for her in *RINALDO* (Armida), Il *PASTOR FIDO* (Amarilli), *TESEO* (Medea) and *AMADIGI* (Melissa). Judging from her arias in these operas she must have been an exceptional and brilliant singer, and she seems to have been ideally suited to playing splendidly dramatic and powerful sorceresses. She probably also sang Metella in *SILLA*. After the 1717 season she left the London stage, and thereafter sang in operas in Germany. Her Venetian husband Giovanni Schiavonetti was a cellist and harpsichordist, and after his death in 1730 she settled at the HANOVER court.

ARTIE HEINRICH

Pinacci (or 'Pinazzi'), Giovanni Battista (b. Florence, 1694–5; d. Florence, 5 June 1750). Italian tenor (compass: c–a′). From 1717 he sang in ROME, Milan, FLORENCE, Genoa, Pistoia, Reggio Emilia, NAPLES, Bologna and VENICE, in operas by Francesco and Michelangelo GASPARINI, Antonio Maria BONONCINI, Giuseppe Maria ORLANDINI, Antonio VIVALDI, Geminiano GIACOMELLI, Antonio Pollarolo, Leonardo VINCI and Francesco Feo. In 1722 he was unanimously enrolled as a singer in the Accademia Filarmonica of Bologna. Pinacci and his wife, the contralto Anna Bagnolesi, were engaged by Handel for the Second Academy's 1731–2 season (OPERA COMPANIES, 3). He probably made his London debut as Bajazet in a revival of *TAMERLANO*, and also sang in revivals of *PORO* (Alessandro), *ADMETO* (Ercole), *GIULIO CESARE* (Sesto), *FLAVIO* (Lotario). He took part in Handel's productions of ARIOSTI's *CORIOLANO* and the pasticcio *LUCIO PAPIRIO DITTATORE*. Prominent dramatic roles composed for Pinacci include Massimo (*EZIO*) and Haliate (*SOSARME*), and the tenor also performed the parts of Silvio and Damon in Handel's revised version of *ACIS AND GALATEA* (HWV 49^b). After only one season in London, Pinacci returned to Italy, where he continued to sing in operas by composers such as Johann Adolf HASSE, Giovanni Battista Pergolesi, Baldassare GALUPPI and Niccolò Jommelli until 1747. His powerful deep-centred register and strong low notes sometimes caused him to be described as a bass.

FRANCESCO LORA (Trans. TERENCE BEST)

Piovene, Count Agostino (b. ?Venice, 17 Oct. 1671; d. after 1721). Italian librettist. He wrote eight librettos for VENICE, including the tragedia per musica *TAMERLANO*, performed in Carnival 1711 (libretto dated '1710' more veneto). A revision by Ippolito Zanelli (Il Bajazet, Reggio Emilia, 1719) reflected dramatic ideas of the lead singer, the tenor Francesco BOROSINI. Handel's opera of 1724, in which Borosini again sang Bajazet, is derived from both these earlier versions.

REINHARD STROHM

Bianconi
M. Bucciarelli, *Italian Opera and European Theatre, 1680–1720*, (Turnhout, 2000)
Strohm

Pirate Editions. See EDITIONS, I

Platzer, (Johann or Jacob ?) Christoph (fl. c.1698–1720). Court painter in Passau about 1720, and presumably identical to Jacob Christoph Platzer in Salzburg. He was the teacher of his better-known nephew Johann Georg Platzer. There are some paintings in churches under his name, for example an altarpiece in the Kajetanerkirche at Salzburg. In about 1710 he made a fine portrait miniature of Handel (Figure 23), which has been lost from the HALLE Händel-Haus (MUSEUMS, I)

EDWIN WERNER

23. A portrait of Handel by Christoph Platzer, c.1710 (now lost).

See also ICONOGRAPHY

W. Kudlich, 'Platzer, Christoph', *Allgemeines Lexikon der Bildenden Künstler von der Antike bis zur Gegenwart*, vol. 27 (Leipzig, 1953)

Plutarch. Biographer, essayist and philosopher from Chaeronea, Greece (b. before AD 50; d. after 120). Plutarch's widely read *Parallel Lives* were available to Handel's contemporaries in DRYDEN's edition (1683–6), and his *Moralia* (*Moral Essays*) as translated by Philemon Holland (1603). Plutarch's firm belief in traditional piety is evident in the nineteen pairs of *Lives*, the stated purpose of which was to exemplify virtue and vice in the lives of great men (*Alexander*, 1). TESEO, SILLA, GIULIO CESARE, ALESSANDRO, PORO, and ALEXANDER'S FEAST adapt elements from Plutarch. His ethical stance generally permeates baroque opera librettos on historical themes. ROBERT KETTERER

Pope, Alexander (b. London, 21 May 1688; d. Twickenham, 30 May 1744). English poet and satirist, whose reputation was formed by *The Rape of the Lock* (1714), *The Dunciad* (1728–43) and the series of 1730s poems updating and adapting Horace's Roman poetry to a contemporary setting called *Imitations of Horace*. Pope was gifted as a lyric and philosophical poet, as evidenced in his lyrics deployed in some librettos that Handel set to music.

Received wisdom on the relationship between Pope and Handel can be expressed syllogistically, thus: Handel wrote opera; Pope hated opera; therefore, Pope hated Handel. This is not true. Notoriously, Pope attacked Italian opera in a passage in his final part of *The Dunciad* (4.45–70, published in 1743); but in that same passage, Handel is represented heroically as opera's main musical opponent. The composer's turn towards oratorio from the later 1730s might render such a rhetorical gambit plausible. Further, Pope certainly collaborated with Handel. Wolfram Windszus, in his HHA edition of *ACIS AND GALATEA* (1718), credits Pope with authorship of seven arias and one piece of recitative, including

'O ruddier than the cherry'. This may result from a somewhat uncritical uptake on Brian Trowell's stylometric test for Pope's hand in the libretto (based on avoiding the juxtaposing of open vowels, which produces a list of eight items in which that stylistic feature does not occur) and greatly exceeds the Twickenham Pope editor's attribution of 'Wretched lovers! Fate has passed' and 'The flocks shall leave the mountains' only. Handel at this time resided at CANNONS, the Edgware home of James Brydges, Duke of CHANDOS, where the 'Scriblerian' collaborators John GAY, Alexander Pope and John ARBUTHNOT were frequent guests (the 'Scriblerians' and the composer had already established social connections through Lord BURLINGTON). The first version of ESTHER dates from the Cannons period, and two sources dated 1732 credit Pope with authorship of its libretto.

For his part, Handel paid rich tribute to Pope when in 1743 (possibly with the assistance of Newburgh HAMILTON), he reworked the CONGREVE/ECCLES SEMELE (c.1707), including lines from the love-complaint of the shepherd Alexis from Pope's pastoral *Summer* that became one of Handel's most famous arias: 'Where'er you walk, cool gales shall fan the glade'. Posthumous tribute was paid to Pope by Thomas MORELL in the libretto of *JEPHTHA* (1752): at the close of Act II, when Jephtha is at his lowest ebb of self-castigation, the Chorus mitigates the harshness of Divine will by using Pope's famous words that close the first Epistle of the *Essay on Man* (1734), 'Whatever is, is Right'.

BREAN S. HAMMOND

M. R. Brownell, 'Ears of an Untoward Make: Pope and Handel', MQ 62/4 (Oct. 1976), 554–70
Mainwaring
A. Pope, *The Twickenham Edition of the Poems of Alexander Pope*, ed. J. Butt and others, 11 vols. (London, 1938–68)
B. Trowell, 'Acis, Galatea and Polyphemus: A "serenata a tre voci"?', *Music and Theatre: Essays in Honour of Winton Dean*, ed. N. Fortune (Cambridge, 1987)

Poro, Rè dell'Indie, HWV 28. Handel's twenty-first opera for the London stage was composed as the only new work for the second season (1730–1) of the so-called Second Academy (OPERA THEATRE, 3). It was first presented at the KING'S THEATRE in the Haymarket on 2 February 1731, only sixteen days after its completion. That it ran for sixteen consecutive performances, with GEORGE II and Queen CAROLINE present on nine occasions, is some indication of its popularity. Although the exotic setting and the strong dramatic plot may have partly accounted for the opera's success, a stronger reason may have been the return to England of the celebrated Italian castrato SENESINO, a favourite of the London public but not of Handel. The first version of *Poro* had the following cast:

Poro	Senesino (castrato)
Alessandro	Annibale Pio FABRI (tenor)
Cleofide	Anna STRADA del Pò (soprano)
Erissena	Antonia Margherita MERIGHI (contralto)
Gandarte	Francesca BERTOLLI (contralto)
Timagene	Giovanni Giuseppe Commano (bass)

This initial success led Handel to revive *Poro* in two later London seasons, in November/December. 1731 (four performances) and December/January

1736–7 (four performances). Both of these revivals included additional or sub-stituted music to accommodate changes in the cast. For the powerful bass, Antonio MONTAGNANA (Timagene, November/December 1731) Handel pro-vided three arias borrowed from *RADAMISTO* (December 1720 version), *SIROE* and *LOTARIO*. In the much-altered third version of *Poro* (1736–7) he intro-duced substituted arias from *Siroe* and *ARIODANTE* for CONTI (Alessandro), whilst ANNIBALI (Poro) was unusually allowed to sing arias from his reper-toire, including two from G. A. Ristori's *Le fate* (DRESDEN, 1736) and one from Vinci's *Flavio Anicio Olibrio* (NAPLES, 1729). In an altered version by TELEMANN, with the title *Der Triumph der Grossmuth und Treue, oder Cleofida, Königen von Indien* and with German recitative text by C. G. Wendt, the opera was presented in HAMBURG, receiving some twenty-seven performances between February 1732 and 1736. It was also performed at the court of BRUNSWICK-WOLFENBÜTTEL in August 1732, again in an altered version (probably by G. K. SCHÜRMANN) but this time entirely in Italian with the title *Poro ed Alessandro*.

The libretto of *Poro* was adapted from METASTASIO's *Alessandro nell'Indie* (1729); it was the second of his three Metastasio operas, the other two being *Siroe* (1728) and *EZIO* (1732). The events in the drama take place during Alexander the Great's invasion and conquest of India in 327–326 BC. The principal action is the celebrated generosity of Alexander (Alessandro) towards Poro, King of part of India, whom he overcame many times in battle, and yet granted him life, liberty and kingdom; with which is interspersed the constant love of Cleofide, Queen of another part of India, Poro's jealousy, and the distress she caused him by using Alessandro's love for her to the advantage of herself and her lover. Compared with Metastasio's original libretto, the text of Handel's *Poro* displays an important shift of dramatic emphasis, moving from the abstract virtues and values of Metastasio's characters to a depth of human experience and feeling that Handel vividly expressed in his music. Whereas Metastasio concentrates on 'the magnanimous Generosity and Clemency of Alexander the Great', Handel appears more interested in the jealousy, the despair and the human frailties of Poro, and in his tempestuous relationship with Cleofide. The change of title would appear to highlight this.

With very few exceptions the arias rank amongst Handel's finest work, widely varied in style and often richly scored. His characterisation of the principal pair of lovers is masterly and convincing: Poro is presented as an impetuous, reckless prince, a character torn by jealousy and hate; Cleofide, by contrast, emerges as a self-sacrificing figure and a symbol of fidelity. Handel's treatment of Alessandro adds a surprising and subtle dimension to the conventional heroic picture of the struggle between love and duty. Erissena is a delightful foil to the serious natures of the principal characters and is provided with engagingly vivacious music.

One unusual feature in Act I is a notable instance of musical recall of a type that is not common in opera seria. In the final bitter and sarcastic scene of the act, Metastasio reintroduced the texts of the vows that the lovers had made to each other earlier on; but he gave them an ironic twist by interchanging their speeches – Poro now scornfully presenting Cleofide's vow of constancy, and she bitterly reminding him of his pledge that he would never again be jealous. Handel deliberately emphasised the different musical identities of the two lovers in their original 'pledge' arias ('Se mai più sarò geloso' and 'Se mai turbo il tuo riposo') so that their diverse musical elements could be brought together and integrated in this duet. This final number of Act I is far more then a mere musical recall; it is a masterly synthesis of melodic, rhythmic and harmonic elements from the two earlier arias which form a new number depicting dramatic conflict and disunity.

Amongst the musical high points in Acts II and III is the tender and expressive duet for Poro and Cleofide, 'Caro, dolce, amico amplesso' (Act II), which is the dramatic antithesis of that at the end of Act I. There are also two simile arias which contain inspired and unusual music – Poro's 'Senza procelle ancora si perde' (Act II), with its elaborate scoring including obbligato parts for pairs of horns and recorders, and Erissena's pastoral 'Son confusa pastorella' (Act III), with its solo flute, musette texture and arresting modulations. BURNEY gave high praise to Poro's 'Dov'è? s'affretti per la morte' (Act III), considering it to be 'not only the best air in the opera, but equal . . . to any of Handel's best productions'; while at the climax of the work Handel provided Cleofide with a profoundly moving aria over a ground bass ('Spirto amato dell'idol mio') which belongs to the great tradition of baroque operatic laments.

GRAHAM H. CUMMINGS

G. H. Cummings, 'A Study of Handel's Opera *Poro* and its History', Ph.D. dissertation (University of Birmingham, 1991)
  'Handel's Compositional Methods in his London Operas of the 1730s, and the Unusual Case of *Poro, rè dell'Indie* (1731)', ML 79/3 (Aug. 1998), 346–67
  'Handel, Telemann and Metastasio, and the Hamburg *Cleofida*', HJb 46 (2000)
  'Handel and the Confus'd Shepherdess: A Case Study of Stylistic Eclecticism', EM 33/4 (Nov. 2005), 575–89
Dean, *Operas*
Harris, *Librettos*
Strohm

Porpora, Nicola Antonio (b. Naples, 17 Aug. 1686; d. Naples, 3 March 1768). Italian composer. The son of a Neapolitan bookseller, he enrolled to study music at his native city's Conservatorio dei Poveri di Gesù Cristo in 1696, and flourished as a composer after Alessandro SCARLATTI left NAPLES for ROME in 1719. Porpora was probably the most celebrated singing teacher in the whole eighteenth century; his pupils included the female soprano Regina Mingotti and the castratos FARINELLI, CAFFARELLI, Felice Salimbeni, Antonio Hubert and Giovanni Bindi (both of the latter were nicknamed 'il Porporino' after their tutor). He also gave musical tuition to the poet METASTASIO, Prince FREDERICK of Wales, Princess Maria Antonia Walpurgis of Saxony and Joseph HAYDN. In a career that spanned six decades, Porpora worked mainly in Naples, Rome, VENICE, London, DRESDEN and Vienna, as a teacher and composer in the service of opera houses and royal courts. At various times he was also *maestro* at three of the Conservatorios in Naples and *maestro di coro* at the three main Venetian Ospedali, but he failed to obtain the posts of *primo maestro* at both St Mark's (Venice) and the Neapolitan Chapel Royal. His large vocal output included some 40 operas, 12 serenatas, 14 oratorios, around 130 cantatas, 60 sacred choral works, 20 solo motets and antiphons, various Lamentations for Holy Week and sacred chamber duets. Despite a pair of fine cello concertos and a printed collection of *Sinfonie da camera* (Op. 2, London, 1736), instrumental music was apparently of minor appeal to him.

Porpora's path crossed with Handel's in at least two cities: in Naples – where he emerged from 1708 as an almost official bard of the new Habsburg regime alongside Alessandro Scarlatti, setting to music several serenatas and cantatas for the viceroyal court and the nobility – and in London, where he was music director and principal composer of the OPERA OF THE NOBILITY from 1733 until 1736. Porpora wrote and performed five operas in direct competition with Handel in London: *Arianna in Nasso* (first performed 29 December 1733, LIN-COLN'S INN FIELDS), *Enea nel Lazio* (11 May 1734, LIF), *Polifemo* (1 February 1735, KING'S THEATRE), *Ifigenia in Aulide* (3 May 1735, KT) and *Mitridate* (24 January 1736, KT). His Italian oratorio *David e Bersabea* (12 March 1734, LIF) and serenata *La festa d'Imeneo* (4 May 1736, KT) were both intended as celebrations of royal weddings for which Handel also produced theatre entertainments (*PARNASSO IN FESTA* and *ATALANTA*). Porpora also directed performances of pasticcio arrangements: *Artaserse* (29 October 1734, KT) and *Orfeo* (March 1736, KT). Most of his original London theatre works were settings of new librettos written by the Opera of the Nobility's Italian secretary Paolo ROLLI, and featured the company's star singers such as SENESINO, CUZZONI, Farinelli (who made his London debut as Aci in *Polifemo*), GISMONDI, MONTAGNANA and BERTOLLI. Porpora's London works are characterised not only by their extravagant virtuoso showpieces, but also by their notable experiments with extended dramatic accompanied recitatives. In summer 1736 Porpora left his position and returned to Italy, although he might have travelled to London again in 1743 to oversee the MIDDLESEX OPERA COMPANY's production of his new opera *Temistocle* (22 February 1743, KT).

Despite international fame during his lifetime, Porpora died in dire poverty. His pension from Saxony was stopped due to the SEVEN YEARS WAR; perhaps aggressive and difficult behaviour, such as that described in Metastasio's correspondence, had alienated from him the sympathies of many patrons. Nevertheless, his former pupil Farinelli provided him with financial aid, while declining to commission new music from him for the Madrid court. Notable BORROWINGS from the Neapolitan composer's music in Handel's works include the ritornello and part of the vocal theme in 'V'adoro pupille' (*GIULIO CESARE*), several themes in *ORLANDO* (including aspects of the title role's 'Fammi combattere', the mad scene, and the coro finale), the style and unison orchestral figures in 'Behold a ghastly band' (*ALEXANDER'S FEAST*), and the unison accompaniment figures in the final chorus of *ISRAEL IN EGYPT*.   CARLO VITALI

N. J. Clapton, 'Scores of Operas by Nicola Porpora in British Libraries', MA dissertation (University of London, 1981)

M. F. Robinson, 'Porpora's Operas for London, 1733–1736', *Soundings* 2 (1971–2), 57–87

Porta, Giovanni (b. Venice or the Veneto, c.1675; d. Munich, 21 May 1755). Italian composer. He studied with GASPARINI in VENICE, and probably worked for Cardinal Pietro OTTOBONI in ROME from 1706 until 1710. After briefly working as *maestro di cappella* at cathedrals in Vicenza and Verona, in 1716 he moved to VENICE, where he became an active opera composer and was *maestro di coro* at the Ospedale della Pietà (1726–37). In 1736 Porta unsuccessfully applied to become *maestro di cappella* at St Mark's, and a year later he left Venice to become Hofkapellmeister at Munich (1737–55). The Royal Academy of Music (OPERA COMPANIES, 2) commissioned Porta's opera *Il Numitore* to open its first season on 2 April 1720 (it was followed on 27 April by Handel's *RADAMISTO*), although it is unknown if Porta visited London. Handel later borrowed a number of themes from *Il Numitore* for *MESSIAH, SAMSON, SOLOMON*, his Organ Concerto in F major (HWV 295, 1739) (ORCHESTRAL WORKS, 5), and an overture composed c.1740–1 (HWV 424). He also used some arias from *Il Numitore* in the pasticcios *ORMISDA, VENCESLAO, SEMIRAMIDE* and *ARBACE*.

KLAUS-PETER KOCH (Trans. ANGELA BAIER)

Dean, *Oratorios*
E. Gibson, *The Royal Academy of Music 1719–1728: The Institution and Its Directors* (New York, 1989)
W. D. Gudger, 'Skizzen und Entwürfe für den Amen-Chor in Händels "Messias" ', HJb 26 (1980)
J. H. Roberts (ed.), *Handel Sources: Materials for the Study of Handel's Borrowing*, vol. 4 (New York, 1986)

Portraits. See ICONOGRAPHY and Appendix 4

Powell, Walter (b. Oxford, 1697; d. Oxford, 6 Nov. 1744). English countertenor who sang for Handel during his week-long visit to OXFORD in July 1733. As clerk at Magdalen College from 1714, he later sang in the choirs of St John's College and Christ Church as well. On 10 July 1733, Powell took part in the first performance of *ATHALIA* (repeated the next day); he was also involved in performances of *ESTHER* (on 5 and 7 July), *ACIS AND GALATEA* (on the 11th), *DEBORAH* (12th), and the music in St Mary's (the university church) on Sunday the 8th. Though restricted by his university duties as 'Superior' (i.e. senior) Bedel in Divinity, Powell also sang at the Three Choirs festival in Gloucester later that same year (FESTIVALS, 1) and was an early supporter of the subscription scheme which eventually led to the building of the Holywell Music Room (opened in 1748).

H. DIACK JOHNSTONE

J. R. Bloxam, *A Register of the Presidents, Fellows . . . Clerks, Choristers and Other Members of Saint Mary College in the University of Oxford*, 8 vols. (Oxford, 1853–85); vol. 2, 87, 128–9; see also *The Gentleman's Magazine* 14 (1744), 619
S. Wollenberg, *Music at Oxford in the Eighteenth and Nineteenth Centuries* (Oxford, 2001)

Pratolino. See FLORENCE; PALAZZI, 2

Protestantism. See BIBLE; CHURCH OF ENGLAND; LUTHERANISM; HANDEL, 12

Publio Cornelio Scipione. See *SCIPIONE*

Purcell, Henry (b. London, ?10 Sept. 1659; d. London, 21 Nov. 1695) and **Daniel** (b. ?London, c.1664; bur. 26 Nov. 1717). Born into a family in service to the CHAPEL ROYAL, Henry Purcell made his way first as a Chapel Royal chorister, then through a variety of court appointments (including one as Gentleman of the Chapel Royal) to serve as one of the establishment's three organists. He also became organist of WESTMINSTER ABBEY, a post he would hold until his death in 1695 at the comparatively young age of thirty-six, leaving a gap in English musical life that has been mourned (not always profitably) ever since. Just before this date, his cousin Daniel (widely thought of as Henry's brother) moved to London from OXFORD, where, after an early career not unlike Henry's, he had lived and worked since about 1689. Once back in the capital, he initially completed Henry's unfinished score for *The Indian Queen* and made his way successfully on the theatre scene in his first years there; his setting of William CONGREVE's *Judgment of Paris* was one of the four finalists in the 'Prize Musick' competition of 1701. However, although Daniel published an important set of Italian-style cantatas with English texts in 1713, he appears to have been unable to adapt to the new vogue for Italian music and opera, and composed little between 1707 and his death in 1717.

Henry Purcell had, by comparison, a very productive career. He remained a court composer until 1690, when William III's cost-cutting and desire that anthems should be accompanied only by the organ except on selected days appear to have driven him to seek employment as a composer in the theatre. He had written stage music from an early date – the first piece was a song in Nathaniel Lee's *Theodosius* written in 1680 – but now there came the operatic spectaculars, including *Dioclesian*, *King Arthur*, *The Fairy-Queen* and *The Indian Queen*, together with a host of other songs, incantations and act tunes; this was the music which was responsible for establishing Purcell's wider reputation. Indeed, when Handel arrived in London in 1710, Henry Purcell was still, musically, 'the greatest Genius we ever had', and one 'who far exceeded all foreigners'.

This public reputation partly rested on his setting of the Te Deum and Jubilate; he chose it to set it for St Cecilia's Day, 1694, the first English setting of the Te Deum with an orchestra. Much admired by Tudway and others, it became customary to perform it on occasions of public thanksgiving, and for many years was the only piece by a dead composer to be included in the SONS OF THE CLERGY Festival. It was such performances that provided a context for the performance of Handel's oratorios, and, ultimately, for the first HANDEL COMMEMORATION in Westminster Abbey in 1784. Van Tassel has pointed out that the Te Deum was quite unlike Purcell's earlier church music; it was public rather than private, dramatic rather than contemplative, and was designed for orchestral forces that were clearly not those of the smaller court band. Purcell's setting inspired BLOW, CROFT and, of course, Handel, and it is generally accepted that Purcell's work was an exemplar for his Utrecht Te Deum of 1713 (TE DEUM, I), which was performed at the public service of thanksgiving at ST PAUL'S CATHEDRAL; Handel's piece finally replaced Purcell's at the Sons of the Clergy Festival in 1734. While it has been argued that Aaron HILL's libretto for Handel's first London opera *RINALDO* was influenced by Purcellian dramatick opera, such influence is confined to aspects of the drama and the scenes and machines; the structure of the libretto is of recitative–da capo form, and sung throughout.

Handel's more direct BORROWINGS from the Purcells appear to be non-existent, although cases have been made (for example, by Zimmermann) for passages and details in Handel's anthem *O sing unto the Lord*, his duet *Beato in ver chi può* (HWV 181) and 'How happy should we mortals prove' from *ALEXANDER BALUS*. Why Handel did not use Purcell's music in the way he used that of others is unclear. Suggestions that Handel did not want the source of his borrowings identified or that he was 'more respectful and circumspect' in relation to Purcell imply both that Handel would have found it in some way 'disrespectful' to a revered composer and that he was embarrassed by the identification of his sources. There is no evidence for either proposition, both of which seem counter to the spirit and intent of Handel's borrowing practices. It is much more likely that the more straightforward music of a STRADELLA or the frothier music of a BONONCINI was more suited to Handel's purposes than the English composer's quirky, inventive, and at times startling music. However, all this is not to say there are not passages of 'scene, mood, atmosphere or affect' in Handel's music that appear to be evocative of Purcell, but it is impossible to establish whether these are 'Purcellian' or simply reflections of a prevailing English style. It is true that their number appears to increase when Handel begins to set works with English texts, and Dean's statement that Purcell was 'the precipitating genius' in the development in England of Handel's choral writing has force.

The few reports that do survive, though, suggest that Handel had a profound respect for the elder Purcell's music, one author mourning that not 'every Man [has] the same Value for our Purcell, as the wonderful Hendel has', while the composer himself was quoted by Mr SAVAGE in R. J. S. Stevens as commenting (when referring to his own oratorio of JEPHTHA) 'O got te teffel. If Purcell had lived he would have composed better music than this.'   MICHAEL BURDEN

M. Burden (ed.), The Purcell Companion (London, 1995)

P. Holman, Purcell (Oxford, 1994)

R. J. S. Stevens (from Mr Savage in 1775), 'Anecdotes', Cambridge, Pendlebury Library of Music MS, fol. 18

W. Weber, The Rise of Musical Classics in Eighteenth-Century England (Oxford, 1992)

F. Zimmerman, 'Purcellian Passages in the Compositions of G. F. Handel', Music in Eighteenth-Century England, ed. C. Hogwood and R. Luckett (Cambridge, 1983)

Q

Qual ti riveggio ('Ero e Leandro'), HWV 150. Hero's complaint over the drowned body of Leander provides a highly dramatic scene in recit.–aria–recit.–aria–recit.–aria–recit. form, scored for solo soprano, two oboes, strings and continuo. In the arias, first violin and cello alternately come to the fore with sophisticated concertato sections. In the 1840s, the autograph collector Aloys FUCHS attributed the poetry to Cardinal OTTOBONI and dated its musical setting to 1707. The latter assumption seems supported by the paper type, the former by close linguistic similarities with a remake of the Greek myth published at VENICE in 1635 by Lucrezia Marinelli (1571–1653), a local poetess-cum-feminist, within her extended poem *Enrico ovvero Bisanzio acquistato* (V.31–56): Enrico celebrated Venice's conquest of Constantinople in 1204 and Ottoboni was born a Venetian nobleman. The fragmentary transmission of the cantata has raised speculations about its integrity. While it is likely that an instrumental overture was originally planned by Handel, the sung text appears perfectly, if unconventionally, closed by three narrative lines of secco recitative, a pattern found elsewhere for the 'cantata in accademia'. For self-BORROWINGS, see *AGRIPPINA*, *FLAVIO*, *EZIO* and various instrumental pieces.   CARLO VITALI

Queen's Chapel, St James's. Completed in 1625 by Inigo Jones for Henrietta Maria, Charles I's Catholic queen, despoiled after the Civil War and refitted in 1662 for Catherine of Braganza with a painted east window and the present concave reredos fronting a small gallery. After James II's flight in 1688 most of the Restoration fittings were removed and the chapel let to the French Protestants. What little fixed seating existed before the nineteenth century was temporarily removed for Princess ANNE's wedding on 14 March 1734, when tiered collegiate seats were built with galleries above and the whole east end filled with musicians on three levels for the anthem *This is the Day* (ANTHEMS, 4).

A fire in 1809 detached the chapel (then Lutheran) from ST JAMES'S PALACE. It was reclaimed as a chapel royal in 1938, when the organ was reinstated on the south recess, and the royal gallery on the west was restored. Further rehabilitation took place after the Second World War.   KERRY DOWNES

Burrows, *Chapel Royal*, Plate V (illustration)

Queen's Library. See GREEN PARK

Queen's Theatre. See KING'S THEATRE; Sir John VANBRUGH

Quinault, Philippe (bap. Paris, 5 June 1632; d. Paris, 26 Nov. 1688). In the 1660s, in the midst of a successful career in the spoken theatre, Quinault began to compose airs and to contribute verses to musical productions at court. In 1672 he devoted himself completely to writing librettos for LULLY's Académie Royale de Musique, to which he contributed eleven librettos between 1673 and 1686. His most direct link to Handel is as the author of *Thésée*, much of which HAYM translated literally in drafting the libretto for *TESEO*. In addition, Antoine HOUDAR DE LA MOTTE's *Amadis de Grèce*, the basis for the libretto of *AMADIGI*, is greatly indebted to Quinault's *Amadis* (1684), and the words Handel set for *ALCESTE* suggest that SMOLLETT's play followed Quinault's *Alceste* (1674) quite closely. It is possible that the librettists of *ADMETO* and *ORLANDO* were familiar with Quinault's *Alceste* and *Roland*, which feature similar characters.

BUFORD NORMAN

B. Norman, *Touched by the Graces: The Libretti of Philippe Quinault in the Context of French Classicism* (Birmingham, AL, 2001)

Racine, Jean (bap. La Ferté-Milon, 22 Dec. 1639; d. Paris, 21 April 1699). The librettos of several of Handel's operas are indebted to Racine's tragedies, which were greatly admired by the creators of opera seria. METASTASIO's *Alessandro nell'Indie*, on which *PORO* is based, draws heavily from Racine's *Alexandre le Grand* (1665), and his *EZIO* features a rivalry similar to the one between Nero and Britannicus in Racine's *Britannicus* (1669). Handel chose these two librettos after abandoning *TITUS L'EMPEREUR* in 1731, a work that, although in Italian, seems based on Racine's *Bérénice* (1670). Several other Handel operas feature characters from Racine's tragedies, but in aspects of their lives which Racine did not dramatise: *Agrippina* (*Britannicus*), *Teseo* (*Phèdre*), *Alessandro* (*Alexandre le Grand*), *Oreste* (*Andromaque*, *Iphigénie*). (The Bajazet of *TAMERLANO* is not the same as the title character of Racine's *Bajazet*, nor is Handel's title heroine in *BERENICE* the same as Racine's.)

Handel's interest in Racine in 1731–2 had an even more direct influence on the oratorios. One cannot say that *Poro* and *Ezio* are based on Racine, but the playwright's biblical tragedies are the obvious inspiration for *ESTHER* and *ATHALIA*. Racine's *Esther* (1689) and *Athalie* (1691), written for the girls' school founded by Mme de Maintenon (the morganatic wife of Louis XIV) at Saint-Cyr, feature *intermèdes* by Jean-Baptiste Moreau (1656–1733) after each act (except for the last of *Athalie*) and within the first and third acts of *Esther*. Some of the lines of these *intermèdes* – written in lines of varying length, as opposed to the alexandrines of the acts – are spoken, but most are sung, mainly by the chorus but also by soloists or small ensembles.

Handel's librettists were clearly familiar with Racine's French texts as well as with the translations by Thomas Brereton (*Esther*, 1715) and William Duncombe (*Athaliah*, 1722). In general, the libretto of *Esther* follows Racine and Brereton fairly closely (in the sections that are included in the oratorio), but it is often difficult to determine if it is following the original or the translation. Nevertheless, some borrowings are clear: Haman's air 'Pluck, root and branch' is clearly from Brereton, but the following passage from scene iii of the libretto is closer to Racine:

> O Jordan, Jordan, sacred tide!
> Shall we no more behold thee glide
> The fertile vales along?

> Ô rives du Jourdain ! Ô champs aimés des Cieux !
> Sacrés monts, fertiles vallées (Racine, I.ii)

> O Banks of Jordan's Stream by Heav'n belov'd (Brereton, I.ii)

Similarly, in the case of *Athalia*, there are similarities between Samuel HUMPHREYS's libretto and Duncombe's translation, but there are more cases in which Humphreys clearly supplied his own translation. When both writers follow Racine closely but do not often use the same words, one can conclude that Humphreys was working directly from Racine's text.

It is interesting to note that, when the Comédie-Française staged *Athalie* in 1939 for the three-hundredth anniversary of Racine's birth, Handel's music was chosen, although several settings of the French text were available.

BUFORD NORMAN

Dean, *Oratorios*
R. Strohm, 'Handel, Metastasio, Racine: The Case of Ezio', MT 118/1617 (1977), 901–3

Radamisto, HWV 12. *Radamisto* was Handel's first opera for the Royal Academy of Music (OPERA COMPANIES, 2). With its heroic subject, the richness of its orchestration, the power and beauty of its arias and the sumptuousness of its staging, it may well have been intended as a spectacular opening of the Academy's first season; but in the event that honour went to Giovanni PORTA's *Numitore*, premiered on 2 April 1720, while *Radamisto* was not given until 27 April.

The libretto was almost certainly by Nicola HAYM, and was based on *L'amor tirannico* by Domenico LALLI, first set by GASPARINI in 1710 in VENICE, then revised for a FLORENCE production in 1712: it was this version which was Haym's source. Lalli's text was derived from an earlier French source (SCUDERY). The story is based on a historical event which took place in Asia Minor in AD 51, recorded in TACITUS's *Annals*. Radamisto, son of Farasmane, King of Thrace, and his wife Zenobia are besieged in their city by Tiridate, King of Armenia, who, despite the love and loyalty of his wife Polissena, Radamisto's sister, is infatuated with Zenobia and wants to possess her. Polissena is in despair; Tigrane, Prince of Pontus and an ally of Tiridate, is in love with her and tries to persuade her to leave her unfaithful husband. Tiridate orders the destruction of the city, and sends his brother Fraarte to parley with Radamisto, threatening to kill Farasmane if Radamisto does not surrender. Encouraged by Farasmane, Radamisto refuses: Fraarte is about to have Farasmane executed, but Tigrane intervenes to prevent it. Tiridate agrees to spare him if Radamisto and Zenobia are brought to him. Tigrane and Fraarte capture the city, and Fraarte reveals that he also loves Zenobia.

In Act II Radamisto and Zenobia have escaped through a tunnel into open country near the River Araxes. As Tigrane's troops approach, Zenobia begs Radamisto to kill her to avoid Tiridate's clutches. In despair he tries to do so, but fails, and she throws herself into the river (this is the incident recorded by Tacitus). Tigrane takes Radamisto prisoner, while Fraarte rescues Zenobia and brings her to Tiridate. Radamisto, disguised as a servant, is brought by Tigrane to Polissena, and brother and sister quarrel over Radamisto's declaration that he will kill Tiridate. Tiridate is trying to force Zenobia to yield to him when Tigrane brings in Radamisto's clothes and announces that he is dead: Radamisto's servant Ismeno will relate what happened. 'Ismeno', who is Radamisto in disguise, is brought in. Zenobia recognises him, but Tiridate does not, and leaves 'Ismeno' with Zenobia, with orders to persuade her to accede to his demands. The couple are reunited in an ecstatic duet.

In Act III Tigrane and Fraarte are determined to make Tiridate abandon his tyrannical attitude. Tiridate offers Zenobia the crown, which she contemptuously rejects; Radamisto enters with Polissena and Farasmane, and threatens Tiridate, but Polissena intervenes. Tiridate orders Radamisto's execution and rejects Polissena's pleas for her brother: she warns him that her loyalty to him may not continue. Tiridate will pardon Radamisto in exchange for possessing Zenobia; in the temple she rejects him and will die with her husband. Polissena comes to announce that Tigrane and Fraarte have led the army to revolt; Tiridate, abandoned by his attendants, repents. Radamisto asks Polissena to pardon him, and says that she and Tiridate may stay on as rulers of Armenia: now he has his Zenobia he has no other desires.

Handel had problems with casting, as the group of international stars whom the Academy wished to recruit had not yet arrived in London. For the first run of performances in April 1720, the cast was:

Radamisto	Margherita DURASTANTI (soprano)
Zenobia	ANASTASIA ROBINSON (alto)
Polissena	ANN TURNER ROBINSON (soprano)
Fraarte	Benedetto Baldassari (castrato)
Tigrane	Caterina Galerati (soprano)
Tiridate	Alexander GORDON (tenor)
Farasmane	John Lagarde (bass)

Baldassari had made a fuss about Fraarte's part being only 'a Captain of the Guard, and a Pimp' (12 March 1720, HHB iv, p. 87), so Handel was instructed by the Directors of the Academy to alter the plot and make him a lover of Zenobia, which somewhat unbalanced the action.

The success of the premiere was immense, and there were nine more performances. For the Academy's second season, which began in November 1720, the long-awaited new cast of singers had arrived. Handel wished to revive *Radamisto*, so he undertook a radical revision of the score to adapt it to the new team. Radamisto became an alto, for SENESINO, Zenobia became a soprano, for Durastanti, who changed roles, and Tiridate became a bass for Giuseppe Maria BOSCHI; Maddalena SALVAI was Polissena. Handel removed eight arias and composed ten new ones, an accompagnato, a duet and a quartet; other arias were revised or allocated to another character. He made one major change to the plot: since Baldassari was no longer in the company (Galerati took over the role), Fraarte was reassigned to his lowlier status as a soldier, not in love with Zenobia; this reduction in the significance of Fraarte was a first step towards his elimination in the revivals of 1721 and 1728. In this second version of the opera, premiered on 28 December 1720, the plot was thus tightened, and the introduction of the magnificent quartet in Act III gave greater dramatic power to the opera's conclusion.

This version was revived in November 1721, without Fraarte, and again in February 1728, with more substantial revisions and transpositions for a largely new cast. Senesino and Boschi retained their roles, while Zenobia was sung by FAUSTINA and Polissena by CUZZONI. One unfortunate consequence of this revival was that as the performing score, which is a primary source for much of the December 1720 version, was being prepared, some of the 1720 material, including all Zenobia's arias, was removed, which has made necessary a certain degree of editorial reconstruction in the HHA edition of the December version.

With *Radamisto* Handel set a high standard for the productions of the Royal Academy, and it remains one of his finest operas. All the characters have some superb arias: Radamisto's lament 'Ombra cara' in Act II, when he believes that he has lost Zenobia for ever, is a masterpiece of pathos; but the most remarkable are those for the two female roles, Polissena and Zenobia: the former's lament 'Sommi Dei', which opens the opera, her tragic 'Tu vuoi ch'io parta' later in Act I, in which she expresses her love for her faithless husband, and her dramatic condemnation of him in Act III with the virtuosic but rather over-elaborate 'Sposo ingrato' in the first version, which was replaced by the more subtle 'Barbaro' in the second; then Zenobia's 'Son contenta di morire' in Act I, 'Quando mai, spietata sorte', 'Già che morir non posso', 'Troppo sofferse' and 'Empio, perverso cor' in Act II, and 'Deggio, dunque, oh Dio, lasciarti' in Act III – these last two are among Handel's greatest arias for a tragic heroine. The plot is well designed, with opportunities for emotional conflict between the principals, and some powerfully dramatic incidents, such as the scene at the River Araxes at the beginning of Act II, in which Zenobia, as in Tacitus's account, throws herself into the river.   TERENCE BEST

T. Best (ed.), *Radamisto* (1. Fassung) [April 1720], HHA II/9.1 (Kassel, 1997)
   (ed.), *Radamisto* (2. Fassung) [later versions], HHA II/9.2 (Kassel, 2000)
Bianconi
M. Bucciarelli, '*Radamisto*'s Theatrical Sources and their Influence on Handel's Creative Process', GHB VII (1998)
Dean and Knapp, *Operas*
Deutsch
B. Edelmann, 'Die zweite Fassung von Händels Oper "Radamisto" (HWV 12^b)', GHB III (1987)
Harris, *Librettos*
HHB iv

Rameau, Jean-Philippe (bap. Dijon, 25 Sept. 1683; d. Paris, 12 Sept. 1764). French composer and theorist. According to HAWKINS, Handel always spoke of Rameau 'in terms of great respect'. His library apparently included unspecified Rameau operas, harpsichord pieces and treatises (HANDEL, 19). Generalised influence apart, however, no evidence has emerged that Handel borrowed from such works, other than in *JOSEPH AND HIS BRETHREN* and *MESSIAH* (neither borrowing indisputable). Handel's direct influence on Rameau is marginally more important. *La princesse de Navarre* (1745) derives themes from *SAMSON* (1742), while the A minor Gavotte with six *doubles*, modelled on Handel's D minor harpsichord variations (HWV 428), set a new trend in the French *clavecin* repertory for multiple pattern-variations.   GRAHAM SADLER

D. Charlton and S. Hibberd, '"My Father was a Poor Parisian Musician": A Memoir (1756) Concerning Rameau, Handel's Library and Sallé', JRMA 128/2 (2003), 161–99
G. Sadler, 'From Themes to Variations: Rameau's Debt to Handel', *L'Esprit français' und die Musik Europas: Entstehung, Einfluss und Grenzen einer ästhetischen Doktrin*, ed. M. Biget-Mainfroy and R. Schmusch (Hildesheim, 2007)
H. Schneider, 'Affinitäten und Differenzen zwischen Rameau und Händel in Opern der Jahre 1735–1737', HJb 50 (2004)

Randall, William (b. c.1728; d. Jan.? 1776). Music publisher, printer and seller. He was a relative of the WALSH family: perhaps he was John Walsh junior's cousin, and related to Peter Randall (Walsh senior's associate, 1706–8). After Walsh junior's death in 1766, William Randall took over his firm in Catharine Street in the Strand, including his extensive stock of printing plates with Handel's music. He worked in association with John Abell until the latter's death in 1768. Randall used Walsh's plates, sometimes with alterations, but sometimes even with the old imprint. The appearance of the firm's prints remained more or less the same and only a few innovations were made. However, Randall and Abell started a series of new full scores to some of Handel's oratorios, including the first printed full score of MESSIAH (1767). After Randall's death, his widow Elizabeth continued the business. She did not publish any new music, but produced reissues made from the old Walsh plates. In 1783 the business came into the possession of H. WRIGHT & Wilkinson.   JENS WEHMANN

See also EDITIONS, 1

C. Humphries and W. C. Smith, *Music Publishing in the British Isles from the Earliest Times to the Middle of the Nineteenth Century: A Dictionary of Engravers, Printers, Publishers and Music Sellers, with a Historical Introduction* (London, 1954)
F. Kidson, 'Handel's Publisher, John Walsh, his Successors and Contemporaries', MQ 6 (1920), 430–50
W. C. Smith, *Handel: A Descriptive Catalogue of the Early Editions*, 2nd edn (London, 1970)

Ranelagh House and Gardens. The Earl of Ranelagh, paymaster of Chelsea Hospital, leased a neighbouring plot in about 1690 for a modest mansion. His daughter was permitted to remain, and in 1717 Ranelagh was the supper destination of the WATER MUSIC excursion. In 1742 speculators developed pleasure gardens and built the remarkable Rotunda, a circular building 150 ft across, with a large central hearth for winter warmth and Michael FESTING as musical director. The level promenade area was ringed by two tiers of boxes, the third storey being windows. In 1752 the tone of the now fashionable Ranelagh was raised, with evening concerts that frequently included music by Handel. After inevitable decline, Rotunda and house were closed in 1803 and the denuded garden reverted to the hospital. Canaletto's painting of the interior is in the National Gallery, London.   KERRY DOWNES

reception of Handel's music

1. Great Britain
2. Germany (including Austria)
3. France
4. Italy
5. Netherlands
6. Scandinavia
7. Switzerland
8. Eastern Europe
9. North America
10. Australasia
11. South Africa
12. Japan

1. Great Britain

Handel was undoubtedly the most successful composer in Britain during the first half of the eighteenth century, with his oratorio-style works popular not only in London but also in regional cities such as BATH, SALISBURY, OXFORD and

DUBLIN. Even after his death in 1759 his music continued to dominate Lenten oratorio seasons. By the beginning of the 1780s interest in his oratorios had diminished, but the 1784 COMMEMORATION considerably revived the general musical public's interest in Handel. Further festivals at WESTMINSTER ABBEY followed in 1785, 1786, 1787, 1790 and 1791, and Samuel ARNOLD commenced his (unfinished) project to publish Handel's complete works (EDITIONS, 2). Handel's music became core repertoire for choral festivals and concert organisations, both in London and in the provinces, in which works by other composers formed a much less significant portion.

By the end of the nineteenth century the three most popular oratorios were *MESSIAH* (Handel), *Elijah* (MENDELSSOHN) and *La Rédemption* (Gounod). In addition to the Three Choirs Festival, choral festivals developed in Birmingham (from 1759), Leeds (from 1858) and BRISTOL (from 1873). During the Victorian era choral festivals and amateur choral societies became firmly established, especially in the provinces. By 1868 Alfred NOVELLO was publishing low-priced music books of the standard sacred Handel works, which were sold as handbooks to audiences. A new phase of the ongoing British tradition of Handel performance had already begun in 1857 with the inauguration of large-scale oratorio festivals at CRYSTAL PALACE (which continued until 1926). Monumental performances of works such as *ISRAEL IN EGYPT* became synonymous with superiority and greatness, which appropriately matched the aspirations and attitudes of the contemporary expansion of the British Empire; also audiences responded enthusiastically to the emotional and ecstatic power of colossal performances of choruses. Britain's subsequent decline as an imperial power coincided with a diminishing interest in established forms of art and culture; perhaps the bombastic aspect of large Handel festivals no longer matched the *Zeitgeist*. The popular fixation on Handel's oratorios decreased and was superseded by new trends, not least after the Bach renaissance gathered momentum in Britain from about 1870.

It was also during the late nineteenth century that the range of Handel's regularly performed works increasingly narrowed. However, it was from 1881 that *Messiah* became established as a popular festive Christmas celebration. Handel's works that were performed reasonably often included *JUDAS MAC-CABAEUS*, *SAUL*, *SAMSON*, *ACIS AND GALATEA*, the Coronation Anthems (ANTHEMS, 3), the Dettingen and Utrecht Te Deums (TE DEUM, 1; 5), *ALEXAN-DER'S FEAST* and the *SONG FOR ST CECILIA'S DAY*. A desire to react against the gargantuan performance style and an increased sensitivity for historically informed PERFORMANCE PRACTICE commenced as early as 1889, when the Royal Choral Society performed *Messiah* in the Royal Albert Hall without the additional accompaniments by MOZART (ARRANGEMENTS, 2) and comparatively reduced forces. In 1900 Ebenezer Prout, August H. MANNS and William H. Cummings tried to reconstruct Handel's original instrumentation and orchestral forces for a performance of *ALEXANDER BALUS* in SCARBOROUGH.

Meanwhile, Handel's operas had been entirely neglected since his lifetime – with the exception of some popular individual arias, usually in ADAPTA-TIONS. The 1754 production of *ADMETO* by Francesco VANNESCHI at the KING'S THEATRE was the last performance of a Handel opera for more than a century. By the early twentieth century baroque *opera seria* was commonly disregarded by both musicians and scholars as an outdated genre. The British renaissance of Handel's operas began in 1927, when the pioneering scholar Edward J. Dent organised an abridged semi-staged performance of GIULIO CESARE at the FOUNDLING HOSPITAL. RINALDO was performed in 1933, and RODELINDA in 1939 (both in English translations). The Handel opera revival gathered momentum in 1955 when the Handel Opera Society was founded by Charles Farncombe (with assistance from Dent) to give annually staged performances of Handel's dramatic works, at first in St Pancras Assembly Rooms, and from 1959 at Sadler's Wells Theatre (the society gave twentyeight productions until it was dissolved in 1985). Interest in Handel's operas was further nurtured in 1959 by Alan Kitching, who founded the Unicorn Opera Group, which gave the first modern staged productions of fifteen Handel operas (in English, some with the arias in Italian) until 1974.

During the second half of the twentieth century a new historically informed approach to performing Handel's music gradually developed. The interest in striving for 'authenticity' gained increasingly widespread acceptance during the 1950s, when John Tobin conducted a complete version of Messiah with the original scoring at the Central Hall in London on 24 February 1951, Alfred Deller led the revival of the art of countertenor singing and conductors such as Anthony Lewis and Charles Mackerras pioneered performances of Handel's stage works. During the 1970s and 1980s musicians such as Christopher Hogwood, Trevor Pinnock, Andrew Parrott, Denys Darlow (founder of the London Handel Festival), John Eliot Gardiner and Robert King established professional period-instrument orchestras and small choirs. These have radically reformed the style of the British Handel performing tradition, have also dramatically expanded the breadth of repertoire on commercially distributed RECORDINGS and have performed in concerts, theatres and festivals (both those devoted to Handel or 'early music' and general international festivals such as the BBC Proms).

2. Germany (including Austria)

Some of Handel's London operas were performed during his lifetime in Germany (with new German recitatives). Between 1715 and 1737 fourteen of his operas were staged at the GÄNSEMARKT in HAMBURG, and between 1723 and 1743 twelve were performed in BRUNSWICK. In 1731 PARTENOPE was staged at SALZDAHLUM. The German reception of his choral works began during the 1760s, at BERLIN, Hamburg, Brunswick and Schwerin. Peripheral phenomena were the performances in Berlin organised by Gottfried van SWIETEN. After his return to Vienna, he initiated an important series of occasional concerts for the Tonkünstlersozietät and the Gesellschaft der Associierten Kavaliere. According to BURNEY and Count Zinzendorf, Alexander's Feast was heard in Vienna in 1771 and 1772. Judas Maccabaeus was performed there in 1779, and during the early 1780s Swieten's friendship with Mozart led to the latter becoming increasingly interested in Handel's music both in small-scale private concerts and with later commissions to make several arrangements of oratorio-style works.

An arrangement of Alexander's Feast by Christian Gottfried Krause, with a German translation by Karl Wilhelm Ramler, was performed at Berlin in 1766 and

1770. *Judas Maccabaeus* and *Messiah* (both in abridged and German versions) were frequently performed from 1772 onwards, and became established as the most popular Handel works in Germany. Additionally, the *Utrecht Te Deum* and *Jubilate* were performed at Berlin in 1770. Handel's music was also performed in GÖTTINGEN, DRESDEN and Weimar. Inspired by the 1784 Handel Commemoration in Westminster Abbey, Johann Adam HILLER organised several large-scale performances of *Messiah* at Berlin (1786), Leipzig (1787) and Breslau (1787). Performances of oratorios became especially popular between 1810 and c.1825, in conjunction with the founding and development of numerous choral societies emulating the *SING-AKADEMIE ZU BERLIN*. Handel's choral works became the core repertoire of newly established music festivals, perhaps because the common perception of their monumentality and patriotic atmosphere appealed to the bourgeoisie.

It was usual to prefer arrangements by Mozart and Ignaz von MOSEL to Handel's original scores: Mosel conducted the first concerts of the Viennese *Gesellschaft der Musikfreunde* (founded 1814), and performed many of his own arrangements of Handel's oratorios (e.g. *Jephtha* in 1819 and *Israel in Egypt* in 1836). Raphael Georg KIESEWETTER also enriched Vienna's concert life with his *Hauskonzerte* reviving ancient music from his collection (SOURCES AND COLLECTIONS, 11). In Heidelberg Anton Friedrich Justus THIBAUT collected a large amount of Handel's works (including late eighteenth-century and early nineteenth-century printed editions) and devoted considerable energy towards rehearsing and performing Handel's vocal compositions with the *Singverein*. The musical activities of Thibaut and his circle strongly influenced such composers as Robert Schumann and MENDELSSOHN.

Although the reception of Handel's music was concentrated in certain regions, his oratorios became widely known and more popular than the works of Bach. The pioneering work of the Handel scholar, editor and arranger Friedrich CHRYSANDER encouraged a remarkable increase in the frequency of oratorio performances from 1860 onwards, but by the end of the century Handel's music became overshadowed by Bach euphoria, and the persistent opinion that Bach is greater than Handel has not yet been fully overcome both in Germany and elsewhere. A sad chapter of Handel oratorio performance history in Germany is the so-called 'Händeloratorien-Renaissance' during the Third Reich (NATIONAL SOCIALIST ARRANGEMENTS).

After 1743 there were no performances of Handel's operas until *Almira* was performed at Leipzig in an abbreviated version (with entirely German text) by Johann Nepomuk Fuchs in 1879 (this was revived at Hamburg in 1885 and 1905). The rediscovery of the operas started at Göttingen in 1920 with Oskar HAGEN's staging of *Rodelinda*. The operas gradually became more frequently performed, but always with German texts and with castrato parts transposed down for basses and tenors. HALLE became an important centre for opera revivals, especially when Göttingen stopped opera productions and instead concentrated on oratorios from 1949 (Göttingen's priorities reversed again in the early 1990s).

During the 1970s interest in historically informed performance practice and the use of 'period' instruments became more widespread, and the 'romantic' sound of orchestras and traditional style of singers began to change, especially with the employment of John Eliot Gardiner at Göttingen and Christian Kluttig at Halle. During the mid-1980s it became more common for castrato roles to be sung by countertenors or women. At present, there are three festivals dedicated to Handel (Göttingen, Halle and Karlsruhe) and numerous professional baroque orchestras which often perform a broad variety of his operatic, choral and instrumental works. In Austria, Nikolaus Harnoncourt's period-instrument group Concentus Musicus Wien made explorative recordings of numerous Handel vocal and instrumental works during the 1970s, and several operas have been performed at Innsbruck.

3. France

The only eighteenth-century performances of Handel operas in France took place in the house of the Parisian patron Pierre Crozat in 1724: *OTTONE* and *Giulio Cesare* were given private concert performances by the London-based Italian singers of the Royal Academy of Music (OPERA COMPANIES, 2). By the end of the century, the interest in Handel's music evident in Berlin and Vienna was absent in France. Likewise, the growing enthusiasm for oratorio during the nineteenth century did not manifest itself very much in France. In 1827 Alexandre Choron performed Part I of *Messiah*, with Latin words and Mozart's orchestral parts. Thirty years later Victor SCHOELCHER stated in the preface of his Handel biography that he 'learnt to admire' the composer's oratorios 'during three previous visits to England, and at home in the constant society of classical amateurs'. Schoelcher hoped to raise French interest in Handel's music so that the oratorios would remedy 'a great deficiency in the culture of Musical Art', and he noted that *Judas Maccabaeus* and *Messiah* had been 'feebly executed three or four times before an audience of subscribers by a society of amateurs' (Schoelcher, *Life of Handel*, p. 417). However, Schoelcher's vision did not come to pass, possibly because concert life in Paris during the second half of the nineteenth century was dominated by Beethoven and Wagner. The first complete public performance of *Messiah* in France eventually took place on 19 December 1873.

In 1935 *Giulio Cesare* was performed in French in Strasbourg, and in 1966 the English Opera Group brought its staged production of *Acis and Galatea* to Lyons. However, during the second half of the 1970s the number of Handel opera performances increased remarkably, and since then numerous French groups devoted to baroque music – especially those directed by Jean-Claude Malgoire, William Christie, Christophe Rousset and Marc Minkowski – have made a vibrant contribution to modern Handel performance. In particular, Handel's music has been frequently performed at festivals in Aix-en-Provence, Ambronay, Beaune and Montpellier, and his operas have been successfully staged in Paris at the Théâtre des Champs-Élysées and the Opéra Garnier.

4. Italy

After Handel left Italy in 1710, his music was not often performed (a pasticcio based on *Rinaldo* was performed at NAPLES under the direction of LEO in 1718). However, the art collector and patron George Nassau Clavering, 3rd Earl Cowper (1738–89) was fond of Handel's music, and spent much time in FLORENCE: he introduced some of Handel's choral music there in 1768, which attracted the attention of Grand Duke Pietro Leopoldo (b. Vienna, 1747; ruler of Tuscany, 1765–90): *Alexander's Feast*, *Messiah*, *Acis and Galatea* and *Judas Maccabaeus*, with their texts translated into Italian, were performed in Florence between 1768 and 1772. The general popularity of Handel's oratorio-style works did not spread to Italy until quite recently: *Acis and Galatea* was staged at Florence in 1940, and *Samson* was staged at Perugia in 1948. *Rinaldo* received a concert performance at ROME in 1947, and from 1950 onwards *Giulio Cesare* has been performed in Naples, Rome and Milan. During the 1980s *AGRIPPINA*, *ORLANDO* and Rinaldo were staged at La Fenice in VENICE, and since the 1990s an increasing number of Italian baroque groups have frequently performed a wide range of Handel's Italian-language compositions.

5. Netherlands
Princess ANNE acquired a large number of copies of Handel's music after she married Prince William IV of Orange, but her library is now lost, and nothing more is currently known about performances of Handel's music in the NETHERLANDS during the eighteenth century. During the nineteenth century his oratorios were often performed (in German) at Amsterdam (*Messiah*, arr. Mozart, 1805) and at festivals in Rotterdam; the impetus for these evidently came from the Dutchman Johannes Josephus Herman Verhulst and the German Friedrich Gernsheim, who had both studied at Leipzig under Schumann and Mendelssohn. Their Handel performance projects included *Israel in Egypt* (arr. Verhulst, cond. Franz Liszt, 1854), *BELSHAZZAR* (1873), *SOLOMON* (arr. Gernsheim, 1878) and *Judas Maccabaeus* (arr. Gernsheim, 1887). Also, the Stichting Toonkunst-Bibliotheek in Amsterdam contains contemporary arrangements of *Saul* (arr. Gernsheim), *JOSHUA* (arr. Julius Rietz), *Samson* (arr. MOSEL) and *Acis and Galatea* (arr. Verhulst). The first performance of a Handel opera in the Netherlands was *Giulio Cesare*, which took place in Amsterdam's Opera Studio in der Stadsschouwburg in 1933. The next was not until 1969 (*Giulio Cesare*, Scheveningen), but since then Handel's operas have been performed more regularly.

6. Scandinavia
Johan Helmich ROMAN introduced several Handel works to Sweden during the early 1730s. Some of these – including the *Water Music* and a Swedish version of *Acis and Galatea* – were occasionally revived later during the reign of Gustavus III (from 1771), along with choruses from *Messiah*. After 1830 oratorios were performed in the circle of the historian Erik Gustaf Geijer in Uppsala, and the organist Jacob Axel Josephson (who had studied in Leipzig) performed Handel's oratorios in Stockholm up to the end of the nineteenth century, but interest in Handel's music was generally restricted to a few places. The first performance of a complete opera took place at Gothenburg in 1932 (*Rodelinda*, in Swedish), and regular performances of Handel's operas at the historic Drottningholm Slottsteater started in 1950 with *Orlando* (in Swedish).

Messiah was first performed in Denmark in 1786, under the influence of the 1784 Westminster Abbey Handel Commemoration. The Danish reception of Handel's operas was influenced by the Germans: in 1923 the Berlin Große Volksoper gave a guest performance of Hagen's version of *Giulio Cesare* in Copenhagen, where a Brunswick production of *PORO* was performed two years later.

The Royal Theatre in Copenhagen staged *Acis and Galatea* (1935) and in 1947 it produced *Giulio Cesare*, which was also staged by the Royal Danish Opera in 2002. Handel's music has not been performed as often in Norway, although a staged production of Il PASTOR FIDO was performed twenty-two times in Oslo between 1979 and 1982.

7. Switzerland

The foundations of choral associations in Switzerland were developed by Hans Georg Nägeli (1773–1836), who founded the Zürich *Singinstitut* in 1805. Swiss choral societies had a wide range of oratorio-style repertoire. For example, the Basler Gesangverein performed *Alexander's Feast, Belshazzar, DEBORAH, HER-CULES, Israel in Egypt, Jephtha, Joshua, Judas Maccabaeus, Messiah* and *Samson*. During the 1920s two of Oskar Hagen's opera productions from Göttingen were performed: *Rodelinda* (Zurich, 1923) and *Giulio Cesare* (Zurich, 1924 and Berne, 1926). His version of *Serse* was also performed at Basle in 1958. At present, the leading Swiss cities for Handel performance are Basle (partly owing to the Schola Cantorum early music conservatoire, but also because the Kammerorchester Basel has made some prominent recordings) and Zurich, where in recent years the opera house has staged Il TRIONFO DEL TEMPO E DEL DISINGANNO (2003), RADAMISTO (2004), SEMELE and *Orlando* (both 2007) and *Rinaldo* (2008).   ANNETTE LANDGRAF

8. Eastern Europe

Travellers to England brought back information about Handel's London performances to their home countries, for example the Russian diplomats Boris Ivanovich Kurakin (in 1711) and Antiokh Dmitriyevich Kantemir (in 1736). Similiar reports were given after 1788 about MOZART's Handel arrangements performed in Vienna, and the Bohemian composer Václav Jan Tomášek heard *Samson* at Vienna in 1814. Interest in Handel's music might have been awakened by the purchase of printed scores or manuscript copies, and often audiences first became acquainted with it through the inclusion of single works in mixed concert programmes. Handel's music came to St Petersburg in 1743 when 'Master Winraw' brought from London a mechanical clock which played pieces by Handel on a rotating cylinder. The earliest manuscript sources in Bohemia date from 1718, including a set of parts for the Utrecht Te Deum, and are now in the collection of the convent of the Knights of the Cross with the Red Star in Prague (not originally part of the Knights' collection, they were perhaps acquired from East Bohemia). An inventory of a music collection amassed between 1752 and 1769 by Thomas Vinciguerra, Count of Collalto and San Salvatore in the southwest Moravian town of Pirnitz (Czech: Brtnice), lists a 'Sinfonia a tre' (i.e. the trio sonata HWV 390^b) (CHAMBER MUSIC) by 'Hendl'. Two performances of Handel operas in ELBING (Polish: Elbląg) in northern Poland are not verifiable, and it also remains uncertain who prepared the pasticcio HERMANN VON BALCKE to commemorate the quincentenary of the town's foundation, but as early as 1743 Johann Jeremias du Grain performed the *Brockes Passion* in Danzig (Polish: Gdańsk).

The peak of Handel reception in Eastern Europe occurred between 1750 and 1800, during which period vocal works by Handel were given new Latin texts and used in Catholic liturgy (for example, this practice was established by the choir of St Vitus Cathedral in Prague from 1765). Choruses and anthems were adapted for the Augustine monastery in Alt-Brünn (Czech: Brno) between 1825 and 1848, and arias, duets and choruses from *Messiah* and *JUDAS MACCABAEUS* were adapted before 1853 in three sources now at the Premonstratensian Strahov Monastery in Prague (similar musical material can also be found in Fünfkirchen (Hungarian: Pécs) in Hungary). It is notable that some Bohemian aristocrats were interested in Handel's vocal works: the Lobkowicz collection in Raudnitz (Czech: Roudnice nad Labem) includes first editions of Handel's printed scores and copies of Mozart's arrangements (only Part III of *Messiah* is extant, reputedly including additions in Mozart's hand). Handeliana in the collection of the Counts Chotek in Kačina and Nové Dvory near Kuttenberg (Czech: Kutná Hora) also dates from around 1800, and during the 1820s Count Heinrich Wilhelm HAUGWITZ commissioned arrangements and performances of Handel's oratorios in Namiescht (Czech: Náměšt' nad Oslavou) in south-western Moravia.

Franz Beinlich performed arrangements of *Judas Maccabaeus* and *Alexander's Feast* before 1777 in the Silesian city of Breslau [Polish: Wrocław], where Johann Adam Hiller performed *Judas Maccabaeus* (1787) and *Messiah* (1788, with 170 instrumentalists and 110 singers). At Königsberg (Russian: Kaliningrad) the local *Kantor* Johann Coelestin Gontkowski performed *Alexander's Feast* in 1783, and in the same year *Samson* was first performed in Moscow.

During the nineteenth century performances of Handel's music in Eastern Europe were mainly related to German communities, and the establishment of German musical societies and male choral societies further sustained this development. By 1850 Handel's music was being performed in Bohemia and Moravia, Lower Silesia, Warsaw, Elbing and Danzig, Riga and Dorpat (Estonian: Tartu), in St Petersburg and Moscow, and also in Hungary, Dalmatia and Transylvania. During the early twentieth century interest grew in his operas, with productions at Prague (1923), Tilsit (Russian: Sovetsk) (1924), Breslau, Königsberg and Stettin (Polish: Szczecin) (1925), etc.

KLAUS-PETER KOCH (Trans. ANGELA BAIER)

9. North America

The earliest verifiable performance of Handel's music on the American continent is a selection from *Messiah* given in George Burns's Music Room in the New York City Tavern on Broadway on 16 January 1770. The HALLELUJAH CHORUS was performed in several concerts during the following decades (including a Boston concert in 1773 celebrating the anniversary of GEORGE III's coronation, and another in the same city when George Washington visited it in 1789). The first performance of *Messiah* in America took place in the hall of the University of Pennsylvania on 9 April 1801. In 1817 Handel's most famous oratorio was performed complete by the Boston Handel and Haydn Society (HANDEL SOCIETIES, 5), but it was spread across three evenings (1, 4 and 6 April) that also featured the corresponding parts of HAYDN's *The Creation*. A performance of *Messiah* given entirely in one evening took place on Christmas Day 1818 in Boston's Boylston Hall.

In 1816 a selection from *Israel in Egypt* was given in New York by the Musical Educational Society, under the direction of George J. Webb and Lowell Mason. There was another incomplete performance of the work on 1 March 1851 in

Boston, where on 10 February 1859 it was performed as a 'complete' two-part oratorio by the Handel and Haydn Society (although the *Boston Courier* made the criticism that 'the labour and expense bestowed upon their preparation are a waste of means, which ought to be lamented rather than encouraged'). In April 1890 the society performed *Israel in Egypt* with about 450 singers, and three years later in the same city a selection from the oratorio was performed by 2,000 singers and 200 instrumentalists (clearly in emulation of the contemporary Crystal Palace Handel Festivals in Britain, but with about half the forces).

According to Johnson's list of American first performances up to 1900, Handel's instrumental and vocal works were also introduced to audiences in Albany, Baltimore, Brooklyn, Charleston, Chicago, Cincinnati, Dayton, Denver, Hartford, Los Angeles, Milwaukee, Minneapolis, Montreal, New Heaven, Pittsburgh, Portland, Salem, San Francisco, St Louis, Toronto, Washington and Worcester. Smaller places established Handelian performance traditions, such as the annual *Messiah* concerts at Lindsborg in Kansas. Large choral festivals developed across the country, such as the May Festival in Cincinnati which featured about 500 singers and 100 instrumentalists, and was modelled on German festivals. A festival at Toronto in 1886 had an audience of approximately 3,000 people. *Acis and Galatea* received the first of many staged productions at New York in 1842. Many oratorio-style works were staged, not only the secular drama *Semele*, but also *Messiah* at Chicago in 1933. Paradoxically, Handel's operas were at first given as concert performances. These were introduced to the USA by Oskar Hagen in 1927 (*Giulio Cesare*, Northampton, MA), 1928 (*Serse*) and 1931 (*Rodelinda*). *Giulio Cesare* has since become popular, with prominent stagings at major opera houses in San Francisco and New York. The New York City Opera's 1966 production and subsequent commercial recording (1967), featuring Beverly Sills as Cleopatra, was a landmark in the popularisation of Handel's operas in America. The first Handel opera performed in Canada was *Rinaldo* (Ottawa, 1982), and *Acis and Galatea* was staged at Montreal in 1967 (by the visiting English Opera Group). The period-instrument movement which revolutionised music-making in Europe during the 1970s has taken much longer to become established in North America. Notable Handel projects have been undertaken by the Maryland Handel Festival, the Toronto-based baroque orchestra Tafelmusik, the Boston Handel and Haydn Society, San Francisco's Philharmonia Baroque Orchestra, and summer opera festivals at Santa Fe, St Louis and Glimmerglass.

10. Australasia

Australian choral societies such as the Musical Union (Perth) and the Philharmonic Society (Melbourne) performed Handel's oratorios with smaller musical forces than was usual in Europe and America during the nineteenth century, when his music was also performed in Sydney and Hobart Town (Tasmania). Productions of *Giulio Cesare* (1970) and *Serse* (1972) at the University of New South Wales, and *Agrippina* at Adelaide (1972), were the first Handel operas to be performed in Australia, and in 1977 *Serse* was also the first of his operas to be performed in New Zealand. The Sydney Opera House's 1981 production of *Alcina* brought an unprecedented amount of public attention to Handel's stage works in Australia (it was revived in 1983 and 1987). Several operas and oratorios were staged at Canberra during the 1980s, and Opera Australia has staged *Giulio*

Cesare (Sydney, 1994; revivals in Brisbane and Melbourne), *Rinaldo* (1999), *Alcina* (2007) and *Orlando* (2008).

11. South Africa

The oratorio repertoire is mostly restricted to *Messiah*, although in the nineteenth century Handel Festivals were held at Grahamstown, and in June 1885 there were celebrations of Handel's bicentenary. *Serse* has been staged at Pretoria (1963) and in Cape Town (1985).

12. Japan

From 1961 to 2002 there were seven performances of Handel operas beginning with *Serse* (Tokyo, 1961). Since 2000 the Handel Institute Japan (HANDEL SOCIETIES, 6) has staged several operas, and the annual Handel Festival Japan (Tokyo) was founded in 2003 to introduce Japanese audiences to less familiar works.   ANNETTE LANDGRAF

See also FESTIVALS; RECORDINGS; Appendix 7: An overview of fifty Handel performers, 1959–2009

V. Cosma, 'Händels Musik in Rumänien', HJb 13/14 (1967/8)
C. Dalhaus, *Die Musik des 19. Jahrhunderts, Neues Handbuch der Musikwissenschaft* 6 (Laaber, 1996)
R. Engländer, 'Händel in der Musik Schwedens', HJb 5 (1959)
M. Freemanová-Kopecká, 'Zur Händel-Rezeption in den böhmischen Ländern in Vergangenheit und Gegenwart', HJb 35 (1989)
A. Gerhard, 'Judas Maccabaeus in der Sprache Racines. Kontroversen um Händels Oratorien im nachrevolutionären Paris', HJb 56 (forthcoming)
R. I. Gruber, 'Händel und die russische Musik', HJb 5 (1959)
J. Heidrich, '"Geistlich" und "weltlich" als musikästhetische Kategorien im Kontext der deutschen Händelrezeption um 1800', HJb 55 (2009)
H. E. Johnson, *First Performances in America to 1900. Works with Orchestra* (Detroit, 1979)
K.-P. Koch, 'Aufführungen von oratorischen Werken Händels im östlichen Europa während des 18. und 19. Jahrhunderts', HJb 55 (2009)
   'Händel-Rezeption bis zum Ende des 18. Jahrhunderts in östlichen Gebieten Europas', *Bach-Händel-Schütz-Ehrung der DDR 1985*, ed. W. Siegmund-Schultze and B. Baselt (Leipzig, 1987)
A. Landgraf, 'Pyramids in Germany: On the German Reception of Handel's Oratorios in the Eighteenth and Nineteenth Centuries', *Handel Studies: A Gedenkschrift for Howard Serwer*, ed. R. G. King (Hillsdale, NY, 2009)
R. Luckett, *Handel's Messiah: A Celebration* (London, 1992)
A. Monheim, *Händel's Oratorien in Nord- und Mitteldeutschland im 18. Jahrhundert* (Eisenach, 1999)
R. Pečman, 'Die Händel-Rezeption in den böhmischen Ländern im 19. Jahrhundert', *Georg Friedrich Händel im Verständnis des 19. Jahrhunderts* (Halle, 1984)
M. Rätzer, *Szenische Aufführungen von Werken Georg Friedrich Händels vom 18. bis 20. Jahrhundert. Eine Dokumentation* (Halle, 2000) (with annual updates in HJb)
P. van Reijen, 'Die Musik Händels in den Niederlanden des 19. Jahrhunderts: Rezeptionsgeschichtliche Aspekte', HJb 53 (2007)
J. A. Rice, 'An Early Handel Revival in Florence', EM 18 (1990)
V. Schoelcher, *The Life of Handel* (London, 1857)
A. Zgorzelecki, 'Händel "alla polacca"', HJb 28 (1982)
E. Zöllner, 'Zur Händel-Rezeption in Skandinavien', HJb 56 (forthcoming)

recorder and **recorder sonatas.** See INSTRUMENTATION, 15 and CHAMBER MUSIC, I

recordings. Commercial sound recordings are currently the most widely influential and accessible method for the dissemination of Handel's music. The earliest known sound recording of Handel's music is fragments of a performance of ISRAEL IN EGYPT made at the CRYSTAL PALACE on 29 June 1888 by George Gouraud (the foreign sales agent for Thomas Alva Edison, the pioneer of sound recording). Nowadays only a ghostly sound can be produced by the three extant yellow paraffin cylinders, but these precious documents of nineteenth-century performance practice confirm that pitch was higher and tempos were much slower than is now usual. In 1894 Emile Berliner started to sell the 'Gramophone', which used flat discs instead of cylinders. The limited capacity of gramophone discs permitted the preservation of only short pieces of music. The first commercial recording to feature music from MESSIAH was a performance of 'Ev'ry valley' by tenor W. D. McFarland (1898; with piano accompaniment). Vocal arias were frequently recorded with simple accompaniment, such as the soprano Nellie Melba's 1904 recording of 'Sweet bird' (from L'ALLEGRO, IL PENSEROSO ED IL MODERATO) with only flute and piano. From the outset 'Ombra mai fu' (the so-called 'Largo' from SERSE) was frequently recorded, often in transposed versions such as those sung by tenors Enrico Caruso (1906; he recorded it again in 1920) and Tito Schipa (1926), and also in instrumental arrangements performed by violinist Fritz Kreisler (1914) and cellist Pablo Casals (1915). 'Lascia ch'io pianga' (RINALDO) was also soon established as a favourite recording vehicle for singers, such as the contralto Ernestine Schumann-Heink (1906), baritone Giuseppe de Luca (1918) and soprano Claudia Muzio (1922). A few early recordings of arias were accompanied by orchestras, such as the tenor Walter Hyde's 'Waft her angels' (JEPHTHA) in 1908, and the contialto Clara Butt's 'Ombra mai fu' (1909; she recorded it again in c.1917 with the New Queen's Hall Orchestra conducted by Henry Wood).

During the 1920s the Handel discography gradually included a wider variety of repertoire. The first gramophone discs of Handel's keyboard music to feature harpsichords began to appear: 'The HARMONIOUS BLACKSMITH' performed by Violet Gordon Woodhouse (1922) was followed by another version played by Wanda Landowska (1923). Also in 1923, a recording was made of Sir Edward Elgar conducting a performance of his arrangement of the overture to the Chandos anthem In the Lord put I my trust (ANTHEMS, 2). Singers continued to record popular arias: Isobel Baillie recorded 'Let the bright Seraphim' (SAMSON), 'O had I Jubal's lyre' (JOSHUA) and 'Angels ever bright and fair' (THEODORA) in 1928. Milestone recordings of excerpts from Messiah were conducted by Malcolm Sargent (at least seven choruses, 1926) and Sir Thomas Beecham (whose abridged version of the entire oratorio was issued on eighteen discs in 1927). Beecham also recorded three extracts from Israel in Egypt in 1934. Handel's instrumental music was less frequently recorded than arias and choruses, although Romanian composer and violinist George Enescu recorded a violin sonata (HWV 371) (CHAMBER MUSIC, I) in 1929 (with piano accompaniment).

Early gramophone discs designed to run at a speed of 78 rpm were heavy and expensive, and record labels issued large works in instalments. The possibility to record longer pieces arose with the gradual development of the long playing ('LP') record, which was first pioneered by Columbia in 1931. Moreover, there was increased interest in recording Handel's instrumental music: the Cologne Chamber Orchestra (conducted by Hermann Abendroth) recorded extracts from

Op. 6, harpsichordist Rudolph Dolmetsch recorded the Passaglia in G minor and the keyboard suite HWV 432 (KEYBOARD MUSIC), and Hamilton Harty recorded his arrangement of the *WATER MUSIC* (all 1933). In 1936 some significant milestones were reached: Marcel Dupré made a recording of an organ concerto (HWV 290) (ORCHESTRAL WORKS, 5), the Boyd Neel Orchestra made the first of its series of concerti grossi recordings (Op. 6 No. 4).

During the early 1940s the development of the recording industry was hindered by the Second World War, although American soprano Lily Pons recorded arias from *FLORIDANTE* and *ALESSANDRO* with the Renaissance Quintet in 1940. There was also German Handelian recording activity during the war: one of Handel's settings of the psalm *Laudaute pueri* (Italian and Latin CHURCH MUSIC) was recorded by the Prussian State Orchestra and Aachen Cathedral Choir in 1943, and in 1944 both the Berlin Philharmonic Orchestra and the Gewandhausorchester Leipzig made recordings of single concertos from Op. 6. The Violin Sonata, HWV 371 was recorded by Yehudi Menuhin (complete, 1944) and Isaac Stern (just the Allegro, 1945), both with piano accompaniment.

In the latter half of the 1940s Columbia began to produce LPs that would play at 33 rpm, which enabled a longer duration of recorded sound, and encouraged labels to issue complete works. In 1946 Sargent conducted an almost complete recording of *Messiah* (featuring the Huddersfield Choral Society and Liverpool Philharmonic Orchestra); it was followed in 1947 by the first complete and uncut LP set of the oratorio conducted by Beecham (albeit using his arrangement of MOZART's orchestral parts, and omitting the da capos of 'He was despised' and 'The trumpet shall sound', which listeners were expected to supply themselves by playing the relevant A sections a second time). The first complete set of all twelve Op. 6 concerti grossi was recorded by the Adolf Busch Chamber Players in 1946, and was soon followed by rival versions by the Bamberger Symphoniker (1952; conducted by Fritz Lehman, and with harpsichord continuo played by Karl Richter) and the English Baroque Orchestra (1954; conducted by Hermann Scherchen). In 1946 Kathleen Ferrier recorded 'Dove sei' from *RODELINDA* in English ('Art thou troubled'); she made an album of various Handel arias with piano accompaniment three years later, and in 1952 she recorded a selection of arias with the London Philharmonic Orchestra conducted by Sir Adrian Boult. In 1956 the LPO and Boult contributed to an album of Handel arias sung by Kirsten Flagstad.

Handel's music theatre works (in something closer to complete form) became more frequently recorded during the mid-1950s. Anthony Lewis conducted a ground-breaking recording of *SOSARME* (1954): not only was it one of the first LPs of a Handel opera, but also it pioneered the use of the original Italian sung texts and had most of the roles performed at approximately the correct pitch. Lewis repeated the innovative feat with his recording of an abridged *SEMELE* (1956). In the meantime Boult recorded *Messiah* (1954) and the *Water Music* (1955), and Sargent made the first comprehensive recording of parts II and III of *Israel in Egypt* (1955). In 1956 Beecham recorded his arrangement of *Solomon*: it was condemned by Winton Dean as 'a sky-scraper of misapplied industry' (*Oratorios*, p. 529), and after this sound recordings gradually reflected musical fashion in turning towards the restoration of Handel's original orchestrations and the incorporation of historically informed principles of PERFORMANCE

PRACTICE. The bicentenary celebration of the composer's death presented an ideal opportunity to offer special commemorative recordings. Perhaps in anticipation of this, Geraint Jones and his eponymous choir and orchestra recorded *Zadok the Priest* (ANTHEMS, 3) and the Utrecht Te Deum and Jubilate (TE DEUM, 1) in 1958. The anniversary year (1959) was commemorated by a flurry of recordings: Sargent and Beecham both rerecorded versions of *Messiah* (the latter used an orchestration by Eugene Goossens), Leonard Bernstein made an LP of the *SONG FOR ST CECILIA'S DAY*, Karl Richter recorded a set of organ concertos, Charles Mackerras revived Handel's original wind-band scoring of the *MUSIC FOR THE ROYAL FIREWORKS*, and Boult recorded *ACIS AND GALATEA* with soprano Joan Sutherland, tenor Peter Pears and bass Owen Brannigan in the leading roles. Sutherland also featured in a radio recording of *ALCINA* (with Cappella Coloniensis, conducted by Ferdinand Leitner) and made an album of arias from the same opera conducted by Anthony Lewis. She later rerecorded *Alcina* with the LSO conducted by Richard Bonynge (1962), and the same team released an album of highlights from *GIULIO CESARE* (1964).

During the 1960s the discography of Handel's oratorio-style works continued to expand. David Willcocks recorded *L'Allegro ed il Penseroso* (without 'Il Moderato') in 1960, and a year later Rudolf Ewerhart directed the premiere recording of *La RESURREZIONE*. German versions of *RADAMISTO* and *PORO* conducted by Horst-Tanu Margraf were issued by the Eterna label. Most notably, *Giulio Cesare* was recorded several times (usually clumsily abridged, and with the castrato parts transposed for bass voice, and often sung in German). Karl Böhm recorded an LP of highlights from the opera (1960); a version performed by New York City Opera featuring soprano Beverly Sills, and conducted by Julius Rudel, was recorded in 1967; and two years later Karl Richter conducted the Munich Bach Orchestra and baritone Dietrich Fischer-Dieskau in a recording for Deutsche Grammophon. However, DG's investment in the emerging 'historically informed' school of performance was evident in its 1967 LPs of a complete performance of the *BROCKES PASSION* by the Schola Cantorum Basiliensis under its pioneering director August Wenzinger. John Moriarty's 1970 recording of *TAMERLANO*, featuring tenor Alexander Young as Bajazet, was a notable milestone because it was almost complete, used Handel's orchestrations and completely eschewed the transposition of the vocal parts.

The period 1970–84 marked a transition regarding both the development of audio technology and also changing ideologies about the performance of baroque music. Companies such as RCA Victor and Philips had promoted tape products such as cassettes during the 1960s, but from 1982 LPs and cassettes were superseded by the 'Compact Disc' (CD) developed by Philips and Sony. The introduction of CD coincided with the consolidation of expert instrumental ensembles playing 'period instruments' (either original historical instruments or modern replicas) and singers becoming more interested in the use of historically informed techniques. In the 1970s both traditional 'modern' chamber orchestras and radical period-instrument groups incorporated scholarly ideas about performance practice into their premiere recordings of complete works. The English Chamber Orchestra's recordings of *SAUL* (under Mackerras, 1972) and *ARIODANTE* (conducted by Raymond Leppard, 1978) were as innovative and important as revolutionary 'early music' efforts including Alan Curtis's

ADMETO (1977), Jean-Claude Malgoire's *Rinaldo* (1977) and Sigiswald Kuijken's *PARTENOPE* (1979). However, rival recordings of *Acis and Galatea* by the modern-instrument Academy of St Martin-in-the-Fields under Neville Marriner (1977) and John's Eliot Gardiner's period-instrument English Baroque Soloists (1978) clearly illustrated that there could be radical differences in stylistic interpretative approaches. In 1980 Malgoire and Christopher Hogwood each recorded 'period' versions of *Messiah* with their own 'authentic' orchestras and English cathedral choirs. Malgoire's version inaccurately claimed to present the original 1742 Dublin first performance version (this was eventually recorded by the Dunedin Consort and Players in 2006), whereas Hogwood's version painstakingly reconstructed the version performed by Handel at the FOUNDLING HOSPITAL in 1754.

In the 1980s recording artists (most notably Gardiner, Hogwood and Trevor Pinnock) frequently directed ambitious recording projects of orchestral and vocal works. Numerous important recordings were produced in connection with the 1985 tercentenary commemoration of Handel's birth: Hogwood's Academy of Ancient Music made premiere recordings of *ESTHER*, *ATHALIA* and several Italian cantatas, Gardiner released an abridged *Solomon* and recorded *Tamerlano*, Pinnock recorded the *Song for St Cecilia's Day*, a Spitalfields production of *Alcina* was recorded under the direction of Richard Hickox, *Alessandro* received its premiere recording (directed by Kuijken) and an abridged *RODELINDA* featured Joan Sutherland in the title role. The pace at which new recordings of operas and oratorio-style works have been produced has barely slowed down since 1985. Period-instrument groups dominate the post-1985 discography, and significant CDs have been made by conductors Fabio Bonizzoni, John Butt, William Christie, Harry Christophers, Laurence Cummings, Christian Curnyn, Alan Curtis, Emmanuelle Haïm, Matthew Halls, René Jacobs, Robert King, Paul McCreesh, Nicholas McGegan, Marc Minkowski, Andrew Parrott, George Petrou and Christophe Rousset. Many of their projects have been premiere recordings that adhere closely to the texts of Handel's first performance versions of large-scale works.

By 2009 most of Handel's chamber instrumental pieces, popular church compositions (e.g. *Dixit Dominus* and Coronation Anthems) and major orchestral compositions have received numerous commercial recordings. Almost every music theatre work (including every extant opera) has been issued on CD at least once, although performances are not always complete, convincing or idiomatic. Singers continue to make albums of Handel arias, albeit with varying degrees of imagination. DVD ('digital versatile disc', launched 1998) has expanded the number of staged opera productions, concerts and documentaries available for domestic viewing, and superseded VHS video cassettes (which were common during the 1980s). Moreover, the current popularity of broadband internet technology enables listeners to source Handel's music through web broadcasts or purchasing downloads. There is still plenty of Handel's music that is not yet represented in the discography, most notably many of his CANTATAS for solo voice and continuo, some of the CHAPEL ROYAL anthems (ANTHEMS, 1), and material from his pre-performance drafts or revivals of works.

Musicians who make noteworthy new contributions to the Handel discography are given formal public recognition and encouragement by the Stanley

Sadie Handel Recording Prize (inaugurated 2002), which is awarded by an international jury of journalists and scholars. Prize-winners have included Il Complesso Barocco, the King's Consort, Sandrine Piau, La Risonanza, the Early Opera Company, and Matthew Halls (up to 2009). DAVID VICKERS

See also Appendix 6: Handel's music on CD and DVD; Appendix 7: An overview of fifty Handel performers, 1959–2009

National Sound Archive, British Library (http://cadensa.bl.uk)

Edelberg Collection, McGill University (http://music.library.mcgill.ca/edelberg.htm)

R. Allorto and R. Ewerhart, 'Discografia ragionata delle musiche italiane di Haendel', *L'approdo musicale* 3/12 (1960), 47–73

P. Beaussant, 'Discographie des oeuvres de Haendel', R. Rolland, *Haendel* (revised edn, Paris, 1975)

F. F. Clough and G. J. Cuming, *The World's Encyclopædia of Recorded Music* (London, 1952) (2nd supplement 1951–2 (London, 1953); 3rd supplement 1953–5 (London, 1957))

W. Dean, 'Handel's Dramatic Music on Records', ML 39 (1958), 57–65

L. Jenkins, 'Beecham's 1947 *Messiah*', *International Classical Record Collector* I/1 (May 1995), 25–30

B. Redfern, 'Selected Recordings of Handel's Music', *Handel: A Biography, with a Survey of Books, Editions and Recordings*, ed. C. Cudworth (London, 1972)

S. Sadie, 'Handel's Orchestral Music on Gramophone', ML 40 (1959), 353–65

'The Operas of Handel', *Opera on Record* 2 (1983), 26–55 (inc. discography by M. Walker)

K. Sasse, 'Verzeichnis der Schallplatten mit Werken von Georg Friedrich Händel in Deutschland für die Jahre 1952–1954', HJb 1 (1955)

T. N. Towe, 'A Collector's *Messiah*: Historic Handel Oratorio Recordings, 1899–1930' (CD booklet note, Koch Historic, 3–7703-2Y6×2, 1993)

'Handel: *Messiah*', *Choral Music on Record*, ed. A. Blyth (Cambridge, 1991)

R. Wigmore, 'Handel's Sacred Oratorios, Part 1', *Gramophone* (Dec. 1999)

'From *Joseph* to *Jephtha*', *Gramophone* (April 2000)

(Periodical discographies are published in GHB and HJb)

Reichardt, Johann Friedrich (b. Kaliningrad (German: Königsberg), 25 Nov. 1752; d. Giebichenstein near Halle, 27 June 1814). Composer and music historian. In the spring of 1774, Reichardt, as an 'attentive traveller', witnessed a performance of JUDAS MACCABAEUS in BERLIN and assessed Johann Joachim Eschenburg's translation of the libretto in detail. He believed that the oratorio's music would help him to find his own artistic individuality. His enthusiasm for Handel is also obvious in his novel *Leben des berühmten Tonkünstlers Heinrich Wilhelm Gulden* (Berlin, 1779). By 1785 he was Royal Prussian Kapellmeister. While visiting London he reported on the HANDEL COMMEMORATION to the Crown Prince Friedrich Wilhelm, and sent him a cantata he had composed on a text by John Lockman (1698–1771) in praise of Handel. The stylistic influence of Handel is apparent in Reichardt's compositions, and he reviewed Handel's music on numerous occasions in the *Musikalisches Kunstmagazin*, praising its 'sense of truth' and its 'innate feeling for expression'. In a review dated 1791 he expressed his high esteem of Handel's opera arias, which by that time were regarded as 'obsolete' in Germany. The music collection he left at his death included Handelian opera and oratorio scores but also three forgeries.

WERNER RACKWITZ (Trans. ANGELA BAIER)

K. Eberl, K. Musketa et al. (eds.), *Johann Friedrich Reichardt (1752– 1814): Zwischen Anpassung und Provokation* (Halle, 2003)

W. Rackwitz, 'Marginalien zur Händel-Rezeption im Umfeld des brandenburgisch-preußischen Hofes im 18. Jahrhundert', HJb 44 (1998)

'J. F. Reichardt und das Händelfest 1785 in London', *Max Schneider zum 85. Geburtstag, Wiss. Ztschr. der Univ. Halle-Wittenberg, Ges. Sprachw.*, vol. 9 (1960), 507–15

J. F. Reichardt, *Autobiographische Schriften*, ed. G. Hartung (Halle, 2002)

W. Salmen, *Johann Friedrich Reichardt*, 2nd edn (Hildesheim, 2002)

Reiche, Johann Gerhard Andreas von (b. ?Hanover, 20 Jan. 1691). *Geheimsekretär* in London of the Hanoverian ministry. A son of Jobst Christoph von Reiche (1656–1740), he was one of GEORGE I's Hanoverian advisers. He received a legacy of £200 under the fourth codicil of Handel's will (HANDEL, 8).   DAVID HUNTER

Reinhold, Henry (Theodore) (d. London, 14 May 1751). Bass singer (range about G–f′). He first sang for Handel in *ATALANTA* (1736), and became his regular bass soloist at *COVENT GARDEN* in 1736–7, when he performed in an extensive and varied programme of operas and oratorios, including the new operas *ARMINIO*, *GIUSTINO* and *BERENICE*. In 1739–41 he sang for Handel in two seasons of opera and oratorio performances at LINCOLN'S INN FIELDS (including the bass solos in L'*ALLEGRO, IL PENSEROSO ED IL MODERATO*). When Handel resumed oratorio performances in 1743 following his return from DUBLIN, Reinhold became his regular bass soloist, receiving roles in every oratorio up to *THEODORA* in 1750. He took part in Handel's abbreviated oratorio season of 1751 and sang in the first of Handel's subsequent performances of *MESSIAH* at the FOUNDLING HOSPITAL, but died before the second performance. His wider career as a theatre singer included success in the role of the dragon in The *DRAGON OF WANTLEY* (CAREY/LAMPE); Handel's decision to cast him as Harapha rather than Manoa in *SAMSON* indicates that he was suited to heavyweight roles. His son Frederick was also a singer, and early in his adult career he was in the chorus for the Foundling Hospital *Messiah* performance in 1758. It is not known which forename the father used.   DONALD BURROWS

Religion. See HANDEL, 12

Resurrezione di Nostro Signor Gesù Cristo, La, HWV 47. Italian oratorio, libretto by Carlo Sigismondo CAPECE. Handel received the commission for *La Resurrezione* from Marchese Francesco Maria RUSPOLI, who by 1707 was hosting semi-public oratorio concerts on Sundays during Lent in his palace, which culminated in a festive performance on Easter Sunday. The idea that *La Resurrezione* was conceived as a counterpart to Alessandro SCARLATTI's *Per la Passione* 'Colpa, Pentimento e Grazia', which had been performed on the Wednesday of Holy Week at Cardinal OTTOBONI's Palazzo della Cancelleria, is no more than an assumption, given that Scarlatti's oratorio had already been performed several times in Rome during the previous years.

Capece's libretto is based on the resurrection narratives in the Gospels; when paraphrasing the text, he divided it into dialogue-based scenes. The action takes place on two consecutive days: from the Harrowing of Hell on the morning of Easter Saturday (after Christ's death and burial on Good Friday), to the morning of Easter Sunday, when Mary Magdalene and Mary Cleophas visit the empty tomb. The action is divided into a number of contrasting 'scenes'. It begins with a brilliant aria for an Angel, who arrives at the gates of Limbo and proclaims Christ's victory. Lucifer is defiant, and summons the infernal powers to rally to him. Mary Magdalene and Mary Cleophas mourn Christ and contemplate the Passion. St John the Evangelist reminds them of the promised resurrection on the third day, and the women decide to visit the tomb. The Angel calls forth the souls of the patriarchs and prophets (led by Adam and Eve) from Limbo, and they break into a jubilant song and chorus. At the beginning of Part II, John interprets the earthquake on Easter morning (after Matthew 28:2) as Hell's last rearing up and the sunrise as a sign of the resurrection, which he confidently expects. The Angel rejoices at the resurrection; Lucifer, who feels vanquished, tries to conceal his defeat from the world, but the Angel shows him the two Marys proceeding to the tomb. Mary Magdalene and Mary Cleophas oscillate between hope and fear and try to reassure each other. Lucifer admits defeat and angrily plunges down to Hell. The women reach the tomb, where the Angel announces Christ's resurrection. The Marys depart to find the risen Jesus: Mary Cleophas tells John about what she has learned at the tomb; Mary Magdalene arrives and reports that she has met Christ in the garden. The oratorio ends with a chorus praising God.

For his libretto Capece draws on many traditions and themes of contemporary oratorio libretto-writing: the linking of reflective and dramatic situations, the simultaneous provision of both entertainment and instruction, the almost kaleidoscopic grouping of contrasting affections and images, the lamento convention as found in contemporary texts and music, the evocation of the Underworld and the stereotyping of the characters of Mary Magdalene, John and Lucifer. Capece cleverly sets two loosely connected strains of action against each other: the 'dramatic' confrontation between the Angel and Lucifer in the Underworld and the more 'lyrical' reflections of Mary Cleophas, Mary Magdalene and John the Evangelist above ground. Capece's text is colourful and rich in images and contrasts and can be regarded as a very successful libretto, which must have issued a challenge to Handel's compositional skills.

Each of the two parts begins with an instrumental sinfonia. Both the 'prima' and the 'seconda parte' alternate between recitatives and arias (the score also includes two duets), and each part ends with a 'coro' sung by the vocal soloists. Mary Magdalene's arias feature some of the oratorio's most enchanting music. Handel sets her 'Ferma l'ali' for two recorders, violini sordini, viola da gamba, and dispenses with harpsichord accompaniment, thereby drawing an evocative picture of the penitent sinner, who, tired from weeping, still resists the wings of sleep in the dead of night. Her unisono aria 'Ho un no so che nel cor', with its blithe and captivating melody, is on the other end of the emotional scale; Handel borrowed the principal motif from a violin sonata by Corelli, and reused the aria in AGRIPPINA (1709). The fact that he was able to use the aria in both oratorio and opera confirms that identical musical language could be equally used to expressive effect in dissimilar contexts and genres.

Handel's notably extravagant score calls for five vocal soloists (SSATB), recorders, flute, oboes, bassoon, trumpets, solo violin, viola da gamba, strings and basso continuo (including theorbo), with the instruments frequently used in unusual and imaginative combinations. He had an exceptionally large orchestra for the first performance of *La Resurrezione*, which took place in Ruspoli's rented Palazzo Bonelli (PALAZZI, 7) in ROME on Easter Sunday, 8 April 1708. Ruspoli's account books show that the orchestra was led by Arcangelo CORELLI, and consisted of about forty-five musicians, including a trombonist (for whom no part has survived, but whose function was probably to double the basso continuo line in passages featuring trumpets). The account books mention only the first names of singers, which means that it is impossible to identify the cast for the first performance with certainty. It might have been:

Angelo	Francesco Finaia (castrato)
Maria Maddalena	Margherita DURASTANTI (soprano)
Maria Cleofe	Pasquale Betti (castrato)
San Giovanni	Vittorio Chiccheri (tenor)
Lucifero	Cristofano Cinotti (bass)

Ruspoli earned a papal reprimand for having had a woman sing in his oratorio, and consequently he may have engaged a castrato to sing Mary Magdalene in the second performance, which took place on Easter Monday. Ruspoli ordered 1,500 copies of the libretto to be printed (some were probably circulated at the three public rehearsals), and lavished considerable sums of money upon the elaborate construction of a temporary theatre in the 'salone' on the palazzo's first floor. Staged performances as we know them today would have been contrary to the conception of oratorio in Italy at that time, but the inclusion of thematically relevant visual elements was not uncommon in special festive performances: a stage was erected with four curved rows of seats for the instrumentalists; ornate new music stands were carved especially for the occasion; above the stage and forming a kind of background prospect was a painting depicting the resurrection by Michelangelo Cerruti, who also provided a tablet upon which the title of the oratorio was illuminated; the whole stage setting was draped with expensive fabrics.

In some respects, *La Resurrezione* is the grandest and boldest of Handel's Roman works. The oratorio has even been called 'the summit of his Italian development' (Hogwood, *Handel*, p. 40), and its masterfully expressive and characterised score certainly demonstrates that by the time of its composition Handel was no longer a northern German apprentice but a fully fledged composer who had completely assimilated contemporary Italian styles and genres.

JULIANE RIEPE (Trans. ANGELA BAIER)

T. Best, 'Handel's word setting in *La Resurrezione*', GHB VII (1998)
    (ed.), *La Resurrezione*, HHA I/3 (Kassel, forthcoming)
W. Breig, '*La Resurrezione* und die Anfänge von Händels Unisono-Arie', HJb 55 (2009)
C. Gianturco, 'The Characterization of Lucifero and Angelo at the Opening of Handel's *La Resurrezione*', GHB VII (1998)
C. Hogwood, *Handel*, rev. edn (London, 2007)
W. and U. Kirkendale, *Music and Meaning: Studies in Music History and the Neighbouring Disciplines* (Florence, 2007)
J. Riepe, 'Händels *La Resurrezione*. Bemerkungen zum Kontext von Werk und Aufführung', *Bericht über die Symposien der Händel-Akademie Karlsruhe 2005–2008*, ed. S. Schmalzriedt and T. Seedorf (forthcoming)
E. Rosand, 'Handel Paints the Resurrection', *Festa musicologica: Essays in Honor of George J. Buelow*, ed. T. J. Mathiesen and B. V. Riviera (Stuyvesant, NY, 1995)

rhetoric. Like all composers of his time, Handel came into contact with humanistic educational traditions, such as the antiquity-based disciplines of the *Trivium*, early in his life and was therefore also acquainted with rhetoric. He probably

537

learned Latin and Greek at Halle's STADTGYMNASIUM, and also the art of free speech and disputation (using the *Institutiones Oratoriae* by Christian Weise) (HANDEL, 13); he signed his youthful mourning poem for his father (1697) as 'der freyen Künste ergebener'('dedicated to the liberal arts'), and it includes exclamations, emphatic repetitions of certain words and expressive metaphors that bear the distinct stamp of baroque rhetoric traditions. Moreover, a number of distinguished scholars trained in antique rhetoric taught at HALLE UNIVERSITY (where Handel enrolled in 1702). His music lessons with ZACHOW were also based on the principles of rhetoric tradition. According to MAINWARING, the young Handel's thoughts were first directed towards the 'art of invention' by Zachow acquainting him with the manifold advantages and disadvantages exemplified in works by various composers, and instructing his pupil to copy interesting pieces and compose new ones modelled on them: thereby his awareness of *loci topici* (the standard rhetorical devices of an expert orator) and *inventio* (i.e. finding an argument) was sharpened. Later on in HAMBURG, he received advice in the 'dramatic style' (with its plot- and *Affekt*-based handling of the text) from MATTHESON and also exchanged ideas with TELEMANN, who consciously used musical-rhetoric devices. Handel was probably already proficient in the fields of textual and musical *dispositio* (ordering an argument) and *elaboratio* (or *elocutio*; the style of the argument). He again came into contact with antique and humanistic traditions and with the principles and expressive gestures of classical rhetoric in the circle of the ARCADIAN ACADEMY in ROME.

Handel's rational handling of the possibilities offered by the *inventio* is not only documented by his numerous BORROWINGS of pieces expressing the right *Affekt* from works by other composers, but also by his careful choice of his own musical effects. For example, in *ACI, GALATEA E POLIFEMO* (NAPLES, 1708) he employed major and minor keys according to their contemporaneous rhetorical meanings, and also used the Lydian ('devilish' because of its pronounced tritone), the Doric or Dorian (majestic or 'divine') and Mixolydian ('lascivious' and based on the 'sun' key of 'sol') modes. In the *dispositio* Handel shows himself to have been influenced by rhetorical-dramaturgic concepts (for example by the rhetorical pattern of 'Exordium, Narratio, Propositio, Confirmatio, Confutatio and Peroratio', emphasised by theorists such as Mattheson) (ARIA, 2). The detailed *elaboratio* of all his compositions is shaped by figures of musical rhetoric, which elucidate and interpret the text. In the short recitative 'Und er trug selbst sein Kreuz' from the *Brockes Passion* he used *hypotyposis* (chiasmus), *exclamatio*, *saltus duriusculus* (tritone) including *katachresis* (in this case a diminished seventh chord), *suspiratio*, *anabasis* and *interrogatio*. Much of Handel's music is pervaded by this semantic vocabulary in a similarly dense form.

HARTMUT KRONES (Trans. ANGELA BAIER)

See also ARIA, 2

G. Fleischhauer, 'Mögliche Begegnungen G. F. Händels mit der literarischen und musikalischen Rhetorik', *Das mitteldeutsche Musikleben vor Händel | Christoph Willibald Gluck (1714–1787)* ed. B. Baselt and W. Siegmund-Schulze, (Halle, 1988)

H. Krones, 'Elemente der musikalischen Rhetorik in Händels *Serenata Aci, Galatea e Polifemo*', *Ausdrucksformen der Musik des Barock. Passionsoratorium – Serenata – Rezitativ*, ed. S. Schmalzriedt (Laaber, 2002)

J. Mattheson, *Der Vollkommene Capellmeister* (Hamburg, 1739)

Riccardo primo, Re d'Inghilterra, HWV 23. Handel's eleventh opera for the Royal Academy of Music (OPERA COMPANIES, 2), composed in 1727. The libretto is by Paolo ROLLI, derived from Isacio tiranno by Francesco BRIANI, which was set by LOTTI and performed in VENICE in 1710. The story is based on a historical event: in 1191 Richard the Lionheart sailed from Sicily with a large fleet to take part in the Third Crusade. With him, but on another ship, was his intended bride, Berengaria of Navarre. Off Cyprus a storm scattered the fleet, and Berengaria's vessel took shelter at Limassol; there she was taken prisoner by Isaac Comnenus, the tyrant of Cyprus. Richard invaded the island, defeated him and rescued Berengaria; they were married in Limassol. Berengaria was renamed Costanza in the librettos, and the plot depends upon a historical improbability, that Berengaria and Richard had never met; this allows Isacio to attempt to pass off his daughter Pulcheria as Costanza.

At the beginning of the opera, after a dramatic storm scene, Costanza and her cousin Berardo have reached the shore; she fears that Riccardo must have perished. Isacio, Pulcheria and her lover Oronte, Isacio's ally, come upon them and receive them graciously. Costanza conceals their real identity, but Isacio is struck by her beauty. Isacio approves the marriage of Pulcheria and Oronte, and orders the destruction of the wrecked English ships. Riccardo is ashore elsewhere, and news reaches him that Costanza is safe; he will go to Isacio, disguised as his own ambassador, and try to recover her. Berardo warns Costanza not to trust Isacio; Oronte pays compliments to Costanza, to Pulcheria's annoyance. Riccardo arrives; Isacio receives him courteously, and promises to surrender Costanza, whose identity he now knows. Riccardo is pleased.

In Act II Costanza is in despair, but hopes that Riccardo knows she is safe. Isacio promises to reunite her with her husband. He tells Pulcheria, who is angry with Oronte, that she must forget him, pretend to be Costanza and go to meet Riccardo as his bride. She is shocked by the deceit, but obeys reluctantly. Riccardo and his army receive her: he is surprised that she is less beautiful than he expected, but he is courteous. Oronte arrives to reveal the deception: Riccardo is furious and swears revenge. Pulcheria is contrite, and Oronte pledges his support to Riccardo. Isacio realises that his trick has failed; Riccardo returns, still in disguise, and demands an explanation. Isacio is defiant and is willing to fight, but Pulcheria pleads with him and he pretends to agree to Riccardo's demands. Pulcheria brings Riccardo to see Costanza, and reveals who he is. Riccardo and Costanza embrace and sing a joyful duet.

As Act III opens, Riccardo has tried to bring Costanza out of the city, but they have been ambushed and Costanza snatched. Oronte joins forces with him and they prepare to attack the city. Riccardo addresses his troops and reminds them of British virtues. Inside, Costanza is once more in despair, and Pulcheria comforts her. Isacio blusters, but says his love is such that he cannot bear to lose her. She begs Berardo to go to Riccardo and tell him she would die rather than submit to Isacio. Riccardo's troops breach the wall, but Isacio appears with Costanza, and threatens to kill her unless the attack stops. Pulcheria threatens suicide if her father will not release Costanza: Isacio still refuses, but is overcome by Oronte and his soldiers. Victory is won, and Riccardo pardons Isacio: all rejoice, Riccardo shall have his Costanza, and Oronte his Pulcheria and the throne of Cyprus.

The compositional history of *Riccardo primo* is unusual: Handel drafted a first version in the spring of 1727, and dated the end of the autograph on 16 May. He had been granted British naturalisation in February, and patriotic pride may have influenced the choice of a libretto whose principal character was one of the most famous of English kings; a more likely reason is that it offered more or less equal parts for two sopranos, a necessity for him because of the presence in his company of the two famous rivals FAUSTINA Bordoni and Francesca CUZZONI. The work may have been intended for performance at the end of that season, which had seen the production of ADMETO; but the rivalry between the two singers (RIVAL QUEENS) caused a riot during a performance of BONONCINI's *Astianatte* on 6 June, which led to the closure of the theatre and the abandonment of the season. On 11 June King GEORGE I died on his way to HANOVER, an event which would have closed the theatres anyway. The accession of GEORGE II, whose CORONATION was scheduled for October, was a happy coincidence for Handel, since he already had in preparation an opera whose subject was one of George's most charismatic predecessors.

The first version had included, as in Briani, a part for Corrado, a confidant of Riccardo; this role was probably intended for Anna DOTTI, but she had now left the company, so the part had to be removed. Handel and Rolli now drastically revised the opera: some of it was totally rewritten, especially Act III. The restructuring involved not only the omission of Corrado but also the introduction of flattering references to the British monarchy, and some alterations in the characterisation; the most significant change was to bring forward to the end of Act II the first meeting between Riccardo and Costanza, which in Briani and the first version occurred late in Act III. Much new music was composed, all of the highest quality. The opera was premiered on 11 November 1727, and there were eleven performances. The cast was:

Riccardo	SENESINO (castrato)	
Costanza	Francesca CUZZONI (soprano)	
Pulcheria	FAUSTINA Bordoni (soprano)	
Isacio	Giuseppe Maria BOSCHI (bass)	
Oronte	Antonio Baldi (castrato)	
Berado	Giovanni Battista Palmerini (bass)	

The work was never revived in Handel's lifetime, and it has had few modern productions; yet the dramatic opening (featuring vivid storm music), the rich orchestration with horns, trumpets, timpani, recorders and a bass flute, and the generally high level of the musical invention, especially that for Costanza, who has some arias of considerable tragic power, make it an effective drama.

TERENCE BEST

T. Best (ed.), *Riccardo primo, Re d'Inghilterra*, HHA II/20 (Kassel, 2005)
Dean, *Operas*
Harris, *Librettos*
J. M. Knapp, 'The Autograph of Handel's *Riccardo primo*', *Studies in Renaissance and Baroque Music in Honor of Arthur Mendel*, ed. R. L. Marshall (1974)
S. Ograjenšek, 'From *Alessandro* (1726) to *Tolomeo* (1728): The Final Royal Academy Operas', Ph.D. dissertation (University of Cambridge, 2005)
Strohm

Rich, John (b. London, bap. 19 May 1692; d. London, 26 Nov. 1761). Dancer, actor, playwright, manager, inherited the third LINCOLN'S INN FIELDS Theatre (LIF) in 1714. For the first few years his company led a precarious existence, but stabilised after he developed the large-scale pantomime between 1717 and 1723. The new form emphasised song, dance and scenic transformations, rather than acting. Many of the early exemplars used a 'classical' or mythological setting accompanied by elevated music, alternating that with a low, often domestic, milieu featuring characters based on the Italian *commedia dell'arte*. Music from *AMADIGI* and *RINALDO* was borrowed as early as 1719, for *Harlequin Hydaspes*. Rich took up dancing as Harlequin in 1717 and under the name 'Lun' performed in many productions until 1752. When Rich became acquainted with Handel is not known, but he subscribed to editions of several of Handel's operas and other compositions, beginning with *RODELINDA* (1725). Rich encouraged the use of many kinds of music at LIF, from popular ballads to 'art' songs. After DRURY LANE had refused *The BEGGAR'S OPERA* (1728), LIF produced what turned out to be the most popular play of the century, which in the contemporaneous quip 'made Gay rich and Rich gay'.

In 1732 Rich built the COVENT GARDEN Theatre, the current version of which is now the Royal Opera House. In 1734, Handel 'engaged with Mr. Rich to carry on the Operas' (Deutsch, p. 369) at Covent Garden two nights a week, though the venture reportedly lost money and ended in 1737. Handel gave his first subscription series of oratorios at Covent Garden in 1743 and continued to use it as his principal venue for the rest of his life. Details of their relationship are lacking, but when Handel died, he left Rich the organ he had installed in the theatre for his oratorios (HANDEL, 8).   JUDITH MILHOUS and ROBERT D. HUME

B. Joncus and J. Barlow (eds.), *The Stage's Glory: John Rich (1692–1761)* (forthcoming)

Riemschneider, Gebhard Julius (b. Halle, 4 April 1687; d. Halle, 1734). Singer and brother of Johann Gottfried Riemschneider. Their father Gebhard Riemschneider was *Kantor* of the Marienkirche (ST MARIEN) in HALLE (from 1683 until 1701). Gebhard Julius studied with Friedrich Wilhelm ZACHOW at the same time as Handel. He was still active as a treble singer at St Marien as late as 1701, and was cantor of the Moritzkirche in HALLE from 1713 until his death.

KLAUS-PETER KOCH (Trans. ANGELA BAIER)

W. Serauky, *Musikgeschichte der Stadt Halle*, vol. 2 (Halle/Berlin, 1939)

Riemschneider, Johann Gottfried (b. Halle, 1691; d. ?). Bass. Between 1722 and 1728 he sang regularly at the HAMBURG opera (GÄNSEMARKT). Handel engaged him for the first season of the Second Academy (1729–30) (OPERA COMPANIES, 3). Mrs Pendarves (later DELANY) called him 'a very good distinct voice, without any harshness', and Paolo ROLLI said he 'sings sweetly in his throat and nose' but disparaged his acting and Italian pronunciation (Deutsch, pp. 247, 250). Riemschneider then returned to Hamburg, where from 1739 to 1741 he served as cantor of the cathedral.   JOHN H. ROBERTS

Rinaldo, HWV 7[a–b]. Handel's first Italian opera for London. The poet Giacomo ROSSI based the libretto on a draft by the Queen's Theatre (KING'S THEATRE) manager

Aaron HILL. The story was taken from Torquato TASSO's *Gerusalemme liberata*, and is set during the First Crusade (which occurred at the end of the eleventh century). The Christian general Goffredo has laid siege to Jerusalem and agrees to his daughter Almirena marrying the army's hero Rinaldo, but only on condition that the city is taken first. The besieged ruler of Jerusalem, Argante, calls for the help of his mistress, the enchantress Armida, who concludes that their only hope of victory is to separate Rinaldo from the crusader army. In order to achieve that goal she uses her magic to abduct Almirena, which forces the desperate Rinaldo to seek for his beloved in an attempt to liberate her. In Act II, Goffredo and his brother Eustazio accompany Rinaldo in search of a Christian magician who can help them to defeat Armida's supernatural powers, but on the way two sirens lure Rinaldo away from his companions and convey him to Armida's palace. Meanwhile Argante has fallen in love with the imprisoned Almirena, but she spurns his advances. The lustful Armida offers the captured Rinaldo her love; when he rejects her, she uses her magic to take the form of Almirena, so that she may seduce him. Rinaldo, although taken in at first, does not fall for her deception; but unfortunately Argante does and Armida becomes furious with jealousy. In Act III, Goffredo and Eustazio find the magician, who helps them to free Rinaldo and Almirena, and destroys Armida's magic. Rinaldo leads the crusaders in a victorious assault on Jerusalem. Armida and Argante are captured, their lives are spared when they convert to Christianity, and the lovers Rinaldo and Almirena are united.

According to MAINWARING, soon after Handel's first arrival in London 'Many of the nobility were impatient for an Opera of his composing'. Rossi's dedication in the printed WORDBOOK claims that the music for *Rinaldo* was composed in only a fortnight. The speed at which the score was produced – probably during January 1711 – was assisted by the composer's copious self-BORROWINGS from operas, oratorios and cantatas that he had recently written in Italy. Almost half of the numbers are based on Italian works which were unfamiliar to London audiences, although Handel often took great care in reworking musical ideas for their new contexts. For example, Argante's entrance aria 'Sibillar gli angui d'Aletto' was taken from Polifemo's aria in *ACI, GALATEA E POLIFEMO*, with only some fleshing out of the orchestral accompaniment; Rinaldo's heroic aria 'Venti turbini, prestate', featuring a florid solo violin part, was borrowed from one of Apollo's arias in *La TERRA È LIBERATA*, and the title hero's 'Abbruggio, avvampo e fremo' was based on musical ideas that Handel had used in both *RODRIGO* and the motet *Saeviat tellus* (Italian and Latin CHURCH MUSIC); Armida's striking lament 'Ah! crudel, il pianto mio' was taken from a cantata (*AH! CRUDEL, NEL PIANTO MIO*); even the seemingly story-specific duets 'Scherzano sul tuo volto' (Rinaldo and Almirena) and 'Fermati! No crudel' (Rinaldo and Armida) were adapted from convenient counterparts in *COR FEDELE, IN VANO SPERI*. Handel transformed ideas from a couple of Italian compositions into Armida's flamboyant 'Vo' far guerra', in which the composer displayed his own performing prowess at the harpsichord. Moreover, the two most famous arias in *Rinaldo* were each influenced by Italian models, albeit to varying extents: the famous sarabande 'Lascia ch'io pianga', in which Almirena pleads for Argante to release her from imprisonment, was taken almost verbatim from Piacere's 'Lascia la spina' in *Il TRIONFO*

DEL TEMPO E DEL DISINGANNO; whereas Rinaldo's emotional lament 'Cara sposa' bears a resemblance to only the vocal part of San Giovanni's 'Cara figlio' in La RESURREZIONE. The newly composed numbers included several impressive highlights, such as Armida's tempestuous first apparition 'Furie terribili' (marked 'Presto furioso'), Almirena's 'Augelletti, che cantate, zefiretti' (with two recorders imitating birdsong), and the title hero's climactic military aria 'Or la tromba' (in which Handel created a splendid rousing effect by introducing four trumpets and drums towards the end of the long opera).

Rinaldo (HWV 7ª) was first performed on 24 February 1711 at the Queen's Theatre, with the following cast:

Rinaldo	NICOLINO (castrato)
Armida	Elisabetta PILOTTI-SCHIAVONETTI (soprano)
Almirena	Isabella Girardeau ('La Isabella') (soprano)
Goffredo	Francesca VANINI-BOSCHI (contralto)
Argante	Giuseppe Maria BOSCHI (bass)
Eustazio	Valentino Urbani (castrato)
Mago	Giuseppe Cassani (castrato)
Sirene	? (sopranos)
Herald	Mr Lawrence (tenor)

The opera was performed fifteen times during its first season and more than thirty times during the next five years. Maybe the popularity of the opera was partly because Aaron Hill designed the lavish staging to be an exuberant spectacle, arguably deriving from the English theatrical tradition of operatic masques (such as those in Henry PURCELL's The Fairy Queen and King Arthur). The audience were entertained by visual effects, particularly regarding Armida's use of magic, which according to the libretto included a 'chariot drawn by two huge Dragons, out of whose Mouths issue Fire and Smoke'. According to satirical reports by Joseph ADDISON and Sir Richard Steele in The Spectator (Deutsch, pp. 35–8), live sparrows and chaffinches flew above the stage, and there was also thunder, lightning, illuminations and fireworks (although Steele wittily alleged that in reality the stage action did not live up to the promises offered by the scene descriptions in the wordbook). Hill's extravagant production of Rinaldo led to a lawsuit from tradesmen who had not been paid, and he was deposed as manager of the Queen's Theatre just nine days after the opera's premiere. However, it seems that the element of visual spectacle was further enhanced by ballets danced between the acts by 'Monsieur du Breil' and 'Mademoiselle le Fevre' on 20 and 24 March 1711.

Rinaldo was revived at the same theatre in 1712 (while Handel was in HANOVER), 1713, 1714–15 and 1717 (when, on 5 June, entr'actes were danced by Marie SALLÉ). Handel did not perform the opera again until he substantially revised it for the Second Academy (OPERA COMPANIES, 3) in 1731. This version (HWV 7ᵇ) omitted the role of Eustazio, the contributions of Armida and Argante were diminished, and every part except Almirena featured changes of pitch. About a quarter of the original 1711 movements were omitted, and only about half a dozen were preserved without musical alteration. All of the other retained arias were either transposed or revised, and eight numbers were inserted from other works (such as GIULIO CESARE and the recent Second

Academy operas *LOTARIO* and *PARTENOPE*). Most of the recitatives and two movements were newly composed, of which the only substantial piece was the extended *accompagnato* 'Orrori menzogneri' (for SENESINO in the title role, III.vii, 1731 version). Certainly Handel's most radical revision of one of his own old operas, HWV 7^b was first performed on 6 April 1731 and ran for six performances. Although he never revived *Rinaldo* again, it was performed fifty-three times in London during his lifetime – a higher total than any of his other operas. It was also the first of his London operas to be performed in Germany: it was presented at HAMBURG in 1715 (in a German version, which was revived during at least six more seasons between 1720 and 1730). A PASTICCIO version with Nicolino in the title role and additional music by Leonardo LEO was performed at Naples in 1718. ARTIE HEINRICH

Burney
Dean and Knapp, *Operas*
Harris, *Librettos*
D. Hunter, 'Bragging on *Rinaldo*. Ten Ways Writers have Trumpeted Handel's Coming to Britain', *GHB* X (2004)
D. Kimbell (ed.), *Rinaldo* (HWV 7^a), HHA II/4.1 (Kassel, 1993)
  (ed.), *Rinaldo* (HWV 7^b), HHA II/4.2 (Kassel, 1996)
R. Kubik, *Händels Rinaldo. Geschichte, Werk, Wirkung* (Neuhausen-Stuttgart, 1982)
J. Milhous and R. D. Hume, 'The Haymarket Opera in 1711', *EM* 17/4 (1989), 523–38
C. Price, 'English Traditions in Handel's *Rinaldo*', *Handel Tercentenary Collection*, ed. S. Sadie and A. Hicks (London, 1987)
Strohm

Rival Queens, The. An epithet for the sopranos Francesca CUZZONI and FAUSTINA Bordoni, who were both engaged by the Royal Academy of Music (OPERA COMPANIES, 2) in London from the middle of the 1725–6 season to the collapse of the Academy in 1728. Cuzzoni had been the prima donna of the company since 1723 when Bordoni arrived in the middle of the 1725–6 season. Their shared London engagement caused a furore between rival soprano factions which has sometimes been thought of as contributing to the Academy's collapse, but this is not supported by hard evidence. Though the furore was of limited duration and restricted to factions within the audience, the image of the two rival sopranos has persisted, largely owing to the powerful connotations of the 'Rival Queens' epithet.

The epithet was induced by the similarities between the first opera in which the sopranos shared the London stage, Handel's *ALESSANDRO*, and the popular tragedy by Nathaniel Lee, *The Rival Queens, or the Death of Alexander the Great* (1677): both their plots are based on the historical figure of Alexander the Great, and in both the hero is torn between two women. It is debatable whether the link between the tragedy and the opera was envisaged on the part of the Academy. The opera is in no way indebted to the tragedy. Furthermore, the Academy was acquiring a second soprano as a competition with continental theatres: engaging both Bordoni and Cuzzoni meant taking over the star soprano pair from the celebrated European opera theatre, Teatro San Giovanni Grisostomo in VENICE, where Cuzzoni and Bordoni had shared the stage in the autumn season of 1718, in the Carnival season of 1719 and in the Carnival season of 1721 (employing pairs of star sopranos and castratos was a habit of those continental opera theatres who could afford it). Also, contrary to modern popular belief, the Academy, operating as a joint-stock company, could not have expected to increase its sales by stimulating celebrity rivalry. A further question is whether the epithet 'The Rival Queens' ever extended further than providing a convenient and amusing tag. The press entertained itself by using both the versions 'The Rival Queens' and 'The Rival Queans', the latter deriving from the title of Colley Cibber's burlesque on Lee's tragedy (1690s/1700s). The epithet first appeared in print in the prologue to the revival of BONONCINI's *Camilla* at LINCOLN'S INN FIELDS THEATRE (printed in *The London Journal*, No. 382, 26 November 1726) and in a satirical notice in *Mist's Weekly Journal* (10 December 1726). 'The Rival Queans' epithet appeared in the title of the farce *The Contre Temps* in July 1727. The epithet has persisted until today and has done more to promote the image of Cuzzoni's and Bordoni's rivalry throughout the centuries than any anecdote, including their infamous, though spurious, stage fight in *Astianatte* (this stage fight actually never happened: in fact, the performance on 6 June 1727 had to be halted because of the audience's misbehaviour in presence of royalty). The persistence of the epithet can be assigned to its interest: it promotes an archetype of professional female rivalry, a pair of self-centred, bad-tempered, jealous divas who are not beyond ravaging each other's elaborate hairpieces on-stage. In this, the epithet tells us more about the audience reception throughout the centuries than about the two sopranos involved.   SUZANA OGRAJENŠEK

E. Gibson, *The Royal Academy of Music 1719–1728: The Institution and its Directors* (New York, 1989)
S. Ograjenšek, 'From *Alessandro* (1726) to *Tolomeo* (1728): The Final Royal Academy Operas', Ph.D. dissertation (University of Cambridge, 2005)

Rivers Gay, Lady Martha (b. London after 1741; d. Winchester, 14 Feb. 1835). Step-daughter of John Christopher SMITH JUNIOR and William COXE's sister. In 1768 she married Revd Sir Peter Rivers Gay, 6th Baronet of Chafford, Kent (1721–90). Smith junior bequeathed to her all of his music books, among which were some of Handel's manuscripts, including most of the composer's performing scores (without *MESSIAH*) (SOURCES AND COLLECTIONS, 2). After the death of her son Sir Henry Rivers Gay these were sold to the bookseller Thomas KERSLAKE in BRISTOL between 1851 and 1856. According to Coxe, she also possessed a book of manuscript music with Handel's initials that was dated 1698, but is now lost.   ANNETTE LANDGRAF

[W. Coxe], *Anecdotes of George Frederick Handel, and John Christopher Smith* (London, 1799; facsimile edn, ed. P. M. Young, New York, 1979), 6n.
W. C. Smith, 'More Handeliana', *ML* 34 (1953), 11–15

Robinson, Anastasia (b. ?Italy, 1692; d. Bath, April 1755). Soprano (compass: $d'-a''$), then from 1720 an alto ($bb-eb''$): She studied singing with William CROFT and Pietro Giuseppe Sandoni (CUZZONI), among others. From 1714 she appeared at the Queen's Theatre (KING'S THEATRE), where she created the part of Oriana in Handel's *AMADIGI*. During the first season of the Royal Academy of Music (1720) (OPERA COMPANIES, 2) she performed the role of Zenobia in *RADAMISTO*, but in the almost all-Italian cast of the following season she sang only minor roles. When Margherita DURASTANTI fell ill during the 1721–2 season, Robinson rose to the rank of prima donna and scored a major success in the title role of BONONCINI's *GRISELDA*. Handel composed roles for her in *MUZIO SCEVOLA* (Irene), *FLORIDANTE* (Elmira), *OTTONE* (Matilda), *FLAVIO*

(Teodata) and *GIULIO CESARE* (Cornelia). Her vocal and dramatic powers seem to have been limited: the part of Elmira, originally written for Durastanti, had to be simplified for her, and she also requested Handel to compose different arias for the role of Matilda. She was a Catholic and close to the Italian circle in London including Bononcini and SENESINO. She retired from the stage in 1724 after her marriage to the Earl of PETERBOROUGH (which was at first kept secret).   HANS DIETER CLAUSEN (Trans. ANGELA BAIER)

> C. S. LaRue, *Handel and his Singers: The Creation of the Royal Academy Operas, 1720–1728* (Oxford, 1995)

Robinson, Ann Turner (b. ?; d. London, 5 Jan. 1741). English soprano (compass: e′–a″). The youngest daughter of the composer and singer Dr William Turner. After her marriage to the composer and organist John Robinson she performed as 'Mrs. Turner Robinson', possibly in order to avoid being confused with ANASTASIA ROBINSON. She sang for the Royal Academy of Music (OPERA COMPANIES, 2) in 1720, and Handel created the part of Polissena in the first version of *RADAMISTO* for her. She was an active concert singer in London during the following years. In 1732 she appeared in Handel's performances of *Acis and Galatea* (HWV 49^b) and *Esther* (HWV 50^b).   ARTIE HEINRICH

Robinson, Miss (fl. 1733–45). Mezzo-soprano (range a–g♯″). Daughter of John and Ann Turner ROBINSON. Little is known about her. Handel engaged her for the oratorio season of 1744–5, when she created the role of Dejanira in *HERCULES*, a role that suggests that she was an accomplished and dramatic singer. Handel's letter to Charles JENNENS of October 1744 (Deutsch, pp. 595–6) indicates that she was to sing the part of Cyrus in *BELSHAZZAR*, but she ultimately took the part of Daniel to replace the ailing Susannah CIBBER. She also appeared in several revivals that season, including *DEBORAH* (Barak), *SEMELE* (Ino), *SAMSON* (Micah, Israelite woman, Philistine woman), *JOSEPH AND HIS BRETHREN* (Phanor), *MESSIAH* and possibly *SAUL*. She sang Handel arias in benefit concerts in April 1745 at COVENT GARDEN and the KING'S THEATRE.
                    DAVID ROSS HURLEY

> Dean, *Oratorios*

Rodelinda, Regina de' Longobardi, HWV 19 (libretto by Antonio SALVI (1710), adapted by Nicola HAYM; Handel's autograph score completed 20 January 1725; first performance 13 February 1725, KING'S THEATRE, Haymarket, London). After the death of Ariberto, the kingdom of Lombardy was divided between his sons: Bertarido ruled in Milan, and Gundeberto in Pavia. To gain control of the whole kingdom, the latter declared war on his brother. He enlisted the support of Grimoaldo, Duke of Benevento, promising him the hand of his sister, Eduige. Gundeberto died; Bertarido fled at the advance of Grimoaldo's forces; Grimoaldo usurped the throne of Milan. So that he could return to Milan incognito and rescue his wife (Rodelinda) and son (Flavio), Bertarido spread a report of his own death.

All these events took place before the beginning of the opera. Crucial elements in the plot are the desire of Grimoaldo to marry Rodelinda and her steadfast rejection of him; the encouragement and assistance given to Grimoaldo by the evil Garibaldo; the latter's ambition to seize the throne for himself; Eduige's fury at being rejected by Grimoaldo; and Unulfo's loyalty to Bertarido. Finding the disguised Bertarido in the graveyard, Unulfo insists that he remain in hiding, in order to ensure the eventual freedom of Rodelinda and Flavio. Bertarido watches as his wife and son grieve at his tomb and as she submits to Garibaldo's harsh demand that, to save Flavio's life, she should marry Grimoaldo. Rodelinda later reveals her stratagem: face-to-face with Grimoaldo, she agrees to marry him only on condition that he kill Flavio, knowing that he could never commit such a deed. Bertarido meets his sister, Eduige, who pledges her support, and is soon reunited with Rodelinda. Their joy is short-lived: Grimoaldo throws Bertarido into prison. Eduige and Unulfo plot his escape: Unulfo has a key to the cell, and will lead Bertarido to safety through an underground passage; Eduige will throw a sword down into the cell. When he hears someone approaching, Bertarido strikes the intruder with the sword, only to find that he has wounded Unulfo. Rodelinda enters the empty cell with Flavio and Eduige; finding Bertarido's clothes and blood on the ground, she fears he has been murdered. Grimoaldo, uncertain whether or not the prisoner really is Bertarido, becomes increasingly delirious; eventually he falls asleep. Garibaldo reveals his treacherous nature: he attempts to murder the sleeping king, but is stopped by Bertarido, who kills him. Grimoaldo acknowledges Bertarido's noble action; he restores Milan to its rightful king, and reunites husband, wife and son; he himself will rule in Pavia with Eduige as his wife.

The libretto, adapted by Nicola HAYM from Antonio SALVI's *Rodelinda, Regina de' Longobardi*, has its ultimate source in the *Gesta Langobardorum* of PAULUS DIACONUS (c.720–99) and a more recent source in Pierre Corneille's *Pertharite, roi des Lombards* (1652). *Rodelinda, Regina de' Longobardi* was first set to music by Giacomo Antonio PERTI and performed at the Pratolino theatre near FLORENCE in 1710. Salvi's libretto is an improvement on Corneille's play, and Haym's revision is a competent piece of work: while the excision of almost 650 lines of recitative leaves one or two obscure references, his cuts and reorderings tighten the drama and sharpen the characterisation. In the Haym/Handel revision hero and heroine dominate the action, while Unulfo, Eduige Garibaldo are less prominent; Grimoaldo remains a 'sheep in wolf's clothing' (Dean and Knapp, p. 577). The omission of Salvi's Unoldo is not a serious dramatic loss, but it caused Handel a slight problem at the beginning of Act III (Jones, 'The Composer as Dramatist', pp. 69–73). Compared with, for example, *OTTONE*, *GIULIO CESARE* and *RICCARDO PRIMO*, the composition history of *Rodelinda* was fairly straightforward, thanks largely to a stable and familiar cast of singers. However, the changes to the libretto that Handel requested while he was composing were substantial and dramatically significant, especially in Act I. Their effect at the beginning of the opera is to engage the audience's attention and sympathy immediately by presenting the emotional nucleus of the opera – the grief and steadfast love of a wife; and in the graveyard scene they not only provide the context (a husband's love for his wife) within which Bertarido's reactions in the following scenes can be understood, but also intensify the drama: rather than hearing of Grimoaldo's desire to marry Rodelinda from Unulfo, he sees it acted out before his eyes. Handel had a strong sense of what he needed from a libretto and of its effect in a dramatic context: Haym wrote a new aria for Rodelinda to replace Salvi's near the beginning of Act II, as she defiantly confronts Grimoaldo and Garibaldo; having set it to music, Handel became dissatisfied, and requested a radically different text; the new aria ('Spietati') vividly depicts Rodelinda's strength of character and creates a powerful effect in the theatre.

Rodelinda was the third of a trio of masterpieces that Handel composed and staged between summer 1723 and early 1725. It received fourteen performances in its first run; the singers were as follows:

Rodelinda	Francesca CUZZONI (soprano)
Bertarido	SENESINO (castrato)
Grimoaldo	Francesco BOROSINI (tenor)
Eduige	Anna Vincenza DOTTI (mezzo-soprano)
Garibaldo	Giuseppe Maria BOSCHI (bass)
Unulfo	Andrea PACINI (castrato)

After attending a rehearsal, the tenor Alexander GORDON wrote that it 'exceeds all I ever heard'; an Italian visitor praised especially Senesino and Cuzzoni. Horace Walpole's famous description of Cuzzoni, reported by Charles BURNEY, is uncomplimentary about her appearance and acting, but provides a rare scrap of information about a contemporary costume: she wore 'a *brown silk gown*, trimmed with silver'.

Particularly impressive are Handel's portrayal of character and his unerring sense of musical drama. By the end of the opera Rodelinda stands before us as a believable human being: angry and defiant in the face of adversity, tender and steadfast in her love for Bertarido, desolate and suicidal when she believes him dead, rapturously joyful when reunited with him. Bertarido wins our sympathy by not being virtuously monochrome: his love for Rodelinda turns to hatred when he thinks her unfaithful. Burney rightly singled out for praise the truncated aria 'Chi di voi', sung by Bertarido in prison. The irregular phrase lengths, tortured lines, dissonant harmonies and interrupted cadences express bitter despair. Scarcely less subtle is Handel's portrayal of Grimoaldo, the usurper who is troubled by a conscience. His greatest moment, dramatically as well as musically, is the accompanied recitative 'Fatto inferno' in Act III: angular melodic lines, disjointed rhythms and chromatic harmonies brilliantly depict a deranged mind. Towards the end of the recitative and in the beautiful siciliano that follows it ('Pastorello d'un povero armento') Grimoaldo longs for respite, and dreams of the peaceful life of a shepherd.

Rodelinda was revived in December 1725 and in 1731, with eight performances each time. For each revival changes in the cast necessitated musical alterations. The first HAMBURG performance, arranged by C. W. Wendt and with recitatives (but not arias) in German, received 'little applause' (Mainwaring); there were four more performances there in 1734–6. Oskar HAGEN, attracted by the excellent libretto, the high quality of Handel's music and the theme of a faithful wife rescuing her husband from prison (which might have reminded him of BEETHOVEN's *Fidelio*), chose *Rodelinda* for performance at GÖTTINGEN in 1920 – the first Handel opera to be staged in the twentieth century.

ANDREW V. JONES

E. Dahnk-Baroffio, 'Nicola Hayms Anteil an Händels Rodelinde-Libretto', Die Musikforschung 7 (1954), 295–300

Dean and Knapp, Operas

U. Etscheit, Händels 'Rodelinda'. Libretto, Komposition, Rezeption (Kassel, 1998)

Harris, Librettos

A. V. Jones (ed.), Rodelinda, Regina de' Longobardi, HHA II/16 (Kassel, 2002)

'The Composer as Dramatist: Handel's Contribution to the Libretto of Rodelinda', ML 88/1 (2007), 49–77

Strohm

Rodrigo (Vincer se stesso è la maggior vittoria), HWV 5. Handel's first opera written in and for Italy. The plot, based on historical events taking place during the reign of the Visigoths in Spain, centres on the confrontation between the Spanish King Rodrigo and his discarded mistress Florinda, who was seduced by the King after having been promised marriage and crown. Dishonoured and pregnant, she vows revenge and allies herself with the mutinous Prince Evanco, who, in his turn, wants to avenge his murdered father Vitizza. Florinda is also supported by her brother Giuliano, a former friend and confidant of Rodrigo. When matters turn against Rodrigo, his selfless and long-suffering wife Esilena manages to save his life. In the end the repentant Rodrigo withdraws into private life and returns the usurped crown to its rightful heir Evanco in accordance with the opera's motto 'Vincer se stesso è la maggior vittoria' or 'To conquer oneself is the greatest victory'.

The first performance probably took place in the Teatro del Cocomero in FLORENCE in autumn 1707 (presumably late October or early November; there is proof of a performance on 9 November 1707). The cast was as follows:

Rodrigo, King of Castile	Stefano Frilli (castrato)
Esilena, his wife	Anna Maria Cecchi Torri (soprano)
Florinda, sister of Giuliano	Aurelia Marcello (soprano)
Giuliano, Count of Cetua	Francesco Guicciardi (tenore)
Evanco, King of Aragon	Caterina Azzolini (soprano)
Fernando, Rodrigo's general	Giuseppe Perini (castrato)

The circumstances leading to the composition and performance of Rodrigo remain obscure to this day. It is unknown when and by whom the opera was commissioned. MAINWARING claimed that at the age of eighteen Handel 'made the Opera of RODRIGO, for which he was presented with 100 sequins, and a service of plate', and also included a detailed amorous anecdote that the young German composer engaged in a liaison with the singer Vittoria TARQUINI, 'who was much admired both as an Actress, and a Singer', and 'bore a principal part in this Opera'. However, Mainwaring's report (published in 1760) is evidently unreliable on two points: Handel was twenty-two years of age in 1707, not eighteen, and Vittoria Tarquini ('La Bombace') is not listed in the printed WORDBOOK cast-list. Another source of information is Voiage historique et politique de Suisse, d'Italie et d'Allemagne (Frankfurt, 1737), probably written by the linen and silk merchant Denis Nolhac from Hanau/Hesse (see Braun and Kirkendale): according to a paragraph entitled 'Histoire du musicien Haindel', Handel was on his way back to Germany via Florence, where he was detained for some time by Cosimo III, Grand Duke of Tuscany, and composed an opera which was much applauded – undoubtedly the opera in question was

Rodrigo, but this account is also unreliable because there is no evidence that Handel planned to return to Germany until his eventual departure from Italy in 1710.

There is no evidence to support the common assumption that Handel received the commission for *Rodrigo* from Ferdinando de' MEDICI: the 1707 wordbook states that the opera was performed 'sotto la protezione del Serenissimo Principe di Toscana' (under the protection of His Highness the Prince of Tuscany), but this was a standardised formula which appeared in all of the librettos of operas performed at the Teatro del Cocomero during the 1707–8 season, and is not an indication of Ferdinando's personal involvement in Handel's opera. Even Mainwaring's claim that Handel had constant free access at court, at least in the days and weeks before the Florentine premiere of *Rodrigo*, cannot be verified. It cannot be proved that Handel ever composed for the Medicis, nor can it be shown that Ferdinando was aware of Handel's opera or admired it. Nor does the printed libretto name the performance venue, librettist or composer.

The text is adapted from Francesco SILVANI's *Il duello d'amore e di vendetta*, first set by Marc'Antonio Ziani (Venice, 1700). Strohm proposed that the version of the text set by Handel was prepared by Antonio SALVI, a librettist held in high esteem by Ferdinando de' Medici. On the other hand, Baselt speculated that the libretto was adapted by an anonymous author of cantatas who collaborated with Handel in ROME (HHB i, p. 75). Both hypotheses have something to be said for them: the commission for the opera presumably came from Florence, and perhaps so did the libretto; whereas it was in Rome that Handel set the text of *Rodrigo* to music – as is attested by the paper-type used and by the involvement of the Roman COPYIST Antonio ANGELINI in the preparation of the score (at least one of the arias is in Angelini's handwriting).

The main extant musical source for *Rodrigo* is Handel's autograph score. However, the autograph version differs markedly from the version presented in Florence in autumn 1707. A direct comparison between the autograph score composed in Rome and the Florentine printed wordbook yields the conclusion that Handel heavily revised the opera before the performance. These changes were not written in his original autograph, but were probably entered directly into the performing materials (now lost): some of the longer recitative passages were heavily cut; two arias were removed and another four were reset. In revising his score, Handel was probably adapting his work to performance conditions that he became better acquainted with after his arrival in Florence, that is, after he had heard the orchestra and singers and formed an opinion about how to best utilise their abilities. Only two of the new arias composed for the premiere have been preserved in contemporary copies.

RAINER HEYINK (Trans. ANGELA BAIER)

Bianconi
W. Braun, 'Händel und der "römische Zauberhut" (1707)', GHB III (1987)
Dean and Knapp, *Operas*
Harris, *Librettos*
R. Heyink, 'Georg Friedrich Händels *Rodrigo*. Anmerkungen zur Entstehungsgeschichte, Quellenlage und Rekonstruktion', HJb 49 (2003)
    (ed.), *Rodrigo*, HHA II/2 (Kassel, 2007)

A. Hicks, 'Handel: Rodrigo', CD booklet note (Virgin Veritas, 5 45897 2, 1999)

U. Kirkendale, 'Orgelspiel im Lateran und andere Erinnerungen an Händel. Ein unbeachteter Bericht in Voiage historique von 1737', *Die Musikforschung* 41 (1988), 1–9

H. J. Marx and S. Voss, 'Eine neue Quelle für Händels Oper Rodrigo', *GHB* X (2004)

Strohm
'Händel in Italia: Nuovi contributi', *Rivista italiana di musicologia* 9 (1974)

Roger, Estienne (b. Caen, 1665 or 1666; d. Amsterdam, 7 July 1722). One of the most important music publishers of the early eighteenth century, he founded his firm in Amsterdam about 1696, and was the first publisher to use serial numbers. From 1716 until 1722 his editions carried the name of his daughter Jeanne, who died shortly after him in the same year; her brother-in-law Michel Charles le Cène took over the business and ran it until his death in 1743. Apart from le Cène's reprint of Handel's first set of harpsichord suites about 1735, the connection of the firm's name with the composer involves three editions which were published with a Jeanne Roger title page, but were prepared piratically by WALSH of London: a volume of KEYBOARD MUSIC, c.1720, and one each of solo and trio sonatas, c.1731–3 (CHAMBER MUSIC).   TERENCE BEST

F. Lesure, *Bibliographie des éditions musicales publiées par Estienne Roger et Michel-Charles Le Cène* (Amsterdam, 1696–1743; Paris, 1969)

Rolland, Romain (b. Clamecy, France, 29 Jan. 1866; d. Vézelay, France, 30 Dec. 1944). French writer, art historian, musicologist and philosopher; 1916 Nobel laureate in literature. He is well known for two monographs on musicians: *La vie de Beethoven* (1903) and *La vie de Handel* (1910). He depicted Handel as a democratic musician, resisting the temptation of acknowledging the composer merely as a church musician, and instead placed greater emphasis on his operas and oratorios. Rolland believed that 'in Handel there dwells the "captivated" Beethoven' (BEETHOVEN).   WALTER KREYSZIG

R. Rolland, *Haendel* (Paris, 1910)

J. Rudolph, 'Romain Rolland und sein Händel-Bild', *HJb* 1 (1955)

Rolli, Paolo Antonio (b. Rome, 13 June 1687; d. Todi, 20 March 1765). Italian librettist. The son of Philippe Rouleau (an architect and merchant from Burgundy) and Marta Arnaldi (from a patrician family of Todi), he studied humanities at the Collegio Romano and under the learned jurist Gianvincenzo Gravina (a founder of the ARCADIAN ACADEMY and the tutor of METASTASIO).) After enrolling in the Arcadian Academy under the nickname of Eulibio Brentiatico, Rolli produced his first publications of poetry in 1708 and 1711, while acquiring a reputation as a singer and an improviser of verses. His first libretto was the serenata *Sacrificio a Venere* for BONONCINI (Rome, 1714). Invited to England by George Dalrymple (the third brother of John, 2nd Earl of Stair), Rolli arrived in London in December 1715 or January 1716. He not only taught Italian and Italian literature to several aristocratic pupils, including Lord BURLINGTON, but also did much to introduce English literature to Italy as a translator and editor.

In 1719 Rolli was appointed as the Italian secretary of the Royal Academy of Music (OPERA COMPANIES, 2) on an annual salary of £200. He prepared most of the librettos performed during the opera company's first three seasons (1720–2), including *MUZIO SCEVOLA* and *FLORIDANTE* (both 1721), and probably supervised their STAGING, but he was dismissed in 1722 following a dispute with the directors (and, apparently, Handel). However, during 1726–7 he revised another three librettos for Handel (*SCIPIONE*, *ALESSANDRO* and *RICCARDO PRIMO*). His publication Di canzonette e di cantate libri due (London, 1727) included three texts that Handel set to music for solo voice and continuo (CANTATAS) during the 1720s: Deh! lasciate e vita e volo (HWV 103), Ho fuggito Amore anch'io (HWV 118) and Son gelsomino (HWV 164^{a-b}). Moreover, Rolli was made a Fellow of the Royal Society in 1729, and published an influential Italian translation of MILTON's Paradise Lost (1729–35).

Correspondence with his friends (notably Giuseppe Riva, SENESINO, Antonio Cocchi and Giovanni Giacomo Zamboni) contains gossip about operatic politics. Rolli satirised Handel's activities during the 'Second Academy' period (1729–34), and in 1733 became the principal poet for the OPERA OF THE NOBILITY. He wrote at least eight librettos for the company until its collapse in 1737, most of them for PORPORA. On 26 September 1736 Rolli was appointed as Italian master to the Princesses CAROLINE and AMELIA, and granted an annual pension ('73 £. 10s') for as long as he stayed in England. After 1737, Rolli prepared a few more operatic texts for London, including the original libretto for Handel's final opera *DEIDAMIA* (1741) and some works for the MIDDLESEX OPERA COMPANY. It has been estimated that he wrote or rewrote librettos for at least thirty-four opera productions in London between 1720 and his eventual departure for Italy on 12 August 1744. After settling in his maternal city Todi, where he had received a patent of nobility in 1735, he had no further involvement in theatrical ventures.

In 1749, on writing to his colleague Carlo Innocenzo FRUGONI, Rolli affected to consider his London librettos as mere 'dramatic skeletons' contrived to meet the audience's poor fluency in Italian, although he boasted that they brought him '200 scudi each' (about £150), plus the sale of wordbooks for his benefit – with the implication that he could produce better work in Italy for less money. However, Frugoni lauded Rolli's 'sturdiness of frank style, strong colours of Poetry, and freedom of veracious and wise thought', as opposed to Metastasio's 'sweet construction of lines both easy and noble'. The bulk of his respectable patrimony was bequeathed to his assistant Samuel Right from Oxfordshire ('Samuele Retti'). Rolli's posthumous collection of epigrams (Marziale in Albion, 1776) uses coded allusions to satirise British society and figures of his time in London.   CARLO VITALI

L. Alcini, 'Paolo Antonio Rolli primo traduttore di Milton: Un poeta, editore, polemista e
      maestro d'italiano nell'Inghilterra del Settecento', Forum Italicum 39/2 (2005), 398–420
Bianconi
C. Caruso (ed.), Paolo Rolli: libretti per musica (Milan, 1993)
Deutsch
G. E. Dorris, Paolo Rolli and the Italian Circle in London, 1715–1744 (The Hague, 1967)
S. Fassini, Il melodramma italiano a Londra nella prima metà del Settecento (Turin, 1914)
Harris, Librettos
L. Lindgren, 'Musicians and Librettists in the Correspondence of Gio. Giacomo Zamboni',
      RMA Research Chronicle 24 (1991)
G. B. Tondini, 'Memorie della vita di Paolo Rolli', prefixed to P. A. Rolli, Marziale in Albion
      (Florence, 1776)

Roman, Johan Helmich (b. Stockholm, 26 Oct. 1694; d. Harasmåla, near Kalmar, 20 Nov. 1758). Swedish violinist, oboist, composer, master of the royal chapel and central figure in Swedish musical culture (epithet 'the Swedish Handel'). He studied for six years in Britain (c.1715–1721) and travelled around Europe (including England) in 1735–7. Inspired by Handel's music, Roman introduced it to his home country: he performed arrangements of the BROCKES PASSION (translated into Swedish, 1731), several ANTHEMS (1733), ACIS AND GALATEA and the WATER MUSIC (both in 1734). Some of his compositions were influenced by Handel's style. ANNETTE LANDGRAF

See also RECEPTION, 6

R. Engländer, 'Händel in der Musik Schwedens', HJb 5 (1959)

Rome. One of the most important Italian musical metropolises, the Holy City was not only the spiritual capital of Roman Catholicism but also the seat of the Papal States' secular government. In addition to the Roman nobility, the papal court attracted diplomatic representatives from European courts, who competed with each other to ensure an adequate public profile in the city. Handel must have been fascinated by the possibility of hearing and performing music in Rome even though the city's public opera houses had been closed by papal decree since 1703. Perhaps he was interested in the city as a centre for church music. The leading composers of sacred music active in Rome were Alessandro SCARLATTI, Ottavio Pittoni and Pietro Paolo Bencini (arguably the single most influential figure in the field of Roman church music in the first half of the eighteenth century). It still remains a desideratum for scholars to focus more closely on possible musical influences on Handel's Italian and Latin CHURCH MUSIC, but, as far as we know, his entire output of sacred music composed in Italy was destined for Rome or for Roman patrons.

The sheer number of musical institutions, potential patrons or occasions for the performance of church music was dazzling. Among the important institutions and patrons were the Cappella Sistina (the papal court chapel), the musical establishments at the three large papal basilicas (i.e. the Cappella Giulia at San Pietro in Vaticano, the Cappella Pia at San Giovanni in Laterano and the Cappella Liberiana at Santa Maria Maggiore), theological seminaries such as the Seminario Romano, confraternities such as the Arciconfraternita della SS Trinità dei Pellegrini or del SS Crocifisso, the Congregazione di S. Filippo Neri (with its two establishments at S. Girolamo della Carità and the Chiesa Nuova), and important aristocratic families who organised concerts in their PALAZZI and family chapels.

The extant information about Handel's stays and compositional activities in Rome is fragmentary, and some of it is of doubtful reliability. However, it is certain that he arrived in Rome during the course of 1706 at the latest. A copy of chamber duets by Agostino STEFFANI and Carlo Luigi Pietro Grua in Handel's handwriting is dated 'Roma 1706'. It is still uncertain to whom Handel applied after his arrival, whom he met and for whom he initially composed. Kirkendale speculates that Handel worked for the Marchese Francesco Maria RUSPOLI – his most important Roman patron – from the turn of the year

1706/7. It was presumably in the early months of 1707 that Handel started composing CANTATAS for Ruspoli. Among the 'virtuosi di canto e suono' employed at Ruspoli's main residence the Palazzo Bonelli were the soprano Margherita DURASTANTI and violinists Pietro CASTRUCCI and Silvestro Rotondi. Music would have been performed on a number of occasions: in addition to the weekly *conversazioni*, which commonly included the performance of a cantata, there were the gatherings of the ARCADIAN ACADEMY in Ruspoli's gardens and the hunting expeditions to his country seats in Vignanello and Cerveteri.

From early 1707 onwards we have more information regarding Handel's movements: the Roman chronicler Valesio mentioned a Saxon, '*eccellente suonatore di cembalo e compositore di musica*', playing the organ in San Giovanni in Laterano (the ecclesiastical seat of the Pope) in January 1707, and from February 1707 at the latest Handel composed works for Cardinal Benedetto PAMPHILIJ. In April he finished the score of *Dixit Dominus* (it is not known who commissioned the work and where it was first performed). A month later Handel corrected the performance materials for his first oratorio Il *TRIONFO DEL TEMPO E DEL DISINGANNO*; although there is no documentation about when and where the oratorio was performed, it was probably commissioned by its librettist Cardinal Pamphilij.

In July 1707 Handel finished two psalm settings (*Laudate pueri* and *Nisi Dominus*), which were probably performed on 15 or 16 July 1707 for the Feast of Our Lady of Mount Carmel in the CARMELITE church of S. Maria di Monte Santo; the costs of the annual festival were defrayed by another Cardinal, Carlo COLONNA. In September 1707 a 'Sassone famoso' performed in the Colonna family's palazzo and in the house of Cardinal Pietro OTTOBONI, vice-chancellor of the Roman Catholic Church and one of the city's most important patrons and lovers of music. Arcangelo CORELLI lived in Ottoboni's official residence, the Palazzo della Cancelleria from 1690, and regularly directed chamber concerts featuring vocal and instrumental music. According to MAINWARING, during one of the gatherings at the Cancelleria, Handel and Domenico SCARLATTI entered into a musical competition on the harpsichord and on the organ. In addition, operas and oratorios were performed in Ottoboni's private theatre, and church music in his titular church S. Lorenzo in Damaso, located within the residential complex of the Cancelleria. Mainwaring claims that Ottoboni commissioned works from Handel, but so far these have not been identified. The Palazzo Colonna also employed a few musicians on a regular basis; additional singers and instrumentalists, who were either passing through Rome or, like Handel, were staying there for longer periods of time, were invited to soirées ('conversazioni'), which took place regularly.

It is not known where Handel spent the winter of 1707/8, but he was certainly in Rome at the end of February 1708, when his name appears in the account books kept by the Ruspoli household. He seems to have lived in Ruspoli's Palazzo Bonelli on the Piazza SS Apostoli, where, after three public rehearsals, his oratorio La *RESURREZIONE* was performed on Easter Sunday and Easter Monday 1708 (8 and 9 April). In mid-June Handel was in NAPLES, but by July he was back in Rome. He is last mentioned in Ruspoli's account books in September 1708, after which his next documented appearance is at

VENICE in December 1709. Handel returned to Rome in 1729 when he was recruiting singers for the Second Academy (OPERA COMPANIES, 3), but there is very little information about this later visit apart from Mainwaring's anecdotal account.   RAINER HEYINK (Trans. ANGELA BAIER)

See also ITALY; PALAZZI

W. Braun, 'Händel und der "römische Zauberhut" (1707)', GHB III (1987)
U. Kirkendale, 'Orgelspiel im Lateran und andere Erinnerungen an Händel. Ein unbeachteter Bericht in Voiage historique von 1737', Die Musikforschung 41 (1988), 1–9
W. and U. Kirkendale, Music and Meaning: Studies in Music History and the Neighbouring Disciplines (Florence, 2007)
J. M. Knapp, 'Handel's Roman Church Music', Händel e gli Scarlatti a Roma, ed. N. Pirrotta and A. Ziino (Florence, 1987)
H. J. Marx, 'Händel in Rom – seine Beziehung zu Benedetto Card. Pamphilj', HJb 29 (1983)
'Händels lateinische Kirchenmusik und ihr gattungsgeschichtlicher Kontext', GHB V (1993)
J. Riepe, 'Kirchenmusik im Rom der Zeit Händels: Institutionen, Auftraggeber, Anlässe. Einige Anmerkungen', HJb 46 (2000)

Rossane (or *Roxana*). A version of Handel's *ALESSANDRO*, probably prepared by Lampugnani and produced for London by the MIDDLESEX OPERA COMPANY in 1743/4. It was revived, with alterations, in 1746/7 and 1747/8. The music included items from other Handel works and insertions not by him. Annotations in Handel's conducting score indicate he loaned it to the company, perhaps in compensation for refusing to write any original works for them. *Rossane* has no connection with the pasticcio *Alessandro nell'Indie* attributed to Lampugnani (1746), with which it has sometimes been confused.   CAROLE TAYLOR

Dean, *Operas*
'"Rossane": Pasticcio or Handel Opera?', GHB VII (1998)
J. M. Knapp, 'Handel/Lampugnani, *Rossane* (1743)', GHB V (1993)

Rossi, Giacomo (fl. 1710–31). Italian librettist. He was commissioned by Aaron HILL to write the Italian verse for Handel's first London opera *RINALDO* (1711). Rossi then produced the librettos of Il *PASTOR FIDO* (1712), of the pasticcio *Ercole* (1712), of *SILLA* (1713) and perhaps further operas. In August 1729 Rossi was engaged as Handel's 'Poet' (Deutsch, p. 235), revising SALVI's *Adelaide* as *LOTARIO* (1729) and possibly further librettos, although specific evidence is lacking. An epigram by Paolo ROLLI, written after 1731, mocks Rossi together with Angelo CORI as 'two friars emigrated from Italy, who exercise their poetic talents where the German harpsichord has banished good sense'.

                                                                        REINHARD STROHM

Dean, *Operas*
S. Fassini, Il melodramma italiano a Londra nella prima metà del settecento (Turin, 1914)
C. Price, 'English Traditions in Handel's Rinaldo', Handel Tercentenary Collection, ed. S. Sadie and A. Hicks (London, 1987)

Rotth, Christian August. See HANDEL, 9

Roubiliac, Louis-François (b. Lyons, bap. 31 Aug. 1702; d. London, 11 Jan. 1762). Sculptor who probably trained under Balthasar Permoser in DRESDEN and Nicolas Coustou in Paris. In about 1732 he moved to England, where his self-confident new style of lively and sometimes theatrical representation of characters attracted attention. He achieved his first great success with the life-size

24. Louis-François Roubiliac's statue of Handel, 1738.

statue of Handel commissioned by Jonathan TYERS for VAUXHALL GARDENS in 1738 (now in the Victoria and Albert Museum; see Figure 24). Associated with this he made a masterly terracotta model (now in the FITZWILLIAM MUSEUM), and in 1739 he sculpted a marble bust which shows the mole on Handel's left cheek (it is now at Windsor). Later he became famous for his dramatic funerary monuments, and his last was Handel's monument in WESTMINSTER ABBEY, unveiled in 1762.   EDWIN WERNER

See also ICONOGRAPHY; MONUMENTS

M. Baker, *Roubiliac and the Eighteenth-Century Monument: Sculpture as Theatre* (New Haven, 1995)

Royal Academy of Music. See OPERA COMPANIES, 2

Royal Fireworks. See GREEN PARK; *MUSIC FOR THE ROYAL FIREWORKS*

Royal Privilege. See COPYRIGHT

Rüdel, Christoph Conrad (fl. Naumburg c.1673). Musician at the Naumburg court of the Dukes of Saxony. On 30 September 1673 he married Handel's cousin Barbara Schweisker at HALLE.   KLAUS-PETER KOCH (Trans. ANGELA BAIER)

See also Appendix 3: Handel's Family Tree

K. Eisenmenger, 'Der junge Händel in Halle. Ein fiktiver Spaziergang im Jahre 1699', *Die Familie Händel und Halle. Zum Stadtjubiläum 1200 Jahre Halle*, ed. Hallische Familienforscher 'Ekkehard' e.V. (Halle, 2006)

Ruspoli, Francesco Maria (Marquis, from 1709 Prince of Cerveteri) (b. 5 March 1672 Rome; d. 12 July 1731 Rome). Italian patron. Heir to his father and his great-uncle, Ruspoli unexpectedly became one of ROME's richest men and from around 1705 tried to consolidate his rise in society by cultivating an adequately grand and glamorous image. Music was an integral part in this self-stylisation. In amicable rivalry with the Cardinals Benedetto PAMPHILIJ and Pietro OTTO-BONI, Ruspoli financed numerous performances of oratorios in his house in the first two decades of the eighteenth century; from 1707 these performances regularly took place on all Sundays during the Lenten season. Between 1707 and 1721 he made his gardens on the Esquiline and Aventine Hills available for the meetings of the ARCADIAN ACADEMY; he was also a member. In 1708 during the War of the SPANISH SUCCESSION, Ruspoli financed a regiment of mercenary soldiers to defend the Papal States against the Emperor's troops. In gratitude Pope Clement XI made Ruspoli the Prince of CERVETERI. After the war had ended and the ban against opera in Rome had been lifted (1709), Ruspoli continued the oratorio performances in his house but also grew more interested in opera. He commissioned operas and later supported the Roman opera houses Alibert and Capranica. In addition, Ruspoli had his own *maestro di cappella* from 1709; until 1716 the post was held by Antonio CALDARA, from 1716 to 1718 by Francesco GASPARINI.

On the basis of the known documents, Ruspoli must be regarded as Handel's most important patron during the composer's Italian years. At no time, however, was Handel one of Ruspoli's official servants (such as Caldara later). It is possible that Handel was in contact with Ruspoli and composed for him from late 1706. In February/March 1707 Handel travelled with Ruspoli to Cerveteri and Civitavecchia, in May/June to Vignanello (where the solo motets *O qualis de coelo sonus*, HWV 239 and *Coelestis dum spirat aura*, HWV 231 and the Marian antiphon *Salve Regina*, HWV 241 were performed) (Italian and Latin CHURCH MUSIC). For Ruspoli's weekly *accademie* Handel regularly composed cantatas and the serenata *OH, COME CHIARE E BELLE*. From February to April 1708, and then probably again from July to September 1708, Handel lived in Ruspoli's residence in Rome, the Palazzo Bonelli (PALAZZI, 7) on Piazza SS Apostoli. This is also where Handel's oratorio La *RESURREZIONE* was first performed on Easter Sunday 1708.   JULIANE RIEPE (Trans. ANGELA BAIER)

S. Franchi, 'Il principe Ruspoli: L'oratorio in Arcadia', *Percorsi dell'oratorio romano: Da 'historia sacra' a melodramma spirituale*, ed. S. Franchi (Rome, 2002)

U. Kirkendale, *Antonio Caldara: Life and Venetian–Roman Oratorios* (Florence, 2007)

W. and U. Kirkendale, *Music and Meaning: Studies in Music History and the Neighbouring Disciplines* (Florence, 2007)

Russell, Mr (fl. 1729; d. London July 1746). COUNTERTENOR, actor and puppeteer. The first David in *SAUL* (16 December 1739), he also performed some music by Handel in a concert at Hickford's Room on 2 April 1740. Lord Wentworth remarked that he 'sings extremely well' (Deutsch, p. 471). As a puppeteer he was a financial failure (Deutsch, pp. 634–5), and died a debtor in the Fleet prison. His range was about a–e″.   NICHOLAS CLAPTON

Saeviat tellus. See Italian and Latin CHURCH MUSIC

St George's Church, Hanover Square. Designed by John James and built 1721–5 under the 1711 New Churches Act to serve the new suburb of Mayfair. James, although an eclectic architect, aspired to 'the greatest plainness' and produced a solid and very mildly baroque variation on the church type developed by Wren and Hawksmoor well suited to early Georgian taste. The interior, which retains its original galleries, has survived quite well apart from rearrangement of the chancel and the darkening effect of stained glass, imported later but good. The six-column temple-front portico was one of the first in London, and indeed this feature, together with a conspicuous chancel and correct orientation, was specified in the 1711 Act. The case of Gerard Smith's original organ survives, augmented by extra towers (1894) and a modern chair organ. Handel, who moved to Brook Street in 1723, was a regular parishioner until his last days.   KERRY DOWNES

St James's Palace. Built by Henry VIII in the 1530s for the Prince of Wales. After the 1698 Whitehall fire St James's became the principal London royal residence, until 1762 when GEORGE III bought Buckingham House for Queen Charlotte and preferred to live there. The south-east quarter burnt down in 1809, and over the next half-century court ceremonies gradually moved to BUCKINGHAM PALACE (as it became). However, embassies are still accredited to the Court of St James's.

Every royal palace has a chapel, and St James's replaced Whitehall as the location for court baptisms and marriages (CHAPEL ROYAL). It is of modest size with a wider ante-chapel beneath the royal gallery. All Handel's Chapel Royal anthems were written for the chapel (ANTHEMS, 1), and the eighteenth-century organ was in a gallery on the north side near the altar. The interior is now largely nineteenth-century but the original wooden coffered ceiling, painted and gilded in 1540 on the latest Renaissance pattern, was restored in 1988.

KERRY DOWNES

See also QUEEN'S CHAPEL

St John Passion. See JOHANNESPASSION

St Lawrence's Church, Whitchurch. Rebuilt for the Duke of CHANDOS by John James, 1714–15. The plain exterior encloses an aisleless nave almost entirely painted in trompe-l'œil architecture. A small organ stands behind the altar in an additional room for musicians and singers, where Handel's *Chandos Anthems* (ANTHEMS, 2) were originally performed, before the chapel at CANNONS was opened in 1720. In the west gallery sat the Duke, framed by Louis Laguerre's adaptation of Raphael's *Transfiguration*: Chandos must have had in mind the chapels of imperial electors he saw in his youth. An annexe, also in *trompe-l'œil*, houses his monument, commissioned from Grinling Gibbons and installed in 1736. The church was restored in the 1980s. KERRY DOWNES

St Maria Magdalenen-Kirche. The church was part of the Franciscan monastery of St Mary Magdalene in HAMBURG, which had been founded by Count Adolf IV of Schauenburg in 1227 in celebration of the military victory against the Danes. The church was enlarged in the early sixteenth century but had to be demolished in 1807 because of its dilapidated state. The loft of the organ, built by Gottfried Fritzsche in 1629/30, was the site of the first meeting between Handel, who had just arrived in Hamburg, and MATTHESON on 9 July 1703.

UTE POETZSCH (Trans. ANGELA BAIER)

H. J. Marx (ed.), J. Mattheson (1681–1764). Lebensbeschreibung des Hamburger Musikers, Schriftstellers und Diplomaten (Hamburg, 1982)
HHB iv

St Marien (Marktkirche). HALLE's four-towered hall church is the baptismal church of Handel and his siblings from his father's second marriage. The houses of his grandfather Valentin (from 1616) and his father Georg (from 1666) both lay within the parish (HANDEL, 9). The church's organist Friedrich Wilhelm ZACHOW was Handel's teacher from 1694 to c.1702, and their lessons probably took place at the positive organ built by Georg Reichel on the eastern loft. The Singakademie, directed by its founder Johann Friedrich Naue, performed the HALLELUJAH CHORUS from *MESSIAH* as part of a service on 19 April 1827, and Robert FRANZ directed a complete performance of the oratorio in the church on 19 March 1857. KLAUS-PETER KOCH (Trans. ANGELA BAIER)

HHB iv
W. Serauky, *Musikgeschichte der Stadt Halle*, vol. 2, part II (Halle, 1942)
B. Weißenborn, *Das Händelhaus in Halle* (Wolfenbüttel/Berlin, 1938)

St Paul's Cathedral. Wren's new cathedral was not officially declared complete until 1710, the year of Handel's first visit to London. However, the annual festival of the Corporation of the SONS OF THE CLERGY had been held in the building since 1697, when the Choir had opened. Recent cleaning has restored its original bright appearance, but the interior is now in many respects very different. There was no seating outside the choir, which was divided from the crossing by the organ screen. New St Paul's quickly became the place for national (rather than royal) services, for example, celebrating the Peace of Utrecht in 1713 (see War of the SPANISH SUCCESSION; TE DEUM, 1). On such occasions the choir floor was seated; all three tiers of stalls were occupied and also the galleries on top, level with the organ loft. Singers and instrumentalists were in galleries flanking the organ. The less privileged stood beyond the screen. Within the choir, acoustics were not a problem even with fewer attenders. Large crowds were rare before the 1851 Great Exhibition, railways, and nave services and the revival of surpliced choirs, which prompted the removal of the screen to make a single space.

According to HAWKINS:

> Handel was very fond of St. Paul's organ . . . a little intreaty was at any time
> sufficient to prevail on him to touch it, but after he had ascended the
> organ-loft, it was with reluctance that he left it; and he has been known, after
> evening service, to play to an audience as great as ever filled the choir. After
> his performance was over it was his practice to adjourn with the principal
> persons of the choir to the Queen's Arms tavern in St. Paul's church-yard,
> where was a great room, with a harpsichord in it; and oftentimes an evening
> was there spent in music and musical conversation. (vol. 2, p. 859)

KERRY DOWNES

Salisbury. Cathedral city in Wiltshire, one of the most flourishing provincial centres of musical activity in eighteenth-century England. Regular subscription concerts were established by the 1730s, with meetings every Thursday evening throughout the year. Local performers, comprising a mixture of professional musicians from the Cathedral and the city with gentlemen amateurs, were supplemented by players from OXFORD and BATH; the concert programmes included both instrumental and vocal items, and took place in the city's successive Assembly Rooms. In 1740 the concert society subscribed to Handel's Op. 6 concertos (ORCHESTRAL WORSK, 2). An annual celebration of St Cecilia's Day in the Cathedral gradually developed into an ambitious music festival during the 1740s, no doubt from the base provided by the concert society. Handel's Dettingen Te Deum (TE DEUM, 5), with orchestral accompaniment, received performances in 1744–6, and in 1748 the Festival blossomed into a two-day event with music at the Cathedral in the mornings and performances of ALEXANDER'S FEAST and ACIS AND GALATEA at the Assembly Room in the evenings. More extensive works followed, including MESSIAH (first performed 1750), SAMSON (1751), JUDAS MACCABAEUS (1752), JOSHUA (1754), HERCULES (1756), SAUL (1758) and JEPHTHA (1760); the Festival also began to employ soloists from London, including Handel's soprano Giulia FRASI in 1758–60. The successful expansion and maintenance of the Festival was the result of the joint leadership of John Stephens (the Cathedral organist from 1746) and James HARRIS, who actively promoted Handel's music and entertained the composer in his Salisbury home in 1739. Harris's personal links with the composer enabled him to borrow Handel's own performing materials for use in Salisbury: it is known that, in addition to the music for the Dettingen Te Deum in 1744, Harris obtained the performing parts for Messiah in the autumn of 1743, though no immediate performance is known.

DONALD BURROWS

Burrows and Dunhill

Sallé, Marie (b. 1709; d. Paris, 27 July 1756). This French choreographer and dancer first performed for Handel when she and her elder brother Francis danced the entr'actes (music unknown) during a benefit of RINALDO at the KING'S THEATRE on 5 June 1717. The children had just completed a highly successful season at John RICH's LINCOLN'S INN FIELDS THEATRE. Writing from Paris in September 1731, Marie expressed a desire to 'join the English Opera' to her patroness, the 2nd Duchess of Richmond. In the autumn of 1734, Sallé collaborated with Handel as a choreographer and leading performer at Rich's COVENT GARDEN Theatre, in an opera season which opened with TERPSI-CORE. Musical sources reveal that all Handel's operas staged this season featured dances (BALLET MUSIC). Their one collaboration which excited critical comment was ALCINA; the Abbé Prévost's well-known account of Sallé being hissed off the stage (allegedly for wearing a travesty costume while dancing as Cupid; see Deutsch, pp. 390-1; HHB iv, 255) is balanced by a neglected letter written by the Duchess of MARLBOROUGH relating a riot at Covent Garden, occasioned by GEORGE II forbidding Sallé an encore in the same opera. Sallé returned to the Paris Opéra in July 1735, retiring from there in 1740. It is thought that she was to have worked with Handel again in 1746, but this plan did not come to fruition. SARAH MCCLEAVE

See also ARIANNA IN CRETA; ARIODANTE; Il PASTOR FIDO; ORESTE

D. Charlton and S. Hibberd, 'My Father was a Poor Parisian Musician: A Memoir (1756) concerning Rameau, Handel's Library, and Sallé', JRMA 128/2 (2003), 161–99
S. McCleave, 'Marie Sallé: A Letter to the Duchess of Richmond', Dance Research 17/1 (Summer 1999), 22–46
'Marie Sallé: A Comparison of English and French Sources for Theatrical Dance', Dance and Music in French Baroque Theatre: Sources and Interpretations, IAMS Study Text 3 (London, 1998), 13–32

Salvai, Maria Maddalena (b. Florence; fl. 1716-33). Italian soprano (compass: e'–bb''). Between 1716 and 1719 she sang in cities across Germany, among others DRESDEN. In 1720 she was recommended by SENESINO for her 'most beautiful voice' and became a cast member of the Royal Academy of Music (OPERA COMPANIES, 2) for two seasons. She appeared as Polissena in RADAMISTO (HWV 12[b]), Fidalma in MUZIO SCEVOLA and Rossane in FLORIDANTE. She also sang in several pasticcios and operas by BONONCINI. After leaving London in 1722 she continued to sing in Italy until 1731, performing at Milan, VENICE, NAPLES and her native Florence; she was engaged at Vienna for the 1732-3 season. ARTIE HEINRICH

Dean, Operas

Salve Regina. See Italian and Latin CHURCH MUSIC

Salvi, Antonio (b. Lucignano nr. Arezzo, 17 Jan. 1664; d. Florence, 21 May 1724). Italian librettist. He served as a physician at the Medici court of FLORENCE under Grand-Duke Cosimo III (d. 1723) and his son Prince Ferdinando de' MEDICI (d. 1713). Salvi wrote some successful intermezzi comici and twenty-one drammi per musica, premiered between 1694 and 1724 in Florence, at the Medici theatre of Pratolino, and elsewhere. Seven drammi were reset by Handel in London: ARMINIO, 1703 → 1737; Publio Cornelio Scipione, 1704 → SCIPIONE, 1726 (revised by Paolo ROLLI); Dionisio re di Portogallo, 1707 → SOSARME, 1732; Ginevra, principessa di Scozia, 1708 → ARIODANTE, 1734; BERENICE, 1709 → 1737; RODELINDA, 1710 →1725; Adelaide, 1722 → LOTARIO, 1729.

Salvi may also have been the reviser of Handel's Florentine RODRIGO in 1707. Handel set Salvi's librettos more often than anybody else's, and more texts by him than any other composer did. He probably owned some of Salvi's librettos and saw productions of them in Florence and Pratolino, c.1707–9, where he may have met the poet. It is unclear why he chose Agostino PIOVENE'S *TAMERLANO* (1724) instead of Salvi's libretto on the same subject.

Salvi's most popular works were *Ginevra/ARIODANTE, Amore e maestà/Arsace* (1715) and *Ipermestra* (1724). A highly respected *poeta drammatico*, he promoted Aristotelian principles of DRAMATURGY, modelling many of his *drammi* after French spoken tragedies (by Jean RACINE, Pierre and Thomas CORNEILLE, Jean Galbert de CAMPISTRON), and using Molière in his *intermezzi comici*. Salvi was a more theatrical and liberal libretto reformer than Apostolo ZENO. In addition to standard heroic (*Gran Tamerlano, Scipione*) and military plots (*Arminio, Dionisio, Scanderbeg, Adelaide*), he draws female characters and love–jealousy relationships (*Rodelinda, Amore e maestà, Arminio*) with considerable psychological insight. A recurring motif is hostage-taking, including that of young children in order to blackmail their mothers. Salvi's letters reveal his concern for the individuality of dramatic characters and performers.   REINHARD STROHM

M. Bucciarelli, *Italian Opera and European Theatre, 1680–1720* (Turnhout, 2000)

F. Giuntini, *I drammi per musica di Antonio Salvi: Aspetti della 'riforma' del libretto nel primo Settecento* (Bologna, 1994)

R. Strohm, *Dramma per musica: Italian Opera Seria of the Eighteenth Century* (New Haven, 1997)

Salzdahlum (Salzthal).Village located 5 kilometres north-east of WOLFENBÜTTEL. Between 1694 and 1813 it was the site of a pleasure palace built by the Dukes of Brunswick-Wolfenbüttel (modelled after Versailles, however, due to lack of funds mainly built of coloured wood) which had its own small stage and after 1715 a new theatre. Ballets, plays and operas were performed under the direction of Hofkapellmeister Georg Caspar SCHÜRMANN, as well as spoken plays. The musical works were composed by Schürmann himself (for example in 1700), Reinhard KEISER (for example in 1695), Carl Heinrich GRAUN (1733), Carlo Francesco POLLAROLO (1699), probably Antonio CALDARA (1711), Agostino STEFFANI (1718) and Francesco GASPARINI (1720). On 12 September 1731 Handel's *PARTENOPE* was performed in the palace's theatre honouring the birthday of the Dowager Duchess Elisabeth Sophie Marie.

KLAUS-PETER KOCH (Trans. ANGELA BAIER)

R. Brockpähler, *Handbuch zur Geschichte der Barockoper in Deutschland* (Emsdetten, 1964)

G. F. Schmidt, *Neue Beiträge zur Geschichte der Musik und des Theaters am Herzoglichen Hofe zu Braunschweig-Wolfenbüttel*, part 1 (Munich, 1929)

Sammartini, Giuseppe (b. Milan, 6 Jan. 1695; d. London, ?17–23 Nov. 1750). Italian oboist and composer, and elder brother of Giovanni Battista Sammartini (also an oboist and composer). He probably studied the oboe with his French father Alexis Saint-Martin, and by 1720 he was employed in the opera orchestra at Milan. He was in London by 21 May 1729, when he performed several of his compositions in a concert at Hickford's Room. He remained in England for the rest of his life, played at CAMBRIDGE when Maurice GREENE was awarded his doctorate in 1730, and joined the KING'S THEATRE opera orchestra. He probably played for the OPERA OF THE NOBILITY in 1734–6, but joined Handel's orchestra at COVENT GARDEN for the 1736–7 season, and performed impressive oboe obbligato parts in *ARMINIO, GIUSTINO* and *BERENICE*. In 1741 Sammartini played an oboe concerto, probably one of his own, in a charity performance of *PARNASSO IN FESTA*. Admired by BURNEY and HAWKINS, and reputed to be the finest oboist in Europe, he was music master to AUGUSTA, Princess of Wales, from 1736 until his death.   DAVID VICKERS

See also INSTRUMENTATION, 13

Samson, HWV 57. English oratorio. The libretto is adapted from John MILTON's closet drama *Samson Agonistes* (published 1671), which, although never intended for the stage, was created after the manner of classical Greek tragedy. Based on Judges 16, Milton's drama concentrates the entire action into the last day in Samson's life: the Israelite hero, once endowed with massive physical strength, has been betrayed by his wife Dalila and fallen into the hands of the enemy Philistines, who have blinded him and are oppressing his people. Milton invented episodes in which Samson's father Manoa, the seemingly penitent Dalila and the bullying Philistine giant Harapha respectively try to buy the hero out of captivity, care for him or provoke him. From his initial self-pity and bitterness, Samson acquires maturity and becomes able to carry out the prophesied heroic deed to liberate his people: when asked to demonstrate his Herculean powers to the assembled goading Philistines, he pulls the temple of Dagon down upon his enemies, although this also costs him his own life.

Handel was probably inspired to set *Samson* during a reading of Milton's closet drama at the Earl of SHAFTESBURY's in 1739; impressed by the poetry he improvised musical interludes on the harpsichord that were 'perfectly adapted to the sublimity of the poem' (Burrows and Dunhill, 80). The libretto was adapted by Newburgh HAMILTON, who divided Milton's text into three acts, condensing it from 1758 lines to 546 (459 in recitative), and by metrically regularising Milton's free iambic metres into blank verse (for recitatives) and rhymed iambic stanzas (for some arias and choruses). The character of Micah was created using choric texts. The texts for the remaining arias and choruses were adapted from Milton's psalm paraphrases and at least fifteen different shorter poems, such as the youthful works *On the Morning of Christ's Nativity* (1629), the *Epitaph on the Marchioness of Winchester* (1631) and *On Time* (c.1632).

Handel commenced composing *Samson* in late summer 1741, soon after he had completed the first draft score of *MESSIAH*. He completed Act I on 29 September, Act II on 11 October, and Act III on 29 October 1741, but the oratorio was not yet fully finished: after he had set the arias and choruses, but only copied out the recitative texts, his work on the score was interrupted by his trip to DUBLIN. After returning from Ireland, he resumed work on the oratorio, and extensively revised it:

1. The part of Micah was extended for the alto Susannah Maria CIBBER, particularly by resetting previously composed choral passages for solo voice and restructuring the aria and chorus 'Return o God of hosts'.
2. He shortened the recitatives by 63 lines.
3. He set the remaining recitatives to music.
4. He added some new arias for anonymous Philistine and Israelite characters for extra singers who had been engaged.
5. The elegy for Samson ('Glorious hero') had originally concluded the oratorio, but Handel added the celebratory aria 'Let the bright seraphims' and

its choral finale 'Let their Celestial chorus all unite' (based on Milton's poem *At a Solemn Musick*, c.1632).

Handel completed *Samson* on 12 October 1742. His decision to set a Miltonic text fulfilled the expectations of some of his admirers that had been raised by his earlier treatment of great English poetry by John DRYDEN and Milton. His ambitious Miltonic oratorio certainly sparked the enthusiasm of the Earl of Shaftesbury, who wrote to James HARRIS on 23 December 1742 that 'Mr Handel has plaid me over his Samson Agonistes. I think I may dare venture to affirm at once hearing only, that it surpasses any of his greatest former performances . . . The whole is inexpressibly great and pathetic' (Burrows and Dunhill, p. 152).

Messiah and *Samson*, both initially drafted within the short space of less than ten weeks, became Handel's most frequently performed oratorios during the second half of the eighteenth century. However, the original constellation of SATB soloists, and his careful notation of note values, rhythms and appoggiaturas in recitatives and changes to some accompaniments (*staccato–sostenuto*) are highly unusual, and suggest that perhaps during the initial COMPOSITIONAL PROCESS he was not yet certain about the practical circumstances under which *Samson* would be first performed. The premiere took place on 18 February 1743 at COVENT GARDEN with the following cast:

Samson	John BEARD (tenor)
Manoa, Father to Samson	William SAVAGE (bass)
Micah, Friend to Samson	Susannah Cibber (alto)
Dalila, Wife of Samson	Kitty CLIVE (soprano)
Harapha, a Philistine Giant	Henry REINHOLD (bass)
Israelite/Philistine Woman	Miss Edwards (soprano)
Israelite/Philistine Woman	Signora AVOGLIO (soprano)
Israelite/Philistine Man	Thomas LOWE (tenor)
An Israelite Officer [or messenger]	Thomas Lowe

The chorus took the roles of Israelites, Philistine Women/Dalila's Virgins and the Priests of Dagon. It was the first in a series of six subscription performances, which were successful enough to persuade Handel to add six more concerts to the season (including two more of *Samson* and the first London performances of *Messiah*). For the last performances of *Samson* during the 1743 season some of his singers were engaged to sing at other London theatres, so it was necessary to use a diminished cast and make heavy cuts to the score.

Handel mostly retained the shortened version of the recitatives for all future performances under his direction, which included revivals in 1744, 1745, 1749, 1750, annually between 1752 and 1755 and in 1759. No extant wordbooks for the 1744 and 1745 revivals have been identified, so it is difficult to determine which version of the score was performed: in 1745 Handel substituted the Israelite Woman's aria 'It is not virtue' with 'Fly from the cleaving mischief' (also on a text based on Milton), which was later included with a different text in the *OCCASIONAL ORATORIO*. Conversely, the aria 'How great and many perils' from the *Occasional Oratorio* was inserted into a performance of *Samson* in 1754.

Samson shows Handel at the height of his powers as an oratorio composer. Hamilton's preface to the wordbook drew a comparison between Milton's archaic use of Greek-style chorus 'after the manner of the Ancients' and Handel's introduction of the oratorio genre, 'a musical Drama, whose Subject must be Scriptural, and in which the Solemnity of Church-Musick is agreeably united with the most pleasing Airs of the Stage'. Most of the roles were taken by native English performers, some of whom were actors by profession rather than singers (Clive and Cibber). This might have influenced Handel to experiment with alternatives to the convention of using da capo arias as showcases for vocal virtuosity, and he created remarkable movements such as Micah's aria 'Return, O God of hosts', in which the aria's choral second part unexpectedly incorporates the soloist's da capo. Another unusual musical device is the confrontational double chorus 'Fix'd in his everlasting seat' in which the worshippers of Jehovah and Dagon (both chorus and all of the named characters) argue for theological supremacy at the end of Act II. Handel took particularly intriguing BORROWINGS from works by other composers: he modelled the Israelites' solemn chorus 'Hear, Jacob's God' on the final part of CARISSIMI's Roman oratorio *Jepthe*, and used part of the overture from PORTA's *Il Numitore* (the first Royal Academy opera; OPERA COMPANIES, 2) to conclude Samson's heroic accompanied recitative 'Then shall I make Jehovah's glory known'.

The casting of a tenor in the title role was unprecedented in Handel's London theatre works (although it subsequently became common during the 1740s), and the character's arias create a clear impression that he is no longer the muscleman who once slew thousands of Philistines with the jawbone of an ass. Samson is a compelling portrait of a character in emotional and spiritual turmoil. He is confronted with a distasteful image of his former self in the giant Harapha, a bass cast in a similar mould to Polyphemus (*ACIS AND GALATEA*), and whose aria 'Honour and arms', puffed up by orchestral unison, is answered by Samson in the contrapuntal 'My strength is from the living God'. When Samson has regained his former strength, he demonstrates it in the surprisingly serene and calm aria 'Thus when the sun'; the blind man's radiant description of a sunrise banishing the shadows of darkness is one of the many instances of imagery alluding to a conflict between darkness and light that pervade the work, spanning from his dejected 'Total eclipse' to the brilliant concluding choral line celebrating an 'endless blaze of light'.

HANS DIETER CLAUSEN (Trans. ANGELA BAIER)

D. Burrows, 'Handel's Use of Soloists in *Samson*: Characterisation versus Practical Necessity', *HJb* 52 (2006)

   (ed.), *Samson* (Novello Handel Edition) (London, 2005)

   'The Word-Books for Handel's *Samson*', *MT* 146/1890 (Spring 2005), 7–15

H. D. Clausen, 'Lässt sich die Urfassung von Händels Oratorium *Samson* rekonstruieren?', *HJb* 52 (2006)

Dean, *Oratorios*

Smith, *Oratorios*

San Giovanni Grisostomo, Teatro. Inaugurated in Carnival 1678 with Carlo Pallavicino's *Il Vespasiano*, it counted as the largest and most fashionable among VENICE's opera houses. The GRIMANI brothers Vincenzo (1652/3–1710) and Giovanni Carlo (1648–1714) had it built in four months over an area in the parish of San Giovanni Grisostomo by Rialto, formerly hosting the Polo family houses. It underwent radical remakes in 1834 and is now the Teatro Malibran, a subsidiary venue of La Fenice.

Its slightly horse-shoed hall was lavishly decorated with gilded boxwood reliefs; the proscenium was about 26 metres deep and 20 metres wide, height may be estimated at 16 metres. According to a French visitor, it could accommodate machinery bearing up to 150 persons. While the original project, tentatively attributed to Tomaso Bezzi or Gasparo Mauro, provided for five tiers of thirty-one boxes each, four more on each side of the stage were soon added to meet growing demand. The total seating, including the parterre, may thus have run in excess of 1,400.

During the first decade of the eighteenth century, the Venetian composers Carlo Francesco Pollarolo, LOTTI and CALDARA monopolised the house's repertoire, with the sole exceptions of Alessandro SCARLATTI (two operas in Carnival 1707) and Handel's *AGRIPPINA*. Steep admission prices witness to the high social level of the audience, as do the librettos' erudite plots, mostly based on ancient or early-medieval history. The physical layout of the hall at that time is documented by an engraving in Vincenzo Coronelli's *I palazzi di Venezia* (Venice, 1709).

CARLO VITALI

San Giovanni in Laterano, Basilica di. See ROME

San Sebastiano, Chiesa di. See Francesco Maria RUSPOLI

Sandoni, Pietro Giuseppe. See CUZZONI

Sanseverino, Aurora (b. Saponara, now Grumento Nova by Potenza, 28 April 1667 or 1669; d. Piedimonte d'Alife, now Piedimonte Matese by Caserta, 2 July 1726). Daughter to Carlo Maria, 10th Prince of Bisignano, and Maria Fardella Gaetani Princess of Paceco. Her second marriage was to Nicola Gaetani dell'Aquila d'Aragona, 9th Duke of Laurenzana.

Her avid patronage and personal practice of music as contralto singer is just one facet of an all-round cultural commitment to literature, high learning and the visual arts that made her a central figure in baroque Italy. Alone or in collaboration with her secretary Nicola GIUVO, she provided a host of composers with texts for cantatas, serenatas and operas, produced lavish performances at her residences in NAPLES and Piedimonte, sponsored virtuosi of both sexes, and received dedications from opera houses nationwide. Textual clues to identification of works originated within her circle are, besides her name Aurora and Arcadian nickname Lucinda, references to the rivers Volturno and Torano (which 'bathe' her husband's possessions), and to the eagle (*aquila*) in the Gaetani noble title and coat of arms. This is notably the case for Handel's continuo cantata *Nel dolce tempo* (HWV 135[a]) and for *ACI, GALATEA E POLIFEMO*.

CARLO VITALI

A. Furnari and C. Vitali, 'Händels Italienreise. Neue Dokumente, Hypothesen und Interpretationen', *GHB* IV (1991)

A. Magaudda and D. Costantini, 'Aurora Sanseverino (1669-1726) e la sua attività di committente musicale nel Regno di Napoli', *Giacomo Francesco Milano ed il ruolo dell'aristocrazia nel patrocinio delle attività musicali nel secolo XVIII*, ed. G. Pitarresi (Reggio Calabria, 2001)

Sans y penser. See SONGS

Santini, Fortunato (b. Rome, 5 Jan. 1778; d. Rome, 14 Sept. 1861). Italian composer and collector of music manuscripts. Raised in an orphanage, he studied music at the Collegio Salviati in ROME, where he also enrolled in classes in philosophy and theology. In 1801 he was ordained into the priesthood. At about this time Santini began assembling a music collection, focusing principally on sacred repertoire. His interest later extended to baroque music, including the works of Handel, and he engaged actively in the purchasing and trading of old music manuscripts (SOURCES AND COLLECTIIONS, 13).   WALTER KREYSZIG

H. J. Marx, 'The Santini Collection', *Handel Collections and their History*, ed. T. Best (Cambridge, 1993)

K. Watanabe, 'Die Kopisten der Handschriften von den Werken Georg Friedrich Händels in der Santini-Bibliothek, Münster', *Ongaku Gaku: Journal of the Japanese Musicological Society* 16 (1970), 225–62

Saul, HWV 53. English oratorio, composed between 23 July and 27 September 1738 and first performed on 16 January 1739, when it opened a season at the KING'S THEATRE which also included *ISRAEL IN EGYPT*, *ALEXANDER'S FEAST*, Il *TRIONFO DEL TEMPO E DELLA VERITÀ* and *GIOVE IN ARGO*. It had six performances, with the following cast:

Saul	Gustavus WALTZ (bass)
David	Mr RUSSELL (countertenor)
Jonathan	John BEARD (tenor)
Michal	FRANCESINA (soprano)
Merab	Cecilia YOUNG (soprano)
High Priest	Kelly (tenor)
Doeg	Butler (bass)
Ghost of Samuel	Hussey (bass)
Amalekite	Stoppelaer (tenor)
Witch	?Marchesini (alto/tenor)

The role of David seems initially to have been intended for a soprano or mezzo. The libretto, by Charles JENNENS, may be the one he sent to Handel in 1735 (Deutsch, p. 394). It is based on the BIBLE (1 Samuel 15–20, 26, 27, 31, and 2 Samuel 1–2) and, as the WORDBOOK (see Figure 25) states, Abraham Cowley's unfinished epic *Davideis* (1656).

In Act I the Israelites, led by Saul, their first king, are threatened by the Philistines. The young shepherd David, inspired by God, kills Goliath, the giant Philistine champion. Saul's younger daughter, Michal, falls in love with David. Saul's son and heir, Jonathan, attracted by David's virtue, declares eternal friendship with him. Saul's elder daughter, Merab, is indignant when Saul promises her to David. The women of Jerusalem celebrate Saul and David, but their song, attributing greater achievements to David, triggers murderous jealousy in Saul. At Michal's suggestion David tries to soothe the King with music, as he has done in the past. But Saul, still enraged, hurls his javelin at David, then commands that he be hunted down. Jonathan, torn between duty to his father and loyalty to his friend, determines to defend 'the God-like David'. The nation prays for David's safety.

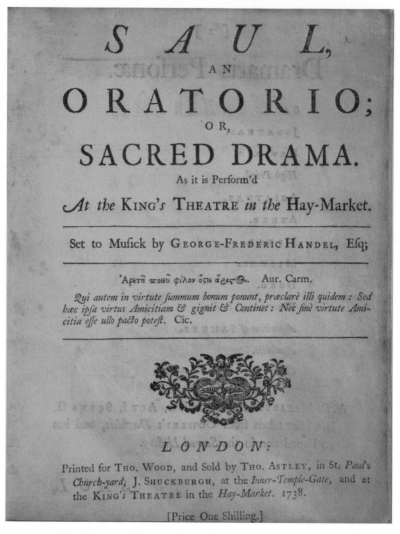

S A U L,

AN

O R A T O R I O;

OR,

SACRED DRAMA.

As it is Perform'd

At the KING's THEATRE *in the* Hay-Market.

Set to Mufick by GEORGE-FREDERIC HANDEL, Efq;

'Ἀρετὴ ποιεῖ φίλον ὅτις ἄρις-Θ.. Aur. Carm.

Qui autem in virtute fummum bonum ponunt, præclarè illi quidem : Sed hæc ipfa virtus Amicitiam & gignit & Continet : Nec fine virtute Amicitia effe ullo paƈƭo poteft. Cic.

L O N D O N:

Printed for THO. WOOD, and Sold by THO. ASTLEY, in St. *Paul's Church-yard,* J. SHUCKBURGH, at the *Inner-Temple-Gate,* and at the KING's THEATRE in the *Hay-Market.* 1738.

[Price One Shilling.]

25. The title page of the wordbook for Saul, an Oratorio, published by T. Wood, 1738.

Act II opens with a chorus decrying the hellish spirit of Envy poisoning Saul. Jonathan assures David of his eternal affection. Saul has withdrawn his offer of Merab to David, who is unconcerned, having been attracted by Michal. Jonathan begs Saul to reflect on David's loyalty. Saul swears to renounce his enmity and reinstates David, giving him Michal in marriage. Alone, Saul reveals that he is sending David to war so that the Philistines will destroy him. Unaware, David and Michal declare their love and happiness. A chorus celebrates David's all-conquering virtue. David returns successful to Michal and relates Saul's response to his victory: another attempt to kill him. Saul's henchmen are at the door, and David escapes through the window. Michal holds off and then defies

Saul's agents. Another of Saul's children turns against him: Merab acknowledges David's virtue and prays for him. At the Feast of the New Moon Saul's murderous plans are frustrated by David's absence. Incensed, Saul turns on Jonathan, who selflessly pleads for David. Saul hurls his javelin at his own son. Jonathan escapes and the surrounding courtiers express horror at their monarch's lawless outrage.

In Act III Saul, now grimly clear-sighted, comes alone in disguise to Endor, to consult the witch there. The witch is afraid to break the King's law against sorcery but Saul swears by Jehovah that she will be unharmed, and asks her to summon the ghost of his mentor Samuel. Samuel rises from the dead and explains to Saul why God has forsaken him: Saul disobeyed God's commands when destroying the enemy Amalekites. The Philistines will destroy Saul and his family and the kingdom will pass to David. In the aftermath of the following battle, David receives news of Philistine victory and the deaths of Saul and Jonathan from the man who gave Saul the *coup de grâce*. David asks his identity: he is an Amalekite. David has him executed for causing the death of the Lord's anointed. In the great elegy which follows, David and the Israelites remember Saul and Jonathan in their heroic prime, and David celebrates Jonathan's love for him. The outpouring of grief is succeeded by acclamation of David as the new king: blessed by God, he will overcome all enemies and unify the nation through his exemplary virtue.

Saul is one of Handel's masterpieces. He expended great effort on it, as the autograph attests: it is one of his most heavily corrected, his pen in places going through the paper. He jettisoned six numbers before the first performance; dropping the aria setting of Saul's recitative at the Feast of the New Moon reduced his part by 60 per cent and ensured his characterisation as a conflicted and frightening presence. Handel invested financial capital too, spending £500 on a new organ, hiring players for three trombones (extremely rare) and commissioning a carillon (keyed glockenspiel, even rarer) which he used for only one number. The HARRIS papers (Burrows and Dunhill, pp. 65–6) record his pride in the INSTRUMENTATION. *Saul* has the most varied orchestral forces of any of his works, and larger forces than any English music theatre work or Italian opera previously performed in England. It is also one of his few dramatic works with a bass title role and the first English oratorio with a male lead; it contains more varied sequences of musical forms than any of his previous works; it is longer, and has more extended scenes, than any previous English music theatre work; and it encompasses a Shakespearian range of emotions and relationships. In his aim, brilliantly accomplished, of bringing ancient Israel's history and people to life for his audience, Handel was probably encouraged by Jennens, for whom the story reflected personal anguish. The replacement of Saul's dynasty by David's was a traditional analogy for modern dynastic changes, and for Jennens expressed his dilemma as a devoted Protestant loyal to the ousted, rightful, but Catholic, Stuart rulers (JACOBITES; NON-JURORS). The autograph, and Jennens's letter about their collaboration (Burrows, pp. 202–3), show Handel accepting some of Jennens's proposed amendments to the score. Handel revived the oratorio in 1740, 1741, 1742 (DUBLIN), 1744, 1745, 1750, and 1754.   RUTH SMITH

Pompeo (Rome, 1683), *Dafni* (Naples, 1700), *Marco Attilio Regolo* (Rome, 1719) and *Griselda* (Rome, 1721). On 17 January 1743 Charles JENNENS wrote to his friend Edward Holdsworth that he had lent some music manuscripts to Handel, whom he had 'formerly' caught 'stealing' from Scarlatti (HHB iv, p. 356).

DAGMAR GLÜXAM (Trans. ANGELA BAIER)

K. Böhmer, '"Tragedia Sacra": Alessandro Scarlattis Oratorien im Palazzo della Cancelleria und ihr Einfluss auf Händel', HJb 55 (2009)

W. Dean, 'Handel and Alessandro Scarlatti', *Händel e gli Scarlatti a Roma: Atti del convegno internazionale di studi* (Florence, 1987)
Operas

E. T. Harris, 'The Italian in Handel', JAMS 33 (1980), 468–500

W and U. Kirkendale, *Music and Meaning: Studies in Music History and the Neighbouring Disciplines* (Florence, 2007)

B. Poensgen, 'Zur Biographie Alessandro Scarlattis während der italienischen Jahre Georg Friedrich Händels. Mögliche Begegnungen, Einflussnahmen und Fehlattributionen', HJb 46 (2000)

J. H. Roberts (ed.), *Handel Sources: Materials for the Study of Handel's Borrowing*, vols. 6–7 (New York, 1986)

J. Steele, 'Dixit Dominus: Alessandro Scarlatti and Handel', *Studies in Music* 7 (1973), 19–27
Strohm
'Händel und Italien – ein intellektuelles Abenteuer', GHB V (1993)
'Händel in Italia: Nuovi contributi', *Rivista italiana di musicologica* 9 (1974), 152–74

Scarlatti, Domenico (b. Naples, 26 Oct. 1685; d. Madrid, 23 July 1757). Italian composer. He was the sixth son of Alessandro Scarlatti. At the age of fifteen he was appointed organist and composer of the royal chapel in NAPLES. He had sporadic work experience in FLORENCE and VENICE, was admired by Prince Ferdinando de' MEDICI, and perfected his skills with Francesco GASPARINI. He had more stable positions in ROME, as *maestro di cappella* of Queen Maria Casimira of Poland (1709–14) and of the Cappella Giulia in St Peter's (1714–19). MAINWARING records that Cardinal OTTOBONI wished him to have a trial of skill with Handel: some gave the preference to Scarlatti on the harpsichord, but even he recognised his opponent's superiority on the organ, and because of his admiration for Handel he followed him all over Italy. With his own instrumental virtuosity Scarlatti in his turn excited the young Thomas Roseingrave, who until 1713 persisted in following him from Venice to Rome and to Naples, later becoming the inspiration behind the English cult of the composer, and organist of ST GEORGE'S, Hanover Square (Handel's London parish).

In 1719 Scarlatti resigned his post in Rome to go to London, but there is no evidence that he ever went there. Instead, at the end of that year, he was introduced to the Lisbon court as a singer, and was later appointed director of the royal chapel by King John V. As music master of the Princess Maria Barbara, he went with her to Madrid after her marriage to Ferdinand IV: so at the Spanish court he worked with FARINELLI, and brought his own composition of keyboard music to new heights.

According to Mainwaring, 'Handel used often to speak of this person [i.e. Scarlatti] with great satisfaction; and indeed there was reason for it; for besides his great talents as an artist, he had the sweetest temper, and the genteelest behaviour. On the other hand, it was mentioned but lately . . . that Scarlatti, as oft as he was admired for his great execution, would mention Handel, and cross himself in token of veneration.' Handel borrowed ideas for his Concerti grossi,

Op. 6 (ORCHESTRAL WORKS, 2) from the first printed edition of Scarlatti's sonatas, *Essercizi per gravicembalo* (sonatas K1–30, London, 1738–9).

FRANCESCO LORA (Trans. TERENCE BEST)

M. Boyd, *Domenico Scarlatti – Master of Music* (London, 1986)
Burney
A. Silbiger, 'Scarlatti Borrowing in Handel's Grand Concertos', MT 125/1692 (1984), 93–5

Schaum, Johann Otto Heinrich (b. Rathenow, 12 Sept. 1763; d. Quedlinburg, 14 April 1834). Editor and translator. One of Prussia's foremost Handel experts, Schaum called for a German edition of the composer's works in 1805. He edited vocal scores of the accompagnato 'Alma del gran Pompeo' from GIULIO CESARE, the aria 'Affanni del pensier' from OTTONE and SEMELE in 1820, and between 1821 and 1825 published editions of the ANTHEMS HWV 253, 251^b, 255, 256^a, 248, 252, 254 and 249^b. In 1830 Schaum published a German version of ACIS AND GALATEA, and from 1830 he arranged the oratorios SOLOMON, ISRAEL IN EGYPT, THEODORA and BELSHAZZAR for the SING-AKADEMIE zu Berlin.

WERNER RACKWITZ (Trans. ANGELA BAIER)

B. Baselt, 'Early German Handel Editions during the Classical Period', *Handel Collections and their History*, ed. T. Best (Oxford, 1993)
S. Flesch, 'Die Händel-Ausgabe von J. O. H. Schaum', HJb 39 (1993)
W. Rackwitz, 'Neues über J. O. H. Schaum', HJb 46 (2000)

Scheidt, Samuel (b. Halle, 4 Nov. 1587; d. Halle, 14 March 1654). Kapellmeister, composer and organist. He is commonly regarded as the most important Hallensian composer before Handel. There is no evidence that Scheidt's music was performed in HALLE after his death, but perhaps his works acquired by the ST MARIENKIRCHE before 1649 were still extant in the church's archives when Handel started training there under Friedrich Wilhelm ZACHOW (a cupboard sold by Scheidt to the church was still there in 1757). Handel's book of manuscript music dated 1698 does not list any music by Scheidt, nor do Scheidt's text incipits correspond with any of Handel's early church music. Moreoever, there are no works by Scheidt included in the music collection sold by Johann Philipp KRIEGER to the Marienkirche (1680), or in the inventory of the estate of the deceased Halle organist Adam Meißner (1718).

KLAUS-PETER KOCH (Trans. ANGELA BAIER)

K.-P. Koch, 'Samuel Scheidt – ein Vorbild für Händel?', *Das mitteldeutsche Musikleben vor Händel/ Christoph Willibald Gluck (1714–1787)*, ed. B. Baselt and W. Siegmund-Schultze (Halle, 1988)
'Reflexion des mitteldeutschen Musiklebens in den schriftlichen Äußerungen von Samuel Scheidt', HJb 51 (2005)

Schiavonetti, Elisabetta. See PILOTTI-SCHIAVONETTI

Schmidt, Johann Christoph. See John Christopher SMITH SENIOR

Schoelcher, Victor (b. Paris, 21 July 1804; d. Houilles, near Paris, 25 Dec. 1893). French writer, politician, collector and music scholar. A significant figure in Handel scholarship of the nineteenth century, he is perhaps better known as a politician and social reformer: in 1848, he wrote, and succeeded in passing, the law that abolished slavery in the French colonies. Schoelcher opposed the *coup d'état* of December 1851 and was exiled. From 1851 to 1870 he lived in England, where he

573

developed a passion for the music of Handel, which occupied him for the rest of his remarkable life.

In 1856 Schoelcher bought Handel's performing (conducting) scores from Thomas KERSLAKE; he eventually sold the majority of them in 1868 to the city of HAMBURG, thus assuring their preservation today in the Staats- und Universitätsbibliothek (SOURCES AND COLLECTIONS, 2). He retained a small part of the collection bought from Kerslake: these volumes, which include autographs of Handel's assistant John Christopher SMITH JUNIOR, are now held by the Bibliothèque nationale and the British Library.

In 1857 Schoelcher published The Life of Handel (London: Trübner), a carefully researched and solidly documented landmark in Handel studies that brought many new sources to light and was long considered the definitive biography in English. Schoelcher's extraordinary Catalogue raisonné of Handel's works (Bibliothèque nationale, Rés. VS 1078³), conceived as a companion to the biography, was never published.

Schoelcher assembled a vast collection of Handelian literature and music, which he donated to the Paris Conservatoire in 1872–3 (his library was transferred in 1964 to the Bibliothèque nationale). The Fonds Schoelcher, as it is called, is an important Handel collection which numbers more than 4,000 items. RICHARD G. KING

R. G. King, 'A Guide to the Uninventoried Parts of the Fonds Schoelcher', Handel Institute Newsletter, vol. 8 (Spring 1997), 7–10
'The Fonds Schoelcher: History and Contents', Notes 53 (1997), 697–721
'New Light on Handel's Musical Library', MQ 81 (1997), 109–38
'Victor Schoelcher's Manuscript Handel Biographies and Catalogues', HJb 48 (2002)

Schulenburg, (Ehrengard) Melusine von der (Duchess of Kendal and Duchess of Munster) (b. Emden 25 Dec. 1667, d. Isleworth, 10 May 1743). Mistress of GEORGE I, Schulenburg was a member of a prominent North German military and courtly family. She moved to HANOVER from Brandenburg in 1690 to become maid of honour to the Duchess Sophia, and the next year became mistress of Sophia's son George Louis, later GEORGE I of Great Britain. They had three daughters, all of whom were officially described as her nieces. She moved to London with George I in 1714, and was made Duchess of Munster in the Irish peerage in 1716, and Duchess of Kendal in the British peerage in 1719.

George's wife had been divorced and imprisoned in Germany in 1694, so Schulenburg acted as hostess at his court, and was a visible presence in London as she regularly accompanied the King on his visits to the opera. Politically, she helped broker arrangements between politicians and the King, but was the focus of controversy for the profits she made from the SOUTH SEA COMPANY and the sale of a patent to produce coins in Ireland.

Schulenburg, Petronilla Melusine von der (Countess of Walsingham and Countess of Chesterfield) (b. 1693; d. London 16 Sept. 1778). The second daughter of Melusine von der Schulenburg and George I. She was a pupil of Handel in London, like her half-niece Princess ANNE. She was made Countess of Walsingham in 1722, and in 1733 married Philip Dormer Stanhope, 4th Earl of Chesterfield, politician and writer. She was one of Handel's most loyal supporters among the nobility, for example supporting *SEMELE* in 1744 when it was deemed unfashionable.   MATTHEW KILBURN

R. Hatton, *George I: Elector and King* (London, 1978)

Schürmann, Georg Caspar (Schurmann; Scheuermann) (b. Idensen near Hanover, 1672/early 1673; d. Wolfenbüttel, 25 Feb. 1751). Singer, Kapellmeister, libretto translator and composer. He started his career as a church and opera singer in HAMBURG (1693–7), and later became Hofkapellmeister at WOLFENBÜTTEL (1697–1703; 1707–51); between 1703 and 1706 he worked in Meiningen. Schürmann wrote church music, operas and ballets, and was a principal collaborator in the development of German-language court opera at BRUNSWICK. He staged various Handel operas between 1723 and 1743 there, and also at Wolfenbüttel and SALZDAHLUM. He translated some of these into German, or included his own texts in others. He borrowed arias from *TESEO* and *RODELINDA* for his opera Clelia (1730).

KLAUS-PETER KOCH (Trans. ANGELA BAIER)

G. F. Schmidt, *Die frühdeutsche Oper und die musikdramatische Kunst Georg Caspar Schürmann's* (Regensburg, 1933)

Scipione (*Publio Cornelio Scipione*), HWV 20. Italian opera. The action is based on an episode known as 'the continence of Scipio', which took place during the Second Punic War while the young Scipio, later called Africanus, was campaigning in Spain. After taking the town of New Carthage (Cartagena), Scipio's men presented him with a beautiful Iberian noblewoman found among the captives. Instead of forcing his attentions on her, Scipio returned her to the local prince to whom she was betrothed, and provided her ransom money as a dowry (LIVY, xxvi.50). This episode is famous from early-modern historical paintings; whether historical or not, Scipione's gesture replicates a similar act of self-control by Alexander with the family of Darius (cf. PLUTARCH, *Alexander*, chapter xxi).

Handel's *Scipione* followed the creative burst that included *GIULIO CESARE, TAMERLANO* and *RODELINDA*. Paolo ROLLI's libretto seems to acknowledge the recent productions of *Giulio Cesare* with the opening aria, in which Scipio makes an anachronistic reference to Roman conquest of Egypt, irrelevant to the war he was fighting against Carthage: 'Our Arms have won, Iberia's vanquish'd; / And so, it seems, the Fates ordain, / Ægypt shall wear Rome's servile Chain.' Both Rolli's libretto and Handel's music were written quickly to fill a gap in the 1725–6 season caused by the delayed arrival in London of FAUSTINA Bordoni, for whom Handel was already composing *ALESSANDRO* (performed later that spring). Handel completed his autograph score on 2 March 1726.

Rolli's libretto notes that 'The first hint of this *Drama*, and some lines from it, are borrow'd; but what, otherwise, relates either to the Plot itself, or the Diction thro' the Whole, is entirely new'. The borrowed text was by Antonio SALVI for a MEDICI production in Livorno in 1704, but the libretto is part of the longer line of *Scipione* operas, beginning with Cavalli's *Scipione affricano* (VENICE, 1665), and when BURNEY ascribes the libretto's origin to Apostolo ZENO (Barcelona,

1710), he is not entirely mistaken. The first performance took place at the KING'S THEATRE on 12 March 1726, with the cast:

Publio Cornelio Scipione	Antonio Baldi (castrato)
Lucejo	SENESINO (castrato)
Berenice	Francesca CUZZONI (soprano)
C. Lelio	Luigi Antinori (tenor)
Ernando	Giuseppe Maria BOSCHI (bass)
Armira	Livia Constantini (soprano)

The scene is New Carthage. Scipio enters in triumph to a March that concludes the overture, and begins to apportion rewards to his soldiers. He is presented with two captive women: Berenice, daughter of Ernando, King of the Balearic Islands, and Armira, the daughter of another Spanish prince. Scipio falls immediately in love with Berenice and entrusts the two women to the protection of his lieutenant Lelio, who falls in love with Armira. Scipio does not know that Berenice was betrothed to Lucejo, who was on his way to the wedding when New Carthage was taken. Disguised as a Roman soldier, Lucejo successfully sneaks into the palace where the women are being kept. As Berenice and Lucejo speak, Scipio enters. To protect Lucejo, Berenice pretends she does not know him. The first act closes with Lucejo's jealousy aria ('Figlia di reo timor'), in which he expresses fear that Berenice is succumbing to Scipio's advances.

In the second act, Berenice's father Ernando arrives to ransom his daughter from the Romans. Scipio learns both of Berenice's parentage and of her engagement to Lucejo (who is still disguised). Scipio pursues his suit to Berenice, though with entirely honourable intentions. The rest of the act is taken up by a series of romantic complications that resolve when Lucejo reveals his identity to Scipio and offers to duel for Berenice. He is disarmed by Scipio's guards. Scipio declares Berenice must marry a Roman, but she ends the act with a vigorous declaration of her constancy ('Scoglio d'immota fronte').

In the third act it appears that Scipio will send Lucejo to Rome, and then pursue Berenice without competition. But Scipio grapples with his conscience and conquers his passions. He reunites the lovers, and a final chorus announces that Spain can be proud to be conquered by such a man. The Roman lieutenant Lelio's desire for the Spanish Princess Armira is only ambiguously resolved, for she has put him off with vague promises, while insisting that there can never be real love between conqueror and captive.

Handel's rapid composition did not deprive *Scipione* of charm or interest, and some informed contemporaries regarded it as equal in quality to *Giulio Cesare* and *Rodelinda*. The March from the overture had an immediate and lasting success. 'The Most celebrated Aires in the Opera of Scipio', arranged for bass line and voice or flute solo and 'sold at the Music Shops', featured five arias sung in the 1726 performances by Senesino, Cuzzoni and Baldi. Notable moments in the opera are Berenice's lilting lament 'Un caro amante' (I.i) and especially her strident conclusion to Act II 'Scoglio d'immota fronte', sung to the accompaniment of oboes and bassoon, which produces a more military sound than anything offered by her soldier-lovers Lucejo and Scipio. Ernando's aria on the civilising force of honour ('Tutta rea la vita umana': III.i) is a vigorous sermon to Scipio about his responsibilities as ruler that stimulates a self-searching accompanied recitative from Scipio – composed, but perhaps not performed in 1726 – that anticipates the agonies of METASTASIO's Emperor Tito.

The opera derived contemporary political relevance due to a perceived threat from Spain, which had made a treaty with the Habsburg emperor in 1725. This, combined with the portrait of Scipio as the ideal ruler, and themes of liberty and honour, gives the opera patriotic and moral qualities that anticipate the oratorios more overtly than Handel's previous serious operas.

Handel offered a considerably revised version of *Scipione* in November 1730. Senesino returned to sing Lucejo after two years' absence from London. Lucejo's arias and most of Berenice's were retained, but the rest of the arias were different, mostly taken from earlier operas. Handel made three changes in vocal pitch that included moving Scipio to the tenor range. The production apparently succeeded with the audiences, but there were only six performances and no further revivals until a production at GÖTTINGEN in 1937.   ROBERT KETTERER

Burney
Dean and Knapp, *Operas*
Harris, *Librettos*
R. Ketterer, 'Handel's *Scipione* and the Neutralization of Politics', *Newsletter of the American Handel Society* 16/1 (April 2001)
Strohm

Scott, Mrs. See Isabella YOUNG

Scudéry, Georges de (b. Le Havre, 22 Aug. 1601; d. Paris, 14 May 1667). One of the circle of French dramatists which included the CORNEILLE brothers. In the 1630s they established a strict form of dramatic composition based on the principles set out in Aristotle's *Poetics*; their influence was profound, both on French theatre and on Italian opera librettos for the next 100 years. Scudéry's tragicomedy *L'amour tyrannique* (1639) was the basis of LALLI's *L'amor tirannico* (1710, 1712), which became the source libretto for Handel's *RADAMISTO*.

                                                    TERENCE BEST

M. Bucciarelli, 'Radamisto's Theatrical Sources and their Influence on Handel's Creative Process', *GHB* VII (1998)

Second Academy. See OPERA COMPANIES, 3

'See the conquering hero comes'. See *JOSHUA*

Semele, HWV 58. Music drama, first performed in the 1744 Lenten oratorio season. The story comes from OVID's *Metamorphoses*. Semele is on the point of marrying Athamas when her lover Jupiter disrupts the wedding with thunder, lightning and rain. After her sister Ino confesses her own love for Athamas, her father Cadmus brings news that Semele has been abducted by an eagle to join Jupiter in 'Endless pleasure'. Juno, in revenge, tricks Semele into demanding that Jupiter make love to her in his divine form. Semele is thus incinerated by his lightning, but Apollo consoles the grieving mortals that the god Bacchus will arise from Semele's ashes.

The libretto was written by William CONGREVE around 1705–6 and set to music by John ECCLES, but their all-sung English opera fell victim to theatrical politics and was not performed. The libretto was published in Congreve's *Complete Works* in 1710, and adapted for Handel by an unknown collaborator. Trowell proposed that the most likely candidate is Newburgh HAMILTON because the adaptation shows some similarities of approach with Hamilton's adaptations of earlier 'great' English poets in *SAMSON* and *ALEXANDER'S FEAST*.

The adapter reduced some longer sections of dialogue, and inserted choruses and arias using text from Congreve's poems *To Sleep*, *The Reconciliation*, *Imitations of Horace*, *Homeric Hymn to Venus*, *Ode on Mrs Arabella Hunt* and *Of Pleasing, an Epistle to Sir Richard Temple*. He inserted 'Where'er you walk' from POPE's *Second Pastoral*, reversified the aria 'With fond desiring', and provided the texts for 'Despair no more shall wound me' and 'Happy, happy shall we be'.

Semele was composed between 3 June and 4 July 1743. Handel made several important revisions during the composition. Athamas was recast from a tenor to a countertenor so his arias were transposed and 'Despair no more shall wound me' was added. Handel also rejected his musical sketch for the final chorus, 'Then Mortals be Merry', and used the fresh words 'Happy, happy shall we be', which ends the work in coronation splendour, rather than with Congreve's unashamed praise of wine. After completion of the autograph, Handel cut Cupid's 'Come Zephyrs come' (and thus the character) and rewrote the arias 'See, she blushing turns her eyes' and 'Behold in this mirror' as recitatives (with the former transferred from Ino to Athamas).

Semele contains self-borrowings from *GIULIO CESARE* and *Fra pensieri quel pensiero* (HWV 115), as well as borrowings from Alessandro SCARLATTI (notably from *Il Pompeo*), PORTA, KEISER and TELEMANN. Noteworthy in the score are the number and quality of accompanied recitatives (a characteristic it shares with *Il Pompeo*), and the sheer variety of style and tempo markings (twenty-three, with nine unique in the English works). The first performance took place at COVENT GARDEN on 10 February 1744. The cast was as follows:

Semele	FRANCESINA (soprano)
Jupiter/Apollo	John BEARD (tenor)
Juno/Ino	Esther YOUNG (alto)
Athamas	Daniel SULLIVAN (countertenor)
Iris	Christina Maria AVOGLIO (soprano)
Cadmus/Somnus	Henry REINHOLD (bass)

Mrs DELANY called it 'a delightful piece of music', but remarked that others were less enthusiastic: 'Semele has a strong party against it, viz. the fine ladies, petit maitres, and *ignoramus's*. All the opera people are enraged at Handel' (HHB iv, pp. 372–3). This was perhaps a reference to supporters (such as Lady BROWN) of the struggling MIDDLESEX OPERA COMPANY, for whom Handel had refused to write. Dr Delany refused to attend a 'profane' work in Lent. The most violent criticisms from Handel's circle came from Charles JENNENS, who requested a subscription to Handel's 1744–5 KING'S THEATRE season with an exemption from *Semele* (Burrows and Dunhill, p. 208), and later wrote in the margin of his copy of MAINWARING's *Memoirs of the Life of the late George Frideric Handel* (1760) that it was 'a baudy Opera'.

Semele was revived only once by Handel, on 1 and 8 December 1744, with several revisions and transpositions. Italian arias from Handel's operas *ARMINIO* and *GIUSTINO* replaced those of Athamas and Juno, an aria 'Somnus rise' (now lost) was added for Iris, and four sections of dialogue containing unambiguous sexual innuendo were cut. In addition to Francesina, Beard and Reinhold, the cast were Miss ROBINSON (Ino, mezzo-soprano), and probably Monticelli (Athamas, castrato); GALLI (Juno, contralto) and Avoglio (Iris, soprano). The only other known eighteenth-century performance, with a tenor Athamas and cut even further, was under J. C. SMITH JUNIOR in 1762.

Congreve's verse is urbane, witty and stylish, whilst his recitatives were, in his own description, 'a more tuneable speaking . . . a kind of Prose in Musick' ('Argument introductory to the Opera of Semele', *Compete Works*). However, the libretto's directness and its portrayal of sexual desire and activity were rooted in a Restoration aesthetic that by the 1740s seemed overly permissive. Handel made several cuts, both before and during composition, to tone down passages of suggestive sexuality, but Jennens's reaction indicates that it remained troublesome for contemporary audiences.

The genre of the work has been the subject of considerable confusion. Handel called it 'The Story of Semele'. Its operatic libretto, da capo arias and borrowings from Il *Pompeo* have led many to classify it as an opera manqué. However, several of its choruses, particularly the finales of Parts II and III are clearly in the oratorio anthem style, and 'Nature to each allots his proper sphere' gives the work a moralising decorum redolent of classical tragedy. Most importantly, several incidents rely for their impact on the audience's imagination, notably Semele's death and insinuations of her sexual relationship with Jupiter. *Semele* is not an 'opera' in an eighteenth-century sense, but its direct treatment of sexually passionate relationships and its fusion of opera, oratorio and classical drama anticipate the grand operas of the nineteenth century.   JOHN K. ANDREWS

J. K. Andrews, 'The Historical Context of Handel's *Semele* (1743)', Ph.D. dissertation (University of Cambridge, 2007)

W. Congreve, *The Works of Mr. William Congreve; in Three Volumes. Containing his Plays and Poems* (London, 1710)

W. Dean, 'Charles Jennens's Marginalia to Mainwaring's Life of Handel', *Essays on Opera* (Oxford, 1990)
Oratorios

A. Hicks, 'Ravishing Semele', MT 114/1561 (March 1973), 275–9

B. Trowell, 'Congreve and the 1744 *Semele* Libretto', MT 111 (1970), 993–4

D. Vickers, 'Handel and "The Story of Semele"' (CD booklet note, Chandos Chaconne CHAN 0745(3), 2007)
(ed.), *Semele*. Novello Handel Edition (forthcoming)

Semiramide riconosciuta (*Semiramis Recognised*), HWV A^8. PASTICCIO opera in three acts, based on Leonardo VINCI's *Semiramide riconosciuta* (ROME, 1729). It was first performed at the KING'S THEATRE on 30 October 1733. METASTASIO wrote the libretto for Vinci, but also allowed PORPORA's setting to be performed in VENICE six days after Vinci's opened in Rome.

The complex plot harks back to seventeenth-century Venetian opera. After the death of Nino, King of Assyria, his wife Semiramide took his place disguised as her son, also named Nino. As the opera opens, Tamiri, a princess under the protection of Semiramide, is preparing to choose among three princes vying for her hand: the uncouth Ircano, the gentle Mirteo, who happens to be Semiramide's long-lost brother, and Scitalce. Years before, in Egypt, Scitalce and Semiramide had been lovers. They intended to elope, but Scitalce, deceived by a letter from his friend Sibari claiming that Semiramide was planning to betray him, stabbed her and threw her body into the Nile. Sibari, who secretly loves Semiramide, is now her confidant. When Tamiri's three suitors are presented, Semiramide and Scitalce immediately recognise each other. Still in love with Scitalce, Semiramide tries to prevent Tamiri from choosing him. Tamiri indicates her choice by offering Scitalce a ceremonial bowl, not knowing it has been poisoned by Sibari, but Scitalce cannot bring himself to accept it in front of Semiramide. Tamiri promises her hand to whoever will avenge his refusal. To protect Scitalce from Ircano and Mirteo, Semiramide puts him in prison. Ircano disgraces himself by trying to abduct Tamiri. Semiramide frees Scitalce and he is reconciled with Tamiri, but Mirteo, informed by Sibari that Scitalce had killed his sister in Egypt, insists on a duel. All is resolved when Scitalce discloses Sibari's letter. The people confirm Semiramide as queen despite her deception, and she marries Scitalce while Tamiri weds Mirteo.

Semiramide opened Handel's first season after most of his singers deserted him for the rival OPERA OF THE NOBILITY. The cast was as follows:

Semiramide	Margherita DURASTANTI (mezzo-soprano)
Tamiri	Anna Maria STRADA del Pò (soprano)
Scitalce	Giovanni CARESTINI (castrato)
Mirteo	Carlo SCALZI (castrato)
Ircano	Maria Caterina NEGRI (alto)
Sibari	Maria Rosa Negri (mezzo-soprano)

Carestini, Scalzi and the Negri sisters were all making their London debut, Durastanti returning after an absence of nine years. Originally Ircano was to have been sung by the bass Gustavus WALTZ and Sibari by Caterina Negri, but Waltz dropped out at the last minute, forcing Handel to recast both roles. It has been supposed that Waltz fell ill; a more likely explanation is that Handel found he had to share his bass with J. F. LAMPE at DRURY LANE, where he mounted a revival of his burlesque The Opera of Operas beginning on 7 November, with Waltz playing the leading role of Grizzle as he had in the original production the previous May–June. The King and his family attended the first performance of Semiramide, and Carestini helped to fill the house, but after the second performance Lady Bristol informed her husband Lord Hervey that the opera was 'dull', the theatre 'empty', and Semiramide lasted only two more nights. Not surprisingly none of the music was published.

Of all Handel's pasticcio arrangements Semiramide has the least music in common with the opera on which it was based. This is partly because Handel apparently worked not from a full score of Vinci's opera but from an aria collection lacking the instrumental movements, choruses, recitatives, and two truncated arias leading directly into recitative. Most of Vinci's arias were also jettisoned in favour of arias by Francesco Corselli, Feo, HASSE, LEO, PORTA, Sarro and Vinci himself, presumably at the request of the singers. Carestini, taking over a role designed by Vinci for a tenor, sang only arias from his own repertory, while Strada seems to have found unacceptable all but one of the arias composed for the novice castrato Pietro Morigi. Although Vinci had written the role of Mirteo for Scalzi, his voice had in the meantime lowered, so his arias had to be transposed downward and in one case replaced. When the role of Ircano was still intended for Waltz, Handel took the extraordinary step of thoroughly recomposing his aria 'Saper bramate' (both versions are printed in full by Strohm). Rough, overbearing and more than slightly absurd, Ircano was conceived by Metastasio and Vinci for the castrato Gaetano BERENSTADT, noted for his blustery manner, and Handel probably reworked this aria, in which Ircano refuses to explain himself to everyone else, in order to make the most of Waltz's gifts as a comic actor. Unfortunately the aria Waltz was to have sung in Act III is lost. One of the arias inserted by Caterina Negri when she took over the role came from Hasse's *Cajo Fabricio*, which Handel would bring out a few weeks after *Semiramide*, but the source appears to have been a copy belonging to the singer rather than the JENNENS score Handel used in preparing his pasticcio. In the conducting score, now in the Staats- und Universitätsbibliothek Hamburg, Handel added a violin line to the vocal portion of Sibari's 'Pensa ad amare', no doubt because the copy supplied by Rosa Negri was incomplete.

In place of the missing overture Handel used the overture from Vinci's *Artaserse*, an opera he would later adapt as the pasticcio ARBACE. The sinfonia in Act II had previously done duty in the pasticcio VENCESLAO (1731), and it cannot be by Handel as suggested by Strohm (p. 186). The final chorus, to which Metastasio's text was rather awkwardly fitted, has not been identified. A short chorus earlier in the same scene hailing Semiramide as queen was fashioned out of the eight-bar ritornello of the final chorus, and Handel later rewrote the bass part, probably so that it could be sung by a tenor (Rochetti?) filling in for Waltz. In setting the recitatives Handel responded strongly to Metastasio's dramatically powerful text. Such scenes as the opening presentation sequence, which unfolds entirely in recitative, and the confrontation between Semiramide and Scitalce near the end of Act II are as finely drawn as anything in the recitatives of his own operas. There is a novel touch in the last scene: Mirteo reads Sibari's crucial letter entirely without accompaniment except for occasional punctuating chords.   JOHN H. ROBERTS

H. D. Clausen, *Händels Direktionspartituren* ('Handexemplare') (Hamburg, 1972)

J. Milhous and R. D. Hume, 'Box Office Reports for Five Operas Mounted by Handel in London, 1732–1734', *Harvard Library Bulletin* 26/3 (1978), 245–66

Strohm

'Senesino' (Francesco Bernardi) (b. 31 Oct. 1686, Siena; fl. 1707-40; d. Siena, 27 Nov. 1758). Castrato (range g–g″). Bernardi, nicknamed 'Senesino', was the son of a Sienese barber who destined both him and his elder brother Giovan Carlo to the career of castrato singers. After an early musical training as boy choristers at Siena Cathedral, Giovan Carlo was castrated in 1696 and Francesco in 1699. However, only Francesco achieved considerable acclaim and wealth (see Figure 26). His first documented operatic appearances were at VENICE's Teatro Sant'Angelo and in nearby Vicenza during the 1707–9 seasons (in operas by Ruggieri, Albinoni and others). Over the next few years he performed at Bologna, Genoa and ROME. From October 1715 until January 1717, Senesino featured in six operas at NAPLES, including several by Alessandro SCARLATTI. At this point of his oratorios were performed. Wren's functional interior allowed a large audience to see and hear well. Reversing the Roman plan, the ceremonies take place in the semicircle with the dignitaries in the tiered seating. The spectacle consists of real, not fictional, events in the auditorium, lit by large windows above the tiered gallery; Wren's ingenious roof structure spans nearly 70ft without internal supports. A small Father Smith organ was introduced in 1671 but Wren provided no gallery; the present instrument, installed in 1876, blocks one of the south windows.

KERRY DOWNES

Siegmund-Schultze, Walther (b. Schweinitz (Elster) 6 July 1916; d. Halle, 6 March 1993). Musicologist, lecturer. He studied at Breslau University (Polish: Wrocław), where he took a doctorate in 1940 with a dissertation on MOZART. After the Second World War he was a teacher in HALLE and a music consultant for the state government of Saxony-Anhalt. In 1951 he completed his *Habilitation* with a thesis on BRAHMS at HALLE UNIVERSITY, where he was lecturer (1951–4), professor (1954–86) and successor of Max Schneider as director of the musicological institute (1956–82). He was a co-founder of both the Halle Handel Festival (FESTIVALS, 4); and the Georg-Friedrich-Händel-Gesellschaft (HANDEL SOCIETIES, 3), serving as the latter's president (1967–90). He was also general editor of the Hallische Händel-Ausgabe (EDITIONS, 7), and an important figure in Handel scholarship and RECEPTION in East Germany.

KLAUS-PETER KOCH (Trans. ANGELA BAIER)

W. Rackwitz, 'Worte des Gedenkens anläßlich der Trauerfeier am 31. März 1993 für Walther Siegmund-Schultze (6.7.1916–6.3.1993)', *HJb* 39 (1993)

'Silent worship'. See *TOLOMEO*

Silete venti. See Italian and Latin CHURCH MUSIC

Silla (*Lucio Cornelio Silla*), HWV 10. Handel's shortest and most perplexing opera is presumed to have been written in the spring or early summer of 1713; no performance is recorded. The libretto is dated 2 June 1713, and its format, larger than usual and with no English translation, suggests that any production that did take place was a private one, most likely in the Queen's Theatre in the Haymarket (KING'S THEATRE), which will have been required for the many spectacular stage effects. The singers, unidentified in the libretto, would presumably have been those who had recently performed in *TESEO*:

Lucio Cornelio Silla, Dictator of Rome	Valentino Urbani (castrato)
Lepido, tribune of the plebs, friend of Silla	Valeriano Pellegrini (castrato)
Claudio, Roman knight and Silla's enemy	Jane Barbier (alto)
Metella, Silla's wife	Elisabetta PILOTTI-SCHIAVONETTI (soprano)
Flavia, Lepido's wife	Margherita de L'EPINE (soprano)
Celia, secretly the beloved of Claudio	Maria Gallia (soprano)
Scabro, favourite of Silla, confidant of Metella	(non-singing role)
The God [in fact the Goddess, Bellona]	Richard Leveridge (bass)

No model has yet been identified for ROSSI's libretto, which acknowledges PLUTARCH as its only source. The action of the opera opens when Sulla (Silla), triumphant from foreign conquests and victorious in a bitter civil war against the followers of Marius, returns with his army to Rome and declares himself perpetual dictator (81 BC). Its exiguous plot is concerned almost exclusively with the savagery and debauchery in which Sulla now indulges himself, and it ends with his abdication (79 BC). The violent pace of the action accelerates into frenzy in the third act as a result of omissions or subsequent cuts in Handel's setting of the text. Because his autograph breaks off after the fourth scene of Act III, we cannot be sure of his real intentions, but the few surviving copies include no music for a duet in Scene ix (Metella and Silla), or for arias in Scenes x (Metella) and xi (Claudio). So meagre are Rossi's efforts to interest the spectator in his characters, so tightly are the preposterous incidents packed together, so ignominiously for the nominal hero do they generally end (Dean and Knapp, p. 263, count seven unsuccessful attempts at indecent assault), that critics have been increasingly inclined to seek not just an allegorical but a malevolent purpose in the opera, the most likely target being the Duke of MARLBOROUGH.

The political context in which Silla was composed must surely be important. The libretto is dedicated to the Duc d'Aumont, who late in 1712 had been appointed Ambassador Extraordinary to Great Britain by the French King, Louis XIV. The War of the SPANISH SUCCESSION, in which France and Great Britain were principal combatants, had dragged on for ten years; and while diplomats in Utrecht negotiated a peace settlement (finally concluded on 11 April 1713), D'Aumont was busy in London impressing the city with his ostentatious magnificence. He is reported to have charged Marlborough, commander-in-chief of the British forces during the war, with responsibility for prolonging it.

The difficulty with arguing for malicious intent is the music. Handel seizes with typical flair the few opportunities for imaginatively designed and impressive musico-dramatic climaxes – in Flavia's prison scene, 'Stelle rubelle', or in the scene in which Bellona, Goddess of War, appears to Silla in a dream to inspire him to 'guerra, stragi e furor'. Throughout the opera a succession of fine arias show the composer in something close to top form. Nine of them subsequently found a home in AMADIGI and a tenth in RADAMISTO. All of them needed to be adapted to their new context in some measure, but – contrary to what has sometimes been implied – nowhere is this due to any weakness or sketchiness in the Silla originals. In short, while the action and the text in which it is embodied give the effect of an unprincipled and titillating piece of propaganda with all the literary finesse of a strip cartoon, Handel's music goes its own distinguished way regardless. By the early years of the twenty-first century exponents of Regie-Theater (producer's opera; STAGING, 2) were beginning to notice that the disconnection between spectacle and music in Silla, hitherto an opera almost entirely ignored, offered a congenial field for their endeavours.   DAVID KIMBELL

Bianconi
D. Chisholm, 'Handel's Lucio Cornelio Silla: Its Problems and Context', EM 14/1 (1986), 64–70
Dean and Knapp, Operas
Harris, Librettos
J. M. Knapp, 'The Libretto of Handel's Silla', ML 50 (1969), 68–75
Strohm

589

Silvani, Francesco (b. Venice, c.1660; fl. until 1716).One of the driving reformers of Italian opera librettos around 1700. Between 1682 and 1716 he wrote at least one libretto each year for Venetian theatres (San Cassiano, San Angelo, SAN GIOVANNI GRISOSTOMO; he also served the Duke of Mantua for a time). His librettos were first set by, among others, Giacomo Antonio PERTI, Marc' Antonio Ziani, Tomaso Albinoni, Francesco GASPARINI and Antonio LOTTI. Some of his poetical subjects are complete inventions even though he claimed that they had historical precedents. Two of his librettos, first set by Ziani, became models for operas by Handel: *La costanza in trionfo* (1696) for *FLORIDANTE* (1721) and *Il duello d'amore, e di vendetta* (1700) for *RODRIGO* (1707).

HANS DIETER CLAUSEN (Trans. ANGELA BAIER)

Sing unto God. See ANTHEMS, 4

Sing-Akademie zu Berlin. Founded on 24 May 1791 by Carl Friedrich Christian Fasch (1736–1800), who started rehearsing choruses from *JUDAS MACCABAEUS* in special 'Singe-Übungen' in 1795, and performed these in the Sing-Akademie's concerts. At around the same time, Carl Friedrich Zelter studied choruses from *ALEXANDER'S FEAST* and *MESSIAH.* Their combined efforts paved the way towards a performance of *Alexanderfest*, with a German text by Karl Wilhelm Ramler, on 13 October 1807. In order to accommodate the Sing-Akademie's style of a cappella singing, Zelter arranged the Utrecht Te Deum (TE DEUM, 1) for two mixed choirs (1806). In 1809 the Dettingen Te Deum (TE DEUM, 5) was performed, followed by *Judas Maccabaeus* (1811, 1814 and 1820), *Alexanderfest* (1821) and *Der Messias* (1822 and 1823, in MOZART's arrangement). Other conductors and arrangers included Johann Otto Heinrich SCHAUM, Felix MENDELSSOHN BARTHOLDY and Gaspare Spontini. In the following decades, especially under Karl Friedrich Rungenhagen (1778–1851) and Eduard Grell (1800–86), Handel's oratorios were at the core of the Sing-Akademie's repertoire. In the 1850s Grell tried to reduce additional unauthentic instrumentation in order to reapproach Handel's original intentions. WERNER RACKWITZ (Trans. ANGELA BAIER)

W. Bollert, 'Die Händelpflege der Berliner Sing-Akademie unter Zelter und Rungenhagen', *Sing-Akademie zu Berlin* (Berlin, 1966)
Die Sing-Akademie zu Berlin und ihre Direktoren (Berlin, 1998)
G. Eberle, *200 Jahre Singakademie zu Berlin* (Berlin, 1991)

Siroe, Re di Persia, HWV 24. The penultimate opera that Handel wrote for the Royal Academy of Music (OPERA COMPANIES, 2), and his first setting of a libretto by METASTASIO. The text was originally set by VINCI for the Teatro di SAN GIOVANNI GRISOSTOMO in VENICE in the Carnival season of 1726; by early 1728 when Handel composed the opera it had already been set by four other composers: by PORTA (two versions), Sarro, PORPORA and VIVALDI. The libretto was adapted for Handel by Nicola HAYM, who used the version set by Sarro for NAPLES in 1727, which had been supervised by Metastasio himself.

The plot draws on the life of the Persian King Khosrau II Parves (Cosroes; r. AD 590–628). He was deposed and murdered by his son Kavadh II (Siroes), who thus prevented the throne passing to his brothers, one of whom was Medarza (Medarses). The historical sources of the story are Zonaras, *Epitome ton istorion* (vol. 14), Elmacinus, *Historia saracenica* (vol. 1), and Baronio *Annalium* (vol. II), drawn from the Theophanes, *Chronographia.* Contemporary plays on which Metastasio could have drawn were Jean de Rotrou's *Cosroès* (1649) and ZENO's *ORMISDA* (1721). The latter deals with a similar plot played out in the same dynasty, a generation earlier. In Metastasio, Cosroe is portrayed as jealous of the valiant Siroe's popularity with the people and excessively fond of his adulating son Medarse. He wishes to circumvent Siroe's right of succession and make Medarse king instead. Cosroe is further disturbed by Siroe's love for Emira, a daughter of his enemy Asbite, the King of Cambaja. Asbite was killed by Cosroe when the latter invaded his kingdom. As the sole survivor of the Cambajan royal family, Emira seeks revenge on Cosroe, having infiltrated herself into his court, disguised as a male courtier, Idaspe. Her real identity is only known to Siroe. The opera begins with Cosroe announcing that he is to make the decision on his successor. Siroe refuses to swear to accept his father's choice and the enraged Cosroe announces that he is going to make Medarse king that very day. Emira urges Siroe to kill Cosroe and thus avenge himself and her father, but he refuses. In anger, Emira tells Laodice, who is Cosroe's favourite but in love with Siroe, that Siroe returns her feelings. When he subsequently rejects her, Laodice decides to avenge herself. Siroe, who wishes to retain his honour and remain constant to both his father and his beloved, decides to inform Cosroe that his life is in danger by writing him an anonymous note. While he is in Cosroe's chamber, the latter's arrival forces him to hide. Siroe thus becomes an unwitting witness of accusations against himself. Laodice complains to Cosroe that Siroe tried to seduce her and threatened to kill her if she refused him; once the anonymous note is discovered, Medarse also grabs the chance to accuse Siroe of planning a patricide. Siroe cannot bear such lies and reveals himself, making his position even worse.

Act II begins with Laodice's regret at her false accusations and an apology to Siroe. He asks Emira either to avenge Asbite by killing him or to forgive Cosroe. She refuses. As Siroe maintains that he will protect Cosroe, she resolves that they must become enemies. Siroe draws his sword to kill himself and Cosroe mistakes the scene as Siroe's attempt to murder 'Idaspe'. Siroe declares that all the accusations against him are true and asks for death. When he is taken away, Emira draws her sword to kill Cosroe, but is interrupted by Medarse; she pretends that she was going to lay the sword in front of the King. Cosroe visits Siroe and offers him Laodice and the kingdom if he talks, otherwise he will die. Siroe leaves it to 'Idaspe' to decide for him and thus finally lets Emira taste the difficulty of his own position.

In Act III, Cosroe orders Siroe's death. Horrified, Laodice confesses that her accusations against Siroe were false. Believing him dead, enraged Emira finally reveals herself as Cosroe's foe, telling him that Siroe was innocent. Heartbroken, Cosroe has her imprisoned, but she is freed by Siroe's friend Arasse, who tells her that Siroe has not yet been executed. She sets off to free him and helps him overcome Medarse, who wishes to kill him. Siroe forgives his repentant brother. In the ensuing combat between the rebels and the royal guards Cosroe falls. Emira wishes to kill him, but Siroe defends his father. Finally, Medarse and Laodice confess their guilt to Cosroe. Siroe magnanimously pardons everybody and Emira is overcome with the example of his virtue. She lays aside her hatred and Cosroe offers her the throne to share with Siroe.

Handel began composing *Siroe* sometime during the 1727–8 season, after abandoning work on GENSERICO. Five of the six arias that he had already composed for *Genserico* were incorporated into Act I of *Siroe*. The autograph score of the opera was completed on 5 February 1728, and the first performance took place at the KING'S THEATRE on 17 February with the following cast:

Siroe	SENESINO (castrato)
Emira	FAUSTINA Bordoni (soprano)
Laodice	Francesca CUZZONI (soprano)
Cosroe	Giuseppe Maria BOSCHI (bass)
Medarse	Antonio Baldi (castrato)
Arasse	Giovanni Battista Palmerini (bass)

Metastasio's libretto resulted in a fine setting by Handel. Haym omitted nearly half of Metastasio's recitatives, but otherwise departed from the source text only in order to augment the roles for the stars and reduce the roles for the secondary singers (in the case of Medarse with detrimental effect). As a consequence, the opera lacks a strong portrayal of the chief villain. Other parts, however, are drawn strongly and in depth. Particular jewels of the score are Siroe's prison lament in Act III, Emira's 'Non vi piacque ingiusti Dei' (II.x) which shows her intimate side, and Cosroe's 'Gelido in ogni vena' (III.iv) as he realises with horror that he ordered the murder of an innocent son. A point of dramaturgical interest is the final chorus, praising love as life's greatest treasure, in which Emira leads the other characters in a responsorial manner, her solo lines harmonised by the *coro*. Notwithstanding Handel's endeavours to provide balanced parts for his two star sopranos ('RIVAL QUEENS'), the curious final *coro* seems to establish Emira as the leading female character.

The reception of *Siroe* has been stigmatised by the triumph of *The* BEGGAR'S OPERA, which was premiered shortly beforehand. Although interest in the Italian opera had been declining, and some of Handel's performances might not have been well attended, the feud between the soprano factions had lost its sting earlier in the season (it had been known at least since November 1727 that the singers were not planning to stay for another season), and it is possible that an interest in Metastasio might have played some part in *Siroe* being performed for eighteen consecutive nights, which was the second longest run of an Academy production in a single season. Handel never revived the opera, but there were two productions of it at BRUNSWICK during the 1730s.

SUZANA OGRAJENŠEK

Dean, *Operas*
Harris, *Librettos*
S. Ograjenšek, 'From *Alessandro* (1726) to *Tolomeo* (1728): The Final Royal Academy Operas', Ph.D. dissertation (University of Cambridge 2005)
Strohm

Smith Collection. See SOURCES AND COLLECTIONS, 16

Smith, John Christopher, senior (Johann Christoph Schmidt) (b. Kitzingen, 3 March 1683; d. London, Jan. 1763). Smith was Handel's friend and principal music COPYIST after Antonio Giuseppe ANGELINI and D. LINICKE. According to COXE, Smith first met Handel at HALLE UNIVERSITY (probably in 1702 although his name cannot be found in the matriculation register). In 1705 he moved to

Nuremberg and then to Ansbach in c.1707. It was there that he renewed contact with Handel during the latter's tour of Germany, probably in 1716, and followed him to London. At first he presumably earned his living by playing the viola. Coxe called him Handel's 'treasurer'. Beginning in 1718/19 he started to learn the task of music-copying (Dean, p. 20). In about 1720 his family followed him to London.

When Handel began archiving his conducting scores (SOURCES AND COLLECTIONS, 2) in late 1720, Smith became involved in this part of Handel's business and was from then on his principal music copyist. The close collaboration on the conducting score of the second version of *RADAMISTO*, which contains an astonishing number of autograph passages, was probably only possible because Handel was working together with a personal friend.

Smith employed a team of other copyists; among them were his son John Christopher (SMITH JUNIOR) and probably his wife Anna Susanna and their other children Charlotte, Judith and ?Frederic. This workshop produced Handel's performing materials, with Smith senior for the most part reserving for himself the right to copy Handel's conducting score. Smith also seems to have acted as a kind of secretary overseeing Handel's scores because anyone who wished to acquire a copy of a score or parts had to apply to him.

Smith also tried his hand at music publishing. In 1720, after the King had granted Handel a royal warrant for the sole right to publication of his music (COPYRIGHT), Smith published *RADAMISTO* and the *Suites pour le Clavecin* (KEYBOARD MUSIC) in collaboration with John CLUER and Richard MEARES, who operated from the 'Hand and Musick Bookshop'. In 1730 he sold printed editions of *RICCARDO PRIMO* and *LOTARIO* for Cluer's widow.

Smith accompanied Handel to DUBLIN in 1741/2. In 1743 he acted as an intermediary between Handel and the MIDDLESEX OPERA COMPANY, which was trying in vain to get Handel to cooperate. This clouded the personal relationship between Handel and the patient Smith (Charles JENNENS called him a 'Toad-eater'). The final rift in their friendship (according to the *Anecdotes*) came in 1755, for petty reasons. Since Smith moved to a new house in the same year, it is presumed that until then he had lived with Handel, after the latter's loss of sight, in the house in Brook Street. However, the younger Smith managed to reconcile the two friends shortly before Handel's death. The elder Smith inherited, among other things, Handel's musical instruments and scores (among them the autograph manuscripts and the conducting scores) (HANDEL, 8).

HANS DIETER CLAUSEN (Trans. ANGELA BAIER)

[W. Coxe], *Anecdotes of George Frederick Handel and John Christopher Smith* (London, 1799; facsimile edn, ed. P. M. Young, New York, 1979)

W. Dean, 'Handel's Early London Copyists', *Essays on Opera* (Oxford, 1990)

J. S. Hall, 'John Christopher Smith, Handel's Friend and Secretary', MT 96/1345 (1955), 132–4

K. Sasse, 'Neue Daten zu Johann Christoph Schmidt', HJb 3 (1957)

Smith, John Christopher, junior (b. Ansbach, 1712; d. Bath, 3 Oct. 1795). Composer (see Figure 27). In about 1720 the elder Smith was joined in London by his family, who also became involved with the Handel circle as musicians or copyists. By 1725 the younger Smith was receiving lessons from Handel in composition and keyboard, and by 1727 he was part of Handel's team of copyists. At

O. E. Deutsch, 'Poetry Preserved in Music. Bibliographical Notes on Smollett and Oswald, Handel and Haydn', *Modern Language Notes* 63 (Feb. 1948), 73–88

R. G. King, 'Who Wrote the Texts for Handel's *Alceste*?', MT 150/1906 (Spring 2009)

L. M. Knapp (ed.), *Tobias Smollett Doctor of Men and Manners* (New York, 1963)

Smyth, James (b. ?1720s; d. London, 8–14 Dec. 1780). A perfumer on Bond Street to whom Handel left a significant bequest of £500 in his will (HANDEL, 8). He was at least twenty-one in 1749 when he voted in the Westminster by-election. The last person outside the household to be with Handel before he died, his letter to Bernard GRANVILLE provides important details about the last hours of 'the great and good Mr. Handel'. ELLEN T. HARRIS

Deutsch

HHB iv

James Smyth's will, PROB 11/1072, fol. 281, The National Archive

Solomon, HWV 67. The libretto of *Solomon* draws upon the Old Testament portrayal of Solomon in 1 Kings 1–10, 1 Chronicles 22; 28–9, and 2 Chronicles 1–9, as well as the Song of Solomon. Each act of the oratorio shows a different aspect of Solomon: his marital bliss, his wisdom and his material wealth. Act I begins with the dedication of the temple, in which Solomon, Zadok, a Levite, and a chorus of Israelites participate. When Solomon's Queen enters, and she and Solomon extol the happiness of married love, culminating in the chorus 'May no rash intruder disturb their soft hours'. The bulk of Act II concerns Solomon's judgement of two women who each claim the same child. In order to identify the real mother, Solomon suggests splitting the babe in half, to which the true mother objects. A chorus celebrates his wisdom. In Act III Solomon shows the splendour of his kingdom to the Queen of Sheba.

Handel composed the score between 5 May and 17 June 1748, and it was first performed at COVENT GARDEN on 17 March 1749. The cast was as follows:

Solomon	Caterina GALLI (alto)
Pharaoh's Daughter	Giulia FRASI (soprano)
1st Harlot	Giulia Frasi
2nd Harlot	Sibilla Gronamann (soprano)
Nicaule, Queen of Sheba	Giulia Frasi
Zadok, the High Priest	Thomas LOWE (tenor)
A Levite	Henry REINHOLD (bass)

The librettist is unknown, but it may be the same anonymous author who wrote *SUSANNA*, which was composed during the same period. The possibility has been raised that Handel had been given the libretto years earlier, but several factors point against this. First, one of the radical revisions of the score has ramifications for the authorship. The extensive musical entertainment in Act III, consisting of a stretch of several choruses performed for the Queen of Sheba, was originally intended for entertainment of Solomon's wife in Act I. This large transfer suggests that Handel was working with a librettist who could not only change Act I but create a third that could accommodate both the original text for Act I and the music Handel had already composed. Handel may have received one act at a time, which implies that he was not working from an old complete libretto, or, if he was, he had an adapter who could make radical changes. Ruth Smith has suggested that the 'cue' for Act III may have come from Arthur Bedford's *The Temple Musick* (1706), who wrote that the temple music under Solomon was the best in the world and that 'one Motive which brought the Queen of Sheba from her Country might be to satisfy her Curiosity . . . and to hear the Musick, as well as see the Temple' (*Oratorios*, p. 91).

Another factor that suggests a recent libretto is the work's appropriateness for 1748–9. At this time England was emerging from a period of wartime, when the Peace of Aix-la-Chapelle (War of the AUSTRIAN SUCCESSION) was being negotiated, and *Solomon* celebrates a country at peace. Solomon is presented as a benevolent ruler without faults; the libretto makes no mention of his hundreds of wives and concubines, or his financial support for the construction of heathen temples – though the original audience would certainly have been aware of the negative side of Solomon presented in the BIBLE.

Much of *Solomon* is in a grand manner with large orchestral forces and large choruses, some of them in eight parts; *Solomon* in fact is the first work since *ISRAEL IN EGYPT* to employ a double chorus with a large orchestra with prominent brass instruments. Some choruses achieve great pomp, such as 'Praise the Lord' in the third act, and some feature antiphonal affects between two choirs, such as 'From the censer curling rise'. The heavy use of the chorus is one of the things that distinguish *Solomon* from the other oratorio of the season, *Susanna*. Handel's use of aria forms also differs from that work: whereas *Susanna* contains a large number of da capo arias, there are just under half a dozen da capos in *Solomon* out of twenty-one arias. Nature is a recurring motive in this work, frequently alluded to in such pieces as 'Haste, haste to the cedar grove', the famous Nightingale chorus, with its depiction of birdsong, 'Beneath the vine', and several others.

Much of the work includes tableaux that are not overtly dramatic in nature. The exception to this is the judgement scene in the heart of the work. Handel provides a great contrast in characterisation between the two women, beginning with a trio that begins with a moving plea from the first woman ('Words are weak to paint my fears'), scorned in quavers by the second woman ('False is all her melting tale'), combined with Solomon's level-headed 'Justice holds the lifted scale'. The contrast in the character of the two women continues throughout the scene. When Solomon orders the child to be split in half, the second woman agrees enthusiastically in her aria with syncopated melody 'Thy sentence, great king, is prudent and wise'. The first woman replies in a heartfelt aria 'Can I see my infant gor'd', which expresses her willingness to give up her child if Solomon will leave it whole. The scene reflects the sort of dramatic sensitivity that Handel had earned from his experience with opera. The scene contrasts vividly with the final act where a lengthy divertissement of choruses in contrasting emotions is presented for the entertainment of the Queen of Sheba.

Solomon is rich in BORROWINGS, particularly from TELEMANN. The nightingale's song in 'May no rash intruder' is a famous borrowed passage, and Telemann material is equally prominent in 'Beneath the vine' and 'Bless'd the day'. Sometimes Handel borrows a ritornello almost intact, as in the opening chorus 'Your harps and cymbals sound', but the rest differs greatly from its source. A handful of sketches for the work exist, which have been analysed in some detail. It was not a popular oratorio during Handel's lifetime. It was performed just three times during its first season, and he revived the work just once, during his last oratorio season ten years later. The 1759 revival altered the score so radically that an entirely new conducting score was prepared.   DAVID ROSS HURLEY

D. Burrows, 'Solomon' (Maryland Handel Festival programme note, 2000)
Burrows and Dunhill
Dean, *Oratorios*
D. R. Hurley, *Handel's Muse: Patterns of Creation in his Oratorios and Musical Dramas, 1743–1751* (Oxford, 2001)
R. Smith, 'Ideal and Reality: The Libretto of *Solomon*' (CD booklet note, Deutsche Grammophon Archiv 0 2894 96882 7, 1999)
   Oratorios
H. E. Smither, *A History of the Oratorio*, vol. 2: *The Oratorio in the Baroque Era: Protestant Germany and England* (Chapel Hill, NC, 1977)
D. Vickers, 'Let the Loud Hosannahs Rise: Handel's *Solomon*' (CD booklet note, Harmonia Mundi HMC 901949.50, 2007)

Somerset House. Old Somerset House was built in 1547–52 by Lord Protector Somerset in the minority of Edward VI and was subsequently used as a London retreat by queens consort or dowager. Inigo Jones built a chapel (1630–5) for Henrietta Maria, and additions including a riverside gallery were made after the Restoration. In the early eighteenth century it accommodated courtiers, including Sir John Stanley, whose niece Mrs DELANY often stayed there in the 1720s, and foreign visitors, including the Prince of Orange in 1733 prior to his wedding to Princess ANNE. The building was demolished in 1776 for the present one, designed as government offices.   KERRY DOWNES

sonatas. See CHAMBER MUSIC

Song for St Cecilia's Day ('From Harmony, heav'nly harmony'), HWV 76. English ode. John DRYDEN's poem was written in 1687, when it was set by Giovanni Battista Draghi (c.1640–1708). Its eight stanzas celebrate the power of music from the beginning to the end of the world. According to the notion of music as the ordering principle of all things (originating in the Middle Ages), the earth was created out of chaos through the harmony of the spheres (stanza 1), and will disintegrate at the sound of the last trump on the Day of Judgement (stanza 8). Stanzas 2–7 record music's power over the emotions and actions of created beings and celebrate notable musicians. In the 'corded shell' of Jubal, biblical original of all musicians, listeners believed they heard God's voice (stanza 2). Trumpet and drums kindle warlike feelings; flute and lute evoke the woes of hopeless love; and 'sharp violins' portray the pangs of jealous passions (stanzas 3–5). Finally, the greatest and purest power of music is personified in St Cecilia: Orpheus could move wild animals and inanimate nature with his lyre, but her organ-playing was so radiant that even an angel mistook it for celestial music (stanzas 6 and 7).

　　According to the autograph score, Handel composed the *Song for St Cecilia's Day* in nine days, between 15 and 24 September 1739, setting it for soprano, tenor and chorus and giving prominent roles to his instrumentalists. The arias concerned with depicting human passions are modelled on the conventional musical rhetoric of opera, but Handel makes charming use of the collocation of specific instrumental colours with particular passions. Jubal's lyre is represented by another kind of 'corded shell', the cello (reserving the lute for its mention in stanza 4), but otherwise Handel writes solos in each stanza for the instruments which Dryden specifies (apart from the third lyre mentioned, Orpheus's), apparently allowing for soloistic display: the cello line at the conclusion of 'What passion cannot Music raise' is marked *ad libitum*, as is the flute part during 'The soft complaining flute'.

Handel's word-painting in the outer movements achieves an extraordinary dramatic impact. Primordial chaos is brilliantly conveyed by inchoate melody and boldly modulating chords; the four temperaments thought to make up human characters are heard to 'leap' into their ordained places with spirited violin figuration; the first chorus contrasts massed 'heavenly harmony' with the single lines of voice and strings, and the 'diapason' note is a wittily emphasised pedal in the midst of the scales which illustrate 'all the compass of the notes'. For the almost scenic depiction of stanzas 6 and 7 Handel used a chorale-like melody and the organ solo (also marked *ad libitum*, and presumably played by the composer) to transport the listener into the realm of church music in the Larghetto 'But oh! what art', which is surprisingly followed by a very secular Hornpipe, alluding to Orpheus's taming of wild animals (heard running after his music in a long melisma). With another sharp contrast, the accompanied recitative 'But bright Cecilia raised' returns to music in a sacred sphere. The final tremendous chorus depicting the Last Judgement, with its declamatory, precentor-like soprano solos and extended fugue writing, seemingly traversing all the harmonies of the *musica universalis*, is clearly modelled on the English anthem.

Handel's two Cecilian odes show Handel using texts written for a uniquely English occasion to experiment with differing stylistic forms of English entertainment. The first performance of the *Song for St Cecilia's Day* formed part of his first ever all-English season, taking place at LINCOLN'S INN FIELDS on 22 November (St Cecilia's Day) 1739, and forming the third part of a concert that also included his 1736 setting of Dryden's Cecilian ode *ALEXANDER'S FEAST*, and thus contributing to the annual St Cecilia's Day festivals which English musicians had been holding each 22 November since the late seventeenth century. The *Song* is the more consciously 'English' work, acknowledging the tradition of Henry PURCELL's Cecilian odes, such as *Hail, bright Cecilia* (1692). Dryden reused 'the double, double, double beat Of the thund'ring drum' (stanza 3) for 'Come if you dare' in his and Purcell's *King Arthur* (1691) and Handel's setting of stanza 3 is especially Purcellian in its economical and varied melodic phrases, the continuity of the soloist's material in the chorus, and the sinfonia-like postlude.

For several movements, including the overture, Handel drew on Johann Gottlieb MUFFAT's harpsichord suites *Componimenti musicali* (published at Augsburg earlier in the same year). He amalgamated the borrowed material and his own musical ideas perfectly: to give just one example, 'But oh! what art' is based on the harmonic structure of a Grave movement from Muffat's Suite No. 3, but in the solo soprano part Handel echoes the German CHORALE 'Wachet auf, ruft uns die Stimme', the third stanza of which praises angelic music, and perhaps in doing so he was personally endorsing the Cecilian legend.

The solo parts were composed for the soprano Elisabeth Duparc ('La FRANCESINA') and the tenor John BEARD. After two performances, the newer ode was paired with *ACIS AND GALATEA* on four occasions during the 1739–40 season, and Handel repeated this double-bill in 1741 and at DUBLIN in 1742. The *Song* was also performed as the third part to L'*ALLEGRO, IL PENSEROSO ED IL MODERATO* – replacing 'il Moderato' – on various occasions between 1741 and 1755. CHRISTINE MARTIN (Trans. ANGELA BAIER)

See also ARRANGEMENTS, 2

Burrows
  (ed.), *Ode for St Cecilia's Day*, Novello Handel Edition (London, 2009)
A. Hicks, 'An *Ode for St Cecilia's Day/Cecilia, volgi un sguardo*' (CD booklet note, Hyperion CDA67463, 2004)
J. Hollander, *The Untuning of the Sky: Ideas of Music in English Poetry 1500–1700* (Princeton, 1961)
H. Jung, 'Caecilia oder die Macht der Affekte. John Drydens Oden und ihre Tradition', *Musik und Dichtung. Festschrift Viktor Pöschl*, ed. M. von Albrecht and W. Schubert (Frankfurt, 1990)
R. Luckett, 'St Cecilia and Music', *Proceedings of the Royal Musical Association* 99 (1972–3), 15–30
  'The Legend of St. Cecilia in English Literature: A Study', Ph.D. dissertation (University of Cambridge, 1972)
H. J. Marx, *Händels Oratorien, Oden und Serenaten* (Göttingen, 1998)
H.-E. Mittig, 'Fortschrittliches in Händels Cäcilienode HWV 76 – aus kunsthistorischer Sicht', *HJb* 53 (2007)
R. M. Myers, *Handel, Dryden and Milton* (London, 1956)
W. Seidel, 'Die Zauberflöte und die Cäcilienode – Über die Macht der Musik in Händels Ode und Mozarts Oper', *HJb* 53 (2007)
W. Siegmund-Schultze, 'Händels Cäcilienode HWV 76. Ihre Stellung im Gesamtwerk', *Kongreßbericht Stuttgart 1985*, vol. 2 (Kassel, 1987)

songs, HWV 218, 226, 228 and HWV Anh. B 011. Songs for solo voice and basso continuo were popular musical entertainments performed in theatres, pleasure gardens (such as VAUXHALL and RANELAGH) and concerts. They could be purchased for domestic use as single-sheet prints or anthologies. Over thirty songs in four different languages (English, German, French and Spanish) have been attributed to Handel. Many of these are ADAPTATIONS based on thematic material taken from his earlier arias or popular instrumental pieces prepared by someone other than the composer. However, Handel did turn some of his arias into songs: song arrangements of a French, Spanish and German aria each from *ALMIRA* and CANTATAS HWV 140 and 155 survive in an autograph entry in a songbook of English provenance; an aria from *ARIODANTE* provided the material for the patriotic song 'From scourging rebellion' (HWV 228[9]). The authenticity of the majority of these songs is unproven: only three have survived as autograph manuscripts (HWV 218, 226 and the chanson 'Quand on suit', HWV Anh. B 011). All others survive in printed editions with attributions to Handel of varying reliability, and it has been proved that HWV 228[12] and HWV 228[20] are spurious.

Most of Handel's songs are simple strophic songs similar to those sung in BALLAD OPERAS. The English-language songs composed for the stage are notable for their musical wit, inventive metrical structure and skilful decoration. 'I like the am'rous youth' (HWV 228[11]), first sung by Kitty CLIVE in *The Universal Passion* (James MILLER's adaptation of Shakespeare's *Much Ado about Nothing*) at DRURY LANE in 1737 has a simple melody but its musical motifs are ingeniously woven together. 'Love's but the frailty of the mind' (HWV 218), written for Clive to sing during William CONGREVE's *The Way of the World* at Drury Lane on

17 March 1740, subtly conveys the text's flippancy by using an independent metrical structure lying underneath the plain surface of the song. The authenticity of the song "Twas when the seas were roaring' ('The Melancholy Nymph', HWV 228[19]) is uncertain; it began to be attributed to Handel from c.1730, and it is a typical ballad with torn-off phrases and an unusual melody which strongly emphasises the words 'roaring' and 'deploring'. This distinctive song was reputedly included in John GAY's burlesque The what d'ye call it (Drury Lane, February 1715), and in 1728 Gay used it again in The BEGGAR'S OPERA with the new text 'How cruel are the traytors' and it became very popular.

At around the time of the JACOBITE rebellion in 1745, Handel composed two patriotic songs for male soloist and unison chorus: 'From scourging rebellion' (HWV 228[9]) celebrates the victory of the Duke of Cumberland (Prince WILLIAM) over the Jacobites in martial trumpet-like motifs, and 'Stand round, my brave boys' (HWV 228[18]) culminates in a sixfold repetition of the call 'Long live the King'. The latter song was premiered by Thomas LOWE during a performance of John VANBRUGH's The Relapse, or, Virtue in Danger (Drury Lane, 14 May 1745). Handel's Hunting Song (1751), featuring imitations of horn fanfares, was inspired by a witty line in a poem by Charles LEGH published in 1747: '"So Ho" cries the huntaman, hark to him "So Ho!"' . . . Such harmony Handel himself never knew.'   CHRISTINE MARTIN (Trans. ANGELA BAIER)

Burrows
   'Four New Handel Songs', MT 128/1730 (April 1987), 199–202
   (ed.), 'G. F. Handel, Songs and Cantatas for Soprano and Continuo' (Oxford, 1988)
O. E. Deutsch, 'Handel's Hunting Song', MT 83/1198 (Dec. 1942), 362–3
A. M. Friedlaender, 'Two Patriotic Songs by Handel', MT 66 (May 1925), 416–19
H. D. Johnstone, 'English Solo Song, c. 1710–1760', JRMA 95/1 (1968), 67–80
H. J. Marx and S. Voss, 'Die Händel zugeschriebenen Kompositionen I (Arien und Lieder, HWV Anh. B 001–033)', GHB XI (2006)
W. Barclay Squire, 'Handel in 1745', Riemann-Festschrift, ed. C. Mennicke (Leipzig, 1909)

Sons of the Clergy, Corporation of the. A charitable corporation established by royal charter in 1678, which celebrated an annual festival in London with a dinner and a church service. From 1697 the new ST PAUL'S CATHEDRAL became the venue for the service, and in 1709 the music there included, probably for the first time, an item with orchestral accompaniment. Works by PURCELL, CROFT and GREENE featured in the following years, but from 1731 the programmes were dominated by Handel's music. By then, both the services and the rehearsals of the music received regular notices in the newspapers.   DONALD BURROWS

Sorge il dì. See ACI, GALATEA E POLIFEMO

Sosarme, Re di Media, HWV 30. Italian opera. Handel completed the score on 4 February 1732, and it was first performed at the KING'S THEATRE on 15 February, only a fortnight after the unpopular EZIO had been withdrawn. The cast was as follows:

Sosarme, King of Media	SENESINO (castrato)
Haliate, King of Lydia	Giovanni Battista PINACCI (tenor)
Elmira, Haliate's daughter	Anna STRADA del Pò (soprano)

Argone, Haliate's estranged son and heir	Antonio CAMPIOLI (castrato)
Erenice, Queen of Lydia	Anna Bagnolesi (alto)
Melo, Haliate's illegitimate son	Francesca BERTOLLI (alto)
Altomaro, Melo's maternal grandfather	Antonio MONTAGNANA (bass)

The libretto was anonymously adapted from Antonio SALVI's *Dionisio, Re di Portogallo*. Handel might have attended a performance of the libretto's first setting by PERTI at Pratolino (PALAZZI, 2) in September 1707, only a few weeks before his his first Italian opera *RODRIGO* was produced in nearby FLORENCE. Perhaps he obtained a copy of the libretto at that time. The WORDBOOK clarifies the plot:

> Sosarmes . . . falling in love with Elmira . . . at the Report he heard of her Beauty, demanded her in Marriage of her Father, who readily assented: But about the Time that Elmira was preparing for her Departure to her Husband, a cruel Rebellion broke out in Lydia, which obliged the Princess to defer her Journey. The author of this Rebellion was Argones, the eldest Son and Successor of Haliates, prompted to it by a Jealousy he entertained, that his Father intended to advance his natural son Melus, whom he tenderly lov'd, to the Throne. When Argones had openly declared himself a Rebel against his Father, the latter was obliged to take up Arms, and besiege the City of Sardis, where his Son and the Rebels had shut themselves up, and by Treachery made themselves Masters of the Palace itself. Both the Besiegers, and those they besieged were equally obstinate, and the Animosity between them rose to such an Extremity, that the Father and Son (deceived by an ambitious Conseller) challenged each other to decide their Differences in a single Combat. Sosarmes, who sometime before had left Media with an Army . . . interposed as an impartial Mediator between the contending Parties; but his good Offices being defeated by the Iniquity of Altomarus, Haliates and Argones at last came to a duel, but Erenice, Melus, Elmira, and Sosarmes, interposing, prevented the Act of Parricide, and undeceiving the Father and Son, re-established them in a perfect Harmony.

Sosarme was performed eleven times. Viscount Percival (later 1st Earl of EGMONT) wrote in his diary that the opera 'takes with the town, and that justly, for it is one of the best I ever heard', while the compiler of COLMAN's *Opera Register* noted that it 'was for many Nights much crowded to some people's admiration'. The pamphlet *See and Seem Blind*, probably written by Aaron HILL, gives us a revealing caricature of a response to Handel's new operas premiered in the 1731–2 season, during which the composer also gave his first public performances of the oratorio *ESTHER*:

> We have likewise had two Operas, Etius and Sosarmes, the first most Masterly, the last most pleasing, and in my mind exceeding pretty: there are two Duetto's which Ravish me, and indeed the whole is vastly Genteel; (I am sorry I am so wicked) but I like one good Opera better than Twenty Oratorio's.

Handel had taken particular care to craft *Ezio* into a serious 'masterly' drama, but, when it failed to excite the London public, it seems that his priority for *Sosarme* was to make it as appealing and 'pleasing' as possible for his AUDIENCE.

The first page of the autograph manuscript reveals that the opera was initially called *Fernando, Re di Castiglia* and was set in Portugal. After completing approximately two-thirds of the score, Handel changed its title, location and most of the characters' names, and revised Acts I and II. The character names from *Fernando* were replaced by the names of their *Sosarme* alter egos: Dionisio (Dinis, or Dionysius, King of Portugal from 1279 to 1325 and founder of the University of Coimbra) was changed to Haliate, his illegitimate son Sancio became Melo, and his disgruntled heir Alfonso became Argone. The King's daughter Elvida became Elmira, and her lover Fernando (King of Castile from 1295 to 1312) became Sosarme. Queen Isabella, based on a historical figure canonised in 1626, became Erenice. Only the villain Altomaro retained his original name. Handel's motivation for making these changes is obscure, but Winton Dean suggested that it might have been done to avoid the libretto causing offence to the Portuguese, who were Britian's oldest political allies.

Handel rejected a substantial amount of essential recitative prior to the first performance, including more than a hundred bars from Act I. Perhaps the unpopularity of METASTASIO's long literary recitatives in *Ezio* caused the composer to hastily over-compensate by removing chunks from eleven scenes in Acts I and II, thereby damaging the contributions of every character. However, the score contains plenty of attractive and imaginative music. Elmira's 'Rendi 'l sereno al ciglio' (I.ii) is the only aria Handel ever composed in B major, and Act I concludes with Elmira's spectacular coloratura aria 'Dite pace', in which contrasting slow and fast sections convey her emotional turmoil as she veers between contemplation and tempestuous indignation. Haliate's venomous 'La turba adulatrice' (I.viii) is an exceptionally incisive and virtuosic rage aria, and Erenice's frustration with the feuding men in her family is potently depicted in II.xii by her launching directly into a presto ('Vado al campo') without an introductory ritornello.

The title hero is almost absent from the first half of the opera. We hear reports of his bravery, but see none of his deeds. Having been led to believe that Sosarme has died in battle, we see him reunited with his fiancée Elmira as he recuperates from minor injuries, and the lovers sing the exquisite reconciliation duet 'Per le porte del tormento' (II.viii). The lovers sing another duet in the final scene ('Tu caro, caro sei'), and Handel's autograph contains a rare indication of how he wanted the basso continuo section to play: Elmira is accompanied by the violins and 'cembalo primo con i suoi bassi' (first harpsichord and bass), Sosarme by four violas in unison and 'cembalo seconda colla teorba, e i suoi bassi' (second harpsichord with theorbo and bass); when the voices sing together the continuo groups combine, but are instructed to play quietly ('mà pp') (INSTRUMENTATION; PERFORMANCE PRACTICE).

BURNEY ranked the score amongst Handel's 'most pleasing theatrical productions', but the composer only revived *Sosarme* in April 1734 for three poorly attended performances, which caused Mrs Pendarves (later DELANY) to lament that it was 'vexatious to have such music neglected'. An abridged recording conducted by Anthony Lewis was issued by L'Oiseau-Lyre in 1955 (RECORDINGS), and the first modern STAGING of the opera was by Unicorn Opera at Abingdon in 1970. Since then it has been infrequently revived, although a version of *Fernando* edited by Alan Curtis was issued on CD in 2007.   DAVID VICKERS

Burney
Dean, *Operas*
   'Handel's *Sosarme*: A Puzzle Opera', *Essays on Opera* (Oxford, 1990)
Deutsch
Harris, *Librettos*
Strohm
D. Vickers 'Handel: *Fernando* (the first *Sosarme*)', CD booklet note (Virgin, 3 65483 2, 2007)

sources and collections. Handel's works have come down to us not only in his autograph manuscripts but also in a large number of secondary manuscripts written by his own COPYISTS, the chief of whom from about 1719 was John Christopher SMITH SENIOR. The most important collection of these copies consists of the scores which Handel used in his performances (known as performing or conducting scores, 'Direktionspartituren' in German), but there are also other collections copied on commission for various patrons who were his friends and admirers. These men wanted to have their own libraries of his music, because with the exception of some of the instrumental works much of the printed material available was inadequate and incomplete – the CLUER and WALSH editions of the operas, for instance, routinely omitted the secco recitatives, and even when advertised as being 'in Score' often left out one or more of the orchestral parts; it was probably also a matter of prestige to have one's own collection.

For no other great composer is there such a quantity of contemporary copies of the music, and while the performing scores are the most important, the others can be significant because they sometimes have music of which the autographs have disappeared (the whole of the *WATER MUSIC* and *ADMETO* are the best-known examples): typical instances of such material are movements inserted for revivals or rewritten for different singers, which just happened to be in the performing score when a particular commission was being fulfilled, but then were lost. Furthermore the copyists, who knew the composer and worked alongside him and so understood what his intentions were, often added dynamics and other details lacking in the principal sources. Editors preparing modern editions are obliged to collate all known copies, and can obtain from them information which clarifies passages which are otherwise confused or obscure. TERENCE BEST

1. Autographs
2. Performing scores
3. The Aylesford Collection
4. The Barrett Lennard Collection
5. The British Library
6. The Chandos Collection
7. The Gerald Coke Handel Collection
8. The Newman Flower Collection
9. The Granville Collection
10. The Hall Collection
11. The Kiesewetter Collection
12. The Malmesbury Collection
13. The Santini Collection
14. The Shaftesbury Collection
15. The Shaw–Hellier Collection
16. The Smith Collection

1. Autographs

Of the major composers, Handel has been one of the most fortunate in the survival of his autograph music. He wrote on good-quality paper and he seems to have taken care to keep his composition-draft scores together, so that it is possible to regard them as a 'collection' from an early stage; the circumstances of transmission following his death largely kept the archive intact. About 7,700 folios of his musical autographs survive, in contrast to the small number of his letters. Of the major works composed in London from 1710 onwards, only the autograph of *Admeto* has been lost completely; AMADIGI and the BROCKES PASSION are represented by fragments, but otherwise the losses have been minimal. It is perhaps not surprising that the serious lacunae involve music written in the early part of his career, before he had a settled home. No autographs from his early HALLE years survive, nor any material from the operas composed for HAMBURG: according to MAINWARING's biography, Handel left two 'chests-full' of music (not necessarily his own compositions) when he departed from that city. Only one autograph, of the early setting of *Laudate pueri Dominum* (HWV 236) (Italian and Latin CHURCH MUSIC), may date from the period before his arrival in Italy; the Italian-period works from 1707 to 1709, apart from Il TRIONFO DEL TEMPO, are surprisingly well represented.

In his will Handel bequeathed his 'Musick Books' to 'Christopher Smith' (HANDEL, 8), and the collection of autographs as it stood in 1759 passed to J. C. SMITH SENIOR, along with the performing scores and probably the remainder of Handel's musical library (HANDEL, 19). On Smith's death in 1763 this passed in turn to his son. The performing scores were a necessary resource for the oratorio seasons that the Smiths continued at the London theatres during the 1760s; it is probable that the autographs were also referred to from time to time, as copy-texts for new library scores or for incidental revisions to the oratorios. It is perhaps remarkable that the opera scores, which had less immediate relevance, were preserved with equal care.

In 1774 Smith junior was involved for the last time in the London performances; he retired to BATH, and the part of his collection that included the autographs was subsequently presented to King GEORGE III. The circumstances of this are uncertain, but the transfer had taken place by 1785, when Charles BURNEY described 'Original Manuscripts in the Possession of his Majesty: Amounting to Eighty-two Volumes'. These volumes seem to have been put into order for binding by Frederic Nicolay, a musical court official; by the mid-nineteenth century they were part of the Royal Music Library at BUCKINGHAM PALACE, an ever-expanding general collection that was housed successively in an upper-storey room and a basement. In March 1911 King George V approved the deposit of the Royal Music Library, as it then stood, on permanent loan to the British Museum, where a special room (completed in 1919) was created for it in a new building. William Barclay SQUIRE, who was in charge of the collections of printed music at the Museum and had probably negotiated the transfer, made some rearrangement of the volume contents and prepared a detailed catalogue. In November 1957 Queen Elizabeth II presented the Library to the Trustees of the British Museum; it passed to the ownership of the British Library in the general transfer of the Museum's library departments in 1973, and moved to the new British Library site at St Pancras which opened in 1997.

The presently known autographs which are not in the Royal Music Library must have become detached during the eighteenth century: Handel may have given away some pages as presentations, but most of the separation was probably accidental. The largest group is that formerly owned by Richard (Viscount) FITZWILLIAM who owned the autograph of one of the Cannons Anthems (ANTHEMS, 2) by 1778, and a further miscellaneous collection (then in six volumes) by 1799. These passed as part of the founder's bequest on the establishment of the FITZWILLIAM MUSEUM in CAMBRIDGE, where they were rearranged and catalogued in the 1890s. Other autographs, none of them comprising more than a few leaves, have been discovered and acquired by collectors and libraries in Britain, Germany Austria, Switzerland and the USA.

Many of the autographs, even of last-draft stages in the music, include revisions that illuminate Handel's COMPOSITIONAL PROCESSES and the circumstances for which particular movements were written. In many cases, however, the music that they record underwent further revision as it came to performance: in that respect, the autographs are authoritative as sources, but not definitive.

DONALD BURROWS

2. Performing scores

('Conducting scores' and 'Harpsichord scores'; known in German as '*Direktionspartituren*'). When rehearsing and conducting his larger vocal works Handel used conducting scores written by copyists. These contained, unlike his compositional autographs, the specific version of a work needed for a particular performance. These manuscripts are (together with the PASTICCIOS performed by Handel) almost completely extant from 1720 onwards. From the years before 1720 there are a number of handwritten scores, which Handel obviously kept in his archives so that he could later revise the works, whereas the conducting scores dating from the years before 1720 seem to have remained with the impresarios responsible for the performances, presumably together with the part-books, and are now lost (with the exception of the Roman oratorios).

From 1720 (beginning with the second season of the Royal Academy of Music (OPERA COMPANIES, 2), when a new agreement with the directors seems to have been made) Handel kept the conducting scores himself. They were now used as archive scores as well. Like those, they contain handwritten annotations by Handel concerning his revisions, in the case of the oratorios also the singers' names, if deemed necessary for copying or arranging the voice parts. They are recognisable as conducting scores because later revisions and replacements are inserted in a particular manner: whereas in other manuscripts cues are sufficient to indicate the exact place where replacing or additional music on separate sheets was to be inserted, in the conducting scores the music is arranged in an easily legible continuous way, in order to avoid leafing back, by pasting over and recopying bars and folding or tacking together sheets. Some of the conducting scores contain handwritten corrections and additions by Handel.

From 1730, approximately from the beginning of the so-called Second Academy (OPERA COMPANIES, 3), Handel also collected the harpsichord scores (*Cembalopartituren*) of his operas. These scores were produced by a number of copyists including John Christopher Smith senior, the main copyist of the conducting scores. They contain at least the bass line of the instrumental and choral parts and arias, in recitatives also the vocal line. In most scores the vocal part of the arias is contained as well. Some harpsichord scores are extended into full scores or at least leave room so that the parts can be filled up later. If the changes in a work for a new performance were too substantial, a new conducting score was prepared.

Handel bequeathed his 'musick books', among them the performing scores, to his friend and principal copyist Smith senior. After Handel's death they were used for the annual oratorio performances until 1774 by John Christopher Smith junior and John STANLEY, until 1786 by Stanley and Thomas Linley, and until 1795 by Linley and Samuel ARNOLD. The no longer needed first conducting score of *MESSIAH*, dated 1742, was probably the first to be auctioned off and is now in the Tenbury collection of the Bodleian Library in OXFORD. Some early archive scores ended up in the Royal Music Library (now in the British Library). The remainder of the collection was handed down in the Smith family (RIVERS) and sold between 1851 and 1856 to the Bristol bookseller Thomas KERSLAKE, who catalogued them. They were purchased by Victor SCHOELCHER in 1856, who catalogued them again. He recognised the importance of the scores to the Händel Gesamtausgabe and, advised by Friedrich CHRYSANDER, sold them, with a few exceptions, to a Hamburg syndicate. These exceptions were some pasticcios compiled by Handel, now in the British Library, and a few harpsichord scores which Schoelcher regarded as doubles but which were bought by Chrysander for his private library later. Today the collection is in the Hamburg Staats- und Universitätsbibliothek 'Carl von Ossietzky'.

HANS DIETER CLAUSEN (Trans. ANGELA BAIER)

3. The Aylesford Collection

The music books once owned by Charles JENNENS. His music library contained copies of Handel's works, a few autographs, early EDITIONS, and a substantial collection of Italian manuscripts by Alessandro SCARLATTI, VIVALDI and many others, which were formerly part of Cardinal OTTOBONI's library. From 1725 to 1727 Jennens was a SUBSCRIBER to Handel's operas, and it seems that he started collecting manuscripts of Handel's works from about 1728. In the mid-1740s he decided to acquire a full set of Handel's works, full scores and sets of parts, although this project was never completed, and the material was never used for performances.

Most of the manuscripts were copied by the Smith circle, mostly by S2. Two were written by Jennens himself. The copies were mainly taken from the autograph, and Jennens was particularly interested in early and rejected versions. He compared his copy with the autograph and other sources, corrected errors and added bass figures, and altered the text underlay in *Messiah* and *L'ALLEGRO*. Jennens had access to Handel's manuscripts, and vice versa: Handel studied Jennens's Italian manuscripts and used material from them in his own works (BORROWINGS).

The manuscripts, which Jennens bequeathed to his relative the 3rd Earl of AYLESFORD, contain unique sources for some works, and occasionally movements and versions that cannot be found in other sources. The instrumental parts preserve important information about the use of oboes and the basso continuo instruments. The former library is now scattered: part of the collection, mainly prints, was sold in 1873; the rest at Sotheby's in 1918. More than 400 volumes are now at Manchester in the Newman Flower Collection (see 8 below), but some manuscripts were purchased by William Barclay SQUIRE (which he donated to the British Museum), and others went to the Fitzwilliam Museum and to the Library of Congress in Washington DC.　　　ANNETTE LANDGRAF

4. The Barrett Lennard Collection

This is named after Henry Barrett LENNARD, its last private owner before it was deposited in the Fitzwilliam Museum in 1902. It consists of sixty-seven bound manuscript volumes, housed in a mahogany bookcase which was said to be Handel's. The ownership of the collection has been traced back to Thomas Greatorex in the early nineteenth century, but its earlier history remains uncertain; the nineteenth-century scholar Victor Schoelcher wrote that the bookcase and its contents passed from Handel to John Christopher Smith senior, but BURNEY reported in 1785 that the publisher Walsh had bought the volumes from Handel, and that Walsh's successor Wright still owned them; there is certainly internal evidence that some of them were used by Wright for the preparation of his editions in the second half of the eighteenth century.

The volumes are bound in leather with four different styles: the first binding style was used for forty-nine of them, whose music pages were copied between about 1736 to 1741, and appear to be a foundation collection; after 1741 there was an interval, and copying was resumed in the 1750s and 1760s; the last binding style dates from the nineteenth century. The contents of the collection are as follows: all the operas (except *ALMIRA*, *AGRIPPINA*, Il *PASTOR FIDO* (1712 version), *IMENEO* and *DEIDAMIA*); all the oratorio-style works (except Il *trionfo del Tempo e del Disinganno*, La *RESURREZIONE*, the Brockes *Passion*, *SEMELE*, the *OCCASIONAL ORATORIO* and The *TRIUMPH OF TIME AND TRUTH*); the ceremonial anthems, four volumes of church music, one each of Italian CHAMBER DUETS and cantatas, two of concertos (including the *Water Music*).

TERENCE BEST

5. The British Library

On its foundation in 1993 the British Library received the collections of manuscripts, printed music and books from the British Museum, which included major collections of Handel material from the Royal Music Library (printed editions and manuscript copies as well as Handel's autographs) and the Granville Collection. These were supplemented by other scores of Handel's music that the Museum had acquired, by gift or purchase, in the course of a century and a half, among them a substantial group of manuscript copies purchased from the collection of Julian Marshall in 1880–1, and some autograph leaves that came as part of the Zweig Collection in 1986. In addition to the Library's rich musical holdings of manuscripts and printed editions, it has many essential items of Handelian relevance in printed books, including original wordbooks for the operas and oratorios, and collections of eighteenth-century newspapers.

DONALD BURROWS

6. The Chandos Collection

James Brydges, Earl of Carnarvon and from April 1719 1st Duke of CHANDOS, compiled a music library that included music by Handel, including works written especially for Brydges's own musicians at CANNONS between 1717 and 1720. The library was catalogued in August 1720 with an addendum in October 1721. The manuscript Handel items appear to have been presentation copies. Some of the manuscript volumes from the Cannons Music Library devolved through Brydges's granddaughter to the Leigh family of Stoneleigh Abbey and survive in the British Library, the Foundling Museum and the Gemeentemuseum at the Hague. These include scores and two instrumental parts for the Cannons Anthems and Te Deum (ANTHEMS, 2; TE DEUM, 3) and a single Italian cantata (HWV 161). Items whose history subsequent to 1721 and present whereabouts cannot be determined with certainty include manuscript copies of *ACIS AND GALATEA*, 'The Oratorium' (*ESTHER*), *Amadigi*, *RADAMISTO*, *MUZIO SCEVOLA*, *ETERNAL SOURCE OF LIGHT DIVINE*, and the *Utrecht Te Deum* (TE DEUM, 1) and Utrecht *JUBILATE*.   GRAYDON BEEKS

7. The Gerald Coke Handel Collection

Gerald COKE's collection was assembled during the greater part of the twentieth century, and includes manuscripts, printed scores, books, librettos, journals and a wealth of ephemeral material including sale catalogues, programmes, handbills and tickets. There is also a significant collection of artworks including oil paintings, ceramics, a ROUBILIAC model for the WESTMINSTER ABBEY monument, drawings and a large number of eighteenth-century prints relating to Handel and his contemporaries. Among the manuscripts are letters from Handel and his contemporaries, as well as the holograph manuscript of Handel's will. Gerald Coke acquired any scores which differed from those already in his collection and thus there are now few important gaps in the printed music before 1800. Coke also acquired the manuscripts of the Shaftesbury Collection (see 15 below), several items from the descendants of Charles Jennens, including the Jennens–Holdsworth correspondence, and the collection of the Handel scholar William C. SMITH. The endowment attached to the Collection, which is now housed and displayed in the Foundling Museum (MUSEUMS, 1) under the auspices of the Gerald Coke Handel Foundation, enables further additions to be made.   KATHARINE HOGG

8. The Newman Flower Collection

When the Aylesford Collection (see 3 above) was sold in 1918, Newman Flower bought the majority of the full scores, instrumental and vocal parts of Handel's works. He subsequently added further manuscripts, early editions and printed WORDBOOKS. In 1965 the collection was incorporated into the Henry Watson Library in Manchester.   ANNETTE LANDGRAF

9. The Granville Collection

Thirty-seven folio-size volumes of manuscript scores of Handel's music, including operas, oratorios, English church music, Italian duets and cantatas, and instrumental music, originally copied in the 1740s for Bernard GRANVILLE, whose London home was near Handel's. The present-day series, which still has its original uniform bindings, matches the description given by Charles Burney in 1785 apart from the loss of one item, of 'single Songs in Eight Parts'. The collection remained in the Granville family until it was purchased by the British Museum in 1915, and is now British Library Egerton MSS 2910–46.

DONALD BURROWS

10. The Hall Collection

Dr James Hall (1899–1973) was a medical practitioner in Deal and Walmer in Kent. He was a Handel enthusiast, and assembled a collection mostly of early printed editions, and a few manuscripts, among which were three copied in the 1740s for FREDERICK, Prince of Wales (*BELSHAZZAR*, *ALEXANDER BALUS*, *JOSEPH AND HIS BRETHREN*). The collection was acquired by Princeton University in 1974.

TERENCE BEST

11. The Kiesewetter Collection

A sizeable collection of sources put together by Raphael Georg KIESEWET-TER (1773–1850) with assistance and support from scholars, critics, composers (MENDELSSOHN) and collectors (Aloys FUCHS, Fortunato SANTINI). His collection included a number of works by Handel, such as *Agrippina*, the Utrecht Te Deum, *JUDAS MACCABAEUS*, and CHAMBER DUETS AND TRIOS. He bequeathed it to the Austrian National Library (*Österreichische Nationalbibliothek*).

WALTER KREYSZIG

12. The Malmesbury Collection

This was assembled by Elizabeth LEGH, and consists of thirty-five volumes which were copied for her between 1715 and 1734, the year of her death (for the acquisition of the collection by the Malmesbury family see her entry). The collection, now deposited at the Hampshire Record Office in Winchester, is one of the most important for scholars and editors, because whatever arrangement Elizabeth had with Handel's copyists meant that she was often the first to receive a copy, sometimes even before the performing score was finalised; consequently her scores have valuable information about the way in which a work was created, and some have music found nowhere else. The collection has all the operas composed in London from *RINALDO* to *ARIANNA* (except *SILLA*), six volumes of vocal works composed between 1713 and 1719, four volumes of keyboard music (both original compositions and arrangements of overtures and other works), and one volume of sonatas and concertos. Two volumes of cantatas are in the Bodleian Library in Oxford, and one of keyboard music is in the Gerald Coke Handel Collection.

13. The Santini Collection

The collection was created in Rome by Fortunato SANTINI in the first half of the nineteenth century. It was described by MENDELSSOHN as 'one of the most complete libraries of ancient Italian music', and was sought after by many major libraries in Europe. Just before Santini's death in 1861 it was purchased on behalf of the Bishop of Münster; and it is now in the Diocesan library of the Bischöfliches Priesterseminar in that city. Twenty-two volumes contain music from Handel's Italian period, and the importance of the collection is that as well as contemporary copies, including the performing score of *La Resurrezione*, there are several works wholly or partly in the composer's autograph, including the complete score of the cantata *AH, CRUDEL, NEL PIANTO MIO*, the motet 'O qualis de coelo' (partly autograph) (Italian and Latin CHURCH MUSIC), and the cantata HENDEL, NON PUÒ MIA MUSA. A number of other manuscripts have annotations by the composer. TERENCE BEST

14. The Shaftesbury Collection

The 4th Earl of SHAFTESBURY (1711–71) was an early patron of Handel who assembled a significant collection of printed and manuscript scores which have remained in an excellent state of preservation since the eighteenth century. Over fifty manuscripts survive, many in the hand of John Christopher Smith senior, representing the full range of Handel's major works. The manuscript scores are now part of the Gerald Coke Collection (see 7 above), although the Shaftesbury family has retained two volumes of particular family interest. The printed scores are part of the Handel House Museum collection (MUSEUMS, 3).

KATHARINE HOGG

15. The Shaw–Hellier Collection

The music collection assembled by Samuel Hellier (1736–84), now at Birmingham University Library, includes a substantial group of early printed editions of Handel's music, manuscript scores (or printed scores with manuscript insertions) from the 1760s, and manuscript performing parts, copied by Oxford-based scribes. The part-books, for oratorios, odes and English church music, may have been intended to serve performances in Worcestershire, where Hellier had an estate, but the pristine state of the original spine-bindings suggests that they remained in his library. The collection also included eighteenth-century musical instruments, which are now in the Russell Collection at Edinburgh.

16. The Smith Collection

A group of large folio-size manuscript scores of Handel's English oratorios, odes and church music, with one matching volume of printed editions, bound in red morocco with gold tooling, some incorporating royal insignia; thirty-two volumes are in the Royal Music Library collection at the British Library; a further three volumes now at Princeton University, and one at the Bodleian Library, Oxford, probably once belonged with them. The 'Smith' title, which has been associated variously with John Christopher Smith junior and the collector Robert Smith (1741–1810), is of doubtful relevance. The earliest fourteen manuscript volumes may have been copied for Frederick, Prince of Wales, in the late 1740s, and the rest were added in the 1760s, probably for King George III. The collection was formalised, with engraved title pages, in 1772–3. DONALD BURROWS

T. Best (ed.), *Handel Collections and their History* (Oxford, 1993) (contains extended essays, with tables of contents, on the following collections: Hamburg (performing scores), Malmesbury, Aylesford, Shaftesbury, Barrett Lennard, Chandos, Shaw–Hellier, Hall, Santini)

D. Burrows, 'The "Granville" and "Smith" Collections of Handel Manuscripts', *Sundry Sorts of Music Books: Essays on the British Library Collections, Presented to O. W. Neighbour on his 70th birthday*, ed. C. Banks, A. Searle and M. Turner (London, 1993)
  'The Royal Music Library and its Handel Collection', *Electronic British Library Journal* (2009): www.bl.uk/eblj/2009articles/article2.html

D. Burrows and M. Ronish, *A Catalogue of Handel's Musical Autographs* (Oxford, 1994)

H. D. Clausen, *Händels Direktionspartituren ('Handexemplare')*, Hamburg, 1972

R. King, 'New Light on Handel's Musical Library', *MQ* 81/1 (Spring 1997), 109–38

A. D. Walker, *George Frideric Handel: The Newman Flower Collection in the Henry Watson Music Library* (Manchester, 1972)

South Sea Company. Founded in 1711, the company was granted a monopoly for trade with Spanish South America. In fact, the company did very little trading. Its main goal was the retirement of the national debt of £9 million by selling shares to individuals who received interest in return. The opening up of a large market for private investment and the extensive promotion of the opportunity led in 1717 to a speculative mania, driving the price of shares unrealistically high. In 1720, the South Sea Bubble burst, ruining many investors and leading to government oversight of trade through the Bank of England. Handel bought £500 of South Sea Stock around autumn of 1715, but he seems to have sold these shares before the crash, as his name appears on no subscription lists from 1720.

ELLEN T. HARRIS

See also HANDEL, 17

J. Carswell, *The South Sea Bubble* (London, 1960)
E. T. Harris, 'Handel the Investor', ML 85/4 (2004), 521–75

Spande ancor a mio dispetto, HWV 165. One of only two instrumental cantatas Handel wrote for bass voice, this is accompanied by violins and basso continuo. Paper evidence of the autograph relates the work, on the one hand, with continuo cantatas that can be tentatively associated with the patronage of Cardinal OTTO-BONI in ROME (1707), and, on the other, with 'Apollo e Dafne' (*La* TERRA È LIBERATA) in VENICE and HANOVER (1709/10). As in the other bass cantata, CUOPRE TALVOLTA IL CIELO, the text describes violent tempests raging in the air and in the singer's heart. Handel depicts the stormy images with angular lines, fast runs and vocal leaps of up to two octaves. ELLEN T. HARRIS

Spanish Succession, War of the (1701–14). The war arose when the last Habsburg King of Spain, Carlos II, died without legitimate issue. The Austrian Habsburgs and French Bourbons both laid claim to Spain and Spanish possessions in the southern Netherlands and Italy. Various attempts had been made to resolve the succession issue prior to Carlos's death through the negotiation of Partition Treaties between Louis XIV and William III, although the death of a compromise candidate before Carlos himself meant these were ultimately fruitless. Louis XIV backed the claims of his grandson, Philip, while the Habsburgs supported those of Archduke Charles. The war was fought in several theatres: the Italian peninsula, the Low Countries, southern Germany, Spain and in America. The main combatants were France, Spain and some of German princes (including the Elector of Bavaria) on one side and Britain, the United Provinces, the Austrian Habsburgs and a collection of German princes including the Electors of Hanover and Brandenburg on the other. The forces of the Grand Alliance, as Louis XIV's opponents were known, enjoyed some early successes. Gibraltar was captured from Spain in 1704. The Duke of MARLBOROUGH and Prince Eugene of Savoy were able to halt the advance of Franco-Bavarian armies marching on Vienna at Blenheim in southern Bavaria in August 1704. The Bavarians subsequently withdrew from the war. The Grand Alliance, directed and largely financed by Britain and the United Provinces, reduced the threat posed by Louis XIV in western Europe. By late 1706, Marlborough had largely conquered the southern Netherlands and Prince Eugene had taken Spanish possessions in northern Italy. The Grand Alliance was much less successful in removing Philip from Spain where he had built up considerable support in Castile. Continuing conflict in Spain delayed an overall settlement – Louis XIV had been willing to negotiate from 1705–6 and the Dutch were keen to settle by 1708. In 1710 a new TORY ministry, led by Robert Harley and Henry St John came to power in Britain. They moved quickly to end the conflict. A peace agreement was signed in April 1713 at Utrecht. Britain and France had the greatest say in shaping the treaty and, consequently, some German princes, including the future GEORGE I, felt betrayed by it. The treaty was celebrated in Handel's Utrecht Te Deum (see Te Deum, 5).   ANDREW C. THOMPSON

H. Kamen, *The War of Succession in Spain, 1700–1715* (London, 1969)

Splenda l'alba in oriente, HWV 166. Italian cantata for alto voice, two recorders, oboe, strings and continuo. The gathering numbers of the autograph suggest that only a fragment has survived, and the paper type indicates that it was composed in London between 1711 and 1713. The extant music consists of two arias linked by a recitative, and the text seems to have been specifically intended for St Cecilia's Day (22 November): the glory of virtue is exalted in a triple-time aria (marked 'A tempo giusto e staccato'), a recitative petitions St Cecilia to grant that her followers will imitate her excellence, and the aria 'La virtute è un vero nume' reiterates the opening aria's literary subject. In 1736 Handel reused the words for parts of CECILIA, VOLGI UN SGUARDO.   DAVID VICKERS

H. J. Marx (ed.), *Kantaten mit Instrumenten III*, HHA V/5 (Kassel, 1999)

Squire, William Barclay (b. London, 16 Oct. 1855; d. London, 13 Jan. 1927). English musical scholar and librarian. In 1885 he was appointed to the staff of the British Museum, with special responsibility for printed music. He retired in 1920, but was subsequently appointed Honorary Curator of the Royal Music Library, which King George V had deposited at the Museum in 1911. Part I of Squire's catalogue of the Library, which covers the Handel manuscripts (including the volumes of autographs) was published in 1927 (SOURCES AND COLLECTIONS, 1; 5); it also includes items from the Aylesford Collection that he had bought at the auction sale in 1918, and had added to the Royal Music Library. Squire was also responsible for catalogues of the music collections (including Handel items) at the British Museum, WESTMINSTER ABBEY and the Royal College of Music.

DONALD BURROWS

Stadtgymnasium. The young Handel was probably instructed in the standard subjects of his time at HALLE's Lutheran Stadtgymnasium. From 1565 it was housed in the former Franciscan monastery which had been dissolved by the sovereign Prince in 1561. The main building of HALLE UNIVERSITY has been located on the same spot since 1834. Only two street names, 'Schulstraße' (School Street) and 'Barfüßerstraße' (Street of the Discalced Monks), provide reminders of the preceding building. The statutes of the Gymnasium, which have been preserved, indicate that music lessons were part of the syllabus. The school also had three choirs, of varying musical quality, which formed the 'Stadtsingechor'. This boys' choir still exists.   GÖTZ TRAXDORF (Trans. ANGELA BAIER)

W. Serauky, *Musikgeschichte der Stadt Halle*, vol. 1 (Halle, 1935)

staging

> 1. Opera production in the eighteenth century
> 2. Handel in the modern theatre

1. Opera production in the eighteenth century

Opera production in the eighteenth century was not 'production' in the manner in which it is understood today. The most important difference is that most eighteenth-century London performances consisted of newly written (or, in the case of pasticcios and local adaptations, newly contrived) pieces; to recognise the full implications of this fact is to recognise the fundamental difference between an opera house of today, and one in which Handel would have worked. In preparing an opera, the question for the theatre was 'how will we make this work?' rather than 'what is it about?' Operas were often reworked and reshaped during the rehearsal process, particularly if it was a PASTICCIO, and/or the singers were exercising 'choice of book' by replacing their arias for ones they felt were more suitable. Just how, when and by whom this was done varied depending on the balance of power in the company; it might be the prima donna, the impresario, the composer, the actor-manager or the prompter: examples of all of these figures in charge of the rehearsal process can be found in operas staged in the eighteenth-century London theatres. Very little is known about the preparation of Handel's own operas, but they escaped such full-scale interference through a combination of the stature of their composer (which gave him authority over the rehearsal process) and the fact that he was, for much of his time in the opera house, also impresario.

As such varied lines of authority suggest, 'stage production' in the modern sense was unknown; the focus was on a singer's individual performance, and on a set of staging conventions which included prescribed flats for entries and exits, stage positions and so on. The singers had, of course, to be able to act; their gestures had to be appropriate, their manner engaging and their ornaments flamboyant (but tasteful!) if they were to be successful on the stage. Further, many production details which are now the preserve of the director were in Handel's time dealt with by the prompter, who was also responsible for actually running the performances, or perhaps by the adapter of the libretto (e.g. HAYM or ROLLI). Some details can be deduced about the staging of Handel's operas from the copious stage directions in the printed librettos (WORDBOOKS), often modified in the composer's autographs, performing scores and copies (SOURCES AND COLLECTIONS).

In terms of design, sets and costumes used in busy eighteenth-century opera houses were visually spectacular but not necessarily opera specific. The theatre possessed a group of stock sets – a temple, say, and a wood, a scene with tents, a cavern and so on – and an impresario would, at the beginning of the opera year, put the sets in order for the coming season. The same applied to the costumes, which for most of the century (and certainly during Handel's time) were, for the heroes, a contemporary costume based in some way on

28. Caricature of Senesino, Cuzzoni and Berenstadt performing at the King's Theatre, etching by John Vanderbank, c.1723.

Roman military dress, with plumed helmets and other accessories, while the heroines' used some of the same accessories, but were a heightened version of contemporary street dress (see Figure 28). There were exceptions; those playing exotic roles such as an oriental despot might have been given a turban, and gods and goddesses frequently carried an associated symbol; Zeus could, for example, carry thunderbolts.

A new opera would, exceptionally, have special sets and costumes both of which would form part of the advertising for that opera; in London, such new designs were usually touted using a version of the phrase 'with entire new Scenes, Dresses and Decorations, both for the Opera and Dances'. But sometimes, halfway through the season, a new opera would sometimes be advertised as having 'a new set', a trifling attempt to attract the public with novelty in the middle of a run. Some operas required special scenic effects, but these were in the minority.

No specific set and designs survive for any Handel opera, and it is doubtful whether any such designs ever existed. In scenographic terms, Handel's operas can be viewed in three phases. Handel's early operas – *RINALDO*, *Il PASTOR FIDO*, *TESEO*, *SILLA* and *AMADIGI* – come from the period during which the work of the Queen's Theatre (from 1714 the KING'S THEATRE) was influenced by English dramatick opera, a genre which from its beginnings in the 1670s had employed spectacular scenes, machines and transformations as its *raison d'être*. From the arrival of Italian opera in 1705 until the mid-1710s, there were attempts to perform dramatick operas alongside the newly imported variety, and this group of early Italian operas contains more spectacle than those in the second and third groups. Marco Ricci is the only designer known to have been associated with the Opera during this period. The scenes used at the Opera in the second group – consisting of some seventeen operas between 1720 and 1728 – can be associated with artists Roberto CLERICI, Giovanni Servandoni, Joseph GOUPY and Pieter Tillemans. The few illustrations of Handel's operas date from this second period, but are mostly caricatures; they suggest that the sets were of a fairly straightforward, symmetrical baroque variety, with nothing specific to the opera supposedly being performed. The evidence of the librettos suggests very little spectacle and few opportunities for machines; the style of the whole repertory during this period has the air of necessity prevailing over luxury. The third group consists of the operas staged through the 1730s to Handel's last, DEIDAMIA, in 1741; only the scene designer John DEVOTO can be associated with the Opera during this period, which did, however, see a return to spectacle (although at a much-diminished level). This return has been attributed to the need to compete with the fantasy-filled pantomimes, and it can be assumed that the efforts of the painters and machinists were either tailored to – or reflected in – the staging indications that can be found in the librettos for Handel's operas during this last period.

2. Handel in the modern theatre

No Handel opera was staged anywhere between 1754 and 1920; this bald statistic has been understood as 'the most remarkable phenomen[on] in the history of art' (Dean, *Operas*). In fact, major works by composers as varied as Monteverdi, Cavalli, GLUCK and MOZART also remained unperformed during the same period, the opera repertory still favouring what was new over what was old. But the 1920s saw productions of many works by these composers; a series of those by Handel was undertaken by Oskar HAGEN in GÖTTINGEN in adaptations to make them 'suitable' for modern performance. These alterations – which included the rewriting of the castrato roles to suit modern voice types, the use of German texts and heavily rearranged scores – are to us drastic, but they did at least put the composer's works back on the stage. Among the landmark productions of Handel's operas in the post-Second World War years have been Zeffirelli's staging at La Fenice of ALCINA with Joan Sutherland in the title role, *Xerxes* (SERSE) directed by Nicholas Hytner at the English National Opera in 1985 (a production still in the repertory over twenty years later) and GIULIO CESARE, again at the English National Opera, with the experienced Handel interpreter Janet Baker in the title role. The post-1920s history of the musical aspects of the operas' staging has roughly followed (or at times, led) trends in historically aware performance: these aspects included the adoption of and interest in the original orchestration, the restoration of the original pitches for the solo characters, the use of period instruments and, eventually, the establishment of the COUNTERTENOR voice as a viable alternative in performing the heroic parts intended for the CASTRATO voice.

Similar attention has been paid in scholarly terms to the history of opera staging, and productions apparently faithful to eighteenth-century originals can be and have been mounted. There is, though, a serious question as to whether they really represent anything like those that would have been seen in Handel's time; one of the few pieces of documentation to survive – a prompt copy of *RADAMISTO* from 1720 – suggests, for example, that the staging involved twenty-six non-singing supernumeraries, something unlikely to be encountered today at a 'baroque staging'. There are also many nuances of singing and acting style of which there is no record whatsoever. It must be accepted that many such stagings are acceptable today because they appeal to modern audiences, not because they can seriously be thought 'authentic'.

As far as contemporary productions are concerned, some of Handel's operas have been staged in numerous modern interpretations, with, predictably, some successes and some failures. Such interpretations have led to attempts to ridicule 'producer's opera', a term which can be broadly defined as a production strategy which provides an 'interpretation' of the work. However, in most cases these attempts have been largely unprofitable; the commentary has failed to address in any meaningful way the production values such authors purport to question, and production details are simply cited (without context) as self-evidently absurd, with little effort being expended in trying to understand precisely what such productions have been trying to achieve. Claims that they damage Handel's standing because an audience will not have the opportunity to see his operas performed 'properly' are misplaced in today's opera climate; a Handel opera that is likely to be given this type of 'producer's treatment' – say *Serse*, *ARIODANTE*, *Giulio Cesare*, or *ORLANDO* – will be a work that will have been and will be performed by another company in another production. And in this, it can be seen that Handel has a secure place in the current opera repertory.

It has to said, however, that the results of the phenomenon of staging Handel's oratorios have been of dubious value. Not only does the staging often work counter to the music – for example, providing action during arias of contemplation – but the productions require the employment of much extra stage business to create an interpretation of an object not meant to be staged in the first place (although stage directions in Handel's autographs and the printed wordbooks show that many of the oratorio-style works were theatrically envisaged to some extent). Nowhere has this problem been demonstrated more forcefully than in *SEMELE*, where the libretto's origins as an opera have led not only to 'stagings' but even to serious efforts to redefine the work's genre (see, for example, Sadie, NG *Opera*); this is in the face of the facts that CONGREVE's libretto was altered to be a similar shape and form as an oratorio, Handel himself set it as work not designed to be staged, and it was originally performed (for whatever reasons) in an oratorio season. This is not to say that productions such as these have not been successful and even engaging on their own terms, but it would be incorrect to suggest that they demonstrate anything other than the fact that Handel well understood the differences between music drama created in oratorio, and dramatic effects created through staged opera.   MICHAEL BURDEN

L. Lindgren, 'The Staging of Handel's operas in London', *Handel Tercentenary Collection*, ed. S. Sadie and A. Hicks (London, 1987)

J. Milhous and R. D. Hume, 'A Prompt Copy of Handel's *Radamisto*', MT 127/1719 (June 1986), 316–21

R. Savage, 'The Staging of Opera', *The Oxford History of Opera*, ed. R. Parker (Oxford, 1994)

Stampiglia, Silvio (b. Civita Lavinia (now Lanuvio), near Rome, 14 March 1664; d. Naples, 27 Jan. 1725). Italian librettist and founder member of the ARCADIAN

ACADEMY (under the name of Palemone Licurio). He worked in NAPLES, ROME and Vienna. Most of his *drammi per musica* use plots from Roman Republican history; many were first set by G. BONONCINI and A. SCARLATTI.

Handel's *SERSE* (1738) is based on Stampiglia's revision of MINATO's *Xerse* (Rome, 1694), and on its music by G. Bononcini. Stampiglia's greatest success was *Il trionfo di Camilla, Regina de' Volsci* (Naples, 1696): Bononcini's setting was often given in London, 1706–27. The libretto of *PARTENOPE* (music by Mancia, Naples, 1699), reset by Handel in 1730, was a fixture on the eighteenth-century stage. *IMENEO* (music by PORPORA, Naples, 1723), was reset by Handel in 1740.

Unlike all other Arcadian librettists, Stampiglia favoured comical, parodistic and erotic innuendoes. The protagonists of his pseudo-historical plots are often females who dominate feeble males (*Camilla, Partenope, Serse*); Rosmene's submission to an unloved suitor in Porpora's wedding serenata *Imeneo* is probably ironical. ZENO's obituary notice (1725) characterised Stampiglia as 'more inventive than learned' and as having had 'more spirit than study'. In 1726 Owen SWINEY deplored the 'depraved taste' of audiences applauding *Partenope* in Italy (Gibson, *Royal Academy*, p. 369).   REINHARD STROHM

E. Gibson, *The Royal Academy of Music, 1718–1728: The Institution and its Directors* (New York, 1989)
Strohm
    Dramma per Musica: Italian Opera Seria of the Eighteenth Century (New Haven, 1997)

Stanley, John (b. London, 17 Jan. 1712; d. London, 19 May 1786). The blind English composer, organist and violinist began his early musical education at the age of seven with John Reading and subsequently Maurice GREENE. In October 1723, shortly before his twelfth birthday, he was appointed organist of All Hallows, Bread Street. He later moved to St Andrew's Holborn (1726) and the Inner Temple (1734), holding both positions until his death. According to his pupil John Allcock, Stanley's organ voluntaries attracted the attention of numerous London musicians, among them Handel. In 1729, he was the youngest person on record to receive an OXFORD B.Mus. degree.

During the 1720s to 1730s Stanley was mostly occupied with performing and writing organ voluntaries, odes and cantatas. It was not until the 1750s that he came into closer contact with Handel's music, directing several performances of oratorio-style works (including *ALEXANDER'S FEAST*, *SAMSON*, *ACIS AND GALATEA* and *L'ALLEGRO*) both in London theatres and privately. He also wrote an oratorio of his own, *Jephtha* (c.1751–7), and, after Handel's death in 1759, took over the running of the Lenten oratorio performances in collaboration with J. C. SMITH JUNIOR. Their programmes were mostly comprised of works by Handel and occasionally their own compositions. Stanley's contribution included two oratorios which follow the Handelian model: *Zimri* (1760) and *The Fall of Egypt* (1774). From 1770 Stanley was a governor of the FOUNDLING HOSPITAL and directed its annual performances of *MESSIAH* between 1775 and 1777.

                    MATTHEW GARDNER

G. A. Williams, 'The Life and Works of John Stanley (1712–86)', Ph.D dissertation (University of Reading, 1977)
E. Zöllner, *English Oratorio after Handel: The London Oratorio Series and its Repertory 1760–1800* (Marburg, 2002)

Steffani, Agostino (b. Castelfranco, Veneto, 25 July 1654; d. Frankfurt am Main, 12 Feb. 1728). Italian composer, diplomat and bishop, who sang as a boy in Padua and VENICE but spent his adult life in Germany. In Munich (1667–88) he sang, played keyboard instruments, became Director of Chamber Music, undertook diplomatic missions and was ordained a priest. In HANOVER (1688–1703) he was both Kapellmeister and a prominent diplomat; at DÜSSELDORF (1703–9) he was appointed a government minister and became Bishop of Spiga (1706). In 1708–9 he pulled off a difficult mission in ROME and was appointed Apostolic Vicar of North Germany. HAWKINS reports that he often sang, presumably during this period, at concerts given by Cardinal Pietro OTTOBONI, but Handel does not appear to have heard him. For the rest of his life Steffani based himself in Hanover. Although music was now a secondary concern, he recommended Benedetta Sorosina for a role in London (she sang Nerina in the January 1725 revival of Handel's *GIULIO CESARE*), and in 1727 he was elected president of the ACADEMY OF ANCIENT MUSIC. As a composer he was known mainly for his chamber duets and his three-act Hanover operas, which were revived in HAMBURG in 1695–9. He first met Handel in either 1703, 1709 or 1710. Handel acquired a manuscript of his duets in 'Roma 1706' (his inscription) and used them as a model for his own. He also borrowed from Steffani's operas, particularly from *La superbia d'Alessandro* (1690) – the basis for *ALESSANDRO* – and the 'divertimento drammatico' *La lotta d'Hercole con Acheloo* (1689), a rich source for *THEODORA*.   COLIN TIMMS

[J. Hawkins], *Memoirs of the Life of Sig. Agostino Steffani, some time Master of the Electoral Chapel at Hanover, and afterwards Bishop of Spiga* [London, c.1750]; repr. *The Gentleman's Magazine*, vol. 31 (1761), 489–92

J. H. Roberts (ed.), *Handel Sources: Materials for the Study of Handel's Borrowing*, vol. 9 (New York, 1986)

C. Timms, *Polymath of the Baroque: Agostino Steffani and His Music* (New York, 2003)

Strada del Pò, Anna Maria (b. Bergamo; fl. 1719–41). Italian soprano. In 1720 and 1721 she created roles in three VIVALDI operas, and from 1724 to 1726 was at the Teatro San Bartolomeo in NAPLES, performing works by LEO, VINCI, PORPORA and PORTA. She was engaged by Handel for the Second Academy (OPERA COMPANIES, 3) making her debut for him as Adelaide in *LOTARIO* (1729). As his leading soprano in opera and oratorio until 1737, she sang more important parts for him than anyone else during the 1730s. Of at least twenty-four opera roles, thirteen more were premieres: the title role in *PARTENOPE* (1730), Cleofide in *PORO* (1731), Fulvia in *EZIO* and Elmira in *SOSARME* (both 1732), Angelica in *ORLANDO* (1733), the title role in *ARIANNA IN CRETA* and Erato in *TERPSICORE* (both 1734), Ginevra in *ARIODANTE* and the title role in *ALCINA* (both 1735), the title role in *ATALANTA* (1736), Tusnelda in *ARMINIO*, Arianna in *GIUSTINO* and the title role in *BERENICE* (all 1737). She also sang for him in eleven revivals and several pasticcios, as well as his revival of ARIOSTI's *CORIOLANO* and BONONCINI's *GRISELDA*. She was Clio in the serenata *PARNASSO IN FESTA* (1734), Galatea in the bilingual *ACIS AND GALATEA* (1732). Handel revised the title role in *ESTHER* for her in 1732, and other oratorio roles included the title role in *DEBORAH* and Josabeth in *ATHALIA* (both 1733). Strada was the soprano soloist in the first performances of *ALEXANDER'S FEAST* (1736), and sang Bellezza in Il *TRIONFO DEL TEMPO E DELLA VERITÀ* (1737).

She was the only one of Handel's singers not to defect to the OPERA OF THE NOBILITY in summer 1733. Perhaps she was faithful to him in recognition of his contribution to her formation as an artist. In BURNEY's opinion, she was 'a singer formed by [Handel], and modelled on his own melodies. She came hither a coarse and aukward [sic] singer with improvable talents, and he at last polished her into reputation and favour' (p. 342). This was perhaps just as well, for it was alleged that her appearance was not such as to recommend her. Burney remarked that 'she was usually called the Pig', and Mrs Pendarves (later DELANY) wrote: 'her person [is] very bad and she makes frightful mouths' (Deutsch, p. 247).

Nonetheless, she was clearly a considerable performer. According to ROLLI, she was 'a copy of Faustina with a better voice and better intonation, but without her charm and brio'. Of her performance in *Lotario*, he remarked, 'Strada pleases mightily . . . [Handel] says that she sings better than the two who have left us, because one of them [Faustina] never pleased him at all and he would like to forget the other [Cuzzoni]. The truth is that she has a penetrating thread of a soprano voice which delights the ear, but oh how far removed from Cuzzona!' (Deutsch, p. 249). This was hardly true vocally, since eight of the roles Handel adapted for Strada in revivals had originally been Cuzzoni's, and both were famous for their trilling ability. Indeed, Strada seems to have combined something of what Tosi, writing of Faustina and Cuzzoni called 'the *Pathetick* of the one, and the *Allegro* of the other' (*Observations in the Florid Song*, trans. Galliard, London, 1742, p. 171). The roles Handel wrote for her demanded considerable emotional depth and expressive power, and a maximum range c'–c'''. Perhaps after financial problems with Handel, Strada left England in 1738. She sang alongside SENESINO in Naples (1739–40), and retired to her home city in 1741.

NICHOLAS CLAPTON

Stradella, Alessandro (b. Nepi, near Viterbo, 3 April 1639; d. Genoa, 25 Feb. 1682). Italian composer. Descended from a noble family, he served from 1653 to 1660 as a page in the Lante palace in ROME. His earliest known composition, an oratorio, dates from 1667. In the next ten years he composed many other oratorios (Latin and Italian), serenatas, cantatas, prologues and intermezzi, often for Roman or Venetian noblemen. In the serenata *Vola, vola in altri petti* (1674) he also pioneered concerto grosso instrumentation – the division of an orchestra into two groups, one smaller than the other. He used this scoring first in arias, to accompany the voice, and later in purely instrumental movements and works. In February 1677 he left Rome for VENICE, where he taught Agnese Van Uffele, the mistress of Alvise Contarini, and in June he eloped with her to Turin, where he was attacked and left for dead. Having recovered, he settled in early 1678 in Genoa, where an unknown assassin stabbed him to death. Stradella excelled in both vocal and instrumental genres. Handel probably heard music by him at OTTOBONI's concerts in Rome and appears to have owned a manuscript of his serenata *Qual prodigio è ch'io miri?*, from which he borrowed extensively in *ISRAEL IN EGYPT* and modestly in *JOSEPH AND HIS BRETHREN*.

COLIN TIMMS

Dean, *Oratorios*

C. Gianturco, *Alessandro Stradella (1639–1682): His Life and Music* (Oxford, 1994)

S. Taylor, The *Indebtedness of Handel to Works by Other Composers: A Presentation of Evidence* (Cambridge, 1906)

Strungk [Strunck], Nicolaus Adam (b. Brunswick, 15 Nov. 1640; d. Dresden, 23 Sept. 1700). Organist, violinist, Kapellmeister, composer. He started his career as a violinist in WOLFENBÜTTEL, Celle and HANOVER, and later undertook journeys to Vienna and Italy. At DRESDEN he was Vizekapellmeister and chamber organist (1688–92) and Hofkapellmeister (1693–6). From 1696 he was music director of the opera house at Leipzig. Handel's book of manuscript music dated 1698 (now lost) included works by Strungk. Handel borrowed from one of Strungk's Capriccio themes in *ISRAEL IN EGYPT*.

KLAUS-PETER KOCH (Trans. ANGELA BAIER)

[W. Coxe], *Anecdotes of George Frederick Handel, and John Christopher Smith* (London, 1799; facsimile edn, ed. P. M. Young, New York, 1979), 6n.

J. Mattheson, *Grundlage einer Ehren-Pforte* (Hamburg, 1740)

Stuart, Charles Edward (known as Bonnie Prince Charlie, the Young Pretender, b. Rome, 31 Dec. 1720; d. Rome, 31 Jan. 1788). Claimant to the English, Scottish and Irish thrones as the elder son of 'James III' (the 'Old Pretender') and grandson of the deposed James II of England, VII of Scotland. Cultivated and charming, he attracted support to the JACOBITE cause, but his 'real political and military gifts' were 'thwarted by his limitations of temperament and by unfortunate father figures' (Pittock, ODNB). France, hostile to England (War of the AUSTRIAN SUCCESSION), fostered plans for Stuart restoration. On 23 July 1745 Charles landed in Scotland, gathered an army, and rapidly penetrated England, causing panic in London. When promised support from France, Spain, Scotland and England failed to materialise he retreated north, pursued by the Duke of Cumberland (Prince WILLIAM), who defeated his remaining army at Culloden on 16 April 1746. After five months on the run in Scotland, Charles was rescued by the French, but in 1749 they agreed to cease supporting him. The last plot to restore him collapsed in 1753.

RUTH SMITH

subscribers

    1. Performances

    2. Publications

1. Performances

A tradition began in the early 1700s of supporting new opera productions in London by raising a subscription. The practice was then extended to cover a whole season. For two payments of 10 guineas a subscriber was entitled to a silver ticket, which permitted access for one person to all performances. In a move designed to reduce fraud, Handel and HEIDEGGER, probably in 1732, required silver-ticket holders to obtain a paper ticket for each performance they wished to attend. Except for certain boxes, seats were not reserved.

    One of the reasons why certain members of the nobility became unhappy with Handel during the 1732–3 season had to do with his requirement that subscribers purchase tickets to the first night of *Deborah*. Effectively, this was

621

Table 1

Season	Company	Number	Comment
1731–2	Second Academy	170	
1732–3	Second Academy	140	
1738–9	Heidegger	133	abandoned
1739–40	MIDDLESEX OPERA COMPANY	78	limited season
1741–2	Middlesex Opera Company	142	
1743–4	Middlesex Opera Company	131	

a doubling of prices but the subscribers resisted and were admitted without purchasing a paper ticket. The policy change mid-season was taken as an arbitrary breaking of the contract, notwithstanding the fact that Handel and Heidegger had much greater expenses for this work due to its larger than usual performing forces.

Handel continued to solicit season subscriptions until 1747. The number of subscribers is known for these KING'S THEATRE opera seasons (Table 1).

An additional layer of financial and descriptive complexity was added with the establishment of the Royal Academy of Music (OPERA COMPANIES, 2) in 1719. As a joint-stock company the Academy initially had sixty-three share-holding investors (called subscribers in the official documents). These persons pledged to pay up to £200 during the life of the Academy to defray expenses, and would receive profits should there be any, and they had managerial as well as fiduciary responsibilities.

2. Publications

Subscribers were solicited by publishers to at least fifteen works of Handel's issued in London during his lifetime. Ten of these are known to have lists. The first such publication was for *RODELINDA* (1725), the last *THEODORA* (1751). The largest number of subscribers was for *ATALANTA* issued by WALSH in 1736 (154 subscribers for 192 copies). The lowest number of subscribers was 57 for *ADMETO* issued by CLUER in 1727, while the lowest number of copies subscribed was 80 for *SCIPIONE*, issued by Cluer in 1726. On the ten lists 539 different persons or groups are named. The largest category of subscribers is Members of Parliament and their wives. Musicians comprise the next largest category. Relatively few members of the royalty and nobility subscribed, and the remaining names are those of government office holders, military officers, gentry, clerics, lawyers, physicians, surgeons and apothecaries. There were, perhaps, fifty individuals in the 1720s and 75–80 in the 1730s who were prepared to support Handel through regular subscription to publication of his operas.

Cluer's *Rodelinda* cost subscribers 15s., half to be paid on subscribing and half on publication. In the case of *FARAMONDO*, Walsh requested the full amount of half a guinea (10s 6d.) upon subscription.   DAVID HUNTER

See also AUDIENCE; EDITIONS, I; OPERA COMPANIES

E. Gibson, *The Royal Academy of Music 1719–1728: The Institution and its Directors* (New York, 1989)

D. Hunter and R. Mason, 'Supporting Handel through Subscription to Publications: The Lists of *Rodelinda* and *Faramondo* Compared', *Notes* 56/1 (Sept. 1999), 23–97

J. Milhous and R. D. Hume, 'Box Office Reports for Five Operas Mounted by Handel in London, 1732–1734', *Harvard Library Bulletin* 26 (1978), 245–66

C. M. Taylor, 'Italian Operagoing in London,1700-1745', Ph.D. dissertation (Syracuse University, 1991)

Suetonius (b. ?AD 70; d. ?130). Roman biographer, whose *Lives of the Twelve Caesars* describes Julius Caesar and the Roman emperors up to Domitian. His simply written essays were composed thematically rather than chronologically and include information about the personal lives of the emperors in sometimes scandalous detail. His analyses nevertheless were based on a popularly established set of expectations of imperial behaviour that accorded well with eighteenth-century notions of moral leadership. Details from *AGRIPPINA*, *GIULIO CESARE* and *ARMINIO* show his influence. ROBERT KETTERER

R. Ketterer, *Ancient Rome in Early Opera* (Urbana and Chicago, 2009)

Suites. See KEYBOARD MUSIC

Sullivan, Daniel (fl. ?early 1730s; d. Dublin, 13 Oct. 1764). Countertenor, who was unusual for having a secular stage career. Engaged for Handel's COVENT GARDEN oratorios in spring 1744, he created Athamas in *SEMELE*, the title role in *JOSEPH AND HIS BRETHREN*, and sang in revivals of *SAMSON* and *SAUL*. Mrs DELANY said he was '*a block with a very fine voice*' (Deutsch, p. 585). From 1755 to 1759 he sang in Handel oratorios and other works at BATH. His range was about g–d″. NICHOLAS CLAPTON

Susanna, HWV 66. English oratorio, which Handel began to compose on 11 July 1748. By 14 August he had drafted the score, and he completed the orchestration on 24 August. Although he began the work about a month after completing *SOLOMON*, it premiered a month earlier than that work, on 10 February 1749 at COVENT GARDEN. The author of the libretto is not known, though Dean has argued that it was probably the same anonymous author who wrote *Solomon*. The original cast included:

Susanna	Giulia FRASI (soprano)
Joacim	Caterina GALLI (mezzo-soprano)
First Elder	Thomas LOWE (tenor)
Second Elder	Henry REINHOLD (bass)
Chelsias	Henry Reinhold
Susanna's Attendant	Sibilla Gronamann (soprano)
Daniel	[unidentified] (boy treble)

According to an eyewitness account the house was full at the first performance, but ultimately there were just four performances of the work in the first season, and Handel revived the work only once, in 1759.

The source for the libretto is the apocryphal story of Susanna and the elders found in chapter 13 of Daniel. The action takes place among the Jews who are exiled in Babylon (hence the opening chorus of lament). The first part of the libretto portrays the loving relationship between Susanna and her husband

Joacim, who is summoned out of the city for a week. During his absence two Elders (community leaders) plan to seduce Susanna when she goes to bathe. Dean remarks that the first Elder's air represents his 'excitement at seeing Susanna in the nude' but Susanna has only expressed her intention of bathing and there is no suggestion that she has disrobed. When Susanna resists them, the Elders decide to threaten her with an accusation of adultery. Susanna is convicted on the elder's lies. Daniel comes to the rescue, however; separately questioning the elders about their account, he shows that their accounts do not match (specifically on the type of tree under which Susanna and her alleged lover were seen). Susanna is cleared and the two elders are condemned to death.

Since the time of its first performance *Susanna* has been recognised as more operatic in character than many of Handel's other biblical oratorios. The Countess of Shaftesbury, in a letter to James HARRIS, remarked that the oratorio 'will not insinuate itself so much into my approbation as most of Handel's performances, as it is in the light operatic style' (Burrows and Dunhill, p. 255). There are several aspects of the work that do point to opera. First, *Susanna* has a greater proportion of da capo arias than any of Handel's oratorios. Additionally, many of the arias are lightweight and galant in character, revealing Handel's interest in the prevailing operatic style. Although we can only speculate as to why this is the case, it is noteworthy that by this time Handel had among his singers two performers who had previously appeared for the MIDDLESEX OPERA COMPANY, Frasi and Galli: Handel may have wished to take advantage of their operatic expertise. Galli frequently sang male roles, and she and Frasi had appeared as two lovers in the pasticcio *L'incostanza delusa* in 1745.

Susanna is not a comic opera, although there is an element of humour in Handel's portrayal of the two elders. As Smither writes, 'the incongruity of youthful passion for a young and beautiful girl in dignified old men was considered inherently humorous (a situation often exploited in comic opera), and Handel underlined the humor in his musical setting, as STRADELLA had previously done in his oratorio *La Susanna*' (*Oratorio*, vol. 2, p. 327). There is a fair amount of contrast in their characterisations. Dean remarked that the first elder whines while the second elder blusters. But there are certainly serious elements as well; the failed rape attempt and the sinister attempts to kill Susanna are not to be taken lightly.

Although *Susanna* contains fewer choruses than usual (this is a point of contrast with its sister oratorio *Solomon*), they do appear periodically and are often serious in content. They function as the Jewish nation, as moral commentator, and once as a crowd witnessing the trial of Susanna ('The cause is decided / the sentence decreed / Susanna is guilty / Susanna must bleed'). The opening chorus, a lament for Israel, is built over a chromatically descending tetrachord bass. 'Tremble, guilt, for thou shalt find' with its flurry of semiquavers graphically depicts the text 'wrath divine outstrips the wind'.

The sources for *Susanna* attest to the fact that Handel made several revisions to the work. For instance, several of the opening numbers were either radically recomposed or replaced with new pieces. The autograph indicates that there were significant changes for both the overture and the opening chorus. Joacim's first aria simply prolonged the mood of lament of the chorus (heartfelt sorrow, constant woe / from our streaming eyes shall flow; / till the Lord has heard our grief, / till the Lord shall send relief); this was replaced with an entirely new aria which bows to the ongoing oppression, but moves to an expression of wedded bliss in its second section. The ensuing duet exists in two versions, the second of which is shorter than the first and utilises a different formal structure. There are several other changes that took place before the first performance, including the addition of the arias 'Would custom bid' and 'Guilt trembling'. One of the choruses that was cut before first performance, 'Righteous Daniel', had begun with a passage borrowed from Handel's previous works, including 'Cara pianta' from La TERRA È LIBERATA, but Handel eliminated much of this borrowing by cutting the opening ritornello before 'filling out' the orchestration. There are several other known BORROWINGS in the work; the overture, for example, draws from the overture of John BLOW's ode Begin the Song (1681) – a rare instance of Handel borrowing from an English composer. When Handel revived the work in 1759 he cut several numbers, but added 'Endless pleasure' (from SEMELE) for Susanna's Attendant, and altered its words to describe Joacim. Very little of the music for the elders was cut.   DAVID ROSS HURLEY

Burrows and Dunhill
Dean, Oratorios
S. Dunlap, 'Susanna and the Male Gaze: The Musical Iconography of a Baroque Heroine',
     Women and Music 5 (2001), 40–60
D. R. Hurley, Handel's Muse: Patterns of Creation in his Oratorios and Musical Dramas, 1743–1751
     (Oxford, 2001)
Smith, Oratorios
H. E. Smither, A History of the Oratorio, vol. 2: The Oratorio in the Baroque Era: Protestant Germany
     and England (Chapel Hill, NC, 1977)
F. Zimmerman, 'Händels Parodie-Ouvertüre zu Susanna: eine neue Ansicht über die
     Entstehungsfrage', HJb 24 (1978)

Swieten, Gottfried Freiherr van (b. Leyden, 29 Oct. 1733; d. Vienna, 29 March 1803). His father, Gerard, was Empress Maria Theresia's personal physician and court librarian from 1745. Gottfried studied philosophy and law (1746–52) and became a diplomat in 1755. He was posted to Brussels, Frankfurt, Paris and Warsaw, visited Switzerland and England, and became imperial envoy of the Holy Roman Emperor Joseph II in BERLIN. In 1777 he was made prefect of the Vienna court library, and in 1781 became president of the Court Commission on Education and Censorship, as which he was instrumental in implementing Emperor Joseph II's educational reforms, called for better education of girls and stressed the importance of including humanistic and artistic subjects in the syllabus. Divested of this office by Leopold II in 1791, van Swieten continued to work in the court library and was made an honorary citizen of Vienna in 1797.

Van Swieten received musical training and composed an opéra comique and further stage works and arias (probably in Paris). In Berlin, where he took lessons in composition with Johann Philipp Kirnberger, he composed a number of symphonies which HAYDN called 'as stiff as he himself'. Even so, MOZART conducted one of these symphonies in 1782. He probably first came into contact with Handel's oratorios in London (summer 1769), and at Berlin (1770–7) he requested help from his friend James Harris junior (the son of James HARRIS) to acquire Handelian works for his library. He led the renewal of

Tacitus, (Publius?) Cornelius (b. ?AD 56; d. after 118). Roman historian whose *Annals* and *Histories* record the reigns of the Roman emperors from Tiberius to Vespasian. He claimed to write unbiased history (*Annals*, 1.1.3), but his mordant reflections on imperial power provided early modern Europe with a critical approach to historiography. Tacitus's cynical accounts affected historical librettos in seventeenth-century VENICE; that influence is still visible in Handel's NERO, AGRIPPINA, ARMINIO, RADAMISTO and the cantata 'Agrippina condotta a morire' (*DUNQUE SARÀ PUR VERO*).   ROBERT KETTERER

W. Heller, 'Poppea's Legacy: The Julio-Claudians on the Venetian Stage', *Journal of Interdisciplinary History* 36/3 (2006), 379–99

R. Ketterer, *Ancient Rome in Early Opera* (Urbana and Chicago, 2009)

Tamerlano, HWV 18. Handel's sixth opera for the Royal Academy of Music (OPERA COMPANIES, 2) composed in 1724. The libretto, by Nicola HAYM, is derived from Agostino PIOVENE's *Tamerlano*, which had been set by GASPARINI and performed in VENICE in 1711; Piovene's source was *Tamerlan, ou la Mort de Bajazet*, by Jacques Pradon, 1672. The story is set in the aftermath of the battle of Angora (Ankara) in 1402, when the Tartar Emperor Timur-i-Leng, or Tamerlane, defeated the Turkish Emperor Bajazet and took him prisoner. Andronico, a Greek prince and ally of Tamerlano, and Bajazet's daughter Asteria, who is imprisoned with her father, are secretly in love. At the beginning of the opera, Andronico comes to release Bajazet from his prison on Tamerlano's orders. Tamerlano tells Andronico that he proposes to reject Irene, Princess of Trebizond, to whom he is betrothed, because he is in love with Asteria, and he has decided that Andronico will marry Irene. Andronico is devastated. Tamerlano tells Asteria of his desires, and promises to spare her father if she accepts; he says that Andronico is willing to persuade Bajazet to agree to it, and will marry Irene. Asteria is angry at what she believes to be Andronico's betrayal; Bajazet reacts furiously to what Andronico tells him and insists that they must all resist Tamerlano. Irene arrives to claim her rights, but is told by Andronico's friend Leone that she cannot see Tamerlano; Andronico advises her to gain access to him by pretending to be a messenger, and bewails his own misfortune.

In Act II Tamerlano tells Andronico that Asteria has accepted his offer. Asteria and Andronico quarrel, and in despair Andronico decides to seek Bajazet's help. Irene, in disguise, rebukes Asteria for usurping her place; Asteria tells Irene not to despair, for things may change. In the throne room Tamerlano tells Asteria to sit beside him; Bajazet throws himself to the floor and challenges her to walk over him; she says she will go to the throne, but by another way. Bajazet disowns her; Irene appears and denounces Tamerlano. Asteria comes down from the throne and reveals the dagger she has concealed: this was to be her marital embrace. Tamerlano is furious, threatens Asteria and Bajazet with death in a trio, and storms out. Bajazet, Andronico and Irene in turn praise Asteria's loyalty and courage, and leave her alone to reflect on her situation.

In Act III, Bajazet hands to Asteria some of the poison he has always carried with him. Tamerlano tells Andronico to pursue once more his offer to Asteria, but Andronico defies him and reveals that he is her lover. Tamerlano declares that Bajazet shall be executed and Asteria handed over to a slave; meanwhile they will wait on him at table, and Andronico is to witness their humiliation. Andronico and Asteria bid farewell in a duet. In the Imperial Hall a supper is prepared. Tamerlano orders Asteria to offer him a cup; she drops the poison into it, but is seen by Irene, who warns Tamerlano not to drink and reveals who she is. Tamerlano softens towards her, and tells Asteria to give the poisoned cup to Andronico or Bajazet. She hesitates, then tries to drink it herself; Andronico knocks the cup to the floor. Asteria rushes out in anger, followed by Andronico, and Bajazet sings an aria of defiance and leaves. Tamerlano and Irene are reconciled. Leone announces that Bajazet is returning: Bajazet says that he has taken poison, and curses Tamerlano, calling on the Furies to avenge them all. Andronico and Asteria help him off stage as he is dying. Tamerlano declares that this spectacle has appeased him, that he will marry Irene, and that Andronico and Asteria may be together. All look for light after the dark night.

The opera was premiered at the KING'S THEATRE on 31 October 1724, and there were twelve performances. The cast was:

Tamerlano	Andrea PACINI (castrato)
Andronico	SENESINO (castrato)
Bajazet	Francesco BOROSINI (tenor)
Asteria	Francesca CUZZONI (soprano)
Irene	Anna DOTTI (alto)
Leone	Giuseppe BOSCHI (bass)

Handel took enormous trouble over *Tamerlano*. The initial act of composition took place between 3 and 23 July 1724, but in the following months substantial revisions were made: first, the role of Irene had been drafted for a soprano, then had to be rewritten for Dotti; second, Handel had composed the part of Bajazet before he had heard Borosini sing, and when he did he found that some of the part lay too high for him, and had to be altered; but Borosini's arrival in September caused a much greater upheaval: he must have brought with him a score and a libretto of a second setting of the Tamerlano story – Il *Bajazet*, which Gasparini had composed for Reggio Emilia in 1719, and in which Borosini had sung Bajazet. Handel realised that this version offered a more dramatic text for the opening and closing scenes of the opera, and rewrote both using the 1719 libretto; most striking is the magnificent *scena* of Bajazet's death. Originally Handel had composed one of the finest arias in the work, 'Cor di padre', for the moment at the end of Act II when Asteria is left to ponder her fate, and in the first scene of Act III there was an aria for Bajazet. He found this aria unsatisfactory, and after three attempts at changing it, including assigning it to Asteria, he hit upon the solution – 'Cor di padre', for Asteria, with its feeling of foreboding, would be ideal, so he moved it there and composed a lighter, more serene replacement for her aria at the end of Act II. Other alterations were made shortly before the premiere, which tightened the drama by cutting superfluous material, including a final scene originally placed between Bajazet's death and the concluding coro. The result of all this revision is a dramatic and musical masterpiece, sometimes spoiled in modern productions by a refusal to accept Handel's last-minute changes, all of which can be shown to represent fine-tuning by a composer of genius. The opera is one of Handel's greatest, consistently serious and even claustrophobic – there are no outdoor scenes – with powerful characterisation and music of the highest quality throughout. *Tamerlano* was briefly revived with an additional aria for Leone in 1731.

TERENCE BEST

T. Best, 'New Light on the Manuscript Copies of *Tamerlano*', GHB IV (1991), 134–45
    (ed.), *Tamerlano*, HHA II/15 (Kassel, 1996)
Dean and Knapp, *Operas*
Harris, *Librettos*
Strohm

Tarquini, Vittoria (b. Venice, c. 1678; d. ?after 1720). Italian soprano. She was said to be a native of VENICE (a possible relative, Rosana Tarquini, sang at Venice's San Salvatore in operas by Legrenzi in 1682–4). The correspondence of G. A. PERTI reveals that Vittoria often visited Venice until 1720, although no operatic appearance there is documented. Her short-lived but successful public career developed in NAPLES (1694–8) and Parma (1699), in operas and serenatas by Giovanni BONONCINI and ALESSANDRO SCARLATTI. From 1697 until at least 1710 she served Grand Prince Ferdinando de' MEDICI as singer, lover and confidante, at first in rivalry with the Roman castrato Francesco 'Checchino' de Castris, whom she supplanted in the Prince's favour in 1703 (the castrato retired to ROME). From 1698 to 1710, Tarquini regularly sang in the autumn seasons at Ferdinando's private theatre in Pratolino (PALAZZI, 2) in operas and pasticcios by Scarlatti, C. F. Pollarolo and Perti; printed librettos do not provide casts, but the Medici papers show that librettist Antonio SALVI was consistently requested to tailor aria texts for her that were grand or pathetic. Indeed, she frequently created royal and noble ladies throughout her career, from Camilla (Bononcini's *Il trionfo di Camilla*, Naples 1696) and Claudia (Scarlatti's *La caduta de' decemviri*, Naples 1697) to Asteria (Scarlatti's *Il gran Tamerlano*, Pratolino 1706) and Rodelinda (Perti's *Rodelinda*, Pratolino 1710).

Judging from extant scores, her vocal style was by turns rhythmically lively and nobly simple, without over-extended coloratura passages, but with firmly intoned leaping intervals and long-sustained breaths. Despite a short vocal range (range: $d'-a''$), her tessitura was high ($e'-g''$) and probably coupled with a softly feminine colour, as her nickname 'La Bombace' (lit. 'cotton wool') may imply.

MAINWARING's narration of Handel's love affair with Tarquini was anticipated five decades earlier in a letter written by Electress Sophia of HANOVER to her granddaughter Sophia Dorothea on 14 June 1710 from HERRENHAUSEN, commenting about Handel's appointment there: 'He is a good-looking man and the gossips say he was the lover of Victoria.' Mainwaring's remark that Tarquini 'was much admired both as an Actress, and a Singer' is confirmed by earlier Italian sources that also credit her with beauty, cleverness in courtly intrigue and 'great courage', but his claim that she sang in Handel's RODRIGO and AGRIPPINA is disproved by documentary evidence. However, Handel may have met her at various times between 1706 and 1709 at FLORENCE, Venice and Rome, and perhaps drew inspiration from her for his cantatas UN'ALMA INNAMORATA (as speculated by U. Kirkendale) and Apollo e Dafne (La TERRA È LIBERATA).   CARLO VITALI

See also HANDEL, 11

W. Kirkendale, The Court Musicians in Florence during the Principate of the Medici: With a Reconstruction of the Artistic Establishment (Florence, 1993)

W. and U. Kirkendale, Music and Meaning: Studies in Music History and the Neighbouring Disciplines (Florence, 2007)

F. Lora, 'I mottetti di Giacomo Antonio Perti per Ferdinando de' Medici principe di Toscana: Ricognizione, cronologia e critica delle fonti', Ph.D. dissertation (University of Bologna, 2005–6)

C. Vitali, 'Un cantante legrenziano e la sua biografia: Francesco De Castris, "musico politico"', Giovanni Legrenzi e la cappella ducale di San Marco, ed. F. Passadore and F. Rossi (Florence, 1994)

R. L. Weaver and N. W. Weaver, A Chronology of Music in the Florentine Theater: Operas, Prologues, Farces, Intermezzos, Concerts, and Plays with Incidental Music, 2 vols. (Detroit, 1978–93)

Tasso, Torquato (b. Sorrento, 11 March 1544; d. Rome, 15 April 1595). Italian poet. Author of Gerusalemme liberata, a late Renaissance epic on the First Crusade, the pastoral drama Aminta, and other poems and prose works. His life and writing were characterised by his struggle to bring a melancholic poetic sensuality into accord with post-Tridentine morality. Several episodes from Gerusalemme liberata became popular themes in musical drama. Handel's only setting of a plot adapted from Tasso is RINALDO, his first London opera.   ROBERT KETTERER

Tate, Nahum (b. Dublin, 1652; d. London, 30 July 1715). Irish poet, librettist and playwright. Educated at Trinity College in DUBLIN from 1668 until 1672, Tate settled in London by 1678. He came in contact with a number of important musicians, including Henry PURCELL, for whom he wrote the libretto of Dido and Aeneas during the 1680s. Tate wrote odes and collaborated on adaptations of the Psalms with Nicholas BRADY; they issued A New Edition of the Psalms of David in 1696, from which Handel later took texts for HWV 247, 251^b and 254 (ANTHEMS, 2).   WALTER KREYSZIG

R. A. Leaver, 'The Failure that Succeeded: The New Version of Tate and Brady', The Hymn 48 (1997), 22–31

C. Spenser, Nahum Tate (New York, 1972)

Taust, Georg. See HANDEL, 9

Te decus virgineum. See Italian and Latin CHURCH MUSIC

Te Deum. The Canticle from the Roman Catholic office of Matins was adopted by the English reformers as the first of the two canticles in the service of Morning Prayer, the other being the JUBILATE. In both versions it had a long-standing association with the celebration of coronations and military victories. In England the use of instruments other than the organ to accompany the Te Deum dated from as recently as 1694 when PURCELL composed his D Major setting for the celebration of St Cecilia's Day. By the time of Handel's arrival in 1710 only a handful of such settings had been made, the most notable being by John BLOW and William CROFT, all of them modelled on Purcell's composition. Handel wrote five settings of which the earliest two are the most influenced by his great predecessor.

1. Utrecht Te Deum and Jubilate in D major, HWV 278–9
2. Caroline Te Deum in D major, HWV 280
3. Cannons Te Deum in B flat major, HWV 281
4. Te Deum in A major, HWV 282
5. Dettingen Te Deum in D major, HWV 283

1. Utrecht Te Deum and Jubilate in D major, HWV 278–9

Handel's first setting of the Te Deum, together with its accompanying canticle for Morning Prayer, the Jubilate, was written to celebrate the Peace of Utrecht that put an end to the War of the SPANISH SUCCESSION. Although the treaty was signed on 31 March 1713, it had been anticipated since late 1712. Handel completed the autograph of the Te Deum on 14 January 1713 and the Jubilate sometime later. They were publicly rehearsed on 5, 7 and 19 March, but the actual Service of Thanksgiving in ST PAUL'S CATHEDRAL was not held until 7 July.

For both the Te Deum and Jubilate Handel clearly took from Purcell's settings the divisions of the texts into movements, the use of five-part chorus with divided sopranos, and even the assignment of certain solo voices (e.g. the alto for 'Vouchsafe, O Lord'). However, his setting is on a grander scale, and his use of wind instruments (with independent oboe parts in the tutti sections and obbligato parts for flute and oboe in the solos), together with the more extended choral sections marked a major stylistic change.

The Utrecht Te Deum and Jubilate, together with Purcell's settings, were popular throughout the eighteenth century, only being gradually eclipsed by the Dettingen Te Deum after 1743. The Utrecht Jubilate was arranged for the smaller forces of the CANNONS CONCERT in 1717 in the form of the anthem *O be Joyful in the Lord* (HWV 246) (ANTHEMS, 2).

2. Caroline Te Deum in D major, HWV 280

Handel's second setting of the Te Deum, scored for soloists, SAATB choruses, flute, trumpet and strings, is the shortest of the five and closest in scale, scoring and external details to Purcell's setting, although the latter had employed double sopranos in his five-part choruses. It was first performed in the CHAPEL ROYAL in ST JAMES'S PALACE at one or both of the services in autumn 1714 that welcomed King GEORGE I and the members of his family to Britain, and is traditionally associated with CAROLINE, Princess of Wales and later Queen of England. It is notable for the outstanding writing for the two original alto soloists, Richard Elford (1677–1714) and Francis Hughes (c.1666–1744), and the lack of imitative counterpoint in the choruses. Handel performed this setting on at least two more occasions in the 1720s and 1740s, each time with modifications.

3. Cannons Te Deum in B flat major, HWV 281

Handel's third setting of the Te Deum was written for his patron James Brydges (1st Duke of CHANDOS) and his private musical establishment, the Cannons Concert, in late 1718 or possibly early 1719. It was first performed in the Church of ST LAWRENCE, Little Stanmore ('Whitchurch') and it has been suggested that it may have been written to celebrate an unidentified event in Brydges's personal life. This setting is scored for a five-part chorus including three tenors, with solos for all but the third tenor, and an instrumental ensemble consisting of strings without violas and single trumpet, oboe and flute. It borrows from portions of the Utrecht Te Deum and Caroline Te Deum that he had not already used in his Cannons anthems (ANTHEMS, 2) but is largely newly composed in a somewhat rambling and long-winded style. The presence of the trumpet seems to have inspired Handel to write a type of rondo-like chorus also seen in the finale to the first version of *ESTHER* (HWV 50^a).

4. Te Deum in A major, HWV 282

Handel's fourth setting of the canticle was almost certainly written to celebrate George I's safe return from HANOVER in early 1726 and performed in the Chapel Royal in St James's Palace together with the Chapel Royal anthem *Let God Arise* (HWV 256^b) (ANTHEMS, 1). Both of these are arrangements and abridgements of their Cannons counterparts HWV 281 and HWV 256^a, both of which were in B flat major, and feature extensive bassoon solos. The orchestra also includes transverse flute and oboe in addition to the usual complement of strings and the solo work is divided between alto and bass as was typical for the Chapel Royal of the time. The need for conciseness forced Handel to impose a tighter structure on his models, generally to the benefit of the music.

5. Dettingen Te Deum in D major, HWV 283

Handel's final setting of the Te Deum was written to celebrate the allied victory over the French at the Battle of DETTINGEN during the War of the AUSTRIAN SUCCESSION, which took place on 27 June 1743. Handel evidently anticipated that there would be a large-scale Service of Thanksgiving in St Paul's Cathedral because it is scored for an orchestra of three trumpets, two oboes, bassoon and strings with a five-part chorus with double sopranos. In the event the service was held in the much smaller Chapel Royal in St James's Palace, paired with the newly composed Dettingen Anthem (HWV 265) (ANTHEMS, 6). Handel borrowed musical ideas from a Latin-texted setting by the Italian composer Francesco Antonio URIO, a source he had already drawn from in *SAUL* and *ISRAEL IN EGYPT*. Handel used relatively short thematic ideas, generally from parallel portions of the text, but there are also references to his own Utrecht setting and to *MESSIAH*, which had received its first London performances earlier in the year. The music of the Dettingen Te Deum is more spacious than that of the Utrecht and also more assertive. There are moments, such as the bellicose opening 'We praise Thee, o God', and the entry of the unaccompanied trumpets following the text 'We believe that thou shalt come to be our judge', that show Handel's masterful command of timing and effect. This setting was immediately popular and in the nineteenth century virtually eclipsed the composer's Utrecht setting.   GRAYDON BEEKS

Burrows, *Chapel Royal*

Telemann, Georg Philipp (b. Magdeburg, 14 March 1681; d. Hamburg, 25 June 1767). German composer. He received an extensive education in Magdeburg, Zellerfeld and Hildesheim, where he became assistant music director at the monastery of St Godehard. From 1701 he studied law in Leipzig, and at around the same time met Handel and Barthold Heinrich BROCKES in HALLE. In 1704 he was appointed music director of the Leipzig Neukirche, in 1705 he became Kapellmeister at Sorau, and in 1708 Konzertmeister and Kapellmeister in Eisenach. In 1712 Telemann moved to Frankfurt, but in 1721 he left for HAMBURG to accept the posts of *Kantor* of the Johanneum and music director of the city's five principal churches. He remained in Hamburg until his death.

Telemann found his talent for music at a very early age, learning to play various instruments and composing vocal and instrumental music. He founded a Collegium musicum in Leipzig, where he composed church music and operas. In Sorau the focus was more on instrumental music (orchestral suites), but in Eisenach he also began regularly to compose church music. At Frankfurt and Hamburg he was primarily responsible for church music, but he also branched out into new fields of interest by organising public concerts. In 1715 he founded a publishing house, which he directed until 1740. From 1721 he became one of the most important opera composers for the Hamburg GÄNSEMARKT opera house. He was a connoisseur of French culture and music, which is reflected in his compositions; his most important journey took him to Paris in 1737–8. Telemann's oeuvre is extremely diverse, stylistically complex and marked by a characteristic individuality. He composed works in all the important musical genres of his time, and remained creative and innovative even into old age (as is evident in his unequalled late work from around 1755, which is also marked by his continued interest in language and literature).

In their youth Handel and Telemann were close friends, exchanged opinions about musical matters and studied 'melodic' settings together (Telemann, *Autobiographie*, p. 201). Two letters in French from Handel to Telemann are extant from later times: the one dated December 1750 (HHB iv, pp. 444–5) implies that Handel had visited Hamburg and the one dated September 1754 (HHB iv, pp. 483–4) announces the delivery of a crate of rare plants to Telemann. Telemann repeatedly spoke of Handel to his pupils, and both set their friend Brockes's Passion oratorio to music (*BROCKES PASSION*). Telemann adapted four of the fourteen London operas by Handel performed at the Gänsemarkt: *TAMERLANO*, *OTTONE*, *RICCARDO PRIMO*, *PORO*, in addition to reviving *ALMIRA* and producing a number of pasticcios including Handel's music. The interest Handel showed in Telemann's music is apparent in his many BORROWINGS of musical themes, motifs or whole movements from cantatas in the *Harmonischer Gottesdienst* (score printed in 1726) and from the important collection of instrumental works *Musique de Table* (parts published in 1733). Handel develops the potential of Telemann's often concise and pointed musical material in ways that are diverse, often extraordinarily subtle and sometimes surprising.

UTE POETZSCH (Trans. ANGELA BAIER)

Dr. Karl Burney's Nachricht von Georg Friedrich Händel's Lebensumständen . . . übersetzt von Johann
    Joachim Eschenburg, Berlin and Stettin, 1785
E. Derr, 'Handel's Procedures for Composing with Materials from Telemann's
    "Harmonischer Gottes-Dienst" in "Solomon"', GHB I (1984)
U. Poetzsch-Seban, 'Musikalische Ausbildung und Sozialisation der Freunde Händel und
    Telemann im Vergleich', HJb 51 (2005)
J. H. Roberts, 'Handel's Borrowings from Telemann: An Inventory', GHB I (1984)
G. P. Telemann, 'Autobiographie', Singen ist das Fundament zur Music in allen Dingen. Eine
    Dokumentensammlung (Leipzig, 1981)

Terpsicore, HWV 8^c. Handel's only opera prologue (to the second revival of Il PASTOR FIDO), it was first staged at COVENT GARDEN on 9 November 1734. Performed a total of five times that month, it was never revived. An anonymous adaptation of the prologue to Louis Fuzelier and composer Colin de Blamont's ballet, *Les festes grecques et romaines* (Paris, 1723), *Terpsicore* features a festival graced by Apollo (sung by CARESTINI), Muse of Music Erato (sung by STRADA), and Muse of Dance Terpsichore (danced by Marie SALLÉ; Sallé's teacher, Françoise Prévost, had performed this role in the premiere of de Blamont's prologue). Handel had the services of Sallé and the entire Covent Garden dance troupe for the 1734–5 opera season; this was his first work to feature them.

    Terpsicore opens with the panegyric chorus, 'I nostri cori dobbiamo offrir' ('Let us our humblest off'rings pay'). This introduces the sun god's entrance with the Muses, and his aria, 'Gran Tonante' ('Grand Thunderer'), calls on Jupiter to bless Erato's new temple. Apollo then comments on Terpsicore's absence. A prelude announces her entry, accompanied by her disciples. (The first dance, a chaconne, is often found in French operas in situations where a solo dancer is featured within a group context.) The remainder of the prologue sees Apollo and Erato introducing, in recitative and aria, the affects which Terpsicore subsequently demonstrates in her dancing. A sarabande represents 'Joy and Mirth' and a gigue, 'ardent' and requited love. The affectively orchestrated duet, 'Tuoi passi son dardi', with its organ and theorbo continuo and prominent obbligato flute part, introduces the metaphor of Cupid's darts and the pleasant wounds they cause. This music is subsequently repeated as an instrumental number for Terpsicore. She later demonstrates the force of Jealousy to an unusual piece of dance music, initially characterised by tirades followed by contrasting rhythmic figures (dotted figures, then triplets) which suggest the essential instability of that emotion. Apollo and Erato then call upon Terpsicore to cease her representation of the passions ('At Will you give of Joy or Pain, Those moving Passions now restrain') before inviting her to demonstrate 'the Swiftness of your Feet' in Apollo's lightly scored aria (it has no bass line), 'Hai tanto rapido'. The music for this (a passepied), is repeated for the dance. Terpsicore joins the other dancers while Apollo and Erato praise her with the duet, 'Vezzi più amabili' ('Where lovelier graces'). The prologue concludes with a chorus honouring Virtue ('Cantiamo lieti della Virtù').

    Neither the autograph nor the conducting score to *Terpsicore* survives; the harpsichord score (Staats- und Universitätsbibliothek Hamburg MA/1041) indicates that the B sections to the first two arias ('Gran Tonante' and 'Di Parnasso') were cancelled. Although Handel worked closely with his model text, he did not follow it slavishly: he cut the part for Clio, Muse of Poetry; he also reversed the dance–aria pairings of the original. Although some of his dances are reminiscent of de Blamont's, he did not tend to use the same dance genres as the French composer to illustrate specific affects within the text.

SARAH MCCLEAVE

See also BALLET MUSIC; DANCE FORMS

terra è liberata, La ('Apollo e Dafne'), HWV 122. A dramatic cantata or short serenata for soprano, bass-baritone, woodwinds (flute, 2 oboes, bassoon), solo violin, solo cello, strings and continuo. Its unattributed libretto mainly draws from OVID's *Metamorphoses* (I.452–567) and Petrarch's *Canzoniere* (XXIX, CCXLVIII). Elated with his victory over the monstrous serpent Python, Apollo extols his own archery skills and vilifies Cupid's golden darts, boasting to be immune from their wounds. His loftiness finds immediate retribution as the beautiful nymph Daphne, a devotee of the virgin goddess Diana, enters the scene. Seized with love for the reluctant maiden, Apollo chases her until she is transformed into a laurel, whose branches will henceforth provide wreaths for the god's head.

The motive of male (heterosexual) desire pushed to the brink of rape, then frustrated through a magical metamorphosis, links this piece to ACI, GALATEA E POLIFEMO, as does the use of the solo bass voice, otherwise rare in Handel's cantata output. It would thus be tempting to assign the inception of 'Apollo e Dafne' to Handel's sojourn (summer 1708) in NAPLES, also because the aria 'Felicissima quest'alma' for Dafne and the duet 'Una guerra ho dentro il seno', both in 12/8, are cast in the typically Neapolitan moulds of siciliana and tarantella, respectively. However, MAINWARING's tantalising allusion to the Venetian flirtations between Handel as Apollo and Vittoria TARQUINI as Daphne – though hardly 'as cruel and obstinate' as the nymph – would rather suggest late 1709 or early 1710, while evidence from the autograph speaks for a composition process spanning over a long period and largely completed in 1710 at HANOVER.

Both singing characters display definite personalities: the vocal writing is more florid, extrovert and eloquent for Apollo, more lyrical and dramatic for Dafne. Lively rhythms, skilful counterpoint, a sensitive rendering of the poetry's meaning through rapid textural shifts, a masterful use of instrumental colour – all contribute to the charm of this fine piece, summing up the experience amassed by Handel since the HAMBURG period and further enhanced during his Italian stay. A wide range of self-BORROWINGS, pointing to the most diverse genres, testify to its high ranking in the composer's opinion. CARLO VITALI

Teseo, HWV 9. Italian opera, and Handel's only music drama in five acts. The plot is based on PLUTARCH's *Life of Theseus*, Pseudo-Apollodorus's *Bibliotheca* and OVID's *Metamorphoses*. At the beginning of the opera Agilea, an orphaned princess living in the Athenian court, enters the temple of Minerva, and asks the goddess for help. She loves the warrior Teseo, and wants to know his fate. Arcane (who is in love with Cleone) has been sent back to Athens to ensure that the ladies are safe. Cleone urges Arcane to return to the battlefield in order to find out about Teseo, but her request makes him jealous. King Egeo's troops return triumphant. Egeo had promised to marry the sorceress Medea in return for her magical assistance in winning the war, but he instead offers his hand in marriage to Agilea and plans to marry Medea to his long-lost son (who is believed to be in Trizene). Agilea does not dare to admit that she wants only Teseo.

Act II is dominated by Medea: she desires Teseo, and is willing to let King Egeo have Agilea. The envious Arcane informs Egeo that the Athenian people have already declared that Teseo is the King's successor. Medea warns Teseo, and he hopes for help from her, but she learns that Teseo loves Agilea and plots revenge. In Act III Cleone and Arcane agree to marry. Teseo returns and is determined to win his beloved Agilea. Egeo sends Arcane to proclaim Agilea as queen. Medea tries to command the defiant Agilea to forsake Teseo, and in order to execute her vengeance she changes the scene into a horrid desert 'full of frightful Monsters'; she allows Arcane and Cleone to go free, but Agilea is carried off by spirits.

In Act IV Arcane reports Medea's actions to Egeo. Agilea is not willing to let Medea have Teseo, but the sorceress threatens to kill the sleeping Teseo (who is brought in by her spirits). Agilea agrees to marry Egeo in order to save Teseo's life, but Medea insists that she must tell Teseo that she no longer loves him; Agilea weeps and cannot. Medea tries another tactic: she offers to support the lovers, but in actual fact plots to destroy Teseo. In the final Act, she tells King Egeo that his absent son will be deprived of the kingdom if Teseo is allowed to reign, and persuades him to present a poisoned cup to the hero. The two pairs of lovers enter for the nuptial ceremony. Egeo tells Teseo that he accepts him as his successor, and gives him the poisoned cup. Teseo takes it, and prepares to swear an oath on his sword, but Egeo recognises that it is the same sword he left as a token with his son many years before. Recognising that he has nearly murdered his own son, he throws the cup down. Medea flees, covering the palace in fire. The goddess Minerva descends in a machine, restores the palace, and bans the infernal powers.

The libretto was adapted by Nicola Francesco HAYM from Philippe QUI-NAULT's *Thésée Tragédie mise en musique* (first set by Lully in 1675). It was the first operatic collaboration between Handel and Haym. The five-act structure of the French *Tragédie lyrique* was preserved, and Haym retained much of Quinault's original text in literal Italian translation. Haym shortened the recitatives, revised the third and fourth acts in order to create a suitable role for Jane Barbier (Arcane), and reshaped the aria texts to suit Italian da capo form. Singers do not customarily exit the stage after their aria as is normally the case in Italianate opera seria, and sometimes characters have two consecutive arias only interrupted by one or two recitatives.

Handel composed the music in London between November and 19 December 1712, possibly at BURLINGTON HOUSE, where he seems to have been the guest of Richard Boyle (3rd Earl of BURLINGTON) from 1712 until 1715. The printed WORDBOOK is dedicated to Burlington, and describes Handel as still employed as 'Maestro di Capella di S. A. E. di Hannover'. The role of Medea's confidante Fedra was cut during the compositional process, but she is mentioned in the stage directions of Act II. Perhaps a decision was made that Fedra would be a 'silent' role: in February and June 1713 HEIDEGGER made payments to Signora

Manina that were notably less than those made to the other singers, and Manina's name appears on the soprano stave in the Act II *coro* in a manuscript copy of the score in the Gerald Coke Handel Collection (SOURCES AND COLLECTIONS, 7). The wordbook contains a lot of lines marked with *virgole* to show that they were omitted in performance. Some of these had been set to music, but were cancelled in the score before the first performance. All such unperformed lines were presumably retained in the wordbook because it was recognised that they were essential for the audience's comprehension of the plot.

The opera was first performed at Queen's Theatre (KING'S THEATRE) on 10 January 1713. The cast was as follows:

Teseo	Valeriano Pellegrini (castrato)
Medea	Elisabetta PILOTTI-SCHIAVONETTI (soprano)
Agilea	Margherita de L'EPINE (soprano)
Egeo	Valentino Urbani (castrato)
Clizia	Maria Gallia (soprano)
Arcane	Jane Barbier (contralto)
Sacredote di Minerva	Richard Leveridge (bass)
Fedra	?Maria Manina (silent role)

Some extra male singers probably sang in the choruses. *Teseo* was performed thirteen times during the 1712–13 season, but after the first two nights (both of which had a full house), the bankrupt theatre manager Owen SWINEY fled the country, having failed to pay for the expensive new scenery, costumes and singers. The singers resolved to continue with the season under the management of Heidegger, but during the fourth performance (21 January) problems with the stage machinery caused an apology to be printed in the *Daily Courant* reassuring the public that the next performance would be given 'in its Perfection, that is to say with all the Scenes, Decorations, Flights, and Machines'. The last performance of the season (16 May) was 'For the Benefit of Mr. Handel . . . with an Addition of several New Songs, and particularly an entertainment for the Harpsichord, Compos'd by Mr. Handel on purpose for that Day'. Handel made £73 10s. 11d. from the occasion, but he never revived the opera.

ANNETTE LANDGRAF

I. A. Alexandre, 'Handel: *Teseo*' (CD booklet note, Erato 2292-45806-2, 1992)
Dean and Knapp, *Operas*
Harris, *Librettos*
D. Kimbell, 'The Libretto of Handel's *Teseo*', ML 44/4 (1963), 371–9
Strohm

Theatre Music. See *ALCESTE*; The *ALCHEMIST*; SONGS

Theatre Royal. See COVENT GARDEN Theatre; DRURY LANE Theatre

Theodora, HWV 68. One of the last of Handel's English oratorios, *Theodora* is the only one, apart from *MESSIAH*, to be based on a Christian subject. It was composed between 28 June and 17 July 1749, after the premiere of *SUSANNA* and *SOLOMON*, the musical celebrations upon the Peace of Aix-la-Chapelle (War of the AUSTRIAN SUCCESSION) and Handel's first FOUNDLING HOSPITAL concert. The full score was completed on 31 July. The composer then went to BATH to take the waters, returning to London to write incidental music to SMOLLETT's ALCESTE and the Organ Concerto in G minor, Op. 7 No. 5 (ORCHESTRAL WORKS, 5).

The libretto was supplied by Thomas MORELL. His principal source was Robert Boyle's short novel, *The Martyrdom of Theodora and Didymus* (1687), which had been published to do good 'by rendering virtue amiable' and had recently been reprinted in his collected works (1744). Another source was PIERRE CORNEILLE's *Théodore, vierge et martyre*, which had been produced in Paris in 1645–6: like Corneille, Morell made Theodora a princess.

The libretto is well crafted and deals with matters of moment. Theodora is the young leader of a Christian community in fourth-century Antioch, a city under Roman rule; she has a companion named Irene. To celebrate the birthday of the Emperor, the governor, Valens, proclaims a festival of Jove in which all must take part. Refusing to acknowledge a Roman god, Theodora is sentenced to solitary confinement, where 'the meanest of my [Valens's] guards with lustful joy shall triumph o'er her boasted chastity'. She is rescued by Didymus, a Roman officer whom she had previously converted to Christianity; when, later, he stands trial for his crime, he in turn is saved by Theodora. To the amazement of Valens and other Romans, both she and Didymus prepare to die for their faith. After the ensuing chorus Morell supplied a conclusion in which Septimius, another Roman officer, is converted to Christianity by their example. Handel did not set it but finished with the chorus, emphasising the nobility of self-sacrifice rather than the possibility of salvation.

Ruth Smith describes *Theodora* as 'the most conspicuously open to interpretation of all Handel's dramas'. For others it demonstrates 'personal faith in a Christian destiny' or 'the necessity of man's subjection to destiny', or displays the influence of Locke's philosophy or WESLEY's Methodism (NONCONFORMITY). Among the primary themes are freedom of conscience and the place of established religion (cf. Didymus: 'Ought we not to leave the free-born mind of man still ever free, since vain is the attempt to force belief with the severest instruments of death?'). The work also casts the hostility between Romans and Christians as a battle of the sexes (proactive, extrovert males versus reactive, introspective females) and raises the ethics of martyrdom and of assisted suicide (Theodora asks Didymus to kill her). She does not respond amorously, however, to the 'virtuous love' with which she has 'inflam'd' his heart: *Theodora* is not a romantic tragedy.

The composition of the oratorio involved extensive borrowing from STEFFANI's 'divertimento drammatico' *La Lotta d'Hercole con Acheloo* (1689) and CLARI's chamber duets, and also from a motet by LEGRENZI, a keyboard suite by MUFFAT, LOTTI's *Missa Sapientiae* and Handel's own *TAMERLANO*, *ISRAEL IN EGYPT* and *HERCULES*. The first performance took place at COVENT GARDEN on Friday, 16 March 1750, with 'a new concerto on the organ'. According to WALSH's edition [1751], the singers were as follows:

Theodora	Giulia FRASI (soprano)
Didymus	Gaetano GUADAGNI (castrato)

Septimius   Thomas LOWE (tenor)
Irene   Caterina GALLI (mezzo-soprano)
Valens   Thomas REINHOLD (bass)

The concerto was probably Op. 7 No. 5, although Roger Fiske argued that it was Op. 7 No. 4. In addition to oboes, bassoons, strings and continuo, the oratorio calls for flutes in Theodora's first 'confinement' scene (II.ii), trumpets and drums in the first Roman chorus and horns in two others.

Although Theodora is an extremely fine work, musically as well as dramatically, it fared worse at the box office than any other of Handel's English oratorios. There were only three performances in 1750 – on 16, 21 and 23 March – and the composer banked only £100. The failure has been attributed to the earthquakes in spring 1750 and the non-biblical nature of the story; Handel is reported to have believed that, being 'Christian' and 'virtuous', the work appealed neither to Jews nor to ladies. It nevertheless occupied a special place in his affections. According to Morell, he 'valued' the libretto (or possibly the oratorio) 'more than any Performance of the Kind' and apparently regarded 'He saw the lovely youth' as his choral masterpiece. He gave only one further performance – at Covent Garden on 5 March 1755 – for which the libretto seems not to have been reprinted. The singers were probably Frasi, Guadagni, BEARD, Christina Passerini and Robert Wass, all of whom appeared in *JUDAS MACCABAEUS* a week later. Handel planned a second revival for 1759, and he may have been assisted by Morell; but although a revised libretto was issued by WATTS and DOD, no performance took place.

It is impossible to establish precisely the versions of Theodora that were prepared in 1750, 1755 or 1759. The 1750 libretto does not reveal whether Reinhold sang the airs 'Go, my faithful soldier, go' and 'Ye ministers of justice' or the recitatives with which Handel replaced them, nor does it tell us exactly which movements were included in the first 'confinement' scene, which the composer revised several times in quick succession. Airs elsewhere were omitted, or shorn of their B section and da capo repeat or shortened by internal cuts, and recitatives were abridged. The changes may have been made – simultaneously or piecemeal – before the first performance or during the opening run. Some could even have been made after the third performance, ready for the revival in 1755. The absence of a 1755 libretto suggests that this version was very similar to the last one performed in 1750.

It also implies that the more numerous and radical amendments found in the 1759 libretto had not been made by 1755. The biggest change was the omission of III.iii – from 'Undaunted in the court' to 'New scenes of joy' (which had already been cut), including the accompanied recitative 'O my Irene' and the duet 'Whither, Princess, do you fly'. Elsewhere, sixteen recitatives were abbreviated (over and above the cuts already made), another air was omitted, one more replaced by a new chorus and a third reduced to its A section. By contrast, a new air ('Lost in anguish, quite despairing', possibly by John Christopher SMITH JUNIOR) was inserted, and another ('The leafy honours of the field', from *BELSHAZZAR*) was added in 1759 or the 1760s.   COLIN TIMMS

Dean, *Oratorios*

D. R. Hurley, 'For Better or Worse? Handel's Revisions in *Theodora*', *Handel Studies: A Gedenkschrift for Howard Serwer*, ed. R. G. King (Hillsdale, NY, 2009)

L. M. M. Robarts, 'Rendering Virtue Amiable: A Study of Some Formal and Intellectual Aspects of Thomas Morell's Libretto and George Frideric Handel's Music for *Theodora*, 1749–50', M.Phil dissertation (Open University, 1997)

D. Schröder, '"A Sect, rebellious to the Gods, and Rome": Händels Oratorium *Theodora* und der Methodismus', *GHB* VI (1996), 101–14

H. W. Shaw (ed.), *Theodora*, Novello Handel Edition (London, 1984)

R. Smith, 'Comprehending Theodora', *Eighteenth-Century Music* 2/1 (2005), 57–90

C. Timms (ed.), *Theodora*, HHA I/29 (Kassel, 2008)

Theorbo. See INSTRUMENTATION, 16

'There in blissful shade and bow'rs'. See COMUS

Thibaut, Anton Friedrich Justus (b. Hameln, 4 Jan. 1772; d. Heidelberg, 28 March 1840). Thibaut was primarily a legal scholar. He studied in GÖTTINGEN (1792–3), Königsberg (1793–4) and Kiel, receiving his doctorate in 1796 and becoming professor in 1798. Thereafter he was law professor in Jena (1802–5) and Heidelberg (1805–40). He was also an amateur musician and theoretician; he began collecting sacred vocal music whilst in Jena and founded the Singverein in Heidelberg. He performed many of Handel's works in Heidelberg, usually involving his own translations of librettos into German. His *Über Reinheit der Tonkunst* (1825) demonstrates further interest in Handel, as does the content of his library, most of which was bought by the Bayrische Staatsbibliothek, Munich, in 1857.   MATTHEW GARDNER

See also RECEPTION

E. Baumstark, *Ant. Friedr. Justus Thibaut* (Leipzig, 1841)

W. Rackwitz, 'A. F. J. Thibauts Beitrag zur Händel-Renaissance im 19. Jahrhundert', *HJb* 26 (1980)

M. Zywietz, 'Das Händel Verständnis von Bernhard Klein und Anton Friedrich Justus Thibaut', *HJb* 44 (1998)

This is the day which the Lord hath made. See ANTHEMS, 4

Three Choirs Festival. See FESTIVALS, 1

Titus, l'Empereur, HWV A⁵. An abandoned opera, probably written during October and November 1731. It is scored for oboes, horns, five-part strings and continuo, and features characters named Tito and Berenice (presumably intended for SENESINO and STRADA respectively), Dalinda and Antioco (for contraltos, probably BERTOLLI and Bagnolesi), Paulino (perhaps for the tenor PINACCI), Oldauro (a secondary tenor role) and Arsete (probably a bass part for MONTAGNANA). Handel's use of a French title for an Italian opera is unusual ('Ouverture pour l'Opera Titus, l'Empereur'), but the dramatis personae and events in I.ii–iii correspond closely to Jean RACINE's play *Bérénice* (1670). No intermediate Italian source libretto has been identified; perhaps Handel unsuccessfully sought to base the opera directly on Racine's drama.

Only an overture and the first three scenes of Act I are extant, including a chorus praising the Emperor (featuring horns) and two arias. The fragment breaks off in the third scene, which lacks an aria. However, the completion of some secco recitatives suggests that Handel might have reached a more advanced stage in his COMPOSITIONAL PROCESS than the surviving fragment reveals. It seems that *Titus* was aborted when he decided to set METASTASIO's *EZIO* instead: he transferred the *Titus* overture to the autograph score of *Ezio*, revised Antioco's 'Mi restano le lagrime' (*Titus*, I.ii) into Onoria's 'Peni tu per un'ingrata' (*Ezio*, III.ii), and possibly modelled Valentiniano's 'Se tu la reggi' (*Ezio*, I.i) on Tito's 'Altra legge nall'amare' (*Titus*, I.i).   DAVID VICKERS

Dean, *Operas*
HHB iii
Strohm

Tobit. See PASTICCIOS, 2

Tolomeo, Re di Egitto (HWV 25). The last opera Handel wrote for the Royal Academy of Music (OPERA COMPANIES, 2) before the company dissolved in 1728. It was also his final collaboration with the librettist Nicola HAYM who died the following year. The libretto is adapted from Carlo Sigismondo CAPECE's *Tolomeo et Alessandro overo La corona disprezzata*, set by DOMENICO SCARLATTI for the domestic theatre of Maria Casimira, the Queen of Poland, in ROME in 1711. It had been set three more times before Handel's version (Fermo 1713, Rome 1724, Jesi 1727); Haym's source was the original version, which he substantially shortened. The story is taken from Justinus's *Historiae Philippicae*. The historical action took place in Egypt in 108 BC: Cleopatra III refused to share the throne with her son Ptolemy Lathyrus (Ptolemy IX Soter II), forced him into exile, abducted his wife Seleuca, and raised her younger son Ptolemy X Alexander to the throne instead. She pursued her elder son to Cyprus and had one of her generals killed because he let him escape, whereupon the younger son abandoned the dangers of the throne. The opera is set in Cyprus, where Tolomeo lives disguised as a simple shepherd, Osmino. Seleuce, believed to have drowned in a shipwreck, sets out to search for Tolomeo, disguised as a shepherdess, Delia. Alessandro, following his mother's command, is also searching for Tolomeo in order to kill him. Capece invented three new characters: the King of Cyprus, Araspe, in love with 'Delia'; his sister Elisa, in love with 'Osmino'; and Araspe's former love, Princess Dorisbe, searching for her faithless lover, disguised as a gardener, Clori. Haym omitted Dorisbe, presumably because there was no singer available for the part.

Act I opens on a sea shore, where Tolomeo is about to commit suicide, but then responds to cries for help from a drowning man. In the unconscious man he recognises Alessandro; he could now have revenge, but refuses to shed fraternal blood. When Alessandro wakes up, his first sight is that of Elisa and he falls in love with her. Her heart, however, burns for the shepherd Osmino, much to her chagrin about being in love with a man of inferior birth. In front of Araspe's villa, situated in a picturesque village of shepherds' cottages, Delia/Seleuce laments the loss of Tolomeo. Araspe attempts to court her, unsuccessfully. Elisa offers the dejected Osmino/Tolomeo a position at court. He would gladly die to avoid her love, but he thinks of Seleuce's unavenged death. Nevertheless, he does not wish to commit a crime against his brother and mother. Weighed down by grief, he falls asleep. Seleuce notices him and tries to identify him by moving his hand which is covering his face. The jealous Araspe, seeing her leaning over

'Osmino', wants to kill Tolomeo, who, however, reassures him that he does not love Delia.

At the beginning of Act II, Tolomeo is prompted by Elisa to reveal his true identity. She is overjoyed to learn that he is of noble blood. Araspe, seeing 'Osmino' again, is enraged. Elisa defends Tolomeo, and Araspe allows her to confront him with 'Delia' to see whether he speaks the truth. Seleuce, however, cautiously refuses to recognise him as her husband Tolomeo. Triumphant, Elisa confesses her love to him and promises to help him regain his throne, but he refuses her. Elisa swears revenge on him. When Alessandro offers his love, she states she will only accept him if he kills Tolomeo and secures the throne. Alessandro would not wish to mount the throne unjustly, but is nevertheless stirred by her words. Meanwhile, Araspe again approaches 'Delia' and tries to forcefully embrace her. Tolomeo steps out to defend her, and his true identity is revealed. Seleuce begs Araspe to show Tolomeo mercy, but in vain. Araspe has Tolomeo put in chains.

In Act III, Alessandro receives news of Cleopatra's death. Araspe advises him to kill Tolomeo rather than take him back to Egypt, but Alessandro refuses. Araspe thus assumes that Alessandro is leaving it to him to kill Tolomeo. In the meantime, Elisa blackmails Seleuce into renouncing Tolomeo in order to save his life, and insists that Seleuce should talk Tolomeo into marrying Elisa. However, the meeting between Tolomeo and Seleuce results in their confirming love for each other. Elisa threatens that both lovers shall die. Alessandro awaits the arrival of his troops in the woods; he intends to enlist their support for Tolomeo. He saves Seleuce, who has been abducted by guards, and sets off to save his brother. Tolomeo has drunk the poison given to him by Elisa. Araspe presents Alessandro with Tolomeo's body, and Alessandro swears his revenge. Repentant Elisa admits to having ordered Seleuce's death. To compensate for this mischief, however, she gave Tolomeo a sleeping potion instead of poison. Tolomeo awakes and is reunited with Seleuce. Alessandro tells Tolomeo that their mother has bequeathed him the throne, and Tolomeo pardons all the wrongs that have been done to him.

Performed after SIROE and its complex plot of courtly intrigue, the quasi-pastoral setting of Tolomeo might have been chosen for a contrast; great efforts were made in the adaptation of the libretto and in the music setting to add nature imagery, which was presumably intended to appeal to the public. As the last new opera in a season during which the Royal Academy's future was looking bleak, Haym's dedicatory preface in the libretto was a manifesto asking for the continued protection of Italian opera in London. The first performance of the opera took place at the KING'S THEATRE on 30 April 1728 with the following cast:

Tolomeo	SENESINO (castrato)
Seleuce	Francesca CUZZONI (soprano)
Elisa	FAUSTINA Bordoni (soprano)
Alessandro	Antonio Baldi (castrato)
Araspe	Giuseppe BOSCHI (bass)

It ran for seven performances. As is the case with Siroe, the opera was arguably hampered by an absence of another star male singer to complement the trio of leading singers (Senesino–Bordoni–Cuzzoni). The roles for the secondary singers were reduced, which has a detrimental effect on the dramatic impact of Alessandro (who was one of the two main characters in Capece's original libretto). Furthermore, Handel's setting with pastoral connotations resulted in an atmosphere with little dynamic contrast in Act I, and the two soprano roles are not consistently differentiated. Nevertheless, each act has a strong conclusion, and the opera contains some exceptionally fine music. Particularly profound is the scene in which Tolomeo drinks the 'poison' (III.vi), with the stirring accompagnato 'Inumano fratel' and the palpitating aria 'Stille amare'. Also notable are Tolomeo's arias 'Torna sol' and 'Tiranni miei pensieri', and the energetic characterisation of Araspe. The opera also contains several moments of dramaturgical invention, most notably the aria *per due* 'Dite, che fa' (II.vi), a complex number in which Tolomeo and Seleuce are looking for each other in the woods, exchanging appearances on and off stage, with Tolomeo's voice echoing Seleuce's from behind the scenes. The most popular aria from the opera today, however, is Alessandro's 'Non lo dirò col labbro', in the English arrangement 'Silent Worship' by Arthur Somervell. Handel produced two substantially revised versions of *Tolomeo* for the Second Academy (OPERA COMPANIES, 3). His first revival of the opera concluded the 1729–30 season, and the second took place in January 1733. The first modern revival of *Tolomeo* was at Göttingen in 1938.   SUZANA OGRAJENŠEK

Dean, *Operas*
Harris, *Librettos*
S. Ograjenšek, 'Handel's Opera *Tolomeo*: A Study of its Genesis and Performances During the Composer's Lifetime', M.Phil. dissertation (University of Cambridge, 2000)
  'From *Alessandro* (1726) to *Tolomeo* (1728): The Final Royal Academy Operas', Ph.D. dissertation (University of Cambridge, 2005)
M. Pacholke (ed.), *Tolomeo, Re di Egitto*, HHA, II/22 (Kassel, 2000)
Strohm

Tonson, Jacob (b. ?1714; d. London, 31 March 1767). There were three generations of booksellers named Jacob Tonson. The third with that name was considered by Dr Johnson as 'a man who is to be praised as often as he is named' (Johnson, *Lives of the Poets*, vol. 1, p. 222). He published WORDBOOKS, printed by John WATTS, for English works by Handel, beginning with *ALEXANDER'S FEAST* in 1736, followed by the *SONG FOR ST CECILIA'S DAY*, *ISRAEL IN EGYPT*, *L'ALLEGRO*, *SAMSON*, *SEMELE*, *HERCULES*, *OCCASIONAL ORATORIO*, *JOSHUA*, *SOLOMON* and *SUSANNA*. When twenty-one, Tonson inherited a fortune and lucrative perpetual copyrights, including those connected with MILTON and DRYDEN. He specialised in publications which promoted British high culture, of which his wordbooks were part. Tonson published the wordbooks for *Hercules* in 1749 and 1752, though they have the name of 'J. Roberts' in their imprint.   LESLIE M. M. ROBARTS

S. Johnson, *Prefaces, Biographical and Critical, to the Works of the English Poets*, vol. 2 (London, 1779), pp. 148–9
K. M. Lynch, *Jacob Tonson Kit-Cat Publisher* (Knoxville, TN, 1971)
L. M. M. Robarts, 'A Bibliographical and Textual Study of the Wordbooks for James Miller's *Joseph and his Brethren* and Thomas Broughton's *Hercules*, Oratorio Librettos Set to Music by George Frideric Handel, 1743–44', Ph.D. dissertation (University of Birmingham, 2008)

Tory. The Tories emerged as the party of the crown and Church in response to the exclusion crisis that had sought to displace the Catholic James, Duke of York, from the line of succession. As with the WHIGS, the name Tory was originally intended as a term of abuse, being that of a particularly notorious gang of Irish (Catholic) brigands. After 1688 some Tories came to be associated with the JACOBITE supporters of the exiled King (and his successors), while others retired from active political life as NON-JURORS: unwilling to take oaths declaring the new regime to be legitimate. The remainder accepted the new order and during the reign of Queen ANNE (1702–14) the party enjoyed its apogee, but the succession of the Hanoverian monarchs spelled doom for the Tories, even though many had aligned themselves very clearly with the German Protestant succession. Within a couple of years of the accession of King GEORGE I no Tories were in positions of any particular significance in government, a situation that was maintained until the accession of GEORGE III. Although Handel was on occasion, rather bizarrely, accused of harbouring Tory-Jacobite sympathies, there seems little reason to give such rumours any credence. He composed a patriotic song to rouse Londoners at the height of the 1745 Jacobite rebellion and another to celebrate the Jacobite defeat at Culloden in 1746.

ROBIN EAGLES

K. Feiling, *A History of the Tory Party, 1640–1714* (Oxford, 1924)
G. Holmes, *British Politics in the Age of Anne*, rev. edn (London, 1987)

Tra le fiamme ('Il consiglio'), HWV 170. A stream of metaphors, involving both stock Arcadian imagery (the moth attracted by the flame to its death) and classical myth (the Phoenix resurrecting from her pyre, Icarus falling into the sea), emphasises such moral concepts as the deceptiveness of beauty and the mortal danger in trespassing the boundaries of nature – Daedalus and the Phoenix being unique exceptions to the general rule. In the concluding aria–recitative sequence, earthly centred flights of fancy on factitious wings are warned against, since Heaven provided man with 'thoughts far swifter and elevated than any feathers' that can raise him to his original destination – Heaven itself.

Cardinal PAMPHILIJ, whose ARCADIAN ACADEMY nickname Fenicio Larisseo hinted at the Phoenix, authored this subtle text. Handel set it to music for soprano and instruments, possibly in mid-1708, during the presence in ROME of his HAMBURG acquaintance Ernst Christian Hesse, a virtuoso gamba player who might also have taken part in the creation of *La RESURREZIONE*. Flamboyant vocal coloratura, extended use of word-painting, lively rhythms, a rich instrumental palette featuring changing combinations of recorders, oboe and gamba, account for the popularity of the piece among modern performers. The final repetition of the opening aria is a structural feature that also occurs in the cantata *ALLA CACCIA* (1707). BORROWINGS: *PARTENOPE, TAMERLANO, RICCARDO PRIMO.*

CARLO VITALI

trio sonatas. See CHAMBER MUSIC, 2

trionfo del Tempo e del Disinganno, Il, HWV 46ᵃ. Italian oratorio, libretto by Cardinal Benedetto PAMPHILIJ. Handel probably composed his first oratorio in the early months of 1707. The copyist Antonio Giuseppe ANGELINI submitted a bill for copying the performing score and the part-books, corrected by Handel himself, to Pamphilij in May 1707. According to MAINWARING, Pamphilij had also commissioned the work from Handel.

If, when and where the work was first performed is unknown; no documents giving definite information have surfaced so far. Pamphilij's account books indicate that the oratorio featured in his music entertainments in 1708 and 1709; copyists were paid for copying revisions and additions to the score and parts, perhaps at the instigation of Carlo CESARINI, Pamphilij's *maestro di cappella*. Cesarini also set Pamphilij's libretto again for a performance in the Collegio Clementino in ROME in 1725.

Handel's oratorio is scored for four vocal soloists (two sopranos, alto and tenor), two recorders, two oboes, strings and basso continuo; the orchestra is divided into concertino and ripieno in some of the movements. The work consists of two parts; the 'prima parte' begins with a three-movement 'sonata': according to Mainwaring, Handel originally intended to have a different overture with a French-style opening part, but changed it because CORELLI complained that he was puzzled about how to play it (some scholars have suggested that perhaps the original overture was HWV 336). Secco recitatives alternate with arias and there are also two accompagnati, two duets and a quartet. The first part ends, as was common at the time, with an ensemble featuring all vocal soloists; the oratorio, like most of the works of Handel's Italian contemporaries, has no choruses (at least not in the sense of Handel's later English oratorio choral movements).

Pamphilij's libretto tells of an allegorical dispute between Bellezza (Beauty, soprano), Piacere (Sensual Pleasure, soprano), Disinganno (Truth or Insight, literally: Dis-Illusionment, alto) and Tempo (Time, tenor). Handel's contemporaries were familiar with allegory as an emblematic art form which represented a close linking of pictorial image, affection and imaginative intellect. Allegory was often used to facilitate grasp of complex and sophisticated matters by making them sensually tangible. The allegory in Pamphilij's libretto should therefore not be regarded as cold, abstract and appealing only to theoretical ideas. It should rather be recognised as a differentiated, vivacious and realistic depiction of an extremely complicated psychological process of gaining wisdom and maturity: the main character Bellezza repents, takes a new direction in life and develops a completely new way of looking at the world. Pamphilij's text explores a pivotal theme that is characteristic of oratorio-writing as a sacred medium, namely that of inner repentance, but does not elaborate on theological disputes. Pamphilij seems to have been more interested in depicting psychomachia, the battle of souls between contrasting inclinations.

At the beginning of Part I Bellezza contemplates herself in the mirror. She is afraid of the transitoriness of her beauty; Piacere cajolingly promises her everlasting beauty. They swear eternal fidelity to each other. Tempo and Disinganno announce that they will demonstrate the evanescence of beauty. A contest is set up to determine the stronger party. Bellezza wants to surround herself with pleasures to arm herself against time. Tempo reassures her that nobody is able to withstand him; in a drastic move, he asks the tombs to open and show them the remains of the beauties interred there. Bellezza and Piacere agree that there is no point in spending the prime of life contemplating gloomy matters since this is a pursuit to be engaged in in old age. Disinganno reminds them that life is short and the time of death uncertain. Bellezza denies the power of time and contends that if time is disregarded, it loses its powers. Piacere introduces his realm which is free from all care. It pleases not only the eye but also the ear: a concerto-like movement for organ, a sort of 'music within the music', is played by a graceful youth who accomplishes (as Bellezza notes) superhuman feats – it is likely that Handel played this organ part himself. Bellezza's triumph is of short duration; she recognises that terrestrial pleasure is always accompanied by pain and that time and truth will not leave her alone. Tempo and Disinganno call Bellezza away from the realm of pleasure into the realm of truth. Piacere warns Bellezza not to leave the flower-strewn path of pleasure.

The second part begins with Tempo introducing Bellezza into the realm of truth. Bellezza is worried; she had expected to find not only pain but also pleasure in truth. Piacere reminds her of her vows of fidelity and says that now that Bellezza has become unfaithful, she suffers deservedly. When asked to make a definite decision, Bellezza wavers and asks for respite. Piacere entreats Bellezza to decide in favour of pleasure and against painful truth ('Lascia la spina', better known as 'Lascia ch'io pianga' in *RINALDO*). But Bellezza, convinced by truth, bids Piacere farewell and asks Disinganno to allow her to look into the mirror of truth. She is dismayed when, instead of beauty, she beholds only ugliness, shame and misery. Bellezza repents, casts away her jewels and decides (like St Mary Magdalene) to live as a hermit. For the sake of her tears which she plans to follow up with good deeds, she hopes the angels in heaven will intercede on her behalf. In the impressive final adagio aria 'Tu del ciel ministro eletto', with a solo violin part presumably composed for Corelli, Bellezza asks her guardian angel to carry her new heart to God. Thus the work ends not triumphantly but *pianissimo*. Linden has interpreted this calculated reduction in the musical structure as a rhetorical means of alluding to the kind of celestial harmony which is unattainable on earth.

Handel's earliest oratorio contains borrowings from at least seven of Reinhard KEISER's operas composed for HAMBURG between 1697 and 1705, but it is anything but a clumsy first effort: he invested a lot of energy in the score, and his satisfaction with the oratorio is suggested by his reuse of more than half of the arias in later works (La *RESURREZIONE*, *AGRIPPINA*, *DEBORAH* and *PARNASSO IN FESTA*, among others), and also by the fact that Il *trionfo del Tempo* is the only one of his major works composed in Italy that he later revived in London.   JULIANE RIEPE (Trans. ANGELA BAIER)

See also Il *TRIONFO DEL TEMPO E DELLA VERITÀ*; The *TRIUMPH OF TIME AND TRUTH*

C. Gianturco, 'Il trionfo del Tempo e del Disinganno: Four Case-Studies in Determining Italian Poetic-Musical Genres', JRMA 119/1 (1994), 43–59
A. Hicks, 'Handel: Il trionfo del Tempo e del Disinganno' (CD booklet note, Virgin 3 63428 2, 2007)
M. Pacholke, 'Dramatische Aspekte in Händels erstem Oratorium Il Trionfo del tempo e del disinganno (HWV 46ª)', HJb 37 (1991)
M. A. Parker, 'Handel's Il trionfo del Tempo e del Disinganno: A Petrarchan Vision in Baroque Style', ML 84/3 (2003), 403–13
R. Smith, 'Psychological Realism in Il Trionfo del Tempo e del Disinganno', HJb 54 (2008)

647

H. Van der Linden, 'Benedetto Pamphilj as librettist: Mary Magdalene and the Harmony of the
Spheres in Handel's Il trionfo del Tempo e del Disinganno', Recercare 16 (2004), 133–60

trionfo del Tempo e della Verità, Il, HWV 46ᵇ. Handel's extensive London revision of his early Italian oratorio Il TRIONFO DEL TEMPO E DEL DISINGANNO. Cardinal Benedetto PAMPHILIJ's original libretto was only slightly reworked: perhaps the allegorical tale of Beauty choosing a spiritual life instead of sensual pleasure was doctrinally unspecific enough to suit Handel's Protestant audience (unlike the strongly Roman Catholic tone of La RESURREZIONE, which the composer never revived in London but frequently used for BORROWINGS). Although Handel could have performed the original 1707 score of Il trionfo with singers he had available during his 1736–7 COVENT GARDEN season, he chose to make extensive changes to the music.

The oratorio was expanded from two to three parts. Thirteen of the 1707 movements were retained, but only seven arias were essentially unchanged, and four were substantially recomposed. Some recitatives were modified from the 1707 originals, but others were new. Handel's decision to add five choruses indicates that choral contributions had become an integral aspect in oratorios; although these were probably sung by the soloists with a few adult singers reinforcing each part (it is unlikely that choirboys from the CHAPEL ROYAL would have been granted permission to participate in an Italian theatre entertainment). Four of these choruses were borrowed from Handel's previous compositions: the splendid opening chorus ('Solo al goder') and the conclusion to Part II ('Pria che sii converta') were both taken from the wedding anthem Sing unto God (ANTHEMS, 4) composed the previous year, the solemn fugue 'Son larve di dolor' (midway through Part I) was based on material from GRAUN'S Passion Kommt her und schaut, and the 'Alleluia' chorus concluding the oratorio was the finale to the organ concerto, Op. 4 No. 4 (ORCHESTRAL WORKS, 5) created for the first London performances of ATHALIA (1735). The other chorus, 'L'uomo sempre se stesso', was a newly composed extension of Bellezza's 1707 aria 'Nasce l'uomo'. Other new compositions written specifically for the 1737 version consist of three spirited sinfonias at the beginning of each part (the first inventively modelled on thematic material from the 1707 overture) and fourteen vocal items (ten arias and two quartets), including entirely new settings of Piacere's arias 'Lascia la spina' (a jaunty intricate piece based on a dance from TERPSICORE; the original 1707 sarabande had in the meantime become popular as 'Lascia ch'io pianga' in RINALDO), 'Un leggiadro giovinetto' (with a solo violin, whereas the 1707 setting had a solo organ part) and 'Come nembo che fugge col vento' (an intense aria di bravua foreshadowing 'Crude furie degl'orridi abissi' in SERSE a year later). Some of the new material was influenced by ideas borrowed from TELEMANN's church cantata collection Der Harmonische Gottes-Dienst (e.g. Tempo's turbulent 'Folle dunque', transformed from its 1707 setting), and Piacere's 'Fosco genio' was based on a solo in Sing unto God. The oratorio's INSTRUMENTATION was enriched by the addition of horns, trumpets and timpani. The violin obbligato in Bellezza's last aria was rewritten for an oboe, presumably to display the abilities of SAMMARTINI.

Handel prepared his autograph manuscript of Il trionfo del Tempo e della Verità between 2 and 14 March 1737. The oratorio was premiered at Covent Garden on 23 March 1737, and another three performances were given during the Lent season. The cast was probably as follows:

Bellezza	Anna STRADA del Pò (soprano)
Piacere	Gioacchino CONTI (castrato)
Tempo	Francesca BERTOLLI (alto)
Disinganno	Maria Caterina NEGRI (alto)

Handel directed only one more revival on 3 March 1739. For this occasion he altered the part of Tempo for a bass (probably Henry REINHOLD), transferred arias between all four characters, added the chorus 'O Tempo, padre di dolor' (using the music of 'O Baal, Monach of the skies' from *DEBORAH*), replaced the solo violin in the Sonatina and 'Un leggiadro giovinetto' with a carillon (INSTRUMENTATION, 3), and reverted to the 1707 original version of 'Lascia la spina'. From 1741 Handel no longer needed to perform Italian texts in London, which caused *Il trionfo del Tempo e della Verità* to fall into obscurity, although most of the choruses and sixteen arias were retained without significant musical change in the 1757 English version The *TRIUMPH OF TIME AND TRUTH*. The 1737 version of the oratorio is in many respects a distinct work from its 1707 predecessor, but it has not yet been published and modern performers seem to favour the Roman original. The first modern revival, which used a performing edition by Anthony Hicks, took place at the London Handel Festival on 30 April 1998. The commercial recording conducted by Joachim Carlos Martini made on 31 May 1998 uses a bizarre composite edition containing movements from the 1707, 1737 and 1739 versions and the 1732 version of *ACIS AND GALATEA* (HWV 49^b).   ARTIE HEINRICH

HHB ii
A. Hicks, '*Il trionfo del Tempo e della Verità*', London Handel Festival programme (1998), 56–8

Triumph of Time and Truth, The, HWV 71. After Handel succumbed to blindness in the early 1750s (HANDEL, 16) he was unable to compose new large-scale works, but in 1757 he presumably instructed his assistant John Christopher SMITH JUNIOR how to adapt Il *TRIONFO DEL TEMPO E DELLA VERITÀ* (HWV 46^h) into an English oratorio. Often described as 'Handel's last oratorio', it is unlikely that he was responsible for undertaking any of the revisions or writing music that seems to be new (e.g. the recitatives, which were probably composed by Smith). The Italian libretto was versified into English by Thomas MORELL, who based his text on George Oldmixon's translation published in the 1737 WORDBOOK. Morell also expanded the oratorio and introduced the new role of Deceit (who joins Pleasure in attempting to persuade Beauty to ignore the advice of Counsel and Time). Four choruses and sixteen arias were brought forward from the 1737 version. Another two arias were revived from the earliest Roman version of the oratorio written fifty years earlier, including one that was substantially recomposed as Pleasure's furious last aria 'Like clouds, stormy winds then impelling' (which peculiarly used Mathan's exit aria 'Hark! his thunders round me roll' from *ATHALIA* as its middle section). Smith enlarged the contribution of the chorus by adding seven movements that drew on music from the Chandos anthem *Have mercy on me* (ANTHEMS, 2), *LOTARIO*, the 1732 version of *ACIS AND GALATEA* (HWV 49^b), *PARNASSO IN FESTA* and the FOUNDLING HOSPITAL anthem *Blessed are they that considereth the poor* (ANTHEMS, 8). The new overture was probably based on an existing piece by Handel that is now lost (perhaps its model was the original 1707 overture, discarded after CORELLI had complained that he did not understand how to interpret its French-style opening).

Smith conducted the premiere of *The Triumph of Time and Truth* on 11 March 1757 at COVENT GARDEN with the following cast:

Beauty	Giulia FRASI (soprano)
Pleasure	John BEARD (tenor)
Deceit	Signora Beralta (soprano)
Counsel/Truth	Isabella YOUNG (ii) (mezzo-soprano)
Time	Samuel Champness (bass)

The oratorio was performed five times. It was revived the following season with some changes, including the addition of five arias based on old Italian period compositions, four of which were to accommodate Cassandra Frederick in the role of Deceit.   ARTIE HEINRICH

Dean, *Oratorios*
HHB ii
A. Hicks, 'The Late Additions to Handel's Oratorios and the Role of the Younger Smith', *Music in Eighteenth-Century England*, ed. C. Hogwood and R. Luckett (Cambridge, 1983)
W. Shaw, 'Handel: *The Triumph of Time and Truth*' (CD booklet note, Hyperion CDD 22050, reissue 2005)

trombone and trumpet. See INSTRUMENTATION, 17; 18

Tu *fedel? tu costante?* HWV 171. According to Giovanni Macchia, the topic of Leporello's catalogue in Da Ponte and MOZART's *Don Giovanni* was ante-dated in both drama and opera at least since the seventeenth century. The unidentified lyricist of *Tu fedel?* enters the thread, describing the 'hundred beauties' wooed by Fileno, a stock pastoral name linked to the Greek verb *fileo* (love). Other ladies quoted for their diverse charms, all impartially coveted by Fileno, are Filli, Licori and Lidia. After reproaching him for his fickleness in an invective-laden text, the (female) singing character finally resolves to leave him for a faithful lover – or stay alone. An effervescent 'Sonata' for two violins and continuo is followed by a furious recitative and a florid minor key *aria di sdegno*. The excitement decreases through the three remaining arias, loosely arranged as a dance suite in French style. From the material of this cantata Handel drew an impressive quantity of self-BORROWINGS. Antonio Giuseppe ANGELINI invoiced RUSPOLI for writing a copy of the cantata on 16 May 1707, thus the premiere may have taken place a few days earlier, perhaps with the vocal part sung by Margherita DURASTANTI.   CARLO VITALI

G. Macchia, *Vita avventure e morte di Don Giovanni* (Bari, 1966)

Tunbridge Wells, Kent. Spa town and fashionable summer 'watering place' in south-east England, developed in the seventeenth century around a chalybeate spring and frequented by Handel from the 1730s. The waters were thought to be effective in relieving nervous conditions and indigestion.

Handel's visits usually took place in July or August, the first for which there is documentary evidence in 1735. In 1737 he went there in search of a cure for the 'Paraletick Disorder' which had deprived him of the use of his right hand earlier in the season — finding one later in the year at AIX-LA-CHAPELLE. During this visit he dined every weekday for a fortnight with the cleric John Upton, a friend of James HARRIS. He returned to Tunbridge Wells in 1748, in which year the artist Thomas Logan drew a group of fashionable visitors on the 'Walks' or 'Pantiles'. Handel is not among them, but the group include Giulia FRASI, who had first sung for him earlier that year, in conversation with David Garrick. There were more visits in 1755 and 1758: during the latter, when Handel's companions included his librettist Thomas MORELL, the itinerant oculist John Taylor operated on his eyes, though without achieving any improvement in his sight (HANDEL, 16). An unsubstantiated anecdote relates that on a visit in the company of his old copyist John Christopher SMITH SENIOR, the two men quarrelled and Smith abandoned the blind composer on the Walks.

According to BURNEY, Handel in later life 'attended public prayers, twice a day . . . both in London and Tunbridge Wells'. In Tunbridge he would have gone to the seventeenth-century Chapel of King Charles the Martyr, happily still standing and not very much altered, though the seating has been turned around. The chapel's upkeep was paid for by the visitors and in 1755 Handel's name appears among the subscribers in the chapel accounts.

JOHN GREENACOMBE and DOROTHEA SCHRÖDER

HHB iv
A. Savidge, *Royal Tunbridge Wells* (Tunbridge Wells, 1975)

Turner Robinson, Ann. See Ann Turner ROBINSON

Tyers, Jonathan (b. Bermondsey 16 April 1702; d. Vauxhall 26 June 1767). Entrepreneur. Tyers, whom Charles BURNEY called 'a man of strong parts & good taste', abandoned his family background in the fellmongering trade to take on, aged twenty-seven, the proprietorship of VAUXHALL GARDENS. As a dedicated supporter of Handel, Tyers ensured that his music was regularly played there by the resident band; and in what the Earl of SHAFTESBURY described as 'a very handsome action' (Burrows and Dunhill, p. 44), Tyers purchased fifty tickets for Handel's 1738 benefit concert (An ORATORIO), just five weeks before the unveiling at Vauxhall of ROUBILIAC's remarkable statue of the composer. The *Vauxhall Observer* (2 June 1823) reported that the composer gave Tyers a precious early piece of his own manuscript composition (then in the possession of the current proprietors), and this rare event suggests ties of friendship between the two men. The 'DEAD MARCH' from *SAUL*, a favourite piece of Tyers, was played annually at Vauxhall to mark the anniversary of his death. DAVID COKE

S. Klima, G. Bowers and K. Grant, *Memoirs of Dr Charles Burney 1726–1769* (Lincoln, NE, 1988)

Un'alma innamorata, HWV 173. An accompanied cantata for soprano, violins and basso continuo, this is among the earliest cantatas Handel wrote after arriving in ROME. Ursula Kirkendale suggests that it was performed at RUSPOLI's country estate in Vignanello no later than 6 June. Indeed, in the bill relating to this and other cantatas that appears in the Ruspoli account books on 30 June 1707, ANGELINI notes that he made the copies in Vignanello. The text warns against becoming a prisoner of love and encourages instead loving more than one heart. Handel provided an appropriately light-hearted setting. The final aria (of three) closes the work with a minuet-inspired dance aria, a common trait in his early cantatas. He reused the music of this aria in the final chorus of Il PASTOR FIDO.

ELLEN T. HARRIS

W. and U. Kirkendale, *Music and Meaning: Studies in Music History and the Neighbouring Disciplines* (Florence, 2007)

Unicorn Opera Group. See Appendix 7: An overview of fifty Handel performers, 1959–2009

University of Halle. See HALLE UNIVERSITY; HANDEL, 13

Urio, Francesco Antonio (b. Milan, ?1631/2; d. Milan, 1719 or later). Italian composer and Franciscan monk. It seems that he did not settle for long in one place. He might be the same person as the forty-year-old Francesco Urio mentioned on a Venetian list of instrumentalists, but by 1679 he was *maestro di cappella* at the cathedral of Spoleto. He was afterwards at Urbino (1681–3), Assisi and Genoa. The title pages of his published works reveal that he was *maestro di cappella* of the Basilica dei Santi Apostoli in ROME by 1690 (when he published a volume of motets dedicated to Cardinal OTTOBONI), of the Frari in VENICE in 1697 (when he published his *Salmi concertati*) and at San Francesco, Milan from 1715 to 1719. Handel borrowed from Urio's Te Deum in SAUL ('The youth inspir'd by thee'/'Our fainting courage', Sinfonie pour le Carillons, 'O fatal consequence of rage', Sinfonia in Act III, 'Gird on thy sword'), ISRAEL IN EGYPT ('The Lord is a man of war'), L'ALLEGRO ('Sweet bird') and the Dettingen Te Deum ('We praise thee', 'All the earth', 'To thee all angels cry', 'To thee Cherubim', 'The glorious company', 'When thou hadst overcome', 'Thou sittest at the right hand', 'We therefore pray thee', 'Day by day we magnify thee') (TE DEUM, 5).

ANNETTE LANDGRAF

Utrecht Te Deum and Jubilate. See TE DEUM, 1; JUBILATE

Utrecht, Treaty of. See War of the SPANISH SUCCESSION

Valeriani, Belisario (fl. 1715–36). Italian librettist. His earliest known libretto, *La Caccia in Etolia* (Ferrara, 1715), was first set to music by Fortunato Chelleri (c.1690–1757), and later served as the source text for Handel's *ATALANTA* (1736). Valeriani was particularly associated with opera projects at Ferrara, Modena and Venice, although his librettos were also revived for productions at Bologna, Florence and Vienna. His last known libretto, *Il Tempo dell'immortalità*, was produced at Ferrara in 1736.   WALTER KREYSZIG and DAVID VICKERS

Sartori
Strohm

Vanbrugh, Sir John (b. London, ?24 Jan. 1664; d. London, 26 March 1726). English playwright, architect and impresario, of Flemish descent. His English mother had kinship connections to noble families. After various unsuccessful ventures he joined the retinue of a kinsman; in Paris in 1688 he was imprisoned as an exchange hostage for over four years.

In November 1696 Vanbrugh surprised the London stage with his successful comedy, *The Relapse*, followed by several other plays and adaptations. His first architectural work (1699) was Castle Howard for his kinsman the 3rd Earl of Carlisle; tutored and assisted by Nicholas Hawksmoor, he became a professional architect. His apparently unpremeditated changes of course were usually well considered. Blenheim (1705) is his most famous building (MARLBOROUGH). He also took seriously his posts of Comptroller of the Queen's Works and Clarenceux Herald, but architecture was his lasting avocation. In 1703 he bought a site in the Haymarket to build a large theatre to his own design. The Queen's Theatre (KING'S THEATRE) opened in April 1705, and as the acoustic favoured music it became an opera house. He abandoned management, but was a director of the Royal Academy of Music (OPERA COMPANIES, 2) in 1719.

Vanbrugh's successful comedies survived through the ensuing centuries when baroque architecture was despised. The dramatic play of shapes, masses and shadows that make Blenheim comparable to contemporaneous continental palaces are now appreciated, and display a genius of great individuality and accomplishment.   KERRY DOWNES

Vanini (Boschi), Francesca ('la Cieca') (b. Bologna; d. Venice, 1744). Italian contralto (compass: g–e″). From 1695 on she performed in numerous operas throughout Italy. Between 1706 and 1709 she sang alongside her husband, the bass Giuseppe Maria BOSCHI, at Genoa, Bologna, Vienna and VENICE, where she sang the male role of Ottone in Handel's *AGRIPPINA*. The couple went to London in

1710 and were part of the cast of Handel's RINALDO a year later, with Vanini again singing a male role (the general Goffredo). She also sang in London performances of operas by Alessandro SCARLATTI and Giovanni BONONCINI, but her voice seems to have deteriorated and she is not known to have made any operatic appearances after 1711. ARTIE HEINRICH

Vanneschi, Francesco (b. ?Florence, early eighteenth century; d. ?London, c.Aug. 1759). Italian impresario. His libretto La commedia in commedia was set to music by Giovanni Chinzer (1698–1749) for the Cocomero in FLORENCE in 1731, and a decade later he was employed by Lord MIDDLESEX as the assistant manager and poet of the MIDDLESEX OPERA COMPANY in London. After Lord Middlesex withdrew from the KING'S THEATRE opera company in 1748, Vanneschi took over as its impresario. His London career was marred by disputes, theft and scandals. It is not clear how much he was involved in the 1754 revival of ADMETO (the last performance of a Handel opera in London during the composer's lifetime). WALTER KREYSZIG

W. C. Smith, 'The 1754 Revival of Handel's "Admeto"', ML 51/2 (April 1970), 141–9
C. Taylor, 'From Losses to Lawsuit: Patronage of the Italian Opera in London by Lord Middlesex, 1739–1745', ML 68/1 (Jan. 1987), 1–25

Vauxhall Gardens. Situated on the Surrey side of the River Thames, south of Lambeth Palace, the New Spring Gardens (as it was then known) was one of the oldest pleasure gardens in or near London. Run by Jonathan TYERS (1702–67) from 1729, the Gardens provided a carefully controlled space for al fresco entertainment from May to September, with striking architectural features, supper boxes, a music pavilion, long walks and numerous art works including paintings and sculpture (Figure 29). Tyers commissioned a statue from the young Louis-François ROUBILIAC to grace an area close to the 'orchestra', the structure where the band and singers were situated on the upper floor. The daringly informal image of Handel in his slippers, elbow resting on a pile of his scores, and playing Apollo's lyre, was unveiled on 1 May 1738 (and can now be seen at the Victoria and Albert Museum). That same year Tyers generously supported Handel's theatrical benefit by buying fifty tickets, and two years later Handel composed a hornpipe for the Vauxhall Gardens orchestra (HWV 356).

As a quid pro quo for offering the use of his lanterns and staff to the peace celebrations in GREEN PARK to be held in April 1749, Tyers was granted the public rehearsal of the MUSIC FOR THE ROYAL FIREWORKS. At great inconvenience and additional cost to Handel and the large band, the rehearsal was held on 21 April. Published reports of 8,000–12,000 persons in attendance are wildly exaggerated; 4,000 is a more plausible upper estimate. The sound of canon was incorporated in the piece and a series of blank charges supplied by the Board of Ordnance for the rehearsal. The gardens remained in the ownership of the Tyers family until 1825, but the attraction eventually fell from fashion, closed in 1859 and was sold to property developers. DAVID HUNTER

D. Hunter, 'Rode the 12,000? Counting Coaches, People, and Errors en route to the Rehearsal of Handel's Music for the Royal Fireworks at Spring Gardens, Vauxhall in 1749', London Journal (forthcoming)

29. *A Perspective View of Vaux Hall Garden by J. Maurer, 1744.*

Venceslao (*Wenceslas*), HWV A⁴. PASTICCIO opera in three acts, first performed at the KING'S THEATRE on 12 January 1726. The libretto is an adaptation of *Venceslao* (1703) by Apostolo ZENO as revised for Parma in 1724 and set by Giovanni Maria Capelli (GIACOMELLI).

Venceslao, King of Poland, has two sons, Casimiro and Alessandro, the first arrogant and violent, the second sweet and mild. Both love Erenice, but Alessandro has concealed his passion, letting his friend Ernando pose as her suitor. Lucinda, Queen of Lithuania, who had previously become secretly engaged to Casimiro, arrives at the Polish court disguised as a man; Casimiro pretends not to recognise her. Although Ernando too loves Erenice, he arranges for her to marry Alessandro in secret, and Casimiro kills his brother on his wedding night, believing him to be Ernando. To fulfil Casimiro's obligation to Lucinda, Venceslao allows them to marry but decrees that Casimiro must die. Incited by Lucinda, the people rise in support of Casimiro, leading Venceslao to abdicate in favour of his son. Erenice consents to wed Ernando. The cast was:

Ernando	Francesca BERTOLLI (alto)
Venceslao	Annibale Pio FABRI (tenor)
Casimiro	SENESINO (castrato)
Alessandro	Giovanni Giuseppe Commano (bass)
Lucinda	Antonia MERIGHI (alto)
Erenice	Anna Maria STRADA del Pò (soprano)
Gismondo	Commano (bass)

Venceslao 'did not take', according to the Colman *Opera Register* (*HJb* 5 (1959), 219) (COLMAN). There were only four performances before it closed on 23 January. Nonetheless WALSH published seven 'favourite songs'.

The history of *Venceslao* is closely connected with that of the pasticcio *ORMISDA*. Like *Ormisda*, it appears to be distantly based on an opera sent to London from VENICE by Owen SWINEY, who hoped it would serve for the debut of FAUSTINA Bordoni. Swiney's letters make clear that he sent a complete score and that the opera was a pasticcio of his own devising. It may have been an arrangement of Capelli's setting, composed for a cast that included Faustina as Lucinda, the same role she would have sung in London. Faustina, however, made her debut in Handel's *ALESSANDRO*, and talk of *Venceslao* being staged in the following season came to nothing, perhaps because Swiney was increasingly distrusted. Handel and Heidegger planned to mount *Venceslao* following *Ormisda* in the spring of 1730, with the role of Casimiro sung by BERNACCHI, but the great success of *Ormisda* caused it to be held back till the next season.

The version of *Venceslao* performed in London in 1730 can have borne little resemblance to the opera prepared by Swiney. Only a few numbers could have been carried over from Swiney's score, such as the overture from LOTTI's *Alessandro Severo* (Venice, 1717) and two choruses from ORLANDINI's *Antigona* (Venice, 1718). New recitatives were composed to a greatly abridged text, probably revised by Giacomo ROSSI. Their style shows them to be the work of the same person as the *Ormisda* recitatives, who cannot have been Handel. As in *Ormisda*, the singers must have chosen most if not all of the arias. Strohm identified the majority as coming from operas by GIACOMELLI, HASSE, LOTTI, Orlandini, PORPORA, PORTA and Vinci. Only one aria from Capelli's setting was included, allotted to a different character than in 1724. The primary architect of both *Ormisda* and *Venceslao* is more likely to have been HEIDEGGER than Handel. Handel owned the conducting and keyboard scores of *Venceslao*, both now in the Staats- und Universitätsbibliothek Hamburg, and these manuscripts contain one alteration possibly in his hand. Otherwise there is no evidence suggesting his involvement in this pasticcio except as a performer.   JOHN H. ROBERTS

H. D. Clausen, *Händels Direktionspartituren ('Handexemplare')* (Hamburg, 1972)
E. Gibson, *The Royal Academy of Music, 1719–1728: The Institution and its Directors* (New York, 1989)
Strohm

Venice. A seaport on the Adriatic Lagoon and the capital of the Republic of St Mark's, whose dominions stretched over several territories in the Italian mainland and the Balkans. At the times Handel visited ITALY, Venice's population stood at around 145,000 inhabitants, thus the same size as ROME, but its traditional industries (such as shipbuilding, the printing press, manufacturing of costly textiles, glass, soap and paper) experienced various degrees of decline and suffered hard competition from France, Great Britain and the NETHERLANDS. Though private banking still flourished, the long-term public debt accrued from 8 million ducats in 1641 to 50 million in 1714. During the War of the SPANISH SUCCESSION between the French and the Habsburg coalitions, the Doge Alvise Mocenigo (in charge 1700–9) declared a policy of strict neutrality, always keeping an eye on Venice's aggressive neighbour, the Ottoman Empire.

According to Rogissart's period handbook for Grand Tourists, the Venetians wanted 'to live in peace with the whole world' and were stubbornly attached to their private liberties, though these included neither the right to 'criticise the government' nor 'to interfere with the affairs of state'. Further statutory limitations were provided for the nobility, the actual ruling class, while the Doge only enjoyed 'the shadow of sovereign power'. Elaborate forms of politeness were in honour among all classes, private homes were 'the cleanest the world over'. Appearances of religion and strict morality prevailed: in 1709 the city numbered 67 parish churches, 54 monasteries, 26 nunneries and 17 'very rich hospitals'; ladies – only excepting *carampane* (prostitutes) – were forbidden to march in the streets unless veiled, modestly dressed and accompanied by a duenna. That would change during the Carnival season, 'when courtesans [prostitutes of higher rank] use to flock in from every corner in Italy and foreign visitors arrive from every part of Europe'.

Montesquieu estimates that tourist inflow around 1708 was 30,000–35,000 each Carnival, but sank to only 150 twenty years later, mainly due to the diffusion of opera outside Venice. 'Up to six or seven operas are staged during the Venice Carnival, to say nothing of comedies,' Rogissart notes – yet he affects to find operas terribly poor in scenery, costumes and lighting. As to comedies, they are nothing else than 'weak and loose farces', since 'the Italian taste for buffoons' is so pronounced that they even introduce one in each opera, who 'shows up in the most serious spots of the piece and performs a hundred jokes, albeit at the climax of tragedy'. Rogissart's dismissive views arguably regard more the minor houses than their elite counterparts such as the San Cassiano (Tron family) or the GRIMANI pool of theatres, including San Giovanni e Paolo and

San Giovanni Grisostomo for opera, plus San Samuele for comedies – and for opera since 1710.

Besides opera houses, important generators of musical activities were the churches, above all the state chapel at St Mark's (first master, Antonio Biffi; deputy master, Carlo Francesco Pollarolo; first organist, Antonio Lotti; second organist, Benedetto Vinaccesi, all of them reputed composers). Also the *scuole* (lay brotherhoods) and the four major *ospedali* or foundling hospitals (Incurabili, Mendicanti, Ospedaletto and La Pietà) provided a combination of instrumental and vocal concerts which attracted large audiences. CARLO VITALI

See also *AGRIPPINA*

Le Sieur de Rogissart, *Les delices de l'Italie, qui contiennent une description exacte du pays, des principales villes* . . . (Leyden, 1706, 2nd edn 1709)
C.-L. Secondat de Montesquieu, *Voyages* (Bordeaux, 1894–6)

Venus and Adonis. The text of 'Venus and Adonis, a Cantata, Set by Mr. Handel' was published in *Poems on Several Occasions . . . by John Hughes Esq.* (1735). Two arias matching HUGHES's text, but without attribution to a composer, are included in a manuscript anthology, principally of arias from stage works performed in London in the period 1707–12. The music of the arias (HWV 85) is insufficiently characteristic to confirm that they were composed by Handel, and the instrumental interludes in the 'B' sections are not in accordance with his practice in operas from his early London years. DONALD BURROWS

See also SONGS

D. Burrows (ed.), *Songs and Cantatas for Soprano and Continuo* (Oxford, 1988)

Veracini, Francesco Maria (b. Florence, 1 Feb. 1690; d. Florence, 31 Oct. 1768). Famous Italian violin virtuoso and composer, whose biography has several intersections with Handel's. Two early duet cantatas by Veracini are preserved with Handel's trio cantata *Quel fior che all'alba ride* (HWV 200, c.1708) in a Florentine manuscript (Conservatorio di Musica Luigi Cherubini, D.II.84, *olim* D.405), which was apparently compiled about the time of Handel's visits to Veracini's native city. From January to December 1714, Veracini played his own and Corelli's sonatas between the acts of operas at the Queen's Theatre (KING'S THEATRE) and in benefit concerts in London. When Handel went to DRESDEN to recruit singers in 1719, Veracini was a court chamber musician there (1717–22). From 1733 to 1738, Veracini composed three operas for the OPERA OF THE NOBILITY, rival to Handel's company in London. During a third visit to the British capital (1741–5), Veracini played a concerto between the acts of a revival of *ACIS AND GALATEA* (1741), composed a fourth opera and played the violin in numerous concerts and dramatic productions. In his unpublished music treatise of c.1758 Veracini, by innuendo, accuses Handel of musical plagiarism. JOHN WALTER HILL

J. W. Hill, 'The Life and Works of Francesco Maria Veracini', Ph.D. dissertation (Harvard University, 1972)

Vienna. See RECEPTION, 2

Vignanello. See PALAZZI, 8; Francesco Maria RUSPOLI

Vincer se stesso è la maggior vittoria. See RODRIGO

Vinci, Leonardo (b. Strongoli, Calabria, ?1696; d. Naples, 27/8 May 1730). Reputedly one of Handel's favourite Italian composers (Strohm, p. 167). Vinci studied at the Conservatorio dei Poveri di Gesù Cristo in NAPLES from 1708 until 1718, after which he briefly served as *maestro di cappella* to Prince Sansevero. His first comic opera, Lo cecato fauzo, was performed at the Teatro dei Fiorentini in Naples in 1719, and during the early 1720s he dominated the Neapolitan comic opera stage. His first opera seria was Publio Cornelio Scipione at the Teatro San Bartolomeo in Naples in 1722, and from 1724 he concentrated on serious operas for theatres in ROME, VENICE and Parma. In 1725 he succeeded Alessandro SCARLATTI as pro-vice-*maestro* at the royal chapel in Naples. Vinci was arguably the most celebrated opera composer in Italy during the 1720s. It was rumoured that his death was caused by poisoning after an illicit love affair.

Vinci was the first composer to set several of Pietro METASTASIO's early librettos, including Siroe (Venice, 1726) and Alessandro nell'Indie (Rome, 1730), which were both later set by Handel for London (*SIROE* and *PORO*). Three of Vinci's other Metastasio settings provided the basis for Handel's pasticcios *DIDONE ABBANDONATA* (composed by Vinci for Rome, 1726), *SEMIRAMIDE RICONOSCIUTA* (Rome, 1729) and *ARBACE* (Artaserse, Rome, 1730). Handel also used music by Vinci in *L'ELPIDIA* (at least fifteen numbers), *ORMISDA* (four numbers), *VENCESLAO* (five numbers), *CATONE* (one aria) and *CAIO FABBRICIO* (one aria).

Handel borrowed manuscript scores of Vinci's Didone abbandonata, Artaserse and Catone in Utica from the library of Charles JENNENS (SOURCES AND COLLECTIONS, 3), who wrote to his friend Edward Holdsworth in January 1743 that he had formerly caught Handel 'stealing' from Vinci (HHB iv, p. 356). Jennens had presumably noticed several BORROWINGS from Didone abbandonata in *GIUSTINO* and *ARMINIO*. Handel also drew musical material from Vinci's Astianatte (Naples, 1725) for the chorus 'Envy! Eldest born of Hell' in *SAUL*.

ANNETTE LANDGRAF and DAVID VICKERS

K. Markstrom, *The Operas of Leonardo Vinci, Napolitano* (Hillsdale, NY, 2007)
J. H. Roberts, 'Handel and Vinci's Didone abbandonata: Revisions and Borrowings', ML 68/2 (1987), 141–50
Strohm

Viol, Viola, Violin, Violetta marina, Violoncello and **Violone.** See INSTRUMENTATION, 19–24

Violin Sonatas. See CHAMBER MUSIC, I

Vivaldi, Antonio (b. Venice, 4 March 1678; d. Vienna, 27/8 July 1741). Italian composer. His L'estro armonico (Op. 3), printed by Estienne ROGER (Amsterdam, 1711), was advertised in London in 1712 and reprinted by John WALSH (c.1715). Vivaldi's concertos were performed in London concerts; Handel's Op. 3, assembled by Walsh (1734), may reflect their influence (ORCHESTRAL WORKS, 2). However, Handel's short organ 'Sonata' in Part I of Il *TRIONFO DEL TEMPO E DEL DISINGANNO* (1707) is already in a solo–tutti form later credited to Vivaldi. A common denominator for Handel's and Vivaldi's solo concerto approach was individual virtuosity on their respective instruments – organ and violin.

VENICE inspired Handel's operatic art, although no Vivaldi opera was given in London. Several opera singers who sang for Vivaldi in Venice later appeared in London under Handel: Diana Vico, Anna DOTTI, Andrea PACINI, Antonia Margherita MERIGHI, Giovanni CARESTINI, Maria Caterina NEGRI and above all Anna Maria STRADA, who began her career under Vivaldi in 1720–1. The two composers shared an abstention from the comic genre, while infusing certain scores with comical elements. They both tackled Ludovico ARIOSTO: Vivaldi with three *Orlando* operas (librettos by Grazio Braccioli) and Antonio SALVI's *Ginevra*. Vivaldi's *Giustino* (1724) was a textual as well as musical model for Handel's (1737). Both composers set Pietro METASTASIO's *SIROE, Re di Persia* (in remarkably similar versions, 1727 and 1728, respectively), Salvi's *Adelaide* (*LOTARIO*) and *Ginevra* (*ARIODANTE*), and Agostino PIOVENE's *TAMERLANO*. Handel performed two or three Vivaldi arias in his pasticcio operas *CATONE IN UTICA* (1732), one in *DIDONE ABBANDONATA* (1737). Vivaldi performed one by Handel ('Già risonar d'intorno' from *EZIO*) in his pasticcio *Rosmira* (1738).

REINHARD STROHM

R. Strohm, 'Vivaldi's and Handel's Settings of "Giustino"', *Music and Theatre: Essays in Honour of Winton Dean*, ed. N. Fortune (Cambridge, 1987)

The Operas of Antonio Vivaldi (Florence, 2008)

Voss, Johann Heinrich (b. Sommerstorf, Mecklenburg, 20 Feb. 1751; d. Heidelberg, 29 March 1826). Translator of classical works and co-founder of the poets' society *Göttinger Hain*. He was friendly with, among others, Friedrich Gottlieb KLOP-STOCK, Johann Friedrich REICHARDT and C. P. E. Bach, whose performance of *MESSIAH* in HAMBURG on 31 December 1775 enthused Voss to remark that Handel's music would endure if it was free of the 'Modegekräusel' (i.e. the fashionable frippery) of its time. He owned a copy of Handel's cantata *La Lucrezia* (CANTATAS).

WERNER RACKWITZ (Trans. ANGELA BAIER)

See also RECEPTION, 2

M. Marx-Weber, 'Hamburger Händel-Pflege im späten 18. Jahrhundert', *Händel und Hamburg*, ed. H. J. Marx (Hamburg, 1981), 135–40

L. Rehm, 'Voß und die Musik', *"Ein Mann wie Voß ..."*, Exhibition catalogue, ed. F. Baudach (Bremen, 2001)

Wake, William (b. Blandford Forum, Dorset, 26 Jan. 1657; d. Lambeth, 24 Jan. 1737). Archbishop of Canterbury. Low-church controversialist. An energetic pastor in Westminster after 1695 and politically active WHIG bishop from 1705, Wake was translated to Canterbury in 1716 as a favourite of the Hanoverian regime. A rift with the ministry over ecclesiastical policy and involvement in the split between GEORGE I and FREDERICK, Prince of Wales, in 1717 left him in political isolation, marginalised, lacking influence and living out his days at Lambeth. In consultation with the Privy Council, however, he was involved in liturgical arrangements for the CORONATION of GEORGE II and Queen CAROLINE in 1727. There is some suggestion that Handel, who was commissioned by George II to compose the anthems, fell into disagreement with Wake over the use of Scripture in the texts and insisted on his own version. In the event, Wake's own annotated copy of the order of service reveals that one anthem was marred by 'the negligence of the choir', another was 'all irregular in the music' and that responses during the Litany were read rather than sung to shorten the service.

BEVERLY ADAMS

C. Burney, 'Sketch of the Life of Handel', *An Account of the Musical Performances . . . in Commemoration of Handel* (London, 1785)
Burrows, *Chapel Royal*
N. Sykes, *William Wake, Archbishop of Canterbury, 1657–1737*, 2 vols. (Cambridge, 1957)

Wales, Prince of. See Prince FREDERICK

Wales, Princess of. See Princess AUGUSTA

Walpole, Robert (b. 26 Aug. 1676; d. 18 March 1745). British prime minister, resident mainly in London and at Houghton in Norfolk. Walpole succeeded his father as Member of Parliament for Castle Rising in 1701, after which he represented King's Lynn from 1702 until the end of his career in the Commons forty years later. A manager in the WHIG Junto under Queen ANNE, although he was in the wilderness following the Whig schism of 1717, he returned to favour in 1722 as a result of the crisis caused by the collapse of the South Sea Bubble (SOUTH SEA COMPANY). His dominance of politics thereafter led to the period being dubbed 'the robinocracy'.

As well as being one of the foremost politicians of the age, Walpole was a committed patron of opera. He was a shareholder in the Royal Academy of Music (OPERA COMPANIES, 2) from 1724, while his wife has been described as 'an avid opera-goer' (McGeary, 'Opera Accounts'). Walpole's regime was parodied in John GAY's The BEGGAR'S OPERA, which some have also seen as an assault to epitomise a view of Handel as publishers' victim. Indeed, *Rinaldo* was one of the few Handel works to be published before 1720 (see Figure 30) even though Handel had written several operas, the *WATER MUSIC* suite, keyboard pieces, the Utrecht Te Deum (TE DEUM, 1), and anthems for Cannons (ANTHEMS, 2) among other works. Walsh published authorised editions of several of Handel's Royal Academy of Music (OPERA COMPANIES, 2) operas between 1722 and 1724, when the composer switched to Cluer.

Walsh senior was buried in the vaults of the church of St Mary-le-Strand (he had been a churchwarden at the Savoy Chapel while the church was under construction). The *Gentleman's Magazine* announced that he had left £30,000, and the *London Daily Post and General Advertiser* put the figure at £20,000.

Walsh, John, junior (b. London, 23 Dec. 1709; d. London, 15 Jan. 1766). Music seller, printer, publisher and instrument maker. He probably assumed control of his father's business about 1730, when the relationship with the HARE family apparently ceased and the numbering of the firm's publications started. On 8 May 1731 Walsh junior succeeded to the appointment of instrument maker to the King. Although John Johnson and other rivals arose, the business continued to prosper and maintained its excellent engraving and paper. Charles BURNEY characterised Walsh junior as 'purveyor general'.

Walsh junior fully developed the firm's relationship with Handel, publishing almost all his works from the early 1730s and in 1739 being granted a monopoly of his music for fourteen years. Handel was paid 25 guineas for each opera published and 20 guineas for oratorios. Some commentators have regarded these figures as low, even exploitative, but, as Burney points out, many of Handel's works were published 'in score, while those of his rivals were suffered to die in silence', which he attributes to 'the different degree of respect in which Handel's compositions were held by the public'. About half of Walsh's output was of Handel compositions. Walsh junior, who, like Handel, never married, was elected a governor of the FOUNDLING HOSPITAL in 1748 (two years before Handel) and may have been responsible for suggesting the performance of *MESSIAH* to raise funds. On Walsh's death the *Public Advertiser* placed his fortune at £40,000.   DAVID HUNTER

See also COPYRIGHT; EDITIONS, 1; William RANDALL

D. Burrows, 'John Walsh and his Handel Editions', *Music and the Book Trade from the Sixteenth to the Twentieth Century*, ed. R. Myers, M. Harris and G. Mandelbrote (New Castle, DE, and London, 2008)

'Walsh's Editions of Handel's Opera 1–5: The Texts and their Sources', *Music in Eighteenth-Century England: Essays in Memory of Charles Cudworth* (Cambridge, 1983)

D. Hunter, 'Handel as Victim: Composer–Publisher Relations and the Discourse of Musicology', *Encomium musicae: Essays in Memory of Robert J. Snow* (Hillsdale, NY, 1997)

Opera and Song Books Published in England 1703–1726: A Descriptive Bibliography (London, 1997)

D. Hunter and R. M. Mason, 'Supporting Handel through Subscription to Publications: The Lists of *Rodelinda* and *Faramondo* Compared', *Notes* 56 (1999), 27–93

R. J. Rabin and S. Zohn, 'Arne, Handel, Walsh, and Music as Intellectual Property: Two Eighteenth-Century Lawsuits', *JRMA* 120 (1995), 112–45

W. C. Smith, *Handel: A Descriptive Catalogue of the Early Editions*, 2nd edn (London, 1970)

Waltz, Gustavus (b. Germany; fl. 1732–59; d. ?London after 1759). English bass (range G – f♮′) of German origin. His first known performance in London was in March 1732 at the LITTLE THEATRE in the Haymarket as Clodomiro in John Frederick LAMPE's *Amelia*. Later that year he sang Polyphemus in an unauthorised performance of *ACIS AND GALATEA*, and he sang at LINCOLN'S INN FIELDS during the 1732–3 season (which included John Christopher SMITH JUNIOR's *Ulysses*). From summer 1733 he replaced MONTAGNANA as Handel's principal bass soloist, and sang in most of the composer's performances until 1739. Roles composed for him include Abner in *ATHALIA*, Minos in *ARIANNA IN CRETA*, Marte in *PARNASSO IN FESTA*, Re in *ARIODANTE*, Melisso in *ALCINA*, Nicandro in *ATALANTA*, the title role in *SAUL* and the bass solos in *ISRAEL IN EGYPT*. He also sang in numerous revivals and pasticcios. From autumn 1739 Handel's regular bass soloist was Henry REINHOLD, but Waltz remained an active singer in London's theatres until 1751. It seems that Handel planned to use him in 1750 as Charon in *ALCESTE*, but the work never reached performance. Waltz took part as a choral singer in Handel's performances of *MESSIAH* at the FOUNDLING HOSPITAL during the 1750s, so he might have sung in Handel's oratorio choirs at other times. According to BURNEY's famous anecdote, Handel criticised GLUCK for knowing 'no more of counterpoint as my cook Waltz', but it cannot be verified that Waltz was Handel's cook. Burney claimed that 'Waltz had but little voice, and his manner was coarse and unpleasant', but this harsh assessment was based on hearing the bass perform in his later years, and is contradicted by the music that Handel composed for him.   ARTIE HEINRICH

W. C. Smith, 'Gustavus Waltz: Was He Handel's Cook?', *Concerning Handel* (London, 1948)

Water Music, HWV 348–50. A suite of twenty-two orchestral movements composed for outdoor performance. The occasion was a royal water party on the River Thames on the evening of 17 July 1717, when King GEORGE I with an entourage embarked on an open barge at Whitehall Stairs and proceeded up river to Chelsea, where the party went ashore and had supper (RANELAGH), then returned the same way to ST JAMES'S PALACE early the next morning. Some fifty musicians were placed in another barge, and played the music by Handel, which was about an hour long; the King was so pleased that he commanded it to be repeated three times. A detailed account of the event was written by the Brandenburg Resident in London, Friedrich Bonet, and the occasion was also reported in the London press. It is unlikely that the complete *Water Music* was ever performed again in such circumstances.

No autograph material for the work has survived, but a number of manuscript copies are extant, of which the most important came to light only in October 2004 in the archive of the Royal Society of Musicians in London; this manuscript full score can be safely dated to 1718. Previously the only known manuscript scores were one in the Newman Flower Collection dating from the early 1730s, and three others dating from about 1738 to 1743 in the Shaftesbury, Barrett Lennard and Granville Collections (SOURCES AND COLLECTIONS). The first printed full score was that published by Samuel ARNOLD in 1788, and it can now be seen to have had the RSM manuscript as its source. Two earlier manuscripts which are keyboard transcriptions date from c.1721 and c.1722, but only the second of these has the whole work.

(1718–37). The erroneous attribution of a flute sonata (HWV 378) to Weiss was caused by a copyist confusing the owner and the composer of the manuscript; probably composed by Handel in Italy, the sonata might have been passed on to Weiss during the former's visit to Düsseldorf (1710). It cannot be verified that his elder brother Sylvius Leopold Weiss met Handel at DRESDEN in autumn 1719. KLAUS-PETER KOCH (Trans. ANGELA BAIER)

L. Hoffmann-Erbrecht, 'Art. Weiß', *Schlesisches Musiklexikon*, ed. L. Hoffman-Erbrecht (Augsburg, 2001)

R. Kubik, 'Zu Händels Solosonaten. Addenda zu einem Aufsatz von Terence Best', *HJb* 26 (1980)

Weissenfels. German town, 30 kilometres south-west of Leipzig. From 1680 until 1746 it was the residence of the Dukes of Saxe-Weissenfels. Duke August, administrator of the Archbishopric of Magdeburg (and from 1656 the 1st Duke of Saxe-Weissenfels), resided at HALLE until his death in 1680, after which his son Duke Johann Adolf I (SAXE-WEISSENFELS) moved the court to Weissenfels. In 1688, Johann Adolf I appointed Georg Händel to the post of Leibchirurg (personal surgeon) of the ducal family and *Geheimer Kammerdiener* (private valet). Some of Handel's relatives lived in Weissenfels. Anna Barbara Metzel, née Händel (1646–80, wife of the Weissenfels surgeon and barber Matthäus Benjamin Metzel), Carl Händel (1649–1713, *Leibchirurg* and *Kammerdiener*), Sophie Rosina Pferstorff, née Händel (1652–1728, wife of Philipp Pferstorff, steward at an estate near Weissenfels). All of them were descendants of Georg Händel's first marriage (HANDEL, 9; Appendix 3: Handel's Family Tree).

After hearing the young Handel play the organ during a visit to Weissenfels (c.1692), the Duke recommended that Georg Händel provide regular music lessons for his son. The Hofkapelle included thirty-six musicians in its prime (1732–6). Several leading musicians hailed from the region and were connected to music at the court: Reinhard KEISER, Johann Christian Schieferdecker (later in HAMBURG and LÜBECK) and Johann David Heinichen (who settled in DRESDEN). There were also connections between Weissenfels and J. S. BACH, TELEMANN and Pantaleon HEBESTREIT. The court had its own German-language opera (e.g. Keiser's *Almira*, 1704). From 1682 to 1685 music dramas were performed on a temporary stage, and thereafter in the 'grosses Theatrum' (until 1736). The repertoire was mainly composed by Hofkapellmeisters Johann Philipp KRIEGER (from 1688 until c.1698) and Johann Augustin Kobelius (between 1696 and 1729), although repertoire and performers were exchanged between Weissenfels, Leipzig, BRUNSWICK and Hamburg. KLAUS-PETER KOCH (Trans. ANGELA BAIER)

T. Fuchs, *Studien zur Musikpflege in der Stadt Weißenfels und am Hofe der Herzöge von Sachsen-Weißenfels* (Lucca, 1997)

K.-P. Koch, 'Die Weißenfelser Hofoper 1682–1736 und ihre Beziehungen zu anderen Bühnen', *Barockes Musiktheater im mitteldeutschen Raum im 17. und 18. Jahrhundert* (Cologne, 1994), pp. 49–59

Wesley, Charles (b. Epworth, Lincs., 18 Dec. 1707; d. London, 29 March 1788). CHURCH OF ENGLAND clergyman, a founder of Methodism (NONCONFORMITY), and a noted hymn writer. Handel set three of Wesley's HYMNS from *Hymns on the Great Festivals* (1746) at the request of Priscilla, third wife of John

RICH the proprietor of COVENT GARDEN. The third tune, 'On the Resurrection' and its text 'Rejoice! The Lord is King' have become a staple pairing in English-language hymnody.

Wesley, John (b. Epworth, Lincs., 17 June 1703; d. London, 2 March 1791). Church of England clergyman and founder of Methodism. While a tutor at Lincoln College, OXFORD, Wesley attended a performance of Handel's ESTHER at the SHELDONIAN THEATRE during the University's official celebrations in July 1733. During the early 1730s he was an active correspondent of Mary Pendarves (later DELANY). In 1758 Wesley attended a performance of MESSIAH in BRISTOL Cathedral soon after the annual Methodist meeting. He noted in his diary: 'I doubt if that congregation was ever so serious at a sermon as they were during this performance. In many parts, especially several of the choruses, it exceeded my expectation.'   DAVID HUNTER

Westminster Abbey. The burial of Edward the Confessor at the beginning of 1066 and the coronation of William the Conqueror at the end of that year, both in the church founded by Edward, sealed the special character of Westminster as a royal building: the majority of sovereigns from Henry III to GEORGE III are buried there, and it is the coronation church. Its layout is unusual for a Latin-cross monastic church, the choir being west of the crossing in what is structurally part of the nave. This leaves the crossing and surrounding aisles free and open as part of the presbytery, which extends into the eastern arm but is separated by the reredos from the apse, which houses the shrine of King Edward, canonised in 1161. For centuries, up to and including the coronation of Elizabeth II in 1953, the central area has made possible the construction of a temporary ceremonial theatre with tiered seating surrounding the throne platform.

The present church was begun by Henry III in 1246 and the eastern arm and the choir were completed in 1272; most of the nave was built a century later, in a consciously archaic uniformity of style rare in Gothic architecture. However, the church was still incomplete at the Dissolution, and the west towers were built to Hawksmoor's design in 1734–45 in a sympathetic and convincing synthesis of Gothic and classical. Westminster is also unique in profile and cross-section, being the tallest and most French-looking great church in England.

In Handel's time the reredos was a classical structure built by Wren for James II's Catholic chapel at Whitehall, dismantled before the fire there and given to the Abbey by Queen ANNE in 1706. A new choir screen designed by Hawksmoor was built in 1728 and the Schrider organ hired for the CORONATION of King GEORGE II and Queen CAROLINE the previous year was installed on it in 1730; the previous organ was on the north side of the choir near the crossing.

Henry VII added the big Lady chapel named after him to the east (1503–c.1510), one of the most spectacular examples of late Gothic fan-vaulting, furnished with collegiate stalls; in the apse is Henry's monument, and the altar (at the west end) was absent between 1644 and 1924. This was the setting for Queen Caroline's funeral in 1737, at which Handel's The ways of Zion do mourn was performed (ANTHEMS, 5).

31. Handel's monument in Westminster Abbe by Louis-François Roubiliac.

Handel's own association with Westminster Abbey did not end with his death. He had been granted burial there but his wish for a private funeral was disregarded. A large crowd attended, and the service was sung by three London choirs combined. He left money for a monument, which was carved by Louis-François ROUBILIAC, the best sculptor of the day (Figure 31). The inscription ante-dates his birth to 1684, then believed to be correct. Thus 1784 was celebrated as his centenary, with performances of his music by a choir and orchestra of 500 with a temporary organ, on staging, at the west end of the nave (HANDEL COMMEMORATION).   KERRY DOWNES

'Where'er you walk'. See Alexander POPE; *SEMELE*

Whig. The Whigs (from the Scottish brigands 'the Whiggamores') emerged from the opposition groupings of the 1670s. Initially, their driving aim was the exclusion of Charles II's Catholic brother, James, Duke of York, but once James had succeeded as king, a number became involved in a series of conspiracies to overthrow James and replace him either with Charles's bastard son, James, Duke of Monmouth or with William of Orange, husband of James's Protestant daughter, Mary. After the Revolution the Whigs vied with the TORY party for supremacy in Parliament, but with the accession of the House of HANOVER in 1714 the Whigs' triumph was assured. Under GEORGE I and GEORGE II all administrations were Whig of one sort or another and it was not until the reign of King GEORGE III that Tories were once again countenanced. At the head of the various Whig factions were a number of noble oligarchs who commanded a greater or lesser degree of influence depending largely on the extent of their electoral interest. Although Handel has occasionally had Tory sympathies attributed to him, his association with the Duke of CHANDOS, a Tory-turned-Whig, and volatile relations with FREDERICK, Prince of Wales, point to his more malleable affiliation to the court rather than to any particular party.   ROBIN EAGLES

See also JACOBITES

H. T. Dickinson, *Liberty and Property: Political Ideology in Eighteenth-Century Britain* (London, 1977)
J. R. Jones, *The First Whigs: The Politics of the Exclusion Crisis, 1678–1683* (London, 1961)

Willes, Edward. See George CARLETON

William Augustus, Prince (Duke of Cumberland) (b. London, 15 April 1721; d. London, 31 Oct. 1765). Second surviving son of GEORGE II and Queen CAROLINE. He received a thorough education, which included learning 'the German flute', although it appears that he was not taught by Handel. He fought alongside George II at the Battle of DETTINGEN (1743), but his greatest fame came in April 1746, when he defeated the JACOBITE army headed by Prince Charles Edward STUART at the Battle of Culloden, thus completely crushing the 1745 Rebellion. Cumberland's triumph over the rebels made him a popular hero despite growing disquiet over his savage treatment of the rebel army. Handel had supported Cumberland's campaign in the winter of 1745–6 by composing the SONGS 'Stand round, my brave boys', 'From Scourging Rebellion', *Song for the Gentlemen Volunteers*, and the *OCCASIONAL ORATORIO*. The composer went on to commemorate Cumberland's victory in *JUDAS MACCABAEUS*. The Duke attended performances of Handel's music, including the *MUSIC FOR THE ROYAL FIREWORKS*, and subscribed to the publication of Handel's *Grand Concertos* (Op. 6) (ORCHESTRAL WORKS, 2). Cumberland was deeply involved in domestic and foreign politics of the 1740s and 1750s, and his cultural patronage of artists such as the Sandby brothers and David Morier reflected his keen military interests. Although military success eluded him in the SEVEN YEARS WAR, he regained importance during the reign of his nephew GEORGE III, dying unmarried at a high point in his political career.   HANNAH SMITH

Wolfenbüttel. Residence of the Dukes of Brunswick-Wolfenbüttel (1283–1754). Duke Anton Ulrich had a new court theatre built in the gardens of his palace, and founded a Hofkapelle which was directed by Georg Caspar SCHÜRMANN (1697–1703; 1707–51). Carl Heinrich GRAUN was Vizekapellmeister (1727–35). Theatre entertainments included Italian pastorals and German arcadian plays, Italian and German operas, ballets and spoken plays. Most opera performances took place at the theatre in BRUNSWICK after it was inaugurated in 1690, but some were also performed at the pleasure palace in SALZDAHLUM after 1694. An Italian-language performance of PARTENOPE was given at Wolfenbüttel in celebration of Emperor Charles VI's birthday on 1 October 1732. Heinrich Bokemeyer, Kantor of the Prinzenschule, wrote to MATTHESON in 1722/3 that he was acquainted with some of Handel's church music, and an undated copy of Laudate Pueri Dominum (HWV 236) is in his handwriting.

KLAUS-PETER KOCH (Trans. ANGELA BAIER)

F. Chrysander, 'Geschichte der Braunschweig-Wolfenbüttelschen Capelle und Oper vom sechszehnten bis zum achtzehnten Jahrhundert', *Jahrbücher für musikalische Wissenschaft*, ed. F. Chrysander, vol. 1 (Leipzig, 1863)
HHB iv

Wolfgang, Georg Andreas ('Wolfgang the Younger') (b. Augsburg, ?1703; d. Gotha, 22 Jan. 1745). Son of the engraver Johann Georg Wolfgang, he studied under his brother-in-law Johann Harper, court painter at BERLIN. As a young man he travelled to Holland and France. In 1726 he first visited England; in 1727 he was in ROME. It is unknown where he produced his first portrait of Handel (now in the Musikmuseet in Stockholm). A portrait drawing (which was engraved by his father) and his well-known miniature (Royal Collection) have been associated with a possible second visit to London in about 1737. In 1742 he became court painter in Gotha, where he died shortly afterwards.

EDWIN WERNER

See also ICONOGRAPHY

J. D., 'Wolfgang, Georg Andreas d. J.', *Allgemeines Lexikon der Bildenden Künstler von der Antike bis zur Gegenwart*, vol. 36 (Leipzig, 1953)
F. Noack, *Das Deutschtum in Rom seit dem Ausgang des Mittelalters*, vol. 2 (Stuttgart, 1927)
J. Simon, *Handel: A Celebration of his Life and Times 1685–1759* (London, 1985)

Wood, Thomas (d. 1748). Printer and principal publisher of the bilingual WORD-BOOKS issued for the Italian operas performed in London in the third and fourth decades of the eighteenth century. Of the thirty-four wordbooks published between 1720 and 1741 for the first performances of new operas by Handel — including his own pasticcios — twenty-two came out under Wood's imprint. In addition Wood issued the wordbooks for at least twenty-two Handel revivals. To these must also be added the bilingual wordbooks for ACIS AND GALATEA, PARNASSO IN FESTA and Il TRIONFO DEL TEMPO E DELLA VERITÀ. Although primarily associated with Italian-language works, Wood did publish a few of the Handel's English oratorios, notably the wordbooks for his first publicly performed oratorio ESTHER (1732) and for the first London performances of MESSIAH (1743). The Messiah wordbook was carefully (and uniquely) set up under the critical eye of the compiler, Charles JENNENS, who, displeased with the quality of the first edition printed in DUBLIN, presumably selected Wood for the job himself. In 1739 Wood had printed Jennens's libretto for *SAUL*, and he may also have printed *ISRAEL IN EGYPT* (possibly also compiled by Jennens) which, however, appeared under the imprint of the KING'S THEATRE. His wordbook for the 1744 revival of *Saul* was his last one for Handel's own performances. Wood's address as given in his imprint from 1720 to the early 1740s was Little Britain, a street off Aldersgate Street. He then moved to Windmill Court, West Smithfield, a street now subsumed in the St Bartholomew's Hospital site.   JOHN GREENACOMBE

wordbooks. For Handel's audiences, the equivalent of a theatre programme was the wordbook or libretto which gave the text of the work being performed, and, when this was in Italian, the wordbooks for English-speaking audiences included a translation on the facing page. There was no dimming of the auditorium lights so the text could be followed during the performance. Wordbooks could usually be purchased at the theatre on the day of the performance or in advance from the publisher or booksellers, and generally cost one shilling – a price which stuck in the craw of one crusty OXFORD cleric in 1733 who complained that the *ESTHER* wordbook was 'not worth 1d.'

In addition to the text, the wordbooks also contain a list of the characters or 'persons represented', the 'argument', which gave often essential background information about the story, and frequently a flowery dedication by the author to some royal or aristocratic personage. The participating singers are usually named in the operas' wordbooks – and exceptionally in the wordbook for the hybrid, bilingual *ACIS* of 1736 – but never in wordbooks for the oratorios or other English-language works. Handel's name appears prominently on the title pages of the English works but only once on the title pages of the operas before the 1730s. The authors' names sometimes appear on the title pages; sometimes they sign the dedication. Very occasionally the scene painter is identified.

Though Handel must have been consulted over the contents, particularly for revivals, the printed text, especially of the first edition, was essentially a matter for the authors and the publishers, and a fastidious author could be quite demanding. Charles JENNENS's libretto for *BELSHAZZAR* appeared in print with all the lines Handel omitted (because they would have made it too long), these lines being indicated in the wordbook by inverted commas.

As considerable care was taken to ensure that the printed text matched what the audiences were hearing, these wordbooks have considerable value in helping to establish the performing text, especially for revivals where changes were frequent. This was achieved either by printing a new edition incorporating the changes, or by 'doctoring' an existing edition. The methods used for the latter ranged from cutting out old pages and inserting new ones to marking up the old edition in ink or pencil. Sometimes slips of paper with the new words were pasted into the existing edition on top of the texts they replaced. Of course, only changes to text not the music could be shown.

The wordbooks are often quite spaciously printed – octavo size for the operas and quarto for the textually shorter oratorios – the title pages frequently having quotations from classical authors appropriate to the theme of the work.

Decoration is confined to a few fairly standard printers' ornaments and ornamental initial letters. The engraved frontispieces occasionally found in some other oratorio wordbooks – like that for PORPORA's *David e Bersabea*, composed for the OPERA OF THE NOBILITY (1734) – are wholly absent. In fact, the only Handel wordbook to include a relevant illustration is that printed in ROME for *La* RESURREZIONE (1708), and paid for by the Marchese RUSPOLI, which has a woodcut of 'Christ rising from the Tomb'.

The following printers/publishers/booksellers issued wordbooks for Handel's own performances: Friedrich Conrad Greflinger (HAMBURG, 1704); Vincenzio Vangelisti (FLORENCE, 1707); Antonio de' Rossi (Rome, 1708): Giovanni Francesco Chracas (Rome, 1708); Marino Rossetti (VENICE, 1709); Thomas HOWLATT (London, 1711); J. GARDYNER (London, 1712); Samuel BUCKLEY (London, 1713); Jacob Tonson, the elder (London, 1715); Thomas WOOD (London and Oxford, 1720–44); John WATTS (London and Oxford, 1733–59); Jacob and Richard TONSON (London, 1736–59); J. CHRICHLEY (London, 1737–41); George FAULKNER (Dublin, 1742).   JOHN GREENACOMBE

See also LIBRETTOS

Smith, *Oratorios*, 23

Wright, Hermond or **Harman** (d. ?London). Music publisher, printer and seller. As successor to Elizabeth RANDALL, Wright took over the publishing house in London's Catharine Street in 1783, including the vast stock of WALSH's printing plates of Handel's music. He seems not to have published any new works but reissued music from the old plates. The name of the firm was initially Wright & Wilkinson, then Wright & Co (1784–5), and afterwards it was H. Wright. The business ceased when Wright sold the plates to Thomas Preston in about 1803.
                                                                JENS WEHMANN

C. Humphries and W. C. Smith, *Music Publishing in the British Isles from the Earliest Times to the Middle of the Nineteenth Century: A Dictionary of Engravers, Printers, Publishers and Music Sellers, with a Historical Introduction* (London, 1954)
W. C. Smith, *Handel: A Descriptive Catalogue of the Early Editions*, 2nd edn (London, 1970)

Wright, Mrs (b. c.1705–10; d. ?1750). English soprano (compass: d'–a''). She played Orinda in the 1728 revival of *ADMETO*, when Handel included a new aria for her. She appeared at LINCOLN'S INN FIELDS, and in 1731 sang Galatea in a benefit performance of *ACIS AND GALATEA* (HWV 49ª, not under Handel's direction). In 1733 she took part in Handel's concert series at OXFORD, where she sang the title role in *ATHALIA* and in revivals of *Acis and Galatea* (HWV 49ᵇ), *DEBORAH* and perhaps *ESTHER* (HWV 50ᵇ). She performed at COVENT GARDEN until 1750.
                                                                ARTIE HEINRICH

Wyche, Cyril (b. c.1695; d. 1756). At the age of nineteen, he was appointed resident at Hamburg by Queen ANNE, and GEORGE I appointed him Minister and Envoy Extraordinary to the Circle of Lower Saxony. In 1729 he was made a Baronet by GEORGE II and continued as resident to the *Hans Towns*. Later he was appointed His Majesty's Envoy Extraordinary to Russia. Handel taught Cyril Wyche for a few lessons (before Mattheson took over), and might have written some of his KEYBOARD MUSIC for him (such as HWV 446). Wyche composed seven additional arias for the Hamburg version of *TAMERLANO*, and also wrote one aria for Mattheson's *Boris Goudenow* and two for *Henrico IV*.   ANNETTE LANDGRAF

J. Burke and J. Bernard, *A Genealogical and Heraldic History of the Extinct and Dormant Baronetcies of England, Ireland and Scotland* (London, 1844)
Burrows, *Handel*
HHB vi
H. J. Marx (ed.), *Händel und Hamburg* (Hamburg, 1985)

Wyche (Wich), John (b. 1671 or 1672; d. 1713). British envoy extraordinary to Bremen, HAMBURG and LÜBECK (1709–13). His secretary was Johann MATTHESON, who dedicated his two operas *Boris Goudenow* (1710) and *Henrico IV* (1711) to 'Johann Wich'. Perhaps the Wyches' home in Hamburg was where Mattheson introduced Handel 'to a certain house where everything was given up to music'.

ANNETTE LANDGRAF

Xerxes. See *SERSE*

Y

Young, Cecilia (b. London, bap. 7 Feb. 1712; d. London, 6 Oct. 1789). English soprano, sister of ISABELLA (1) and ESTHER YOUNG. Making her public debut in a concert organised by her teacher Francesco GEMINIANI in 1730, Young quickly made a name for herself in opera as well as concert performances. Handel engaged her for his operas and oratorios at COVENT GARDEN in the seasons of 1734–6, and composed roles for her in *ARIODANTE* (Dalinda) and *ALCINA* (Morgana); she took part in the first London performance of *ATHALIA* in 1735, and a year later might have performed 'War, he sung is toil and trouble' in the premiere of *ALEXANDER'S FEAST*. In 1739, by which time Handel had moved his oratorio series to the KING'S THEATRE, Young sang the role of Merab in the premiere of *SAUL*.

In 1737 Cecilia Young married Thomas Augustine ARNE and in ensuing years she frequently appeared in productions of compositions by her husband, such as *The Tempest* and *Comus*. Probably prompted by Handel's example, in 1742 the Arnes left for DUBLIN in order to establish musical connections and a career there, staying for two years. A second trip to Dublin followed in 1748–9; this time Cecilia went without Arne, but was accompanied by her sister Isabella. While in Ireland, she performed in several of Handel's oratorios, *ESTHER*, *SOLOMON* and *ACIS AND GALATEA*. Back in London, she sang at Covent Garden in the seasons of 1750–1 and 1751–2. During a third Dublin stay from 1755–6 – this time with an extended party which apart from Cecilia and her husband included her two nieces as well as Arne's pupil Charlotte BRENT – the marriage deteriorated dramatically, causing Arne to return to London, together with Brent. Young was left behind in Ireland with her niece Polly Barthélemon. Left to her own devices, Cecilia took employment as a singing teacher, before returning to London again in 1762. However, her public career as a singer was virtually over. Shortly before Arne's death in 1778, the couple were reconciled. Young spent her later years with the Barthélemon family. EVA ZÖLLNER

Young, Esther (b. London, 14 Feb. 1717; d. London, buried 6 June 1795). English alto, sister of CECILIA and ISABELLA (1) YOUNG. Appearing in concerts from 1736, she sang in LAMPE's *The DRAGON OF WANTLEY* in 1737, and she was Handel's first Juno and Ino in *SEMELE* in 1744. In 1762 she married the music publisher and bookseller Charles Jones. She was a regular performer at COVENT GARDEN until her retirement in 1776, but her last years were troubled by poor health and financial difficulties, forcing her to appeal to the Royal Society of Musicians for funding. EVA ZÖLLNER

Young, Isabella (i) (?bap. 3 Jan. 1716; d. London, 5 Jan. 1795). English soprano, sister of CECILIA and ESTHER YOUNG. She enjoyed a successful career as a singer but never performed for Handel. She married the composer John Frederick LAMPE in 1737.   EVA ZÖLLNER

Young, Isabella (ii) (b. ?London ?1741; d. London, 17 Aug. 1791). English mezzo-soprano, niece of CECILIA, ESTHER and ISABELLA (i) YOUNG. A student of Gustavus WALTZ, she first appeared in one of Waltz's concerts in 1751. In Handel's last years, she was repeatedly engaged in performances of his works, being part of his COVENT GARDEN company from 1756. Young was Handel's first Counsel (Truth) in The TRIUMPH OF TIME AND TRUTH and she was also numbered among the soloists in the FOUNDLING HOSPITAL performances of MESSIAH in the 1750s. After her marriage to the Hon. John Scott in 1757, she appeared alternately as Miss Young and Mrs Scott.   EVA ZÖLLNER

Z

Zachow (Zachau), Friedrich Wilhelm (b. Leipzig, 14 Nov. 1663; d. Halle, 7 Aug. 1712). Organist, music teacher, composer. Zachow came from Leipzig, via Eilenburg, to HALLE where he was organist and *Director musices* at the Marienkirche (1684–1712). According to Walther, Zachow taught Handel keyboard and organ as well as composition in around 1694. MAINWARING's claim that the boy Handel started his training with Zachow at an even earlier time is unlikely to be true (WEISSENFELS). A book of manuscript music (dated 1698) bearing Handel's initials – which he presumably compiled during the time he studied with Zachow – existed at least until 1799, when it was mentioned by COXE (it is now lost). The book contained compositions by Zachau (Zachow), ALBERTI, Frobergher (FROBERGER), KRIEGER, Kerl (KERLL), EBNER and Strunch (STRUNGK).

It was probably on Zachow's recommendation that Handel, although a Lutheran, became organist at the German reformed community church (formerly Hofkirche or DOM) in Halle (HALLE) at an unknown date between 13 March 1702 and his departure for HAMBURG in July 1703. The influence of Zachow's teaching upon Handel cannot be properly assessed because only the titles of several church pieces (HWV 229/1–7) (German CHURCH MUSIC) are known. However, MATTHESON noted that Handel was already a masterful performer on all keyboard instruments when he arrived in Hamburg, and expressed the criticism that his early compositions, whilst being too long and deficient in melodic invention, were already noteworthy for their 'perfect harmony' and excellent counterpoint. In 1710 Handel visited Zachow in Halle, and afterwards made various borrowings from his old teacher in *ACIS AND GALATEA* (HWV 49ᵃ), *SAUL*, *ISRAEL IN EGYPT*, Op. 6 No. 12 (ORCHESTRAL WORKS, 2) and *MESSIAH*. KLAUS-PETER KOCH (Trans. ANGELA BAIER)

[W. Coxe], *Anecdotes of George Frederick Handel and John Christopher Smith* (London, 1799; facsimile edn, ed. P. M. Young, New York, 1979), 6n.

HHB ii, 151, 164; iii, 94

J. Mattheson, *Grundlage einer Ehren-Pforte* (Hamburg, 1740), 93

M. Seiffert, 'Händels Verhältnis zu Tonwerken älterer deutscher Meister', *Jahrbuch der Musikbibliothek Peters für 1907* 14 (Leipzig, 1908), 54–5

W. Serauky, *Musikgeschichte der Stadt Halle*, vol. 2, part I (Halle and Berlin, 1939), 393, 404

G. Thomas, *Friedrich Wilhelm Zachow* (Regensburg, 1966)

Zadok the Priest, HWV 258. The most famous of the four anthems composed for the CORONATION of King GEORGE II (ANTHEMS, 3). Handel paraphrased the text from the King James BIBLE (1 Kings 1:38–40). This powerful and dazzling composition in three linked sections – sung at the Unction, by means of which the king attains a messianic status – has been performed at every British coronation from 1727 to the present day.

FRANCESCO LORA (Trans. TERENCE BEST)

Zeno, Apostolo (b. Venice, 11 Dec. 1668; d. Venice, 11 Nov. 1750). Italian poet and librettist. He spent his earlier career in VENICE; from 1718 to 1729 he was imperial court poet in Vienna, where he was succeeded by Pietro METASTASIO. As an influential Arcadian writer (ARCADIAN ACADEMY), historian and tremendously successful author of about fifty opera librettos, Zeno left his personal imprint on eighteenth-century Italian opera. He intended to 'reform' the genre by imitating literary tragedy and Aristotelian DRAMATURGY; he aimed at (relative) historical accuracy, moral integrity, formal clarity and credible imitation of human nature. Although he was a man of the theatre and not only interested in the literary aspect (as Sala di Felice maintains in NG), Zeno had little sense of *poesia per musica* and felt beleaguered by the demands of musicians. Handel used Zeno's librettos for *FARAMONDO* (1738) and for the pasticcio operas *ALESSANDRO SEVERO* (1738), *ELPIDIA* (1725, based on I *rivali generosi*), *ORMISDA* (1730), *VENCESLAO* (1731) and *LUCIO PAPIRIO DITTATORE* (1732). James MILLER's oratorio *JOSEPH AND HIS BRETHREN*, set by Handel in 1744, partially draws on Zeno's sacred drama *Giuseppe*. REINHARD STROHM

D. Chisholm, 'New Sources for the Libretto of Handel's Joseph', *Handel Tercentenary Collection*, ed. S. Sadie and A. Hicks (London, 1987)

R. Strohm, *Dramma per musica: Italian Opera Seria of the Eighteenth Century* (New Haven and London, 1997)

Zweig, Stephan (b. Vienna, 28. Nov. 1881; d. Petrópolis, Brazil, 22. Feb. 1942). Austrian writer and collector of manuscripts. His Jewish heritage required him to escape from the Nazis to London. He became a British citizen in 1940 (although he later lived in Brazil). With his literary contributions including essays, fiction, historical biography, poetry and reviews, Zweig was a respected writer during the first half of the twentieth century. His admiration for musicians triggered his miniature The Lord gave the Word (Original title: *Georg Friedrich Händels Auferstehung*) in the volume The Tide of Fortune (Original title: *Sternstunden der Menschheit*, English trans. 1940), where he gives a highly romanticised account from the time of Handel's recovering from the 'paraletick disorder' (1737) (HANDEL, 16) until the composition of *MESSIAH* (1741). Zweig was an enthusiastic collector of manuscripts, within the realms of both literature and music. A substantial portion of Zweig's collection, containing a few Handel autographs, was bequeathed to the British Library in 1986 (SOURCES AND COLLECTIONS, 1; 5).

WALTER KREYSZIG

H. Arens, *Stefan Zweig* (Esslingen, 1949)

H. Lunzer and G. Renner, *Stefan Zweig, 1881–1981: Aufsätze und Dokumente* (Vienna, 1981)

U. Weinzierl, *Stefan Zweig, Triumph und Tragik. Aufsätze, Tagebuchnotizen, Briefe* (Frankfurt, 1992)

Appendix 1: Worklist

ANNETTE LANDGRAF AND DAVID VICKERS

HHA volume numbers indicated in square brackets are not yet published.

Operas

HWV	Title (Libretto)	Scoring	First performance	HHA	Remarks
1	Almira [Der in Krohnen erlangte Glückswechsel, oder: Almira, Königin von Kastilien] (F. C. Feustking, after G. Pancieri)	3 S, 2 T, 2 B, SATB, 2 rec, 2 ob, bn, 2 clarini, pricipale, timp, 3 vn, va. da braccio solo, va, vc, bc	8 Jan. 1705, Hamburg, Theater am Gänsemarkt	II/1	Autograph lost, the aria 'Ingrato, spietato' recently rediscovered, music lost
2	Nero [Die durch Blut und Mord erlangte Liebe] (F. C. Feustking)		25 Feb. 1705, Hamburg, Theater am Gänsemarkt		
3, 4	Der beglückte Florindo; Die verwandelte Daphne (H. Hinsch)		Jan. 1708, Hamburg, Theater am Gänsemarkt		Handel must have started composing the work in 1706, music mainly lost
5	Rodrigo [Vincer se stesso è la maggior vittoria] (after F. Silvani)	4 S, A, T, 2 rec, 2 ob, vn solo, 3 vn, va, bc	? 9 Nov. 1707, Florence, Cocomero	II/2	
6	Agrippina (attr. V. Grimani)	3 S, 3 A, 3 B, 2 rec, 2 ob, 2 tpt, timp, 3 va (violetta), 2 vc, bc	26 Dec. 1709, Venice, Teatro San Giovanni Grisostomo	[II/3]	
7[a]	Rinaldo (G. Rossi/A. Hill after T. Tasso)	5 S, MS, 2 A, T, B, flageoletto, 2 fl. dolce 2 ob, bn, 4 tpt, timp, vn solo, 3 vn, 2 va (violetta), vc, cemb solo, bc	24 Feb. 1711, London, Queen's Theatre	II/4.1	Revised versions 1717 and 1731 (HWV 7[b], HHA II/4.2)

(cont.)

Operas (cont.)

HWV	Title (Libretto)	Scoring	First performance	HHA	Remarks
8ᵃ	Il pastor fido (G. Rossi, after B. Guarini)	3 S, 2 A, B, SATB, 2 trav, 2 ob, bn, 2 vn, va, vc, bc	22 Nov. 1712, London, Queen's Theatre	[II/5]	Revised and expanded version performed May 1734 (HWV 8ᵇ). The ballet Terpsicore (HWV8ᶜ) added Nov. 1734
9	Teseo (N. F. Haym, after P. Quinault)	5 S, 2 A, b, SDATB, 2 rec, 2 fl, 2 ob, bn, 2 tpt, 3 vn, 2 va, vc, bc	10 Jan. 1713, London, Queen's Theatre	[II/6]	
10	Silla [Lucio Cornelio Silla] (G. Rossi)	4 S, 2 MS, B, silent part, 2 rec, 2 ob, bn, tpt, 2 vn, va, vc, bc	?June or July 1713, London	[II/7]	No documented performance; Libr. dated 2 June 1713
11	Amadigi di Gaula (after A. H. de Lamotte)	3 S, MS, A, SATB, 2 rec, 2 ob, tpt, 2 vn, va, bc	25 May 1715, London, King's Theatre	II/8	
12ᵃ	Radamisto (after D. Lalli/G. de Scudéry)	4 S, A, T, B, fl, 2 ob, bn, 2 hn, 2 tpt, vn solo, 2 vn, va, vc solo, bc	27 April 1720, London, King's Theatre	II/9.1	Revised version performed Dec. 1720 (HWV 12ᵇ, HHA II/9.2)
13	Muzio Scevola (P. A. Rolli, after Livy)	4 S, MS, A, B, 2 ob, bn, 2 hn, 2 tpt, 3 vn, va, vc, bc	15 April 1721, London, King's Theatre	[II/10]	Only Act III by Handel
14	Il Floridante (Rolli, after Silvani)	2 S, MS, 2B, [2 rec], 2 ob, 2 bn, 2 hn, 2 tpt, 3 vn, va, bc	9 Dec. 1721, London, King's Theatre	II/11	
15	Ottone, Re di Germania (Haym, after S. B. Pallavicino)	2 S, MS, 2 A, B, fl. dolce, 2 ob, 2 bn, 3 vn, va, bc	12 Jan. 1723, London, King's Theatre	II/12	
16	Flavio, Re de' Longobardi (Haym, after M. Noris)	2 S, MS, 2 A, T, B, rec, fl, 2 ob, bn, 3 vn, va, vc, bc	14 May 1723, London, King's Theatre	II/13	Initially titled Emilia

No.	Title (librettist)	Scoring	Date, place	Ref.	Notes
17	Giulio Cesare in Egitto (Haym, after G. F. Bussani)	2 S, MS, 3 A, 2 B, 2 rec, 2 fl, 2 ob, bn, 4 hn, tpt (1725), vn solo, 3 vn, va da gamba, vc, harp, theorbo, bc	20 Feb. 1724, London, King's Theatre	[II/14]	
18	Tamerlano (Haym, after A. Piovene/J. N. Pradon)	2 S, MS, A, T, B, 2 rec, 2 fl, 2 ob, bn, 2 cornetto, 2 vn, va, bc	31 Oct. 1724, London, King's Theatre	II/15	
19	Rodelinda, Regina de' Longobardi (Haym, after A. Salvi/P. Corneille)	S, MS, A, T, B, silent part, 2 rec, 2 fl, 2 ob, bn, 2 hn, 3 vn, va, bc	13 Feb. 1725, London, King's Theatre	II/16	
20	Scipione [Publio Cornelio Scipione] (Rolli, adapted from A. Salvi)	3 S, A, T (1730: 2 S, 2 A, T, B), 2 rec, 2 fl, 2 ob, bn, 2 hn, 2 vn, va, bc	12 March 1726, London, King's Theatre	[II/17]	
21	Alessandro (Rolli, after O. Mauro)	2 S, MS, 2 A, T, B, 2 rec, 2 ob, bn, 2 hn, 2 tpt, 3 vn, va, vc, bc	5 May 1726, London, King's Theatre	[II/18]	
22	Admeto, Re di Tessaglia (after A. Aureli / O. Mauro)	2 S, MS, 2 A, 2 B, trav, 2 ob, fg, 2 hn, 3 vn, va, vc, bc	31 Jan. 1727, London, King's Theatre	[II/19]	Autograph and performing score lost
23	Riccardo primo, Re d'Inghilterra (Rolli, after F. Briani)	2 S, MS, A, 2 B, fl piccolo, rec, trav basso, 2 ob, 2 chalumeaux, fg, 2 hn, 3 tpt, timp, 3 vn, va, bc	11 Nov. 1727, London, King's Theatre	II/20	
24	Siroe, Re di Persia (Haym, after P. Metastasio)	2 S, MS, A, 2 B, 2 ob, 3 vn, va, bc	17 Feb. 1728, London, King's Theatre	[II/21]	
25	Tolomeo, Re d'Egitto (Haym, after C. S. Capece)	2 S, MS, A, B, 2 rec, fl, 2 ob, bn, 2 hn, 2 vn, va, bc	30 April 1728, London, King's Theatre	II/22	
26	Lotario (after A. Salvi)	S, MS, 2 A, T, B, 2 ob, bn, 2 hn, tpt, 3 vn, va, bc	2 Dec. 1729, London, King's Theatre	II/23	
27	Partenope (after S. Stampiglia)	S, MS, 2 A, T, B (1737: 2 S, MS, 2 A, T), 2 fl, 2 ob, bn, 2 hn, tpt, 3 vn, va, theorbo, bc	24 Feb. 1730, London, King's Theatre	[II/24]	

(cont.)

Operas (cont.)

HWV	Title (Libretto)	Scoring	First performance	HHA	Remarks
28	*Poro, Re dell'Indie* (after P. Metastasio)	S, MS, 2 A, T, B, 2 rec, fl, 2 ob, bn, 2 hn, tpt, vn solo, 3 vn, va, bc	2 Feb. 1731, London, King's Theatre	[II/25]	
29	*Ezio* (after P. Metastasio)	S, MS, 2 A, T, B, 2 rec, 2 fl, 2 ob, 2 bn, 2 hn, tpt, 3 vn, 2 va, vc, bc	15 Jan. 1732, London, King's Theatre	II/26	
30	*Sosarme, Re di Media* (after A. Salvi)	S, MS, 3 A, T, B, 2 ob, bn, 2 hn, 2 tpt, vn solo, 3 vn, va, vc, theorbo, bc	15 Feb. 1732, London, King's Theatre	[II/27]	Initially titled *Fernando*
31	*Orlando* (after C. S. Capece/L. Ariosto)	S, 2 MS, A, B, 2 rec, 2 ob, bn, 2 hn, 3 vn, va, 2 violetta marina, bc	27 Jan. 1733, London, King's Theatre	II/28	
32	*Arianna in Creta* (after P. Pariati)	2 S, 2 MS, A, 2 B, fl, 2 ob, bn, 2 hn, 2 vn, va, vc, bc	26 Jan. 1734, London, King's Theatre	[II/29]	
A[11]	*Oreste* (after G. Barlocci)	2 S, MS, A, T, B, SATB, 2 ob, 2 hn, 3 vn, lute, bc	18 Dec. 1734, London, Covent Garden	II/Suppl.1	Self-pasticcio
33	*Ariodante* (after A. Salvi/L. Ariosto)	2 S, MS, A, 2 T, B, SATB, 2 rec, fl, 2 ob, bn, 2 hn, 2 tpt, vn solo, 3vn, va, vc, bc	8 Jan. 1735, London, Covent Garden	II/32	
34	*Alcina* (after L. Ariosto)	3 S, MS, A, T, B, SSATB, fl piccolo, 2 rec, 2 ob, bn, 2 hn, vn solo, 2 vn, va, vc solo, bc	16 April 1735, London, Covent Garden	II/33	
35	*Atalanta* (after B. Valeriano)	2 S, A, T, 2 B, SATB, 2 ob, 2 hn, 3 tpt, timp, 2 vn, va, vc, bc	12 May 1736, London, Covent Garden	[II/34]	
36	*Arminio* (after A. Salvi)	2 S, MS, 2 A, T, B, SATB, 2 rec, 2 ob, 2 hn, 3 vn, va, bc	12 Jan. 1737, London, Covent Garden	[II/35]	

No.	Title (librettist)	Scoring	Date, place	Ref.	Notes
37	Giustino (after N. Beregan / P. Pariati)	3 S, MS, 2 A, T, 2 B, SATB, 2 rec, basso de' flauti, ob solo, 2 ob, bn, 2 hn, 2 tpt 3 vn, va, bc	15 Feb. 1737, London, Covent Garden	[II/36]	
38	Berenice, Regina d'Egitto (after A. Salvi)	2 S, MS, 2 A, T, B, SATB, 2 ob, 3 vn, va, bc	18 May 1737, London, Covent Garden	[II/37]	
39	Faramondo (after A. Zeno)	4 S, MS, A, 2 B, SATB, fl, 2 ob, 2 hn, 3 vn, va, bc	3 Jan. 1738, London, King's Theatre	[II/38]	
A13	Alessandro Severo (after A. Zeno)	3 S, MS, A, 2 B, SATB, 2 rec, 2 ob, 2 hn, tpt, 3 vn, va, bc	25 Feb. 1738, London, King's Theatre	[II/Suppl.]	Self-pasticcio
40	Serse (after N. Minato / S. Stampiglia)	2 S, MS, 2 B, SATB, 2 ob, 3 vn, va, bc	15 April 1738, London, King's Theatre	II/39	
A14	Giove in Argo (after A. M. Lucchini)	3 S, T, 2 B, SATB, 2 fl, 2 ob, bn, 2 hn, 2 vn, va, bc	1 May 1739, London, King's Theatre	[II/Suppl.]	Self-pasticcio
41	Imeneo (after S. Stampiglia)	2 S, MS, 2 B, SATB, 2 ob, 3 vn, va, bc	22 Nov. 1740, London, Lincoln's Inn Fields	II/40	
42	Deidamia (P. Rolli)	4 S, 2 B, SATB, 2 ob, bn, 2 hn, 2 tpt, timp, 3 vn, va, vc, bc	10 Jan. 1741, London, Lincoln's Inn Fields	II/41	

Oratorios (cont.)

HWV	Title (Libretto)	Scoring	First performance	HHA	Remarks
66	Susanna (anon.)	3 S, MS, T, 3 B, SATB, 2 ob, bn, 2 tpt, 2 vn, 2 va, bc	10 Feb. 1749, London, Covent Garden	II/28	
67	Solomon (anon.)	4 S, A, 2 T, B, SSAATTBB, 2 fl, 2 ob, 2 bn, 2 hn, 2 tpt, timp, 2 vn, 2 va, vc, org, bc	17 March 1749, London, Covent Garden	[II/27]	
68	Theodora (T. Morell)	S, 2 A, 2 T, B, 2 fl, 2 ob, bn, 2 hn, 2 tpt, timp, 2 vn, va, vc, bc	16 March 1750, London, Covent Garden	II/29	
70	Jephtha (T. Morell)	2 S, MS, A, T, B, SSATB, fl, 2 ob, 2 bn, 2 hn, 2 tpt, 3 vn, va, bc	26 Feb. 1752, London, Covent Garden	[II/30]	
71	The Triumph of Time and Truth (T. Morell, after B. Pamphilij)	2 S, A, T, B, SSSSAATB, 2 rec, 2 fl, 2ob, 2 bn, 2 hn, 2 tpt, timp, 3 vn, va, vc, bc	11 March 1757, London, Covent Garden	[II/32]	English version of HWV 46[b]

Oratorios – uncertain, doubtful, spurious

HWV	Title (Libretto)	Scoring	First performance	HHA	Remarks
deest	*Passion nach dem Evangelisten Johannes* (St John passion)	S, S, A, A,T, T, T, B, SATTB, 2 ob, 2 vn, va, bc	1704, Hamburg	I/2	poss. by Georg Böhm, Reinhard Keiser or Christian Ritter

Serenatas, masques, odes, English Dramas

HWV	Title (Libretto)	Scoring	First performance	HHA	Remarks
72	Aci, Galatea e Polifemo (N. Giuvo)	S, A, B, rec, 2 ob, 2 tpt, 2 vn, va, 2 vc, bc	? 19 July 1708, Naples	I/5	Score completed 16 June 1708, Naples
74	Eternal source of light divine [Birthday Ode for Queen Anne] (A. Philips)	S, A, B, SATB, 2 ob, 2 tpt, 2 vn, va, bc	[no documented performance]	I/6	Probably comp. early 1713 for prospective performance on 6 February
49^{a}	Acis and Galatea (attr. J. Gay, A. Pope and J. Hughes, after Ovid)	S, 2 T, B, STTTB, fl piccolo, 2 rec, 2 ob, 2 vn, va, vc, bc	1718, Cannons	I/9	Revised and expanded bilingual version first performed at the King's Theatre, 10 June 1732 (HWV 49^{b})
73	Parnasso in festa [Parnasso in festa, per li sponsali di Teti e Peleo] (anon.)	2 S, MS, 4 A, 2 B, SSATB, 2 fl, 2 ob, bn, 2 hn 2 tpt, timp, 2 vn, va, vc, bc	13 March 1734, London, King's Theatre	[II/30]	Celebration of the wedding of Princess Anne to Prince William of Orange
75	Alexander's Feast, or The Power of Music (J. Dryden, adapted N. Hamilton)	S, A, T, B SSATBB, 2 hn, 2 tpt, timp, 3 vn, 2 va, vc, org, bc	19 Feb. 1736, London, Covent Garden	I/1	
76	Song for St Cecilia's Day (J. Dryden)		22 Nov. 1739, London, Lincoln's Inn Fields	[I/15]	
55	L'Allegro, il Penseroso ed il Moderato (Parts I and II adapted from J. Milton by J. Harris and C. Jennens; Part III by Jennens)	S, A, T, B, SATB, 2 fl, 2 ob, 2 bn, hn, 2 tpt, caril on, vn solo/vc solo, 3 vn, va, org, bc	27 Feb. 1740, London, Lincoln's Inn Fields	I/16	

(cont.)

Serenatas, masques, odes, English Dramas (cont.)

HWV	Title (Libretto)	Scoring	First performance	HHA	Remarks
58	Semele (W. Congreve, anon. adaptation)	2 S, 3 A, 2 T, 3 B, SATB, 2 ob, 2 bn, 2 hn, 2 tpt, timp, 3 vn, va, 2 vc, org, bc	10 Feb. 1744, London, Covent Garden	[I/19]	
60	Hercules (T. Broughton, after Sophocles/Ovid)	3 S, A, T, 3 B, SATB, 2 ob, 2 hn, 2 tpt, timp, 3 vn, va, bc	5 Jan. 1745, London, King's Theatre	[I/22]	
44	Comus	S, S, B, 2 ob, 2 vn, org, bc	June 1745, Exton, Leicestershire	[I/Suppl.]	3 songs and a trio for a private domestic performance of Milton's masque
45	Alceste (song texts by T. Morell)	2 S, A, T, B, fl, 2 ob, bn, 2 tpt, 3 vn, va, bc	[unperformed]	[I/Suppl.]	Comp. Dec. 1749–Jan. 1750 for an aborted theatre collaboration with T. Smollett (whose spoken text is lost)
69	The Choice of Hercules (T. Morell after R. Lowth)	2 S, MS, T, SATB, 2 fl, 2 ob, bn, 2 hn, 2 tpt, 2 vn, va, bc	1 March 1751, London, Covent Garden	I/31	Music adapted from Alceste

German, Latin and Italian sacred music

HWV	Title (Text)	Scoring	Date, place	HHA	Remarks
229[1]	Das ganze Haupt ist krank		c.1700–3		Lost
229[2]	Es ist der alte Bund		c.1700–3		Lost
229[3]	Fürwahr, er trug unsere Krankheit		c.1700–3		Lost
229[4]	Thue Rechnung von deinem Haußhalten		c.1700–3		Lost
229[5]	Victoria. Der Tod ist verschlungen in den Sieg		c.1700–3		Lost
229[6]	Was werden wir essen		c.1700–3		Lost
229[7]	Wer ist der, so von Edom kömmt		c.1700–3		Lost
230	Ah che troppo ineguali / O del ciel Maria Regina (anon.)	S, 2 vn, va, bc	? perf. 17 Aug. 1707, Rome, Palazzo della Cancelleria	III/2	poss. comp. for Ottoboni
231	Coelestis dum spirat aura (anon.)	S, 2 vn, bc	? comp. May/June 1707, Rome: ? perf. Vignanello, 13 June 1707, S. Sebastiano	III/2	autograph lost, comp. for Ruspoli; poss. for the Feast of St Anthony of Padua
232	Dixit Dominus Domino meo (Psalm 109)	S, A, SSATB, 2 vn, 2 va, bc	comp. April 1707, Rome	III/1	Details of performance and commission unknown
233	Donna, che in ciel (anon.)	S, SATB, 2 vn, va, bc	? perf. 2 Feb. 1707, Rome	III/2	autograph lost; poss. comp. to commemorate the earthquakes of winter 1702/3
235	Haec est regina virginum (anon.)	S, 2 vn, va, bc	? perf. 15 July 1707, Rome, S. Maria di Monte Santo	III/2	poss. for the annual feast of Our Lady of Mount Carmel (patron C. Colonna)
236	Laudate pueri Dominum (Psalm 112)	S, 2 vn, bc	? Hamburg 1703–5	III/2	

(cont.)

German, Latin and Italian sacred music (cont.)

HWV	Title (Text)	Scoring	Date, place	HHA	Remarks
237	Laudate pueri Dominum (2nd setting) (Psalm 112)	S, SATB, 2 ob, 2 vn, 2 va, org, bc	comp. 8 July 1707, Rome; ? perf. 15 July 1707, Rome, S. Maria di Monte Santo	III/2	poss. for the annual feast of Our Lady of Mount Carmel (patron C. Colonna)
238	Nisi Dominus (Psalm 126)	A, T, B, SATB, SATB, 2 vn, va, bc, 2 vn, va, org, db, bc	comp. 13 July 1707, Rome; ? perf. 16 July 1707, Rome, S. Maria di Monte Santo	III/2	poss. for the annual feast of Our Lady of Mount Carmel (patron C. Colonna); autograph destroyed in a fire in 1860
239	O qualis de coelo sonus (1707) (anon.)	S, 2 vn, bc	? perf. 12 June 1707 (Whit Sunday), Vignanello, S. Sebastiano	III/2	comp. for Ruspoli
240	Saeviat tellus inter rigores (anon.)	S, S, 2 ob, 2 vn, va, bc	? perf. 16 July 1707, Rome, S. Maria di Monte Santo	III/2	autograph lost; poss. for the annual feast of Our Lady of Mount Carmel (patron C. Colonna)
241	Salve regina (attrib. to Hermann v. Vehringen)	S, 2 vn, vc, org.	? perf. 19 June 1707 (Trinity Sunday), Vignanello, S. Sebastiano	III/2	comp. for Ruspoli
242	Silete venti (anon.)	2 ob, bn, 2 vn, va, bc	comp. in London, poss. mid-1720s, and no later than 1732	III/2	
243	Te decus virgineum (anon.)	A, 2 vn, va, bc	? perf. 15 July 1707, Rome, S. Maria di Monte Santo	III/2	poss. for the annual feast of Our Lady of Mount Carmel (patron C. Colonna)

German, Latin and Italian sacred music – uncertain, doubtful, spurious

HWV	Title (Text)	Scoring	Date, place	HHA	Remarks
234	Il Pianto di Maria: Giunta l'ora fatal (anon.)	S, 4 vn, va, bc	1709		by G. Ferrandini
244	Kyrie eleison	SATB, 2 vn, 2 va, bc	1746–8		by Antonio Lotti
245	Gloria in excelsis deo	SSATTB, ob, tpt, 2 vn, 2 va, org, bc	1746–8		by Lotti
deest	Gloria	S, 2 vn, bc		[III/2, Anhang]	

English church music

HWV	Title	Scoring	Date, place	HHA	Remarks
246	O be joyful in the Lord	S, T, B, STB, ob, bn, 2 vn, vc, bc	c.1717, Cannons	III/4	HG Anthem I
247	In the Lord put I my trust	T, STB, ob, bn, 2 vn, vc, db, org	c.1717, Cannons	III/4	HG Anthem II
248	Have mercy upon me	S, T, STB, ob, bn, 2 vn, vc, db, org	c.1717, Cannons	III/4	HG Anthem III
249^a	O sing unto the Lord a new song	A, B SATB, fl, 2 ob, 2 tpt, 2 vn, va, bc	perf. 26 Sept 1714, London, Chapel Royal	III/9	HG Anthem IV^A
249^b	O sing unto the Lord a new song	S, T, STB, ob, bn, 2 vn, vc, db, org	c.1717, Cannons	III/4	HG Anthem IV
250^a	I will magnify thee	S, T STB, ob, bn, 2 vn, vc, db, org	c.1717, Cannons	III/5	HG Anthem V^A
250^b	I will magnify thee	S, A, B, SATB, ob, 2 vn, va, bc	after 1718, London, Chapel Royal	III/9	HG Anthem V^B
251^a	As pants the hart	S, A, A, T, B, B, SAATBB, vc, db, org	before Oct. 1714, London, Chapel Royal	III/9	HG Anthem VI^C
251^b	As pants the hart	S, T, STB, ob, bn, 2 vn, vc, db, org	c.1717, Cannons	III/5	HG Anthem VI^A
251^c	As pants the hart	A, T, B, SAATBB, 2 ob, 2 vn, va, vc, db, org	after 1720, London, Chapel Royal	III/9	HG Anthem VI^B
251^d	As pants the hart	A, A, B, SAATBB, vc, db, org	c.1721, London, Chapel Royal	III/9	HG Anthem VI^D
252	My song shall be alway	S, A, T, B, SATB, ob, bn, 2 vn, vc, db, org	c.1717, Cannons	III/5	HG Anthem VII
253	O come let us sing unto the Lord	S, T, STTB, ob, 2 vn, bc	c.1718, Cannons	III/5	HG Anthem VIII
254	O praise the Lord with one consent	S, T, T, B, SATB, ob, 2 vn, bc	c.1718, Cannons	III/5	HG Anthem IX
255	The Lord is my light	S, T, T, STTTB, 2 rec, ob, 2 vn, bc	c.1718, Cannons	III/6	HG Anthem X

No.	Title	Scoring	Date/place		
256ª	Let God arise	S, T, SATB, ob, bn, 2 vn, db, org	c.1717, Cannons	III/6	HG Anthem XIᴬ
256ᵇ	Let God arise	A, B, SATB, ob, bn, 2 vn, va, vc, db, org	? perf. 5 Jan. 1724, London, Chapel Royal	III/9	HG Anthem XIᴮ
258	Zadok the Priest	SSAATBB, 2 ob, 2 br, 3 tpt, timp, 3 vn, va, vc, db, org	comp. Aug./Sept. 1727, London; perf. 11 Oct 1727, London, Westminster Abbey	[III/10]	Anthem for the coronation of King George II and Queen Caroline
259	Let thy hand be strengthened	SAATB, 2 ob, 2 vn, va, bc	comp. Aug./Sept. 1727, London; perf. 11 Oct 1727, London, Westminster Abbey	[III/10]	Coronation anthem
260	The King shall rejoice	SAATBB, 2 ob, 3 tpt, timp, 3 vn, va, bc	comp. Aug./Sept. 1727, London; perf. 11 Oct 1727, London, Westminster Abbey	[III/10]	Coronation anthem
261	My heart is inditing	SAATBB, 2 ob, 3 tpt, timp, 2 vn, va, bc	comp. Aug./Sept. 1727, London; perf. 11 Oct 1727, London, Westminster Abbey	[III/10]	Coronation anthem
262	This is the day which the Lord hath made	S, A, T, B, SSAATTBB, 2 fl, 2 ob, bn, 2 tpt, timp, 2 vn, va, vc, db, archlute, org, cemb	perf. 14 March 1734, London, Queen's Chapel	[III/11]	Wedding anthem for Princess Anne and Prince William of Orange
263	Sing unto God, ye kingdoms of the earth	S, A, T, B, SATB, 2 ob, 2 tpt, 2 timp, 2 vn, va, bc	perf. 27 April 1736, London, Chapel Royal	[III/11]	Wedding anthem for Prince Frederick of Wales and Princess Augusta of Saxe-Gotha
264	The ways of Zion do mourn ('Anthem for the funeral of Queen Caroline')	SSAATB, 2 ob, bn, 2 vn, va, bc, org	comp. 5–12 Dec. 1737, London; perf. 17 Dec. 1737, London, Henry VII Chapel, Westminster Abbey	III/12	
265	The King shall rejoice (Dettingen Anthem)	A, B, SSATB, 2 ob, bn, 2 tpt, principale, timp, 2 vn, va, bc	comp. 30 July–3 Aug. 1743, London; perf. 27 Nov. 1743, London, Chapel Royal	[III/13]	

(cont.)

English church music (cont.)

HWV	Title	Scoring	Date, place	HHA	Remarks
266	*How beautiful are the feet* (Anthem on the Peace)	S, A, A, SATB, fl, ob, bn, 2 tpt, timp, 2 vn, va, bc	perf. 25 April 1749, London, Chapel Royal	[III/14]	
267	*How beautiful are the feet*	S, SATB, 2 ob, bn, 2 tpt, timp, 2 vn, va, bc	c.1749	[III/14]	fragment, poss. draft for HWV 266
268	*Blessed are they that considereth the poor* (Founding Hospital Anthem)	S, S, A, T, B, SSATB, 2 ob, bn, 2 tpt, timp, 2 vn, va, bc	perf. 27 May 1749, London, Foundling Hospital Chapel	[III/14]	
269	*Amen, halleluja*	S, bc	c.1745–7, London	[III/15]	
270	*Amen*	S, bc	c.1732–9, London	[III/15]	
271	*Amen*	S, bc	c.1732–9, London	[III/15]	
272	*Alleluja, amen*	S, bc	c.1738–41, London	[III/15]	
273	*Alleluja, amen*	S, bc	c.1738–41, London	[III/15]	
274	*Alleluja, amen*	S, bc	c.1738–41, London	[III/15]	
275	*Amen, alleluia*	S, bc	c.1732–9, London	[III/15]	autograph without verbal text
276	*Amen*	S, bc	c.1743–7, London	[III/15]	
277	*Hallelujah, amen*	S, bc	c.1745–7, London	[III/15]	
278	Utrecht Te Deum	S, S, A, A, T, B, SSAATTB, fl, 2 ob, bn, 2 tpt, 3 vn, va, vc, bc, org	finished 14 Jan. 1713, London; perf. 7 July 1713, London, St Paul's Cathedral	III/3	

HWV	Title	Scoring			
279	Utrecht Jubilate	A, A, B, SSAATTBB, 2 ob, bn, 2 tpt, 3 vn, va, vc, bc, org	perf. 7 July 1713, London, St Paul's Cathedral	III/3	
280	Caroline Te Deum in D major	A, B, SAATB, fl, 2 tpt, 2 vn, va, bc	? perf. 26 Sept. 1714 London, Chapel Royal	[III/8]	revised 1749 for the Thanksgiving service for the Peace of Aix-la-Chapelle
281	Chandos Te Deum in B major	S, T, T, B, STTTB: rec, ob, tpt, 2 va, bc	c.1718, Cannons	[III/7]	
282	Te Deum in A major	A, T, B, SAATBBB: fl, ob, bn, 2 vn, va, vc, db, org	? perf. 5 Jan. 1724, London, Chapel Royal	[III/8]	
283	Dettingen Te Deum	A, T, B, SSATB, 2 ob, bn, 2 tpt, principale, timp, 2 vn, va, vc, db, bc, org	comp. 17 July–end July 1743, London; perf. 27 Nov. 1743, London, Chapel Royal	[III/13]	
284	The invitation: Sinners obey the Gospel word	S, bc	c.1746–7, London	[III/15]	Hymn
285	Desiring to love: O love divine, how sweet thou art	S, bc	c.1746–7, London	[III/15]	Hymn
286	On the resurrection: Rejoice, the Lord is King	S, bc	c.1746–7, London	[III/15]	Hymn

English church music – uncertain, doubtful, spurious

HWV	Title	Scoring		Remarks
257	O praise the Lord, ye angels of his	A, B, SATB, 2 ob, 2 tpt, 2 vn, va, vc, bc		published by Arnold, now attr. Maurice Greene

Secular cantatas with instruments – uncertain, doubtful, spurious

HWV	Title (Text)	Scoring	Remarks
85	'Venus and Adonis' (John Hughes)	S, [vn], bc	c.1711, London; no proof of authenticity
–	Three English dialogue cantatas: *To lonely shades; With roving and ranging; So pleasing the pain is*	S, T, B, 2 vn, bc	Three English dialogue cantatas, arranged from music in *Ottone, Flavio* and *Giulio Cesare* (probably by William Hayes)

Secular cantatas with basso continuo

HWV	Title (Text)	Scoring	Date, place	HHA	Remarks
77	Ah! Che pur troppo è vero (anon.)	S, bc	c.1707. Florence	[V/1]	
80	Allor ch'io dissi: Addio (anon.)	S, bc	1707–9, ?Rome	[V/1]	
84	Aure soavi, e lieti (anon.)	S, bc	May 1707, Rome	[V/1]	
86	Bella ma ritrosetta (anon.)	S, bc	after 1710, London	[V/1]	
88	Care selve, aure grate (anon.)	S, bc	1707–8, Rome	[V/1]	
90	Chi rapì la pace al core (anon.)	S, bc	c.1706–7, Florence	[V/1]	
91ª	Clori, degli occhi miei (anon.)	A, bc	end of 1707, Florence	[V/1]	transposed by Handel in autograph
91ᵇ	Clori, degli occhi miei (anon.)	S, bc	after 1710, London	[V/1]	autograph lost; music used in Rinaldo (1711)
93	Clori, ove sei? (anon.)	S, bc	1707–8, Italy	[V/1]	
95	Clori, vezzosa Clori (anon.)	S, bc	July/Aug. 1708, Rome	[V/1]	autograph lost; copied by Angelini on 9 Aug. 1708 (poss. for Ruspoli)
100	Da sete ardente afflitto (anon.)	S, bc	1708–9, Italy	[V/1]	autograph lost; copied by Lanciani in Aug. 1709 for Ruspoli
102ª	Dalla guerra amorosa (anon.)	B, bc	1708–9, Italy	[V/1]	autograph lost
102ᵇ	Dalla guerra amorosa (anon.) (original version)	S, bc	1708–9, Italy	[V/1]	autograph lost; copied by Lanciani in Aug. 1709 for Ruspoli
103	Deh! lasciate e vita e volo (P. Rolli)	A, bc	after 1720, London	[V/1]	poss. comp. for Senesino
104	Del bel[l']idolo mio (anon.)	S, bc	1708–9, Rome	[V/1]	
106	Dimmi, o mio cor (anon.)	S, bc	1707–9, Italy	[V/1]	
107	Dite, mie piante (anon.)	S, bc	July/Aug. 1708, Rome	[V/1]	autograph lost, Angelini made two copies for Ruspoli on 9 and 28 Aug. 1708

(cont.)

Secular cantatas with basso continuo (cont.)

HWV	Title (Text)	Scoring	Date, place	HHA	Remarks
109[a]	Dolce pur d'amor l'affanno (anon.)	A, bc	after 1710, London	[V/1]	autograph with ornamentation
109[b]	Dolce pur d'amor l'affanno (anon.)	S, bc	after 1730, London	[V/1]	probably by Handel
111[a]	E partirai, mia vita? (anon.)	S, bc	1707–9, Italy	[V/1]	original version
111[b]	E partirai, mia vita? (anon.)	S, bc	after 1710, London	[V/1]	autograph, transposed version
112	Figli del mesto cor (anon.)	A, bc	? 1707–9, Italy	[V/1]	autograph lost
114	Filli adorata e cara (anon.)	S, bc	1707–8, Rome	[V/1]	
115	Fra pensieri quel pensiero (anon.)	A, bc	1707–8, Italy	[V/1]	autograph lost; not for Ruspoli
116	Fra tante pene (anon.)	S, bc	1706–7, Italy	[V/1]	autograph; same text also set by A. Scarlatti
117	Hendel, non può mia musa (B. Pamphilij)	S, bc	July/August 1708, Rome	[V/1]	
118	Ho fuggito Amore anch'io (P. Rolli)	A, bc	after 1720, London	[V/1]	
120	Irene, idolo mio (anon.)	S, bc	?1707–9, Italy	[V/1]	autograph lost
120[b]	Irene, idolo mio (anon.)	A, bc	after 1710, London	[V/1]	transposed, no autograph
121[a]	L'aure grate, il fresco rio ('La Solitudine') (anon.)	A, bc	c.1721–3, London	[V/1]	autograph lacks recitative
121[b]	L'aure grate, il fresco rio ('La Solitudine') (anon.)	A, bc	c.1718, London	[V/1]	no autograph; copies contain recitative; first aria is different from its counterpart in HWV 121[a]
125[a]	Lungi da me, pensier tiranno (anon.)	S, bc	1707–9, Italy	[V/1]	autograph lost, copied by Lanciani Aug. 1709 for Ruspoli
125[b]	Lungi da me, pensier tiranno (anon.)	A, bc	after 1710, London	[V/1]	no autograph; transposed
126[a]	Lungi da voi, che siete poli (anon.)	S, bc	July/Aug. 1708, Rome	[V/1]	authenticity uncertain; parts were copied by Angelini in Aug. 1708 for Ruspoli (alternative version HWV 126[b] of uncertain authenticity)

No.	Title	Scoring	Date, place		Notes
126[c]	Lungi da voi, che siete poli (anon.)	A, bc	after 1710, London	[V/1]	authenticity uncertain
127[a]	Lungi dal mio bel nume (anon.)	S, bc	3 March 1708, Rome	[V/1]	
127[c]	Lungi dal mio bel nume (anon.)	S, bc	c.1724–5, London	[V/1]	
128	Lungi n'andò Fileno (anon.)	S,, bc	Aug. 1708. Rome	[V/1]	
129	Manca pur quanto sai (anon.)	S, bc	July/Aug. 1708, Rome	[V/1]	
130	Mentre il tutto è in furore (anon.)	S, bc	Aug. 1708. Rome	[V/1]	
131	Menzognere speranze (anon.)	S, bc	Sept. 1707, Rome	[V/1]	
132[a]	Mi palpita il cor (anon.)	S, bc	after 1710, London	[V/1]	Revised by Handel; arioso added
133	Ne' tuoi lumi, o bella Clori (anon.)	S, bc	Sept. 1707, Rome	[V/1]	autograph lost; copied by Angelini for Ruspoli; same text also set/comp. by A. Scarlatti
135[a]	Nel dolce tempo (anon.)	S, bc	? June/July 1708, Naples	[V/1]	autograph lost, text also comp./set by A. Scarlatti
135[b]	Nel dolce tempo (anon.)	A, bc	after 1710. London	[V/1]	autograph lost
136[a]	Nell'africane selve (anon.)	B, bc	June/July 1708, Naples	[V/1]	
137	Nella stagion che di viole e rose (anon.)	S, bc	April/May 1707, Rome	[V/1]	
138	Nice, che fa? che pensa? (anon.)	S, bc	1707–9, Italy	[V/2]	
139[a]	Ninfe e pastori (anon.)	S, bc	1707–9, Rome	[V/2]	
139[c]	Ninfe e pastori (anon.)	S, bc	c.1727, London	[V/2]	
141	Non sospirar, non piangere (anon.)	S, bc	autumn 1707, Florence	[V/2]	
144	O lucenti, o sereni occhi (anon.)	S, bc	1707–9, Rome	[V/2]	autograph lost
145	O numi eterni ('La Lucrezia') (anon.)	S, bc	1706–7, Florence	[V/2]	
146	Occhi miei che faceste? (anon.)	S, bc	1707–8, Rome	[V/2]	
147	Parti, l'idolo mio (anon.)	S, bc	after 1710, London	[V/2]	autograph lost

(cont.)

Secular cantatas with basso continuo (cont.)

HWV	Title (Text)	Scoring	Date, place	HHA	Remarks
148	Poiché giuraro amore (anon.)	S, bc	spring 1707, Rome	[V/2]	
151	Qualor crudele sì, ma vaga Dori (anon.)	A, bc	after 1710, London	[V/2]	autograph lost
152	Qualor l'egre pupille (anon.)	S, bc	Sept. 1707, Rome	[V/2]	autograph lost; copied by Angelini in Sept. 1707 for Ruspoli
153	Quando sperasti, o core (anon.)	S, bc	? June/July 1708, Naples	[V/2]	
154	Quel fior che all'alba ride (anon.)	S, bc	c.1738–40, London	[V/2]	
155	Sans y penser (anon.)	S, S, bc	Sept. 1707, Rome	[V/2]	
156	Sarai contenta un dì (anon.)	S, bc	1706–7, Florence	[V/2]	
157	Sarei troppo felice (B. Pamphilij)	S, bc	Sept. 1707, Rome	[V/2]	autograph lost; copied by Angelini in Sept. 1707 and Aug. 1708 for Ruspoli; same text also set by A. Scarlatti
158/1	Se pari è la tua fè ((anon.)	S, bc		[V/2]	Handel's original version, but autograph lost and only extant in copies
158ᵃ	Se pari è la tua fè (anon.)	S, bc	1708, Rome	[V/2]	2nd version, copied by Angelini Aug. 1708 for Ruspoli
158ᶜ	Se pari è la tua fè (anon.)	S, bc	c.1724–7, London	[V/2]	
159	Se per fatal destino (anon.)	S, bc	spring 1707, Rome	[V/2]	
160ᵃ	Sei pur bella, pur vezzosa ('La bianca rosa') (anon.)	S, bc	spring 1707, Rome	[V/2]	autograph lost; copied by Angelini in May 1707 for Ruspoli
160ᵇ	Sei pur bella, pur vezzosa ('La bianca rosa') (anon.)	S, bc	c.1724–7, London	[V/2]	
160ᶜ	Sei pur bella, pur vezzosa ('La bianca rosa') (anon.)	S, bc	c.1724–30, London	[V/2]	autograph incomplete
161ᵇ	Sento là che ristretto (anon.)	A, bc	? June/July 1708, Naples	[V/2]	

161[c]	Sento là che ristretto (anon.)	S, bc	? c.1717–20, Cannons	[V/2]	
162	Siete rose ruggiadose (anon.)	A, bc	c.1711–12, London	[V/2]	autograph lost
163	Solitudini care, amata libertà (anon.)	S, bc	after 1710, London	[V/2]	
164[a]	Son gelsomino ('Il Gelsomino') (P. Rolli)	S, bc	c.1720–7, London	[V/2]	
164[b]	Son gelsomino ('Il Gelsomino') (P. Rolli)	A, bc	after 1717–18, London	[V/2]	
167[a]	Stanco di più soffrire (anon.)	A, bc	1707–8. Italy	[V/2]	autograph lost
167[b]	Stanco di più soffrire (anon.)	S, bc	July/August 1708, Rome	[V/2]	autograph lost
168	Stelle, perfide stelle ('Partenza di G.B.') (anon.)	S, bc	Rome	[V/2]	autograph lost
169	Torna il core al suo diletto (anon.)	S, bc	? 1707–8, Rome	[V/2]	autograph lost
172	Udite il mio consiglio (anon.)	S, bc	April/May 1707, Rome	[V/2]	
174	Un sospir a chi si muore (anon.)	S, bc	autumn 1707, Florence	[V/2]	
175	Vedendo Amor (anon.)	A, bc	1707–8, Rome	[V/2]	A manuscript in the Fitzwilliam Museum has HWV 175 and 176, with some additional material of uncertain authenticity, collected together as one extended cantata entitled Amore uccellatore
176	Venne voglia ad Amore (anon.)	A, bc	1707–8, Rome	[V/2]	
177	Zeffiretto, arresta il volo (anon.)	S, bc	1707–9, Italy	[V/2]	

Secular cantatas with basso continuo – uncertain, doubtful, spurious

HWV	Title (Text)	Scoring	Remarks
94	*Clori, sì, ch'io t'adoro* (anon.)	S, bc	almost certainly spurious
101^a	*Dal fatale momento* (anon.)	S, bc	comp. by Mancini
101^b	*Dal fatale momento* (anon.)	B, bc	comp. by Mancini
108	*Dolce mio ben, s'io taccio* (anon.)	S, bc	poss. spurious
126^b	*Lungi da voi, che siete poli* (anon)	S, bc	Rome, 1708
127^b	*Lungi dal mio bel nume* (anon.)	A, bc	transposed, but not by Handel
136^b	*Nell'africane selve* (anon.)	B, bc	poss. spurious
139^b	*Ninfe e pastori* (anon.)	A, bc	transposed, but not by Handel
149	*Qual sento io non conosciuto* (anon.)	S, bc	almost certainly spurious
158^b	*Se pari è la tua fè* (anon.)	S, bc	garbled inauthentic version
161^a	*Sento là che ristretto* (anon.)	S, bc	poss. inauthentic transposition from HWV 161^b

Chamber duets and trios

HWV	Title (Text)	Scoring	Date, place	HHA	Remarks
178	A mirarvi io son intento (?O. Mauro)	S, A, bc	c.1711, Hanover	[V/7]	
179	Ahi, nelle sorti umane (anon.)	S, S, bc	31 Aug. 1745, London	[V/7]	
180	Amor gioie mi porge (anon.)	S, S, bc	1707–9, Italy	[V/7]	
181	Beato in ver chi può (Quintus Horatius Flaccus)	S, A, bc	31 Oct. 1742, London	[V/7]	
182ᵃ	Caro autor di mia doglia (anon.)	S, T, bc	1707–9, Italy	[V/7]	
182ᵇ	Caro autor di mia doglia (anon.)	A, A, bc	c.1742, London	[V/7]	
184	Che vai pensando, folle pensier (?O. Mauro)	S, B, bc	1707–9, Italy	[V/7]	
185	Conservate, raddoppiate (?O. Mauro)	S, A, bc	c.1711, Hanover	[V/7]	
186	Fronda leggiera e mobile (anon.)	S, A, bc	c.1745, London	[V/7]	
187	Giù nei Tartarei regni (anon.)	S, B, bc	1707–9, Italy	[V/7]	
188	Langue, geme, sospira (G. D. de Totis)	S, A, bc	1720s, London	[V/7]	
189	No, di voi non vuò fidarmi (anon.)	S, S, bc	3 July 1741, London	[V/7]	thematic ideas used in Messiah
190	No, di voi non vuò fidarmi (anon.)	S, A, bc	2 Nov. 1742, London	[V/7]	
191	Quando in calma ride (?O. Mauro)	S, B, bc	1707–11, Italy or Hanover	[V/7]	
192	Quel fior che all'alba ride (anon.)	S, S, bc	1 July 1741, London	[V/7]	thematic ideas used in Messiah
193	Se tu non lasci amore (anon.)	S, A, bc	London, 1720s	[V/7]	thematic ideas used in Messiah
194	Sono liete, fortunate (?O. Mauro)	S, A, bc	c.1711, Hanover	[V/7]	
196	Tacete, ohimè, tacete (Francesco de' Lemme)	S, B, bc	1707–9, Italy	[V/7]	
197	Tanti strali al sen mi scocchi (?O. Mauro)	A, A, bc	1710–12, Hanover	[V/7]	
198	Troppo cruda, troppo fiera (?O. Mauro)	S, A, bc	c.1711, Hanover	[V/7]	
199	Va', speme infida (?O. Mauro)	S, S, bc	c.1711, Italy	[V/7]	
200	Quel fior che all'alba ride (anon.)	S, S, B, bc	1707–9, Italy	[V/7]	
201	Se tu non lasci amore (anon.)	S, S, B bc	12 July 1708, Naples	[V/7]	

Chamber duets and trios – uncertain, doubtful, spurious

HWV	Title (Text)	Scoring	Remarks
183	Caro autor di mia doglia (anon.)	S, S, bc	comp. by Keiser
195	Spero indarno (anon.)	S, B, bc	doubtful

Miscellaneous arias

HWV	Title (Text)	Scoring	Date, place	HHA	Remarks
202	Künfft'ger Zeiten eitler Kummer (B. H. Brockes)	S, instr. (?vn, ob or fl), bc	c.1724–5, London	[V/6]	HWV 202–10: 'Neun Deutsche Arien' ('Nine German Arias')
203	Das zitternde Glänzen der spielenden Wellen (B. H. Brockes)	S, instr. (?vn, ob or fl), bc	c.1724–6, London	[V/6]	
204	Süßer Blumen Ambraflocken (B. H. Brockes)	S, instr. (?vn, ob or fl), bc	c.1724–6, London	[V/6]	
205	Süße Stille, sanfte Quelle ruhiger Gelassenheit (B. H. Brockes)	S, instr. (?vn, ob or fl), bc	c.1724–6, London	[V/6]	
206	Singe, Seele, Gott zum Preise (B. H. Brockes)	S, instr. (?vn, ob or fl), bc	c.1724–6, London	[V/6]	
207	Meine Seele hört im Sehen (B. H. Brockes)	S, instr. (?vn, ob or fl), bc	c.1724–6, London	[V/6]	
208	Die ihr aus dunklen Grüften (B. H. Brockes)	S, instr. (?vn, ob or fl), bc	c.1724–6, London	[V/6]	
209	In den angenehmen Büschen (B. H. Brockes)	S, instr. (?vn, ob or fl), bc	c.1724–6, London	[V/6]	
210	Flammende Zierde der Erden (B. H. Brockes)	S, instr. (?vn, ob or fl), bc	c.1724–6, London	[V/6]	
211	Aure dolci, deh, spirate (anon.)	A, 2 vn, va, bc	c.1722–6, London	[V/6]	
212	Con doppia gloria mia (anon.)	S, 2 vn, bc	c.1722–6, London	[V/6]	
213	Con lacrime sì belle (anon.)	A, 2 ob, 2 vn, vc, bc	c.1717–18, London	[V/6]	
214	Dell'onda instabile (anon.)	A, fl, bc	c.1749, London	[V/6]	
215	Col valor del vostro brando (anon.)	S, 2 vn, vc, bn, db, cemb	c.1711–13, London	[V/6]	
216	Impari del mio core (anon.)	S, bc	c.1749, London	[V/6]	
217	L'odio, sì, ma poi ritrovo (anon.)	A, 2 vn, bc	c.1722–6, London	[V/6]	
219	Non so se avrai mai bene (anon.)	S, bc	c.1710–18, London	[V/6]	
220	Per dar pace al mio tormento (anon.)	S, bc	c.1749, London	[V/6]	
221	Quant'invidio tua fortuna (anon.)	S, bc	c.1749, London	[V/6]	
222	Quanto più amara fu sorte crudele (anon.)	S, 2vn, va, bc	c.1721–3, London	[V/6]	
223	S'un dì m'appaga, la mia crudele (anon.)	S, 2vn, bc	c.1738–41, London	[V/6]	
224	Sì, crudel, tornerà (anon.)	S, 2 vn, bc	c.1738–41, London	[V/6]	
225	Spera chi sa, perché la sorte (anon.)	A, 2 ob, 2 vn, va, bc	c.1717–18, London	[V/6]	
227	Vo' cercando tra fiori (anon.)	S, 2 vn, bc	c.1726, London	[V/6]	
Anh. B 023	Lusinga questo cor (anon.)	S, ob, 2 vn, va, bc	c.1736–40, London	[V/6]	poss. for An Oratorio (1738)
Anh. B 025	Mi palpita il cor (anon.)	S, bc	? 1738, London	V/4	
Anh. B 027	No, così presto no (anon.)	S, bc	c.1749–51, London	[V/6]	
Anh. B 028	No, non così severe (anon.)	A, rec, 2 vn, va, bc	?c.1719, London	II/4,1	fragment, poss. a draft
deest	Sa perché pena il cor (anon.)	A, ob, 2vn, va, bc	?c.1712–17, London	[V/6]	

Miscellaneous arias – uncertain, doubtful, spurious

HWV	Title (text)	Scoring	Remarks
Anh. B 010	*Par les charmes d'un doux mensonge* (anon.)	S	Printed in 1737; possibly by Handel
Anh. B 012	*Agitata è l'alma mia* (anon.)	B, 2 vn, va, bc	doubtful
Anh. B 024	*M'avrai crudele* (anon.)	B, 2 vn, va, bc	doubtful
Anh. B 031	*Per delitto di donna incostante* (anon.)	S, bc	attr. to Handel; poss. from the repertoire of a singer in London, c.1725–32
Anh. B 032	*Se tu meco in campo scendi* (anon.)	S, 2 vn, va, bc	poss. Handel, c.1738; thematic ideas appear in Saul

Songs

HWV	Title (Text)	Scoring	Date, place	HHA	Remarks
218	Love's but the frailty of the mind (W. Congreve)	S, bc	1740, London	[II/4]	perf. 17 March 1740 by Kitty Clive
226	The morning is charming ('Hunting song') (Charles Legh)	T, bc	1751, London	[V/6]	autograph presented to Charles Legh in 1751
228⁹	From scourging rebellion (John Lockman)	T, bc	1746, London	[II/4]	perf. 15 May 1746 by Thomas Lowe
228¹¹	I like the am'rous youth that's free (James Miller)	S, bc	1737, London	[II/4]	perf. 28 Feb. 1737 by Kitty Clive
228¹⁸	Stand round, my brave boys (anon.)	T, bc	1745, London	[V/6]	'A Song made for the Gentlemen Volunteers of the City of London'; perf. 14 Nov. 1745 by Thomas Lowe
Anh. B 011	Quand on suit (anon.)	S, bc	c.1738–41, London	[V/6]	

Songs – uncertain, doubtful, spurious
Note: Some may be authentic, some may be spurious or pirated arrangements.

HWV	Title (Text)	Scoring	Remarks
228[1]	As Celia's fatal arrows flew ('The unhappy lovers') (anon.)	S, bc	c.1730; attr. to Handel in contemporary prints
228[2]	Ask not the cause ('Charming Cloris') / The sun was sunk beneath the hill ('The poor shepherd') (J. Gay)	S, bc	c.1730; attr. to Handel in contemporary prints
228[3]	As on a sunshine summer's day (B. Griffin)	S	c.1729; attr. to Handel in contemporary prints, used in *The Village Opera* and in the ballad opera *The Chamber Maid*
228[4]	Bacchus one day gayly striding ('Bacchus's speech in praise of wine') (Phillips)	S, bc	c.1730; attr. to Handel in contemporary prints, also in the ballad opera *Devil to Pay*
228[5]	Charming is your shape and air ('The Polish minuet' or 'Miss Kitty Grevil's delight') (anon.)	S, bc	c.1720; attr. to Handel in contemporary prints, also in the ballad opera *Silvia*
228[6]	Come and listen to my ditty ('The sailor's complaint') / As near Portobello lying ('Hosier's ghost')	S, bc	c.1735; attr. to Handel in contemporary prints
228[7]	Di godere ha speranza il mio core ('Oh, my dearest, my lovely creature') (anon.)	S, bc	c.1719; attr. to Handel in contemporary prints
228[8]	Faithless ungrateful ('The forsaken maid's complaint') / Cloe proves false ('The slighted swain') (anon.)	S, bc	c.1728; attr. to Handel in contemporary prints, melody from *Floridante*
228[10]	Guardian angels now protect me ('The forsaken nymph') (anon.)	S, bc	c.1735; attr. to Handel in contemporary prints
228[12]	My fair, ye swains, is gone astray ('Phillis')	S, bc	c.1725; comp. by T. Arne
228[13]	Not, Cloe, that I better am (anon.)	S, bc	c.1730; attributed to Handel in a contemporary print
228[14]	Oh cruel tyrant love ('Strephon's complaint of love') (anon.)	S, bc	c.1730; attr. to Handel in contemporary prints, melody from the ballad opera *The Fashionable Lady* by J. Ralph

(cont.)

Songs – uncertain, doubtful, spurious (*cont.*)

HWV	Title (Text)	Scoring	Remarks
228¹⁵	On the shore of a low ebbing sea / Ye swains that are courting a maid ('The satyr's advice to a Stock Jobber') / Says my uncle I pray you discover ('Minory mogg') (anon.)	S, bc	c.1730; attr. to Handel in contemporary prints
228¹⁶	Phillis be kind and hear me (Mr Paratt)	S, bc	c.1730; melody from Menuet, HWV 545, attr. to Handel in a contemporary print
228¹⁷	Phillis the lovely, turn to your swain ('Phillis advised') (anon.)	S, bc	c.1739; attr. to Handel in a contemporary print
228¹⁹	'Twas when the seas were roaring ('The faithful maid' or 'The melancholy nymph') (J. Gay)	S, bc	c.1725; by c.1730 attr. to Handel; used in *The Beggar's Opera*
228²⁰/ Anh. B 009	When I survey Clarinda's charms / Venus now leaves her Paphian dwelling ('The rapture' or 'Matchless Clorinda') (B. [?Bradley])	S, bc	c.1725; Handel or F. Geminiani
228²¹	When Phoebus the tops of the hills does adorn ('The death of the stag') (anon.)	2 S (2 vn, 2 fl, 2 hn), bc	c.1740; attr. to Handel in contemporary prints and later manuscript copies
228²²	Who to win a woman's favour (anon.)	S, bc	c.1746; attr. to Handel in a contemporary print, melody from *Almira*
228²³	Ye winds to whom Collin complains ('An answer to Collin's complaint') (anon.)	S	c.1716; attr. to Handel in a contemporary print
228²⁴	Yes, I'm in love (W. Whitehead)	S, bc	c.1740; attr. to Handel in contemporary prints

Concertos

HWV	Type	Key	Scoring	Date, place	HHA	Remarks
287	Concerto for oboe and orchestra	g	ob solo, 2 vn, va, bc	? c.1703–6, Hamburg	IV/12	no autograph, one early MS copy
288	Sonata a 5	Bb	vn solo, 2 ob, 2 vn, va, bc	c.1707, Italy	IV/12	poss. for Corelli
289	Concerto for organ and orchestra (Op. 4 No. 1)	g	org solo, 2 ob, 2 vn, va, bc	1st perf. 19 Feb. 1736, Covent Garden	IV/2	HWV 289–94: Six Organ Concertos, Op. 4; No. 1 perf. with *Alexander's Feast*
290	Concerto for organ and orchestra (Op. 4 No. 2)	Bb	org solo, 2 ob, 2 vn, va, bc	1st perf. 5 March 1735, Covent Garden	IV/2	performed with revival of *Esther* (HWV 50[b])
291	Concerto for organ and orchestra (Op. 4 No. 3)	g	org solo, vn solo, vc solo, 2 ob, 2 vn, va, bc	1st perf. 5 March 1735, Covent Garden	IV/2	perf. with revival of *Esther* (HWV 50[b])
292	Concerto for organ and orchestra (Op. 4 No. 4)	F	org solo, 2 ob, 2 vn, va, bc	completed 25 March 1735; 1st perf. 1 April 1735, Covent Garden	IV/2	perf. with revival of *Athalia*; last movement originally featured an 'Alleluja' chorus
293	Concerto for organ and orchestra (Op. 4 No. 5)	F	org solo, 2 ob, 2 vn, va, bc	?1st perf. 26 March 1735, Covent Garden	IV/2	poss. perf. with revival of *Deborah*; adapted from HWV 369
294	Concerto for harp and orchestra (Op. 4 No. 6)	Bb	harp solo, 2 rec, 2 vn, va, bc	1st perf. 19 Feb. 1736, Covent Garden	IV/2	perf with *Alexander's Feast*; orig. for harp, later arr. for org.
295	Concerto for organ and orchestra	F	org solo, 2 ob, 2 vn, va, bc	completed 2 April 1739; 1st perf. 4 April 1739, King's Theatre	IV/8	HWV 295–300: Six Organ Concertos, 'Second Set'; HWV 295 first perf. with *Israel in Egypt*
296[a]	Concerto for organ and orchestra	A	org solo, 2 ob, 3 vn, va, bc	?1st perf. 20 March 1739, King's Theatre	IV/8	?perf with revival of *Alexander's Feast*

(cont.)

Concertos (cont.)

HWV	Type	Key	Scoring	Date, place	HHA	Remarks
296[b]	Concerto for organ and orchestra	A	org solo, 2 ob, 2 vn, va, bc	after Feb. 1743, London		'Pasticcio' concerto; no proof of performance, arr. by Handel from HWV 296[a], 294, 307
302[a]	Concerto for oboe and orchestra	B♭	ob. solo, 2 vn, va, bc	after 1718, London	IV/12	arr. from Cannons anthem ouvertures; printed 1740, London
302[b]	Suite de Pièces	F	2 ob, 2 hn, 2 vn, va ad lib, bc	c.1737–8, London	VI12	
303	Adagio	d	org. solo, 2 vn, va, 2 vc, 2 bn, bc, org	c.1737–9, London	VI/12	later published as 1st movement in HWV 309
304	Concerto for organ and orchestra	d	org solo, 3 vn, va, bc	?1st perf. 14 Feb. 1746, Covent Garden	VI/12	? perf. with *Occasional Oratorio*
305[a]	Concerto for organ and orchestra	F	org solo, [2 ob], 2 vn, bc	c.1748, London	VI/16	arr. by Handel from HWV 334 and March in F major from *Judas Maccabaeus*
305[b]	Concerto for organ solo	F	org solo	after 1747, London	VI/16	rearranged by Handel
306	Concerto for organ and orchestra (Op. 7 No. 1)	B♭	org solo, 2 ob, 2 bn, 3 vn, va, bc	completed 17 Feb. 1740; 1st perf. 27 Feb. 1740, Lincoln's Inn Fields	VI/8	HWV 306–11: Six Organ Concertos, Op. 7; HWV 306 perf. with *L'Allegro*
307	Concerto for organ and orchestra (Op. 7 No. 2)	A	org solo, 2 ob, 3 vn, va, bc	completed 5 Feb. 1743; 1st perf. London 18 Feb. 1743, Covent Garden	VI/8	perf. with *Samson*
308	Concerto for organ and orchestra (Op. 7 No. 3)	B♭	org solo, 2 ob, 3 vn, va, bc	comp. 1–4 Jan. 1751; ?1st perf. 1 March 1751, Covent Garden	VI/8	?perf. with revival of *Alexander's Feast*; last concerto before blindness

309	Concerto for organ and orchestra (Op. 7 No. 4)	d	org solo, 2 ob, 3 vn, va, 2 vc, 2 bn org or cemb, db	c.1740–6, London	VI/8	?compilation
310	Concerto for organ and orchestra (Op. 7 No. 5)	g	org solo, 2 ob, 3 vn, va, bc (with cbn)	completed 31 Jan. 1750; 1st perf. 16 March 1750, Covent Garden	VI/8	perf. with *Theodora*
311	Concerto for organ and orchestra (Op. 7 No. 6)	B♭	org solo, 2 ob, 3 vn, va, bc	c.1748–9, London; perf. 1749	VI/8	
312	Concerto grosso (Op. 3 No. 1)	B♭	conc.: 2 rec, 2 ob, 2 bn, vn rip.: 2 vn, 2 va, **bc**	?c.1710, Hanover	VI/11	HWV 312–17: Six Concerti grossi, Op. 3
313	Concerto grosso (Op. 3 No. 2]	B♭	conc.: 2 ob, 2 vn, 2 vc rip.: 2 vn, 2va, bc	c.1715–18, London	VI/11	
314	Concerto grosso (Op. 3 No. 3)	G	conc.: fl/ob, vn rip.: 2vn, va, bc	c.1717–18, London	VI/11	? arr. by Walsh
315	Concerto grosso (Op. 3 No. 4)	F	conc.: 2 ob, v1 rip.: 2 ob, bn, 2 vn, va, bc	c. May–June 1716, London; 1st perf. 20 June 1716, King's Theatre	VI/11	'Orchestra Concerto' perf. with *Amadigi*, benefit night for the orchestra
316	'Concerto grosso' (Op. 3 No. 5)	d	2 ob, 2 vn, va, bc	c.1717–18, London	VI/11	arr. from sinfonias to Cannons anthems
317	Concerto grosso (Op. 3 No. 6)	D/d	conc.: 2 ob, bn, org/cemb rip.: 2 vn, va, vc, bn, bc	c.1722, London	VI/11	1st mov. probably perf. with *Ottone*; 2nd mov. = HWV 309; 3rd mov. ?assembled by Walsh
318	Concerto grosso ('Alexander's Feast concerto')	C	conc.: 2 vn, vc rip.: 2 ob, 2 vn, va, bc	completed 25 Jan 1736; 1st perf. 19 Feb. 1736 Covent Garden	VI/11	perf. with *Alexander's Feast*
319	Concerto grosso (Op. 6 No. 1)	g	conc.: 2 vn, vc rip.: [2 ob], 2 vn, va, bc	completed 29 Sept. 1739, London	IV/14	HWV 319–30: Twelve Grand Concertos (later called Op. 6) oboes in autograph added later

(cont.)

Concertos – uncertain, doubtful, spurious

HWV	Type / Key	Key	Scoring	Remarks
297	Concerto for organ	d	org. solo	1739, London; arr. from HWV 328 (Op. 6 No. 10)
298	Concerto for organ	G	org. solo	1739, London; arr. from HWV 319 (Op. 6 No. 1)
299	Concerto for organ	D	org. solo	1739, London; arr. from HWV 323 (Op. 6 No. 5)
300	Concerto for organ	g	org. solo	1739, London; arr. from HWV 324 (Op. 6 No. 6)
301	Concerto for oboe and orchestra	B♭	ob solo, 2 vn, va, bc	printed London 1740; authenticity uncertain; included in HHA IV/12

Suites, overtures, individual movements

HWV	Type	Key	Scoring	Date, place	HHA	Remarks
336	Ouverture	B♭	2 ob, bn, 2 vn, va, bc	c.1705–6, Hamburg or Italy	IV/15	autograph lost; theory that this might have been the original overture for Il trionfo del Tempo (HWV 46ᵃ) is speculative
337	Ouverture	D	2 ob, bn, 3 vn, bc	c.1722, London	IV/15	poss. 1st draft overture for Giulio Cesare
338¹⁻²	Adagio / Allegro	b / D	Adagio: fl, vn solo, lute, vc, db – 2 vn, vc, bc / Allegro: 2 ob, 2 vn, va, bc	c.1722, London	IV/15	poss. comp. at around the same time as 1st movt of HWV 317, published as Op. 3 No. 6
339	Sinfonia	B♭	2 vn, bc	c.1706–7, Hamburg or Italy	IV/15	
340	Allegro	G	2 vn, bc	c.1715, London	IV/19	
342	Ouverture	F	2 ob, 2 hn, 2 va, va, bc	c.1733–4, London		orig. for 1734 revival of Il pastor fido (HWV 8ᵇ)
343ᵃ⁻ᵇ	Ritornellos for a Chaconne	G	2 ob, 2 vn, va, bc	HWV 343ᵇ: March/April 1739, London	IV/19	written to complement HWV 435
344	Coro and Minuet	D	str, bc	c.1706	IV/19	from Florindo
345	Marche	D	tpt, 2 vn, bc	before 1738, London	IV/19	
347	Sinfonia	B♭	2 ob, str, bc	c.1747, London	IV/19	
348–50	Water Music		rec picc, fl, 2 ob, bn, 2 hn, 2 tpt, 2 vn conc, 3 vn, va, vc, db, bc	c.1715, London	IV/13 Neuausgabe	scholars now believe that there were not originally three separate suites, but only one long suite

Suites, overtures, individual movements (cont.)

HWV	Type	Key	Scoring	Date place	HHA	Remarks
351	*Music for the Royal Fireworks*		2 fl, 3 ob, 3 hn, 3 tpt, timpani e tamburi militari, 2 vn, va, 2 bn, serpentone, cbn, vc, db	March/April 1749, London; perf. April 1749, Green Park	IV/13	comp. to precede fireworks display celebrating the Treaty of Aix-la-Chapelle
352[1–4]	Suite	Bb	2 ob, 2 vn, va, bc	c.1703–6, Hamburg	IV/19	from *Daphne*
353[1–4]	Suite	G	2 ob, 2 vn, va, bc	c.1703–6, Hamburg	IV/19	from *Daphne*
354[1–4]	Suite	Bb	2 vn, va, bc	c.1703–6, Hamburg	IV/19	from *Florindo*
355	Aria (Hornpipe)	c	2 vn, va, bc	not later than 1732	IV/19	
356	Hornpipe	D	2 vn, va, bc	c.1740, London	IV/19	'compos'd for the Concert at Vauxhall 1740'
406	Adagio-Allegro	A	vn solo, other instr. (2 vn), bc	c.1750, London	IV/19	instr. not specified
407	Allegro	G	vn solo	1738, London	IV/19	instr. not specified
408	Allegro	c	vn, bc	c.1725, London	IV/19	instr. not specified
409	Aria (Andante)	d	rec, bc	c.1725–6, London	IV/18 (Anhang)	early version of the Andante from Sonata HWV 367[a]
412	Aria (Andante)	a	vn, bc	c.1724–5, London	IV/19	instr. not specified
413	Gigue	Bb	vn, va, bc	1736, London	IV/19	similarities to the Gigue in the *Berenice* overture

HWV	Type	Key	Scoring		HHA	Remarks
419[1]	March	G	fl/ob/vn, bc	c.1710–20, London	IV/19	'March in Ptolomy'; survived in early editions
419[2]	March	G	fl/ob/vn, bc	c.1710–20, London	IV/19	'Ld. Loudon's March'; survived in early editions
419[3]	March	G	fl/ob/vn, bc	c.1710–20, London	IV/19	'Admiral Boscowin's March'; survived in early editions
419[4]	March	F	fl/ob/vn, bc	c.1710–2c, London	IV/19	survived in early editions
419[5]	March	C	fl/ob/vn, bc	c.1710–20, London	IV/19	survived in early editions
419[6]	March	C	fl/vn, bc	c.1710–20, London	IV/19	survived in early editions
420	Menuet	D	fl/vn, bc	c.1743, London	IV/19	instr. not specified
421	Menuet	D	fl/vn, bc	London, c.1744	IV/19	instr. not specified
425	Air (Sarabande)	E	vn, bc	c.1750, St Giles, Wimborne, Dorset	IV/19	instr. not specified

Suites, overtures, individual movements – uncertain, doubtful, spurious

HWV	Type	Key	Scoring	HHA	Remarks
341	Ouverture ('Handel's Water Piece')	D	tpt, 2 vn, va, bc	IV/13 Appendix	authenticity doubtful, perhaps comp. by F. Geminiani

Music for wind ensembles

HWV	Type	Key	Scoring	Date, place	HHA	Remarks
346	Marche	F	2 ob, 2 hn, bc	c.1728–9, London	IV/19	'March in Ptolomy'
410	Aria	F	2 ob, 2 hunting hn, bn	c.1725, London	IV/19	
411	Aria	F	2 ob, 2 hunting hn, bn	c.1725, London	IV/19	
414	Marche for the Fife	C	fife, bn	c.1747, London	IV/19	subject used for Introduzione to Joshua
415	Marche for the Fife	D	fife, bn	c.1747, London	IV/19	subject used for Joshua ('See the conquering hero comes')
416	Marche allegro	D	2 ob, bn, tpt	c.1734, London	IV/19	'Dragoon's March'; autograph placed among the ballets for revival of Il pastor fido in 1734 (HWV 8^b)
417	March (La Marche)	D	bn, 2 hn	c.1746–7, London	IV/19	used for Alexander Balus ('Flushed with conquest')
418	March	G	2 ob, bn	c.1741, London	IV/19	instr. not specified, autograph among sketches for Messiah
422	Menuet	G	2 ob, bn, 2 hn	c.1746–7, London	IV/19	revised for the 2nd minuet in the Music for the Royal Fireworks
423	Menuet	G	2 ob, bn, 2 hn	c.1746–7, London	IV/19	
424	Ouverture	D	2 cl, hunting hn	c.1740–1, London	IV/15	

Trio sonatas

HWV	Type	Key	Scoring	Date, place	HHA	Remarks
386[a]	Sonata (Op. 2 No. 1[a])	c	rec/ob, vn, bc	c.1718, London	IV/10/1 (Anhang)	original version
386[b]	Sonata (Op. 2 No. 1[b])	b	rec/ob, vn, bc	c.1726–32, London	IV/10/1	transposition, poss. authentic
387	Sonata (Op. 2 No. 2)	g	2 vn, bc	? c.1700, Halle	IV/10/1	
388	Sonata (Op. 2 No. 3)	Bb	2 vn (2 ob/rec, vn), bc	c.1718, London	IV/10/1	
389	Sonata (Op. 2 No. 4)	F	fl (rec, ob, vn), vn (fl), bc	c.1718, London	IV/10/1	
390[a]	Sonata (Op. 2 No. 5[a])	g	2 vn, bc	c.1718, London	IV/10/1	
391	Sonata (Op. 2 No. 6)	g	2 vn, bc	c.1707–10, Italy	IV/10/1	
392	Sonata	F	2 vn, bc	c.1706–9, Italy	IV/10/1	
396	Sonata (Op. 5 No. 1)	A	2 vn, bc	c.1737–8, London	IV/10/2	
397	Sonata (Op. 5 No. 2)	D	2 vn, bc	c.1737–8, London	IV/10/2	
398	Sonata (Op. 5 No. 3)	e	2 vn, bc	c.1737–8, London	IV/10/2	
399	Sonata (Op. 5 No. 4)	G	2 vn, (va ad lib.) bc	c.1737–8, London	IV/10/2	taken from other compositions, arr. possibly not Handel's
400	Sonata (Op. 5 No. 5)	g	2 vn, bc	c.1737–8, London	IV/10/2	
401	Sonata (Op. 5 No. 6)	F	2 vn, bc	c.1737–8, London	IV/10/2	
402	Sonata (Op. 5 No. 7)	Bb	2 vn, bc	c.1737–8, London	IV/10/2	
403	Sonata	C	2 vn, bc	c.1738, London	I/13	material also appears in overture for Saul
404	Sonata	g	ob/vn, vn, bc	? c.1718–20, Cannons	IV/15	poss. item no. 117 in the 'Cannons Catalogue'
405	Sonata	F	2 rec, bc	c.1707–9, Italy	IV/19	

Trio sonatas – uncertain, doubtful, spurious

HWV	Type	Key	Scoring	Remarks
380	Sonata I	B♭	ob, vn, bc	doubtful
381	Sonata II	d	ob, vn, bc	doubtful
382	Sonata III	E♭	ob, vn, bc	doubtful
383	Sonata IV	F	ob, vn, bc	doubtful
384	Sonata V	G	ob, vn, bc	doubtful
385	Sonata VI	D	ob, vn, bc	doubtful
390[b]	Sonata (Op. 2 No. 5[b])	g	2 vn, vc, cemb, org	possibly not Handel's arrangement
393	Sonata	g	2 vn, bc	doubtful
394	Sonata	E	2 vn, bc	spurious
395	Sonata	e	2 trav, bc	doubtful, poss. comp. by Hasse

Solo sonatas

HWV	Type	Key	Scoring	Date, place	HHA	Remarks
357	Sonata	B♭	ob, bc	c.1707–9, Italy	IV/18	'Sonata pour l'Hautbois solo'
358	Sonata	G	vn, bc	c.1707–9, Italy	IV/18	
359[a]	Sonata	d	vn, bc	c.1724, London	IV/18	original version
359[b]	Sonata (Op. 1 No. 1[b])	e	fl, t:c	c.1726–32, London	IV/3	
360	Sonata (Op. 1 No. 2)	g	rec, bc	c.1725–6, London	IV/3	
361	Sonata (Op. 1 No. 3)	A	vn, bc	c.1725–6, London	IV/3	'Sonata a Flauto e Cembalo'
362	Sonata(Op. 1 No. 4)	a	rec, bc	c.1725–6, London	IV/3	
363[a]	Sonata (Op. 1 No. 5)	F	fl, t:c	c.1712–16, London	IV/18	original version
363[b]	Sonata	G	trav, bc	c.1726–32, London	IV/3	
364[a]	Sonata (Op. 1 No. 6)	g	vn (ob), bc	c.1724, London	IV/18	solo instrument poss. violin or oboe
364[b]	Sonata	g	viola da gamba, bc	c.1724, London		authentic adaptation of HWV 364[a]
365	Sonata (Op. 1 No. 7)	C	rec, bc	c.1725–6, London	IV/3	
366	Sonata (Op. 1 No. 8)	c	ob, bc	c.1710–11, London	IV/18	
367[a]	Sonata	d	rec, bc	c.1724, London	IV/18	'Fitzwilliam Sonata III'
367[b]	Sonata (Op. 1 No. 9)	b	fl, bc	c.1726–32, London	IV/3	
369	Sonata (Op. 1 No. 11)	F	rec, bc	c.1725–6, London	IV/3	'Sonata a Flauto e Cembalo'
371	Sonata (Op. 1 No. 13)	D	vn, bc	c.1750, London	IV/4	'Sonata a Violino Solo e Cembalo'
377	Sonata	B♭	rec, bc	c.1724–5, London	IV/18	'Fitzwilliam Sonata I'
378	Sonata	D	fl, bc	c.1707–10, Italy	IV/18	formerly attributed to J. S. Weiß
379	Sonata (Op. 1 No. 1[a])	e	fl, bc	c.1727–8, London	IV/3	'Sonata a Traversa e Basso'

Solo sonatas – uncertain, doubtful, spurious

HWV	Type	Key	Scoring	Remarks
368	Violin sonata	g	vn, bc	published as Op. 1 No. 10 doubtful
370	Violin sonata	F	vn, bc	published as Op. 1 No. 12 doubtful
372	Violin sonata	A	vn, bc	published as Op. 1 No. 14 doubtful
373	Violin sonata	E	vn, bc	published as Op. 1 No. 15 doubtful
374	Flute sonata	a	fl, bc	'Hallenser Sonate I'
375	Flute sonata	e	fl, bc	'Hallenser Sonate II'
376	Flute sonata	b	fl, bc	'Hallenser Sonate III'

Keyboard music

HWV	Type	Key	Date, place	HHA	Remarks
426	Suite No. 1	A	c.1710–17, London	IV/1	HWV 426–33: Eight Suites de Pièces, Walsh's 'Premier Volume' (printed 1720)
427	Suite No. 2	F	c.1710–17, London	IV/1	
428	Suite No. 3	d	c.1710–17, London	IV/1	
429	Suite No. 4	e	c.1710–17, London	IV/1	
430	Suite No. 5	E	c.1710–17, London	IV/1	'The Harmonious Blacksmith'
431	Suite No. 6	f♯	c.1710–17, London	IV/1	
432	Suite No. 7	g	c.1710–17, London	IV/1	
433	Suite No. 8	f	c.1710–17, London	IV/1	
434	(Suite No. 1)	B♭	c.1710–17, London	IV/5	HWV 433–42: Nine Suites de Pièces, Walsh's 'Second Volume' (printed c.1733–4)
435	(Suite No. 2) Chaconne	G	c.1705–7	IV/5	21 variations
436	(Suite No. 3)	d	c.1721–6, London	IV/5	
437	(Suite No. 4)	d	? c.1703–6, Hamburg	IV/5	
438	(Suite No. 5)	e	? c.1710–17, London	IV/5	
439	(Suite No. 6)	g	? c.1703–6, Hamburg	IV/5	
440	(Suite No. 7)	B♭	? c.1703–6, Hamburg, rev. 1717–18	IV/5	
441	(Suite No. 8)	G	? c.1703–6, Hamburg	IV/5	partly spurious
442	(Suite No. 9) Prelude and Chaconne	G	? c.1703–6, Hamburg	IV/5	62 variations
443	Suite	C	? c.1703–6, Hamburg	IV/17	includes Chaconne (26 variations)
444	Partita	c	? c.1705–6, Hamburg	IV/17	
445	Suite	c	? c.1705–6, Hamburg	IV/17	
446	Suite deux clavecins	c	? c.1703–6, Hamburg	IV/19	music for only 1 harpsichord survived
447	Suite	d	c.1738–9, London	IV/6	for Princess Louisa

(cont.)

Keyboard music (cont.)

HWV	Type	Key	Date, place	HHA	Remarks
448	Suite	d	? c.1705–6, Hamburg	IV/17	
449	Suite	d	? c.1705, Hamburg	IV/17	
450	Partita	G	c.1700–5	IV/17	
451	Suite	g	? c.1703–6, Hamburg	IV/19	
452	Suite	g	c.1738–9, London	IV/6	for Princess Louisa
453	Suite	g	? c.1705–6, Hamburg	IV/17 and IV/19	
454	Partita	A	? c.1703–6, Hamburg	IV/6	
455	Suite	Bb	? c.1706, Hamburg	IV/6	keyboard version of HWV 336 and 354
456[1]	Ouverture (Il pastor fido, 1st version)	d	c.1720–7, London	IV/19	authentic keyboard arrangement
456[2]	Ouverture (Amadigi)	c	c.1720–7, London	IV/19	authentic keyboard arrangement
456[3]	Ouverture (Flavio)	g	c.1720–7, London	IV/19	authentic keyboard arrangement
456[4]	Ouverture (Rodelinda)	C	c.1720–7, London	IV/19	authentic keyboard arrangement
456[5]	Ouverture (Riccardo primo)	D	c.1720–7, London	IV/19	authentic keyboard arrangement
457	Aria	C	c.1720–1, London	IV/19	
460	Air (March)	D	c.1720–1, London	IV/19	
461	Air (Hornpipe)	d	c.1717–18, London	IV/19	
462	Air en menuet	d	c.1724–6, London	IV/19	
463	Air	F	c.1707–9, Italy	IV/19	
464	Air	F	c.1710–20, London	IV/13, Anhang	keyboard arr. of Air from Water Music
465	Air and 2 Doubles	F	c.1710–20, London	IV/17	
466	Air for 2-manual harpsichord	g	c.1710–20, London	IV/17	poss. for organ
467	Air (Lentement)	g	c.1710–20, London	IV/17	
468	Air	A	c.1727–8, London	IV/6	for organ or harpsichord
469	Air	Bb	c.1738, London	IV/19	reused in HWV 347, 311

470	Air for 2-manual harpsichord	Bb	c.1710–20, London	IV/17	
471	Air	Bb	c.1710–20, London	IV/17	
472	Allegro	C	?c.1705, Hamburg	IV/17	
474	Air	G	c.1733–5, London	IV/19	'O the pleasure of the plains' (*Acis and Galatea*) for organ
475	Allegro	d	c.1710–20, London	IV/17	
476	Allemande	F	c.1730–5, London	IV/6	
477	Allemande	A	c.1724–6, London	IV/6	
478	Allemande	a	?c.1705, Hamburg	IV/17	
479	Allemande	b	c.1721–2, London	IV/15	
480	Chorale 'Jesu meine Freude'	g	c.1736–40, London	IV/19	pcss. for organ
481	Capriccio	F	?c.1703–6, Hamburg	IV/6	
482[1]	Aria dell'opera *Rinaldo*	C	c.1717–24, London	IV/19	'Molto voglio', authentic keyboard arrangement
482[2]	Aria dell'opera *Floridante*	Eb	c.1722, London	IV/19	'Sventurato, godi, o core abbandonato', authentic keyboard arrangement
482[3]	Aria dell'opera *Radamisto*	g	c.1720–5, London	IV/19, Anhang II	'Ombra cara' no autograph
482[4]	Aria dell'opera *Muzio Scevola*	F	c.1720–5, London	IV/19, Anhang II	'Pupille sdegnose' no autograph
482[5]	Aria dell'opera *Muzio Scevola*	G	c.1720–5, London	IV/19, Anhang II	'Come se ti vedrò' no autograph
483	Capriccio	g	c.1720–1, London	IV/6	
484	Chaconne with 49 variations	C	c.1700–5, Halle/Hamburg	IV/17	version of Chaconne in HWV 443
485	Chaconne for 2-manual harpsichord	F	?c.1705, Hamburg	IV/17	
486	Chaconne	g	?c.1705, Hamburg	IV/17	
487	Concerto	G	c.1710–20, London	IV/17	
488	Allegro (Courante)	F	c.1717–8, London	IV/5	
489	Courante	b	c.1722, London	IV/17	

(cont.)

Keyboard music (cont.)

HWV	Type	Key	Date, place	HHA	Remarks
544	Menuet	A	c.1710–20, London	IV/19	
545	Menuet	A	c.1710–20, London	IV/19	
546	Menuet	A	c.1710–17, London	IV/19	'Water Music'
547	Menuet	a	c.1710–17, London	IV/19	
548	Menuet	a	c.1710–20, London	IV/19	
549	Menuet	a	c.1710–20, London	IV/19	
550	Menuet ('Florindo')	B♭	c.1705–6, Hamburg	IV/19	
551	Menuet	B♭	c.1710–20, London	IV/19	
552	Menuet	B♭	c.1710–20, London	IV/19	
553	Menuet	B♭	c.1710–20, London	IV/19	
554	Menuet	B♭	c.1710–20, London	IV/19	
555a–b	Menuet (1st/2nd version)	B♭	c.1710–20, London	IV/19	
556	Menuet	B♭	c.1710–20, London	IV/19	
557	Menuet	B♭	c.1710–20, London	IV/19	
558	Menuet	b	c.1707–8, Rome	IV/19	from *Poro*
559	Passepied	C	c.1721–2, London	IV/19	
560	Passepied	A	? c.1705, Hamburg	IV/19	
561	Prélude	d	c.1705–6, Hamburg	IV/5, 2nd edn	= HWV 437, 1st
562	Prélude 'Harpeggio'	d	c.1711–12, London	IV/6	
563	Prélude	d	? c.1700–3, Halle	IV/17	
564	Preludio	d	? c.1705, Hamburg	IV/17	
565	Prélude	d	c.1710–20, London	IV/1, 2nd edn, Anhang	early version of Prelude to HWV 428

566	Preludio	E	c.1710–20, London	IV/17	
567	Preludium	F	c.1710–20, London	IV/17	
568	Preludium	f	c.1710–20, London	IV/17	
570	Prélude (Harpeggio)	f♯	c.1717–18, London	IV/6	
571	Prélude e Capriccio (Allegro)	G	? c.1703–6, Hamburg	IV/17	
572	Prélude	g	c.1710–17, London	IV/6	
573	Prélude (Harpeggio)	g	? c.1705, Hamburg	IV/17	
574	Preludio ed Allegro (Sonata)	g	? c.1705, Hamburg	IV/6	
575	Prélude (Harpeggio)	a	c.1717–18, London	IV/6	
576	Preludio ed Allegro	a	? c.1705–6, Hamburg	IV/17	
577	Sonata (Fantasie)	C	? c.1703–5, Hamburg	IV/6	
579	Sonata for a 2-manual harpsichord	G	? c.1707–10, Italy	IV/6	
580	Sonata (Larghetto)	g	? c.1707–10, Italy	IV/17	
581	Sonatina	d	? c.1705, Hamburg	IV/17	
582	Sonatina (Fuga)	G	c.1721–2, London	IV/6	
583	Sonatina	g	c.1722, London	IV/17	
585	Sonatina	B♭	c.1721–2, London	IV/6	
586	Toccata	g	c.1710–20, London	IV/17	
605	Fugue No. 1	g	c.1711–18, London	IV/6	HWV 605–10: Six Fugues or Voluntaries for the Organ or Harpsichord (printed 1735, London)
606	Fugue No. 2	G	c.1711–18, London	IV/6	
607	Fugue No. 3	B♭	c.1711–18, London	IV/6	
608	Fugue No. 4	b	c.1711–18, London	IV/6	
609	Fugue No. 5	a	c.1711–18, London	IV/6	
610	Fugue No. 6	c	c.1711–18, London	IV/6	
611	Fugue	F	c.1705	IV/17	no autograph
612	Fugue	E		IV/19	no autograph, prob. authentic

Pasticcios and opera fragments

HWV	Title (Libretto)	Scoring	First performance	Remarks
A[1]	L'Elpidia, ovvero Li rivali generosi (?N. F. Haym, after A. Zeno))	S, MS, 2 A, T, B, 2 ob, 2 tpt, 2 va, bc	11 May 1725, London, King's Theatre	arias by Vinci, Orlandini, Lotti, Capelli, Sarro
A[2]	Genserico (?N. F. Haym after N. Berengani)	3 S, MS, A, 2 B, 2 ob, 2 hn, 3 vn, va, bc		fragment; only part of Act I comp., probably late 1727
A[3]	Ormisda (?G. Rossi after A. Zeno)	S, MS, 2 A, T, B, 2 ob, 2 tpt, 2 vn, bc	4 April 1730, London, King's Theatre	arias by Orlandini, Vinci, Hasse, Leo, Sarro, Fiore
A[4]	Venceslao (?G. Rossi after A. Zeno)	S, MS, 2 S, T, 2 B, SATB, 2 ob, 2 bn, 2 hunting hn, tpt, 2 vn, va, bc	12 Jan. 1731, London, King's Theatre	arias by Vinci, Hasse, Lotti, Porpora, Orlandini, Capelli, Giacomelli, Porta
A[5]	Titus l'Empereur (?after Berenice by J. Racine)	S, MS, 3 A, T, B, 2 ob, 2 hn, 3 vn, va, bc		fragment, only part of Act I comp., Oct.–Nov. 1731
A[6]	Lucio Papirio Dittatore (?G. Rossi after A. Zeno/ C. I. Frugoni)	S, 2 MS, 2 A, T, B, SSATB, 2 ob, 2 hn, 2 tpt, 2 vn, va, bc	23 May 1732, London, King's Theatre	arias by Giacomelli, Porpora
A[7]	Catone (after P. Metastasio)	2 S, MS, A, B, 2 ob, 2 hn, 2 tpt, 2 vn, va, bc	4 Nov. 1732, London, King's Theatre	arias by Leo, Hasse, Porpora, Vivaldi, Vinci
A[8]	Semiramide riconosciuta (after P. Metastasio)	4 S, MS, A, SSAB, 2 ob, 2 hn, 2 tpt, timp, 2 vn, va, bc	10 Oct. 1733, London, King's Theatre	arias by Vinci, Hasse, Feo, Leo, Sarro
A[9]	Cajo Fabbricio (after A. Zeno)	4 S, MS, A, B, 2 ob, 2 hn, 2 vn, va, bc	4 Dec. 1733, London, King's Theatre	arias by Hasse, Vinci, Leo
A[10]	Arbace (after P. Metastasio)	4 S, MS, A, SST, 2 ob, bn, 2 hn, tpt, 2 vn, va, bc	5 Jan. 1734, London, King's Theatre	arias by Vinci, Hasse, Porta
A[12]	Didone abbandonata (after P. Metastasio)	2 S, MS, 2 A, T, 2 ob, 2 hn, 2 tpt, 2 vn, 2 va, bc	13 April 1737, London, Covent Garden	arias by Vinci, Hasse, Giacomelli, Vivaldi

Appendix 2: Chronology

DONALD BURROWS and DAVID VICKERS

Year	Biography	Music and musicians
1685	Handel born, 23 February, at Halle, son of Georg Händel and his second wife Dorothea (née Taust)	J. S. Bach born at Eisenach, 21 March D. Scarlatti born at Naples, 26 October
1686		Porpora born
1687		Lully dies
		Geminiani and Galliard born
1688		
1689		
1690		Muffat born
		Legrenzi dies
1691		Purcell, *King Arthur*
1692	Begins to study under Zachow in Halle, following a visit to Weissenfels	Purcell, *The Fairy Queen*
1693		
1694		Purcell, D major Te Deum and Jubilate
1695		Giuseppe Sammartini born
		Purcell dies
1696	?Visit to Prussian court at Berlin	Greene born
1697	Handel's father dies	Blow's anthem *I was glad* written for the opening of the choir at Wren's new St Paul's Cathedral
		Quantz born
1698		Metastasio born
1699		Hasse born
1700		Giovanni Battista Sammartini born
		N. A. Strungk dies
		Bartolomeo Cristofori builds first fortepianos
1701	Takes first communion at Marktkirche, Halle ?First contact with Telemann in Leipzig	
1702	Registers as a student at Halle University Appointed organist at 'Domkirche' in Halle	
1703	Moves to Hamburg, where he is befriended by Mattheson Begins career at Hamburg opera house as a back-desk violinist	

(cont.)

Year	Biography	Music and musicians
1739	Gives mixed season of English and Italian works at King's Theatre Trio Sonatas, Op. 5 published by Walsh Composes *Song for St Cecilia's Day* and Concerti grossi, Op. 6 Begins season of performances of English works at Lincoln's Inn Fields Theatre	Hickford's Concert Room 'removes' from Poulton St. to Brewer St.: raffle of Clay (musical) clock, and picture of Handel set up in the new room Dittersdorf born
1740	Composes *L'Allegro, Il Penseroso ed il Moderato* and Organ Concerto, HWV 306 (with obbligato pedal part) Op. 6 Concerti grossi published Travels to continent in summer: on return to London, revises *Imeneo* and composes *Deidamia*, for new season at Lincoln's Inn Fields 'Second Set' of organ concertos published	Lotti dies J. S. Bach visits Halle Samuel Arnold and Paisiello born Arne, *Alfred* Mattheson's *Grundlage einer Ehren-Pforte* published in Hamburg
1741	Gives his last performance of Italian opera in London Composes *Messiah*, *Samson* and Italian duets Attends first performance of the new 'Middlesex' opera company Leaves London for Dublin, travelling via Chester and Holyhead Begins first subscription concert series at Dublin with *L'Allegro*	Fux and Vivaldi die Gluck's first opera, *Artaserse* Grétry born
1742	Completes two six-concert subscription series in Dublin, followed by first performances of *Messiah* Returns to London Completes score of *Samson*	
1743	Presents oratorio season at Covent Garden Composes *Semele*, Dettingen Te Deum and Anthem, and *Joseph and his Brethren*	'Middlesex' Italian opera company opens at King's Theatre, with *Rossane*, a version of Handel's *Alessandro*. Boccherini born
1744	Presents second oratorio season at Covent Garden Composes *Hercules* and *Belshazzar* Begins ambitious oratorio subscription season at King's Theatre for 1744–5	'Middlesex' opera company collapses
1745	Oratorio season meets difficulties, but continues Visits 'the country' in the summer	

Year	Biography	Music and musicians
1746	Composes *Occasional Oratorio* and *Judas Maccabaeus*	Re-formed 'Middlesex' company opens with Gluck's opera *La Caduta de' Giganti*: Gluck in London
		W. F. Bach appointed organist at the Marktkirche, Halle
1747	Presents first non-subscription oratorio season at Covent Garden	J. S. Bach visits Friedrich II at Potsdam
	Galli joins Handel's company	Bononcini dies
	Composes *Alexander Balus* and *Joshua*	
1748	Composes *Solomon* and *Susanna*	J. G. Walther dies
		Holywell Music Room, Oxford, built
1749	New leading soprano, Frasi, joins Handel's company	Galliard and Heidegger die
		Cimarosa born
	Composes *Fireworks Music*	
	Gives first charity performance for Foundling Hospital	
	Composes *Theodora*	
	Visits Bath	
	Writes incidental music for projected production of Smollett's play *Alceste*	
1750	Covent Garden cast includes new castrato, Guadagni	J. S. Bach dies
	Handel's first *Messiah* performances at Foundling Hospital	Giuseppe Sammartini dies (in London)
	Makes his will	Salieri born
	Reuses much of the music from *Alceste* in *The Choice of Hercules*	
	Visits continent: plays organs in the Netherlands	
1751	Composes last instrumental work, Organ Concerto, HWV 308	Albinoni dies
	Composition of *Jephtha* interrupted by problems with eyesight	
	Travels to Bath and Cheltenham	
	Handel's pupil J. C. Smith junior returns to London to assist with management of oratorio seasons	
1752	Remaining eyesight deteriorates	Pepusch dies
		J. F. Reichardt born
		Avison publishes *Essay on Musical Expression*
1753	At Foundling Hospital *Messiah* performance plays 'voluntary' on organ – the last newspaper report of him playing in public	
1754	First surviving account list for Foundling Hospital performances	Martín y Soler born
	Dictates and signs letter to Telemann	

(cont.)

Year	Biography	Music and musicians
1755	Attains seventieth birthday	*The Fairies* (J. C. Smith, jun.) produced at Drury Lane Greene dies
1756	Plays the organ during Lenten oratorio season – last known public performances. Adds first codicil to will, with bequests to Morell and Hamilton	Mozart born
1757	Handel possibly more active, and collaborates with Morell over adaptation of *Il trionfo del Tempo* into *The Triumph of Time and Truth* Adds further codicil to will: bequests to John Rich and Jennens, and copies of *Messiah* (score and parts) to Foundling Hospital	J. Stamitz and D. Scarlatti die
1758	Visits Tunbridge Wells, possibly with Morell	
1759	Attends *Messiah* performance on 6 April and intends to travel to Bath, but is too ill to do so Adds 4th (final) codicil to will: bequests include £1,000 to Decay'd Musicians Fund and £600 provision for a monument at Westminster Abbey Dies at his home in Brook Street at about 8 a.m. on 14 April (Easter Saturday); funeral at Westminster Abbey, 20 April	Earliest known reference to Haydn's Symphony No. 1 in D major (possibly composed earlier)

Appendix 3: Handel's family tree

ANNETTE LANDGRAF

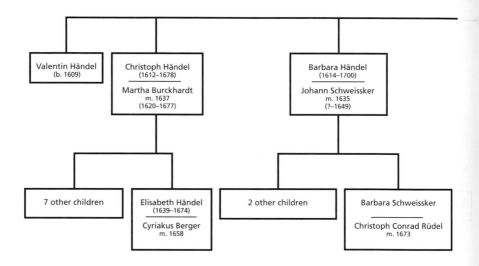

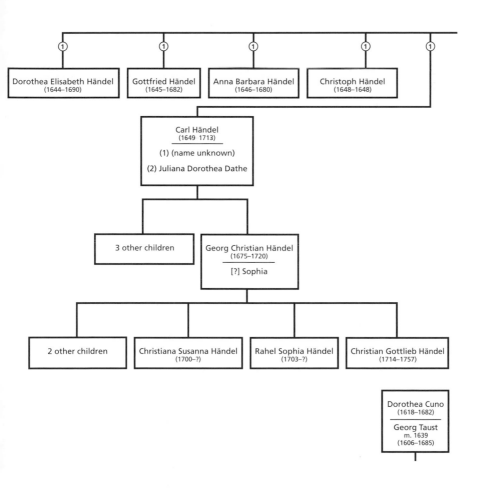

Valentin Händel
(1582–1636)

Anna Beichling
m. 1608
(1587–1670)

① Dorothea Elisabeth Händel
(1644–1690)

① Gottfried Händel
(1645–1682)

① Anna Barbara Händel
(1646–1680)

① Christoph Händel
(1648–1648)

① Carl Händel
(1649 1713)

(1) (name unknown)

(2) Juliana Dorothea Dathe

3 other children

Georg Christian Händel
(1675–1720)

[?] Sophia

2 other children

Christiana Susanna Händel
(1700–?)

Rahel Sophia Händel
(1703–?)

Christian Gottlieb Händel
(1714–1757)

Dorothea Cuno
(1618–1682)

Georg Taust
m. 1639
(1606–1685)

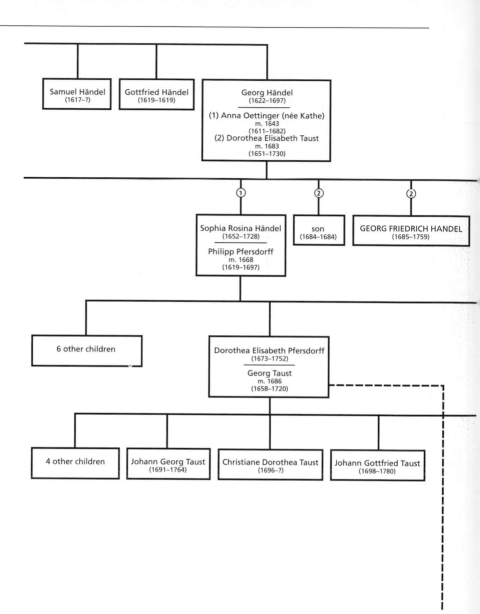

Samuel Händel
(1617–?)

Gottfried Händel
(1619–1619)

Georg Händel
(1622–1697)
_____
(1) Anna Oettinger (née Kathe)
m. 1643
(1611–1682)
(2) Dorothea Elisabeth Taust
m. 1683
(1651–1730)

① Sophia Rosina Händel
(1652–1728)
_____
Philipp Pfersdorff
m. 1668
(1619–1697)

② son
(1684–1684)

② GEORG FRIEDRICH HANDEL
(1685–1759)

6 other children

Dorothea Elisabeth Pfersdorff
(1673–1752)
_____
Georg Taust
m. 1686
(1658–1720)

4 other children

Johann Georg Taust
(1691–1764)

Christiane Dorothea Taust
(1696–?)

Johann Gottfried Taust
(1698–1780)

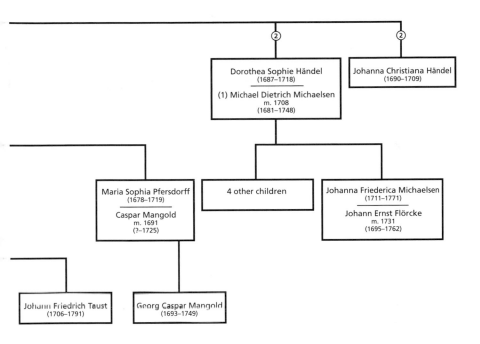

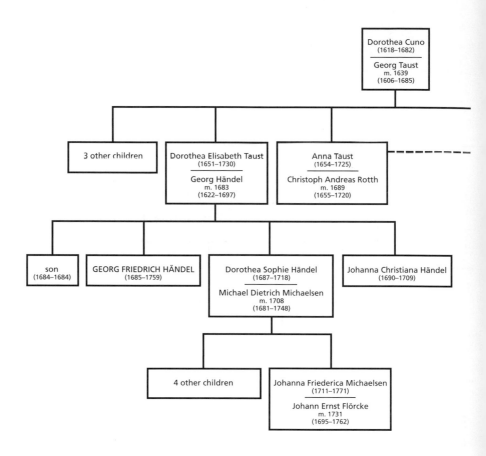

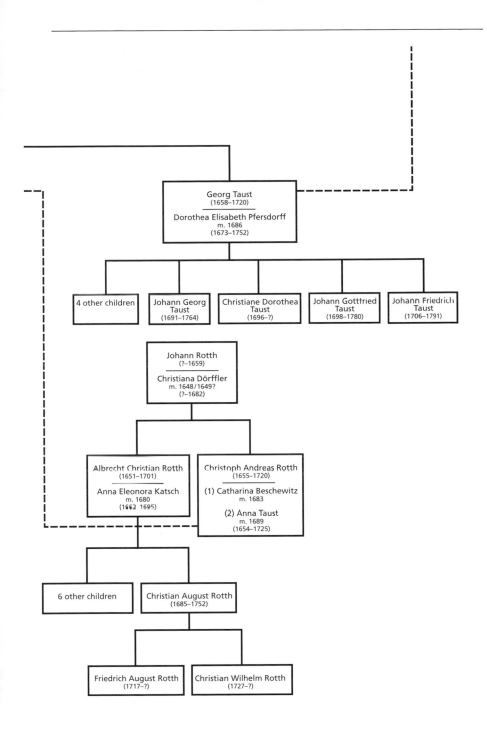

Appendix 4: Handel iconography

EDWIN WERNER

Portraits considered to be authentic

Date	Artist (or attributed to)	Medium, size (cm)	Present owner or location	Documentation (selection)
c.1710	(Johann oder Jacob) Christoph Platzer	Miniature, on vellum, 6.77 × 4.78 oval	Händel-Haus, Halle (missing)	E. Werner, 'Georg Friedrich Händel: Miniatur von Georg Platzer, um 1710', Händel-Hausmitteilungen 1 (1992), 22–3
c.1720	Anonymous (in the past attributed to James Thornhill)	Oil on canvas, 102.2 × 87.7	Fitzwilliam Museum, Cambridge	J. W. Goodison, Catalogue of Paintings in the Fitzwilliam Museum, Cambridge, vol. 3: British School (Cambridge, 1977), 32–3
? c.1725	Bartholomew Dandridge (1691–c.1755) (?)	Oil on canvas, 118.4 × 94	Fitzwilliam Museum, Cambridge	Goodison, Catalogue of Paintings, 64–5
before 1730	Anon.	Engraving, 30.2 × 21.9	Royal College of Music, London	J. Simon (ed.), Handel: A Celebration of his Life and Times 1685–1759 (London, 1985), 37
1727–8	Balthasar Denner (1685–1749)	Oil on canvas, 74.9 × 62.6	National Portrait Gallery, London	D. Saywell and J. Simon (eds.), Complete Illustrated Catalogue, National Portrait Gallery (London, 2004), 277
c.1730	William Hogarth (1697–1764)	Oil on canvas, 7.5 × 7.1	Burghley House Collection, Stamford, Lincs.	J. Barlow, The Enraged Musician: Hogarth's Musical Imagery (Aldershot, 2005), 12, 14, 339
1733	Balthasar Denner	Oil on canvas, 76 × 63.5	Deutsches Historisches Museum, Berlin	Bilder und Zeugnisse aus der deutschen Geschichte . . . , vol. 1 (Berlin, 1997), 202
?1731	attr. Georg Andreas Wolfgang junior (1703–45)	Oil on canvas, c. 61 × 73	Musikmuseet Stockholm	P. A. Scholes, 'Burney's will', The Great Dr. Burney, vol. 2 (London, 1948), 269–70; letters from the owner 1974

Date	Artist	Medium and dimensions	Location	Reference
1730–5	Philip Mercier (1689–1760)	Oil on canvas, 127 × 101.6	Trustees of the Viscount FitzHarris	R. A. Raines, 'A Catalogue of the Paintings, Drawings and Etchings of Philippe Mercier', *The Walpole Society* 46 (1976–8), 24, No. 51
?1736	Anon. (previously attr. Denner)	Oil on canvas, 66 × 61	National Trust (Lord Sackville, Knole House, Sevenoaks, Kent	J. F. Kerslake, *Early Georgian Portraits*, vol. I (London, 1977), 121; Simon, *A Celebration*, 36
1737	Georg Andreas Wolfgang junior	Black crayon and sepia on parchment, 14.5 × 12.5	Musikbibliothek Peters, Leipzig (missing)	*Jahrbuch der Musikbibliothek Peters*, 3. Jahrgang, 1896 (Leipzig, 1897), frontispiece
1737–9	Johann Georg Wolfgang (1662–1744) after G. A. Wolfgang junior	Engraving		W. C. Smith, *Concerning Handel: His Life and Works* (London, 1948); Simon, *A Celebration*, 39
1737–9	G. A. Wolfgang junior	Watercolour on ivory, 17 × 13.4	The Royal Collection, London	Simon, *A Celebration*, pp. 38–9
1737/8	Louis-François Roubiliac (1702–62)	Terracotta, h (whole): 47.2	Fitzwilliam Museum, Cambridge	*Victoria & Albert Museum Bulletin* 1/4 (1965), 1–14
1737–8	Jacobus Houbraken (1698–1780)	Copper engraving, 35.6 × 22.1	National Portrait Gallery, London	*The Craftsman*, 22 April 1738 (HHB vi, 294); Simon, *A Celebration*, 32, 38
1738	Louis-François Roubiliac	Marble statue, h: 135.3	Victoria & Albert Museum, London	D. Bilbey, *British Sculpture 1470 to 2000: A Concise Catalogue of the Collection at the Victoria & Albert Museum* (London, 2002), 114–15
1739	Louis-François Roubiliac	Terracotta, h: 71	Coram Foundation, London	J. F. Kerslake, 'Roubiliac's "Handel": A Terracotta Restored', *Burlington Magazine* 108 (1966), 475
1739	Louis-François Roubiliac	Marble bust, h: 71	The Royal Collection, London	*George III & Queen Charlotte: Patronage, Collecting and Court Taste* (London, 2004)
1740	John Theodore Heins (1697–1756)	Oil on canvas, 123 × 98	Sparkassenstiftung Halle-Saalkreis	E. Werner, 'G. F. Händel freundlich und gelassen – ein neu entdecktes Porträt', *Händel-Hausmitteilungen* 15/2 (2006) 40

(cont.)

Portraits considered to be authentic (cont.)

Date	Artist (or attributed to)	Medium, size (cm)	Present owner or location	Documentation (selection)
? c.1745	attr. Francis van der Myn (?) (1719–83)	Oil on canvas, 77 × 64.3	The Royal Society of Musicians of Great Britain	Simon, *A Celebration*, 42–3; R. Elkin, *The Old Concert Rooms of London* (1955), 89; Kerslake, *Early Georgian Portraits*, 125–6
1748/9	Thomas Hudson (1701–79)	Oil on canvas, 121 × 100.5	Staats- und Universitätsbibliothek, Hamburg	H. J. Marx (ed.), *Händel und Hamburg* (Hamburg, 1985), 166–8
1756	Thomas Hudson	Oil on canvas, 238.8 × 146.1	National Portrait Gallery, London	Saywell and Simon, *Complete Illustrated Catalogue*, 277; W. Schenkluhn, 'Zwischen Repräsentation und Selbstdarstellung – Die späten Händelporträts von Thomas Hudson', *HJb* 49 (2003)
after 1756	Louis-François Roubiliac	Marble bust, 71 × 8 × 26	The Royal Collection, London	Simon, *A Celebration*, 47
? 1759	Louis-François Roubiliac	Mask, plaster	private owner	Simon, *A Celebration*, 45–6
? 1759	Louis-François Roubiliac	Terracotta, h: 71	Grimsthorpe and Drummond Castle Trustees	Simon, *A Celebration*, 46–7
? 1759	Louis-François Roubiliac	Terracotta, model of the Monument in Westm. Abbey, h: 34	Foundling Museum, Coke Handel Collection, London	K. Esdaile, *The Life and Works of Louis François Roubiliac* (London, 1928), 223
1759–60	Louis-François Roubiliac	Terracotta, model of the Monument in Westminster Abbey, h: 98	Ashmolean Museum, Oxford	Simon, *A Celebration*, 47
1759–62	Louis-François Roubiliac	Marble Monument	Westminster Abbey	Simon, *A Celebration*, 47; S. Aspden, '"Fam'd Handel Breathing, tho' Transformed to Stone": The Composer as Monument', *JAMS* 55/1 (2002), 67ff.

Portraits of doubtful authenticity painted in Handel's lifetime (selection)

1720–30	Anon. (previously attr. Denner)	Oil on canvas, 64 × 54 (?)	? (last in the possession of Newman Flower)	K.-E. Henrici and L. Liepmannssohn, 'Musiker-Bildnisse aus der Sammlung Wilhelm Heyer in Köln, Antiquariat (12/13 Sept. 1927), No. 206
?before 1730	Anon.	Oil on canvas, 76.2 × 63;5	Coram Foundation, London	J. M. Coopersmith, 'A List of Portraits, Sculptures, etc. of Georg Friedrich Händel', ML 13/2 (1932), 159, No. 34
? c.1725	John Vander Bank (1694–1739)	Oil on canvas	City of Hanover	Coopersmith, 'List of Portraits' 160, No. 41
?1737–51	William Hoare of Bath (1707–92)	Oil on canvas, 59 × 71	Foundling Museum, Coke Handel Collection, London	The Gerald Coke Handel Collection: Exhibition, Jenkyn Place (Bentley, 1985), 37
c.1750–99	Anon.	Oil on canvas	Ulf Wagner, Radebeul, on loan to the Händel-Haus, Halle	Coopersmith, 'List of Portraits', 157, No. 3; E. Werner, Das Händel-Haus in Halle (Halle, 2007), 68

Replicas and copies (selection)

18th C	Anon. after Denner	Oil on canvas, 124.5 × 101	Museo internazionale e biblioteca della musica di Bologna	Connoisseur 215 (Feb. 1985), 94
1737–9	Anon. after Wolfgang junior	Oil on canvas, 121.5 × 98	Foundling Museum, Coke Handel Collection, London	Musica 8 (1956), 9, plate 18
1742	Francis Kyte (fl. 1710–45)	Oil on canvas, 18.4 × 14	National Portrait Gallery, on loan to the Handel House Museum, London	Saywell and Simon, Complete Illustrated Catalogue, 277
? c.1750	Anon. after Hudson	Oil on canvas	University of Oxford	Mrs Reginald Lane Poole (ed.), Catalogue of Portraits in the Possession of the University, Colleges, City, and County of Oxford, vol. 1 (Oxford, 1912–25), No. 257; Simon, A Celebration, 44
after 1756	Anon. after Hudson	Oil on canvas, 70 × 60	Royal College of Music, London	Coopersmith, 'List of Portraits', 159, No. 26
c.1756–60	Anon. after Hudson	Oil on canvas, 80.6 × 72.1	Royal Collection, on loan to the Handel House Museum, London	Handel House Museum Companion (London, 2001), 49
after 1756	Anon. after Hudson	Oil on canvas, 17.8 × 20.3	Fitzwilliam Museum, Cambridge	Goodison, Catalogue of Paintings, 122–3

Imaginary portraits (selection)

1815	Johann Gottfried Schadow (1764–1850)	Pencil on paper	Staatliche Museen zu Berlin, Alte Nationalgalerie	H. Mackowsky, 'Gottfried Schadows Familienalbum', *Die graphischen Künste* (Vienna, 1919), 30, fol. 11, no. 30
1819/20	Johann Gottfried Schadow	Plaster with coat of paint	Schauspielhaus Berlin (destroyed)	H. Mackowsky, *Die Bildwerke Gottfried Schadows* (Berlin, 1951), 237, no. 253
1870/1	Carl Jaeger (1833–87)	Oil on canvas (Grisaille), 46 × 54	Händel-Haus, Halle	G. Richter, 'Das Händelporträt von Carl Jaeger', *Händel-Hausmitteilungen* 2 (1994), 25–8

Monuments after 1762

1815/16	Rudolf Schadow (1786–1822)	Marble bust	Walhalla, Donaustauf	
1859	Hermann Rudolf Heidel (1810–65)	Monument, bronze, h: 320	Stadt Halle	W. Piechocki, 'Zur Geschichte des Händel-Denkmals in Halle', HJb 31 (1985); U. Krenzlin, *Halle an der Saale: Händel-Denkmal* (Regensburg, 2003)
1864–75	George Gilbert Scott (1811–78); Henry Hugh Armstead (1828–1905)	Relief figure, sandstone	The Royal Collection	L. Handley-Read, *British Sculpture 1850–1914: A Loan Exhibition of Sculpture and Medals Sponsored by The Victorian Society* (London, 1968), 7
1887/8	Jean-Jules Salmson (1823–1902)	Marble	Théâtre de l'Opéra, Paris	Coopersmith, 'List of Portraits', 166

Appendix 5: Genealogical table of the ruling houses of Britain and Hanover

RUTH SMITH

Names in bold are British monarchs; dates in bold show reigns

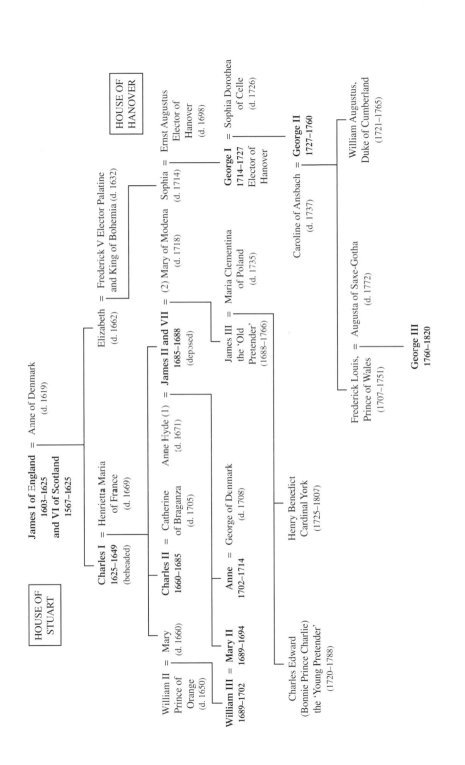

HOUSE OF STUART

James I of England 1603–1625 and VI of Scotland 1567–1625 = Anne of Denmark (d. 1619)

HOUSE OF HANOVER

Elizabeth (d. 1662) = Frederick V Elector Palatine and King of Bohemia (d. 1632)

Sophia (d. 1714) = Ernst Augustus Elector of Hanover (d. 1698)

George I 1714–1727 Elector of Hanover = Sophia Dorothea of Celle (d. 1726)

Charles I 1625–1649 (beheaded) = Henrietta Maria of France (d. 1669)

Charles II 1660–1685 = Catherine of Braganza (d. 1705)

Anne Hyde (1) (d. 1671) = James II and VII 1685–1688 (deposed) = (2) Mary of Modena (d. 1718)

James III the 'Old Pretender' (1688–1766) = Maria Clementina of Poland (d. 1735)

Caroline of Ansbach (d. 1737) = George II 1727–1760

William Augustus, Duke of Cumberland (1721–1765)

Anne 1702–1714 = George of Denmark (d. 1708)

Henry Benedict Cardinal York (1725–1807)

Frederick Louis, Prince of Wales (1707–1751) = Augusta of Saxe-Gotha (d. 1772)

George III 1760–1820

William II Prince of Orange (d. 1650) = Mary (d. 1660)

William III 1689–1702 = Mary II 1689–1694

Charles Edward (Bonnie Prince Charlie) the 'Young Pretender' (1720–1788) the Philharmonia Baroque Orchestra, was made available for download from Magnatune.com in 2006)

Berenice, HWV 38. J. Baird (Berenice), J. Lane (Demetrio), D'A. Fortunato (Selene), A. Matthews (Alessandro), D. Minter (Arsace), J. McMaster (Fabio), J. Opalach (Aristoboldo), Brewer Chamber Orchestra, R. Palmer (cond); recorded 1994; Newport Classic, NPD 85620/3 (3 CDs), 1995

Deidamia, HWV 42. S. Kermes (Deidamia), A. Bonitatibus (Ulisse), A. M. Panzarella (Achille), D. Labelle (Nerea), A. Abete (Lycomede), F. Zanasi (Fenice), Il Complesso Barocco, A. Curtis (cond); recorded 2002; Virgin Veritas, 5 45550 2 (3 CDs), 2003

Ezio, HWV 29. A. Hallenberg (Ezio), K. Gauvin (Fulvia), S. Prina (Valentiniano), M. Andersen (Onoria), V. Priante (Varo), A. Z. Giustiniani (Massimo), Il Complesso Barocco, A. Curtis (cond); recorded 2008; Deutsche Grammophon Archiv, 477 8073 (3 CDs), 2009

Faramondo, HWV 39. M.-E. Cencic (Faramondo), S. Kärthauser (Clotilde), M. de Liso (Rosimonda), P. Jaroussky (Adolfo), I.-S. Sim (Gustavo), X. Sabata (Gernando), T. Whey (Childerico), F. Bettin (Teobaldo), Coro della Radio Svizzera, I Barocchisti, O. Fasolis (cond); recorded 2008; Virgin, 5099921661129 (3 CDs), 2009

Flavio, HWV 16. J. Gall (Flavio), D. L. Ragin (Guido), L. Lootens (Emilia), B. Fink (Teodata), C. Högman (Vitige), G. Fagotto (Ugone), U. Messthaler (Lotario), Ensemble 415, R. Jacobs (cond); recorded 1989; Harmonia Mundi (France), HMC 901312.13 (2 CDs), 1990 (incorporates short extracts from other works)

Floridante, Il, HWV 14. M. Mijanović (Floridante), R. Invernizzi (Timante), V. Priante (Oronte), R. Novaro (Coralbo), J. DiDonato (Elmira), Sharon Rostorf-Zamir (Rossane), Il Complesso Barocco, A. Curtis (cond); recorded 2005; Deutsche Grammophon Archiv, 477 6566 (3 CDs), 2007

Giulio Cesare, HWV 17. J. Larmore (Cesare), B. Schlick (Cleopatra), M. Rørholm (Sesto), B. Fink (Cornelia), D. L. Ragin (Tolomeo), F. Zanasi (Achilla), D. Visse (Nireno), O. Lallouette (Curio), Concerto Köln, R. Jacobs (cond); recorded 1991; Harmonia Mundi (France), HMC 901385.87 (4 CDs), 1991

Giustino, HWV 37. M. Chance (Giustino), D. Röschmann (Arianna), D. Kotoski (Anastasio), J. Lane (Leocasta), M. Padmore (Vitaliano), D. Minter (Amanzio), J. Gondek (Fortuna), D. Ely (Polidarte, Voce di dentro), Freiburger Barockorchester, N. McGegan (cond); recorded 1994; Harmonia Mundi (USA), HMU 907130.32 (3 CDs), 1995

Imeneo, HWV 41. K. Stiefermann (Imeneo), J. Stojkovic (Rosmene), A. Hallenberg (Tirinto), S. K. Thornhill (Clomiri), L. Chung (Argenio), Vokalensemble Köln, Capella Augustina, A. Spering; recorded 2002; CPO, 999 915–2 (2 CDs), 2003

Lotario, HWV 26. S. Mingardo (Lotario), S. Kermes (Adelaide), S. Davislim (Berengario), H. Summers (Matilde), S. Prina (Idelberto), V. Priante (Clodomiro), Il Complesso Barocco, A. Curtis (cond); recorded 2004; Deutsche Harmonia Mundi, 82876 58797 2 (2 CDs), 2004

Muzio Scevola, HWV 13. D'A. Fortunato (Muzio), J. Baird (Clelia), E. Mills (Orazio), A. Matthews (Fidalma), J. Lane (Irene), F. Urrey (Tarquinio), Brewer Baroque Chamber Orchestra, R. Palmer (cond); recorded 1991; Newport Classics, NPD 85540 (2 CDs, including excerpts from Bononcini's Act 2), 1992

Orlando, HWV 31. P. Bardon (Orlando), R. Mannion (Dorinda), H. Summers (Medoro), R. Joshua (Angelica), H. van der Kamp (Zoroastro), Les Arts Florissants, W. Christie (cond); recorded 1996; Erato, 0630–14636-2 (3 CDs), 1996

Ottone, HWV 15. D. Minter (Ottone), L. Saffer (Teofane), R. Popken (Adelberto), J. Gondek (Gismonda), M. Dean (Emireno), P. Spence (Matilda), Freiburger Barockorchester, N. McGegan (cond); recorded 1992; Harmonia Mundi (USA), HMU 907073.75 (3 CDs), 1993

Partenope, HWV 27. R. Joshua (Partenope), L. Zazzo (Arsace), H. Summers (Rosmira), S. Wallace (Armindo), K. Streit (Emilio), A. Foster-Williams (Ormonte), Early Opera Company, C. Curnyn (cond); recorded 2004; Chandos Chaconne, CHAN719-3 (3 CDs), 2005

pastor fido, Il, HWV 8^b (composite of May and November 1734 versions). P. Esswood (Mirtillo), K. Farkas (Amarilli), M. Lukin (Dorinda), G. Kállay (Silvio), M. Flohr (Eurilla), J. Gregor (Tirenio), Savaria Vocal Ensemble, Capella Savaria, N. McGegan (cond); recorded 1988; Hungaroton, HCD 12912–13 (2 CDs), 1995 (see **Terpsicore**)

Poro, HWV 28. G. Banditelli (Poro), R. Bertini (Cleofide), B. Fink (Erissena), G. Lesne (Gandarte), S. Naglia (Alessandro), R. Abbondanza (Timagene), Europa Galante, F. Biondi (cond); recorded 1994; Opus 111 (Naïve), OPS 30–113/115 (3 CDs), 1994 (an alternative performance by the Akademie für alte Musik Berlin, conducted by K. Junghänel, was made available on CD to members of the Göttingen Handel Society in 2006)

Radamisto, April 1720 version, HWV 12^a. J. DiDonato (Radamisto), M. Beaumont (Zenobia), P. Cioñ (Polissena), L. Cherici (Tigrane), D. Labelle (Fraarte), Z. Stains (Tiridate), C. Lepore (Farasmane), Il Complesso Barocco, A. Curtis (cond); recorded 2003; Virgin, 5 45673 2 (3 CDs), 2005

December 1720 version, HWV 12^b. R. Popken (Radamisto), J. Gondek (Zenobia), L. Saffer (Polissena), D. Hanchard (Tigrane), M. Frimmer (Fraarte), M. Dean (Tiridate), N. Cavallier (Farasmane), Freiburger Barockorchester, N. McGegan (cond); recorded 1993; Harmonia Mundi (USA), HMU 907111.13 (3 CDs), 1994

Riccardo primo, HWV 23. L. Zazzo (Riccardo), N. Rial (Costanza), G. McGreevy (Pulcheria), D. Wilson-Johnson (Isacio), T. Mead (Oronte), C. Streetman (Berardo), Kammerorchester Basel, P. Goodwin (cond); recorded 2007; Deutsche Harmonia Mundi, 88697174212 (3 CDs), 2008

Rinaldo, HWV 7^a. D. Daniels (Rinaldo), C. Bartoli (Almirena), L. Orgonasova (Armida), G. Finley (Argante), B. Fink (Goffredo), D. Taylor (Eustazio), B. Mehta (Mago cristiano), C. Bott (Sirena), A.-M. Rincon (Sirena, Donna), M. Padmore (Araldo), the Academy of Ancient Music, C. Hogwood (cond); recorded 1999; Decca L'Oiseau-Lyre, 467 087–2 (3 CDs), 2000 (an alternative performance by Concerto

Köln, conducted by N. McGegan, was made available on CD to members of the Göttingen Handel Society in 2004)

Rodelinda, HWV 19. S. Kermes (Rodelinda), M. Mijanović (Bertarido), S. Davislim (Grimoaldo), S. Prina (Eduige), M. N. Lemieux (Unulfo), V. Priante (Garibaldo), Il Complesso Barocco, A. Curtis (cond); recorded 2004; Deutsche Grammophon Archiv, 477 5391 (3 CDs), 2005 (an alternative performance by Concerto Köln, conducted by N. McGegan, was made available on CD to members of the Göttingen Handel Society in 2000)

Rodrigo, HWV 5. M. R. Wesseling (Rodrigo), M. Bayo (Esilena), S. Rostorf-Zamir (Florinda), K. van Rensburg (Giuliano), A.-C. Gillet (Evanco), M. E. Cencic (Fernando), Al Ayre Español, E. Lopéz Banzo (cond); recorded 2007; Ambroisie, AM 132 (3 CDs), 2008

Serse, HWV 40. A. S. von Otter (Serse), E. Norberg-Schulz (Romilda), L. Zazzo (Arsamene), S. Piau (Atalanta), S. Tro Santafé (Amastre), G. Furlanetto (Ariodate), A. Abete (Elviro), Les Arts Florissants, W. Christie (cond); recorded 2003; Virgin 5 45711 2 (3 CDs), 2004

Scipione, HWV 20. D. L. Ragin (Scipione), S. Piau (Berenice), D. Lamprecht (Lucejo), O. Lallouette (Ernando), V. Tabery (Armira), G. Flechter (Lelio), Les Talens Lyriques, C. Rousset (cond); recorded 1993; Fnac, 592245 (3 CDs), 1994

Silla, HWV 10. J. Bowman (Silla), J. Lunn (Lepido), S. Baker (Claudio), R. Nicholls (Metella), N. Marsh (Flavia), E. Cragg (Celia), C. Dixon (il Dio), the London Handel Orchestra, D. Darlow (cond); recorded 2000; Somm, SOMMCD 227–8 (2 CDs), 2000

Siroe, HWV 24. A. Hallenberg (Siroe), J. Stojkovic (Emira), S. Im (Laodice), G. Schmid (Medarse), S. Noack (Cosroe), T. de Jong (Arasse), Cappella Coloniensis, A. Spering (cond); recorded 2003; Harmonia Mundi (France), HMC 901826.27 (2 CDs), 2004

Sosarme, HWV 30. D'A. Fortunato (Sosarme), J. Baird (Elmira), D. Minter (Melo), J. Lane (Erenice), J. Aler (Haliate), N. Watson (Altomaro), R. Pellerin (Argone), AmorArtis Orchestra, J. Somary (cond); recorded 1993; Newport Classic, NPD 85575 (2 CDs), 1994 (an attempt to reconstruct Handel's aborted first draft of this opera led to a CD recording of *Fernando* by Il Complesso Barocco, conducted by A. Curtis, issued by Virgin in 2007)

Tamerlano, HWV 18. N. Spanos (Tamerlano), M.-E. Nesi (Adronico), T. Christoyannis (Bajazet), M. Katsuli (Asteria), I Karaianni (Irene), P. Magoulas (Leone), Orchestra of Patras, G. Petrou (cond); recorded 2006; MDG, 609 1457–2 (3 CDs), 2007

Terpsicore, HWV 8^b (prologue to November 1734 version of **Il pastor fido**). D. L. Ragin (Apollo), K. Farkas (Erato), Capella Savaria, N. McGegan (cond); Hungaroton, HCD 31193 (1 CD), 1993 (+ orchestral movements and dances from HWV 33–4)

Teseo, HWV 9. E. James (Teseo), D. Jones (Medea), J. Gooding (Agilea), D. L. Ragin (Egeo), C. Napoli (Clizia), J. Gall (Arcane), Les Musiciens du Louvre, M. Minkowski (cond); recorded 1992; Erato, 2292–45806-2 (2 CDs), 1992

Tolomeo, HWV 25. A. Hallenberg (Tolomeo), K. Gauvin (Seleuce), A. Bonitatibus (Elisa), R. Basso (Alessandro), P. Spagnoli (Araspe), Il Complesso Barocco, A. Curtis (cond); recorded 2006; Deutsche Grammophon Archiv, 477 7106 (3 CDs), 2008

ORATORIOS

Alexander Balus, HWV 65. C. Denley (Alexander Balus), L. Dawson (Cleopatra), M. George (Ptolomee), C. Daniels (Jonathan), C. McFadden (Aspasia), Choir of New College Oxford, Choir of the King's Consort, the King's Consort, R. King (cond); recorded 1997; Hyperion, CDA 67241/2 (2 CDs), 1997

Athalia, HWV 52. S. Kermes (Athalia), O. Pasychnyk (Josabeth), M. Oro (Joas), T. W. Lund (Joad), T. Cooley (Mathan), W. M. Friedrich (Abner), Kölner Kammerchor, Collegium Cartusianum, P. Neumann (cond); recorded 2003; MDG, 332 1276–2 (2 CDs), 2004

Belshazzar, HWV 61. A. Rolfe-Johnson (Belshazzar), A. Augér (Nitocris), C. Robbin (Cyrus), J. Bowman (Daniel), D. Wilson-Johnson (Gobrias), the English Concert, T. Pinnock (cond); recorded 1990; Deutsche Grammophon Archiv, 477 037–2 (reissue, 3 CDs), 2004

Brockes Passion, HWV 48. M. Klietmann (Evangelist), I. Gáti (Jesus), M. Zádori (Tochter Zion), K. Farkas (s), D. Minter (ct), G. de Mey (t), J. Bándi (t), G. Burzynski (b), Stadtsingechor Halle, Capella Savaria, N. McGegan (cond); recorded 1985; Hungaroton, HCD 12734–36 (3 CDs), 1994

Deborah, HWV 51. Y. Kenny (Deborah), S. Gritton (Jael, Israelite woman), C. Denley (Sisera), J. Bowman (Barak), M. George (Abinoam), Choir of New College Oxford, Choristers of Salisbury Cathedral, the King's Consort, R. King (cond); recorded 1993; Hyperion, CDA 66841/2 (2 CDs), 1993

Esther, 'Cannons' version, HWV 50ª. L. Russell (Esther), T. Randle (Ahasuerus), M. Padmore (Mordecai), M. George (Haman), N. Argenta (Israelite Woman), M. Chance (Priest), the Sixteen, the Symphony of Harmony and Invention, H. Christophers (cond); recorded 1995; Coro, 16019 (reissue, 2 CDs), 2004
    1732 version, HWV 50ᵇ. R. Joshua (Esther), J. Bowman (Ahasuerus), S. Bickley (Mordecai), C. Purves (Hamam), R. Outram (Israelite Woman), London Handel Festival Chorus and Orchestra, L. Cummings (cond); recorded 2002; Somm, SOMMCD 238–9 (2 CDs), 2007

Israel in Egypt, HWV 54. N. Argenta (s), E. van Evera (s), T. Wilson (ct), A. Rolfe-Jonhson (t), D. Thomas (b), J. White (b), Taverner Choir and Players, A. Parrott (cond); recorded 1989; Virgin Veritas, 5 62155 2 (reissue, 2 CDs), 2003

Jephtha, HWV 70. N. Robson (Jephtha), L. Dawson (Iphis), A. S. von Otter (Storgè), M. Chance (Hamor), S. Varcoe (Zebul), R. Holton (Angel), Monteverdi Choir, English Baroque Soloists, J. E. Gardiner (cond); recorded 1988; Philips 478 039–8 (reissue, 3 CDs), 2008 (an alternative performance by the English Concert and Winchester Cathedral Choir, conducted by N. McGegan, was made available on CD to members of the Göttingen Handel Society in 2003)

Joseph and his Brethren, HWV 59. J. Bowman (Joseph), Y. Kenny (Asenath), J. M. Ainsley (Simeon, Judah), C. Denley (Potiphera, Phanor), M. George (Pharaoh, Reuben), C. Burrowes (Benjamin), Choir of New College Oxford, King's Consort, R. King (cond); recorded 1996; Hyperion, CDA 67171/3 (3 CDs), 1996

Joshua, HWV 64. A. Clayton (Joshua), C. Manley (Achsah), A. Gibson (Othniel), G. Humphreys (Caleb), Richard Rowntree (Angel), London Handel Singers, London Handel Orchestra, L. Cummings (cond); recorded 2008; Somm, 240–2 (2 CDs), 2009

Judas Maccabaeus, HWV 63. J. McDougall (Judas Maccabaeus), E. Kirkby (Israelite woman), C. Denley (Israelite man), M. George (Simon), J. Bowman (Messenger, Priest), S. Birchall (Eupolemus), Choir of New College Oxford, King's Consort, R. King (cond); recorded 1992; Hyperion, CDA 66641/2 (2 CDs), 1992

Messiah, HWV 54, 1742 Dublin version. S. Hamilton (s), H. Cairncross (s), A. Gill (a), C. Wilkinson (a), N. Mulroy (t), M. Brook (b), E. Caswell (b), Dunedin Consort and Players, J. Butt (cond); recorded 2006; Linn, CKD 285 (2 CDs), 2007

 1754 Foundling Hospital version. J. Nelson (s), E. Kirkby (s), C. Watkinson (a), P. Elliott (t), D. Thomas (b), Choir of Christ Church Cathedral Oxford, Academy of Ancient Music, C. Hogwood (cond); recorded 1980; Decca L'Oiseau-Lyre 430 488–2 (reissue, 2 CDs), 1991

 Composite version. A. Augér (s), A. S. von Otter (ms), M. Chance (ct), H. Crook (t), J. Tomlinson (b), English Concert, T. Pinnock (cond); recorded 1988; Deutsche Grammophon Archiv, 477 590–4 (reissue, 2 CDs), 2006

Occasional Oratorio, HWV 62. S. Gritton (s), L. Milne (s), J. Bowman (ct), J. M. Ainsley (t), M. George (b), Choir of New College Oxford, Choristers and Choir of the King's Consort, King's Consort, R. King (cond); recorded 1994; Hyperion, CDA 66961/2 (2 CDs), 1995

Resurrezione, La, HWV 47. J. Smith (Maddalena), A. Massis (Angelo), L. Maguire (Cleofe), J. M. Ainsley (Giovanni), L. Naouri (Lucifero), Les Musiciens du Louvre, M. Minkowski (cond); recorded 1995; Deutsche Grammophon Archiv, 447 767–2 (2 CDs), 1996

Samson, 1743 version, HWV 57. T. Randle (Samson), L. Russell (Dalila), L. Dawson (Israelite Woman, Philistine Woman, Virgin), C. Wyn-Rogers (Micah), M. George (Manoa), J. Best (Harapha), M. Padmore (Philistine Man, Israelite Man), The Sixteen, Symphony of Harmony and Invention, H. Christophers (cond); recorded 1996; Coro, COR 16008 (reissue, 3 CDs), 2002

 1753 version. T. Cooley (Samson), S. Daneman (Philistine Woman, Israelite Woman, Dalila), F. Gottwald (Micah), W. Berger (Manoa), W. M. Friedrich (Harapha), M. Slattery (Philistine Man, Israelite Man), NDR Chor, FestspielOrchester Göttingen, N. McGegan (cond); recorded 2008; Carus, 83.425 (3 CDs), 2009

Saul, HWV 53. A. Miles (Saul), D. Brown (Merab), L. Dawson (Michal), J. M. Ainsley (Jonathan), D. L. Ragin (David), R. Savage (Samuel), N. Mackie (High Priest), P. Salmon (Witch of Endor), P. Slane (Abner, Amalekite), S. Oberst (Doeg),

R. Hotlon (s), Monteverdi Choir, English Baroque Soloists, J. E. Gardiner (cond); recorded 1989; Philips, 478 8256 4 (reissue, 3 CDs), 2007

Solomon, HWV 67. A. Scholl (Solomon), I. Dam-Jensen (Queen), S. Gritton (Queen of Sheba), A. Hagley (1st Harlot), S. Bickley (2nd Harlot), P. Agnew (Zadok), P. Harvey (a Levite), Gabrieli Consort and Players, P. McCreesh (cond); recorded 1998; Deutsche Grammophon Archiv, 459 688–2 (3 CDs), 1999

Susanna, HWV 66. L. Hunt (Susanna), D. Minter (Joacim), J. Feldman (Daniel, an attendant), J. Thomas (first Elder), D. Thomas (second Elder), W. Parker (Chelsias, Judge), U. C. Berkeley Chamber Choir, Philamonia Baroque Orchestra, N. McGegan (cond); recorded 1989; Harmonia Mundi (USA), HMU 907030.32 (3 CDs), 1990

Theodora, HWV 68. S. Daneman (Theodora), D. Taylor (Didymus), J. Galstian (Irene), R. Croft (Septimius), N. Berg (Valens), L. Slaars (Messenger), Les Arts Florissants, W. Christie (cond); recorded 2000; Erato, 0927 43181–2 (3 CDs), 2003

trionfo del Tempo e del Disinganno, Il, HWV 46^a. D. York (Bellezza), G. Bertagnolli (Piacere), S. Mingardo (Disinganno), N. Sears (Tempo), Concerto Italiano, R. Alessandrini (cond); recorded 2000; Opus 111 (Naïve), OP 30440 (reissue, 2 CDs), 2007

trionfo del Tempo e della Verità, Il, HWV 46^b. C. McFadden (Bellezza), E. Scholl (Piacere), P. Abilgaard (Disinganno), N. Hariades (Tempo), Junge Kantorei, Barockorchester Frankfurt, J. C. Martini (cond); recorded 1998; Naxos, 8.554440–42 (3 CDs), 2000 (performing edition presents a composite version including movements from HWV 46^a, the 1739 revival of HWV 46^b and HWV 49^b)

Triumph of Time and Truth, The, HWV 71. I. Partridge (Pleasure), S. Varcoe (Time), London Handel Choir and Orchestra, D. Darlow (cond); recorded 1982; Hyperion, CDD 22050 (reissue, 2 CDs), 2005

SERENATAS, MASQUES, ODES, ENGLISH DRAMAS

Aci, Galatea e Polifemo, HWV 72. S. Piau (Aci), S. Mingardo (Galatea), L. Naouri (Polifemo), Le Concert d'Astrée, E. Haïm (cond); recorded 2002; Virgin Veritas, 5 45557 2 (2 CDs), 2003

Acis and Galatea, 1718 Cannons version, HWV 49^a. S. Hamilton (Galatea), N. Mulroy (Acis), M. Brook (Polyphemus), T. Hobbs (Damon), N. Hurndall-Smith (Coridon), Dunedin Consort and Players, J. Butt (cond); recorded 2008; Linn, CKD 319 (2 CDs), 2008

  composite version. S. Daneman (Galatea), P. Agnew (Acis), A. Ewing (Polyphemus), P. Petibon (Damon), J. Cornwell (Coridon), Les Arts Florissants, W. Christie (cond); recorded 1998; Erato, 3984–25505-2 (2 CDs), 1999

Alceste, HWV 45. E. Kirkby (s), J. Nelson (s), Margaret Cable (ms), P. Elliot (t), D. Thomas (b), Academy of Ancient Music, C. Hogwood (cond); recorded 1979; Decca L'Oiseau-Lyre, 443 183–2 (reissue, 1 CD), 1994

Alexander's Feast, HWV 75. 1736 version (including Organ Concerto, Op. 4 No. 1 and Harp Concerto, Op. 4 No. 6). N. Argenta (s), I. Partridge (t), M. George (b),

The Sixteen, Symphony of Harmony and Invention, H. Christophers (cond); recorded 1990; Coro, COR16028 (2 CDs), 2005

    1739 version (including *Ode for St Cecilla's Day*, HWV 76). S. Kermes (s), V. Hartinger (t), K. Wolff (b), Kölner Kammerchor, Collegium Cartusianum, P. Neumann (cond); recorded 2008; Carus, 83.424 (2 CDs), 2009

    1751 version. D. Brown (s), C. Watkinson (a), A. Stafford (ct), N. Robson (t), S. Varcoe (b), Monteverdi Choir, English Baroque Soloists, J. E. Gardiner (cond); recorded 1987; Philips (reissue, 2 CDs), 2006

Allegro, il Penseroso, ed il Moderato, L', HWV 55. S. Gritton (s), L. Anderson (s), C. McFadden (s), P. Agnew (t), N. Davies (b), Choir of the King's Consort, King's Consort, R. King (cond); recorded 1999; Hyperion, CDA 67283/4 (2 CDs), 1999

Choice of Hercules, The, HWV 69. R. Blaze (Hercules), S. Gritton (Pleasure), A. Coote (Virtue), C. Daniels (attendant of Pleasure), King's Consort, R. King (cond); recorded 2001; Hyperion, CDA 67298 (1 CD), 2002

Comus, HWV 44. P. Kwella (s), Margaret Cable (ms), D. Thomas (b), Academy of Ancient Music, C. Hogwood (cond); recorded 1980; Decca L'Oiseau-Lyre, 443 183–2 (reissue, 1 CD), 1994

Eternal source of light divine, HWV 74. S. Gritton (s), R. Blaze (ct), M. George (b), Choir of King's College Cambridge, Academy of Ancient Music, S. Cleobury (cond); recorded 2001; EMI, 5 57140 2 (1 CD), 2001 (+ *Coronation Anthems*)

Hercules, HWV 60. G. Saks (Hercules), A. S. von Otter (Dejanira), R. Croft (Hyllus), L. Dawson (Iole), D. Daniels (Lichas), M. Pujol (Priest of Jupiter), Les Musiciens du Louvre, M. Minkowski (cond); recorded 2000; Deutsche Grammophon Archiv, 469 532–2 (3 CDs), 2002

Parnasso in festa, HWV 73. D. Moore (Apollo, Euterpe), C. Sampson (Clio), L. Crowe (Orfeo), R. Outram (Calliope), R. Massey (Clori), P. Harvey (Marte), Choir of the King's Consort, King's Consort, M. Halls (cond); recorded 2008; Hyperion, CDA67701/2 (2 CDs), 2008

Semele, HWV 58. R. Joshua (Semele), R. Croft (Jupiter, Apollo), H. Summers (Juno, Ino), S. Wallace (Athamus), G. Pearson (Iris), B. Sherratt (Somnus, Cadmus), Early Opera Company, C. Curnyn (cond); recorded 2007, Chandos Chaconne, CHAN 0745(3) (3 CDs), 2007

Song for St Cecilia's Day ('An Ode for St Cecilia's Day'), HWV 76. C. Sampson (s), J. Gilchrist (t), Choir of the King's Consort, King's Consort, R. King (cond); recorded 2003; Hyperion, CDA67463 (1 CD), 2004 (+ HWV 89)

CANTATAS

Agrippina condotta a morire ('Dunque sarà pur vero'), HWV 110. V. Gens (s), Les Basses Réunies; recorded 1996–7; Virgin Veritas, 5 45283 2 (1 CD), 1999 (+ HWV 105, 145)

Ah! crudel, nel pianto mio, HWV 78. R. Milanesi (s), La Risonanza, F. Bonizzoni (cond); recorded 2007; Glossa, GCD 921523 (1 CD), 2007 (+ HWV 140, 150, 165)

Alla caccia ('Diana cacciatrice'), HWV 79. R. Invernizzi (s), La Risonanza, F. Bonizzoni (cond); recorded 2005; Glossa, GCD 921522 (1 CD), 2007 (+ HWV 105, 142, 171, 173)

Alpestre monte, HWV 81. E. Kirkby (s), Academy of Ancient Music, C. Hogwood (cond); recorded 1985; Decca L'Oiseau-Lyre, 414 473–2 (1 CD), 1985 (+ HWV 132^a, 170, 171)

Aminta e Fillide ('Arresta il passo'), HWV 83. M. G. Schiavo (s), N. Rial (s), La Risonanza, F. Bonizzoni (cond); recorded 2007; Glossa, GCD 921524 (1 CD), 2008 (+ HWV 92)

Apollo e Dafne ('La terra è liberata'), HWV 122. K. Gauvin (s), R. Braun (b), Les Violons du Roy, B. Labadie (cond); recorded 2000; Dorian, xCD-90288 (1 CD), 2000 (+ HWV 242)

Armida abbandonata ('Dietro l'orme fugaci'), HWV 105. E. Galli (s), La Risonanza, F. Bonizzoni (cond); recorded 2005; Glossa, GCD 921522 (1 CD), 2007 (+ HWV 79, 142, 171, 173)

Cecilia, volgi un sguardo, HWV 89. C. Sampson (s), J. Gilchrist (t), King's Consort, R. King (cond); recorded 2003; Hyperion, SACDA67463 (1 CD), 2004 (+ HWV 76)

Clori, mia bella Clori, HWV 92. M. G. Schiavo (s), La Risonanza, F. Bonizzoni (cond); recorded 2007; Glossa, GCD 921524 (1 CD), 2008 (+ HWV 83)

Clori, Tirsi e Fileno ('Cor fedele, in vano speri'), HWV 96. R. Invernizzi(s), Y. A. Fernández (s), R. Bassa (a), La Risonanza, F. Bonnizoni (cond); recorded 2008; Glossa, GCD 921 525 (1 CD), 2008

Crudel tiranno Amor, HWV 97. N. Argenta (s), Collegium Musicum 90, S. Standage (cond); recorded 1994; Chandos Chaconne, CHAN 0583 (1 CD), 1995 (+ HWV 122)

Cuopre tal volta il cielo, HWV 98. J.-L. Bindi (b), Artificii Musicali, G. Delvaux (cond); recorded 1995; Stradivarius, STR 33425 (1 CD), 1996 (+ HWV 102, 136^a, 165)

delirio amoroso, Il ('Da quel giorno fatale'), HWV 99. R. Invernizzi (s), La Risonanza, F. Bonizzoni (cond); recorded 2005; Glossa, GCD 921521 (1 CD), 2006 (+ HWV 113, 134, 170)

duello amoroso, Il ('Amarilli vezzosa'), HWV 82. A. Scholl (ct), H. Guilmette (s), Accademia Bizantina, O. Dantone (cond); recorded 2005; Harmonia Mundi (France), HMC 901957 (1 CD), 2007 (+ HWV 132^c, 135^b, 175)

Ero e Leandro ('Qual ti riveggio'), HWV 150. R. Milanesi (s), La Risonanza, F. Bonizzoni (cond); recorded 2007; Glossa, GCD 921523 (1 CD), 2007 (+ HWV 78, 140, 165)

Figlio d'alte speranze, HWV 113. R. Invernizzi (s), La Risonanza, F. Bonizzoni (cond); recorded 2005; Glossa, GCD 921521 (1 CD), 2006 (+ HWV 99, 134, 170)

Languia di bocca lusinghiera, HWV 123. D. York (s), Bruges Collegium Instrumentale, P. Peire (cond); recorded 1999; Eufoda, 1297 (1 CD), 1999 (+ HWV 78, 79, 99)

Look down, harmonious Saint ('The Praise of Harmony'), HWV 124. J. M. Ainsley (t), King's Consort, R. King (cond); recorded 1989; Hyperion, 66361/2 (2 CDs), 1990 (+ HWV 49[a])

Lucrezia ('Oh Numi eterni'), HWV 145. V. Gens (s), Les Basses Réunies; recorded 1996–7; Virgin Veritas, 5 45283 2 (1 CD), 1999 (+ HWV 105, 110, 145)

Mi palpita il cor, soprano version, HWV 132[a]. E. Kirkby (s), Academy of Ancient Music, C. Hogwood (cond); recorded 1985; Decca L'Oiseau-Lyre, 414 473–2 (1 CD), 1985 (+ HWV 81, 170, 171)
     alto version, 132[c]. A. Scholl (ct), Accademia Bizantina, O. Dantone (cond); recorded 2005; Harmonia Mundi (France), HMC 901957 (1 CD), 2007 (+ HWV 82, 135[b], 175)

Nel dolce dell'oblio ('Pensieri notturni di Filli'), HWV 134. R. Invernizzi (s), La Risonanza, F. Bonizzoni (cond); recorded 2005; Glossa, GCD 921521 (1 CD), 2006 (+ HWV 99, 113, 170)

No se emenderá jamás, HWV 140. R. Milanesi (s), La Risonanza, F. Bonizzoni (cond); recorded 2007; Glossa, GCD 921523 (1 CD), 2007 (+ HWV 78, 150, 165)

Notte placida e cheta, HWV 142. E. Galli (s), La Risonanza, F. Bonizzoni (cond); recorded 2005; Glossa, GCD 921522 (1 CD), 2007 (+ HWV 79, 105, 171, 173)

Oh, come chiare e belle ('Olinto pastore, Tebro fiume, Gloria'), HWV 143. P. Kwella (s), G. Fisher (s), London Handel Orchestra, D. Darlow (cond); recorded 1984; Hyperion, CDH55136 (reissue 1 CD), 2003

Spande ancor a mio dispetto, HWV 165. S. Vitale (b), La Risonanza, F. Bonizzoni (cond); recorded 2007; Glossa, GCD 921523 (1 CD), 2007 (+ HWV 78, 140, 150)

Splenda l'alba in oriente, HWV 166. G. Lesne (ct/cond), Il Seminario Musicale; recorded 1990; Virgin Veritas, 5 61803 2 (reissue, 2 CDs), 2000 (+ HWV 87, 132[c], 145 and cantatas by Alessandro Scarlatti)

Tra le fiamme, HWV 170. R. Invernizzi (s), La Risonanza, F. Bonizzoni (cond); recorded 2005; Glossa, GCD 921521 (1 CD), 2006 (+ HWV 99, 113, 134)

Tu fedel? Tu costante?, HWV 171. E. Galli (s), La Risonanza, F. Bonizzoni (cond); recorded 2005; Glossa, GCD 921522 (1 CD), 2007 (+ HWV 79, 105, 142, 173)

Un'alma innamorata, HWV 173. E. Galli (s), La Risonanza, F. Bonizzoni (cond); recorded 2005; Glossa, GCD 921522 (1 CD), 2007 (+ HWV 79, 105, 142, 171)

Vedendo Amor, HWV 175. A. Scholl (ct), H. Guilmette (s), Accademia Bizantina, O. Dantone (cond); recorded 2005; Harmonia Mundi (France), HMC 901957 (1 CD), 2007 (+ HWV 132[c], 135b, 175)

OTHER VOCAL CHAMBER MUSIC

Arcadian Duets, L. Claycomb (s), N. Dessay (s), V. Gens (s), J. Lascarro (s), A. M. Panzarella (s), P. Petibon (s), M. Mijanović (a), S. Mingardo (a), B. Asawa (ct), P. Agnew (t), Le Concert d'Astrée, E. Haïm (cond); recorded 2001; Virgin Veritas, 5 45524 2 (1 CD), 2002 (includes HWV 178, 185, 186, 188, 190, 192, 194, 197, 198)

Italian Duets, G. Fisher (s), J. Bowman (ct), King's Consort; recorded 1990; Hyperion, CDA66440 (1 CD), 1990 (includes HWV 178, 181, 185, 186, 188, 190, 193, 194, 197, 198)

Nine German Arias, HWV 202–10. C. Sampson (s), S.-M. Degand (vn), King's Consort; recorded 2006; Hyperion, CDA67627 (1 CD), 2007 (+ HWV 357, 363^a, 366)

Occasional Songs, The, E. Kirkby (s), C. Daniels (t), P. Nicholson (hpd); recorded 2000; Somm, SOMMCD 226 (1 CD), 2001 (contains a miscellaneous selection of songs, including English songs from HWV 228 and French airs HWV 155)

CHURCH AND DEVOTIONAL VOCAL MUSIC

Ah! che troppo ineguali, HWV 230. A. Mellon (s), Arion, M. Huggett (cond); recorded 2003; early~music.com, EMCCD-7757 (1 CD), 2003

Blessed are they that considereth the poor ('Foundling Hospital Anthem'), HWV 268. Winchester Cathedral Choir, Brandenburg Consort, D. Hill (cond); recorded 1993; Argo (Decca), 440 946–2 (1 CD), 1994 (+ *Coronation Anthems*)

'Carmelite Vespers (1707)', J. Feldman (s), E. Kirkby (s), E. van Evera (s), M. Cable (a), M. Nichols (a), J. Cornwell (t), D. Thomas (b), Taverner Choir, Taverner Players, A. Parrott (cond); recorded 1987; Virgin Veritas, 5615792 (reissue, 2 CDs), 1999 (speculative programme of how Handel's Latin church music composed in Rome could have been performed within the Vespers liturgy, includes HWV 232, 235, 237–8, 240–1, 243)

Chandos Anthems, HWV 246–8, 249^b, 250^a, 251^b, 252–6^a. L. Dawson (s), P. Kwella (s), J. Bowman (ct), I. Partridge (t), M. George (b), The Sixteen Choir and Orchestra, H. Christophers (cond); recorded 1987–9; Chandos Chaconne, CHAN 0554–7 (reissue 4 CDs), 1994

Chandos Te Deum, HWV 281. Vocalsolisten Frankfurt, Drottningholms Baroque Ensemble, G. Jenemann (cond); recorded 1994; Arte Nova, 74321 59228 2 (1 CD), 1998

Coelestis dum spirat aura, HWV 231. E. Kirkby (s), London Baroque, C. Medlam (cond); recorded 1999; BIS, CD-1065 (1 CD), 2001 (+ HWV 236, 239, 241)

Coronation Anthems, HWV 258–61. Choir of King's College Cambridge, Academy of Ancient Music, S. Cleobury (cond); recorded 2001; EMI, 5 57140 2 (1 CD), 2001 (+ HWV 74)

Dettingen Anthem, HWV 284. Choir of Westminster Abbey, English Concert, S. Preston (cond); recorded 1982–3; Deutsche Grammophon Archiv, 410 647–2 (1 CD), 1984 (+ HWV 283)

Dettingen Te Deum, HWV 283. Choir of Trinity College Cambridge, Academy of Ancient Music, S. Layton (cond); recorded 2007; Hyperion, CDA67678 (1 CD), 2008 (+ HWV 258, 296^a)

Dixit Dominus, HWV 232. Balthasar-Neumann-Chor, Balthasar-Neumann-Ensemble, T. Hengelbrock (cond); recorded 2003; Deutsche Harmonia Mundi (BMG),

82876 58792 2 (1 CD), 2004 (+ *Missa Dolorosa* and *Crucifixus* by Caldara; see **'Carmelite Vespers'**)

Donna, che in ciel di tanta luce splendi, HWV 233. A. S. von Otter (ms), Musica Antiqua Köln, R. Goebel (cond); recorded 1993; Deutsche Grammophon Archiv, 439 866–2 (1 CD), 1994 (+ HWV 230, 235)

Gloria, HWV deest, attr. Handel. M. Léger (s), RosaSolis; recorded 2008; Musica Ficta, MF8008 (1 CD), 2009 (+ HWV 231, 241, 393, 401)

Laudate pueri dominum, HWV 236. E. Kirkby (s), London Baroque, C. Medlam (cond); recorded 1999; BIS, CD-1065 (1 CD), 2001 (+ HWV 231, 239, 241)

Laudate pueri dominum, HWV 237. S. McNair (s), Monteverdi Choir, English Baroque Soloists, J. E. Gardiner (cond); recorded 1992; Philips, 434 920–2 (1 CD), 1993 (+ HWV 242 and Mozart's *Exsultate jubilate*; see **'Carmelite Vespers'**)

Music for the Chapel Royal, including HWV 249^a, 250^b, 251^a, two movements from 251^d, 256^b. Choir of the Chapel Royal, Musicians Extra-ordinary, A. Gant (cond); recorded 2005; Naxos, 8.557935 (1 CD), 2007

Nisi Dominus, HWV 238 (see **'Carmelite Vespers'**)

O quails de coelo sonus, HWV 239. E. Kirkby (s), London Baroque, C. Medlam (cond); recorded 1999; BIS, CD-1065 (1 CD), 2001 (+ HWV 231, 236, 241)

Saeviat tellus, HWV 240 (also see 'Carmelite Vespers'). A. Massis (s), Les Musiciens du Louvre, M. Minkowski (cond); recorded 1998; Deutsche Grammophon Archiv, 459 627–2 (1 CD), 1999 (+ HWV 232, 237, 241; see **'Carmelite Vespers'**)

Salve regina, HWV 241. E. Kirkby (s), London Baroque, C. Medlam (cond); recorded 1999; BIS, CD-1065 (1 CD), 2001 (+ HWV 231, 236, 239; see **'Carmelite Vespers'**)

Silete venti, HWV 242. S. McNair (s), English Baroque Soloists, J. E. Gardiner (cond); recorded 1992; Philips, 434 920–2 (1 CD), 1993 (+ HWV 237 and Mozart's *Exsultate jubilate*)

Sing unto God (Wedding Anthem), HWV 263. G. Fisher (s), J. Bowman (ct), J. M. Ainsley (t), M. George (b), Choir of New College Oxford, King's Consort, R. King (cond); recorded 1988; Hyperion CDA66315 (1 CD), 1989 (+ HWV 74, 280)

Te Deum in A major, HWV 282. U. Andersen (a), M. Wilde (t), C. Dixon (b), Alsfeder Vokalsensemble, Concerto Polacco, W. Helbich (cond); recorded 1999; Naxos 8.554753 (1 CD), 2001 (+ HWV 283)

Utrecht Te Deum and Jubilate, HWV 278–9. Choir of St Paul's Cathedral, Parley of Instruments, J. Scott (cond); recorded 1997; Hyperion, CDA67009 (1 CD), 1998 (+ music composed for St Paul's by Blow and Boyce)

ways of Zion do mourn, The (Funeral Anthem), HWV 264. Alsfeder Vokalsensemble, Barockorchester Bremen, W. Helbich (cond); recorded 1993; CPO, 999 244–2 (1 CD), 1995 (+ HWV 280)

ORCHESTRAL MUSIC

Concerti a due cori, HWV 332–4. Zefiro, A. Bernadini (cond); recorded 2006; Sony, 88697367912 (1 CD), 2008 (+ HWV 351)

Concerti grossi, Op. 3, HWV 312–7. Tafelmusik, J. Lamon (cond); Recorded 1991; Sony Vivarte, SK 52 553 (1 CD), 1993

Concerti grossi, Op. 6, HWV 319–30. Academy of Ancient Music, A. Manze (cond); recorded 1997; Harmonia Mundi (USA), HMU 907228.29 (2 CDs), 1998

Harp Concerto, HWV 294. A. Lawrence-King (hp), Tragicomedia, Symphony of Harmony and Invention, H. Christophers (cond); recorded 1990; Coro, COR16028 (2 CDs), 2005 (+ HWV 75)

Music for the Royal Fireworks, HWV 351. Original windband orchestration. English Concert, T. Pinnock (cond); recorded 1996; Deutsche Grammophon Archiv, 453 451–2 (1 CD), 1997
  Revised scoring with strings. Tafelmusik, J. Lamon (cond); recorded 1997; Sony, SK 63073 (1 CD), 1998 (+ HWV 332–4)

Oboe Concertos, HWV 287, 301, 302^a. D. Reichenberg (ob), English Concert, T. Pinnock (cond); recorded 1984; Deutsche Grammophon Archiv, 415 291–2 (1 CD), 1985 (+ HWV 288, 318)

Organ Concertos, HWV 295–6, 304, 305^a. Orchestra of the Age of Enlightenment, B. van Asperen (org/cond); recorded 1996; Virgin Veritas, 5 45236 2 (2 CDs), 1997 (+ Op. 7)

Organ Concertos, Op. 4, HWV 289–94. F. Kelly (hp), P. Nicholson (org), Brandenburg Consort, R. Goodman (cond); recorded 1996; Hyperion, CDD22052 (reissue 2 CDs), 2005 (+ Op. 7)

Organ Concertos, Op. 7, HWV 306–11. P. Nicholson (org), Brandenburg Consort, R. Goodman (cond); recorded 1996; Hyperion, CDD22052 (reissue 2 CDs), 2005 (+ Op. 4)

Sonata a 5 ('Violin concerto'), HWV 288. P. Beznosiuk (vn), Academy of Ancient Music, R. Egarr (cond); recorded 2006; Harmonia Mundi (USA), HMU 907415 (1 CD), 2007 (+ Op. 3)

Water Music, HWV 348–50. Tafelmusik, J. Lamon (cond); recorded 1995; Sony, SK 68257 (1 CD), 1996 (+ suite of dances from HWV 8^c)

Orchestral Works, including *Water Music*, HWV 348–50, *Music for the Royal Fireworks*, HWV 351, *Concerti a due cori*, Nos. 2–3, HWV 333–4, *Concerti grossi*, Op. 3, HWV 312–17, *Concerto grosso in C* ('Alexander's Feast'), HWV 318, *Concerti grossi*, Op. 6, HWV 319–30. English Concert, T. Pinnock (cond); recorded 1981–4; Deutsche Grammophon Archiv, 463 094–2 (reissue, 6 CDs), 1999

INSTRUMENTAL CHAMBER MUSIC

Das Gesamtwerk für Cembalo. E. Kraus (hpd); recorded 1972; EBS Records, EBS 6111 (10 CDs); 1995 (the only attempt to record Handel's complete solo keyboard works issued on CD)

Eight Harpsichord Suites, The, HWV 426–33. P. Nicholson (hpd); recorded 1994; Hyperion, CDD22045 (reissue, 2 CDs), 2002 (+ HWV 605–12)

Harpsichord Works, volume 1, HWV 434–9. S. Yates (hpd); recorded 1998; Chandos Chaconne, CHAN 0644 (1 CD), 1999

Harpsichord Works, volume 2, HWV 426–30. S. Yates (hpd); recorded 2000–1; Chandos Chaconne, CHAN 0669 (1 CD), 2001

Harpsichord Works, volume 3, HWV 431–33, 440–1, Prelude from HWV 442. S. Yates (hpd); recorded 2001; Chandos Chaconne, CHAN 0688 (1 CD), 2002

Op. 1 Sonatas, HWV 357–62, 363^b, 364^a, 365–77, 379. E. Wallfisch (vn), P. Goodwin (ob), L. Beznosiuk (fl), R. Beckett (r), R. Tunnicliffe (vc), P. Nicholson (hpd); recorded 1994; Hyperion, CDA66921/3 (3 CDs), 1995

Op. 2 Trio Sonatas, HWV 386^b, 387–9, 390^a, 391. Sonnerie; recorded 2002; Avie, AV0033 (1 CD), 2003

Op. 5 Trio Sonatas, HWV 396–402. Brook Street Band; recorded 2005; Avie, AV2068 (1 CD), 2005

Sonatas, Flute, HWV 359^b, 363^b, 367^b, 374–9. L. Beznosiuk (fl); recorded 1994 and 2001; Hyperion, CDA67278 (1 CD), 2001

Sonatas, Oboe, HWV 357, 363^a, 366. A. Bellamy (ob), King's Consort; recorded 2006; Hyperion, CDA67627 (1 CD), 2007 (+ HWV 202–10)

Sonatas, Recorder, HWV 360, 362, 365, 367^a, 369, 377. P. Thorby (r); recorded 2003; Linn, CKD 223 (1 CD), 2004

Sonatas, Violin, HWV 358, 359, 361, 364, 367, 371, 406–8, 412. A. Butterfield (vn); recorded 2007; Somm, SOMMCD 068 (1 CD), 2007 (+ Sonatina in A from HWV 46b)

The Chamber Music, including flute sonatas, violin sonatas, oboe sonatas, Op. 2, Op. 5, Trio sonatas for 2 violins and continuo (HWV 392–4), recorder sonatas. S. Preston (fl), J. Holloway (vn), M. Comberti (vn), D. Reichenberg (ob), P. Pickett (r), L'École d'Orphée; [n.d.]; CRD, 5002 (reissue 6 CDs), 2001

VOCAL RECITALS

As steals the morn: Handel arias and scenes for tenor. M. Padmore (t), L. Crowe (s), R. Blaze (ct), the English Concert, A. Manze (vn/dir.); recorded 2006; Harmonia Mundi (USA), HMU 907422 (1 CD), 2007

Between Heaven and Earth. S. Piau (s), T. Lehtipuu (t), Accademia Bizantina, S. Montanari (cond); recorded 2008; Naïve, OP 30484 (1 CD), 2009

Duetti Amorosi. N. Rial (s), L. Zazzo (ct), Kammerorchester Basel, L. Cummings (cond); recorded 2007; Deutsche Harmonia Mundi, 88697214722 (1 CD), 2008

Furore. J. DiDonato (ms), Les Talens Lyriques, C. Rousset (cond.); recorded 2008; Virgin, 5 19038 2 (1 CD), 2008

Great Handel Arias. A. Murray (ms), Orchestra of the Age of Enlightenment, C. Mackerras (cond); recorded 1994; Forlane, UCD 16738 (1 CD), 1995

Great Oratorio Duets. C. Sampson (s), R. Blaze (ct), Orchestra of the Age of Enlighten-ment, N. Kraemer (cond); recorded 2005; BIS, BIS-SACD-1436 (1 CD), 2006

Handel. S. Piau (s), S. Mingardo (a), Concerto Italiano, R. Alessandrini (cond); recorded 2008; Naïve, OP 304 83 (1 CD), 2008 (opera arias and duets)

Handel Arias. L. Hunt-Lieberson (ms), Orchestra of the Age of Enlightenment, H. Bicket (cond); recorded 2003–4; Avie, AV0030 (1 CD), 2004

Handel Arias: Love and Madness. J. Zomer (s), B. Schneemann (ob), Musica Amphion, P.-J. Belder (cond); recorded 2008; Channel Classics, CCS SA 29209 (1 CD), 2009

Handel Arie per basso. L. Regazzo (b), Concerto Italiano, R. Alessandrini (cond); recorded 2008; Naïve, OP 30472 (1 CD), 2009

Handel English Arias. J. Bowman (ct), King's Consort, R. King (cond); recorded 1995; Hyperion, CDA66797 (1 CD), 1995

Handel Heroic Arias. J. Bowman (ct), King's Consort, R. King (cond); recorded 1990; Hyperion, CDA66483 (1 CD), 1991

Handel Opera Arias. N. Stutzmann (a), Hanover Band, R. Goodman (cond); recorded 1991; RCA Victor Red Seal, 09026 61205 2 (1 CD), 1992

Handel Opera Arias. E. Kirkby (s), C. Bott (s), Brandenburg Consort, R. Goodman (cond); recorded 1995 (vol. 1), 1997 (vol. 2), 1999 (vol. 3); Hyperion, CDS44271/3 (reissue, 3 CDs), 2007 (Disc 1: 'Arias and Overtures from the first part of Han-del's operatic career, 1704–1726'; Disc 2: 'Arias and Duets from the era of "The Rival Queens", 1726–1728'; Disc 3: 'Arias and Overtures from the latter part of Handel's operatic career, 1729–1741')

Handel Operatic Arias. D. Daniels (ct), Orchestra of the Age of Enlightenment, R. Nor-rington (cond); recorded 1998; Virgin Veritas, 5 45326 2 (1 CD), 1998

Handel Oratorio Arias. D. Daniels (ct), Ensemble Orchestral de Paris, J. Nelson (cond); recorded 2000; Virgin, 5 45497 2 (1 CD), 2002

Heroes and Heroines. S. Connolly (ms), Symphony of Harmony and Invention, H. Christophers (cond); [n.d.]; Coro, COR16025 (1 CD), 2004

La Diva: Arias for Cuzzoni. S. Kermes (s), Lautten Compagney, W. Katschner (cond); recorded 2008, Berlin Classics, 0016422BC (1 CD), 2009

Ombra mai fù. A. Scholl (ct), Akademie für Alte Musik Berlin; recorded 1998; Harmonia Mundi (France), HMC 901685 (1 CD), 1999

Opera Seria. S. Piau (s), Les Talens Lyriques, C. Rousset (cond); recorded 2004; Naïve, E 8928 (reissue, 1 CD), 2009

DVDs

A Night with Handel. J. M. Ainsley (t), S. Connolly (ms), C. McFadden (s), R. Mannion (s), A. Miles (b), C. Robson (ct), Orchestra of the Age of Enlightenment, H. Bicket (cond); (n.d., documentary/film broadcast by Channel 4, 1996); NVC Arts (Warner Music Vision), 0630–15900-2, 1999

Admeto, HWV 22. M. Rexroth (Admeto), R. Lichtenstein (Alceste), R. Nolte (Ercole), M. Hirsch (Orindo), T. Mead (Trasimede), M. Bach (Antigona), G. Vogel (Meraspe), Händelfestspieleorchester, H. Arman (cond), A. Köhler (dir); recorded 2006; Arthaus, 101 257 (2 DVD +2 CD), 2007

Giulio Cesare, HWV 17. A. Scholl (Cesare), I. Dam-Jensen (Cleopatra), T. Semmingsen (Sesto), R. Stene (Cornelia), C. Robson (Tolomeo), P. Knudsen (Achilla), J. Lundgren (Curio), M. Maniaci (Nireno), Concerto Copenhagen, L. U. Mortensen (cond), F. Negrin (dir); recorded 2005; Harmonia Mundi (France), HMD 9909008.09 (2 DVDs), 2007

Hercules, HWV 60. W. Shimell (Hercules), J. Di Donato (Dejanira), T. Spence (Hyllus), I. Bohlin (Iole), M. Ernman (Lichas), S. Kirkbride (Priest of Jupiter), Les Arts Florissants, W. Christie (cond), L. Bondy (dir); recorded 2004; Bel Air Classiques, BAC013 (2 DVDs), 2005

Partenope, HWV 27. I. Dam-Jensen (Partenope), A. Scholl (Arsace), T. Semmingsen (Rosmira), C. Dumaux (Armindo), B. K. Jensen (Emilio), P. Knudsen (Ormonte), Concerto Copenhagen, L. U. Mortensen (cond), F. Negrin (dir); recorded 2008; Decca, 074 3348 5 (2 DVDs), 2009

Rinaldo, HWV 7^a. D. Daniels (Rinaldo), D. York (Almirena, Sirena), N. Nadelman (Armida, Sirena), E. Silins (Argante), D. Walker (Goffredo), A. Köhler (Eustazio), C. Maxwell (Mago cristiano, Donna, Araldo), Bavarian State Orchestra, H. Bicket (cond), D. Alden (dir); recorded 2001; Arthaus 100 388 (2 DVDs), 2003

Rodelinda, HWV 19. A. C. Antonacci (Rodelinda), A. Scholl (Bertarido), K. Streit (Grimoaldo), L. Winter (Eduige), A. Stefanowicz (Unulfo), U. Chiummo (Garibaldo), Orchestra of the Age of Enlightenment, W. Christie (cond), J.-M. Villégier (dir); recorded 1998; NVC Arts (Warner Music Vision), 3984–23024–3 (1 DVD), 2005

Serse, HWV 40. P. Rasmussen (Serse), I. Bayrakdarian (Romilda), A. Hallenberg (Arsamene), P. Bardon (Amastre), M. Lippi (Ariodate), S. Piau (Atalanta), M. Peirone (Elviro), Les Talens Lyriques, C. Rousset (cond), M. Hampe (dir); recorded 2000; TDK, DV-OPSER (1 DVD), 2005

Tamerlano, HWV 18. M. Bacelli (Tamerlano), S. Mingardo (Adronico), P. Domingo (Bajazet), I. Bohlin (Asteria), J. Holloway (Irene), L. de Donato (Leone), Orchestra of the Teatro Real, P. McCreesh (cond), G. Vick (dir); recorded 2008; Opus Arte, OA 1006 D (3 DVDs), 2009

Teseo, HWV 9. J. Laszczkowski (Teseo), M. R. Wesseling (Medea), S. Rostorf-Zamir (Agilea), J. Maldonado (Egeo), M. Meyer (Clizia), T. Diestler (Arcane), Lautten Compagney, W. Katschner (cond), A. Köhler (dir); recorded 2004; Arthaus, 100 708 (1 DVD), 2005

Theodora, HWV 68. D. Upshaw (Theodora), D. Daniels (Didymus), L. Hunt (Irene), R. Croft (Septimius), F. Olsen (Valens), Orchestra of the Age of Enlightenment, W. Christie (cond), P. Sellars (dir); recorded 1996; NVC Arts (Warner Music Vision), 0630–15481–2 (1 DVD), [n.d.]

Appendix 7: An overview of fifty Handel performers, 1959–2009

DAVID VICKERS

This is a concise overview of fifty performers (including orchestras) that have left an indelible mark on the way we hear the composer's music since the bicentenary anniversary of his death (it also includes a few of the emerging generation who might be on the road towards making such an impact). It is impossible to include a fully comprehensive survey of all the singers, instrumentalists, conductors, stage directors and companies that have made a sustained, informed or influential contribution to modern performances of Handel's works. Moreover, if such a list were to be compiled again eighteen months' time after the time of writing, or by another editor, it might look very different. It is hoped that the reader will not be offended by any omissions, or the subjectiveness of such an exercise. However, the inclusion (or exclusion) of particular performers should not be interpreted as evidence of the editor's personal taste. Cross-references only indicate other entries in this appendix.

Academy of Ancient Music, The. English period-instrument ensemble. Founded in 1973, the AAM varies in size from a group small enough to perform baroque trio sonatas to an orchestra and chorus large enough to tackle oratorios. Christopher HOGWOOD founded the ensemble (of which he is now Emeritus Director) in order to explore historically informed approaches to performing music, after becoming frustrated at the limited interest shown by conventional chamber orchestras and mainstream conductors in reconstructing the original size, constitution and interpretative styles of musical ensembles in the seventeenth and eighteenth centuries. Investigating less commonly heard repertoire was also a priority for the early AAM, which performed instrumental music by Boyce and Arne, and theatre music by Purcell. In the late 1970s the orchestra began to challenge received thinking about Mozart's symphonies, and it has also performed and recorded a considerable amount of music by Haydn and Beethoven. Handel has always been a cornerstone of the AAM, from its ground-breaking reconstruction of the 1754 Foundling Hospital version of *Messiah* (released by Decca's early music label L'Oiseau-Lyre in 1980) to the first complete recordings of *La Resurrezione*, *Rinaldo*, *Esther*, *Orlando*, *Athalia* and *Alceste*. Under the direction of violinist Andrew Manze (Associate Director, 1996–2003), the AAM made a benchmark recording of *Concerti grossi*, *Opus* 6 (Harmonia Mundi, USA). Under guest directors such as Simon Preston, Paul Goodwin, Stephen Cleobury and Stephen Layton, the AAM has made a substantial contribution to reviving interest in Handel's English church music. In 2007 the AAM embarked on two new Handel projects: to perform several operas in concerts around Europe (including

Amadigi, Flavio and *Arianna in Creta*) under Hogwood, and to record concertos and chamber sonatas under the direction of harpsichordist Richard Egarr.

Arman, Howard (b. London, 1954). English conductor. He studied at Trinity College of Music in London, and established a conducting career in Germany and Austria, working extensively with choirs in Hamburg, Salzburg, Vienna, Stuttgart, Berlin and Leipzig. Between 1993 and 1996 he trained the resident orchestra of the Halle Handel Festival to play on period instruments, for which he was awarded the city's Handel Prize in 1996. He has conducted productions of *Ezio*, *Orlando*, *Tolomeo* and *Admeto* at Halle, and *Partenope* at Innsbruck.

Augér, Arleen (b. Long Beach, California, 13 Sept. 1939; d. Leusden, Netherlands, 10 June 1993). American soprano. Her early musical training was in a local church choir. In 1967 she won a scholarship to study in Vienna, where an impressed conductor, Josef Krips, engaged her to make her debut as the Queen of the Night in *Die Zauberflöte* at the Staatsoper. Regarded as the finest Mozart soprano of her generation, Augér's lyrical clarity and skill at conveying a wide range of emotional characters suited her increasing interest in singing Monteverdi, Bach, Handel and lieder. She gave memorable performances as Angelica in *Orlando* (with the AAM), the title role in *Alcina* at the 1985 Spitalfields Festival (recorded by EMI), and made outstanding recordings with Trevor PINNOCK (*Belshazzar* and *Messiah*) and of the 'Nine German Arias' (for the Berlin Classics label).

Baker, Dame Janet (b. Hatfield, Yorks., 21 Aug. 1933). English mezzo-soprano, and one the greatest singers to pioneer the revival of Handel's operas in the mid-twentieth century. In the bicentenary of Handel's death (1959), she sang Eduige in the HANDEL OPERA SOCIETY's *Rodelinda*, and other acclaimed roles included the title roles in *Ariodante* (1964; she later recorded the role under Raymond Leppard for Philips), *Orlando* (at the Barber Institute of Fine Arts, University of Birmingham) and *Julius Caesar* (at ENO; later recorded and filmed for television). Her Handel collaborations with Sir Anthony LEWIS (*Admeto* in 1968), Sir Charles MACKERRAS (e.g. *Julius Caesar*, *Judas Maccabaeus*) and Sir Roger Norrington (*Radamisto* in 1984) placed her at the forefront of the modern Handel revolution for nearly three decades. She also performed Dejanira in *Hercules* at the Aldeburgh Festival. A remarkable singer, she retired from the stage in 1982.

Bonizzoni, Fabio (b. Milan, 2 April 1965). Italian harpsichordist, organist and conductor. After studying under Ton Koopman, he played in several early music groups (Koopman's Amsterdam Baroque Orchestra, Jordi Savall's Le Concert des Nations, Fabio Biondi's Europa Galante, and La Venexiana). In 1995 he founded the vocal and instrumental ensemble La Risonanza, which focuses on late Italian baroque music. In 2005 Bonizzoni and La Risonanza commenced an ambitious project to research, perform and record all of Handel's Italian *cantate con strumenti* for the Spanish early music label Glossa. The first volume, *Cantate per il Cardinal Pamphilij*, which featured the Italian soprano Roberta Invernizzi, won the 2007 Stanley Sadie Handel Recording Prize. Bonizzoni is harpsichord professor at the Royal Conservatory of The Hague (Holland), and founder of the Associazione Hendel, a society devoted to the study and performance of Handel's music in Italy.

Bowman, James (b. Oxford, 6 Nov. 1941). English countertenor. Renowned as a concert and oratorio singer, he was also one of the first countertenors to enjoy a prominent stage career. After studying at Oxford, he made his opera debut at Paris in 1967, and in subsequent years sang numerous title roles (Scipione, Ottone and Giustino) for the HANDEL OPERA SOCIETY in London. He sang the title role in the first unabridged production of *Giulio Cesare* in modern times (Barber Institute of Fine Arts, 1977; he later recorded the role under Jean-Claude MALGOIRE). He participated in pioneering performances of *Ariodante* (under Raymond Leppard) and *Admeto* (under Alan CURTIS), and also sang the title role in *Orlando* for Scottish Opera and with the ACADEMY OF ANCIENT MUSIC. A prolific recording artist, Bowman's Handel discography most notably includes *Saul* (under MACKERRAS), *Athalia* (under HOGWOOD), *Belshazzar* (under PINNOCK), *Eternal Source of Light Divine* and *Deborah* (under Robert King), the *Choice of Hercules* (under Philip Ledger), and several anthologies of arias and chamber duets with the KING'S CONSORT. Although now retired, he sings with the choir of the Chapel Royal.

Cambridge Handel Opera Group. Founded in 1985 by Andrew Jones, the Cambridge Handel Opera Group produces a fully staged Handel opera (sung in English) every two years at the university's Faculty of Music, based on a new performing edition prepared from the original sources. The group aims to perform in a style that respects the composer's intentions and expectations not only in the musical aspects but also in the visual aspects of the production. So far thirteen operas have been revived, including both well-known operas (such as *Orlando* and *Serse*) and neglected works (*Floridante* and *Berenice*).

Chance, Michael (b. Penn, Bucks., 7 March 1955). English countertenor. Studied as a choral scholar at King's College, Cambridge, and quickly gained a reputation as an outstanding singer working in groups such as the Monteverdi Choir and the Tallis Scholars. Following in the footsteps of James BOWMAN as a countertenor dividing work between the theatre and the concert hall, Chance became widely known as a countertenor soloist of remarkable vocal purity and beauty in a series of highly acclaimed Bach projects with John Eliot GARDINER, who cast him as Andronico in a production of *Tamerlano* (1985). Admired for his communication of the literary, sentimental and intellectual qualities of baroque repertoire, he contributed to several important recordings during the 1980s and early 1990s, inlcuding *Jephtha* and *Agrippina* (under Gardiner), *Giustino* (under McGEGAN), *Semele* (under John Nelson) and *Messiah* (under PINNOCK).

Christie, William (b. Buffalo, NY, 19 Dec. 1944). American conductor. Studied Art History at Harvard, and harpsichord with Ralph Kirkpatrick at Yale. In 1971 he moved to Paris, and regularly collaborated with singers René JACOBS and Judith Nelson in the group Concerto Vocale. He founded his own group, Les Arts Florissants (LAF), in 1979 in order to explore the neglected French baroque vocal repertoire of Lully, Charpentier and Rameau. Known for a highly theatrical and vibrant style, Christie revolutionsed the French early music scene, although his affection for a wide range of seventeenth- and eighteenth-century repertoire has led to important recordings of Purcell, Mozart and Haydn. LAF came to Handelian prominence with recordings of *Messiah* and *Orlando*, and Christie has evident in his world premiere recordings of *The Triumph of Time and Truth* and *Silla*.

English Chamber Orchestra. Originally named the Goldsborough Orchestra, it was formed by Arnold Goldsborough to perform baroque orchestral music. Renamed the English Chamber Orchestra in 1960, it has made a significant contribution to Handelian performance, especially during the 1970s with recordings of *Saul* (under Sir Charles MACKERRAS, and again under Philip Ledger), *Alexander's Feast* and *The Choice of Hercules* (under Ledger), *Ariodante* and *Samson* (under Raymond Leppard), and orchestral concertos. In 1990 the orchestra recorded *Semele* (under John Nelson). Its repertoire has evolved wider than Goldsborough's focus upon baroque music, not least since the surge in period-instrument bands, but the ECO continues to maintain its status as one of the world's foremost modern chamber orchestras.

English Concert, The. Period-instrument orchestra founded by Trevor PINNOCK. The ensemble gave its debut at the English Bach Festival in 1973, after which it commenced an extensive series of ground-breaking recordings for Deutsche Grammophon, which included orchestral music by Vivaldi, Telemann, Bach, Fasch, C. P. E. Bach, Haydn and Mozart. Pinnock also directed performances of operas, oratorios, odes and church music by Purcell and Handel. Several projects of Handel's Italian and English church music were performed and recorded with the Choir of Westminster Abbey under Simon Preston. The English Concert has appeared at many festivals across the world, such as both Halle and Göttingen (including performances of *Jephtha* under Nicholas McGEGAN in 2003). It appointed violinist Andrew Manze as music director in 2003, under whom it performed several Handel recitals with Mark PADMORE (which led to a recital disc for Harmonia Mundi). In 2007 the orchestra appointed the harpsichordist Harry Bicket as its new director, although it also works with an increasing number of international guest conductors.

Farncombe, Charles (b. London, 29 July 1919; d. London, 30 June 2006). English conductor. After studying engineering, he trained as a musician at the Royal School of Church Music and the Royal Academy of Music. With the assistance of Edward J. Dent, he founded the HANDEL OPERA SOCIETY in 1955, and was its musical director for thirty years. In addition to performances of works by Cavalieri, Rameau, J. C. Smith, Arne, Haydn and Mozart, Farncombe conducted the modern premieres of many Handel operas, including *Rinaldo*, *Alcina* and *Deidamia*. The society's productions were toured to Göttingen, Halle, Liège and Drottningholm (where Farncombe was music director, 1970–9). He also conducted staged productions of Handel's oratorios (including a composite version of *Esther* in 1980), and directed performances of Handel's music at Karlsruhe. An important pioneer in the revival of Handel's operas, he was made a CBE in 1977, and only a year before his death conducted a revival of *Parnasso in festa* at St John's Smith Square.

Gardiner, Sir John Eliot (b. Fontmell Magna, Dorset, 20 April 1943). English conductor. Studied History and Arabic at King's College, Cambridge, where he founded the Monteverdi Choir. He went on to study music with Thurston Dart and Nadia Boulanger, and during the late 1960s gained a reputation for exploring baroque repertoire (most notably Monteverdi's *Vespers*). Several recordings of Handel's music were made in the early 1970s with the modern-instrument Monteverdi Orchestra, but by the end of the decade Gardiner became interested in using period instruments to enhance his theatrical style of historically informed performing. In 1978 he founded the English Baroque Soloists (their debut recording was *Acis and Galatea* for Deutsche Grammophon). He was artistic director of the Göttingen Handel Festival (1981–90), where he made a series of landmark recordings for Philips (most notably *Solomon*, *Alexander's Feast*, *Saul* and *Jephtha*), and performed *Tamerlano* (a co-production with Opéra de Lyon, recorded by Erato). During the 1980s, Gardiner also made revelatory recordings of *L'Allegro, il Penseroso ed il Moderato*, *Semele*, *Messiah* and *Hercules*, in which the articulate polish of the Monteverdi Choir was combined with superbly characterised playing from the English Baroque Soloists. His Handel projects often featured outstanding singers such as Anthony Rolfe JOHNSON, Michael CHANCE, Anne Sofie von Otter, Carolyn Watkinson, Lynne Dawson, Alastair Miles, Nancy Argenta and Della Jones. Gardiner's exploration of other composers – such as Mozart's operas, Beethoven's symphonies (for which he founded the Orchestre Révolutionnaire et Romantique in 1990), Berlioz, Schumann, Brahms, and, above all, Bach's cantatas – has led him to perform Handel less often since the early 1990s (although concert performances of *Agrippina* and *Dixit Dominus* led to recordings for Philips).

Handel Opera Society, The. An organisation founded in 1955 by Charles FARNCOMBE and Edward J. Dent for reviving professional stage performances of Handel's dramatic works (which included both Italian operas and English-text works such as *Hercules*). The annual productions were often given in English translations by Farncombe, Dent, Arthur Jacobs and others. From 1959 the society's productions were performed at Sadler's Wells, and notable performances during the 1950s included Joan SUTHERLAND as Alcina (1957), and Janet BAKER as Eduige in *Rodelinda* (1959). The society staged twenty-eight productions. Its final project was *Rodrigo* in 1985.

Hogwood, Christopher (b. Nottingham, 10 Sept. 1941). English conductor, keyboard player and scholar. He read Classics and Music at Pembroke College, Cambridge, and studied harpsichord with Mary Potts and Gustav Leonhardt. He was a founder member of David Munrow's Early Music Consort in 1967, and six years later founded the ACADEMY OF ANCIENT MUSIC. As director of the AAM, Hogwood explored a wide range of baroque, classical and early romantic repertoire, often orchestral, but sometimes oratorio, opera and sacred music. Hogwood is now Emeritus Director of the AAM, and is also Conductor Laureate of the Handel and Haydn Society of Boston, with whom he recorded the Opus 3 and Opus 6 Concerti grossi, and Mozart's arrangements of Handel's *Acis and Galatea*, *Alexander's Feast*, and the *Song for St Cecilia's Day*. Hogwood has recently revised his Thames & Hudson biography of Handel, written a book about the *Water Music* and the *Music for the Royal Fireworks* (CUP), and made a recording of Handel's keyboard music using clavichords.

Horne, Marilyn (b. Bradford, PA, 16 Jan. 1929). American mezzo-soprano. After studying at the University of Southern California, she worked at leading opera houses

Krapp, Edgar (b. Bamberg, 3 June 1947). German keyboardist. He received early musical training as a chorister at the Regensburg 'Domspatzen', and later studied organ and harpsichord at the Musikhochschule in Munich (where he became a lecturer in 1972, and professor in 1993). A distinguished teacher and organist, he is one of the few harpsichordists to have attempted recording a complete survey of Handel's keyboard music.

Lewis, Sir Anthony (b. Bermuda, 2 March 1915; d. Haslemere, 5 June 1983). English conductor and musicologist. Studied with Edward J. Dent at Peterhouse in Cambridge, and afterwards with Nadia Boulanger. He joined the BBC in 1935, and three years later devised the series *Handel in Rome*. A prime mover in the development of Radio 3, he was elected Peyton and Barber Professor of Music at Birmingham University in 1947. He remained Professor there for twenty-one years, during which time he conducted pioneering revivals of Handel operas. He co-edited *Semele* with Sir Charles MACKERRAS, and made a recording of *Sosarme* which, in its use of voices in the correct vocal ranges singing in Italian, was far ahead of its time. He was also a champion for Monteverdi and Purcell, founded the edition *Musica Britannica* in 1951, and was principal of the Royal Academy of Music until his retirement in 1982.

McCreesh, Paul (b. London, 24 May 1960). English conductor. After studying music at the University of Manchester, he founded the Gabrieli Consort and Players in 1982. The ensemble initially specialised in late Renaissance and early baroque music, particularly Gabrieli, Monteverdi, Carissimi, Praetorius, Morales, Victoria, and often placed the music within conceptual programmes based on liturgical context. During the 1990s McCreesh became more interested in performing later baroque and classical repertoire, including church music and oratorios by Bach, Mozart and Haydn. Handel oratorio performances at the BBC Proms and around Europe have led to important complete recordings of the 1754 Foundling Hospital version of *Messiah* (1997), *Solomon* (1999), *Theodora* (2000) and *Saul* (2004). McCreesh has also conducted numerous other Handel oratorios and operas (*Alcina* and *Rodelinda* at the Beaune Festival), and has recently increased his involvement as a guest conductor of staged operatic productions: he was music director for Welsh National Opera's staging of *Jephtha* (2003), and in 2008 conducted productions of *Tamerlano* (featuring Placido Domingo as Bajazet) and *Il trionfo del Tempo e del Disinganno* at the Teatro Real in Madrid.

McGegan, Nicholas (b. Sawbridgeworth, Herts., 14 Jan. 1950). British conductor. After studying at Oxford and Cambridge, he pursued a career as a baroque flautist. In the late 1970s he gained attention as a conductor of baroque opera with a series of Rameau performances for the English Bach Festival, and developed a close collaboration with the Hungarian period-instrument group Capella Savaria (with whom he made a series of world-premiere Handel recordings, including *Terpsicore*, *Floridante* and *Atalanta*). In 1985 he was appointed the first music director of the newly founded Philharmonia Baroque Orchestra in Berkeley, California. A passionate advocate for performing Handel's operas in a variety of 'authentic' and modern stagings, McGegan has conducted *Teseo* at the Boston Early Music Festival, *Ariodante* at ENO, and was principal conductor of the Drottningholm Slottstheater (1983–5). In 1991 he succeeded John Eliot

GARDINER as artistic director of the Göttingen Handel Festival, and under his direction the festival has grown increasingly international, and now revolves around staged opera productions. Many of these productions have led to recordings, either released commercially (e.g. *Giustino*, *Ottone*, *Ariodante*) or through the Göttingen Handel Society (e.g. *Arianna in Creta*, *Rodelinda*, *Rinaldo*, *Orlando*). McGegan has also extensively performed Handel's oratorios with a variety of orchestras and choirs, and formed an ensemble (the 'Arcadian Academy') to explore Italian baroque chamber cantatas. His performances feature wittily characterised rhythms, attention to instrumental detail, and a fine awareness of how to support and accompany solo singers. In 2006 he formed the Göttingen Handel Festival Orchestra, which consists of leading instrumentalists from all over the world.

Mackerras, Sir Charles (b. Schenectady, NY, 17 Nov. 1925). Australian conductor. He studied at the New South Wales Conservatorium in Sydney, and came to Europe in 1947. He studied in Prague, where he developed a lasting attachment to Slavonic music (particularly Janáček). Renowned as an excellent interpreter of orchestral and choral music of many periods, much of Mackerras's career has been devoted to the opera house. He made his London operatic debut in 1948. In comparison to his prolific output of Mozart and Janáček recordings, Mackerras has committed relatively few complete Handel works to disc (a notable example is *Saul* for Deutsche Grammophon), but he was one of the first modern 'mainstream' conductors to pursue a serious interest in historically informed performance of appoggiaturas and ornamentation in eighteenth-century music, and to convey the dance-like exuberance and dramatic power of Handel's theatrical works. Moreover, in 1959 he made a pioneering recording of the *Music for the Royal Fireworks* using Handel's original wind-band scoring. Notable productions have included *Semele* (using an edition that he prepared with Sir Anthony LEWIS), *Julius Caesar* (with Dame Janet BAKER), *Xerxes* (an ENO production by Nicholas Hytner), *Ariodante* (with Ann Murray), and *Orlando* (in a thoughtful production by Francisco Negrin). Now into his mid-eighties, Mackerras continues to collaborate with the Scottish Chamber Orchestra, the Orchestra of the Age of Enlightenment, English National Opera and the Royal Opera House.

Malgoire, Jean-Claude (b. Avignon, 25 Nov. 1940). French conductor. He studied in Avignon and at the Paris Conservatoire, and in 1966 founded La Grande Écurie et la Chambre du Roy to perform baroque music. A pioneer in the revival of operas by Campra, Lully and Rameau, and one of the first serious proponents of early music performance in France, Malgoire was one of the first conductors to make a period-instrument recording of *Messiah*. Although some of his opera recordings were clumsily cut (e.g. *Tamerlano*), his best achievements (such as an enthusiastic interpretation of *Rinaldo*) paved the way for subsequent generations of French musicians to discover Handel's dramatic music.

Minkowski, Marc (b. Paris, 4 Oct. 1962). French conductor. After pursuing a career as a baroque bassoonist in leading French and Belgian groups, he founded Les Musiciens du Louvre in 1984. Known for fast tempi, extremity of rhetorical affect, and colourful instrumental accompaniments, Minkowski has revived several Handel operas and dramatic oratorios to thrilling effect. Occasionally maverick and often controversial for his musical decisions, Minkowski's work is exuberant and dramatic. In recent years he has devoted greater attention to later French operatic repertoire such as Gluck, Offenbach and Bizet.

Neumann, Peter (b. Karlsruhe, 8 March 1940). German conductor. Founder of the Kölner Kammerchor (since 1970) and the period-instrument orchestra Collegium Cartusianum (since 1988), his Cologne concerts since the early 1980s have included most of Handel's English-language works. From 1999 until 2002 he directed the series '250 years of Handel Oratorio', which included nine works that Handel gave during his oratorio seasons 1749–52. Neumann is equally at home in music from Schütz to Mozart, but he is probably the leading German interpreter of Handel's oratorios. His performances are impressive for the excellent English pronunciation and communication of his choir, the lean dramatic playing of his orchestra, and his generally excellent pacing of large-scale scores. His recordings of *Athalia*, *Saul* and *Alexander's Feast* rival any of those by native English-speaking groups.

Nicholson, Paul (b. London, 31 Dec. 1952). English conductor, harpsichordist and organist. He studied at Dartington College of Arts and the University of York, and played continuo with many of the leading British early music groups. He was associate musical director of the London Handel Festival (1994–7), frequently directed the Parley of Instruments in performances of eighteenth-century English music, and was a member of the chamber ensemble Convivium. His tasteful and judicious musicianship can be heard on recordings of Handel's harpsichord suites and organ concertos (on the Hyperion label). In 2002 he resigned from his musical positions, including principal keyboardist of the Orchestra of the Age of Enlightenment, to become a full-time Anglican priest.

Padmore, Mark (b. London, 8 March 1961). English tenor. After studying as a choral scholar at King's College, Cambridge, he was a lay clerk at Westminster Abbey for two years. He sang in leading early music groups the Tallis Scholars, the Sixteen, the Monteverdi Choir, the Taverner Consort and the Hilliard Ensemble, gained valuable experience performing 'haute-contre' roles for William CHRISTIE in operas by Purcell, Charpentier and Rameau, and became a regular soloist in Bach projects under Philippe Herreweghe. He appears as a soloist on three very different recordings of *Messiah*, under Christie (1994), Sir Colin Davis (2007) and Harry CHRISTOPHERS (2008). He has sung the title roles of *Belshazzar* at Halle (2002), *Jephtha* with Welsh National Opera (2003), *Samson* at San Francisco (under Nicholas McGEGAN, 2005), and in 2007 recorded a thoughtful recital disc *As steals the morn* with the ENGLISH CONCERT.

Piau, Sandrine (b. Issy-les-Moulineaux, 5 June 1965). French soprano. Studied the harp at Paris Conservatoire, and early music with William CHRISTIE. She became a leading proponent of French baroque opera as a regular soloist in performances by Les Arts Florissants. Her virtuosity, spectacular coloratura and strong melodic awareness led Christophe ROUSSET to cast her in Handel prima donna roles in *Scipione*, *Tamerlano*, *Giulio Cesare* and *Riccardo primo*. She has made outstanding contributions to productions and concert performances of *Aci, Galatea e Polifemo*, *Serse* and *Arianna in Creta*. One of the foremost Handel opera sopranos working today, Piau's recital disc *Opera Seria* (under Rousset) won the Stanley Sadie Handel Recording Prize in 2005.

Pinnock, Trevor (b. Canterbury, 16 Dec. 1946). English harpsichordist and conductor. He was a chorister at Canterbury Cathedral and studied keyboard at the Royal College of Music. He founded the ENGLISH CONCERT in 1973, with whom he made an outstanding contribution to historically informed performances of Handel's music. Important recordings have included a radiant performance of the *Song for St Cecilia's Day*, sonorous accounts of *Messiah* and *Belshazzar*, a disc of cantatas featuring *Cecilia, volgi un sguardo*, fine interpretations of both sets of concerti grossi (Op. 3 and Op. 6), a selection of overtures, the *Water Music*, and the *Music for the Royal Fireworks* (both in the conventional chamber orchestral scoring, and Handel's original wind-band version). Pinnock has directed most of these from the keyboard, with remarkable warmth, finesse and integrity. In 2001 he conducted Jonathan Miller's production of *Tamerlano* at Halle and Sadler's Wells (the Halle performances were released on CD and DVD). He has also pioneered period-instrument performances of orchestral and vocal music by Purcell, Haydn and Mozart. Since standing down as the English Concert's director in 2003, Pinnock has concentrated most fully on a career as a solo harpsichordist, although he founded the European Brandenburg Ensemble to celebrate his sixtieth birthday in 2006. In addition to critically acclaimed performances of keyboard music of Handel, Scarlatti, Rameau and Bach, Pinnock has been a guest conductor for Handel stagings in New York (*Giulio Cesare*, 1988), Karlsruhe (*Rodelinda*, 1998) and Sydney (*Rinaldo*, 2005).

Rolfe-Johnson, Anthony (b. Tackley, Northants., 5 Nov. 1940). One of the most versatile and respected British tenors of his generation. After working as a farmer, he studied at the Guildhall, and made his opera debut in 1973. A fine Evangelist in Bach's Passions and an impeccably stylish Mozart singer, he also excelled at singing earlier music, often in collaboration with John Eliot GARDINER, Christopher HOGWOOD, Trevor PINNOCK, Nikolaus Harnoncourt and Sir Charles MACKERRAS. He sang many parts in Handel's English works, most notably Jupiter in *Semele* (which he recorded with Gardiner, and later performed at the Royal Opera House), the title role in *Jephtha* (which he recorded with Sir Neville Marriner), and the tenor solos in Trevor Pinnock's seminal recording of the *Song for St Cecilia's Day*.

Rousset, Christophe (b. Montfavet, nr. Avignon, 12 April 1961). French harpsichordist and conductor. Whilst a teenage harpsichord student, he was inspired to explore Handel's operas after witnessing a production of *Alcina* at Aix-en-Provence. He studied at The Hague under Bob van Asperen, the Kuijken brothers and Gustav Leonhardt. He was harpsichordist with William CHRISTIE's Les Arts Florissants from 1986, but in 1991 he founded his own ensemble Les Talens Lyriques. As well as a flourishing career as a solo harpsichordist, which has included several guest appearances playing Bach with the ACADEMY OF ANCIENT MUSIC, he is an energetic champion of French and Italian opera of the seventeenth and eighteenth centuries, often advocating the revival of forgotten works by Lully, Mondonville, Jommelli, Traetta, Martin y Soler and Salieri. He has led Les Talens

Lyriques in performances of many Handel operas, including vibrant premiere recordings of *Scipione* and *Riccardo primo*, and concert performances or staged productions of *Admeto, Tamerlano, Giulio Cesare, Serse, Alcina, Arianna in Creta, Ariodante* and *Parterope*. His contribution to the soundtrack of the film *Farinelli: il Castrato* (1994) helped to popularise arias from *Rinaldo* for a new audience (although the historical Farinelli never sang them). He has collaborated on Handel aria recital projects with Joyce DiDonato and Sandrine PIAU which have been notable for imaginative programming and spirited performances.

Sampson, Carolyn (b. Bedford, 18 May 1974). English soprano. Studied music at Birmingham University, where she joined the early music choir Ex Cathedra. Whilst working in choirs such as Polyphony and the Sixteen, she swiftly developed a reputation as an 'early music' soprano, regularly appearing as a soloist with the KING'S CONSORT, Bach Collegium Japan, the Gabrieli Consort, Collegium Vocale Gent, the ENGLISH CONCERT, and conductors such as Trevor PIN-NOCK and Laurence CUMMINGS. Staged opera performances have included Asteria in *Tamerlano* under Emmanuelle Haïm, and the title role in *Semele* at ENO. Sampson's stylistic awareness and sweet delivery of text are well represented on the King's Consort's recordings of the *Nine German Arias, Cecilia, volgi un sguardo* and *Parnasso in festa*.

Scholl, Andreas (b. Eltville, 10 Nov. 1967). German countertenor. Studied at the Schola Cantorum Basiliensis, where one of his teachers was René JACOBS. Initially known best as a singer of lute songs and church music (particularly Bach under Philippe Herreweghe), he has become a popular interpreter of Handel's operas, oratorios and chamber cantatas. He sang all of the alto solos on William CHRISTIE's highly acclaimed recording of *Messiah* (1994), and made his major opera house debut as Bertarido in *Rodelinda* at Glyndebourne (1998). In addition to recording several aria anthologies, including one exploring the career of Senesino, Scholl has performed the title role in *Giulio Cesare* (2005) and Arsace in *Partenope* (2008) at the Danish Royal Opera. Arguably at his most impressive in gentler poetic music, his contributions to *Solomon* and *Saul* (both with the Gabrieli Consort and Players under McCREESH) ideally suit his intimate and cerebral musicianship.

Steele-Perkins, Crispian (b. Exeter, 18 Dec. 1944). English trumpeter. He studied at the Guildhall School of Music, and began his career as an orchestral trumpeter with Sadler's Wells Opera (later ENO) and the Royal Philharmonic Orchestra. Inspired by the early-music pioneer David Munrow, he became passionately interested in using historical trumpets for performances of baroque and classical repertoire. A respected restorer of natural and early mechanical trumpets, he used them when playing with many leading period-instrument orchestras, including the ACADEMY OF ANCIENT MUSIC, John Eliot GARDINER's English Baroque Soloists, the ENGLISH CONCERT, Andrew Parrott's the Taverner Players, the KING'S CONSORT, Tafelmusik, the Amsterdam Baroque Orchestra and Collegium Musicum 90. In addition to pioneering work in music by Purcell, Bach and Haydn, he has performed and recorded most of Handel's important trumpet parts, including 'The trumpet shall sound' on at least five different well-known recordings of *Messiah*.

Sutherland, Dame Joan (b. Sydney, 7 Nov. 1926). Australian soprano. She was taught by her mother until she was nineteen, and then received formal musical training in Sydney. In August 1947 she sang her first baroque opera role in a concert of Purcell's *Dido and Aeneas*. In 1951 she went to study in London at the Royal College of Music, and a year later gave her Royal Opera House debut as the First Lady in *Die Zauberflöte*. Encouraged by her conductor husband Richard Bonynge, Sutherland developed a specialism for nineteenth-century bel canto opera, but also devoted considerable effort to reviving Handel roles, singing Alcina for the HANDEL OPERA SOCIETY in 1957, Rodelinda for Anthony LEWIS in 1959 and Cleopatra at Sadler's Wells (later ENO) in 1963. She made a vital contribution to popularising the revival of Handel's operas on the stage, was made a DBE in 1979, and retired in 1990.

Weißenborn, Günther (b. Coburg, 2 June 1911; d. Detmold, 25 Feb. 2001). German pianist and conductor. He studied at the Hochschule für Musik in Berlin, where one of his teachers was Paul Hindemith. After the Second World War he studied at Hanover, and worked at the Hamburg Staatsoper. In summer 1950 he performed with an orchestra in plays and ballets at the Deutsches Theatre in Göttingen. When this group was dissolved, he founded the Göttinger Symphonie Orchester. In 1960 he became the artistic director of the Göttingen Handel Festival, and during his twenty years at the helm of the festival he conducted numerous performances of works by Handel (usually abridged, transposed and in German). He was perhaps best known as a pianist accompanying lieder recitals by singers such as Dietrich Fischer-Dieskau.

Zazzo, Lawrence (b. Philadelphia, 15 Dec. 1970). American countertenor. He graduated in Music and English from Yale and King's College, Cambridge, and completed his vocal studies at the Royal College of Music, where he sang in the London Handel Festival's productions of *Arminio* and *Alessandro Severo*. He has performed in prominent Handel projects conducted by William CHRISTIE (Arsamene in *Serse*), Alan CURTIS (title role in *Fernando/Sosarme*), Trevor PINNOCK (Didymus in *Theodora*), Christian CURNYN (title role in *Partenope*), Christopher HOGWOOD (title role in *Amadigi*), Paul Goodwin (title roles in *Lotario* and *Riccardo primo*) and Laurence CUMMINGS (a Handel duets recording with soprano Nuria Rial). One of the most prolific modern Handelian artists in both the opera house and on CD, Zazzo has regularly collaborated with René JACOBS (Goffredo in *Rinaldo*, Ottone in *Agrippina*, David in *Saul*, the title role in *Giulio Cesare*), and was the first countertenor soloist to sing in the Huddersfield Choral Society's famous annual performances of *Messiah*.

Appendix 8: Handel organisations and websites

American Handel Society, The. School of Music, University of Maryland, College Park, Maryland 20742, USA; e-mail info@americanhandelsociety.org, website http://americanhandelsociety.org/

Associazione Hendel (Milan). E-mail info@associazionehendel.it, website www.associazionehendel.it/

Cambridge Handel Opera Group. Miss Elisabeth Fleming (Company Manager), Cambridge Handel Opera Group, c/o Dr A. V. Jones, Selwyn College, Cambridge, CB3 9DQ, United Kingdom; e-mail elisabeth@chog.co.uk, website www.chog.co.uk/

Czech Handel Society, The. Na Manínách 11/795, 170 00, Praha 7, Czech Republic; e-mail info@haendel.cz, website www.haendel.cz/

Georg Friederich Händel-Gesellschaft e.V. (Halle). c/o Händel-Haus, Große Nikolaistraße 5, D-06108 Halle (Saale), Germany; e-mail gesellschaft@haendelhaus.de, website www.haendel-in-halle.de/

Gerald Coke Handel Collection. The Foundling Museum, 40 Brunswick Square, London, WC1N 1AZ, United Kingdom; e-mail handel@foundlingmuseum.org.uk, website www.foundlingmuseum.org.uk/exhibit_handel.php

GFHandel.org. http://gfhandel.org/

Göttinger Händel-Gesellschaft. Hainholzweg 3/5, 37085 Göttingen, Germany; e-mail info@haendel-festspiele.de, website www.haendel-festspiele.de/

Haendel.it. www.haendel.it/

Hallische Händel-Ausgabe. c/o Händel-Haus, Große Nikolaistraße 5, 06108 Halle, Germany

Händel-Gesellschaft Karlsruhe. Paul-Ehrlich-Str. 7, D-76133 Karlsruhe, Germany; e-mail Haendel-KA@web.de, website www.haendel-karlsruhe.de

Händel-Haus (Halle). Große Nikolaistraße 5, 06108 Halle (Saale), Germany; website www.haendelhaus.de/de

Handel House Museum, The. 25 Brook Street, Mayfair, London, W1K 4HB, United Kingdom; e-mail mail@handelhouse.org, website www.handelhouse.org/

Handel Institute, The. Malcolm London (Treasurer), 42 Falcon Point, Hopton Street, London, SE1 9JW, United Kingdom; website http://gfhandel.org/

Handel Institute of Japan, The. E-mail fwnd6030@mb.infoweb.ne.jp, website http://www.handel-institute-japan.org/

Handel-L (internet discussion group). http://launch.groups.yahoo.com/group/handel-l/

London Handel Society (London Handel Festival). Horton House, 8 Ditton Street, Ilminster, Somerset TA19 0BQ, United Kingdom; e-mail c-hodgson@btconnect.com, website www.london-handel-festival.com/

Stanley Sadie Handel Recording Prize. E-mail info@gfhandel.org, website http://gfhandel.org/

Select bibliography

FREQUENTLY CITED JOURNALS

Early Music, quarterly (London, 1973–).

Göttinger Händel-Beiträge, approximately every two years (Kassel, 1984–93; Göttingen, 1996–).

Händel-Jahrbuch, annual (Leipzig, 1928–33; 2nd series Leipzig, 1955–91; Cologne, 1992–5; Kassel, 1997–).

Music & Letters, quarterly (London, later Oxford, 1920–).

Musical Times, monthly/quarterly (London, 1843–).

GENERAL REFERENCE

A Biographical Dictionary of Actors, Actresses, Musicians, Dancers, Managers, and Other Stage Personnel in London, 1660–1800, ed. P. H. Highfill, K. A. Burnim and E. A. Langhans (Carbondale, IL, 1973–93).

Die Musik in Geschichte und Gegenwart (MGG), 2nd edn (Kassel etc., 1994–2008).

London Stage, 1660–1800: A Calendar of Plays, Entertainments & Afterpieces, Together with Casts, Box-Receipts and Contemporary Comment, The, Part II: 1700–1729, ed. L. E. Avery (Carbondale, IL, 1960).

London Stage 1660–1800: A Calendar of Plays, Entertainments & Afterpieces, Together with Casts, Box-Receipts and Contemporary Comment, The, Part III: 1729–1747, ed. A. H. Scouten (Carbondale, IL, 1961).

New Grove Dictionary of Music and Musicians, 2nd edn, ed. S. Sadie and J. Tyrrell (London, 2001) (online version www.oxfordmusic.com).

New Grove Dictionary of Opera, ed. S. Sadie and C. Bashford (London, 1992) (online version www.oxfordmusic.com).

Oxford Dictionary of National Biography (Oxford, 2004) (online version www.oxforddnb.com).

CATALOGUES, DOCUMENTS AND LIBRETTOS

Barclay Squire, W., *Catalogue of the King's Music Library. Part I: The Handel Manuscripts* (London, 1927).

Baselt, B., 'Verzeichnis der Werke Georg Friedrich Handels' (the 'HWV' catalogue of Handel's works), *Händel-Handbuch* (Leipzig and Kassel), vol. 1: *Bühnenwerke* (1978); vol. 2: *Oratorische Werke, Vokale Kammermusik, Kirchenmusik* (1984); vol. 3: *Instrumentalmusik, Pasticci und Fragmente* (1986); (vol. 4: see Deutsch).

Bianconi, L., and Bianconi, G. (eds.), *I libretti italiani di Georg Friedrich Händel e le loro fonti*, 1* & 1** (Florence, 1992).

Burrows, D. (ed.), *Handel's Will: Facsimiles and Commentary* (London 2009).

Burrows, D., and Dunhill, R., *Music and Theatre in Handel's World: The Family Papers of James Harris, 1732–1780* (Oxford, 2002).

Burrows, D., and Ronish, M. J., *A Catalogue of Handel's Musical Autographs* (Oxford, 1994).

Clausen, H. D., *Händels Direktionspartituren (Handexemplare)* (Hamburg: Verlag der Musikalienhandlung, Karl Dieter Wagner, 1972).

Deutsch, O. E., *Handel: A Documentary Biography* (New York and London, 1955); see also *Händel-Handbuch* (HHB) iv: *Dokumente zu Leben und Schaffen* (Kassel and Leipzig, 1985).

Fuller-Maitland, J. A. , and Mann, A. H., *Catalogue of the Music in the Fitzwilliam Museum, Cambridge* (London, 1893).

Harris, E. T., *The Librettos of Handel's Operas*, 13 vols. (New York, 1989).

Marx, H. J., (ed.), *Händel und Hamburg* (Hamburg, 1985).

(ed.), *An International Handel Bibliography/Internationale Händel-Bibliographie (1959–2009)* (Göttingen, 2009).

Parker, M. A., G. F. Handel: A Guide to Research, 2nd edn (New York and London, 2005).

Sartori, C., *I libretti italiani a stampa dalle origini al 1800*, 7 vols. (Cuneo, 1990–4).

Smith, W. C., *Handel: A Descriptive Catalogue of the Early Editions* (London, 1960).

Walker, A. D., *George Frideric Handel: The Newman Flower Collection in the Henry Watson Music Library* (Manchester, 1972).

ARTICLES, BOOKS AND COLLECTIONS OF ESSAYS

Abraham, G. (ed.), *Handel: A Symposium* (London, 1954).

Best, T. (ed.), *Handel Collections and their History* (Oxford, 1993).

Blakeman, E., *The Faber Pocket Guide to Handel* (London, 2009).

Burney, C , A General History of Music: From the Earliest Ages to the Present Period (1789), vol. 4, ed. F. Mercer (London, 1789; repr. 1935).

An Account of the Musical Performances in Westminster Abbey and the Pantheon . . . in Commemoration of Handel (London, 1785) (includes 'Sketch of the Life of Handel').

Burrows, D. (ed.), *The Cambridge Companion to Handel* (Cambridge, 1997).

Handel (Oxford, 1994).

Handel and the English Chapel Royal (Oxford, 2005).

Handel: Messiah (Cambridge, 1991).

Chrysander, F., *G. F. Händel* (Leipzig, 1858–67).

[Coxe, W.], *Anecdotes of George Frederick Handel and John Christopher Smith* (London, 1799; facsimile edn, ed. P. M. Young, New York, 1979).

Dean, W., *Essays on Opera* (Oxford, 1990).

Handel and the Opera Seria (Berkeley, 1969).

Handel's Dramatic Oratorios and Masques, paperback edn (Oxford, 1990).

Handel's Operas 1726–1741 (Woodbridge, 2006).

Dean, W., and Hicks, A., *The New Grove Handel* (London, 1983).

Dean, W., and Knapp, J. M., *Handel's Operas 1704–1726*, rev. edn (Oxford, 1995).

Fiske, R., *English Theatre Music in the Eighteenth Century*, 2nd edn (Oxford, 1986).

Fortune, N. (ed.), *Music and Theatre: Essays in Honour of Winton Dean* (Cambridge, 1987).

Gibson, E., *The Royal Academy of Music 1719–1728: The Institution and its Directors* (New York, 1989).

Harris, E. T., *Handel and the Pastoral Tradition* (Oxford, 1980).
Handel as Orpheus (Harvard, 2001).

Hawkins, J., *A General History of the Science and Practice of Music* (London, 1776).

Hicks, A., 'Handel's Early Musical Development', *Proceedings of the Royal Musical Association* 103 (1976–7).

Hogwood, C., *Handel*, rev. edn (London, 2007).
Water Music and Music for the Royal Fireworks (Cambridge, 2005).

Hogwood, C., and Luckett, R. (eds.), *Music in Eighteenth-Century England: Essays in Memory of Charles Cudworth* (Cambridge, 1983).

Hortschansky K., and Musketa K., (eds.), *Georg Friedrich Händel – Ein Lebensinhalt: Gedenkschrift für Bernd Baselt (1934–1993)* (Kassel and Halle, 1995).

Hurley, D. R., *Handel's Muse: Patterns of Creation in his Oratorios and Musical Dramas, 1743–1751* (Oxford, 2001).

Keates, J., *Handel: The Man and his Music*, 2nd edn (London, 2008).

King, R. G. (ed.), *Handel Studies: A Gedenkschrift for Howard Serwer* (Hillsdale, NY, 2009).

Kirkendale, W. and U., *Music and Meaning. Studies in Music History and the Neighbouring Disciplines* (Florence, 2007).

Lang, P. H., *George Frideric Handel* (New York: Norton, 1966).

Larue, C. S., *Handel and his Singers: The Creation of the Royal Academy Operas, 1720–1728* (Oxford, 1995).

Mainwaring, J., *Memoirs of the Life of the Late George Frederic Handel* (London, 1760).

Mann, A., *Handel: The Orchestral Music* (New York, 1996).

Marx, H. J. (ed.), *Händel und seine Zeitgenossen. Eine biographische Enzyklopädie*, 2 vols. (Laaber, 2009).

Mattheson, J., *Critica musica* (Hamburg, 1723).
Grundlage einer Ehren-Pforte (Hamburg, 1740).
Der musicalische Patriot (Hamburg, 1728).

Mattheson, J., and Scheibe, J. A., *Critischer Musikus* (Leipzig, 1745)

Pirrotta, N., and Ziino, A. (eds.), *Händel e gli Scarlatti a Roma* (Florence, 1987).

Rätzer, M., *Szenische Aufführungen von Werken Georg Friedrich Händels vom 18. bis 20. Jahrhundert: Eine Dokumentation* (Halle, 2000) (with annual updates published in HJb).

Roberts, J. H., (ed.), *Handel Sources: Materials for the Study of Handel's Borrowing*, 9 vols. (New York, 1986).

Sadie, S., *Handel Concertos* (London, 1972).

Sadie, S., and Hicks, A. (eds.), *Handel Tercentenary Collection* (London, 1987).

Schoelcher, V., *The Life of Handel* (London, 1857).

Simon, J., (ed.), *Handel: A Celebration of his Life and Times* (London, 1985).

Smith, R., *Handel's Oratorios and Eighteenth-Century Thought* (Cambridge, 1995).

Smither, H. E., *A History of the Oratorio*, vol. 2: *The Oratorio in the Baroque Era – Protestant Germany and England* (Chapel Hill, NC, 1977).

Streatfield, R. A., *Handel* (London, 1909).

Strohm, R., *Essays on Handel and Italian Opera* (Cambridge, 1985).

    Dramma per Musica: Italian Opera Seria of the Eighteenth Century (New Haven, 1997).

Walther, J. G., *Musicalisches Lexicon* (Leipzig, 1732).

Williams, P. (ed.), *Bach, Handel, Scarlatti: Tercentenary Essays* (Cambridge, 1985).

Zöllner, E., *English Oratorio after Handel: The London Oratorio Series and its Repertory, 1760–1800* (Marburg, 2002).

General index

Pachelbel, Johann 372
Pacini, Andrea 128, 211, 450, 478, 548, 629, 660
Paganini, Niccolò 269
Palestrina, Giovanni 1
Palladianism 109, 110
Palladio, Andrea 109
Pallavicini, Stefano Benedetto 410, 471, 473, 484
Pallavicino, Carlo 273, 316, 347, 484, 565
Palmer (née Peacock), Elizabeth 298, 484
Palmer, Ralph 484
Palmerini, Giovanni Battista 7, 540, 592
Pampani, Antonio Gaetano 163
Pamphilij family 480
Pamphilij, Anna 480
Pamphilij, Benedetto, Cardinal 33, 37, 50, 119, 131, 167, 179, 251, 286, 322, 354, 480, 484–5, 554, 557, 571, 645, 646, 648
Pamphilij, Camillo 480
Pamphilij, Giovan Battista, see Innocent X
Pancieri, Giulio 30, 485
Paolo Demidoff, Prince 479
Paradies, Domenico 99
Pariati, Pietro 55, 90, 162, 167, 265, 384, 485
Parker, Thomas 79
Parkgate 142, 199, 304
Parrott, Andrew 522, 533
Pasini, Nicola 12, 13
Pasquini, Bernardo 50, 157, 251, 484
Pasquini, Giovanni Claudio 316, 485
Passerini, Christina 22, 84, 640
Passerini, Giuseppe 84
Paulus Diaconus 169, 497
Pears, Peter 532
Pelham Holles (née Godolphin), Henrietta, Duchess of Newcastle-upon-Tyne 167
Peli, Francesco 212
Pellegrin, Abbé Simon-Joseph 359
Pellegrini, Giovanni Antonio 407
Pellegrini, Valeriano 12, 13, 496, 588, 638
Pendarves, Alexander 187
Pendarves, Mrs, see Delany
Pepusch, Johann Christoph (John Christopher) 1, 86, 117, 140, 213, 330, 381, 498, 570, 594
Perceval (Percival), John, 1st Earl of Egmont 1, 198, 210, 214, 220, 458, 498, 602
Perceval (Percival), Martha 198, 498
Perceval (Percival), Philip 192, 198, 199, 210, 498–9
Perez, David 163
performing scores 606–7
Pergolesi, Giovanni 110, 163, 505

Perini, Giuseppe 549
Permoser, Balhasar 555
Perrault, Charles 194
Perti, Giacomo Antonio 2, 30, 57, 91, 479, 504, 547, 590, 602, 630
Pescetti, Giovanni Battista 113, 163, 170, 249, 452
Peter III, Emperor of Russia 586
Peterborough, 3rd Earl of, see Mordaunt, Charles 586
Petrarca, Francesco 273
Petrou, George 533
Pfersdorff, Maria Sophie, see Mangold
Pfersdorff, Philipp 668
Pfersdorff (née Händel), Sophie Rosina 299, 668
Philip V of Spain, Philippe de France, fils de France and duc d'Anjou 12, 224, 353, 612, 613
Philip of Hesse-Darmstadt 353, 407
Philips, Ambrose 216
Piau, Sandrine 534
Piedimonte 2
Piedimonte d'Alife, family 483
Pietragrua, Carlo Luigi 275, 410, 553
Pietro Leopoldo of Habsburg-Lorraine, Grand Duke 525
Pilotti-Schiavonetti, Elisabetta 34, 496, 504–5, 543, 588, 638
Pinacci (Pinazzi), Giovanni Battista 9, 217, 403, 451, 505, 601, 641
Pine, John 307
Pinnock, Trevor 522, 533
Pinto, Thomas 103
Piovene, Agostino, Count 194, 505, 562, 628, 660
Pippard, Luke 662
Pisendel, Johann Georg 196
Pistocchi, Francesco Antonio Massimiliano 220, 222
Pitt, William junior 310
Pittoni, Ottavio 553
Pius V, Pope 481
Platen und Hallermund, Franz Ernst, Baron von 375
Platzer, (Johann or Jacob?) Christoph 333, 505
Platzer, Johann Georg 505
Pluche, Noël Antoine 331
Plutarch 506, 575, 589, 636
Pohle, David 278
Polka, Pawel 312
Pollarolo, Carlo Francesco 113, 177, 201, 222, 225, 505, 562, 566, 630, 658
Pons, Lily 531